MERGENT'S DIVIDEND ACHIEVERS

2003 Summer Edition

MERGENT

MERGENT'S DIVIDEND ACHIEVERS

Mergent, Inc.

PUBLISHER: Jonathan Worrall

ASSOCIATE PUBLISHER: Thomas Wecera

Staff for *MERGENT'S DIVIDEND ACHIEVERS*

EDITORS: Brad A. Armbruster, Stacy M. Cleeland

ASSOCIATE EDITORS: Reggie D. Cain, Kevin D. Heckert

SENIOR BUSINESS ANALYSTS: Christalyn Y. Daniel, Richard K. Dee, Jr., Melissa A. Francis, Andrew J. Kalinski

BUSINESS ANALYSTS: Ava A. Alexander, Troy Gaunt, Anthony E. Harp, Talvi S. Young

TABLE OF CONTENTS

Page

INTRODUCTION

With the era of consistent gains in the equity markets somewhat a memory of the past and volatility becoming more of the norm, many investors have found themselves back on their heels seeking an approach that would assist them in making confident investment decisions. If you add in the effects of uncertain global conditions, ramifications resulting from the war in Iraq and the overwhelming fear of terrorist acts, it only makes sense for investors to search for a safer place to allocate their capital.

Going back to late 2002, speculation about the potential elimination of taxes on dividends has cast a light on a group of companies that are frequently overlooked by investors in their search for the quick payoff. Corporations that consistently pay dividends often persevere even when the road gets difficult to maneuver. With the recent signing of a bill to cut the tax rate paid by individuals on corporate dividends to 15%, those companies become even more appealing as a portfolio addition.

Since 1979, MERGENT has been singling out companies with exceptionally strong dividend records. For the summer 2003 edition, MERGENT has identified 284 companies with at least ten consecutive years of annual dividend growth. This elite group of companies referred to as *MERGENT's Dividend Achievers* represents 2.5% of the 11,400-plus U.S.-listed dividend-paying stocks in Mergent's database.

The list of Dividend Achievers in the following pages is ranked by 10-year average annual compound increases in dividends for the period ended 2002. For the fifth year in a row New York-based **Paychex, Inc.**, a payroll and benefits services provider, holds the honor as the company with the fastest-growing dividend with a ten-year average annual increase rate of 45.25%. In second place is **Linear Technology Corporation**, a manufacturer of high performance integrated circuits, with 40.70%. The third runner up is Vermont-based **Chittenden Corporation**, a bank holding company, with 29.63%.

For the twelve months ended 4/30/03, the average of the Dividend Achievers' annual total returns was negative -7.3%. By comparison, the return for Standard and Poor's 500 declined by a wider margin of negative -14.9% over the same period. Out of the Dividend Achiever companies, approximately 32% produced a positive return for the one-year period ending 4/30/03.

Leading this group of companies was Puerto Rico-based **Doral Financial Corporation**, a financial services provider, which posted a one-year return of 74.4%. Other notables include men's shoe manufacturer **Weyco Group, Inc.** with a return of 69.5%, and natural gas distributor **UGI Corporation**, with a return of 56.0%. **Raven Industries, Inc.**, which held the top honor for calendar 2002 and 2001, slipped backed slightly in the rankings with a still very strong one-year return of 42.1%. Complete one-, three- and five-year total return information begins on page 15a.

We were once again forced to pass along the distinction of the longest record of consecutive annual dividend increases following the acquisition of Household International, Inc. by HSBC Holdings, plc in March 2003. The honor is now being held in a three-way tie between **American States Water Company, Diebold, Inc.** and **The Procter & Gamble Company**, as all three have recorded 49 years of consecutive increases. A remarkable achievement to say the least.

At midyear, the major indexes were starting to demonstrate some upside momentum, with the Dow Jones Industrial Average up 7.7% year-to-date as of 6/27/03. However, a rally in the markets is not guaranteed given the roller-coaster ride that investors experienced during the first six months of 2003. Readers should keep an eye out for the fall edition of *Mergent's Dividend Achievers*. Provided some good fortune and a continued turnaround in the economy, supported by the Federal Reserve Board's decision to reduce interest rates in June, this group of companies could offer a promising investment opportunity in the second half of the year.

Ranking the 2003 Dividend Achievers

Companies are listed by the ten-year average annual compound growth rate of their dividends. Also shown are total numbers of consecutive years of dividend growth.

Rank	Company	10-Year Growth Rate %	No. of Yrs.
1.	[2] Paychex, Inc. (NS)	45.25	14
2.	[2] Linear Technology Corp. (NS)	40.70	10
3.	[1] Chittenden Corp. (NY)	29.63	10
4.	[1] Citigroup Inc. (NY)	27.85	16
5.	[1] Home Depot, Inc. (NY)	27.62	15
6.	[1] Roper Industries, Inc. (NY)	27.10	10
7.	[1] Pier 1 Imports, Inc. (NY)	25.86	11
8.	[1] TCF Financial Corp. (NY)	25.49	11
9.	[2] First Financial Corp. (NS)	24.93	10
10.	[2] SEI Investments Co. (NS)	24.29	11
11.	[1] Doral Financial Corp. (NY)	23.72	13
12.	[2] Stryker Corp. (NY)	23.11	10
13.	[2] CVB Financial Corp. (NS)	22.88	12
14.	[1] Charter One Financial, Inc. (NY)	22.32	14
15.	[1] Medtronic, Inc. (NY)	22.13	25
16.	[1] Washington Mutual Inc. (NY)	21.76	13
17.	[2] T. Rowe Price Group, Inc. (NS)	21.67	16
18.	[2] Arrow International, Inc. (NS)	21.48	10
19.	[1] Cintas Corp. (NS)	21.15	20
20.	[2] Republic Bancorp Inc. (NS)	20.92	10
21.	[1] Eaton Vance Corp. (NY)	20.79	21
22.	[2] Virco Manufacturing Corp. (AM)	20.75	20
23.	[1] M&T Bank Corp. (NY)	20.70	22
24.	[1] Sysco Corp. (NY)	20.67	26
25.	[2] First Federal Capital Corp (NS)	20.42	11
26.	[1] Synovus Financial Corp. (NY)	20.41	26
27.	[1] Nuveen Investments, Inc. (NY)	20.11	10
28.	[1] Praxair, Inc. (NY)	19.78	10
29.	[2] Applebee's International, Inc. (NS)	19.60	11
30.	[1] Wal-Mart Stores, Inc. (NY)	19.42	21
31.	[2] Jack Henry & Associates, Inc. (NS)	18.93	12
32.	[2] Fifth Third Bancorp (NS)	18.78	30
33.	[1] Hudson United Bancorp (NY)	18.55	12
34.	[1] National Commerce Financial (NY)	18.52	28
35.	[1] Irwin Financial Corp. (NY)	18.369	13
36.	[2] WestAmerica Bancorporation (NS)	18.367	13
37.	[1] Nucor Corp. (NY)	18.33	30
38.	[1] Tootsie Roll Industries, Inc. (NY)	18.30	39
39.	[1] Archer-Daniels-Midland Co. (NY)	18.17	28
40.	[2] First Indiana Corp. (NS)	18.07	11
41.	[2] Pacific Capital Bancorp (NS)	17.94	33
42.	[2] S&T Bancorp, Inc. (NS)	17.74	13
43.	[2] F.N.B. Corp. (NS)	17.62	18
44.	[2] First Financial Holdings, Inc. (NS)	17.46	10
45.	[1] Commerce Bancorp, Inc. (NY)	17.42	11
46.	[2] Trustco Bank Corp NY (NS)	17.41	26
47.	[2] Glacier Bancorp, Inc. (NS)	17.22	11
48.	[1] Superior Industries Int'l, Inc. (NY)	17.13	17
49.	[1] Mercury General Corp. (NY)	16.98	16
50.	[2] Community First Bankshares (NS)	16.75	11
51.	[1] Freddie Mac (NY)	16.57	12
52.	[2] Park National Corp. (AM)	16.55	15
53.	[1] Fidelity National Financial (NY)	16.27	15
54.	[1] BB&T Corp. (NY)	15.97	31
55.	[1] Leggett & Platt, Inc. (NY)	15.85	33
56.	[1] Automatic Data Processing (NY)	15.65	27
	[1] State Street Corp. (NY)	15.65	22
58.	[2] Northern Trust Corp. (NS)	15.57	17
59.	[1] Pfizer Inc. (NY)	15.48	35
60.	[1] Wells Fargo & Co. (NY)	15.08	15
61.	[1] Brady Corp. (NY)	15.02	18
62.	[2] Harleysville National Corp. (NS)	14.99	16
63.	[1] AFLAC Inc. (NY)	14.91	20
64.	[1] Bank of New York Co. (NY)	14.87	10
	[2] Popular, Inc. (NS)	14.87	10
66.	[1] Illinois Tool Works Inc. (NY)	14.74	40
67.	[1] Golden West Financial Corp. (NY)	14.71	19
68.	[2] McGrath Rentcorp (NS)	14.54	12
69.	[2] First Charter Corp. (NS)	14.48	10
70.	[1] General Electric Co. (NY)	14.45	27
71.	[2] United Mobile Homes, Inc. (AM)	14.42	12
72.	[1] Fannie Mae (NY)	14.36	17
73.	[2] SouthTrust Corp. (NS)	14.35	32
74.	[1] Legg Mason, Inc. (NY)	13.96	19
75.	[1] Transatlantic Holdings, Inc. (NY)	13.90	12
76.	[1] Gallagher (Arthur J.) & Co. (NY)	13.74	18
77.	[1] Old Republic Intl. Corp. (NY)	13.70	21
78.	[2] Associated Banc-Corp. (NS)	13.67	32
79.	[1] Cousins Properties Inc. (NY)	13.60	11
80.	[1] Schering-Plough Corp. (NY)	13.581	17
81.	[1] Johnson & Johnson (NY)	13.580	40
82.	[1] Morgan (J.P.) Chase & Co. (NY)	13.50	11
83.	[1] FleetBoston Financial Corp. (NY)	13.35	10
84.	[2] National Penn Bancshares (NS)	13.309	24
85.	[1] MBNA Corp. (NY)	13.307	11
86.	[1] El Paso Corp. (NY)	13.22	10
87.	[2] Trustmark Corp. (NS)	13.14	29
88.	[1] Teleflex Inc. (NY)	13.09	25
89.	[2] Compass Bancshares, Inc. (NS)	13.05	21
90.	[1] ConAgra Foods, Inc. (NY)	13.02	25
91.	[2] Badger Meter, Inc. (AM)	12.93	10
92.	[1] SunTrust Banks, Inc. (NY)	12.82	17
93.	[1] Avery Dennison Corp. (NY)	12.66	27
94.	[1] General Dynamics Corp. (NY)	12.53	11
95.	[1] Myers Industries, Inc. (NY)	12.52	26
96.	[2] 1st Source Corp. (NS)	12.49	15

Rank	Company	10-Year Growth Rate %	No. of Yrs.
97.	[1] Bank of America Corp. (NY)	12.45	25
98.	[1] Franklin Resources, Inc. (NY)	12.44	13
99.	[1] Altria Group, Inc. (NY)	12.37	37
100.	[2] Lancaster Colony Corp. (NS)	12.33	33
101.	[1] American International Grp. (NY)	12.30	17
102.	[1] Abbott Laboratories (NY)	12.27	30
103.	[1] Kimco Realty Corp. (NY)	12.22	10
104.	[2] Chemical Financial Corp. (NS)	12.10	27
105.	[1] Valspar Corp. (NY)	12.02	24
106.	[1] Ecolab Inc. (NY)	11.93	10
107.	[1] Jefferson-Pilot Corp. (NY)	11.87	35
108.	[1] Merck & Co., Inc. (NY)	11.853	19
109.	[2] First Midwest Bancorp (NS)	11.851	10
110.	[1] Family Dollar Stores, Inc. (NY)	11.83	26
111.	[2] Mercantile Bankshares Corp. (NS)	11.80	26
112.	[1] Pitney Bowes Inc. (NY)	11.71	19
113.	[1] Unitrin, Inc. (NY)	11.68	12
114.	[2] Raven Industries, Inc. (NS)	11.613	15
115.	[1] Alberto-Culver Co. (NY)	11.612	18
	[1] Comerica, Inc. (NY)	11.612	19
117.	[1] Webster Financial Corp. (NY)	11.54	10
118.	[2] Unizan Financial Corp. (NS)	11.44	18
119.	[1] Procter & Gamble Co. (NY)	11.39	49
120.	[1] ABM Industries Inc. (NY)	11.38	38
121.	[2] Cincinnati Financial Corp. (NS)	11.24	42
122.	[1] Coca-Cola Co. (NY)	11.07	40
	[1] First Commonwealth Finl. (NY)	11.07	15
124.	[1] AmSouth Bancorporation (NY)	11.06	32
125.	[1] SLM Corporation (NY)	10.98	22
126.	[2] Corus Bankshares, Inc. (NS)	10.84	16
127.	[1] Ambac Financial Group, Inc. (NY)	10.77	11
128.	[1] BancorpSouth, Inc. (NY)	10.69	16
129.	[1] MBIA Inc. (NY)	10.65	15
130.	[2] Commerce Bancshares, Inc. (NS)	10.59	34
131.	[1] Sherwin-Williams Co. (NY)	10.55	23
132.	[2] Sigma-Aldrich Corp. (NS)	10.52	21
133.	[1] HON INDUSTRIES Inc. (NY)	10.45	14
134.	[2] State Auto Financial Corp. (NS)	10.44	11
135.	[1] Valley National Bancorp (NY)	10.43	11
136.	[1] Hillenbrand Industries, Inc. (NY)	10.38	32
137.	[2] Donegal Group Inc. (NS)	10.17	13
138.	[1] Protective Life Corp. (NY)	10.120	13
139.	[2] First Financial Bancorp. (NS)	10.119	19
140.	[1] Community Bank System (NY)	10.11	11
141.	[1] Federal Signal Corp. (NY)	10.10	15
142.	[1] Marshall & Ilsley Corp. (NY)	10.04	30
143.	[1] Becton, Dickinson & Co. (NY)	10.03	30
	[1] Rouse Company (NY)	10.03	10
145.	[1] Wrigley (Wm.) Jr. Co. (NY)	10.01	22
146.	[2] Nordson Corp. (NS)	9.99	22
147.	[1] Carlisle Companies Inc. (NY)	9.92	26
148.	[2] Sterling Financial Corp. (NS)	9.839	15
149.	[1] Regions Financial Corp. (NY)	9.837	31
150.	[2] National City Corp. (NS)	9.83	10
151.	[1] First Virginia Banks, Inc. (NY)	9.69	25
152.	[1] Dover Corp. (NY)	9.65	47
153.	[1] Colgate-Palmolive Co. (NY)	9.61	40
154.	[1] Anheuser-Busch Cos., Inc. (NY)	9.60	28
155.	[2] Fulton Financial Corp. (NS)	9.51	29
156.	[1] Marsh & McLennan Cos. (NY)	9.45	41
157.	[1] Citizens Banking Corp. (NS)	9.40	19
158.	[2] Alfa Corp. (NS)	9.39	17
159.	[1] KeyCorp (NY)	9.37	23
160.	[1] Hershey Foods Corp. (NY)	9.36	28
161.	[2] Harleysville Group Inc. (NS)	9.25	16
162.	[1] Sara Lee Corp. (NY)	9.15	26
163.	[1] McDonald's Corp. (NY)	9.08	26
164.	[2] FirstMerit Corp. (NS)	9.07	20
165.	[1] Banta Corp. (NY)	8.974	24
166.	[1] PepsiCo, Inc. (NY)	8.966	31
167.	[1] Vulcan Materials Co. (NY)	8.92	10
168.	[2] Washington Federal, Inc. (NS)	8.91	19
169.	[1] Beckman Coulter, Inc. (NY)	8.84	11
170.	[1] Lowe's Cos., Inc. (NY)	8.62	41
171.	[1] Wilmington Trust Corp. (NY)	8.61	21
172.	[1] Pentair, Inc. (NY)	8.52	26
173.	[1] Bemis Co., Inc. (NY)	8.50	19
174.	[1] Lilly (Eli) & Co. (NY)	8.47	35
175.	[1] Emerson Electric Co. (NY)	8.35	46
176.	[2] United Bankshares, Inc. (NS)	8.27	21
177.	[1] McCormick & Co., Inc. (NY)	8.26	16
178.	[2] Community Trust Bancorp (NS)	8.24	14
179.	[2] Weyco Group, Inc. (NS)	8.23	22
180.	[1] Grainger (W.W.), Inc. (NY)	8.20	31
181.	[2] Mine Safety Appliances Co. (AM)	8.16	32
182.	[1] Heinz (H.J.) Co. (NY)	8.15	39
183.	[1] Hormel Foods Corp. (NY)	8.04	35
	[1] Walgreen Co. (NY)	8.04	27
185.	[1] RLI Corp. (NY)	7.89	26
	[1] TEPPCO Partners, L.P. (NY)	7.89	10
187.	[1] Avon Products, Inc. (NY)	7.87	12
188.	[1] Bandag, Inc. (NY)	7.70	26
189.	[2] Midland Co. (NS)	7.69	16
190.	[1] Old National Bancorp (NY)	7.67	19
191.	[2] Susquehanna Bancshares, Inc. (NS)	7.64	32
192.	[1] Clorox Co. (NY)	7.62	26
193.	[2] National Security Group, Inc. (NS)	7.55	12
194.	[1] Johnson Controls, Inc. (NY)	7.51	27
195.	[1] Smith (A.O.) Corp. (NY)	7.31	10
196.	[2] WesBanco, Inc. (NS)	7.22	17
197.	[1] Stepan Co. (NY)	7.14	36
198.	[1] Diebold, Inc. (NY)	7.12	49
199.	[1] Air Products & Chemicals (NY)	7.11	20
200.	[1] Cedar Fair, L.P. (NY)	7.10	15
201.	[1] GATX Corp. (NY)	7.01	17
202.	[1] Sonoco Products Co. (NY)	6.94	19
203.	[1] La-Z-Boy Inc. (NY)	6.91	21
204.	[1] West Pharmaceutical Services (NY)	6.77	10

Rank	Company	10-Year Growth Rate %	No. of Yrs.	Rank	Company	10-Year Growth Rate %	No. of Yrs.
205.	[1] Rohm & Haas Co. (NY)	6.750	25	245.	[1] Stanley Works (NY)	4.46	35
206.	[1] Donnelley (R.R.) & Sons Co. (NY)	6.749	33	246.	[2] American National Insurance (NS)	4.42	29
207.	[1] Target Corp. (NY)	6.60	31	247.	[1] NACCO Industries, Inc. (NY)	4.33	19
208.	[1] Health Care Prop. Investors (NY)	6.57	17	248.	[1] Progressive Corp. (NY)	4.31	33
209.	[1] Fuller (H.B.) Co. (NY)	6.56	35	249.	[1] SuperValu Inc. (NY)	4.18	30
210.	[1] Eastgroup Properties, Inc. (NY)	6.38	10	250.	[1] Quaker Chemical Corp. (NY)	4.08	31
211.	[1] ALLTEL Corp. (NY)	6.27	42	251.	[1] Gannett Co., Inc. (NY)	4.05	31
212.	[2] Frisch's Restaurants, Inc. (AM)	6.20	19	252.	[1] SBC Communications Inc. (NY)	3.93	18
213.	[1] McGraw-Hill Cos., Inc. (NY)	6.18	29	253.	[2] Wesco Financial Corp. (AM)	3.75	31
214.	[2] Telephone & Data Systems (AM)	6.13	28	254.	[1] MDU Resources Group, Inc. (NY)	3.74	12
215.	[1] PPG Industries, Inc. (NY)	6.10	31	255.	[1] Kimberly-Clark Corp. (NY)	3.71	28
216.	[1] Masco Corp. (NY)	5.98	44	256.	[2] Gorman-Rupp Co. (AM)	3.62	30
217.	[1] Chubb Corp. (NY)	5.88	38	257.	[1] Atmos Energy Corp. (NY)	3.59	15
218.	[1] Lincoln National Corp. (NY)	5.78	19	258.	[2] Florida Public Utilities Co. (AM)	3.53	34
219.	[1] V.F. Corp. (NY)	5.742	30	259.	[1] Vectren Corporation (NY)	3.47	27
220.	[1] Genuine Parts Co. (NY)	5.738	46	260.	[1] Black Hills Power, Inc. (NY)	3.45	31
221.	[1] Hilb, Rogal & Hamilton Co. (NY)	5.72	16	261.	[1] Questar Corp. (NY)	3.379	23
222.	[1] Piedmont Natural Gas Co. (NY)	5.71	23	262.	[2] SJW Corp. (AM)	3.377	36
223.	[1] RPM International Inc. (NY)	5.65	29	263.	[1] Energen Corp. (NY)	3.36	20
224.	[1] Bank of Hawaii Corp. (NY)	5.621	25	264.	[1] National Fuel Gas Co. (NY)	3.31	31
225.	[1] May Department Stores Co. (NY)	5.619	27	265.	[1] Progress Energy, Inc. (NY)	3.27	14
226.	[1] Haverty Furniture Cos., Inc. (NY)	5.61	32	266.	[1] Tennant Co. (NY)	3.00	30
227.	[1] Brown-Forman Corp. (NY)	5.58	18	267.	[2] Middlesex Water Co. (NS)	2.711	30
228.	[1] Bard (C.R.), Inc. (NY)	5.573	31	268.	[1] CLECO Corp. (NY)	2.710	21
229.	[2] Energy West Inc. (NS)	5.566	16	269.	[1] Exxon Mobil Corp. (NY)	2.66	20
230.	[1] St. Paul Cos., Inc. (NY)	5.51	16	270.	[2] Otter Tail Corp. (NS)	2.60	27
231.	[1] Universal Corp. (NY)	5.45	32	271.	[1] UGI Corp. (NY)	2.50	15
232.	[1] ChevronTexaco Corp. (NY)	5.43	15	272.	[1] Federal Realty Invest. Trust (NY)	2.36	35
233.	[1] United Dominion Rlty. Trust (NY)	5.34	17	273.	[1] WPS Resources Corp. (NY)	2.11	44
234.	[1] Washington R.E.I.T. (NY)	5.21	41	274.	[1] Clarcor Inc. (NY)	1.89	22
235.	[1] Weingarten Realty Investors (NY)	5.02	14	275.	[1] California Water Service Co. (NY)	1.88	35
236.	[1] Bristol-Myers Squibb Co. (NY)	4.96	30	276.	[1] WGL Holdings, Inc. (NY)	1.76	26
237.	[1] CenturyTel, Inc. (NY)	4.913	29	277.	[1] Peoples Energy Corp. (NY)	1.69	19
238.	[1] Philadelphia Suburban Corp. (NY)	4.911	11	278.	[1] Universal Health Rlty. Inc. Tr. (NY)	1.651	15
239.	[1] ServiceMaster Co. (NY)	4.79	32	279.	[2] EnergySouth, Inc. (NS)	1.650	25
240.	[2] Bowl America Inc. (AM)	4.77	30	280.	[1] Commercial Net Lease Realty (NY)	1.63	13
241.	[1] TECO Energy, Inc. (NY)	4.62	43	281.	[1] Consolidated Edison, Inc. (NY)	1.57	28
242.	[1] Briggs & Stratton Corp. (NY)	4.60	11	282.	[2] Connecticut Water Service (NS)	1.30	27
243.	[1] Nicor Inc. (NY)	4.56	15	283.	[1] American States Water Co. (NY)	1.29	49
244.	[1] 3M Company (NY)	4.48	44	284.	[2] MGE Energy, Inc. (NS)	1.15	27

[1] Appears in Mergent's Handbook of Common Stocks   [2] Appears in Mergent's Handbook of Nasdaq Stocks
(NY) New York Stock Exchange   (NS) Nasdaq Stock Market   (AM) American Stock Exchange

Longest Records of Dividend Achievement

These Dividend Achievers boast the longest records of consecutive annual dividend increases.

Rank	Company	No. of Yrs.	Rank	Company	No. of Yrs.
1.	American States Water Co.	49		Lancaster Colony Corp.	33
	Diebold, Inc.	49		Leggett & Platt, Inc.	33
	Procter & Gamble Co.	49		Pacific Capital Bancorp	33
4.	Dover Corp.	47		Progressive Corp.	33
5.	Emerson Electric Co.	46	42.	AmSouth Bancorporation	32
	Genuine Parts Co.	46		Associated Banc-Corp.	32
7.	3M Company	44		Haverty Furniture Cos., Inc.	32
	Masco Corp.	44		Hillenbrand Industries, Inc.	32
	WPS Resources Corp.	44		Mine Safety Appliances Co.	32
10.	TECO Energy, Inc.	43		ServiceMaster Co.	32
11.	ALLTEL Corp.	42		SouthTrust Corp.	32
	Cincinnati Financial Corp.	42		Susquehanna Bancshares, Inc.	32
13.	Lowe's Cos., Inc.	41		Universal Corp.	32
	Marsh & McLennan Cos., Inc.	41	51.	Bard (C.R.), Inc.	31
	Washington R.E.I.T.	41		BB&T Corp.	31
16.	Coca-Cola Co.	40		Gannett Co., Inc.	31
	Colgate-Palmolive Co.	40		Grainger (W.W.), Inc.	31
	Illinois Tool Works Inc.	40		National Fuel Gas Co.	31
	Johnson & Johnson	40		PepsiCo, Inc.	31
20.	Heinz (H.J.) Co.	39		PPG Industries, Inc.	31
	Tootsie Roll Industries, Inc.	39		Quaker Chemical Corp.	31
22.	ABM Industries Inc.	38		Regions Financial Corp.	31
	Chubb Corp.	38		Target Corp.	31
24.	Altria Group, Inc.	37		Wesco Financial Corp.	31
25.	SJW Corp.	36	62.	Abbott Laboratories	30
	Stepan Co.	36		Becton, Dickinson & Co.	30
27.	California Water Service Co.	35		Bowl America Inc.	30
	Federal Realty Invest. Trust	35		Bristol-Myers Squibb Co.	30
	Fuller (H.B.) Co.	35		Fifth Third Bancorp	30
	Hormel Foods Corp.	35		Gorman-Rupp Co.	30
	Jefferson-Pilot Corp.	35		Marshall & Ilsley Corp.	30
	Lilly (Eli) & Co.	35		Middlesex Water Co.	30
	Pfizer Inc.	35		Nucor Corp.	30
	Stanley Works	35		SuperValu Inc.	30
35.	Commerce Bancshares, Inc.	34		Tennant Co.	30
	Florida Public Utilities Co.	34		V.F. Corp.	30
37.	Donnelley (R.R.) & Sons Co.	33			

Dividend Achiever Arrivals

The following companies, which recorded at least ten consecutive years of dividend increases in 2002, mark their debut as Dividend Achievers.

Ambac Financial Group, Inc.
Arrow International, Inc.
Badger Meter, Inc.
Bank of New York Co., Inc. (The)
Chittenden Corp.
Doral Financial Corp.
Eastgroup Properties, Inc.
Ecolab Inc.
El Paso Corp.
First Charter Corp.
First Financial Corp.
First Financial Holdings, Inc.
First Midwest Bancorp, Inc.
FleetBoston Financial Corp.
Glacier Bancorp, Inc.
Harleysville National Corp.
Kimco Realty Corp.
Linear Technology Corp.

National City Corp.
Nuveen Investments, Inc.
Popular, Inc.
Praxair, Inc.
Republic Bancorp Inc.
Roper Industries, Inc.
Rouse Company (The)
Smith (A.O) Corp.
Sterling Financial Corp.
Stryker Corp.
TCF Financial Corp.
TEPPCO Partners, L.P.
Unizan Financial Corp.
Vulcan Materials Co.
Washington Federal, Inc.
Webster Financial Corp.
West Pharmaceutical Services, Inc.

Dividend Achiever Departures

According to Mergent's database, the following former Dividend Achievers did not increase their regular cash dividends in 2002 and dropped from the list.

Albertson's, Inc. 30
Aon Corp. 50
Baldor Electric Co. 18
Belo Corp. 14
Cohu, Inc. 14
Crawford & Company 21
Dollar General Corp. 11
DQE, Inc. 12
Gillette Company (The) 24
Health Care REIT, Inc. 12
Hubbell, Inc. 41
Huntington Bancshares, Inc. 35
Interpublic Group of Companies, Inc. 20
Kaydon Corp. 14
Kellogg Company 45

Lee Enterprises, Inc. 41
Merrill Lynch & Co., Inc. 10
Modine Manufacturing Co. 15
NiSource, Inc. 13
North Pittsburgh Systems, Inc. 39
Pall Corp. 21
PNC Financial Services Group, Inc 10
Raymond James Financial, Inc. 15
Schwab (Charles) Corp. 12
SEMCO Energy, Inc. 23
United Fire & Casualty Co. 16
Wausau-Mosinee Paper Mills Corp. 17
Weis Markets, Inc. 27
Worthington Industries, Inc. 19
XCEL Energy, Inc. 26

The following former Dividend Achiever company has been acquired.

American Water Works Company, Inc.

Dividend Achiever Name Changes

The following companies have changed their names in the last year.

Old Name	New Name
Madison Gas & Electric Company	MGE Energy, Inc.
Minnesota Mining & Manufacturing Company	3M Company
Nuveen (John) Company (The)	Nuveen Investments, Inc.
Pacific Century Financial Corporation	Bank of Hawaii Corporation
Philip Morris Companies, Inc.	Altria Group, Inc.
RPM, Inc.	RPM International Inc.
USA Education, Inc.	SLM Corporation

Dividend Achiever Latest Developments

The following companies have beeen dropped from the Summer 2003 Edition of Mergent's Dividend Achievers

Household International, Inc. —The Company was acquired by HSBC Holdings, plc on 3/28/03.

NorthWestern Corp. — The Company suspended its dividend payment in February 2003.

Top 20 by Total Assets

Rank	Company	Assets ($Mil.)	Rank	Company	Assets ($Mil.)
1.	Citigroup Inc.	1,097,190.0	11.	Exxon Mobil Corp.	152,644.0
2.	Fannie Mae	887,515.0	12.	National City Corp.	118,258.4
3.	Morgan (J.P.) Chase & Co.	758,800.0	13.	SunTrust Banks, Inc.	117,322.5
4.	Freddie Mac	717,340.0	14.	SBC Communications Inc.	95,057.0
5.	Bank of America Corp.	660,458.0	15.	Wal-Mart Stores, Inc.	94,685.0
6.	General Electric Co.	575,244.0	16.	Lincoln National Corp.	93,133.3
7.	American International Grp.	561,229.0	17.	Altria Group, Inc.	87,540.0
8.	Wells Fargo & Co.	349,259.0	18.	State Street Corp.	85,794.0
9.	Washington Mutual Inc.	268,298.0	19.	KeyCorp	85,202.0
10.	FleetBoston Financial Corp.	190,453.0	20.	Fifth Third Bancorp	80,893.7

Top 20 by Return on Equity

Rank	Company	Return on Equity %	Rank	Company	Return on Equity %
1.	Colgate-Palmolive Co.	367.8	11.	PepsiCo, Inc.	35.6
2.	Sara Lee Corp.	65.8	12.	Coca-Cola Co.	33.7
3.	Anheuser-Busch Cos., Inc.	63.4	13.	3M Company	32.9
4.	Altria Group, Inc.	57.0	14.	Lilly (Eli) & Co.	32.7
5.	Pitney Bowes Inc.	51.3		Nuveen Investments, Inc.	32.7
6.	Heinz (H.J.) Co.	48.5	16.	Eaton Vance Corp.	32.5
	SEI Investments Co.	48.5	17.	Sysco Corp.	31.9
8.	Pfizer Inc.	46.0	18.	Procter & Gamble Co.	31.8
9.	SLM Corporation	39.6	19.	McCormick & Co., Inc.	30.4
10.	Merck & Co., Inc.	39.3	20.	Kimberly-Clark Corp.	29.8

Top 20 by Return on Assets

Rank	Company	Return on Assets %	Rank	Company	Return on Assets %
1.	SEI Investments Co.	30.3		Nuveen Investments, Inc.	15.0
2.	Pfizer Inc.	19.8	12.	Lancaster Colony Corp.	14.9
3.	Eaton Vance Corp.	19.6	13.	Applebee's International, Inc.	14.7
4.	Wrigley (Wm.) Jr. Co.	19.0	14.	Lilly (Eli) & Co.	14.2
5.	Colgate-Palmolive Co.	18.2		T. Rowe Price Group, Inc.	14.2
6.	Johnson & Johnson	16.3	16.	PepsiCo, Inc.	14.1
7.	Coca-Cola Co.	16.2	17.	Schering-Plough Corp.	14.0
8.	Avon Products, Inc.	16.1	18.	Anheuser-Busch Cos., Inc.	13.7
9.	Raven Industries, Inc.	15.4	19.	Pier 1 Imports, Inc.	13.4
10.	Merck & Co., Inc.	15.0		Sigma-Aldrich Corp.	13.4

Top 20 by Current Yield

Based on closing prices on 5/31/03

Rank	Company	Current Yield %	Rank	Company	Current Yield %
1.	Health Care Property Investors	8.5	11.	Altria Group, Inc.	6.2
2.	Commercial Net Lease Realty	7.6		National Security Group	6.2
3.	GATX Corp.	7.5	13.	Federal Realty Invest. Trust	5.9
4.	TEPPCO Partners, L.P.	7.3		TECO Energy, Inc.	5.9
	Universal Health Realty Inc. Tr.	7.3	15.	Kimco Realty Corp.	5.8
6.	EastGroup Properties, Inc.	7.0	16.	United Mobile Homes, Inc.	5.7
7.	United Dominion Realty Tr.	6.7		Weingarten Realty Investors	5.7
8.	Cedar Fair, L.P.	6.4	18.	Cousins Properties Inc.	5.5
	Energy West Inc.	6.4	19.	Washington Real Estate Inc.	5.4
10.	Unitrin, Inc.	6.3	20.	Atmos Energy Corp.	5.3

Highest Price/Earnings Ratios

Based on closing prices on 5/31/03

Rank	Company	P/E Ratio	Rank	Company	P/E Ratio
1.	Lincoln National Corp.	165.7	11.	Stryker Corp.	37.2
2.	United Dominion Realty Trust	81.4		Medtronic, Inc.	37.2
3.	American National Insurance	76.5	13.	Nordson Corp.	37.1
4.	Citizens Banking Corp.	75.7	14.	St. Paul Cos., Inc.	35.9
5.	GATX Corp.	70.8		West Pharmaceutical Services	35.9
6.	Linear Technology Corp.	51.3	16.	National Security Group	35.6
7.	Chubb Corp.	45.1	17.	Eastgroup Properties, Inc.	34.5
8.	Wesco Financial Corp.	42.5	18.	Rohm & Haas Co.	33.1
9.	Federal Realty Invest. Trust	41.3	19.	Morgan (J.P.) Chase & Co.	32.9
10.	Paychex, Inc.	39.6	20.	Mercury General Corp.	32.7

Lowest Price/Earnings Ratios

Based on closing prices on 5/31/03

Rank	Company	P/E Ratio	Rank	Company	P/E Ratio
1.	Fidelity National Financial, Inc.	6.7	11.	Republic Bancorp Inc.	10.5
2.	Freddie Mac	7.6	12.	Frisch's Restaurants, Inc.	10.8
3.	Altria Group, Inc.	8.0	13.	Protective Life Corp.	10.9
4.	Donegal Group Inc.	9.1	14.	Washington Federal, Inc.	11.1
5.	TECO Energy, Inc.	9.2	15.	First Federal Capital Corp.	11.2
6.	Washington Mutual Inc.	9.9		Nicor Inc.	11.2
7.	SBC Communications Inc.	10.2		V.F. Corp.	11.2
8.	NACCO Industries, Inc.	10.3		Webster Financial Corp.	11.2
	SuperValu Inc.	10.3	19.	MBIA Inc.	11.3
10.	Old Republic International Corp.	10.4	20.	Universal Corp.	11.4

Highest Seven-Year Price Scores

Scores cover a seven-year period ending 5/31/03. Definitions of price scores may be found on page 35a.

Rank	Company	Price Score	Rank	Company	Price Score
1.	Hilb, Rogal & Hamilton Co.	245.6	11.	Applebee's International, Inc.	180.2
2.	Doral Financial Corp.	237.9	12.	Sysco Corp.	172.5
3.	Raven Industries, Inc.	215.3	13.	Weyco Group, Inc.	172.2
4.	SLM Corporation	205.3	14.	Nuveen Investments, Inc.	172.1
5.	CVB Financial Corp.	194.6	15.	Family Dollar Stores, Inc.	170.9
6.	Commerce Bancorp, Inc.	192.2	16.	Clarcor Inc.	169.8
7.	Stryker Corp.	190.2	17.	Pier 1 Imports, Inc.	168.8
8.	Golden West Financial Corp.	185.1	18.	M&T Bank Corp.	167.9
9.	Fidelity National Financial, Inc.	183.1	19.	Gallagher (Arthur J.) & Co.	167.7
10.	Lowe's Cos., Inc.	182.6		Eaton Vance Corp.	167.7

Highest Twelve-Month Price Scores

Scores cover twelve months ending 5/31/03. Definitions of price scores may be found on page 35a.

Rank	Company	Price Score	Rank	Company	Price Score
1.	Doral Financial Corp.	130.4	11.	Energen Corp.	114.0
2.	Weyco Group, Inc.	125.8		Linear Technology Corp.	114.0
3.	Irwin Financial Corp.	123.7	13.	Morgan (J.P.) Chase & Co.	113.8
4.	Applebee's International, Inc.	122.8	14.	Legg Mason, Inc.	112.7
5.	UGI Corp.	121.8	15.	Clarcor Inc.	112.2
6.	Progressive Corp.	119.4	16.	Kimco Realty Corp.	111.7
7.	State Auto Financial Corp.	118.0	17.	Donegal Group Inc.	111.4
8.	Pacific Capital Bancorp	117.8		Federal Realty Invest. Trust	111.4
9.	Questar Corp.	115.6		Fidelity National Financial, Inc.	111.4
10.	MDU Resources Group, Inc.	114.3	20.	Avon Products, Inc.	111.2

Top 20 by Revenues

Rank	Company	Rev. ($Mil.)	Rank	Company	Rev. ($Mil.)
1.	Wal-Mart Stores, Inc.	246,525.0	11.	Bank of America Corp.	45,732.0
2.	Exxon Mobil Corp.	204,506.0	12.	Target Corp.	43,917.0
3.	General Electric Co.	131,698.0	13.	Morgan (J.P) Chase & Co.	43,372.0
4.	ChevronTexaco Corp.	99,049.0	14.	SBC Communications Inc.	43,138.0
5.	Citigroup Inc.	92,556.0	15.	Procter & Gamble Co.	40,238.0
6.	Altria Group, Inc.	80,408.0	16.	Freddie Mac	38,684.0
7.	American International Grp.	67,482.0	17.	Johnson & Johnson	36,298.0
8.	Home Depot, Inc.	58,247.0	18.	Pfizer Inc.	32,373.0
9.	Fannie Mae	52,901.0	19.	Walgreen Co.	28,681.0
10.	Merck & Co., Inc.	51,790.3	20.	Wells Fargo & Co.	28,473.0

Top 20 by Net Income

Rank	Company	Net Inc. ($Mil.)	Rank	Company	Net Inc. ($Mil.)
1.	General Electric Co.	15,133.0	11.	Freddie Mac	5,764.0
2.	Citigroup Inc.	13,448.0	12.	Wells Fargo & Co.	5,710.0
3.	Altria Group, Inc.	11,102.0	13.	American International Grp.	5,519.0
4.	Exxon Mobil Corp.	11,011.0	14.	Fannie Mae	4,619.0
5.	Bank of America Corp.	9,249.0	15.	Procter & Gamble Co.	4,352.0
6.	Pfizer Inc.	9,181.0	16.	Coca-Cola Co.	3,976.0
7.	Wal-Mart Stores, Inc.	8,039.0	17.	Washington Mutual Inc.	3,896.0
8.	SBC Communications Inc.	7,473.0	18.	Home Depot, Inc.	3,664.0
9.	Merck & Co., Inc.	7,149.5	19.	PepsiCo, Inc.	3,313.0
10.	Johnson & Johnson	6,597.0	20.	Abbott Laboratories	2,793.7

Ranking the Dividend Achievers
by Total Returns

Based on 1, 3 & 5 year periods ending 4/30/03. For information about total returns, please see page 22a.

1-yr. Rank	Company Name	1-yr. Tot. Return %	3-yr. Tot. Return %	3-yr. Rank	5-yr. Tot. Return %	5-yr. Rank
1.	Doral Financial Corp.	74.4	430.7	1	274.6	2
2.	Weyco Group, Inc.	69.5	118.7	15	119.8	16
3.	UGI Corp.	56.0	166.6	6	123.3	14
4.	Raven Industries, Inc.	42.1	299.5	2	195.7	4
5.	Glacier Bancorp, Inc.	32.5	137.3	10	56.7	69
6.	Popular, Inc.	26.9	93.8	29	15.6	150
7.	Pacific Capital Bancorp	26.0	70.8	71	77.3	42
8.	Stryker Corp.	25.5	87.3	35	200.6	3
9.	Irwin Financial Corp.	24.9	46.0	121	-8.9	220
10.	Fidelity National Financial, Inc.	24.5	195.4	5	34.3	102
11.	Donegal Group Inc.	24.4	40.6	136	-41.9	272
12.	Sterling Financial Corp.	20.9	88.7	34	25.3	119
13.	CVB Financial Corp.	20.6	132.0	11	119.0	17
14.	Federal Realty Invest. Trust	20.3	75.9	60	79.3	40
15.	Energen Corp.	19.2	92.5	31	69.4	51
16.	National Penn Bancshares, Inc.	19.1	80.9	55	51.9	74
17.	Ecolab Inc.	18.9	40.4	137	81.4	38
18.	Kimco Realty Corp.	18.7	59.9	92	93.7	27
19.	Progressive Corp.	18.5	213.9	4	52.5	73
20.	Bank of Hawaii Corp.	18.3	75.0	61	55.6	70
21.	Cedar Fair, L.P.	18.1	62.8	88	32.3	109
22.	SLM Corporation (USA Education)	17.9	269.1	3	178.7	5
23.	Clarcor Inc.	17.4	118.7	15	84.5	33
	Community Trust Bancorp, Inc.	17.4	84.1	45	32.6	107
25.	Bard (C.R.), Inc.	17.1	52.6	102	91.8	28
26.	Weingarten Realty Investors	16.3	72.3	69	86.6	32
27.	State Auto Financial Corp.	16.2	92.7	30	7.9	174
28.	California Water Service Co.	15.1	31.9	154	24.3	122
29.	Carlisle Companies Inc.	14.2	16.8	198	-2.1	206
30.	Harleysville National Corp.	13.0	113.5	20	64.2	54
	Lancaster Colony Corp.	13.0	73.2	68	22.2	131
32.	Universal Health Realty Inc. Trust	12.7	99.9	24	90.1	31
33.	Commercial Net Lease Realty	12.5	82.0	52	47.5	81
34.	Rouse Company	11.8	68.9	76	41.2	91
35.	Questar Corp.	10.9	73.4	66	61.5	60
36.	First Financial Corp.	10.8	67.7	80	11.7	164
	Golden West Financial Corp.	10.8	124.0	14	120.4	15
38.	AFLAC Inc.	10.3	36.8	142	108.7	21
39.	Briggs & Stratton Corp.	10.2	28.0	164	13.9	157
40.	Eastgroup Properties, Inc.	10.0	49.6	108	80.8	39

Total Returns (cont.)

1-yr. Rank	Company Name	1-yr. Tot. Return %	3-yr. Tot. Return %	3-yr. Rank	5-yr. Tot. Return %	5-yr. Rank
41.	First Virginia Banks, Inc.	9.9	83.4	47	26.9	115
42.	Merck & Co., Inc.	9.7	-11.0	248	5.9	184
43.	Colgate-Palmolive Co.	9.3	3.9	220	35.5	101
44.	Fulton Financial Corp.	9.0	52.5	103	25.6	118
	Legg Mason, Inc.	9.0	47.0	117	91.8	28
46.	United Mobile Homes, Inc.	8.8	111.0	21	71.7	50
47.	F.N.B. Corp.	8.4	85.4	40	14.6	153
	Hudson United Bancorp	8.4	81.4	53	25.7	117
49.	Washington Mutual Inc.	7.6	150.9	8	45.4	84
50.	Diebold, Inc.	7.5	46.1	120	7.2	180
51.	Medtronic, Inc.	7.4	-6.7	243	84.3	34
52.	CenturyTel, Inc.	7.1	22.4	183	6.7	181
53.	S&T Bancorp, Inc.	6.1	74.5	62	25.2	121
	WesBanco, Inc.	6.1	22.3	184	11.0	166
55.	MGE Energy, Inc.	6.0	82.9	50	72.6	49
56.	Community Bank System, Inc.	5.9	69.2	74	16.3	146
	Sigma-Aldrich Corp.	5.9	73.3	67	30.2	112
	TEPPCO Partners, L.P.	5.9	86.2	36	57.0	68
59.	Avon Products, Inc.	5.7	46.9	118	53.9	72
60.	MDU Resources Group, Inc.	5.5	49.5	109	51.0	76
61.	Bank of America Corp.	5.4	67.8	79	14.6	153
62.	Applebee's International, Inc.	5.3	70.2	72	151.3	10
	United Dominion Realty Trust	5.3	100.9	23	76.9	43
64.	Citigroup Inc.	4.8	4.7	217	57.6	66
65.	Gannett Co., Inc.	4.6	23.3	179	18.5	142
	Wrigley (Wm.) Jr. Co.	4.6	63.9	85	38.3	94
67.	Clorox Co.	4.3	31.0	157	18.4	143
	Peoples Energy Corp.	4.3	43.6	127	36.7	97
69.	Piedmont Natural Gas Co., Inc.	4.2	49.1	111	34.2	103
70.	Lowe's Cos., Inc.	4.0	78.6	59	154.1	9
71.	RLI Corp.	3.9	91.6	32	46.3	83
72.	Florida Public Utilities Co.	3.8	51.0	106	83.7	35
	WGL Holdings, Inc.	3.8	19.2	192	23.0	127
74.	SouthTrust Corp.	3.6	144.1	9	43.1	87
75.	Praxair, Inc.	3.1	36.1	144	23.5	125
76.	Procter & Gamble Co.	2.8	61.6	91	20.7	139
77.	American States Water Co.	2.6	42.5	131	101.3	23
	National Fuel Gas Co.	2.6	10.4	212	23.2	126
79.	SJW Corp.	2.4	-24.4	261	61.6	59
80.	Cousins Properties Inc.	2.3	15.4	201	64.8	53
81.	Virco Manufacturing Corp.	2.2	27.1	169	-35.9	267
82.	3M Company	2.0	54.4	100	49.0	78
83.	Wal-Mart Stores, Inc.	1.4	3.3	221	128.3	13
84.	WPS Resources Corp.	1.0	56.2	98	60.5	61
85.	Community First Bankshares, Inc.	0.6	73.8	64	22.7	128

Total Returns (cont.)

1-yr. Rank	Company Name	1-yr. Tot. Return %	3-yr. Tot. Return %	3-yr. Rank	5-yr. Tot. Return %	5-yr. Rank
	HON INDUSTRIES Inc.	0.6	25.0	174	0.4	197
	Park National Corp.	0.6	17.9	195	22.1	132
88.	Valley National Bancorp	0.5	59.9	92	48.2	79
89.	Quaker Chemical Corp.	0.4	48.2	114	38.1	95
	Sysco Corp.	0.4	58.2	96	156.7	6
91.	M&T Bank Corp.	0.2	99.9	24	75.5	45
92.	WestAmerica Bancorporation	-0.2	84.2	44	44.8	85
93.	Family Dollar Stores, Inc.	-0.3	84.4	43	111.3	19
94.	Chemical Financial Corp.	-0.5	23.9	178	13.9	157
	National City Corp.	-0.5	98.2	27	4.4	189
96.	Atmos Energy Corp.	-0.6	64.8	82	-3.1	209
97.	Brown-Forman Corp.	-0.8	48.8	112	49.1	77
98.	Regions Financial Corp.	-0.9	81.3	54	-9.8	223
99.	Republic Bancorp Inc.	-1.1	89.6	33	39.5	92
100.	Lilly (Eli) & Co.	-1.4	-13.3	251	-1.5	201
101.	McCormick & Co., Inc.	-1.7	67.9	78	59.7	63
102.	Smith (A.O.) Corp.	-2.3	56.0	99	11.0	166
103.	Emerson Electric Co.	-2.4	-0.5	231	-10.6	225
	Hershey Foods Corp.	-2.4	51.4	105	-2.8	208
105.	Hilb, Rogal & Hamilton Co.	-2.5	160.9	7	339.1	1
106.	ALLTEL Corp.	-2.7	-24.6	263	22.6	130
	Trustmark Corp.	-2.7	43.2	128	18.7	141
108.	Washington R.E.I.T.	-2.9	85.0	41	97.5	25
109.	Associated Banc-Corp.	-3.0	83.0	49	19.8	140
	Vectren Corporation	-3.0	30.5	161	----	----
111.	Johnson Controls, Inc.	-3.1	36.8	142	51.1	75
112.	Compass Bancshares, Inc.	-3.4	99.0	26	21.5	137
	First Federal Capital Corp	-3.4	80.5	56	22.0	134
	Health Care Property Investors	-3.4	64.5	83	58.4	64
	Webster Financial Corp.	-3.4	85.9	39	21.8	136
116.	Marsh & McLennan Cos., Inc.	-3.5	2.6	223	77.9	41
117.	Wells Fargo & Co.	-3.6	25.0	174	33.9	104
118.	Becton, Dickinson & Co.	-3.7	42.9	130	7.3	178
	Bowl America Inc.	-3.7	82.4	51	75.7	44
120.	AmSouth Bancorporation	-3.8	63.3	86	-8.9	220
	Philadelphia Suburban Corp.	-3.8	58.5	95	91.1	30
122.	McGrath Rentcorp	-4.0	66.9	81	42.2	89
123.	General Electric Co.	-4.1	-40.7	273	12.3	163
124.	Mercantile Bankshares Corp.	-4.2	45.8	122	14.4	155
125.	Genuine Parts Co.	-4.4	35.6	145	5.9	184
126.	Old National Bancorp	-4.5	-16.4	256	-1.6	202
	PPG Industries, Inc.	-4.5	-2.4	235	-21.2	249
128.	Anheuser-Busch Cos., Inc.	-4.6	47.8	116	136.0	11
129.	EnergySouth, Inc.	-4.8	62.9	87	42.6	88
	Susquehanna Bancshares, Inc.	-4.8	83.5	46	13.9	157

Total Returns (cont.)

1-yr. Rank	Company Name	1-yr. Tot. Return %	3-yr. Tot. Return %	3-yr. Rank	5-yr. Tot. Return %	5-yr. Rank
131.	Valspar Corp.	-5.0	25.5	172	16.2	147
132.	Universal Corp.	-5.1	129.1	12	26.0	116
133.	Washington Federal, Inc.	-5.2	84.5	42	36.3	99
134.	Hormel Foods Corp.	-5.3	58.7	94	47.7	80
135.	BancorpSouth, Inc.	-5.7	43.2	128	4.8	187
	Marshall & Ilsley Corp.	-5.7	34.7	146	10.4	169
137.	Brady Corp.	-6.1	21.6	187	22.7	128
	Old Republic International Corp.	-6.1	127.2	13	12.9	160
139.	First Commonwealth Financial	-6.4	18.8	194	7.5	176
140.	Fannie Mae	-6.5	26.2	170	31.2	110
141.	Ambac Financial Group, Inc.	-6.6	86.0	38	59.8	62
142.	Bandag, Inc.	-6.7	61.8	90	-25.5	257
143.	Consolidated Edison, Inc.	-6.9	27.7	165	9.4	170
144.	United Bankshares, Inc.	-7.1	45.0	123	28.9	113
145.	First Financial Holdings, Inc.	-7.2	114.9	17	28.4	114
146.	McGraw-Hill Cos., Inc.	-7.3	16.6	199	63.6	56
	Middlesex Water Co.	-7.3	30.6	160	94.0	26
148.	First Midwest Bancorp	-7.4	48.8	112	12.4	162
149.	Bristol-Myers Squibb Co.	-7.5	-42.0	277	-40.8	271
	Sherwin-Williams Co.	-7.5	19.5	191	-13.4	233
151.	V.F. Corp.	-8.0	50.0	107	-14.7	238
152.	Protective Life Corp.	-8.1	27.5	167	-16.0	243
	Stepan Co.	-8.1	25.9	171	-10.0	224
	Wesco Financial Corp.	-8.1	25.4	173	-19.3	245
155.	Air Products & Chemicals	-8.8	46.3	119	8.9	171
	Rohm & Haas Co.	-8.8	-0.6	232	2.4	193
157.	Alberto-Culver Co.	-9.1	113.7	19	75.0	46
	Commerce Bancshares, Inc.	-9.1	49.3	110	6.6	182
159.	National Security Group, Inc.	-9.2	64.4	84	8.7	172
160.	Arrow International, Inc.	-9.5	27.6	166	33.9	104
	Badger Meter, Inc.	-9.5	-3.5	240	-11.2	226
162.	Mercury General Corp.	-9.6	74.5	62	-22.5	253
163.	Illinois Tool Works Inc.	-10.0	4.0	219	-3.7	211
164.	First Charter Corp.	-10.1	40.9	135	-20.4	247
	Freddie Mac	-10.1	30.7	158	32.6	107
166.	Exxon Mobil Corp.	-10.3	-3.4	238	7.3	178
167.	ConAgra Foods, Inc.	-10.4	24.2	177	-14.9	241
168.	Johnson & Johnson	-10.5	42.1	132	68.1	52
169.	Heinz (H.J.) Co.	-10.7	19.1	193	-20.7	248
170.	KeyCorp	-10.8	48.2	114	-26.0	259
	Linear Technology Corp.	-10.8	-38.9	272	74.5	48
172.	Connecticut Water Service, Inc.	-11.2	52.2	104	99.0	24
173.	Charter One Financial, Inc.	-11.6	79.3	57	23.9	123
	T. Rowe Price Group, Inc.	-11.6	-16.5	257	-13.6	234
175.	BB&T Corp.	-11.8	33.3	150	10.5	168

Total Returns (cont.)

1-yr. Rank	Company Name	1-yr. Tot. Return %	3-yr. Tot. Return %	3-yr. Rank	5-yr. Tot. Return %	5-yr. Rank
176.	West Pharmaceutical Services	-11.9	6.7	215	-12.1	228
177.	Morgan (J.P.) Chase & Co.	-12.1	-31.9	269	-25.9	258
178.	Midland Co.	-12.3	69.8	73	41.8	90
	Wilmington Trust Corp.	-12.3	34.1	148	7.5	176
180.	Bemis Co., Inc.	-12.5	32.7	151	15.3	151
181.	Mine Safety Appliances Co.	-13.2	86.1	37	74.9	47
182.	Corus Bankshares, Inc.	-13.4	79.2	58	3.3	191
183.	First Indiana Corp.	-13.5	21.9	186	-5.3	215
184.	SunTrust Banks, Inc.	-13.6	21.5	188	-21.3	250
185.	Nuveen Investments, Inc.	-13.9	96.3	28	128.5	12
186.	Pfizer Inc.	-14.1	-24.4	261	-14.7	238
187.	Pitney Bowes Inc.	-14.2	-1.8	234	-13.3	232
188.	Unizan Financial Corp.	-14.4	44.3	125	-0.6	199
189.	First Financial Bancorp.	-14.5	-3.4	238	-23.2	254
190.	Archer-Daniels-Midland Co.	-15.1	29.0	163	-32.5	265
	Black Hills Power, Inc.	-15.1	37.4	140	63.7	55
192.	Paychex, Inc.	-15.3	-8.1	245	103.4	22
193.	Avery Dennison Corp.	-15.5	-14.2	254	11.3	165
	PepsiCo, Inc.	-15.5	22.5	182	16.6	145
195.	Chittenden Corp.	-15.6	39.5	138	3.8	190
196.	Trustco Bank Corp NY	-15.7	31.6	155	35.9	100
197.	MBIA Inc.	-15.8	41.1	134	-3.9	212
198.	American International Group	-15.9	-20.2	260	25.3	119
	Banta Corp.	-15.9	68.8	77	8.4	173
200.	Progress Energy, Inc.	-16.0	30.1	162	22.0	134
201.	Franklin Resources, Inc.	-16.1	10.5	211	-32.8	266
202.	Commerce Bancorp, Inc.	-16.5	114.6	18	111.0	20
	Frisch's Restaurants, Inc.	-16.5	110.6	22	63.0	57
204.	Grainger (W.W.), Inc.	-16.6	11.5	207	-8.8	219
	Nordson Corp.	-16.6	20.2	190	18.4	143
206.	Otter Tail Corp.	-16.7	17.0	197	83.0	36
207.	American National Insurance	-17.1	72.0	70	-11.8	227
208.	Eaton Vance Corp.	-17.6	44.6	124	155.4	7
209.	Alfa Corp.	-17.8	54.1	101	63.0	57
	Beckman Coulter, Inc.	-17.8	23.2	181	46.9	82
	Jefferson-Pilot Corp.	-17.8	-3.1	237	14.2	156
212.	Walgreen Co.	-17.9	11.0	208	82.9	37
213.	Sara Lee Corp.	-18.6	20.9	189	-36.4	269
214.	MBNA Corp.	-18.8	10.6	210	33.1	106
215.	Transatlantic Holdings, Inc.	-18.9	24.9	176	36.5	98
216.	Pentair, Inc.	-19.0	7.2	214	-2.1	206
217.	Cincinnati Financial Corp.	-19.6	-2.7	236	-4.2	213
218.	Leggett & Platt, Inc.	-19.8	2.9	222	-12.6	230
219.	Fuller (H.B.) Co.	-19.9	34.5	147	-15.0	242
220.	Harleysville Group Inc.	-20.0	56.6	97	-1.6	202

Total Returns (cont.)

1-yr. Rank	Company Name	1-yr. Tot. Return %	3-yr. Tot. Return %	3-yr. Rank	5-yr. Tot. Return %	5-yr. Rank
221.	FleetBoston Financial Corp.	-21.4	-17.6	258	-28.2	263
222.	Dover Corp.	-21.5	-41.1	274	-22.4	251
	Hillenbrand Industries, Inc.	-21.5	73.7	65	-12.9	231
224.	Pier 1 Imports, Inc.	-21.6	69.2	74	12.7	161
	SBC Communications Inc.	-21.6	-41.9	276	-36.1	268
	SEI Investments Co.	-21.6	33.4	149	118.6	18
	TCF Financial Corp.	-21.6	83.1	48	38.5	93
228.	Kimberly-Clark Corp.	-21.9	-9.2	246	7.8	175
229.	Federal Signal Corp.	-22.0	-6.6	242	-5.2	214
	Sonoco Products Co.	-22.0	15.2	202	-30.5	264
231.	Vulcan Materials Co.	-22.2	-15.3	255	0.2	198
232.	Superior Industries Int'l, Inc.	-22.4	27.2	168	30.8	111
233.	Abbott Laboratories	-22.9	11.7	206	21.2	138
	Target Corp.	-22.9	2.4	224	58.4	64
235.	Masco Corp.	-23.1	0.7	225	-19.4	246
236.	Tennant Co.	-23.4	0.2	227	-13.9	236
237.	Gorman-Rupp Co.	-23.5	32.6	152	15.7	149
238.	Haverty Furniture Cos., Inc.	-24.5	30.7	158	37.2	96
239.	RPM International Inc.	-24.7	37.0	141	-13.7	235
240.	ChevronTexaco Corp.	-25.1	-19.3	259	-12.1	228
241.	FirstMerit Corp.	-25.2	39.3	139	-14.7	238
242.	National Commerce Financial	-25.6	32.3	153	0.7	196
243.	Bank of New York Co.	-25.7	-31.7	268	-2.0	205
244.	ABM Industries Inc.	-26.0	17.1	196	6.6	182
	Coca-Cola Co.	-26.0	-10.6	247	-43.2	274
246.	Synovus Financial Corp.	-26.1	11.8	205	-8.4	218
247.	Fifth Third Bancorp	-27.1	22.1	185	43.7	86
248.	NACCO Industries, Inc.	-27.3	23.3	179	-66.3	282
249.	Citizens Banking Corp.	-27.8	44.2	126	-22.4	251
250.	Comerica, Inc.	-28.2	12.6	204	-24.9	255
251.	Nucor Corp.	-28.9	-0.4	229	-27.0	261
	St. Paul Cos., Inc.	-28.9	4.1	218	-7.1	217
253.	Gallagher (Arthur J.) & Co.	-29.3	41.5	133	155.2	8
254.	Chubb Corp.	-29.4	-11.8	249	-26.1	260
255.	Myers Industries, Inc.	-29.5	14.2	203	-27.6	262
256.	Cintas Corp.	-30.3	-8.0	244	15.8	148
257.	State Street Corp.	-30.6	-25.7	265	2.3	194
258.	Lincoln National Corp.	-30.8	0.1	228	-17.5	244
259.	Teleflex Inc.	-31.1	16.1	200	-3.2	210
260.	Schering-Plough Corp.	-31.2	-52.1	281	-50.9	280
261.	Nicor Inc.	-32.7	0.7	225	-9.7	222
262.	Northern Trust Corp.	-32.8	-43.3	279	1.9	195
	Roper Industries, Inc.	-32.8	-0.4	229	3.3	191
264.	ServiceMaster Co.	-33.0	-26.6	266	-45.2	275
265.	Automatic Data Processing	-33.1	-35.9	271	4.7	188

Total Returns (cont.)

1-yr. Rank	Company Name	1-yr. Tot. Return %	3-yr. Tot. Return %	3-yr. Rank	5-yr. Tot. Return %	5-yr. Rank
266.	La-Z-Boy Inc.	-34.0	31.3	156	22.1	132
	Tootsie Roll Industries, Inc.	-34.0	7.9	213	-1.6	202
268.	Donnelley (R.R.) & Sons Co.	-34.6	5.1	216	-46.7	278
269.	General Dynamics Corp.	-35.1	11.0	208	57.2	67
270.	May Department Stores Co.	-35.5	-14.1	253	-39.9	270
271.	CLECO Corp.	-36.4	-1.5	233	15.0	152
272.	Unitrin, Inc.	-38.1	-5.9	241	-0.8	200
273.	GATX Corp.	-38.2	-41.2	275	-46.1	276
274.	Home Depot, Inc.	-38.9	-49.5	280	23.6	124
275.	McDonald's Corp.	-39.0	-53.8	282	-42.7	273
276.	Altria Group, Inc.	-40.7	62.0	89	5.6	186
277.	1st Source Corp.	-42.9	-25.5	264	-56.1	281
278.	Jack Henry & Associates, Inc.	-43.6	-32.8	270	55.2	71
	SuperValu Inc.	-43.6	-13.5	252	-14.1	237
280.	Energy West Inc.	-45.3	-28.0	267	-25.4	256
281.	Stanley Works	-46.9	-11.9	250	-46.4	277
282.	Telephone & Data Systems	-49.3	-56.9	283	-5.9	216
283.	TECO Energy, Inc.	-58.5	-42.3	278	-47.0	279
284.	El Paso Corp.	-80.2	-80.8	284	-76.9	283

Note: The five-year return for Vectren Corp. does not appear as sufficient pricing data was not available

About Total Return

Total return represents one of the best measures of how well an investor in any given stock has fared because it reflects both dividend payments and price appreciation. Mergent has calculated total return for each Dividend Achiever company on the basis that cash dividends of each stock were reinvested in that company's shares on the ex-dividend date of each dividend paid. Thus the preceding table demonstrates the effect of compounding as well as each stock's performance and the level of dividends paid. Figures have been adjusted for splits, stock dividends and spin-offs. In the case of a spin-off, shares in the spun-off company were assumed to be converted to cash and reinvested in the original company's stock.

How to read the rankings: On the preceding pages the Dividend Achiever companies are listed by one-year total return for the twelve months ended 4/30/03. For example, an investor who bought shares at the end of April, 2002 in Doral Financial Corp., and sold them at the end of April, 2003, would have realized a 74.4% gain on the original investment. Following each company's one-year total return is its three-year total return and ranking and five-year total return and ranking. The three-year total return is based on an investment made at the end of April, 2000, and the five-year total return on an investment made at the end of April, 1998. The three- and five-year total-return percentages represent cumulative totals. Thus an investment made in Doral Financial at the end of April, 2000, would have increased 430.7% if the stock were sold at the end of April, 2003. If an investor had bought shares in Doral Financial at the end of April, 1998, and sold them at the end of April, 2003, his investment would have grown by 274.6%.

Dividend Reinvestment Plan & Web Site Information

Company	Dividend Reinvestment Plan	Web Site
Abbott Laboratories	Yes	www.abbott.com
ABM Industries Inc.	No	www.abm.com
AFLAC Inc.	Yes	www.aflac.com
Air Products & Chemicals	Yes	www.airproducts.com
Alberto-Culver Co.	No	www.alberto.com
Alfa Corp.	Yes	www.alfains.com
ALLTEL Corp.	Yes	www.alltel.com
Altria Group, Inc.	Yes	www.altria.com
Ambac Financial Group, Inc.	No	www.ambac.com
American International Group	No	www.aig.com
American National Insurance	No	www.anico.com
American States Water Co.	Yes	www.aswater.com
AmSouth Bancorporation	Yes	www.amsouth.com
Anheuser-Busch Cos., Inc.	Yes	www.anheuser-busch.com
Applebee's International, Inc.	No	www.applebees.com
Archer-Daniels-Midland Co.	Yes	www.admworld.com
Arrow International, Inc.	No	www.arrowintl.com
Associated Banc-Corp.	Yes	www.associatedbank.com
Atmos Energy Corp.	Yes	www.atmosenergy.com
Automatic Data Processing	No	www.adp.com
Avery Dennison Corp.	Yes	www.averydennison.com
Avon Products, Inc.	Yes	www.avon.com
Badger Meter, Inc.	Yes	www.badgermeter.com
BancorpSouth, Inc.	Yes	www.bancorpsouth.com
Bandag, Inc.	Yes	www.bandag.com
Bank of America Corp.	Yes	www.bankofamerica.com
Bank of Hawaii Corp.	Yes	www.boh.com
Bank of New York Co. (The)	Yes	www.bankofny.com
Banta Corp.	Yes	www.banta.com
Bard (C.R.), Inc.	Yes	www.crbard.com
BB&T Corp.	Yes	www.bbandt.com
Beckman Coulter, Inc.	Yes	www.beckmancoulter.com
Becton, Dickinson & Co.	Yes	www.bd.com
Bemis Co., Inc.	Yes	www.bemis.com
Black Hills Power, Inc.	Yes	www.blackhillscorp.com
Bowl America Inc.	No	N/A

Dividend Reinvestment Plan & Web Site Information (cont.)

Company	Dividend Reinvestment Plan	Web Site
Brady Corp.	Yes	www.bradycorp.com
Briggs & Stratton Corp.	Yes	www.briggsandstratton.com
Bristol-Myers Squibb Co.	Yes	www.bms.com
Brown-Forman Corp.	Yes	www.brown-forman.com
California Water Service Co.	Yes	www.calwater.com
Carlisle Companies Inc.	Yes	www.carlisle.com
Cedar Fair, L.P.	Yes	www.cedarfair.com
CenturyTel, Inc.	Yes	www.centurytel.com
Charter One Financial, Inc.	Yes	www.charterone.com
Chemical Financial Corp.	Yes	www.chemicalbankmi.com
ChevronTexaco Corp.	Yes	www.chevrontexaco.com
Chittenden Corp.	Yes	www.chittendencorp.com
Chubb Corp.	Yes	www.chubb.com
Cincinnati Financial Corp.	Yes	www.cinfin.com
Cintas Corp.	No	www.cintas-corp.com
Citigroup Inc.	No	www.citigroup.com
Citizens Banking Corp.	Yes	www.cbclientsfirst.com
Clarcor Inc.	Yes	www.clarcor.com
CLECO Corp.	Yes	www.cleco.com
Clorox Co. (The)	Yes	www.clorox.com
Coca-Cola Co. (The)	Yes	www.coca-cola.com
Colgate-Palmolive Co.	Yes	www.colgate.com
Comerica, Inc.	Yes	www.comerica.com
Commerce Bancorp, Inc.	No	www.commerceonline.com
Commerce Bancshares, Inc.	Yes	www.commercebank.com
Commercial Net Lease Realty	Yes	www.cnlreit.com
Community Bank System, Inc.	Yes	www.communitybankna.com
Community First Bankshares, Inc.	Yes	www.communityfirst.com
Community Trust Bancorp, Inc.	Yes	www.ctbi.com
Compass Bancshares, Inc.	Yes	www.compassweb.com
ConAgra Foods, Inc.	Yes	www.conagra.com
Connecticut Water Service, Inc.	Yes	www.ctwater.com
Consolidated Edison, Inc.	Yes	www.conedison.com
Corus Bankshares, Inc.	No	www.corusbank.com
Cousins Properties Inc.	No	www.cousinsproperties.com
CVB Financial Corp.	No	www.cvbcorp.com

Dividend Reinvestment Plan & Web Site Information (cont.)

Company	Dividend Reinvestment Plan	Web Site
Diebold, Inc.	Yes	www.diebold.com
Donegal Group Inc.	Yes	www.donegalgroup.com
Donnelley (R.R.) & Sons Co.	Yes	www.rrdonnelley.com
Doral Financial Corp.	No	www.doralfinancial.com
Dover Corp.	Yes	www.dovercorporation.com
Eastgroup Properties, Inc.	Yes	www.eastgroup.net
Eaton Vance Corp.	No	www.eatonvance.com
Ecolab Inc.	Yes	www.ecolab.com
El Paso Corp.	Yes	www.elpaso.com
Emerson Electric Co.	Yes	www.gotoemerson.com
Energen Corp.	Yes	www.energen.com
Energy West Inc.	Yes	www.ewst.com
EnergySouth, Inc.	Yes	www.energysouth.com
Exxon Mobil Corp.	Yes	www.exxonmobil.com
F.N.B. Corp.	Yes	www.fnbcorporation.com
Family Dollar Stores, Inc.	No	www.familydollar.com
Fannie Mae	Yes	www.fanniemae.com
Federal Realty Investment Trust	Yes	www.federalrealty.com
Federal Signal Corp.	Yes	www.federalsignal.com
Fidelity National Financial, Inc.	No	www.fnf.com
Fifth Third Bancorp	Yes	www.53.com
First Charter Corp.	Yes	www.firstcharter.com
First Commonwealth Financial	Yes	www.fcfbank.com
First Federal Capital Corp	Yes	www.firstfed.com
First Financial Bancorp.	Yes	www.ffbc-oh.com
First Financial Corp.	No	www.first-online.com
First Financial Holdings, Inc.	Yes	www.firstfinancialholdings.com
First Indiana Corp.	Yes	www.firstindiana.com
First Midwest Bancorp, Inc.	Yes	www.firstmidwest.com
1st Source Corp.	No	www.1stsource.com
First Virginia Banks, Inc.	Yes	www.firstvirginia.com
FirstMerit Corp.	Yes	www.firstmerit.com
FleetBoston Financial Corp.	Yes	www.fleet.com
Florida Public Utilities Co.	Yes	www.fpuc.com
Franklin Resources, Inc.	Yes	www.franklintempleton.com
Freddie Mac	Yes	www.freddiemac.com

Dividend Reinvestment Plan & Web Site Information (cont.)

Company	Dividend Reinvestment Plan	Web Site
Frisch's Restaurants, Inc.	No	www.frischs.com
Fuller (H.B.) Co.	Yes	www.hbfuller.com
Fulton Financial Corp.	Yes	www.fult.com
Gallagher (Arthur J.) & Co.	No	www.ajg.com
Gannett Co., Inc.	Yes	www.gannett.com
GATX Corp.	Yes	www.gatx.com
General Dynamics Corp.	No	www.generaldynamics.com
General Electric Co.	Yes	www.ge.com
Genuine Parts Co.	Yes	www.genpt.com
Glacier Bancorp, Inc.	Yes	www.glacierbancorp.com
Golden West Financial Corp.	No	www.worldsavings.com
Gorman-Rupp Co. (The)	Yes	www.gormanrupp.com
Grainger, (W.W.) Inc.	No	www.grainger.com
Harleysville Group Inc.	Yes	www.harleysvillegroup.com
Harleysville National Corp.	Yes	www.hncbank.com
Haverty Furniture Cos., Inc.	No	www.havertys.com
Health Care Property Investors	Yes	www.hcpi.com
Heinz (H.J.) Co.	Yes	www.heinz.com
Hershey Foods Corp.	Yes	www.hersheys.com
Hilb, Rogal & Hamilton Co.	No	www.hrh.com
Hillenbrand Industries, Inc.	Yes	www.hillenbrand.com
Home Depot, Inc. (The)	Yes	www.homedepot.com
HON INDUSTRIES Inc.	No	www. honi.com
Hormel Foods Corp.	Yes	www.hormel.com
Hudson United Bancorp	Yes	www.hudsonunitedbank.com
Illinois Tool Works Inc.	Yes	www.itw.com
Irwin Financial Corp.	Yes	www.irwinfinancial.com
Jack Henry & Associates, Inc.	Yes	www.jackhenry.com
Jefferson-Pilot Corp.	Yes	www.jpfinancial.com
Johnson & Johnson	Yes	www.jnj.com
Johnson Controls, Inc.	Yes	www.johnsoncontrols.com
KeyCorp	Yes	www.key.com
Kimberly-Clark Corp.	Yes	www.kimberly-clark.com
Kimco Realty Corp.	Yes	www.kimcorealty.com
Lancaster Colony Corp.	Yes	www.lancastercolony.com
La-Z-Boy Inc.	Yes	www.la-z-boy.com

Dividend Reinvestment Plan & Web Site Information (cont.)

Company	Dividend Reinvestment Plan	Web Site
Legg Mason, Inc.	No	www.leggmason.com
Leggett & Platt, Inc.	No	www.leggett.com
Lilly (Eli) & Co.	Yes	www.lilly.com
Lincoln National Corp.	Yes	www.lfg.com
Linear Technology Corp.	No	www.linear.com
Lowe's Cos., Inc.	Yes	www.lowes.com
M&T Bank Corp.	Yes	www.mandtbank.com
Marsh & McLennan Cos., Inc.	Yes	www.mmc.com
Marshall & Ilsley Corp.	Yes	www.micorp.com
Masco Corp.	Yes	www.masco.com
May Department Stores (The)	Yes	www.maycompany.com
MBIA Inc.	No	www.mbia.com
MBNA Corp.	No	www.mbna.com
McCormick & Co., Inc.	Yes	www.mccormick.com
McDonald's Corp.	Yes	www.mcdonalds.com
McGrath Rentcorp	No	www.mgrc.com
McGraw-Hill Cos., Inc. (The)	Yes	www.mcgraw-hill.com
MDU Resources Group, Inc.	Yes	www.mdu.com
Medtronic, Inc.	Yes	www.medtronic.com
Mercantile Bankshares Corp.	Yes	www.mrbk.com
Merck & Co., Inc.	Yes	www.merck.com
Mercury General Corp.	Yes	www.mercuryinsurance.com
MGE Energy, Inc.	Yes	www.mge.com
Middlesex Water Co.	Yes	www.middlesexwater.com
Midland Co. (The)	Yes	www.midlandcompany.com
Mine Safety Appliances Co.	Yes	www.msanet.com
Morgan (J.P.) Chase & Co.	Yes	www.jpmorganchase.com
Myers Industries, Inc.	Yes	www.myersind.com
NACCO Industries, Inc.	No	www.nacco.com
National City Corp.	Yes	www.nationalcity.com
National Commerce Financial	Yes	www.ncbccorp.com
National Fuel Gas Co.	Yes	www.natfuel.com
National Penn Bancshares, Inc.	Yes	www.nationalpennbancshares.com
National Security Group (The)	No	www.nationalsecuritygroup.com
NICOR Inc.	Yes	www.nicorinc.com
Nordson Corp.	Yes	www.nordson.com

Dividend Reinvestment Plan & Web Site Information (cont.)

Company	Dividend Reinvestment Plan	Web Site
Northern Trust Corp.	No	www.northerntrust.com
Nucor Corp.	Yes	www.nucor.com
Nuveen Investments, Inc.	No	www.nuveen.com
Old National Bancorp	Yes	www.oldnational.com
Old Republic International Corp.	Yes	www.oldrepublic.com
Otter Tail Corp.	Yes	www.ottertail.com
Pacific Capital Bancorp	No	www.pcbancorp.com
Park National Corp.	Yes	www.parknationalcorp.com
Paychex, Inc.	Yes	www.paychex.com
Pentair, Inc.	Yes	www.pentair.com
Peoples Energy Corp.	Yes	www.pecorp.com
PepsiCo, Inc.	Yes	www.pepsico.com
Pfizer Inc.	Yes	www.pfizer.com
Philadelphia Suburban Corp.	Yes	www.suburbanwater.com
Piedmont Natural Gas Co., Inc.	Yes	www.piedmontng.com
Pier 1 Imports, Inc.	Yes	www.pier1.com
Pitney Bowes Inc.	Yes	www.pb.com
Popular, Inc.	Yes	www.popularinc.com
PPG Industries, Inc.	Yes	www.ppg.com
Praxair, Inc.	Yes	www.praxair.com
Procter & Gamble Co. (The)	Yes	www.pg.com
Progress Energy, Inc.	Yes	www.progress-energy.com
Progressive Corp. (The)	No	www.progressive.com
Protective Life Corp.	Yes	www.protective.com
Quaker Chemical Corp.	Yes	www.quakerchem.com
Questar Corp.	Yes	www.questar.com
Raven Industries, Inc.	Yes	www.ravenind.com
Regions Financial Corp.	Yes	www.regions.com
Republic Bancorp Inc.	Yes	www.republicbancorp.com
RLI Corp.	Yes	www.rlicorp.com
Rohm & Haas Co.	Yes	www.rohmhaas.com
Roper Industries, Inc.	No	www.roperind.com
Rouse Company (The)	Yes	www.therousecompany.com
RPM International Inc.	Yes	www.rpminc.com
S&T Bancorp, Inc.	Yes	www.stbank.com
Sara Lee Corp.	Yes	www.saralee.com

Dividend Reinvestment Plan & Web Site Information (cont.)

Company	Dividend Reinvestment Plan	Web Site
SBC Communications Inc.	Yes	www.sbc.com
Schering-Plough Corp.	Yes	www.schering-plough.com
SEI Investments Co.	No	www.seic.com
ServiceMaster Co. (The)	Yes	www.servicemaster.com
Sherwin-Williams Co. (The)	Yes	www.sherwin.com
Sigma-Aldrich Corp.	No	www.sigma-aldrich.com
SJW Corp.	No	www.sjwater.com
SLM Corporation	Yes	www.salliemae.com
Smith (A.O.) Corp.	Yes	www.aosmith.com
Sonoco Products Co.	Yes	www.sonoco.com
SouthTrust Corp.	Yes	www.southtrust.com
St. Paul Cos., Inc. (The)	Yes	www.stpaul.com
Stanley Works (The)	Yes	www.stanleyworks.com
State Auto Financial Corp.	Yes	www.stauto.com
State Street Corp.	Yes	www.statestreet.com
Stepan Co.	No	www.stephan.com
Sterling Financial Corp.	Yes	www.sterlingfi.com
Stryker Corp.	No	www.strykercorp.com
SunTrust Banks, Inc.	Yes	www.suntrust.com
Superior Industries Int'l, Inc.	Yes	www.supind.com
SuperValu Inc.	Yes	www.supervalu.com
Susquehanna Bancshares, Inc.	Yes	www.susqbanc.com
Synovus Financial Corp.	Yes	www.synovus.com
Sysco Corp.	Yes	www.sysco.com
T. Rowe Price Group, Inc.	Yes	www.troweprice.com
Target Corp.	Yes	www.target.com
TCF Financial Corp.	Yes	www.tcfbank.com
TECO Energy, Inc.	Yes	www.tecoenergy.com
Teleflex Inc.	Yes	www.teleflex.com
Telephone & Data Systems	Yes	www.teldta.com
Tennant Co.	Yes	www.tennantco.com
TEPPCO Partners, L.P.	No	www.teppco.com
3M Company	Yes	www.3m.com
Tootsie Roll Industries, Inc.	No	www.tootsie.com
Transatlantic Holdings, Inc.	No	www.transre.com
Trustco Bank Corp NY	Yes	www.trustcobank.com

Dividend Reinvestment Plan & Web Site Information (cont.)

Company	Dividend Reinvestment Plan	Web Site
Trustmark Corp.	Yes	www.trustmark.com
UGI Corp.	Yes	www.ugicorp.com
United Bankshares, Inc.	Yes	www.ubsi-wv.com
United Dominion Realty Trust	Yes	www.udrt.com
United Mobile Homes, Inc.	Yes	www.umh.com
Unitrin, Inc.	No	www.unitrin.com
Universal Corp.	Yes	www.universalcorp.com
Universal Health Realty Inc. Trust	Yes	www.uhrit.com
Unizan Financial Corp.	Yes	www.unbcorp.com
Valley National Bancorp	Yes	www.valleynationalbank.com
Valspar Corp. (The)	Yes	www.valspar.com
Vectren Corporation	Yes	www.vectren.com
V.F. Corp.	Yes	www.vfc.com
Virco Manufacturing Corp.	No	www.virco.com
Vulcan Materials Co.	Yes	www.vulcanmaterials.com
Walgreen Co.	Yes	www.walgreens.com
Wal-Mart Stores, Inc.	Yes	www.wal-mart.com
Washington Federal, Inc.	No	www.washingtonfederal.com
Washington Mutual, Inc.	Yes	www.wamu.com
Washington R.E.I.T.	Yes	www.writ.com
Webster Financial Corp.	Yes	www.websterbank.com
Weingarten Realty Investors	Yes	www.weingarten.com
Wells Fargo & Co.	Yes	www.wellsfargo.com
WesBanco, Inc.	Yes	www.wesbanco.com
Wesco Financial Corp.	No	N/A
West Pharmaceutical Services	Yes	www.westpharma.com
WestAmerica Bancorporation	Yes	www.westamerica.com
Weyco Group, Inc.	No	www.weycogroup.com
WGL Holdings, Inc.	Yes	www.washgas.com
Wilmington Trust Corp.	Yes	www.wilmingtontrust.com
WPS Resources Corp.	Yes	www.wpsr.com
Wrigley (Wm.) Jr. Co.	Yes	www.wrigley.com

AMUSEMENTS
Bowl America Inc.

APPAREL
* V.F. Corp.

AUTOMOBILE PARTS
* Clarcor Inc.
* Genuine Parts Co.
* Myers Industries, Inc.
* Superior Industries International, Inc.

BANKS - MAJOR
* Bank of America Corp.
* Bank of New York Co., Inc. (The)
* FleetBoston Financial Corp.
  MBNA Corp.
* Morgan (J.P.) Chase & Co.

BANKS - MID-ATLANTIC
* Community Trust Bancorp, Inc.
* First Commonwealth Financial Corp.
* First Virginia Banks, Inc.
* F.N.B. Corp.
* Fulton Financial Corp.
* Marshall & Ilsley Corp.
* Mercantile Bankshares Corp.
* Susquehanna Bancshares, Inc.
* WesBanco, Inc.

BANKS - MIDWEST
* Associated Banc-Corp.
* Charter One Financial, Inc.
* Citizens Banking Corp.
* Comerica Inc.
* Commerce Bancshares, Inc.
* Community First Bankshares, Inc.
  Corus Bankshares, Inc.
* Fifth Third Bancorp
* First Financial Bancorp.
  First Financial Corp.
* First Midwest Bancorp., Inc.
  1st Source Corp.
* FirstMerit Corp.
* Irwin Financial Corp.
* KeyCorp
* National City Corp.
  Northern Trust Corp.
* Old National Bancorp
* Park National Corp.
* Republic Bancorp Inc.
* TCF Financial Corp.
* United Bankshares, Inc.
* Unizan Financial Corp.
* Wells Fargo & Co.

BANKS - NORTHEAST
* Chemical Financial Corp.
* Chittenden Corp.
  Commerce Bancorp, Inc.
* Community Bank System, Inc.
* Harleysville National Corp.
* Hudson United Bancorp
* M&T Bank Corp.

* National Penn Bancshares, Inc.
* S&T Bancorp, Inc.
* State Street Corp.
* Sterling Financial Corp.
* Trustco Bank Corp NY
* Valley National Bancorp
* Webster Financial Corp.
* Wilmington Trust Corporation

BANKS - PUERTO RICO
Doral Financial Corp.
* Popular, Inc.

BANKS - SOUTH
* AmSouth Bancorporation
* BancorpSouth, Inc.
* BB&T Corp.
* Compass Bancshares, Inc.
* First Charter Corp.
* National Commerce Financial Corp.
* Regions Financial Corp.
* SouthTrust Corp.
* SunTrust Banks, Inc.
* Synovus Financial Corp.
* Trustmark Corp.

BANKS - WEST
CVB Financial Corp.
* Bank of Hawaii Corp.
* Glacier Bancorp, Inc.
  Pacific Capital Bancorp
* WestAmerica Bancorporation

BREWING
* Anheuser-Busch Companies, Inc.

BUILDING MATERIALS & EQUIPMENT
* Vulcan Materials Co.

CANDY & GUM
* Hershey Foods Corporation
  Tootsie Roll Industries, Inc.
* Wrigley (Wm.) Jr. Co.

CHEMICALS
* Air Products & Chemicals, Inc.
* Brady Corp.
* Fuller (H.B.) Company
* PPG Industries, Inc.
* Praxair, Inc.
* Quaker Chemical Corp.
* Rohm & Haas Co.
  Sigma-Aldrich Corporation
  Stepan Co.

COMPUTERS - SERVICES
Automatic Data Processing, Inc.
* Jack Henry & Associates, Inc.

CONGLOMERATES
* Carlisle Companies Inc.
* Hillenbrand Industries, Inc.
* 3M Company

COSMETICS & TOILETRIES
Alberto-Culver Co.
* Avon Products, Inc.

DEFENSE SYSTEMS & EQUIPMENT
General Dynamics Corp.

DISTILLING
* Brown-Forman Corp.

DRUGS
* Bristol-Myers Squibb Co.
* Lilly (Eli) & Co.
* Merck & Co., Inc.
* Pfizer Inc.
* Schering-Plough Corp.

ELECTRIC POWER - CENTRAL & SOUTHEASTERN REGIONS
* CLECO Corp.
* MGE Energy, Inc.
* Progress Energy, Inc.
* TECO Energy, Inc.
* WPS Resources Corp.

ELECTRIC POWER - NORTHEASTERN REGION
* Consolidated Edison, Inc.

ELECTRIC POWER - WESTERN REGION
* Black Hills Power, Inc.
* Otter Tail Corp.

ELECTRICAL EQUIPMENT
* Emerson Electric Co.
* General Electric Co.
* Raven Industries, Inc.
* Smith (A.O.) Corp.

ELECTRONIC COMPONENTS
Linear Technology Corp.

ENGINEERING & CONSTRUCTION
* Masco Corp.

EQUIPMENT LEASING
McGrath Rentcorp

FINANCE
* Fannie Mae
* Freddie Mac
* SLM Corporation

FINANCIAL SERVICES
Eaton Vance Corp.
* T. Rowe Price Group, Inc.
Citigroup Inc.

FOOD - GRAIN & AGRICULTURE
* Archer-Daniels-Midland Co.
* ConAgra Foods, Inc.

FOOD PROCESSING
* Heinz (H.J.) Co.
* Hormel Foods Corp.
* Lancaster Colony Corp.
* McCormick & Co., Inc.
* Sara Lee Corp.

FOOD WHOLESALERS
* SuperValu Inc.
* Sysco Corp.

FURNITURE & FIXTURES
* La-Z-Boy Inc.
Leggett & Platt, Inc.
Virco Manufacturing Corp.

HARDWARE & TOOLS
* Illinois Tool Works Inc.
* Stanley Works (The)

INSURANCE - BROKERAGE
Gallagher (Arthur J.) & Co.
Hilb, Rogal & Hamilton Co.
* Marsh & McLennan Companies, Inc.

INSURANCE - COMBINED
American International Group, Inc.
* Cincinnati Financial Corp.
* Jefferson-Pilot Corp.
* Lincoln National Corp.
* Midland Co. (The)
* Old Republic International Corp.
Progressive Corp. (The)

INSURANCE - LIFE
* AFLAC Inc.
American National Insurance Co.
Protective Life Corp.

INSURANCE - PROPERTY & CASUALTY
* Alfa Corp.
Ambac Financial Group, Inc.
* Chubb Corp.
* Donegal Group Inc.
* Harleysville Group Inc.
* Mercury General Corp.
National Security Group, Inc. (The)
* RLI Corp.
* St. Paul Cos., Inc. (The)
* State Auto Financial Corp.
Transatlantic Holdings, Inc.
Unitrin, Inc.

INSURANCE - SPECIALTY
Fidelity National Financial, Inc.
MBIA Inc.

MACHINERY & EQUIPMENT
* Briggs & Stratton Corp.
* Dover Corp.
* Federal Signal Corp.
* Gorman-Rupp Co. (The)
NACCO Industries, Inc.
* Nordson Corp.
* Tennant Co.

MAINTENANCE & SECURITY SERVICES
ABM Industries Inc.

MEASURING & CONTROL INSTRUMENTS
* Badger Meter, Inc.
* Johnson Controls, Inc.
Roper Industries, Inc.
* Teleflex Inc.

MEDICAL & DENTAL EQUIPMENT & SUPPLIES
* Abbott Laboratories
  Arrow International, Inc.
* Bard (C.R.), Inc.
* Beckman Coulter, Inc.
* Becton, Dickinson & Co.
* Johnson & Johnson
* Medtronic, Inc.
* Mine Safety Appliances Co.
  Stryker Corp.

NATURAL GAS
* El Paso Corp.
* MDU Resources Group, Inc.
* National Fuel Gas Co.
* Peoples Energy Corp.
* Vectren Corp.

NATURAL GAS - DISTRIBUTORS
* Atmos Energy Corp.
* Energen Corp.
* Energy West Inc.
* EnergySouth, Inc.
* Florida Public Utilities Co.
* Nicor Inc.
* Piedmont Natural Gas Co., Inc.
* Questar Corp.
* UGI Corp.
* WGL Holdings, Inc.

NEWSPAPERS
* Gannett Co., Inc.

OFFICE EQUIPMENT & SUPPLIES
* Avery Dennison Corp.
* Diebold, Inc.
  HON INDUSTRIES Inc.
* Pitney Bowes Inc.

OIL
* ChevronTexaco Corp.
* Exxon Mobil Corp.

OIL SERVICES & EQUIPMENT
  TEPPCO Partners, L.P.

PAINTS & RELATED PRODUCTS
* RPM International Inc.
* Sherwin-Williams Co. (The)
* Valspar Corp. (The)

PAPER
* Bemis Co., Inc.
* Kimberly-Clark Corp.
* Pentair, Inc.
* Sonoco Products Co.

PLASTICS & PLASTIC PRODUCTS
* West Pharmaceutical Services, Inc.

PRINTING & ENGRAVING
* Banta Corp.
* Donnelley (R. R.) & Sons Co.

PUBLISHING
* McGraw-Hill Companies, Inc. (The)

RAILROAD EQUIPMENT
* GATX Corp.

REAL ESTATE INVESTMENT TRUSTS
* Commercial Net Lease Realty, Inc.
  Cousins Properties Inc.
* Eastgroup Properties, Inc.
* Federal Realty Investment Trust
* Health Care Property Investors, Inc.
* Kimco Realty Corp.
* Rouse Company (The)
* United Dominion Realty Trust, Inc.
* United Mobile Homes, Inc.
* Universal Health Realty Income Trust
* Washington Real Estate Investment Trust
* Weingarten Realty Investors

RECREATION
* Cedar Fair, L.P.

RESTAURANTS
  Applebee's International, Inc.
  Frisch's Restaurants, Inc.
* McDonald's Corp.

RETAIL DEPARTMENT STORES
* May Department Stores Co. (The)
* Target Corp.

RETAIL - DISCOUNT & VARIETY STORES
  Family Dollar Stores, Inc.
* Wal-Mart Stores, Inc.

RETAIL - DRUG STORES
* Walgreen Co.

RETAIL - SPECIALTY STORES
  Haverty Furniture Companies, Inc.
* Home Depot, Inc. (The)
* Lowe's Companies, Inc.
* Pier 1 Imports, Inc.

SAVINGS & LOAN
* First Federal Capital Corp
* First Financial Holdings, Inc.
* First Indiana Corp.
  Golden West Financial Corp.
  Washington Federal, Inc.
* Washington Mutual, Inc.
  Wesco Financial Corp.

SECURITIES BROKERAGE
* Franklin Resources, Inc.
  Legg Mason, Inc.
  Nuveen Investments, Inc.
  SEI Investments Co.

SERVICES
Cintas Corporation
* Paychex, Inc.
* ServiceMaster Co. (The)

SHOE MANUFACTURING
Weyco Group, Inc.

SOAPS & CLEANERS
* Clorox Co. (The)
* Colgate-Palmolive Co.
* Ecolab Inc.
* Procter & Gamble Co. (The)

SOFT DRINKS
* Coca-Cola Co. (The)
* PepsiCo, Inc.

STEEL
* Nucor Corp.

TELECOMMUNICATIONS
* ALLTEL Corp.
* CenturyTel, Inc.
* SBC Communications Inc.
* Telephone & Data Systems, Inc.

TIRES & RUBBER GOODS
* Bandag, Inc.

TOBACCO
* Altria Group, Inc.
* Universal Corp.

WATER COMPANIES
* American States Water Co.
* California Water Service Co.
* Connecticut Water Service, Inc.
* Middlesex Water Company
* Philadelphia Suburban Corp.
SJW Corp.

WHOLESALERS - DISTRIBUTORS - JOBBERS
Grainger (W.W.), Inc.

*Designates companies offering dividend reinvestment plans

MERGENT'S *Dividend Achievers* is a compact, easy-to-use reference that provides basic financial and business information on 284 companies that have increased their cash dividends annually over at least the past ten calendar years. The presentation of background information plus current and historical data provides the answers to three basic questions for each company:

1. What does the company do?
   (See G.)
2. How has it done in the past?
   (See B, D, E, I, J.)
3. How is it doing now?
   (See D, E, F, H.)

The following information is highlighted:

A. CAPSULE STOCK INFORMATION – This section shows the stock symbol, plus the approximate yield afforded by the indicated dividend, based on a recent price, and the price earnings ratio calculated on earnings from the most recent four quarters.

B. LONG-TERM PRICE CHART – This chart illustrates the pattern of monthly stock price movements, fully adjusted for stock dividends and splits. The chart points out the degree of volatility in the price movement of the company's stock and reveals its long-term trend. It indicates areas of price support and resistance, plus other technical points to be considered by the investor. The bars at the base of the long-term price chart indicate the monthly trading volume.

C. PRICE SCORES – Below each company's price/volume chart are its *Mergent's Price Scores*. These are basic measures of the stock's performance. Each stock is measured against the New York Stock Exchange Composite Index.

A score of 100 indicates that the stock did as well as the New York Stock Exchange Composite Index during the time period. A score of less than 100 means that the stock did not do as well; a score of more than 100 means that the stock outperformed the NYSE Com-

posite Index. All stock prices are adjusted for splits and stock dividends. The time periods measured for each company conclude with the date of the recent price shown in the top-left corner of each company's profile.

The **SEVEN-YEAR PRICE SCORE** mirrors the common stock's price growth over the previous seven years. The higher the price score, the better the relative performance. It is based on the ratio of the latest twelve-month average price to the current seven year average. This ratio is then indexed against the same ratio for the market as a whole (the New York Stock Exchange Composite Index), which is taken as 100.

The **TWELVE-MONTH PRICE SCORE** is a similar measurement but for a shorter period of time. It is based on the ratio of the latest two-month average price to the current twelve-month average. As was done for the Seven-Year Price Score, this ratio is also indexed to the same ratio for the market as a whole.

In both cases, all prices are adjusted for all stock dividends and splits.

D. INTERIM EARNINGS (Per Share) – Figures are reported before extraordinary items, discontinued operations and the cumulative effects of accounting changes (unless otherwise noted). Each figure is for the quarterly period indicated, unless otherwise noted. Prior to 12/15/97, primary earnings per share are shown. After that date, diluted earnings per share are displayed, as described in Financial Accounting Standards Board Statement 128. Figures are adjusted for all stock dividends and splits. See 'Earnings Per Share' below.

E. INTERIM DIVIDENDS (Per Share) – The cash dividends are the actual dollar amounts declared by the company. No adjustments have been made for stock dividends and splits. **Ex-Dividend Date**: a stockholder must purchase the stock prior to this date in order to be entitled to the dividend. The **Record Date** indicates the date on which the

ILLUSTRATIVE INC.

YIELD 0.2%
P/E RATIO 18.1

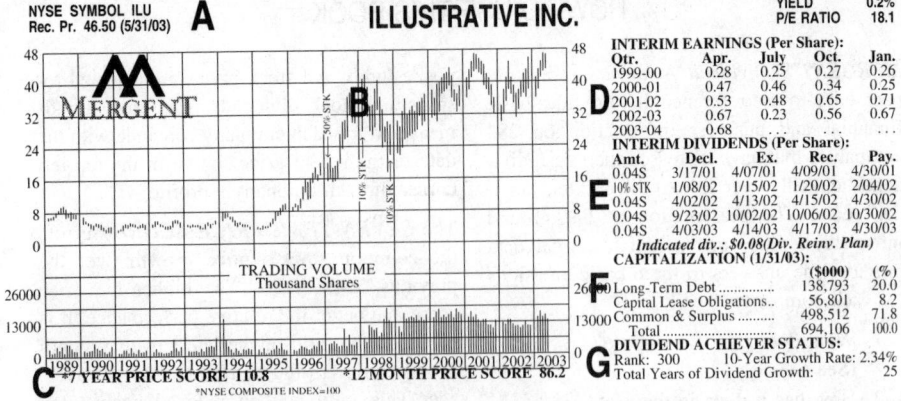

C *7 YEAR PRICE SCORE 110.8*   *12 MONTH PRICE SCORE 86.2*

103.2   *NYSE COMPOSITE INDEX=100*

INTERIM EARNINGS (Per Share):

Qtr.	Apr.	July	Oct.	Jan.
1999-00	0.28	0.25	0.27	0.26
2000-01	0.47	0.46	0.34	0.25
2001-02	0.53	0.48	0.65	0.71
2002-03	0.67	0.23	0.56	0.67
2003-04	0.68	...	...	...

INTERIM DIVIDENDS (Per Share):

Amt.	Decl.	Ex.	Rec.	Pay.
0.04$	3/17/01	4/07/01	4/09/01	4/30/01
10% STK	1/08/02	1/15/02	1/20/02	2/04/02
0.04$	4/02/02	4/13/02	4/15/02	4/30/02
0.04$	9/23/02	10/02/02	10/06/02	10/30/02
0.04$	4/03/03	4/14/03	4/17/03	4/30/03

Indicated div.: $0.08(Div. Reinv. Plan)

CAPITALIZATION (1/31/03):

	($000)	(%)
Long-Term Debt	138,793	20.0
Capital Lease Obligations..	56,801	8.2
Common & Surplus	498,512	71.8
Total	694,106	100.0

DIVIDEND ACHIEVER STATUS:

Rank: 300   10-Year Growth Rate: 2.34%
Total Years of Dividend Growth: 25

RECENT DEVELOPMENTS: For the quarter ended 4/30/03, net income before an extraordinary gain improved to $13.8 million compared with net income of $10.3 million the year before. Total revenues increased to $288.0 million from $157.1 million the year before. Increased revenues are contributing to improving margins at Bill's Burgers, Salads a Go Go, and Pizza Galore chains. Revenues from Company-owned restaurants climbed to $205.0 million from $137.8 million.

PROSPECTS: Growing revenues per restaurant across all the Company's chains bode well for future results. The Company is planning to open an additional 60 Bill's Burgers restaurants in 2003, and another 90 in 2004. Meanwhile, 80 Pizza Galore and 40 Salad a Go Go restaurants are planned to open in the Midwest in the second half of 2003. The Company is predicting earnings per share of $1.10 to $1.20 for the current fiscal year.

H BUSINESS

ILLUSTRATIVE INC., through its subsidiaries and franchisees, owns and/or operates 1,576 Bill's Burgers restaurants, featuring the Company's patented vegetarian Bill Burgers. The restaurants are located in all 50 states. In addition, the Company owns 582 Salad a Go Go restaurants and take-out facilities in 14 eastern and southeastern states. The Company also owns and operates 312 Pizza Galore restaurants and 12 Seafood Symphony restaurants in North and South Carolina.

REVENUES

(01/31/03)	($000)	(%)
Co.-operated restaurants	1,022,453	88.9
Franchised & licensed	127,206	11.1
Total	1,149,659	100.0

J ANNUAL FINANCIAL DATA

	1/31/03	1/31/02	1/31/01	1/31/00	1/31/99	1/25/98	1/27/97
Earnings Per Share	2.37	1.52	1.06	0.66	0.54	0.51	0.48
Cash Flow Per Share	1.76	1.34	0.95	0.71	0.81	0.68	1.20
Tang. Book Val. Per Share	8.86	5.34	3.01	2.67	2.72	2.58	2.76
Dividends Per Share	0.07	0.06	0.05	0.04	0.03	0.02	0.01
Dividend Payout %	3.0	3.9	4.7	6.1	5.6	3.9	2.1
INCOME STATEMENT (IN MILLIONS):							
Total Revenues	1,149.7	614.1	465.4	443.7	460.4	502.6	533.6
Costs & Expenses	1,017.1	545.0	418.3	412.4	427.0	484.7	487.0
Depreciation & Amort.	46.4	27.1	21.4	22.8	22.8	25.2	26.6
Operating Income	86.2	42.0	25.7	8.6	10.5	d7.3	20.0
Net Interest Inc./(Exp.)	d16.9	d9.9	d10.0	d9.2	d10.4	d13.6	d16.7
Income Before Income Taxes	76.6	36.7	18.0	2.4	6.3	d7.3	18.9
Income Taxes	29.9	14.4	7.0	1.1	1.8	cr4.2	5.8
Net Income	46.8	22.3	11.0	1.3	4.4	d3.1	13.0
Cash Flow	93.2	49.4	32.3	24.0	27.3	22.1	39.6
Average Shs. Outstg. (000)	52,934	36,801	33,902	33,971	33,699	32,732	33,018
BALANCE SHEET (IN MILLIONS):							
Cash & Cash Equivalents	30.4	39.8	25.9	18.2	26.1	44.4	36.7
Total Current Assets	92.2	72.9	56.8	56.8	69.4	90.6	83.8
Net Property	674.6	242.9	155.7	163.8	146.8	150.6	175.0
Total Assets	957.4	401.2	246.8	244.3	242.1	268.9	292.6
Total Current Liabilities	176.5	83.9	61.3	71.6	66.6	91.4	92.3
Long-Term Obligations	195.6	81.9	70.6	69.9	63.3	80.3	102.1
Net Stockholders' Equity	498.5	214.8	101.2	88.5	92.1	84.7	89.7
Net Working Capital	d84.3	d11.0	d4.5	d14.7	2.9	d0.9	d8.5
Year-end Shs. Outstg. (000)	56,293	40,195	33,632	33,133	33,899	32,835	32,521
STATISTICAL RECORD:							
Operating Profit Margin %	7.5	6.8	5.5	1.9	2.3	...	3.8
Net Profit Margin %	4.1	3.6	2.4	0.3	1.0	...	2.4
Return on Equity %	9.4	10.4	10.8	1.4	4.8	...	14.5
Return on Assets %	4.9	5.6	4.4	0.5	1.8	...	4.5
Debt/Total Assets %	20.4	20.4	28.6	28.6	26.1	29.8	34.9
Price Range	47.50-32	42.50-31	37.13-21.75	42-17.50	37.50-15.19	19.97-7.99	9.25-4.50
P/E Ratio	20-13.5	28-20.4	35-20.5	63.6-26.5	69.4-28.1	...	19.3-9.4
Average Yield %	0.2	0.2	0.2	0.1	0.1	0.2	0.2

Statistics are as originally reported. Adj. for stk. splits: 10% div., 1/99, 2/98; 3-for-2, 1/97

shareholder had to have been a holder of record in order to have qualified for the dividend. The **Payable Date** indicates the date the company paid or intends to pay the dividend. The cash amount shown in the first column is followed by a letter (example "Q" for quarterly) to indicate the frequency of the dividend.

Indicated Dividend – This is the annualized amount (fully adjusted for splits) of the latest regular cash dividend. If the company has a dividend reinvestment plan, it is indicated here.

F. CAPITALIZATION – These are certain items in the company's capital account. Both the dollar amounts and their respective percentages are given.

Long-term Debt is the total amount of debt owed by the company which is due beyond one year.

Capital Lease Obligations is shown as a separate caption when indicated on the balance sheet as such.

Deferred Income Taxes represents the company's tax liability arising from accelerated depreciation and investment tax credit.

Preferred Stock is the sum of equity issues, exclusive of common stock, the holders of which have a prior claim, ahead of the common shareholders, to the income of the company while it continues to operate and to the assets in the event of dissolution.

Minority Interest in this instance is a capital item which reflects the share of ownership by an outside party in a consolidated subsidiary of the company.

Common and Surplus is the sum of the stated or par value of the common stock, plus additional paid-in capital and retained earnings less the dollar amount of treasury shares.

G. DIVIDEND ACHIEVER STATUS – The company's rank among the Dividend Achievers for dividend growth is indicated. Each company is ranked by its ten-year compound annual average cash dividend growth rate, which is also shown here, along with the total consecutive years of increases.

H. COMPANY BUSINESS – This section explains what the company does: the products or services it sells, its markets and production facilities.

I. RECENT DEVELOPMENTS – This section keeps you up to date on what has happened in the most recent quarter or fiscal year for which results are available. It provides analysis of recently released sales and earnings figures, including special charges and credits, and may also include results by sector, expense trends and ratios, and other current information.

J. ANNUAL FINANCIAL DATA – These figures are fully adjusted for all stock dividends and stock splits.

Earnings Per Share are as reported by the company except for adjustment for certain items as footnoted. Earnings per share reported after 12/15/97 are presented on a diluted basis, as described by Financial Accounting Standards Board Statement 128. Earnings per share reported prior to that date are shown on a primary basis.

Cash Flow Per Share is computed by dividing the total of net income and non-cash depreciation and amortization charges, less preferred dividends, by average shares outstanding.

Tangible Book Value Per Share is calculated by dividing stockholders equity minus intangibles by shares outstanding at fiscal year end. It demonstrates the underlying value of each common share if the company were to be liquidated as of that date.

Dividends Per Share represent the sum of all cash payments on a calendar year basis. Any fiscal year ending prior to June 30, for example, is shown with dividends for the prior calendar year.

Dividend Payout % is the percentage of cash paid out of **Earnings Per Share**.

K. INCOME STATEMENT, BALANCE SHEET AND STATISTICAL RECORD – Here is pertinent earnings and balance sheet information essential to analyzing a corporation's performance. The comparisons, each

HOW TO USE THIS BOOK (Continued)

year shown as originally reported, provide the necessary historical perspective to intelligently review the various operating and financial trends. Generic definitions follow.

INCOME STATEMENT:

Total Revenues is the total income from operations including non-operating revenues.

Costs and Expenses is the total of all costs related to the operation of the business – including cost of sales, selling, and general and administrative expenses. Excluded items are depreciation, interest and non-operating expenses.

Depreciation and Amortization includes all non-cash charges such as depletion and amortization as well as depreciation.

Operating Income is the profit remaining after deducting depreciation as well as all operating costs and expenses from the company's net sales and revenues. This figure is *before* interest expenses, extraordinary gains and charges, and income and expense items of a non-operating nature.

Net Interest Income/(Expense) is the net amount of interest paid and received by a company during the fiscal year.

Income Before Income Taxes is the remaining income *after* deducting all costs, expenses, property charges, interest, etc. but *before* deducting income taxes.

Equity Earnings/Minority Interest is the net amount of profits allocated to minority owners or affiliates.

Income Taxes are shown as reported by the company and include both the amount of current taxes actually paid out and the amount deferred to future years.

Net Income is as reported by the corporation, before extraordinary gains and losses, discontinued operations and accounting changes, which are appropriately footnoted.

Cash Flow is the sum of net income and non-cash depreciation and amortization charges, less preferred dividends.

Average Shares Outstanding is the weighted average number of shares including common equivalent shares outstanding during the year, as reported by the corporation and fully adjusted for all stock dividends and splits. The use of *average shares* minimizes the distortion in *earnings per share* which could result from issuance of a large amount of stock or the company's purchase of a large amount of its own stock during the year.

BALANCE SHEET:

All balance sheet items are shown as reported by the corporation in its annual report. Because of the limited amount of space available and in an effort to simplify and standardize accounts, some items have been combined.

Cash & Cash Equivalents comprise unrestricted cash and temporary investments in marketable securities, such as U.S. Government securities, certificates of deposit and short-term investments.

Total Current Assets are all of the company's short-term assets, including cash, marketable securities, inventories, certain receivables, etc., as reported.

Net Property is total fixed assets, including all property, land, plants, buildings, equipment, fixtures, etc., less accumulated depreciation.

Total Assets represent the sum of all tangible and intangible assets as reported by the company.

Total Current Liabilities are all of the obligations of the company due within one year, as reported.

Long-term Obligations are total long-term debts (due beyond one year) reported by the company, including bonds, capital lease obligations, notes, mortgages, debentures, etc.

Net Stockholders' Equity is the sum of all capital stock accounts – stated values of preferred and common stock, paid-in capital, earned surplus (retained earnings), etc., net of all treasury stock.

Net Working Capital is derived by subtracting Current Liabilities from Current Assets.

Year-end Shares Outstanding are the number of shares outstanding as of the date of the company's annual report, exclusive of treasury stock and adjusted for subsequent stock dividends and splits.

STATISTICAL RECORD:

Operating Profit Margin indicates operating profit as a percentage of net sales or revenues.

Net Profit Margin is the percentage of total revenues remaining after the deduction of all non-extraordinary costs, including interest and taxes.

Return on Equity is one of several measures of profitability. It is the ratio of net income to net stockholders' equity, expressed as a percentage. This ratio illustrates how effectively the investment of the stockholders is being utilized to earn a profit.

Return on Assets is another means of measuring profitability. It is the ratio of net income to total assets, expressed as a percentage. This indicates how effectively the corporate assets are being used to generate profits.

Debt/Total Assets represents the ratio of long-term obligations to total assets as a percentage.

Price/Earnings Ratio is shown as a range. The figures are calculated by dividing the stock's highest price for the year and its lowest price by the year's earnings per share. Prices are for calendar years. Earnings used in the calculation for a particular calendar year are for the fiscal year in which the majority of the company's business took place. As a rule, for companies whose fiscal years end before June 30, the ratio is calculated by using the price range of the prior calendar year. For those with fiscal years ending on June 30 or later, the current year's price range is used.

Average Yield is the ratio (expressed as a percentage) of the annual dividend to the mean price of the common stock (average of the high and low for the year). Both prices and dividends are for calendar years.

EDITOR'S NOTE: In order to preserve the historical relationships between prices, earnings and dividends, figures are not restated to reflect subsequent events.

L. ADDITIONAL INFORMATION – For each stock, listings are provided for the company's officers, date of incorporation, its address, telephone number, fax number and website (when available), annual meeting date, the number of employees, the number of stockholders, institutional holdings, and transfer agent.

Institutional Holdings indicates the number of institutions holding the stock and the total number of shares held as last reported. Coverage includes investment companies, mutual funds, insurance companies, and banks. The percentage of shares outstanding held by institutions is also provided.

ABBREVIATIONS
AND
SYMBOLS

d	Deficit
E	Extra
M	Monthly
N.M.	Not Meaningful
p	Preliminary
P.F.	Pro Forma
Q	Quarterly
r	Revised
S	Semi-annual
Sp	Special Dividend
Y	Year-end Dividend

ABBOTT LABORATORIES

YIELD 2.2%
P/E RATIO 25.5

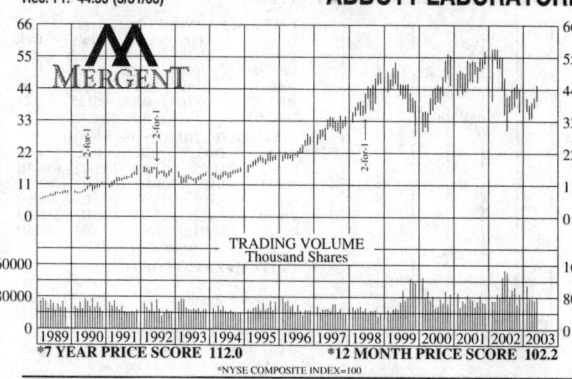

TRADING VOLUME
Thousand Shares

*7 YEAR PRICE SCORE 112.0   *12 MONTH PRICE SCORE 102.2
*NYSE COMPOSITE INDEX=100

INTERIM EARNINGS (Per Share):

Qtr.	Mar.	June	Sept.	Dec.
1999	0.43	0.42	0.38	0.43
2000	0.44	0.44	0.42	0.48
2001	0.06	0.34	0.40	0.39
2002	0.54	0.38	0.46	0.40
2003	0.51	...	...	...

INTERIM DIVIDENDS (Per Share):

Amt.	Decl.	Ex.	Rec.	Pay.
0.235Q	2/15/02	4/11/02	4/15/02	5/15/02
0.235Q	6/06/02	7/11/02	7/15/02	8/15/02
0.235Q	9/13/02	10/10/02	10/15/02	11/15/02
0.235Q	12/13/02	1/13/03	1/15/03	2/15/03
0.245Q	2/14/03	4/11/03	4/15/03	5/15/03

Indicated div.: $0.98 (Div. Reinv. Plan)

CAPITALIZATION (12/31/02):

	($000)	(%)
Long-Term Debt	4,273,973	28.6
Common & Surplus	10,664,553	71.4
Total	14,938,526	100.0

DIVIDEND ACHIEVER STATUS:
Rank: 102   10-Year Growth Rate: 12.27%
Total Years of Dividend Growth: 30

RECENT DEVELOPMENTS: For the quarter ended 3/31/03, net earnings declined 6.2% to $801.0 million versus $854.3 million in the equivalent perido of the prior year. The decrease in earnings was primarily attributed to accelerated spending for the launch of HUMIRA, used for reducing the signs and symptoms and inhibiting the progression of structural damage in adults with moderate to severe active rheumatoid arthritis. Net sales improved 9.3% to $4.58 billion from $4.19 billion the year before.

PROSPECTS: The Company announced that it will phase out all I.V. sets that contain or require needles, as part of its continued commitment to improving patient and health care worker safety. As a result, ABT expects millions of needles to be eliminated from the U.S. health care system. ABT will use a needle-free technology across its entire line of infusion therapy products. Separately, ABT launched its DEXAMET™ stent system in Europe during February 2003.

BUSINESS

ABBOTT LABORATORIES' principal business is the discovery, development, manufacture, and sale of pharmaceuticals, nutritionals, and medical products, including devices and diagnostics. Pharmaceutical products include adult and pediatric pharmaceuticals and vitamins. This segment also includes consumer products, agricultural and chemical products, and bulk pharmaceuticals. Products in the hospital and laboratory segment include diagnostic systems, intravenous and irrigating fluids and related administration equipment, anesthetics, critical care equipment, and other specialty products. Products in the Ross segment include nutritional products such as SIMILAC and ENSURE. ABT owns 50.0% of the joint venture, TAP Pharmaceutical Products Inc. On 2/8/01, ABT acquired BASF's pharmaceutical business, including the global operations of Knoll, for $6.90 billion in cash.

ANNUAL FINANCIAL DATA

	12/31/02	12/31/01	12/31/00	12/31/99	12/31/98	12/31/97	12/31/96
Earnings Per Share	③ 1.78	③ 0.99	② 1.78	① 1.57	1.51	1.34	1.21
Cash Flow Per Share	2.52	1.74	2.31	2.10	2.02	1.81	1.64
Tang. Book Val. Per Share	1.93	1.14	4.54	3.70	2.88	2.54	2.48
Dividends Per Share	0.92	0.82	0.74	0.66	0.58	0.53	0.47
Dividend Payout %	51.4	82.8	41.6	42.0	38.7	39.2	38.6
INCOME STATEMENT (IN MILLIONS):							
Total Revenues	17,684.7	16,285.2	13,745.9	13,177.6	12,477.8	11,883.5	11,013.5
Costs & Expenses	12,977.2	13,223.2	9,517.9	9,200.2	8,575.7	8,305.3	7,710.3
Depreciation & Amort.	1,177.3	1,168.0	827.4	828.0	784.2	727.8	686.1
Operating Income	3,530.1	1,894.0	3,400.6	3,149.4	3,117.9	2,850.4	2,617.1
Net Interest Inc./(Exp.)	d205.2	d234.8	d23.2	d81.8	d104.1	d86.8	d50.9
Income Before Income Taxes	3,673.4	1,883.1	3,816.4	3,396.9	3,240.6	2,949.9	2,669.6
Income Taxes	879.7	332.8	1,030.4	951.1	907.4	855.5	787.5
Net Income	③ 2,793.7	③ 1,550.4	② 2,786.0	① 2,445.8	2,333.2	2,094.5	1,882.0
Cash Flow	3,971.0	2,718.4	3,613.4	3,273.8	3,117.5	2,822.2	2,568.1
Average Shs. Outstg. (000)	1,573,293	1,565,963	1,565,579	1,557,655	1,545,658	1,561,462	1,562,494
BALANCE SHEET (IN MILLIONS):							
Cash & Cash Equivalents	966.1	713.5	1,156.7	723.3	383.3	259.0	123.1
Total Current Assets	9,121.8	8,419.2	7,376.2	6,419.8	5,553.1	5,038.2	4,480.9
Net Property	5,828.1	5,551.5	4,816.9	4,770.1	4,738.8	4,569.7	4,461.5
Total Assets	24,259.1	23,296.4	15,283.3	14,471.0	13,216.2	12,061.4	11,125.6
Total Current Liabilities	7,002.2	7,926.8	4,297.5	4,516.7	4,962.1	5,034.5	4,343.7
Long-Term Obligations	4,274.0	4,335.5	1,076.4	1,336.8	1,339.7	938.0	932.9
Net Stockholders' Equity	10,664.6	9,059.4	8,570.9	7,427.6	5,713.7	4,998.7	4,820.2
Net Working Capital	2,119.6	492.4	3,078.7	1,903.0	591.0	3.7	137.2
Year-end Shs. Outstg. (000)	1,563,060	1,554,530	1,545,934	1,547,020	1,516,063	1,528,188	1,548,898
STATISTICAL RECORD:							
Operating Profit Margin %	20.0	11.6	24.7	23.9	25.0	24.0	23.8
Net Profit Margin %	15.8	9.5	20.3	18.6	18.7	17.6	17.1
Return on Equity %	26.2	17.1	32.5	32.9	40.8	41.9	39.0
Return on Assets %	11.5	6.7	18.2	16.9	17.7	17.4	16.9
Debt/Total Assets %	17.6	18.6	7.0	9.2	10.1	7.8	8.4
Price Range	58.00-29.80	57.17-42.00	56.25-29.38	53.31-27.94	50.06-32.53	34.88-24.88	28.69-19.06
P/E Ratio	32.6-16.7	57.7-42.4	31.6-16.5	34.0-17.8	33.2-21.5	26.0-18.6	23.8-15.8
Average Yield %	2.1	1.7	1.7	1.6	1.4	1.8	1.9

Statistics are as originally reported. Adjusted for 2-for-1 stock split, 5/98. ① Incl. a nonrecurring pre-tax charge of $168.0 million relating to an FDA consent decree. ② Incl. pre-tax gain of $138.5 mill. on sale of bus. ③ Incl. pre-tax acq. in-process research & dev. chrg. of $107.7 mill.; 12/02; $1.33 bill., 12/01.

OFFICERS:
M. D. White, Chmn., C.E.O.
T. C. Freyman, Sr. V.P., C.F.O.
T. C. Kearney, V.P., Treas.

INVESTOR CONTACT: Investor Relations, (847) 937-6400

PRINCIPAL OFFICE: 100 Abbott Park Road, Abbott Park, IL 60064-6400

TELEPHONE NUMBER: (847) 937-6100
FAX: (847) 937-1511
WEB: www.abbott.com

NO. OF EMPLOYEES: 71,819 (avg.)

SHAREHOLDERS: 94,687

ANNUAL MEETING: In Apr.

INCORPORATED: IL, Mar., 1900

INSTITUTIONAL HOLDINGS:
No. of Institutions: 1,044
Shares Held: 910,947,461
% Held: 58.3

INDUSTRY: Pharmaceutical preparations (SIC: 2834)

TRANSFER AGENT(S): EquiServe, Providence, RI

NYSE SYMBOL ABM
Rec. Pr. 14.78 (5/31/03)

ABM INDUSTRIES INCORPORATED

YIELD 2.6%
P/E RATIO 18.9

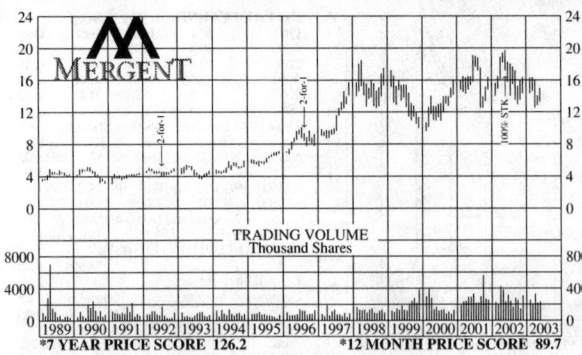

TRADING VOLUME
Thousand Shares

*7 YEAR PRICE SCORE 126.2   *12 MONTH PRICE SCORE 89.7

*NYSE COMPOSITE INDEX=100

INTERIM EARNINGS (Per Share):

Qtr.	Jan.	April	July	Oct.
1998-99	0.15	0.18	0.23	0.28
1999-00	0.16	0.21	0.26	0.30
2000-01	0.17	0.24	0.26	d0.02
2001-02	0.16	0.27	0.25	0.24
2002-03	0.09	0.20	...	...

INTERIM DIVIDENDS (Per Share):

Amt.	Decl.	Ex.	Rec.	Pay.
0.09Q	6/11/02	7/11/02	7/15/02	8/05/02
0.09Q	9/10/02	10/10/02	10/15/02	11/05/02
0.095Q	12/10/02	1/15/03	1/17/03	2/05/03
0.095Q	3/11/03	4/15/03	4/18/03	5/05/03
0.095Q	6/10/03	7/10/03	7/14/03	8/04/03

Indicated div.: $0.38

CAPITALIZATION (10/31/02):

	($000)	(%)
Common & Surplus	386,670	100.0
Total	386,670	100.0

DIVIDEND ACHIEVER STATUS:
Rank: 120   10-Year Growth Rate: 11.38%
Total Years of Dividend Growth: 38

RECENT DEVELOPMENTS: For the quarter ended 4/30/03, net income fell 29.3% to $9.9 million compared with $14.0 million in the equivalent 2002 quarter, due to high office vacancies, downturn in travel stemming from severe acute respiratory syndrome and the war in Iraq. Total revenues rose 11.3% to $589.8 million from $530.2 million a year earlier. Results included contributions from ABM Lakeside Building Maintenance, which was acquired in July 2002, and Horizon's self-performed janitorial operations, which was acquired in January 2003.

PROSPECTS: On 5/9/03, ABM's subsidiary, Ampco System Parking, acquired selected assets of Valet Parking Services based in Culver city California. Assets acquired by Ampco include 93 contracts for commercial parking structures, surface lots and hotel valet business throughout Los Angeles County and Las Vegas, Nevada. Annual revenues from the acquisition are about $23.0 million. Meanwhile, on 4/16/03, ABM's subsidiary, Amtech Elevator Services, was awarded a multi-year, multi-million dollar contract with Wells Fargo.

BUSINESS

ABM INDUSTRIES INCORPO-RATED is a facility services contractor. The Company provides elevator, engineering, janitorial, lighting, parking, security, mechanical and network services for thousands of commercial, industrial, institutional and retail facilities in hundreds of cities across North America. The ABM Family of Services includes ABM Janitorial, Ampco System Parking, American Commercial Security (ACSS), ABM Engineering, Amtech Elevator, Amtech Lighting, CommAir Mechanical, ABM Service Network and ABM Lakeside Building Maintenance. Contributions to sales for fiscal 2002 were as follows: ABM Janitorial, 58.0%; Ampco System Parking, 16.5%; ABM Engineering, 7.7%; ACSS, 6.5%; Amtech Lighting, 6.0%; and Amtech Elevator, 5.3%.

ANNUAL FINANCIAL DATA

	10/31/02	10/31/01	10/31/00	10/31/99	10/31/98	10/31/97	10/31/96
Earnings Per Share	③ 0.92	① 0.65	0.93	0.83	0.72	0.67	0.56
Cash Flow Per Share	1.21	1.18	1.43	1.27	1.16	1.08	0.92
Tang. Book Val. Per Share	4.46	5.08	4.48	3.82	3.12	2.38	2.26
Dividends Per Share	0.36	0.33	0.31	0.28	0.24	0.20	0.17
Dividend Payout %	39.1	50.8	33.5	33.9	33.3	30.1	31.5
INCOME STATEMENT (IN MILLIONS):							
Total Revenues	② 2,192.0	1,950.0	1,807.6	1,629.7	1,501.8	1,252.5	1,086.9
Costs & Expenses	2,107.4	1,870.8	1,711.3	1,541.8	1,424.7	1,189.4	1,035.2
Depreciation & Amort.	15.2	26.3	23.5	20.7	19.6	16.1	13.7
Income Before Income Taxes	69.3	52.9	72.7	67.2	57.5	47.0	38.1
Income Taxes	22.6	20.1	28.4	27.6	23.6	19.7	16.4
Net Income	③ 46.7	① 32.8	44.3	39.7	33.9	27.2	21.7
Cash Flow	61.9	58.7	67.4	59.9	53.0	42.8	34.9
Average Shs. Outstg. (000)	51,015	50,020	47,418	47,496	46,322	40,286	38,246
BALANCE SHEET (IN MILLIONS):							
Cash & Cash Equivalents	19.4	3.1	2.0	2.1	1.8	1.8	1.6
Total Current Assets	437.8	465.5	436.8	367.6	324.3	291.5	233.8
Net Property	36.3	42.9	40.7	35.2	27.3	26.6	22.6
Total Assets	704.9	683.1	642.0	563.4	501.4	464.3	379.8
Total Current Liabilities	227.1	236.0	212.6	183.3	157.8	153.8	113.8
Long-Term Obligations	...	0.9	36.8	28.9	33.7	38.4	33.7
Net Stockholders' Equity	386.7	361.2	316.3	277.0	237.5	197.8	164.3
Net Working Capital	210.7	229.5	224.2	184.3	166.5	137.8	120.0
Year-end Shs. Outstg. (000)	48,997	48,778	45,998	44,814	43,202	40,928	38,978
STATISTICAL RECORD:							
Operating Profit Margin %	3.2	2.7	4.0	4.1	3.8	3.7	3.5
Net Profit Margin %	2.1	1.7	2.5	2.4	2.3	2.2	2.0
Return on Equity %	12.1	9.1	14.0	14.3	14.3	13.8	13.2
Return on Assets %	6.6	4.8	6.9	7.0	6.8	5.9	5.7
Debt/Total Assets %	...	0.1	5.7	5.1	6.7	8.3	8.9
Price Range	19.75-12.92	19.10-12.48	16.06-9.63	17.25-10.00	18.50-12.50	15.75-8.69	10.09-6.75
P/E Ratio	21.5-14.0	29.4-19.2	17.4-10.4	20.9-12.1	25.7-17.4	23.7-13.1	18.2-12.2
Average Yield %	2.2	2.1	2.4	2.1	1.5	1.6	2.1

Statistics are as originally reported. Adj. for stk. split: 2-for-1, 8/96 & 5/02. ① Incl. a pre-tax charge of $20.0 million to strengthen the Company's self-insurance. ② Incl. $10.0 mill. gain on insurance claims. ③ Incl. $6.4 mill. after-tax gains rel. to World Trade Center business interruption.

OFFICERS:
M. H. Mandles, Chmn., C.A.O.
H. Slipsager, Pres., C.E.O.
G. B. Sundby, Sr. V.P., C.F.O.

INVESTOR CONTACT: George B. Sundby, Sr.
V.P., C.F.O., (415) 733-4000

PRINCIPAL OFFICE: 160 Pacific Avenue,
Suite 222, San Francisco, CA 94111

TELEPHONE NUMBER: (415) 733-4000
FAX: (415) 733-7333
WEB: www.abm.com
NO. OF EMPLOYEES: 62,000 (approx.)
SHAREHOLDERS: 4,451 (approx.)
ANNUAL MEETING: In Mar.
INCORPORATED: CA, Apr., 1955; reincorp., DE, May, 1985

INSTITUTIONAL HOLDINGS:
No. of Institutions: 118
Shares Held: 32,663,922
% Held: 66.7

INDUSTRY: Building maintenance services, nec (SIC: 7349)

TRANSFER AGENT(S): Mellon Investor Services LLC, San Franscisco, CA

AFLAC INCORPORATED

YIELD 0.9%
P/E RATIO 19.9

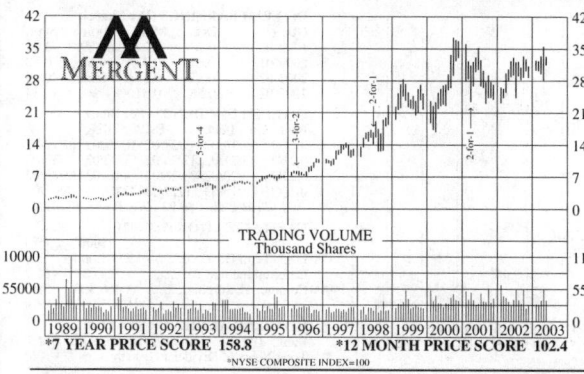

TRADING VOLUME
Thousand Shares

*7 YEAR PRICE SCORE 158.8   *12 MONTH PRICE SCORE 102.4
*NYSE COMPOSITE INDEX=100

INTERIM EARNINGS (Per Share):

Qtr.	Mar.	June	Sept.	Dec.
2000	0.29	0.37	0.30	0.31
2001	0.33	0.28	0.36	0.31
2002	0.34	0.40	0.45	0.35
2003	0.45	...	...	...

INTERIM DIVIDENDS (Per Share):

Amt.	Decl.	Ex.	Rec.	Pay.
0.07Q	1/30/03	2/12/03	2/14/03	3/03/03
0.07Q	4/23/03	5/13/03	5/15/03	6/02/03
0.07Q	...	8/12/03	8/14/03	9/02/03
0.07Q	...	11/10/03	11/13/03	12/01/03

Indicated div.: $0.28 (Div. Reinv. Plan)

CAPITALIZATION (12/31/02):

	($000)	(%)
Long-Term Debt	1,283,000	12.7
Capital Lease Obligations..	29,000	0.3
Deferred Income Tax	2,364,000	23.5
Common & Surplus	6,394,000	63.5
Total	10,070,000	100.0

DIVIDEND ACHIEVER STATUS:
Rank: 63   10-Year Growth Rate: 14.91%
Total Years of Dividend Growth: 20

RECENT DEVELOPMENTS: For the quarter ended 3/31/03, net income was $237.0 million, up 26.7% versus income of $187.0 million, before an accounting change charge of $4.0 million, in the equivalent 2002 quarter. Results for 2003 and 2002 included realized losses from investments of $7.0 million and $5.0 million. Revenues grew 18.4% to $2.81 billion reflecting a 12.1% increase to $227.0 million in new annualized premium sales at AFLAC Japan.

PROSPECTS: Looking ahead, the Company believes the aging population in Japan will lead to continued strong demand for AFL's insurance products. For 2003, the Company expects AFLAC Japan's new annualized premium sales will grow in the range of 5.0% to 10.0% in yen currency terms. Meanwhile, in the U.S., AFL is making sales organizational changes that are expected to result in short-term disruption.

BUSINESS

AFLAC INCORPORATED is an international insurance organization whose principal subsidiary is American Family Life Assurance Company of Columbus. In addition to life, and health & accident insurance, AFL has pioneered cancer-expense and intensive-care insurance coverage. AFLAC's subsidiary Communicorp specializes in printing, advertising, audio-visuals, sales incentives, business meetings and mailings. As of 4/23/03, AFL insured more than 40.0 million people worldwide, and offered policies to employees through 258,800 payroll accounts. Also, the Company insures one out of four Japanese households and is the second largest life insurer in Japan in terms of individual policies in force.

ANNUAL FINANCIAL DATA

	12/31/02	12/31/01	12/31/00	12/31/99	12/31/98	12/31/97	12/31/96
Earnings Per Share	1.55	1.28	[2] 1.26	1.04	0.88	[1] 1.04	[1] 0.69
Tang. Book Val. Per Share	12.43	10.40	8.87	7.28	7.09	6.44	3.57
Dividends Per Share	0.23	0.19	0.17	0.14	0.13	0.11	0.10
Dividend Payout %	14.8	15.0	13.1	14.0	14.3	10.7	14.1
INCOME STATEMENT (IN MILLIONS):							
Total Premium Income	8,595.0	8,061.0	8,239.0	7,264.0	5,943.0	5,873.7	5,910.0
Net Investment Income	1,614.0	1,550.0	1,550.0	1,369.0	1,138.0	1,077.7	1,022.0
Other Income	48.0	d13.0	d69.0	7.0	23.0	299.3	168.2
Total Revenues	10,257.0	9,598.0	9,720.0	8,640.0	7,104.0	7,250.7	7,100.2
Policyholder Benefits	6,589.0	6,303.0	6,618.0	5,885.0	4,877.0	4,833.1	4,895.5
Income Before Income Taxes	1,259.0	1,081.0	1,012.0	778.0	551.0	864.8	650.0
Income Taxes	438.0	394.0	325.0	207.0	64.0	279.8	255.6
Net Income	821.0	687.0	[2] 687.0	571.0	487.0	[1] 585.0	[1] 394.4
Average Shs. Outstg. (000)	528,326	537,380	544,906	550,846	551,744	563,192	578,048
BALANCE SHEET (IN MILLIONS):							
Cash & Cash Equivalents	1,379.0	852.0	609.0	616.0	374.0	279.0	261.7
Premiums Due	435.0	347.0	301.0	270.0	272.0	215.7	227.0
Invst. Assets: Fixed-term	31,053.0	25,817.0	25,817.0	25,248.0	21,564.0	22,437.8	20,327.0
Invst. Assets: Equities	258.0	245.0	236.0	215.0	177.0	146.3	136.3
Invst. Assets: Loans	...	...	...	...	...	16.7	17.8
Invst. Assets: Total	37,768.0	31,941.0	31,558.0	31,408.0	26,620.0	22,644.2	20,746.5
Total Assets	45,058.0	37,860.0	37,232.0	37,041.0	31,183.0	29,454.0	25,022.8
Long-Term Obligations	1,312.0	1,207.0	1,079.0	1,111.0	596.0	523.2	353.5
Net Stockholders' Equity	6,394.0	5,425.0	4,694.0	3,868.0	3,770.0	3,430.5	2,125.6
Year-end Shs. Outstg. (000)	514,439	521,615	529,210	531,482	531,368	532,872	578,048
STATISTICAL RECORD:							
Return on Revenues %	8.0	7.2	7.1	6.6	6.9	8.1	5.6
Return on Equity %	12.8	12.7	14.6	14.8	12.9	17.1	18.6
Return on Assets %	1.8	1.8	1.8	1.5	1.6	2.0	1.6
Price Range	33.45-23.10	36.09-23.00	37.47-16.78	28.38-19.50	22.66-11.34	14.47-9.38	11.00-7.06
P/E Ratio	21.6-14.9	28.2-18.0	29.7-13.3	27.4-18.8	25.7-12.9	13.9-9.0	16.1-10.3
Average Yield %	0.8	0.7	0.6	0.6	0.7	0.9	1.1

Statistics are as originally reported. Adj. for stk. splits: 2-for-1, 3/01 & 6/98; 3-for-2, 3/96 [1] Incl. non-recurr. credit $267.2 mill., 12/97; $60.3 mill., 12/96 [2] Incl. one-time benefit of $99.0 mill. & realized invest. loss of $69.0 mill.

OFFICERS:
D. P. Amos, Chmn., C.E.O.
K. Cloninger III, Pres., C.F.O., Treas.

INVESTOR CONTACT: Kenneth S. Janke, Jr., Sr. V.P., Inv. Rel., (800) 235-2667

PRINCIPAL OFFICE: 1932 Wynnton Road, Columbus, GA 31999

TELEPHONE NUMBER: (706) 323-3431
FAX: (706) 596-3488
WEB: www.aflac.com

NO. OF EMPLOYEES: 6,086

SHAREHOLDERS: 73,887 (registered)

ANNUAL MEETING: In May

INCORPORATED: GA, 1973

INSTITUTIONAL HOLDINGS:
No. of Institutions: 520
Shares Held: 272,812,734
% Held: 53.0

INDUSTRY: Accident and health insurance (SIC: 6321)

TRANSFER AGENT(S): AFLAC Incorporated, Columbus, GA

AIR PRODUCTS & CHEMICALS, INC.

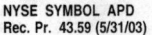
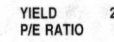
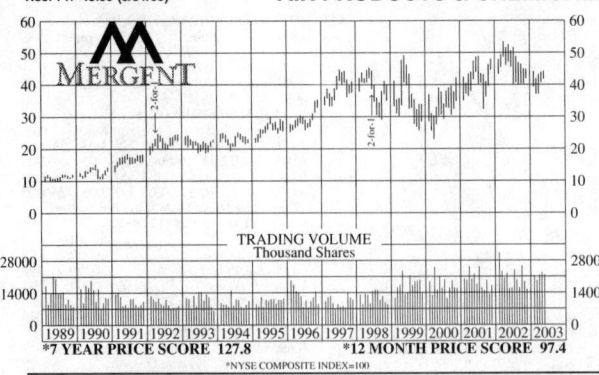

INTERIM EARNINGS (Per Share):

Qtr.	Dec.	Mar.	June	Sept.
1999-00	0.23	0.22	d0.89	1.01
2000-01	0.62	0.43	0.60	0.68
2001-02	0.52	0.57	0.63	0.65
2002-03	0.58	0.51	...	...

INTERIM DIVIDENDS (Per Share):

Amt.	Decl.	Ex.	Rec.	Pay.
0.21Q	9/19/02	9/27/02	10/01/02	11/12/02
0.21Q	11/21/02	12/30/02	1/02/03	2/10/03
0.21Q	3/20/03	3/28/03	4/01/03	5/12/03
0.23Q	5/15/03	6/27/03	7/01/03	8/11/03

Indicated div.: *$0.92 (Div. Reinv. Plan)*

CAPITALIZATION (9/30/02):

	($000)	(%)
Long-Term Debt	2,041,000	32.8
Deferred Income Tax	725,600	11.7
Common & Surplus	3,460,400	55.6
Total	6,227,000	100.0

DIVIDEND ACHIEVER STATUS:

Rank: 199   10-Year Growth Rate: 7.11%
Total Years of Dividend Growth: 20

TRADING VOLUME
Thousand Shares

*7 YEAR PRICE SCORE 127.8   *12 MONTH PRICE SCORE 97.4

*NYSE COMPOSITE INDEX=100

RECENT DEVELOPMENTS: For the three months ended 3/31/03, net income slipped 9.9% to $113.6 million compared with $126.1 million in the equivalent period of 2002. Results for 2002 included an after-tax gain of $25.7 million for the sale of APD's U.S. packaged gas business and an after-tax charge of $18.9 million for a global cost-reduction plan. Sales amounted to $1.58 billion, up 20.2% from $1.31 billion in the prior-year period.

PROSPECTS: The slowdown in demand across manufacturing industries is hampering APD's North American gas and performance polymers volumes. Meanwhile, increased energy and raw material costs are hampering APD's chemicals segment and its gases segment. Also, delays in new liquid natural gas heat exchanger orders and reduced activity in air separation plants are decreasing expectations for equipment segment profitability.

BUSINESS

AIR PRODUCTS & CHEMICALS, INC. is an international supplier of industrial and specialty gas products.

Principal products of the industrial gases segment (68.0% of 2002 revenues) are oxygen, nitrogen, argon, hydrogen, carbon monoxide, carbon dioxide, synthesis gas and helium.

The chemicals segment (26.9%) consists of performance materials, and chemical intermediates. The equipment segment (5.1%) designs and manufactures cryogenic and gas processing equipment for air separation, gas processing, natural gas liquefaction, and hydrogen purification. This segment also designs and builds cryogenic transportation containers for liquid helium and hydrogen.

ANNUAL FINANCIAL DATA

	9/30/02	9/30/01	9/30/00	9/30/99	9/30/98	9/30/97	9/30/96
Earnings Per Share	6 2.36	5 2.33	4 0.57	3 2.09	1 2 2.48	1.95	1 1.86
Cash Flow Per Share	4.97	4.58	3.24	4.53	4.71	4.04	3.71
Tang. Book Val. Per Share	13.33	13.67	9.07	11.39	11.08	20.08	11.22
Dividends Per Share	0.82	0.78	0.74	0.70	0.64	0.57	0.54
Dividend Payout %	34.7	33.5	129.8	33.5	25.8	29.5	28.8
INCOME STATEMENT (IN MILLIONS):							
Total Revenues	5,401.2	5,722.7	5,495.5	5,039.8	4,933.8	4,662.0	4,033.0
Costs & Expenses	4,045.3	4,404.3	4,089.0	3,787.9	3,599.4	3,477.5	3,030.0
Depreciation & Amort.	581.0	573.0	575.7	527.2	489.4	459.1	412.0
Operating Income	774.9	745.4	830.8	724.7	845.0	725.4	591.0
Net Interest Inc./(Exp.)	d122.3	d191.2	d196.7	d159.1	d162.8	d161.3	d129.0
Income Before Income Taxes	784.5	737.0	118.1	669.0	823.7	630.4	610.0
Income Taxes	240.8	219.0	cr13.7	203.4	276.9	201.1	193.0
Equity Earnings/Minority Int.	d18.3	76.1	d7.6	d15.1	38.0	66.3	81.0
Net Income	6 525.4	5 431.7	4 124.2	3 450.5	1 2 546.8	429.3	1 417.0
Cash Flow	1,106.4	1,085.9	699.9	977.7	1,036.2	888.4	829.0
Average Shs. Outstg. (000)	222,700	219,300	216,200	216,000	220,100	220,100	223,400
BALANCE SHEET (IN MILLIONS):							
Cash & Cash Equivalents	253.7	66.2	94.1	132.0	61.5	52.5	79.0
Total Current Assets	1,909.3	1,684.8	1,805.0	1,782.4	1,641.7	1,624.3	1,375.0
Net Property	5,377.8	5,118.5	5,256.7	5,192.9	4,786.1	4,441.2	3,959.0
Total Assets	8,495.0	8,084.1	8,270.5	8,235.5	7,489.6	7,244.1	6,522.0
Total Current Liabilities	1,256.2	1,352.4	1,374.8	1,857.8	1,265.6	1,124.6	1,263.0
Long-Term Obligations	2,041.0	2,027.5	2,615.8	1,961.6	2,274.3	2,291.7	1,739.0
Net Stockholders' Equity	3,460.4	3,105.8	2,821.3	2,961.6	2,667.3	2,648.1	2,574.0
Net Working Capital	653.1	332.4	430.2	d75.4	376.1	499.7	112.0
Year-end Shs. Outstg. (000)	227,219	227,186	229,305	229,305	211,500	119,500	222,000
STATISTICAL RECORD:							
Operating Profit Margin %	14.3	13.0	15.1	14.4	17.1	15.6	14.7
Net Profit Margin %	9.7	7.5	2.3	8.9	11.1	9.2	10.3
Return on Equity %	15.2	13.9	4.4	15.2	20.5	16.2	16.2
Return on Assets %	6.2	5.3	1.5	5.5	7.3	5.9	6.4
Debt/Total Assets %	24.0	25.1	31.6	23.8	30.4	31.6	26.7
Price Range	53.52-40.00	49.00-32.5	42.25-23.00	49.25-25.69	45.34-29.00	44.81-33.19	35.31-25.19
P/E Ratio	22.7-16.9	21.0-13.8	74.1-40.3	23.6-12.3	18.3-11.7	23.0-17.0	19.0-13.5
Average Yield %	1.8	1.9	2.3	1.9	1.7	1.5	1.8

Statistics are as originally reported. Adj. for 2-for-1 split, 6/98. ☐ Incl $35.0 mil aft-tx gn, 1998; aft-tx gn $41.0 mil, 1996. ☐ Incl $58.1 mil. aft-tx gn fr. sale of bus. ☐ Incl $28.3 mil. net chgs & $23.6 mil. net gn. ☐ Incl $456.5 mil. aft-tx loss fr. curr. hedge & $126.8 mil. gn fr. sale of bus. ☐ Incl $67.3 mil. aft-tx chg, $3.7 mil. aft-tax lit. chg, $64.6 mil. aft-tax gn, & excl $28.5 mil. aft-tax extra loss. ☐ Incl $25.7 mil. aft-tx gn on sale of bus. & $18.9 mil. aft-tx chg.

OFFICERS:
J. P. Jones III, Chmn., Pres., C.E.O.
J. R. Owings, V.P., C.F.O.

INVESTOR CONTACT: Alexander W. Massetti, Dir., Inv. Rel., (610) 481-5775

PRINCIPAL OFFICE: 7201 Hamilton Boulevard, Allentown, PA 18195-1501

TELEPHONE NUMBER: (610) 481-4911
FAX: (610) 481-5900
WEB: www.airproducts.com
NO. OF EMPLOYEES: 17,200 (approx.)
SHAREHOLDERS: 11,433
ANNUAL MEETING: In Jan.
INCORPORATED: MI, Oct., 1940; reincorp., DE, June, 1940

INSTITUTIONAL HOLDINGS:
No. of Institutions: 458
Shares Held: 180,243,801
% Held: 79.4

INDUSTRY: Industrial gases (SIC: 2813)

TRANSFER AGENT(S): American Stock Transfer & Trust Company, New York, NY

ALBERTO-CULVER COMPANY

YIELD 0.8%
P/E RATIO 20.4

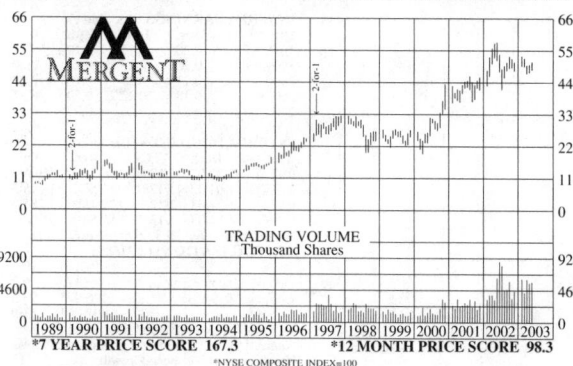

*7 YEAR PRICE SCORE 167.3   *12 MONTH PRICE SCORE 98.3
*NYSE COMPOSITE INDEX=100

TRADING VOLUME
Thousand Shares

INTERIM EARNINGS (Per Share):

Qtr.	Dec.	Mar.	June	Sept.
1998-99	0.32	0.35	0.40	0.44
1999-00	0.37	0.40	0.45	0.50
2000-01	0.41	0.45	0.50	0.55
2001-02	0.50	0.55	0.61	0.66
2002-03	0.60	0.63	...	...

INTERIM DIVIDENDS (Per Share):

Amt.	Decl.	Ex.	Rec.	Pay.
0.09Q	4/25/02	5/02/02	5/06/02	5/20/02
0.09Q	7/25/02	8/01/02	8/05/02	8/20/02
0.09Q	10/24/02	10/31/02	11/04/02	11/20/02
0.105Q	1/23/03	1/30/03	2/03/03	2/20/03
0.105Q	4/24/03	5/01/03	5/05/03	5/20/03

Indicated div.: $0.42

CAPITALIZATION (9/30/02):

	($000)	(%)
Long-Term Debt	320,181	26.2
Deferred Income Tax	38,337	3.1
Common & Surplus	862,459	70.6
Total	1,220,977	100.0

DIVIDEND ACHIEVER STATUS:

Rank: 115   10-Year Growth Rate: 11.61%
Total Years of Dividend Growth: 18

RECENT DEVELOPMENTS: For the quarter ended 3/31/03, net earnings advanced 15.9% to $37.9 million from $32.7 million in the corresponding prior-year period. Net sales grew 7.5% to $707.0 million from $657.8 million the previous year. Gross profit climbed 11.5% to $357.9 million from $320.9 million a year earlier. Operating income amounted to $64.9 million, up 15.1% from $50.2 million the year before.

PROSPECTS: ACV continues to perform well despite a slowdown in retail traffic due to harsh winter weather conditions and the war in Iraq. Worldwide consumer product sales and profits were each up in double-digits for the quarter, and the Sally and Beauty Systems Group continues to grow steadily as well. Going forward, ACV will continue to focus on controlling costs and using the contributions from those efforts to reinvest in its businesses.

BUSINESS

ALBERTO-CULVER COMPANY is engaged in developing, manufacturing, distributing and marketing branded consumer products worldwide. The Company has three primary business segments. Specialty Distribution -Sally (62.1% of fiscal 2002 revenues), consists of Sally Beauty Company, a specialty distributor of professional beauty supplies with 2,740 stores as of 4/21/03, in the U.S., Germany, the United Kingdom, Canada, Japan and Mexico, and its Beauty Systems Group, which sells professional beauty products through over 1,000 professional distributor sales consultants. Alberto-Culver North America (23.0%) includes ACV's consumer products in the U.S. and Canada, while Alberto-Culver International (14.9%) sells consumer products in more than 120 other countries. Brands sold by ACV include ALBERTO VO5, ST. IVES SWISS FORMULA and TRESEMME hair and skin beauty care products.

ANNUAL FINANCIAL DATA

	9/30/02	9/30/01	9/30/00	9/30/99	9/30/98	9/30/97	9/30/96
Earnings Per Share	2.32	1.91	⑪ 1.83	1.51	1.37	⑪ 1.49	⑪ 1.11
Cash Flow Per Share	3.12	2.80	2.71	2.25	1.94	2.17	1.70
Tang. Book Val. Per Share	7.55	6.90	5.16	5.81	5.75	5.57	4.33
Dividends Per Share	0.36	0.33	0.30	0.26	0.24	0.20	0.18
Dividend Payout %	15.5	17.3	16.4	17.2	17.5	13.4	16.2
INCOME STATEMENT (IN MILLIONS):							
Total Revenues	2,651.0	2,494.2	2,247.2	1,975.9	1,834.7	1,775.3	1,590.4
Costs & Expenses	2,369.3	2,253.7	2,024.0	1,787.3	1,655.6	1,592.0	1,445.4
Depreciation & Amort.	47.2	51.4	49.6	42.2	38.1	38.9	32.9
Operating Income	234.4	189.1	173.5	146.5	141.0	144.4	112.1
Net Interest Inc./(Exp.)	d22.6	d21.8	d19.2	d12.7	d8.6	d8.2	d12.1
Income Before Income Taxes	211.8	167.2	154.3	133.8	132.4	136.1	100.0
Income Taxes	74.1	56.9	51.1	47.5	49.3	50.7	37.3
Net Income	137.7	110.4	⑪ 103.2	86.3	83.1	⑪ 85.4	⑪ 62.7
Cash Flow	184.9	161.8	152.8	128.5	121.2	124.4	95.7
Average Shs. Outstg. (000)	59,214	57,838	56,410	57,162	62,420	57,202	56,426
BALANCE SHEET (IN MILLIONS):							
Cash & Cash Equivalents	217.5	202.8	115.0	57.8	73.3	87.6	71.6
Total Current Assets	984.2	876.9	740.5	645.6	591.6	580.3	512.7
Net Property	247.9	235.8	240.1	238.8	223.5	191.0	175.9
Total Assets	1,729.5	1,516.5	1,389.8	1,184.5	1,068.2	1,000.1	909.3
Total Current Liabilities	460.4	390.3	340.8	336.4	313.6	311.3	286.6
Long-Term Obligations	320.2	321.2	340.9	225.2	171.8	149.4	161.5
Net Stockholders' Equity	862.5	736.0	635.5	568.8	534.0	497.0	425.1
Net Working Capital	523.8	486.6	399.7	309.2	277.9	269.0	226.1
Year-end Shs. Outstg. (000)	58,179	56,828	55,939	55,726	57,210	56,142	55,630
STATISTICAL RECORD:							
Operating Profit Margin %	8.8	7.6	7.7	7.4	7.7	8.1	7.0
Net Profit Margin %	5.2	4.4	4.6	4.4	4.5	4.8	3.9
Return on Equity %	16.0	15.0	16.2	15.2	15.6	17.2	14.8
Return on Assets %	8.0	7.3	7.4	7.3	7.8	8.5	6.9
Debt/Total Assets %	18.5	21.2	24.5	19.0	16.1	14.9	17.8
Price Range	57.91-41.55	46.26-36.88	43.50-19.38	27.88-21.56	32.44-19.75	32.56-23.56	25.00-16.25
P/E Ratio	25.0-17.9	24.2-19.3	23.8-10.6	18.5-14.3	23.7-14.4	21.9-15.8	22.5-14.6
Average Yield %	0.7	0.8	1.0	1.1	0.9	0.7	0.9

Statistics are as originally reported. Adj. for stk. splits: 2-for-1, 2/97. ⑪ Incl. non-recurr. gain 2000, $6.0 mill.; credit 1997, $15.6 mill., 1996, $9.8 mill.

OFFICERS:
L. H. Lavin, Chmn.
B. E. Lavin, Vice-Chmn., Treas., Sec.
H. B. Bernick, Pres., C.E.O.

INVESTOR CONTACT: Wesley C. Davidson, V.P., Invest. Rel., (708) 450-3145

PRINCIPAL OFFICE: 2525 Armitage Avenue, Melrose Park, IL 60160

TELEPHONE NUMBER: (708) 450-3000
FAX: (708) 450-3419
WEB: www.alberto.com

NO. OF EMPLOYEES: 16,900 (approx.)

SHAREHOLDERS: 877 (CL. A); 865 (CL. B)

ANNUAL MEETING: In Jan.

INCORPORATED: DE, Jan., 1961

INSTITUTIONAL HOLDINGS:
No. of Institutions: 225
Shares Held: 22,490,998
% Held: 38.8

INDUSTRY: Toilet preparations (SIC: 2844)

TRANSFER AGENT(S): EquiServe L.P., Providence, RI

ALFA CORPORATION

YIELD 2.5%
P/E RATIO 14.3

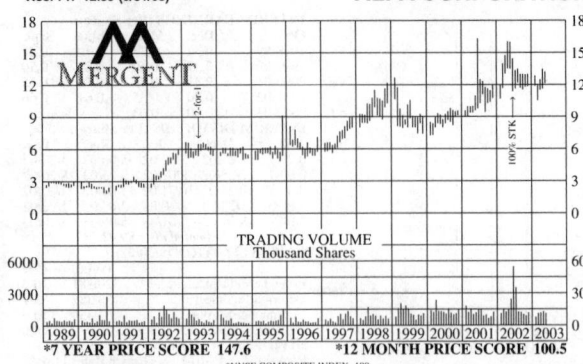

7 YEAR PRICE SCORE 147.6   **12 MONTH PRICE SCORE 100.5**

*NYSE COMPOSITE INDEX=100

INTERIM EARNINGS (Per Share):

Qtr.	Mar.	June	Sept.	Dec.
1998	0.20	0.15	0.19	0.17
1999	0.20	0.20	0.21	0.20
2000	0.21	0.27	0.18	0.20
2001	0.18	0.22	0.24	0.25
2002	0.23	0.20	0.22	0.25
2003	0.23	...	...	...

INTERIM DIVIDENDS (Per Share):

Amt.	Decl.	Ex.	Rec.	Pay.
0.075Q	7/30/02	8/13/02	8/15/02	8/30/02
0.075Q	11/04/02	11/13/02	11/15/02	11/29/02
0.075Q	1/21/03	2/12/03	2/14/03	2/28/03
0.08Q	4/24/03	5/13/03	5/15/03	5/30/03

Indicated div.: $0.32 (Div. Reinv. Plan)

CAPITALIZATION (12/31/02):

	($000)	(%)
Deferred Income Tax	40,970	6.7
Common & Surplus	566,098	93.3
Total	607,067	100.0

DIVIDEND ACHIEVER STATUS:
Rank: 158   10-Year Growth Rate: 9.39%
Total Years of Dividend Growth: 17

RECENT DEVELOPMENTS: For the quarter ended 3/31/03, net income rose 1.4% to $18.7 million from $18.5 million in the equivalent prior-year quarter. Total revenues grew 4.8% to $149.6 million from $142.7 million the previous year. Revenues included realized investment losses of $1.8 million in 2003 versus realized investment gains of $906,225 in 2002. Property and casualty premiums climbed 7.8% to $111.5 million from $103.4 million in 2002. Life insurance premiums advanced 18.3% to $9.0 million, while life insurance policy charges improved 2.5% to $8.7 mil-

lion. Net investment income slipped 2.1% to $21.7 million. Benefits and settlement expenses amounted to $88.0 million, up 7.0% from $82.2 million a year earlier. Looking ahead to the second quarter, earnings are likely to be hampered by higher-than-normal storm-related losses due to a series of storm systems that passed through the Southeastern U.S. in April and May. The impact of these claims, after reinsurance and taxes, are expected to be about $0.06 per diluted share.

BUSINESS

ALFA CORPORATION is a financial services holding company with total investments of $1.71 billion as of 3/31/03. The Company and its subsidiaries together with Alfa Mutual Companies comprise the Alfa Group. Alfa's primary business is personal lines of property and casualty insurance and life insurance. Alfa's subsidiaries write life insurance in Alabama, Georgia and Mississippi and casualty insurance in Georgia and Mississippi. The Company's noninsurance subsidiaries are engaged in consumer financing, leasing, real estate investments, residential and commercial construction and real estate sales.

ANNUAL FINANCIAL DATA

	12/31/02	12/31/01	12/31/00	12/31/99	12/31/98	12/31/97	12/31/96
Earnings Per Share	0.90	①0.89	0.85	0.80	0.69	0.65	0.40
Tang. Book Val. Per Share	7.09	6.50	6.05	5.17	5.31	4.82	3.96
Dividends Per Share	0.30	0.28	0.26	0.24	0.22	0.20	0.19
Dividend Payout %	33.1	31.9	30.0	29.5	31.7	30.8	49.0
INCOME STATEMENT (IN MILLIONS):							
Total Premium Income	491.1	452.9	429.2	405.3	391.8	371.0	337.2
Net Investment Income	88.5	84.7	72.9	67.8	62.5	57.5	54.2
Other Income	7.9	8.7	8.2	9.1	6.6	5.5	5.0
Total Revenues	587.5	546.3	510.3	482.3	461.0	434.0	396.3
Policyholder Benefits	346.5	312.9	295.9	281.7	277.9	266.1	267.3
Income Before Income Taxes	99.3	98.1	94.7	92.1	83.3	76.8	45.9
Income Taxes	27.6	28.1	27.9	27.5	26.5	24.0	13.7
Net Income	71.7	①70.0	66.8	64.6	56.7	52.8	32.2
Average Shs. Outstg. (000)	79,547	78,963	78,814	80,471	82,297	81,862	81,573
BALANCE SHEET (IN MILLIONS):							
Cash & Cash Equivalents	111.5	160.5	60.4	60.0	60.6	30.9	44.6
Premiums Due	18.3	25.7	22.6	17.3	26.2	15.1	13.9
Invst. Assets: Fixed-term	1,130.2	960.9	946.9	813.9	775.8	733.6	613.1
Invst. Assets: Equities	65.3	74.7	114.6	113.2	103.1	116.1	96.0
Invst. Assets: Loans	158.8	138.6	116.6	43.1	39.0	35.5	32.5
Invst. Assets: Total	1,569.4	1,491.2	1,355.0	1,155.2	1,084.1	1,027.7	886.0
Total Assets	1,884.1	1,697.6	1,546.3	1,335.3	1,246.7	1,170.1	1,019.3
Net Stockholders' Equity	566.1	509.1	473.6	408.7	423.6	382.9	323.3
Year-end Shs. Outstg. (000)	79,278	78,359	78,297	79,085	79,737	79,376	81,573
STATISTICAL RECORD:							
Return on Revenues %	12.2	12.8	13.1	13.4	12.3	12.2	8.1
Return on Equity %	12.7	13.7	14.1	15.8	13.4	13.8	10.0
Return on Assets %	3.8	4.1	4.3	4.8	4.5	4.5	3.2
Price Range	16.05-10.68	16.35-9.06	9.81-7.25	12.69-7.41	12.19-8.00	9.06-5.63	8.13-5.13
P/E Ratio	17.8-11.9	18.5-10.2	11.5-8.5	15.9-9.3	17.7-11.6	14.0-8.7	20.6-13.0
Average Yield %	2.2	2.2	3.0	2.4	2.2	2.7	2.9

Statistics are as originally reported. Adj. for stk. split: 100% div., 6/17/02 ① Bef. acctg. loss of $456,328

OFFICERS:
J. A. Newby, Chmn., Pres., C.E.O.
S. G. Rutledge, Sr. V.P., C.F.O.

INVESTOR CONTACT: Steve Rutledge, Sr. V.P., C.F.O., (334) 288-3900

PRINCIPAL OFFICE: 2108 East South Blvd., P.O. Box 11000, Montgomery, AL 36116

TELEPHONE NUMBER: (334) 288-3900
FAX: (334) 288-0905
WEB: www.alfains.com

NO. OF EMPLOYEES: 618 (avg.)

SHAREHOLDERS: 2,800 (approx.)

ANNUAL MEETING: In April
INCORPORATED: DE, 1974

INSTITUTIONAL HOLDINGS:
No. of Institutions: 63
Shares Held: 6,980,729
% Held: 9.3

INDUSTRY: Fire, marine, and casualty insurance (SIC: 6331)

REGISTRAR(S): American Stock Transfer & Trust Company, New York, NY

ALLTEL CORPORATION

YIELD 2.9%
P/E RATIO 15.1

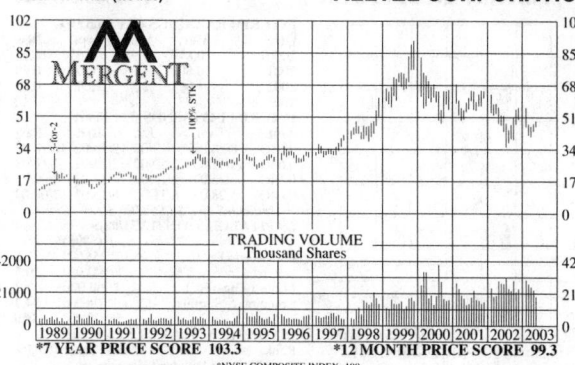

TRADING VOLUME
Thousand Shares

*7 YEAR PRICE SCORE 103.3   *12 MONTH PRICE SCORE 99.3
*NYSE COMPOSITE INDEX=100

INTERIM EARNINGS (Per Share):

Qtr.	Mar.	June	Sept.	Dec.
2000	0.68	3.15	1.53	0.83
2001	1.19	0.70	0.71	0.74
2002	0.68	0.69	0.76	0.82
2003	0.90	...	...	...

INTERIM DIVIDENDS (Per Share):

Amt.	Decl.	Ex.	Rec.	Pay.
0.34Q	7/25/02	9/05/02	9/09/02	10/03/02
0.35Q	10/24/02	12/05/02	12/09/02	1/03/03
0.35Q	1/23/03	2/20/03	2/24/03	4/03/03
0.35Q	4/24/03	6/05/03	6/09/03	7/03/03

Indicated div.: $1.40 (Div. Reinv. Plan)

CAPITALIZATION (12/31/02):

	($000)	(%)
Long-Term Debt	6,145,500	46.2
Deferred Income Tax	1,158,500	8.7
Preferred Stock	400	0.0
Common & Surplus	5,997,700	45.1
Total	13,302,100	100.0

DIVIDEND ACHIEVER STATUS:

Rank: 211   10-Year Growth Rate: 6.27%
Total Years of Dividend Growth: 42

RECENT DEVELOPMENTS: For the quarter ended 3/31/03, income from continuing operations was $227.6 million compared with income from continuing operations of $194.9 million in the corresponding year-earlier period. Results for 2002 included integration expenses and other charges of $42.8 million. Total revenues and sales rose 17.4% to $1.91 billion. Operating income climbed 23.3% to $466.0 million versus $377.9 million the year before.

PROSPECTS: AT's near-term outlook appears solid, reflecting the Company's growing wireless and wireline businesses. Separately, on 4/1/03, AT completed the sale of the financial services division of ALLTEL Information Services to Fidelity National Financial Inc. for $775.0 million in cash and $275.0 million in Fidelity National common stock. The telecommunication services division of ALLTEL Information Services will remain with AT.

BUSINESS

ALLTEL CORPORATION, with more than 12.0 million communication customers in 26 states as of 4/24/03, provides wireless and wireline local, long-distance, network access and Internet services, wide-area paging service and information processing management services and advanced application software. Telecommunications products are warehoused and sold by AT's distribution subsidiary. A subsidiary also publishes telephone directories for affiliates and other independent telephone companies. On 7/1/98, AT acquired 360 Communications Company. On 7/2/99, AT acquired Aliant Communications Inc. for $1.80 billion. In August 2002, AT purchased certain local telephone properties from Verizon for $1.90 billion and selected wireless properties from CenturyTel Inc. for $1.57 billion.

ANNUAL FINANCIAL DATA

	12/31/02	12/31/01	12/31/00	12/31/99	12/31/98	12/31/97	12/31/96
Earnings Per Share	[7] 2.96	[5][6] 3.34	[4][6] 6.20	[3] 2.47	[1] 1.89	[2] 2.70	[2] 1.53
Cash Flow Per Share	6.73	7.07	9.31	5.19	4.44	5.10	3.75
Tang. Book Val. Per Share	...	6.87	5.92	7.03	5.82	8.67	8.88
Dividends Per Share	1.36	1.32	1.28	1.22	1.16	1.10	1.04
Dividend Payout %	45.9	39.5	20.6	49.4	61.4	40.7	68.0
INCOME STATEMENT (IN MILLIONS)							
Total Revenues	7,983.4	7,598.9	7,067.0	6,302.3	5,194.0	3,263.6	3,192.4
Costs & Expenses	4,989.2	4,766.5	4,411.1	3,915.0	3,597.9	2,065.8	2,176.7
Depreciation & Amort.	1,178.6	1,167.7	988.4	862.2	707.1	450.8	424.1
Operating Income	1,815.6	1,664.7	1,667.5	1,525.1	889.0	[2] 747.0	[2] 591.6
Net Interest Inc./(Exp.)	d349.4	d288.9	d310.8	d280.2	d263.7	d130.2	d130.8
Income Before Income Taxes	1,465.5	1,751.8	3,350.7	1,330.9	972.3	828.7	461.4
Income Taxes	541.2	704.3	1,385.3	547.2	446.9	320.8	169.7
Net Income	[7] 924.3	[5][6] 1,047.5	[4][6] 1,965.4	[3] 783.6	[1] 525.5	[2] 507.9	[2] 291.7
Cash Flow	2,102.8	2,215.1	2,953.7	1,644.9	1,231.7	957.6	714.8
Average Shs. Outstg. (000)	312,300	313,500	317,200	316,814	277,276	187,689	190,370
BALANCE SHEET (IN MILLIONS)							
Cash & Cash Equivalents	155.5	85.3	67.2	17.6	55.5	16.2	13.9
Total Current Assets	1,646.0	1,767.8	1,780.7	1,167.2	980.8	665.8	709.5
Net Property	7,708.7	6,781.3	6,549.0	5,734.5	4,828.1	3,190.5	3,041.5
Total Assets	16,389.1	12,609.0	12,182.0	10,774.2	9,374.2	5,633.4	5,359.2
Total Current Liabilities	1,819.2	1,285.1	1,515.9	1,194.0	1,206.5	637.3	590.7
Long-Term Obligations	6,145.5	3,861.5	4,611.7	3,750.4	3,491.8	1,874.2	1,756.1
Net Stockholders' Equity	5,998.1	5,565.8	5,095.4	4,205.7	3,270.9	2,208.5	2,097.1
Net Working Capital	d173.2	482.7	264.8	d26.8	d225.7	28.6	118.8
Year-end Shs. Outstg. (000)	311,183	310,530	312,984	314,258	281,198	183,673	187,200
STATISTICAL RECORD:							
Operating Profit Margin %	22.7	21.9	23.6	24.2	17.1	22.9	18.5
Net Profit Margin %	11.6	13.8	27.8	12.4	10.1	15.6	9.1
Return on Equity %	15.4	18.8	38.6	18.6	16.1	23.0	13.9
Return on Assets %	5.6	8.3	16.1	7.3	5.6	9.0	5.4
Debt/Total Assets %	37.5	30.6	37.9	34.8	37.2	33.3	32.8
Price Range	63.25-35.33	68.69-49.43	82.94-47.75	91.81-56.31	61.38-38.25	41.63-29.75	35.63-26.63
P/E Ratio	21.4-11.9	20.6-14.8	13.4-7.7	37.2-22.8	32.5-20.2	15.4-11.0	23.3-17.4
Average Yield %	2.8	2.2	2.0	1.6	2.3	3.1	3.3

Statistics are as originally reported. [1] Incl. net chrg. of $10.8 mill. [2] Incl. non-recurr. chrg. 12/31/97: $189.7 mill.; chrg. 12/31/96: $74.2 mill. [3] Incl. chrgs. of $90.5 mill. [4] Incl. chrgs. of $25.4 mill. & gain on disp. of assets & oth. non-recurr. items of $1.93 bill. [5] Incl. chrgs. of $92.2 mill. & gain on disp. of assets & oth. non-recurr. items of $357.6 mill. [6] Bef. acctg. chge. cr. 12/31/01: $19.5 mill.; chrg. 12/31/00: $36.6 mill. [7] Incl. chrgs. of $115.1 mill. & gain on disp. of assets & oth. non-recurr. items of $985,000.

OFFICERS:
J. T. Ford, Chmn.
S. T. Ford, Pres., C.E.O.
J. R. Gardner, Exec. V.P., C.F.O.

INVESTOR CONTACT: Rob Clancy, Investor Relations, (501) 905-8991

PRINCIPAL OFFICE: One Allied Drive, Little Rock, AR 72202

TELEPHONE NUMBER: (501) 905-8000
FAX: (501) 905-0962
WEB: www.alltel.com
NO. OF EMPLOYEES: 25,348 (avg.)
SHAREHOLDERS: 254,521 (approx.)
ANNUAL MEETING: In Apr.
INCORPORATED: OH, June, 1960; reincorp., DE, 1990

INSTITUTIONAL HOLDINGS:
No. of Institutions: 553
Shares Held: 181,867,533
% Held: 58.5

INDUSTRY: Telephone communications, exc. radio (SIC: 4813)

TRANSFER AGENT(S): Wachovia Bank, Charlotte, NC

ALTRIA GROUP, INC.

YIELD 6.2%
P/E RATIO 8.0

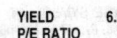
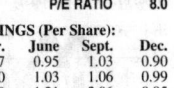

TRADING VOLUME
Thousand Shares

7 YEAR PRICE SCORE 114.7   *12 MONTH PRICE SCORE 81.8*

NYSE COMPOSITE INDEX=100

INTERIM EARNINGS (Per Share):

Qtr.	Mar.	June	Sept.	Dec.
2000	0.87	0.95	1.03	0.90
2001	0.80	1.03	1.06	0.99
2002	1.09	1.21	2.06	0.85
2003	1.07	...	...	...

INTERIM DIVIDENDS (Per Share):

Amt.	Decl.	Ex.	Rec.	Pay.
0.64Q	8/28/02	9/12/02	9/16/02	10/10/02
0.64Q	12/11/02	12/19/02	12/23/02	1/10/03
0.64Q	2/26/03	3/12/03	3/14/03	4/09/03
0.64Q	5/28/03	6/11/03	6/13/03	7/08/03

Indicated div.: $2.56 (Div. Reinv. Plan)

CAPITALIZATION (12/31/02):

	($000)	(%)
Long-Term Debt	21,355,000	37.6
Deferred Income Tax	11,633,000	20.5
Minority Interest	4,366,000	7.7
Common & Surplus	19,478,000	34.3
Total	56,832,000	100.0

DIVIDEND ACHIEVER STATUS:
Rank: 99   10-Year Growth Rate: 12.37%
Total Years of Dividend Growth: 37

RECENT DEVELOPMENTS: For the quarter ended 3/31/03, net earnings were $2.19 billion versus $2.37 billion in the corresponding year-earlier period. Results for 2002 included non-recurring charges of $192.0 million for various items. Net revenues fell 5.7% to $19.37 billion due primarily to the sale of MO's Miller Brewing Co. business and a $1.20 billion drop in domestic tobacco net revenues. Operating income slid 7.4% to $3.86 billion.

PROSPECTS: On 3/21/03, the judge in an Illinois class action, the Price case, found in favor of the plaintiff class and awarded about $7.10 billion in compensatory damages and $3.00 billion in punitive damages. Plaintiffs in the case alleged, among other things, that Philip Morris U.S.A.'s use of the terms "Lights" and/or "Ultra Lights" constituted deceptive and unfair trade practices. The Illinois class action case is not related to the state settlement agreements.

BUSINESS

ALTRIA GROUP, INC. (formerly Philip Morris Companies, Inc.) is one of the world's largest consumer products companies. Tobacco is manufactured and sold through Philip Morris U.S.A. (23.5% of 2002 operating revenues) and Philip Morris International Inc. (35.7%). Retail packaged foods are processed and marketed through Kraft Foods North America (26.7%) in the U.S. and Canada and Kraft Foods International (10.2%) in Europe and the Asia/Pacific region. Philip Morris Capital Corporation (0.6%) engages in financing and investment activities. On 7/9/02, MO combined its Miller Brewing Co. (3.3%) with South African Breweries plc, forming SABMiller plc. As of 12/31/02, MO maintained a 36.0% economic interest in SABMiller. As of 4/16/03, MO owned about 84.0% of Kraft Foods Inc.

ANNUAL FINANCIAL DATA

	12/31/02	12/31/01	12/31/00	12/31/99	12/31/98	12/31/97	12/31/96
Earnings Per Share	⑤ 5.21	④ 3.88	⑤ 3.75	② 3.19	① 2.20	① 2.58	2.56
Cash Flow Per Share	5.84	4.93	4.50	3.90	2.89	3.25	3.25
Dividends Per Share	2.38	2.17	1.97	1.80	1.64	1.60	1.40
Dividend Payout %	45.7	55.9	52.5	56.4	74.5	62.0	54.7

INCOME STATEMENT (IN MILLIONS):

Total Revenues	80,408.0	89,924.0	80,356.0	78,596.0	74,391.0	72,055.0	69,204.0
Costs & Expenses	62,476.0	71,885.0	63,960.0	63,404.0	62,724.0	58,763.0	55,744.0
Depreciation & Amort.	1,331.0	2,337.0	1,717.0	1,702.0	1,690.0	1,629.0	1,691.0
Operating Income	16,601.0	15,702.0	14,679.0	13,490.0	9,977.0	11,663.0	11,769.0
Net Interest Inc./(Exp.)	d1,134.0	d1,418.0	d719.0	d795.0	d890.0	d1,052.0	d1,086.0
Income Before Income Taxes	18,098.0	14,284.0	13,960.0	12,695.0	9,087.0	10,611.0	10,683.0
Income Taxes	6,424.0	5,407.0	5,450.0	5,020.0	3,715.0	4,301.0	4,380.0
Equity Earnings/Minority Int.	d572.0	d311.0	...	...	...	...	...
Net Income	⑪ 11,102.0	④ 8,566.0	③ 8,510.0	② 7,675.0	① 5,372.0	① 6,310.0	6,303.0
Cash Flow	12,433.0	10,903.0	10,227.0	9,377.0	7,062.0	7,939.0	7,994.0
Average Shs. Outstg. (000)	2,129,000	2,210,000	2,272,000	2,403,000	2,446,000	2,442,000	2,463,327

BALANCE SHEET (IN MILLIONS):

Cash & Cash Equivalents	565.0	453.0	937.0	5,100.0	4,081.0	2,282.0	240.0
Total Current Assets	17,441.0	17,275.0	17,238.0	20,895.0	20,230.0	17,440.0	15,190.0
Net Property	14,846.0	15,137.0	15,303.0	12,271.0	12,335.0	11,621.0	11,751.0
Total Assets	87,540.0	84,968.0	79,067.0	61,381.0	59,920.0	55,947.0	54,871.0
Total Current Liabilities	19,082.0	20,653.0	26,976.0	18,017.0	16,379.0	15,071.0	15,040.0
Long-Term Obligations	21,355.0	18,651.0	19,154.0	12,226.0	12,615.0	12,430.0	12,961.0
Net Stockholders' Equity	19,478.0	19,620.0	15,005.0	15,305.0	16,197.0	14,920.0	14,218.0
Net Working Capital	d1,641.0	d3,378.0	d9,738.0	2,878.0	3,851.0	2,369.0	150.0
Year-end Shs. Outstg. (000)	2,039,260	2,152,503	2,208,896	2,338,520	2,430,535	2,425,487	2,431,347

STATISTICAL RECORD:

Operating Profit Margin %	20.6	17.5	18.3	17.2	13.4	16.2	17.0
Net Profit Margin %	13.8	9.5	10.6	9.8	7.2	8.8	9.1
Return on Equity %	57.0	43.7	56.7	50.1	33.2	42.3	44.3
Return on Assets %	12.7	10.1	10.8	12.5	9.0	11.3	11.5
Debt/Total Assets %	24.4	22.0	24.2	19.9	21.1	22.2	23.6
Price Range	57.79-35.40	53.88-38.75	45.94-18.69	55.56-21.25	59.50-34.75	48.13-36.00	39.67-28.54
P/E Ratio	11.1-6.8	13.9-10.0	12.2-5.0	17.4-6.7	27.0-15.8	18.7-14.0	15.5-11.1
Average Yield %	5.1	4.7	6.1	4.7	3.5	3.8	4.1

Statistics are as originally reported. Adj. for 3-for-1 stk. split, 4/97. ① Incl. non-recurr. chrg. 12/31/98, $3.38 bill.; 12/31/97, $1.46 bill. ② Incl. chrgs. of $476.0 mill. for separation programs. ③ Incl. gain of $139.0 mill. on sale of a French confectionery business & $100.0 mill. gain on sale of beer rights. ④ Incl. non-recurr. chrg. of $19.0 mill. & loss of $82.0 mill. rel. to sale of factory and integr. costs; bef. acctg. chge. chrg. of $6.0 mill. ⑤ Incl. non-recurr. chrgs. of $624.0 mill., business sales gains of $80.0 mill. & gain of $2.63 bill. on Miller transaction.

OFFICERS:
L. C. Camilleri, Chmn., C.E.O.
D. S. Devitre, Sr. V.P., C.F.O.
A. J. Engel, V.P., Treas.

INVESTOR CONTACT: Nicholas M. Rolli, Investor Relations, (917) 663-3460

PRINCIPAL OFFICE: 120 Park Avenue, New York, NY 10017

TELEPHONE NUMBER: (917) 663-5000
FAX: (917) 878-2167
WEB: www.altria.com
NO. OF EMPLOYEES: 166,000 (approx.)
SHAREHOLDERS: 129,700 (approx.)
ANNUAL MEETING: In Apr.
INCORPORATED: VA, Mar., 1985

INSTITUTIONAL HOLDINGS:
No. of Institutions: 838
Shares Held: 1,360,025,591
% Held: 66.9

INDUSTRY: Cigarettes (SIC: 2111)

TRANSFER AGENT(S): First Chicago Trust Company, Jersey City, NJ

AMBAC FINANCIAL GROUP, INC.

YIELD 0.6%
P/E RATIO 16.0

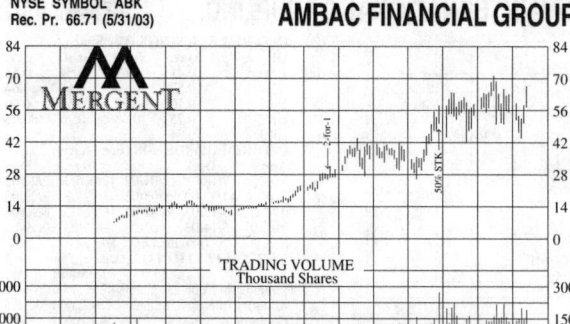

TRADING VOLUME
Thousand Shares

*7 YEAR PRICE SCORE 158.1 *12 MONTH PRICE SCORE 100.2
*NYSE COMPOSITE INDEX=100

INTERIM EARNINGS (Per Share):

Qtr.	Mar.	June	Sept.	Dec.
1999	0.69	0.67	0.75	0.79
2000	0.80	0.87	0.85	0.89
2001	0.90	0.99	1.02	1.07
2002	1.07	1.09	1.21	0.59
2003	1.27	...	...	...

INTERIM DIVIDENDS (Per Share):

Amt.	Decl.	Ex.	Rec.	Pay.
0.09Q	5/07/02	5/16/02	5/20/02	6/05/02
0.10Q	7/17/02	8/08/02	8/12/02	9/04/02
0.10Q	10/16/02	11/06/02	11/11/02	12/04/02
0.10Q	1/23/03	2/06/03	2/10/03	3/05/03
0.10Q	5/06/03	5/15/03	5/19/03	6/04/03

Indicated div.: $0.40

CAPITALIZATION (12/31/02):

	($000)	(%)
Long-Term Debt	616,715	13.9
Deferred Income Tax	185,641	4.2
Common & Surplus	3,625,179	81.9
Total	4,427,535	100.0

DIVIDEND ACHIEVER STATUS:
Rank: 127   10-Year Growth Rate: 10.77%
Total Years of Dividend Growth: 11

RECENT DEVELOPMENTS: For the quarter ended 3/31/03, net income increased 17.9% to $137.9 million from $117.0 million in the same period of the prior year. Total revenues grew 17.0% to $293.7 million. Revenues included a net realized investment gain of $14.3 million in 2003 and a realized investment loss of $309,000 in 2002. Also, revenues for 2003 and 2002 included mark-to-market losses on derivative hedge contracts of $11.5 million and $3.9 million, respectively.

PROSPECTS: Business activity remains robust as the low interest rate environment continues to fuel bond issues in all its markets. In public finance, ABK continues to benefit from the high level of municipal issuance. Structured finance growth was spurred by strong activity in both the consumer and commercial asset-backed segments. Meanwhile, in international finance, deal activity remains strong as the Company was able to close three large transportation transactions during the quarter.

BUSINESS

AMBAC FINANCIAL GROUP, Inc. is a holding company whose subsidiaries provide financial guarantee products and other financial services to clients in both the public and private sectors. The Company provides financial guarantees for public finance and structured finance obligations through its principal operating subsidiary, Ambac Assurance Corporation. Through its financial services subsidiaries, the Company provides financial and investment products including investment agreements, interest rate and total return swaps, funding conduits, investment advisory and cash management services. These products are sold principally to the Company's financial guarantee clients, which include municipalities and their authorities, school districts, health care organizations and asset-backed issuers.

ANNUAL FINANCIAL DATA

	12/31/02	12/31/01	12/31/00	12/31/99	12/31/98	12/31/97	12/31/96
Earnings Per Share	3.97	3.97	3.41	2.87	2.37	2.09	2.63
Cash Flow Per Share	4.08	3.86	3.32	2.86	1.43	1.14	1.74
Tang. Book Val. Per Share	34.20	28.26	24.60	19.23	19.98	17.85	15.34
Dividends Per Share	0.38	0.34	0.31	0.28	0.25	0.23	0.20
Dividend Payout %	9.6	8.6	9.0	9.7	10.7	11.0	7.8
INCOME STATEMENT (IN MILLIONS):							
Total Revenues	971.8	724.9	621.3	533.3	358.3	282.1	193.5
Costs & Expenses	351.6	122.2	104.4	61.3	55.2	44.9	40.6
Depreciation & Amort.	12.3	d12.4	d9.4	d1.5	d2.5	d1.3	0.4
Operating Income	607.9	615.1	526.3	473.5	305.6	238.5	152.6
Net Interest Inc./(Exp.)	d43.7	d40.4	d37.5	d62.3	d68.3	d49.3	d31.9
Income Before Income Taxes	564.2	568.7	482.1	404.7	230.1	186.3	280.8
Income Taxes	131.6	135.8	116.0	96.7	74.9	63.0	99.2
Net Income	432.6	432.9	366.2	307.9	155.2	123.3	181.6
Cash Flow	444.9	420.5	356.8	306.4	152.7	122.0	182.0
Average Shs. Outstg. (000)	109,066	108,948	107,415	107,049	106,995	106,841	104,895
BALANCE SHEET (IN MILLIONS):							
Cash & Cash Equivalents	682.4	502.8	554.7	337.5	380.1	231.0	321.4
Total Current Assets	1,132.9	930.2	848.5	1,462.9	1,548.9	786.7	607.9
Total Assets	15,355.5	12,267.7	10,120.3	11,345.1	11,212.3	8,249.7	5,876.0
Total Current Liabilities	353.4	680.4	131.0	941.2	917.3	339.7	93.3
Long-Term Obligations	616.7	619.3	424.1	424.0	423.9	223.9	223.8
Net Stockholders' Equity	3,625.2	2,983.7	2,596.1	2,018.5	2,096.1	1,872.5	1,615.0
Net Working Capital	779.5	249.8	717.5	521.8	631.6	447.0	514.5
Year-end Shs. Outstg. (000)	105,991	105,584	105,551	104,937	104,913	104,921	105,270
STATISTICAL RECORD:							
Operating Profit Margin %	62.6	84.9	84.7	88.8	85.3	84.6	78.8
Net Profit Margin %	44.5	59.7	58.9	57.7	43.3	43.7	93.9
Return on Equity %	11.9	14.5	14.1	15.3	7.4	6.6	11.2
Return on Assets %	2.8	3.5	3.6	2.7	1.4	1.5	3.1
Debt/Total Assets %	4.0	5.0	4.2	3.7	3.8	2.7	3.8
Price Range	71.25-49.86	64.00-42.20	58.31-25.92	42.00-29.79	43.96-27.25	31.71-20.67	23.17-15.17
P/E Ratio	17.9-12.6	16.1-10.6	17.1-7.6	14.6-10.4	18.5-11.5	15.2-9.9	8.8-5.8
Average Yield %	0.6	0.6	0.7	0.8	0.7	0.9	1.1

Statistics are as originally reported. Adj. for stk. splits: 50% div., 12/00; 2-for-1, 9/97

OFFICERS:
P. B. Lassiter, Chmn., Pres., C.E.O.
R. Genader, Pres., C.O.O.
T. J. Gandolfo, C.F.O., Contr.

INVESTOR CONTACT: Peter R. Poillon, Investor Relations, (212) 208-3333

PRINCIPAL OFFICE: One State Street Plaza, New York, NY 10004

TELEPHONE NUMBER: (212) 668-0340
FAX: (212) 509-9190
WEB: www.ambac.com
NO. OF EMPLOYEES: 391 (avg.)
SHAREHOLDERS: 78
ANNUAL MEETING: In May
INCORPORATED: DE, Apr., 1991

INSTITUTIONAL HOLDINGS:
No. of Institutions: 389
Shares Held: 100,922,354
% Held: 95.2

INDUSTRY: Surety insurance (SIC: 6351)

TRANSFER AGENT(S): Citibank, N.A., New York, NY

AMERICAN INTERNATIONAL GROUP, INC.

YIELD 0.4%
P/E RATIO 27.7

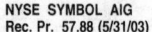
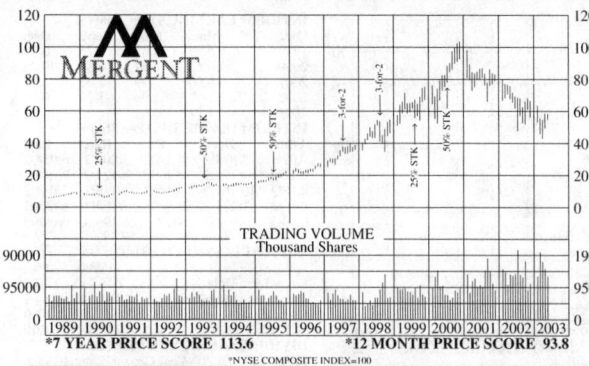

TRADING VOLUME
Thousand Shares

*7 YEAR PRICE SCORE 113.6   *12 MONTH PRICE SCORE 93.8
*NYSE COMPOSITE INDEX=100

INTERIM EARNINGS (Per Share):

Qtr.	Mar.	June	Sept.	Dec.
1999	0.41	0.67	0.54	0.56
2000	0.57	0.90	0.60	0.64
2001	0.70	0.50	0.15	0.70
2002	0.75	0.68	0.70	d0.03
2003	0.74	...	...	...

INTERIM DIVIDENDS (Per Share):

Amt.	Decl.	Ex.	Rec.	Pay.
0.047Q	9/18/02	12/04/02	12/06/02	12/20/02
0.047Q	11/13/02	3/05/03	3/07/03	3/21/03
0.047Q	3/12/03	6/04/03	6/06/03	6/20/03
0.052Q	5/14/03	9/03/03	9/05/03	9/19/03

Indicated div.: $0.21

CAPITALIZATION (12/31/02):

	($000)	(%)
Long-Term Debt	47,923,000	44.1
Minority Interest	1,580,000	1.5
Common & Surplus	59,103,000	54.4
Total	108,606,000	100.0

DIVIDEND ACHIEVER STATUS:

Rank: 101   10-Year Growth Rate: 12.30%
Total Years of Dividend Growth: 17

RECENT DEVELOPMENTS: For the quarter ended 3/31/03, net income declined 1.3% to $1.95 billion from $1.98 billion in the corresponding prior-year quarter. Results for 2003 and 2002 included after-tax realized capital losses of $412.8 million and $150.4 million, respectively. Total revenues increased 17.3% to $18.93 billion from $16.14 billion the previous year. Premiums and other considerations advanced 25.8% to $12.95 billion from $10.29 billion in 2002. Net investment income grew 10.3% to $4.02 billion from $3.65 billion the year before.

PROSPECTS: Going forward, AIG expects premium rates to continue to strengthen in 2003, both domestically and in key international markets. Meanwhile, in the life insurance segment, AIG expects continued growth with respect to its domestic individual fixed annuity operation. Internationally, AIG's life insurance operations are expected to achieve double-digit growth as it further expands its operations in China to include Beijing, Suzhou, Dongguan and Jiangmen. AIG also expects additional growth opportunities in India and Vietnam.

BUSINESS

AMERICAN INTERNATIONAL GROUP, INC. is a holding company that, through its subsidiaries, is engaged in a broad range of insurance and insurance-related activities in the United States and internationally. AIG's primary activities include general and life insurance operations. Other significant activities include financial services, and retirement savings and asset management. AIG's general insurance subsidiaries are multiple line companies writing substantially all lines of property and casualty insurance. On 1/1/99, AIG acquired SunAmerica Inc. for $18.00 billion. On 8/28/01, the Company acquired American General Corporation for approximately $23.00 billion.

ANNUAL FINANCIAL DATA

	12/31/02	②12/31/01	12/31/00	12/31/99	12/31/98	12/31/97	12/31/96
Earnings Per Share	③2.10	⑤2.07	2.41	2.15	1.90	1.68	1.46
Tang. Book Val. Per Share	20.32	19.94	16.98	14.33	13.78	12.20	11.13
Dividends Per Share	0.18	0.16	0.14	0.13	0.11	0.10	0.09
Dividend Payout %	8.5	7.6	5.8	5.9	5.9	6.0	6.0

INCOME STATEMENT (IN MILLIONS):

Total Premium Income	44,589.0	38,608.0	31,017.0	27,486.0	24,345.0	22,346.7	20,833.1
Other Income	67,482.0	16,851.0	11,423.0	10,265.0	6,507.0	5,600.7	5,041.2
Total Revenues	67,482.0	55,459.0	42,440.0	37,751.0	30,852.0	27,947.4	25,874.3
Policyholder Benefits	12,917.0	13,863.0	7,186.0	6,919.0	6,036.0	5,607.0	5,451.1
Income Before Income Taxes	8,142.0	8,139.0	8,349.0	7,512.0	5,472.0	4,617.2	3,957.1
Income Taxes	2,328.0	2,339.0	2,458.0	2,219.0	1,594.0	1,366.6	1,116.0
Equity Earnings/Minority Int.	d295.0	d301.0	d255.0	d238.0	d112.0	81.7	56.1
Net Income	⑤5,519.0	①5,499.0	5,636.0	5,055.0	3,766.0	3,332.3	2,897.3
Average Shs. Outstg. (000)	2,634,000	2,650,000	2,343,000	2,350,500	1,978,125	1,982,768	1,987,221

BALANCE SHEET (IN MILLIONS):

Cash & Cash Equivalents	70,517.0	65,150.0	53,692.0	43,995.0	36,784.0	28,972.3	22,963.9
Premiums Due	63,613.0	60,954.0	42,012.0	37,898.0	35,652.0	33,109.0	29,937.1
Invst. Assets: Fixed-term	243,366.0	200,616.0	102,010.0	90,142.0	61,906.0	51,326.7	48,148.0
Invst. Assets: Equities	5,482.0	6,188.0	6,125.0	6,002.0	5,565.0	5,209.3	5,989.6
Invst. Assets: Loans	19,928.0	18,092.0	12,243.0	12,134.0	8,247.0	7,919.8	7,876.8
Invst. Assets: Total	328,306.0	297,855.0	173,524.0	152,204.0	114,526.0	94,970.6	87,696.9
Total Assets	561,229.0	492,982.0	306,577.0	268,238.0	194,398.0	163,970.7	148,431.0
Long-Term Obligations	47,923.0	37,447.0	20,672.0	2,344.0	1,620.0	13,885.4	13,299.3
Net Stockholders' Equity	59,103.0	52,150.0	39,619.0	33,306.0	27,131.0	24,001.1	22,044.2
Year-end Shs. Outstg. (000)	2,609,600	2,615,432	2,332,713	2,323,692	1,968,750	1,967,394	1,980,454

STATISTICAL RECORD:

Return on Revenues %	8.2	9.9	13.3	13.4	12.2	11.9	11.2
Return on Equity %	9.3	10.5	14.2	15.2	13.9	13.9	13.1
Return on Assets %	1.0	1.1	1.8	1.9	1.9	2.0	2.0
Price Range	80.00-47.61	98.31-66.00	103.75-52.38	75.25-51.00	54.74-34.60	40.02-25.25	27.59-20.89
P/E Ratio	38.1-22.7	47.5-31.9	43.0-21.7	35.0-23.7	28.7-18.2	23.8-15.0	18.9-14.3
Average Yield %	0.3	0.2	0.2	0.2	0.3	0.3	0.4

Statistics are as originally reported. Adj. for stk. splits: 25% div., 7/30/99; 3-for-2, 7/98, 7/97. ① Bef. acctg. change chrg. $136.2 mill.; Incl. after-tax acquisition chrgs. $1.38 bill.; a realized capital loss $541.7 mill. & after-tax loss of $33.0 mill. related to the terrorist attacks on 9/11/01. ② Refl. acq. of American General Corp. on 8/28/01 ③ Incl. after-tax reserve chrg. of $1.79 bill.

OFFICERS:
M. R. Greenberg, Chmn., C.E.O.
M. J. Sullivan, Co-Vice-Chmn., C.O.O.
H. I. Smith, Vice-Chmn., C.F.O.

INVESTOR CONTACT: Charlene M. Hamrah, Inv. Relations, (212) 770-3144

PRINCIPAL OFFICE: 70 Pine Street, New York, NY 10270

TELEPHONE NUMBER: (212) 770-7000
FAX: (212) 344-6828
WEB: www.aig.com

NO. OF EMPLOYEES: 80,000 (approx.)

SHAREHOLDERS: 60,000 (approx.)

ANNUAL MEETING: In May

INCORPORATED: DE, June, 1967

INSTITUTIONAL HOLDINGS:
No. of Institutions: 1,218
Shares Held: 1,536,141,605
% Held: 58.9

INDUSTRY: Fire, marine, and casualty insurance (SIC: 6331)

TRANSFER AGENT(S): EquiServe Trust Company, N.A., Jersey City, NJ

AMERICAN NATIONAL INSURANCE COMPANY

YIELD 3.5%
P/E RATIO 76.5

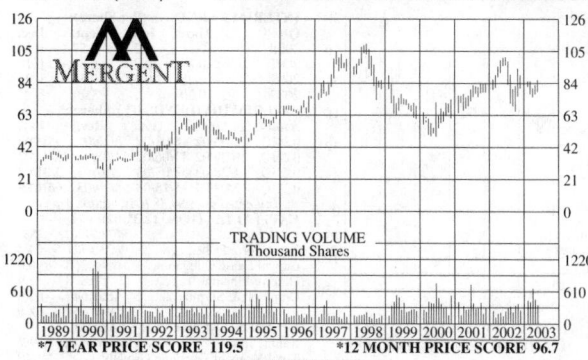

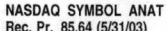

7 YEAR PRICE SCORE 119.5   **12 MONTH PRICE SCORE 96.7**

*NYSE COMPOSITE INDEX=100

TRADING VOLUME
Thousand Shares

INTERIM EARNINGS (Per Share):

Qtr.	Mar.	June	Sept.	Dec.
1999	4.20	1.55	1.73	2.60
2000	2.36	1.56	1.45	d0.08
2001	1.39	1.56	d0.17	d0.33
2002	1.59	0.79	1.19	d2.37
2003	1.51	...	...	...

INTERIM DIVIDENDS (Per Share):

Amt.	Decl.	Ex.	Rec.	Pay.
0.74Q	7/25/02	9/04/02	9/06/02	9/20/02
0.74Q	11/01/02	12/04/02	12/06/02	12/20/02
0.74Q	2/27/03	3/05/03	3/07/03	3/21/03
0.74Q	4/25/03	6/04/03	6/06/03	6/20/03

Indicated div.: $2.96

CAPITALIZATION (12/31/02):

	($000)	(%)
Long-Term Debt	204,128	6.5
Deferred Income Tax	47,710	1.5
Minority Interest	8,982	0.3
Common & Surplus	2,873,729	91.7
Total	3,134,549	100.0

DIVIDEND ACHIEVER STATUS:
Rank: 246   10-Year Growth Rate: 4.42%
Total Years of Dividend Growth: 29

RECENT DEVELOPMENTS: For the quarter ended 3/31/03, net income declined 4.8% to $40.1 million compared with $42.1 million in the equivalent 2002 quarter. The decline in earnings was primarily attributed to $15.5 million of an other-than-temporary impairment of marketable securities on an after-tax basis, partially offset by an after-tax realized capital gain of $12.6 million. Revenues rose 5.2% to $620.0 million from $589.6 million a year earlier mainly

due to higher premiums, which grew 8.6% versus the same period of 2002. Property and casualty premiums grew to $238.8 million from $198.3 million the year before. Net investment income amounted to $143.5 million versus $137.0 million in 2002. Revenues included a net loss of $4.4 million and a net gain of $8.6 million in 2003 and 2002, respectively, on the sale of investments.

BUSINESS

AMERICAN NATIONAL INSURANCE COMPANY served more than 3.3 million policy holders in 49 states, the District of Columbia, Mexico, Puerto Rico, Guam, American Samoa and Western Europe as of 12/31/02. ANAT offers a broad line of insurance coverages including: life, health, and annuities; group life and health; personal lines property and casualty and credit insurance. ANAT also offers investment and advisory services through its subsidiary broker-dealer, Securities Management and Research, Inc. ANAT's major insurance subsidiary companies include American National Life Insurance Co. of Texas, American National Property and Casualty Co., American National de Mexico, Compania de Seguros de Vida, S.A. de C.V., Garden State Life Insurance Co., Farm Family Life Insurance Co., Farm Family Casualty Insurance Co., United Farm Family Insurance Co. and Standard Life and Accident Insurance Co.

ANNUAL FINANCIAL DATA

	12/31/02	12/31/01	12/31/00	12/31/99	12/31/98	12/31/97	12/31/96
Earnings Per Share	0.64	① 2.45	5.29	10.07	7.45	9.38	8.14
Tang. Book Val. Per Share	108.53	110.89	114.19	115.68	110.07	102.17	93.43
Dividends Per Share	2.96	2.93	2.86	2.78	2.70	2.62	2.54
Dividend Payout %	462.4	119.6	54.1	27.6	36.2	27.9	31.2
INCOME STATEMENT (IN MILLIONS)							
Total Premium Income	1,747.2	1,546.0	1,292.0	1,230.9	1,193.7	1,140.5	1,034.9
Net Investment Income	563.5	529.1	479.1	473.9	475.2	472.9	435.7
Other Income	d69.4	59.2	63.4	184.7	75.7	126.5	79.4
Total Revenues	2,241.3	2,134.4	1,834.5	1,889.6	1,744.7	1,739.9	1,550.0
Policyholder Benefits	1,320.4	1,202.9	963.5	866.1	828.6	895.9	831.1
Income Before Income Taxes	26.8	105.1	206.9	388.7	273.9	373.0	305.5
Income Taxes	10.0	40.2	66.8	122.1	76.5	124.7	89.9
Net Income	16.9	① 64.9	140.2	266.6	197.4	248.4	215.6
Average Shs. Outstg. (000)	26,480	26,479	26,479	26,479	26,479	26,479	26,479
BALANCE SHEET (IN MILLIONS)							
Cash & Cash Equivalents	631.4	443.5	297.3	109.7	112.6	132.2	19.0
Premiums Due	1,106.9	1,033.4	572.2	395.9	328.3	274.9	223.6
Invst. Assets: Fixed-term	4,497.0	3,811.6	3,534.5	3,636.8	3,566.0	3,605.9	3,430.7
Invst. Assets: Equities	758.3	889.1	844.9	963.3	1,051.9	882.9	754.0
Invst. Assets: Loans	1,351.7	1,332.5	1,318.6	1,326.6	1,321.8	1,403.9	1,401.9
Invst. Assets: Total	9,175.0	8,453.7	7,148.2	7,372.9	7,263.6	7,082.8	6,661.8
Total Assets	12,139.2	11,258.1	9,270.4	9,090.5	8,815.7	8,483.0	7,988.5
Long-Term Obligations	204.1	204.4	...	...	...	...	...
Net Stockholders' Equity	2,873.7	2,936.3	3,023.7	3,063.1	2,914.6	2,705.4	2,473.9
Year-end Shs. Outstg. (000)	26,480	26,480	26,479	26,479	26,479	26,479	26,479
STATISTICAL RECORD:							
Return on Revenues %	0.8	3.0	7.6	14.1	11.3	14.3	13.9
Return on Equity %	0.6	2.2	4.6	8.7	6.8	9.2	8.7
Return on Assets %	0.1	0.6	1.5	2.9	2.2	2.9	2.7
Price Range	101.38-65.56	84.10-64.50	73.50-49.00	89.38-60.63	109.88-73.00	105.00-73.00	75.50-63.00
P/E Ratio	158.4-102.4	34.3-26.3	13.9-9.3	8.9-6.0	14.7-9.8	11.2-7.8	9.3-7.7
Average Yield %	3.5	3.9	4.7	3.7	3.0	2.9	3.7

Statistics are as originally reported. ① Incl. chrgs. of $21.1 mill. rel. to the events of 9/11/01 & start-up costs of $6.5 mill.

OFFICERS:
R. L. Moody, Chmn., C.E.O.
G. R. Ferdinandtsen, Pres., C.O.O.
V. J. Krc, Asst. Treas.
J. M. Flippin, Sec.

INVESTOR CONTACT: Investor Relations, (409) 763-4661

PRINCIPAL OFFICE: One Moody Plaza, Galveston, TX 77550-7999

TELEPHONE NUMBER: (409) 763-4661
FAX: (409) 766-6502
WEB: www.anico.com

NO. OF EMPLOYEES: 1,500

SHAREHOLDERS: 1,557 (approx.)

ANNUAL MEETING: In Apr.

INCORPORATED: TX, Mar., 1905

INSTITUTIONAL HOLDINGS:
No. of Institutions: 81
Shares Held: 14,973,853
% Held: 57.6

INDUSTRY: Life insurance (SIC: 6311)

TRANSFER AGENT(S): Mellon Investor Services LLC, South Hackensack, NJ

AMERICAN STATES WATER COMPANY

YIELD 3.5%
P/E RATIO 19.9

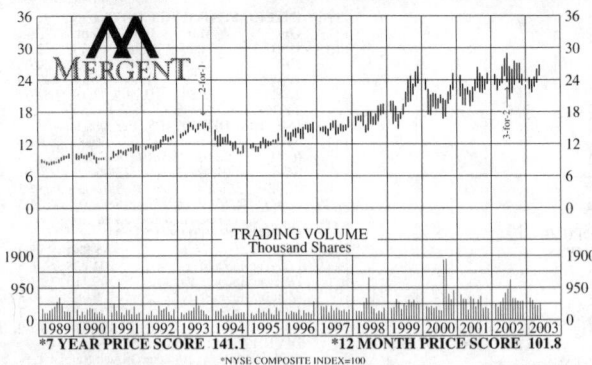

INTERIM EARNINGS (Per Share):

Qtr.	Mar.	June	Sept.	Dec.
2000	0.21	0.29	0.57	0.20
2001	0.20	0.33	0.62	0.18
2002	0.25	0.35	0.50	0.23
2003	0.20	...	...	...

INTERIM DIVIDENDS (Per Share):

Amt.	Decl.	Ex.	Rec.	Pay.
0.217Q	8/06/02	8/08/02	8/12/02	9/01/02
0.221Q	10/29/02	11/06/02	11/08/02	12/01/02
0.221Q	1/28/03	2/05/03	2/07/03	3/01/03
0.221Q	5/08/03	5/15/03	5/19/03	6/01/03

Indicated div.: $0.88 (Div. Reinv. Plan)

CAPITALIZATION (12/31/02):

	($000)	(%)
Long-Term Debt	230,721	24.4
Capital Lease Obligations..	368	0.0
Deferred Income Tax	55,828	5.9
Common & Surplus	657,647	69.6
Total	944,564	100.0

TRADING VOLUME
Thousand Shares

*7 YEAR PRICE SCORE 141.1   *12 MONTH PRICE SCORE 101.8
*NYSE COMPOSITE INDEX=100

DIVIDEND ACHIEVER STATUS:

Rank: 283   10-Year Growth Rate: 1.29%
Total Years of Dividend Growth: 49

RECENT DEVELOPMENTS: For the quarter ended 3/31/03, net income fell 21.5% to $3.0 million versus $3.8 million in the equivalent 2002 quarter due to the effects of delayed rate increases and the California Public Utility Commission's (CPUC) elimination of an earnings impact protection from increasing supply costs at AWR's largest water utility unit. Revenues grew 4.9% to $46.7 million due to electric rate increases during 2002 at AWR's Bear Valley Electric division.

PROSPECTS: Looking ahead, AWR's subsidiary, Southern California Water Company (SCW), has approved anticipated net capital expenditures of about $81.6 million, principally reflecting the 2003 infrastructure replacement program in SCW's metropolitan customer service area, a water treatment plant upgrade, water supply related projects, and security-related costs. However, approved capital expenditures may be limited pending CPUC approval of SCW's generate rate case filings.

BUSINESS

AMERICAN STATES WATER COMPANY is a public utility engaged principally in the purchase, production, distribution, and sale of water, and distribution of electricity through its primary subsidiary Southern California Water Company (SCW). SCW is organized into three water service regions and one electric customer service area operating within 75 communities in 10 counties in California and provides water service in 21 customer service areas. As of 5/13/03, SCW served approximately 22,000 electric customers. Through its American States Utility Services (ASUS) subsidiary, the Company contracts to lease, operate and maintain government-owned water and wastewater systems and to provide other services to local governments to assist them in the operation and maintenance of their water and wastewater systems. ASUS has approximately 91,500 accounts under contract. Through its Chaparral City Water Company, the Company serves approximately 12,000 customers in the town of Fountain Hills, Arizona and a portion of the City of Scottsdale, Arizona.

ANNUAL FINANCIAL DATA

	12/31/02	12/31/01	12/31/00	12/31/99	12/31/98	12/31/97	12/31/96
Earnings Per Share	1.34	1.33	1.27	1.19	1.08	1.04	1.13
Cash Flow Per Share	2.55	2.51	2.36	2.26	2.04	1.89	2.01
Tang. Book Val. Per Share	43.32	42.83	37.31	36.25	32.11	31.21	30.22
Dividends Per Share	0.871	0.867	0.86	0.85	0.84	0.83	0.82
Dividend Payout %	65.0	65.2	67.3	71.5	77.8	79.8	72.5
INCOME STATEMENT (IN THOUSANDS):							
Total Revenues	209,205	197,514	183,960	173,421	148,060	153,755	151,529
Costs & Expenses	153,255	142,871	136,314	130,543	110,120	118,910	117,711
Depreciation & Amort.	18,302	17,951	15,339	14,364	12,929	11,387	10,389
Operating Income	37,648	36,692	32,307	28,514	25,011	23,458	23,429
Net Interest Inc./(Exp.)	d17,699	d15,735	d14,122	d12,945	d11,207	d10,157	d10,500
Income Before Income Taxes	20,339	20,447	18,086	16,101	14,573	14,059	13,460
Net Income	20,339	20,447	18,086	16,101	14,573	14,059	13,460
Cash Flow	38,612	38,314	33,339	30,377	27,412	25,354	23,755
Average Shs. Outstg.	15,157	15,257	14,117	13,437	13,437	13,436	11,837
BALANCE SHEET (IN THOUSANDS):							
Cash & Cash Equivalents	18,397	30,496	5,808	2,189	620	4,186	3,783
Total Current Assets	51,846	87,789	52,480	44,340	39,288	44,494	43,762
Net Property	563,311	539,842	509,096	449,595	414,753	383,623	357,776
Total Assets	701,650	763,764	616,646	533,181	484,671	457,074	430,922
Total Current Liabilities	79,520	63,636	80,217	54,965	63,768	56,180	44,688
Long-Term Obligations	231,089	245,692	176,452	167,363	120,809	115,286	107,190
Net Stockholders' Equity	657,647	649,136	565,418	488,615	433,007	421,032	404,402
Net Working Capital	d27,674	24,153	d27,737	d10,625	d24,480	d11,686	d926
Year-end Shs. Outstg.	15,181	15,119	15,113	13,437	13,437	13,437	13,329
STATISTICAL RECORD:							
Operating Profit Margin %	18.0	18.6	17.6	16.4	16.9	15.3	15.5
Net Profit Margin %	9.7	10.4	9.8	9.3	9.8	9.1	8.9
Return on Equity %	3.1	3.1	3.2	3.3	3.4	3.3	3.3
Return on Assets %	2.9	3.0	3.0	3.0	3.0	3.1	3.1
Debt/Total Assets %	32.9	35.9	28.6	31.4	24.9	25.2	24.9
Price Range	29.01-20.25	26.40-19.00	25.29-16.67	26.50-14.79	19.50-14.08	18.13-13.50	16.08-12.50
P/E Ratio	21.6-15.1	19.8-14.3	19.9-13.1	22.2-12.4	18.1-13.0	16.4-13.0	14.3-11.1
Average Yield %	3.5	3.8	4.1	4.1	5.0	5.4	5.7

Statistics are as originally reported. Adj. for stk. split: 3-for-2, 6/02.

OFFICERS:
L. E. Ross, Chmn.
F. E. Wicks, Pres., C.E.O.
M. Harris, III, Sr. V.P., C.F.O., Treas., Sec.

INVESTOR CONTACT: M. Harris, III, (909) 394-3000 ext. 705

PRINCIPAL OFFICE: 630 East Foothill Blvd., San Dimas, CA 91773-1212

TELEPHONE NUMBER: (909) 394-3600
FAX: (909) 394-0711
WEB: www.aswater.com

NO. OF EMPLOYEES: 503 (avg.)

SHAREHOLDERS: 3,438

ANNUAL MEETING: In Apr.

INCORPORATED: CA, Dec., 1929

INSTITUTIONAL HOLDINGS:
No. of Institutions: 101
Shares Held: 5,283,786
% Held: 35.2

INDUSTRY: Water supply (SIC: 4941)

TRANSFER AGENT(S): Mellon Investor Services, L.L.C., Ridgefield Park, NJ

AMSOUTH BANCORPORATION

YIELD 4.1%
P/E RATIO 12.9

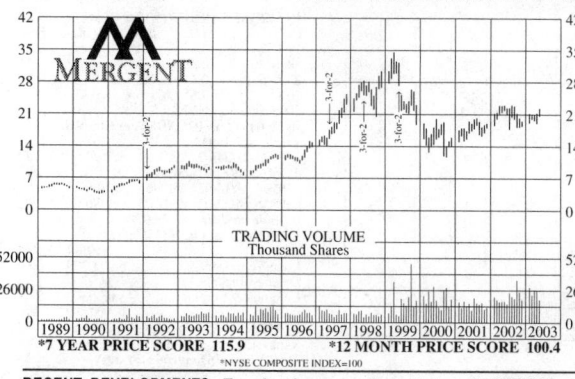

TRADING VOLUME
Thousand Shares

*7 YEAR PRICE SCORE 115.9   *12 MONTH PRICE SCORE 100.4
*NYSE COMPOSITE INDEX=100

INTERIM EARNINGS (Per Share):

Qtr.	Mar.	June	Sept.	Dec.
2000	0.35	0.26	d0.10	0.34
2001	0.34	0.36	0.37	0.38
2002	0.40	0.42	0.43	0.44
2003	0.44	...	...	...

INTERIM DIVIDENDS (Per Share):

Amt.	Decl.	Ex.	Rec.	Pay.
0.22Q	7/18/02	9/13/02	9/17/02	10/01/02
0.23Q	10/17/02	12/17/02	12/19/02	1/02/03
0.23Q	1/16/03	3/14/03	3/18/03	4/01/03
0.23Q	4/17/03	6/13/03	6/17/03	7/01/03

Indicated div.: $0.92 (Div. Reinv. Plan)

CAPITALIZATION (12/31/02):

	($000)	(%)
Total Deposits	27,315,624	73.2
Long-Term Debt	6,888,700	18.5
Capital Lease Obligations	583	0.0
Common & Surplus	3,115,997	8.3
Total	37,320,904	100.0

DIVIDEND ACHIEVER STATUS:

Rank: 124   10-Year Growth Rate: 11.06%
Total Years of Dividend Growth: 32

RECENT DEVELOPMENTS: For the three months ended 3/31/03, net income grew 6.7% to $155.4 million from $145.6 million in the same period of the previous year. Net interest income slipped 2.3% to $363.0 million from $371.7 million a year earlier. Provision for loan losses fell 20.3% to $44.7 million from $56.1 million the year before. Non-interest revenues climbed 8.6% to $192.9 million, while non-interest expenses rose 0.9% to $289.6 million.

PROSPECTS: Results are being positively affected by continued loan growth, fueled by strength in the commercial middle market and increased residential mortgages, along with total deposit growth. Meanwhile, operating profitability is benefiting from improved credit quality, as net charge-offs continue to decline in the Company's consumer and commercial loan portfolios.

BUSINESS

AMSOUTH BANCORPORATION is a regional bank holding company headquartered in Birmingham, Alabama. As of 3/31/03, ASO had assets of $42.10 billion and operated 600 branch banking offices and more than 1,200 ATMs in the following southeastern states: Alabama, Florida, Tennessee, Mississippi, Georgia, and Louisiana. ASO's affiliates, AmSouth N.A., AmSouth Bank of Florida, AmSouth Bank of Tennessee, AmSouth Bank of Georgia and AmSouth Bank of Alabama, AmSouth Investment Services and AmSouth Leasing Corporation, provide a full line of traditional and non-traditional financial services including consumer and commercial banking, small business banking, mortgage lending, equipment leasing, annuity and mutual fund sales, and trust and investment management services. On 10/1/99, ASO acquired First American Corporation.

ANNUAL FINANCIAL DATA

	12/31/02	12/31/01	12/31/00	12/31/99	12/31/98	12/31/97	12/31/96
Earnings Per Share	1.68	1.45	④ 0.86	③ 0.86	② 1.45	1.21	① 0.96
Tang. Book Val. Per Share	8.82	8.14	7.53	7.56	8.05	7.64	7.38
Dividends Per Share	0.88	0.84	0.80	0.67	0.53	0.50	0.47
Dividend Payout %	52.4	57.9	93.0	78.3	36.9	41.0	49.5
INCOME STATEMENT (IN MILLIONS):							
Total Interest Income	2,254.1	2,634.5	3,070.4	2,932.8	1,462.5	1,377.8	1,353.8
Total Interest Expense	781.5	1,239.7	1,691.3	1,424.8	763.6	701.5	701.4
Net Interest Income	1,472.6	1,394.9	1,379.1	1,507.9	699.0	676.3	652.4
Provision for Loan Losses	213.6	187.1	227.6	165.6	58.1	67.4	65.2
Non-Interest Income	739.4	748.2	669.5	847.6	346.6	266.0	235.3
Non-Interest Expense	1,126.6	1,185.4	1,366.4	1,648.5	582.1	526.2	534.2
Income Before Taxes	871.8	770.6	454.6	541.4	405.3	348.7	288.3
Net Income	609.1	536.3	④ 329.1	③ 340.5	② 262.7	226.2	① 182.7
Average Shs. Outstg. (000)	362,329	370,948	384,677	396,515	181,922	186,179	191,042
BALANCE SHEET (IN MILLIONS):							
Cash & Due from Banks	1,220.0	1,441.6	1,278.7	1,563.3	619.6	658.5	648.5
Securities Avail. for Sale	4,792.8	4,842.5	1,920.9	6,016.7	3,033.5	2,509.1	2,294.4
Total Loans & Leases	27,350.9	25,124.5	24,616.4	26,436.4	12,869.9	12,342.8	12,168.6
Allowance for Credit Losses	1,093.1	1,091.3	852.2	533.1	283.7	284.4	267.4
Net Loans & Leases	26,969.3	24,033.2	23,764.3	25,903.3	12,586.2	12,058.5	11,901.2
Total Assets	40,571.3	38,600.4	38,936.0	43,406.6	19,901.7	18,622.3	18,407.3
Total Deposits	27,315.6	26,167.0	26,623.3	27,912.4	13,283.8	12,945.2	12,467.6
Long-Term Obligations	6,889.3	6,102.3	5,883.4	5,603.5	3,239.8	1,633.2	1,435.7
Total Liabilities	37,455.3	35,645.3	36,122.6	40,447.3	18,474.1	17,237.0	17,011.4
Net Stockholders' Equity	3,116.0	2,955.1	2,813.4	2,959.2	1,427.6	1,385.2	1,395.8
Year-end Shs. Outstg. (000)	353,424	363,035	373,807	391,374	177,377	181,208	189,081
STATISTICAL RECORD:							
Return on Equity %	19.5	18.1	11.7	11.5	18.4	16.3	13.1
Return on Assets %	1.5	1.4	0.8	0.8	1.3	1.2	1.0
Equity/Assets %	7.7	7.7	7.2	6.8	7.2	7.4	7.6
Non-Int. Exp./Tot. Inc. %	50.9	55.3	66.7	70.0	55.7	55.8	60.2
Price Range	23.06-17.75	20.24-15.00	20.06-11.69	34.59-18.75	30.42-20.46	25.36-14.00	15.07-10.19
P/E Ratio	13.7-10.6	14.0-10.3	23.3-13.6	40.2-21.8	21.0-14.1	20.9-11.5	15.8-10.6
Average Yield %	4.3	4.8	5.0	2.5	2.1	2.5	3.8

Statistics are as originally reported. Adj. for 3-for-2 splits 5/99, 4/98, 4/97. ① Incl. SAIF pre-tax chrg. of $24.2 mill. ② Incl. $28.0 mill. gain fr. sale of assets. ③ Incl. net gain fr. sale of businesses of $8.6 mill. & merger-rel. chrgs. of $301.4 mill. ④ Incl. pre-tax merger-rel. costs of $110.2 mill. & a gain of $538,000 on the sale of businesses.

OFFICERS:
C. D. Ritter, Chmn., Pres., C.E.O.
S. D. Gibson, Vice-Chmn., C.F.O.
S. A. Yoder, Exec. V.P., Gen. Couns., Sec.

INVESTOR CONTACT: M. List Underwood, Jr., Exec. V.P.-Corp. Fin., (205) 801-0265

PRINCIPAL OFFICE: 1900 Fifth Avenue North, Birmingham, AL 35203

TELEPHONE NUMBER: (205) 320-7151
FAX: (205) 326-4072
WEB: www.amsouth.com

NO. OF EMPLOYEES: 11,600 (approx.)

SHAREHOLDERS: 33,630 (approx.)

ANNUAL MEETING: In Apr.

INCORPORATED: DE, Nov., 1970

INSTITUTIONAL HOLDINGS:
No. of Institutions: 343
Shares Held: 145,767,342
% Held: 41.1

INDUSTRY: State commercial banks (SIC: 6022)

TRANSFER AGENT(S): The Bank of New York, New York, NY

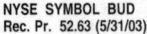
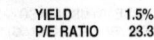

NYSE SYMBOL BUD
Rec. Pr. 52.63 (5/31/03)

ANHEUSER-BUSCH COMPANIES, INC.

YIELD 1.5%
P/E RATIO 23.3

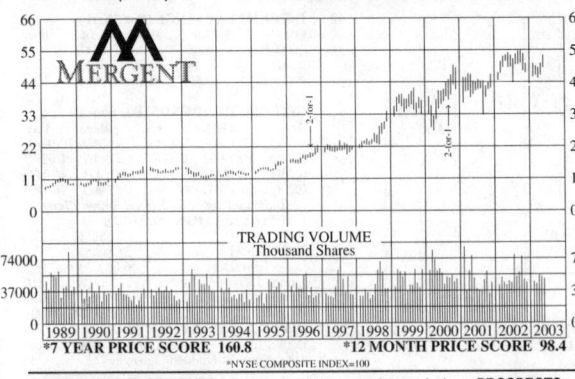

TRADING VOLUME
Thousand Shares

| 1989 | 1990 | 1991 | 1992 | 1993 | 1994 | 1995 | 1996 | 1997 | 1998 | 1999 | 2000 | 2001 | 2002 | 2003 |

*7 YEAR PRICE SCORE 160.8   ***12 MONTH PRICE SCORE 98.4**
*NYSE COMPOSITE INDEX=100

INTERIM EARNINGS (Per Share):

Qtr.	Mar.	June	Sept.	Dec.
1999	0.33	0.45	0.49	0.21
2000	0.38	0.52	0.56	0.23
2001	0.43	0.58	0.62	0.26
2002	0.51	0.66	0.71	0.32
2003	0.57	...	...	...

INTERIM DIVIDENDS (Per Share):

Amt.	Decl.	Ex.	Rec.	Pay.
0.195Q	7/24/02	8/07/02	8/09/02	9/09/02
0.195Q	10/23/02	11/06/02	11/11/02	12/09/02
0.195Q	1/14/03	2/06/03	2/10/03	3/10/03
0.195Q	4/23/03	5/07/03	5/09/03	6/09/03

Indicated div.: $0.78 (Div. Reinv. Plan)

CAPITALIZATION (12/31/02):

	($000)	(%)
Long-Term Debt	6,603,200	60.0
Deferred Income Tax	1,345,100	12.2
Common & Surplus	3,052,300	27.7
Total	11,000,600	100.0

DIVIDEND ACHIEVER STATUS:
Rank: 154   10-Year Growth Rate: 9.60%
Total Years of Dividend Growth: 28

RECENT DEVELOPMENTS: For the three months ended 3/31/03, net income climbed 6.3% to $484.8 million compared with $456.1 million in the corresponding quarter of the previous year. Net sales rose 4.6% to $3.28 billion from $3.14 billion in the year-earlier period. Domestic beer net sales grew 4.0% to $2.65 billion, due to strong sales of BUD LIGHT and MICHELOB ULTRA. International net sales increased 14.2% to $140.0 million, reflecting volume growth in China.

PROSPECTS: On 4/3/03, the Company and Tsingtao Brewery Co., Ltd. announced that they have closed their agreement under which BUD's ownership in Tsingtao will increase to 27.0% over a period of up to seven years. Meanwhile, the Company should continue to benefit from strong growth in domestic revenue per barrel. However, volume related to BUD's ownership in Grupo Medelo was down 5.0% in the recent quarter reflecting weak economic conditions in Mexico.

BUSINESS

ANHEUSER-BUSCH COMPANIES, INC. is a diversified corporation whose chief subsidiary is Anheuser-Busch, Inc., the world's largest brewer. Beer is sold under brand names including BUDWEISER, MICHELOB, BUSCH, and NATURAL LIGHT. Additionally, theme park operations are conducted through BUD's subsidiary, Busch Entertainment Corporation, which owned nine theme parks as of 12/31/02. BUD also engages in packaging, malt and rice production, international beer, non-beer beverages, real estate development, marketing communications, and transportation services. As of 12/31/02, BUD owned approximately 50.2% of Grupo Modelo, S.A. de C.V., a Mexican brewer.

ANNUAL FINANCIAL DATA

	12/31/02	12/31/01	12/31/00	12/31/99	12/31/98	12/31/97	12/31/96
Earnings Per Share	2.20	③ 1.89	1.69	1.47	1.27	① 1.18	② 1.14
Cash Flow Per Share	3.16	2.82	2.56	2.29	2.02	1.86	1.73
Tang. Book Val. Per Share	3.61	4.62	4.11	4.25	4.42	4.15	4.05
Dividends Per Share	0.75	0.69	0.63	0.58	0.54	0.50	0.46
Dividend Payout %	34.1	36.5	37.3	39.5	42.7	42.4	40.3
INCOME STATEMENT (IN MILLIONS)							
Total Revenues	13,566.4	12,911.5	12,261.8	11,703.7	11,245.8	11,066.2	10,883.7
Costs & Expenses	9,739.4	9,371.8	8,963.6	8,624.4	8,382.1	8,329.5	8,260.7
Depreciation & Amort.	847.3	834.5	803.5	777.0	738.4	683.7	593.9
Operating Income	2,979.7	2,705.2	2,494.7	2,302.3	2,125.3	2,053.0	2,029.1
Net Interest Inc./(Exp.)	d349.7	d333.2	d313.8	d285.3	d259.7	d211.2	d187.9
Income Before Income Taxes	2,623.6	2,359.8	2,179.9	2,007.6	1,852.6	1,832.5	1,892.9
Income Taxes	1,041.5	913.2	828.3	762.9	704.3	703.6	736.8
Equity Earnings/Minority Int.	351.7	240.1	200.0	157.5	85.0	50.3	...
Net Income	1,933.8	③1,704.5	1,551.6	1,402.2	1,233.3	①1,179.2	②1,156.1
Cash Flow	2,781.1	2,539.0	2,355.1	2,179.2	1,971.7	1,862.9	1,750.0
Average Shs. Outstg. (000)	878,900	901,600	919,700	953,600	975,000	999,400	1,011,600
BALANCE SHEET (IN MILLIONS):							
Cash & Cash Equivalents	188.9	162.6	159.9	152.1	224.8	147.3	93.6
Total Current Assets	1,504.7	1,550.4	1,547.9	1,600.6	1,640.4	1,583.9	1,465.8
Net Property	8,363.9	8,314.0	8,243.8	7,964.6	7,849.0	7,750.6	7,208.2
Total Assets	14,119.5	13,862.0	13,084.5	12,640.4	12,484.3	11,727.1	10,463.6
Total Current Liabilities	1,787.1	1,732.3	1,675.7	1,987.2	1,733.3	1,500.7	1,430.9
Long-Term Obligations	6,603.2	5,983.9	5,374.5	4,880.6	4,718.6	4,365.6	3,270.9
Net Stockholders' Equity	3,052.3	4,061.5	4,128.9	3,921.5	4,216.0	4,041.8	4,029.1
Net Working Capital	d283.0	d181.9	d127.8	d386.6	d89.9	83.2	34.9
Year-end Shs. Outstg. (000)	846,600	879,100	903,600	922,200	953,200	974,040	994,714
STATISTICAL RECORD:							
Operating Profit Margin %	22.0	21.1	20.3	19.7	18.9	18.6	19.1
Net Profit Margin %	14.3	13.2	12.7	12.0	11.0	10.7	10.6
Return on Equity %	63.4	42.0	37.6	35.8	29.3	29.2	28.7
Return on Assets %	13.7	12.3	11.9	11.1	9.9	10.1	11.0
Debt/Total Assets %	46.8	43.2	41.1	38.6	37.8	37.2	31.3
Price Range	55.00-43.65	46.95-32.60	49.88-27.31	42.00-32.22	34.13-21.47	24.13-19.25	22.50-16.19
P/E Ratio	25.0-19.8	24.8-17.2	29.5-16.2	28.6-21.9	27.0-17.0	20.4-16.3	19.7-14.2
Average Yield %	1.5	1.7	1.6	1.6	1.9	2.3	2.4

Statistics are as originally reported. Adj. for 2-for-1 stk. split, 9/00 & 9/96. ① Bef. acctg. cange chrge. of $10.0 mill. ② Incl. $54.7 mill. gain fr. the sale of the St. Louis Cardinals & bef. disc. oper. gain of $33.8 mill. ③ Incl. a pre-tax gain on the sale of SeaWorld Cleveland of $17.8 mill.

OFFICERS:
A. A. Busch III, Chmn.
P. T. Stokes, Pres., C.E.O.
W. R. Baker, V.P., C.F.O.
INVESTOR CONTACT: Carlos Ramierz, Investor Relations, (314) 577-9629
PRINCIPAL OFFICE: One Busch Place, St. Louis, MO 63118

TELEPHONE NUMBER: (314) 577-2000
FAX: (314) 577-2900
WEB: www.anheuser-busch.com
NO. OF EMPLOYEES: 23,176
SHAREHOLDERS: 57,259
ANNUAL MEETING: In Apr.
INCORPORATED: DE, Apr., 1979

INSTITUTIONAL HOLDINGS:
No. of Institutions: 764
Shares Held: 508,410,442
% Held: 60.0

INDUSTRY: Malt beverages (SIC: 2082)

TRANSFER AGENT(S): Mellon Investor Services, Ridgefield Park, NJ

APPLEBEE'S INTERNATIONAL, INC.

YIELD 0.2%
P/E RATIO 20.0

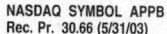
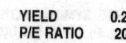
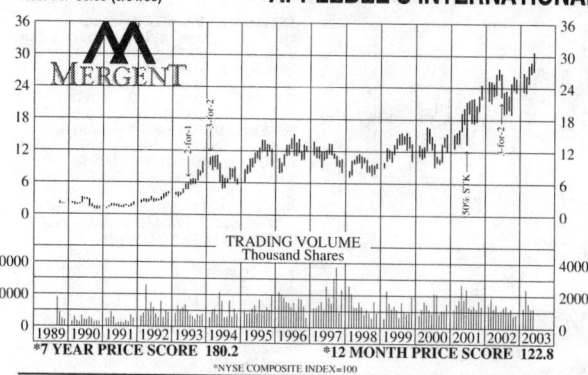

*7 YEAR PRICE SCORE 180.2   *NYSE COMPOSITE INDEX=100   ***12 MONTH PRICE SCORE 122.8**

TRADING VOLUME
Thousand Shares

INTERIM EARNINGS (Per Share):

Qtr.	Mar.	June	Sept.	Dec.
1999	0.11	0.23	0.23	0.27
2000	0.25	0.27	0.27	0.28
2001	0.30	0.31	0.29	0.25
2002	0.35	0.37	0.37	0.36
2003	0.43	...	...	...

INTERIM DIVIDENDS (Per Share):

Amt.	Decl.	Ex.	Rec.	Pay.
50% STK	5/10/01	6/13/01	5/25/01	6/12/01
0.08A	12/14/01	12/21/01	12/26/01	1/29/02
3-for-2	5/09/02	6/12/02	5/24/02	6/11/02
0.06A	12/12/02	12/24/02	12/27/02	1/30/03

Indicated div.: $0.06

CAPITALIZATION (12/29/02):

	($000)	(%)
Long-Term Debt	47,948	10.8
Capital Lease Obligations..	4,238	1.0
Common & Surplus	392,581	88.3
Total	444,767	100.0

DIVIDEND ACHIEVER STATUS:

Rank: 29   10-Year Growth Rate: 19.60%
Total Years of Dividend Growth: 11

RECENT DEVELOPMENTS: For the first quarter ended 3/30/03, net earnings advanced 21.3% to $24.6 million compared with $20.3 million in the corresponding prior-year quarter. Results for 2003 and 2002 included pre-opening expenses of $221,000 and $335,000, and losses on disposition of restaurants and equipment of $467,000 and $294,000, respectively. Total revenues increased 19.1% to $238.2 million from $199.9 million a year earlier. Company restaurant sales climbed 19.1% to $208.4 million,

while franchise royalties and fee income improved 9.4% to $27.2 million. Other franchise income amounted to $2.6 million versus $134,000 in the 2002 period. System-wide comparable store sales increased 3.3% for the quarter. Operating earnings jumped 20.2% to $38.5 million from $32.1 million the year before. Looking ahead, the Company expects to open approximately 100 new restaurants in 2003, including 25 company restaurants and 70 to 80 franchise restaurants.

BUSINESS

APPLEBEE'S INTERNATIONAL, INC. develops, franchises and operates a national chain of casual dining restaurants under the trademark of "Applebee's Neighborhood Grill & Bar." Each of the restaurants is designed as a neighborhood establishment featuring a selection of moderately-priced food and beverage items with full service luncheon and evening dining. As of 4/27/03, there were 1,517 Applebee's restaurants in 49 states and nine countries. On 4/13/99, the Company completed the sale of its Rio Bravo International division, comprised of 40 Company and 25 franchised restaurants, to Chevys Inc.

ANNUAL FINANCIAL DATA

	12/29/02	12/30/01	12/31/00	12/26/99	12/27/98	12/28/97	12/29/96
Earnings Per Share	② 1.46	② 1.15	② 1.07	② 0.84	① 0.74	0.64	0.54
Cash Flow Per Share	2.09	1.83	1.69	1.40	1.26	0.97	0.80
Tang. Book Val. Per Share	5.46	4.39	3.45	2.70	2.90	3.36	3.08
Dividends Per Share	0.053	0.049	0.044	0.040	0.036	0.031	0.027
Dividend Payout %	3.7	4.2	4.2	4.8	4.8	4.9	4.9
INCOME STATEMENT (IN THOUSANDS):							
Total Revenues	826,796	744,344	690,152	669,584	647,562	515,820	413,131
Costs & Expenses	661,402	593,638	546,069	539,069	523,850	420,352	336,353
Depreciation & Amort.	35,686	38,279	36,876	35,605	35,150	24,185	17,945
Operating Income	129,708	112,427	107,207	94,910	88,562	71,283	58,833
Net Interest Inc./(Exp.)	d2,168	d7,456	d9,304	d10,814	d9,922	d1,705	d1,571
Income Before Income Taxes	130,136	103,877	99,938	85,735	80,409	71,801	60,725
Income Taxes	47,109	38,227	36,777	31,537	29,753	26,710	22,711
Net Income	② 83,027	② 65,650	② 63,161	② 54,198	① 50,656	45,091	38,014
Cash Flow	118,713	103,929	100,037	89,803	85,806	69,276	55,959
Average Shs. Outstg.	56,922	56,877	59,171	64,352	68,366	71,190	70,173
BALANCE SHEET (IN THOUSANDS):							
Cash & Cash Equivalents	15,672	22,747	12,075	3,982	6,646	19,814	57,410
Total Current Assets	69,579	67,999	53,181	34,211	34,909	43,954	83,992
Net Property	383,002	330,924	314,216	300,140	364,058	276,082	196,950
Total Assets	566,114	500,411	471,707	442,216	510,904	377,474	314,111
Total Current Liabilities	115,186	97,746	93,835	77,662	65,951	62,488	41,843
Long-Term Obligations	52,186	74,525	90,461	106,293	145,522	22,579	24,435
Net Stockholders' Equity	392,581	325,183	281,718	253,873	296,053	290,443	244,764
Net Working Capital	d45,607	d29,747	d40,654	d43,451	d31,042	d18,534	42,149
Year-end Shs. Outstg.	55,388	55,816	56,745	59,844	66,465	70,835	70,423
STATISTICAL RECORD:							
Operating Profit Margin %	15.7	15.1	15.5	14.2	13.7	13.8	14.2
Net Profit Margin %	10.0	8.8	9.2	8.1	7.8	8.7	9.2
Return on Equity %	21.1	20.2	22.4	21.3	17.1	15.5	15.5
Return on Assets %	14.7	13.1	13.4	12.3	9.9	11.9	12.1
Debt/Total Assets %	9.2	14.9	19.2	24.0	28.5	6.0	7.8
Price Range	27.67-19.03	24.59-12.61	16.70-9.08	15.56-8.95	11.56-7.17	13.83-8.00	15.22-7.89
P/E Ratio	18.9-13.0	21.3-10.9	15.6-8.5	18.5-10.6	15.6-9.7	21.7-12.6	28.1-14.6
Average Yield %	0.2	0.3	0.3	0.3	0.4	0.3	0.2

Statistics are as originally reported. Adj. for stk. splits: 50%, 6/01; 3-for-2, 6/02 ① Bef. extraord. chrg. $641,000 ② Incl. loss on disposition of restaurant & equipment: $1.1 mill., 12/02; $1.3 mill., 12/00; 5.6 mill., 12/99

OFFICERS:
L. L. Hill, Chmn., Pres., C.E.O.
S. K. Lumpkin, Exec. V.P., C.F.O., Treas.

INVESTOR CONTACT: Carol DiRamo, Investor Relations, (913) 967-4109

PRINCIPAL OFFICE: 4551 W. 107th Street, Suite 100, Overland Park, KS 66207

TELEPHONE NUMBER: (913) 967-4000
FAX: (913) 341-1694
WEB: www.applebees.com

NO. OF EMPLOYEES: 23,500 (avg.)

SHAREHOLDERS: 1,203 (record)

ANNUAL MEETING: In May

INCORPORATED: DE, 1983

INSTITUTIONAL HOLDINGS:
No. of Institutions: 205
Shares Held: 44,738,755
% Held: 81.3

INDUSTRY: Eating places (SIC: 5812)

TRANSFER AGENT(S): American Stock Transfer & Trust Company, New York, NY

ARCHER DANIELS MIDLAND COMPANY

YIELD 2.0%
P/E RATIO 16.6

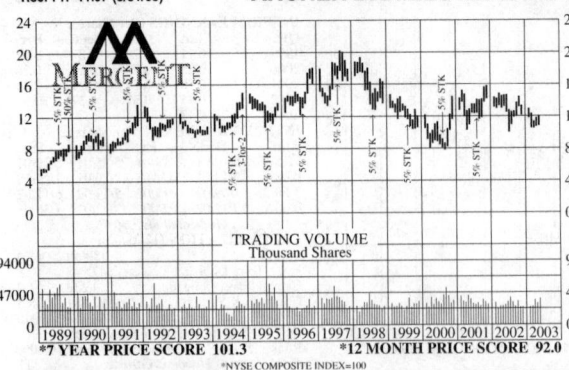

TRADING VOLUME
Thousand Shares

*7 YEAR PRICE SCORE 101.3   *12 MONTH PRICE SCORE 92.0
*NYSE COMPOSITE INDEX=100

INTERIM EARNINGS (Per Share):

Qtr.	Sept.	Dec.	Mar.	June
1998-99	0.17	0.16	0.02	0.07
1999-00	0.06	0.15	0.15	0.10
2000-01	0.16	0.19	0.14	0.09
2001-02	0.20	0.23	0.18	0.17
2002-03	0.17	0.20	0.18	...

INTERIM DIVIDENDS (Per Share):

Amt.	Decl.	Ex.	Rec.	Pay.
0.06Q	8/08/02	8/15/02	8/19/02	9/09/02
0.06Q	11/07/02	11/15/02	11/19/02	12/12/02
0.06Q	1/28/03	2/05/03	2/07/03	3/04/03
0.06Q	5/01/03	5/07/03	5/09/03	6/02/03

Indicated div.: $0.24 (Div. Reinv. Plan)

CAPITALIZATION (6/30/02):

	($000)	(%)
Long-Term Debt	3,111,294	29.6
Deferred Income Tax	631,923	6.0
Common & Surplus	6,754,821	64.3
Total	10,498,038	100.0

DIVIDEND ACHIEVER STATUS:
Rank: 39   10-Year Growth Rate: 18.17%
Total Years of Dividend Growth: 28

RECENT DEVELOPMENTS: For the quarter ended 3/31/03, net earnings totaled $116.8 million, down 0.3% compared with $117.2 million in the corresponding prior-year period. Results for 2003 and 2002 included gains of $15,000 and $1.9 million, respectively, from securities transactions. Net sales and other operating income climbed 52.4% to $7.91 billion from $5.19 billion the year before.

PROSPECTS: Strong earnings from the Company's corn processing operations are being fueled by higher prices for corn-based products such as ethanol, a gasoline additive, and high fructose corn syrup, an ingredient used to sweeten soft drinks. Higher demand for ethanol in the U.S. is being driven by increased use by refiners in California, which began blending ethanol in their gasoline this year.

BUSINESS

ARCHER DANIELS MIDLAND COMPANY is engaged in procuring, transporting, storing, processing and merchandising agricultural commodities and products. The Company processes soybeans, cottonseed, sunflower seeds, canola, peanuts, flaxseed and corn germ into vegetable oils and meals primarily for the food and feed industries. In addition, ADM's corn milling operations produce products for the food and beverage industry, along with ethyl alcohol, or ethanol, which is used as a gasoline additive. The Company also processes wheat, corn and milo into flour. Sales (and operating profit) for fiscal 2002 were derived as follows: oilseeds processing, 38.3% (37.3%); agricultural services, 35.3% (16.3%); corn processing, 8.3% (20.7%); wheat processing, 5.8% (7.6%); and other, 12.3% (18.1%).

ANNUAL FINANCIAL DATA

	6/30/02	6/30/01	6/30/00	6/30/99	6/30/98	6/30/97	6/30/96
Earnings Per Share	[7] 0.78	[6] 0.58	[4] 0.45	[3] 0.41	[2] 0.59	[2] 0.54	[1] 0.99
Cash Flow Per Share	1.71	1.51	1.42	1.32	1.40	1.24	1.59
Tang. Book Val. Per Share	10.60	9.64	9.39	9.13	9.47	8.92	8.82
Dividends Per Share	0.22	0.193	0.184	0.175	0.167	0.159	0.151
Dividend Payout %	28.2	33.3	40.9	42.7	28.3	29.4	15.3

INCOME STATEMENT (IN MILLIONS):

Total Revenues	23,453.6	[8] 20,051.4	12,876.8	14,283.3	16,108.6	13,853.3	13,314.0
Costs & Expenses	21,983.0	18,728.7	11,739.0	13,130.2	14,828.3	12,752.3	11,980.4
Depreciation & Amort.	614.1	622.0	647.6	622.2	560.1	475.5	419.2
Operating Income	856.5	700.8	490.2	531.0	720.3	625.4	914.4
Income Before Income Taxes	718.9	521.9	353.2	419.8	610.0	644.4	1,054.4
Income Taxes	207.8	138.6	52.3	138.5	206.4	267.1	358.5
Net Income	[7] 511.1	[5] 383.3	[4] 300.9	[3] 281.3	[2] 403.6	[2] 377.3	[1] 695.9
Cash Flow	1,125.2	1,005.3	948.5	903.5	963.7	852.8	1,115.1
Average Shs. Outstg. (000)	656,955	664,507	669,279	685,328	686,047	690,352	702,012

BALANCE SHEET (IN MILLIONS):

Cash & Cash Equivalents	978.7	817.8	931.4	903.6	725.5	728.0	1,354.8
Total Current Assets	7,363.2	6,150.3	6,162.4	5,789.6	5,451.7	4,284.3	4,384.7
Net Property	4,890.2	4,920.4	5,277.1	5,567.2	5,322.7	4,708.6	4,114.3
Total Assets	15,416.3	14,339.9	14,423.1	14,029.9	13,833.5	11,354.4	10,449.9
Total Current Liabilities	4,719.3	3,867.0	4,332.9	3,840.3	3,717.3	2,248.8	1,633.6
Long-Term Obligations	3,111.3	3,351.1	3,277.2	3,191.9	2,847.1	2,344.9	2,003.0
Net Stockholders' Equity	6,754.8	6,331.7	6,110.2	6,240.6	6,504.9	6,050.1	6,144.8
Net Working Capital	2,643.9	2,283.3	1,829.4	1,949.3	1,734.4	2,035.6	2,751.1
Year-end Shs. Outstg. (000)	637,175	656,853	650,683	683,341	686,612	677,955	696,621

STATISTICAL RECORD:

Operating Profit Margin %	3.7	3.5	3.8	3.7	4.5	4.5	6.9
Net Profit Margin %	2.2	1.9	2.3	2.0	2.5	2.7	5.2
Return on Equity %	7.6	6.1	4.9	4.5	6.2	6.2	11.3
Return on Assets %	3.3	2.7	2.1	2.0	2.9	3.3	6.7
Debt/Total Assets %	20.2	23.4	22.7	22.8	20.6	20.7	19.2
Price Range	14.85-10.00	15.80-10.24	14.47-7.80	14.74-10.38	19.44-12.80	20.26-13.32	18.12-12.22
P/E Ratio	19.0-12.8	27.2-17.6	32.3-17.4	36.1-25.4	32.9-21.7	37.3-24.5	18.4-12.4
Average Yield %	1.8	1.5	1.7	1.4	1.0	0.9	1.0

Statistics are as originally reported. Adj. for all stk. divs. & splits through 9/01. [1] Incl. $0.04/sh net chg. [2] Incl. $48 mil chg. for fines & litig. costs & $0.04/sh gain fr secs. trans., 1998; & $0.18/sh net chg., 1997. [3] Excl. $15.3 mil extraord. chg. & incl. $63.0 mil gain fr. secs. trans. [4] Incl. $72.0 mil chg. for plant closings, $60.0 mil tax cr. & $6.0 mil after-tax gain fr. secs. trans. [5] Incl. $0.09/sh gain fr. secs. trans. & $0.03/sh loss fr. invests. [6] Refl. adoption of new acctg. standards rel. to recog. sales. [7] Incl. $38.3 mil gain fr. secs. trans., a $147.0 mil gain fr. a litigation settlement, and a $83.0 mil chg. fr. asset write down.

OFFICERS:
G. A. Andreas, Chmn., C.E.O.
P. B. Mulhollem, Pres., C.O.O.
D. J. Schmalz, Sr. V.P., C.F.O.

INVESTOR CONTACT: Dwight Grimestad, V.P., Inv. Rel., (217) 424-4586

PRINCIPAL OFFICE: 4666 Faries Parkway, Box 1470, Decatur, IL 62525

TELEPHONE NUMBER: (217) 424-5200
FAX: (217) 424-5381
WEB: www.admworld.com

NO. OF EMPLOYEES: 24,746 (avg.)

SHAREHOLDERS: 26,715

ANNUAL MEETING: In Nov.

INCORPORATED: DE, May, 1923

INSTITUTIONAL HOLDINGS:
No. of Institutions: 354
Shares Held: 403,986,661
% Held: 62.5

INDUSTRY: Soybean oil mills (SIC: 2075)

TRANSFER AGENT(S): Hickory Point Bank & Trust, Decatur, IL

ARROW INTERNATIONAL, INC.

YIELD 0.7%
P/E RATIO 26.1

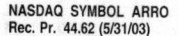
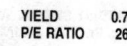
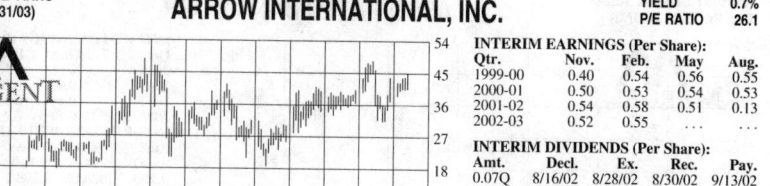

7 YEAR PRICE SCORE 130.9 **12 MONTH PRICE SCORE 107.7**
NYSE COMPOSITE INDEX=100

INTERIM EARNINGS (Per Share):

Qtr.	Nov.	Feb.	May	Aug.
1999-00	0.40	0.54	0.56	0.55
2000-01	0.50	0.53	0.54	0.53
2001-02	0.54	0.58	0.51	0.13
2002-03	0.52	0.55	...	...

INTERIM DIVIDENDS (Per Share):

Amt.	Decl.	Ex.	Rec.	Pay.
0.07Q	8/16/02	8/28/02	8/30/02	9/13/02
0.07Q	11/15/02	11/26/02	11/29/02	12/13/02
0.08Q	2/14/03	2/26/03	2/28/03	3/14/03
0.08Q	5/16/03	5/28/03	5/30/03	6/13/03

Indicated div.: $0.32

CAPITALIZATION (8/31/02):

	($000)	(%)
Long-Term Debt	300	0.1
Common & Surplus	360,356	99.9
Total	360,656	100.0

DIVIDEND ACHIEVER STATUS:
Rank: 18   10-Year Dividend Growth Rate: 21.48%
Total Years of Dividend Growth: 10

RECENT DEVELOPMENTS: For the quarter ended 2/28/03, net income decreased 6.1% to $11.9 million compared with $12.7 million in the equivalent period of the previous year. The decrease in earnings reflected lower margins realized on the sale of the ARRO products, which were purchased as part of its acquisition of the net assets of Stepic Medical, ARRO's former New York City distributor, on 9/3/02. Net sales climbed 8.1% to $92.8 million from $85.8 million in the year-earlier period. Sales of critical care products increased 8.7% to $78.5 million from $72.2 million, while

sales of cardiac care products rose 5.1% to $14.3 million from $13.6 million in the prior-year quarter. International sales advanced 9.3% to $30.6 million from $28.0 million the year before. Gross profit grew 3.1% to $45.7 million from $44.4 million, but slipped as a percentage of net sales to 49.3% from 51.7% in 2002. Operating income fell 8.3% to $17.6 million from $19.2 million the year before. Meanwhile, ARRO expects sales growth of 9.0% and earnings per share to range from $2.46 to $2.50 for fiscal 2003.

BUSINESS

ARROW INTERNATIONAL, INC. develops, manufactures and markets a range of disposable catheters and related products for critical and cardiac care. The Company's critical care products are primarily used for central vascular access for the administration of fluids, drugs and blood products, patient monitoring and diagnostic purposes, and for pain management. The Company's products are used by anesthesiologists, critical care specialists, surgeons, emergency and trauma physicians, cardiologists, interventional radiologists, electrophysiologists and other health care providers. On 11/25/02, the Company purchased substantially all of the assets of Diatek Corporation, an early stage developer of chronic hemodialysis catheters, for $10.8 million.

ANNUAL FINANCIAL DATA

	8/31/02	8/31/01	8/31/00	8/31/99	8/31/98	8/31/97	8/31/96
Earnings Per Share	1.78	2.10	② 2.05	1.54	① 0.37	1.58	1.41
Cash Flow Per Share	2.75	3.13	2.98	2.34	1.04	2.25	2.00
Tang. Book Val. Per Share	13.42	10.98	9.32	9.06	8.33	7.88	6.07
Dividends Per Share	0.28	0.26	0.24	0.22	0.20	0.18	0.16
Dividend Payout %	15.7	12.4	11.7	14.3	54.0	11.4	11.3

INCOME STATEMENT (IN THOUSANDS):

Total Revenues	340,759	334,042	320,340	295,946	260,890	245,889	229,945
Costs & Expenses	260,508	239,585	227,814	225,220	216,047	168,574	161,939
Depreciation & Amort.	21,693	22,696	20,931	18,606	15,623	15,552	13,593
Operating Income	58,558	71,761	71,595	52,120	29,220	61,763	54,413
Net Interest Inc./(Exp.)	d392	d1,897	d1,945	d975	d328	d3	d1,238
Income Before Income Taxes	57,777	69,470	69,450	55,341	27,582	59,732	52,113
Income Taxes	18,777	22,925	23,266	19,646	19,010	22,997	19,282
Net Income	39,000	46,545	② 46,184	35,695	① 8,572	36,735	32,831
Cash Flow	60,693	69,241	67,115	54,301	24,195	52,287	46,424
Average Shs. Outstg.	22,106	22,120	22,519	23,195	23,226	23,227	23,230

BALANCE SHEET (IN THOUSANDS):

Cash & Cash Equivalents	33,103	2,968	3,959	3,939	4,652	6,276	4,807
Total Current Assets	224,873	203,985	179,651	166,627	154,617	135,973	110,693
Net Property	130,323	126,260	121,440	116,934	111,368	110,593	108,999
Total Assets	425,680	417,710	385,814	357,484	322,881	320,373	299,422
Total Current Liabilities	50,425	78,429	89,601	58,256	54,341	54,513	55,608
Long-Term Obligations	300	600	900	11,105	11,686	12,043	15,988
Net Stockholders' Equity	360,356	326,089	285,204	278,167	247,868	245,917	219,773
Net Working Capital	174,448	125,556	90,050	107,901	100,256	81,460	55,085
Year-end Shs. Outstg.	21,908	22,001	22,001	23,058	23,224	23,226	23,229

STATISTICAL RECORD:

Operating Profit Margin %	17.2	21.5	22.3	17.6	11.2	25.1	23.7
Net Profit Margin %	11.4	13.9	14.4	12.1	3.3	14.9	14.3
Return on Equity %	10.8	14.3	16.2	12.8	3.5	14.9	14.9
Return on Assets %	9.2	11.1	12.0	10.0	2.7	11.5	11.0
Debt/Total Assets %	0.1	0.1	0.2	3.1	3.6	3.8	5.3
Price Range	48.50-31.28	40.32-33.00	41.13-28.00	31.38-18.63	41.75-20.88	39.75-26.75	46.75-21.00
P/E Ratio	27.2-17.6	19.2-15.7	20.1-13.7	20.4-12.1	112.8-56.4	25.2-16.9	33.2-14.9
Average Yield %	0.7	0.7	0.7	0.9	0.6	0.5	0.5

Statistics are as originally reported. ① Incl. non-recurr. chrg. $36.2 mill. ② Incl. special chrg. $3.3 mill.

OFFICERS:
M. J. Miller Jr., Chmn., C.E.O.
C. G. Anderson Jr., Vice-Chmn
P. B. Fleck, Pres., C.O.O.

INVESTOR CONTACT: Investor Relations, (610) 478-3116

PRINCIPAL OFFICE: 2400 Bernville Road, Reading, PA 19605

TELEPHONE NUMBER: (610) 378-0131
FAX: (610) 374-5360
WEB: www.arrowintl.com

NO. OF EMPLOYEES: 3,005

SHAREHOLDERS: 559 (approx.)

ANNUAL MEETING: In Jan.

INCORPORATED: PA, 1975

INSTITUTIONAL HOLDINGS:
No. of Institutions: 76
Shares Held: 6,890,346
% Held: 31.3

INDUSTRY: Surgical and medical instruments (SIC: 3841)

TRANSFER AGENT(S): First Chicago Trust Division of EquiServe, Jersey City, NJ

NASDAQ SYMBOL ASBC
Rec. Pr. 37.40 (5/31/03)

ASSOCIATED BANC-CORP

YIELD 3.6%
P/E RATIO 13.1

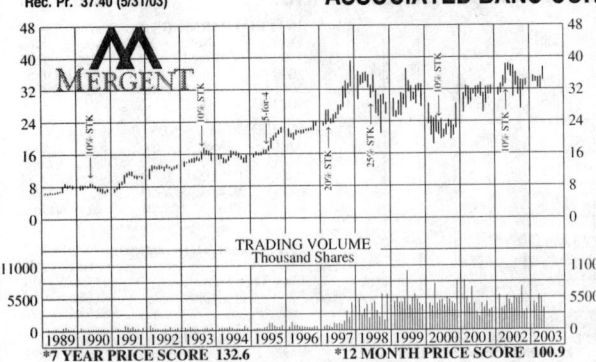

*7 YEAR PRICE SCORE 132.6   *12 MONTH PRICE SCORE 100.9
*NYSE COMPOSITE INDEX=100

INTERIM EARNINGS (Per Share):

Qtr.	Mar.	June	Sept.	Dec.
2000	0.56	0.57	0.55	0.55
2001	0.57	0.63	0.62	0.64
2002	0.69	0.68	0.70	0.71
2003	0.77	...	...	...

INTERIM DIVIDENDS (Per Share):

Amt.	Decl.	Ex.	Rec.	Pay.
0.31Q	4/24/02	5/01/02	5/03/02	5/15/02
0.31Q	7/24/02	7/30/02	8/01/02	8/15/02
0.31Q	10/23/02	10/30/02	11/01/02	11/15/02
0.31Q	1/22/03	1/30/03	2/03/03	2/13/03
0.34Q	4/23/03	4/29/03	5/01/03	5/15/03

Indicated div.: $1.36 (Div. Reinv. Plan)

CAPITALIZATION (12/31/02):

	($000)	(%)
Total Deposits	9,124,852	73.0
Long-Term Debt	1,906,845	15.3
Redeemable Pfd. Stock	190,111	1.5
Common & Surplus	1,272,183	10.2
Total	12,493,991	100.0

DIVIDEND ACHIEVER STATUS:
Rank: 78   10-Year Growth Rate: 13.67%
Total Years of Dividend Growth: 32

RECENT DEVELOPMENTS: For the quarter ended 3/31/03, net income rose 12.7% to $58.0 million versus $51.5 million in the corresponding prior-year period. Results for 2003 and 2002 included net asset sale gains of $122,000 and $331,000, respectively. Net interest income grew 8.5% to $127.5 million. Provision for loan losses increased 15.2% to $13.0 million. Total non-interest income climbed 37.6% to $65.2 million, while total non-interest expense rose 19.1% to $98.2 million. Separately, on 4/1/03, ASBC

agreed to acquire Minnesota-based CFG Insurance Services, Inc. When combined with ASBC's existing insurance agency, Associated Insurance Management Group, Inc., the agency is expected to rank among the top 60 insurance agencies in the U.S., with about $28.0 million in revenues in 2002. Looking ahead, ASBC remains cautiously optimistic about achieving its earnings per share growth goal of about 10.0% in 2003.

BUSINESS

ASSOCIATED BANC-CORP is a multi-bank holding company headquartered in Green Bay, Wisconsin. ASBC provides advice and specialized services to its affiliates in banking policy and operations, including auditing, data processing, marketing/advertising, investing, legal/compliance, personnel services, trust services, risk management, facilities management, security, corporate-wide purchasing, treasury, finance, accounting, and other financial services functionally related to banking. Through its affiliates, ASBC provides a wide range of banking services to individuals and small- to medium-sized businesses. As of 3/31/03, ASBC had total assets of $15.09 billion and more than 200 banking offices serving over 150 communities in Wisconsin, Illinois and Minnesota. On 12/19/98, ASBC acquired Citizens Bankshares Inc. On 2/28/02, ASBC acquired Signal Financial Corporation.

ANNUAL FINANCIAL DATA

	12/31/02	12/31/01	12/31/00	12/31/99	12/31/98	12/31/97	12/31/96
Earnings Per Share	2.79	2.46	2.24	2.12	2.03	☐ 0.67	1.72
Tang. Book Val. Per Share	13.71	16.38	13.32	11.90	11.55	10.68	11.80
Dividends Per Share	1.21	1.11	1.01	0.96	0.86	0.73	0.63
Dividend Payout %	43.4	45.2	45.0	45.1	42.4	109.0	36.5
INCOME STATEMENT (IN MILLIONS):							
Total Interest Income	792.1	880.6	931.2	814.5	785.8	787.2	311.7
Total Interest Expense	290.8	458.6	547.6	418.8	411.0	411.6	142.5
Net Interest Income	501.3	422.0	383.6	395.7	374.7	375.6	169.3
Provision for Loan Losses	50.7	28.2	20.2	19.2	14.7	31.7	4.7
Non-Interest Income	220.3	195.6	184.2	165.9	168.0	96.0	65.1
Non-Interest Expense	374.5	338.4	317.7	305.1	295.0	323.6	140.4
Income Before Taxes	296.3	251.0	229.8	237.3	233.0	116.3	89.3
Net Income	210.7	179.5	168.0	164.9	157.0	☐ 52.4	57.2
Average Shs. Outstg. (000)	75,493	73,168	75,251	77,514	77,185	77,361	33,328
BALANCE SHEET (IN MILLIONS):							
Cash & Due from Banks	430.7	588.0	368.2	284.7	331.5	288.0	236.3
Securities Avail. for Sale	3,362.7	3,197.0	2,891.6	2,841.5	2,357.0	2,167.7	437.4
Total Loans & Leases	10,303.2	9,019.9	8,913.4	8,357.9	7,272.7	7,076.6	3,159.9
Allowance for Credit Losses	162.5	128.2	120.2	113.2	99.7	92.7	47.4
Net Loans & Leases	10,140.7	8,891.7	8,793.1	8,244.8	7,173.0	6,983.8	3,112.4
Total Assets	15,043.3	13,604.4	13,128.4	12,519.9	11,250.7	10,691.4	4,419.1
Total Deposits	9,124.9	8,612.6	9,291.6	8,691.8	8,557.8	8,364.1	3,508.0
Long-Term Obligations	1,906.8	1,103.4	122.4	24.3	26.0	15.3	21.1
Total Liabilities	13,771.1	12,534.0	12,159.7	11,610.1	10,371.9	9,877.7	4,025.9
Net Stockholders' Equity	1,272.2	1,070.4	968.7	909.8	878.7	813.7	393.1
Year-end Shs. Outstg. (000)	74,283	65,335	72,728	76,472	76,093	76,194	33,325
STATISTICAL RECORD:							
Return on Equity %	16.6	16.8	17.3	18.1	17.9	6.4	14.6
Return on Assets %	1.4	1.3	1.3	1.3	1.4	0.5	1.3
Equity/Assets %	8.5	7.9	7.4	7.3	7.8	7.6	8.9
Non-Int. Exp./Tot. Inc. %	51.9	54.9	55.2	54.6	55.0	64.2	60.1
Price Range	38.45-27.01	33.61-26.14	28.41-18.29	37.19-24.95	36.53-20.97	39.17-22.86	24.10-19.42
P/E Ratio	13.8-9.7	13.7-10.6	12.7-8.2	17.5-11.7	18.0-10.3	58.1-33.9	14.0-11.3
Average Yield %	3.7	3.7	4.3	3.1	3.0	2.4	2.9

Statistics are as originally reported. Adj. for stk. splits: 10% div., 5/02 & 6/00; 25% div., 6/12/98; 20% div., 3/17/97; 5-for-4, 6/15/95. ☐ Incl. non-recurr. chrg. $103.7 mill.

OFFICERS:
R. C. Gallagher, Chmn.
P. S. Beideman, Pres., C.E.O.
J. B. Selner, C.F.O.
INVESTOR CONTACT: Joe Selner, C.F.O., (920) 491-7120
PRINCIPAL OFFICE: 1200 Hansen Road, Green Bay, WI 54304

TELEPHONE NUMBER: (920) 491-7000
FAX: (920) 433-3261
WEB: www.associatedbank.com
NO. OF EMPLOYEES: 4,085
SHAREHOLDERS: 9,807
ANNUAL MEETING: In April
INCORPORATED: WI, 1964

INSTITUTIONAL HOLDINGS:
No. of Institutions: 181
Shares Held: 28,410,365
% Held: 38.4
INDUSTRY: State commercial banks (SIC: 6022)
TRANSFER AGENT(S): National City Bank, Cleveland, OH

ATMOS ENERGY CORPORATION

YIELD 5.3%
P/E RATIO 12.8

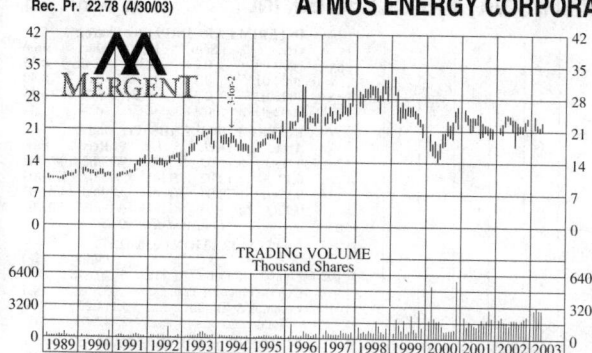
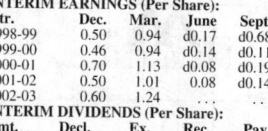

TRADING VOLUME
Thousand Shares

*7 YEAR PRICE SCORE 103.5   *12 MONTH PRICE SCORE 104.0
*NYSE COMPOSITE INDEX=100

INTERIM EARNINGS (Per Share):

Qtr.	Dec.	Mar.	June	Sept.
1998-99	0.50	0.94	d0.17	d0.68
1999-00	0.46	0.94	d0.14	d0.11
2000-01	0.70	1.13	d0.08	d0.19
2001-02	0.50	1.01	0.08	d0.14
2002-03	0.60	1.24	...	...

INTERIM DIVIDENDS (Per Share):

Amt.	Decl.	Ex.	Rec.	Pay.
0.295Q	5/15/02	5/23/02	5/28/02	6/10/02
0.295Q	8/14/02	8/22/02	8/26/02	9/10/02
0.30Q	11/13/02	11/21/02	11/25/02	12/10/02
0.30Q	2/11/03	2/21/03	2/25/03	3/10/03
0.30Q	5/13/03	5/22/03	5/27/03	6/10/03

Indicated div.: $1.20 (Div. Reinv. Plan)

CAPITALIZATION (9/30/02):

	($000)	(%)
Long-Term Debt	670,463	48.6
Deferred Income Tax	134,540	9.8
Common & Surplus	573,235	41.6
Total	1,378,238	100.0

DIVIDEND ACHIEVER STATUS:
Rank: 257   10-Year Growth Rate: 3.59%
Total Years of Dividend Growth: 15

RECENT DEVELOPMENTS: For the quarter ended 3/31/03, ATO reported income of $56.3 million, before an accounting change charge of $7.8 million, versus net income of $41.4 million in the equivalent 2002 quarter. Earnings benefited from a strong performance from the gas utility operations, which more than offset lower results from nonutility gas operations, primarily due to higher natural gas costs. Operating revenues surged 84.6% to $700.4 million from $379.5 million a year earlier.

PROSPECTS: The Company expects full-year 2003 earnings to range from $1.52 to $1.58 per share. Over the long-term, ATO is committed to growing its earnings between 5.0% and 7.0% annually. Going forward, the Company anticipates taking steps that will be designed to eliminate or minimize any future negative effects of the events that caused the lower-than-expected earnings from its natural gas marketing segment.

BUSINESS

ATMOS ENERGY CORPORATION is engaged in the natural gas utility business (97.4% of revenues in fiscal 2002) as well as certain non-regulated businesses (2.6%). ATO distributes natural gas through sales and transportation arrangements to approximately 1.7 million residential, commercial public authority and industrial customers through its regulated utility operations in twelve states. ATO also transports natural gas through its distribution system for others. ATO's non-regulated businesses provide natural gas storage services and own an interest in storage fields in Kansas, Kentucky and Louisiana. ATO also provides energy management and gas marketing services and electrical power generation as well as markets gas to wholesale customers in Texas and Louisiana. ATO also holds an indirect equity interest in Heritage Propane Partners, L.P. On 12/3/02, ATO acquired Mississippi Valley Gas Company.

ANNUAL FINANCIAL DATA

	9/30/02	9/30/01	9/30/00	9/30/99	9/30/98 ②	9/30/97	9/30/96
Earnings Per Share	1.45	1.47	1.14	0.58	1.84	①0.81	1.51
Cash Flow Per Share	3.48	3.31	3.25	2.58	3.62	2.25	3.04
Tang. Book Val. Per Share	9.19	12.43	12.28	12.09	12.21	11.04	10.75
Dividends Per Share	1.19	1.17	1.15	1.11	1.07	1.02	0.97
Dividend Payout %	81.7	79.2	100.4	191.3	58.1	125.9	64.2
INCOME STATEMENT (IN THOUSANDS):							
Total Revenues	950,849	1,442,275	850,152	690,196	848,208	906,835	483,744
Costs & Expenses	711,597	1,235,644	690,268	565,142	671,635	786,045	402,862
Depreciation & Amort.	83,921	70,470	66,920	61,674	53,416	42,207	24,417
Maintenance Exp.	...	6,368	7,648	9,141	10,278	11,974	4,212
Operating Income	155,331	130,281	85,316	54,239	112,879	66,609	52,253
Net Interest Inc./(Exp.)	d59,174	d47,011	d43,823	d36,298	d30,149	d28,185	d14,585
Income Taxes	35,180	33,368	20,319	9,503	31,806	14,298	13,310
Net Income	59,656	56,090	35,918	17,744	55,265	①23,838	23,949
Cash Flow	143,577	126,560	102,838	79,418	108,681	66,045	48,366
Average Shs. Outstg.	41,250	38,247	31,594	30,819	30,031	29,409	15,892
BALANCE SHEET (IN THOUSANDS):							
Gross Property	2,127,827	2,109,867	1,579,803	1,549,258	1,446,420	1,332,672	666,438
Accumulated Depreciation	827,507	774,469	597,457	583,476	528,560	483,545	252,871
Net Property	1,300,320	1,335,398	982,346	965,782	917,860	849,127	413,567
Total Assets	1,980,221	2,036,180	1,348,758	1,230,537	1,141,390	1,088,311	501,861
Long-Term Obligations	670,463	692,399	363,198	377,483	398,548	302,981	122,303
Net Stockholders' Equity	573,235	583,864	392,466	377,663	371,158	327,260	172,298
Year-end Shs. Outstg.	41,676	40,792	31,952	31,248	30,398	29,642	16,021
STATISTICAL RECORD:							
Operating Profit Margin %	16.3	9.0	10.0	7.9	13.3	7.3	10.8
Net Profit Margin %	6.3	3.9	4.2	2.6	6.5	2.6	5.0
Net Inc./Net Property %	4.6	4.2	3.7	1.8	6.0	2.8	5.8
Net Inc./Tot. Capital %	4.3	4.0	4.0	2.0	6.5	3.3	7.2
Return on Equity %	10.4	9.6	9.2	4.7	14.9	7.3	13.9
Accum. Depr./Gross Prop. %	38.9	36.7	37.8	37.7	36.5	36.3	37.9
Price Range	24.55-17.56	25.75-19.45	26.25-14.25	33.00-19.63	32.25-24.75	30.50-22.13	31.00-20.88
P/E Ratio	16.9-12.1	17.5-13.2	23.0-12.5	56.9-33.8	17.5-13.5	37.6-27.3	20.5-13.8
Average Yield %	5.6	5.2	5.7	4.2	3.8	3.9	3.7

Statistics are as originally reported. ① Incl. a non-recurr. after-tax chg. of $2.8 mill. related to mgmt. changes & an after-tax charge of $12.6 mill. for merger & integration exps. ② Incl. results of United Cities Gas Company

OFFICERS:
R. W. Best, Chmn., Pres., C.E.O.
J. P. Reddy, Sr. V.P., C.F.O.
L. P. Gregory, Sr. V.P., Gen. Couns.
INVESTOR CONTACT: Susan C. Kappes, V.P. Investor Relations, (972) 855-3729
PRINCIPAL OFFICE: 3 Lincoln Centre, Ste. 1800, 5430 LBJ Freeway, Dallas, TX 75240

TELEPHONE NUMBER: (972) 934-9227
FAX: (972) 855-3075
WEB: www.atmosenergy.com
NO. OF EMPLOYEES: 2,338 (avg.)
SHAREHOLDERS: 28,829
ANNUAL MEETING: In Feb.
INCORPORATED: TX, Oct., 1983

INSTITUTIONAL HOLDINGS:
No. of Institutions: 127
Shares Held: 16,450,548
% Held: 36.6
INDUSTRY: Natural gas transmission (SIC: 4922)
TRANSFER AGENT(S): EquiServe Trust Company, N.A., Providence, RI

AUTOMATIC DATA PROCESSING, INC.

YIELD	1.4%
P/E RATIO	19.7

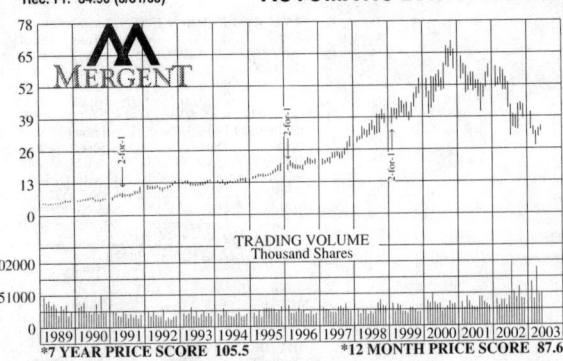

INTERIM EARNINGS (Per Share):

Qtr.	Sept.	Dec.	Mar.	June
1999-00	0.23	0.31	0.42	0.35
2000-01	0.27	0.32	0.45	0.40
2001-02	0.31	0.42	0.56	0.46
2002-03	0.34	0.43	0.54	...

INTERIM DIVIDENDS (Per Share):

Amt.	Decl.	Ex.	Rec.	Pay.
0.115Q	8/12/02	9/11/02	9/13/02	10/01/02
0.12Q	11/12/02	12/11/02	12/13/02	1/01/03
0.12Q	1/28/03	3/12/03	3/14/03	4/01/03
0.12Q	5/13/03	6/11/03	6/13/03	7/01/03

Indicated div.: $0.48

CAPITALIZATION (6/30/02):

	($000)	(%)
Long-Term Debt	90,648	1.7
Deferred Income Tax	237,633	4.4
Common & Surplus	5,114,205	94.0
Total	5,442,486	100.0

DIVIDEND ACHIEVER STATUS:

Rank: 56   10-Year Growth Rate: 15.65%
Total Years of Dividend Growth: 27

TRADING VOLUME
Thousand Shares

*7 YEAR PRICE SCORE 105.5   *12 MONTH PRICE SCORE 87.6

*NYSE COMPOSITE INDEX=100

RECENT DEVELOPMENTS: For the quarter ended 3/31/03, net earnings slipped 6.5% to $329.4 million versus $352.3 million in the same period of 2002. Total revenues climbed 1.9% to $1.91 billion versus $1.87 billion in the prior-year period. Revenue in the Employer Services segment grew 6.1% to $1.25 billion from $1.17 billion, while revenues in the Dealer Services segment rose 15.3% to $203.0 million from $176.0 million. Revenues in the Brokerage Services segment declined 13.9% to $396.0 million.

PROSPECTS: On 3/13/03, ADP announced that it lowered its earnings per share guidance for fiscal 2003 to a range of $1.68 to $1.73 and expects revenues to be flat versus fiscal 2002. The change in guidance was due to the effects of ongoing weak economic conditions on the Employer and Brokerage Services segments, as well as acceleration of investment in three areas, including attractive growth initiatives, the exiting of certain product lines and the retention of employees.

BUSINESS

AUTOMATIC DATA PROCESSING, INC. is an independent computer services firm with over 500,000 clients. ADP's Employer Services group (62.9% of fiscal 2002 revenues) provides employers with payroll, human resources, tax deposit and reporting services. Brokerage Services (26.5% of revenues) provides securities transaction processing, investor support tools, market data services, and investor communications-related services to the financial community worldwide. ADP Dealer Services (10.6% of revenues) is a major provider of computing, data and professional services to auto and truck dealers in the U.S., Canada, Europe, Asia and Latin America.

ANNUAL FINANCIAL DATA

	6/30/02	6/30/01	6/30/00	6/30/99	6/30/98	6/30/97	6/30/96
Earnings Per Share	1.75	③ 1.44	1.31	② 1.10	0.99	① 0.88	0.79
Cash Flow Per Share	2.19	1.93	1.74	1.52	1.37	1.27	1.14
Tang. Book Val. Per Share	5.25	4.97	4.71	3.97	2.90	2.30	1.86
Dividends Per Share	0.46	0.41	0.35	0.30	0.27	0.23	0.20
Dividend Payout %	26.3	28.5	26.7	27.7	26.8	26.1	25.5
INCOME STATEMENT (IN MILLIONS):							
Total Revenues	7,004.3	7,017.6	6,287.5	5,540.1	4,798.1	4,112.2	3,566.6
Costs & Expenses	5,052.2	5,079.9	4,668.1	4,163.7	3,645.2	3,136.9	2,699.8
Depreciation & Amort.	279.1	320.9	284.3	272.8	244.6	223.4	201.6
Operating Income	1,673.0	1,616.9	1,335.1	1,103.6	908.2	751.8	665.1
Net Interest Inc./(Exp.)	...	d14.3	d13.1	d19.1	d24.0	d27.8	d29.7
Income Before Income Taxes	1,787.0	1,525.0	1,289.6	1,084.5	884.2	724.0	635.4
Income Taxes	686.2	600.3	448.8	387.7	278.9	210.5	180.7
Net Income	1,100.8	③ 924.7	840.8	② 696.8	605.3	① 513.5	454.7
Cash Flow	1,379.8	1,245.6	1,125.1	969.6	849.9	736.9	656.3
Average Shs. Outstg. (000)	630,579	645,989	646,098	636,892	620,822	581,980	577,934
BALANCE SHEET (IN MILLIONS):							
Cash & Cash Equivalents	1,475.8	1,790.6	1,824.4	1,092.5	897.2	1,024.9	636.2
Total Current Assets	2,817.3	3,083.5	3,064.5	2,194.3	1,829.3	1,805.3	1,454.3
Net Property	596.5	614.7	597.3	579.3	583.7	519.3	468.3
Total Assets	18,276.5	17,889.1	16,850.8	5,824.8	5,175.4	4,382.8	3,839.9
Total Current Liabilities	1,411.1	1,336.3	1,296.7	1,286.4	1,221.0	1,019.9	835.6
Long-Term Obligations	90.6	110.2	132.0	145.8	192.1	401.2	403.7
Net Stockholders' Equity	5,114.2	4,701.0	4,582.8	4,007.9	3,406.5	2,660.6	2,315.3
Net Working Capital	1,406.2	1,747.2	1,767.8	907.9	608.3	785.5	618.7
Year-end Shs. Outstg. (000)	616,317	623,936	628,746	623,627	604,212	585,698	575,242
STATISTICAL RECORD:							
Operating Profit Margin %	23.9	23.0	21.2	19.9	18.9	18.3	18.6
Net Profit Margin %	15.7	13.2	13.4	12.6	12.6	12.5	12.7
Return on Equity %	21.5	19.7	18.3	17.4	17.8	19.3	19.6
Return on Assets %	6.0	5.2	5.0	12.0	11.7	11.7	11.8
Debt/Total Assets %	0.5	0.6	0.8	2.5	3.7	9.2	10.5
Price Range	59.53-31.15	63.56-41.00	69.94-40.00	54.81-36.25	42.16-28.78	31.34-19.75	22.88-17.81
P/E Ratio	34.0-17.8	44.1-28.5	53.4-30.5	49.8-33.0	42.6-29.1	35.6-22.4	29.1-22.7
Average Yield %	1.0	0.8	0.6	0.7	0.7	0.9	1.0

Statistics are as originally reported. Adj. for 2-for-1 stk. split, 1/99 & 1/96. ① Incl. non-recur. chg. of $11.7 mill. ② Incl. about $37.0 pre-tax gain, $40.0 mill. provision for taxes, & $14.0 mill. net non-recur. adjustment. ③ Incl. $54.0 mill. non-cash, non-recur. write-off of investment.

OFFICERS: A. F. Weinbach, Chmn., C.E.O. G. C. Butler, Pres., C.O.O. K. E. Dykstra, V.P., Fin. **INVESTOR CONTACT:** Karen E. Dykstra, V.P., Fin., (973) 974-5000 **PRINCIPAL OFFICE:** One ADP Boulevard, Roseland, NJ 07068	**TELEPHONE NUMBER:** (973) 974-5000 **FAX:** (973) 974-5390 **WEB:** www.adp.com **NO. OF EMPLOYEES:** 40,000 (approx.) **SHAREHOLDERS:** 34,536 (approx. record) **ANNUAL MEETING:** In Nov. **INCORPORATED:** DE, June, 1961

INSTITUTIONAL HOLDINGS:
No. of Institutions: 771
Shares Held: 427,002,235
% Held: 71.2

INDUSTRY: Data processing and preparation (SIC: 7374)

TRANSFER AGENT(S): Mellon Investor Services, Ridgefield Park, NJ

AVERY DENNISON CORPORATION

YIELD 2.6%
P/E RATIO 20.9

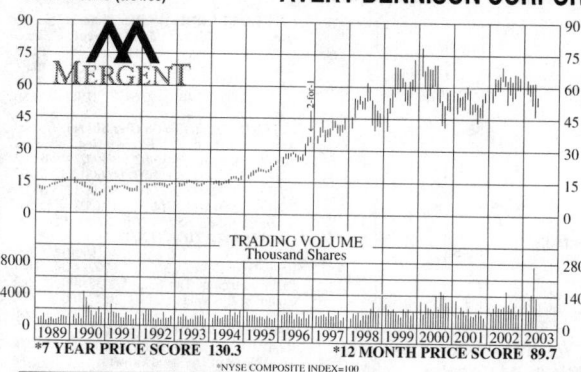

TRADING VOLUME
Thousand Shares

*7 YEAR PRICE SCORE 130.3 *12 MONTH PRICE SCORE 89.7
*NYSE COMPOSITE INDEX=100

INTERIM EARNINGS (Per Share):

Qtr.	Mar.	June	Sept.	Dec.
1999	0.18	0.63	0.65	0.67
2000	0.70	0.73	0.73	0.69
2001	0.65	0.61	0.63	0.59
2002	0.66	0.74	0.64	0.56
2003	0.71	...	...	...

INTERIM DIVIDENDS (Per Share):

Amt.	Decl.	Ex.	Rec.	Pay.
0.33Q	7/25/02	8/30/02	9/04/02	9/18/02
0.36Q	10/24/02	12/02/02	12/04/02	12/18/02
0.36Q	1/30/03	3/03/03	3/05/03	3/19/03
0.36Q	4/24/03	6/02/03	6/04/03	6/18/03

Indicated div.: $1.44 (Div. Reinv. Plan)

CAPITALIZATION (12/28/02):

	($000)	(%)
Long-Term Debt	837,200	42.5
Deferred Income Tax	74,000	3.8
Common & Surplus	1,056,400	53.7
Total	1,967,600	100.0

DIVIDEND ACHIEVER STATUS:
Rank: 93   10-Year Growth Rate: 12.66%
Total Years of Dividend Growth: 27

RECENT DEVELOPMENTS: For the three months ended 3/29/03, net income climbed 9.3% to $70.8 million compared with income of $64.8 million in the corresponding quarter of 2002. Net sales were $1.15 billion, up 23.6% from $930.8 million in the prior-year period. Sales benefited from acquisitions and the positive effect of currency exchange rates. Sales for the pressure-sensitive adhesives and materials segment jumped 31.6% to $724.3 million.

PROSPECTS: Going forward, the Company should continue to benefit from solid sales and earnings growth despite the challenging economic and geopolitical climate. However, AVY has reduced its previously announced full-year 2003 earnings per share estimate by $0.05. As a result, earnings per share for full-year 2003 are now expected in the range of $3.00 to $3.20.

BUSINESS

AVERY DENNISON CORPORATION is a worldwide manufacturer of pressure-sensitive adhesives and materials, office products and converted products. A portion of self-adhesive material is converted into labels and other products through embossing, printing, stamping and die-cutting, and some are sold in unconverted form as base materials, tapes and reflective sheeting. AVY also manufactures and sells a variety of office products and other items not involving pressure-sensitive components, such as notebooks, three-ring binders, organization systems, felt-tip markers, glues, fasteners, business forms, tickets, tags, and imprinting equipment. Sales for 2002 were derived: pressure-sensitive adhesives and materials, 58.6%; and consumer and converted products, 41.4%.

ANNUAL FINANCIAL DATA

	12/28/02	12/29/01	12/30/00	1/1/00	1/2/99	12/27/97	12/28/96
Earnings Per Share	④ 2.59	③ 2.47	2.84	② 2.13	2.15	1.93	① 1.68
Cash Flow Per Share	4.12	4.05	4.41	3.61	3.37	3.03	2.76
Tang. Book Val. Per Share	2.53	4.70	4.35	4.18	6.88	6.87	6.72
Dividends Per Share	1.35	1.23	1.11	0.99	0.87	0.72	0.62
Dividend Payout %	52.1	49.8	39.1	46.5	40.5	37.3	36.9
INCOME STATEMENT (IN MILLIONS):							
Total Revenues	4,206.9	3,803.3	3,893.5	3,768.2	3,459.9	3,345.7	3,222.5
Costs & Expenses	3,613.5	3,237.6	3,255.7	3,244.0	2,961.4	2,886.0	2,801.1
Depreciation & Amort.	152.8	156.0	156.9	150.4	127.2	116.8	113.4
Operating Income	440.6	409.7	480.9	373.8	371.3	342.9	308.0
Net Interest Inc./(Exp.)	d43.7	d50.2	d54.6	d43.4	d34.6	d31.7	d37.4
Income Before Income Taxes	364.8	359.8	426.3	330.4	336.7	311.2	270.6
Income Taxes	107.6	116.4	142.8	115.0	113.4	106.4	94.7
Net Income	④ 257.2	③ 243.4	283.5	② 215.4	223.3	205.3	① 175.9
Cash Flow	410.0	399.4	440.4	365.8	350.5	321.6	289.3
Average Shs. Outstg. (000)	99,400	98,600	99,800	101,300	104,100	106,100	105,000
BALANCE SHEET (IN MILLIONS):							
Cash & Cash Equivalents	22.8	19.1	11.4	6.9	18.5	3.3	3.8
Total Current Assets	1,215.5	982.5	982.4	956.0	802.0	793.5	804.5
Net Property	1,199.2	1,074.6	1,079.0	1,043.5	1,035.6	985.3	962.7
Total Assets	3,652.4	2,819.2	2,699.1	2,592.5	2,142.6	2,046.5	2,036.7
Total Current Liabilities	1,296.1	951.3	800.7	850.4	664.3	629.9	693.9
Long-Term Obligations	837.2	626.7	772.9	617.5	465.9	404.1	370.7
Net Stockholders' Equity	1,056.4	929.4	828.1	809.9	833.3	837.2	832.0
Net Working Capital	d80.6	31.2	181.7	105.6	137.7	163.6	110.6
Year-end Shs. Outstg. (000)	110,467	109,891	110,245	98,800	100,000	102,400	103,600
STATISTICAL RECORD:							
Operating Profit Margin %	10.5	10.8	12.4	9.9	10.7	10.2	9.6
Net Profit Margin %	6.1	6.4	7.3	5.7	6.5	6.1	5.5
Return on Equity %	24.3	26.2	34.2	26.6	26.8	24.5	21.1
Return on Assets %	7.0	8.6	10.5	8.3	10.4	10.0	8.6
Debt/Total Assets %	22.9	22.2	28.6	23.8	21.7	19.7	18.2
Price Range	69.70-52.06	60.50-43.25	78.50-41.13	73.00-39.38	62.06-39.44	45.31-33.38	36.50-23.75
P/E Ratio	26.9-20.1	24.5-17.5	27.6-14.5	34.3-18.5	28.9-18.3	23.5-17.3	21.7-14.1
Average Yield %	2.2	2.4	1.9	1.8	1.7	1.8	2.1

Statistics are as originally reported. Adj. for 2-for-1 split, 12/96. ① Incl. non-recur. chgs. of $2.1 mill. ② Incl. $65.0 mill. one-time restr. chg. ③ Excl. $200,000 acct. chg. ④ Incl. $32.1 mill. asset impair. chg., lease cancel. costs, & restr. costs.

OFFICERS:
P. M. Neal, Chmn., C.E.O.
D. A. Scarborough, Pres., C.O.O.
D. R. O'Bryant, Sr. V.P., C.F.O

INVESTOR CONTACT: Cynthia S. Guenther, V.P., Investor Relations, (626) 304-2204

PRINCIPAL OFFICE: 150 North Orange Grove Boulevard, Pasadena, CA 91103

TELEPHONE NUMBER: (626) 304-2000
FAX: (626) 792-7312
WEB: www.averydennison.com

NO. OF EMPLOYEES: 20,500 (avg.)

SHAREHOLDERS: 11,765 (record)

ANNUAL MEETING: In Apr.

INCORPORATED: DE, Sept., 1946

INSTITUTIONAL HOLDINGS:
No. of Institutions: 420
Shares Held: 76,297,988
% Held: 77.1

INDUSTRY: Paper coated and laminated, nec (SIC: 2672)

TRANSFER AGENT(S): First Chicago Trust Company of New York, Jersey City, NJ

AVON PRODUCTS, INC.

YIELD	1.4%
P/E RATIO	27.2

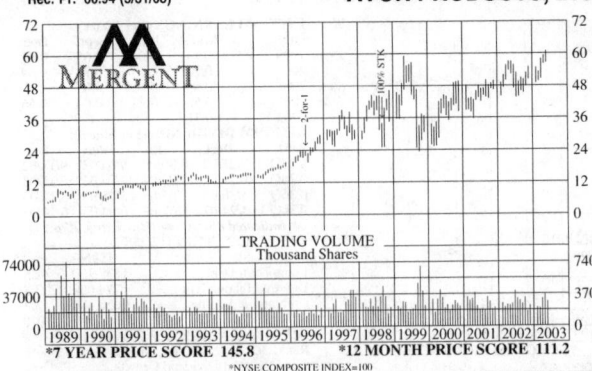

INTERIM EARNINGS (Per Share):

Qtr.	Mar.	June	Sept.	Dec.
1999	d0.19	0.46	0.34	0.58
2000	0.31	0.52	0.39	0.81
2001	0.34	0.57	0.42	0.46
2002	0.40	0.64	0.38	0.80
2003	0.42	...	...	...

INTERIM DIVIDENDS (Per Share):

Amt.	Decl.	Ex.	Rec.	Pay.
0.20Q	8/08/02	8/15/02	8/19/02	9/03/02
0.20Q	11/07/02	11/14/02	11/18/02	12/02/02
0.21Q	1/30/03	2/12/03	2/14/03	3/03/03
0.21Q	5/01/03	5/14/03	5/16/03	6/02/03

Indicated div.: $0.84 (Div. Reinv. Plan)

CAPITALIZATION (12/31/02):

	($000)	(%)
Long-Term Debt	767,000	113.7
Deferred Income Tax	35,400	5.2
Common & Surplus	d127,700	-18.9
Total	674,700	100.0

DIVIDEND ACHIEVER STATUS:
Rank: 187   10-Year Growth Rate: 7.87%
Total Years of Dividend Growth: 12

TRADING VOLUME
Thousand Shares

*7 YEAR PRICE SCORE 145.8   *12 MONTH PRICE SCORE 111.2

*NYSE COMPOSITE INDEX=100

RECENT DEVELOPMENTS: For the quarter ended 3/31/03, net income grew 2.7% to $98.9 million from $96.3 million in the equivalent 2002 quarter. Results for 2003 included a pre-tax charge of $18.0 million for the repositioning of AVP's BECOMING product line. Total revenue rose 7.1% to $1.48 billion, reflecting an 11.0% increase in beauty products, as well as increases in both unit volume and active representatives, which were up 10.0% and 13.0%, respectively. All geographic regions posting solid gains.

PROSPECTS: Looking ahead, the Company expects overall sales in the second quarter of 2003 to increase the same rate as the first quarter. U.S. sales growth is anticipated to be approximately 3.0%, with further acceleration in the second half of the year due to the launch of its new MARK. brand and pipeline of new beauty products in its core business. Meanwhile, operating profit is expected to grow in the low-teens range with earnings per share in the mid-single-digit range.

BUSINESS

AVON PRODUCTS, INC. is a global manufacturer and marketer of beauty and related products. AVP's products fall into four product categories: Beauty, which consists of cosmetics, fragrance and toiletries; Beauty Plus, which consists of jewelry, watches and apparel and accessories; Beyond Beauty, which consists of home products, gifts and candles; and women's health and wellness, which consists of vitamins and nutrition supplements, exercise and fitness items, and self-care and stress relief products. Avon product lines include such brands as AVON COLOR, ANEW, SKIN-SO-SOFT, ADVANCE TECHNIQUES HAIR CARE, BECOMING and AVON WELLNESS. As of 4/25/03, the Company had operations in 58 countries and its products were distributed in 85 more for coverage in 143 countries. Sales are made principally by approximately 3.9 million independent Avon representatives. In 2002, net sales by geographic area consisted of: North America, 39.1%; Latin America, 27.6%; Europe, 19.9% and Pacific, 13.4%.

ANNUAL FINANCIAL DATA

	12/31/02	12/31/01	12/31/00	12/31/99	12/31/98	12/31/97	12/31/96
Earnings Per Share	⑤ 2.22	②④ 1.79	② 2.02	③ 1.17	① 1.02	1.27	1.19
Cash Flow Per Share	2.76	2.25	2.40	1.49	1.29	1.54	1.43
Tang. Book Val. Per Share	...	...	...	...	1.09	1.08	0.91
Dividends Per Share	0.80	0.76	0.74	0.72	0.68	0.63	0.58
Dividend Payout %	36.0	42.5	36.6	61.5	66.7	49.6	48.7
INCOME STATEMENT (IN MILLIONS):							
Total Revenues	6,228.3	5,994.5	5,714.6	5,289.1	5,212.7	5,079.4	4,814.2
Costs & Expenses	5,215.4	5,121.1	4,828.8	4,656.7	4,667.5	4,469.5	4,204.9
Depreciation & Amort.	142.9	124.0	97.1	83.0	72.0	72.1	64.5
Operating Income	870.0	749.4	788.7	549.4	473.2	537.8	544.8
Net Interest Inc./(Exp.)	d36.8	d56.7	d76.2	d32.1	d18.8	d18.8	d25.5
Income Before Income Taxes	835.6	665.7	691.0	506.6	455.9	534.9	510.4
Income Taxes	292.3	230.9	201.7	204.2	190.8	197.9	191.4
Equity Earnings/Minority Int.	d8.7	d4.5	d4.2	...	4.9	1.8	d1.1
Net Income	⑤ 534.6	②④ 430.3	② 485.1	③ 302.4	① 270.0	338.8	317.9
Cash Flow	677.5	554.3	582.2	385.4	342.0	410.9	382.4
Average Shs. Outstg. (000)	245,470	246,050	242,950	259,370	265,950	267,000	267,400
BALANCE SHEET (IN MILLIONS):							
Cash & Cash Equivalents	606.8	508.5	122.7	117.4	105.6	141.9	184.5
Total Current Assets	2,048.2	1,889.1	1,545.7	1,337.8	1,341.4	1,344.0	1,349.6
Net Property	769.1	774.9	768.4	734.8	669.9	611.0	566.6
Total Assets	3,327.5	3,193.1	2,826.4	2,528.6	2,433.5	2,272.9	2,222.4
Total Current Liabilities	1,975.5	1,461.0	1,359.3	1,712.8	1,329.5	1,355.9	1,391.3
Long-Term Obligations	767.0	1,236.3	1,108.2	701.4	201.0	102.2	104.5
Net Stockholders' Equity	d127.7	d74.6	d215.8	d406.1	285.1	285.0	241.7
Net Working Capital	72.7	428.1	186.4	d375.0	11.9	d11.9	d41.7
Year-end Shs. Outstg. (000)	235,258	236,681	238,162	237,895	262,520	263,628	265,640
STATISTICAL RECORD:							
Operating Profit Margin %	14.0	12.5	13.8	10.4	9.1	10.6	11.3
Net Profit Margin %	8.6	7.2	8.5	5.7	5.2	6.7	6.6
Return on Equity %	...	...	...	...	94.7	118.9	131.5
Return on Assets %	16.1	13.5	17.2	12.0	11.1	14.9	14.3
Debt/Total Assets %	23.1	38.7	39.2	27.7	8.3	4.5	4.7
Price Range	57.10-43.49	50.12-35.55	49.75-25.25	59.13-23.31	46.25-25.00	39.00-25.31	29.75-18.16
P/E Ratio	25.7-19.6	28.0-19.9	24.6-12.5	50.5-19.9	45.3-24.5	30.7-19.9	25.0-15.3
Average Yield %	1.6	1.8	2.0	1.7	1.9	2.0	2.4

Statistics are as originally reported. Adj. for stk. splits: 2-for-1, 9/98; 6/96. ① Incl. non-recur. chrg. $70.5 mill. ② Bef. acctg. change chrg. $300,000, 12/01; $6.7 mill., 12/00. ③ Incl. pre-tax special chrg. of $105.2 mill. ④ Incl. after-tax cash settlement gain $15.7 mill.; after-tax tax liab. chrg. $3.4 mill.; asset impair. chrg. $14.5 mill.; after-tax spec. chrg. $68.3 mill. ⑤ Incl. a net after-tax chrg. of $25.2 mill. for bus. trans.

OFFICERS:
A. Jung, Chmn., C.E.O.
S. J. Kropf, Pres., C.O.O.
R. J. Corti, Exec. V.P., C.F.O.

PRINCIPAL OFFICE: 1345 Avenue of the Americas, New York, NY 10105-0196

TELEPHONE NUMBER: (212) 282-5000
FAX: (212) 282-6035
WEB: www.avon.com
NO. OF EMPLOYEES: 45,000 (approx.)
SHAREHOLDERS: 20,852
ANNUAL MEETING: In May
INCORPORATED: NY, Jan., 1916

INSTITUTIONAL HOLDINGS:
No. of Institutions: 450
Shares Held: 198,546,683
% Held: 84.5

INDUSTRY: Toilet preparations (SIC: 2844)

TRANSFER AGENT(S): EquiServe, Jersey City, NJ

BADGER METER, INC.

YIELD 3.6%
P/E RATIO 15.1

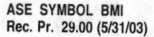
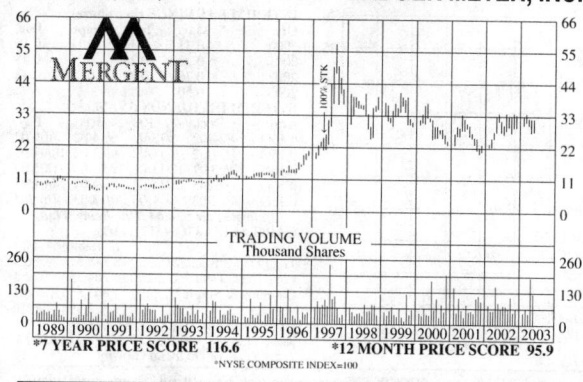

*7 YEAR PRICE SCORE 116.6
*12 MONTH PRICE SCORE 95.9
NYSE COMPOSITE INDEX=100

TRADING VOLUME
Thousand Shares

INTERIM EARNINGS (Per Share):

Qtr.	Mar.	June	Sept.	Dec.
2000	0.67	0.44	0.56	0.32
2001	0.28	0.16	0.29	0.29
2002	0.49	0.70	0.70	0.31
2003	0.21	...	...	...

INTERIM DIVIDENDS (Per Share):

Amt.	Decl.	Ex.	Rec.	Pay.
0.25Q	5/17/02	5/29/02	5/31/02	6/14/02
0.26Q	8/16/02	8/28/02	8/30/02	9/13/02
0.26Q	11/08/02	11/26/02	11/29/02	12/13/02
0.26Q	2/14/03	2/26/03	2/28/03	3/14/03
0.26Q	5/02/03	5/28/03	5/30/03	6/13/03

Indicated div.: $1.04 (Div. Reinv. Plan)

CAPITALIZATION (12/31/02):

	($000)	(%)
Long-Term Debt	12,857	19.5
Capital Lease Obligations	189	0.3
Deferred Income Tax	4,710	7.2
Common & Surplus	48,095	73.0
Total	65,851	100.0

DIVIDEND ACHIEVER STATUS:
Rank: 91   10-Year Growth Rate: 12.93%
Total Years of Dividend Growth: 10

RECENT DEVELOPMENTS: For the quarter ended 3/31/03, net income dropped 56.1% to $706,000 versus $1.6 million in the corresponding quarter of 2002. Results were negatively affected by soft economic conditions, the war in Iraq and terrorism. Net sales climbed 5.7% to $39.6 million from $37.5 million in the prior-year period. Market conditions hampered sales of residential water meters and metering systems. In addition, the Company is experiencing a longer sales cycle for purchases by water utilities as they evaluate requirements and costs of higher security and lower budgets from governments. This was partially offset by the introduction of the Orion® radio frequency system, which is an automated drive-by radio frequency meter reading system for water utilities, and increased sales of products, including automotive fluid meters, electromagnetic flowmeters and research control valves. Gross profit amounted to $12.9 million, or 32.7% of net sales, versus $12.8 million, or 34.1% of net sales, in 2002.

BUSINESS

BADGER METER, INC. is a global marketer and manufacturer of products and a provider of services using flow measurement and control technologies. The Company's products are sold to water utilities, original equipment manufacturers and a range of industrial customers primarily in the markets of water, wastewater and process waters; energy and petroleum; food and beverage; pharmaceutical; chemical; and concrete. The Company operates five product lines: residential and commercial water meters, automotive fluid meters and systems, small precision valves and industrial process meters. Water meters and related systems produce the majority of the Company's sales. BMI's products are primarily manufactured and assembled in its Milwaukee, Wisconsin, Tulsa, Oklahoma, Rio Rico, Arizona, Mattapoisett, Massachusetts and Brno, Czech Republic facilities. Assembly is also done in the Nogales, Mexico, Stuttgart, Germany and Nancy, France facilities.

ANNUAL FINANCIAL DATA

	12/31/02	12/31/01	12/31/00	12/31/99	12/31/98	12/31/97	12/31/96
Earnings Per Share	2.20	1.03	2.00	2.60	2.12	1.65	1.36
Cash Flow Per Share	4.62	3.10	3.75	4.11	3.32	2.64	2.50
Tang. Book Val. Per Share	12.82	13.28	13.17	12.55	12.73	11.43	10.07
Dividends Per Share	1.02	1.00	0.86	0.72	0.60	0.48	0.43
Dividend Payout %	46.4	97.1	43.0	27.7	28.3	29.2	31.6
INCOME STATEMENT (IN MILLIONS):							
Total Revenues	167.3	138.5	146.4	150.9	143.8	130.8	116.0
Costs & Expenses	146.1	125.7	129.3	128.6	125.1	115.9	103.1
Depreciation & Amort.	8.0	6.8	6.1	5.6	4.7	4.0	4.1
Operating Income	13.2	6.1	11.0	16.7	14.0	11.0	8.8
Net Interest Inc./(Exp.)	d1.8	d1.4	d2.2	d1.3	d0.6	d0.5	d0.4
Income Before Income Taxes	11.4	5.0	10.7	15.7	13.4	10.2	8.2
Income Taxes	4.2	1.6	3.8	6.0	5.1	3.7	3.0
Net Income	7.3	3.4	6.9	9.7	8.2	6.5	5.1
Cash Flow	15.3	10.2	13.0	15.3	12.9	10.5	9.2
Average Shs. Outstg. (000)	3,304	3,275	3,470	3,728	3,896	3,961	3,698
BALANCE SHEET (IN MILLIONS):							
Cash & Cash Equivalents	3.8	3.4	4.2	3.8	2.4	1.1	1.1
Total Current Assets	55.4	44.4	44.5	43.0	45.7	42.5	35.0
Net Property	43.5	41.1	42.6	42.1	37.4	24.0	19.4
Total Assets	126.5	98.8	98.7	103.1	96.9	82.3	66.1
Total Current Liabilities	48.6	23.8	37.7	36.8	34.9	28.7	17.4
Long-Term Obligations	13.0	20.5	5.9	11.5	2.6	0.9	1.1
Net Stockholders' Equity	48.1	43.0	43.3	43.0	47.8	41.5	36.6
Net Working Capital	6.8	20.6	6.8	11.2	10.8	13.9	17.6
Year-end Shs. Outstg. (000)	3,221	3,180	3,207	3,340	3,646	3,571	3,552
STATISTICAL RECORD:							
Operating Profit Margin %	7.9	4.4	7.5	11.0	9.7	8.4	7.5
Net Profit Margin %	4.3	2.4	4.7	6.4	5.7	5.0	4.4
Return on Equity %	15.1	7.8	16.0	22.6	17.2	15.7	14.0
Return on Assets %	5.7	3.4	7.0	9.4	8.5	7.9	7.8
Debt/Total Assets %	10.3	20.7	6.0	11.1	2.7	1.1	1.6
Price Range	34.00-22.30	33.50-20.00	37.38-23.00	41.00-29.38	40.63-25.00	57.50-18.13	20.81-12.38
P/E Ratio	15.5-10.1	32.5-19.4	18.7-11.5	15.8-11.3	19.2-11.8	34.8-11.0	15.0-8.9
Average Yield %	3.6	3.7	2.8	2.0	1.8	1.3	2.6

Statistics are as originally reported.

OFFICERS:
J. L. Forbes, Chmn.
R. A. Meeusen, Pres., C.E.O.
R. E. Johnson, V.P., C.F.O., Treas.

INVESTOR CONTACT: Joan C. Zimmer, Investor Relations, (414) 371-5702

PRINCIPAL OFFICE: 4545 W. Brown Deer Road, Milwaukee, WI 53223

TELEPHONE NUMBER: (414) 355-0400
FAX: (414) 355-7499
WEB: www.badgermeter.com

NO. OF EMPLOYEES: 1,025
SHAREHOLDERS: 494
ANNUAL MEETING: In May
INCORPORATED: WI, Mar., 1905

INSTITUTIONAL HOLDINGS:
No. of Institutions: 22
Shares Held: 1,224,768
% Held: 40.8

INDUSTRY: Fluid meters and counting devices (SIC: 3824)

TRANSFER AGENT(S): U.S. Bank, N.A., Milwaukee, WI

BANCORPSOUTH, INC.

YIELD 2.9%
P/E RATIO 14.3

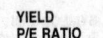

INTERIM EARNINGS (Per Share):

Qtr.	Mar.	June	Sept.	Dec.
2000	0.31	0.31	0.11	0.15
2001	0.27	0.28	0.26	0.38
2002	0.36	0.38	0.33	0.33
2003	0.50	...	...	...

INTERIM DIVIDENDS (Per Share):

Amt.	Decl.	Ex.	Rec.	Pay.
0.15Q	4/24/02	6/12/02	6/14/02	7/01/02
0.15Q	7/24/02	9/11/02	9/13/02	10/01/02
0.16Q	10/23/02	12/11/02	12/13/02	1/02/03
0.16Q	1/22/03	3/12/03	3/14/03	4/01/03
0.16Q	4/23/03	6/11/03	6/13/03	7/01/03

Indicated div.: $0.64 (Div. Reinv. Plan)

CAPITALIZATION (12/31/02):

	($000)	(%)
Total Deposits	8,548,918	88.9
Long-Term Debt	264,757	2.8
Common & Surplus	807,823	8.4
Total	9,621,498	100.0

DIVIDEND ACHIEVER STATUS:
Rank: 128   10-Year Growth Rate: 10.69%
Total Years of Dividend Growth: 16

TRADING VOLUME
Thousand Shares

*7 YEAR PRICE SCORE 131.2   *12 MONTH PRICE SCORE 102.2
*NYSE COMPOSITE INDEX=100

RECENT DEVELOPMENTS: For the quarter ended 3/31/03, net income climbed 33.2% to $39.1 million from $29.4 million in the prior year. Results for 2003 included an $8.4 million after-tax gain from the sale of securities. Net interest revenue decreased 2.5% to $90.1 million from $92.4 million a year earlier. Net interest margin was 3.97% compared with 4.31% in 2002. Provision for credit losses declined 3.5% to $6.5 million. Total non-interest revenue jumped 57.5% to $55.0 million, while total non-interest expense rose 3.2% to $79.6 million.

PROSPECTS: Results are benefiting from significantly higher sales of non-interest bearing products, partially offset by lower net interest revenue stemming from lower interest rates and weaker demand for loans due to uncertain economic conditions. Going forward, the Company plans to boost non-interest revenue through increased sales of fee-income products to existing customers in Mississippi, Alabama and Tennessee, as well as from the ongoing launch of these products in newer markets in Arkansas, Louisiana and Texas.

BUSINESS

BANCORPSOUTH, INC. is a bank holding company headquartered in Tupelo, Mississippi with assets of $10.34 billion and total deposits of $8.69 billion as of 3/31/03. BXS operates approximately 250 commercial banking, insurance, trust, broker/dealer and consumer finance locations in Alabama, Arkansas, Louisiana, Mississippi, Tennessee and Texas. BXS and its subsidiaries provide a range of financial services to individuals and small-to-medium size businesses. BXS operates investment services, consumer finance, credit life insurance and insurance agency subsidiaries. BXS trust department offers a variety of services including personal trust and estate services, and certain employee benefit accounts and plans. On 2/28/02, BXS completed its acquisition of Pinnacle Bancshares, Inc.

ANNUAL FINANCIAL DATA

	12/31/02	12/31/01	12/31/00	12/31/99	12/31/98	12/31/97	12/31/96
Earnings Per Share	1.39	1.19	① 0.88	1.20	1.01	1.02	1.01
Tang. Book Val. Per Share	10.40	9.92	9.39	8.68	8.48	8.09	7.50
Dividends Per Share	0.60	0.56	0.52	0.48	0.44	0.38	0.34
Dividend Payout %	43.2	47.1	59.1	40.0	43.6	37.4	33.7
INCOME STATEMENT (IN MILLIONS):							
Total Interest Income	590.4	665.8	674.0	414.2	383.5	307.1	277.9
Total Interest Expense	218.9	331.1	346.9	196.7	187.4	144.1	126.5
Net Interest Income	371.5	334.7	327.2	217.5	196.1	163.0	151.4
Provision for Loan Losses	29.4	22.3	26.2	14.7	15.0	9.0	8.8
Non-Interest Income	132.2	128.6	85.6	79.3	53.0	43.7	40.7
Non-Interest Expense	312.4	295.3	274.2	183.0	152.1	132.0	118.5
Income Before Taxes	162.0	145.8	112.3	99.1	82.0	65.7	64.9
Net Income	112.0	98.5	① 74.4	69.0	54.5	45.4	42.9
Average Shs. Outstg. (000)	80,481	82,979	84,811	57,524	53,871	44,788	42,426
BALANCE SHEET (IN MILLIONS):							
Cash & Due from Banks	357.0	341.5	314.9	217.3	175.4	286.3	153.1
Securities Avail. for Sale	1,642.2	1,083.2	857.4	345.3	549.8	406.2	230.7
Total Loans & Leases	6,435.3	6,127.0	6,161.1	4,131.4	3,561.4	2,852.9	2,554.1
Allowance for Credit Losses	133.8	137.0	147.5	133.4	142.3	133.7	122.1
Net Loans & Leases	6,301.5	5,990.1	6,013.6	3,998.0	3,419.1	2,719.2	2,432.1
Total Assets	10,189.2	9,395.4	9,044.0	5,776.9	5,203.7	4,180.1	3,617.2
Total Deposits	8,548.9	7,856.8	7,480.9	4,815.4	4,441.9	3,540.3	3,161.4
Long-Term Obligations	264.8	140.9	152.0	138.6	178.3	47.5	55.8
Total Liabilities	9,381.4	8,590.0	8,254.5	5,279.5	4,747.4	3,819.7	3,301.9
Net Stockholders' Equity	807.8	805.4	789.6	497.4	456.4	360.4	315.3
Year-end Shs. Outstg. (000)	77,681	81,226	84,043	57,304	53,833	44,542	42,026
STATISTICAL RECORD:							
Return on Equity %	13.9	12.2	9.4	13.9	11.9	12.6	13.6
Return on Assets %	1.1	1.0	0.8	1.2	1.0	1.1	1.2
Equity/Assets %	7.9	8.6	8.7	8.6	8.8	8.6	8.7
Non-Int. Exp./Tot. Inc. %	62.7	65.2	64.0	62.5	61.3	64.2	61.7
Price Range	22.21-15.90	17.00-12.06	17.25-11.88	19.44-15.38	24.00-16.81	23.78-13.25	14.25-10.06
P/E Ratio	16.0-11.4	14.3-10.1	19.6-13.5	16.2-12.8	23.8-16.6	23.4-13.1	14.1-10.0
Average Yield %	3.1	3.9	3.6	2.8	2.2	2.1	2.8

Statistics are as originally reported. Adj. for 2-for-1 split, 5/98. ① Incl. after-tax merger-related charges of $22.5 mill.

OFFICERS:
A. B. Patterson, Chmn., C.E.O.
J. V. Kelley, Pres., C.O.O.
L. N. Allen, Jr., C.F.O., Treas.
INVESTOR CONTACT: Investor Relations, (662) 680-2000
PRINCIPAL OFFICE: One Mississippi Plaza, 201 South Spring Street, Tupelo, MS 38804

TELEPHONE NUMBER: (662) 680-2000
FAX: (662) 680-2570
WEB: www.bancorpsouth.com
NO. OF EMPLOYEES: 3,828
SHAREHOLDERS: 9,017
ANNUAL MEETING: In Apr.
INCORPORATED: MS, July, 1982

INSTITUTIONAL HOLDINGS:
No. of Institutions: 94
Shares Held: 12,345,606
% Held: 15.8
INDUSTRY: State commercial banks (SIC: 6022)
TRANSFER AGENT(S): SunTrust Bank, Atlanta, GA

BANDAG, INC.

YIELD 3.5%
P/E RATIO 13.8

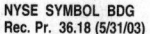

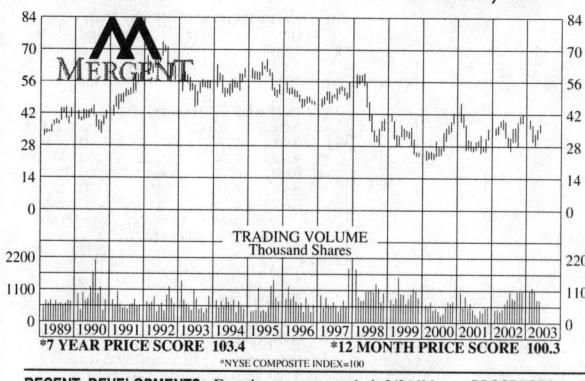

*7 YEAR PRICE SCORE 103.4   *12 MONTH PRICE SCORE 100.3
*NYSE COMPOSITE INDEX=100

TRADING VOLUME
Thousand Shares

INTERIM EARNINGS (Per Share):

Qtr.	Mar.	June	Sept.	Dec.
1999	0.46	0.73	0.82	0.38
2000	0.48	0.85	0.86	0.71
2001	0.11	0.46	0.71	0.84
2002	0.06	0.57	1.02	0.91
2003	0.12	...	...	...

INTERIM DIVIDENDS (Per Share):

Amt.	Decl.	Ex.	Rec.	Pay.
0.315Q	5/14/02	6/17/02	6/19/02	7/19/02
0.315Q	8/27/02	9/17/02	9/19/02	10/18/02
0.32Q	11/12/02	12/17/02	12/19/02	1/17/03
0.32Q	3/11/03	3/19/03	3/21/03	4/17/03
0.32Q	5/13/03	6/16/03	6/18/03	7/18/03

Indicated div.: $1.28 (Div. Reinv. Plan)

CAPITALIZATION (12/31/02):

	($000)	(%)
Long-Term Debt	45,373	9.7
Common & Surplus	424,593	90.3
Total	469,966	100.0

DIVIDEND ACHIEVER STATUS:

Rank: 188   10-Year Growth Rate: 7.70%
Total Years of Dividend Growth: 26

RECENT DEVELOPMENTS: For the quarter ended 3/31/03, net income was $2.4 million versus income of $1.2 million, before an accounting charge of $47.3 million, in the prior-year quarter. Net sales declined 8.9% to $175.3 million from $192.5 million a year earlier. Net sales for Tire Distribution Systems, Inc. dropped 21.4% to $63.6 million, while net sales for the traditional retread business improved 0.1% to $111.7 million.

PROSPECTS: Although the Company's near-term economic outlook remains uncertain, BDG is encouraged by continuing progress at Tire Distribution Systems, Inc. In addition, the Company's dealers and fleet customers have responded positively to recent advancements in BDG's processes as an innovative service provider for commercial tire dealers and the transportation industry.

BUSINESS

BANDAG, INC. is engaged in the manufacture of pre-cured tread rubber, equipment, and supplies primarily for the re-treading of truck and bus tires by a patented cold-bonding reaction process. The Company also does some custom processing of rubber compounds. As of 5/13/03, revenues were generated by more than 1,100 franchised dealers in the U.S. and abroad who are licensed to produce and market cold process retreads utilizing the Bandag process. BDG's wholly-owned subsidiary, Tire Management Solutions, Inc., provides tire management systems outsourcing for commercial truck fleets. Tire Distribution Systems, Inc., also a wholly-owned subsidiary, sells and services new and retread tires. In 2002, the traditional retread rubber, equipment and supplier for re-treading accounted for 62.1% of net sales and Tire Distribution Systems accounted for 37.9% of net sales.

ANNUAL FINANCIAL DATA

	12/31/02	12/31/01	12/31/00	12/31/99	12/31/98	12/31/97	12/31/96
Earnings Per Share	③ 2.52	② 2.12	2.90	② 2.40	② 2.63	① 5.33	3.44
Cash Flow Per Share	4.14	4.35	5.33	4.87	4.91	6.93	4.89
Tang. Book Val. Per Share	21.97	21.22	20.03	18.62	19.14	17.00	17.85
Dividends Per Share	1.26	1.22	1.18	1.14	1.10	1.00	0.90
Dividend Payout %	50.0	57.5	40.7	47.5	41.8	18.8	26.2
INCOME STATEMENT (IN MILLIONS):							
Total Revenues	912.0	982.2	1,013.4	1,027.9	1,079.5	931.7	769.0
Costs & Expenses	801.2	862.2	854.9	872.3	917.8	688.6	602.4
Depreciation & Amort.	32.3	46.2	50.5	53.8	51.4	36.9	34.6
Operating Income	91.4	73.9	108.1	101.8	110.3	206.3	132.0
Net Interest Inc./(Exp.)	d6.9	d7.4	d8.7	d9.7	d10.8	d3.3	d1.2
Income Before Income Taxes	71.5	66.5	99.4	92.1	99.5	202.9	130.8
Income Taxes	21.5	22.7	39.0	39.8	40.2	80.9	49.2
Net Income	③ 50.1	② 43.8	60.3	② 52.3	② 59.3	① 122.0	81.6
Cash Flow	82.4	90.0	110.8	106.1	110.7	158.9	116.2
Average Shs. Outstg. (000)	19,888	20,686	20,778	21,764	22,559	22,908	23,746
BALANCE SHEET (IN MILLIONS):							
Cash & Cash Equivalents	143.7	155.0	93.4	60.1	47.6	198.0	33.5
Total Current Assets	416.1	450.2	427.2	428.1	439.1	599.0	341.7
Net Property	134.7	158.0	177.2	198.0	213.0	197.6	145.1
Total Assets	617.8	718.6	714.5	722.4	784.2	899.9	588.3
Total Current Liabilities	147.9	186.1	132.7	154.1	174.9	306.5	139.2
Long-Term Obligations	45.4	40.9	105.2	111.2	108.9	123.2	10.1
Net Stockholders' Equity	424.6	489.0	474.2	454.1	495.7	463.4	410.9
Net Working Capital	268.2	264.1	294.4	274.1	264.2	292.5	202.5
Year-end Shs. Outstg. (000)	19,152	20,642	20,562	20,771	21,955	22,813	22,923
STATISTICAL RECORD:							
Operating Profit Margin %	10.0	7.5	10.7	9.9	10.2	22.1	17.2
Net Profit Margin %	5.5	4.5	6.0	5.1	5.5	13.1	10.6
Return on Equity %	11.8	9.0	12.7	11.5	12.0	26.3	19.9
Return on Assets %	8.1	6.1	8.4	7.2	7.6	13.6	13.9
Debt/Total Assets %	7.3	5.7	14.7	15.4	14.0	13.7	1.7
Price Range	42.01-26.00	46.75-25.01	42.63-21.88	41.63-23.50	59.75-28.31	55.75-45.00	55.88-44.50
P/E Ratio	16.7-10.3	22.1-11.8	14.7-7.5	17.3-9.8	22.7-10.8	10.5-8.4	16.2-12.9
Average Yield %	3.7	3.4	3.7	3.5	2.5	2.0	1.8

Statistics are as originally reported. ① Incl. nonrecurr. gain of $78.6 mill. on sale of secur. ② Incl. nonrecurr. chrg. of $2.0 mill., 2001; $13.5 mill., 1999; $4.2 mill., 1998. ③ Bef. an acctg. chng. chrg. of $47.3 mill.; incl. litigation chrg. of $10.7 mill.

OFFICERS:
M. G. Carver, Chmn., Pres., C.E.O.
W. W. Heidbreder, V.P., C.F.O., Sec.
J. C. Pattison, V.P., Treas.

INVESTOR CONTACT: Investor Relations,
(563) 262-1260

PRINCIPAL OFFICE: 2905 North Highway 61, Muscatine, IA 52761-5886

TELEPHONE NUMBER: (563) 262-1400
FAX: (563) 262-1284
WEB: www.bandag.com

NO. OF EMPLOYEES: 3,715 (approx.)

SHAREHOLDERS: 1,819 (record); 1,017 (class A); 196 (class B)

ANNUAL MEETING: In May

INCORPORATED: IA, Dec., 1957

INSTITUTIONAL HOLDINGS:
No. of Institutions: 105
Shares Held: 5,184,463
% Held: 27.3

INDUSTRY: Tires and inner tubes (SIC: 3011)

TRANSFER AGENT(S): EquiServe Trust Company, N.A., Providence, RI

BANK OF AMERICA CORPORATION

YIELD 3.5%
P/E RATIO 12.1

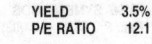
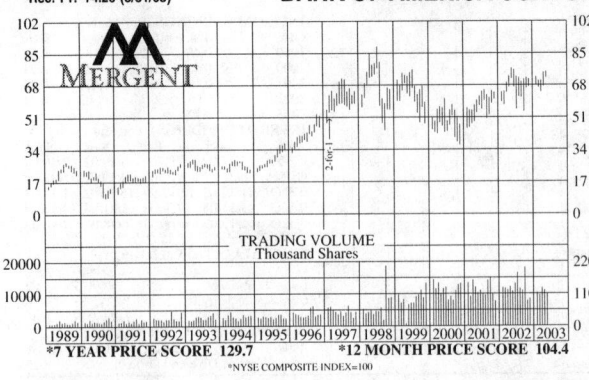

TRADING VOLUME
Thousand Shares

7 YEAR PRICE SCORE 129.7   *12 MONTH PRICE SCORE 104.4*

*NYSE COMPOSITE INDEX=100

INTERIM EARNINGS (Per Share):

Qtr.	Mar.	June	Sept.	Dec.
2000	1.33	1.23	1.10	0.85
2001	1.15	1.24	0.51	1.28
2002	1.38	1.40	1.45	1.69
2003	1.59	...	...	...

INTERIM DIVIDENDS (Per Share):

Amt.	Decl.	Ex.	Rec.	Pay.
0.60Q	4/24/02	6/05/02	6/07/02	6/28/02
0.60Q	7/24/02	9/04/02	9/06/02	9/27/02
0.64Q	10/23/02	12/04/02	12/06/02	12/27/02
0.64Q	1/22/03	3/05/03	3/07/03	3/28/03
0.64Q	4/30/03	6/04/03	6/06/03	6/27/03

Indicated div.: $2.56 (Div. Reinv. Plan)

CAPITALIZATION (12/31/02):

	($000)	(%)
Total Deposits	386,458,000	77.6
Long-Term Debt	61,145,000	12.3
Preferred Stock	58,000	0.0
Common & Surplus	50,261,000	10.1
Total	497,922,000	100.0

DIVIDEND ACHIEVER STATUS:

Rank: 97   10-Year Growth Rate: 12.45%
Total Years of Dividend Growth: 25

RECENT DEVELOPMENTS: For the first quarter ended 3/31/03, net income increased 11.2% to $2.42 billion compared with $2.18 billion in the corresponding prior-year quarter. Results for 2003 and 2002 included gains on sales of securities of $273.0 million and $44.0 million, respectively. Net interest income rose 1.1% to $5.21 billion from $5.15 billion a year earlier, primarily due to strong mortgage sales, further penetration in debit and credit cards and growth in deposits and loans.

PROSPECTS: Looking ahead, the Company plans to open up to 550 new banking centers over three years, including 15 in Chicago during 2003. Meanwhile, the BAC expects that its recent acquisition of a 24.9% stake in Grupo Financiero Santander Serfin will enable the Company to better understand its Hispanic customers. The acquisition should enhance its products and services and position BAC as a bank of choice for the Mexican-American population in key markets.

BUSINESS

BANK OF AMERICA CORPORA-TION (formerly NationsBank Corporation) is a bank holding company with $679.77 billion in total assets as of 3/31/03. The Company was formed on 9/30/98 as a result of BankAmerica's merging into NationsBank. The Company adopted its present name on 4/29/99. As of 3/31/03, BAC provides financial products and services through 4,202 banking centers and 13,266 automatic teller machines, as well as 30 international offices serving clients in 150 countries, and an Internet Web site that provides on-line access for 5.2 million active users, including 2.0 million active bill pay users. BAC maintains full-service operations in 21 states and the District of Columbia.

ANNUAL FINANCIAL DATA

	12/31/02	12/31/01	12/31/00	12/31/99	⑤ 12/31/98	12/31/97	⑤ 12/31/96
Earnings Per Share	5.91	④ 4.18	③ 4.52	③ 4.48	② 2.90	4.17	① 4.00
Tang. Book Val. Per Share	23.77	20.79	19.00	15.66	16.68	14.86	18.43
Dividends Per Share	2.44	2.28	2.06	1.85	1.59	1.37	1.20
Dividend Payout %	41.3	54.5	45.6	41.3	54.8	32.9	30.0

INCOME STATEMENT (IN MILLIONS):

Total Interest Income	32,161.0	38,293.0	43,258.0	37,323.0	38,588.0	16,579.0	13,796.0
Total Interest Expense	11,238.0	18,003.0	24,816.0	19,086.0	20,290.0	8,681.0	7,467.0
Net Interest Income	20,923.0	20,290.0	18,442.0	18,237.0	18,298.0	7,898.0	6,329.0
Provision for Loan Losses	3,697.0	4,287.0	2,535.0	1,820.0	2,920.0	800.0	605.0
Non-Interest Income	13,571.0	14,348.0	14,514.0	14,309.0	13,206.0	5,155.0	3,713.0
Non-Interest Expense	21,503.0	24,521.0	18,633.0	18,511.0	20,536.0	7,457.0	5,803.0
Income Before Taxes	12,991.0	10,117.0	11,788.0	12,215.0	8,048.0	4,796.0	3,634.0
Net Income	9,249.0	④ 6,792.0	③ 7,517.0	③ 7,882.0	⑤ 5,165.0	3,077.0	① 2,375.0
Average Shs. Outstg. (000)	1,565,467	1,625,654	1,664,929	1,760,058	1,775,760	737,791	590,216

BALANCE SHEET (IN MILLIONS):

Securities Avail. for Sale	70,809.0	53,276.0	48,489.0	43,298.0	46,352.0	26,073.0	20,532.0
Total Loans & Leases	342,755.0	329,153.0	392,193.0	370,662.0	357,328.0	146,417.0	125,031.0
Allowance for Credit Losses	6,851.0	6,875.0	6,838.0	6,828.0	7,122.0	5,407.0	4,716.0
Net Loans & Leases	335,904.0	322,278.0	385,355.0	363,834.0	350,206.0	141,010.0	120,315.0
Total Assets	660,458.0	621,764.0	642,191.0	632,574.0	617,679.0	264,562.0	185,794.0
Total Deposits	386,458.0	373,495.0	364,244.0	347,273.0	357,260.0	138,194.0	106,498.0
Long-Term Obligations	61,145.0	62,496.0	67,547.0	55,486.0	45,888.0	27,204.0	22,985.0
Total Liabilities	610,139.0	573,244.0	594,563.0	588,142.0	571,741.0	243,225.0	172,085.0
Net Stockholders' Equity	50,319.0	48,520.0	47,628.0	44,432.0	45,938.0	21,337.0	13,709.0
Year-end Shs. Outstg. (000)	1,500,691	1,559,297	1,613,632	1,677,273	1,724,484	712,188	573,000

STATISTICAL RECORD:

Return on Equity %	18.4	14.0	15.8	17.7	11.2	14.4	17.3
Return on Assets %	1.4	1.1	1.2	1.2	0.8	1.2	1.3
Equity/Assets %	7.6	7.8	7.4	7.0	7.4	8.1	7.4
Non-Int. Exp./Tot. Inc. %	62.3	70.8	56.5	56.9	65.2	57.1	57.8
Price Range	77.09-53.95	65.54-45.00	61.00-36.31	76.38-47.63	88.44-44.00	71.69-48.00	52.63-32.19
P/E Ratio	13.0-9.1	15.7-10.8	13.5-8.0	17.0-10.6	30.5-15.2	17.2-11.5	13.2-8.0
Average Yield %	3.7	4.1	4.2	3.0	2.4	2.3	2.8

Statistics are as originally reported. Adj. for 2-for-1 stk. split, 2/97. ① Bef. acctg. cred. of $200.0 mill. ② Incl. merg.-rel. & restr. chgs. of $346.0 mill., 2000; $358.0 mill., 1999; $1.80 bill., 1998. ③ Refl. merger of NationsBank Corp. & BankAmerica Corp. on 9/30/98. ④ Incl. a loss of $1.30 bill. rel. to the exit of certain consumer finance businesses; restruct. chrgs. of $550.0 mill.; and a loss of $231.0 mill. assoc. with Co.'s credit exposure to Enron.

OFFICERS:
K. D. Lewis, Chmn., Pres., C.E.O.
J. H. Hance Jr., Vice-Chmn., C.F.O.

INVESTOR CONTACT: Kevin Stitt, Investor Relations, (704) 386-5667

PRINCIPAL OFFICE: Bank of America Corporate Center, Charlotte, NC 28255

TELEPHONE NUMBER: (704) 386-8486
FAX: (704) 386-6699
WEB: www.bankofamerica.com
NO. OF EMPLOYEES: 133,944
SHAREHOLDERS: 237,080
ANNUAL MEETING: In April
INCORPORATED: NC. July, 1968; reincorp., DE, Sept., 1998

INSTITUTIONAL HOLDINGS:
No. of Institutions: 970
Shares Held: 893,925,821
% Held: 59.7

INDUSTRY: National commercial banks (SIC: 6021)

TRANSFER AGENT(S): Mellon Investor Services LLC, South Hackensack, NJ

BANK OF HAWAII CORPORATION

YIELD 2.2%
P/E RATIO 19.8

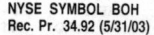
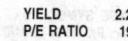
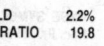

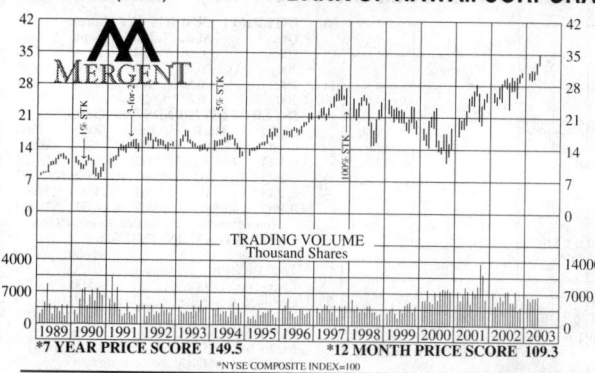

TRADING VOLUME
Thousand Shares

*7 YEAR PRICE SCORE 149.5   ***12 MONTH PRICE SCORE 109.3**
*NYSE COMPOSITE INDEX=100

INTERIM EARNINGS (Per Share):

Qtr.	Mar.	June	Sept.	Dec.
2000	0.50	0.08	0.44	0.41
2001	0.42	0.32	0.37	0.34
2002	0.41	0.42	0.43	0.44
2003	0.47	...	...	...

INTERIM DIVIDENDS (Per Share):

Amt.	Decl.	Ex.	Rec.	Pay.
0.18Q	4/22/02	5/22/02	5/24/02	6/14/02
0.18Q	7/22/02	8/21/02	8/23/02	9/16/02
0.19Q	10/23/02	11/20/02	11/22/02	12/13/02
0.19Q	1/27/03	2/20/03	2/24/03	3/14/03
0.19Q	4/21/03	5/21/03	5/23/03	6/13/03

Indicated div.: $0.76 (Div. Reinv. Plan)

CAPITALIZATION (12/31/02):

	($000)	(%)
Total Deposits	6,920,161	84.3
Long-Term Debt	275,004	3.3
Common & Surplus	1,015,759	12.4
Total	8,210,924	100.0

DIVIDEND ACHIEVER STATUS:

Rank: 224   10-Year Growth Rate: 5.62%
Total Years of Dividend Growth: 25

RECENT DEVELOPMENTS: For the first quarter ended 3/31/03, net income decreased 4.0% to $29.8 million compared with $31.1 million in the corresponding prior-year quarter. Results for 2003 included an information technology systems replacement charge of $7.4 million. Results for 2002 included a provision for loan and lease losses of $8.3 million and a restructuring charge of $2.0 million. Net interest income declined 4.1% to $91.0 million from $94.9 million a year earlier, primarily due to lower interest rates.

PROSPECTS: Results should continue to be enhanced by reduced unemployment and tourism, which rose 4.1% as measured by passenger arrivals in the first quarter of 2003 versus the year-earlier quarter. Meanwhile, BOH expects full-year 2003 earnings of about $131.0 million. Separately, BOH is continuing to transition to its new information technology systems, which should be operational in the third quarter of 2003. The systems should result in annual cost savings of over $17.0 million.

BUSINESS

BANK OF HAWAII CORPORA-TION (formerly Pacific Century Financial Corporation), with assets of $9.41 billion as of 3/31/03, is a bank holding company. BOH operates in Hawaii, the West Pacific, and American Samoa. BOH's principal subsidiary is the Bank of Hawaii. The Retail banking segment (50.9% of 2002 net income) offers loan, lease and deposit products to consumers and small businesses. The Commercial banking segment (27.5%) provides corporate banking and commercial real estate loans, lease financing, auto dealer financing, deposit and cash management products to middle-market and large companies. The Investment Services group (7.5%) includes private banking, trust services, asset management, institutional investment advice and retail brokerage. The Treasury and Other Corporate segment (14.1%) provides corporate asset and liability management activities.

ANNUAL FINANCIAL DATA

	12/31/02	12/31/01	12/31/00	12/31/99	12/31/98	12/31/97	12/31/96
Earnings Per Share	④ 1.70	③ 1.46	② 1.42	① 1.64	① 1.32	1.72	1.63
Tang. Book Val. Per Share	15.09	16.16	13.93	12.57	12.07	11.47	12.13
Dividends Per Share	0.73	0.72	0.71	0.68	0.66	0.63	0.58
Dividend Payout %	42.9	49.3	50.0	41.5	49.8	36.3	35.6
INCOME STATEMENT (IN MILLIONS):							
Total Interest Income	516.5	828.3	1,057.5	1,026.5	1,099.8	1,062.6	982.1
Total Interest Expense	146.3	368.6	501.3	451.8	523.2	526.3	499.8
Net Interest Income	370.2	459.7	556.2	574.7	576.6	536.3	482.3
Provision for Loan Losses	11.6	74.3	142.9	60.9	84.0	30.3	22.2
Non-Interest Income	199.9	439.3	263.4	265.6	211.8	187.8	164.5
Non-Interest Expense	370.8	584.3	496.4	553.2	540.3	474.3	419.8
Income Before Taxes	187.7	240.0	180.0	225.7	163.6	218.0	203.3
Net Income	④ 121.2	③ 117.8	② 113.7	① 133.0	① 107.0	139.5	133.1
Average Shs. Outstg. (000)	71,447	80,578	79,813	80,045	81,142	80,946	81,596
BALANCE SHEET (IN MILLIONS):							
Cash & Due from Banks	374.4	406.0	524.0	639.9	564.2	795.3	581.2
Securities Avail. for Sale	2,287.2	2,001.4	2,507.1	2,542.2	3,018.4	2,651.3	2,306.6
Total Loans & Leases	5,399.1	6,125.5	9,668.5	9,717.6	9,854.0	9,498.4	8,699.3
Allowance for Credit Losses	142.9	159.0	500.2	436.7	437.2	384.1	351.4
Net Loans & Leases	5,256.3	5,966.5	9,168.1	9,280.8	9,416.8	9,114.3	8,347.9
Total Assets	9,516.4	10,627.8	14,013.8	14,440.3	15,016.6	14,995.5	14,009.2
Total Deposits	6,920.2	6,673.6	9,080.6	9,394.2	9,576.3	9,621.3	8,684.1
Long-Term Obligations	275.0	469.7	997.2	727.7	585.6	705.8	932.1
Total Liabilities	8,500.7	9,380.8	12,712.5	13,228.0	13,831.0	13,878.3	12,943.0
Net Stockholders' Equity	1,015.8	1,247.0	1,301.4	1,212.3	1,185.6	1,117.2	1,066.1
Year-end Shs. Outstg. (000)	63,015	73,218	79,612	80,036	80,326	79,685	79,918
STATISTICAL RECORD:							
Return on Equity %	11.9	9.4	8.7	11.0	9.0	12.5	12.5
Return on Assets %	1.3	1.1	0.8	0.9	0.7	0.9	1.0
Equity/Assets %	10.7	11.7	9.3	8.4	7.9	7.5	7.6
Non-Int. Exp./Tot. Inc. %	65.1	67.5	60.4	67.0	68.9	65.8	65.0
Price Range	31.05-22.79	28.30-16.88	23.19-11.06	24.94-17.38	25.88-14.75	28.06-20.31	22.00-16.56
P/E Ratio	18.3-13.4	19.4-11.6	16.3-7.8	15.2-10.6	19.6-11.2	16.3-11.8	13.5-10.2
Average Yield %	2.7	3.2	4.1	3.2	3.2	2.6	3.0

Statistics are as originally reported. Adj. for stk. split: 100% div., 12/97. ① Incl. a restruct. chrg. of $22.5 mill., 1999; $19.4 mill., 1998. ② Incl. a pre-tax gain of $11.9 mill. on the settlement of pension obligations. ③ Incl. a pre-tax gain of $173.4 mill. on the sale of banking ops. & venture invest. loss & pre-tax restr. & oth. rel. costs of $104.8 mill. ④ Incl. pre-tax restr. chrg. of $2.4 mill. and info. tech. systems replacement chrg. of $13.6 mill.

OFFICERS:
M. E. O'Neill, Chmn., C.E.O.
A. R. Landon, Vice-Chmn., C.F.O.
J. T. Kiefer, Exec. V.P., Gen. Couns.

INVESTOR CONTACT: Cindy G. Wyrick, Sr. V.P., Investor Relations, (808) 537-8430

PRINCIPAL OFFICE: 130 Merchant Street, Honolulu, HI 96813

TELEPHONE NUMBER: (808) 538-4727
FAX: (808) 538-4007
WEB: www.boh.com
NO. OF EMPLOYEES: 2,900 (approx.)
SHAREHOLDERS: 10,030
ANNUAL MEETING: In April
INCORPORATED: HI, Aug., 1971; reincorp., DE, April, 1998

INSTITUTIONAL HOLDINGS:
No. of Institutions: 158
Shares Held: 42,022,135
% Held: 68.9

INDUSTRY: State commercial banks (SIC: 6022)

TRANSFER AGENT(S): Continental Stock Transfer & Trust Company, New York, NY

BANK OF NEW YORK COMPANY, INC. (THE)

YIELD 2.6%
P/E RATIO 24.9

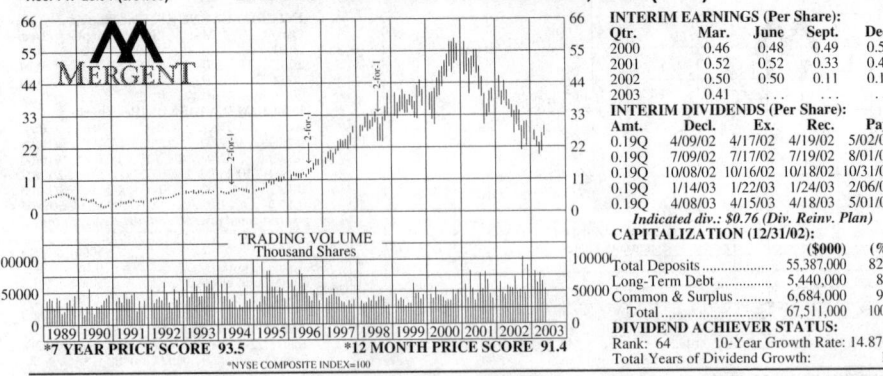

| | 1989 | 1990 | 1991 | 1992 | 1993 | 1994 | 1995 | 1996 | 1997 | 1998 | 1999 | 2000 | 2001 | 2002 | 2003 |

TRADING VOLUME Thousand Shares

*7 YEAR PRICE SCORE 93.5   *12 MONTH PRICE SCORE 91.4
*NYSE COMPOSITE INDEX=100

INTERIM EARNINGS (Per Share):

Qtr.	Mar.	June	Sept.	Dec.
2000	0.46	0.48	0.49	0.50
2001	0.52	0.52	0.33	0.45
2002	0.50	0.50	0.11	0.14
2003	0.41	...	...	...

INTERIM DIVIDENDS (Per Share):

Amt.	Decl.	Ex.	Rec.	Pay.
0.19Q	4/09/02	4/17/02	4/19/02	5/02/02
0.19Q	7/09/02	7/17/02	7/19/02	8/01/02
0.19Q	10/08/02	10/16/02	10/18/02	10/31/02
0.19Q	1/14/03	1/22/03	1/24/03	2/06/03
0.19Q	4/08/03	4/15/03	4/18/03	5/01/03

Indicated div.: $0.76 (Div. Reinv. Plan)

CAPITALIZATION (12/31/02):

	($000)	(%)
Total Deposits	55,387,000	82.0
Long-Term Debt	5,440,000	8.1
Common & Surplus	6,684,000	9.9
Total	67,511,000	100.0

DIVIDEND ACHIEVER STATUS:

Rank: 64   10-Year Growth Rate: 14.87%
Total Years of Dividend Growth: 10

RECENT DEVELOPMENTS: For the first quarter ended 3/31/03, net income declined 18.5% to $295.0 million compared with $362.0 million in the same period the year before. Earnings for 2003 were adversely affected by declines in equity prices and trading volumes, as well as capital markets activity, associated with the weak global economy and recent geopolitical developments. Net interest income was down 6.3% to $386.0 million from $412.0 million a year earlier. Provision for credit losses climbed 14.3% to $40.0 million.

PROSPECTS: On 5/1/03, the Company announced the completion of the acquisition of Pershing LLC, the broker clearing services unit of Credit Suisse First Boston, for $2.00 billion. Meanwhile, during the first quarter of 2003, BK acquired Capital Resource Financial Services, a Chicago-based provider of commission recapture, transition management and third-party services to plan sponsors and investment managers. Separately, to reduce risk BK has lowered total exposures to corporate clients by over $1.50 billion.

BUSINESS

THE BANK OF NEW YORK COMPANY, INC. is a bank holding company with assets of $79.55 billion and total deposits of $57.12 billion as of 3/31/03. BK provides a broad range of banking and other financial services to corporations and individuals worldwide through its basic businesses, including securities servicing and global payment services, corporate banking, BNY asset management and private client services, retail banking and global market services. BK's primary subsidiaries are the Bank of New York, BNY Holdings (Delaware) Corporation, and The Bank of New York (Delaware). BK has operating centers in London, Brussels, Dublin, Singapore and Luxembourg and 28 non-U.S. branch and representative offices in 25 countries and provides securities servicing in over 100 markets.

ANNUAL FINANCIAL DATA

	12/31/02	12/31/01	12/31/00	12/31/99	12/31/98	12/31/97	12/31/96
Earnings Per Share	1.24	[1] 1.81	1.92	[2] 2.27	1.53	[1] 1.36	1.24
Tang. Book Val. Per Share	5.66	5.80	8.30	6.95	7.05	6.67	6.50
Dividends Per Share	0.76	0.72	0.66	0.58	0.54	0.49	0.42
Dividend Payout %	61.3	39.8	34.4	25.5	35.3	36.2	34.0
INCOME STATEMENT (IN MILLIONS):							
Total Interest Income	2,613.0	3,620.0	4,377.0	3,473.0	3,510.0	3,560.0	3,583.0
Total Interest Expense	948.0	1,939.0	2,507.0	1,772.0	1,859.0	1,705.0	1,622.0
Net Interest Income	1,665.0	1,681.0	1,870.0	1,701.0	1,651.0	1,855.0	1,961.0
Provision for Loan Losses	685.0	375.0	105.0	135.0	20.0	280.0	600.0
Non-Interest Income	3,143.0	3,540.0	3,109.0	3,493.0	2,283.0	2,137.0	2,130.0
Non-Interest Expense	2,751.0	2,788.0	2,510.0	2,107.0	1,928.0	1,874.0	1,835.0
Income Before Taxes	1,372.0	2,058.0	2,364.0	2,952.0	1,986.0	1,838.0	1,656.0
Equity Earnings/Minority Int.	...	...	d113.0	d112.0	d95.0	d65.0	d2.0
Net Income	902.0	[3] 1,343.0	1,429.0	[2] 1,739.0	1,192.0	[1] 1,104.0	1,020.0
Average Shs. Outstg. (000)	728,000	741,000	745,000	765,000	781,000	808,000	840,000
BALANCE SHEET (IN MILLIONS):							
Cash & Due from Banks	4,748.0	3,222.0	3,125.0	3,276.0	3,999.0	5,769.0	6,032.0
Securities Avail. for Sale	24,655.0	19,921.0	18,700.0	14,743.0	7,088.0	8,117.0	5,430.0
Total Loans & Leases	31,339.0	35,747.0	36,261.0	37,547.0	38,386.0	35,127.0	37,006.0
Allowance for Credit Losses	831.0	616.0	616.0	595.0	636.0	641.0	901.0
Net Loans & Leases	30,508.0	35,131.0	35,645.0	36,952.0	37,750.0	34,486.0	36,105.0
Total Assets	77,564.0	81,025.0	77,114.0	74,756.0	63,503.0	59,961.0	55,765.0
Total Deposits	55,387.0	55,711.0	56,376.0	55,751.0	44,632.0	41,357.0	39,343.0
Long-Term Obligations	5,440.0	4,976.0	3,036.0	2,811.0	2,086.0	1,809.0	1,816.0
Total Liabilities	70,880.0	74,708.0	69,462.0	68,113.0	56,755.0	53,959.0	50,038.0
Net Stockholders' Equity	6,684.0	6,317.0	6,152.0	5,143.0	5,448.0	5,002.0	5,127.0
Year-end Shs. Outstg. (000)	726,456	730,324	741,068	740,214	773,119	750,000	772,000
STATISTICAL RECORD:							
Return on Equity %	13.5	21.3	23.2	33.8	21.9	22.1	19.9
Return on Assets %	1.2	1.7	1.9	2.3	1.9	1.8	1.8
Equity/Assets %	8.6	7.8	8.0	6.9	8.6	8.3	9.2
Non-Int. Exp./Tot. Inc. %	57.2	53.4	50.4	40.6	49.0	46.9	44.9
Price Range	46.50-20.85	58.13-29.75	59.38-29.75	45.19-31.81	40.56-24.00	29.28-16.38	18.06-10.88
P/E Ratio	37.5-16.8	32.1-16.4	30.9-15.5	19.9-14.0	26.5-15.7	21.6-12.1	14.6-8.5
Average Yield %	2.3	1.6	1.5	1.5	1.7	2.1	2.9

Statistics are as originally reported. Adj. for 2-for-1 split, 8/98. [1] Incl. a pre-tax gain of $177.0 mill. fr. sale of BK's credit card operations & a $100.0 mill. prov. for credit losses. [2] Incl. a pre-tax gain of $1.02 bill. on sale of BNY Fin'l. Corp. [3] Incl. a pre-tax one-time special chrg. of $235.0 mill. & a pre-tax inv. recovery of $175.0 mill.

OFFICERS:
T. A. Renyi, Chmn., C.E.O.
A. R. Griffith, Vice-Chmn.
G. L. Hassell, Pres.
INVESTOR CONTACT: John M. Roy, (212) 635-8005
PRINCIPAL OFFICE: One Wall Street, New York, NY 10286

TELEPHONE NUMBER: (212) 495-1784
FAX: (212) 495-2546
WEB: www.bankofny.com
NO. OF EMPLOYEES: 19,435 (avg.)
SHAREHOLDERS: 27,589
ANNUAL MEETING: In May
INCORPORATED: NY, July, 1968

INSTITUTIONAL HOLDINGS:
No. of Institutions: 601
Shares Held: 462,801,943
% Held: 63.4
INDUSTRY: State commercial banks (SIC: 6022)
TRANSFER AGENT(S): The Bank of New York, New York, NY

BANTA CORPORATION

YIELD 2.0%
P/E RATIO 19.9

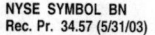
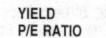
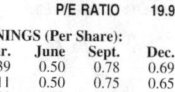
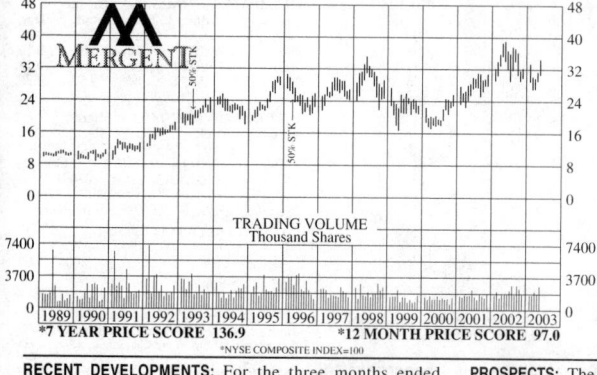

INTERIM EARNINGS (Per Share):

Qtr.	Mar.	June	Sept.	Dec.
2000	0.39	0.50	0.78	0.69
2001	0.11	0.50	0.75	0.65
2002	0.41	0.52	0.76	0.02
2003	0.44	...	...	...

INTERIM DIVIDENDS (Per Share):

Amt.	Decl.	Ex.	Rec.	Pay.
0.16Q	7/30/02	10/16/02	10/18/02	11/01/02
0.16Q	12/10/02	1/15/03	1/17/03	2/03/03
0.16Q	1/28/03	4/15/03	4/18/03	5/01/03
0.17Q	4/29/03	7/16/03	7/18/03	8/01/03

Indicated div.: $0.68 (Div. Reinv. Plan)

CAPITALIZATION (12/28/02):

	($000)	(%)
Long-Term Debt	110,779	19.2
Capital Lease Obligations..	710	0.1
Deferred Income Tax	13,679	2.4
Common & Surplus	453,113	78.4
Total	578,281	100.0

DIVIDEND ACHIEVER STATUS:
Rank: 165   10-Year Growth Rate: 8.97%
Total Years of Dividend Growth: 24

*7 YEAR PRICE SCORE 136.9   *12 MONTH PRICE SCORE 97.0

*NYSE COMPOSITE INDEX=100

RECENT DEVELOPMENTS: For the three months ended 3/31/03, net income climbed 7.2% to $11.2 million compared with $10.5 million in the equivalent quarter of 2002. Results reflected improved performance from BN's supply-chain management business. Results for 2002 included an after-tax restructuring charge of $565,000 related to the restructuring and realignment of BN's consumer catalog and other facilities. Net sales were $336.4 million, up 1.1% from $332.8 million in 2002.

PROSPECTS: The Company continues to perform relatively well, despite lower advertising and promotional spending, the difficult print environment and persistent weakness in economic conditions. Much of the improvement is attributable to ongoing cost-controls and greater operating efficiency. Looking ahead, the Company expects earnings per share for 2003 to range between $2.36 and $2.48, before restructuring charges. Separately, on 2/24/03, the Company acquired Qualipak Incorporated.

BUSINESS

BANTA CORPORATION provides a broad range of printing and digital imaging services. BN operates in three business segments: print, turnkey services, and healthcare. The print segment provides products and services to publishers of educational and general books and special interest magazines. The print segment also supplies direct marketing materials and consumer and business catalogs. The turnkey services segment provides supply-chain management, product assembly, fulfillment and product localization services to technology companies. The healthcare products are primarily engaged in the production of disposable products used in outpatient clinics, dental offices and hospitals. Sales (and operating income) for 2002 were derived: printing and digital imaging, 71.5% (69.9%); supply-chain management, 21.4% (22.0%); and healthcare, 7.1% (8.1%).

ANNUAL FINANCIAL DATA

	12/28/02	12/29/01	12/30/00	1/1/00	1/2/99	1/3/98	12/28/96
Earnings Per Share	③ 1.71	② 2.01	2.35	① 0.59	1.80	① 1.44	1.63
Cash Flow Per Share	4.78	5.04	5.38	3.10	4.06	3.50	3.49
Tang. Book Val. Per Share	15.46	13.89	12.41	12.31	11.83	11.80	12.29
Dividends Per Share	0.64	0.61	0.60	0.56	0.51	0.47	0.44
Dividend Payout %	37.4	30.3	25.5	94.9	28.3	32.6	26.8

INCOME STATEMENT (IN MILLIONS):

	12/28/02	12/29/01	12/30/00	1/1/00	1/2/99	1/3/98	12/28/96
Total Revenues	1,366.5	1,457.9	1,537.7	1,278.3	1,335.8	1,202.5	1,083.8
Costs & Expenses	1,206.4	1,274.1	1,347.2	1,161.7	1,171.4	1,060.8	933.3
Depreciation & Amort.	78.4	75.4	75.7	68.2	66.9	62.1	58.3
Operating Income	81.6	108.4	114.8	48.4	97.5	79.5	92.2
Net Interest Inc./(Exp.)	d11.3	d13.7	d16.8	d12.4	d10.8	d11.1	d10.2
Income Before Income Taxes	71.8	82.2	96.6	34.6	86.1	70.8	84.2
Income Taxes	28.0	32.2	37.9	18.6	33.2	27.5	33.3
Net Income	③ 43.8	② 50.0	58.7	① 16.0	52.9	① 43.3	50.9
Cash Flow	122.2	125.4	134.5	84.2	119.8	105.4	109.2
Average Shs. Outstg. (000)	25,566	24,857	24,980	27,177	29,475	30,113	31,249

BALANCE SHEET (IN MILLIONS):

	12/28/02	12/29/01	12/30/00	1/1/00	1/2/99	1/3/98	12/28/96
Cash & Cash Equivalents	154.8	66.0	27.7	27.7	26.6	16.4	57.4
Total Current Assets	460.2	357.5	406.7	355.9	354.6	365.7	347.5
Net Property	278.0	325.0	344.3	327.4	318.6	338.4	319.9
Total Assets	805.3	788.0	854.5	773.3	770.0	781.2	719.2
Total Current Liabilities	185.8	184.8	240.3	245.4	196.5	200.4	127.8
Long-Term Obligations	111.5	131.0	179.2	113.5	120.6	130.1	133.7
Net Stockholders' Equity	453.1	407.3	370.9	353.8	409.9	414.1	420.6
Net Working Capital	274.4	172.7	166.4	110.5	158.1	165.3	219.6
Year-end Shs. Outstg. (000)	25,247	24,730	24,567	23,943	28,261	29,793	30,969

STATISTICAL RECORD:

	12/28/02	12/29/01	12/30/00	1/1/00	1/2/99	1/3/98	12/28/96
Operating Profit Margin %	6.0	7.4	7.5	3.8	7.3	6.6	8.5
Net Profit Margin %	3.2	3.4	3.8	1.3	4.0	3.6	4.7
Return on Equity %	9.7	12.3	15.8	4.5	12.9	10.5	12.1
Return on Assets %	5.4	6.3	6.9	2.1	6.9	5.5	7.1
Debt/Total Assets %	13.8	16.6	21.0	14.7	15.7	16.6	18.6
Price Range	39.10-29.05	31.04-22.49	25.70-17.19	27.38-16.75	35.25-21.81	29.88-21.63	30.67-20.50
P/E Ratio	22.9-17.0	15.4-11.2	10.9-7.3	46.4-28.4	19.6-12.1	20.7-15.0	18.8-12.6
Average Yield %	1.9	2.3	2.8	2.5	1.8	1.8	1.7

Statistics are as originally reported. Adj. for 50% stk. div., 3/1/96. ① Incl. restr. charges of $55.0 mill., 1/00; $13.5 mill., 1/98. ② Incl. $12.5 mill. write-down of invest. ③ Incl. $26.8 mill. asset impair. chg.

OFFICERS:
D. D. Belcher, Chmn.
S. A. Streeter, Pres., C.E.O.
G. A. Hensler, Exec. V.P., C.F.O.

INVESTOR CONTACT: Gerald A. Henseler, Exec. V.P., C.F.O., (920) 751-7777

PRINCIPAL OFFICE: 225 Main Street, Menasha, WI 54952

TELEPHONE NUMBER: (920) 751-7777
FAX: (920) 751-7790
WEB: www.banta.com

NO. OF EMPLOYEES: 8,300 (approx.)

SHAREHOLDERS: 1,812 (record)

ANNUAL MEETING: In Apr.

INCORPORATED: WI, 1901

INSTITUTIONAL HOLDINGS:
No. of Institutions: 165
Shares Held: 19,022,089
% Held: 76.1

INDUSTRY: Commercial printing, nec (SIC: 2759)

TRANSFER AGENT(S): Firstar Bank, N.A., Milwaukee, Wisc.

BARD (C.R.), INC.

YIELD	1.3%
P/E RATIO	22.1

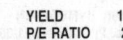

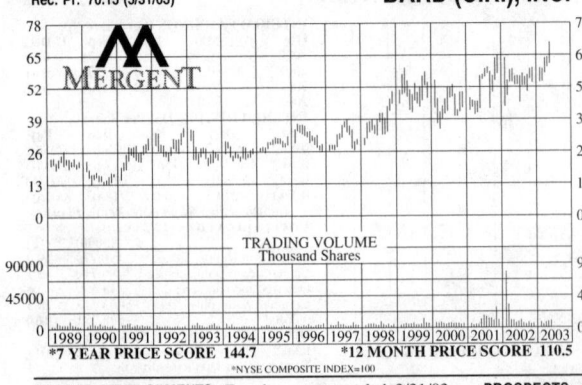

TRADING VOLUME
Thousand Shares

90000
45000
0

1989 | 1990 | 1991 | 1992 | 1993 | 1994 | 1995 | 1996 | 1997 | 1998 | 1999 | 2000 | 2001 | 2002 | 2003

*7 YEAR PRICE SCORE 144.7   *12 MONTH PRICE SCORE 110.5
*NYSE COMPOSITE INDEX=100

INTERIM EARNINGS (Per Share):

Qtr.	Mar.	June	Sept.	Dec.
1999	0.51	0.55	0.58	0.64
2000	0.62	0.65	0.66	0.16
2001	0.65	0.68	0.68	0.74
2002	0.65	0.83	0.57	0.89
2003	0.89	...	...	...

INTERIM DIVIDENDS (Per Share):

Amt.	Decl.	Ex.	Rec.	Pay.
0.22Q	7/10/02	7/18/02	7/22/02	8/02/02
0.22Q	10/09/02	10/17/02	10/21/02	11/01/02
0.22Q	12/11/02	1/15/03	1/20/03	1/31/03
0.22Q	4/16/03	4/24/03	4/28/03	5/09/03

Indicated div.: $0.88 (Div. Reinv. Plan)

CAPITALIZATION (12/31/02):

	($000)	(%)
Long-Term Debt	152,200	14.7
Common & Surplus	880,400	85.3
Total	1,032,600	100.0

DIVIDEND ACHIEVER STATUS:
Rank: 228   10-Year Growth Rate: 5.57%
Total Years of Dividend Growth: 31

RECENT DEVELOPMENTS: For the quarter ended 3/31/03, net income jumped 35.2% to $46.9 million compared with $34.7 million in the corresponding period of the previous year. Results for 2002 included an after-tax non-recurring charge of $9.9 million for various items and an after-tax credit of $3.0 million for the reversal of certain legal accruals. Net sales advanced 11.3% to $335.9 million, supported by higher sales from BCR's vascular, urology, oncology and surgery divisions.

PROSPECTS: BCR should continue to benefit from its realignment efforts in 2002. Meanwhile, the Company's gross margins, which have improved significantly, should continue to allow BCR to meaningfully add to its research and development portfolio, while also generating a strong bottom line. Separately, BCR will continue with its acquisition strategy that targets small research or developing companies as well as larger established companies with strong market positions.

BUSINESS

BARD (C.R.), INC. is a major multinational developer, manufacturer and marketer of health care products. The Company engages in the design, manufacture, packaging, distribution and sale of medical, surgical, diagnostic and patient-care devices. Bard holds strong positions in the fields of vascular, urology and surgical specialty products. BCR's products are marketed worldwide to hospitals, individual health care professionals, extended care facilities, alternate site facilities and the home, employing a combination of direct delivery and medical specialty distributors. The Vascular Group accounted for 20.4% of 2002 sales; Urology, 32.9%; Oncology, 23.5%; Surgery, 18.0%; and other, 5.2%.

ANNUAL FINANCIAL DATA

	12/31/02	12/31/01	12/31/00	12/31/99	12/31/98	12/31/97	12/31/96
Earnings Per Share	⑥ 2.94	2.75	⑤ 2.09	④ 2.28	③ 4.51	② 1.26	① 1.62
Cash Flow Per Share	3.74	3.78	3.06	3.22	5.56	2.26	2.63
Tang. Book Val. Per Share	9.67	7.94	5.06	4.67	4.05	2.62	2.71
Dividends Per Share	0.86	0.84	0.82	0.78	0.74	0.70	0.66
Dividend Payout %	29.3	30.5	39.2	34.2	16.4	55.6	40.7
INCOME STATEMENT (IN MILLIONS):							
Total Revenues	1,273.8	1,181.3	1,098.8	1,036.5	1,164.7	1,213.5	1,194.4
Costs & Expenses	1,020.5	914.9	854.9	797.5	947.3	991.8	976.0
Depreciation & Amort.	42.3	53.2	49.6	49.1	58.7	57.3	57.4
Operating Income	211.0	213.2	194.3	189.9	158.7	164.4	161.0
Net Interest Inc./(Exp.)	d12.6	d14.2	d19.3	d19.3	d26.4	d32.9	d26.4
Income Before Income Taxes	211.0	204.9	154.0	173.3	464.4	104.9	102.7
Income Taxes	56.0	61.7	47.1	55.2	212.1	32.6	10.2
Net Income	⑥ 155.0	143.2	⑤ 106.9	④ 118.1	③ 252.3	② 72.3	① 92.5
Cash Flow	197.3	196.4	156.5	167.2	311.0	129.6	149.9
Average Shs. Outstg. (000)	52,800	52,001	51,222	51,882	55,970	57,273	57,090
BALANCE SHEET (IN MILLIONS):							
Cash & Cash Equivalents	383.2	271.0	119.7	95.9	42.4	60.7	78.0
Total Current Assets	758.0	647.4	526.6	529.1	488.5	563.5	576.9
Net Property	168.0	157.9	155.5	169.7	172.7	206.4	226.1
Total Assets	1,416.7	1,231.1	1,089.2	1,126.4	1,079.8	1,279.3	1,332.5
Total Current Liabilities	316.9	234.5	224.5	352.5	302.8	310.6	336.2
Long-Term Obligations	152.2	156.4	204.3	158.4	160.0	340.7	342.8
Net Stockholders' Equity	880.4	788.7	613.9	574.3	567.6	573.1	601.5
Net Working Capital	441.1	412.9	302.1	176.6	185.7	252.9	240.7
Year-end Shs. Outstg. (000)	51,603	52,384	50,909	50,782	51,498	56,785	56,986
STATISTICAL RECORD:							
Operating Profit Margin %	16.6	18.0	17.7	18.3	13.6	13.5	13.5
Net Profit Margin %	12.2	12.1	9.7	11.4	21.7	6.0	7.7
Return on Equity %	17.6	18.2	17.4	20.6	44.5	12.6	15.4
Return on Assets %	10.9	11.6	9.8	10.5	23.4	5.7	6.9
Debt/Total Assets %	10.7	12.7	18.8	14.1	14.8	26.6	25.7
Price Range	63.94-44.10	64.95-40.86	54.94-35.00	59.88-41.69	50.25-28.50	39.00-26.38	37.38-25.88
P/E Ratio	21.7-15.0	23.6-14.9	26.3-16.7	26.3-18.3	11.1-6.3	30.9-20.9	23.1-16.0
Average Yield %	1.6	1.6	1.8	1.5	1.9	2.1	2.1

Statistics are as originally reported. ① Incl. net nonrecurr. chgs. of $12.9 mill. ② Incl. pre-tax restruct chg. of $44.1 mill. & a nonrecurr. net gain of $3.9 mill. ③ Incl. net gain of $163.8 mill. fr. the sale of cardiology bus. & several nonrecur. chgs. total. $25.9 mill. ④ Incl. gain of $9.2 mill. fr. the sale cardiology bus. ⑤ Incl. gain of $15.4 mill. fr. the sale cardiology bus. ⑥ Incl. pre-tax non-recurring chrgs. of $34.9 mill. & pre-tax credit of $3.5 mill.

OFFICERS:
W. H. Longfield, Chmn., C.E.O.
C. P. Slacik, Sr. V.P., C.F.O.
N. J. Bernstein, V.P., Gen. Couns., Sec.

INVESTOR CONTACT: Eric J. Shick, Investor Relations, (908) 277-8413

PRINCIPAL OFFICE: 730 Central Avenue, Murray Hill, NJ 07974

TELEPHONE NUMBER: (908) 277-8000
FAX: (908) 277-8278
WEB: www.crbard.com
NO. OF EMPLOYEES: 7,700 (approx.)
SHAREHOLDERS: 5,427
ANNUAL MEETING: In Apr.
INCORPORATED: NJ, Feb., 1923

INSTITUTIONAL HOLDINGS:
No. of Institutions: 292
Shares Held: 43,328,358
% Held: 83.3

INDUSTRY: Surgical and medical instruments (SIC: 3841)

TRANSFER AGENT(S): EquiServe, Jersey City, NJ

BB&T CORPORATION

YIELD 3.4%
P/E RATIO 12.4

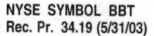
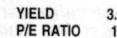
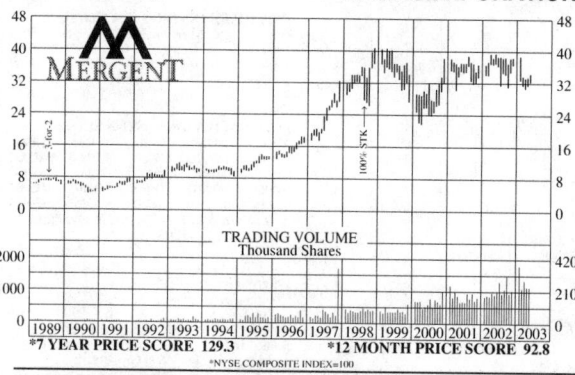

TRADING VOLUME
Thousand Shares

*7 YEAR PRICE SCORE 129.3   *12 MONTH PRICE SCORE 92.8
*NYSE COMPOSITE INDEX=100

INTERIM EARNINGS (Per Share):

Qtr.	Mar.	June	Sept.	Dec.
2000	0.46	0.48	0.12	0.56
2001	0.53	0.54	0.48	0.61
2002	0.64	0.68	0.68	0.70
2003	0.69	...	...	...

INTERIM DIVIDENDS (Per Share):

Amt.	Decl.	Ex.	Rec.	Pay.
0.29Q	6/25/02	7/10/02	7/12/02	8/01/02
0.29Q	8/27/02	10/09/02	10/11/02	11/01/02
0.29Q	12/17/02	1/15/03	1/17/03	2/03/03
0.29Q	2/25/03	4/09/03	4/11/03	5/01/03

Indicated div.: *$1.16* (Div. Reinv. Plan)

CAPITALIZATION (12/31/02):

	($000)	(%)
Total Deposits	51,280,016	71.0
Long-Term Debt	13,586,037	18.8
Capital Lease Obligations	1,804	0.0
Common & Surplus	7,387,914	10.2
Total	72,255,771	100.0

DIVIDEND ACHIEVER STATUS:
Rank: 54   10-Year Growth Rate: 15.97%
Total Years of Dividend Growth: 31

RECENT DEVELOPMENTS: For the quarter ended 3/31/03, net income rose 9.3% to $327.7 million versus income of $299.9 million, before a $9.8 million accounting change charge, a year ago. Results for 2003 and 2002 included after-tax merger-related charges of $3.1 million and $9.4 million, respectively. Net interest income grew 6.9% to $692.2 million from $647.3 million in 2002. Non-interest income jumped 24.4% to $444.9 million, while non-interest expense rose 13.7% to $604.1 million.

PROSPECTS: On 1/21/03, BBT announced plans to acquire First Virginia Banks Inc. for approximately $3.38 billion. First Virginia, which had $11.20 billion in assets as of 12/31/02, is the parent company of eight community banks and 364 branches in Virginia, Maryland and Tennessee. The transaction is expected to be completed in the third quarter of 2003. On 4/1/03, BBT completed its acquisition of Southeastern Fidelity Corporation, an insurance premium finance company based in Tallahassee, Florida.

BUSINESS

BB&T CORPORATION, a multibank holding company with assets of $79.65 billion as of 3/31/03, owns 1,118 banking offices in the Carolinas, Virginia, West Virginia, Tennessee, Kentucky, Georgia, Maryland, Florida, Alabama, Indiana and Washington, D.C. BBT's largest subsidiary is Branch Banking and Trust Company (BB&T-NC). BB&T-NC's subsidiaries include BB&T Leasing Corp., BB&T Investment Services, and BB&T Insurance Services. BBT's other subsidiaries include Branch Banking and Trust Co. of South Carolina, Branch Banking and Trust Co. of Virginia, and Fidelity Service Corporation. On 3/26/99, BBT acquired Scott & Stringfellow Financial, Inc. On 1/13/00, BBT acquired Premier Bancshares, Inc. On 7/7/00, BBT acquired One Valley Bancorp Inc. On 9/16/02, the Company acquired Regional Financial Corporation.

ANNUAL FINANCIAL DATA

	12/31/02	12/31/01	12/31/00	12/31/99	12/31/98	12/31/97	12/31/96
Earnings Per Share	⑥2.70	⑤2.12	⑤1.55	④1.83	③1.71	②1.30	①1.28
Tang. Book Val. Per Share	12.04	13.50	11.91	9.66	9.51	8.22	7.91
Dividends Per Share	1.10	0.98	0.86	0.75	0.66	0.58	0.50
Dividend Payout %	40.7	46.2	55.5	41.0	38.6	44.6	39.1
INCOME STATEMENT (IN MILLIONS):							
Total Interest Income	4,434.0	4,849.5	4,339.7	3,115.8	2,481.2	2,122.9	1,606.6
Total Interest Expense	1,686.6	2,415.1	2,322.0	1,534.1	1,233.8	1,023.4	778.1
Net Interest Income	2,747.5	2,434.5	2,017.6	1,581.7	1,247.4	1,099.5	828.5
Provision for Loan Losses	263.7	224.3	127.4	92.1	80.3	89.9	53.7
Non-Interest Income	1,692.5	1,378.7	777.0	761.4	528.0	474.9	297.4
Non-Interest Expense	2,385.5	2,228.4	1,761.5	1,346.9	961.4	937.1	654.1
Income Before Taxes	1,790.7	1,360.4	905.7	904.1	733.7	547.4	418.2
Net Income	1,293.2	⑤973.6	⑤626.4	④612.8	③501.8	②359.9	①283.7
Average Shs. Outstg. (000)	478,793	459,290	398,916	335,298	293,571	276,440	220,972
BALANCE SHEET (IN MILLIONS):							
Cash & Due from Banks	1,929.7	1,871.4	1,471.0	1,138.8	938.8	839.6	638.7
Securities Avail. for Sale	17,748.0	16,719.4	13,878.6	10,575.3	8,031.8	6,549.4	5,136.8
Total Loans & Leases	53,945.6	48,404.6	41,933.8	30,152.2	23,375.2	20,012.0	14,524.6
Allowance for Credit Losses	3,528.9	3,513.3	3,001.5	1,627.8	1,024.6	495.2	344.0
Net Loans & Leases	50,416.6	44,891.3	38,932.4	28,524.5	22,350.7	19,516.9	14,180.7
Total Assets	80,216.8	70,869.9	59,340.2	43,481.0	34,427.2	29,177.6	21,246.6
Total Deposits	51,280.0	44,733.3	38,014.5	27,251.1	23,046.9	20,210.1	14,953.9
Long-Term Obligations	13,587.8	11,721.1	8,354.7	5,491.7	4,736.9	3,283.0	2,051.8
Total Liabilities	72,828.9	64,719.7	54,554.3	40,281.8	31,668.7	26,940.0	19,517.4
Net Stockholders' Equity	7,387.9	6,150.2	4,785.9	3,199.2	2,758.5	2,237.6	1,729.2
Year-end Shs. Outstg. (000)	470,452	455,683	401,679	331,170	290,211	272,104	218,594
STATISTICAL RECORD:							
Return on Equity %	17.5	15.8	13.1	19.2	18.2	16.1	16.4
Return on Assets %	1.6	1.4	1.1	1.4	1.5	1.2	1.3
Equity/Assets %	9.2	8.7	8.1	7.4	8.0	7.7	8.1
Non-Int. Exp./Tot. Inc. %	55.9	60.4	58.5	57.4	54.4	59.6	58.3
Price Range	39.47-31.03	38.84-30.24	38.25-21.69	40.63-27.19	40.75-26.25	32.50-17.50	18.50-12.88
P/E Ratio	14.6-11.5	18.3-14.3	24.7-14.0	22.2-14.9	23.8-15.3	25.0-13.5	14.5-10.1
Average Yield %	3.1	2.8	2.9	2.2	2.0	2.3	3.2

Statistics are as originally reported. Adj. for 100% stock div., 8/98. ① Incl. one-time after-tax SAIF chg. of $21.3 mill. ② Incl. $2.7 mill. in after-tax UCB merger-rel. chgs. ③ Incl. after-tax merger costs of $10.9 mill. ④ Incl. non-recur. chrg. of $46.2 mill. ⑤ Incl. aft.-tax nonrecur. chrgs. of $126.5 mill., 12/01; $248.6 mill., 12/00. ⑥ Bef. $9.8 mill. acctg. gain & incl. $14.9 mill. after-tax nonrecur. chrg.

OFFICERS:
J. A. Allison IV, Chmn., C.E.O.
K. S. King, Pres.
S. E. Reed, Sr. Exec. V.P., C.F.O.
H. G. Williamson, C.O.O.

INVESTOR CONTACT: Thomas A. Nicholson Jr., Senior Vice Pres, (336) 733-3058

PRINCIPAL OFFICE: 200 West Second Street, Winston-Salem, NC 27101

TELEPHONE NUMBER: (336) 733-2000
FAX: (336) 671-2399
WEB: www.bbandt.com
NO. OF EMPLOYEES: 22,500 (approx.)
SHAREHOLDERS: 145,174
ANNUAL MEETING: In Apr.
INCORPORATED: NC, 1897; reincorp., NC, 1968

INSTITUTIONAL HOLDINGS:
No. of Institutions: 377
Shares Held: 127,410,364
% Held: 27.0

INDUSTRY: National commercial banks (SIC: 6021)

TRANSFER AGENT(S): Branch Banking & Trust Company, Wilson, NC

BECKMAN COULTER, INC.

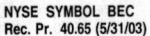

YIELD		0.9%
P/E RATIO		17.2

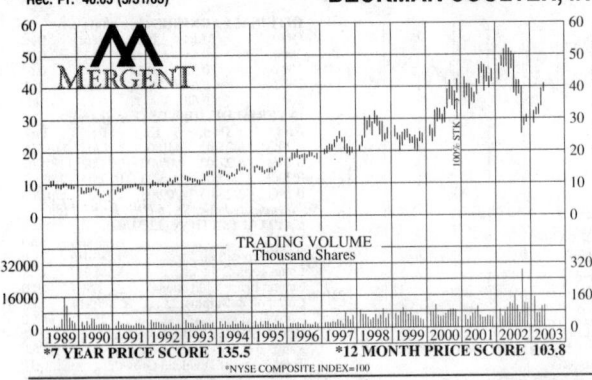

TRADING VOLUME
Thousand Shares

*7 YEAR PRICE SCORE 135.5	*12 MONTH PRICE SCORE 103.8

*NYSE COMPOSITE INDEX=100

INTERIM EARNINGS (Per Share):

Qtr.	Mar.	June	Sept.	Dec.
1999	0.29	0.44	0.41	0.65
2000	0.35	0.53	0.47	0.69
2001	0.37	0.58	0.52	0.75
2002	0.43	0.64	0.49	0.53
2003	0.70	...	...	...

INTERIM DIVIDENDS (Per Share):

Amt.	Decl.	Ex.	Rec.	Pay.
0.09Q	7/26/02	8/14/02	8/16/02	9/05/02
0.09Q	10/03/02	10/16/02	10/18/02	11/07/02
0.09Q	2/06/03	2/19/03	2/21/03	3/13/03
0.09Q	...	5/07/03	5/09/03	5/29/03

Indicated div.: $0.36 (Div. Reinv. Plan)

CAPITALIZATION (12/31/02):

	($000)	(%)
Long-Term Debt	626,600	49.7
Deferred Income Tax	41,700	3.3
Common & Surplus	592,100	47.0
Total	1,260,400	100.0

DIVIDEND ACHIEVER STATUS:

Rank: 169   10-Year Growth Rate: 8.84%
Total Years of Dividend Growth: 11

RECENT DEVELOPMENTS: For the quarter ended 3/31/03, net earnings advanced 59.3% to $44.6 million compared with $28.0 million in the corresponding period of the previous year. Results for 2003 included a net credit of $26.9 million before taxes related to litigation settlement and related expenses and a pre-tax restructuring charge of $18.5 million. Sales grew 4.6% to $467.3 million from $446.7 million in 2002.

PROSPECTS: The Company expects the second half of the year to have stronger sales and earnings growth, driven by easier sales comparisons in its Biomedical Research division and new product introductions across the Company. BEC continues to expect total year sales to increase in the 5.5% to 6.5% range. Diluted earnings per share growth for the year should be in the 11.0% to 14.0% range, before non-recurring items.

BUSINESS

BECKMAN COULTER, INC. (formerly Beckman Instruments Inc.) designs, manufactures, sells, and services laboratory systems for biological analysis and investigation into life processes. The Company targets three markets: the life sciences laboratory market, specialty testing and the hospital and clinical diagnostic laboratory market. Customers such as universities, research institutions, pharmaceutical companies, hospitals and clinical laboratories use BEC's products across the entire spectrum of biologically-based endeavors, from basic scientific research to daily analysis of blood samples. Beckman Coulter markets its products in approximately 130 countries. BEC's products are used in all phases of the battle against disease to improve methodologies for biological discovery and diagnosis.

ANNUAL FINANCIAL DATA

	12/31/02	12/31/01	12/31/00	12/31/99	12/31/98	12/31/97	12/31/96
Earnings Per Share	⑤ 2.08	④ 2.21	③ 2.03	③ 1.79	② 0.57	① d4.79	1.29
Cash Flow Per Share	3.77	4.19	4.23	4.20	3.17	d2.81	2.81
Tang. Book Val. Per Share	...	...	...	...	...	...	7.13
Dividends Per Share	0.35	0.34	0.33	0.32	0.31	0.30	0.26
Dividend Payout %	16.8	15.4	16.0	17.9	53.5	...	20.2
INCOME STATEMENT (IN MILLIONS):							
Total Revenues	2,059.4	1,984.0	1,886.9	1,808.7	1,718.2	1,198.0	1,028.0
Costs & Expenses	1,726.1	1,618.0	1,518.2	1,448.5	1,451.0	1,325.9	817.7
Depreciation & Amort.	109.8	126.4	136.1	143.7	152.4	109.1	87.8
Operating Income	223.5	239.6	232.6	216.5	114.8	d237.0	122.5
Net Interest Inc./(Exp.)	d37.9	d46.9	d65.6	d66.0	d74.4	d23.3	d12.3
Income Before Income Taxes	178.9	205.0	181.9	154.7	46.6	d251.9	111.5
Income Taxes	43.4	63.5	56.4	48.7	13.1	12.5	36.8
Net Income	⑦ 135.5	⑥ 141.5	⑤ 125.5	⑤ 106.0	④ 33.5	③ d264.4	74.7
Cash Flow	245.3	267.9	261.6	249.7	185.9	d155.3	162.5
Average Shs. Outstg. (000)	65,060	64,011	61,800	59,400	58,600	55,200	57,800
BALANCE SHEET (IN MILLIONS):							
Cash & Cash Equivalents	91.4	36.0	29.6	34.4	24.7	33.5	42.7
Total Current Assets	1,056.2	1,035.6	927.8	966.4	956.6	976.7	579.4
Net Property	370.8	347.4	298.2	305.9	309.4	410.9	263.5
Total Assets	2,263.6	2,178.0	2,018.2	2,110.8	2,133.3	2,331.0	960.1
Total Current Liabilities	611.6	509.9	501.1	575.9	719.3	894.9	279.3
Long-Term Obligations	626.6	760.3	862.8	980.7	982.2	1,181.3	176.6
Net Stockholders' Equity	592.1	518.2	343.9	227.9	126.9	81.8	398.9
Net Working Capital	444.6	525.7	426.7	390.5	237.3	81.8	300.1
Year-end Shs. Outstg. (000)	61,000	61,200	59,700	58,000	56,800	55,200	55,952
STATISTICAL RECORD:							
Operating Profit Margin %	10.9	12.1	12.3	12.0	6.7	...	11.9
Net Profit Margin %	6.6	7.1	6.7	5.9	1.9	...	7.3
Return on Equity %	22.9	27.3	36.5	46.5	26.4	...	18.7
Return on Assets %	6.0	6.5	6.2	5.0	1.6	...	7.8
Debt/Total Assets %	27.7	34.9	42.8	46.5	46.0	50.7	18.4
Price Range	53.00-25.20	47.60-32.80	42.44-22.78	27.88-19.75	32.47-20.03	26.16-18.69	20.56-16.00
P/E Ratio	25.5-12.1	21.5-14.8	20.9-11.2	15.6-11.1	57.0-35.1	...	15.9-12.4
Average Yield %	0.9	0.8	1.0	1.3	1.2	1.3	1.4

Statistics are as originally reported. Adj. for 2-for-1 stk. split., 12/00. ① Incl. a $0.05 per sh. dil. for exps. assoc./w the acq. of the Access® immunoassay product line & incl. after-tax chgs. totaling $318.4 mill. ② Incl. after-tax chrgs. of $110.9 mill. ③ Incl. a pre-tax restruct. gain of $2.4 mill., 2000; $200,000, 1999. ④ Bef. acctg. chrg. of $3.1 mill.; incl. restruct. credit of $500,000. ⑤ Incl. pre-tax litig. settlement & other exps. of $39.3 mill.

OFFICERS:
J. P. Wareham, Chmn., Pres., C.E.O.
A. I. Khalifa, V.P., C.F.O.
J. T. Glover, V.P., Treas.

INVESTOR CONTACT: Jeanie Herbert, Investor Relations, (714) 773-7620

PRINCIPAL OFFICE: 4300 N. Harbor Boulevard, Fullerton, CA 92834-3100

TELEPHONE NUMBER: (714) 871-4848
FAX: (714) 773-8283
WEB: www.beckmancoulter.com

NO. OF EMPLOYEES: 10,094 (approx.)

SHAREHOLDERS: 6,239 (approx.)

ANNUAL MEETING: In Apr.

INCORPORATED: DE, July, 1988

INSTITUTIONAL HOLDINGS:
No. of Institutions: 245
Shares Held: 49,375,645
% Held: 80.9

INDUSTRY: Analytical instruments (SIC: 3826)

TRANSFER AGENT(S): First Chicago Trust Company of New York, Jersey City, NJ

BECTON, DICKINSON AND COMPANY

YIELD	1.0%
P/E RATIO	20.9

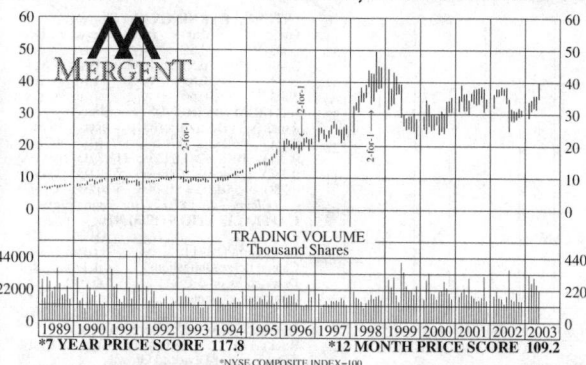

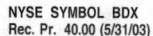

INTERIM EARNINGS (Per Share):

Qtr.	Dec.	Mar.	June	Sept.
1999-00	0.29	0.45	0.43	0.32
2000-01	0.23	0.44	0.46	0.49
2001-02	0.37	0.48	0.44	0.50
2002-03	0.43	0.54	...	...

INTERIM DIVIDENDS (Per Share):

Amt.	Decl.	Ex.	Rec.	Pay.
0.098Q	7/23/02	9/05/02	9/09/02	9/30/02
0.10Q	11/26/02	12/10/02	12/12/02	1/02/03
0.10Q	1/28/03	3/06/03	3/10/03	3/31/03
0.10Q	5/20/03	6/05/03	6/09/03	6/30/03

Indicated div.: $0.40 (Div. Reinv. Plan)

CAPITALIZATION (9/30/02):

	($000)	(%)
Long-Term Debt	802,967	23.6
Deferred Income Tax	105,459	3.1
Preferred Stock	37,945	1.1
Common & Surplus	2,450,029	72.1
Total	3,396,400	100.0

DIVIDEND ACHIEVER STATUS:
Rank: 143   10-Year Growth Rate: 10.03%
Total Years of Dividend Growth: 30

TRADING VOLUME
Thousand Shares

*7 YEAR PRICE SCORE 117.8   *12 MONTH PRICE SCORE 109.2
*NYSE COMPOSITE INDEX=100

RECENT DEVELOPMENTS: For the quarter ended 3/31/03, net income climbed 9.9% to $142.0 million compared with $129.2 million in the corresponding period of the previous year. Results for 2002 included pre-tax special charges of $9.9 million. Revenues advanced 12.0% to $1.13 billion from $1.01 billion in the prior-year quarter. Notably, revenues in the medical systems segment climbed 13.5% to $601.8 million from $530.4 million the year before.

PROSPECTS: The Company announced plans to discontinue U.S. sales of many conventional needles and other ''sharp'' devices across a range of product categories. These actions reflect the significant progress made by the U.S. healthcare facilities in transitioning to safety-engineered designs from conventional devices. Meanwhile, the Company should continue to benefit from recent product launches, particularly those of safety-engineered devices.

BUSINESS

BECTON, DICKINSON AND COMPANY is principally engaged in the manufacture and sale of a broad line of medical supplies and devices and diagnostic systems used by healthcare professionals, medical research institutions and the general public. BDX's operations consist of three worldwide business segments: Medical Systems, (53.3% of 2002 revenues); Clinical Laboratory Solutions, (30.7%); and Biosciences, (16.0%). Major products in the Medical Systems segment are hypodermic products, specially designed devices for diabetes care, prefillable drug delivery systems, infusion therapy products, elastic support products and thermometers. Major products in the Clinical Laboratory Solutions segment are specimen collection products and services. Major products in the Biosciences segment are clinical and industrial microbiology products, sample collection products, cellular analysis systems, and hematology instruments.

ANNUAL FINANCIAL DATA

	9/30/02	9/30/01	9/30/00	9/30/99	9/30/98	9/30/97	9/30/96
Earnings Per Share	⑤ 1.79	① 1.63	④ 1.49	1.04	②③ 0.90	1.21	1.10
Cash Flow Per Share	2.93	2.76	2.59	2.02	1.78	2.08	1.91
Tang. Book Val. Per Share	4.95	5.35	3.80	2.74	3.30	4.11	4.43
Dividends Per Share	0.39	0.38	0.37	0.34	0.29	0.26	0.23
Dividend Payout %	21.8	23.3	24.8	32.7	32.2	21.5	20.9
INCOME STATEMENT (IN MILLIONS):							
Total Revenues	4,033.1	3,754.3	3,618.3	3,418.4	3,116.9	2,810.5	2,769.8
Costs & Expenses	3,052.5	2,802.7	2,815.3	2,714.3	2,482.7	2,150.2	2,138.0
Depreciation & Amort.	304.9	305.7	288.3	258.9	228.7	209.8	200.5
Operating Income	675.7	645.9	514.8	445.2	405.4	450.5	431.2
Net Interest Inc./(Exp.)	d33.3	d55.4	d74.2	d72.1	d56.3	d39.4	d37.4
Income Before Income Taxes	628.6	576.8	519.9	372.7	340.9	422.6	393.7
Income Taxes	148.6	138.3	127.0	96.9	104.3	122.6	110.2
Net Income	⑤ 480.0	① 438.4	④ 392.9	275.7	②③ 236.6	300.1	283.4
Cash Flow	784.8	741.4	678.7	532.0	462.7	507.2	481.3
Average Shs. Outstg. (000)	268,183	268,833	263,239	264,580	262,128	245,230	253,418
BALANCE SHEET (IN MILLIONS):							
Cash & Cash Equivalents	245.0	86.7	54.8	64.6	90.6	141.0	165.1
Total Current Assets	1,928.7	1,762.9	1,660.7	1,683.7	1,542.8	1,312.6	1,276.8
Net Property	1,765.7	1,716.0	1,576.1	1,431.1	1,302.7	1,250.7	1,244.1
Total Assets	5,040.5	4,802.3	4,505.1	4,437.0	3,846.0	3,080.3	2,889.8
Total Current Liabilities	1,252.5	1,264.7	1,353.5	1,329.3	1,091.9	678.2	766.1
Long-Term Obligations	803.0	783.0	779.6	954.2	765.2	665.4	468.2
Net Stockholders' Equity	2,488.0	2,328.8	1,956.0	1,768.7	1,613.8	1,385.4	1,325.2
Net Working Capital	676.3	498.3	307.1	354.4	450.8	634.4	510.7
Year-end Shs. Outstg. (000)	255,530	259,237	253,496	250,798	247,843	244,168	247,220
STATISTICAL RECORD:							
Operating Profit Margin %	16.8	17.2	14.2	13.0	13.0	16.0	15.6
Net Profit Margin %	11.9	11.7	10.9	8.1	7.6	10.7	10.2
Return on Equity %	19.3	18.8	20.1	15.6	14.7	21.7	21.4
Return on Assets %	9.5	9.1	8.7	6.2	6.2	9.7	9.8
Debt/Total Assets %	15.9	16.3	17.3	21.5	19.9	21.6	16.2
Price Range	38.60-24.70	39.25-29.96	35.31-23.75	44.19-22.38	49.63-24.38	27.81-20.94	22.75-17.69
P/E Ratio	21.6-13.8	24.1-18.4	23.7-15.9	42.5-21.5	55.1-27.1	23.0-17.3	20.7-16.1
Average Yield %	1.2	1.1	1.3	1.0	0.8	1.1	1.1

Statistics are as originally reported. Adj. for 2-for-1 stk. split, 8/96 & 8/98. ① Bef. acctg. adj. chrg. of $36.8 mill., 2001. ② Incl. a one-time chg. of $7.0 mill. for in-prog. res. & dev. rel. to two recent acqs. and incl. a spec. pre-tax chg. of $90.9 mill. ③ Incl. a one-time gain of $7.0 mill. and net pre-tax chrgs. of $103.0 mill. ④ Incl. a one-time pre-tax spec. chrg. of $57.5 mill. and net gains on invest. of $76.2 mill. ⑤ Incl. a one-time spec. chrg. of $21.5 mill.

OFFICERS:
E. J. Ludwig, Chmn., Pres., C.E.O.
J. R. Considine, Exec. V.P., C.F.O.
B. M. Healy, V.P., Gen. Couns., Sec.

INVESTOR CONTACT: Dean J. Paranicas, Investors Relations, (201) 847-7102

PRINCIPAL OFFICE: 1 Becton Drive, Franklin Lakes, NJ 07417-1880

TELEPHONE NUMBER: (201) 847-6800
FAX: (201) 847-6475
WEB: www.bd.com

NO. OF EMPLOYEES: 25,249 (avg.)

SHAREHOLDERS: 10,035 (approx. record)

ANNUAL MEETING: In Feb.

INCORPORATED: NJ, Nov., 1906

INSTITUTIONAL HOLDINGS:
No. of Institutions: 418
Shares Held: 211,908,609
% Held: 83.1

INDUSTRY: Surgical and medical instruments (SIC: 3841)

TRANSFER AGENT(S): First Chicago Trust Company of New York, Jersey City, NJ

BEMIS COMPANY, INC.

YIELD 2.4%
P/E RATIO 14.8

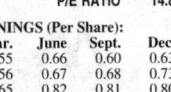

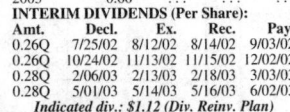

INTERIM EARNINGS (Per Share):

Qtr.	Mar.	June	Sept.	Dec.
2000	0.55	0.66	0.60	0.63
2001	0.56	0.67	0.68	0.73
2002	0.65	0.82	0.81	0.80
2003	0.66	...	...	...

INTERIM DIVIDENDS (Per Share):

Amt.	Decl.	Ex.	Rec.	Pay.
0.26Q	7/25/02	8/12/02	8/14/02	9/03/02
0.26Q	10/24/02	11/13/02	11/15/02	12/02/02
0.28Q	2/06/03	2/13/03	2/18/03	3/03/03
0.28Q	5/01/03	5/14/03	5/16/03	6/02/03

Indicated div.: $1.12 (Div. Reinv. Plan)

CAPITALIZATION (12/31/02):

	($000)	(%)
Long-Term Debt Ⅰ	717,162	40.2
Capital Lease Obligations..	1,115	0.1
Deferred Income Tax	106,050	5.9
Common & Surplus	958,974	53.8
Total	1,783,301	100.0

DIVIDEND ACHIEVER STATUS:
Rank: 173   10-Year Growth Rate: 8.50%
Total Years of Dividend Growth: 19

TRADING VOLUME
Thousand Shares

| 1989 | 1990 | 1991 | 1992 | 1993 | 1994 | 1995 | 1996 | 1997 | 1998 | 1999 | 2000 | 2001 | 2002 | 2003 |

*7 YEAR PRICE SCORE 135.0   ***12 MONTH PRICE SCORE 93.1**
*NYSE COMPOSITE INDEX=100

RECENT DEVELOPMENTS: For the quarter ended 3/31/03, net income rose 1.7% to $35.5 million compared with $34.9 million in the equivalent 2002 quarter. Net sales climbed 15.5% to $638.6 million from $552.7 million a year earlier. Operating profit of the flexible packaging segment grew 4.1% to $67.0 million, reflecting acquisitions, and, to a lesser extent, organic sales volume growth, partially offset by higher resin costs and pension expense.

PROSPECTS: On 4/15/03, the U.S. Department of Justice filed a civil complaint to block the proposed sale of the pressure-sensitive materials segment to UPM-Kymmene, citing concern that the sale would reduce competition in the production of bulk paper labelstock for use in variable information printing and prime labeling. On 4/23/03, UPM-Kymmene announced its intent to challenge this civil action. A court date is set for early June 2003.

BUSINESS

BEMIS COMPANY, INC. is a manufacturer of flexible packaging products and pressure-sensitive materials used by food, consumer products, manufacturing, and other companies worldwide. Flexible packaging products include a broad range of consumer and industrial packaging consisting of high-barrier products that include advanced multi-layer coextruded, coated and laminated film structures; polyethylene products; and paper products. Pressure-Sensitive Materials include roll label products, graphics and distribution products, and technical and industrial products.

As of 4/23/03, the Company manufactured from 56 facilities in ten countries. In 2002, sales were as follows: flexible packaging, 80.0%, and pressure-sensitive materials, 20.0%.

ANNUAL FINANCIAL DATA

	12/31/02	12/31/01	12/31/00	12/31/99	12/31/98	12/31/97	12/31/96
Earnings Per Share	3.08	2.64	2.44	2.18	2.09	2.00	1.90
Cash Flow Per Share	5.30	4.98	4.46	4.04	3.76	3.46	3.14
Tang. Book Val. Per Share	8.21	8.78	9.52	13.91	12.83	12.08	10.83
Dividends Per Share	1.04	1.00	0.96	0.92	0.88	0.80	0.72
Dividend Payout %	33.8	37.9	39.3	42.2	42.1	40.0	37.9
INCOME STATEMENT (IN MILLIONS):							
Total Revenues	2,369.0	2,293.1	2,164.6	1,918.0	1,848.0	1,877.2	1,655.4
Costs & Expenses	1,967.7	1,908.8	1,811.5	1,602.1	1,550.5	1,603.1	1,413.9
Depreciation & Amort.	119.2	124.1	108.1	97.7	88.9	78.9	66.2
Operating Income	282.2	260.2	245.0	218.2	208.5	195.3	175.4
Net Interest Inc./(Exp.)	d15.4	d30.3	d31.6	d21.2	d21.9	d18.9	d13.4
Income Before Income Taxes	267.0	227.4	211.5	185.9	181.9	175.0	162.8
Income Taxes	101.5	87.1	80.9	71.1	70.5	67.4	61.7
Equity Earnings/Minority Int.	d0.9	d0.6	d0.5	d4.2	d4.4	d5.4	d4.7
Net Income	165.5	140.3	130.6	114.8	111.4	107.6	101.1
Cash Flow	284.7	264.5	238.7	212.5	200.3	186.4	167.3
Average Shs. Outstg. (000)	53,746	53,122	53,553	52,657	53,324	53,880	53,252
BALANCE SHEET (IN MILLIONS):							
Cash & Cash Equivalents	56.4	35.1	28.9	18.2	23.7	13.8	10.2
Total Current Assets	721.7	586.9	640.0	583.6	517.9	516.4	466.9
Net Property	910.0	852.7	825.8	776.2	740.1	685.2	583.5
Total Assets	2,256.7	1,923.0	1,888.6	1,532.1	1,453.1	1,362.6	1,168.8
Total Current Liabilities	325.9	238.2	495.1	253.3	242.8	251.2	214.4
Long-Term Obligations	718.3	595.2	438.0	372.3	371.4	316.8	241.1
Net Stockholders' Equity	959.0	886.1	798.8	725.9	670.8	639.9	567.1
Net Working Capital	395.8	348.7	144.9	330.3	275.2	265.2	252.5
Year-end Shs. Outstg. (000)	52,944	52,870	52,602	52,189	52,269	52,968	52,361
STATISTICAL RECORD:							
Operating Profit Margin %	11.9	11.3	11.3	11.4	11.3	10.4	10.6
Net Profit Margin %	7.0	6.1	6.0	6.0	6.0	5.7	6.1
Return on Equity %	17.3	15.8	16.4	15.8	16.6	16.8	17.8
Return on Assets %	7.3	7.3	6.9	7.5	7.7	7.9	8.6
Debt/Total Assets %	31.8	31.0	23.2	24.3	25.6	23.2	20.6
Price Range	58.24-39.40	52.47-28.69	39.31-22.94	40.38-30.19	46.94-33.50	47.94-33.63	37.63-25.63
P/E Ratio	18.9-12.8	19.9-10.9	16.1-9.4	18.5-13.8	22.5-16.0	24.0-16.8	19.8-13.5
Average Yield %	2.1	2.5	3.1	2.6	2.2	2.0	2.3

Statistics are as originally reported. Ⅰ Incl. capital lease obligations.

OFFICERS:
J. H. Roe, Chmn.
J. H. Curler, Pres., C.E.O.
B. R. Field, III, Sr. V.P., C.F.O., Treas.

INVESTOR CONTACT: Melanie E.R. Miller, Dir., Investor Relations, (612) 376-3000

PRINCIPAL OFFICE: 222 South 9th Street, Suite 2300, Minneapolis, MN 55402-4099

TELEPHONE NUMBER: (612) 376-3000
FAX: (612) 340-6174
WEB: www.bemis.com

NO. OF EMPLOYEES: 11,837 (avg.)

SHAREHOLDERS: 4,542

ANNUAL MEETING: In May

INCORPORATED: MO, May, 1885

INSTITUTIONAL HOLDINGS:
No. of Institutions: 255
Shares Held: 30,847,207
% Held: 58.2

INDUSTRY: Paper coated & laminated, packaging (SIC: 2671)

TRANSFER AGENT(S): Wells Fargo Shareowner Services, South St. Paul, MN

BLACK HILLS CORPORATION

YIELD 4.0%
P/E RATIO 12.6

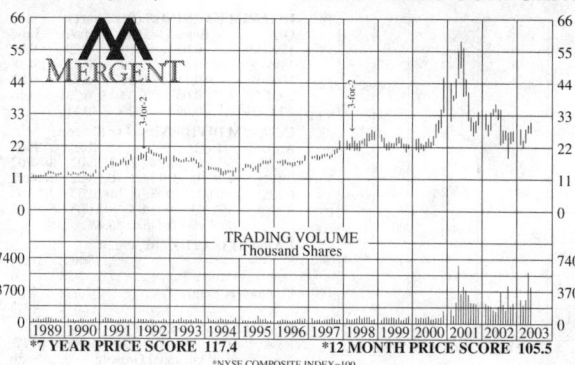

TRADING VOLUME
Thousand Shares

*7 YEAR PRICE SCORE 117.4   *12 MONTH PRICE SCORE 105.5
*NYSE COMPOSITE INDEX=100

INTERIM EARNINGS (Per Share):

Qtr.	Mar.	June	Sept.	Dec.
2000	0.42	0.38	0.71	0.83
2001	1.37	1.34	0.61	0.18
2002	0.52	0.54	0.64	0.59
2003	0.62	...	...	...

INTERIM DIVIDENDS (Per Share):

Amt.	Decl.	Ex.	Rec.	Pay.
0.29Q	7/22/02	8/14/02	8/16/02	9/01/02
0.29Q	10/29/02	11/13/02	11/15/02	12/01/02
0.30Q	1/29/03	2/12/03	2/14/03	3/01/03
0.30Q	4/29/03	5/16/03	5/20/03	6/01/03

Indicated div.: $1.20 (Div. Reinv. Plan)

CAPITALIZATION (12/31/02):

	($000)	(%)
Long-Term Debt	618,862	47.9
Deferred Income Tax	132,270	10.2
Minority Interest	6,454	0.5
Preferred Stock	5,549	0.4
Common & Surplus	529,614	41.0
Total	1,292,749	100.0

DIVIDEND ACHIEVER STATUS:
Rank: 260   10-Year Growth Rate: 3.45%
Total Years of Dividend Growth: 31

RECENT DEVELOPMENTS: For the quarter ended 3/31/03, income was $16.9 million versus $14.9 million, before a loss from discontinued operations of $1.7 million, in the prior-year quarter. Earnings excluded a charge of $2.7 million in 2003 and a gain of $896,000 in 2002 from accounting changes. Revenues climbed 75.4% to $299.3 million from $170.6 million a year earlier. Integrated Energy group revenue surged 96.1% to $246.9 million, primarily due to higher prices and volumes of crude oil marketed.

PROSPECTS: On 3/10/03, BKH announced the acquisition of Mallon Resources Corporation for total consideration of approximately $53.0 million. Mallon Resources' proved reserves are estimated at about 86.00 billion cubic feet of gas as of 12/31/02. The oil and gas leases of the acquisition total more than 66,500 gross acres, most of which are contained in a contiguous block that is in the early stages of development. The acquisition should increase BKH's gas and oil production by nearly 50.0%.

BUSINESS

BLACK HILLS CORPORATION is an energy and communications company with three business groups. Black Hills Energy, Inc. (54.0% of 2002 revenues) is the integrated energy unit that generates electricity, produces natural gas, oil and coal and markets energy. BHE produces coal natural gas and crude oil primarily in the Rocky Mountain region, which it sells nationwide. Black Hills Power, Inc. (38.3%) is an electric utility serving customers in western South Dakota, northeastern Wyoming and southeastern Montana. Black Hills FiberCom, LLC (7.7%) provides broadband communications to residential and business customers in Rapid City and the northern Black Hills region of South Dakota. Broadband offerings include bundled telephone, high speed Internet and cable entertainment services.

ANNUAL FINANCIAL DATA

	12/31/02	12/31/01	12/31/00	12/31/99	12/31/98	12/31/97	12/31/96
Earnings Per Share	② 2.33	3.42	2.37	1.73	① 1.19	1.49	1.40
Cash Flow Per Share	4.88	5.49	3.84	2.89	2.30	2.52	2.45
Tang. Book Val. Per Share	15.42	14.67	10.45	10.14	9.52	9.46	8.91
Dividends Per Share	1.16	1.12	1.08	1.04	1.00	0.95	0.92
Dividend Payout %	49.8	32.7	45.6	60.1	84.0	63.5	65.7
INCOME STATEMENT (IN MILLIONS):							
Total Revenues	③ 423.9	1,558.6	1,623.8	791.9	679.3	313.7	162.6
Costs & Expenses	221.6	1,334.3	1,476.2	704.9	606.0	232.4	85.5
Depreciation & Amort.	69.7	54.1	32.9	25.1	24.0	22.3	22.8
Operating Income	132.6	170.2	114.8	61.9	49.2	58.9	54.3
Net Interest Inc./(Exp.)	d40.6	d37.2	d23.3	d11.8	d11.8	d11.8	d12.2
Income Taxes	29.7	50.5	30.4	15.8	11.7	14.3	13.6
Equity Earnings/Minority Int.	d3.2	d4.2	d11.3	...	...	...	...
Net Income	② 63.2	88.1	52.8	37.1	① 25.8	32.4	30.3
Cash Flow	132.7	141.6	85.6	62.1	49.8	54.7	53.0
Average Shs. Outstg. (000)	27,167	25,771	22,281	21,482	21,665	21,706	21,660
BALANCE SHEET (IN MILLIONS):							
Gross Property	993.8	737.9	961.6	659.9	619.5	598.3	581.5
Accumulated Depreciation	414.0	328.4	277.8	246.3	229.9	197.2	181.1
Net Property	730.9	539.2	794.3	464.2	389.6	401.1	400.4
Total Assets	2,035.2	1,658.8	1,320.3	674.8	559.4	508.7	467.4
Long-Term Obligations	618.9	415.8	307.1	160.7	162.0	163.4	164.7
Net Stockholders' Equity	535.2	515.2	282.3	216.6	206.7	205.4	193.2
Year-end Shs. Outstg. (000)	27,102	26,891	22,921	21,372	21,719	21,705	21,675
STATISTICAL RECORD:							
Operating Profit Margin %	31.3	10.9	7.1	7.8	7.2	18.8	33.4
Net Profit Margin %	14.9	5.7	3.3	4.7	3.8	10.3	18.6
Net Inc./Net Property %	8.6	16.3	6.7	8.0	6.6	8.1	7.6
Net Inc./Tot. Capital %	4.9	8.6	7.7	8.5	6.1	7.7	7.4
Return on Equity %	11.8	17.1	18.7	17.1	12.5	15.8	15.7
Accum. Depr./Gross Prop. %	41.7	44.5	28.9	37.3	37.1	33.0	31.1
Price Range	36.90-18.35	58.50-26.00	46.06-20.44	26.50-20.31	27.94-20.69	24.29-17.50	19.17-15.17
P/E Ratio	15.8-7.9	17.1-7.6	19.4-8.6	15.3-11.7	23.5-17.4	16.3-11.7	13.7-10.8
Average Yield %	4.2	2.7	3.2	4.4	4.1	4.5	5.4

Statistics are as originally reported. Adj. for 3-for-2 stk. split, 3/98 ① Inc. non-recurr. chrg. $8.8 mill. ② Bef. acctg. change gain of $896,000 and loss fr. discont. opers. of $2.6 mill. ③ Reflects new reporting requirement to show trading rev. net of exp.

OFFICERS:
D. P. Landguth, Chmn., C.E.O.
E. E. Hoyt, Pres., C.O.O.
M. T. Thies, Exec. V.P., C.F.O.
INVESTOR CONTACT: Dale T. Jahr., Dir., Investor Relations, (605) 721-2326
PRINCIPAL OFFICE: 625 Ninth Street, Rapid City, SD 57701

TELEPHONE NUMBER: (605) 721-1700
FAX: (605) 721-2599
WEB: www.blackhillscorp.com
NO. OF EMPLOYEES: 840
SHAREHOLDERS: 5,350 (record); 16,000 (approx. benef.)
ANNUAL MEETING: In May
INCORPORATED: SD, Aug., 1941

INSTITUTIONAL HOLDINGS:
No. of Institutions: 150
Shares Held: 12,103,102
% Held: 44.8

INDUSTRY: Electric services (SIC: 4911)

TRANSFER AGENT(S): Wells Fargo Shareowner Services, St. Paul, MN

ASE SYMBOL BWLA
Rec. Pr. 11.33 (5/31/03)

BOWL AMERICA INC.

YIELD 4.2%
P/E RATIO 17.2

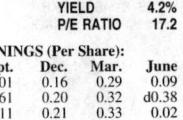

TRADING VOLUME
Thousand Shares

| 1989 | 1990 | 1991 | 1992 | 1993 | 1994 | 1995 | 1996 | 1997 | 1998 | 1999 | 2000 | 2001 | 2002 | 2003 |

*7 YEAR PRICE SCORE 159.8   ***12 MONTH PRICE SCORE 96.8**

*NYSE COMPOSITE INDEX=100

INTERIM EARNINGS (Per Share):

Qtr.	Sept.	Dec.	Mar.	June
1998-99	0.01	0.16	0.29	0.09
1999-00	0.61	0.20	0.32	d0.38
2000-01	0.11	0.21	0.33	0.02
2001-02	0.08	0.23	0.33	0.10
2002-03	0.05	0.20	0.31	…

INTERIM DIVIDENDS (Per Share):

Amt.	Decl.	Ex.	Rec.	Pay.
0.12Q	6/25/02	7/24/02	7/26/02	8/14/02
0.12Q	9/26/02	10/11/02	10/16/02	11/14/02
0.12Q	12/03/02	1/08/03	1/10/03	2/12/03
0.12Q	3/18/03	4/21/03	4/23/03	5/14/03

Indicated div.: $0.48

CAPITALIZATION (6/30/02):

	($000)	(%)
Deferred Income Tax	1,928	5.6
Common & Surplus	32,682	94.4
Total	34,610	100.0

DIVIDEND ACHIEVER STATUS:

Rank: 240   10-Year Growth Rate: 4.77%
Total Years of Dividend Growth: 30

RECENT DEVELOPMENTS: For the quarter ended 3/30/03, net income declined 5.6% to $1.6 million compared with $1.7 million in the equivalent 2002 quarter. The decline in earnings was primarily attributed to BWLA operating one fewer center than last year. In addition, heavy snow storms resulted in closings at all of the Company's northern centers. Operating revenues fell 1.7% to $8.8 million from $9.0 million a year earlier. Bowling and other revenues slid 2.2% to $6.2 million from $6.3 million the year before.

Food, beverage and merchandise sales decreased 0.5% to $2.6 million compared with $2.7 million in 2002. Operating income slid 3.9% to $2.4 million from $2.5 million a year earlier. During the quarter, promotional pricing succeeded in increasing games bowled by 2.0%, and in comparable centers, by 6.0%, at the cost of a reduced average game rate. Looking ahead, the Company expects to close on the sale of a bowling center for $2.3 million prior to 8/30/03.

BUSINESS

BOWL AMERICA INC. operated 18 bowling centers in Maryland, Virginia and Florida as of 5/14/03. These bowling centers are fully air-conditioned with facilities for the service of food and beverages, game rooms, rental lockers and playroom facilities. All centers provide shoes for rental and bowling balls are provided free. In addition, each center retails bowling accessories.

ANNUAL FINANCIAL DATA

	6/30/02	7/1/01	7/2/00	6/27/99	6/28/98	6/29/97	6/30/96
Earnings Per Share	0.74	0.74	0.75	0.55	0.49	0.40	0.41
Cash Flow Per Share	1.09	1.11	1.13	0.93	0.86	0.73	0.73
Tang. Book Val. Per Share	6.35	6.66	6.78	6.12	5.66	5.35	5.25
Dividends Per Share	0.47	0.45	0.41	0.38	0.363	0.358	0.34
Dividend Payout %	63.5	60.8	54.7	69.1	74.1	89.5	82.9
INCOME STATEMENT (IN THOUSANDS):							
Total Revenues	29,810	29,401	28,902	27,547	27,087	26,995	27,327
Costs & Expenses	22,652	22,568	21,051	20,727	20,661	21,475	21,795
Depreciation & Amort.	1,764	1,940	2,100	2,268	2,323	2,111	2,035
Operating Income	5,394	4,893	5,751	4,552	4,103	3,410	3,497
Net Interest Inc./(Exp.)	599	1,036	823	685	675	633	664
Income Before Income Taxes	5,993	5,928	6,574	5,237	4,778	4,042	4,161
Income Taxes	2,174	2,060	2,361	1,902	1,716	1,552	1,567
Net Income	3,819	3,868	4,213	3,335	3,062	2,490	2,594
Cash Flow	5,582	5,809	6,313	5,603	5,385	4,601	4,629
Average Shs. Outstg.	5,132	5,223	5,588	6,026	6,240	6,263	6,315
BALANCE SHEET (IN THOUSANDS):							
Cash & Cash Equivalents	9,818	7,575	10,397	9,248	9,986	8,173	8,881
Total Current Assets	11,538	9,613	11,495	10,453	11,194	9,366	10,508
Net Property	20,506	21,079	19,368	20,909	22,223	23,455	22,681
Total Assets	36,563	37,598	40,711	41,748	40,435	38,003	37,901
Total Current Liabilities	1,820	2,407	2,165	2,064	1,968	2,286	2,855
Net Stockholders' Equity	32,682	32,703	34,868	35,477	35,292	33,382	32,904
Net Working Capital	9,718	7,206	9,330	8,389	9,226	7,080	7,653
Year-end Shs. Outstg.	5,150	4,908	5,140	5,794	6,236	6,243	6,265
STATISTICAL RECORD:							
Operating Profit Margin %	18.1	16.6	19.9	16.5	15.1	12.6	12.8
Net Profit Margin %	12.8	13.2	14.6	12.1	11.3	9.2	9.5
Return on Equity %	11.7	11.8	12.1	9.4	8.7	7.5	7.9
Return on Assets %	10.4	10.3	10.3	8.0	7.6	6.6	6.8
Price Range	12.25-10.68	11.30-7.62	8.69-6.24	7.37-5.78	8.50-6.24	8.62-5.90	7.37-5.67
P/E Ratio	16.6-14.4	15.3-10.3	11.6-8.3	13.3-10.5	17.4-12.7	21.6-14.8	18.1-13.8
Average Yield %	4.1	4.7	5.5	5.8	4.9	4.9	5.3

Statistics are as originally reported. Adj. for 5.0% stk. split 7/26/00, 7/26/01.

OFFICERS:
L. H. Goldberg, Pres., C.E.O., C.O.O.
R. E. Macklin, Sr. V.P., Treas.
C. A. Dragoo, C.F.O., Contr., Asst. Treas.
A. J. Levy, Sr. V.P., Sec.

INVESTOR CONTACT: Investor Relations, (703) 941-6300

PRINCIPAL OFFICE: 6446 Edsall Road, Alexandria, VA 22312

TELEPHONE NUMBER: (703) 941-6300
FAX: (703) 256-2430

NO. OF EMPLOYEES: 700 (approx.)

SHAREHOLDERS: 445 (approx. class A com.); 31 (approx. class B com.)

ANNUAL MEETING: In Dec.

INCORPORATED: MD, July, 1958

INSTITUTIONAL HOLDINGS:
No. of Institutions: 13
Shares Held: 586,126
% Held: 11.7

INDUSTRY: Bowling centers (SIC: 7933)

TRANSFER AGENT(S): American Stock Transfer & Trust Co., New York, NY

BRADY CORPORATION

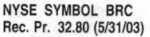
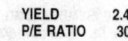

YIELD 2.4%
P/E RATIO 30.4

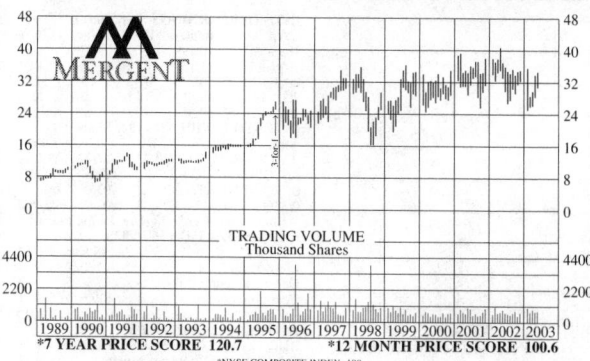

TRADING VOLUME
Thousand Shares

1989|1990|1991|1992|1993|1994|1995|1996|1997|1998|1999|2000|2001|2002|2003
*7 YEAR PRICE SCORE 120.7   ***12 MONTH PRICE SCORE 100.6**
*NYSE COMPOSITE INDEX=100

INTERIM EARNINGS (Per Share):

Qtr.	Oct.	Jan.	Apr.	July
1999-00	0.54	0.43	0.51	0.57
2000-01	0.49	0.37	0.44	d0.12
2001-02	0.34	0.26	0.36	0.24
2002-03	0.35	0.12	0.37	...

INTERIM DIVIDENDS (Per Share):

Amt.	Decl.	Ex.	Rec.	Pay.
0.19Q	5/14/02	7/09/02	7/11/02	7/31/02
0.20Q	9/10/02	10/09/02	10/11/02	10/31/02
0.20Q	11/14/02	1/08/03	1/11/03	1/31/03
0.20Q	2/18/03	4/08/03	4/10/03	4/30/03
0.20Q	5/20/03	7/08/03	7/10/03	7/31/03

Indicated div.: $0.80 (Div. Reinv. Plan)

CAPITALIZATION (7/31/02):

	($000)	(%)
Long-Term Debt	3,751	1.1
Preferred Stock.................	2,855	0.9
Common & Surplus	321,387	98.0
Total	327,993	100.0

DIVIDEND ACHIEVER STATUS:
Rank: 61   10-Year Growth Rate: 15.02%
Total Years of Dividend Growth: 18

RECENT DEVELOPMENTS: For the quarter ended 4/30/03, net income totaled $8.6 million, up 1.4% compared with $8.5 million in the corresponding prior-year period. Net sales climbed 8.8% to $142.0 million from $130.5 million a year earlier. Cost of products sold increased 8.4% to $68.8 million from $63.5 million the year before, while selling, general and administrative expenses rose 12.3% to $55.9 million from $49.8 million the previous year. Operating income slipped 5.0% to $12.1 million.

PROSPECTS: The Company is expanding its operations in Europe through acquisitions. BRC acquired Cleere Advantage, a safety and facility identification products dealer in the United Kingdom in April 2003. Meanwhile, on 5/5/03, the Company announced that it had completed the acquisition of Etimark GmbH, a provider of barcode products, including labels, printers, applicators and software in Germany. Separately, BRC is taking steps to combine its sales and marketing operations in North America and Europe.

BUSINESS

BRADY CORPORATION (formerly W.H. Brady Co.) is an international manufacturer and marketer of identification products and specialty coated materials, which are designed to help companies improve safety, security, productivity and performance. BRC's array of labels are used in applications ranging from marking wires and cables in facilities, electrical, telecommunication and transportation equipment to marking electronic components and printed circuit boards that require identification for purposes such as maintenance, work-in-process or asset tracking. Offerings ranging from signs, pipemakers, lockout/tagout devices, labels and tags to services including consulting, product installation and training enable companies to comply with safety and environmental regulations.

ANNUAL FINANCIAL DATA

	7/31/02	7/31/01	7/31/00	7/31/99	7/31/98	7/31/97	7/31/96
Earnings Per Share	⬚ 1.20	⬚ 1.18	2.05	⬚ 1.73	⬚ 1.23	1.44	1.27
Cash Flow Per Share	1.92	2.17	2.84	2.41	1.83	1.05	0.88
Tang. Book Val. Per Share	9.23	8.89	8.25	8.17	7.87	7.64	6.96
Dividends Per Share	0.77	0.73	0.69	0.65	0.61	0.54	0.43
Dividend Payout %	64.2	61.9	33.7	37.6	49.6	37.5	33.9
INCOME STATEMENT (IN THOUSANDS):							
Total Revenues	516,962	545,944	541,077	470,862	455,150	426,081	359,542
Costs & Expenses	458,829	478,776	453,953	391,941	395,932	361,562	307,775
Depreciation & Amort.	16,630	22,646	17,833	15,149	13,288	14,151	10,602
Operating Income	41,503	44,522	69,291	63,772	45,930	50,368	41,165
Net Interest Inc./(Exp.)	d82	d418	d578	d445	d403	d256	d302
Income Before Income Taxes	43,135	44,790	76,131	64,782	46,165	51,271	45,433
Income Taxes	14,882	17,244	28,930	25,198	18,129	19,564	17,406
Net Income	⬚ 28,253	⬚ 27,546	47,201	⬚ 39,584	⬚ 28,036	31,707	28,027
Cash Flow	44,624	49,933	64,775	54,474	41,065	45,599	38,370
Average Shs. Outstg.	23,340	23,107	22,933	22,683	22,602	43,816	43,694
BALANCE SHEET (IN THOUSANDS):							
Cash & Cash Equivalents	75,969	62,811	60,784	75,466	65,609	65,329	49,281
Total Current Assets	210,026	194,993	203,183	203,169	184,053	187,969	156,111
Net Property	80,891	84,533	80,660	66,984	67,165	62,442	65,649
Total Assets	420,525	392,476	398,134	351,120	311,824	291,662	261,835
Total Current Liabilities	74,262	71,163	87,099	73,285	58,667	57,245	46,423
Long-Term Obligations	3,751	4,144	4,157	1,402	3,716	3,890	1,809
Net Stockholders' Equity	324,242	302,579	291,224	260,564	233,373	206,547	189,263
Net Working Capital	135,764	123,830	116,084	129,884	125,386	130,724	109,688
Year-end Shs. Outstg.	23,121	22,914	22,731	22,605	22,496	21,941	21,863
STATISTICAL RECORD:							
Operating Profit Margin %	8.0	8.2	12.8	13.5	10.1	11.8	11.4
Net Profit Margin %	5.5	5.0	8.7	8.4	6.2	7.4	7.8
Return on Equity %	8.7	9.1	16.2	15.2	12.0	15.4	14.8
Return on Assets %	6.7	7.0	11.9	11.3	9.0	10.9	10.7
Debt/Total Assets %	0.9	1.1	1.0	0.4	1.2	1.3	0.7
Price Range	40.70-26.70	39.24-25.55	34.94-24.50	36.31-19.50	35.75-26.13	35.00-21.63	27.50-18.00
P/E Ratio	33.9-22.2	33.3-21.7	17.0-12.0	21.0-11.3	29.1-13.2	24.3-15.0	21.7-14.2
Average Yield %	2.3	2.3	2.3	2.3	2.3	1.9	1.9

Statistics are as originally reported. ⬚ Incl. non-recur. pre-tax chrg. in 2002 of $2.7 mill.; 2001, $9.6 mill.; gain of $611,000, 1999; $5.4 mill. chrg., 1998.

OFFICERS:
K. M. Hudson, Chmn.
F. M. Jaehnert, Pres., C.E.O.
D. W. Schroeder, Sr. V.P., C.F.O.
D. Rearic, Sr. V.P., Treas., Asst. Sec.

INVESTOR CONTACT: Barbara Bolens, Dir., Invest. Rel., (414) 438-6940

PRINCIPAL OFFICE: 6555 West Good Hope Road, Milwaukee, WI 53223-0571

TELEPHONE NUMBER: (414) 358-6600
FAX: (414) 438-6910
WEB: www.bradycorp.com

NO. OF EMPLOYEES: 3,200 (approx.)

SHAREHOLDERS: 350 (class A); 3 (class B)

ANNUAL MEETING: In Nov.

INCORPORATED: WI, 1939

INSTITUTIONAL HOLDINGS:
No. of Institutions: 88
Shares Held: 16,195,878
% Held: 70.4

INDUSTRY: Signs and advertising specialities (SIC: 3993)

TRANSFER AGENT(S): Wells Fargo Shareowner Services, St. Paul, MN

BRIGGS & STRATTON CORPORATION

YIELD 2.8%
P/E RATIO 13.9

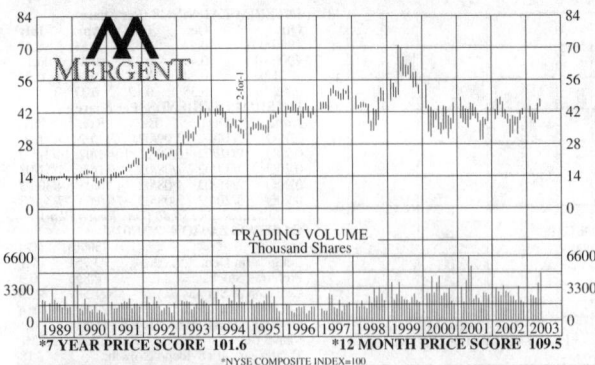

INTERIM EARNINGS (Per Share):

Qtr.	Sept.	Dec.	Mar.	June
1998-99	0.19	1.05	1.79	1.51
1999-00	1.10	1.77	1.84	1.24
2000-01	d0.29	0.92	1.38	0.21
2001-02	d0.81	0.11	1.58	1.30
2002-03	d0.32	0.53	1.81	...

INTERIM DIVIDENDS (Per Share):

Amt.	Decl.	Ex.	Rec.	Pay.
0.32Q	8/07/02	8/20/02	8/22/02	10/01/02
0.32Q	10/16/02	11/27/02	12/02/02	1/02/03
0.32Q	1/15/03	2/27/03	3/03/03	4/01/03
0.32Q	4/16/03	5/29/03	6/02/03	6/27/03

Indicated div.: $1.28 (Div. Reinv. Plan)

CAPITALIZATION (6/30/02):

	($000)	(%)
Long-Term Debt	499,022	51.1
Deferred Income Tax	27,405	2.8
Common & Surplus	449,646	46.1
Total	976,073	100.0

DIVIDEND ACHIEVER STATUS:
Rank: 242   10-Year Growth Rate: 4.60%
Total Years of Dividend Growth: 11

TRADING VOLUME
Thousand Shares

*7 YEAR PRICE SCORE 101.6   *12 MONTH PRICE SCORE 109.5

*NYSE COMPOSITE INDEX=100

RECENT DEVELOPMENTS: For the quarter ended 3/31/03, net income rose 14.3% to $43.0 million versus $37.6 million in the corresponding year-earlier period. BGG attributed the improvement in earnings to increased power products segment sales volume, increased margins from export sales due to a stronger Euro, better utilization of production facilities, a lower effective tax rate and lower interest expense. Net sales grew 8.3% to $560.4 million. Gross profit on sales amounted to $116.6 million, or 20.8% of net sales, versus $103.0 million, or 19.9% of net sales, in 2002.

PROSPECTS: Ample rainfall across all of BGG's major market areas, which should fuel consumer demand for lawn and garden equipment as spring progresses, reinforces the Company's favorable near-term outlook. Consequently, BGG expects full-year fiscal 2003 consolidated sales will be 4.0% higher than the previous year and gross margins will approximate 19.6%. Full-year fiscal 2003 net income, including an effective tax rate of 32.0%, is expected to range between $74.0 million and $76.0 million.

BUSINESS

BRIGGS & STRATTON CORPORATION is a producer of air-cooled gasoline engines for outdoor power equipment. The Company designs, manufactures, markets and services these products for original equipment manufacturers (OEMs) worldwide. These engines are primarily aluminum alloy gasoline engines ranging from 3 through 25 horsepower. BGG's engines are used primarily by the lawn and garden equipment industry. Major lawn and garden equipment applications include walk-behind lawn mowers, riding lawn mowers and garden tillers. Briggs & Stratton engines are marketed under various brand names including CLASSIC™, SPRINT™, QUATTRO™, QUANTUM®, INTEK™, I/C®, INDUSTRIAL PLUS™ and VANGUARD™. BGG also designs, manufactures and markets portable generators, pressure washers and related accessories. On 5/15/01, BGG acquired Generac Portable Products for net cash of $267.0 million. Dividends have been paid since 1929.

ANNUAL FINANCIAL DATA

	6/30/02	7/1/01	7/2/00	6/27/99	6/28/98	6/29/97	6/30/96
Earnings Per Share	2.36	2.21	① 5.97	4.52	2.85	2.16	3.19
Cash Flow Per Share	4.87	4.90	8.22	6.64	4.78	3.68	4.68
Tang. Book Val. Per Share	13.34	11.53	18.51	15.45	12.87	13.40	17.17
Dividends Per Share	1.27	1.24	1.21	1.17	1.13	1.10	1.06
Dividend Payout %	53.8	56.1	20.3	25.9	39.6	50.9	33.2

INCOME STATEMENT (IN MILLIONS):

Total Revenues	1,529.4	1,312.4	1,590.6	1,501.7	1,327.6	1,316.4	1,287.0
Costs & Expenses	1,345.0	1,153.6	1,334.0	1,272.0	1,155.2	1,169.3	1,090.6
Depreciation & Amort.	66.0	59.7	51.4	49.6	47.7	43.4	43.0
Operating Income	118.4	99.1	205.2	180.1	124.7	103.7	153.4
Net Interest Inc./(Exp.)	d44.4	d30.7	d21.3	d17.0	d19.4	d9.9	d10.1
Income Before Income Taxes	80.5	71.9	216.6	169.8	113.1	99.3	149.1
Income Taxes	27.4	23.9	80.2	63.7	42.5	37.7	56.6
Net Income	53.1	48.0	① 136.5	106.1	70.6	61.6	92.4
Cash Flow	119.1	107.7	187.8	155.7	118.4	104.9	135.4
Average Shs. Outstg. (000)	24,452	21,966	22,842	23,459	24,775	28,551	28,927

BALANCE SHEET (IN MILLIONS):

Cash & Cash Equivalents	215.9	88.7	17.0	60.8	84.5	112.9	150.6
Total Current Assets	669.9	613.4	472.0	459.1	382.0	418.4	452.7
Net Property	395.2	416.4	395.6	404.5	391.9	396.3	374.2
Total Assets	1,349.0	1,296.2	930.2	875.9	793.4	842.2	838.2
Total Current Liabilities	266.0	242.2	312.8	282.5	222.9	214.0	190.2
Long-Term Obligations	499.0	508.1	98.5	113.3	128.1	142.9	60.0
Net Stockholders' Equity	449.6	422.8	409.5	365.9	316.5	351.1	500.5
Net Working Capital	403.9	371.2	159.2	176.6	159.1	204.4	262.5
Year-end Shs. Outstg. (000)	21,639	21,599	21,746	23,200	23,824	25,414	28,927

STATISTICAL RECORD:

Operating Profit Margin %	7.7	7.6	12.9	12.0	9.4	7.9	11.9
Net Profit Margin %	3.5	3.7	8.6	7.1	5.3	4.7	7.2
Return on Equity %	11.8	11.4	33.3	29.0	22.3	17.5	18.5
Return on Assets %	3.9	3.7	14.7	12.1	8.9	7.3	11.0
Debt/Total Assets %	37.0	39.2	10.6	12.9	16.1	17.0	7.2
Price Range	48.39-30.75	48.38-29.65	53.88-30.38	71.13-46.69	52.44-33.63	53.63-42.63	46.88-36.50
P/E Ratio	20.5-13.0	21.9-13.4	9.0-5.1	15.7-10.3	18.4-11.8	24.8-19.7	14.7-11.4
Average Yield %	3.2	3.2	2.9	2.0	2.6	2.3	2.5

Statistics are as originally reported. ① Incl. non-recurr. gain $16.5 mill.

OFFICERS:
J. S. Shiely, Chmn., Pres., C.E.O.
J. E. Brenn, Sr. V.P., C.F.O.
C. R. Twinem, Treas.
INVESTOR CONTACT: G. R. Thompson, V.P., Corp. Comm., (414) 259-5312
PRINCIPAL OFFICE: 12301 West Wirth Street, Wauwatosa, WI 53222

TELEPHONE NUMBER: (414) 259-5333
FAX: (414) 259-9594
WEB: www.briggsandstratton.com
NO. OF EMPLOYEES: 7,019 (avg.)
SHAREHOLDERS: 4,669 (record)
ANNUAL MEETING: In Oct.
INCORPORATED: DE, June, 1924; reincorp., WI, Oct., 1992

INSTITUTIONAL HOLDINGS:
No. of Institutions: 173
Shares Held: 17,528,585
% Held: 79.7
INDUSTRY: Internal combustion engines, nec (SIC: 3519)
TRANSFER AGENT(S): U.S. Bank, N.A., Milwaukee, WI

BRISTOL-MYERS SQUIBB COMPANY

YIELD 4.4%
P/E RATIO 25.6

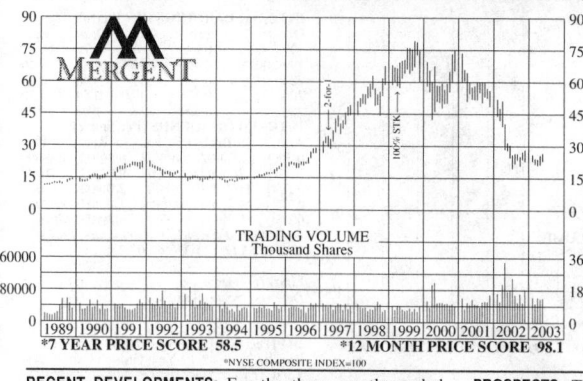

7 YEAR PRICE SCORE 58.5   **12 MONTH PRICE SCORE 98.1**
*NYSE COMPOSITE INDEX=100

INTERIM EARNINGS (Per Share):

Qtr.	Mar.	June	Sept.	Dec.
1999	0.53	0.47	0.54	0.52
2000	0.56	0.50	0.45	0.54
2001	0.63	0.56	0.63	d0.54
2002	0.43	0.25	0.17	0.19
2003	0.39	...	...	...

INTERIM DIVIDENDS (Per Share):

Amt.	Decl.	Ex.	Rec.	Pay.
0.28Q	9/10/02	10/02/02	10/04/02	11/01/02
0.28Q	12/03/02	12/31/02	1/03/03	2/01/03
0.28Q	3/04/03	4/02/03	4/04/03	5/01/03
0.28Q	6/10/03	7/01/03	7/03/03	8/01/03

Indicated div.: $1.12 (Div. Reinv. Plan)

CAPITALIZATION (12/31/02):

	($000)	(%)
Long-Term Debt	6,248,000	41.0
Capital Lease Obligations..	13,000	0.1
Common & Surplus	8,967,000	58.9
Total	15,228,000	100.0

DIVIDEND ACHIEVER STATUS:
Rank: 236   10-Year Growth Rate: 4.96%
Total Years of Dividend Growth: 30

RECENT DEVELOPMENTS: For the three months ended 3/31/03, net income was $761.0 million compared with income of $842.0 million, before a gain of $14.0 million from discontinued operations, in the corresponding quarter of the previous year. Results for 2003 included a pre-tax provision for restructuring and other items of $12.0 million and pre-tax litigation settlement income of $21.0 million. Net sales rose 1.1% to $4.71 billion from $4.66 billion in the year-earlier period.

PROSPECTS: The Company announced that it has signed a purchase agreement with OPR Development, L.P. to acquire CAFCIT® Injection and Oral Suspension, the only drug approved by the U.S. FDA for the short-term treatment of apnea of prematurity in infants between 28 and 33 weeks gestational age. Separately, BMY announced that the U.S. FDA has approved the GLUCOPHAGE® XR 750 mg tablet, a new dosage strength for the treatment of type 2 diabetes.

BUSINESS

BRISTOL-MYERS SQUIBB COMPANY, through its divisions and subsidiaries, is a major producer and distributor of medicines. Major products include PRAVACHOL® (12.5% of 2002 sales), a cholesterol-lowering agent; PLAVIX® (10.4%), a platelet aggregation inhibitor; and GLUCOPHAGE® (1.6%), an oral medication for treatment of non-insulin dependent (type 2) diabetes. The Company also produces and distributes infant formulas, ostomy products and wound care products. In August 2001, BMY completed the tax-free spin-off of its Zimmer business. On 11/15/01, the Company sold its Clairol beauty care subsidiary for $4.95 billion.

ANNUAL FINANCIAL DATA

	12/31/02	12/31/01	12/31/00	12/31/99	12/31/98	12/31/97	12/31/96
Earnings Per Share	5️⃣ 1.05	4️⃣ 1.29	3️⃣ 2.05	2.06	2️⃣ 1.55	1️⃣ 1.57	1.42
Cash Flow Per Share	1.43	1.68	2.42	2.39	1.85	1.86	1.68
Tang. Book Val. Per Share	1.12	1.70	3.96	3.61	3.01	2.82	2.53
Dividends Per Share	1.12	1.10	0.98	0.86	0.78	0.76	0.75
Dividend Payout %	106.7	85.3	47.8	41.7	50.3	48.4	52.8
INCOME STATEMENT (IN MILLIONS):							
Total Revenues	18,119.0	19,423.0	18,216.0	20,222.0	18,284.0	16,701.0	15,065.0
Costs & Expenses	14,310.0	15,914.0	11,992.0	13,691.0	12,337.0	11,897.0	10,593.0
Depreciation & Amort.	735.0	781.0	746.0	678.0	625.0	591.0	519.0
Operating Income	3,074.0	2,728.0	5,478.0	5,853.0	5,322.0	4,213.0	3,953.0
Net Interest Inc./(Exp.)	d410.0	...	...	...	d67.0	d12.0	17.0
Income Before Income Taxes	2,647.0	2,986.0	5,478.0	5,767.0	4,268.0	4,482.0	4,013.0
Income Taxes	435.0	459.0	1,382.0	1,600.0	1,127.0	1,277.0	1,163.0
Net Income	5️⃣ 2,034.0	3️⃣ 4,096.0	4,167.0	2️⃣ 3,141.0	1️⃣ 3,205.0	2,850.0	
Cash Flow	2,769.0	3,308.0	4,842.0	4,845.0	3,766.0	3,796.0	3,369.0
Average Shs. Outstg. (000)	1,942,000	1,965,000	1,997,000	2,027,000	2,031,000	2,042,000	2,008,000
BALANCE SHEET (IN MILLIONS):							
Cash & Cash Equivalents	3,989.0	5,654.0	3,385.0	2,957.0	2,529.0	1,794.0	2,185.0
Total Current Assets	9,975.0	12,349.0	9,824.0	9,267.0	8,782.0	7,736.0	7,528.0
Net Property	5,321.0	4,879.0	4,548.0	4,621.0	4,429.0	4,156.0	3,964.0
Total Assets	24,874.0	27,057.0	17,578.0	17,114.0	16,272.0	14,977.0	14,685.0
Total Current Liabilities	8,220.0	8,826.0	5,632.0	5,537.0	5,791.0	5,032.0	5,050.0
Long-Term Obligations	6,261.0	6,237.0	1,336.0	1,342.0	1,364.0	1,279.0	966.0
Net Stockholders' Equity	8,967.0	10,736.0	9,180.0	8,645.0	7,576.0	7,219.0	6,570.0
Net Working Capital	1,755.0	3,523.0	4,192.0	3,730.0	2,991.0	2,704.0	2,478.0
Year-end Shs. Outstg. (000)	1,963,829	1,935,621	1,953,535	1,980,806	1,988,000	1,986,000	2,002,000
STATISTICAL RECORD:							
Operating Profit Margin %	17.0	14.0	30.1	28.9	29.1	25.2	26.2
Net Profit Margin %	11.2	13.0	22.5	20.6	17.2	19.2	18.9
Return on Equity %	22.7	23.5	44.6	48.2	41.5	44.4	43.4
Return on Assets %	8.2	9.3	23.3	24.3	19.3	21.4	19.4
Debt/Total Assets %	25.2	23.1	7.6	7.8	8.4	8.5	6.6
Price Range	51.95-19.49	73.50-48.50	74.88-42.44	79.25-57.25	67.63-44.16	49.09-26.63	29.09-19.50
P/E Ratio	49.5-18.6	57.0-37.6	36.5-20.7	38.5-27.8	43.6-28.5	31.3-17.0	20.5-13.7
Average Yield %	3.1	1.8	1.7	1.3	1.4	2.0	3.1

Statistics are as originally reported. Adj. for 2-for-1 stk. split, 2/97 & 2/99. 1️⃣ Incl. pre-tax prov. of $225.0 mill. for restr. & $225.0 mill. gain on sale of a bus. 2️⃣ Incl. spec. chg. of $800.0 mill. 3️⃣ Bef. gain fr. disc. ops. of $615.0 mill.; incl. a pre-tax chrgs. of $226.0 mill. 4️⃣ Bef. gain fr. disc. ops. of $2.72 bill.; incl. net pre-tax chrgs. of $3.13 bill. 5️⃣ Bef. a gain of $2.72 bill. & incl. pre-tax non-recurr. chrgs. of $3.41 bill.

OFFICERS:
P. R. Dolan, Chmn., C.E.O.
R. J. Lane, Sr. V.P., C.F.O.

INVESTOR CONTACT: Timothy Costs, Investor Relations, (212) 546-4103

PRINCIPAL OFFICE: 345 Park Avenue, New York, NY 10154-0037

TELEPHONE NUMBER: (212) 546-4000
FAX: (212) 546-4020
WEB: www.bms.com

NO. OF EMPLOYEES: 44,000 (approx.)

SHAREHOLDERS: 101,954 (approx.)

ANNUAL MEETING: In May

INCORPORATED: DE, Aug., 1933

INSTITUTIONAL HOLDINGS:
No. of Institutions: 1,060
Shares Held: 1,246,438,820
% Held: 64.3

INDUSTRY: Pharmaceutical preparations (SIC: 2834)

TRANSFER AGENT(S): Mellon Investor Services, Ridgefield Park, NJ

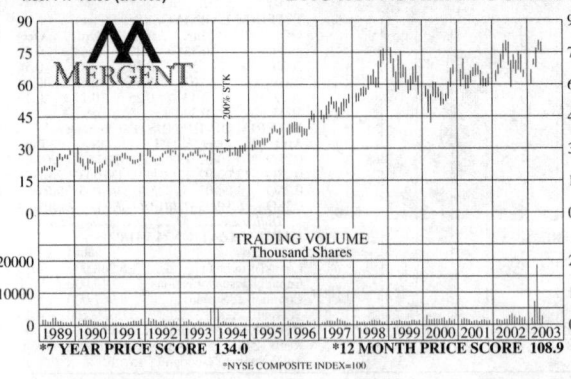

NYSE SYMBOL BFB
Rec. Pr. 78.86 (5/31/03)

BROWN-FORMAN CORPORATION

YIELD 1.9%
P/E RATIO 21.7

INTERIM EARNINGS (Per Share):

Qtr.	July	Oct.	Jan.	Apr.
1998-99	0.54	0.97	0.72	0.70
1999-00	0.56	1.06	0.80	0.76
2000-01	0.62	1.17	0.80	0.79
2001-02	0.57	1.17	0.84	0.75
2002-03	0.53	1.18	1.02	0.90

INTERIM DIVIDENDS (Per Share):

Amt.	Decl.	Ex.	Rec.	Pay.
0.35Q	5/23/02	6/04/02	6/06/02	7/01/02
0.35Q	7/25/02	8/30/02	9/04/02	10/01/02
0.375Q	11/21/02	12/04/02	12/06/02	1/01/03
0.375Q	1/23/03	2/28/03	3/04/03	4/01/03
0.375Q	5/29/03	6/05/03	6/09/03	7/01/03

Indicated div.: $1.50 (Div. Reinv. Plan)

CAPITALIZATION (4/30/02):

	($000)	(%)
Long-Term Debt	40,000	2.8
Deferred Income Tax	58,000	4.1
Common & Surplus	1,311,000	93.0
Total	1,409,000	100.0

TRADING VOLUME
Thousand Shares

7 YEAR PRICE SCORE 134.0   *12 MONTH PRICE SCORE 108.9*
NYSE COMPOSITE INDEX=100

DIVIDEND ACHIEVER STATUS:
Rank: 227   10-Year Growth Rate: 5.58%
Total Years of Dividend Growth: 18

RECENT DEVELOPMENTS: For the year ended 4/30/03, net income improved 7.7% to $245.3 million from $227.8 million the year before, reflecting stonger demand for JACK DANIEL's and SOUTHERN COMFORT, increased profitability in the U.K. from a new distribution arrangement, and favorable currency translation, partially offset by significantly lower profits for the Company's wine brands. Net sales grew 6.9% to $2.38 billion from $2.22 billion.

PROSPECTS: BFB completed its Business Improvement Program, spending a total of $0.29 per share over the past two fiscal years. The series of initiatives were designed to streamline procurement and production practices. BFB anticipates that benefits will strengthen long-term cash flow and earnings for both the Beverages and Consumer Durables segments. Looking ahead, earnings per share for fiscal 2004 are expected to range from $4.10 to $4.30.

BUSINESS

BROWN-FORMAN CORPORA-TION, with assets as of 4/30/03 of $2.26 billion, operates in two business segments: wines and spirits and consumer durables. The wines and spirits segment includes the production, importing and marketing of wines and distilled spirits under brand names of JACK DANIEL's, SOUTHERN COMFORT, FINLANDIA Vodka, CANADIAN MIST, KORBEL CALIFORNIA champagnes, and FETZER and BOLLA wines. The Company's consumer durables segment includes tableware and flatware sold under the LENOX, GORHAM and DANSK brand names, as well as HARTMANN luggage. In fiscal 2002, sales (operating income) were as follows: 73.4% (95.2%), wine and spirits; 26.6% (4.8%) consumer durables.

ANNUAL FINANCIAL DATA

	p4/30/03	4/30/02	4/30/01	4/30/00	4/30/99	4/30/98	4/30/97
Earnings Per Share	3.63	3.33	3.40	3.18	2.93	2.67	2.45
Cash Flow Per Share	...	4.13	4.33	4.08	3.74	3.42	3.17
Tang. Book Val. Per Share	...	15.58	13.50	11.36	9.53	8.04	6.73
Dividends Per Share	1.40	1.32	1.24	1.18	1.12	1.08	1.04
Dividend Payout %	38.6	39.6	36.5	37.1	38.2	40.4	42.4
INCOME STATEMENT (IN MILLIONS):							
Total Revenues	2,378.1	2,208.0	2,180.0	2,134.0	2,030.0	1,924.0	1,841.0
Costs & Expenses	...	1,800.0	1,742.0	1,724.0	1,653.0	1,566.0	1,504.0
Depreciation & Amort.	...	55.0	64.0	62.0	55.0	51.0	50.0
Operating Income	378.4	353.0	374.0	348.0	322.0	307.0	287.0
Net Interest Inc./(Exp.)	...	d5.0	d8.0	d5.0	d4.0	d11.0	d14.0
Income Before Income Taxes	...	348.0	366.0	343.0	318.0	296.0	273.0
Income Taxes	...	120.0	133.0	125.0	116.0	111.0	104.0
Net Income	245.3	228.0	233.0	218.0	202.0	185.0	169.0
Cash Flow	...	283.0	297.0	280.0	257.0	235.0	218.0
Average Shs. Outstg. (000)	...	68,500	68,600	68,600	68,700	69,000	69,014
BALANCE SHEET (IN MILLIONS):							
Cash & Cash Equivalents	...	116.0	86.0	180.0	171.0	78.0	58.0
Total Current Assets	...	1,029.0	994.0	1,020.0	999.0	869.0	802.0
Net Property	506.0	437.0	424.0	376.0	348.0	281.0	292.0
Total Assets	2,263.6	2,016.0	1,939.0	1,802.0	1,735.0	1,494.0	1,428.0
Total Current Liabilities	...	495.0	538.0	522.0	517.0	382.0	399.0
Long-Term Obligations	...	40.0	40.0	41.0	53.0	50.0	63.0
Net Stockholders' Equity	840.1	1,311.0	1,187.0	1,048.0	917.0	817.0	730.0
Net Working Capital	...	534.0	456.0	498.0	482.0	487.0	403.0
Year-end Shs. Outstg. (000)	...	68,348	68,459	68,512	68,506	68,996	68,996
STATISTICAL RECORD:							
Operating Profit Margin %	15.9	16.0	17.2	16.3	15.9	16.0	15.6
Net Profit Margin %	10.3	10.3	10.7	10.2	10.0	9.6	9.2
Return on Equity %	29.2	17.4	19.6	20.8	22.0	22.6	23.2
Return on Assets %	10.8	11.3	12.0	12.1	11.6	12.4	11.8
Debt/Total Assets %	...	2.0	2.1	2.3	3.1	3.3	4.4
Price Range	80.54-58.69	72.00-57.65	69.25-41.88	77.25-54.94	76.88-51.75	55.38-42.00	47.50-35.25
P/E Ratio	22.2-16.2	21.6-17.3	20.4-12.3	24.3-17.3	26.2-17.7	20.7-15.7	19.4-14.4
Average Yield %	2.0	2.0	2.2	1.8	1.7	2.2	2.5

Statistics are as originally reported.

OFFICERS:
O. Brown II, Chmn., C.E.O.
W. M. Street, Pres.
P. A. Wood, Exec. V.P., C.F.O.

INVESTOR CONTACT: Phil Lynch, V.P. & Dir. of Corp. Comm., (502) 774-7928

PRINCIPAL OFFICE: 850 Dixie Highway, Louisville, KY 40210

TELEPHONE NUMBER: (502) 585-1100
FAX: (502) 774-7876
WEB: www.brown-forman.com
NO. OF EMPLOYEES: 5,400 full-time (approx.); 1,600 part-time (approx.)
SHAREHOLDERS: 3,734 (class A common); 4,453 (class B common)
ANNUAL MEETING: In July
INCORPORATED: KY, 1901; reincorp., DE, 1933

INSTITUTIONAL HOLDINGS:
No. of Institutions: 194
Shares Held: 28,794,322
% Held: 42.3

INDUSTRY: Wines, brandy, and brandy spirits (SIC: 2084)

TRANSFER AGENT(S): National City Bank, Cleveland, OH

CALIFORNIA WATER SERVICE GROUP

YIELD 4.0%
P/E RATIO 26.4

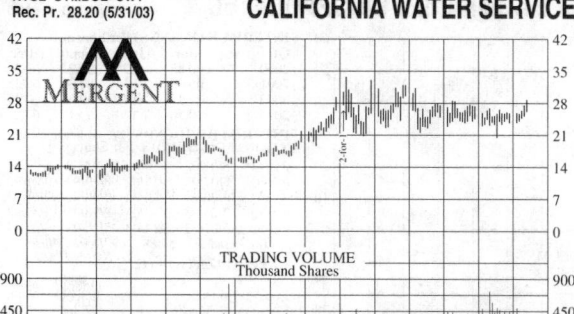

*7 YEAR PRICE SCORE 115.0 ***12 MONTH PRICE SCORE 105.8**
*NYSE COMPOSITE INDEX=100

INTERIM EARNINGS (Per Share):

Qtr.	Mar.	June	Sept.	Dec.
2000	0.09	0.38	0.60	0.23
2001	0.01	0.37	0.39	0.20
2002	0.12	0.43	0.50	0.19
2003	d0.05	...	...	...

INTERIM DIVIDENDS (Per Share):

Amt.	Decl.	Ex.	Rec.	Pay.
0.28Q	7/24/02	8/01/02	8/05/02	8/19/02
0.28Q	10/23/02	10/31/02	11/04/02	11/18/02
0.281Q	1/29/03	2/05/03	2/07/03	2/21/03
0.281Q	4/23/03	4/30/03	5/02/03	5/16/03

Indicated div.: $1.13 (Div. Reinv. Plan)

CAPITALIZATION (12/31/02):

	($000)	(%)
Long-Term Debt	165,665	41.4
Deferred Income Tax	31,371	7.8
Preferred Stock	3,475	0.9
Common & Surplus	199,217	49.8
Total	399,728	100.0

DIVIDEND ACHIEVER STATUS:
Rank: 275   10-Year Growth Rate: 1.88%
Total Years of Dividend Growth: 35

RECENT DEVELOPMENTS: For the quarter ended 3/31/03, the Company reported a net loss of $768,000 compared with net income of $1.9 million in the equivalent 2002 quarter. The decline in earnings was primarily attributed to lower customer usage due to unfavorable weather conditions and delays in receiving rate relief from the California Public Utilities Commission (CPUC). Operating revenue slid 0.6% to $51.3 million, reflecting a decrease in water sales to existing customers, partially offset by rate increases and elevated sales to new customers.

PROSPECTS: With regard to the second of three filings related to the Bakersfield Treatment Plant, CWT received authorization in April 2003 to recover costs incurred for construction of that plant. The two filings will add an estimated $1.5 million to 2003 revenues. Meanwhile, in May 2003, the Company was authorized to recover $5.4 million in higher costs, primarily due to increases in power rates, incurred in eight of its operating districts prior to 11/29/01. The $5.4 million will be recovered over the next 12 to 24 months through surcharges on ratepayer bills.

BUSINESS

CALIFORNIA WATER SERVICE GROUP is a public utility water company that provides regulated and non-regulated water utility services to more than 2.0 million customers in 98 communities in California, Washington and New Mexico as of 4/23/03. CWT is the parent company of California Water Service Company, Washington Water Service Company, New Mexico Water Service Company and CWS Utility Services. The sole business of the Company consists of the production, purchase, storage, purification, distribution and sale of water for domestic, industrial, public, and irrigation uses, and for fire protection. Annual water production totaled nearly 132.00 billion gallons for 2002.

ANNUAL FINANCIAL DATA

	12/31/02	12/31/01	12/31/00	12/31/99	12/31/98	12/31/97	12/31/96
Earnings Per Share	①1.25	0.97	1.31	1.53	1.45	1.83	1.51
Cash Flow Per Share	2.65	2.24	2.53	2.76	2.61	2.93	2.52
Tang. Book Val. Per Share	13.12	12.95	13.13	13.70	13.38	13.00	12.22
Dividends Per Share	1.12	1.11	1.10	1.08	1.07	1.05	1.04
Dividend Payout %	89.6	114.9	84.0	70.9	73.8	57.6	69.1

INCOME STATEMENT (IN THOUSANDS):

Total Revenues	263,151	246,820	244,806	206,440	186,273	195,324	182,764
Costs & Expenses	200,029	190,312	181,650	150,845	132,606	137,986	131,415
Depreciation & Amort.	21,238	19,226	18,368	15,802	14,563	13,670	12,665
Maintenance Exp.	11,587	12,131	11,592	9,183	9,030	9,319	8,317
Operating Income	30,297	25,151	33,196	30,610	30,074	34,349	30,367
Net Interest Inc./(Exp.)	d16,841	d16,029	d14,646	d13,201	d12,446	d11,922	d11,907
Net Income	①19,073	14,965	19,963	19,919	18,395	23,305	19,067
Cash Flow	40,158	34,038	38,179	35,568	32,805	36,822	31,579
Average Shs. Outstg.	15,185	15,285	15,173	12,936	12,619	12,619	12,580

BALANCE SHEET (IN THOUSANDS):

Gross Property	1,001,310	909,658	851,281	737,352	680,690	647,648	618,432
Accumulated Depreciation	304,322	285,316	269,273	221,998	202,385	187,241	174,844
Net Property	696,988	624,342	582,008	515,354	478,305	460,407	443,588
Total Assets	715,882	710,214	666,605	587,618	548,499	531,297	512,390
Long-Term Obligations	165,665	202,600	187,098	156,572	136,345	139,205	142,153
Net Stockholders' Equity	202,692	200,094	202,309	180,657	172,279	167,540	157,701
Year-end Shs. Outstg.	15,182	15,182	15,146	12,936	12,619	12,619	12,620

STATISTICAL RECORD:

Operating Profit Margin %	11.5	10.2	13.6	14.8	16.1	17.6	16.6
Net Profit Margin %	7.2	6.1	8.2	9.6	9.9	11.9	10.4
Net Inc./Net Property %	2.7	2.4	3.4	3.9	3.8	5.1	4.3
Net Inc./Tot. Capital %	4.8	3.5	4.8	5.6	5.5	7.0	5.9
Return on Equity %	9.4	7.5	9.9	11.0	10.7	13.9	12.1
Accum. Depr./Gross Prop. %	30.4	31.4	31.6	30.1	29.7	28.9	28.3
Price Range	26.89-20.45	28.60-22.88	31.38-21.50	32.00-22.56	33.75-20.75	29.38-18.63	21.88-16.25
P/E Ratio	21.5-16.4	29.5-23.6	23.9-16.4	20.9-14.7	23.3-14.3	16.1-10.2	14.5-10.8
Average Yield %	4.7	4.3	4.2	4.0	3.9	4.4	5.5

Statistics are as originally reported. Adj. for stk. split: 2-for-1, 1/98 ① Incl. gain of $3.0 mill. on sale of non-utility property.

OFFICERS:
R. W. Foy, Chmn.
P. C. Nelson, Pres., C.E.O.
G. F. Feeney, V.P., C.F.O., Treas.
INVESTOR CONTACT: Richard Nye, (408) 367-8216
PRINCIPAL OFFICE: 1720 North First Street, San Jose, CA 95112

TELEPHONE NUMBER: (408) 367-8200
FAX: (408) 437-9185
WEB: www.calwater.com
NO. OF EMPLOYEES: 802 (avg.)
SHAREHOLDERS: 11,000 (approx.)
ANNUAL MEETING: In Apr.
INCORPORATED: CA, Dec., 1926

CARLISLE COMPANIES INCORPORATED

YIELD 1.9%
P/E RATIO 18.0

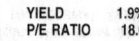
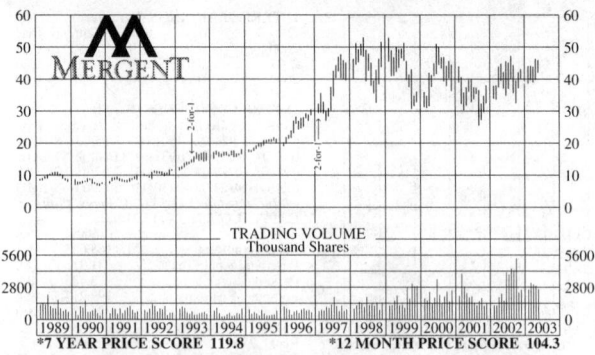

TRADING VOLUME
Thousand Shares

*7 YEAR PRICE SCORE 119.8   *12 MONTH PRICE SCORE 104.3
*NYSE COMPOSITE INDEX=100

INTERIM EARNINGS (Per Share):

Qtr.	Mar.	June	Sept.	Dec.
2000	0.83	1.04	0.92	0.35
2001	d0.33	0.54	0.36	0.25
2002	0.42	0.81	0.65	0.49
2003	0.56	...	...	...

INTERIM DIVIDENDS (Per Share):

Amt.	Decl.	Ex.	Rec.	Pay.
0.21Q	5/01/02	5/15/02	5/17/02	6/01/02
0.215Q	8/07/02	8/15/02	8/19/02	9/01/02
0.215Q	11/06/02	11/14/02	11/18/02	12/01/02
0.215Q	2/05/03	2/13/03	2/18/03	3/01/03
0.215Q	5/01/03	5/14/03	5/16/03	6/01/03

Indicated div.: $0.86 (Div. Reinv. Plan)

CAPITALIZATION (12/31/02):

	($000)	(%)
Long-Term Debt	293,124	34.6
Common & Surplus	553,077	65.4
Total	846,201	100.0

DIVIDEND ACHIEVER STATUS:
Rank: 147   10-Year Growth Rate: 9.92%
Total Years of Dividend Growth: 26

RECENT DEVELOPMENTS: For the quarter ended 3/31/03, CSL reported net income of $17.1 million versus income of $12.8 million, before an accounting charge of $43.8 million, in 2002. Net sales increased 4.5% to $475.5 million. Industrial component sales rose 4.3% to $165.3 million, while construction material sales jumped 15.9% to $98.4 million, primarily due to acquisitions in 2002. Specialty product sales grew 3.6% to $31.6 million, and transportation product sales inched up 1.8% to $28.1 million.

PROSPECTS: On 6/2/03, the Company announced the acquisition of Flo-Pac Corporation, a manufacturer of brooms, brushes, rotary brushes and cleaning tools for the sanitary maintenance industry. Terms of the deal were not disclosed. Meanwhile, new products and cost-reduction efforts are expected to support sales and earnings growth in 2003. For 2003, the Company expects earnings to range from $2.60 to $2.80 per share.

BUSINESS

CARLISLE COMPANIES INCORPORATED produces and sells a diverse line of products in six industry segments. The Industrial Components segment (31.5% of 2002 revenue) manufactures and distributes tire and wheel assemblies and high-performance wire/cable and cable assemblies. The Construction Materials segment (24.8%) manufactures membranes and accessories for rubber and plastic roofing systems for non-residential flat roofs. The General Industry segment (20.3%) consists of several businesses with products, including stainless steel in-plant processing equipment, food service products and cheese making systems. The Automotive Components segment (12.0%) manufactures highly engineered plastic and rubber components for the automotive industry. The Transportation Products segment (6.1%) produces specialty and high-payload trailers and dump bodies. The Specialty Products segment (5.3%) manufactures heavy-duty friction and braking systems for trucks and off-highway equipment.

ANNUAL FINANCIAL DATA

	12/31/02	12/31/01	12/31/00	12/31/99	12/31/98	12/31/97	12/31/96
Earnings Per Share	③ 2.37	② 0.82	3.14	① 3.13	2.77	2.28	1.80
Cash Flow Per Share	4.23	2.92	5.09	4.67	4.24	3.53	2.76
Tang. Book Val. Per Share	8.09	6.72	9.79	10.63	8.85	7.48	6.55
Dividends Per Share	0.85	0.82	0.76	0.68	0.60	0.53	0.47
Dividend Payout %	35.9	100.0	24.2	21.7	21.7	23.0	25.8

INCOME STATEMENT (IN MILLIONS):

Total Revenues	1,971.3	1,849.5	1,771.1	1,611.3	1,517.5	1,260.6	1,017.5
Costs & Expenses	1,786.5	1,720.9	1,536.1	1,396.0	1,320.7	1,094.4	890.6
Depreciation & Amort.	57.0	64.0	59.5	47.4	45.2	38.8	29.8
Operating Income	127.7	64.6	175.4	167.9	151.6	127.4	97.1
Net Interest Inc./(Exp.)	d17.2	d29.1	d28.0	d19.2	d22.7	d16.5	d9.1
Income Before Income Taxes	110.5	37.9	150.9	155.5	140.3	116.8	92.0
Income Taxes	38.1	13.1	54.7	59.7	55.4	46.1	36.4
Net Income	③ 72.4	② 24.8	96.2	① 95.8	84.9	70.7	55.7
Cash Flow	129.4	88.8	155.7	143.2	130.1	109.4	85.4
Average Shs. Outstg. (000)	30,583	30,450	30,599	30,635	30,674	31,025	30,953

BALANCE SHEET (IN MILLIONS):

Cash & Cash Equivalents	23.0	15.6	9.0	10.4	3.9	1.7	8.3
Total Current Assets	481.5	553.3	576.5	541.0	478.5	417.5	345.9
Net Property	448.0	447.7	402.6	349.5	354.8	294.2	264.2
Total Assets	1,315.9	1,398.0	1,305.7	1,080.7	1,022.9	861.2	866.8
Total Current Liabilities	324.3	273.8	399.9	240.4	255.3	226.1	170.6
Long-Term Obligations	293.1	461.7	281.9	281.7	273.5	209.6	191.2
Net Stockholders' Equity	553.1	540.3	547.9	478.1	406.9	348.8	307.5
Net Working Capital	157.2	279.5	176.5	300.7	223.2	191.4	175.3
Year-end Shs. Outstg. (000)	30,598	30,263	30,251	30,128	30,179	30,351	30,351

STATISTICAL RECORD:

Operating Profit Margin %	6.5	3.5	9.9	10.4	10.0	10.1	9.5
Net Profit Margin %	3.7	1.3	5.4	5.9	5.6	5.6	5.5
Return on Equity %	13.1	4.6	17.6	20.0	20.9	20.3	18.1
Return on Assets %	5.5	1.8	7.4	8.9	8.3	8.2	6.4
Debt/Total Assets %	22.3	33.0	21.6	26.1	26.7	24.3	25.7
Price Range	47.23-32.36	44.00-25.50	51.00-30.94	52.94-30.63	53.06-32.56	47.75-27.00	30.50-19.00
P/E Ratio	19.9-13.7	53.7-31.1	16.2-9.9	16.9-9.8	19.2-11.8	20.9-11.8	16.9-10.6
Average Yield %	2.1	2.4	1.9	1.6	1.4	1.4	1.9

Statistics are as originally reported. Adj. for stk. split: 2-for-1, 1/97 ① Incl. non-recurr. gain of $685,000. ② Incl. after-tax restructuring chrg. of $21.5 mill. ③ Bef. acctg. change chrg. of $43.8 mill.

OFFICERS:
S. P. Munn, Chmn.
R. D. McKinnish, Pres., C.E.O.
K. F. Vincent, V.P., C.F.O.

INVESTOR CONTACT: Kirk F. Vincent, V.P., C.F.O., (704) 501-1100

PRINCIPAL OFFICE: 13925 Ballantyne Corporate Place, Suite 400, Charlotte, NC 28277

TELEPHONE NUMBER: (704) 501-1100
FAX: (704) 501-1190
WEB: www.carlisle.com

NO. OF EMPLOYEES: 11,631 (avg.)

SHAREHOLDERS: 2,170 (record)

ANNUAL MEETING: In April

INCORPORATED: DE, Sept., 1917; reincorp., DE, May, 1986

INSTITUTIONAL HOLDINGS:
No. of Institutions: 158
Shares Held: 18,809,006
% Held: 60.7

INDUSTRY: Tires and inner tubes (SIC: 3011)

TRANSFER AGENT(S): Computershare Investor Services, Chicago, IL

CEDAR FAIR, L.P.

YIELD	6.4%
P/E RATIO	17.9

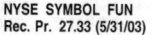

TRADING VOLUME
Thousand Shares

| 1989 | 1990 | 1991 | 1992 | 1993 | 1994 | 1995 | 1996 | 1997 | 1998 | 1999 | 2000 | 2001 | 2002 | 2003 |

*7 YEAR PRICE SCORE 121.1   ***12 MONTH PRICE SCORE 109.2**

*NYSE COMPOSITE INDEX=100

INTERIM EARNINGS (Per Share):

Qtr.	Mar.	June	Sept.	Dec.
1999	d0.41	0.37	1.83	d0.15
2000	d0.51	0.36	1.83	d0.17
2001	d0.60	0.13	2.10	d0.50
2002	d0.63	0.40	2.01	d0.26
2003	d0.62	...	...	...

INTERIM DIVIDENDS (Per Share):

Amt.	Decl.	Ex.	Rec.	Pay.
0.41Q	3/11/02	4/01/02	4/03/02	5/15/02
0.41Q	6/17/02	7/01/02	7/03/02	8/15/02
0.42Q	9/26/02	10/01/02	10/03/02	11/15/02
0.42Q	12/19/02	1/02/03	1/06/03	2/14/03
0.44Q	3/10/03	4/01/03	4/03/03	5/15/03

Indicated div.: 1.76 (Div. Reinv. Plan)

CAPITALIZATION (12/31/02):

	($000)	(%)
Long-Term Debt	365,150	54.5
Common & Surplus	305,320	45.5
Total	670,470	100.0

DIVIDEND ACHIEVER STATUS:
Rank: 200   10-Year Growth Rate: 7.10%
Total Years of Dividend Growth: 15

RECENT DEVELOPMENTS: For the quarter ended 3/30/03, the Company reported a loss of $31.5 million compared with a net loss of $34.0 million in the equivalent 2002 quarter. The decline in earnings was primarily attributed to lower early-season attendance at Knott's Berry Farm versus last year's first quarter. Results for 2002 included a provision for losses on the retirement of assets of $3.2 million. Net revenues declined 10.2% to $21.5 million.

PROSPECTS: The Company remains optimistic that it can generate 3.0% to 5.0% of internal growth in net revenues this season and improve its adjusted earnings before interest, taxes, depreciation and amortization due to the level of public interest in FUN's new rides and attractions. Attractions being added for the 2003 season include family-oriented water attractions at both Dorney Park and Worlds of Fun, which are on budget and on schedule.

BUSINESS

CEDAR FAIR, L.P. is a limited partnership managed by Cedar Fair Management Company. The partnership owns and operates six amusement parks: Cedar Point, located on Lake Erie in Sandusky, OH; Knott's Berry Farm, located in Buena Park, CA; Dorney Park & Wildwater Kingdom, near Allentown, PA; Valleyfair, located near Minneapolis, MN; Worlds of Fun, located in Kansas City, MO; and Michigan's Adventure, located near Muskegon, MI. The partnership's five water parks are located near San Diego and Palm Springs, CA, and adjacent to Cedar Point, Knott's Berry Farm and Worlds of Fun. All principal rides and attractions are owned and operated by the partnership. FUN owns and operates four hotel facilities. FUN also operates Knott's Camp Snoopy at the Mall of America in Bloomington, MN under a management contract.

ANNUAL FINANCIAL DATA

	12/31/02	12/31/01	12/31/00	12/31/99	12/31/98	12/31/97	12/31/96
Earnings Per Share	② ③ 1.39	② 1.13	① 1.50	1.63	1.58	1.47	1.59
Cash Flow Per Share	2.21	1.96	2.27	2.31	2.20	1.95	2.02
Tang. Book Val. Per Share	5.81	5.88	6.31	6.56	6.38	5.24	3.47
Dividends Per Share	1.65	1.58	1.50	1.39	1.28	1.26	1.18
Dividend Payout %	118.7	139.8	100.2	85.1	81.3	85.5	73.9
INCOME STATEMENT (IN THOUSANDS):							
Total Revenues	502,851	477,256	472,920	438,001	419,500	264,137	250,523
Costs & Expenses	339,977	336,213	317,832	286,194	274,827	166,306	150,330
Depreciation & Amort.	41,682	42,486	39,572	35,082	32,065	21,528	19,072
Operating Income	121,192	98,557	115,516	116,725	112,608	76,303	81,121
Net Interest Inc./(Exp.)	d24,967	d24,143	d21,357	d15,371	d14,660	d7,845	d6,942
Income Before Income Taxes	88,576	74,414	94,159	101,354	97,948	68,458	74,179
Income Taxes	17,159	16,520	16,353	15,580	14,507	...	...
Net Income	② ③ 71,417	② 57,894	① 77,806	85,774	83,441	68,458	74,179
Cash Flow	113,099	100,380	117,378	120,856	115,506	89,986	93,251
Average Shs. Outstg.	51,263	51,113	51,679	52,390	52,414	46,265	46,116
BALANCE SHEET (IN THOUSANDS):							
Cash & Cash Equivalents	2,171	2,280	2,392	638	1,137	2,520	1,279
Total Current Assets	29,237	26,868	25,378	24,184	20,967	21,954	11,730
Net Property	781,502	771,918	728,919	674,640	600,044	567,137	281,638
Total Assets	822,257	810,231	764,143	708,961	631,325	599,619	304,104
Total Current Liabilities	106,338	96,700	114,024	86,559	77,231	62,426	39,241
Long-Term Obligations	365,150	373,000	300,000	261,200	200,350	189,750	87,600
Net Stockholders' Equity	305,320	308,250	330,589	349,986	341,991	285,381	169,994
Net Working Capital	d77,101	d69,832	d88,646	d62,375	d56,264	d40,472	d27,511
Year-end Shs. Outstg.	50,549	50,514	50,813	51,798	51,980	52,403	45,920
STATISTICAL RECORD:							
Operating Profit Margin %	24.1	20.7	24.4	26.7	26.8	28.9	32.4
Net Profit Margin %	14.2	14.1	16.5	19.6	19.9	25.9	29.6
Return on Equity %	23.4	18.8	23.5	24.5	24.4	24.0	43.6
Return on Assets %	8.7	7.1	10.2	12.1	13.2	11.4	24.4
Debt/Total Assets %	44.4	46.0	39.3	36.8	31.7	31.6	28.8
Price Range	24.80-19.59	25.00-17.80	20.88-17.44	26.00-18.44	30.13-21.75	28.25-17.69	19.50-16.13
P/E Ratio	17.8-14.1	22.1-15.8	13.9-11.6	15.9-11.3	19.1-13.8	19.2-12.0	12.3-10.1
Average Yield %	7.4	7.4	7.8	6.2	5.0	5.5	6.6

Statistics are as originally reported. Adj. for stk. split: 2-for-1, 11/7/97. ① Incl. nonrecurr. chrg. of $7.8 mill. to terminate general partner fees. ② Incl. non-cash unit option exp. of $4.0 mill., 2002; $11.7 mill., 2001. ③ Incl. prov. for losses on retirement of assets of $3.2 mill.

OFFICERS:
R. L. Kinzel, Pres., C.E.O.
B. A. Jackson, V.P., C.F.O.
T. W. Salamone, Treas.

INVESTOR CONTACT: Brian C. Witherow, Corporate Director - Investor Relations, (419) 627-2233

PRINCIPAL OFFICE: One Cedar Point Drive, Sandusky, OH 44870-5259

TELEPHONE NUMBER: (419) 626-0830
FAX: (419) 627-2234
WEB: www.cedarfair.com

NO. OF EMPLOYEES: 1,400 (approx.)

SHAREHOLDERS: 10,000 (approx.).

ANNUAL MEETING: N/A

INCORPORATED: MN, 1983; reincorp., 1987

INSTITUTIONAL HOLDINGS:
No. of Institutions: 109
Shares Held: 9,494,195
% Held: 18.6

INDUSTRY: Amusement parks (SIC: 7996)

TRANSFER AGENT(S): American Stock Transfer & Trust Company, New York, NY

CENTURYTEL, INC.

YIELD 0.7%
P/E RATIO 20.9

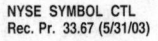

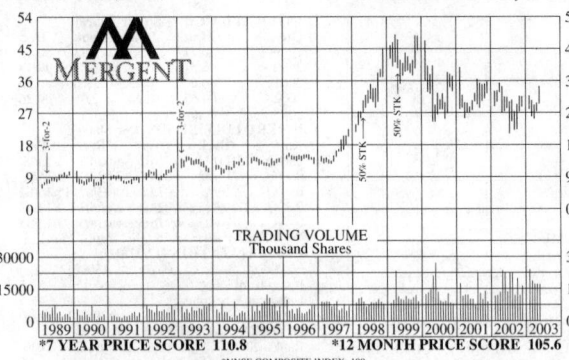

| 1989 | 1990 | 1991 | 1992 | 1993 | 1994 | 1995 | 1996 | 1997 | 1998 | 1999 | 2000 | 2001 | 2002 | 2003 |

TRADING VOLUME
Thousand Shares

*7 YEAR PRICE SCORE 110.8   ***12 MONTH PRICE SCORE 105.6**
*NYSE COMPOSITE INDEX=100

INTERIM EARNINGS (Per Share):

Qtr.	Mar.	June	Sept.	Dec.
1999	0.43	0.38	0.46	0.43
2000	0.35	0.41	0.47	0.40
2001	0.33	1.09	0.65	0.35
2002	0.30	0.28	0.45	0.30
2003	0.58	...	...	...

INTERIM DIVIDENDS (Per Share):

Amt.	Decl.	Ex.	Rec.	Pay.
0.052Q	8/27/02	9/05/02	9/09/02	9/20/02
0.052Q	11/21/02	11/27/02	12/02/02	12/13/02
0.055Q	2/25/03	3/06/03	3/10/03	3/21/03
0.055Q	5/29/03	6/05/03	6/09/03	6/20/03
Indicated div.: $0.22 (Div. Reinv. Plan)				

CAPITALIZATION (12/31/02):

	($000)	(%)
Long-Term Debt	3,578,132	53.7
Preferred Stock	7,975	0.1
Common & Surplus	3,080,029	46.2
Total	6,666,136	100.0

DIVIDEND ACHIEVER STATUS:
Rank: 237   10-Year Growth Rate: 4.91%
Total Years of Dividend Growth: 29

RECENT DEVELOPMENTS: For the quarter ended 3/31/03, net income was $83.9 million compared with income from continuing operations of $43.1 million in the corresponding year-earlier period. Earnings for 2003 included a nonrecurring gain of $5.0 million from the partial recovery of amounts previously written off in connection with the WorldCom bankruptcy. Earnings for 2002 included a nonrecurring charge of $3.0 million. Total revenues increased 37.3% to $580.5 million.

PROSPECTS: CTL has raised its full-year 2003 earnings guidance to between $2.14 and $2.22 per diluted share, up from its previous estimate of between $2.05 and $2.15 per share. CTL attributed the increase to higher revenues, successful cost and resource management and lower depreciation expenses from its acquired properties than previously anticipated. Meanwhile, CTL is posting solid revenue gains outside its local exchange telephone services business.

BUSINESS

CENTURYTEL, INC. (formerly Century Telephone Enterprises, Inc.) is a regional telecommunications company that is primarily engaged in providing local exchange telephone services. CTL also provides long distance, Internet access, competitive local exchange carrier, fiber network, security monitoring, and other communications and business information services in certain local and regional markets. As of 12/31/02, CTL's local exchange telephone subsidiaries operated about 2.4 million telephone access lines, primarily in rural, suburban and small urban areas in 22 states, with the largest customer bases located in Wisconsin, Missouri, Alabama, Arkansas, Washington, Michigan, Louisiana, Colorado, Ohio and Oregon. On 8/1/02, CTL sold its wireless business to ALLTEL for $1.57 billion. On 7/1/02 and 8/31/02, CTL acquired a total of approximately 654,000 telephone access lines from Verizon for about $2.16 billion.

ANNUAL FINANCIAL DATA

	12/31/02	12/31/01	12/31/00	12/31/99	12/31/98	12/31/97	12/31/96
Earnings Per Share	⑤1.33	④2.41	③1.63	③1.70	①1.64	②1.87	②0.96
Cash Flow Per Share	4.21	5.63	4.37	4.16	3.98	3.02	1.94
Tang. Book Val. Per Share	...	...	...	1.45	...	...	3.61
Dividends Per Share	0.21	0.20	0.19	0.18	0.17	0.165	0.16
Dividend Payout %	15.8	8.3	11.7	10.6	10.6	8.8	16.7
INCOME STATEMENT (IN MILLIONS):							
Total Revenues	1,972.0	2,117.5	1,845.9	1,676.7	1,577.1	901.5	749.7
Costs & Expenses	985.0	1,086.2	932.5	819.8	768.7	474.3	394.4
Depreciation & Amort.	411.6	473.4	388.1	348.8	328.6	159.5	132.0
Operating Income	575.4	557.9	525.4	508.1	479.8	267.8	223.3
Net Interest Inc./(Exp.)	d221.8	d225.5	d183.3	d150.6	d167.6	d56.5	d44.7
Income Before Income Taxes	293.5	553.1	386.2	429.3	387.5	408.3	203.6
Income Taxes	103.5	210.0	154.7	189.5	158.7	152.4	74.6
Net Income	⑤189.9	④343.0	③231.5	③239.8	①228.8	②256.0	②129.1
Cash Flow	601.1	816.0	619.1	588.2	556.9	415.0	260.7
Average Shs. Outstg. (000)	142,879	142,307	141,864	141,432	140,105	137,412	134,829
BALANCE SHEET (IN MILLIONS):							
Cash & Cash Equivalents	3.7	13.4	19.0	56.6	5.7	26.0	8.4
Total Current Assets	295.9	300.3	376.5	286.1	226.2	283.5	109.2
Net Property	3,531.6	2,999.6	2,959.3	2,256.5	2,351.5	2,258.4	1,149.0
Total Assets	7,770.4	6,318.7	6,393.3	4,705.4	4,935.5	5,187.1	2,258.8
Total Current Liabilities	388.1	1,294.0	743.4	309.2	304.8	322.1	144.1
Long-Term Obligations	3,578.1	2,087.5	3,050.5	2,078.3	2,558.0	2,609.5	625.9
Net Stockholders' Equity	3,088.0	2,337.4	2,032.1	1,848.0	1,531.5	1,300.3	1,028.2
Net Working Capital	d92.2	d993.7	d366.9	d23.1	d78.6	d38.6	d34.9
Year-end Shs. Outstg. (000)	142,956	141,233	140,667	139,946	138,083	136,656	134,683
STATISTICAL RECORD:							
Operating Profit Margin %	29.2	26.3	28.5	30.3	30.4	29.7	29.8
Net Profit Margin %	9.6	16.2	12.5	14.3	14.5	28.4	17.2
Return on Equity %	6.2	14.7	11.4	13.0	14.9	19.7	12.6
Return on Assets %	2.4	5.4	3.6	5.1	4.6	5.4	6.4
Debt/Total Assets %	46.0	33.0	47.7	44.2	51.8	55.4	30.9
Price Range	35.50-21.13	39.88-25.45	47.31-24.44	49.00-35.19	45.17-21.56	22.42-12.67	15.78-12.67
P/E Ratio	26.7-15.9	16.5-10.6	29.0-15.0	28.8-20.7	27.5-13.1	12.0-6.8	16.5-13.2
Average Yield %	0.7	0.6	0.5	0.4	0.5	0.9	1.1

Statistics are as originally reported. Adj. for 50% stk. div., 3/99 & 3/98. ① Incl. non-recurr. pre-tax credit of $49.9 mill. ② Incl. pre-tax credit 12/31/97: $169.9 mill.; credit 12/31/96, $815,000. ③ Incl. pre-tax gain on sales of assets of $20.6 mill., 2000; $62.8 mill., 1999. ④ Incl. pre-tax non-recurr. gain of $200.0 mill. ⑤ Incl. pre-tax non-recurr. gain of $3.7 mill.; bef. inc. fr. disc. ops. of $611.7 mill.

OFFICERS:
G. F. Post III, Chmn., C.E.O.
K. A. Puckett, Pres., C.O.O.
R. S. Ewing, Jr., Exec. V.P., C.F.O.

INVESTOR CONTACT: Tony Davis, Inv. Rel., (318) 388-9525

PRINCIPAL OFFICE: 100 CenturyTel Drive, Monroe, LA 71203

TELEPHONE NUMBER: (318) 388-9000
FAX: (318) 789-8656
WEB: www.centurytel.com

NO. OF EMPLOYEES: 6,960 (approx.)

SHAREHOLDERS: 4,890 (approx.)

ANNUAL MEETING: In May

INCORPORATED: LA, Apr., 1968

INSTITUTIONAL HOLDINGS:
No. of Institutions: 343
Shares Held: 113,741,583
% Held: 79.5

INDUSTRY: Telephone communications, exc. radio (SIC: 4813)

TRANSFER AGENT(S): Computershare Investor Services, LLC, Chicago, IL

CHARTER ONE FINANCIAL, INC.

YIELD 3.2%
P/E RATIO 12.3

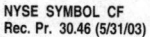

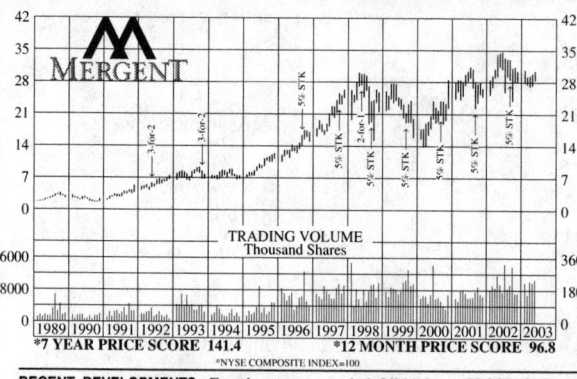

TRADING VOLUME
Thousand Shares

| | 1989 | 1990 | 1991 | 1992 | 1993 | 1994 | 1995 | 1996 | 1997 | 1998 | 1999 | 2000 | 2001 | 2002 | 2003 |

*7 YEAR PRICE SCORE 141.4   *12 MONTH PRICE SCORE 96.8

*NYSE COMPOSITE INDEX=100

INTERIM EARNINGS (Per Share):

Qtr.	Mar.	June	Sept.	Dec.
1999	0.41	0.43	0.42	0.09
2000	0.46	0.43	0.47	0.48
2001	0.49	0.54	0.54	0.56
2002	0.59	0.60	0.61	0.63
2003	0.64	...	...	...

INTERIM DIVIDENDS (Per Share):

Amt.	Decl.	Ex.	Rec.	Pay.
5% STK	7/17/02	9/11/02	9/13/02	9/30/02
0.22Q	10/23/02	11/04/02	11/06/02	11/20/02
0.22Q	1/21/03	2/04/03	2/06/03	2/20/03
0.24Q	4/22/03	5/02/03	5/06/03	5/20/03

Indicated div.: $0.96 (Div. Reinv. Plan)

CAPITALIZATION (12/31/02):

	($000)	(%)
Total Deposits	27,527,843	68.2
Long-Term Debt	9,746,778	24.2
Common & Surplus	3,083,825	7.6
Total	40,358,446	100.0

DIVIDEND ACHIEVER STATUS:

Rank: 14   10-Year Growth Rate: 22.32%
Total Years of Dividend Growth: 14

RECENT DEVELOPMENTS: For the quarter ended 3/31/03, net income increased 3.5% to $147.5 million in the corresponding prior-year period. Earnings for 2003 and 2002 included pre-tax non-recurring net gains of $76.7 million and $21.7 million, respectively. Net interest income improved 5.6% to $299.0 million. Provision for loan and lease losses more than doubled to $61.5 million from $28.7 million in 2001.

PROSPECTS: In early 2003, the Company announced plans for aggressive de novo expansion during 2003 and 2004. The expansion is expected to include 125 new banking centers, with 97 in-store and 28 traditional locations. The 2003 goal is to open approximately 85 new banking centers, with 69 in-store and 16 traditional locations. During the quarter, the Company opened 16 banking centers, increasing its in-store franchise to 64 banking centers.

BUSINESS

CHARTER ONE FINANCIAL, INC. is a bank holding company whose principal line of business is consumer banking, which includes retail banking, mortgage banking and other related financial services. As of 3/31/03, Charter One Bank, N.A., with $43.25 billion in total assets, had 475 branch locations in Ohio, Michigan, Illinois, New York, Massachusetts and Vermont, and operated 918 automated teller machines at various banking offices. As of 12/31/02, Charter One Mortgage Corp., CF's mortgage banking subsidiary, operated 26 loan production offices nationwide. On 10/1/99, CF acquired St. Paul Bancorp, Inc. On 11/5/99, CF acquired fourteen Vermont National Bank offices from Chittenden Corporation. On 7/2/01, CF acquired Alliance Bancorp.

ANNUAL FINANCIAL DATA

	12/31/02	12/31/01	12/31/00	12/31/99	12/31/98	12/31/97	12/31/96
Earnings Per Share	④ 2.45	④ 2.11	③ 1.81	①② 1.32	①② 1.33	①② 0.91	1.05
Tang. Book Val. Per Share	12.00	10.94	9.95	9.12	8.54	7.76	7.29
Dividends Per Share	0.83	0.72	0.61	0.52	0.43	0.37	0.32
Dividend Payout %	33.9	34.0	33.8	39.1	32.4	40.6	30.6
INCOME STATEMENT (IN MILLIONS):							
Total Interest Income	2,286.5	2,378.2	2,247.1	2,128.5	1,760.4	1,377.7	1,004.5
Total Interest Expense	1,116.6	1,387.8	1,344.1	1,194.4	1,031.3	850.7	621.1
Net Interest Income	1,169.8	990.4	903.0	934.1	729.1	527.0	383.4
Provision for Loan Losses	192.0	100.8	54.2	35.2	29.5	40.9	4.0
Non-Interest Income	547.5	473.6	392.9	230.6	211.6	110.8	57.1
Non-Interest Expense	679.0	629.7	604.0	633.3	492.5	373.9	244.0
Income Before Taxes	846.4	733.6	637.7	496.1	418.7	223.0	192.5
Net Income	④ 577.7	④ 500.7	③ 434.0	①② 335.5	①② 277.0	①② 151.1	127.7
Average Shs. Outstg. (000)	236,116	238,383	239,895	252,184	207,533	165,291	122,309
BALANCE SHEET (IN MILLIONS):							
Cash & Due from Banks	...	...	530.8	689.1	334.1	214.7	152.3
Securities Avail. for Sale	11,536.9	8,030.5	4,087.2	4,193.1	2,299.2	1,070.2	265.4
Total Loans & Leases	26,401.4	25,842.1	24,297.4	22,545.8	17,688.0	12,360.1	8,295.0
Allowance for Credit Losses	548.6	446.0	347.3	268.9	185.3	...	194.6
Net Loans & Leases	25,852.8	25,396.1	23,950.2	22,276.9	17,502.7	12,360.1	8,100.3
Total Assets	41,896.1	38,174.5	32,971.4	31,819.1	24,467.3	19,760.3	13,904.6
Total Deposits	27,527.8	25,123.3	19,605.7	19,074.0	15,165.1	10,219.2	7,841.2
Long-Term Obligations	9,746.8	8,657.2	9,636.3	9,226.2	6,186.1	5,370.5	3,194.3
Total Liabilities	38,812.2	35,246.0	30,515.2	29,421.4	22,592.1	18,383.4	12,975.9
Net Stockholders' Equity	3,083.8	2,928.5	2,456.2	2,397.7	1,875.1	1,376.9	928.7
Year-end Shs. Outstg. (000)	224,790	235,557	229,572	242,242	201,044	165,809	118,549
STATISTICAL RECORD:							
Return on Equity %	18.7	17.1	17.7	14.0	14.8	11.0	13.8
Return on Assets %	1.4	1.3	1.3	1.1	1.1	0.8	0.9
Equity/Assets %	7.4	7.7	7.4	7.5	7.7	7.0	6.7
Non-Int. Exp./Tot. Inc. %	39.5	43.0	46.6	54.4	52.4	58.6	55.4
Price Range	34.77-23.89	31.41-22.29	28.57-13.83	27.75-15.87	30.13-15.23	26.33-16.11	17.53-10.54
P/E Ratio	14.2-9.8	14.9-10.6	15.7-7.6	21.0-12.0	22.6-11.4	28.8-17.6	16.8-10.1
Average Yield %	2.8	2.7	2.9	2.4	1.9	1.7	2.3

Statistics are as originally reported. Adj. for stk. splits: 5% stk. div., 9/02; 9/01; 9/00, 9/99; 9/98; 2-for-1, 5/98; 5% stk. div., 10/97. ① Incl. non-recurr. chrg. $60.6 mill., 1997; $55.7 mill., 1998; $63.5 mill., 1999. ② Bef. extraord. chrg. $2.7 mill., 1997; chrg. $61.7 mill., 1998; chrg. $1.6 mill., 1999. ③ Incl. pre-tax merger expenses of $29.5 mill. & non-recurr. net gains of $9.3 mill. ④ Incl. pre-tax nonrecurr. net gains of $205.0 mill., 2002; $114.3 mill., 2001.

OFFICERS:
C. J. Koch, Chmn., Pres., C.E.O.
H. G. Chorbajian, Vice-Chmn.
J. L. Schostak, Vice-Chmn.
R. W. Neu, Exec. V.P., C.F.O.

INVESTOR CONTACT: Ellen L. Batkie, Senior V.P., (800) 262-6301

PRINCIPAL OFFICE: 1215 Superior Avenue, Cleveland, OH 44114

TELEPHONE NUMBER: (216) 566-5300
FAX: (216) 566-1465
WEB: www.charterone.com

NO. OF EMPLOYEES: 7,198

SHAREHOLDERS: 20,000 (approx.)

ANNUAL MEETING: In April

INCORPORATED: DE, 1987

INSTITUTIONAL HOLDINGS:
No. of Institutions: 387
Shares Held: 136,140,141
% Held: 60.5

INDUSTRY: Federal savings institutions (SIC: 6035)

TRANSFER AGENT(S): EquiServe, Providence, RI

CHEMICAL FINANCIAL CORPORATION

YIELD 3.2%
P/E RATIO 13.4

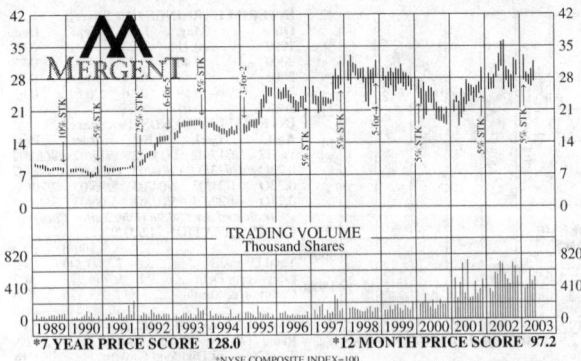

INTERIM EARNINGS (Per Share):

Qtr.	Mar.	June	Sept.	Dec.
1999	0.41	0.43	0.45	0.48
2000	0.44	0.47	0.47	0.50
2001	0.16	0.50	0.55	0.58
2002	0.58	0.57	0.59	0.57
2003	0.59	...	...	...

INTERIM DIVIDENDS (Per Share):

Amt.	Decl.	Ex.	Rec.	Pay.
0.24Q	7/15/02	9/04/02	9/06/02	9/20/02
0.24Q	10/21/02	12/04/02	12/06/02	12/20/02
5% STK	12/09/02	1/02/03	1/06/03	1/24/03
0.25Q	1/21/03	3/05/03	3/07/03	3/21/03
0.25Q	4/21/03	6/04/03	6/06/03	6/20/03

Indicated div.: $1.00 (Div. Reinv. Plan)

CAPITALIZATION (12/31/02):

	($000)	(%)
Total Deposits	2,847,272	82.9
Long-Term Debt	157,393	4.6
Common & Surplus	430,339	12.5
Total	3,435,004	100.0

DIVIDEND ACHIEVER STATUS:
Rank: 104   10-Year Growth Rate: 12.10%
Total Years of Dividend Growth: 27

RECENT DEVELOPMENTS: For the quarter ended 3/31/03, net income rose 2.2% to $14.0 million from $13.7 million in the corresponding period of the year before. Net interest income slipped 3.0% to $35.1 million, due to the low interest rate environment and the decrease in the yield on earning assets, which offset the decrease in CHFC's cost of funds. Provision for loan losses decreased 54.8% to $295,000. Total non-interest income improved 7.4% to $9.3 million, while total non-interest expense slid 2.8% to $23.0 million. Total deposits rose 2.8% to $2.90 billion from $2.82 billion the year before. Total loans rose 2.2% to $2.13 billion, primarily due to growth in residential real estate loans, which was undertaken to achieve the Company's desired mix of residential loans to total loans.

BUSINESS

CHEMICAL FINANCIAL CORPORATION is a bank holding company headquartered in Midland, Michigan, with total assets of $3.61 billion as of 3/31/03. The Company's three subsidiary banks, Chemical Bank and Trust Company, Chemical Bank Shoreline and Chemical Bank West, operate 129 Chemical Bank offices and two loan production offices throughout 32 counties in the lower peninsula of Michigan. Non-bank subsidiaries include CFC Data Corp., a provider of data processing services, CFC Financial Services, an insurance company operating under the Chemical Financial Insurance Agency and CFC Investment Center names, and CFC Title Services, an issuer of title insurance to buyers and sellers of residential and commercial mortgage properties.

QUARTERLY DATA

(12/31/2002)($000)	REV	INC
1st Quarter	54,241	13,710
2nd Quarter	53,292	13,535
3rd Quarter	52,475	14,018
4th Quarter	51,036	13,682

ANNUAL FINANCIAL DATA

	12/31/02	12/31/01	12/31/00	12/31/99	12/31/98	12/31/97	12/31/96
Earnings Per Share	2.31	① 1.80	1.87	1.76	1.65	1.52	1.40
Tang. Book Val. Per Share	16.46	14.67	18.28	16.86	16.25	14.39	13.36
Dividends Per Share	0.91	0.87	0.80	0.73	0.66	0.58	0.50
Dividend Payout %	39.6	48.4	42.7	41.2	40.2	38.1	35.8
INCOME STATEMENT (IN MILLIONS):							
Total Interest Income	211.0	219.3	131.1	121.9	121.6	117.3	113.3
Total Interest Expense	65.4	89.2	54.0	47.1	49.1	48.3	46.2
Net Interest Income	145.7	130.1	77.0	74.8	72.5	69.0	67.1
Provision for Loan Losses	3.8	2.0	0.5	0.5	1.0	1.0	1.1
Non-Interest Income	34.5	31.9	17.4	16.0	15.6	13.1	12.2
Non-Interest Expense	93.5	94.6	50.9	49.0	48.3	45.7	45.1
Income Before Taxes	82.9	65.3	43.1	41.4	38.8	35.4	33.0
Net Income	54.9	① 42.7	29.0	27.7	26.0	23.9	22.0
Average Shs. Outstg. (000)	23,742	23,692	15,527	15,723	15,786	15,728	15,723
BALANCE SHEET (IN MILLIONS):							
Cash & Due from Banks	148.1	150.5	95.0	98.8	98.5	95.8	89.5
Securities Avail. for Sale	858.7	731.4	433.3	428.0	489.0	494.2	441.8
Total Loans & Leases	2,075.2	2,182.5	1,085.9	1,009.0	898.3	845.6	807.7
Allowance for Credit Losses	30.7	31.0	18.2	18.2	18.1	17.4	16.6
Net Loans & Leases	2,044.5	2,151.5	1,067.6	990.8	880.2	828.2	791.0
Total Assets	3,568.9	3,488.3	1,973.4	1,890.4	1,872.6	1,765.1	1,698.8
Total Deposits	2,847.3	2,789.5	1,606.2	1,561.7	1,554.3	1,475.8	1,429.9
Long-Term Obligations	157.4	167.9	0.2	0.2	8.0	9.0	10.0
Total Liabilities	3,138.6	3,098.9	1,704.7	1,640.8	1,630.8	1,541.2	1,491.5
Net Stockholders' Equity	430.3	389.5	268.7	249.6	241.8	223.9	207.3
Year-end Shs. Outstg. (000)	23,684	23,640	14,704	14,800	14,880	15,560	15,513
STATISTICAL RECORD:							
Return on Equity %	12.8	11.0	10.8	11.1	10.8	10.7	10.6
Return on Assets %	1.5	1.2	1.5	1.5	1.4	1.4	1.3
Equity/Assets %	12.1	11.2	13.6	13.2	12.9	12.7	12.2
Non-Int. Exp./Tot. Inc. %	51.9	58.4	54.0	54.4	55.8	55.8	57.0
Price Range	36.25-24.86	30.33-17.52	27.64-17.74	31.10-24.08	33.17-21.77	31.79-20.40	26.64-20.69
P/E Ratio	15.7-10.8	16.9-9.7	14.8-9.5	17.7-13.7	20.1-13.2	20.9-13.4	19.0-14.8
Average Yield %	3.0	3.6	3.5	2.6	2.4	2.2	2.1

Statistics are as originally reported. Adj for stk. splits: 5% div., 1/03, 12/01, 1/00, 12/97, 12/96 & 5-for-4, 12/98. ① Incl. $7.1 mill. after-tax merger and restructuring charge.

OFFICERS:
A. J. Oliver, Chmn.
D. B. Ramaker, Pres., C.E.O.
L. A. Gwizdala, Exec. V.P., C.F.O., Treas.

INVESTOR CONTACT: Lori A Gwizdala, C.F.O., (989) 839-5350

PRINCIPAL OFFICE: 333 East Main Street, Midland, MI 48640-0569

TELEPHONE NUMBER: (989) 839-5350
FAX: (989) 839-5255
WEB: www.chemicalbankmi.com

NO. OF EMPLOYEES: 1,412

SHAREHOLDERS: 9,100 (approx.)

ANNUAL MEETING: In April

INCORPORATED: MI, Aug., 1974

INSTITUTIONAL HOLDINGS:
No. of Institutions: 69
Shares Held: 5,053,821
% Held: 21.1

INDUSTRY: State commercial banks (SIC: 6022)

TRANSFER AGENT(S): Computershare Investor Services, LLC, Chicago, IL

CHEVRONTEXACO CORP.

YIELD 3.9%
P/E RATIO 29.8

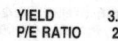
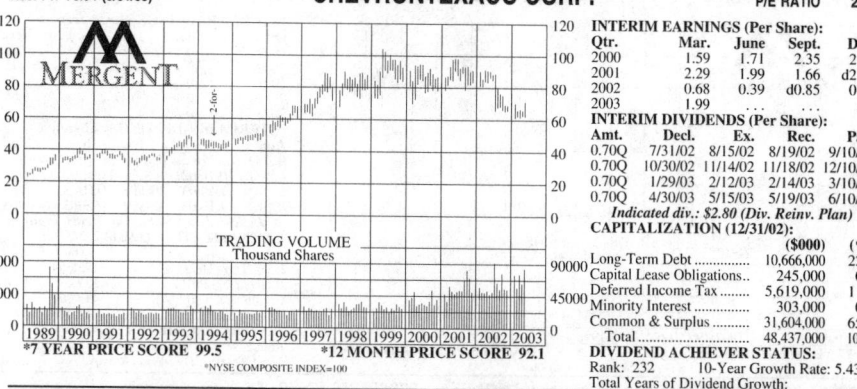

*7 YEAR PRICE SCORE 99.5 ***12 MONTH PRICE SCORE 92.1**
*NYSE COMPOSITE INDEX=100

INTERIM EARNINGS (Per Share):

Qtr.	Mar.	June	Sept.	Dec.
2000	1.59	1.71	2.35	2.32
2001	2.29	1.99	1.66	d2.24
2002	0.68	0.39	d0.85	0.85
2003	1.99	...	...	...

INTERIM DIVIDENDS (Per Share):

Amt.	Decl.	Ex.	Rec.	Pay.
0.70Q	7/31/02	8/15/02	8/19/02	9/10/02
0.70Q	10/30/02	11/14/02	11/18/02	12/10/02
0.70Q	1/29/03	2/12/03	2/14/03	3/10/03
0.70Q	4/30/03	5/15/03	5/19/03	6/10/03

Indicated div.: $2.80 (Div. Reinv. Plan)

CAPITALIZATION (12/31/02):

	($000)	(%)
Long-Term Debt	10,666,000	22.0
Capital Lease Obligations	245,000	0.5
Deferred Income Tax	5,619,000	11.6
Minority Interest	303,000	0.6
Common & Surplus	31,604,000	65.2
Total	48,437,000	100.0

DIVIDEND ACHIEVER STATUS:
Rank: 232   10-Year Growth Rate: 5.43%
Total Years of Dividend Growth: 15

RECENT DEVELOPMENTS: For the quarter ended 3/31/03, income was $2.12 billion, before an accounting change charge of $196.0 million, versus net income of $725.0 million the previous year. Results for 2002 included merger-related expenses of $183.0 million. Earnings were fueled by strong crude oil and natural gas prices, as well as improved worldwide refining and marketing margins. Total revenue and other income rose 41.0% to $30.97 billion.

PROSPECTS: On 4/23/03, CVX announced that it will offer to sell more than 100 producing properties throughout North America in several regional packages. CVX expects to complete the sale of all properties by 9/30/03. Also, on 4/10/03, CVX announced plans to sell its interests and resign operatorship of its Papua New Guinea joint ventures as part of the Company's efforts to focus on assets more aligned with strategic growth objectives.

BUSINESS

CHEVRONTEXACO CORP. (formerly Chevron Corp.) is a global energy company engaged in the exploration and production, refining, marketing and transportation of crude oil, natural gas and natural gas liquids. CVX is also engaged in chemicals manufacturing and sales, and holds investments in power generation and gasification businesses. Formed as a result of the acquisition by Chevron Corporation of Texaco Inc. on 10/9/01, CVX operates in the U.S. and about 180 other countries. As of 12/31/02, net proved reserves of natural gas were 19,335.00 billion cubic feet and net proved reserves of crude oil, condensate and natural gas liquids totaled 8,668.0 million barrels.

ANNUAL FINANCIAL DATA

	12/31/02	12/31/01	12/31/00	12/31/99	12/31/98	12/31/97	12/31/96
Earnings Per Share	8 1.07	5 3.70	9 7.97	3 3.14	2.04	4.95	1 3.99
Cash Flow Per Share	5.98	10.34	12.34	7.48	5.57	8.44	7.39
Tang. Book Val. Per Share	29.59	31.82	31.08	27.04	25.81	26.64	23.82
Dividends Per Share	2.80	2.65	2.60	2.48	2.44	2.28	2.08
Dividend Payout %	261.7	71.6	32.6	79.0	119.6	46.1	52.1

INCOME STATEMENT (IN MILLIONS):

Total Revenues	99,049.0	106,245.0	52,129.0	36,586.0	30,557.0	41,950.0	43,893.0
Costs & Expenses	89,040.0	89,941.0	39,551.0	29,600.0	25,998.0	33,836.0	36,573.0
Depreciation & Amort.	5,231.0	7,059.0	2,848.0	2,866.0	2,320.0	2,300.0	2,216.0
Operating Income	4,778.0	9,245.0	9,730.0	4,120.0	2,239.0	5,814.0	5,104.0
Net Interest Inc./(Exp.)	d565.0	d833.0	d460.0	d472.0	d405.0	d312.0	d364.0
Income Before Income Taxes	4,156.0	8,291.0	9,270.0	3,648.0	1,834.0	5,502.0	4,740.0
Income Taxes	3,024.0	4,360.0	4,085.0	1,578.0	495.0	2,246.0	2,133.0
Net Income	8 1,132.0	3 3,931.0	9 5,185.0	2 2,070.0	1,339.0	3,256.0	1 2,607.0
Cash Flow	6,363.0	10,984.0	8,033.0	4,936.0	3,659.0	5,556.0	4,823.0
Average Shs. Outstg. (000)	1,063,400	1,062,900	651,100	659,500	657,100	658,400	653,000

BALANCE SHEET (IN MILLIONS):

Cash & Cash Equivalents	3,781.0	3,150.0	2,630.0	2,032.0	1,413.0	1,670.0	1,637.0
Total Current Assets	17,776.0	18,327.0	8,213.0	8,297.0	6,297.0	7,006.0	7,942.0
Net Property	44,155.0	43,233.0	22,894.0	25,317.0	23,729.0	22,671.0	21,496.0
Total Assets	77,359.0	77,572.0	41,264.0	40,668.0	36,540.0	35,473.0	34,854.0
Total Current Liabilities	19,876.0	20,654.0	7,674.0	8,889.0	7,166.0	6,946.0	8,907.0
Long-Term Obligations	10,911.0	8,989.0	5,153.0	5,485.0	4,393.0	4,431.0	3,988.0
Net Stockholders' Equity	31,604.0	33,958.0	19,925.0	17,749.0	17,034.0	17,472.0	15,623.0
Net Working Capital	d2,100.0	d2,327.0	539.0	d592.0	d869.0	60.0	d965.0
Year-end Shs. Outstg. (000)	1,068,137	1,067,221	641,060	636,346	660,000	655,900	656,000

STATISTICAL RECORD:

Operating Profit Margin %	4.8	8.7	18.7	11.3	7.3	13.9	11.6
Net Profit Margin %	1.1	3.7	9.9	5.7	4.4	7.8	5.9
Return on Equity %	3.6	11.6	26.0	11.7	7.9	18.6	16.7
Return on Assets %	1.5	5.1	12.6	5.1	3.7	9.2	7.5
Debt/Total Assets %	14.1	11.6	12.5	13.5	12.0	12.5	11.4
Price Range	91.60-65.41	98.49-78.44	94.88-69.94	104.44-73.13	90.19-61.75	89.19-61.75	68.38-51.00
P/E Ratio	85.6-61.1	26.6-21.2	11.9-8.8	33.3-23.3	44.2-33.2	18.0-12.5	17.1-12.8
Average Yield %	3.6	3.0	3.2	2.8	3.1	3.0	3.5

Statistics are as originally reported. The financial data for 12/31/00 and prior years reflects the former operations of Chevron Corporation only. ① Incl. nonrecurr. chrg. of $44.0 mill. ② Incl. spec. chrgs. of $216.0 mill. ③ Incl. spec. chrgs. of $252.0 mill. ④ Refl. acq. of Texaco Inc. ⑤ Incl. spec. chrgs. of $1.74 bill. & merger-rel. chrgs. of $1.78 bill.; bef. extraord. loss of $643.0 mill. ⑥ Incl. merger-rel. chrgs. of $386.0 mill. & oth. spec. chrgs. of $2.25 bill.

OFFICERS:
D. J. O'Reilly, Chmn., C.E.O.
P. J. Robertson, Vice-Chmn., V.P.
J. S. Watson, V.P., C.F.O.

INVESTOR CONTACT: Pierre Breber, Mgr., Inv. Rel., (925) 842-3523

PRINCIPAL OFFICE: 6001 Bollinger Canyon Road, San Ramon, CA 94583-2324

TELEPHONE NUMBER: (925) 842-1000
WEB: www.chevrontexaco.com

NO. OF EMPLOYEES: 53,014 (avg.)

SHAREHOLDERS: 250,000 (approx.)

ANNUAL MEETING: In May

INCORPORATED: DE, Jan., 1926

INSTITUTIONAL HOLDINGS:
No. of Institutions: 1,068
Shares Held: 617,997,719
% Held: 57.9

INDUSTRY: Petroleum refining (SIC: 2911)

TRANSFER AGENT(S): Mellon Investor Services, Ridgefield Park, NJ

CHITTENDEN CORPORATION

YIELD 2.9%
P/E RATIO 13.9

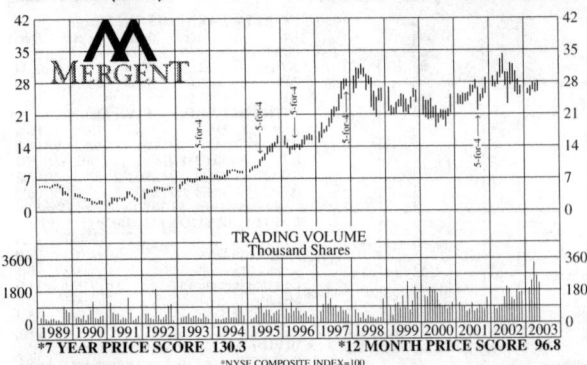

TRADING VOLUME
Thousand Shares

*7 YEAR PRICE SCORE 130.3   *12 MONTH PRICE SCORE 96.8
*NYSE COMPOSITE INDEX=100

INTERIM EARNINGS (Per Share):

Qtr.	Mar.	June	Sept.	Dec.
1999	0.34	d1.26	0.44	0.39
2000	0.41	0.42	0.44	0.45
2001	0.44	0.44	0.46	0.46
2002	0.46	0.47	0.48	0.55
2003	0.49	...	...	...

INTERIM DIVIDENDS (Per Share):

Amt.	Decl.	Ex.	Rec.	Pay.
0.20Q	7/17/02	7/31/02	8/02/02	8/16/02
0.20Q	10/16/02	10/30/02	11/01/02	11/15/02
0.20Q	1/15/03	1/29/03	1/31/03	2/14/03
0.20Q	4/16/03	4/30/03	5/02/03	5/16/03

Indicated div.: $0.80 (Div. Reinv. Plan)

CAPITALIZATION (12/31/02):

	($000)	(%)
Long-Term Debt	173,654	24.2
Redeemable Pfd. Stock	125,000	17.4
Common & Surplus	418,792	58.4
Total	717,446	100.0

DIVIDEND ACHIEVER STATUS:
Rank: 3   10-Year Growth Rate: 29.63%
Total Years of Dividend Growth: 10

RECENT DEVELOPMENTS: For the quarter ended 3/31/03, net income grew 11.9% to $16.6 million from $14.8 million in the equivalent 2002 quarter. Net interest income rose 14.5% to $50.9 million from $44.5 million in 2002. Provision for loan losses was essentially unchanged at $2.1 million versus the prior year period. Net gains on sales of loans increased 61.0% to $4.4 million primarily due to heavy mortgage refinancing activity and the acquisition of Granite Bank on 2/28/03, which contributed $319,000 to mortgage gains.

PROSPECTS: On 2/28/03, the Company completed the acquisition of Granite Bank, a $1.10 billion commercial bank headquartered in Keene, New Hampshire, for $123.0 million in cash and about 4.4 million in shares of CHZ stock valued at $116.0 million. Looking ahead, the Company should continue to experience a decline in nonperforming assets as a percentage of total loans as a result of the Granite acquisition. In addition, the Granite acquisition will likely lead to an increase in securities available for sale.

BUSINESS

CHITTENDEN CORPORATION is a bank holding company with total assets of $6.00 billion at March 31, 2003. The Company's subsidiary banks are Chittenden Bank, The Bank of Western Massachusetts, Flagship Bank and Trust Company, Maine Bank & Trust Company, Ocean National Bank and Granite Bank. Chittenden Bank also operates under the name Mortgage Service Center, and it owns Chittenden Insurance Group and Chittenden Securities, Inc. The Company offers a broad range of financial products and services, including deposit accounts and services; consumer, commercial, and public sector loans; insurance; brokerage; and investment and trust services to individuals, businesses, and the public sector. On 2/28/03, CHZ acquired Granite Bank.

ANNUAL FINANCIAL DATA

	12/31/02	12/31/01	12/31/00	12/31/99	12/31/98	12/31/97	12/31/96
Earnings Per Share	1.96	1.80	①1.72	①d0.07	1.67	1.55	1.37
Tang. Book Val. Per Share	9.90	9.44	9.13	9.69	9.18	8.23	8.56
Dividends Per Share	0.79	0.77	0.75	0.69	0.62	②1.03	0.46
Dividend Payout %	40.3	42.6	43.7	...	37.3	66.4	33.6
INCOME STATEMENT (IN MILLIONS):							
Net Investment Income	259.0	266.5	288.1	288.2	151.5	150.2	142.6
Other Income	65.1	63.7	54.8	64.2	32.4	28.2	24.9
Total Revenues	324.1	330.2	342.9	352.4	183.9	178.4	167.5
Income Before Income Taxes	97.8	90.2	86.7	26.6	46.5	44.7	40.2
Income Taxes	34.2	31.7	28.0	29.1	15.9	15.3	13.5
Net Income	63.6	58.5	①58.7	①d2.5	30.7	29.4	26.7
Average Shs. Outstg. (000)	32,495	32,547	34,100	35,795	18,354	18,958	19,482
BALANCE SHEET (IN MILLIONS):							
Cash & Cash Equivalents	1,689.3	1,134.5	763.9	799.9	638.4	506.7	588.8
Invst. Assets: Loans	2,919.7	2,739.8	2,719.6	2,760.8	1,293.0	1,326.6	1,255.5
Invst. Assets: Total	4,528.9	3,630.8	3,362.7	3,430.5	1,829.0	1,712.6	1,631.7
Total Assets	4,920.5	4,153.7	3,769.9	3,827.3	2,122.0	1,977.2	1,988.7
Long-Term Obligations	173.7	44.4	93.8	197.1	23.4	25.5	26.5
Net Stockholders' Equity	418.8	370.7	342.1	362.5	175.1	162.3	174.4
Year-end Shs. Outstg. (000)	35,749	35,743	35,737	35,473	17,728	18,027	19,181
STATISTICAL RECORD:							
Return on Revenues %	19.6	17.7	17.1	...	16.7	16.5	16.0
Return on Equity %	15.2	15.8	17.2	...	17.5	18.1	15.3
Return on Assets %	1.3	1.4	1.6	...	1.4	1.5	1.3
Price Range	34.18-23.18	28.99-21.75	25.25-18.05	26.90-20.80	32.00-20.35	28.80-14.80	16.80-12.29
P/E Ratio	17.4-11.8	16.1-12.1	14.7-10.5	...	19.1-12.2	18.6-9.5	12.3-9.0
Average Yield %	2.8	3.0	3.5	2.9	2.4	4.7	3.2

Statistics are as originally reported. ① Incl. special chrgs. of $833,000, 2000; $58.5 mill., 1999. ② Incl. special div. of $0.48 per share.

OFFICERS:
P. A. Perrault, Chmn., Pres., C.E.O.
K. W. Walters, Exec. V.P., C.F.O., Treas.
F. S. Prentice, Sr. V.P., Gen. Couns., Sec.
INVESTOR CONTACT: F. Sheldon Prentice, Sec., (802) 660-1412
PRINCIPAL OFFICE: Two Burlington Square, Burlington, VT 05401

TELEPHONE NUMBER: (802) 658-4000
FAX: (802) 660-1591
WEB: www.chittendencorp.com
NO. OF EMPLOYEES: 1,779
SHAREHOLDERS: 4,633
ANNUAL MEETING: In Apr.
INCORPORATED: VT, 1971

INSTITUTIONAL HOLDINGS:
No. of Institutions: 112
Shares Held: 17,563,687
% Held: 54.9
INDUSTRY: State commercial banks (SIC: 6022)
TRANSFER AGENT(S): BankBoston, N.A., Boston, MA

NYSE SYMBOL CB
Rec. Pr. 64.03 (5/31/03)

CHUBB CORPORATION (THE)

YIELD 2.2%
P/E RATIO 45.1

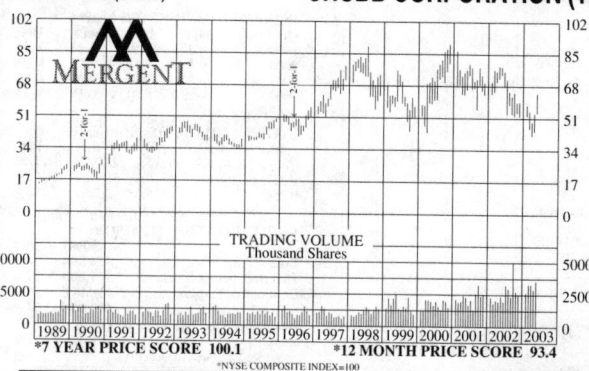

*7 YEAR PRICE SCORE 100.1   *12 MONTH PRICE SCORE 93.4
*NYSE COMPOSITE INDEX=100

INTERIM EARNINGS (Per Share):

Qtr.	Mar.	June	Sept.	Dec.
1999	1.14	1.18	0.44	0.93
2000	0.87	1.02	1.17	0.95
2001	0.97	0.83	d1.40	0.16
2002	1.15	1.20	d1.42	0.33
2003	1.31	...	...	...

INTERIM DIVIDENDS (Per Share):

Amt.	Decl.	Ex.	Rec.	Pay.
0.35Q	9/06/02	9/18/02	9/20/02	10/08/02
0.35Q	12/05/02	12/17/02	12/19/02	1/07/03
0.36Q	3/24/03	4/01/03	4/03/03	4/11/03
0.36Q	6/06/03	6/18/03	6/20/03	7/08/03

Indicated div.: $1.44 (Div. Reinv. Plan)

CAPITALIZATION (12/31/02):

	($000)	(%)
Long-Term Debt	1,959,100	22.2
Common & Surplus	6,859,200	77.8
Total	8,818,300	100.0

DIVIDEND ACHIEVER STATUS:
Rank: 217   10-Year Growth Rate: 5.88%
Total Years of Dividend Growth: 38

RECENT DEVELOPMENTS: For the quarter ended 3/31/03, net income increased 13.3% to $224.6 million from $198.2 million in the equivalent 2002 quarter. Results for 2003 included an after-tax charge of about $13.7 million related to the expensing of stock options. Results also included an after-tax realized investment gain of $2.9 million in 2003 and an after-tax realized investment loss of $6.1 million in 2002. Net premiums earned climbed 25.3% to $2.33 billion from $1.86 billion the year before.

PROSPECTS: Going forward, CB will continue to maintain underwriting discipline, while results should continue to benefit from higher earned premiums, better risk selection and favorable terms and conditions. Meanwhile, the Company announced that it has undertaken a restructuring plan to improve performance in Europe, including several actions to significantly reduce operating expenses. Premiums in Europe are expected to grow at a double-digit rate in 2003.

BUSINESS

THE CHUBB CORPORATION is a holding company with subsidiaries principally engaged in the property and casualty insurance business. The property and casualty insurance subsidiaries provide insurance coverages principally in North America, Europe, Latin America, Asia and Australia. CB also has investments in high quality bonds, U.S. Treasury, government agency, mortgage-backed securities and corporate issues as well as equity securities. CB has a real estate group that is composed of Bellemead Development Corporation and its subsidiaries. The group's activities involve commercial development primarily in New Jersey and residential development activities primarily in central Florida. In 2002, the combined loss and expense ratio after policy holder's dividends was 106.7%.

ANNUAL FINANCIAL DATA

	12/31/02	12/31/01	12/31/00	12/31/99	12/31/98	12/31/97	12/31/96
Earnings Per Share	③ 1.29	② 0.63	4.01	3.66	4.19	4.39	① 2.75
Tang. Book Val. Per Share	37.33	35.62	37.13	32.85	34.78	32.11	31.24
Dividends Per Share	1.39	1.35	1.31	1.27	1.22	1.14	1.05
Dividend Payout %	107.7	214.3	32.7	34.8	29.1	26.0	38.4
INCOME STATEMENT (IN MILLIONS):							
Total Premium Income	8,085.3	6,656.4	6,145.9	5,652.0	5,303.8	5,157.4	4,569.3
Other Income	1,055.0	1,097.6	1,105.6	1,077.6	1,046.0	1,506.6	1,111.3
Total Revenues	9,140.3	7,754.0	7,251.5	6,729.6	6,349.8	6,664.0	5,680.5
Policyholder Benefits	6,064.6	5,357.4	4,127.7	3,942.0	3,493.7	3,307.0	3,010.8
Income Before Income Taxes	168.4	d66.0	851.0	710.1	849.7	974.1	546.9
Income Taxes	cr54.5	cr177.5	136.4	89.0	142.7	204.6	60.7
Net Income	③ 222.9	② 111.5	714.6	621.1	707.0	769.5	① 486.2
Average Shs. Outstg. (000)	172,900	175,800	178,300	169,800	168,600	176,200	174,402
BALANCE SHEET (IN MILLIONS):							
Cash & Cash Equivalents	3,153.4	1,400.1	1,079.1	1,223.3	352.5	736.6	280.6
Premiums Due	2,040.6	1,692.8	1,409.8	1,234.7	1,199.3	1,464.6	984.9
Invst. Assets: Fixed-term	18,263.5	16,116.7	15,564.4	14,519.1	13,318.9	12,453.4	11,158.8
Invst. Assets: Equities	992.2	710.4	830.6	769.2	1,092.6	871.1	646.3
Invst. Assets: Total	23,236.8	19,234.2	18,128.8	17,188.3	15,501.3	14,839.6	13,685.0
Total Assets	34,114.4	29,449.0	25,026.7	23,537.0	20,746.0	19,615.6	19,938.9
Long-Term Obligations	1,959.1	1,351.0	753.8	759.2	607.5	398.6	1,070.5
Net Stockholders' Equity	6,859.2	6,525.3	6,981.7	6,271.8	5,644.1	5,657.1	5,462.9
Year-end Shs. Outstg. (000)	171,202	170,071	174,919	175,490	162,267	176,200	174,861
STATISTICAL RECORD:							
Return on Revenues %	2.4	1.4	9.9	9.2	11.1	11.5	8.6
Return on Equity %	3.2	1.7	10.2	9.9	12.5	13.6	8.9
Return on Assets %	0.7	0.4	2.9	2.6	3.4	3.9	2.4
Price Range	78.64-51.91	86.63-55.54	90.25-43.25	76.38-44.00	88.81-55.38	78.50-51.13	56.25-40.88
P/E Ratio	61.0-40.2	137.5-88.1	22.5-10.8	20.9-12.0	21.2-13.2	17.9-11.6	20.5-14.9
Average Yield %	2.1	1.9	2.0	2.1	1.7	1.8	2.2

Statistics are as originally reported. Adj. for stk. split: 2-for-1, 5/96 ① Bef. disc. oper. gain $26.5 mill. ② Incl. after-tax chrg. of $143.0 mill. fr. 9/11/01 attacks & after-tax chrgs. of $143.0 mill. from Enron. ③ Incl. a pre-tax chrg. of $700.0 mill. for asbestos claims, a pre-tax tax valuation allowance of $40.0 mill., & a pre-tax settlement gain of $88.0 mill.

OFFICERS:
J. J. Cohen, Chmn.
J. D. Finnegan, Pres., C.E.O.
M. O'Reilly, Vice-Chmn., C.F.O.

INVESTOR CONTACT: Mary Jane Murphy, Asst. Sec., (908) 903-3579

PRINCIPAL OFFICE: 15 Mountain View Road, P.O. Box 1615, Warren, NJ 07061-1615

TELEPHONE NUMBER: (908) 903-2000
FAX: (908) 903-2003
WEB: www.chubb.com

NO. OF EMPLOYEES: 12,600 (approx.)

SHAREHOLDERS: 6,300 (approx.)

ANNUAL MEETING: In April

INCORPORATED: NJ, June, 1967

INSTITUTIONAL HOLDINGS:
No. of Institutions: 466
Shares Held: 139,333,571
% Held: 81.5

INDUSTRY: Fire, marine, and casualty insurance (SIC: 6331)

TRANSFER AGENT(S): EquiServe Trust Company, N.A., Jersey City, NJ

CINCINNATI FINANCIAL CORPORATION

YIELD 2.7%
P/E RATIO 27.5

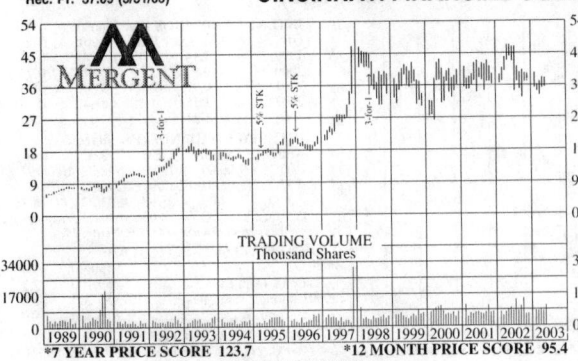

INTERIM EARNINGS (Per Share):

Qtr.	Mar.	June	Sept.	Dec.
1999	0.38	0.52	0.34	0.28
2000	0.48	0.45	0.03	d0.26
2001	0.44	0.30	0.22	0.22
2002	0.46	0.21	0.44	0.35
2003	0.35	...	...	...

INTERIM DIVIDENDS (Per Share):

Amt.	Decl.	Ex.	Rec.	Pay.
0.223Q	11/15/02	12/23/02	12/26/02	1/15/03
0.25Q	2/01/03	3/24/03	3/26/03	4/15/03
0.25Q	5/23/03	6/23/03	6/25/03	7/15/03

Indicated div.: $1.00 (Div. Reinv. Plan)

CAPITALIZATION (12/31/02):

	($000)	(%)
Long-Term Debt	420,000	5.4
Deferred Income Tax	1,737,000	22.4
Common & Surplus	5,598,000	72.2
Total	7,755,000	100.0

DIVIDEND ACHIEVER STATUS:
Rank: 121   10-Year Growth Rate: 11.24%
Total Years of Dividend Growth: 42

*7 YEAR PRICE SCORE 123.7   ***12 MONTH PRICE SCORE 95.4**
*NYSE COMPOSITE INDEX=100

RECENT DEVELOPMENTS: For the quarter ended 3/31/03, net income dropped 24.0% to $57.0 million from $75.0 million in the equivalent prior-year quarter. Total revenues rose 2.9% to $707.0 million from $687.0 million a year earlier. Revenues for 2003 and 2002 included realized investment losses of $62.0 million and $8.0 million, respectively. Net earned premiums in the property casualty insurance group climbed 12.5% to $629.0 million from $559.0 million the previous year. CINF's combined ratio improved 3.7 percentage points to 95.1% from 98.8% the year before.

Net premiums earned in the life insurance group grew 6.4% to $21.0 million. Net investment income rose 6.4% to $116.0 million. Separately, CINF announced that it expects to incur pre-tax catastrophe losses of about $48.0 million resulting from severe weather across the Midwestern and Mid-Atlantic states. The storm losses are expected to add a total of about 7.5 percentage points to the second quarter property casualty combined ratio. CINF noted that the after-tax impact on earnings for the second quarter are expected to be about $0.19 per share.

BUSINESS

CINCINNATI FINANCIAL CORPORATION, through six subsidiaries, sells insurance primarily in the Midwest and Southeast regions of the U.S. through a network of local independent agents. Insurance products include fire, automobile, casualty, bonds and all related forms of property casualty insurance as well as a full line of life insurance products. Cincinnati Insurance Company operates in 31 states and is licensed for the sale of property casualty insurance. Cincinnati Casualty Company seeks to provide flexibility in underwriting, pricing and billing. Cincinnati Indemnity Company writes nonstandard personal and casualty lines of insurance in 31 states. Cincinnati Life Insurance Company markets life, disability income and long-term care insurance and annuities, while CFC Investment Company complements the insurance subsidiaries with leasing and financing services. CinFin Capital Management offers investment management services to corporations, insurance agencies and companies, institutions, pension plans and high net worth individuals.

ANNUAL FINANCIAL DATA

	12/31/02	12/31/01	12/31/00	12/31/99	12/31/98	12/31/97	12/31/96
Earnings Per Share	1.46	1.19	① 0.73	1.52	1.41	1.77	1.31
Tang. Book Val. Per Share	34.56	37.02	37.26	33.46	33.72	28.35	18.95
Dividends Per Share	0.88	0.82	0.74	0.66	0.60	0.53	0.47
Dividend Payout %	60.1	68.9	101.4	43.6	42.3	30.1	36.1
INCOME STATEMENT (IN MILLIONS):							
Total Premium Income	2,478.0	2,152.0	1,906.9	1,732.0	1,612.7	1,516.4	1,422.9
Net Investment Income	445.0	421.0	415.3	386.8	368.0	348.6	327.3
Other Income	d80.0	d12.0	8.8	9.5	73.6	77.4	58.5
Total Revenues	2,843.0	2,561.0	2,331.0	2,128.2	2,054.3	1,942.4	1,808.7
Policyholder Benefits	1,826.0	1,663.0	1,581.1	1,254.4	1,221.1	1,054.9	1,087.1
Income Before Income Taxes	279.0	221.0	126.8	321.6	307.1	394.6	282.4
Income Taxes	41.0	28.0	cr9.7	66.9	65.5	95.2	58.7
Net Income	238.0	193.0	① 118.4	254.7	241.6	299.4	223.8
Average Shs. Outstg. (000)	163,193	162,000	163,921	168,615	172,078	170,795	173,349
BALANCE SHEET (IN MILLIONS):							
Cash & Cash Equivalents	112.0	93.0	60.3	339.6	58.6	80.2	59.9
Premiums Due	1,516.0	1,274.0	897.6	358.7	332.5	299.4	304.8
Invst. Assets: Fixed-term	3,305.0	3,010.0	2,721.3	2,617.4	2,812.2	2,751.2	2,561.8
Invst. Assets: Equities	7,884.0	8,495.0	8,526.0	7,510.9	7,454.8	5,999.3	3,740.2
Invst. Assets: Total	11,257.0	11,571.0	11,315.8	10,194.2	10,325.0	8,797.1	6,355.0
Total Assets	14,059.0	13,959.0	13,287.1	11,380.2	11,086.5	9,493.4	7,045.5
Long-Term Obligations	420.0	426.0	449.2	456.4	471.5	58.4	79.8
Net Stockholders' Equity	5,598.0	5,998.0	5,995.0	5,421.3	5,620.9	4,717.0	3,162.9
Year-end Shs. Outstg. (000)	162,000	162,000	160,891	162,021	166,681	166,356	166,908
STATISTICAL RECORD:							
Return on Revenues %	8.4	7.5	5.1	12.0	11.8	15.4	12.4
Return on Equity %	4.3	3.2	2.0	4.7	4.3	6.3	7.1
Return on Assets %	1.7	1.4	0.9	2.2	2.2	3.2	3.2
Price Range	47.30-32.43	42.93-34.00	43.31-26.19	42.50-30.13	46.92-30.50	47.08-20.67	21.83-17.75
P/E Ratio	32.4-22.2	36.1-28.6	59.3-35.9	28.0-19.8	33.3-21.6	26.6-11.7	16.7-13.6
Average Yield %	2.2	2.1	2.1	1.8	1.5	1.6	2.4

Statistics are as originally reported. Adj. for stk. splits: 3-for-1, 5/15/98; 5% div., 4/30/96; 5% div., 4/28/95 ① Incl. one-time asset impair. chrg. of $39.1 mill.

OFFICERS:
J. J. Schiff, Jr., Chmn., Pres., C.E.O.
J. E. Benoski, Vice-Chmn., Sr. V.P.
K. W. Stecher, Sr. V.P., C.F.O., Treas., Sec.
INVESTOR CONTACT: Kenneth W. Stecher, (513) 870-2639
PRINCIPAL OFFICE: 6200 S. Gilmore Road, Fairfield, OH 45014-5141

TELEPHONE NUMBER: (513) 870-2000
FAX: (513) 870-2066
WEB: www.cinfin.com
NO. OF EMPLOYEES: 3,511 (avg.)
SHAREHOLDERS: 11,486
ANNUAL MEETING: In April
INCORPORATED: OH, Sept., 1968

INSTITUTIONAL HOLDINGS:
No. of Institutions: 278
Shares Held: 71,665,104
% Held: 44.5
INDUSTRY: Fire, marine, and casualty insurance (SIC: 6331)
TRANSFER AGENT(S): Cincinnati Financial Corporation, Fairfield, OH

CINTAS CORPORATION

YIELD 0.7%
P/E RATIO 25.7

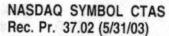
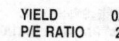
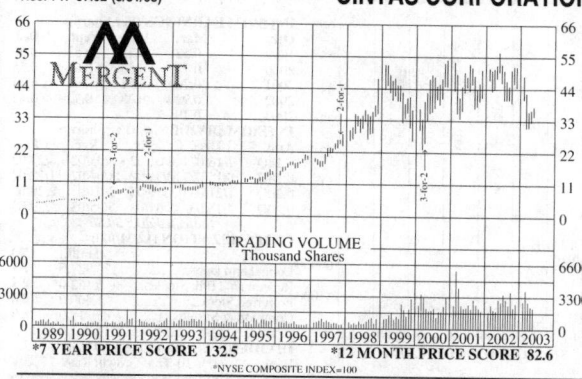

*7 YEAR PRICE SCORE 132.5   *12 MONTH PRICE SCORE 82.6
*NYSE COMPOSITE INDEX=100

INTERIM EARNINGS (Per Share):

Qtr.	Aug.	Nov.	Feb.	May
1997-98	0.17	0.19	0.18	0.20
1998-99	0.21	0.25	0.23	0.11
1999-00	0.25	0.29	0.29	0.31
2000-01	0.30	0.33	0.32	0.35
2001-02	0.33	0.34	0.32	0.37
2002-03	0.36	0.37	0.34	...

INTERIM DIVIDENDS (Per Share):

Amt.	Decl.	Ex.	Rec.	Pay.
0.25A	1/31/02	2/13/02	2/15/02	4/08/02
0.27A	1/24/03	2/05/03	2/07/03	3/14/03

Indicated div.: $0.27

CAPITALIZATION (5/31/02):

	($mill.)	(%)
Long-Term Debt	703.3	31.9
Deferred Income Tax	79.6	3.6
Common & Surplus	1,423.8	64.5
Total	2,206.6	100.0

DIVIDEND ACHIEVER STATUS:
Rank: 19   10-Year Dividend Growth Rate: 21.15%
Total Years of Dividend Growth: 20

RECENT DEVELOPMENTS: For the quarter ended 2/28/03, net income increased 6.2% to $59.1 million from $55.6 million in the comparable prior-year quarter. Total revenue advanced 21.7% to $663.8 million from $545.5 million the previous year, primarily due to the Company's May 2002 acquisition of Omni Services, Inc. and growth in its customer base. The increased revenues were somewhat mitigated by increased lost business and reductions in existing business, attributable to the current sluggish economy and the resulting reduction in the labor force. Rentals revenue

increased 23.0% to $523.2 million from $425.3 million in 2002, aided by a 17.0% increase in uniform sales. Other services revenue rose 16.9% to $140.6 million. Cost of rentals grew 27.5% to $293.9 million, while cost of other services rose 11.6% to $95.4 million. Separately, due to continued market pressure on the Company's sales, CTAS has revised its forecast for fiscal 2003. Revenues are expected to be in a range of $2.68 billion to $2.73 billion. Earnings per share are forecasted to range from $1.43 to $1.50.

BUSINESS

CINTAS CORPORATION rents and sells uniforms. CTAS provides services to businesses of all types, from small service and manufacturing companies to major corporations. The Company classifies its businesses into two operating segments: Rentals and Other Services. The Rental operating segment (77.2% of fiscal 2002 revenues) designs and manufactures corporate identity uniforms, which it rents, along with other items, to its customers. The Other Services operating segment (22.8%) involves the design, manufacture and direct sale of uniforms to its customers as well as the sale of ancillary services including sanitation supplies, first aid products and services and cleanroom supplies. As of 11/30/02, the Company operated seven distribution facilities and 14 wholly-owned manufacturing facilities, which provide for a substantial amount of its standard uniform needs. Additional products are purchased from several outside suppliers. In March 1999, CTAS acquired Unitog Company, based in Kansas City, Missouri. In April 1999, the Company acquired Chicago-based Uniforms To You. On 5/13/02, CTAS acquired Omni Services, Inc. for about $660.0 million including assumed debt.

ANNUAL FINANCIAL DATA

	5/31/02	5/31/01	5/31/00	5/31/99	5/31/98	5/31/97	5/31/96
Earnings Per Share	1.36	1.30	1.14	⊡ 0.82	⊡ 0.79	0.64	0.53
Cash Flow Per Share	2.06	1.95	1.72	1.35	1.16	0.97	0.84
Tang. Book Val. Per Share	4.39	7.27	6.20	5.24	4.17	2.83	2.29
Dividends Per Share	0.22	0.19	0.15	0.12	0.10	0.08	0.07
Dividend Payout %	16.2	14.4	12.9	14.6	12.6	13.1	12.5
INCOME STATEMENT (IN MILLIONS):							
Total Revenues	2,271.1	2,160.7	1,902.0	1,751.6	1,198.3	839.9	730.1
Costs & Expenses	1,774.1	1,680.7	1,478.7	1,380.1	940.2	641.8	558.2
Depreciation & Amort.	120.0	112.1	99.5	90.2	57.2	47.7	43.1
Operating Income	376.9	367.9	323.8	281.3	200.9	150.4	128.8
Net Interest Inc./(Exp.)	d5.3	d10.7	d11.2	d11.8	d4.4	d3.8	d6.6
Income Before Income Taxes	371.6	356.5	311.8	224.0	179.4	146.6	122.2
Income Taxes	137.3	134.0	118.4	85.1	56.6	55.8	47.0
Net Income	234.3	222.5	193.4	⊡ 138.9	⊡ 122.9	90.8	75.2
Cash Flow	354.3	334.5	292.9	229.2	180.1	138.6	118.3
Average Shs. Outstg. (000)	172,244	171,629	169,987	169,341	155,435	142,893	141,297
BALANCE SHEET (IN MILLIONS):							
Cash & Cash Equivalents	85.1	110.2	109.8	88.1	100.9	102.9	82.5
Total Current Assets	853.3	819.7	721.5	634.5	508.6	356.0	297.5
Net Property	778.4	701.1	642.5	573.1	367.1	287.4	252.6
Total Assets	2,519.2	1,752.2	1,581.3	1,407.8	1,017.8	761.8	668.8
Total Current Liabilities	312.6	250.9	235.4	212.1	159.0	116.1	102.6
Long-Term Obligations	703.3	220.9	254.4	283.6	180.0	111.5	117.9
Net Stockholders' Equity	1,423.8	1,231.3	1,042.9	871.4	654.5	512.4	429.5
Net Working Capital	540.6	568.8	486.1	422.4	349.6	239.8	194.9
Year-end Shs. Outstg. (000)	169,930	169,371	168,282	166,424	156,917	144,801	141,597
STATISTICAL RECORD:							
Operating Profit Margin %	16.6	17.0	17.0	16.1	16.8	17.9	17.6
Net Profit Margin %	10.3	10.3	10.2	7.9	10.3	10.8	10.3
Return on Equity %	16.5	18.1	18.5	15.9	18.8	17.7	17.5
Return on Assets %	9.3	12.7	12.2	9.9	12.1	11.9	11.2
Debt/Total Assets %	27.9	12.6	16.1	20.1	17.7	14.6	17.6
Price Range	53.25-33.75	54.00-23.17	52.25-26.00	47.50-26.00	28.33-17.00	21.17-13.92	16.00-11.17
P/E Ratio	39.2-24.8	41.5-17.8	45.8-22.8	57.9-31.7	35.7-21.4	33.2-21.8	30.0-20.9
Average Yield %	0.5	0.5	0.4	0.3	0.4	0.4	0.5

Statistics are as originally reported. Adj. for stk. splits: 3-for-2, 3/7/00; 2-for-1, 11/18/97.
⊡ Incl. non-recur. chrg. $11.3 mill., 5/99; credit $17.1 mill., 5/98.

OFFICERS:
R. T. Farmer, Chmn.
S. D. Farmer, Pres., C.O.O.
R. J. Kohlhepp, C.E.O.

INVESTOR CONTACT: William C. Gale,
V.P., C.F.O., (513) 459-1200

PRINCIPAL OFFICE: 6800 Cintas Blvd., P.O.
Box 625737, Cincinnati, OH 45262-5737

TELEPHONE NUMBER: (513) 459-1200
FAX: (513) 573-4030
WEB: www.cintas-corp.com
NO. OF EMPLOYEES: 27,000 (approx.)
SHAREHOLDERS: 2,100 (approx.)
ANNUAL MEETING: In Oct.
INCORPORATED: OH, 1968; reincorp., WA,
Dec., 1986

INSTITUTIONAL HOLDINGS:
No. of Institutions: 369
Shares Held: 94,542,941
% Held: 55.6

INDUSTRY: Men's and boys' work clothing
(SIC: 2326)

TRANSFER AGENT(S): The Fifth Third Bank,
Cincinnati, OH

CITIGROUP INC.

	YIELD	2.0%
	P/E RATIO	14.9

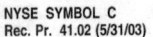

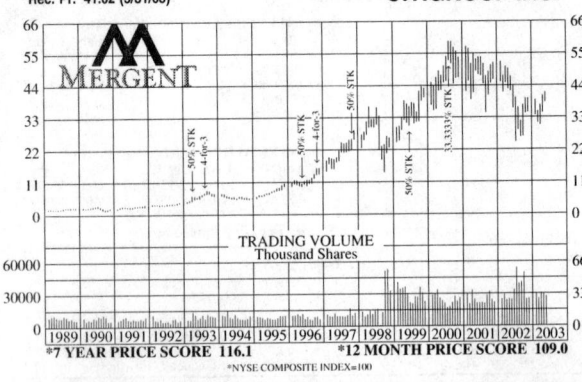

TRADING VOLUME
Thousand Shares

| 1989 | 1990 | 1991 | 1992 | 1993 | 1994 | 1995 | 1996 | 1997 | 1998 | 1999 | 2000 | 2001 | 2002 | 2003 |

*7 YEAR PRICE SCORE 116.1   *12 MONTH PRICE SCORE 109.0

*NYSE COMPOSITE INDEX=100

INTERIM EARNINGS (Per Share):

Qtr.	Mar.	June	Sept.	Dec.
1999	0.52	0.53	0.53	0.56
2000	0.78	0.65	0.67	0.55
2001	0.70	0.71	0.61	0.74
2002	0.93	0.78	0.72	0.47
2003	0.79	...	...	...

INTERIM DIVIDENDS (Per Share):

Amt.	Decl.	Ex.	Rec.	Pay.
0.18Q	7/16/02	8/01/02	8/05/02	8/23/02
0.18Q	10/15/02	10/31/02	11/04/02	11/22/02
0.20Q	1/21/03	1/30/03	2/03/03	2/28/03
0.20Q	4/15/03	5/01/03	5/05/03	5/23/03

Indicated div.: $0.80

CAPITALIZATION (12/31/02):

	($mill.)	(%)
Long-Term Debt	126,927.0	57.7
Redeemable Pfd. Stock	6,152.0	2.8
Preferred Stock	1,400.0	0.6
Common & Surplus	85,318.0	38.8
Total	219,797.0	100.0

DIVIDEND ACHIEVER STATUS:
Rank: 4   10-Year Growth Rate: 27.85%
Total Years of Dividend Growth: 16

RECENT DEVELOPMENTS: For the quarter ended 3/31/03, net income rose 17.8% to $4.1 million compared with income of $3.5 million in the equivalent 2002 quarter. Results for 2003 included a gain of $13.0 million and a loss of $46.0 million in 2002 for restructuring-related items. Results for 2002 included various charges totaling $858.0 million stemming from the economic situation in Argentina. Total revenues climbed 2.4% to $23.2 million.

PROSPECTS: Looking ahead, the Company believes it has a solid basis to bring a recovery claim as a result of various actions of the Argentine government, including abandoning the country's fixed U.S. dollar-to-peso exchange rate. As the economic situation and legal and regulatory issues in Argentina remain unsettled, the Company continues to work with the government and its customers and monitor conditions closely in an attempt to minimize losses.

BUSINESS

CITIGROUP INC., (formerly Travelers Group Inc.) was formed on 10/8/98 by the merger of Travelers and Citicorp. The Company consists of businesses that produce a broad range of financial services -- consumer banking and credit, corporate and investment banking, insurance, securities brokerage, and asset management -- and use diverse channels to make them available to consumers, governments and institutions around the world. Major brand names include CITIBANK, CITIFINANCIAL, PRIMERICA, SALOMON SMITH BARNEY, BANAMEX, and TRAVELERS LIFE and ANNUITY. On 8/6/01, the Company acquired Grupo Financiero Banamex-Accival for approximately $12.48 billion. On 8/20/02, the Company completed the spin-off of a $7.00 billion tax-free distribution to its stockholders of a majority portion of its remaining ownership in Travelers Property Casualty Corp. On 11/6/02, the Company acquired Golden State Bancorp in a transaction valued at about $5.80 billion.

ANNUAL FINANCIAL DATA

	12/31/02	12/31/01	12/31/00	12/31/99	5 12/31/98	6 12/31/97	12/31/96
Earnings Per Share	7 2.59	4 6 2.75	3 2.62	2 4 2.15	4 1.22	1.27	1 1.15
Tang. Book Val. Per Share	9.70	15.57	12.84	10.64	8.94	6.99	4.95
Dividends Per Share	0.70	0.60	0.52	0.41	0.28	0.20	0.15
Dividend Payout %	27.0	21.8	19.8	18.9	22.8	15.7	13.0
INCOME STATEMENT (IN BILLIONS):							
Net Investment Income	62.35	80.03	77.37	55.34	56.09	26.61	14.35
Other Income	30.21	32.00	34.46	26.66	20.34	11.00	7.00
Total Revenues	92.56	112.02	111.83	82.01	76.43	37.61	21.35
Policyholder Benefits	3.48	11.76	10.15	8.67	8.37	7.71	7.37
Income Before Income Taxes	20.54	21.90	21.14	15.95	9.27	5.01	3.40
Income Taxes	7.00	7.53	7.53	5.70	3.23	1.70	1.05
Equity Earnings/Minority Int.	d0.09	d0.09	d0.10	d0.25	d0.23	d0.21	d0.05
Net Income	7 13.45	4 6 14.28	3 13.52	2 4 9.99	4 5.81	3.10	1 2.30
Average Shs. Outstg. (000)	5,166,200	5,147,000	5,122,200	4,591,332	4,630,399	2,359,799	1,916,400
BALANCE SHEET (IN BILLIONS):							
Cash & Cash Equivalents	312.48	298.23	253.01	235.97	228.51	253.50	83.61
Premiums Due	29.71	47.53	36.24	32.68	30.91	30.94	22.41
Invst. Assets: Equities	...	...	...	...	...	...	1.16
Invst. Assets: Loans	432.32	375.17	354.74	240.34	221.96	10.82	13.79
Invst. Assets: Total	757.05	680.92	607.37	462.63	445.48	212.38	77.28
Total Assets	1,097.19	1,051.50	902.21	716.94	668.64	386.56	151.07
Long-Term Obligations	126.93	121.63	111.78	47.09	48.67	28.35	11.33
Net Stockholders' Equity	86.72	81.25	66.21	49.69	42.71	20.89	13.09
Year-end Shs. Outstg. (000)	5,140,682	5,118,689	5,022,222	4,490,032	4,515,999	2,289,999	1,912,800
STATISTICAL RECORD:							
Return on Revenues %	14.5	12.8	12.1	12.2	7.6	8.3	10.8
Return on Equity %	15.5	17.6	20.4	20.1	13.6	14.9	17.6
Return on Assets %	1.2	1.4	1.5	1.4	0.9	0.8	1.5
Price Range	52.20-24.48	57.38-34.51	59.13-35.34	43.69-24.50	36.75-14.25	28.69-14.58	15.83-9.42
P/E Ratio	20.2-9.5	20.9-12.5	22.6-13.5	20.4-11.4	30.2-11.7	22.6-11.5	13.8-8.2
Average Yield %	1.8	1.3	1.1	1.2	1.1	0.9	1.2

Statistics are as originally reported. Adj. for stk. splits: 33.3% stk. div., 8/25/00; 3-for-2, 5/99; 11/97; 4-for-3, 8/00, 11/96; 3-for-2, 5/96 ① Bef. disc. oper. gain $31.0 mill. ② Bef. acctg. chrgs. $127.0 mill. ③ Results reflect the acquisition of Salomon Inc. in 11/97. ④ Incl. non-recurr. chrg. 2001, $621.0 mill.; credit 1999, $47.0 mill.; 1998, $795.0 mill.; chrg. 1997, $255.4 mill.; credit 1996, $397.0 mill.; 1995, $117.0 mill.; 1994, $88.7 mill. ⑤ Results prior to fourth quarter of 1998 are for Travelers Group. ⑥ Incl. restruct. & merger related items 2001, $285.0 mill.; 2000, $621.0 mill. ⑦ Bef. disc. oper. gain $1.88 bill., acctg. chrgs. $47.0 mill., but incl. non-recurr. chrg. $225.0 mill.

OFFICERS:
S. I. Weill, Chmn., C.E.O.
W. R. Rhodes, Sr. Vice-Chmn.
M. T. Masin, Vice-Chmn, C.O.O.
R. B. Willumstad, Pres.

INVESTOR CONTACT: Sheri Ptachek, Investor Relations, (212) 559-9446

PRINCIPAL OFFICE: 399 Park Avenue, New York, NY 10043

TELEPHONE NUMBER: (212) 559-1000
FAX: (212) 816-8913
WEB: www.citigroup.com

NO. OF EMPLOYEES: 250,000 full-time (approx.); 5,000 part-time (approx.)

SHAREHOLDERS: 216,500 (approx.)

ANNUAL MEETING: In Apr.

INCORPORATED: DE, Dec., 1993

INSTITUTIONAL HOLDINGS:
No. of Institutions: 1,257
Shares Held: N/A
% Held: 61.9

INDUSTRY: National commercial banks (SIC: 6021)

TRANSFER AGENT(S): Citibank Shareholder Services, Jersey City, NJ

CITIZENS BANKING CORP.

YIELD 4.3%
P/E RATIO 75.7

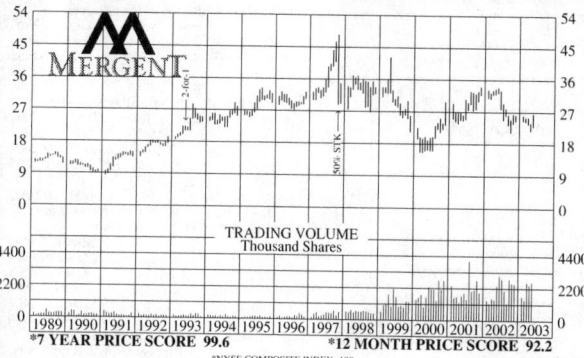

TRADING VOLUME
Thousand Shares

7 YEAR PRICE SCORE 99.6   **12 MONTH PRICE SCORE 92.2**

*NYSE COMPOSITE INDEX=100

INTERIM EARNINGS (Per Share):

Qtr.	Mar.	June	Sept.	Dec.
1999	0.47	0.50	0.49	d0.19
2000	0.46	0.47	0.54	0.44
2001	0.51	0.59	0.60	0.56
2002	0.53	0.56	d1.03	0.48
2003	0.34	...	...	...

INTERIM DIVIDENDS (Per Share):

Amt.	Decl.	Ex.	Rec.	Pay.
0.285Q	4/16/02	4/24/02	4/26/02	5/08/02
0.285Q	7/19/02	7/24/02	7/26/02	8/07/02
0.285Q	10/18/02	10/23/02	10/25/02	11/06/02
0.285Q	1/16/03	1/22/03	1/24/03	2/05/03
0.285Q	4/15/03	4/23/03	4/25/03	5/07/03

Indicated div.: $1.14 (Div. Reinv. Plan)

CAPITALIZATION (12/31/02):

	($000)	(%)
Total Deposits	5,936,913	82.6
Long-Term Debt	599,313	8.3
Common & Surplus	650,469	9.1
Total	7,186,695	100.0

DIVIDEND ACHIEVER STATUS:
Rank: 157   10-Year Growth Rate: 9.40%
Total Years of Dividend Growth: 19

RECENT DEVELOPMENTS: For the quarter ended 3/31/03, net income dropped 37.5% to $15.1 million from $24.1 million in the corresponding prior-year period. Earnings for 2003 included a loan charge-off of $11.5 million. Net interest income slid 4.6% to $71.5 million due to a lower average volume of earning assets. Provision for loan losses totaled $19.0 million versus $5.3 million in 2002. Total non-interest income slipped 5.8% to $23.3 million, while total non-interest expense declined 7.5% to $56.6 million.

For the remainder of 2003, deposits are anticipated to grow at a modest pace, while total loans are expected to decline slightly. CBCF expects a decrease in noninterest income for 2003 compared to 2002 due primarily to the sale of the merchant business in 2002. Moreover, CBCF expects charge-offs for the remainder of the year to trend downward from first quarter 2003 levels. Accordingly, earnings per share for 2003 are expected to be less than the previously-announced $2.02 to $2.08 range.

BUSINESS

CITIZENS BANKING CORP. is a multibank holding company, which directly or indirectly owns four banking subsidiaries and four nonbanking subsidiaries, with total assets of $7.77 billion as of 3/31/03. The Company's subsidiary banks are full-service commercial banks offering a variety of financial services to corporate, commercial, correspondent and individual bank customers. These services include commercial, mortgage and consumer lending, demand and time deposits, trust services, investment services, retirement planning, asset management, insurance services, safe deposit facilities, and other financial products and services. Citizens operated 188 branch, private banking, and financial center locations throughout Michigan, Wisconsin, Iowa, and Illinois as of 4/14/03.

ANNUAL FINANCIAL DATA

	12/31/02	12/31/01	12/31/00	12/31/99	12/31/98	12/31/97	12/31/96
Earnings Per Share	④ 0.56	⑤ 2.25	② 1.91	① 1.28	1.98	① 1.11	1.28
Tang. Book Val. Per Share	13.18	13.70	12.67	11.28	13.76	12.47	8.73
Dividends Per Share	1.13	1.08	1.01	0.92	0.82	0.74	0.67
Dividend Payout %	201.7	48.2	53.1	71.5	41.4	67.0	52.8
INCOME STATEMENT (IN MILLIONS):							
Total Interest Income	463.4	573.6	622.0	542.4	339.9	335.9	255.9
Total Interest Expense	161.6	265.6	307.1	231.9	142.0	144.0	109.8
Net Interest Income	301.8	308.0	314.9	310.5	197.8	191.8	146.1
Provision for Loan Losses	120.2	26.4	21.0	24.7	14.1	15.3	8.3
Non-Interest Income	101.8	117.5	90.3	79.8	56.3	46.7	40.5
Non-Interest Expense	246.0	251.2	242.2	236.8	158.3	153.4	126.0
Income Before Taxes	24.0	147.9	126.5	90.0	81.7	46.0	52.3
Net Income	④ 25.0	③ 104.7	② 90.7	① 62.0	56.8	① 31.5	37.4
Average Shs. Outstg. (000)	45,077	46,590	47,543	48,617	28,743	28,420	29,332
BALANCE SHEET (IN MILLIONS):							
Cash & Due from Banks	171.9	224.4	318.1	250.7	140.5	168.4	137.9
Securities Avail. for Sale	...	38.2	...	...	...	...	...
Total Loans & Leases	5,432.6	5,922.4	6,422.8	5,917.5	3,584.5	3,541.6	2,620.7
Allowance for Credit Losses	109.5	80.3	80.1	76.4	46.4	45.9	36.0
Net Loans & Leases	5,323.1	5,842.1	6,342.7	5,841.1	3,538.1	3,495.7	2,584.7
Total Assets	7,522.0	7,678.9	8,405.1	7,899.4	4,501.4	4,439.3	3,483.9
Total Deposits	5,936.9	5,965.1	6,244.1	6,129.0	3,764.4	3,694.3	2,864.8
Long-Term Obligations	599.3	629.1	471.1	127.1	130.9	108.2	84.1
Total Liabilities	6,871.6	6,981.4	7,725.1	7,265.7	4,060.3	4,029.4	3,168.6
Net Stockholders' Equity	650.5	697.5	680.0	633.7	441.1	409.8	315.2
Year-end Shs. Outstg. (000)	43,702	45,098	46,510	47,568	28,100	28,048	28,680
STATISTICAL RECORD:							
Return on Equity %	3.8	15.0	13.3	9.8	12.9	7.7	11.9
Return on Assets %	0.3	1.4	1.1	0.8	1.3	0.7	1.1
Equity/Assets %	8.6	9.1	8.1	8.0	9.8	9.2	9.0
Non-Int. Exp./Tot. Inc. %	61.0	59.0	59.8	60.7	62.3	64.3	67.5
Price Range	33.88-21.25	34.02-23.69	29.81-15.50	42.25-21.25	37.13-26.75	48.50-28.75	32.25-27.25
P/E Ratio	60.5-37.9	15.1-10.5	15.6-8.1	33.0-16.6	18.7-13.5	43.7-25.9	25.3-21.4
Average Yield %	4.1	3.8	4.5	2.9	2.6	1.9	2.3

Statistics are as originally reported. Adj. for stk. splits: 50% div., 11/18/97. ① Incl. aftertax chrg. $28.4 mill., 12/99; $17.3 mill., 12/97. ② Incl. special chrg. of $15.5 mill. ③ Incl. net gain of $20.6 mill. rel. to various items. ④ Incl. a special chrg. of $13.4 mill. & a gain on sale of assets of $5.4 mill.

OFFICERS:
W. R. Hartman, Chmn., Pres., C.E.O.
C. D. Christy, Exec. V.P., C.F.O.
T. W. Gallagher, Sr. V.P., Sec., Gen. Couns.

INVESTOR CONTACT: Ryan P. Mathews, Investor Relations, (810) 257-2489

PRINCIPAL OFFICE: 328 S. Saginaw Street, Flint, MI 48502

TELEPHONE NUMBER: (810) 766-7500
FAX: (810) 766-7503
WEB: www.cbclientsfirst.com

NO. OF EMPLOYEES: 2,520

SHAREHOLDERS: 6,177

ANNUAL MEETING: In April

INCORPORATED: MI, Jan., 1982

INSTITUTIONAL HOLDINGS:
No. of Institutions: 91
Shares Held: 11,673,903
% Held: 27.1

INDUSTRY: National commercial banks (SIC: 6021)

TRANSFER AGENT(S): Computershare Investor Services, Chicago, IL

CLARCOR INC.

YIELD	1.3%
P/E RATIO	19.2

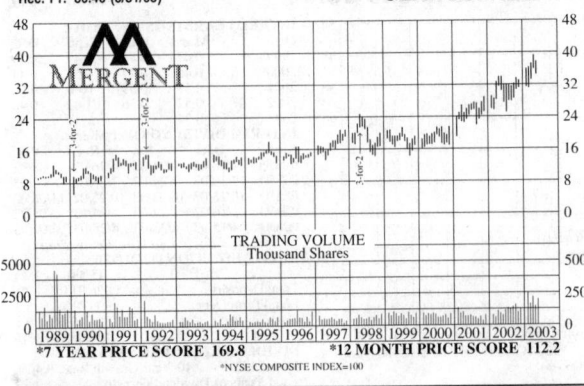

INTERIM EARNINGS (Per Share):

Qtr.	Feb.	May	Aug.	Nov.
2000	0.29	0.41	0.41	0.53
2001	0.40	0.36	0.41	0.51
2002	0.32	0.42	0.48	0.62
2003	0.38	...	...	...

INTERIM DIVIDENDS (Per Share):

Amt.	Decl.	Ex.	Rec.	Pay.
0.12Q	3/19/02	4/10/02	4/12/02	4/26/02
0.12Q	6/24/02	7/10/02	7/12/02	7/26/02
0.122Q	9/23/02	10/09/02	10/11/02	10/25/02
0.122Q	12/16/02	1/15/03	1/17/03	1/31/03
0.122Q	3/24/03	4/09/03	4/11/03	4/25/03

Indicated div.: $0.49 (Div. Reinv. Plan)

CAPITALIZATION (11/30/02):

	($000)	(%)
Long-Term Debt	22,648	6.3
Deferred Income Tax	19,045	5.3
Minority Interest	536	0.1
Common & Surplus	315,461	88.2
Total	357,690	100.0

DIVIDEND ACHIEVER STATUS:

Rank: 274	10-Year Growth Rate: 1.89%
Total Years of Dividend Growth:	22

7 YEAR PRICE SCORE 169.8   **12 MONTH PRICE SCORE 112.2**
*NYSE COMPOSITE INDEX=100

RECENT DEVELOPMENTS: For the quarter ended 3/1/03, net earnings advanced 20.0% to $9.6 million versus $8.0 million in the equivalent 2002 quarter. Net sales increased 8.4% to $171.5 million from $158.3 million a year earlier. Engine/Mobile Filtration segment sales climbed 15.5% to $66.8 million, while Industrial/Environmental Filtration segment sales rose 5.1% to $90.4 million. Packaging segment sales decreased 0.9% to $14.3 million. Gross profit improved 8.1% to $48.3 million.

PROSPECTS: The impact of the Total Filtration Program, which provides a range of filtration products and services from a single source, should become evident as it is introduced to current and new customers. Meanwhile, sales of air quality equipment and filtration systems and sales to the aerospace market are not expected to improve in the near term. However, sales growth is expected for the Packaging segment in 2003. As a result, CLC expects 2003 earnings to range from $1.92 to $2.02 per diluted share.

BUSINESS

CLARCOR INC. manufactures mobile, industrial and environmental filtration products and consumer and industrial packaging products for domestic and international markets. The Industrial/Environmental Filtration segment (53.6% of fiscal 2002 net sales) includes products used primarily for commercial, residential and industrial applications. The segment markets commercial and industrial air filters and systems, electrostatic contamination control equipment and electrostatic high precision spraying equipment. The Engine/Mobile Filtration segment (36.8%) markets a full line of oil, air, fuel, coolant and hydraulic fluid filters. The Packaging segment (9.6%) includes a variety of custom styled containers and packaging items used primarily by the food, confectionery, spice, drug, toiletries and chemical specialties industries. In June 2001, CLC acquired Total Filtration Systems, Inc. for $33.3 million.

ANNUAL FINANCIAL DATA

	11/30/02	11/30/01	11/30/00	11/27/99	11/28/98	11/29/97	11/30/96
Earnings Per Share	1.85	1.68	1.64	1.46	1.30	[1] 1.11	1.12
Cash Flow Per Share	2.64	2.56	2.50	2.09	1.80	1.60	1.56
Tang. Book Val. Per Share	7.74	6.40	5.75	4.98	6.90	6.41	5.87
Dividends Per Share	0.48	0.47	0.46	0.45	0.44	0.437	0.43
Dividend Payout %	26.1	28.1	28.2	31.0	34.0	39.1	38.2
INCOME STATEMENT (IN THOUSANDS):							
Total Revenues	715,563	666,964	652,148	477,869	426,773	394,264	333,388
Costs & Expenses	618,028	569,304	555,082	406,420	362,730	338,240	283,073
Depreciation & Amort.	19,760	21,850	21,079	15,372	12,380	11,600	9,785
Operating Income	77,775	75,810	75,987	56,077	51,663	[1] 44,424	40,530
Net Interest Inc./(Exp.)	d5,612	d9,616	d10,836	d2,200	d1,053	d2,759	d3,243
Income Before Income Taxes	71,450	65,734	63,487	55,615	51,347	44,192	40,019
Income Taxes	24,773	23,804	23,201	20,137	19,262	17,164	14,896
Equity Earnings/Minority Int.	d76	d37	d49	d66	d6	d110	d145
Net Income	46,601	41,893	40,237	35,412	32,079	[1] 26,918	24,978
Cash Flow	66,361	63,743	61,316	50,784	44,459	38,518	34,763
Average Shs. Outstg.	25,172	24,892	24,506	24,314	24,649	24,134	22,289
BALANCE SHEET (IN THOUSANDS):							
Cash & Cash Equivalents	13,747	7,418	10,864	14,745	33,321	30,324	17,372
Total Current Assets	259,746	244,350	230,479	227,670	168,173	160,527	124,379
Net Property	132,892	137,316	140,121	126,026	86,389	82,905	78,586
Total Assets	546,119	530,617	501,930	472,991	305,766	282,519	243,964
Total Current Liabilities	174,255	94,931	97,826	97,475	61,183	54,237	45,156
Long-Term Obligations	22,648	135,203	141,486	145,981	36,419	37,656	35,522
Net Stockholders' Equity	315,461	274,261	242,093	210,718	186,807	171,162	146,059
Net Working Capital	85,491	149,419	132,653	130,195	106,990	106,290	79,223
Year-end Shs. Outstg.	24,919	24,626	24,381	24,020	23,949	24,243	22,313
STATISTICAL RECORD:							
Operating Profit Margin %	10.9	11.4	11.7	11.7	12.1	11.3	12.2
Net Profit Margin %	6.5	6.3	6.2	7.4	7.5	6.8	7.5
Return on Equity %	14.8	15.3	16.6	16.8	17.2	15.7	17.1
Return on Assets %	8.5	7.9	8.0	7.5	10.5	9.5	10.2
Debt/Total Assets %	4.1	25.5	28.2	30.9	11.9	13.3	14.5
Price Range	34.00-25.03	28.88-19.00	21.50-16.06	21.38-14.25	24.67-14.25	20.83-13.23	16.75-12.42
P/E Ratio	18.4-13.5	17.2-11.3	13.1-9.8	14.6-9.8	19.0-11.0	18.7-12.0	15.0-11.1
Average Yield %	1.6	2.0	2.5	2.5	2.3	2.5	2.9

Statistics are as originally reported. Adj. for stk. split: 3-for-2, 4/98 [1] Incl. non-recurr. credit of $1.7 mill. & non-recurr. chrg. of $3.0 mill.

OFFICERS:
N. E. Johnson, Chmn., Pres., C.E.O.
B. A. Klein, V.P., C.F.O.
D. J. Boyd, V.P., Sec., Gen. Couns.

INVESTOR CONTACT: Bruce A. Klein, V.P., C.F.O., (815) 962-8867

PRINCIPAL OFFICE: 2323 Sixth Street, P.O. Box 7007, Rockford, IL 61125

TELEPHONE NUMBER: (815) 962-8867
FAX: (815) 962-0417
WEB: www.clarcor.com
NO. OF EMPLOYEES: 4,594 (approx.)
SHAREHOLDERS: 1,300 (approx. record)
ANNUAL MEETING: In March
INCORPORATED: IL, 1904; reincorp., DE, 1969

INSTITUTIONAL HOLDINGS:
No. of Institutions: 153
Shares Held: 17,058,485
% Held: 68.2

INDUSTRY: Motor vehicle parts and accessories (SIC: 3714)

TRANSFER AGENT(S): EquiServe, First Chicago Trust Division, Jersey City, NJ

CLECO CORPORATION

YIELD 5.2%
P/E RATIO 11.4

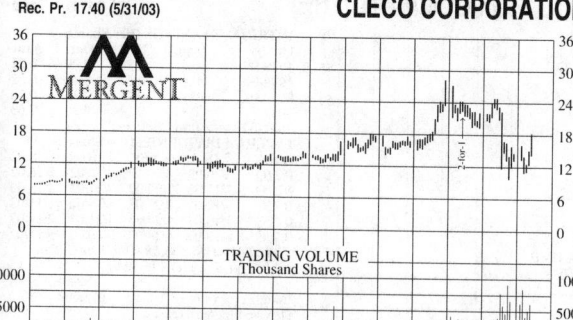
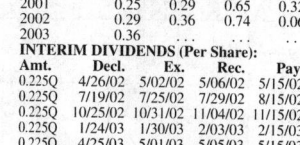

*7 YEAR PRICE SCORE 99.4 ***12 MONTH PRICE SCORE 99.6**

*NYSE COMPOSITE INDEX=100

INTERIM EARNINGS (Per Share):

Qtr.	Mar.	June	Sept.	Dec.
2000	0.22	0.36	0.63	0.18
2001	0.25	0.29	0.65	0.32
2002	0.29	0.36	0.74	0.06
2003	0.36	...	...	...

INTERIM DIVIDENDS (Per Share):

Amt.	Decl.	Ex.	Rec.	Pay.
0.225Q	4/26/02	5/02/02	5/06/02	5/15/02
0.225Q	7/19/02	7/25/02	7/29/02	8/15/02
0.225Q	10/25/02	10/31/02	11/04/02	11/15/02
0.225Q	1/24/03	1/30/03	2/03/03	2/15/03
0.225Q	4/25/03	5/01/03	5/05/03	5/15/03

Indicated div.: $0.90 (Div. Reinv. Plan)

CAPITALIZATION (12/31/02):

	($000)	(%)
Long-Term Debt	868,684	49.7
Deferred Income Tax	299,019	17.1
Preferred Stock	17,508	1.0
Common & Surplus	562,470	32.2
Total	1,747,681	100.0

DIVIDEND ACHIEVER STATUS:
Rank: 268   10-Year Growth Rate: 2.71%
Total Years of Dividend Growth: 21

RECENT DEVELOPMENTS: For the quarter ended 3/31/03, net income advanced 27.6% to $17.3 million versus $13.6 million in the prior-year quarter. Total revenue increased 25.2% to $187.4 million. Revenues included a net loss of $194,000 in 2003 and a net gain of $1.0 million in 2002 from energy trading contracts. Electric operations revenue climbed 13.9% to $138.9 million, while tolling operations revenue surged 104.6% to $23.8 million. Energy operations revenue jumped 117.4% to $18.7 million.

PROSPECTS: The Company's ongoing goals for 2003 are to reinforce its balance sheet and improve liquidity, reduce risk associated with the Midstream generating projects through either asset sales or contract restructuring, and build on the strengths of its utility business. Also, CNL recently agreed to sell its 725-megawatt power plant in Perryville, Louisiana to a subsidiary of Entergy. Proceeds will be used to eliminate all Perryville project debt as well as some corporate debt.

BUSINESS

CLECO CORPORATION, under an energy services holding structure, is the parent company of Cleco Power LLC and Cleco Midstream Resources LLC. Cleco Power LLC (78.7% of 2002 revenues) is a regulated electric utility company that provided electricity to approximately 260,000 customers in Louisiana as of 5/8/03. Cleco Midstream Resources LLC (16.9%) is a nonregulated regional energy services group that develops and operates electric power generation facilities, invests in and develops natural gas pipelines and other gas-related assets, and provides energy services to organizations that operate electric utility systems. The other segment (4.4%) consists of a shared services subsidiary and an investment subsidiary.

ANNUAL FINANCIAL DATA

	12/31/02	12/31/01	12/31/00	12/31/99	12/31/98	12/31/97	12/31/96
Earnings Per Share	③ 1.47	② 1.51	① 1.46	1.19	1.12	1.09	1.12
Cash Flow Per Share	2.86	2.73	2.57	2.19	2.11	2.02	2.07
Tang. Book Val. Per Share	11.96	10.94	10.33	9.77	9.45	9.10	8.76
Dividends Per Share	0.90	0.87	0.84	0.83	0.81	0.79	0.77
Dividend Payout %	60.9	57.6	58.1	69.7	72.3	72.5	68.8
INCOME STATEMENT (IN MILLIONS):							
Total Revenues	721.2	1,058.6	820.0	768.2	515.2	456.2	435.4
Costs & Expenses	459.7	818.3	582.3	576.2	328.9	280.5	264.6
Depreciation & Amort.	69.4	60.0	55.2	49.5	49.1	45.9	42.7
Maintenance Exp.	35.1	30.7	35.3	29.9	30.3	23.3	23.5
Operating Income	157.0	149.5	147.2	112.5	107.0	106.5	104.6
Net Interest Inc./(Exp.)	d59.0	d40.0	d42.7	d27.9	d27.0	d28.2	d27.8
Income Taxes	42.2	38.4	35.0	27.2	26.7	27.7	26.2
Net Income	③ 71.9	② 72.3	① 69.3	56.8	53.8	52.5	52.1
Cash Flow	139.4	130.4	122.7	104.3	100.7	96.3	92.8
Average Shs. Outstg. (000)	48,772	47,764	47,655	47,697	47,734	47,728	44,906
BALANCE SHEET (IN MILLIONS):							
Gross Property	2,280.3	1,880.4	1,836.9	1,767.3	1,641.5	1,544.2	1,428.1
Accumulated Depreciation	714.2	655.8	604.1	555.7	551.7	518.7	475.2
Net Property	1,566.2	1,224.7	1,232.8	1,211.6	1,089.8	1,025.6	952.9
Total Assets	2,344.6	1,768.1	1,845.7	1,704.7	1,429.0	1,361.0	1,321.8
Long-Term Obligations	868.7	626.8	659.1	579.6	343.0	365.9	340.9
Net Stockholders' Equity	580.0	508.0	480.0	452.5	437.5	420.1	402.9
Year-end Shs. Outstg. (000)	47,035	44,961	44,991	44,884	44,962	44,926	44,906
STATISTICAL RECORD:							
Operating Profit Margin %	21.8	14.1	18.0	14.6	20.8	23.4	24.0
Net Profit Margin %	10.0	6.8	8.5	7.4	10.4	11.5	12.0
Net Inc./Net Property %	4.6	5.9	5.6	4.7	4.9	5.1	5.5
Net Inc./Tot. Capital %	4.1	5.4	4.8	3.9	4.7	4.6	4.8
Return on Equity %	12.4	14.2	14.4	12.5	12.3	12.5	12.9
Accum. Depr./Gross Prop. %	31.3	34.9	32.9	31.4	33.6	33.6	33.3
Price Range	24.90-9.74	27.25-19.25	28.25-15.06	17.75-14.13	18.06-14.31	16.56-12.38	14.63-12.56
P/E Ratio	16.9-6.6	18.0-12.7	19.4-10.4	15.0-11.9	16.1-12.8	15.2-11.4	13.1-11.3
Average Yield %	5.2	3.7	3.9	5.2	5.0	5.5	5.7

Statistics are as originally reported. Adj. for 2-for-1 stock split 5/21/01. ① Bef. extraord. gain of $2.5 mill. & disc. opers. loss $6.9 mill. ② Bef. a loss from discont. opers. of $2.0 mill. ③ Incl. restr. chrg. of $10.2 mill. and asset impair. chrg. of $3.6 mill.

OFFICERS:
D. M. Eppler, Pres., C.E.O.
D. Samil, Sr. V.P., C.F.O.
K. F. Nolen, Treas.

INVESTOR CONTACT: Rodney J. Hamilton, Investor Relations, (318) 484-7593

PRINCIPAL OFFICE: 2030 Donahue Ferry Road, Pineville, LA 71360-5226

TELEPHONE NUMBER: (318) 484-7400
FAX: (318) 484-7465
WEB: www.cleco.com

NO. OF EMPLOYEES: 1,214 (avg.)

SHAREHOLDERS: 8,990 (common)

ANNUAL MEETING: In April

INCORPORATED: LA, Dec., 1932

INSTITUTIONAL HOLDINGS:
No. of Institutions: 159
Shares Held: 27,065,417
% Held: 57.6

INDUSTRY: Electric services (SIC: 4911)

TRANSFER AGENT(S): EquiServe Trust Company, N.A., Providence, RI

CLOROX COMPANY (THE)

YIELD 2.0%
P/E RATIO 19.9

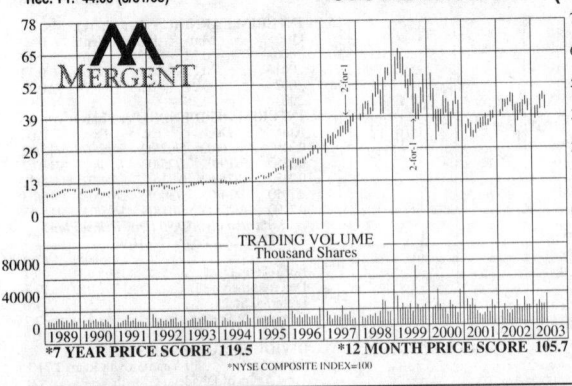

INTERIM EARNINGS (Per Share):

Qtr.	Sept.	Dec.	Mar.	June
1998-99	0.41	0.28	0.09	0.21
1999-00	0.36	0.32	0.44	0.52
2000-01	0.42	0.27	0.33	0.34
2001-02	0.45	0.22	0.20	0.63
2002-03	0.71	0.39	0.51	...

INTERIM DIVIDENDS (Per Share):

Amt.	Decl.	Ex.	Rec.	Pay.
0.21Q	3/20/02	4/26/02	4/30/02	5/15/02
0.22Q	7/17/02	7/29/02	7/31/02	8/15/02
0.22Q	9/18/02	10/29/02	10/31/02	11/15/02
0.22Q	1/15/03	1/29/03	1/31/03	2/14/03
0.22Q	3/19/03	4/28/03	4/30/03	5/15/03

Indicated div.: $0.88 (Div. Reinv. Plan)

CAPITALIZATION (6/30/02):

	($000)	(%)
Long-Term Debt	678,000	31.2
Deferred Income Tax	142,000	6.5
Common & Surplus	1,354,000	62.3
Total	2,174,000	100.0

DIVIDEND ACHIEVER STATUS:
Rank: 192   10-Year Growth Rate: 7.62%
Total Years of Dividend Growth: 26

TRADING VOLUME
Thousand Shares

*7 YEAR PRICE SCORE 119.5   *12 MONTH PRICE SCORE 105.7
^NYSE COMPOSITE INDEX=100

RECENT DEVELOPMENTS: For the quarter ended 3/31/03, income was $112.0 million, before a loss from discontinued operations of $2.0 million, versus income of $50.0 million, before a loss from discontinued operations of $4.0 million, in the equivalent 2002 period. Earnings for 2003 a charge of $7.0 million for stock-performance incentive plan. Results for 2002 included a non-recurring charge of $100.0 million and a gain of $33.0 million from the sale of assets. Net sales slipped 0.4% to $1.02 billion.

PROSPECTS: For fiscal 2003, CLX continues to expect low-single-digit volume and sales growth and earnings per diluted share in the range of $2.22 to $2.25. Looking ahead, first quarter for fiscal 2004 are expected to be hurt by significant increases in spending to launch new products, such as GLAD® PRESS 'N SEAL™, as well as higher raw-material costs and research and development investments. Despite the shortfall, earnings per share are expected in the range of $2.47 to $2.57 for fiscal 2004.

BUSINESS

THE CLOROX COMPANY is a manufacturer and marketer of household products, both domestically and internationally, and products for institutional markets. CLX operates in three business segments. The Household Products North America segment (54.1% of fiscal 2002 sales) includes products such as SOFT SCRUB, CLOROX, TUFFY, FORMULA 409, LIQUID PLUMR, PINE - SOL, TILEX, and SOS. The Specialty Products segment (32.1%) includes brand names such as ARMOR ALL, STP and KINGSFORD CHARCOAL, HIDDEN VALLEY and K C MASTERPIECE dressings and sauces, GLAD, and GLADWARE businesses and SCOOP AWAY, and FRESH STEP cat litters. The Household Products Latin America/Other segment (13.8%), includes CLX's overseas operations, excluding the European automotive care business. This business primarily focuses on the laundry, household cleaning and insecticide categories. On 1/29/99, the Company acquired First Brands Corp. for $2.00 billion.

ANNUAL FINANCIAL DATA

	6/30/02	6/30/01	6/30/00	③ 6/30/99	6/30/98	6/30/97	6/30/96
Earnings Per Share	③1.37	①③1.36	③1.64	③1.03	1.41	1.21	1.07
Cash Flow Per Share	2.18	2.30	2.48	1.87	2.06	1.82	1.63
Tang. Book Val. Per Share	0.24	1.38	1.10	0.31	...	...	1.11
Dividends Per Share	0.86	0.84	0.82	0.76	0.68	0.61	0.56
Dividend Payout %	62.8	61.8	50.0	73.8	48.2	50.6	51.9
INCOME STATEMENT (IN MILLIONS)							
Total Revenues	4,061.0	3,903.0	4,083.0	4,003.0	2,741.3	2,532.7	2,217.8
Costs & Expenses	3,360.0	3,067.0	3,138.0	3,250.0	2,065.6	1,939.9	1,686.3
Depreciation & Amort.	190.0	225.0	201.0	202.0	137.6	126.4	116.5
Operating Income	511.0	611.0	744.0	551.0	538.1	466.4	415.0
Net Interest Inc./(Exp.)	d39.0	d88.0	d98.0	d97.0	d69.7	d55.6	d38.3
Income Before Income Taxes	498.0	487.0	622.0	430.0	471.9	416.0	370.4
Income Taxes	176.0	162.0	228.0	184.0	174.0	166.6	148.3
Net Income	③ 322.0	①③ 325.0	③ 394.0	③ 246.0	298.0	249.4	222.1
Cash Flow	512.0	550.0	595.0	448.0	435.5	375.8	338.6
Average Shs. Outstg. (000)	234,704	239,483	239,614	240,002	211,270	206,584	207,740
BALANCE SHEET (IN MILLIONS)							
Cash & Cash Equivalents	177.0	251.0	245.0	132.0	89.7	101.0	90.8
Total Current Assets	1,002.0	1,103.0	1,454.0	1,116.0	798.7	673.5	573.8
Net Property	922.0	1,046.0	1,079.0	1,054.0	596.3	570.6	551.4
Total Assets	3,630.0	3,995.0	4,353.0	4,132.0	3,030.0	2,778.0	2,178.9
Total Current Liabilities	1,225.0	1,069.0	1,541.0	1,368.0	1,225.1	892.7	623.9
Long-Term Obligations	678.0	685.0	590.0	702.0	316.3	565.9	356.3
Net Stockholders' Equity	1,354.0	1,900.0	1,794.0	1,570.0	1,085.2	1,036.0	932.8
Net Working Capital	d223.0	34.0	d87.0	d252.0	d426.4	d219.2	d50.0
Year-end Shs. Outstg. (000)	223,010	236,691	235,361	235,311	207,370	206,390	205,032
STATISTICAL RECORD:							
Operating Profit Margin %	12.6	15.7	18.2	13.8	19.6	18.4	18.7
Net Profit Margin %	7.9	8.3	9.6	6.1	10.9	9.8	10.0
Return on Equity %	23.8	17.1	22.0	15.7	27.5	24.1	23.8
Return on Assets %	8.9	8.1	9.1	6.0	9.8	9.0	10.2
Debt/Total Assets %	18.7	17.1	13.6	17.0	10.4	20.4	16.4
Price Range	47.95-31.92	40.85-29.95	56.38-28.38	66.47-37.50	58.75-37.19	40.19-24.31	27.56-17.50
P/E Ratio	35.0-23.3	30.0-22.0	34.4-17.3	64.5-36.4	41.7-26.4	33.3-20.2	25.8-16.4
Average Yield %	2.2	2.4	1.9	1.5	1.4	1.9	2.5

Statistics are as originally reported. Adj. for stk. splits: 2-for-1, 8/99 and 9/97. ① Bef. acctg. change chrg. $2.0 mill., 6/01 ② Incl. results of First Brands Corp. ③ Incl. one-time chrgs. $241.0 mill., 6/02; $98.0 mill., 6/01; $21.0 mill., 6/00; $180.0 mill., 6/99.

OFFICERS:
G. C. Sullivan, Chmn., C.E.O.
G. E. Johnston, Pres., C.O.O.
K. M. Rose, V.P., C.F.O.
INVESTOR CONTACT: Doug Hughes, Investor Relations, (510) 271-2270
PRINCIPAL OFFICE: 1221 Broadway, Oakland, CA 94612-1888

TELEPHONE NUMBER: (510) 271-7000
FAX: (510) 832-1463
WEB: www.clorox.com
NO. OF EMPLOYEES: 9,500 (approx.)
SHAREHOLDERS: 15,023 (approx.)
ANNUAL MEETING: In Nov.
INCORPORATED: CA, 1913; reincorp., DE, Sept., 1986

INSTITUTIONAL HOLDINGS:
No. of Institutions: 428
Shares Held: 110,266,959
% Held: 50.8
INDUSTRY: Polishes and sanitation goods (SIC: 2842)
TRANSFER AGENT(S): EquiServe Trust Company, N.A., Providence, RI

COCA-COLA COMPANY (THE)

YIELD 1.9%
P/E RATIO 27.6

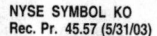

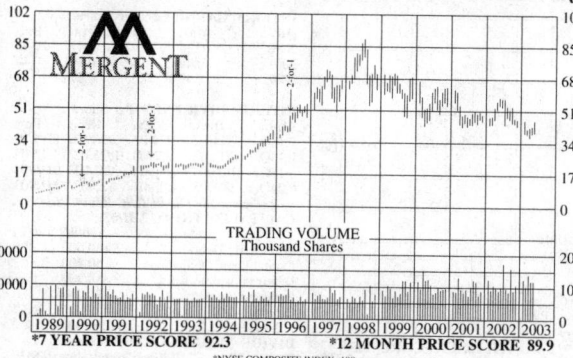

INTERIM EARNINGS (Per Share):

Qtr.	Mar.	June	Sept.	Dec.
1999	0.30	0.38	0.32	d0.02
2000	d0.02	0.37	0.43	0.10
2001	0.35	0.45	0.43	0.37
2002	0.29	0.44	0.44	0.38
2003	0.34	...	...	...

INTERIM DIVIDENDS (Per Share):

Amt.	Decl.	Ex.	Rec.	Pay.
0.20Q	7/18/02	9/11/02	9/15/02	10/01/02
0.20Q	10/17/02	11/26/02	12/01/02	12/15/02
0.22Q	2/20/03	3/12/03	3/15/03	4/01/03
0.22Q	4/16/03	6/11/03	6/15/03	7/01/03

Indicated div.: $0.88 (Div. Reinv. Plan)

CAPITALIZATION (12/31/02):

	($000)	(%)
Long-Term Debt	2,701,000	18.1
Deferred Income Tax	399,000	2.7
Common & Surplus	11,800,000	79.2
Total	14,900,000	100.0

DIVIDEND ACHIEVER STATUS:
Rank: 122 10-Year Dividend Rate: 11.07%
Total Years of Dividend Growth: 40

*7 YEAR PRICE SCORE 92.3 ***12 MONTH PRICE SCORE 89.9**
*NYSE COMPOSITE INDEX=100

RECENT DEVELOPMENTS: For the quarter ended 3/31/03, net income was $835.0 million versus income of $732.0 million, before an accounting change charge of $926.0 million, the previous year. Results for 2003 included a charge of $159.0 million related to streamlining initiatives. Results for 2002 included a non-recurring gain of about $52.0 million. Net operating revenues rose 10.3% to $4.50 billion. Worldwide unit case volume grew 4.0%, reflecting 3.0% volume growth in North America and 4.0% internationally.

PROSPECTS: KO's prospects appear reasonably positive. For instance, the Company's results going forward should benefit from continued healthy growth from its non-carbonated beverage lineup, which includes DASANI, POWERADE, and MINUTE MAID. In addition, KO's large exposure to foreign markets, as evidenced by 67.6% of its 2002 revenues being generated outside of North America, provides for significant growth opportunities.

BUSINESS

THE COCA-COLA COMPANY is engaged in the manufacturing, distributing and marketing of soft drink concentrates and syrups. Principal beverage products include: COCA-COLA, COCA-COLA CLASSIC, DIET COKE, CHERRY COKE, FANTA, SPRITE, MR. PIBB, MELLO YELLOW, BARQ'S ROOT BEER, POWERADE, FRUITOPIA, DASANI plus other assorted diet and caffeine-free versions. The Company also produces juice and juice-drink products. Brands include MINUTE MAID, SIMPLY ORANGE, ODWALLA, SAMANTHA, FIVE ALIVE, BACARDI brand tropical fruit mixers and HI-C. Coca-Cola Nestle Refreshments, KO's joint venture with Nestle S.A., markets ready-to-drink teas and coffees in certain countries. In 2002, sales were derived: North America, 32.4%; Europe, Eurasia & Middle East, 27.2%; Asia, 26.1%; Latin America, 10.8%; and Africa, 3.5%. As of 12/31/02, KO held an approximate 38.0% interest in Coca-Cola Enterprises, Inc.

ANNUAL FINANCIAL DATA

	12/31/02	12/31/01	12/31/00	12/31/99	12/31/98	12/31/97	12/31/96
Earnings Per Share	⑤ 1.60	④ 1.60	③ 0.88	② 0.98	1.42	① 1.64	1.40
Cash Flow Per Share	1.93	1.92	1.19	1.30	1.67	1.89	1.59
Tang. Book Val. Per Share	3.34	3.53	2.98	3.06	3.19	2.66	2.18
Dividends Per Share	0.80	0.72	0.68	0.64	0.60	0.56	0.50
Dividend Payout %	50.0	45.0	77.3	65.3	42.3	34.1	35.7
INCOME STATEMENT (IN MILLIONS):							
Total Revenues	19,564.0	20,092.0	20,458.0	19,805.0	18,813.0	18,868.0	18,546.0
Costs & Expenses	13,300.0	13,937.0	15,994.0	15,031.0	13,201.0	13,241.0	14,152.0
Depreciation & Amort.	806.0	803.0	773.0	792.0	645.0	626.0	479.0
Operating Income	5,458.0	5,352.0	3,691.0	3,982.0	4,967.0	5,001.0	3,915.0
Net Interest Inc./(Exp.)	10.0	36.0	d102.0	d77.0	d58.0	d47.0	d48.0
Income Before Income Taxes	5,499.0	5,670.0	3,399.0	3,819.0	5,198.0	6,055.0	4,596.0
Income Taxes	1,523.0	1,691.0	1,222.0	1,388.0	1,665.0	1,926.0	1,104.0
Net Income	⑤ 3,976.0	⑤ 3,979.0	④ 2,177.0	③ 2,431.0	3,533.0	① 4,129.0	3,492.0
Cash Flow	4,782.0	4,782.0	2,950.0	3,223.0	4,178.0	4,755.0	3,971.0
Average Shs. Outstg. (000)	2,483,000	2,487,000	2,487,000	2,487,000	2,496,000	2,515,000	2,494,000
BALANCE SHEET (IN MILLIONS):							
Cash & Cash Equivalents	2,345.0	1,934.0	1,892.0	1,812.0	1,807.0	1,843.0	1,658.0
Total Current Assets	7,352.0	7,171.0	6,620.0	6,480.0	6,380.0	5,969.0	5,910.0
Net Property	5,911.0	4,453.0	4,168.0	4,267.0	3,669.0	3,743.0	3,550.0
Total Assets	24,501.0	22,417.0	20,834.0	21,623.0	19,145.0	16,940.0	16,161.0
Total Current Liabilities	7,341.0	8,429.0	9,321.0	9,856.0	8,640.0	7,379.0	7,406.0
Long-Term Obligations	2,701.0	1,219.0	835.0	854.0	687.0	801.0	1,116.0
Net Stockholders' Equity	11,800.0	11,366.0	9,316.0	9,513.0	8,403.0	7,311.0	6,156.0
Net Working Capital	11.0	d1,258.0	d2,701.0	d3,376.0	d2,260.0	d1,410.0	d1,496.0
Year-end Shs. Outstg. (000)	2,470,979	2,486,227	2,484,761	2,471,575	2,466,000	2,471,000	2,481,000
STATISTICAL RECORD:							
Operating Profit Margin %	27.9	26.6	18.0	20.1	26.4	26.5	21.1
Net Profit Margin %	20.3	19.8	10.6	12.3	18.8	21.9	18.8
Return on Equity %	33.7	35.0	23.4	25.6	42.0	56.5	56.7
Return on Assets %	16.2	17.7	10.4	11.2	18.5	24.4	21.6
Debt/Total Assets %	11.0	5.4	4.0	3.9	3.6	4.7	6.9
Price Range	57.91-42.90	62.19-42.37	66.88-42.88	70.88-47.31	88.94-53.63	72.63-50.00	54.25-36.06
P/E Ratio	36.2-26.8	38.9-26.5	76.0-48.7	72.3-48.3	62.6-37.8	44.3-30.5	38.7-25.8
Average Yield %	1.6	1.4	1.2	1.1	0.8	0.9	1.1

Statistics are as originally reported. ① Incl. non-recurr. net gain of $290.0 mill. ② Incl. non-recurr. chrg. of $813.0 mill. ③ Incl. non-recurr. chrgs. of $1.04 bill. & asset writedown of $405.0 mill. ④ Incl. non-recurr. gain of $91.0 mill.; bef. acctg. chge. chrg. of $10.0 mill. ⑤ Incl. non-recurr. chrg. of $157.0 mill.; bef. acctg. chge. chrg. of $926.0 mill.

OFFICERS:
D. N. Daft, Chmn., C.E.O.
B. G. Dyson, Vice-Chmn.
S. J. Heyer, Pres., C.O.O.

INVESTOR CONTACT: Institutional Investor Inquires, (404) 676-5766

PRINCIPAL OFFICE: One Coca-Cola Plaza, Atlanta, GA 30313

TELEPHONE NUMBER: (404) 676-2121
FAX: (404) 676-6792
WEB: www.coca-cola.com

NO. OF EMPLOYEES: 56,000 (approx.)

SHAREHOLDERS: 365,189

ANNUAL MEETING: In Apr.

INCORPORATED: DE, Sept., 1919

INSTITUTIONAL HOLDINGS:
No. of Institutions: 1,002
Shares Held: 1,393,598,840
% Held: 56.6

INDUSTRY: Bottled and canned soft drinks (SIC: 2086)

TRANSFER AGENT(S): EquiServe, Jersey City, NJ

COLGATE-PALMOLIVE COMPANY

YIELD 1.6%
P/E RATIO 26.3

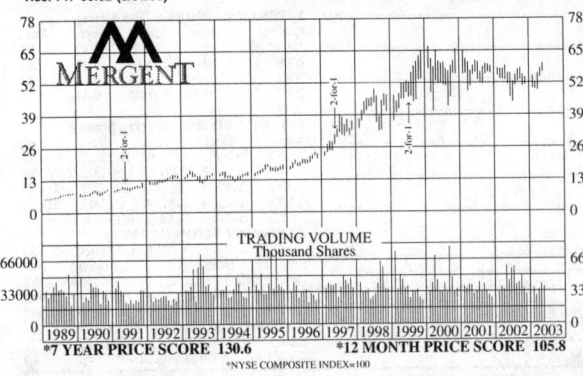

INTERIM EARNINGS (Per Share):

Qtr.	Mar.	June	Sept.	Dec.
2000	0.38	0.42	0.44	0.46
2001	0.44	0.42	0.49	0.49
2002	0.49	0.55	0.57	0.59
2003	0.56	...	...	...

INTERIM DIVIDENDS (Per Share):

Amt.	Decl.	Ex.	Rec.	Pay.
0.18Q	7/11/02	7/24/02	7/26/02	8/15/02
0.18Q	10/10/02	10/23/02	10/25/02	11/15/02
0.18Q	1/09/03	1/30/03	2/03/03	2/14/03
0.24Q	2/06/03	4/23/03	4/25/03	5/15/03

Indicated div.: $0.96 (Div. Reinv. Plan)

CAPITALIZATION (12/31/02):

	($000)	(%)
Long-Term Debt	3,160,600	78.0
Capital Lease Obligations..	50,200	1.2
Deferred Income Tax	488,800	12.1
Preferred Stock	323,000	8.0
Common & Surplus	27,300	0.7
Total	4,049,900	100.0

DIVIDEND ACHIEVER STATUS:
Rank: 153 10-Year Growth Rate: 9.61%
Total Years of Dividend Growth: 40

TRADING VOLUME
Thousand Shares

*7 YEAR PRICE SCORE 130.6 *12 MONTH PRICE SCORE 105.8
*NYSE COMPOSITE INDEX=100

RECENT DEVELOPMENTS: For the quarter ended 3/31/03, net income grew 11.8% to $324.0 million from $289.7 million in the equivalent 2002 quarter. Net sales advanced 7.0% to $2.35 billion from $2.20 billion the previous year. Worldwide unit volume grew 6.0% from the year-earlier period, with every operating division contributing strong gains. Gross profit improved 7.9% to $1.30 billion. Operating income rose 10.8% to $510.5 million.

PROSPECTS: The Company's first quarter results set the stage for what should be a very profitable year. Sales growth and record gross profit margin during the first quarter funded a substantial increase in commercial and media investment. The increased commercial and media investment is expected to support a number of new products around the globe, which in turn should help drive market share increases in key categories.

BUSINESS

COLGATE-PALMOLIVE COMPANY is a consumer products company that markets its products in over 200 countries. The Company operates five segments. Oral, Personal, Fabric and Household Surface Care accounted for 86.0% of 2002 revenues and consists of tooth pastes, toothbrushes, soaps, shampoos, baby products, deodorants, detergents, cleaners, shave products and other similar items under brand names including COLGATE, PALMOLIVE, MENNEN, SOFT SOAP, IRISH SPRING, PROTEX, SORRISO, KOLYNOS, AJAX, AXION, SOUPLINE, SUAVITEL and FAB. Pet Nutrition, 14.0%, consists of pet food products manufactured and marketed by Hill's Pet Nutrition. Hill's markets pet foods primarily under SCIENCE DIET, which is sold by authorized pet supply retailers, breeders and veterinarians for every day nutritional needs, and PRESCRIPTION DIET for dogs and cats with disease conditions.

ANNUAL FINANCIAL DATA

	12/31/02	12/31/01	12/31/00	12/31/99	12/31/98	12/31/97	12/31/96
Earnings Per Share	2.19	☐ 1.89	1.70	1.47	1.31	1.14	1.05
Cash Flow Per Share	2.65	2.40	2.20	1.97	1.79	1.60	1.59
Dividends Per Share	0.72	0.68	0.63	0.59	0.55	0.53	0.47
Dividend Payout %	32.9	35.7	37.1	40.1	42.1	46.7	44.8
INCOME STATEMENT (IN MILLIONS):							
Total Revenues	9,294.3	9,427.8	9,357.9	9,118.2	8,971.6	9,056.7	8,749.0
Costs & Expenses	6,984.7	7,256.8	7,279.6	7,211.8	7,218.3	7,451.0	7,280.7
Depreciation & Amort.	296.5	336.2	337.8	340.2	330.3	319.9	316.3
Operating Income	2,013.1	1,834.8	1,740.5	1,566.2	1,423.0	1,285.8	1,152.0
Net Interest Inc./(Exp.)	d142.8	d166.1	d173.3	d171.6	d172.9	d183.5	d197.4
Income Before Income Taxes	1,870.3	1,668.7	1,567.2	1,394.6	1,250.1	1,102.3	954.6
Income Taxes	582.0	522.1	503.4	457.3	401.5	361.9	319.6
Net Income	1,288.3	☐ 1,146.6	1,063.8	937.3	848.6	740.4	635.0
Cash Flow	1,562.9	1,461.1	1,380.9	1,256.5	1,158.0	1,039.2	929.9
Average Shs. Outstg. (000)	589,100	607,700	627,300	638,800	648,400	650,200	586,400
BALANCE SHEET (IN MILLIONS):							
Cash & Cash Equivalents	167.9	172.7	212.5	235.2	194.5	205.3	307.8
Total Current Assets	2,228.1	2,203.4	2,347.2	2,354.8	2,244.9	2,196.5	2,372.3
Net Property	2,491.3	2,513.5	2,528.3	2,551.1	2,589.2	2,441.0	2,428.9
Total Assets	7,087.2	6,984.8	7,252.3	7,423.1	7,685.2	7,538.7	7,901.5
Total Current Liabilities	2,148.7	2,123.5	2,244.1	2,273.5	2,114.4	1,959.5	1,904.3
Long-Term Obligations	3,210.8	2,812.0	2,536.9	2,243.3	2,300.6	2,340.3	2,786.8
Net Stockholders' Equity	350.3	846.4	1,468.1	1,833.7	2,085.6	2,178.6	2,034.1
Net Working Capital	79.4	79.9	103.1	81.3	130.5	237.0	468.0
Year-end Shs. Outstg. (000)	535,980	550,700	566,656	578,863	585,420	591,280	588,536
STATISTICAL RECORD:							
Operating Profit Margin %	21.7	19.5	18.6	17.2	15.9	14.2	13.2
Net Profit Margin %	13.9	12.2	11.4	10.3	9.5	8.2	7.3
Return on Equity %	367.8	135.5	72.5	51.1	40.7	34.0	31.2
Return on Assets %	18.2	16.4	14.7	12.6	11.0	9.8	8.0
Debt/Total Assets %	45.3	40.3	35.0	30.2	29.9	31.0	35.3
Price Range	58.86-44.05	64.75-48.50	66.75-40.50	65.00-36.56	49.44-32.53	39.34-22.50	24.13-17.22
P/E Ratio	26.9-20.1	34.3-25.7	39.3-23.8	44.2-24.9	37.9-24.9	34.7-19.8	23.0-16.4
Average Yield %	1.4	1.2	1.2	1.2	1.3	1.7	2.3

Statistics are as originally reported. Adj. for stk. splits: 2-for-1, 6/99 & 5/97 ☐ Incl. non-recurr. chrgs. $15.0 mill.

OFFICERS:
R. Mark, Chmn., C.E.O.
W. S. Shanahan, Pres., C.O.O.
S. C. Patrick, C.F.O.

INVESTOR CONTACT: Bina Thompson, Inv. Rel., (212) 310-3072

PRINCIPAL OFFICE: 300 Park Ave., New York, NY 10022-7499

TELEPHONE NUMBER: (212) 310-2000
FAX: (212) 310-3284
WEB: www.colgate.com

NO. OF EMPLOYEES: 37,700 (avg.)

SHAREHOLDERS: 38,800 (avg.); 215 (pfr.)

ANNUAL MEETING: In May

INCORPORATED: DE, July, 1923

INSTITUTIONAL HOLDINGS:
No. of Institutions: 756
Shares Held: 374,049,276
% Held: 69.7

INDUSTRY: Toilet preparations (SIC: 2844)

TRANSFER AGENT(S): First Chicago Trust Company of New York, Jersey City, NJ

COMERICA, INC.

YIELD 4.3%
P/E RATIO 13.8

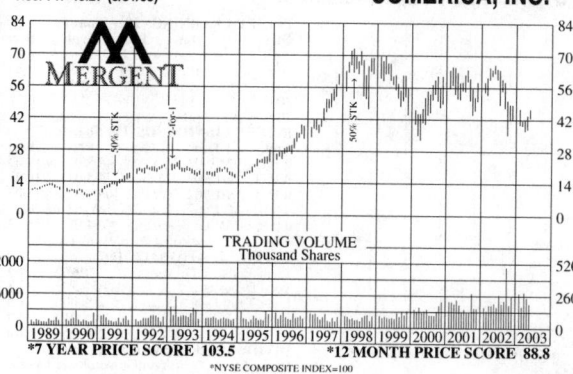

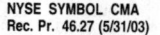

INTERIM EARNINGS (Per Share):

Qtr.	Mar.	June	Sept.	Dec.
1999	0.98	1.03	1.05	1.08
2000	1.10	1.15	1.18	1.20
2001	0.50	1.13	1.14	1.11
2002	1.20	1.03	0.14	1.18
2003	1.00	...	...	...

INTERIM DIVIDENDS (Per Share):

Amt.	Decl.	Ex.	Rec.	Pay.
0.48Q	5/21/02	6/12/02	6/15/02	7/01/02
0.48Q	7/24/02	9/11/02	9/15/02	10/01/02
0.48Q	11/26/02	12/11/02	12/15/02	1/01/03
0.50Q	1/28/03	3/12/03	3/15/03	4/01/03
0.50Q	5/20/03	6/11/03	6/15/03	7/01/03

Indicated div.: $2.00 (Div. Reinv. Plan)

CAPITALIZATION (12/31/02):

	($000)	(%)
Total Deposits	41,775,000	80.4
Long-Term Debt	5,216,000	10.0
Common & Surplus	4,947,000	9.5
Total	51,938,000	100.0

TRADING VOLUME
Thousand Shares

7 YEAR PRICE SCORE 103.5

NYSE COMPOSITE INDEX=100

12 MONTH PRICE SCORE 88.8

DIVIDEND ACHIEVER STATUS:
Rank: 115   10-Year Growth Rate: 11.61%
Total Years of Dividend Growth: 19

RECENT DEVELOPMENTS: For the quarter ended 3/31/03, net income decreased 17.8% to $176.0 million versus $214.0 million in the corresponding period of the year before. Earnings included a gain of $13.0 million in 2003 and a loss of $1.0 million in 2002 from securities transactions. Earnings for 2002 also included a warrant gain of $2.0 million. Net interest income slipped 5.4% to $511.0 million from $540.0 million the year before.

PROSPECTS: The Company remains focused on its strategy of relationship-based middle market lending. Additionally, CMA will concentrate on growing individual and investment banks to meet the needs of its small business and private banking customers by building new branches and refurbishing existing ones. Looking ahead, the Company expects modest loan growth and a lower net interest margin for the second quarter of 2003.

BUSINESS

COMERICA, INC. is a bank holding company headquartered in Detroit, Michigan. The Company, as of 3/31/03, had assets of $55.81 billion and total deposits of $44.37 billion. CMA operates banking subsidiaries in Michigan, Texas and California, banking operations in Florida, and businesses in several other states. CMA is a diversified financial services provider, offering a broad range of financial products and services for businesses and individuals. CMA has an investment services affiliate, Munder Capital Management, and operates banking subsidiaries in Canada and Mexico. On 1/30/01, CMA acquired Imperial Bancorp in a transaction valued at $1.30 billion.

QUARTERLY DATA

12/31/2002($000)	REV	INC
1st Quarter	921,000	214,000
2nd Quarter	936,000	157,000
3rd Quarter	916,000	24,000
4th Quarter	883,000	206,000

ANNUAL FINANCIAL DATA

	12/31/02	12/31/01	12/31/00	12/31/99	12/31/98	12/31/97	12/31/96
Earnings Per Share	④ 3.40	②③ 3.88	② 4.63	4.14	① 3.72	3.19	① 2.37
Tang. Book Val. Per Share	28.30	27.15	23.94	20.60	17.94	16.02	14.77
Dividends Per Share	1.88	1.72	1.56	1.40	1.25	1.12	0.99
Dividend Payout %	55.3	44.3	33.7	33.8	33.5	35.1	41.7
INCOME STATEMENT (IN MILLIONS):							
Total Interest Income	2,797.0	3,393.5	3,261.6	2,672.7	2,616.8	2,647.4	2,562.8
Total Interest Expense	665.0	1,291.2	1,602.8	1,125.6	1,155.5	1,204.6	1,150.5
Net Interest Income	2,132.0	2,102.3	1,658.9	1,547.1	1,461.3	1,442.8	1,412.3
Provision for Loan Losses	635.0	236.0	145.0	114.0	113.0	146.0	114.0
Non-Interest Income	900.0	803.3	825.9	716.9	603.1	528.0	507.0
Non-Interest Expense	1,515.0	1,559.0	1,188.4	1,117.0	1,020.0	1,008.0	1,159.0
Income Before Taxes	882.0	1,110.6	1,151.4	1,033.1	931.4	816.7	646.2
Net Income	④ 601.0	②③ 709.6	② 749.3	672.6	① 607.1	530.5	① 417.2
Average Shs. Outstg. (000)	177,000	177,665	156,398	158,397	158,757	161,040	172,281
BALANCE SHEET (IN MILLIONS):							
Cash & Due from Banks	1,902.0	1,925.3	1,496.7	1,202.0	1,773.1	1,927.1	1,901.8
Securities Avail. for Sale	5,499.0	5,369.5	2,843.1	3,352.4	2,821.8	4,208.9	4,800.0
Total Loans & Leases	42,281.0	41,196.3	36,060.3	32,693.3	30,604.9	28,895.0	26,206.7
Allowance for Credit Losses	791.0	655.1	538.1	476.5	452.4	424.1	367.2
Net Loans & Leases	41,490.0	40,541.2	35,522.2	32,216.8	30,152.5	28,470.9	25,839.5
Total Assets	53,301.0	50,732.0	41,985.2	38,653.3	36,600.8	36,292.4	34,206.1
Total Deposits	41,775.0	37,570.4	27,168.0	23,291.4	24,313.1	22,586.3	22,367.2
Long-Term Obligations	5,216.0	5,502.5	8,088.7	8,579.9	5,282.3	7,286.4	4,241.8
Total Liabilities	48,354.0	45,924.5	37,977.9	35,178.7	33,554.2	33,530.6	31,590.5
Net Stockholders' Equity	4,947.0	4,807.5	4,007.3	3,474.6	3,046.6	2,761.8	2,615.6
Year-end Shs. Outstg. (000)	174,775	177,075	156,944	156,518	155,881	156,815	160,211
STATISTICAL RECORD:							
Return on Equity %	12.1	14.8	18.7	19.4	19.9	19.2	15.9
Return on Assets %	1.1	1.4	1.8	1.7	1.7	1.5	1.2
Equity/Assets %	9.3	9.5	9.5	9.0	8.3	7.6	7.6
Non-Int. Exp./Tot. Inc. %	50.0	53.7	47.8	49.3	49.4	51.1	60.4
Price Range	66.09-35.20	65.15-44.02	61.13-32.94	70.00-44.00	73.00-46.50	61.88-34.17	39.58-24.17
P/E Ratio	19.4-10.4	16.8-11.3	13.2-7.1	16.9-10.6	19.6-12.5	19.4-10.7	16.7-10.2
Average Yield %	3.7	3.2	3.3	2.5	2.1	2.3	3.1

Statistics are as originally reported. Adj. for 50% stk. div., 4/98. ① Incl. merger-related or restructuring charges: $6.8 mill., 1998; $90.0 mill., 1996. ② Incl. a pre-tax net gain on the sales of businesses of $31.2 mill., 2001; $47.6 mill., 2000. ③ Incl. pre-tax restr. chrg. of $151.7 mill. ④ Incl. pre-tax net gain on the sales of businesses of $12.0 mill. & goodwill impairment losses of $86.0 mill.

OFFICERS:
R. W. Babb Jr., Chmn., Pres., C.E.O.
J. D. Lewis, Vice-Chmn.
E. S. Acton, Exec. V.P., C.F.O.

INVESTOR CONTACT: Judith S. Love, Investor Relations, (313) 222-2840

PRINCIPAL OFFICE: Comerica Tower at Detroit Center, 500 Woodward Avenue, MC 3391, Detroit, MI 48226-3509

TELEPHONE NUMBER: (313) 222-9743
FAX: (313) 222-6091
WEB: www.comerica.com
NO. OF EMPLOYEES: 10,368 full-time; 1,440 part-time
SHAREHOLDERS: 16,534 (approx.)
ANNUAL MEETING: In May
INCORPORATED: DE, 1973

INSTITUTIONAL HOLDINGS:
No. of Institutions: 374
Shares Held: 111,602,049
% Held: 63.8

INDUSTRY: National commercial banks (SIC: 6021)

TRANSFER AGENT(S): Wells Fargo Shareowner Services, South St. Paul, MN

COMMERCE BANCORP, INC.

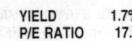

YIELD	1.7%
P/E RATIO	17.4

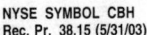

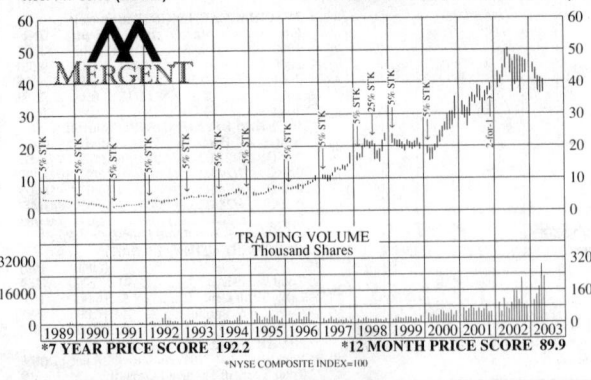

TRADING VOLUME
Thousand Shares

*7 YEAR PRICE SCORE 192.2   ***12 MONTH PRICE SCORE 89.9**

*NYSE COMPOSITE INDEX=100

INTERIM EARNINGS (Per Share):

Qtr.	Mar.	June	Sept.	Dec.
1999	---------------- 1.09 ----------------			
2000	0.29	0.31	0.32	0.33
2001	0.35	0.37	0.38	0.41
2002	0.45	0.49	0.53	0.57
2003	0.60	...	...	...

INTERIM DIVIDENDS (Per Share):

Amt.	Decl.	Ex.	Rec.	Pay.
0.15Q	3/19/02	4/03/02	4/05/02	4/19/02
0.15Q	6/18/02	7/02/02	7/05/02	7/19/02
0.15Q	9/17/02	10/02/02	10/04/02	10/18/02
0.165Q	12/17/02	1/02/03	1/06/03	1/20/03
0.165Q	3/19/03	4/02/03	4/04/03	4/18/03

Indicated div.: $0.66

CAPITALIZATION (12/31/02):

	($000)	(%)
Total Deposits	14,548,841	92.9
Long-Term Debt	200,000	1.3
Common & Surplus	918,010	5.9
Total	15,666,851	100.0

DIVIDEND ACHIEVER STATUS:

Rank: 45	10-Year Growth Rate: 17.42%	
Total Years of Dividend Growth:		11

RECENT DEVELOPMENTS: For the quarter ended 3/31/03, net income increased 35.1% to $42.9 million compared with $31.8 million in the corresponding period of the prior year. Net interest income advanced 34.9% to $167.3 million from $124.1 million the year before. Net interest margin was 4.59% versus 4.85% in 2001. Provision for loan losses remained the same at $6.9 million compared with the previous year.

PROSPECTS: The Company continues to produce strong gains in revenue driven by healthy deposit growth. Looking ahead, the Company expects growth in revenue, net income and deposits of 25.0%, and earnings per share growth of 20.0% in 2003. Meanwhile, the Company has plans to open approximately 13 branch offices in metropolitan Philadelphia and 33 branch offices in metropolitan New York in 2003.

BUSINESS

COMMERCE BANCORP, INC., with assets of $17.80 billion as of 3/31/03, is a bank holding company primarily serving the Metropolitan Philadelphia, New Jersey, Delaware and New York markets. The Company operates five bank subsidiaries including, Commerce Bank, N.A., Commerce Bank/Pennsylvania, N.A., Commerce Bank/Shore, N.A., Commerce Bank/Delaware, N.A. and Commerce Bank/North. As of 12/31/02, these banks provided a full range of retail and commercial banking services for consumers and small and mid-sized companies through 224 retail branch offices. In addition, CBH operates non-banking subsidiaries Commerce Capital Markets, Inc., which is engaged in various securities, investment banking and brokerage activities, and Commerce National Insurance Services, Inc., which operates an insurance brokerage agency concentrating on commercial property, casualty and surety as well as personal lines of insurance.

QUARTERLY DATA

(12/31/2002)($000)	REV	INC
1st Quarter	202,024	40,574
2nd Quarter	196,775	37,689
3rd Quarter	188,368	34,802
4th Quarter	168,204	31,750

ANNUAL FINANCIAL DATA

	12/31/02	12/31/01	12/31/00	12/31/99	12/31/98	12/31/97	12/31/96
Earnings Per Share	2.04	1.51	1.25	1.09	0.94	0.81	0.76
Tang. Book Val. Per Share	13.53	9.67	7.75	5.98	5.97	5.28	4.93
Dividends Per Share	0.60	0.55	0.48	0.41	⊡ 0.44	0.28	0.23
Dividend Payout %	29.4	36.4	38.9	38.2	46.3	34.3	30.1
INCOME STATEMENT (IN MILLIONS):							
Total Interest Income	755.4	604.4	505.3	386.4	289.3	244.2	179.4
Total Interest Expense	182.6	203.0	208.4	142.1	115.6	97.0	70.9
Net Interest Income	572.8	401.3	296.9	244.4	173.7	147.1	108.5
Provision for Loan Losses	33.2	26.4	13.9	9.2	5.9	4.7	3.0
Non-Interest Income	257.5	196.8	150.8	114.6	88.9	57.4	30.0
Non-Interest Expense	579.2	420.0	315.4	252.5	182.0	137.9	94.1
Income Before Taxes	217.9	151.7	118.4	97.3	74.8	61.9	41.5
Net Income	144.8	103.0	80.0	66.0	49.3	40.3	26.6
Average Shs. Outstg. (000)	70,903	68,102	64,222	60,930	52,397	49,951	34,594
BALANCE SHEET (IN MILLIONS):							
Cash & Due from Banks	811.4	557.7	443.9	317.6	245.4	167.9	159.6
Securities Avail. for Sale	8,133.3	4,435.5	2,130.6	1,782.1	1,368.9	1,323.0	741.2
Total Loans & Leases	5,822.6	4,583.4	3,687.3	2,961.1	1,931.4	1,411.3	1,096.2
Allowance for Credit Losses	90.7	67.0	48.7	38.4	26.4	21.3	14.3
Net Loans & Leases	5,731.9	4,516.4	3,638.6	2,922.7	1,905.0	1,390.0	1,081.8
Total Assets	16,404.0	11,363.7	8,296.5	6,635.8	4,894.1	3,939.0	2,862.0
Total Deposits	14,548.8	10,185.6	7,387.6	5,608.9	4,435.1	3,369.4	2,573.4
Long-Term Obligations	200.0	80.5	80.5	80.5	80.5	80.5	23.0
Total Liabilities	15,486.0	10,727.1	7,804.3	6,279.0	4,593.3	3,688.2	2,680.6
Net Stockholders' Equity	918.0	636.6	492.2	356.8	300.7	250.8	181.4
Year-end Shs. Outstg. (000)	67,833	65,833	63,523	59,689	50,411	46,029	35,261
STATISTICAL RECORD:							
Return on Equity %	15.8	16.2	16.3	18.5	16.4	16.1	14.7
Return on Assets %	0.9	0.9	1.0	1.0	1.0	1.0	0.9
Equity/Assets %	5.6	5.6	5.9	5.4	6.1	6.4	6.3
Non-Int. Exp./Tot. Inc. %	69.8	70.2	70.4	70.3	69.3	67.4	67.9
Price Range	50.49-36.10	39.60-26.00	35.41-15.44	23.81-18.45	24.04-15.05	17.95-9.03	10.94-6.62
P/E Ratio	24.7-17.7	26.2-17.2	28.4-12.4	21.9-17.0	25.5-16.0	22.3-11.2	14.5-8.8
Average Yield %	1.4	1.7	1.9	2.0	2.2	2.0	2.6

Statistics are as originally reported. Adjusted for stk. splits: 2-for-1, 12/01; 5%, 1/97, 1/98, 1/99, 1/00; 25%, 7/98. ⊡ Includes special dividend of $0.09 per share.

OFFICERS:
V. W. Hill II, Chmn., Pres., C.E.O.
D. J. Pauls, Sr. V.P., C.F.O.
P. M. Musumeci Jr., Exec. V.P., Treas., Asst. Sec.

INVESTOR CONTACT: C. Edward Jordan, Jr., Exec. Vice-Pres., (888) 751-9000

PRINCIPAL OFFICE: Commerce Atrium, 1701 Route 70 East, Cherry Hill, NJ 08034-5400

TELEPHONE NUMBER: (856) 751-9000
FAX: (856) 751-9260
WEB: www.commerceonline.com

NO. OF EMPLOYEES: 6,800 (approx.)

SHAREHOLDERS: 52,000 (approx.)

ANNUAL MEETING: In May

INCORPORATED: NJ, Dec., 1982

INSTITUTIONAL HOLDINGS:
No. of Institutions: 246
Shares Held: 44,415,310
% Held: 64.4

INDUSTRY: National commercial banks (SIC: 6021)

TRANSFER AGENT(S): Mellon Investor Services, LLP, New York, NY

COMMERCE BANCSHARES, INC.

YIELD 1.6%
P/E RATIO 14.2

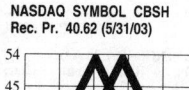

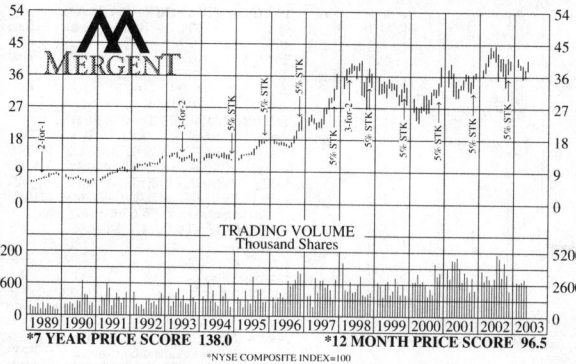

TRADING VOLUME
Thousand Shares

*7 YEAR PRICE SCORE 138.0 *12 MONTH PRICE SCORE 96.5

*NYSE COMPOSITE INDEX=100

INTERIM EARNINGS (Per Share):

Qtr.	Mar.	June	Sept.	Dec.
1999	0.53	0.59	0.59	0.61
2000	0.57	0.64	0.64	0.66
2001	0.63	0.65	0.65	0.68
2002	0.68	0.71	0.74	0.72
2003	0.70	...	...	...

INTERIM DIVIDENDS (Per Share):

Amt.	Decl.	Ex.	Rec.	Pay.
0.163Q	7/26/02	9/11/02	9/13/02	9/27/02
0.163Q	10/25/02	11/26/02	11/29/02	12/13/02
5% STK	10/25/02	11/26/02	11/29/02	12/13/02
0.165Q	1/31/03	3/05/03	3/07/03	3/27/03
0.165Q	4/16/03	6/04/03	6/06/03	6/26/03

Indicated div.: $0.66 (Div. Reinv. Plan)

CAPITALIZATION (12/31/02):

	($000)	(%)
Total Deposits	9,913,311	85.0
Long-Term Debt	338,457	2.9
Common & Surplus	1,416,337	12.1
Total	11,668,105	100.0

DIVIDEND ACHIEVER STATUS:
Rank: 130   10-Year Growth Rate: 10.59%
Total Years of Dividend Growth: 34

RECENT DEVELOPMENTS: For the quarter ended 3/31/03, net income increased 3.8% to $47.2 million compared with $45.5 million in the corresponding period the previous year. Total interest income slipped 5.0% to $155.6 million from $163.8 million the prior year. Net interest income amounted to $124.2 million, up 2.9% from $120.7 million a year earlier, reflecting higher total earning assets, partially offset by low interest rates and weak loan demand. Provi-

sion for loan losses grew 35.4% to $10.0 million. Total non-interest income rose 8.0% to $74.6 million due to growth in bankcard, bond and deposit fee revenues. Total non-interest expense increased 3.8% to $120.7 million. Total loans rose 5.0% to $7.99 billion from $7.61 billion the year before. Total deposits increased 3.2% to $10.28 billion compared with $9.96 billion a year earlier.

BUSINESS

COMMERCE BANCSHARES, INC., with assets of $13.44 billion as of 3/31/03, is a bank holding company that operates in 330 banking locations. The Company presently owns all of the outstanding capital stock of four national banking associations, which are headquartered in Missouri, Illinois, Kansas, and Nebraska. The Nebraska bank is limited in its activities to the issuance of credit cards. The remaining three banking subsidiaries engage in general banking business, providing a broad range of retail, corporate, investment and private banking products and services to individuals and businesses. The Company also owns, directly or through its banking subsidiaries, various nonbanking subsidiaries. Their activities include owning real estate leased to the Companys banking subsidiaries, underwriting credit life and credit accident and health insurance, selling property and casualty insurance (relating to consumer loans made by the banking subsidiaries), venture capital investment, securities brokerage, mortgage banking, and leasing activities.

ANNUAL FINANCIAL DATA

	12/31/02	12/31/01	12/31/00	12/31/99	12/31/98	12/31/97	12/31/96
Earnings Per Share	2.89	2.60	2.50	2.24	1.99	① 1.76	1.55
Tang. Book Val. Per Share	20.40	17.78	15.73	14.01	13.50	12.10	11.13
Dividends Per Share	0.62	0.58	0.54	0.49	0.45	0.41	0.36
Dividend Payout %	21.4	22.3	21.4	22.1	22.8	23.2	23.3
INCOME STATEMENT (IN MILLIONS):							
Total Interest Income	652.6	751.0	812.2	750.6	728.5	682.9	647.6
Total Interest Expense	152.6	283.1	331.5	284.6	300.7	285.1	281.9
Net Interest Income	500.0	467.9	480.7	466.0	427.7	397.8	365.7
Provision for Loan Losses	34.1	36.4	35.2	35.3	36.9	31.4	24.5
Non-Interest Income	280.6	277.5	252.8	236.2	214.0	180.1	159.2
Non-Interest Expense	452.9	439.6	430.4	419.0	379.3	344.4	318.0
Income Before Taxes	293.5	269.4	267.9	247.9	225.6	202.1	182.4
Net Income	199.5	182.0	178.6	166.2	150.1	① 132.7	119.5
Average Shs. Outstg. (000)	69,038	70,058	71,282	73,448	75,488	75,664	77,290
BALANCE SHEET (IN MILLIONS):							
Cash & Due from Banks	710.4	824.2	616.7	685.2	738.7	978.2	833.3
Securities Avail. for Sale	4,213.1	3,667.2	1,885.7	2,475.4	3,002.4	2,620.5	2,681.7
Total Loans & Leases	7,875.9	7,638.5	7,906.7	7,576.9	7,046.9	6,224.4	5,472.3
Allowance for Credit Losses	130.6	130.0	128.4	123.0	117.1	105.9	98.2
Net Loans & Leases	7,745.3	7,508.5	7,778.2	7,453.9	6,929.8	6,118.5	5,374.1
Total Assets	13,308.4	12,902.8	11,115.1	11,400.9	11,402.0	10,306.9	9,698.2
Total Deposits	9,913.3	10,032.0	9,081.7	9,164.1	9,530.2	8,700.6	8,166.4
Long-Term Obligations	338.5	392.6	224.7	25.7	27.1	7.2	14.1
Total Liabilities	11,892.1	11,630.3	9,971.4	10,321.1	10,321.2	9,326.2	8,773.9
Net Stockholders' Equity	1,416.3	1,272.5	1,143.8	1,079.8	1,080.8	980.8	924.3
Year-end Shs. Outstg. (000)	67,102	68,709	68,992	72,206	74,340	73,987	75,133
STATISTICAL RECORD:							
Return on Equity %	14.1	14.3	15.6	15.4	13.9	13.5	12.9
Return on Assets %	1.5	1.4	1.6	1.5	1.3	1.3	1.2
Equity/Assets %	10.6	9.9	10.3	9.5	9.5	9.5	9.5
Non-Int. Exp./Tot. Inc. %	58.0	59.0	58.7	59.7	59.1	59.6	60.6
Price Range	44.62-32.97	39.57-29.86	38.78-22.79	35.89-27.82	40.45-26.64	36.70-20.90	24.63-15.76
P/E Ratio	15.4-11.4	15.2-11.5	15.5-9.1	16.0-12.4	20.3-13.4	20.9-11.9	15.9-10.2
Average Yield %	1.6	1.7	1.7	1.5	1.4	1.4	1.8

Statistics are as originally reported. Adj. for stk. split: 5% div., 12/02, 12/01, 12/00, 12/98, 12/97 & 12/96; 3-for-2, 3/98. ① Incl. non-recurr. credit $3.3 mill.

OFFICERS:
D. W. Kemper, Chmn., Pres., C.E.O.
J. M. Kemper, Vice-Chmn.
A. B. Clark, Exec. V.P., C.F.O., Treas.

INVESTOR CONTACT: Jeffrey Aberdeen, Controller, (816) 234-2081

PRINCIPAL OFFICE: 1000 Walnut, Kansas City, MO 64106

TELEPHONE NUMBER: (816) 234-2000
FAX: (816) 234-2369
WEB: www.commercebank.com

NO. OF EMPLOYEES: 4,437 full-time; 773 part-time

SHAREHOLDERS: 5,081

ANNUAL MEETING: In April

INCORPORATED: MO, Aug., 1966

INSTITUTIONAL HOLDINGS:
No. of Institutions: 179
Shares Held: 23,442,957
% Held: 35.5

INDUSTRY: State commercial banks (SIC: 6022)

TRANSFER AGENT(S): EquiServe Trust Company, N.A., Jersey City, NJ

COMMERCIAL NET LEASE REALTY, INC.

YIELD 7.6%
P/E RATIO 17.1

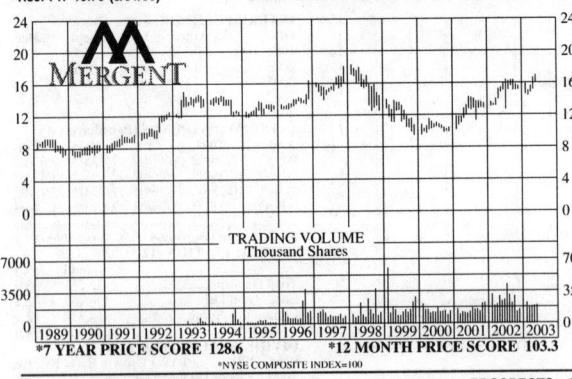

*7 YEAR PRICE SCORE 128.6   *12 MONTH PRICE SCORE 103.3
*NYSE COMPOSITE INDEX=100

TRADING VOLUME
Thousand Shares

INTERIM EARNINGS (Per Share):

Qtr.	Mar.	June	Sept.	Dec.
1999	0.32	0.23	0.29	0.31
2000	0.28	0.28	0.28	0.41
2001	0.38	0.34	0.24	d0.01
2002	0.29	0.27	0.23	0.27
2003	0.21	...	...	...

INTERIM DIVIDENDS (Per Share):

Amt.	Decl.	Ex.	Rec.	Pay.
0.32Q	7/15/02	7/29/02	7/31/02	8/15/02
0.32Q	10/15/02	10/29/02	10/31/02	11/15/02
0.32Q	1/16/03	1/29/03	1/31/03	2/14/03
0.32Q	4/15/03	4/28/03	4/30/03	5/15/03

Indicated div.: $1.28 (Div. Reinv. Plan)

CAPITALIZATION (12/31/02):

	($000)	(%)
Long-Term Debt	345,689	38.6
Preferred Stock	44,551	5.0
Common & Surplus	504,590	56.4
Total	894,830	100.0

DIVIDEND ACHIEVER STATUS:
Rank: 280   10-Year Growth Rate: 1.63%
Total Years of Dividend Growth: 13

RECENT DEVELOPMENTS: For the three months ended 3/31/03, income from continuing operations was $9.6 million compared with income of $12.0 million in the corresponding quarter of the previous year. Results for 2003 included a pre-tax dissenting shareholders' settlement charge of $2.4 million. Results for 2003 and 2002 excluded gains of $572,000 and $731,000, respectively, from discontinued operations. Total revenues were $23.6 million.

PROSPECTS: Operating results should continue to benefit from contributions from newer properties. During the first quarter of 2003, the Company and its affiliated subsidiaries invested $17.6 million in additional properties and construction in progress. The Company also announced that it disposed of seven properties generating net proceeds of $12.1 million. As of 3/31/03, the Company's occupancy (based on gross leasable area) was 95.8%.

BUSINESS

COMMERCIAL NET LEASE REALTY, INC. is a fully integrated, self-administered real estate investment trust that acquires, owns, manages and indirectly develops a diversified portfolio of freestanding properties. The Company invests in single-tenant, freestanding retail properties that are located in intensive commercial corridors with purchase prices up to $8.0 million. As of 5/6/03, the Company owned 345 properties in 39 states that are generally leased to major retail businesses under long-term commercial net leases. These businesses include Barnes & Noble, Best Buy, Eckerd and OfficeMax. On 12/1/01, NNN acquired Captec Net Lease Realty, Inc.

ANNUAL FINANCIAL DATA

	12/31/02	12/31/01	12/31/00	12/31/99	12/31/98	12/31/97	12/31/96
Earnings Per Share	③ 1.04	③ 0.91	① ② 1.27	① 1.16	① 1.10	① 1.25	① 1.18
Tang. Book Val. Per Share	12.49	12.68	12.93	12.94	13.00	12.96	15.04
Dividends Per Share	1.27	1.26	1.25	1.24	1.23	1.20	1.18
Dividend Payout %	122.1	138.4	98.0	106.9	111.8	96.0	100.0
INCOME STATEMENT (IN THOUSANDS):							
Rental Income	73,874	58,092	60,591	58,417	48,935	38,143	25,140
Interest Income	18,397	20,550	19,147	16,243	13,476	11,992	8,229
Total Income	93,827	80,526	80,891	76,543	64,773	50,135	33,369
Costs & Expenses	39,558	20,573	6,768	16,436	13,835	3,723	2,844
Depreciation	11,425	9,211	9,088	8,634	6,759	5,302	3,553
Income Before Income Taxes	46,060	30,438	42,598	36,277	32,074	30,283	19,839
Net Income	③ 46,060	③ 28,963	① ② 38,618	① 35,311	① 32,441	① 30,385	① 19,839
Average Shs. Outstg.	40,589	31,717	30,408	30,408	29,397	24,221	16,799
BALANCE SHEET (IN THOUSANDS):							
Cash & Cash Equivalents	1,737	6,974	2,190	3,329	1,442	2,160	1,410
Total Real Estate Investments	703,465	706,280	514,962	546,193	519,948	400,977	269,031
Total Assets	954,108	1,006,628	761,611	749,789	685,595	537,014	370,953
Long-Term Obligations	345,689	435,333	360,381	350,971	292,907	171,836	116,956
Total Liabilities	404,967	441,988	367,710	358,427	301,705	174,870	118,379
Net Stockholders' Equity	549,141	564,640	393,901	391,362	383,890	362,144	252,574
Year-end Shs. Outstg.	40,404	40,599	30,457	30,256	29,521	27,954	16,799
STATISTICAL RECORD:							
Net Inc.+Depr./Assets %	6.0	3.8	6.3	5.9	5.7	6.6	6.3
Return on Equity %	8.4	5.1	9.8	9.0	8.5	8.4	7.9
Return on Assets %	4.8	2.9	5.1	4.7	4.7	5.7	5.3
Price Range	16.40-12.60	14.25-10.13	11.50-9.50	13.94-9.44	18.31-12.50	18.13-13.88	16.38-12.75
P/E Ratio	15.8-12.1	15.7-11.1	9.1-7.5	12.0-8.1	16.6-11.4	14.5-11.1	13.9-10.8
Average Yield %	8.8	10.3	11.9	10.6	8.0	7.5	8.1

Statistics are as originally reported. ① Incl. gain on sale of investment $4.6 mill., 2001; $4.1 mill., 2000; $6.7 mill., 1999; $1.4 mill., 1998; $651,000, 1997; $73,000, 1996; $374,000, 1993. ② Excl. acctg. chg. of $367,000. ③ Excl. disc. oper. of $2.0 mill. & incl. pre-tax prov. of $1.9 mill. for loss on the impair. of real estate.

OFFICERS:
J. M. Seneff Jr., Chmn., C.E.O.
R. A. Bourne, Vice-Chmn.
G. M. Ralston, Pres., C.O.O.

INVESTOR CONTACT: Kevin B. Habicht, Investor Relations, (407) 265-7348

PRINCIPAL OFFICE: 450 South Orange Avenue, Orlando, FL 32801

TELEPHONE NUMBER: (407) 265-7348
FAX: (407) 423-2894
WEB: www.cnlreit.com

NO. OF EMPLOYEES: 36

SHAREHOLDERS: 1,255 (common); 48 (preferred)

ANNUAL MEETING: In May

INCORPORATED: DE, June, 1984; reincorp., MD, June, 1994

INSTITUTIONAL HOLDINGS:
No. of Institutions: 100
Shares Held: 12,077,543
% Held: 30.2

INDUSTRY: Real estate investment trusts (SIC: 6798)

TRANSFER AGENT(S): First Union National Bank, Charlotte, NC

COMMUNITY BANK SYSTEM, INC.

YIELD 3.0%
P/E RATIO 12.8

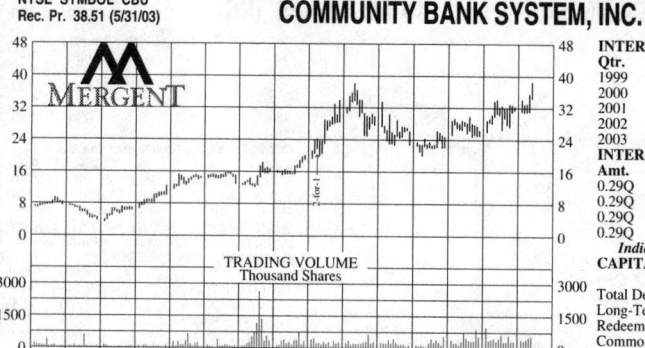

TRADING VOLUME
Thousand Shares

| | 1989 | 1990 | 1991 | 1992 | 1993 | 1994 | 1995 | 1996 | 1997 | 1998 | 1999 | 2000 | 2001 | 2002 | 2003 |

*7 YEAR PRICE SCORE 134.5   *12 MONTH PRICE SCORE 108.3
*NYSE COMPOSITE INDEX=100

INTERIM EARNINGS (Per Share):

Qtr.	Mar.	June	Sept.	Dec.
1999	0.50	0.55	0.68	0.69
2000	0.70	0.72	0.72	0.70
2001	0.50	0.18	0.55	0.39
2002	0.65	0.70	0.84	0.73
2003	0.75	...	...	...

INTERIM DIVIDENDS (Per Share):

Amt.	Decl.	Ex.	Rec.	Pay.
0.29Q	8/22/02	9/12/02	9/16/02	10/10/02
0.29Q	11/21/02	12/12/02	12/16/02	1/10/03
0.29Q	2/20/03	3/12/03	3/14/03	4/10/03
0.29Q	5/29/03	6/12/03	6/16/03	7/10/03

Indicated div.: $1.16 (Div. Reinv. Plan)

CAPITALIZATION (12/31/02):

	($000)	(%)
Total Deposits	2,505,356	75.1
Long-Term Debt	430,000	12.9
Redeemable Pfd. Stock	77,375	2.3
Common & Surplus	325,038	9.7
Total	3,337,769	100.0

DIVIDEND ACHIEVER STATUS:

Rank: 140   10-Year Growth Rate: 10.11%
Total Years of Dividend Growth: 11

RECENT DEVELOPMENTS: For the quarter ended 3/31/03, net income was $9.9 million compared with $8.6 million in the corresponding year-earlier period. Earnings for 2002 included pre-tax acquisition and unusual expenses of $592,000. Net interest income rose 7.7% to $32.5 million. Loan loss provision was $3.4 million versus $1.5 million the year before. Total noninterest income climbed 16.9% to $9.0 million, primarily due to general banking revenues that climbed 45.4% to $6.0 million.

PROSPECTS: CBU expects full-year 2003 earnings to approximate $2.96 per share, consistent with its previous guidance. CBU noted that it believes that non-interest income and non-interest expenses will continue to be favorable to previous guidance, effectively offsetting a higher than anticipated provision for loan losses. CBU anticipates loan growth for 2003 in the low single digits, reflecting continued commercial loan growth and a restoration of installment loan growth.

BUSINESS

COMMUNITY BANK SYSTEM, INC. is a bank holding company with $3.37 billion in assets as of 3/31/03. As of 12/31/02, CBU's wholly-owned community banking subsidiary, Community Bank, N.A., operated 116 customer facilities and 85 automated teller machines located from Northern New York to the Southern Tier, west to Lake Erie, and in Northeastern Pennsylvania. Other subsidiaries include Elias Asset Management, Inc., an investment management firm; Benefit Plans Administrative Services, Inc., a pension administration and consulting firm serving sponsors of defined benefit and defined contribution plans; and Community Investment Services, Inc., a broker-dealer delivering financial products, including mutual funds, annuities, individual stocks and bonds, and long-term health care and other selected insurance products.

ANNUAL FINANCIAL DATA

	12/31/02	12/31/01	12/31/00	12/31/99	12/31/98	12/31/97	12/31/96
Earnings Per Share	③ 2.93	② 1.62	2.85	2.42	① 2.05	2.02	1.84
Tang. Book Val. Per Share	14.66	9.74	12.64	8.09	9.01	7.82	9.85
Dividends Per Share	1.10	1.08	1.02	0.94	0.83	0.74	0.68
Dividend Payout %	37.5	66.7	35.8	38.8	40.5	36.6	36.8
INCOME STATEMENT (IN MILLIONS):							
Total Interest Income	204.9	197.9	145.2	123.9	122.9	117.6	97.7
Total Interest Expense	77.0	101.2	74.0	55.9	58.5	54.8	42.4
Net Interest Income	127.8	96.7	71.2	67.9	64.4	62.9	55.3
Provision for Loan Losses	12.2	7.1	7.2	5.1	5.1	4.5	2.9
Non-Interest Income	32.6	29.1	21.0	15.5	17.0	11.8	8.9
Non-Interest Expense	95.8	89.0	56.0	52.7	51.9	45.8	37.4
Income Before Taxes	52.4	29.6	29.0	25.6	24.4	24.4	23.8
Net Income	③ 38.5	② 20.7	20.3	17.6	① 15.5	15.6	14.1
Average Shs. Outstg. (000)	13,167	11,825	7,136	7,295	7,671	7,676	6,943
BALANCE SHEET (IN MILLIONS):							
Cash & Due from Banks	113.5	106.6	59.3	76.5	...	82.1	52.5
Total Loans & Leases	1,807.0	1,733.1	1,093.8	1,006.1	916.0	845.0	658.4
Allowance for Credit Losses	26.4	24.1	9.7	10.3	11.3	14.2	14.0
Net Loans & Leases	1,780.6	1,709.0	1,084.1	995.8	904.8	830.8	644.3
Total Assets	3,434.2	3,210.8	2,022.6	1,840.7	1,680.7	1,633.7	1,343.9
Total Deposits	2,505.4	2,546.0	1,457.7	1,360.3	1,378.1	1,345.7	1,027.2
Long-Term Obligations	430.0	263.1	331.1	324.0	...	...	...
Total Liabilities	3,109.2	2,942.9	1,883.3	1,732.2	1,560.5	1,515.5	1,234.5
Net Stockholders' Equity	325.0	268.0	139.4	108.5	120.2	118.0	109.4
Year-end Shs. Outstg. (000)	12,979	12,903	6,993	7,296	7,296	7,587	7,474
STATISTICAL RECORD:							
Return on Equity %	11.8	7.7	14.6	16.3	12.9	13.2	12.9
Return on Assets %	1.1	0.6	1.0	1.0	0.9	1.0	1.1
Equity/Assets %	9.5	8.3	6.9	5.9	7.1	7.2	8.1
Non-Int. Exp./Tot. Inc. %	59.7	70.8	60.7	63.2	63.7	61.3	58.4
Price Range	34.21-25.91	29.85-24.75	26.25-20.00	33.63-22.63	38.25-24.81	34.00-19.25	20.13-15.13
P/E Ratio	11.7-8.8	18.4-15.3	9.2-7.0	13.9-9.3	18.7-12.1	16.8-9.5	11.0-8.2
Average Yield %	3.7	4.0	4.4	3.3	2.6	2.8	3.8

Statistics are as originally reported. Adj. for 2-for-1 stk. split, 3/97. ① Bef. acctg. chg. credit of $193,860. ② Incl. acquisition & unusual exp. of $8.2 mill.; bef. extraord. loss of $1.6 mill. ③ Incl. acquisition & unusual exp. of $700,000.

OFFICERS:
J. A. Gabriel, Chmn.
S. A. Belden, Pres., C.E.O.
D. G. Wallace, Exec. V.P., C.F.O.

INVESTOR CONTACT: David G. Wallace, Exec. V.P., C.F.O., (315) 445-2282

PRINCIPAL OFFICE: 5790 Widewaters Parkway, DeWitt, NY 13214-1883

TELEPHONE NUMBER: (315) 445-2282
FAX: (315) 445-2997
WEB: www.communitybankna.com

NO. OF EMPLOYEES: 1,120

SHAREHOLDERS: 9,000 (approx. record)

ANNUAL MEETING: In May

INCORPORATED: DE, Apr., 1983

INSTITUTIONAL HOLDINGS:
No. of Institutions: 89
Shares Held: 4,252,770
% Held: 32.7

INDUSTRY: National commercial banks (SIC: 6021)

TRANSFER AGENT(S): Mellon Investor Services, L.L.C., Ridgefield Park, NJ

COMMUNITY FIRST BANKSHARES, INC.

YIELD 3.2%
P/E RATIO 13.9

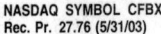

*7 YEAR PRICE SCORE 143.7   *12 MONTH PRICE SCORE 100.6
*NYSE COMPOSITE INDEX=100

INTERIM EARNINGS (Per Share):

Qtr.	Mar.	June	Sept.	Dec.
1999	0.36	0.38	0.39	0.35
2000	0.37	0.38	0.40	0.40
2001	0.24	0.43	0.45	0.46
2002	0.47	0.49	0.51	0.50
2003	0.50	...	...	...

INTERIM DIVIDENDS (Per Share):

Amt.	Decl.	Ex.	Rec.	Pay.
0.21Q	8/13/02	8/28/02	9/01/02	9/15/02
0.21Q	10/29/02	11/26/02	12/01/02	12/15/02
0.22Q	2/05/03	2/26/03	3/01/03	3/15/03
0.22Q	4/25/03	5/28/03	6/01/03	6/15/03

Indicated div.: $0.88 (Div. Reinv. Plan)

CAPITALIZATION (12/31/02):

	($000)	(%)
Total Deposits	4,669,746	90.2
Long-Term Debt	127,500	2.5
Common & Surplus	378,449	7.3
Total	5,175,695	100.0

DIVIDEND ACHIEVER STATUS:
Rank: 50   10-Year Growth Rate: 16.75%
Total Years of Dividend Growth: 11

RECENT DEVELOPMENTS: For the three months ended 3/31/03, net income increased to $19.4 million compared with $19.3 million in the corresponding year-earlier period. Net interest income declined 2.5% to $64.9 million from $66.6 million the previous year. Provision for loan losses was $3.5 million versus $3.3 million the year before. Total non-interest income grew 10.1% to $20.9 million, while non-interest expense inched up to $53.5 million from $53.1

million in 2002. Separately, on 5/1/03, CFBX announced that it has acquired Kraft Insurance Service, Inc., located in Grand Junction, Colorado. On 6/2/03, CFBX announced the acquisition of Larry Levitt Insurance, Inc., located in Rock Springs, Wyoming. The Company noted that it will continue to seek opportunities for additional expansion of its insurance offerings through both future agency acquisitions and organic growth.

BUSINESS

COMMUNITY FIRST BANK-SHARES, INC. is a bank holding company that as of 6/2/03 operated through one bank subsidiary with banking offices in 136 communities in Arizona, California, Colorado, Iowa, Minnesota, Nebraska, New Mexico, North Dakota, South Dakota, Utah, Wisconsin and Wyoming. The banks are community banks that provide a range of commercial and consumer banking services primarily to individuals and businesses in small and medium-sized communities and surrounding market areas. The Company provides the banks with access to lines of financial services including trust products and administration, insurance and investment services, data processing services, credit policy formulation and review, investment management and specialized staff support.

ANNUAL FINANCIAL DATA

	12/31/02	12/31/01	12/31/00	12/31/99	12/31/98	12/31/97	12/31/96
Earnings Per Share	1.97	①1.57	1.54	②1.48	②③0.98	②④1.20	②0.90
Tang. Book Val. Per Share	7.32	6.44	5.50	5.96	5.77	5.95	5.32
Dividends Per Share	0.80	0.68	0.60	0.56	0.44	0.35	0.29
Dividend Payout %	40.6	43.3	39.0	37.8	44.9	29.2	31.3
INCOME STATEMENT (IN MILLIONS):							
Total Interest Income	358.2	434.0	477.6	465.2	449.2	278.6	229.4
Total Interest Expense	89.9	162.2	210.3	185.8	188.5	117.3	95.2
Net Interest Income	268.3	271.8	267.3	279.4	260.8	161.3	134.2
Provision for Loan Losses	13.3	17.5	15.8	20.2	22.5	5.4	6.8
Non-Interest Income	81.3	76.7	75.2	72.5	60.3	36.6	27.4
Non-Interest Expense	217.6	232.4	219.3	218.2	230.1	125.2	104.3
Income Before Taxes	118.8	98.5	107.4	113.5	68.4	67.4	50.5
Net Income	79.2	①65.1	71.6	②74.9	②③47.0	②④45.9	②32.5
Average Shs. Outstg. (000)	40,243	41,471	46,579	50,671	47,882	38,138	33,398
BALANCE SHEET (IN MILLIONS):							
Cash & Due from Banks	242.9	248.3	256.1	247.1	251.0	222.1	175.7
Total Loans & Leases	3,577.9	3,736.7	3,738.2	3,690.4	3,386.1	2,637.1	2,064.1
Allowance for Credit Losses	56.2	55.0	52.2	48.9	50.2	36.2	26.2
Net Loans & Leases	3,521.7	3,681.7	3,686.0	3,641.5	3,336.0	2,600.9	2,037.9
Total Assets	5,827.2	5,772.3	6,089.7	6,302.2	6,003.0	4,855.5	3,116.4
Total Deposits	4,669.7	4,750.8	5,019.9	4,909.9	4,884.7	3,619.3	2,537.4
Long-Term Obligations	127.5	136.8	124.0	75.6	93.5	116.5	46.8
Total Liabilities	5,328.7	5,295.6	5,624.3	5,775.0	5,477.7	4,396.2	2,870.5
Net Stockholders' Equity	378.4	356.7	345.4	407.3	405.2	339.3	244.6
Year-end Shs. Outstg. (000)	38,679	40,246	41,867	47,118	47,119	40,646	34,304
STATISTICAL RECORD:							
Return on Equity %	20.9	18.2	20.7	18.4	11.6	13.5	13.3
Return on Assets %	1.4	1.1	1.2	1.2	0.8	0.9	1.0
Equity/Assets %	6.5	6.2	5.7	6.5	6.8	7.0	7.8
Non-Int. Exp./Tot. Inc. %	62.2	66.7	64.0	62.0	71.7	63.3	64.5
Price Range	28.45-21.80	27.00-17.13	19.19-12.38	24.06-13.63	27.25-13.50	28.13-13.63	14.50-10.00
P/E Ratio	14.4-11.1	17.2-10.9	12.5-8.0	16.3-9.2	27.8-13.8	23.4-11.4	15.7-10.8
Average Yield %	3.2	3.1	3.8	3.0	2.2	1.7	2.4

Statistics are as originally reported. Adj. for 2-for-1 stk. split, 5/98. ① Incl. restruct. chrg. of $7.7 mill. ② Incl. acquisition, integration & conforming chrgs. of $3.1 mill., 12/99; $3.7 mill., 12/98; $398,000, 12/97; $2.9 mill., 12/96. ③ Bef. loss fr. disc. ops. of $3.9 mill. ④ Bef. inc. fr. disc. ops. of $967,000 & extraord. loss of $265,000.

OFFICERS:
R. K. Strand, Vice-Chmn., C.O.O.
M. A. Anderson, Pres., C.E.O.
C. A. Weiss, Exec. V.P., C.F.O.

INVESTOR CONTACT: Community First Shareholder Services, (701) 298-5601

PRINCIPAL OFFICE: 520 Main Avenue, Fargo, ND 58124

TELEPHONE NUMBER: (701) 298-5600
FAX: (701) 237-4517
WEB: www.communityfirst.com
NO. OF EMPLOYEES: 1,919 full-time; 441 part-time
SHAREHOLDERS: 2,105 (record); 9,000 (approx. beneficial)
ANNUAL MEETING: In Apr.
INCORPORATED: DE, 1989

INSTITUTIONAL HOLDINGS:
No. of Institutions: 142
Shares Held: 21,914,710
% Held: 57.7

INDUSTRY: State commercial banks (SIC: 6022)

TRANSFER AGENT(S): Wells Fargo Shareowner Services, South St. Paul, MN

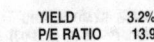

NASDAQ SYMBOL CTBI
Rec. Pr. 29.52 (5/31/03)

COMMUNITY TRUST BANCORP, INC.

YIELD 2.8%
P/E RATIO 13.1

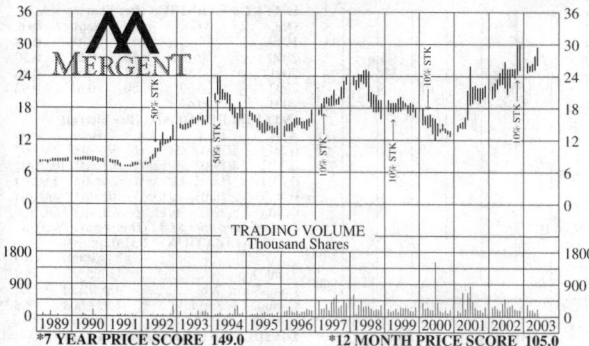

TRADING VOLUME
Thousand Shares

*7 YEAR PRICE SCORE 149.0   ***12 MONTH PRICE SCORE 105.0**
*NYSE COMPOSITE INDEX=100

INTERIM EARNINGS (Per Share):

Qtr.	Mar.	June	Sept.	Dec.
1999	0.42	0.45	0.45	0.46
2000	0.38	0.44	0.44	0.45
2001	0.41	0.46	0.42	0.46
2002	0.50	0.50	0.63	0.56
2003	0.56	...	...	...

INTERIM DIVIDENDS (Per Share):

Amt.	Decl.	Ex.	Rec.	Pay.
10% STK	10/22/02	11/26/02	12/01/02	12/15/02
0.21Q	10/22/02	12/11/02	12/15/02	1/01/03
0.21Q	1/28/03	3/12/03	3/15/03	4/01/03
0.21Q	4/29/03	6/11/03	6/15/03	7/01/03

Indicated div.: $0.84 (Div. Reinv. Plan)

CAPITALIZATION (12/31/02):

	($000)	(%)
Total Deposits	2,127,716	90.8
Long-Term Debt	6,721	0.3
Common & Surplus	209,419	8.9
Total	2,343,856	100.0

DIVIDEND ACHIEVER STATUS:
Rank: 178   10-Year Growth Rate: 8.24%
Total Years of Dividend Growth: 14

RECENT DEVELOPMENTS: For the three months ended 3/31/03, net income rose 10.6% to $7.0 million compared with $6.3 million in the equivalent period of 2002. Results for 2003 and 2002 included gains on sales of loans of $1.5 million and $859,000, respectively. Results for 2003 also included securities gains of $979,000. Net interest income slipped 8.5% to $20.5 million from $22.4 million the previous year. Provision for loan losses dropped 43.6% to $1.5 million versus $2.7 million a year earlier. Non-interest

income was $8.5 million, up 52.8% from $5.6 million the year before due to increased deposit service charge revenue, increased gains on sales of residential real estate loans and increased gains on sales of securities. Non-interest expense grew 6.5% to $17.6 million from $16.5 million in 2002. Total deposits slipped 2.2% to $2.10 billion from $2.15 billion, while loans declined 3.9% to $1.62 billion from $1.69 billion.

BUSINESS

COMMUNITY TRUST BANCORP, INC. is a bank holding company with assets of $2.47 billion as of 3/31/03 that currently owns all the capital stock of two commercial banks and one trust company, serving small and mid-sized communities in eastern, central, south central Kentucky, and southern West Virginia. The commercial banks are Community Trust Bank, NA, Pikeville, Kentucky and Citizens National Bank & Trust, Hazard. The trust company, Trust Company of Kentucky, NA, Lexington, purchased the trust operations of its subsidiary banks and has additional offices in Pikeville, Ashland, Middlesboro and Versailles, Kentucky. The Company operates 69 banking locations across eastern and central Kentucky, and 5 banking locations in West Virginia. On 12/29/00, the Company merged its thrift subsidiary, Community Trust Bank, FSB, into the Bank. On 1/26/01, Community Trust Bank, NA, acquired the deposits, loans, and fixed assets of The Bank of Mt. Vernon, Inc.

ANNUAL FINANCIAL DATA

	12/31/02	12/31/01	12/31/00	12/31/99	12/31/98	12/31/97	12/31/96
Earnings Per Share	2.19	1.76	1.70	1.79	1.14	☐ 1.31	1.41
Tang. Book Val. Per Share	11.73	10.11	9.76	9.30	8.40	10.47	9.35
Dividends Per Share	0.76	0.73	0.68	0.65	0.60	0.54	0.49
Dividend Payout %	34.9	41.4	39.8	36.1	52.9	41.6	34.9
INCOME STATEMENT (IN MILLIONS):							
Total Interest Income	146.6	176.8	175.7	163.5	160.6	150.6	144.4
Total Interest Expense	57.3	93.7	91.5	79.7	84.0	74.1	69.1
Net Interest Income	89.3	83.1	84.2	83.8	76.6	76.5	75.4
Provision for Loan Losses	10.1	9.2	9.2	9.1	16.0	11.2	7.3
Non-Interest Income	27.9	23.8	19.5	21.0	19.5	18.4	14.4
Non-Interest Expense	67.3	64.9	61.9	64.4	62.2	59.9	55.2
Income Before Taxes	39.8	32.8	32.6	31.3	17.9	23.9	27.3
Net Income	27.6	22.3	22.3	21.8	14.0	☐ 16.0	18.8
Average Shs. Outstg. (000)	12,607	12,725	13,150	12,198	12,176	12,245	13,379
BALANCE SHEET (IN MILLIONS):							
Cash & Due from Banks	93.0	96.2	72.7	99.8	98.1	61.4	63.9
Securities Avail. for Sale	527.3	367.2	236.6	270.3	301.1	165.6	230.0
Total Loans & Leases	1,634.6	1,711.1	1,694.5	1,619.5	1,502.4	1,428.4	1,309.6
Allowance for Credit Losses	23.3	23.6	25.9	25.1	26.1	20.5	18.8
Net Loans & Leases	1,611.3	1,687.4	1,668.6	1,594.4	1,476.3	1,408.0	1,290.8
Total Assets	2,487.9	2,503.9	2,262.0	2,176.1	2,248.0	1,852.7	1,840.0
Total Deposits	2,127.7	2,155.8	1,943.9	1,877.3	1,921.1	1,465.0	1,480.8
Long-Term Obligations	6.7	23.0	61.4	70.6	105.2	155.3	130.1
Total Liabilities	2,278.5	2,312.3	2,080.1	2,003.7	2,083.2	1,694.6	1,695.3
Net Stockholders' Equity	209.4	191.6	181.9	172.4	164.8	158.0	144.8
Year-end Shs. Outstg. (000)	12,348	12,568	12,871	12,148	12,179	13,393	13,366
STATISTICAL RECORD:							
Return on Equity %	13.2	11.6	12.3	12.7	8.5	10.1	13.0
Return on Assets %	1.1	0.9	1.0	1.0	0.6	0.9	1.0
Equity/Assets %	8.4	7.7	8.0	7.9	7.3	8.5	7.9
Non-Int. Exp./Tot. Inc. %	57.5	60.8	59.7	61.4	64.7	63.1	61.5
Price Range	30.00-19.79	28.50-15.00	19.77-13.13	22.16-17.95	27.84-17.56	26.34-18.41	19.53-13.90
P/E Ratio	13.7-9.0	14.8-7.8	10.6-7.0	11.2-9.1	22.3-14.1	18.3-12.5	12.6-9.0
Average Yield %	3.1	3.7	4.5	3.5	2.9	2.7	

Statistics are as originally reported. Adj. for 10% stk. splits, 12/15/02, 4/15/00, 4/15/99, 4/15/97. ☐ Bef. extraord. gain of $3.1 mill.

OFFICERS:
B. Coleman, Chmn.
J. R. Hale, Vice-Chmn., Pres., C.E.O.
M. A. Gooch, Exec. V.P., Treas.

INVESTOR CONTACT: Investor Relations,
(606) 432-1414

PRINCIPAL OFFICE: 346 North Mayo Trail,
Pikeville, KY 41501-2947

TELEPHONE NUMBER: (606) 432-1414
FAX: (606) 437-3345
WEB: www.ctbi.com

NO. OF EMPLOYEES: 874

SHAREHOLDERS: 1,636 (approx.)

ANNUAL MEETING: In Apr.

INCORPORATED: KY, Aug., 1980

INSTITUTIONAL HOLDINGS:
No. of Institutions: 44
Shares Held: 3,150,404
% Held: 26.3

INDUSTRY: National commercial banks
(SIC: 6021)

TRANSFER AGENT(S): Community Trust
Bancorp, Inc., Pikeville, KY

COMPASS BANCSHARES, INC.

YIELD	3.1%
P/E RATIO	14.7

INTERIM EARNINGS (Per Share):

Qtr.	Mar.	June	Sept.	Dec.
1999	0.45	0.47	0.48	0.48
2000	0.48	0.50	0.52	0.50
2001	0.50	0.52	0.53	0.56
2002	0.59	0.60	0.61	0.62
2003	0.64	...	...	...

INTERIM DIVIDENDS (Per Share):

Amt.	Decl.	Ex.	Rec.	Pay.
0.25Q	5/20/02	6/12/02	6/14/02	7/01/02
0.25Q	8/19/02	9/12/02	9/16/02	10/01/02
0.25Q	11/15/02	12/12/02	12/16/02	1/02/03
0.28Q	2/18/03	3/12/03	3/14/03	4/01/03
0.28Q	5/22/03	6/11/03	6/13/03	7/01/03

Indicated div.: $1.12 (Div. Reinv. Plan)

CAPITALIZATION (12/31/02):

	($000)	(%)
Total Deposits	15,135,387	68.9
Long-Term Debt	4,900,132	22.3
Common & Surplus	1,931,502	8.8
Total	21,967,021	100.0

DIVIDEND ACHIEVER STATUS:

Rank: 89	10-Year Growth Rate: 13.05%

Total Years of Dividend Growth: 21

*7 YEAR PRICE SCORE 144.8   *12 MONTH PRICE SCORE 104.7

*NYSE COMPOSITE INDEX=100

RECENT DEVELOPMENTS: For the three months ended 3/31/03, net income climbed 7.7% to $82.1 million from $76.2 million in the corresponding prior-year period. Earnings for 2003 and 2002 included merger and integration costs of $466,000 and $768,000, respectively. Net interest income slipped 2.8% to $227.2 million from $233.8 million a year earlier. Provision for loan losses declined 1.8% to $29.8 million from $30.3 million in 2002. Total non-interest income advanced 29.6% to $123.1 million, while total non-interest expense rose 7.2% to $196.1 million. As of 3/31/03, total assets were up 6.3% year-over-year to $24.32 billion. During the first quarter, the Company acquired two full-line general insurance companies, including Tucson, Arizona-based Mueller & Associates, Inc. on 3/12/03 and Dallas, Texas-based Maxson-Mahoney-Turner, Inc. on 3/17/03.

BUSINESS

COMPASS BANCSHARES, INC. (formerly Central Bancshares of the South, Inc.) is a bank holding company headquartered in Birmingham, Alabama, with total assets of $24.32 billion as of 3/31/03. Principal subsidiaries include Compass Bank; Compass Banks of Texas, Inc., a Delaware bank holding company, which owns Compass Bank, a Texas state bank headquartered in Houston, Texas; Central Bank of the South, an Alabama banking corporation headquartered in Anniston, Alabama; Arizona Bank; and Western Bancshares, Inc., in Albuquerque, New Mexico. In fiscal 2000, the Company expanded into New Mexico and Colorado with the acquisitions of Albuquerque-based Western Bancshares, Inc. and Denver-based MegaBank Financial Corp., Inc. In January 2001, the Company expanded into Nebraska with the acquisition of FirsTier Corporation. As of 3/31/03, Compass Bank conducted general commercial banking and trust services at 357 full-service bank offices, including 123 in Texas, 90 in Alabama, 67 in Arizona, 42 in Florida, 24 in Colorado, nine in New Mexico and two in Nebraska.

ANNUAL FINANCIAL DATA

	12/31/02	12/31/01	12/31/00	12/31/99	12/31/98	12/31/97	12/31/96
Earnings Per Share	① 2.42	① 2.11	① 2.00	① 1.88	1.57	1.56	1.42
Tang. Book Val. Per Share	13.06	13.53	12.24	10.52	10.30	9.70	8.81
Dividends Per Share	0.98	0.91	0.86	0.78	0.68	0.62	0.55
Dividend Payout %	40.5	43.1	43.0	41.2	43.6	39.5	38.9
INCOME STATEMENT (IN MILLIONS):							
Total Interest Income	1,386.9	1,517.7	1,432.8	1,247.6	1,134.5	949.0	820.4
Total Interest Expense	462.1	691.9	752.0	608.4	555.2	473.9	417.9
Net Interest Income	924.9	825.9	680.8	639.2	579.4	475.2	402.4
Provision for Loan Losses	136.3	106.2	53.5	31.1	38.4	22.4	17.6
Non-Interest Income	441.1	376.4	298.9	241.1	222.5	181.5	154.7
Non-Interest Expense	752.4	685.8	569.6	517.9	491.0	395.7	337.5
Income Before Taxes	477.2	410.2	356.6	331.2	272.4	238.5	202.1
Net Income	① 314.4	① 270.4	① 240.6	① 217.0	180.9	155.6	128.9
Average Shs. Outstg. (000)	129,850	129,138	120,454	114,441	113,745	99,771	90,835
BALANCE SHEET (IN MILLIONS):							
Cash & Due from Banks	734.5	716.0	719.5	684.5	831.6	693.7	670.4
Securities Avail. for Sale	4,806.4	6,585.0	5,049.5	4,243.8	3,773.4	2,422.2	2,132.6
Total Loans & Leases	16,481.3	15,926.4	11,494.5	10,789.5	10,103.2	8,677.0	7,459.8
Allowance for Credit Losses	232.8	2,410.5	153.6	143.6	138.6	127.4	121.2
Net Loans & Leases	16,248.5	13,515.9	11,340.9	10,645.8	9,964.6	8,549.5	7,338.7
Total Assets	23,884.7	23,015.0	19,992.2	18,150.8	17,288.9	13,459.6	11,814.2
Total Deposits	15,135.4	13,735.2	14,033.2	12,808.9	12,013.4	9,632.5	9,220.6
Long-Term Obligations	4,900.1	3,837.5	2,529.3	2,564.3	2,046.0	1,387.1	701.5
Total Liabilities	21,953.2	21,299.4	18,511.8	16,954.5	16,092.8	12,499.5	11,011.2
Net Stockholders' Equity	1,931.5	1,715.6	1,480.5	1,196.2	1,196.1	960.0	803.1
Year-end Shs. Outstg. (000)	126,116	126,801	120,972	113,709	113,351	98,987	91,181
STATISTICAL RECORD:							
Return on Equity %	16.3	15.8	16.3	18.1	15.1	16.2	16.1
Return on Assets %	1.3	1.2	1.2	1.2	1.0	1.2	1.1
Equity/Assets %	8.1	7.5	7.4	6.6	6.9	7.1	6.8
Non-Int. Exp./Tot. Inc. %	55.1	57.0	58.1	58.8	61.2	60.3	60.6
Price Range	36.12-26.00	29.46-18.75	24.44-15.50	30.75-20.50	36.00-18.75	31.67-17.22	17.83-13.67
P/E Ratio	14.9-10.7	14.0-8.9	12.2-7.7	16.4-10.9	23.0-12.0	20.3-11.0	12.6-9.6
Average Yield %	3.2	3.8	4.3	3.0	2.5	2.5	3.5

Statistics are as originally reported. Adj. for stk. splits: 3-for-2, 4/2/99 & 4/2/97. ① Incl. merger-related chrg. $2.8 mill., 12/02; $7.1 mill., 12/01; $8.9 mill., 12/00; $5.1 mill., 12/99.

OFFICERS:
D. P. Jones, Jr., Chmn., C.E.O.
G. R. Hegel, C.F.O.
J. W. Powell, Sec., Gen. Couns.

INVESTOR CONTACT: Ed Bilek, Dir., Investor Relations, (205) 297-3331

PRINCIPAL OFFICE: 15 South 20th St., Birmingham, AL 35233

TELEPHONE NUMBER: (205) 297-3000
FAX: (205) 933-3043
WEB: www.compassweb.com

NO. OF EMPLOYEES: 7,200 (approx.)

SHAREHOLDERS: 6,100 (approx.)

ANNUAL MEETING: In Apr.

INCORPORATED: DE, 1970

INSTITUTIONAL HOLDINGS:
No. of Institutions: 242
Shares Held: 45,501,201
% Held: 36.1

INDUSTRY: National commercial banks (SIC: 6021)

TRANSFER AGENT(S): Continental Stock Transfer & Trust Company, New York, NY

CONAGRA FOODS, INC.

YIELD 4.1%
P/E RATIO 16.0

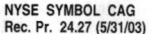
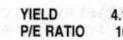
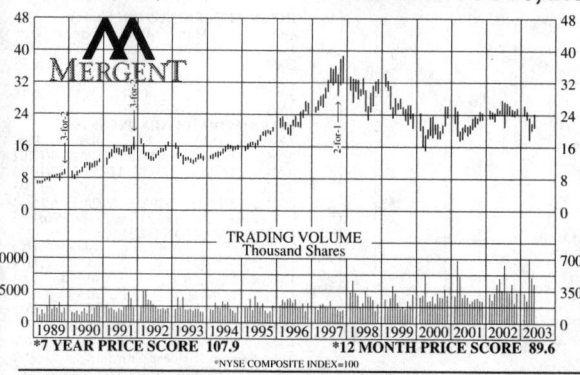

7 YEAR PRICE SCORE 107.9 *NYSE COMPOSITE INDEX=100* **12 MONTH PRICE SCORE 89.6**

INTERIM EARNINGS (Per Share):

Qtr.	Aug.	Nov.	Feb.	May
1998-99	0.23	0.46	0.36	d0.30
1999-00	0.21	0.39	0.30	d0.04
2000-01	0.30	0.58	0.19	0.23
2001-02	0.36	0.44	0.31	0.36
2002-03	0.42	0.44	0.30	...

INTERIM DIVIDENDS (Per Share):

Amt.	Decl.	Ex.	Rec.	Pay.
0.235Q	4/08/02	5/01/02	5/03/02	6/01/02
0.235Q	7/12/02	7/31/02	8/02/02	9/01/02
0.247Q	9/26/02	10/30/02	11/01/02	12/01/02
0.247Q	12/05/02	1/29/03	1/31/03	3/01/03
0.247Q	4/08/03	4/30/03	5/02/03	6/01/03

Indicated div.: $0.99 (Div. Reinv. Plan)

CAPITALIZATION (5/26/02):

	($000)	(%)
Long-Term Debt	5,743,700	57.1
Common & Surplus	4,308,200	42.9
Total	10,051,900	100.0

DIVIDEND ACHIEVER STATUS:
Rank: 90   10-Year Growth Rate: 13.02%
Total Years of Dividend Growth: 25

RECENT DEVELOPMENTS: For the 13 weeks ended 2/23/03, net income totaled $161.0 million, down 5.7% compared with $170.8 million in the corresponding prior-year period. Net sales fell 28.8% to $4.45 billion from $6.24 billion the year earlier, primarily reflecting the 9/19/02 divestiture of the Company's fresh beef and pork processing business, partially offset by higher sales in the Food Ingredients segment. Operating profit slid 15.8% to $385.3 million from $457.8 million in the previous year.

PROSPECTS: On 6/9/03, the Company announced that it has agreed to sell its chicken processing business, which has annual revenue of about $2.00 billion, to Pilgrim's Pride Corporation for approximately $590.0 million. The transaction is expected to be completed in the summer of 2003. Separately, on 5/19/03, CAG announced that it completed the sale of its BUMBLE BEE canned seafood business and other seafood assets. Terms of the transaction were not disclosed.

BUSINESS

CONAGRA FOODS, INC. (formerly ConAgra, Inc.) operates in four industry segments: Packaged Foods (44.8% of sales and 78.2% of operating profit in fiscal 2002) includes branded shelf-stable, frozen and refrigerated products for retail and foodservice markets. Meat Processing (36.3%, 13.1%) includes the Company's fresh beef, pork and poultry operations. Agricultural Products (12.9%, 0.9%) includes CAG's crop inputs distribution business and its agricultural merchandising operations. Food Ingredients (6.0%, 7.8%) includes spices, grain milling and ingredients for food products. The Company's major brands include: HEALTHY CHOICE, BANQUET, CHEF BOYARDEE, WESSON, HUNT'S, ORVILLE REDENBACHER'S, SLIM JIM, PETER PAN, PARKAY, VAN CAMP'S, PAM, SWISS MISS, LOUIS KEMP, REDDI-WIP, ACT II, BUTTERBALL, LA CHOY and ARMOUR.

ANNUAL FINANCIAL DATA

	5/26/02	5/27/01	5/28/00	5/30/99	5/31/98	5/25/97	5/26/96
Earnings Per Share	① 1.47	① 1.33	② 0.86	② 0.75	① 1.36	1.34	② 0.40
Cash Flow Per Share	2.67	2.48	1.98	1.80	2.33	2.24	1.28
Tang. Book Val. Per Share	...	...	1.22	1.02	0.85	0.08	...
Dividends Per Share	0.91	0.84	0.74	0.65	0.56	0.49	0.43
Dividend Payout %	61.9	62.8	85.9	86.3	41.5	36.8	108.8

INCOME STATEMENT (IN MILLIONS):

Total Revenues	27,629.6	27,194.2	25,385.8	24,594.3	23,840.5	24,002.1	24,821.6
Costs & Expenses	25,336.7	25,073.9	23,557.6	22,654.8	22,073.8	22,293.4	23,192.4
Depreciation & Amort.	623.2	592.9	536.5	499.8	446.3	413.8	407.9
Operating Income	1,669.7	1,527.4	1,291.7	1,439.7	1,320.4	1,294.9	1,221.3
Net Interest Inc./(Exp.)	d401.5	d423.3	d303.4	d316.6	d299.3	d277.2	d304.9
Income Before Income Taxes	1,268.2	1,104.1	666.1	682.3	1,021.1	1,017.7	408.6
Income Taxes	483.2	421.6	253.1	323.9	393.1	402.7	219.7
Net Income	① 785.0	① 682.5	② 413.0	② 358.4	① 628.0	615.0	② 188.9
Cash Flow	1,408.2	1,275.4	949.5	858.2	1,074.3	1,028.8	588.2
Average Shs. Outstg. (000)	528,000	514,300	478,600	476,700	461,300	459,000	459,000

BALANCE SHEET (IN MILLIONS):

Cash & Cash Equivalents	157.9	198.1	157.6	62.8	95.2	105.8	113.7
Total Current Assets	6,433.9	7,362.6	5,966.5	5,656.1	5,473.8	5,077.5	5,444.2
Net Property	3,893.9	3,884.7	3,584.0	3,614.2	3,395.8	3,242.5	2,820.5
Total Assets	15,496.2	16,480.8	12,295.8	12,146.1	11,702.8	11,277.1	11,196.6
Total Current Liabilities	4,313.4	6,935.6	5,489.2	5,386.4	5,070.2	4,989.6	5,193.7
Long-Term Obligations	5,743.7	4,109.5	2,566.8	2,543.1	2,487.4	2,355.7	2,262.9
Net Stockholders' Equity	4,308.2	3,983.2	2,964.1	2,908.8	2,778.9	2,471.7	2,255.5
Net Working Capital	2,120.5	427.0	477.3	269.7	403.6	87.9	250.5
Year-end Shs. Outstg. (000)	537,040	537,067	492,212	488,173	459,076	476,126	486,312

STATISTICAL RECORD:

Operating Profit Margin %	6.0	5.6	5.1	5.9	5.5	5.4	4.9
Net Profit Margin %	2.8	2.5	1.6	1.5	2.6	2.6	0.8
Return on Equity %	18.2	17.1	13.9	12.3	22.6	24.9	8.4
Return on Assets %	5.1	4.1	3.4	3.0	5.4	5.5	1.7
Debt/Total Assets %	37.1	24.9	20.9	20.9	21.3	20.9	20.2
Price Range	26.00-17.50	26.19-15.06	34.38-20.63	33.63-22.56	38.75-24.50	27.38-18.81	20.88-14.88
P/E Ratio	17.7-11.9	19.7-11.3	40.0-24.0	44.8-30.1	28.5-18.0	20.4-14.0	52.8-37.6
Average Yield %	4.2	4.1	2.7	2.3	1.8	2.1	2.4

Statistics are as originally reported. Adj. for 2-for-1 stk. split, 10/97. ① Bef. $2.0 mil acctg. chg., 2002; $43.9 mil ($0.09/sh), 2001; & $14.8 mil ($0.03/sh), 1998. ② Incl. $621.4 mil pre-tax, non-recur. chg., 2000; $337.9 mil ($0.71/sh) after-tax, non-recur chg., 1999; & $356.3 mil ($0.78/sh) after-tax, non-recur. chg., 1996.

OFFICERS:
B. C. Rohde, Chmn., Pres., C.E.O.
J. P. O'Donnell, Exec. V.P., C.F.O., Sec.
K. W. Gerhardt, Sr. V.P., Chief Info. Off.

INVESTOR CONTACT: Shareholder Services, (800) 214-0349

PRINCIPAL OFFICE: One ConAgra Drive, Omaha, NE 68102-5001

TELEPHONE NUMBER: (402) 595-4000
FAX: (402) 595-4707
WEB: www.conagra.com
NO. OF EMPLOYEES: 89,000 (approx.)
SHAREHOLDERS: 34,000 (record); 190,000 (approx. beneficial)
ANNUAL MEETING: In Sept.
INCORPORATED: NE, Sept., 1919; reincorp., DE, Dec., 1975

INSTITUTIONAL HOLDINGS:
No. of Institutions: 480
Shares Held: 326,235,492
% Held: 60.8

INDUSTRY: Meat packing plants (SIC: 2011)

TRANSFER AGENT(S): Wells Fargo Shareowner Services, St. Paul, MN

CONNECTICUT WATER SERVICE, INC.

YIELD 3.2%
P/E RATIO 21.8

INTERIM EARNINGS (Per Share):

Qtr.	Mar.	June	Sept.	Dec.
1999	0.21	0.25	0.37	0.20
2000	0.21	0.25	0.37	0.25
2001	0.30	0.37	0.38	0.16
2002	0.20	0.24	0.50	0.18
2003	0.26	...	...	...

INTERIM DIVIDENDS (Per Share):

Amt.	Decl.	Ex.	Rec.	Pay.
0.205Q	8/14/02	8/29/02	9/03/02	9/17/02
0.205Q	11/13/02	11/27/02	12/02/02	12/16/02
0.205Q	1/08/03	2/27/03	3/03/03	3/17/03
0.205Q	3/14/03	5/29/03	6/02/03	6/16/03

Indicated div.: $0.82 (Div. Reinv. Plan)

CAPITALIZATION (12/31/02):

	($000)	(%)
Long-Term Debt	64,734	36.8
Deferred Income Tax	30,504	17.3
Common & Surplus	80,822	45.9
Total	176,060	100.0

DIVIDEND ACHIEVER STATUS:
Rank: 282   10-Year Growth Rate: 1.30%
Total Years of Dividend Growth: 27

TRADING VOLUME
Thousand Shares

1989 | 1990 | 1991 | 1992 | 1993 | 1994 | 1995 | 1996 | 1997 | 1998 | 1999 | 2000 | 2001 | 2002 | 2003
*7 YEAR PRICE SCORE 151.2   *12 MONTH PRICE SCORE 97.4
*NYSE COMPOSITE INDEX=100

RECENT DEVELOPMENTS: For the quarter ended 3/31/03, net income increased 36.7% to $2.1 million compared with $1.5 million in the equivalent 2002 quarter. Results for 2003 included a net gain of $943,000 on property transactions. Operating revenues grew 6.0% to $10.9 million from $10.3 million in 2002 due in part to a 55.0% increase in non-water sales reflecting the Company's Linebacker™ service line maintenance program and antenna leases. Util-ity operating income fell 19.3% to $2.0 million from $2.5 million a year earlier. This reduction reflected increases in wages, pension and insurance expense, and maintenance expense due to numerous main breaks in the first quarter of 2003. Looking ahead, the Company intends to donate approximately 133 acres to the Town of Killingly, Con-necticut in 2004.

BUSINESS

CONNECTICUT WATER SER-VICE, INC. is the parent company of five regulated water (90.0% of 2002 earnings) companies that supplied water to 85,536 customers for residen-tial, commercial, industrial and municipal purposes in 42 towns in Connecticut and Massachusetts as of 12/31/02. The Company and its sub-sidiaries represent the largest domes-tic investor-owned water system in the state of Connecticut in terms of operating revenues and utility plant investment. The area served has an estimated population of 300,000 as of 5/14/03. In addition, the Company had six unregulated water companies (10.0%) as of 12/31/02. Water supply sources vary among the individual systems, but from the systems as a whole, about 42.0% of the total dependable yield comes from reser-voirs and 58.0% from wells as of 12/31/02.

ANNUAL FINANCIAL DATA

	12/31/02	12/31/01	12/31/00	12/31/99	12/31/98	12/31/97	12/31/96
Earnings Per Share	1.12	①1.10	②1.09	②1.03	②1.02	②1.00	0.97
Cash Flow Per Share	1.81	1.75	1.72	1.65	1.60	1.53	1.48
Tang. Book Val. Per Share	9.73	9.25	8.92	8.61	8.52	8.26	8.03
Dividends Per Share	0.81	0.804	0.80	0.79	0.78	0.77	0.76
Dividend Payout %	72.7	73.1	73.2	76.6	76.2	77.2	77.6
INCOME STATEMENT (IN THOUSANDS):							
Total Revenues	45,830	45,392	41,512	42,624	37,924	38,501	38,592
Costs & Expenses	28,645	29,072	25,687	26,883	21,584	22,591	23,380
Depreciation & Amort.	5,351	5,006	4,666	4,514	3,981	3,624	3,420
Maintenance Exp.	...	...	...	...	2,055	1,952	1,664
Operating Income	11,834	11,314	11,159	11,227	10,304	10,334	10,128
Net Interest Inc./(Exp.)	d4,534	d4,632	d4,541	d4,391	d4,177	d4,182	d3,788
Income Taxes	...	...	...	57	262	215	21
Net Income	8,780	①8,439	②7,963	②7,494	②6,965	②6,804	6,603
Cash Flow	14,093	13,407	12,591	11,970	10,908	10,390	9,985
Average Shs. Outstg.	7,771	7,662	7,308	7,272	6,803	6,786	6,743
BALANCE SHEET (IN THOUSANDS):							
Gross Property	316,699	279,027	254,612	244,653	223,661	216,103	202,957
Accumulated Depreciation	87,602	76,697	67,641	63,311	56,335	52,346	49,059
Net Property	229,097	202,330	186,971	181,342	167,326	163,757	153,898
Total Assets	264,799	231,714	215,399	210,885	194,586	189,277	184,640
Long-Term Obligations	64,734	63,953	64,658	65,399	62,501	54,532	54,430
Net Stockholders' Equity	80,822	70,783	65,678	63,267	58,717	56,841	55,167
Year-end Shs. Outstg.	7,940	7,649	7,279	7,258	6,804	6,791	6,777
STATISTICAL RECORD:							
Operating Profit Margin %	25.8	24.9	26.9	26.3	27.2	26.8	26.2
Net Profit Margin %	19.2	18.6	19.2	17.6	18.4	17.7	17.1
Net Inc./Net Property %	3.8	4.2	4.3	4.1	4.2	4.2	4.3
Net Inc./Tot. Capital %	5.0	5.2	5.1	4.9	4.8	5.1	5.0
Return on Equity %	10.9	11.8	12.1	11.8	11.9	12.0	12.0
Accum. Depr./Gross Prop. %	27.7	27.5	26.6	25.9	25.2	24.2	24.2
Price Range	31.09-20.35	32.21-19.50	23.50-17.04	24.67-12.67	19.00-13.33	14.33-12.22	13.56-11.00
P/E Ratio	27.8-18.2	29.3-17.7	21.6-15.6	24.0-12.3	18.6-13.1	14.4-12.3	13.9-11.3
Average Yield %	3.2	3.1	3.9	4.2	4.8	5.8	6.2

Statistics are as originally reported. Adj. for stk. split: 3-for-2, 9/7/01; 3-for-2, 9/15/98 ① Incls. gain of $1.1 mill. from prop. transaction & merger costs of $352,000. ② Incls. gain on prop. trans. of $440,000, 12/02; $534,000, 12/00; $161,000, 12/99; $475,000, 12/98; $183,000, 12/97.

OFFICERS:
M. T. Chiaraluce, Chmn., Pres., C.E.O.
D. C. Benoit, V.P., C.F.O. Treas.
P. J. Bancroft, Asst. Treas., Contr.
M. G. DiAcri, Corp. Sec.

INVESTOR CONTACT: David C. Benoit, (800) 669-8630 ext. 3030

PRINCIPAL OFFICE: 93 West Main Street, Clinton, CT 06413-1600

TELEPHONE NUMBER: (860) 669-8636
FAX: (860) 669-9326
WEB: www.ctwater.com

NO. OF EMPLOYEES: 191 (avg.)

SHAREHOLDERS: 4,976 (approx.)

ANNUAL MEETING: In Apr.

INCORPORATED: CT, Feb., 1956

INSTITUTIONAL HOLDINGS:
No. of Institutions: 40
Shares Held: 1,164,644
% Held: 14.6

INDUSTRY: Water supply (SIC: 4941)

TRANSFER AGENT(S): State Street Bank and Trust Company EquiServe, Boston, MA

NYSE SYMBOL ED
Rec. Pr. 42.99 (5/31/03)

CONSOLIDATED EDISON, INC.

YIELD 5.2%
P/E RATIO 14.0

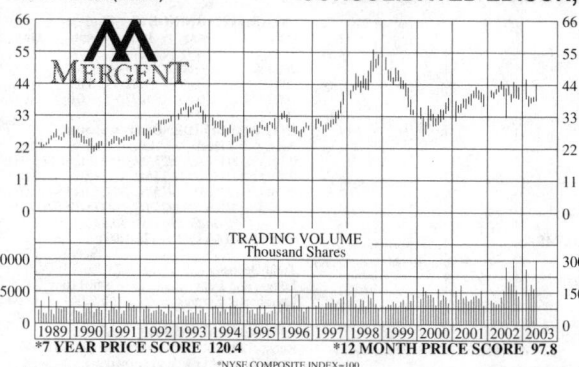

TRADING VOLUME
Thousand Shares

| | 1989 | 1990 | 1991 | 1992 | 1993 | 1994 | 1995 | 1996 | 1997 | 1998 | 1999 | 2000 | 2001 | 2002 | 2003 |

*7 YEAR PRICE SCORE 120.4   ***12 MONTH PRICE SCORE 97.8**
*NYSE COMPOSITE INDEX=100

INTERIM EARNINGS (Per Share):

Qtr.	Mar.	June	Sept.	Dec.
2000	0.88	0.33	1.32	0.30
2001	0.84	0.48	1.30	0.59
2002	0.78	0.46	1.33	0.56
2003	0.72	...	...	...

INTERIM DIVIDENDS (Per Share):

Amt.	Decl.	Ex.	Rec.	Pay.
0.555Q	7/18/02	8/12/02	8/14/02	9/15/02
0.555Q	10/17/02	11/08/02	11/13/02	12/15/02
0.56Q	1/16/03	2/10/03	2/12/03	3/15/03
0.56Q	4/17/03	5/12/03	5/14/03	6/15/03

Indicated div.: $2.24 (Div. Reinv. Plan)

CAPITALIZATION (12/31/02):

	($000)	(%)
Long-Term Debt	6,168,430	42.0
Capital Lease Obligations..	38,487	0.3
Deferred Income Tax	2,575,646	17.5
Common & Surplus	5,921,079	40.3
Total	14,703,642	100.0

DIVIDEND ACHIEVER STATUS:
Rank: 281   10-Year Growth Rate: 1.57%
Total Years of Dividend Growth: 28

RECENT DEVELOPMENTS: For the three months ended 3/31/03, net income slipped 7.2% to $154.0 million compared with income of $166.0 million, before an accounting change charge of $20.0 million, in the same period of 2002. Results for 2002 included a one-time goodwill impairment charge of $20.0 million related to certain unregulated generating assets. Total operating revenues increased 27.8% to $2.60 billion from $2.04 billion in the prior-year period.

PROSPECTS: The Company confimed its forecast of earnings per share for 2003 in the range of $2.90 to $3.05. This estimate reflects ED's expectations for the timing of the economic recovery from the current downturn. Separately, on 3/17/03, Con Edison Communications, a subsidiary of ED, introduced two new service offerings, PowerNet Internet and PowerCall Voice Services. The new services mark the Company's entrance into the small and medium business markets.

BUSINESS

CONSOLIDATED EDISON, INC. (formerly Consolidated Edison Company of New York) provides a range of energy-related products and services through six subsidiaries. Consolidated Edison Company of New York is a regulated utility providing electric, gas and steam service to New York City and Westchester County, New York. Orange and Rockland Utilities, Inc. is a regulated utility serving customers in southeastern New York state and adjacent sections of New Jersey and northeastern Pennsylvania. Con Edison Solutions is a retail energy services company and Con Edison Energy is a wholesale energy supply company. Con Edison Development is an infrastructure development company and Con Edison Communications is a telecommunications infrastructure company. Sales for 2002 were derived: electric, 73.7%; gas, 14.2%; steam, 4.8%; and non-utility, 7.3%.

ANNUAL FINANCIAL DATA

	12/31/02	12/31/01	12/31/00	12/31/99	12/31/98	12/31/97	12/31/96
Earnings Per Share	② 3.13	3.21	① 2.74	3.13	3.04	2.95	2.93
Cash Flow Per Share	5.49	5.68	5.51	5.49	5.25	5.09	5.04
Tang. Book Val. Per Share	25.40	30.66	26.39	25.90	25.88	25.18	24.37
Dividends Per Share	2.22	2.20	2.18	2.14	2.12	2.10	2.08
Dividend Payout %	70.9	68.5	79.6	68.4	69.7	71.2	71.0
INCOME STATEMENT (IN MILLIONS):							
Total Revenues	8,481.9	9,634.0	9,431.4	7,491.3	7,093.0	7,121.3	6,959.7
Costs & Expenses	6,539.9	7,550.0	7,370.8	5,507.4	5,043.8	5,098.3	4,991.1
Depreciation & Amort.	494.6	526.2	586.4	526.2	518.5	502.8	496.4
Maintenance Exp.	387.3	430.3	458.0	438.0	477.4	474.8	458.6
Operating Income	1,060.1	1,127.5	1,016.1	1,019.8	1,053.3	1,045.4	1,013.6
Net Interest Inc./(Exp.)	d441.6	d430.9	d407.4	d337.6	d325.8	d331.1	d323.5
Income Taxes	cr21.7	cr21.9	cr10.6	cr26.9	cr2.2	cr3.2	cr1.0
Net Income	② 668.1	695.8	① 596.4	714.2	729.7	712.8	694.1
Cash Flow	1,162.2	1,208.5	1,169.2	1,226.8	1,231.3	1,197.3	1,184.6
Average Shs. Outstg. (000)	214,050	212,920	212,186	223,442	234,308	235,082	234,977
BALANCE SHEET (IN MILLIONS):							
Gross Property	17,998.9	16,317.9	17,020.5	16,002.8	16,033.9	15,557.2	15,251.6
Accumulated Depreciation	4,669.7	4,473.0	5,234.7	4,733.6	4,726.2	4,392.4	4,285.7
Net Property	13,329.2	12,248.4	11,893.4	11,353.8	11,406.5	11,267.1	11,067.3
Total Assets	18,820.3	16,996.1	16,767.2	15,531.5	14,381.4	14,722.5	14,057.2
Long-Term Obligations	6,206.9	5,542.3	5,446.9	4,559.1	4,087.4	4,228.8	4,281.3
Net Stockholders' Equity	5,921.1	5,878.8	5,685.0	5,624.6	6,238.2	6,163.5	5,965.7
Year-end Shs. Outstg. (000)	213,933	188,916	188,816	192,452	232,833	235,490	234,994
STATISTICAL RECORD:							
Operating Profit Margin %	12.5	11.7	10.8	13.6	14.9	14.7	14.6
Net Profit Margin %	8.0	7.2	6.3	9.5	10.3	10.0	10.0
Net Inc./Net Property %	5.1	5.7	5.0	6.3	6.4	6.3	6.3
Net Inc./Tot. Capital %	4.6	5.1	4.4	5.7	5.7	5.6	5.5
Return on Equity %	11.5	11.8	10.5	12.7	11.7	11.6	11.6
Accum. Depr./Gross Prop. %	25.9	27.4	30.8	29.6	29.5	28.2	28.1
Price Range	45.40-32.65	43.37-31.44	39.50-26.19	53.44-33.56	56.13-39.06	41.50-27.00	34.75-25.88
P/E Ratio	14.5-10.4	13.5-9.8	14.4-9.6	17.1-10.7	18.5-12.8	14.1-9.2	11.9-8.8
Average Yield %	5.7	5.9	6.6	4.9	4.5	6.1	6.9

Statistics are as originally reported. ① Incl. approx. $84.9 mill. chg. fr. replacement power costs. ② Excl. $22.1 mill. acctg. change chg.

OFFICERS:
E. R. McGrath, Chmn., Pres., C.E.O.
J. S. Freilich, Exec. V.P., C.F.O.
C. E. McTiernan, Jr., Gen. Couns.

INVESTOR CONTACT: Jan C. Childress, Dir. of Inv. Rel., (212) 460-6611

PRINCIPAL OFFICE: 4 Irving Place, New York, NY 10003

TELEPHONE NUMBER: (212) 460-4600
FAX: (212) 475-0734
WEB: www.conedison.com

NO. OF EMPLOYEES: 14,293 (approx.)

SHAREHOLDERS: 97,987 (record)

ANNUAL MEETING: In May

INCORPORATED: NY, Nov., 1884

INSTITUTIONAL HOLDINGS:
No. of Institutions: 366
Shares Held: 81,741,633
% Held: 38.2

INDUSTRY: Electric and other services combined (SIC 4931)

TRANSFER AGENT(S): The Bank of New York, New York, NY

CORUS BANKSHARES, INC.

YIELD	1.3%
P/E RATIO	13.8

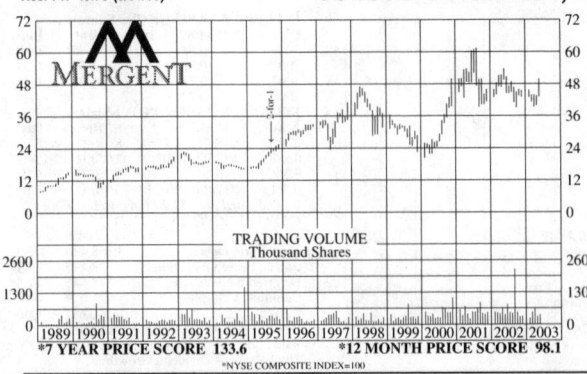

TRADING VOLUME
Thousand Shares

| 1989 | 1990 | 1991 | 1992 | 1993 | 1994 | 1995 | 1996 | 1997 | 1998 | 1999 | 2000 | 2001 | 2002 | 2003 |

*7 YEAR PRICE SCORE 133.6   ***12 MONTH PRICE SCORE 98.1**

*NYSE COMPOSITE INDEX=100

INTERIM EARNINGS (Per Share):

Qtr.	Mar.	June	Sept.	Dec.
1999	0.71	0.74	0.76	0.59
2000	0.80	1.28	1.11	2.02
2001	0.99	1.02	0.83	0.93
2002	0.73	0.97	1.01	0.74
2003	0.88	...	...	...

INTERIM DIVIDENDS (Per Share):

Amt.	Decl.	Ex.	Rec.	Pay.
0.16Q	8/14/02	9/25/02	9/27/02	10/10/02
0.16Q	11/12/02	12/24/02	12/27/02	1/10/03
0.16Q	2/24/03	3/25/03	3/27/03	4/10/03
0.165Q	4/10/03	6/25/03	6/27/03	7/10/03
	Indicated div.: $0.66			

CAPITALIZATION (12/31/02):

	($000)	(%)
Total Deposits	2,059,773	79.5
Long-Term Debt	48,110	1.9
Common & Surplus	482,041	18.6
Total	2,589,924	100.0

DIVIDEND ACHIEVER STATUS:
Rank: 126   10-Year Growth Rate: 10.84%
Total Years of Dividend Growth: 16

RECENT DEVELOPMENTS: For the quarter ended 3/31/03, net income rose 19.1% to $12.5 million compared with $10.5 million in the corresponding year-earlier period. Net interest income climbed 18.1% to $26.8 million from $22.7 million the previous year. Provision for loan losses amounted to nil in 2003 and 2002. Total noninterest income fell 30.6% to $3.6 million, primarily due to net securities losses of $101,000 in 2003 versus net securities gains of $1.6 million in 2002. Total noninterest expense slid 4.8% to

$11.7 million. Total nonperforming assets increased to $16.1 million, or 0.88% of total loans, versus $5.5 million, or 0.26% of total loans, a year earlier. CORS attributed the rise to an increase in commercial real estate troubled debt restructurings (TDR). CORS defines a TDR as a loan that was restructured in such a way as to provide the borrower with some form of concession relative to market absent a concession from the borrower that is deemed to be approximately proportionate to the lender's concession.

BUSINESS

CORUS BANKSHARES, INC. is a bank holding company with total assets of $2.60 billion as of 3/31/03. CORS provides consumer and corporate banking products and services through its wholly-owned banking subsidiary, Corus Bank, N.A. The two main business activities for CORS are commercial real estate lending and deposit gathering. The third, and smaller, business is servicing the check cashing industry. The bank has eleven branches in the Chicago metropolitan area and offers general banking services such as checking, savings, money market and time deposit accounts, as well as safe deposit boxes and a variety of additional services. On 12/31/00, the Company's subsidiary, Bancorp operations Company merged with CORS.

REVENUES

(12/31/02)	($000)	(%)
Loan - Taxable	127,998	72.7
Loan - Tax-advanced.	222	0.1
Federal Funds Sold....	7,486	4.3
Taxable Securities	11,847	6.7
Tax-advanced Securities	66	0.1
Dividend Securities ...	4,810	2.7
Trading Accounts Securities	449	0.3
Other Noninterest Income	23,079	13.1
Total	175,957	100.0

ANNUAL FINANCIAL DATA

	12/31/02	12/31/01	12/31/00	12/31/99	12/31/98	12/31/97	12/31/96
Earnings Per Share	3.45	3.79	⑪ 5.23	2.82	2.75	2.63	2.93
Tang. Book Val. Per Share	33.82	31.52	28.06	22.19	21.15	19.25	15.07
Dividends Per Share	0.63	0.61	0.59	0.57	0.55	0.52	0.45
Dividend Payout %	18.3	16.1	11.3	20.2	20.0	19.8	15.4
INCOME STATEMENT (IN MILLIONS):							
Total Interest Income	152.9	188.6	223.7	196.6	187.5	183.9	191.0
Total Interest Expense	54.6	80.9	102.6	90.4	89.3	82.7	79.6
Net Interest Income	98.3	107.7	121.1	106.1	98.2	101.3	111.3
Provision for Loan Losses	...	...	...	...	10.0	16.0	16.0
Non-Interest Income	23.1	25.7	45.5	18.9	25.7	26.9	22.8
Non-Interest Expense	47.5	51.1	52.9	63.1	51.9	51.7	50.2
Income Before Taxes	73.9	82.3	113.7	62.0	62.0	60.5	67.9
Net Income	49.3	54.2	⑪ 74.8	40.7	40.6	39.4	43.9
Average Shs. Outstg. (000)	14,295	14,309	14,302	14,464	14,773	14,966	14,994
BALANCE SHEET (IN MILLIONS):							
Cash & Due from Banks	61.6	58.5	111.1	72.3	72.1	62.2	57.5
Total Loans & Leases	1,742.0	1,475.2	1,551.9	1,727.4	1,551.6	1,546.0	1,623.1
Allowance for Credit Losses	36.6	40.5	39.6	32.1	35.8	30.7	32.7
Net Loans & Leases	1,705.3	1,434.8	1,512.3	1,695.3	1,515.8	1,515.3	1,590.5
Total Assets	2,617.1	2,659.3	2,598.5	2,388.2	2,589.4	2,251.9	2,218.5
Total Deposits	2,059.8	2,121.5	2,107.6	1,964.4	2,154.7	1,863.1	1,900.7
Long-Term Obligations	48.1	55.8	41.1	46.9	64.9	49.3	46.3
Total Liabilities	2,135.0	2,208.4	2,196.1	2,060.4	2,271.3	1,960.3	1,982.9
Net Stockholders' Equity	482.0	450.9	402.4	327.8	318.1	291.6	235.6
Year-end Shs. Outstg. (000)	14,119	14,160	14,143	14,369	14,551	14,681	14,820
STATISTICAL RECORD:							
Return on Equity %	10.2	12.0	18.6	12.4	12.8	13.5	18.6
Return on Assets %	1.9	2.0	2.9	1.7	1.6	1.7	2.0
Equity/Assets %	18.4	17.0	15.5	13.7	12.3	13.0	10.6
Non-Int. Exp./Tot. Inc. %	41.6	40.7	33.6	49.9	43.7	42.0	38.4
Price Range	53.80-38.95	61.50-39.20	50.00-20.25	36.44-22.50	47.13-28.63	41.00-23.50	33.00-24.75
P/E Ratio	15.6-11.3	16.2-10.3	9.6-3.9	12.9-8.0	17.1-10.4	15.6-8.9	11.3-8.4
Average Yield %	1.4	1.2	1.7	1.9	1.5	1.6	1.6

Statistics are as originally reported. ⑪ Incl. a $22.5 mill. gain on sale of student loans.

OFFICERS:
J. C. Glickman, Chmn.
R. J. Glickman, Pres., C.E.O.
T. H. Taylor, Exec. V.P., C.F.O.

INVESTOR CONTACT:

INVESTOR CONTACT: Tim Taylor, Exec. V.P., C.F.O., (773) 832-3470

PRINCIPAL OFFICE: 3959 N. Lincoln Avenue, Chicago, IL 60613-2431

TELEPHONE NUMBER: (773) 549-7100
FAX: (773) 549-0734
WEB: www.corusbank.com

NO. OF EMPLOYEES: 475

SHAREHOLDERS: 2,500 (approx.)

ANNUAL MEETING: In Apr.

INCORPORATED: MN, Oct., 1958

INSTITUTIONAL HOLDINGS:
No. of Institutions: 75
Shares Held: 4,385,819
% Held: 31.3

INDUSTRY: State commercial banks (SIC: 6022)

TRANSFER AGENT(S): Mellon Investor Services, LLC, Ridgefield Park, NJ

COUSINS PROPERTIES INCORPORATED

YIELD 5.5%
P/E RATIO 20.9

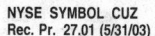

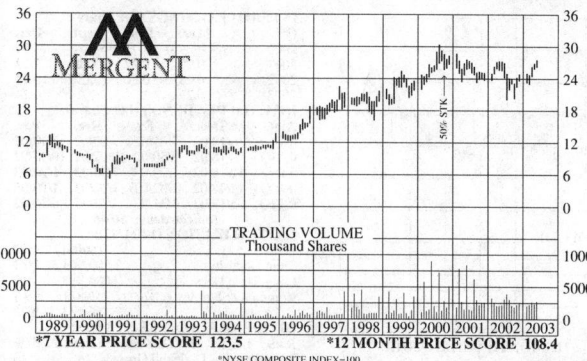

INTERIM EARNINGS (Per Share):

Qtr.	Mar.	June	Sept.	Dec.
1999	0.31	1.29	0.26	0.26
2000	0.43	0.27	0.27	0.29
2001	0.62	0.25	0.27	0.27
2002	0.25	0.25	0.24	0.26
2003	0.54	...	...	...

INTERIM DIVIDENDS (Per Share):

Amt.	Decl.	Ex.	Rec.	Pay.
0.37Q	5/01/02	5/15/02	5/17/02	5/30/02
0.37Q	7/30/02	8/08/02	8/12/02	8/26/02
0.37Q	11/20/02	12/04/02	12/06/02	12/20/02
0.37Q	1/27/03	2/06/03	2/10/03	2/24/03
0.37Q	5/06/03	5/15/03	5/19/03	5/30/03

Indicated div.: $1.48

CAPITALIZATION (12/31/02):

	($000)	(%)
Long-Term Debt	669,792	62.1
Common & Surplus	408,884	37.9
Total	1,078,676	100.0

DIVIDEND ACHIEVER STATUS:
Rank: 79   10-Year Growth Rate: 13.60%
Total Years of Dividend Growth: 11

RECENT DEVELOPMENTS: For the quarter ended 3/31/03, income from continuing operations amounted to $26.2 million versus $8.0 million in the equivalent 2002 quarter. Results included after-tax gains of $1.0 million in both 2003 and 2002. Results for 2002 also included a loss on debt extinguishment of $3.5 million. Total revenues advanced 45.7% to $67.0 million. Notably, rental property revenues jumped 60.7% to $58.1 million, primarily due to lease termination fees of $21.1 million.

PROSPECTS: On 6/2/03, CUZ announced the sale of Mira Mesa MarketCenter, a 464,000 square-foot retail project in Mira Mesa, California, to DBS Properties for $87.0 million. Separately CUZ's aggressive leasing efforts have allowed it to sign several significant leases in the office market despite high vacancy rates in most of its markets. Meanwhile, CUZ's retail operations have received commitments for 70.0% of a 206,000 square foot retail specialty center under construction in suburban Atlanta.

BUSINESS

COUSINS PROPERTIES INCORPORATED is a fully-integrated, self-administered equity real estate investment trust. The Company has three reportable segments. The Office division develops, leases and manages office buildings. The Retail division develops, leases and manages retail centers. The Land division owns various tracts of land being held for future development. Also, the Land division develops single-family residential communities which are parceled into lots and sold to home builders. As of 5/5/03, the Company's portfolio consisted of interests in 13.3 million square feet of office space, 3.3 million square feet of retail space and 900,000 square feet of medical office space, and more than 300 acres of strategically located land for future commercial development. CUZ also provides leasing and management services to third-party investors.

ANNUAL FINANCIAL DATA

	12/31/02	12/31/01	12/31/00	12/31/99	12/31/98	12/31/97	12/31/96
Earnings Per Share	[4] 1.00	[3] 1.41	[2] 1.26	[2] 2.12	[1] 0.94	[1] 0.84	[1] 0.96
Tang. Book Val. Per Share	8.45	9.36	9.24	9.07	7.94	7.85	6.90
Dividends Per Share	1.48	1.39	1.24	1.12	0.99	0.86	0.75
Dividend Payout %	148.0	98.6	98.4	52.8	105.7	102.4	77.8
INCOME STATEMENT (IN MILLIONS):							
Rental Income	168.0	145.5	114.0	62.5	67.7	62.3	33.1
Total Income	199.8	177.7	144.6	97.8	98.3	86.0	58.5
Costs & Expenses	84.7	77.2	64.1	49.9	47.5	40.8	33.9
Depreciation	54.2	44.7	32.8	16.9	15.2	14.0	7.2
Interest Expense	37.4	27.6	13.6	0.6	11.6	14.1	6.5
Income Before Income Taxes	45.2	46.8	49.6	47.8	41.2	29.8	26.5
Income Taxes	1.5	cr0.6	cr1.1	2.4	cr0.1	cr1.5	cr1.7
Equity Earnings/Minority Int.	6.3	23.5	11.9	58.8	3.9	6.0	12.8
Net Income	[4] 50.0	[3] 70.8	[2] 62.6	[1] 104.1	[1] 45.3	[1] 37.3	[1] 41.0
Average Shs. Outstg. (000)	49,937	50,280	49,731	49,031	48,060	44,540	42,780
BALANCE SHEET (IN MILLIONS):							
Cash & Cash Equivalents	9.5	10.6	1.7	1.5	1.3	32.7	1.6
Total Real Estate Investments	965.2	939.8	884.4	732.9	438.7	416.0	357.3
Total Assets	1,248.1	1,212.0	1,115.8	932.9	752.9	617.7	556.6
Long-Term Obligations	669.8	585.3	485.1	312.3	198.9	226.3	231.8
Total Liabilities	708.7	614.8	518.8	347.9	373.0	247.1	257.5
Net Stockholders' Equity	408.9	462.7	454.5	437.7	379.9	370.7	299.2
Year-end Shs. Outstg. (000)	48,386	49,425	49,211	48,262	47,831	47,208	43,380
STATISTICAL RECORD:							
Net Inc.+Depr./Assets %	8.4	9.5	8.5	13.0	8.0	8.3	8.7
Return on Equity %	12.2	15.3	13.8	23.8	11.9	10.1	13.7
Return on Assets %	4.0	5.8	5.6	11.2	6.0	6.0	7.4
Price Range	27.32-20.05	28.75-23.30	30.42-21.92	25.50-19.04	21.71-16.13	22.50-16.17	18.75-12.25
P/E Ratio	27.3-20.0	20.4-16.5	24.1-17.4	12.0-9.0	23.1-17.2	26.8-19.2	19.5-12.8
Average Yield %	6.2	5.3	4.7	5.0	5.3	4.4	4.8

Statistics are as originally reported. Adj. for 3-for-2 stk. split, 10/00. [1] Incl. gains on sales of prop. of $12.8 mill., 1996; $6.0 mill., 1997; $3.9 mill., 1998; $58.8 mill., 1999. [2] Bef. acctg. chng. chrg. of $566,000; incl. gain of $11.9 mill. on sale of prop. [3] Incl. gain of $23.5 mill. on the sale of invest. prop. [4] Bef. extraord. loss of $3.5 mill. and gain fr. disc. opers. of $1.4 mill.; incl. aft.-tax gain on sale of invest. prop. of $6.3 mill.

OFFICERS:
T. G. Cousins, Chmn.
T. D. Bell Jr., Vice-Chmn., Pres., C.E.O.
T. G. Charlesworth, Exec. V.P., C.F.O.

INVESTOR CONTACT: Mark A. Russell, Dir., Inv. Rel., (770) 857-2449

PRINCIPAL OFFICE: 2500 Windy Ridge Pkwy., Atlanta, GA 30339-5683

TELEPHONE NUMBER: (770) 955-2200
FAX: (770) 857-2360
WEB: www.cousinsproperties.com
NO. OF EMPLOYEES: 403 (avg.)
SHAREHOLDERS: 1,137
ANNUAL MEETING: In May
INCORPORATED: GA, Nov., 1961; reincorp., GA, June, 1972

INSTITUTIONAL HOLDINGS:
No. of Institutions: 125
Shares Held: 18,952,334
% Held: 39.5

INDUSTRY: Real estate investment trusts (SIC: 6798)

TRANSFER AGENT(S): Wachovia Bank, N.A., Charlotte, NC

CVB FINANCIAL CORPORATION

YIELD	2.3%
P/E RATIO	18.9

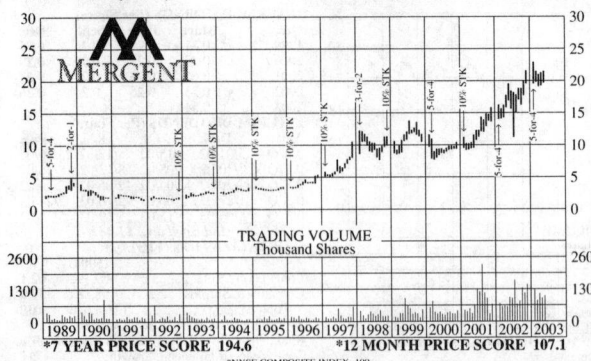

TRADING VOLUME
Thousand Shares

|1989|1990|1991|1992|1993|1994|1995|1996|1997|1998|1999|2000|2001|2002|2003|

7 YEAR PRICE SCORE 194.6   **12 MONTH PRICE SCORE 107.1**

*NYSE COMPOSITE INDEX=100

INTERIM EARNINGS (Per Share):

Qtr.	Mar.	June	Sept.	Dec.
2000		0.79		
2001	0.20	0.22	0.24	0.24
2002	0.28	0.26	0.30	0.28
2003	0.29	...	...	...

INTERIM DIVIDENDS (Per Share):

Amt.	Decl.	Ex.	Rec.	Pay.
0.14Q	6/19/02	7/01/02	7/03/02	7/18/02
0.14Q	9/18/02	9/30/02	10/02/02	10/17/02
5-for-4	12/18/02	1/22/03	1/03/03	1/21/03
0.12Q	12/18/02	1/02/03	1/06/03	1/21/03
0.12Q	3/19/03	3/31/03	4/02/03	4/16/03

Indicated div.: $0.48

CAPITALIZATION (12/31/02):

	($000)	(%)
Total Deposits	2,309,964	80.9
Long-Term Debt	286,888	10.0
Common & Surplus	259,821	9.1
Total	2,856,673	100.0

DIVIDEND ACHIEVER STATUS:
Rank: 13   10-Year Growth Rate: 22.88%
Total Years of Dividend Growth: 12

RECENT DEVELOPMENTS: For the first quarter ended 3/31/03, net earnings increased 3.1% to $12.7 million compared with $12.3 million in the corresponding prior-year quarter. Results for 2003 and 2002 included net after-tax gains on the sale of securities of $460,000 and $1.8 million, respectively. Net interest income advanced 17.3% to $31.2 million from $26.6 million a year earlier. Total interest income climbed 10.1% to $40.3 million, while total interest expense declined 8.9% to $9.1 million. Non-interest

income fell 18.8% to $6.9 million from $8.5 million the year before. Non-interest expense grew 14.5% to $17.7 million from $15.5 million in the 2002 quarter. Meanwhile, on 5/12/03, the Company announced the execution of a definitive agreement to acquire Kaweah National Bank for $15.5 million in cash, stock or a combination of both at the election of Kaweah shareholders. The transaction is expected to be completed by the end of the third quarter of 2003.

BUSINESS

CVB FINANCIAL CORPORATION is a bank holding company, with assets, as of 3/31/03, totaling $3.40 billion. The Company's largest subsidiary, Citizens Business Bank, operates 33 business financial centers located in the Inland Empire, Los Angeles County, Orange County, and the Central Valley areas of California. The Company provides a full complement of all business banking products and services, including asset management services. CVBF owns 100% of Community Trust Deed Services, which prepares and files notices of default, reconveyances and related documents and acts as a trustee under deeds of trust. The Company also owns 100% of CVB Ventures Inc., which charges fees and collects commissions for acting as an intermediary for emerging growth companies in obtaining capital, loans, leases and other financing. On 10/4/99, CVBF acquired Orange National Bancorporation. On 6/28/02, CVBF acquired Western Security Bank, N.A. for $6.2 million.

QUARTERLY DATA

(12/31/2002)	REV	INC
1st Quarter	12,317	26,638
2nd Quarter	11,639	27,447
3rd Quarter	13,196	29,371
4th Quarter	12,593	30,428

ANNUAL FINANCIAL DATA

	12/31/02	12/31/01	12/31/00	12/31/99	12/31/98	12/31/97	12/31/96
Earnings Per Share	④ 1.11	0.90	③ 0.79	① 0.59	0.56	0.47	② 0.55
Tang. Book Val. Per Share	5.61	4.93	4.19	3.11	2.99	2.84	3.28
Dividends Per Share	0.44	0.35	0.28	0.22	0.17	0.11	0.08
Dividend Payout %	39.6	38.9	35.5	37.6	30.0	23.4	14.6
INCOME STATEMENT (IN MILLIONS):							
Total Interest Income	154.3	155.9	150.9	128.5	96.8	84.7	74.9
Total Interest Expense	40.4	52.8	56.8	38.5	31.2	25.0	21.5
Net Interest Income	113.9	103.1	94.1	90.0	65.6	59.7	53.4
Provision for Loan Losses	...	1.8	2.8	2.7	2.5	2.7	2.9
Non-Interest Income	29.0	22.2	19.0	18.6	15.0	13.8	14.3
Non-Interest Expense	66.1	60.2	56.3	64.7	45.0	42.9	41.9
Income Before Taxes	76.8	63.4	54.0	41.2	33.0	27.9	22.9
Net Income	④ 49.7	40.0	③ 34.7	① 26.0	20.8	17.4	② 13.3
Average Shs. Outstg. (000)	44,578	44,269	44,009	43,770	36,997	36,941	24,293
BALANCE SHEET (IN MILLIONS):							
Cash & Due from Banks	125.0	82.7	130.3	118.4	100.0	107.7	142.5
Securities Avail. for Sale	1,452.5	1,181.5	1,070.1	877.3	676.2	434.1	333.3
Total Loans & Leases	1,450.2	1,190.9	1,054.8	956.1	691.4	619.6	592.2
Allowance for Credit Losses	25.8	23.9	22.5	20.3	15.7	14.1	15.5
Net Loans & Leases	1,424.3	1,167.1	1,032.3	935.8	675.7	605.5	576.7
Total Assets	3,123.4	2,514.1	2,308.0	2,010.8	1,555.2	1,258.8	1,160.4
Total Deposits	2,310.0	1,877.0	1,595.0	1,501.1	1,215.3	1,075.7	990.6
Long-Term Obligations	286.9	335.0	11.2	17.0	0.1	7.9	12.6
Total Liabilities	2,863.6	2,293.4	2,119.4	1,870.0	1,439.5	1,156.7	1,071.3
Net Stockholders' Equity	259.8	220.7	188.6	140.8	115.7	102.1	89.1
Year-end Shs. Outstg. (000)	43,533	43,478	43,218	42,482	35,519	32,172	23,569
STATISTICAL RECORD:							
Return on Equity %	19.1	18.1	18.4	18.4	18.0	17.0	15.0
Return on Assets %	1.6	1.6	1.5	1.3	1.3	1.4	1.1
Equity/Assets %	8.3	8.8	8.2	7.0	7.4	8.1	7.7
Non-Int. Exp./Tot. Inc. %	46.2	48.0	49.8	59.6	55.9	58.4	61.9
Price Range	21.59-11.19	15.83-9.20	11.64-7.17	13.79-8.55	12.27-7.67	10.54-4.97	5.39-3.27
P/E Ratio	19.5-10.1	17.5-10.2	14.8-9.8	23.2-14.4	21.8-13.6	22.4-10.6	9.8-5.9
Average Yield %	2.7	2.8	2.9	2.0	1.7	1.4	1.9

Statistics are as originally reported. Adj. for stk. splits: 5-for-4, 1/03 & 1/02; 10% div., 1/01; 5-for-4, 1/00; 10% div., 1/99; 3-for-2, 1/98; 10% div., 1/97. ① Incl. acquisition-related costs of $4.9 mill. ② Incl. litigation settlement gain $2.1 mill. ③ Incl. a loss of $218,000 on the sale of securities & gain of $223,000 on the sale of other real estate owned. ④ Incl. after-tax gain on sale of securs. of $3.2 mill.

OFFICERS:
G. A. Borba, Chmn.
D. L. Wiley, Pres., C.E.O.
E. J. Biebrich Jr., C.F.O.

INVESTOR CONTACT: D. Linn Wiley, Pres., C.E.O., (909) 980-4030

PRINCIPAL OFFICE: 701 North Haven Avenue, Suite 350, Ontario, CA 91764

TELEPHONE NUMBER: (909) 980-4030
FAX: (909) 481-2130
WEB: www.cvbcorp.com

NO. OF EMPLOYEES: 417 full-time; 201 part-time

SHAREHOLDERS: 1,471 (approx.)

ANNUAL MEETING: In May

INCORPORATED: CA, April, 1981

DIEBOLD, INC.

YIELD 1.7%
P/E RATIO 21.9

66 55 44 33 22 11 0

MERGENT

TRADING VOLUME
Thousand Shares

2000 1000 0

1989 1990 1991 1992 1993 1994 1995 1996 1997 1998 1999 2000 2001 2002 2003

*7 YEAR PRICE SCORE 121.8   *12 MONTH PRICE SCORE 103.5
*NYSE COMPOSITE INDEX=100

INTERIM EARNINGS (Per Share):

Qtr.	Mar.	June	Sept.	Dec.
2000	0.44	0.50	0.49	0.49
2001	0.11	0.39	0.20	0.24
2002	0.37	0.55	0.61	0.30
2003	0.36	...	...	...

INTERIM DIVIDENDS (Per Share):

Amt.	Decl.	Ex.	Rec.	Pay.
0.165Q	4/25/02	5/15/02	5/17/02	6/07/02
0.165Q	8/07/02	8/14/02	8/16/02	9/06/02
0.165Q	10/09/02	11/13/02	11/15/02	12/06/02
0.17Q	2/05/03	2/12/03	2/14/03	3/07/03
0.17Q	4/24/03	5/14/03	5/16/03	6/06/03

Indicated div.: $0.68 (Div. Reinv. Plan)

CAPITALIZATION (12/31/02):

	($000)	(%)
Minority Interest	14,323	1.5
Common & Surplus	940,823	98.5
Total	955,146	100.0

DIVIDEND ACHIEVER STATUS:
Rank: 198   10-Year Growth Rate: 7.12%
Total Years of Dividend Growth: 49

RECENT DEVELOPMENTS: For the three months ended 3/31/03, net income totaled $25.9 million compared with income of $26.5 million, before a $33.1 million accounting change charge, in the corresponding prior-year quarter. Total net sales rose 2.3% to $410.2 million from $401.0 million a year earlier. Gross profit was $124.2 million, or 30.3% of net sales, versus $117.8 million, or 29.4% of net sales, the previous year. Operating profit increased 3.9% to $41.8 million from $40.2 million in 2002.

PROSPECTS: The Company is targeting full-year 2003 revenue growth of between 5.0% and 8.0%, fueled by strong revenue growth of its voting systems and security products and services, and full-year 2003 earnings in the range of $2.32 to $2.42 per share. Revenue growth is being driven by strong demand for the Company's security products in the financial industry, government and retail markets, partially offset by unfavorable foreign currency exchange rates.

BUSINESS

DIEBOLD, INC. provides card-based transaction systems, security products, and customer service solutions to the financial, education, and healthcare industries. The Company develops, manufactures, sells and services the following products: automated teller machines, electronic and physical security systems, bank facility equipment, electronic voting systems, software and integrated systems for global financial and commercial markets. The products segment accounted for 51.2% of revenues, while the services segment accounted for 48.8% for the year ended 12/31/02.

ANNUAL FINANCIAL DATA

	12/31/02	12/31/01	12/31/00	12/31/99	12/31/98	12/31/97	12/31/96
Earnings Per Share	② 1.83	① 0.93	1.92	① 1.85	① 1.10	1.76	1.42
Cash Flow Per Share	2.68	1.57	2.42	2.35	1.47	2.03	1.72
Tang. Book Val. Per Share	9.32	8.79	8.94	9.63	9.87	9.69	8.36
Dividends Per Share	0.66	0.64	0.62	0.60	0.56	0.50	0.45
Dividend Payout %	36.1	68.8	32.3	32.4	50.9	28.4	31.9

INCOME STATEMENT (IN MILLIONS):

Total Revenues	1,940.2	1,760.3	1,743.6	1,259.2	1,185.7	1,226.9	1,030.2
Costs & Expenses	1,637.7	1,575.9	1,478.8	1,038.3	1,053.8	1,024.4	868.8
Depreciation & Amort.	61.3	45.5	35.9	34.7	25.6	18.7	21.0
Operating Income	241.2	138.9	229.0	186.1	106.2	183.9	140.4
Net Interest Inc./(Exp.)	d26.7	d12.7	d17.7	...	...	...	...
Income Before Income Taxes	218.6	99.8	204.4	201.3	119.8	185.7	146.5
Income Taxes	86.3	32.9	67.4	72.5	43.7	63.1	49.1
Net Income	② 132.3	① 66.9	136.9	① 128.9	① 76.1	122.5	97.4
Cash Flow	193.6	112.3	172.8	163.6	101.8	141.2	118.4
Average Shs. Outstg. (000)	72,297	71,783	71,479	69,562	69,310	69,490	68,796

BALANCE SHEET (IN MILLIONS):

Cash & Cash Equivalents	163.4	125.7	126.5	84.6	80.0	56.8	65.1
Total Current Assets	924.9	952.4	804.4	647.9	543.5	549.8	479.6
Net Property	219.6	190.2	174.9	160.7	147.1	143.9	95.9
Total Assets	1,625.1	1,651.9	1,585.4	1,298.8	1,004.2	991.1	859.1
Total Current Liabilities	565.0	658.0	566.8	382.4	235.5	242.1	228.2
Long-Term Obligations	...	20.8	20.8	20.8	20.8	20.8	...
Net Stockholders' Equity	940.8	903.1	936.1	844.4	699.1	668.6	575.6
Net Working Capital	359.9	294.4	237.6	265.5	308.0	307.8	251.4
Year-end Shs. Outstg. (000)	72,111	71,357	71,547	71,096	68,881	69,005	68,841

STATISTICAL RECORD:

Operating Profit Margin %	12.4	7.9	13.1	14.8	9.0	15.0	13.6
Net Profit Margin %	6.8	3.8	7.9	10.2	6.4	10.0	9.5
Return on Equity %	14.1	7.4	14.6	15.3	10.9	18.3	16.9
Return on Assets %	8.1	4.0	8.6	9.9	7.6	12.4	11.3
Debt/Total Assets %	...	1.3	1.3	1.6	2.1	2.1	...
Price Range	43.55-30.30	41.50-25.75	34.75-21.50	39.88-19.69	55.31-19.13	50.63-28.00	42.33-22.45
P/E Ratio	23.8-16.6	44.6-27.7	18.1-11.2	21.6-10.6	50.3-17.4	28.8-15.9	29.8-15.8
Average Yield %	1.8	1.9	2.2	2.0	1.5	1.3	1.4

Statistics are as originally reported. Adj. for 3-for-2 stk. split, 2/97. ① Incl. $73.7 mil pre-tax chrg. for realignment and other special charges, 2001; $1.2 mil one-time pre-tax chg., 1999; $41.9 mil ($0.60/sh) after-tax chrg. for realignment program, 1998. ② Bef. $33.1 mil ($0.46/sh) acctg. change chrg.

OFFICERS:
W. W. O'Dell, Chmn., Pres., C.E.O.
G. T. Geswein, Sr. V.P., C.F.O.
R. J. Warren, V.P., Treas.

INVESTOR CONTACT: Sandy K. Upperman, Mgr., Inv. Rel., (800) 766-5859

PRINCIPAL OFFICE: 5995 Mayfair Road, P.O. Box 3077, North Canton, OH 44720-8077

TELEPHONE NUMBER: (330) 490-4000
FAX: (330) 588-3794
WEB: www.diebold.com

NO. OF EMPLOYEES: 13,072 (avg.)

SHAREHOLDERS: 72,309

ANNUAL MEETING: In Apr.

INCORPORATED: OH, Aug., 1876

INSTITUTIONAL HOLDINGS:
No. of Institutions: 302
Shares Held: 49,828,478
% Held: 69.2

INDUSTRY: Calculating and accounting equipment (SIC: 3578)

TRANSFER AGENT(S): The Bank of New York, New York, NY

NASDAQ SYMBOL DGICA
Rec. Pr. 13.47 (5/31/03)

DONEGAL GROUP INC.

YIELD 3.3%
P/E RATIO 9.1

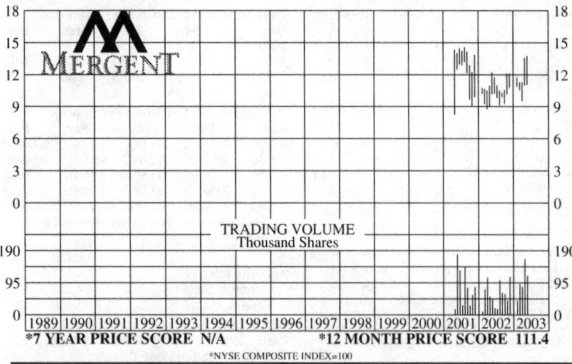

TRADING VOLUME
Thousand Shares

*7 YEAR PRICE SCORE N/A *12 MONTH PRICE SCORE 111.4
*NYSE COMPOSITE INDEX=100

INTERIM EARNINGS (Per Share):

Qtr.	Mar.	June	Sept.	Dec.
1999	0.26	0.16	d0.29	0.67
2000	0.15	0.28	0.30	0.29
2001	0.33	0.30	0.11	d0.10
2002	0.24	0.35	0.33	0.39
2003	0.41	...	...	...

INTERIM DIVIDENDS (Per Share):

Amt.	Decl.	Ex.	Rec.	Pay.
0.10Q	4/19/02	4/29/02	5/01/02	5/15/02
0.10Q	7/22/02	7/31/02	8/02/02	8/15/02
0.10Q	10/22/02	10/30/02	11/01/02	11/15/02
0.10Q	12/20/02	1/30/03	2/03/03	2/17/03
0.11Q	4/17/03	4/29/03	5/01/03	5/15/03

Indicated div.: $0.44 (Div. Reinv. Plan)

CAPITALIZATION (12/31/02):

	($000)	(%)
Long-Term Debt	19,800	12.9
Common & Surplus	133,183	87.1
Total	152,983	100.0

DIVIDEND ACHIEVER STATUS:
Rank: 137   10-Year Growth Rate: 10.17%
Total Years of Dividend Growth: 13

RECENT DEVELOPMENTS: For the quarter ended 3/31/03, net income leapt 76.3% to $3.8 million from $2.2 million in the corresponding prior-year quarter. Results reflected rate increases taken over the past two years, coupled with improved underwriting and strict expense control. Total revenues increased 4.3% to $52.2 million from $50.0 million the previous year. Revenues included a loss of $130,480 in 2003 and a gain of $126,778 in 2002 for realized investments. Net written premiums rose 4.2% to

$50.3 million. Net premiums earned grew 5.4% to $47.9 million from $45.5 million a year earlier. Net investment income dropped 9.8% to $3.4 million due to the low interest rate environment. The Company's loss ratio, or the ratio of direct claims incurred to direct premiums earned, improved 2.4 percentage points to 66.5% from 68.9% in the equivalent 2002 period. The Company's expense ratio, or the ratio of underwriting expenses to net premiums earned, improved to 30.2% from 31.9% the year before.

BUSINESS

DONEGAL GROUP INC. is an insurance holding company, which through its subsidiaries, Atlantic States Insurance Company and Southern Insurance Company of Virginia, engages in the property and casualty insurance business in 14 mid-Atlantic and southeastern states. The Company has three reportable operating segments, which consist of the investment function, the personal lines of insurance and the commercial lines of insurance. Products offered in the personal lines of insurance consist primarily of homeowners and private passenger automobile policies. Products offered in the commercial lines of insurance consist primarily of commercial automobile, commercial multiple peril and workers' compensation policies.

ANNUAL FINANCIAL DATA

	12/31/02	12/31/01	12/31/00	12/31/99	12/31/98	12/31/97	12/31/96
Earnings Per Share	1.31	☐0.64	1.02	0.80	1.09	1.32	1.10
Cash Flow Per Share	1.44	0.78	1.11	0.91	1.16	1.37	1.17
Tang. Book Val. Per Share	14.52	13.44	12.84	12.24	12.27	15.19	13.64
Dividends Per Share	0.40	0.39	0.36	0.35	0.33	0.28	0.24
Dividend Payout %	30.5	60.9	35.3	43.8	30.3	21.2	21.8
INCOME STATEMENT (IN THOUSANDS):							
Total Revenues	203,804	185,164	168,223	159,711	130,586	121,328	112,519
Costs & Expenses	184,953	174,697	152,276	153,610	117,096	105,853	100,662
Depreciation & Amort.	1,237	1,128	839	936	521	391	236
Operating Income	17,614	9,339	15,108	5,164	12,970	15,084	11,622
Net Interest Inc./(Exp.)	d1,119	d2,247	d3,285	d1,535	d1,293	d910	d375
Income Before Income Taxes	16,495	7,092	11,823	3,629	11,677	14,174	11,246
Income Taxes	4,492	1,274	2,936	cr3,028	2,659	3,532	2,350
Net Income	12,003	☐5,818	8,887	6,657	9,018	10,641	8,896
Cash Flow	13,239	6,946	9,726	7,593	9,539	11,032	9,132
Average Shs. Outstg.	9,193	9,078	8,737	8,327	8,250	8,036	7,815
BALANCE SHEET (IN THOUSANDS):							
Cash & Cash Equivalents	224,886	201,868	135,760	119,961	129,275	83,857	73,708
Total Current Assets	338,341	297,973	224,778	195,423	201,161	139,309	123,958
Net Property	4,430	4,569	5,017	5,517	5,920	4,939	2,169
Total Assets	501,218	456,632	439,101	399,733	385,232	304,105	273,129
Total Current Liabilities	15,131	12,910	8,842	10,963	10,084	12,245	7,144
Long-Term Obligations	19,800	27,600	40,000	37,000	37,500	10,500	8,500
Net Stockholders' Equity	133,183	120,928	113,745	103,415	100,631	91,597	81,277
Net Working Capital	323,210	285,063	215,936	184,461	191,076	127,065	116,814
Year-end Shs. Outstg.	9,172	8,997	8,859	8,452	8,203	8,031	5,961
STATISTICAL RECORD:							
Operating Profit Margin %	8.6	5.0	9.0	3.2	9.9	12.4	10.3
Net Profit Margin %	5.9	3.1	5.3	4.2	6.9	8.8	7.9
Return on Equity %	9.0	4.8	7.8	6.4	9.0	11.6	10.9
Return on Assets %	2.4	1.3	2.0	1.7	2.3	3.5	3.3
Debt/Total Assets %	4.0	6.0	9.1	9.3	9.7	3.5	3.1
Price Range	12.25-8.75	13.10-8.50	13.94-5.75	16.25-5.75	22.79-12.63	16.88-11.26	11.68-9.15
P/E Ratio	9.4-6.7	61.4-39.8	13.7-5.6	20.3-7.2	20.9-11.6	12.8-8.5	10.6-8.3
Average Yield %	3.8	3.7	3.2	1.9	2.0	2.3	2.4

Statistics are as originally reported. Adj. for 1-for-3 stk. split & 200% stk. div., 4/20/01. Share and per share amounts reflect B shares prior to 4/20/01. ☐Incl. $4.2 mill. for reserve strengthing & $543,000 rel. to the insolvency of Reliance Insurance Co.

OFFICERS:	TELEPHONE NUMBER: (717) 426-1931	INSTITUTIONAL HOLDINGS:
P. H. Glatfelter, II, Chmn.	FAX: (717) 426-7009	No. of Institutions: 16
D. H. Nikolaus, Pres., C.E.O.	WEB: www.donegalgroup.com	Shares Held: 1,164,078
R. G. Spontak, Sr. V.P., C.F.O., Sec.		% Held: 0.0
	NO. OF EMPLOYEES: 410 (avg.)	
INVESTOR CONTACT: Ralph G. Spontak, Sr. V.P. & C.F.O., (717) 426-1931	SHAREHOLDERS: 613 (Cl. A); 513 (Cl. B)	INDUSTRY: Fire, marine, and casualty insurance (SIC: 6331)
	ANNUAL MEETING: In April	
PRINCIPAL OFFICE: 1195 River Road, P.O. Box 302, Marietta, PA 17547-0302	INCORPORATED: DE, Aug., 1986	TRANSFER AGENT(S): EquiServe Trust Company, N.A., Jersey City, NJ

DONNELLEY (R.R.) & SONS CO.

YIELD 4.0%
P/E RATIO 21.0

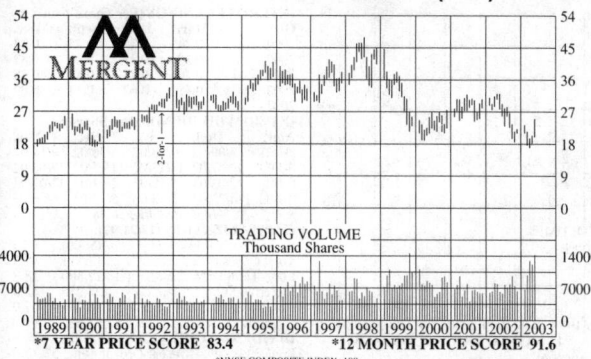

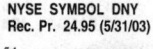

INTERIM EARNINGS (Per Share):

Qtr.	Mar.	June	Sept.	Dec.
2000	0.38	0.46	0.75	0.58
2001	0.12	0.05	0.36	d0.33
2002	0.20	0.30	0.42	0.42
2003	0.05	...	...	...

INTERIM DIVIDENDS (Per Share):

Amt.	Decl.	Ex.	Rec.	Pay.
0.25Q	7/25/02	8/08/02	8/12/02	8/31/02
0.25Q	9/26/02	11/06/02	11/08/02	11/30/02
0.25Q	1/23/03	2/03/03	2/05/03	3/01/03
0.25Q	3/27/03	5/07/03	5/09/03	5/31/03

Indicated div.: $1.00 (Div. Reinv. Plan)

CAPITALIZATION (12/31/02):

	($000)	(%)
Long-Term Debt	752,870	40.0
Deferred Income Tax	214,112	11.4
Common & Surplus	914,594	48.6
Total	1,881,576	100.0

TRADING VOLUME
Thousand Shares

*7 YEAR PRICE SCORE 83.4   *12 MONTH PRICE SCORE 91.6
*NYSE COMPOSITE INDEX=100

DIVIDEND ACHIEVER STATUS:
Rank: 206   10-Year Growth Rate: 6.75%
Total Years of Dividend Growth: 33

RECENT DEVELOPMENTS: For the three months ended 3/31/03, net income dropped 74.8% to $5.7 million compared with $22.7 million in the equivalent quarter of 2002. Results for 2003 and 2002 included after-tax restructuring and impairment charges of $2.0 million and $17.0 million, respectively. Results for 2002 also included an after-tax gain of $30.0 million from the reversal of excess tax reserves. Net sales were $1.07 billion, down 1.8% from $1.09 billion in the prior-year period.

PROSPECTS: The Company reaffirmed its earnings per share guidance for 2003 of $1.25 to $1.40, which includes $0.06 per share for expected restructuring activity. In addition, this estimate includes the effect of weak print demand and an unfavorable pricing environment, partially offset by ongoing cost-reduction and productivity efforts. Capital spending for 2003 is expected to be below $250.0 million. Separately, DNY is expanding its printing operations in Lancaster, PA and Spartanburg, SC.

BUSINESS

DONNELLEY (R.R.) & SONS CO. provides comprehensive, integrated communications applications that produce, manage and deliver its customers' content, regardless of the communication medium. The Company's services include content creation, digital content management, production and distribution. The Company operates primarily in two business segments, commercial print and logistic services. DNY serves the following end-markets: long-run magazines, catalogs and inserts; telecommunications; book publishing services; and financial services. The Company also operates through specialized publishing services, RRD Direct, Premedia Technologies, and R.R. Donnelley Logistics. DNY operates facilities in North and South America, Europe and the Asia/Pacific Basin. Sales for 2002 industry segment data were derived: print solutions, 65.0%; logistics services, 16.5%; and other, 18.5%.

ANNUAL FINANCIAL DATA

	12/31/02	12/31/01	12/31/00	12/31/99	12/31/98	12/31/97	12/31/96
Earnings Per Share	[6] 1.24	[6] 0.21	[5] 2.17	[4] 2.40	[3] 2.08	[2] 1.40	[1] d1.04
Cash Flow Per Share	4.32	3.41	5.34	5.29	4.67	3.91	1.53
Tang. Book Val. Per Share	4.51	3.15	5.88	6.01	6.85	8.31	7.49
Dividends Per Share	0.98	0.94	0.90	0.86	0.82	0.78	0.74
Dividend Payout %	79.0	447.4	41.5	35.8	39.4	55.7	...

INCOME STATEMENT (IN MILLIONS):

	12/31/02	12/31/01	12/31/00	12/31/99	12/31/98	12/31/97	12/31/96
Total Revenues	4,754.9	5,297.8	5,764.3	5,183.4	5,018.4	4,850.0	6,599.0
Costs & Expenses	4,157.6	4,771.8	4,872.9	4,278.6	4,242.3	4,110.8	6,345.8
Depreciation & Amort.	352.4	378.7	390.4	374.4	367.8	370.4	389.1
Operating Income	244.9	147.3	501.0	530.4	408.4	368.8	d136.0
Net Interest Inc./(Exp.)	d62.8	d71.2	d89.6	d88.2	d78.2	d90.8	d95.5
Income Before Income Taxes	175.7	74.9	434.0	506.5	509.3	303.8	d110.5
Income Taxes	33.5	49.9	167.1	195.0	214.7	97.2	47.1
Net Income	[6] 142.2	[6] 25.0	[5] 266.9	[4] 311.5	[3] 294.6	[2] 206.5	[1] d157.6
Cash Flow	494.6	403.7	657.3	685.9	662.4	577.0	231.5
Average Shs. Outstg. (000)	114,372	118,498	123,093	129,566	141,865	147,508	151,800

BALANCE SHEET (IN MILLIONS):

	12/31/02	12/31/01	12/31/00	12/31/99	12/31/98	12/31/97	12/31/96
Cash & Cash Equivalents	60.5	48.6	60.9	41.9	66.2	47.8	31.1
Total Current Assets	866.4	940.2	1,206.4	1,229.9	1,145.0	1,146.6	1,752.9
Net Property	1,411.0	1,490.1	1,620.6	1,710.7	1,700.9	1,788.1	1,944.7
Total Assets	3,151.8	3,400.0	3,914.2	3,853.5	3,787.8	4,134.2	4,849.0
Total Current Liabilities	954.7	984.3	1,190.6	1,203.5	898.3	812.6	1,147.5
Long-Term Obligations	752.9	881.3	739.2	748.5	999.0	1,153.2	1,430.7
Net Stockholders' Equity	914.6	888.4	1,232.5	1,138.3	1,300.9	1,591.5	1,631.3
Net Working Capital	d88.3	d44.1	15.9	26.4	246.7	333.9	605.3
Year-end Shs. Outstg. (000)	113,124	140,889	121,055	123,237	134,322	145,118	145,554

STATISTICAL RECORD:

	12/31/02	12/31/01	12/31/00	12/31/99	12/31/98	12/31/97	12/31/96
Operating Profit Margin %	5.2	2.8	8.7	10.2	8.1	7.6	...
Net Profit Margin %	3.0	0.5	4.6	6.0	5.9	4.3	...
Return on Equity %	15.6	2.8	21.7	27.4	22.6	13.0	...
Return on Assets %	4.5	0.7	6.8	8.1	7.8	5.0	...
Debt/Total Assets %	23.9	25.9	18.9	19.4	26.4	27.9	29.5
Price Range	32.10-18.50	31.90-24.30	27.50-19.00	44.75-21.50	48.00-33.75	41.75-29.50	39.88-29.38
P/E Ratio	25.9-14.9	151.8-115.7	12.7-8.8	18.6-9.0	23.1-16.2	29.8-21.1	...
Average Yield %	3.9	3.3	4.0	2.6	2.0	2.2	2.1

Statistics are as originally reported. [1] Incl. $560.6 mill. pre-tax restr. chg. & $80.0 mill. gains from IPO's. [2] Bef. loss fr. disc. ops. of $76.9 mill. & incl. $70.7 mill. pre-tax restr. chg. [3] Incl. $168.9 mill. gain fr. sale of sub. & $80.1 mill. loss fr. bus. held for sale. [4] Incl. $42.8 mill. gain fr. sale of bus. & excl. $3.2 mill. loss fr. disc. ops. [5] Excl. $13.0 mill. pre-tax gain fr. sale of shares. [6] Incl. $88.9 mill. restr. & impair. chgs., 2002; $195.5 mill., 2001.

OFFICERS:
W. L. Davis, Chmn., Pres., C.E.O.
G. A. Stoklosa, Exec. V.P., C.F.O.
M. M. Fohrman, Sr. V.P., Sec., Gen. Couns.

INVESTOR CONTACT: Christopher Curtis, Director, Investor Relations, (312) 326-8313

PRINCIPAL OFFICE: 77 West Wacker Drive, Chicago, IL 60601

TELEPHONE NUMBER: (312) 326-8000
FAX: (312) 326-8543
WEB: www.rrdonnelley.com
NO. OF EMPLOYEES: 31,000 (approx.)
SHAREHOLDERS: 8,388
ANNUAL MEETING: In Mar.
INCORPORATED: DE, May, 1956

INSTITUTIONAL HOLDINGS:
No. of Institutions: 299
Shares Held: 85,496,939
% Held: 75.7

INDUSTRY: Commercial printing, lithographic (SIC: 2752)

TRANSFER AGENT(S): EquiServe Trust Company, N.A., Jersey City, NJ

DORAL FINANCIAL CORPORATION

YIELD	1.3%
P/E RATIO	13.5

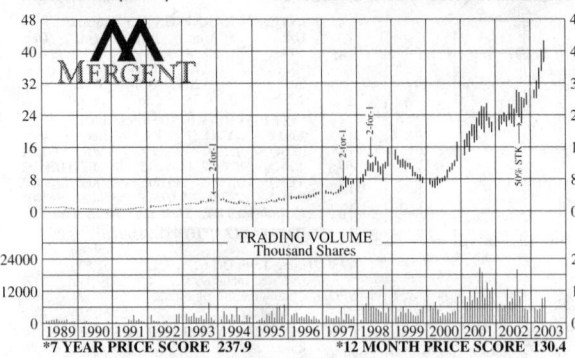

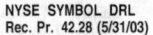

INTERIM EARNINGS (Per Share):

Qtr	Mar.	June	Sept.	Dec.
1999	0.24	0.25	0.25	0.26
2000	0.30	0.31	0.31	0.32
2001	0.40	0.43	0.49	0.55
2002	0.61	0.67	0.74	0.82
2003	0.90	...	...	...

INTERIM DIVIDENDS (Per Share):

Amt.	Decl.	Ex.	Rec.	Pay.
50% STK	8/09/02	9/16/02	8/30/02	9/14/02
0.11Q	10/07/02	11/13/02	11/15/02	12/06/02
0.14Q	2/03/03	2/12/03	2/17/03	3/07/03
0.14Q	4/23/03	5/13/03	5/15/03	6/06/03

Indicated div.: $0.56

CAPITALIZATION (12/31/02):

	($000)	(%)
Total Deposits	2,217,211	48.5
Long-Term Debt	1,311,500	28.7
Preferred Stock	228,250	5.0
Common & Surplus	816,721	17.9
Total	4,573,682	100.0

DIVIDEND ACHIEVER STATUS:

Rank: 11	10-Year Growth Rate: 23.72%
Total Years of Dividend Growth:	13

TRADING VOLUME
Thousand Shares

*7 YEAR PRICE SCORE 237.9   *12 MONTH PRICE SCORE 130.4
*NYSE COMPOSITE INDEX=100

RECENT DEVELOPMENTS: For the quarter ended 3/31/03, net income rose 50.4% to $70.0 million versus $46.5 million in the corresponding year-earlier period. Net interest income grew 15.0% to $41.3 million from $35.9 million the previous year. Provision for loan losses was $4.8 million versus $748,000 in 2002. Total non-interest income climbed 84.3% to $91.4 million, due largely to net gains on mortgage loans sales and fees. DRL attributed this increase principally to higher sales volume and favorable pricing.

PROSPECTS: The high demand for new housing in Puerto Rico, coupled with refinancing activity consistent with DRL's historical experience, strengthens the Company's near-term outlook. Meanwhile, DRL intends to continue to explore opportunities to expand geographically within the mainland U.S., chiefly within the New York City metropolitan area and other areas with large Hispanic or minority populations.

BUSINESS

DORAL FINANCIAL CORPORATION (formerly First Financial Caribbean Corporation) is a diversified financial services company engaged in mortgage banking, banking, institutional broker-dealer and investment banking activities and insurance agency activities. DRL's activities are principally conducted in Puerto Rico and in the New York City metropolitan area. The Company conducts its mortgage banking activities in Puerto Rico primarily through its HF Mortgage Bankers division, and through its subsidiaries, Doral Mortgage Corporation, Centro Hipotecario de Puerto Rico, Inc. and Sana Investment Mortgage Bankers, Inc. In the U.S., DRL conducts its mortgage banking activities through its subsidiary, Doral Money, Inc. As of 12/31/02, DRL operated 54 mortgage banking offices in Puerto Rico and one office on the United States mainland. The Company's insurance agency activities are conducted through Doral Insurance Agency. As of 3/31/03, DRL had consolidated assets of $8.77 billion and deposits of $2.47 billion.

ANNUAL FINANCIAL DATA

	12/31/02	12/31/01	12/31/00	12/31/99	12/31/98	12/31/97	12/31/96
Earnings Per Share	2.84	[1] 1.88	1.23	1.00	0.84	[2] 0.57	0.50
Tang. Book Val. Per Share	11.37	8.89	5.84	6.16	4.35	3.27	2.63
Dividends Per Share	0.42	0.32	0.25	0.20	0.15	0.13	0.11
Dividend Payout %	14.8	16.8	20.5	20.0	18.3	22.6	22.1
INCOME STATEMENT (IN THOUSANDS):							
Total Interest Income	415,600	356,095	325,545	211,679	148,051	90,131	66,987
Total Interest Expense	263,178	271,668	283,241	161,795	114,786	61,438	...
Net Interest Income	152,422	84,427	42,304	49,884	33,265	28,693	66,987
Provision for Loan Losses	7,429	4,445	4,078	2,626	883	600	...
Non-Interest Income	255,393	191,132	164,585	126,911	88,340	45,286	40,846
Non-Interest Expense	139,410	112,854	106,659	97,556	60,883	35,582	76,554
Income Before Taxes	260,976	158,260	96,152	76,613	59,839	37,797	31,279
Net Income	220,968	[1] 137,922	84,656	67,926	52,832	[2] 32,548	27,041
Average Shs. Outstg.	72,959	68,254	63,140	63,632	62,892	58,093	54,399
BALANCE SHEET (IN THOUSANDS):							
Cash & Due from Banks	156,137	45,970	28,999	25,793	31,945	17,390	...
Securities Avail. for Sale	...	253,403	125,815	102,796	140,469	62,542	...
Total Loans & Leases	1,059,876	669,899	440,639	277,550	216,866	134,618	130,046
Allowance for Credit Losses	37,534	25,786	42,448	46,366	49,879	1,563	1,280
Net Loans & Leases	1,022,342	644,113	398,191	231,184	166,987	133,055	128,766
Total Assets	8,421,689	6,694,283	5,463,386	4,537,343	2,918,113	1,857,789	1,101,955
Total Deposits	2,217,211	1,669,909	1,303,525	1,010,424	533,113	300,494	158,902
Long-Term Obligations	1,311,500	687,500	389,000	134,000	32,000	32,000	25,000
Total Liabilities	7,376,718	5,932,163	4,957,676	4,152,361	2,648,554	1,670,834	951,424
Net Stockholders' Equity	1,044,971	762,120	505,710	384,982	269,559	186,955	150,531
Year-end Shs. Outstg.	71,841	71,716	63,590	60,643	60,643	55,192	54,667
STATISTICAL RECORD:							
Return on Equity %	21.1	18.1	16.7	17.6	19.6	17.4	18.0
Return on Assets %	2.6	2.1	1.5	1.5	1.8	1.8	2.5
Equity/Assets %	12.4	11.4	9.3	8.5	9.2	10.1	13.7
Non-Int. Exp./Tot. Inc. %	34.2	41.0	51.6	55.2	50.1	48.1	71.0
Price Range	30.26-20.18	26.93-13.88	17.33-5.75	15.38-7.00	15.83-6.83	8.67-4.04	4.79-2.96
P/E Ratio	10.7-7.1	14.3-7.4	14.1-4.7	15.4-7.0	18.8-8.1	15.3-7.1	9.6-6.0
Average Yield %	1.7	1.6	2.2	1.8	1.4	2.0	2.8

Statistics are as originally reported. Adj. for stk. splits: 50% div., 9/02; 2-for-1, 5/98, 8/97. [1] Excl. acctg. change credit $5.9 mill. [2] Excl. extraord. chrg. $12.3 mill.

OFFICERS:
S. Levis, Chmn., C.E.O.
Z. Lewis, Pres., C.O.O.

INVESTOR CONTACT: Richard F. Bonini, Sr. V.P., C.F.O., Treas., (212) 329-3729

PRINCIPAL OFFICE: 1451 Franklin D. Roosevelt Avenue, San Juan, Puerto Rico 00920-2717

TELEPHONE NUMBER: (787) 474-6700
FAX: (787) 749-8267
WEB: www.doralfinancial.com
NO. OF EMPLOYEES: 1,930 (avg.)
SHAREHOLDERS: 582 Approx.
ANNUAL MEETING: In Mar.
INCORPORATED: PRI, Dec., 1972

INSTITUTIONAL HOLDINGS:
No. of Institutions: 168
Shares Held: 43,290,775
% Held: 60.1

INDUSTRY: Mortgage bankers and correspondents (SIC: 6162)

TRANSFER AGENT(S): Mellon Investor Services, LLC, Ridgefield Park, NJ

DOVER CORPORATION

YIELD 1.8%
P/E RATIO 27.8

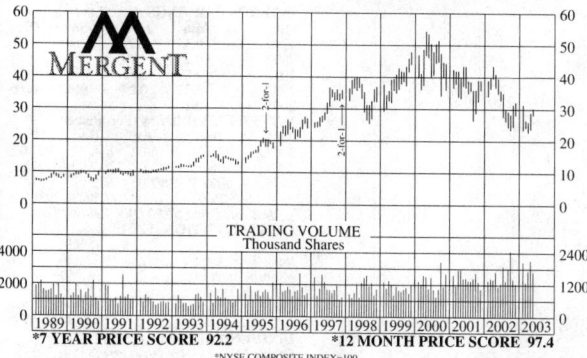

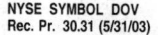

INTERIM EARNINGS (Per Share):

Qtr.	Mar.	June	Sept.	Dec.
1999	0.32	0.44	0.58	0.58
2000	0.57	0.67	0.71	0.66
2001	0.38	0.24	0.02	0.18
2002	0.24	0.32	0.29	0.19
2003	0.29	...	...	...

INTERIM DIVIDENDS (Per Share):

Amt.	Decl.	Ex.	Rec.	Pay.
0.135Q	8/01/02	8/28/02	8/30/02	9/13/02
0.135Q	11/07/02	11/26/02	11/29/02	12/13/02
0.135Q	2/13/03	2/26/03	2/28/03	3/14/03
0.135Q	5/08/03	5/28/03	5/30/03	6/13/03

Indicated div.: $0.54 (Div. Reinv. Plan)

CAPITALIZATION (12/31/02):

	($000)	(%)
Long-Term Debt	1,030,299	28.9
Deferred Income Tax	136,469	3.8
Common & Surplus	2,394,623	67.2
Total	3,561,391	100.0

TRADING VOLUME
Thousand Shares

*7 YEAR PRICE SCORE 92.2   *12 MONTH PRICE SCORE 97.4

*NYSE COMPOSITE INDEX=100

DIVIDEND ACHIEVER STATUS:
Rank: 152   10-Year Growth Rate: 9.65%
Total Years of Dividend Growth: 47

RECENT DEVELOPMENTS: For the quarter ended 3/31/03, earnings from continuing operations were $58.5 million versus earnings from continuing operations of $48.4 million in the corresponding year-earlier period. Sales rose 3.3% to $1.03 billion. Operating profit increased 11.1% to $102.1 million, reflecting gains across the Company's industry segments with the exception of Dover Industries, which reported a 30.6% decline in operating income to $27.2 million due to poor market conditions.

PROSPECTS: DOV's near-term prospects are clouded by the uncertain economic outlook that is restraining both top and bottom line growth. Separately, on 3/20/03, DOV acquired the assets of the Airborne and Arell business units of Standard Automotive, which manufactures precision aero engine components, landing gear and aircraft structure components. Also, during the quarter ended 3/31/03, the Company sold the Wittemann business of Dover Resources Inc.

BUSINESS

DOVER CORPORATION is a diversified industrial manufacturing corporation encompassing over 50 operating companies. Dover Diversified (28.5% of 2002 revenues), builds packaging and printing machinery, heat transfer equipment, food refrigeration and display cases, specialized bearings, construction and agricultural cabs, as well as products for use in the defense, aerospace and automotive industries. Dover Industries (26.8%) makes products for use in the waste handling, bulk transport, automotive service, commercial food service and packaging, welding, cash dispenser and construction industries. Dover Technologies (24.7%) builds automated assembly and testing equipment and specialized electronic components for the electronics industry, and industrial printers for coding and marking. Dover Resources Inc. (20.0%), manufactures products primarily for the automotive, fluid handling, petroleum, winch and chemical equipment industries. On 1/5/99, DOV sold Dover Elevator for $1.16 billion.

ANNUAL FINANCIAL DATA

	12/31/02	12/31/01	12/31/00	12/31/99	12/31/98	12/31/97	12/31/96
Earnings Per Share	⑥ 1.04	⑤ 0.82	④ 2.61	③ 1.92	① 1.45	② 1.79	② 1.73
Cash Flow Per Share	1.83	1.90	3.60	2.79	2.20	2.54	2.27
Tang. Book Val. Per Share	2.65	1.97	1.79	1.07	2.11	2.66	2.29
Dividends Per Share	0.54	0.52	0.48	0.44	0.40	0.36	0.32
Dividend Payout %	51.9	63.4	18.4	22.9	27.6	20.1	18.5
INCOME STATEMENT (IN MILLIONS):							
Total Revenues	4,183.7	4,459.7	5,400.7	4,446.4	3,977.7	4,547.7	4,076.3
Costs & Expenses	3,681.0	3,940.7	4,354.1	3,627.8	3,278.0	3,764.3	3,412.5
Depreciation & Amort.	161.0	220.0	203.4	183.2	167.7	170.7	125.1
Operating Income	341.6	299.0	843.2	635.4	532.0	② 612.7	② 538.7
Net Interest Inc./(Exp.)	d64.8	d75.3	d88.5	d34.9	d46.4	d37.0	d23.5
Income Before Income Taxes	269.7	238.4	772.3	615.0	488.6	616.8	588.7
Income Taxes	58.5	71.6	239.1	210.0	162.2	211.4	198.5
Net Income	⑥ 211.1	⑤ 166.8	④ 533.2	③ 405.1	① 326.4	② 405.4	② 390.2
Cash Flow	372.2	386.8	736.6	588.3	494.1	576.1	515.3
Average Shs. Outstg. (000)	203,346	204,013	204,677	210,679	224,386	226,815	226,524
BALANCE SHEET (IN MILLIONS):							
Cash & Cash Equivalents	295.0	176.9	186.7	138.0	96.8	146.7	217.8
Total Current Assets	1,658.0	1,654.9	1,974.8	1,611.6	1,304.5	1,591.3	1,489.8
Net Property	704.9	761.4	755.5	646.5	572.0	570.6	494.9
Total Assets	4,437.4	4,602.2	4,892.1	4,131.9	3,627.3	3,277.5	2,993.4
Total Current Liabilities	696.9	819.2	1,604.6	1,334.9	989.7	1,196.6	1,139.1
Long-Term Obligations	1,030.3	1,033.2	631.8	608.0	610.1	262.6	253.0
Net Stockholders' Equity	2,394.6	2,519.5	2,441.6	2,038.8	1,910.9	1,703.6	1,489.7
Net Working Capital	961.1	835.8	370.2	276.7	314.8	394.8	350.7
Year-end Shs. Outstg. (000)	202,402	202,579	203,184	204,629	220,407	234,507	225,060
STATISTICAL RECORD:							
Operating Profit Margin %	8.2	6.7	15.6	14.3	13.4	13.5	13.2
Net Profit Margin %	5.0	3.7	9.9	9.1	8.2	8.9	9.6
Return on Equity %	8.8	6.6	21.8	19.9	17.1	23.8	26.2
Return on Assets %	4.8	3.6	10.9	9.8	9.0	12.4	13.0
Debt/Total Assets %	23.2	22.5	12.9	14.7	16.8	8.0	8.5
Price Range	43.55-23.54	43.55-26.40	54.38-34.13	47.94-29.31	39.94-25.50	36.69-24.13	27.56-18.31
P/E Ratio	41.9-22.6	53.1-32.2	20.8-13.1	25.0-15.3	27.5-17.6	20.5-13.5	16.0-10.6
Average Yield %	1.6	1.5	1.1	1.1	1.2	1.2	1.4

Statistics are as originally reported. Adj. for 2-for-1 stk. split, 12/97. ① Bef. inc. fr. disc. ops. of $52.4 mill. ② Incl. pre-tax cr. 12/31/97: $3.2 mill.; cr. 12/31/96: $75.1 mill. ③ Incl. non-recurr. gain of $10.5 mill.; bef. gain fr. disc. ops. of $523.9 mill. ④ Incl. non-recurr. gain of $10.5 mill.; bef. loss fr. disc. ops. of $13.6 mill. ⑤ Bef. inc. fr. disc. ops. of $81.7 mill. ⑥ Bef. loss fr. disc. ops of $39.4 mill. & acctg. chg. chrg. of $293.0 mill.

OFFICERS:
T. L. Reece, Chmn., Pres., C.E.O.
R. G. Kuhbach, V.P., C.F.O., Treas.
J. W. Schmidt, V.P., Sec., Gen. Couns.

INVESTOR CONTACT: John F. McNiff, Vice President, (212) 922-1640

PRINCIPAL OFFICE: 280 Park Avenue, New York, NY 10017

TELEPHONE NUMBER: (212) 922-1640
FAX: (212) 922-1656
WEB: www.dovercorporation.com

NO. OF EMPLOYEES: 25,000 (approx.)

SHAREHOLDERS: 16,000 (approx.)

ANNUAL MEETING: In Apr.

INCORPORATED: DE, 1947

INSTITUTIONAL HOLDINGS:
No. of Institutions: 372
Shares Held: 156,331,804
% Held: 77.0

INDUSTRY: Construction machinery (SIC: 3531)

TRANSFER AGENT(S): Mellon Investor Services, Ridgefield Park, NJ

EASTGROUP PROPERTIES, INC.

YIELD	7.0%
P/E RATIO	34.5

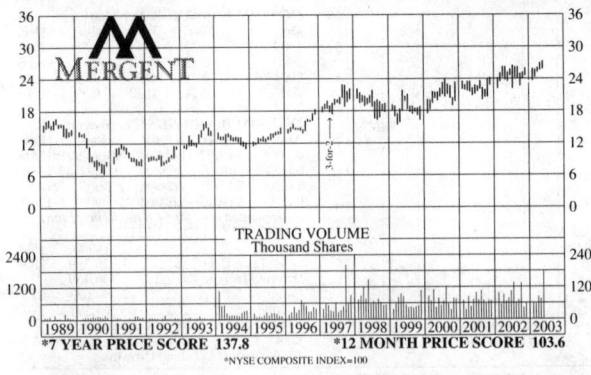

INTERIM EARNINGS (Per Share):

Qtr.	Mar.	June	Sept.	Dec.
1999	0.33	0.29	1.11	0.24
2000	0.28	0.29	0.29	0.76
2001	0.27	0.53	0.38	0.32
2002	0.22	0.27	0.16	0.18
2003	0.18	...	...	...

INTERIM DIVIDENDS (Per Share):

Amt.	Decl.	Ex.	Rec.	Pay.
0.47Q	9/05/02	9/16/02	9/18/02	9/27/02
0.47Q	12/06/02	12/13/02	12/17/02	12/27/02
0.475Q	3/06/03	3/17/03	3/19/03	3/31/03
0.475Q	5/29/03	6/16/03	6/18/03	6/30/03

Indicated div.: $1.90 (Div. Reinv. Plan)

CAPITALIZATION (12/31/02):

	($000)	(%)
Long-Term Debt	322,300	47.4
Minority Interest	1,759	0.3
Preferred Stock	108,535	15.9
Common & Surplus	247,950	36.4
Total	680,544	100.0

DIVIDEND ACHIEVER STATUS:
Rank: 210   10-Year Growth Rate: 6.38%
Total Years of Dividend Growth: 10

RECENT DEVELOPMENTS: For the three months ended 3/31/03, income from continuing operations was $5.6 million compared with income of $6.1 million in the corresponding quarter of the previous year. Results for 2002 included a pre-tax gain on the sale of real estate investments of $93,000. Results for 2003 and 2002 excluded gains of $104,000 and $12,000, respectively, from discontinued operations. Revenues rose 5.0% to $26.8 million.

PROSPECTS: The Company narrowed its funds from operations guidance for 2003 to a range of $2.42 to $2.50 per share. Moreover, the Company expects earnings for fiscal 2003 in the range of $0.60 to $0.70 per share. Separately, during the first quarter, the Company purchased 9.9 acres of land for new development in the World Houston International Business Center for approximately $901,000.

BUSINESS

EASTGROUP PROPERTIES, INC. is a self-administered, equity real estate investment trust focused on the acquisition, operation and development of industrial properties in major sunbelt markets throughout the United States. The Company's strategy for growth is based on its property portfolio orientation toward premier distribution facilities located near major transportation centers. The Company's portfolio includes 18.7 million square feet with an additional 510,000 square feet of properties under development as of 4/22/03.

ANNUAL FINANCIAL DATA

	12/31/02	12/31/01	12/31/00	12/31/99	12/31/98	12/31/97	12/31/96
Earnings Per Share	☑ 0.84	1.51	1.68	☐ 1.99	1.66	1.56	0.96
Tang. Book Val. Per Share	15.40	16.48	16.84	16.76	16.25	15.88	9.18
Dividends Per Share	1.88	1.80	1.58	1.48	1.40	1.34	1.28
Dividend Payout %	223.8	119.2	94.0	74.4	84.3	85.7	133.3
INCOME STATEMENT (IN MILLIONS):							
Interest Income	...	0.6	0.1	0.2	0.2	0.6	0.1
Total Income	105.8	105.3	98.1	86.2	76.7	53.6	39.8
Costs & Expenses	34.5	30.6	28.3	25.0	23.6	28.3	15.6
Depreciation	30.3	27.0	23.4	20.2	16.6	10.4	7.8
Interest Expense	17.4	17.8	18.6	17.7	16.9	...	8.9
Income Before Income Taxes	23.7	34.2	36.5	38.8	29.3	21.3	12.8
Equity Earnings/Minority Int.	...	...	...	...	...	d0.5	d0.3
Net Income	☑ 23.7	34.2	36.5	☐ 38.8	29.3	20.8	12.5
Average Shs. Outstg. (000)	16,237	16,046	15,798	17,362	16,432	13,338	...
BALANCE SHEET (IN MILLIONS):							
Cash & Cash Equivalents	1.4	1.8	2.9	2.7	2.8	1.3	0.4
Total Real Estate Investments	672.7	644.0	624.5	589.5	531.4	376.7	260.9
Total Assets	702.3	683.8	666.2	632.2	567.5	413.1	281.5
Long-Term Obligations	322.3	205.0	168.7	148.7	122.5	105.4	115.1
Total Liabilities	345.9	311.3	289.1	260.5	248.8	153.4	133.0
Net Stockholders' Equity	356.5	370.7	375.4	369.3	316.0	257.3	145.3
Year-end Shs. Outstg. (000)	16,104	15,912	15,849	15,556	16,308	16,205	15,824
STATISTICAL RECORD:							
Net Inc.+Depr./Assets %	7.7	9.0	9.0	9.3	8.1	7.5	7.2
Return on Equity %	6.6	9.2	9.7	10.5	9.3	8.1	8.6
Return on Assets %	3.4	5.0	5.5	6.1	5.2	5.0	4.4
Price Range	26.50-22.09	24.25-20.00	24.00-17.50	21.88-15.38	22.13-16.31	22.94-17.38	18.33-13.83
P/E Ratio	31.5-26.3	16.1-13.2	14.3-10.4	11.0-7.7	13.3-9.8	14.7-11.1	19.1-14.4
Average Yield %	7.7	8.1	7.6	7.9	7.3	6.6	8.0

Statistics are as originally reported. Adj. for 3-for-2 stk. spl., 4/97. ☐ Bef. acctg. chrg. of $418,000. ☑ Bef. loss from disc. opers. of $79,000.

OFFICERS:
L. R. Speed, Chmn.
D. H. Hoster II, Pres., C.E.O.
N. K. McKey, Exec. V.P., C.F.O., Sec.

INVESTOR CONTACT: Investor Relations, (601) 354-3555

PRINCIPAL OFFICE: 300 One Jackson Place, 188 East Capitol St., Jackson, MS 39201

TELEPHONE NUMBER: (601) 354-3555
FAX: (601) 352-1441
WEB: www.eastgroup.net

NO. OF EMPLOYEES: 54 full-time; 3 part-time

SHAREHOLDERS: 1,200 (approx.)

ANNUAL MEETING: In June

INCORPORATED: MD, July, 1969

INSTITUTIONAL HOLDINGS:
No. of Institutions: 94
Shares Held: 6,720,281
% Held: 42.0

INDUSTRY: Real estate investment trusts (SIC: 6798)

TRANSFER AGENT(S): First Chicago Trust Company of New York, Jersey City, NJ

EATON VANCE CORPORATION

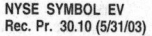
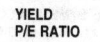

YIELD 1.1%
P/E RATIO 19.9

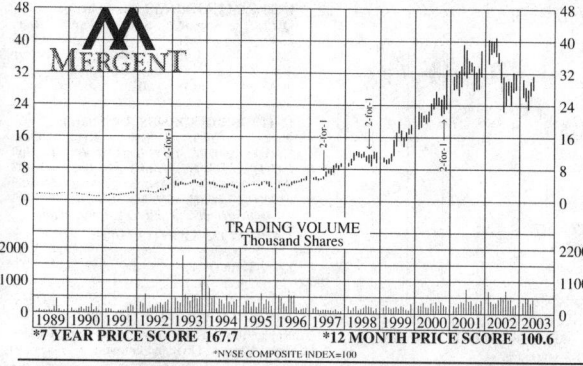

INTERIM EARNINGS (Per Share):

Qtr.	Jan.	Apr.	July	Oct.
1999-00	0.39	0.40	0.33	0.42
2000-01	0.44	0.29	0.44	0.44
2001-02	0.46	0.46	0.44	0.34
2002-03	0.37	0.36	...	...

INTERIM DIVIDENDS (Per Share):

Amt.	Decl.	Ex.	Rec.	Pay.
0.072Q	7/10/02	7/29/02	7/31/02	8/12/02
0.08Q	10/16/02	10/29/02	10/31/02	11/11/02
0.08Q	1/15/03	1/29/03	1/31/03	2/10/03
0.08Q	4/16/03	4/28/03	4/30/03	5/12/03

Indicated div.: $0.32

CAPITALIZATION (10/31/02):

	($000)	(%)
Long-Term Debt	124,118	22.7
Deferred Income Tax	50,531	9.2
Common & Surplus	372,302	68.1
Total	546,951	100.0

DIVIDEND ACHIEVER STATUS:
Rank: 21   10-Year Growth Rate: 20.79%
Total Years of Dividend Growth: 21

*7 YEAR PRICE SCORE 167.7   *12 MONTH PRICE SCORE 100.6
*NYSE COMPOSITE INDEX=100

RECENT DEVELOPMENTS: For the quarter ended 4/30/03, net income declined 23.8% to $25.0 million compared with $32.8 million in the equivalent 2002 quarter. Results for 2003 included a gain of $76,000 on investments. Total revenues decreased 9.0% to $120.9 million from $132.8 million a year earlier, reflecting lower average assets under management and changes in product mix. Total expenses slid 0.8% to $82.3 million from $82.9 million in 2002.

PROSPECTS: As a result of prolonged weakness in the equity markets, EV continues to focus on areas that support long-term growth. Initiatives continue to center on increasing EV's market share, strengthening its competitive position and making significant progress toward long-term goals. In recent months, EV has completed the build-out of its marketing organization and broadened its access to broker/dealer managed account programs.

BUSINESS

EATON VANCE CORPORATION creates, markets and manages mutual funds and provides management and counseling services to institutions and individuals. The Company conducts its investment management and counseling business through two wholly-owned subsidiaries, Eaton Vance Management and Boston Management and Research. As of 10/31/02, the Company provided investment advisory or administration services to 180 funds, 1,370 separately managed individual and institutional accounts, and participated in 40 managed account broker/dealer programs. EV's funds consist of money markets, equities, bank loans, and taxable and non-taxable fixed income. As of 4/30/03, assets under management totaled $57.89 billion.

ANNUAL FINANCIAL DATA

	10/31/02	10/31/01	10/31/00	10/31/99	10/31/98	10/31/97	10/31/96
Earnings Per Share	④ 1.70	④⑤ 1.60	④ 1.58	②④ 0.71	③ 0.41	0.52	① 0.47
Cash Flow Per Share	2.94	2.67	2.74	1.58	1.29	1.26	1.19
Tang. Book Val. Per Share	3.83	2.81	3.65	2.73	2.94	3.03	2.77
Dividends Per Share	0.30	0.25	0.20	0.16	0.13	0.10	0.09
Dividend Payout %	17.5	15.8	12.8	22.7	31.5	20.2	19.0
INCOME STATEMENT (IN THOUSANDS):							
Total Revenues	522,985	486,372	429,566	348,950	249,987	200,910	181,361
Costs & Expenses	250,262	218,533	161,959	205,380	134,591	79,941	67,335
Depreciation & Amort.	88,800	76,946	84,943	65,666	66,744	57,064	55,005
Operating Income	183,923	190,893	182,664	77,904	48,652	63,905	59,021
Net Interest Inc./(Exp.)	1,921	4,556	3,652	671	1,791	d380	d7
Income Before Income Taxes	186,241	178,489	187,179	85,910	50,038	67,470	59,922
Income Taxes	65,184	62,469	71,128	33,505	19,515	27,236	24,088
Net Income	④ 121,057	⑤⑥ 116,020	④ 116,051	⑥④ 52,405	③ 30,523	40,234	① 35,834
Cash Flow	209,857	192,966	200,994	118,071	97,267	97,298	90,839
Average Shs. Outstg.	71,412	72,300	73,222	74,494	75,514	77,396	76,616
BALANCE SHEET (IN THOUSANDS):							
Cash & Cash Equivalents	187,964	210,709	102,479	77,395	96,435	140,520	116,375
Total Current Assets	213,567	237,480	120,242	90,488	130,433	164,168	130,072
Net Property	13,897	14,938	13,161	12,459	2,696	2,537	2,828
Total Assets	616,619	675,301	432,989	358,229	380,260	387,513	360,262
Total Current Liabilities	68,270	83,844	61,793	48,890	48,957	39,968	24,081
Long-Term Obligations	124,118	215,488	21,429	28,571	35,714	50,964	54,549
Net Stockholders' Equity	372,302	301,126	254,950	194,268	211,809	226,280	210,780
Net Working Capital	145,297	153,636	58,449	41,598	81,476	124,200	105,991
Year-end Shs. Outstg.	69,257	68,617	69,544	70,520	71,332	73,876	75,072
STATISTICAL RECORD:							
Operating Profit Margin %	35.2	39.2	42.5	22.3	19.5	31.8	32.5
Net Profit Margin %	23.1	23.9	27.0	15.0	12.2	20.0	19.8
Return on Equity %	32.5	38.5	45.5	27.0	14.4	17.8	17.0
Return on Assets %	19.6	17.2	26.8	14.6	8.0	10.4	9.9
Debt/Total Assets %	20.1	31.9	4.9	8.0	9.4	13.2	15.1
Price Range	41.00-22.46	39.22-26.50	32.94-18.13	20.00-9.34	12.55-8.72	9.50-5.22	6.22-3.25
P/E Ratio	24.1-13.2	24.5-16.6	20.8-11.5	28.4-13.3	31.0-21.5	18.3-10.0	13.3-6.9
Average Yield %	0.9	0.8	0.8	1.1	1.2	1.4	1.9

Statistics are as originally reported. Adj. for 2-for-1 stk. split: 11/00, 8/98 & 5/97. ① Bef. extraord. credit $1.6 mill. ② Bef. acct. chrg. of $36.6 mill., 10/31/99. ③ Incl. an impairment loss on real estate of $2.6 mill. & a gain of $2.1 mill. from the sale of an investment. ④ Incl. a gain on the sale of investments of $1.3 mill., 10/31/02; loss of $2.6 mill., 10/31/01; gain of $226,000, 10/31/00; gain of $7.3 mill., 10/31/99. ⑤ Incl. an impairment loss on investments of $15.1 mill.

OFFICERS:
J. B. Hawkes, Chmn., Pres., C.E.O.
W. M. Steul, V.P., C.F.O., Treas.
A. R. Dynner, V.P., Sec.

INVESTOR CONTACT: William M. Steul, C.F.O., (617) 482-8260

PRINCIPAL OFFICE: 255 State Street, Boston, MA 02109

TELEPHONE NUMBER: (617) 482-8260
FAX: (617) 482-2396
WEB: www.eatonvance.com
NO. OF EMPLOYEES: 575
SHAREHOLDERS: 1,100 (approx. non-voting common); 11 (voting common)
ANNUAL MEETING: In May
INCORPORATED: MD, May, 1959; reincorp., MD, Feb., 1981

INSTITUTIONAL HOLDINGS:
No. of Institutions: 184
Shares Held: 34,305,446
% Held: 49.7

INDUSTRY: Investment advice (SIC: 6282)

TRANSFER AGENT(S): EquiServe Trust Company, N.A., Providence, RI

ECOLAB, INC.

YIELD 1.1%
P/E RATIO 30.2

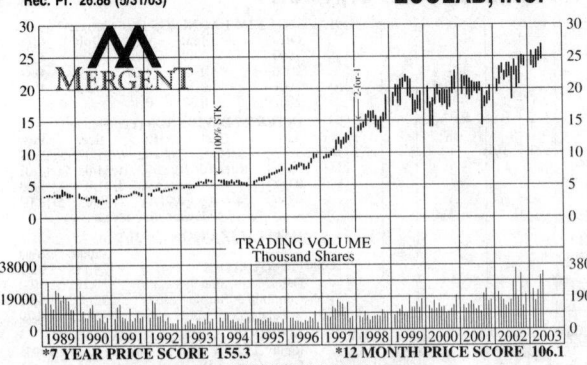

*7 YEAR PRICE SCORE 155.3   *12 MONTH PRICE SCORE 106.1
*NYSE COMPOSITE INDEX=100

INTERIM EARNINGS (Per Share):

Qtr.	Mar.	June	Sept.	Dec.
1999	0.13	0.16	0.21	0.16
2000	0.16	0.18	0.23	0.20
2001	0.17	0.19	0.22	0.15
2002	0.14	0.20	0.28	0.20
2003	0.21	...	...	...

INTERIM DIVIDENDS (Per Share):

Amt.	Decl.	Ex.	Rec.	Pay.
0.145Q	12/05/02	12/19/02	12/23/02	1/15/03
0.145Q	2/24/03	3/14/03	3/18/03	4/15/03
100% STK	5/09/03	6/09/03	5/23/03	6/06/03
0.072Q	5/09/03	6/13/03	6/17/03	7/15/03

Indicated div.: $0.29 (Div. Reinv. Plan)

CAPITALIZATION (12/31/02):

	($000)	(%)
Long-Term Debt	539,743	32.9
Common & Surplus	1,099,751	67.1
Total	1,639,494	100.0

DIVIDEND ACHIEVER STATUS:
Rank: 106   10-Year Growth Rate: 11.93%
Total Years of Dividend Growth: 10

RECENT DEVELOPMENTS: For the quarter ended 3/31/03, net income was $55.3 million versus income of $37.0 million, before a gain from discontinued operations of $1.9 million and an accounting change charge of $4.0 million, in the previous year. Results included one-time items that resulted in a net gain of $242,000 in 2003 and a net loss of $17.2 million in 2002. Net sales increased 11.4% to $875.9 million. Domestic sale rose 6.0% to $490.6 million. International sales grew 5.8% to $360.6 million.

PROSPECTS: The Company's outlook is promising as it continues to build its product and service offerings. Moreover, ECL should benefit from focused sales efforts on new and existing markets, continued cost control and savings from restructuring initiatives. For the second quarter of 2003, ECL anticipates earnings in the range of $0.48 to $0.52 per share. For the full-year, ECL remains confident that it can achieve earnings growth of 10.0% to 13.0%, with earnings per share of approximately $2.05.

BUSINESS

ECOLAB, INC. develops and markets cleaning, sanitizing, pest elimination, maintenance and repair products and services. The Cleaning and Sanitizing segment (47.5% of revenue in 2002) consists of seven business units and offers cleaners, sanitizers, detergents, lubricants, chemical cleaning, animal health, water treatment, infection control and janitorial products to customers in the U.S. Other U.S. Services (9.0%) consists of two business units focused on the elimination and prevention of pests, and the manufacturing of dishwashing and customized machines for the foodservice industry. The International segment (43.5%) serves customers in Europe, Asia Pacific, Canada, Latin America, the Middle East and Africa. Customers include hotels and restaurants, foodservice, healthcare and educational facilities, commercial laundries, light industry, and food processors. On 11/30/01, the Company acquired the remaining 50.0% of its Henkel-Ecolab joint venture for approximately $430.0 million.

ANNUAL FINANCIAL DATA

	12/31/02	12/31/01	12/31/00	12/31/99	12/31/98	12/31/97	12/31/96
Earnings Per Share	④ 0.81	③ 0.73	② 0.79	0.66	① 0.58	0.50	0.88
Cash Flow Per Share	1.66	1.35	1.35	1.15	1.03	0.88	1.57
Tang. Book Val. Per Share	0.83	0.41	2.98	2.94	2.67	2.14	4.01
Dividends Per Share	0.27	0.26	0.24	0.21	0.19	0.16	0.14
Dividend Payout %	33.3	35.9	30.4	32.1	33.0	32.0	16.0
INCOME STATEMENT (IN MILLIONS):							
Total Revenues	3,403.6	2,354.7	2,264.3	2,080.0	1,888.2	1,640.4	1,490.0
Costs & Expenses	2,784.3	1,873.6	1,772.7	1,655.5	1,504.3	1,321.0	1,215.2
Depreciation & Amort.	223.4	163.0	148.4	134.5	122.0	100.9	89.5
Operating Income	395.9	318.2	343.1	290.0	262.0	218.5	185.3
Net Interest Inc./(Exp.)	d43.9	d28.4	d24.6	d22.7	d21.7	d12.6	d14.4
Income Before Income Taxes	352.0	289.7	318.5	267.2	240.2	205.9	170.9
Income Taxes	140.1	117.4	129.5	109.8	101.8	85.3	70.8
Equity Earnings/Minority Int.	...	15.8	19.5	18.3	16.1	13.4	13.0
Net Income	④ 211.9	③ 188.2	② 208.6	175.8	① 154.5	134.0	113.2
Cash Flow	435.3	351.2	357.0	310.3	276.5	234.8	202.7
Average Shs. Outstg. (000)	261,574	259,856	263,892	268,838	268,094	267,644	128,992
BALANCE SHEET (IN MILLIONS):							
Cash & Cash Equivalents	49.2	41.8	44.0	47.7	28.4	61.2	69.3
Total Current Assets	1,015.9	929.6	600.6	577.3	503.5	509.5	435.5
Net Property	680.3	644.3	501.6	448.1	420.2	395.6	332.3
Total Assets	2,878.4	2,525.0	1,714.0	1,585.9	1,471.0	1,416.3	1,208.4
Total Current Liabilities	866.4	828.0	532.0	470.7	399.8	404.5	327.8
Long-Term Obligations	539.7	512.3	234.4	169.0	227.0	259.4	148.7
Net Stockholders' Equity	1,099.8	880.4	757.0	762.0	690.5	551.7	520.0
Net Working Capital	149.6	101.6	68.5	106.6	103.7	105.0	107.7
Year-end Shs. Outstg. (000)	259,880	255,800	254,322	258,832	258,958	258,254	129,600
STATISTICAL RECORD:							
Operating Profit Margin %	11.6	13.5	15.2	13.9	13.9	13.3	12.4
Net Profit Margin %	6.2	8.0	9.2	8.5	8.2	8.2	7.6
Return on Equity %	19.3	21.4	27.5	23.1	22.4	24.3	21.8
Return on Assets %	7.4	7.5	12.2	11.1	10.5	9.5	9.4
Debt/Total Assets %	18.8	20.3	13.7	10.7	15.4	18.3	12.3
Price Range	25.20-18.27	22.09-14.25	22.84-14.00	22.22-15.84	19.00-13.06	13.91-9.06	9.88-7.28
P/E Ratio	31.1-22.5	30.5-19.7	28.9-17.7	33.9-24.2	33.0-22.7	27.8-18.1	11.3-8.3
Average Yield %	1.2	1.4	1.3	1.1	1.2	1.4	1.6

Statistics are as originally reported. Adj. for stk. splits: 100% div., 6/03; 2-for-1, 1/98. ① Excl. disc. opers. gain of $38.0 mill. ② Bef. acctg. chrg., $2.4 mill.; incl. gain on sale of business of $25.9 mill. & restruct. chrg. of $5.2 mill. ③ Incl. net non-recurr. chrg. of $824,000 ④ Excl. disc. opers. gain $1.9 mill & acctg. chrg. $4.0 mill.; Incl. net spec. chrgs. $37.0 mill.

OFFICERS:
A. L. Schuman, Chmn., Pres., C.E.O.
S. L. Fritze, Sr. V.P., C.F.O.
L. T. Bell, Sr. V.P., Gen. Counsel

INVESTOR CONTACT: Michael J. Monahan, V.P., Ext. Rel., (651) 293-2809

PRINCIPAL OFFICE: 370 Wabasha Street North, St. Paul, MN 55102-2233

TELEPHONE NUMBER: (651) 293-2233
FAX: (651) 293-2092
WEB: www.ecolab.com
NO. OF EMPLOYEES: 20,417 (avg.)
SHAREHOLDERS: 5,018
ANNUAL MEETING: In May
INCORPORATED: DE, Feb., 1924

INSTITUTIONAL HOLDINGS:
No. of Institutions: 332
Shares Held: 138,635,206 (Adj.)
% Held: 53.3

INDUSTRY: Polishes and sanitation goods (SIC: 2842)

TRANSFER AGENT(S): EquiServe Trust Company, N.A., Canton, MA

EL PASO CORPORATION

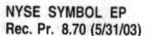

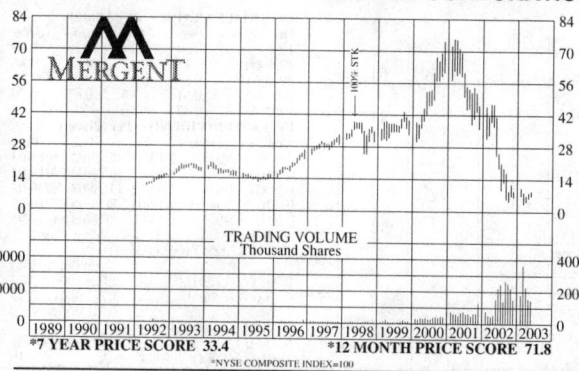

INTERIM EARNINGS (Per Share):

Qtr.	Mar.	June	Sept.	Dec.
2000	0.70	0.56	0.57	0.61
2001	d0.78	d0.26	0.42	0.72
2002	0.46	0.02	d0.06	d2.55
2003	0.63	...	...	...

INTERIM DIVIDENDS (Per Share):

Amt.	Decl.	Ex.	Rec.	Pay.
0.217Q	7/17/02	9/04/02	9/06/02	10/07/02
0.217Q	11/07/02	12/04/02	12/06/02	1/06/03
0.04Q	2/05/03	3/05/03	3/07/03	4/07/03
0.04Q	4/29/03	6/04/03	6/06/03	7/07/03

Indicated div.: $0.16 (Div. Reinv. Plan)

CAPITALIZATION (12/31/02):

	($000)	(%)
Long-Term Debt	16,307,000	57.7
Deferred Income Tax	3,576,000	12.7
Common & Surplus	8,377,000	29.6
Total	28,260,000	100.0

7 YEAR PRICE SCORE 33.4   **12 MONTH PRICE SCORE 71.8**
*NYSE COMPOSITE INDEX=100

DIVIDEND ACHIEVER STATUS:
Rank: 86   10-Year Growth Rate: 13.22%
Total Years of Dividend Growth: 10

RECENT DEVELOPMENTS: For the quarter ended 3/31/03, EP posted a loss from continuing operations of $375.0 million versus income of $248.0 million in 2002. Results included a loss of $318.0 million for 2003 and a gain of $15.0 million for 2002 related to long-lived assets. Results for 2003 and 2002 also included other nonrecurring charges of $75.0 million and $33.0 million, respectively. Operating revenues rose 6.7% to $4.02 billion.

PROSPECTS: On 4/30/03, EP announced that it has signed a letter of intent with Sunoco, Inc. to sell its Eagle Point refinery and related assets for $130.0 million. Also, in April 2003, EP executed agreements to sell various Mid-Continent and Northern Louisiana midstream assets for about $120.0 million and all of the common interests in East Coast Power, L.L.C. for $456.0 million.

BUSINESS

EL PASO CORPORATION (formerly El Paso Energy Corp.) operates through four primary business segments: Pipelines (21.4% of 2002 revenues), Production (17.4%), Field Services (16.6%) and Merchant Energy (45.8%). Corporate and eliminations comprise the balance (-1.2%). The Pipelines segment owns or has interests in about 60,000 miles of interstate natural gas pipelines in the U.S. and internationally. EP's Production segment conducts its natural gas and oil exploration and production activities. The Field Services segment conducts EP's midstream activities. The Merchant Energy segment consists of three primary divisions: global power, petroleum and energy trading. On 2/5/03, EP announced its intent to sell its remaining petroleum and chemicals assets. On 11/8/02, EP announced its plan to exit the energy trading business and pursue an orderly liquidation of its trading portfolio.

ANNUAL FINANCIAL DATA

	12/31/02	12/31/01	12/31/00	12/31/99	12/31/98	12/31/97	12/31/96
Earnings Per Share	⑨ d2.30	⑦ 0.13	⑤ 2.44	③ d1.06	1.85	1.59	② 0.53
Cash Flow Per Share	0.21	2.76	4.82	1.65	4.11	3.74	1.93
Tang. Book Val. Per Share	11.69	17.63	15.20	10.47	13.09	16.32	14.82
Dividends Per Share	0.86	0.84	0.82	0.79	0.76	0.72	0.69
Dividend Payout %	...	648.3	33.5	...	40.9	45.4	129.5

INCOME STATEMENT (IN MILLIONS):

Total Revenues	⑩ 12,194.0	⑥ 57,475.0	⑧ 21,950.0	④ 10,581.0	5,782.0	5,638.0	① 3,010.0
Costs & Expenses	10,861.0	55,283.0	20,030.0	9,999.0	4,983.0	4,862.0	2,739.0
Depreciation & Amort.	1,405.0	1,359.0	589.0	618.0	293.0	255.0	101.0
Operating Income	d72.0	833.0	1,331.0	d36.0	506.0	521.0	170.0
Net Interest Inc./(Exp.)	d1,400.0	d1,155.0	d538.0	d405.0	d267.0	d238.0	d110.0
Income Taxes	cr495.0	182.0	286.0	cr81.0	127.0	129.0	25.0
Net Income	⑨ d1,289.0	⑦ 67.0	⑤ 582.0	③ d242.0	225.0	186.0	② 38.0
Cash Flow	116.0	1,426.0	1,171.0	376.0	518.0	441.0	139.0
Average Shs. Outstg. (000)	560,000	516,000	243,000	228,000	126,000	118,000	72,000

BALANCE SHEET (IN MILLIONS):

Gross Property	38,355.0	38,970.0	17,073.0	15,468.0	6,406.0	6,004.0	...
Accumulated Depreciation	14,745.0	14,379.0	7,777.0	7,656.0	1,546.0	1,395.0	...
Net Property	23,610.0	24,591.0	11,659.0	10,261.0	7,341.0	7,116.0	5,938.0
Total Assets	46,224.0	48,171.0	27,445.0	16,657.0	10,069.0	9,532.0	8,712.0
Long-Term Obligations	16,307.0	13,184.0	5,949.0	5,223.0	2,552.0	2,119.0	2,215.0
Net Stockholders' Equity	8,377.0	9,356.0	3,569.0	2,947.0	2,108.0	1,959.0	1,638.0
Year-end Shs. Outstg. (000)	599,568	530,735	234,780	229,597	120,000	120,000	110,550

STATISTICAL RECORD:

Operating Profit Margin %	...	1.4	6.1	...	8.8	9.2	5.6
Net Profit Margin %	...	0.1	2.7	...	3.9	3.3	1.3
Net Inc./Net Property %	...	0.3	5.0	...	3.1	2.6	0.6
Net Inc./Tot. Capital %	...	0.2	5.0	...	3.6	3.3	0.8
Return on Equity %	...	0.7	16.3	...	10.7	9.5	2.3
Accum. Depr./Gross Prop. %	38.4	36.9	45.6	49.5	24.1	23.2	...
Price Range	46.89-4.39	75.30-36.00	74.25-30.31	43.44-30.69	38.94-24.69	33.38-24.44	26.63-14.31
P/E Ratio	...	578.8-276.7	30.4-12.4	...	21.0-13.3	21.0-15.4	50.2-27.0
Average Yield %	3.4	1.5	1.6	2.1	2.4	2.5	3.4

Statistics are as originally reported. Adj. for 100% stk. div., 4/98 ① Refl. acq. of Tenneco ② Incl. chrgs. of $64.6 mill. ③ Incl. chrgs. of $909.0 mill.; bef. acctg. chge. chrg. of $13.0 mill. ④ Refl. acq. of Sonat Inc. in 10/99. ⑤ Incl. merger rel. costs & asset impair. chrgs. of $91.0 mill.; bef. extraord. gain of $70.0 mill. ⑥ Refl. growth of energy commodities revs. ⑦ Incl. nonrecur. chrgs. of $1.84 bill. & ceiling test chrg. of $135.0 mill.; bef. extraord. gain of $26.0 mill. ⑧ Refl. acq. of The Coastal Corp. on 1/29/01. ⑨ Incl. nonrecur. chrgs. of $81.0 mill., ceiling test chrg. of $269.0 mill. & settlmnt. chrg. of $899.0 mill.; bef. loss fr. disc. ops. of $124.0 mill. & acctg. chrg. chg. of $54.0 mill. ⑩ Refl. adopt. of Emerging Issues Task Force Issue No. 02-3.

OFFICERS:
R. L. Kuehn, Jr., Chmn., C.E.O.
H. B. Austin, Pres., C.O.O.
D. D. Scott, Exec. V.P., C.F.O.

INVESTOR CONTACT: Bruce Connery, V.P., Investor Relations, (713) 420-5855

PRINCIPAL OFFICE: 1001 Louisiana Street, Houston, TX 77002

TELEPHONE NUMBER: (713) 420-2600
FAX: (713) 420-4417
WEB: www.elpaso.com

NO. OF EMPLOYEES: 11,855 (approx.)

SHAREHOLDERS: 52,489

ANNUAL MEETING: In June

INCORPORATED: DE, 1928

INSTITUTIONAL HOLDINGS:
No. of Institutions: 433
Shares Held: 460,825,681
% Held: 76.9

INDUSTRY: Natural gas transmission (SIC: 4922)

TRANSFER AGENT(S): Fleet National Bank c/o EquiServe, Providence, RI

EMERSON ELECTRIC CO.

YIELD 3.0%
P/E RATIO 22.4

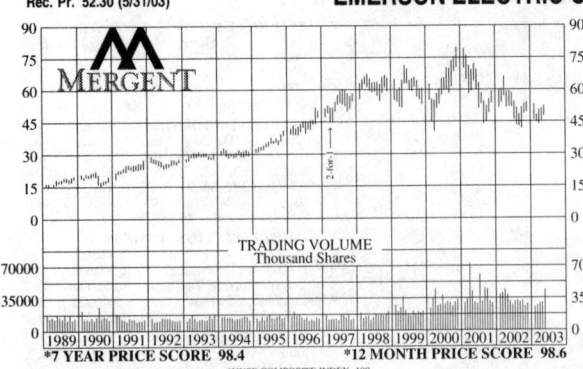

INTERIM EARNINGS (Per Share):

Qtr.	Dec.	Mar.	June	Sept.
1998-99	0.69	0.74	0.79	0.78
1999-00	0.75	0.82	0.87	0.86
2000-01	0.83	0.83	0.77	d0.03
2001-02	0.61	0.65	0.67	0.59
2002-03	0.52	0.56	...	...

INTERIM DIVIDENDS (Per Share):

Amt.	Decl.	Ex.	Rec.	Pay.
0.388Q	5/07/02	5/15/02	5/17/02	6/10/02
0.388Q	8/06/02	8/14/02	8/16/02	9/10/02
0.393Q	11/05/02	11/13/02	11/15/02	12/10/02
0.393Q	2/04/03	2/12/03	2/14/03	3/10/03
0.393Q	5/06/03	5/14/03	5/16/03	6/10/03

Indicated div.: $1.57 (Div. Reinv. Plan)

CAPITALIZATION (9/30/02):

	($000)	(%)
Long-Term Debt	2,990,000	34.2
Common & Surplus	5,741,000	65.8
Total	8,731,000	100.0

DIVIDEND ACHIEVER STATUS:
Rank: 175   10-Year Growth Rate: 8.35%
Total Years of Dividend Growth: 46

TRADING VOLUME
Thousand Shares

*7 YEAR PRICE SCORE 98.4   *12 MONTH PRICE SCORE 98.6

*NYSE COMPOSITE INDEX=100

RECENT DEVELOPMENTS: For the second quarter ended 3/31/03, net earnings declined 14.3% to $236.0 million compared with $275.0 million in equivalent 2002 quarter. Results for 2003 and 2002 included rationalization charges of $36.0 million and $55.0 million, respectively. Results for 2002 also included a gain from divestitures of $93.0 million. Net sales increased 1.7% to $3.48 billion from $3.42 billion a year earlier.

PROSPECTS: The weak economic environment and uncertainty continues to dampen business investment and capital spending in many of the industries the Company serves. Meanwhile, the Company's directors have approved a plan to divest Dura-Line, the fiber-optic conduit unit of EMR's electronics and telecommunications segment. Looking ahead, EMR's earnings should benefit from continuing restructuring actions and various international contracts.

BUSINESS

EMERSON ELECTRIC CO. is a global manufacturer of electrical, electromechanical and electronic products and systems sold through independent distributors and to original equipment manufacturers. The appliance and tools segment (24.2% of 2002 sales) provides motors, controls and other components for appliances, refrigeration and comfort control applications as well as disposers, tools and storage products. The process control segment (23.9%) provides measurement and fluid flow instrumentation, valves and control systems as well as services for process and industrial applications. The industrial automation segment (17.6%) provides industrial motors, drives, controls and equipment. The electronics and telecommunications segment (17.4%) provides power supplies and power distribution, protection and conversion equipment, and fiber optic conduits. The heating, ventilating and air conditioning (HVAC) segment (16.9%) provides components and systems for refrigeration and comfort control markets.

ANNUAL FINANCIAL DATA

	9/30/02	9/30/01	9/30/00	9/30/99	9/30/98	9/30/97	9/30/96
Earnings Per Share	☑ 2.52	☑ 2.40	3.30	3.00	2.77	2.52	2.27
Cash Flow Per Share	3.80	4.05	4.87	4.45	4.03	3.67	3.31
Tang. Book Val. Per Share	1.98	2.22	2.53	4.43	4.79	5.23	5.75
Dividends Per Share	1.56	1.54	1.46	1.33	1.21	1.10	1.00
Dividend Payout %	61.7	64.0	44.1	44.4	43.7	43.8	44.3
INCOME STATEMENT (IN MILLIONS)							
Total Revenues	13,824.0	15,479.6	15,544.8	14,269.5	13,447.2	12,298.6	11,149.9
Costs & Expenses	11,485.0	12,878.2	12,400.4	11,421.4	10,809.5	9,882.5	8,949.4
Depreciation & Amort.	541.0	708.5	678.5	637.5	562.5	511.6	464.6
Operating Income	1,798.0	1,892.9	2,465.9	2,210.6	2,075.2	1,904.5	1,735.9
Net Interest Inc./(Exp.)	d233.0	d304.3	d287.6	d189.7	d151.7	d120.9	d126.9
Income Before Income Taxes	1,565.0	1,588.6	2,178.3	2,020.9	1,923.5	1,783.6	1,609.0
Income Taxes	505.0	556.8	755.9	707.3	694.9	661.7	590.5
Net Income	☑ 1,060.0	☑ 1,031.8	1,422.4	1,313.6	1,228.6	1,121.9	1,018.5
Cash Flow	1,601.0	1,740.3	2,100.9	1,951.1	1,791.1	1,633.5	1,483.1
Average Shs. Outstg. (000)	420,900	429,500	431,400	438,400	444,100	445,000	448,096
BALANCE SHEET (IN MILLIONS)							
Cash & Cash Equivalents	381.0	355.7	280.8	266.1	209.7	221.1	149.0
Total Current Assets	4,961.0	5,320.1	5,482.7	5,124.4	5,001.3	4,716.8	4,187.2
Net Property	3,116.0	3,288.0	3,243.4	3,154.4	3,011.6	2,735.4	2,450.8
Total Assets	14,545.0	15,046.4	15,164.3	13,623.5	12,659.8	11,463.3	10,481.0
Total Current Liabilities	4,400.0	5,379.1	5,218.8	4,590.4	4,021.7	3,842.4	3,021.1
Long-Term Obligations	2,990.0	2,255.6	2,247.7	1,317.1	1,056.6	570.7	772.6
Net Stockholders' Equity	5,741.0	6,114.0	6,402.8	6,180.5	5,803.3	5,420.7	5,353.4
Net Working Capital	561.0	d59.0	263.9	534.0	979.6	874.4	1,166.1
Year-end Shs. Outstg. (000)	420,710	419,626	427,477	433,044	438,224	440,804	447,440
STATISTICAL RECORD:							
Operating Profit Margin %	13.0	12.2	15.8	15.5	15.4	15.5	15.6
Net Profit Margin %	7.7	6.7	9.2	9.2	9.1	9.1	9.1
Return on Equity %	18.5	16.9	22.2	21.3	21.2	20.7	19.0
Return on Assets %	7.3	6.9	9.4	9.6	9.7	9.8	9.7
Debt/Total Assets %	20.6	15.0	14.8	9.7	8.3	5.0	7.4
Price Range	66.09-41.74	79.25-44.04	79.75-40.50	71.44-51.44	67.44-54.50	60.38-45.00	51.75-38.75
P/E Ratio	26.2-16.6	33.0-18.3	24.2-12.3	23.8-17.1	24.3-19.7	24.0-17.9	22.8-17.1
Average Yield %	2.9	2.5	2.4	2.2	2.0	2.1	2.2

Statistics are as originally reported. Adjusted for 2-for-1 stock split 11/96. ☐ Incl. pre-tax rationalization chrg. of $377.0 mill. ☑ Bef. acctg. change chrg. of $938.0 mill.; incl. divestiture gain of $231.0 mill. and rational. chrg. of $207.0 mill.

OFFICERS:
C. F. Knight, Chmn.
D. N. Farr, C.E.O.
J. G. Berges, Pres.

INVESTOR CONTACT: Mark Polzin, (314) 982-1700

PRINCIPAL OFFICE: 8000 West Florissant Avenue, P.O. Box 4100, St. Louis, MO 63136

TELEPHONE NUMBER: (314) 553-2000
FAX: (314) 553-3527
WEB: www.gotoemerson.com

NO. OF EMPLOYEES: 111,500 (approx.)

SHAREHOLDERS: 32,700 (approx.)

ANNUAL MEETING: Feb.

INCORPORATED: MO, Sept., 1890

INSTITUTIONAL HOLDINGS:
No. of Institutions: 775
Shares Held: 283,795,545
% Held: 67.4

INDUSTRY: Process control instruments (SIC: 3823)

TRANSFER AGENT(S): Mellon Investor Services, LLC, South Hackensack, NJ

ENERGEN CORPORATION

YIELD 2.2%
P/E RATIO 13.4

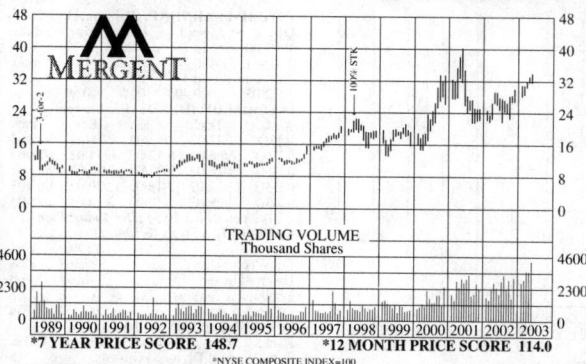

7 YEAR PRICE SCORE 148.7   **12 MONTH PRICE SCORE 114.0**

NYSE COMPOSITE INDEX=100

INTERIM EARNINGS (Per Share):

Qtr.	Dec.	Mar.	June	Sept.
1999-00	0.30	1.36	0.15	d0.06
2000-01	0.44	1.52	0.33	d0.10

Qtr.	Mar.	June	Sept.	Dec.
2001	...	...	...	0.12
2002	1.24	0.37	0.01	0.54
2003	1.52	...	...	...

INTERIM DIVIDENDS (Per Share):

Amt.	Decl.	Ex.	Rec.	Pay.
0.18Q	7/31/02	8/13/02	8/15/02	9/03/02
0.18Q	10/30/02	11/13/02	11/15/02	12/02/02
0.18Q	1/29/03	2/12/03	2/14/03	3/03/03
0.18Q	4/23/03	5/13/03	5/15/03	6/02/03

Indicated div.: $0.72 (Div. Reinv. Plan)

CAPITALIZATION (12/31/02):

	($000)	(%)
Long-Term Debt	512,954	46.8
Common & Surplus	582,810	53.2
Total	1,095,764	100.0

DIVIDEND ACHIEVER STATUS:
Rank: 263   10-Year Growth Rate: 3.36%
Total Years of Dividend Growth: 20

RECENT DEVELOPMENTS: For the quarter ended 3/31/03, income from continuing operations was $53.2 million compared with income of $38.9 million, before an accounting change charge of $2.2 million, in the equivalent period of the previous year. Results for 2003 and 2002 excluded gains of $1.3 million and $25,000, respectively, from discontinued operations. Total operating revenues improved 28.2% to $310.1 million from $242.0 million in the year-earlier quarter.

PROSPECTS: EGN is benefiting from the positive impact of higher commodity prices and increased production at Energen Resources, as well as the improved performance of its natural gas utility. Moreover, as a result of the Company's substantial hedge position in the first quarter of 2003, EGN raised its earnings guidance for 2003 to a range of between $2.65 and $2.75 per diluted share from its previous range of $2.40 to $2.50 per diluted share.

BUSINESS

ENERGEN CORPORATION is a diversified energy holding company engaged in the business of natural gas distribution and oil and gas exploration and production. EGN provides natural gas to residential, commercial and industrial customers located in Alabama. Alagasco, EGN's principal subsidiary, is the largest natural gas distribution utility in the State of Alabama. EGN's utility operations are subject to regulation by the Alabama Public Service Commission. The oil and gas exploration and production arm of EGN is Energen Resources, which conducts its activities in the Gulf of Mexico. In fiscal 2002, revenues were derived: 62.7% natural gas distribution and 37.3% oil and gas production activities.

ANNUAL FINANCIAL DATA

	12/31/02 ⑤	12/31/01	9/30/01	9/30/00	9/30/99	9/30/98	9/30/97
Earnings Per Share	④ 2.09	② 0.12	2.18	① 1.75	1.38	1.23	1.16
Cash Flow Per Share	5.36	...	4.98	4.61	4.35	3.98	3.53
Tang. Book Val. Per Share	16.77	...	15.61	13.21	12.09	11.23	13.49
Dividends Per Share	0.71	0.69	0.69	0.67	0.65	0.63	0.61
Dividend Payout %	34.0	...	31.6	38.3	47.1	51.2	52.8

INCOME STATEMENT (IN THOUSANDS):

Total Revenues	677,175	147,328	784,973	555,595	497,517	502,627	448,230
Costs & Expenses	430,322	136,330	573,989	372,721	331,519	360,143	325,444
Depreciation & Amort.	110,767	25,184	86,975	87,073	88,615	80,999	59,688
Maintenance Exp.	...	...	...	...	...	...	11,112
Operating Income	136,086	10,998	124,009	95,801	77,383	61,485	51,986
Net Interest Inc./(Exp.)	d43,713	d10,634	d42,070	d37,769	d37,173	d30,001	d22,906
Income Taxes	20,509	cr3,325	15,976	6,789	135	cr2,221	3,097
Net Income	④ 70,586	② 3,658	67,896	① 53,018	41,410	36,249	28,997
Cash Flow	181,353	...	154,871	140,091	130,025	117,248	88,685
Average Shs. Outstg.	33,838	31,277	31,084	30,359	29,921	29,438	25,126

BALANCE SHEET (IN THOUSANDS):

Gross Property	1,928,893	1,618,976	1,581,330	1,422,770	1,315,581	1,148,205	1,037,840
Accumulated Depreciation	677,781	613,297	587,669	519,444	458,614	395,794	375,303
Net Property	1,256,803	1,005,679	998,334	907,829	861,107	756,344	667,003
Total Assets	1,530,891	1,240,356	1,223,879	1,203,041	1,184,895	993,455	919,797
Long-Term Obligations	512,954	544,133	544,110	353,932	371,824	372,782	279,602
Net Stockholders' Equity	582,810	474,205	480,767	400,860	361,504	329,249	301,143
Year-end Shs. Outstg.	34,745	31,249	30,799	30,351	29,904	29,327	22,336

STATISTICAL RECORD:

Operating Profit Margin %	20.1	7.5	15.8	17.2	15.6	12.2	11.6
Net Profit Margin %	10.4	2.5	8.6	9.5	8.3	7.2	6.5
Net Inc./Net Property %	5.6	0.4	6.8	5.8	4.8	4.8	4.3
Net Inc./Tot. Capital %	6.4	0.4	6.6	7.0	5.6	5.2	5.0
Return on Equity %	12.1	0.8	14.1	13.2	11.5	11.0	9.6
Accum. Depr./Gross Prop. %	35.1	38.0	37.2	36.5	34.9	34.5	36.2
Price Range	29.99-21.65	...	40.25-21.50	33.56-14.69	21.25-13.13	22.50-15.13	20.63-14.50
P/E Ratio	14.3-10.4	...	18.5-9.9	19.2-8.4	15.4-9.5	18.3-12.3	17.9-12.6
Average Yield %	2.7	...	2.2	2.8	3.8	3.3	3.5

Statistics are as originally reported. Adjusted for 2-for-1 stock split, 3/98. ① Incl. an after-tax gain of $1.9 mill. on the sale of offshore properties. ② Excl. one-time, non-cash exp. of $5.5 mill. assoc. w/the oil and gas unit's open hedge contracts w/Enron Corporation. ③ For 3 mos. ended due to change in fiscal year-end date. ④ Excl. acctg. chrg. of $2.2 mill. & income of $273,000 from disc. oper.

OFFICERS:
W. M. Warren Jr., Chmn., Pres., C.E.O.
G. C. Ketcham, Exec. V.P., C.F.O., Treas.
J. D. Woodruff, Jr., Gen. Couns., Sec.
INVESTOR CONTACT: Julie S. Ryland, Asst. V.P., Inv. Rel., (800) 654-3206
PRINCIPAL OFFICE: 605 Richard Arrington Jr. Boulevard North, Birmingham, AL 35203-2707

TELEPHONE NUMBER: (205) 326-2700
FAX: (205) 326-2704
WEB: www.energen.com
NO. OF EMPLOYEES: 1,533
SHAREHOLDERS: 7,930 (approx., record).
ANNUAL MEETING: In Apr.
INCORPORATED: AL, Jan., 1978

INSTITUTIONAL HOLDINGS:
No. of Institutions: 174
Shares Held: 20,671,134
% Held: 59.1
INDUSTRY: Natural gas distribution (SIC: 4924)
TRANSFER AGENT(S): EquiServe Trust Company, Jersey City, NJ

ENERGY WEST INCORPORATED

YIELD 6.4%
P/E RATIO 24.1

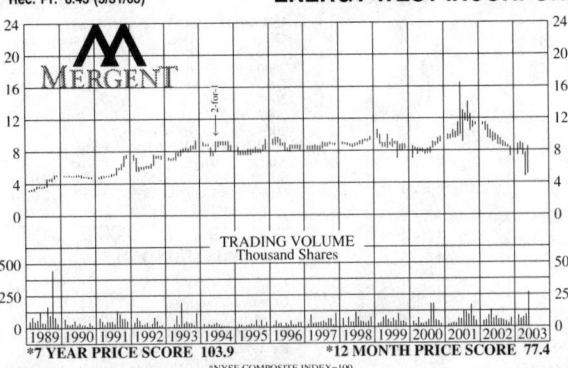

INTERIM EARNINGS (Per Share):

Qtr.	Sept.	Dec.	Mar.	June
1999-00	d0.27	0.20	0.59	0.01
2000-01	d0.24	0.52	1.04	0.22
2001-02	d0.17	0.25	0.46	0.01
2002-03	d0.40	0.05	0.69	...

INTERIM DIVIDENDS (Per Share):

Amt.	Decl.	Ex.	Rec.	Pay.
0.13Q	2/22/02	3/13/02	3/15/02	3/29/02
0.135Q	6/06/02	6/12/02	6/14/02	6/28/02
0.135Q	9/16/02	9/23/02	9/20/02	9/27/02
0.135Q	11/27/02	12/18/02	12/20/02	1/03/03
0.135Q	2/28/03	3/12/03	3/14/03	3/28/03

Indicated div.: $0.54 (Div. Reinv. Plan)

CAPITALIZATION (6/30/02):

	($000)	(%)
Long-Term Debt	15,367	22.8
Deferred Income Tax	4,043	6.0
Common & Surplus	47,912	71.2
Total	67,323	100.0

DIVIDEND ACHIEVER STATUS:
Rank: 229   10-Year Growth Rate: 5.57%
Total Years of Dividend Growth: 16

TRADING VOLUME
Thousand Shares

*7 YEAR PRICE SCORE 103.9   *12 MONTH PRICE SCORE 77.4
*NYSE COMPOSITE INDEX=100

RECENT DEVELOPMENTS: For the third quarter ended 3/31/03, net income advanced 51.6% to $1.8 million compared with $1.2 million in the corresponding prior-year quarter. Total revenue decreased 14.5% to $31.6 million from $36.9 million a year earlier. Revenues for 2003 included pipeline revenues of $101,481. Natural gas operations revenue fell 17.4% to $12.6 million, while gas and electric-wholesale revenue dropped 19.8% to $13.3 million.

Propane operations revenue increased 10.4% to $5.5 million. Gross profit increased 27.2% to $6.8 million from $5.3 million the year before, primarily due to the selling of natural gas storage inventories by the marketing and wholesale operations and contributions from the pipeline operations. Operating income jumped 55.9% to $3.3 million from $2.1 million a year earlier.

BUSINESS

ENERGY WEST INCORPORATED is a regulated public utility involved in the distribution and sale of natural gas to the public in and around Great Falls and West Yellowstone, Montana and Cody, Wyoming, and the distribution and sale of propane to the public through underground propane vapor systems in and around Payson, Arizona and Cascade, Montana. Energy West, Propane, Inc. (EWP); Energy West Resources, Inc. (EWR); and Energy West Development, Inc. (EWD) are non-regulated, non-utility subsidiaries. EWP is engaged in the wholesale and retail distribution of bulk propane. EWR markets gas and electricity, and EWD owns a parcel of real estate, operates a gas appliance retail business and conducts pipeline operations. Operating revenues for fiscal 2002 were derived as follows: marketing and wholesale, 52.8%; natural gas, 37.0%; and propane, 10.2%.

ANNUAL FINANCIAL DATA

	6/30/02	6/30/01	6/30/00	6/30/99	6/30/98	6/30/97	6/30/96
Earnings Per Share	0.55	1.10	0.53	① 0.66	0.64	0.55	0.61
Cash Flow Per Share	1.46	2.05	1.41	1.46	1.47	1.35	1.41
Tang. Book Val. Per Share	18.62	18.74	17.90	18.04	17.85	14.29	14.27
Dividends Per Share	0.53	0.51	0.49	0.47	0.45	0.43	0.41
Dividend Payout %	96.3	46.4	92.4	71.2	70.3	78.2	67.2
INCOME STATEMENT (IN THOUSANDS):							
Total Revenues	99,635	119,940	72,196	53,461	43,064	38,215	31,318
Costs & Expenses	93,986	111,559	66,886	48,272	37,324	33,127	26,520
Depreciation & Amort.	2,327	2,379	2,170	1,948	1,986	1,893	1,834
Operating Income	3,321	6,002	3,140	3,240	3,753	3,195	2,965
Net Interest Inc./(Exp.)	d1,047	d2,097	d1,674	d1,493	d1,583	d1,525	d1,243
Income Before Income Taxes	2,275	4,341	2,047	2,564	2,312	1,996	2,173
Income Taxes	874	1,575	750	977	792	703	766
Net Income	1,401	2,765	1,297	① 1,587	1,520	1,293	1,407
Cash Flow	3,728	5,144	3,466	3,536	3,506	3,186	3,241
Average Shs. Outstg.	2,559	2,510	2,457	2,419	2,391	2,357	2,299
BALANCE SHEET (IN THOUSANDS):							
Cash & Cash Equivalents	368	221	112	226	58	149	893
Total Current Assets	19,091	26,621	16,287	11,429	12,326	12,398	9,092
Net Property	36,519	32,999	31,804	29,372	27,572	27,398	26,090
Total Assets	57,869	62,278	51,547	44,201	43,335	42,856	37,495
Total Current Liabilities	19,899	24,416	14,841	7,230	6,745	15,317	11,088
Long-Term Obligations	15,367	15,881	16,395	16,840	17,228	9,684	10,046
Net Stockholders' Equity	47,912	47,108	44,318	43,904	42,901	33,678	33,126
Net Working Capital	d808	2,205	1,446	4,199	5,581	d2,919	d1,995
Year-end Shs. Outstg.	2,573	2,513	2,475	2,434	2,403	2,357	2,321
STATISTICAL RECORD:							
Operating Profit Margin %	3.3	5.0	4.3	6.1	8.7	8.4	9.5
Net Profit Margin %	1.4	2.3	1.8	3.0	3.5	3.4	4.5
Return on Equity %	2.9	5.9	2.9	3.6	3.5	3.8	4.2
Return on Assets %	2.4	4.4	2.5	3.6	3.5	3.0	3.8
Debt/Total Assets %	26.6	25.5	31.8	38.1	39.9	22.6	26.8
Price Range	11.50-7.25	16.50-9.05	9.75-7.00	10.63-7.00	9.75-8.38	9.13-8.13	9.75-7.88
P/E Ratio	20.9-13.2	15.0-8.2	18.4-13.2	16.1-10.6	15.2-13.1	16.6-14.8	16.0-12.9
Average Yield %	5.7	4.0	5.9	5.3	5.0	5.0	4.7

Statistics are as originally reported. ① Incls. gain of $236,291 from sales of assets.

OFFICERS:
E. J. Bernica, Pres., C.E.O.
J. C. Allen, V.P., Sec., Gen. Couns.
J. S. Hogan, Asst. V.P., Treas.

INVESTOR CONTACT: JoAnn S. Hogan, Financial Comm., (406) 791-7555

PRINCIPAL OFFICE: 1 First Avenue South, Great Falls, MT 59401

TELEPHONE NUMBER: (406) 791-7500
FAX: (406) 791-7560
WEB: www.ewst.com

NO. OF EMPLOYEES: 131 (avg.)

SHAREHOLDERS: 493

ANNUAL MEETING: In Nov.

INCORPORATED: MT, 1909

INSTITUTIONAL HOLDINGS:
No. of Institutions: 6
Shares Held: 40,333
% Held: 1.3

INDUSTRY: Natural gas distribution (SIC: 4924)

TRANSFER AGENT(S): Computershare Trust Company, Golden, CO

ENERGYSOUTH, INC.

YIELD 4.1%
P/E RATIO 13.3

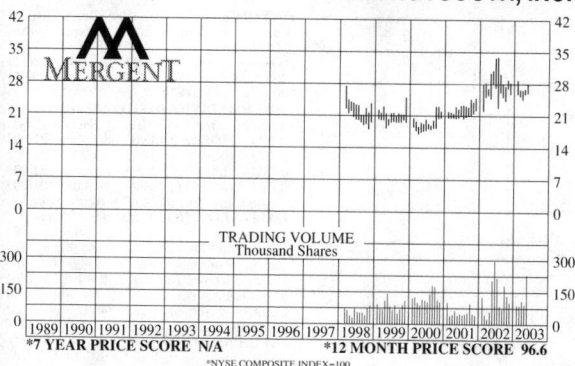

TRADING VOLUME
Thousand Shares

| 1989 | 1990 | 1991 | 1992 | 1993 | 1994 | 1995 | 1996 | 1997 | 1998 | 1999 | 2000 | 2001 | 2002 | 2003 |

*7 YEAR PRICE SCORE N/A   *12 MONTH PRICE SCORE 96.6
*NYSE COMPOSITE INDEX=100

INTERIM EARNINGS (Per Share):

Qtr.	Dec.	Mar.	June	Sept.
1998-99	0.59	0.76	0.22	0.18
1999-00	0.54	0.84	0.21	0.18
2000-01	0.55	0.73	0.10	0.14
2001-02	0.75	0.93	0.18	0.17
2002-03	0.66	1.09	...	...

INTERIM DIVIDENDS (Per Share):

Amt.	Decl.	Ex.	Rec.	Pay.
0.27Q	4/26/02	6/12/02	6/14/02	7/01/02
0.27Q	7/26/02	9/12/02	9/16/02	10/01/02
0.27Q	10/25/02	12/05/02	12/09/02	1/01/03
0.27Q	1/31/03	3/12/03	3/14/03	4/01/03
0.285Q	4/25/03	6/12/03	6/16/03	7/01/03

Indicated div.: $1.14 (Div. Reinv. Plan)

CAPITALIZATION (9/30/02):

	($000)	(%)
Long-Term Debt	98,645	51.6
Deferred Income Tax	15,275	8.0
Common & Surplus	77,283	40.4
Total	191,203	100.0

DIVIDEND ACHIEVER STATUS:
Rank: 279   10-Year Growth Rate: 1.65%
Total Years of Dividend Growth: 25

RECENT DEVELOPMENTS: For the quarter ended 3/31/03, net income increased 18.3% to $5.6 million from $4.7 million in the equivalent 2002 quarter. Results benefited from increased earnings in both Mobile Gas' distribution business and Bay Gas' storage business. Mobile Gas' earnings were positively affected by increased margins resulting from higher consumption and a rate adjustment which was effective 12/1/02. Offsetting the positive impact from increased margins was an increase in operations and main-

tenance expense and depreciation expense due to an additional plant placed in service. Bay Gas' earnings benefited from increased transportation and storage revenues received from additional customers, partially offset by increased operations and maintenance costs and an increase in depreciation expense and property taxes. Operating revenues advanced 13.8% to $35.6 million. Operating expenses climbed 13.8% to $25.0 million. Operating income grew 14.0% to $10.6 million.

BUSINESS

ENERGYSOUTH, INC. is the holding Company for Mobile Gas Service Corporation (MGS), a natural gas utility, and its subsidiaries. MGS is engaged in the purchase, distribution, sale and transportation of natural gas to approximately 100,000 residential, commercial and industrial customers in Mobile, Alabama and surrounding areas. The Company also provides merchandise sales, services and financing. EnergySouth Services, Inc. engages in contract and consulting work for other utilities and industrial customers. As of 12/31/02, MGS Storage Services, Inc. held a general partnership interest of 90.9% in Bay Gas Storage Company, Ltd., which provides underground storage and delivery of natural gas for MGS and other customers. The Company also owns MGS Marketing Services, Inc., which provides gas acquisition services for utilities and industrial customers. Southern Gas Transmission is engaged in the intrastate transportation of natural gas.

ANNUAL FINANCIAL DATA

	9/30/02	9/30/01	9/30/00	9/30/99	9/30/98	9/30/97	9/30/96
Earnings Per Share	2.03	②1.52	1.78	①1.75	1.71	1.67	1.79
Cash Flow Per Share	3.74	3.06	3.21	3.13	3.05	2.84	2.90
Tang. Book Val. Per Share	15.31	14.20	13.95	13.11	12.29	11.36	10.43
Dividends Per Share	1.06	1.02	0.97	0.91	0.84	0.77	0.73
Dividend Payout %	52.2	67.1	54.5	52.0	49.1	46.1	40.8
INCOME STATEMENT (IN THOUSANDS):							
Total Revenues	86,419	107,759	74,097	68,060	74,022	72,670	71,378
Costs & Expenses	31,031	61,483	27,546	40,698	47,743	47,410	45,562
Depreciation & Amort.	8,619	7,696	7,079	6,795	6,596	5,740	5,406
Maintenance Exp.	24,025	20,981	20,218	1,579	1,533	1,542	1,945
Operating Income	22,744	17,599	19,254	18,988	18,150	17,978	18,465
Net Interest Inc./(Exp.)	d5,791	d4,783	d4,424	d4,850	d4,240	d4,624	d4,390
Income Taxes	5,983	4,604	5,270	5,003	4,967	4,712	5,013
Equity Earnings/Minority Int.	d739	d651	d768	d511	d526	d516	d431
Net Income	10,231	②7,561	8,792	①8,624	8,417	8,126	8,631
Cash Flow	18,850	15,257	15,871	15,419	15,013	13,866	14,037
Average Shs. Outstg.	5,046	4,987	4,944	4,933	4,926	4,883	4,838
BALANCE SHEET (IN THOUSANDS):							
Gross Property	254,735	231,445	189,162	179,531	172,000	166,154	155,579
Accumulated Depreciation	66,912	60,853	54,811	49,855	44,872	40,289	36,099
Net Property	187,823	170,592	134,351	129,676	127,128	125,865	119,480
Total Assets	221,474	218,852	167,380	173,635	166,541	161,867	152,118
Long-Term Obligations	98,645	90,592	55,222	58,017	58,979	63,580	54,509
Net Stockholders' Equity	77,283	70,124	68,544	64,154	59,895	55,177	50,400
Year-end Shs. Outstg.	5,048	4,937	4,912	4,894	4,872	4,856	4,833
STATISTICAL RECORD:							
Operating Profit Margin %	26.3	16.3	26.0	27.9	24.5	24.7	25.9
Net Profit Margin %	11.8	7.0	11.9	12.7	11.4	11.2	12.1
Net Inc./Net Property %	5.4	4.4	6.5	6.7	6.6	6.5	7.2
Net Inc./Tot. Capital %	5.3	4.3	6.3	6.7	6.3	6.2	7.4
Return on Equity %	13.2	10.8	12.8	13.4	14.1	14.7	17.1
Accum. Depr./Gross Prop. %	26.3	26.3	29.0	27.8	26.1	24.2	23.2
Price Range	33.95-22.05	24.86-20.36	23.00-17.00	25.00-18.25	27.50-18.00	...	...
P/E Ratio	16.7-10.9	16.4-13.4	12.9-9.6	14.3-10.4	16.1-10.5	...	...
Average Yield %	3.8	4.5	4.8	4.2	3.7	...	...

Statistics are as originally reported. Adj. to reflect 3-for-2 conversion of stock from Mobile Gas Service Corp. to EnergySouth, Inc. ① Bef. net acctg. chng. chrg. of $349,000. ② Bef. extraord. loss of $1.4 million.

OFFICERS:
J. C. Hope III, Chmn.
W. L. Hovell, Vice-Chmn.
J. S. Davis, Pres., C.E.O.

INVESTOR CONTACT: Charles P. Huffman, Sr. V.P., C.F.O., (251) 476-2720

PRINCIPAL OFFICE: 2828 Dauphin Street, Mobile, AL 36606

TELEPHONE NUMBER: (251) 450-4774
FAX: (251) 478-5817
WEB: www.energysouth.com

NO. OF EMPLOYEES: 294

SHAREHOLDERS: 1,438

ANNUAL MEETING: In Jan.

INCORPORATED: AL, May, 1933

INSTITUTIONAL HOLDINGS:
No. of Institutions: 33
Shares Held: 901,279
% Held: 18.0

INDUSTRY: Natural gas distribution (SIC: 4924)

TRANSFER AGENT(S): BankBoston, N.A., Boston, MA

EXXON MOBIL CORPORATION

YIELD 2.7%
P/E RATIO 15.9

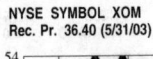
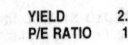
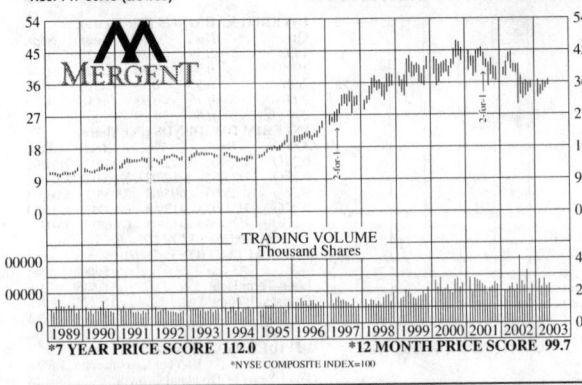

MERGENT

TRADING VOLUME
Thousand Shares

| 1989 | 1990 | 1991 | 1992 | 1993 | 1994 | 1995 | 1996 | 1997 | 1998 | 1999 | 2000 | 2001 | 2002 | 2003 |

*7 YEAR PRICE SCORE 112.0   ***12 MONTH PRICE SCORE 99.7**

*NYSE COMPOSITE INDEX=100

INTERIM EARNINGS (Per Share):

Qtr.	Mar.	June	Sept.	Dec.
2000	0.44	0.58	0.59	0.71
2001	0.71	0.65	0.46	0.39
2002	0.30	0.39	0.39	0.54
2003	0.97	...	...	...

INTERIM DIVIDENDS (Per Share):

Amt.	Decl.	Ex.	Rec.	Pay.
0.23Q	7/31/02	8/09/02	8/13/02	9/10/02
0.23Q	10/30/02	11/07/02	11/12/02	12/10/02
0.23Q	1/29/03	2/06/03	2/10/03	3/10/03
0.25Q	4/30/03	5/09/03	5/13/03	6/10/03

Indicated div.: $1.00 (Div. Reinv. Plan)

CAPITALIZATION (12/31/02):

	($000)	(%)
Long-Term Debt	6,361,000	6.3
Capital Lease Obligations..	294,000	0.3
Deferred Income Tax	16,484,000	16.4
Minority Interest	2,768,000	2.8
Common & Surplus	74,597,000	74.2
Total	100,504,000	100.0

DIVIDEND ACHIEVER STATUS:
Rank: 269   10-Year Growth Rate: 2.66%
Total Years of Dividend Growth: 20

RECENT DEVELOPMENTS: For the quarter ended 3/31/03, income was $6.49 billion, before an accounting change gain of $550.0 million, versus income from continuing operations of $2.06 billion the previous year. Results for 2002 included merger expenses of $60.0 million. XOM's results were fueled by increased realizations on sales of crude oil and natural gas and higher refining and marketing margins. Total revenues rose 47.0% to $63.78 billion.

PROSPECTS: XOM's near-term results should benefit from the year-over-year improvement in natural gas and crude oil prices, despite its lackluster production growth. For instance, for the quarter ended 3/31/03, oil-equivalent production was essentially flat at 4.5 million oil equivalent barrels daily. However, plans for long-term capacity gains remain on track as evidenced by the 17.6% rise in capital and exploration expenditures to $3.50 billion.

BUSINESS

EXXON MOBIL CORPORATION'S principal business is energy, involving exploration for, and production of, crude oil and natural gas, manufacturing of petroleum products and transportation and sale of crude oil, natural gas and petroleum products. Exxon Mobil is a major manufacturer and marketer of basic petrochemicals, including olefins, aromatics, polyethylene and polypropylene plastics and a wide variety of specialty products. Exxon Mobil also has interests in electric power generation facilities. As of 12/31/02, XOM owned 69.6% of Imperial Oil Limited. In 2002, worldwide proved reserves were: crude oil and natural gas liquids, 11,823 million barrels; and natural gas, 55,718 billion cubic feet. On 11/30/99, Exxon Corp. acquired Mobil Corporation in a transaction valued at $81.00 billion.

ANNUAL FINANCIAL DATA

	12/31/02	12/31/01	⑥ 12/31/00	12/31/99	12/31/98	12/31/97	12/31/96
Earnings Per Share	② 1.61	③ 2.18	④ 2.28	⑤ 1.13	⑥ 1.31	⑦ 1.69	1.51
Cash Flow Per Share	2.84	3.32	3.43	2.35	2.43	2.78	2.58
Tang. Book Val. Per Share	11.13	10.74	10.21	9.12	8.99	8.85	8.70
Dividends Per Share	0.92	0.91	0.88	0.83	0.82	0.81	0.78
Dividend Payout %	57.1	41.7	38.7	74.2	62.8	48.2	51.8

INCOME STATEMENT (IN MILLIONS):

Total Revenues	204,506.0	213,488.0	232,748.0	185,527.0	117,772.0	137,242.0	134,249.0
Costs & Expenses	178,079.0	181,132.0	196,948.0	165,378.0	103,276.0	118,555.0	116,540.0
Depreciation & Amort.	8,310.0	7,944.0	8,130.0	8,304.0	5,340.0	5,474.0	5,329.0
Operating Income	18,117.0	24,412.0	27,670.0	11,845.0	9,156.0	13,213.0	12,380.0
Net Interest Inc./(Exp.)	d398.0	d293.0	d589.0	d695.0	d100.0	d415.0	d464.0
Income Before Income Taxes	17,510.0	24,119.0	27,081.0	11,150.0	9,056.0	12,798.0	11,916.0
Income Taxes	6,499.0	9,014.0	11,091.0	3,240.0	2,616.0	4,338.0	4,406.0
Net Income	② 11,011.0	③ 15,105.0	④ 15,990.0	⑤ 7,910.0	⑥ 6,440.0	⑦ 8,460.0	⑦ 7,510.0
Cash Flow	19,321.0	23,049.0	24,120.0	16,214.0	11,780.0	13,934.0	12,839.0
Average Shs. Outstg. (000)	6,803,000	6,941,000	7,034,000	6,906,000	4,856,000	5,010,000	4,968,000

BALANCE SHEET (IN MILLIONS):

Cash & Cash Equivalents	7,229.0	6,547.0	7,081.0	1,761.0	1,461.0	4,062.0	2,969.0
Total Current Assets	38,291.0	35,681.0	40,399.0	31,141.0	17,593.0	21,192.0	19,910.0
Net Property	94,940.0	89,602.0	89,829.0	94,043.0	65,199.0	66,414.0	66,607.0
Total Assets	152,644.0	143,174.0	149,000.0	144,521.0	92,630.0	96,064.0	95,527.0
Total Current Liabilities	33,175.0	30,114.0	38,191.0	38,733.0	19,412.0	19,654.0	19,505.0
Long-Term Obligations	6,655.0	7,099.0	7,280.0	8,402.0	4,530.0	7,050.0	7,236.0
Net Stockholders' Equity	74,597.0	73,161.0	70,757.0	63,466.0	43,750.0	43,660.0	43,542.0
Net Working Capital	5,116.0	5,567.0	2,208.0	d7,592.0	d1,819.0	1,538.0	405.0
Year-end Shs. Outstg. (000)	6,700,000	6,809,000	6,930,000	6,959,784	4,856,000	4,914,000	4,968,000

STATISTICAL RECORD:

Operating Profit Margin %	8.9	11.4	11.9	6.4	7.8	9.6	9.2
Net Profit Margin %	5.4	7.1	6.9	4.3	5.5	6.2	5.6
Return on Equity %	14.8	20.6	22.6	12.5	14.7	19.4	17.2
Return on Assets %	7.2	10.6	10.7	5.5	7.0	8.8	7.9
Debt/Total Assets %	4.4	5.0	4.9	5.8	4.9	7.3	7.6
Price Range	44.58-29.75	45.84-35.01	47.72-34.94	43.63-32.16	38.66-28.31	33.63-24.13	25.31-19.41
P/E Ratio	27.7-18.5	21.0-16.1	21.0-15.4	38.8-28.6	29.6-21.7	20.0-14.3	16.8-12.9
Average Yield %	2.5	2.3	2.1	2.2	2.4	2.8	3.5

Statistics are as originally reported. Adj. for stk. splits: 2-for-1, 4/97 & 7/01. ① Bef. acctg. chrg. of $70.0 mill. ② Incl. cr. 12/31/97: $305.0 mill.; cr. 12/31/96: $90.0 mill. ③ Incl. chrg. of $625.0 mill. ④ Incl. merger-rel. exp. of $1.41 bill.; bef. extraord. gain of $1.73 bill. ⑤ Incl. results of Mobil Corporation. ⑥ Incl. merger-rel. exp. of $748.0 mill.; bef. extraord. gain of $215.0 mill. ⑦ Incl. merger-rel. exp. of $410.0 mill.; bef. inc. fr. disc. ops. of $449.0 mill.

OFFICERS:
L. R. Raymond, Chmn.
H. J. Longwell, Exec. V.P.
E. G. Galante, Exec. V.P.

INVESTOR CONTACT: Media Relations,
(972) 444-1109

PRINCIPAL OFFICE: 5959 Las Colinas Blvd.,
Irving, TX 75039-2298

TELEPHONE NUMBER: (972) 444-1000
FAX: (972) 444-1348
WEB: www.exxonmobil.com
NO. OF EMPLOYEES: 92,500 (approx.)
SHAREHOLDERS: 679,211
ANNUAL MEETING: In May
INCORPORATED: NJ, Aug., 1882

INSTITUTIONAL HOLDINGS:
No. of Institutions: 1,272
Shares Held: 3,311,492,000
% Held: 49.5

INDUSTRY: Petroleum refining (SIC: 2911)

TRANSFER AGENT(S): ExxonMobil Shareholder Services c/o EquiServe Trust Company, NA, Boston, MA

F.N.B. CORPORATION

YIELD 3.2%
P/E RATIO 14.8

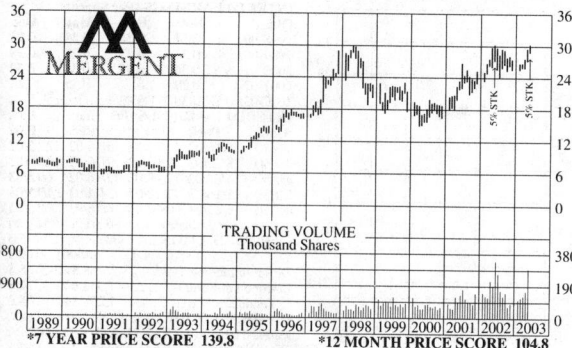

TRADING VOLUME
Thousand Shares

*7 YEAR PRICE SCORE 139.8   *12 MONTH PRICE SCORE 104.8

*NYSE COMPOSITE INDEX=100

INTERIM EARNINGS (Per Share):

Qtr.	Mar.	June	Sept.	Dec.
1999	0.33	0.37	0.39	0.39
2000	0.38	0.40	0.42	0.44
2001	0.22	0.37	0.47	0.48
2002	d0.19	0.50	0.51	0.52
2003	0.50	...	...	...

INTERIM DIVIDENDS (Per Share):

Amt.	Decl.	Ex.	Rec.	Pay.
0.22Q	11/21/02	11/27/02	12/02/02	12/15/02
0.22Q	2/25/03	3/04/03	3/06/03	3/15/03
5% STK	4/28/03	5/13/03	5/15/03	5/30/03
0.24Q	4/28/03	5/29/03	6/02/03	6/15/03

Indicated div.: $0.96 (Div. Reinv. Plan)

CAPITALIZATION (12/31/02):

	($000)	(%)
Total Deposits	5,426,157	83.8
Long-Term Debt	450,647	7.0
Preferred Stock	1	0.0
Common & Surplus	598,595	9.2
Total	6,475,400	100.0

DIVIDEND ACHIEVER STATUS:
Rank: 43   10-Year Growth Rate: 17.62%
Total Years of Dividend Growth: 18

RECENT DEVELOPMENTS: For the three months ended 3/31/03, net income jumped to $23.3 million compared with a net loss of $8.9 million in the corresponding period of 2002. Results benefited from solid revenue and loan growth, particularly in the Florida market. Results for 2003 and 2002 included amortization of intangibles of $821,000 and $837,000, merger expenses of $1.0 million and $41.9 million, and gains on the sale of securities of $693,000 and $175,000, respectively. Net interest income rose 8.3% to $73.1 million from $67.5 million a year earlier. Provision for loan losses increased 39.8% to $5.9 million versus $4.2 million the year before. Total non-interest income advanced 14.6% to $32.0 million from $27.9 million, while total non-interest expense decreased 35.9% to $65.5 million from $102.2 million in 2002. Separately, on 3/31/03, the Company announced it has completed the acquisition of Charter Banking Corporation, the holding company for Southern Exchange Bank in Tampa, Florida.

BUSINESS

F.N.B. CORPORATION, with assets of $7.13 billion as of 3/31/03, is a financial holding company that provides a full range of financial services to consumers and small- to medium-size businesses in its market areas. FBAN's bank subsidiaries offer traditional full-service commercial banking services, including commercial and individual demand and time deposit accounts and commercial, mortgage and individual installment loans. In addition, the bank subsidiaries offer various alternative investment products, including mutual funds and annuities. The consumer finance subsidiary offers personal installment loans to individuals and purchase installment sales finance contracts from retail merchants. As of 1/16/03, the Company owned and operated community banks, insurance agencies, a consumer finance company and First National Trust Company with offices located in Florida, Pennsylvania, Ohio and Tennessee. On 1/18/02, FBAN acquired Promistar Financial Corporation.

ANNUAL FINANCIAL DATA

	12/31/02	12/31/01	12/31/00	12/31/99	12/31/98	12/31/97	12/31/96
Earnings Per Share	④ 1.34	③ 1.52	② 1.62	① 1.48	① 1.32	① 1.63	① 1.37
Tang. Book Val. Per Share	11.08	13.02	12.51	11.35	11.77	11.61	11.68
Dividends Per Share	0.81	0.69	0.65	0.62	0.58	0.50	0.48
Dividend Payout %	60.4	45.4	40.1	41.9	43.9	30.7	35.0
INCOME STATEMENT (IN MILLIONS):							
Total Interest Income	426.8	296.7	290.9	254.9	236.0	195.5	139.0
Total Interest Expense	145.7	125.7	135.3	106.5	103.4	84.5	58.2
Net Interest Income	281.1	171.0	155.6	148.4	132.6	111.0	80.7
Provision for Loan Losses	19.1	12.9	10.9	9.2	7.3	10.6	6.1
Non-Interest Income	120.9	82.8	55.6	46.9	31.7	23.1	15.3
Non-Interest Expense	289.4	174.8	137.5	129.7	109.2	88.2	62.8
Income Before Taxes	93.4	66.1	62.9	56.5	47.9	35.4	27.1
Net Income	④ 63.3	③ 44.6	② 42.8	① 39.3	① 31.9	① 24.3	① 18.4
Average Shs. Outstg. (000)	47,074	29,311	25,484	26,468	24,266	20,323	12,788
BALANCE SHEET (IN MILLIONS):							
Cash & Due from Banks	246.8	155.9	141.8	171.4	128.9	87.9	70.3
Total Loans & Leases	5,296.3	3,246.9	3,024.8	2,865.8	2,360.7	1,905.8	1,327.1
Allowance for Credit Losses	144.2	85.2	101.5	98.3	61.9	47.6	45.7
Net Loans & Leases	5,152.1	3,161.7	2,923.3	2,767.5	2,298.8	1,858.2	1,281.4
Total Assets	7,090.2	4,129.1	3,886.5	3,706.2	3,250.7	2,649.5	1,726.7
Total Deposits	5,426.2	3,292.4	3,102.9	2,909.4	2,708.6	2,192.7	1,429.7
Long-Term Obligations	450.6	103.0	116.1	117.6	69.5	67.2	34.2
Total Liabilities	6,491.6	3,759.9	3,565.3	3,415.9	2,978.5	2,418.9	1,572.0
Net Stockholders' Equity	598.6	369.2	321.2	290.3	272.2	230.6	154.8
Year-end Shs. Outstg. (000)	46,055	28,347	25,541	25,385	22,929	19,612	12,947
STATISTICAL RECORD:							
Return on Equity %	10.6	12.1	13.3	13.5	11.7	10.5	11.9
Return on Assets %	0.9	1.1	1.1	1.1	1.0	0.9	1.1
Equity/Assets %	8.4	8.9	8.3	7.8	8.4	8.7	9.0
Non-Int. Exp./Tot. Inc. %	72.0	68.9	65.1	66.4	66.4	65.8	65.4
Price Range	30.24-23.36	26.76-17.93	19.87-14.91	23.04-17.24	29.97-18.81	29.01-16.35	17.95-13.54
P/E Ratio	22.5-17.4	17.6-11.8	12.2-9.2	15.6-11.6	22.8-14.3	17.8-10.0	13.1-9.9
Average Yield %	3.0	3.1	3.7	3.1	2.4	2.2	3.0

Statistics are as originally reported. Adj. for stk. splits: 5% div., 5/96, 5/97, 5/98, 5/99, 5/00, 5/01, 5/02 & 5/03. ① Incl. non-recur. chg. $1.8 mill., 1999; $5.5 mill., 1998; $13.4 mill., 1997, $1.9 mill., 1996. ② Incl. chg. of $2.1 mill. fr. amort. of intang. ③ Incl. one-time legal expense chg. of $4.0 mill., merger-rel. chg. of $3.8 mill. and restr. chg. of $3.2 mill. ④ Incl. $43.2 mill. merg.-rel chg. & $1.9 mill. gain fr. sale of sec.

OFFICERS:
P. Mortensen, Chmn.
S. J. Gurgovits, Vice-Chmn.
G. L. Tice, Pres., C.E.O.
INVESTOR CONTACT: Investor Relations, (239) 262-7600
PRINCIPAL OFFICE: 2150 Goodlette Road North, Naples, FL 34102

TELEPHONE NUMBER: (239) 262-7600
WEB: www.fnbcorporation.com
NO. OF EMPLOYEES: 2,586 full-time; 599 part-time
SHAREHOLDERS: 6,921 (approx.)
ANNUAL MEETING: In April
INCORPORATED: PA, June, 1974; reincorp., FL, June, 2001

INSTITUTIONAL HOLDINGS:
No. of Institutions: 95
Shares Held: 12,079,761
% Held: 27.5
INDUSTRY: National commercial banks (SIC: 6021)
TRANSFER AGENT(S): F.N.B. Shareholder Services, Naples, FL

FAMILY DOLLAR STORES, INC.

YIELD	0.8%
P/E RATIO	27.2

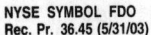
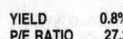
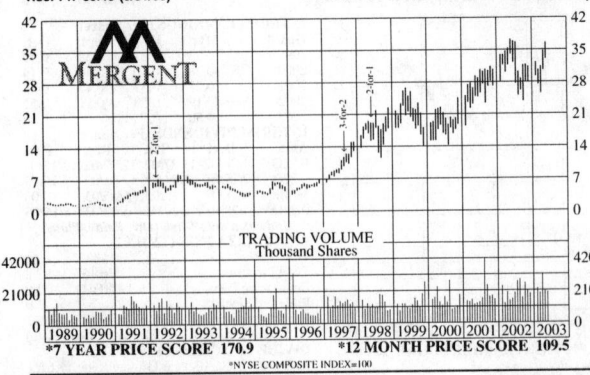

INTERIM EARNINGS (Per Share):

Qtr.	Nov.	Feb.	May	Aug.
1998-99	0.17	0.24	0.24	0.16
1999-00	0.21	0.32	0.29	0.18
2000-01	0.24	0.35	0.31	0.20
2001-02	0.29	0.37	0.35	0.24
2002-03	0.33	0.42	...	...

INTERIM DIVIDENDS (Per Share):

Amt.	Decl.	Ex.	Rec.	Pay.
0.065Q	5/16/02	6/12/02	6/14/02	7/15/02
0.065Q	8/20/02	9/12/02	9/16/02	10/15/02
0.065Q	11/07/02	12/12/02	12/16/02	1/15/03
0.075Q	1/16/03	3/12/03	3/14/03	4/15/03
0.075Q	5/15/03	6/12/03	6/16/03	7/15/03

Indicated div.: $0.30

CAPITALIZATION (8/31/02):

	($000)	(%)
Deferred Income Tax	68,891	5.6
Common & Surplus	1,154,948	94.4
Total	1,223,839	100.0

DIVIDEND ACHIEVER STATUS:
Rank: 110   10-Year Growth Rate: 11.83%
Total Years of Dividend Growth: 26

TRADING VOLUME
Thousand Shares

*7 YEAR PRICE SCORE 170.9   *12 MONTH PRICE SCORE 109.5
*NYSE COMPOSITE INDEX=100

RECENT DEVELOPMENTS: For the three months ended 3/1/03, net income climbed 14.0% to $72.7 million from $63.8 million in the corresponding prior-year period. Net sales totaled $1.26 billion, up 13.7% compared with $1.11 billion the previous year. Results for fiscal 2002 benefited from a 2.9% increase in existing-store sales and sales from new stores opened as part of the Company's store expansion program. Gross margin advanced 14.5% to $417.5 million from $364.7 million the year before.

PROSPECTS: Higher energy and insurance costs are being offset by improved gross profit margin driven by the implementation of supply chain improvements. During the current fiscal year, the Company expects to open between 475 and 500 new stores and close approximately 65 existing locations. Meanwhile, FDO is targeting earnings per share growth in the range of 14.0% to 16.0%, along with existing-store sales growth of between 3.0% and 5.0% during the second half of the current fiscal year.

BUSINESS

FAMILY DOLLAR STORES, INC. operated 4,776 discount stores as of 4/10/03. The stores are located in a contiguous 42-state area ranging as far northwest as South Dakota, northeast to Maine, southeast to Florida and southwest to Arizona. The stores' relatively small size, generally 7,500 to 9,500 square feet, gives FDO flexibility to open them in various markets from small rural towns to large urban centers. The stores are located in strip shopping centers or as freestanding buildings convenient to FDO's low- and middle-income customer base. The merchandise, which is generally priced under $10.00, is sold in a no-frills, low overhead, self-service environment.

ANNUAL FINANCIAL DATA

	8/31/02	9/1/01	8/26/00	8/29/99	8/29/98	8/31/97	8/31/96
Earnings Per Share	1.25	1.10	1.00	0.81	0.60	0.44	0.35
Cash Flow Per Share	1.69	1.49	1.31	1.07	0.80	0.61	0.50
Tang. Book Val. Per Share	6.66	5.57	4.66	4.00	3.36	2.75	2.61
Dividends Per Share	0.26	0.23	0.21	0.20	0.17	0.16	0.14
Dividend Payout %	20.4	21.4	21.5	24.1	29.2	36.0	40.9
INCOME STATEMENT (IN MILLIONS):							
Total Revenues	4,162.7	3,665.4	3,132.6	2,751.2	2,361.9	1,995.0	1,714.6
Costs & Expenses	3,744.0	3,299.3	2,807.2	2,484.7	2,161.1	1,844.4	1,591.2
Depreciation & Amort.	77.0	67.7	54.5	43.8	34.8	29.1	24.6
Operating Income	341.6	298.4	270.9	222.7	166.0	121.5	98.8
Income Before Income Taxes	341.6	298.4	270.9	222.7	166.0	121.5	98.8
Income Taxes	124.7	108.9	98.9	82.6	62.7	46.8	38.2
Net Income	216.9	189.5	172.0	140.1	103.3	74.7	60.6
Cash Flow	293.9	257.2	226.5	183.9	138.1	103.8	85.2
Average Shs. Outstg. (000)	174,049	172,774	172,649	172,511	173,224	171,187	170,441
BALANCE SHEET (IN MILLIONS):							
Cash & Cash Equivalents	220.3	21.8	43.6	95.3	134.2	42.5	18.8
Total Current Assets	1,055.9	807.3	750.7	720.0	646.6	544.7	507.9
Net Property	685.6	580.9	487.6	371.1	291.8	231.2	184.6
Total Assets	1,754.6	1,399.7	1,243.7	1,095.3	942.2	780.3	696.8
Total Current Liabilities	530.8	390.3	412.0	378.5	343.3	261.2	234.2
Net Stockholders' Equity	1,154.9	959.0	798.0	690.7	578.2	500.2	445.0
Net Working Capital	525.1	417.0	338.7	341.4	303.4	283.5	273.7
Year-end Shs. Outstg. (000)	173,329	172,036	171,132	172,751	172,204	182,063	170,606
STATISTICAL RECORD:							
Operating Profit Margin %	8.2	8.1	8.6	8.1	7.0	6.1	5.8
Net Profit Margin %	5.2	5.2	5.5	5.1	4.4	3.7	3.5
Return on Equity %	18.8	19.8	21.6	20.3	17.9	14.9	13.6
Return on Assets %	12.4	13.5	13.8	12.8	11.0	9.6	8.7
Price Range	37.25-23.75	31.35-18.38	24.50-14.25	26.75-14.00	22.44-11.50	15.06-6.25	7.00-3.67
P/E Ratio	29.8-19.0	28.5-16.7	24.5-14.2	33.0-17.3	37.4-19.2	34.6-14.4	20.0-10.5
Average Yield %	0.8	0.9	1.1	1.0	1.0	1.5	2.7

Statistics are as originally reported. Adj. for 2-for-1 stk. split, 4/98 & 3-for-2 stk. split, 7/97.

OFFICERS:
H. R. Levine, Chmn., C.E.O.
R. J. Kelly, Vice-Chmn., C.F.O.
R. D. Alexander, Jr., Pres., C.O.O.

INVESTOR CONTACT: George R. Mahoney, Jr., (704) 814-3252

PRINCIPAL OFFICE: 10401 Old Monroe Road, P.O. Box 1017, Charlotte, NC 28201

TELEPHONE NUMBER: (704) 847-6961
FAX: (704) 847-5534
WEB: www.familydollar.com

NO. OF EMPLOYEES: 22,800 full-time (approx.); 16,600 part-time (approx.)
SHAREHOLDERS: 1,875 (approx.)
ANNUAL MEETING: In Jan.
INCORPORATED: DE, Nov., 1969

INSTITUTIONAL HOLDINGS:
No. of Institutions: 309
Shares Held: 144,149,216
% Held: 83.8

INDUSTRY: Variety stores (SIC: 5331)

TRANSFER AGENT(S): Mellon Investor Services, Ridgefield Park, NJ

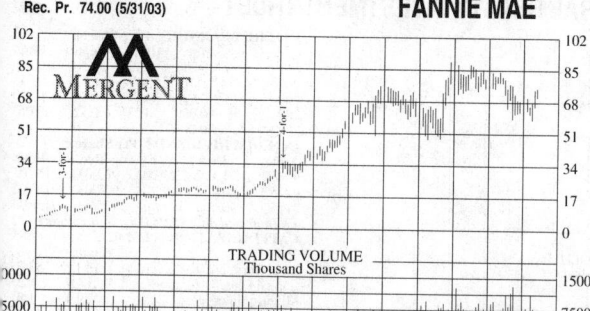

NYSE SYMBOL FNM
Rec. Pr. 74.00 (5/31/03)

FANNIE MAE

YIELD 2.1%
P/E RATIO 14.0

INTERIM EARNINGS (Per Share):

Qtr.	Mar.	June	Sept.	Dec.
1999	0.88	0.91	0.94	0.99
2000	1.02	1.02	1.09	1.13
2001	1.14	1.45	1.32	1.98
2002	1.17	1.44	0.98	0.94
2003	1.93	…	…	…

INTERIM DIVIDENDS (Per Share):

Amt.	Decl.	Ex.	Rec.	Pay.
0.33Q	4/16/02	4/26/02	4/30/02	5/25/02
0.33Q	7/16/02	7/29/02	7/31/02	8/25/02
0.33Q	10/15/02	10/29/02	10/31/02	11/25/02
0.39Q	1/21/03	1/29/03	1/31/03	2/25/03
0.39Q	4/15/03	4/28/03	4/30/03	5/25/03

Indicated div.: $1.56 (Div. Reinv. Plan)

CAPITALIZATION (12/31/02):

	($000)	(%)
Long-Term Debt	468,570,000	96.6
Preferred Stock	2,678,000	0.6
Common & Surplus	13,610,000	2.8
Total	484,858,000	100.0

TRADING VOLUME
Thousand Shares

*7 YEAR PRICE SCORE 123.7   *12 MONTH PRICE SCORE 102.9
*NYSE COMPOSITE INDEX=100

DIVIDEND ACHIEVER STATUS:
Rank: 72   10-Year Growth Rate: 14.36%
Total Years of Dividend Growth: 17

RECENT DEVELOPMENTS: For the quarter ended 3/31/03, net income climbed 60.6% to $1.94 billion from $1.21 billion in the equivalent 2002 quarter. Results are attributed to a surge in net interest income, primarily due to an 11.7% improvement in average net investment balance and a 29 basis point increase in the net interest yield. Results for 2003 and 2002 included purchased options expenses of $624.6 million and $787.2 million, respectively. Net interest income advanced 38.6% to $3.37 billion.

PROSPECTS: Going forward, in light of higher-than-expected first quarter earnings, FNM raised its outlook for 2003 growth in core operating earnings. FNM now expects a moderate increase in its previous projection of 12.0% to 13.0%. FNM expects the pattern of change in its net interest margin to result in stronger quarterly growth in the first half of the year than in the second half. Meanwhile, FMN continues to anticipate that its credit-related losses will rise moderately in 2003.

BUSINESS

FANNIE MAE (formerly Federal National Mortgage Association) is the largest investor in home mortgage loans in the U.S. The Company was established in 1938 as a U.S. government agency to provide supplemental liquidity to the mortgage market and was transformed into a stockholder-owned and privately-managed company by legislation enacted in 1968. FNM provides funds to the mortgage market by purchasing mortgage loans from lenders, thereby replenishing their funds for additional lending. FNM also issues mortgage-backed securities (MBS), primarily in exchange for pools of mortgage loans from lenders, which also increases the liquidity of residential mortgage loans. FNM receives guaranty fees for its guaranty of timely payment of principal of and interest on MBS certificates.

ANNUAL FINANCIAL DATA

	12/31/02	12/31/01	12/31/00	12/31/99	12/31/98	12/31/97	12/31/96
Earnings Per Share	4.53	①②5.89	①4.26	①3.73	①3.26	①2.84	②2.50
Tang. Book Val. Per Share	13.76	15.86	18.58	16.02	13.95	12.34	11.10
Dividends Per Share	1.32	1.20	1.12	1.08	0.96	0.84	0.76
Dividend Payout %	29.1	20.4	26.3	29.0	29.4	29.6	30.4

INCOME STATEMENT (IN MILLIONS):

Total Interest Income	50,853.0	49,170.0	42,781.0	35,495.0	29,995.0	26,378.0	23,772.0
Total Interest Expense	40,287.0	41,080.0	37,107.0	30,601.0	25,885.0	22,429.0	20,180.0
Net Interest Income	10,566.0	8,090.0	5,674.0	4,894.0	4,110.0	3,949.0	3,592.0
Provision for Loan Losses	128.0	cr115.0	cr120.0	cr120.0	cr50.0	100.0	195.0
Non-Interest Income	2,048.0	1,633.0	1,307.0	1,473.0	1,504.0	1,399.0	1,282.0
Non-Interest Expense	5,764.0	1,547.0	1,119.0	1,047.0	1,019.0	911.0	774.0
Income Before Taxes	6,048.0	8,291.0	5,982.0	5,440.0	4,645.0	4,337.0	3,905.0
Net Income	4,619.0	①②6,067.0	①4,416.0	①3,921.0	①3,444.0	①3,068.0	②2,754.0
Average Shs. Outstg. (000)	997,000	1,006,000	1,009,000	1,031,000	1,037,000	1,056,000	1,083,000

BALANCE SHEET (IN MILLIONS):

Securities Avail. For Sale	36,794.0	35,833.0	21,136.0	18,091.0	16,216.0	5,906.0	3,500.0
Total Loans & Leases	185,797.0	707,476.0	610,122.0	523,941.0	414,515.0	316,378.0	286,259.0
Allowance for Credit Losses	cr258.0	2,309.0	2,723.0	1,161.0	cr708.0	362.0	…
Net Loans & Leases	186,055.0	705,167.0	607,399.0	522,780.0	415,223.0	316,016.0	286,259.0
Total Assets	887,515.0	799,791.0	675,072.0	575,167.0	485,014.0	391,673.0	351,041.0
Long-Term Obligations	468,570.0	419,975.0	362,360.0	321,037.0	254,878.0	194,374.0	171,370.0
Total Liabilities	871,227.0	781,673.0	654,234.0	557,538.0	469,561.0	377,880.0	338,268.0
Net Stockholders' Equity	16,288.0	18,118.0	20,838.0	17,629.0	15,453.0	13,793.0	12,773.0
Year-end Shs. Outstg. (000)	989,000	997,000	999,000	1,019,000	1,025,000	1,037,000	1,061,000

STATISTICAL RECORD:

Return on Equity %	28.4	33.5	21.2	22.2	22.3	22.2	21.6
Return on Assets %	0.5	0.8	0.7	0.7	0.7	0.8	0.8
Equity/Assets %	1.8	2.3	3.1	3.1	3.2	3.5	3.6
Non-Int. Exp./Tot. Inc. %	45.7	15.9	16.0	16.4	18.2	17.0	15.9
Price Range	84.10-58.85	87.94-72.08	89.38-47.88	75.88-58.56	76.19-49.56	57.31-36.13	41.63-27.50
P/E Ratio	18.6-13.0	14.9-12.2	21.0-11.2	20.3-15.7	23.4-15.2	20.2-12.7	16.6-11.0
Average Yield %	1.8	1.5	1.6	1.6	1.5	1.8	2.2

Statistics are as originally reported. Adj. for stk. split: 4-for-1, 1/96. ① Bef. extraord. chrg. $340.5 mill.; 12/01; gain $31.5 mill., 12/00; chrg., $9.2 mill.,12/99; $10.7 mill., 12/98; $12.8 mill., 12/97; $29.0 mill., 12/96; $11.4 mill. ② Bef. acctg. gain of $167.9 mill.

OFFICERS:
F. D. Raines, Chmn., C.E.O.
D. H. Mudd, Vice-Chmn., C.O.O.
J. T. Howard, Exec. V.P., C.F.O.
INVESTOR CONTACT: Janis Smith, Inv. Rel. (202) 752-6673
PRINCIPAL OFFICE: 3900 Wisconsin Ave., N.W., Washington, DC 20016-2892

TELEPHONE NUMBER: (202) 752-7000
FAX: (202) 752-4934
WEB: www.fanniemae.com
NO. OF EMPLOYEES: 4,800 (approx.)
SHAREHOLDERS: 26,000 (approx.)
ANNUAL MEETING: In May
INCORPORATED: 1938

INSTITUTIONAL HOLDINGS:
No. of Institutions: 992
Shares Held: 807,454,818
% Held: 81.8
INDUSTRY: Federal & fed.-sponsored credit (SIC: 6111)
TRANSFER AGENT(S): First Chicago Trust Company of New York, Jersey City, NJ

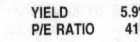

NYSE SYMBOL FRT
Rec. Pr. 33.00 (5/31/03)

FEDERAL REALTY INVESTMENT TRUST

YIELD 5.9%
P/E RATIO 41.3

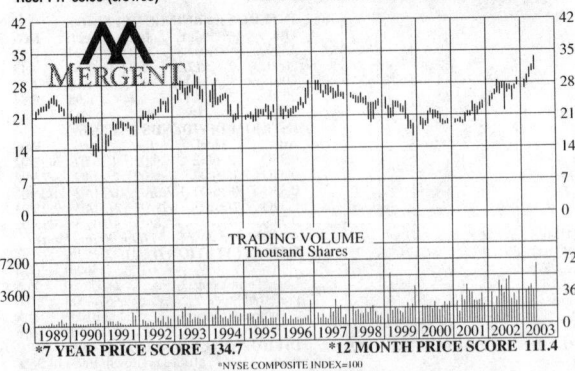

7 YEAR PRICE SCORE 134.7   **12 MONTH PRICE SCORE 111.4**
*NYSE COMPOSITE INDEX=100

INTERIM EARNINGS (Per Share):

Qtr.	Mar.	June	Sept.	Dec.
1999	0.29	0.12	0.30	0.30
2000	0.31	0.51	0.32	0.31
2001	0.32	0.51	0.33	0.35
2002	0.08	0.27	0.32	d0.05
2003	0.26	...	...	...

INTERIM DIVIDENDS (Per Share):

Amt.	Decl.	Ex.	Rec.	Pay.
0.485Q	12/13/02	12/30/02	1/02/03	1/15/03
0.485Q	3/04/03	3/25/03	3/27/03	4/15/03
0.485Q	6/03/03	6/23/03	6/25/03	7/15/03

Indicated div.: $1.94 (Div. Reinv. Plan)

CAPITALIZATION (12/31/02):

	($mill.)	(%)
Long-Term Debt	898.8	53.6
Capital Lease Obligations..	104.4	6.2
Minority Interest	29.4	1.8
Preferred Stock.................	235.0	14.0
Common & Surplus	409.3	24.4
Total	1,676.9	100.0

DIVIDEND ACHIEVER STATUS:
Rank: 272   10-Year Growth Rate: 2.36%
Total Years of Dividend Growth: 35

RECENT DEVELOPMENTS: For the quarter ended 3/31/03, net income was $16.4 million versus income of $7.5 million, before a loss from discontinued operations of $8.8 million, in the equivalent prior-year quarter. Results for 2002 included a restructuring charge of $8.5 million. Total revenues increased 13.4% to $85.3 million. Rental income grew 13.5% to $80.0 million. Same-center property income increased 4.8% year-over-year. FRT reported an occupancy rate of 94.3% at 3/31/03 versus 95.5% at 3/31/02.

PROSPECTS: Going forward, FMT is projecting earnings per diluted share for 2003 of $0.99, with funds from operations of $2.60 per share. Separately, FRT recently announced the status of its three Kmart locations that were closed following the retailer's Chapter 11 bankruptcy filing. Kohl's Corporation is assuming the previous Kmart lease at Fresh Meadows located in Queens, New York. Meanwhile, FMT will re-claim the leases for both the Flourtown, Pennsylvania and Leesburg, Virginia locations.

BUSINESS

FEDERAL REALTY INVESTMENT TRUST is an equity real estate investment trust specializing in the ownership, management, development and redevelopment of shopping centers and street retail properties. As of 5/7/03, the Company's portfolio contained over 15.7 million square feet located in major metropolitan markets across the United States. As of 3/31/03, the operating portfolio was 94.3% occupied by over 2,000 national, regional and local retailers, with no single tenant accounting for more than 2.5% of rental revenue.

ANNUAL FINANCIAL DATA

	12/31/02	12/31/01	12/31/00	12/31/99	12/31/98	12/31/97	12/31/96
Earnings Per Share	① 0.82	1.52	1.35	1.02	0.94	1.14	0.86
Tang. Book Val. Per Share	9.40	8.92	9.31	10.00	10.73	11.59	10.84
Dividends Per Share	1.93	1.89	1.82	1.77	1.73	1.69	1.65
Dividend Payout %	321.7	124.3	134.8	173.5	184.0	148.2	191.8
INCOME STATEMENT (IN MILLIONS):							
Rental Income	298.1	279.9	260.7	245.8	222.2	188.5	164.9
Interest Income	5.2	6.6	7.5	7.6	5.9	6.0	4.4
Total Income	318.8	300.5	279.3	264.7	238.5	204.3	179.1
Costs & Expenses	140.8	106.5	96.2	93.8	89.2	74.1	66.2
Depreciation	64.3	59.9	53.3	50.0	46.0	41.4	38.2
Interest Expense	65.1	69.3	66.4	61.5	55.1	47.3	45.6
Income Before Income Taxes	58.1	73.9	67.1	52.3	48.1	47.8	29.1
Equity Earnings/Minority Int.	d4.1	d5.2	d6.5	d3.9	d3.1	d1.3	d0.4
Net Income	① 54.0	68.8	60.5	48.4	45.0	46.5	28.7
Average Shs. Outstg. (000)	42,882	40,266	39,910	40,638	40,080	38,988	33,573
BALANCE SHEET (IN MILLIONS):							
Cash & Cash Equivalents	23.1	17.6	11.4	11.7	17.2	17.0	11.0
Total Real Estate Investments	1,856.1	1,708.5	1,503.7	1,403.5	1,356.1	1,206.1	924.3
Total Assets	1,999.4	1,838.0	1,621.1	1,534.0	1,484.3	1,316.6	1,035.3
Long-Term Obligations	1,003.2	935.6	809.2	757.9	583.8	551.9	519.5
Total Liabilities	1,355.1	1,245.6	1,153.4	1,032.2	954.4	762.8	646.4
Net Stockholders' Equity	644.3	592.4	467.7	501.8	529.9	553.8	388.9
Year-end Shs. Outstg. (000)	43,535	40,071	39,469	40,201	40,080	39,148	35,886
STATISTICAL RECORD:							
Net Inc.+Depr./Assets %	5.9	7.0	7.0	6.4	6.1	6.7	6.5
Return on Equity %	8.4	11.6	12.9	9.7	8.5	8.4	7.4
Return on Assets %	2.7	3.7	3.7	3.2	3.0	3.5	2.8
Price Range	28.92-21.83	23.96-18.97	22.31-17.75	24.88-16.38	25.94-19.38	28.75-24.50	28.75-20.25
P/E Ratio	35.3-26.6	15.8-12.5	16.5-13.1	24.4-16.1	27.6-20.6	25.2-21.5	33.4-23.5
Average Yield %	7.6	8.8	9.1	6.4	7.6	6.3	6.7

Statistics are as originally reported. ① Excl. inc. fr. disc. opers. of $1.3 mill. & a gain fr. sales of real estate of $9.5 mill.; Incl. restruct. chrg. $22.3 mill.

OFFICERS:
M. S. Ordan, Chmn.
D. C. Wood, Pres., C.E.O.
L. E. Finger, Sr. V.P., C.F.O., Treas.

INVESTOR CONTACT: Andrew Blocher,
V.P., Investor Relations, (301) 998-8166

PRINCIPAL OFFICE: 1626 East Jefferson
Street, Rockville, MD 20852-4041

TELEPHONE NUMBER: (301) 998-8100
FAX: (301) 998-3700
WEB: www.federalrealty.com
NO. OF EMPLOYEES: 270
SHAREHOLDERS: 35,787 (approx.)
ANNUAL MEETING: In May
INCORPORATED: DC, 1962; reincorp., MD,
June, 1999

INSTITUTIONAL HOLDINGS:
No. of Institutions: 147
Shares Held: 27,063,855
% Held: 60.1

INDUSTRY: Real estate investment trusts
(SIC: 6798)

TRANSFER AGENT(S): American Stock
Transfer & Trust Company, New York, NY

FEDERAL SIGNAL CORP.

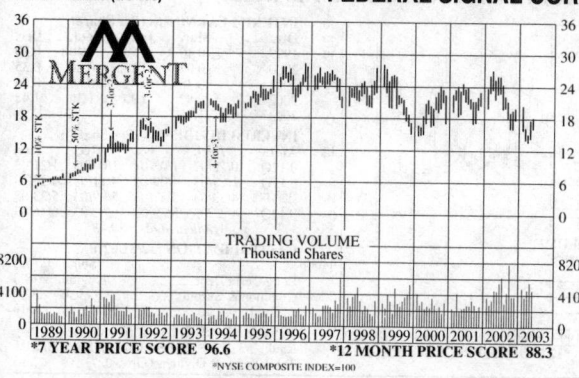

*7 YEAR PRICE SCORE 96.6 *12 MONTH PRICE SCORE 88.3

*NYSE COMPOSITE INDEX=100

INTERIM EARNINGS (Per Share):

Qtr.	Mar.	June	Sept.	Dec.
1999	0.29	0.30	0.30	0.37
2000	0.30	0.36	0.32	0.29
2001	0.26	0.37	0.20	0.21
2002	0.22	0.24	0.28	0.28
2003	0.14	...	...	...

INTERIM DIVIDENDS (Per Share):

Amt.	Decl.	Ex.	Rec.	Pay.
0.20Q	7/18/02	9/10/02	9/12/02	10/01/02
0.20Q	10/17/02	12/11/02	12/13/02	1/03/03
0.20Q	2/06/03	3/11/03	3/13/03	4/01/03
0.20Q	4/17/03	6/10/03	6/12/03	7/01/03

Indicated div.: $0.80 (Div. Reinv. Plan)

CAPITALIZATION (12/31/02):

	($000)	(%)
Long-Term Debt	481,566	52.7
Deferred Income Tax	33,495	3.7
Minority Interest	744	0.1
Common & Surplus	398,065	43.6
Total	913,870	100.0

DIVIDEND ACHIEVER STATUS:
Rank: 141   10-Year Growth Rate: 10.10%
Total Years of Dividend Growth: 15

RECENT DEVELOPMENTS: For the three months ended 3/31/03, net income was $6.5 million compared with income of $9.8 million, before an accounting change charge of $8.0 million, in the corresponding quarter of the previous year. Revenues increased 18.9% to $292.0 million from $245.6 million in the year-earlier period. Environmental Products Group sales improved 13.3% to $84.7 million from $74.8 million the year before.

PROSPECTS: Earnings are being pressured by lower operating margins for Environmental Products and Safety Products, due to weak municipal lawn care sales and a lower margin sales mix. However, FSS is benefiting from higher North American sales of fire rescue equipment and the addition of sales associated with the two refuse truck body acquisitions made during the latter part of 2002.

BUSINESS

FEDERAL SIGNAL CORP. is a manufacturer and worldwide supplier of public safety, signaling and communications equipment, fire trucks, emergency and street sweeping vehicles, parking control equipment, custom on-premise signage, carbide cutting tools, precision punches and related die components. The Environmental Products Group manufactures street sweeping, industrial vacuuming and municipal catch basin/sewer cleaning vehicles, hydroexcavation equipment, glycol recovery vehicles and high-pressure water blasting equipment. The Fire Rescue Group makes commercial fire apparatus and rescue vehicles. The Safety Products Group provides warning, signal and communication products. Standard and special die components and precision parts are manufactured by the Tool Group. Revenues for 2002 were derived: fire rescue; 31.6%, environmental products, 28.0%; safety products, 25.6%; and tool group, 14.8%.

ANNUAL FINANCIAL DATA

	12/31/02	12/31/01	12/31/00	12/31/99	12/31/98	12/31/97	12/31/96
Earnings Per Share	④ 1.01	③ 1.03	② 1.27	1.25	1.30	1.29	① 1.35
Cash Flow Per Share	1.53	1.69	1.90	1.84	1.81	1.73	1.75
Tang. Book Val. Per Share	1.04	1.74	1.82	1.67	1.98	2.45	2.36
Dividends Per Share	0.80	0.78	0.76	0.73	0.70	0.65	0.56
Dividend Payout %	78.7	75.2	59.4	58.6	53.8	50.2	41.5
INCOME STATEMENT (IN MILLIONS):							
Total Revenues	1,057.2	1,072.2	1,106.1	1,061.9	1,002.8	924.9	896.4
Costs & Expenses	951.3	949.9	960.4	928.2	877.5	804.7	775.1
Depreciation & Amort.	24.0	30.3	29.1	27.2	23.6	20.5	18.4
Operating Income	81.9	92.0	116.7	106.5	101.8	99.7	102.9
Income Before Income Taxes	61.1	64.5	84.4	84.4	86.2	84.8	93.4
Income Taxes	14.9	17.9	26.8	26.9	26.8	25.9	31.4
Net Income	④ 46.2	③ 46.6	② 57.7	57.5	59.4	59.0	① 62.0
Cash Flow	70.2	76.8	86.7	84.8	83.0	79.5	80.4
Average Shs. Outstg. (000)	45,939	45,443	45,521	45,958	45,846	45,840	45,952
BALANCE SHEET (IN MILLIONS):							
Cash & Cash Equivalents	9.8	16.9	13.6	8.8	15.3	10.7	12.4
Total Current Assets	394.8	342.3	348.9	346.1	311.2	268.6	267.0
Net Property	143.9	113.7	112.6	115.4	97.4	84.7	82.8
Total Assets	1,168.4	1,014.7	991.1	961.0	836.0	727.9	703.9
Total Current Liabilities	221.9	179.4	288.9	269.5	195.2	227.0	374.6
Long-Term Obligations	481.6	446.6	316.9	307.0	288.8	177.5	34.3
Net Stockholders' Equity	398.1	359.4	357.4	354.0	321.8	299.8	272.8
Net Working Capital	172.9	162.9	60.0	76.7	116.0	41.6	d107.6
Year-end Shs. Outstg. (000)	47,660	45,129	45,304	46,114	45,329	45,606	45,318
STATISTICAL RECORD:							
Operating Profit Margin %	7.8	8.6	10.5	10.0	10.1	10.8	11.5
Net Profit Margin %	4.4	4.3	5.2	5.4	5.9	6.4	6.9
Return on Equity %	11.6	13.0	16.1	16.3	18.5	19.7	22.7
Return on Assets %	4.0	4.6	5.8	6.0	7.1	8.1	8.8
Debt/Total Assets %	41.2	44.0	32.0	31.9	34.5	24.4	4.9
Price Range	27.07-16.00	24.63-17.00	24.13-14.75	28.13-15.06	27.50-20.00	27.50-19.88	28.25-20.88
P/E Ratio	26.8-15.8	23.9-16.5	19.0-11.6	22.5-12.0	21.2-15.4	21.3-15.4	20.9-15.5
Average Yield %	3.7	3.7	3.9	3.4	2.9	2.7	2.3

Statistics are as originally reported. ① Incl. $2.8 mill. after-tax gain on sale of assets. ② Bef. inc. from disc. opers. of $726,000 and accts. change chrg. of $844,000 & incl. pre-tax restruct. chrg. of $3.7 mill. ③ Bef. income from disc. oper. of $983,000 & incl. pre-tax restruct. chrg. of $2.3 mill. ④ Bef. acctg. chng. chrg. of $8.0 mill.

OFFICERS:
J. J. Ross, Chmn., C.E.O.
S. K. Kushner, V.P., C.F.O.

INVESTOR CONTACT: Stephanie K. Kushner, V.P., C.F.O., (630) 954-2020

PRINCIPAL OFFICE: 1415 West 22nd Street, Oak Brook, IL 60523-2004

TELEPHONE NUMBER: (630) 954-2000
FAX: (630) 954-2030
WEB: www.federalsignal.com
NO. OF EMPLOYEES: 7,378 (avg.)
SHAREHOLDERS: 3,716
ANNUAL MEETING: In Apr.
INCORPORATED: IL, Mar., 1901; reincorp., DE, Mar., 1969

INSTITUTIONAL HOLDINGS:
No. of Institutions: 156
Shares Held: 31,798,117
% Held: 66.2

INDUSTRY: Motor vehicles and car bodies (SIC: 3711)

TRANSFER AGENT(S): EquiServe Trust Company, Providence, RI

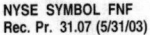

NYSE SYMBOL FNF
Rec. Pr. 31.07 (5/31/03)

FIDELITY NATIONAL FINANCIAL, INC.

| YIELD | 1.5% |
| P/E RATIO | 6.7 |

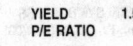

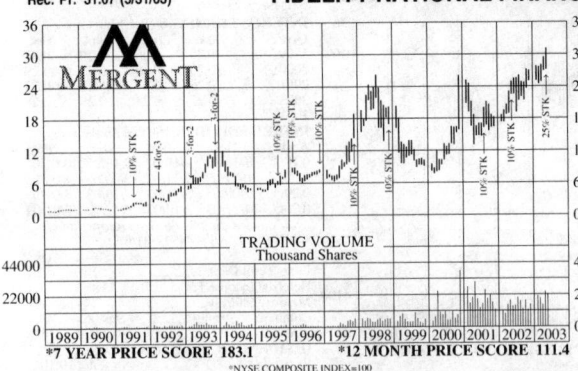

INTERIM EARNINGS (Per Share):

Qtr.	Mar.	June	Sept.	Dec.
1999	0.40	0.50	0.40	0.20
2000	0.04	0.30	0.36	0.35
2001	0.38	0.74	0.69	0.76
2002	0.82	0.90	1.16	1.42
2003	1.15	...	...	...

INTERIM DIVIDENDS (Per Share):

Amt.	Decl.	Ex.	Rec.	Pay.
0.12Q	10/22/02	1/03/03	1/07/03	1/21/03
0.15Q	1/29/03	4/09/03	4/11/03	4/25/03
2% STK	4/23/03	5/27/03	5/09/03	5/23/03
0.12Q	4/23/03	5/29/03	6/02/03	6/16/03

Indicated div.: $0.48

CAPITALIZATION (12/31/02):

	($000)	(%)
Long-Term Debt	493,458	18.0
Common & Surplus	2,253,936	82.0
Total	2,747,394	100.0

DIVIDEND ACHIEVER STATUS:
Rank: 53   10-Year Growth Rate: 16.27%
Total Years of Dividend Growth: 15

*7 YEAR PRICE SCORE 183.1   ***12 MONTH PRICE SCORE 111.4**

*NYSE COMPOSITE INDEX=100

RECENT DEVELOPMENTS: For the quarter ended 3/31/03, net income rose 42.2% to $143.6 million versus $101.0 million in the same period a year-earlier. Total revenues climbed 34.7% to $1.44 billion. Total title premiums grew 32.7% to $967.7 million. Real estate related services jumped 50.3% to $174.2 million. Separately, on 4/22/03, FNF entered into a definitive agreement to acquire the flood insurance business of Mutual of Omaha's subsidiary, Omaha Property and Casualty Insurance Company.

PROSPECTS: On 4/1/03, the Company acquired the financial services division of ALLTEL Information Services, a wholly-owned subsidiary of ALLTEL Corporation, for $775.0 million in cash and $275.0 million in stock. Also, on 3/28/03, FNF signed a definitive agreement to acquire 100.0% of the outstanding common stock of Key Title Company. Lastly, on 3/26/03, FNF completed the acquisition of ANFI, Inc., a provider of title insurance and other real estate related services.

BUSINESS

FIDELITY NATIONAL FINANCIAL, INC., through its principal subsidiaries, is a major U.S. title insurance and diversified real estate-related services company. FNF's title insurance underwriters are Fidelity National Title, Chicago Title, Ticor Title, Security Union Title and Alamo Title. As of 12/31/02, FNF provided title insurance in 49 states, the District of Columbia, Guam, Mexico, Puerto Rico, the U.S. Virgin Islands and Canada. FNF also performs other real estate-related services such as escrow, default management, mortgage loan fulfillment, exchange intermediary services, and homeowners, flood and home warranty insurance. FNF also provides information-based technology applications and processing services to the mortgage and financial services industries through its subsidiary Fidelity Information Services. On 3/20/00, FNF acquired Chicago Title Corporation.

ANNUAL FINANCIAL DATA

	12/31/02	12/31/01	12/31/00	12/31/99	12/31/98	12/31/97	12/31/96
Earnings Per Share	4.30	③ 2.58	1.18	1.50	② 2.14	① 1.25	0.93
Tang. Book Val. Per Share	10.51	13.91	11.58	10.52	9.08	6.55	4.33
Dividends Per Share	0.32	0.27	0.26	0.19	0.17	0.15	0.14
Dividend Payout %	7.5	10.5	22.4	12.3	7.9	12.2	14.9
INCOME STATEMENT (IN MILLIONS):							
Total Premium Income	3,547.7	2,694.5	1,946.2	939.5	910.3	533.2	476.0
Other Income	1,534.9	1,179.6	795.8	412.8	378.2	213.5	161.0
Total Revenues	5,082.6	3,874.1	2,742.0	1,352.2	1,288.5	746.7	636.9
Policyholder Benefits	177.4	134.7	97.3	52.7	59.3	38.7	33.3
Income Before Income Taxes	851.3	518.6	194.1	117.8	175.1	73.4	40.6
Income Taxes	306.5	207.5	85.8	47.0	69.4	32.0	16.2
Equity Earnings/Minority Int.	d13.1	...	...	...	...	...	...
Net Income	531.7	③ 311.2	108.3	70.9	② 105.7	① 41.5	24.3
Average Shs. Outstg. (000)	123,519	121,081	92,166	47,396	50,629	35,742	26,107
BALANCE SHEET (IN MILLIONS):							
Cash & Cash Equivalents	482.6	542.6	263.0	38.6	51.3	54.0	64.0
Premiums Due	233.2	992.7	936.4	79.1	86.7	61.5	65.7
Invst. Assets: Fixed-term	1,564.2	1,216.2	1,188.7	347.1	330.1	217.0	166.3
Invst. Assets: Total	2,565.6	1,803.8	1,685.3	506.9	510.5	326.3	227.7
Total Assets	5,245.7	4,416.0	3,834.0	1,029.2	969.5	600.6	509.3
Long-Term Obligations	493.5	565.7	791.4	226.4	214.6	123.0	148.9
Net Stockholders' Equity	2,253.9	1,638.9	1,106.7	432.5	396.7	196.3	110.3
Year-end Shs. Outstg. (000)	119,632	117,811	95,562	41,122	43,704	29,971	25,477
STATISTICAL RECORD:							
Return on Revenues %	10.5	8.0	4.0	5.2	8.2	5.6	3.8
Return on Equity %	23.6	19.0	9.8	16.4	26.6	21.1	22.1
Return on Assets %	10.1	7.0	2.8	6.9	10.9	6.9	4.8
Price Range	27.18-17.24	25.21-13.03	26.03-7.69	20.33-8.88	26.22-13.79	18.90-6.28	8.94-5.96
P/E Ratio	6.3-4.0	9.8-5.1	22.1-6.5	13.5-5.9	12.3-6.5	15.1-5.0	9.6-6.4
Average Yield %	1.4	1.4	1.6	1.3	0.8	1.2	1.9

Statistics are as originally reported. Adjusted for 5-for-4 stk. split, 5/03; 10.0% stk. div., 5/02, 8/01, 12/98, 12/97. ① Excl. net extraord. loss of $1.7 mill. ② Incl. $7.3 mil in pre-tax merger-related expenses. ③ Excl. acctg. chrg. $5.7 mill.; Incl. after-tax non-recurr. chrgs. $10.0 mill.

OFFICERS:
W. P. Foley II, Chmn., C.E.O.
R. R. Quick, Pres.
A. L. Stinson, Exec. V.P., C.F.O.

INVESTOR CONTACT: Dan Murphy, Dir., Inv. Rel., (949) 622-4333

PRINCIPAL OFFICE: 17911 Von Karman Avenue, Suite 300, Irvine, CA 92614

TELEPHONE NUMBER: (949) 622-4333
FAX: (949) 622-4153
WEB: www.fnf.com

NO. OF EMPLOYEES: 20,800 (approx.)

SHAREHOLDERS: 1,730 (approx.)

ANNUAL MEETING: In June

INCORPORATED: DE, Nov., 1984

FIFTH THIRD BANCORP

YIELD 1.8%
P/E RATIO 20.4

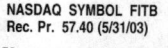

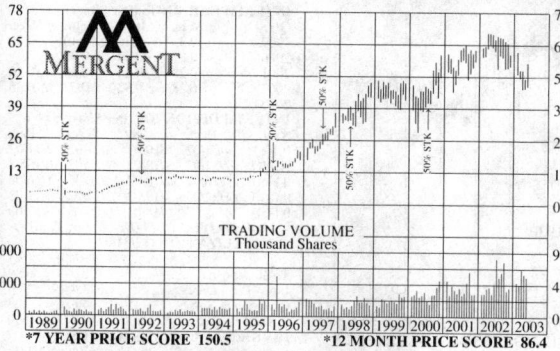

TRADING VOLUME
Thousand Shares

| 1989 | 1990 | 1991 | 1992 | 1993 | 1994 | 1995 | 1996 | 1997 | 1998 | 1999 | 2000 | 2001 | 2002 | 2003 |

*7 YEAR PRICE SCORE 150.5 ***12 MONTH PRICE SCORE 86.4**
*NYSE COMPOSITE INDEX=100

INTERIM EARNINGS (Per Share):

Qtr.	Mar.	June	Sept.	Dec.
2000	0.44	0.41	0.48	0.50
2001	0.51	0.22	0.47	0.65
2002	0.66	0.68	0.70	0.72
2003	0.72	...	...	...

INTERIM DIVIDENDS (Per Share):

Amt.	Decl.	Ex.	Rec.	Pay.
0.23Q	6/18/02	6/26/02	6/28/02	7/16/02
0.26Q	9/17/02	9/26/02	9/30/02	10/15/02
0.26Q	12/17/02	12/27/02	12/31/02	1/15/03
0.26Q	3/18/03	3/27/03	3/31/03	4/15/03

Indicated div.: $1.04 (Div. Reinv. Plan)

CAPITALIZATION (12/31/02):

	($000)	(%)
Total Deposits	52,208,000	75.8
Long-Term Debt	8,178,700	11.9
Preferred Stock	9,000	0.0
Common & Surplus	8,466,000	12.3
Total	68,861,700	100.0

DIVIDEND ACHIEVER STATUS:

Rank: 32 10-Year Growth Rate: 18.78%
Total Years of Dividend Growth: 30

RECENT DEVELOPMENTS:

For the quarter ended 3/31/03, net income increased 7.4% to $419.0 million from $390.2 million in the corresponding prior-year period. Earnings for 2003 and 2002 included net securities gains of $24.9 million and $9.3 million, respectively. Total interest income slipped 1.7% to $1.00 billion. Interest and fees on loans and leases slid 3.2% to $676.1 million. Net interest income rose 9.3% to $706.4 million due to strong earning asset growth. Provision for credit losses increased 54.3% to $84.8 million. Total other operating income improved 18.5% to $588.0 billion, while total operating expenses grew 14.2% to $579.8 million. Results for 2003 were driven by solid loan growth. Separately, on 3/27/03, FITB announced an amendment that extends the termination date of its agreement to acquire Franklin Financial Corporation to 6/30/04. Furthermore, in the event that the Board of Governors of the Federal Reserve System has not granted regulatory approval for the merger on or before 5/31/04, Franklin will have the right to terminate the agreement and receive a termination fee of $27.0 million from FITB.

BUSINESS

FIFTH THIRD BANCORP is a bank holding company headquartered in Cincinnati, Ohio. As of 3/31/03, the Company had $84.29 billion in assets and operated 17 affiliates with 941 full-service banking centers, including 132 Bank Mart® locations open seven days a week inside select grocery stores and 1,880 Jeanie® ATMs in Ohio, Kentucky, Indiana, Florida, Michigan, Illinois, Tennessee and West Virginia. The Company operates four main businesses: Retail, Commercial, Investment Advisors and Fifth Third Processing Solutions. On 3/9/01, FITB acquired Capital Holdings, Inc. On 4/2/01, FITB acquired Old Kent Financial Corporation for about $5.50 billion. On 10/31/01, FITB acquired USB, Inc., a provider of payment processing services.

ANNUAL FINANCIAL DATA

	12/31/02	12/31/01	12/31/00	12/31/99	12/31/98	12/31/97	12/31/96
Earnings Per Share	2.76	② 1.86	① 1.83	① 1.43	① 1.17	1.13	① 0.95
Tang. Book Val. Per Share	12.65	13.09	10.50	8.80	7.94	6.52	6.00
Dividends Per Share	0.95	0.78	0.68	0.56	0.44	0.37	0.32
Dividend Payout %	34.4	41.9	37.2	39.1	37.3	32.5	33.2
INCOME STATEMENT (IN MILLIONS):							
Total Interest Income	4,129.0	4,709.0	3,263.0	2,738.0	2,018.7	1,478.4	1,385.1
Total Interest Expense	1,429.0	2,276.0	1,793.0	1,333.0	1,015.9	733.4	695.9
Net Interest Income	2,700.0	2,433.0	1,470.0	1,405.0	1,002.8	745.0	689.2
Provision for Loan Losses	246.0	236.0	89.0	134.0	109.2	80.3	64.0
Non-Interest Income	2,194.0	1,797.0	1,013.0	877.0	636.2	445.5	368.4
Non-Interest Expense	2,216.0	2,341.0	1,119.0	1,122.0	803.6	506.2	493.3
Income Before Taxes	2,432.0	1,653.0	1,275.0	1,026.0	726.3	603.9	500.3
Equity Earnings/Minority Int.	d38.0	d2.0	...	...	...	...	...
Net Income	1,635.0	① 1,101.0	① 863.0	① 668.0	① 476.1	401.2	① 335.1
Average Shs. Outstg. (000)	592,020	591,316	475,978	471,855	398,007	354,789	350,980
BALANCE SHEET (IN MILLIONS):							
Cash & Due from Banks	1,891.0	2,301.0	985.0	1,213.0	819.9	720.1	808.9
Securities Avail. for Sale	25,776.0	20,732.0	15,800.0	13,043.0	8,453.2	6,426.5	6,268.5
Total Loans & Leases	47,190.0	42,459.0	26,936.0	25,887.0	18,468.2	13,985.8	12,963.0
Allowance for Credit Losses	1,945.0	1,535.0	1,367.0	1,290.0	956.1	748.1	635.4
Net Loans & Leases	45,245.0	40,924.0	25,569.0	24,597.0	17,512.2	13,237.8	12,327.5
Total Assets	80,893.7	71,025.9	45,857.0	41,589.0	28,921.8	21,375.1	20,549.0
Total Deposits	52,208.0	45,854.0	30,948.0	26,083.0	18,780.4	14,914.1	14,374.7
Long-Term Obligations	8,178.7	7,029.9	4,034.0	1,977.0	2,288.2	457.9	277.7
Total Liabilities	71,957.7	62,965.9	40,966.0	37,512.0	25,743.3	19,097.6	18,404.9
Net Stockholders' Equity	8,475.0	7,639.0	4,891.0	4,077.0	3,178.5	2,277.4	2,144.1
Year-end Shs. Outstg. (000)	574,355	582,675	465,652	463,330	400,377	349,256	357,389
STATISTICAL RECORD:							
Return on Equity %	19.3	14.4	17.6	16.4	15.0	17.6	15.6
Return on Assets %	2.0	1.6	1.9	1.6	1.6	1.9	1.6
Equity/Assets %	10.5	10.8	10.7	9.8	11.0	10.7	10.4
Non-Int. Exp./Tot. Inc. %	45.3	55.3	45.1	49.2	49.0	42.5	46.6
Price Range	69.70-55.26	64.77-45.69	60.88-29.53	50.29-38.59	49.42-31.67	37.11-18.00	22.00-12.89
P/E Ratio	25.3-20.0	34.8-24.6	33.3-16.0	35.1-26.9	42.1-27.0	32.9-15.9	23.1-13.5
Average Yield %	1.5	1.4	1.5	1.3	1.1	1.3	1.8

Statistics are as originally reported. Adj. for 50% stk. div.: 7/00, 4/98, 7/97 & 1/96. ① Incl. non-recurr. chrg. $34.0 mill., 12/00; $82.0 mill., 12/99; $89.7 mill., 12/98; $16.6 mill., 12/96. ② Bef. acctg. chrg. $6.8 mill.; incl. pre-tax merg-rel. chrg. $348.6 mill.

OFFICERS:
G. A. Schaefer Jr., Pres., C.E.O.
N. E. Arnold, Exec. V.P., C.F.O.

INVESTOR CONTACT: Neal E. Arnold, Exec. V.P. & C.F.O., (513) 579-4356

PRINCIPAL OFFICE: 38 Fountain Sq. Plaza, Fifth Third Ctr., Cincinnati, OH 45263

TELEPHONE NUMBER: (513) 534-5300
FAX: (513) 579-6246
WEB: www.53.com
NO. OF EMPLOYEES: 20,569 (avg.)
SHAREHOLDERS: 56,300 (approx.)
ANNUAL MEETING: In Mar.
INCORPORATED: OH, 1974

FIRST CHARTER CORPORATION

YIELD	3.8%
P/E RATIO	14.6

*7 YEAR PRICE SCORE 108.4   *12 MONTH PRICE SCORE 102.0
*NYSE COMPOSITE INDEX=100

INTERIM EARNINGS (Per Share):

Qtr.	Mar.	June	Sept.	Dec.
1999	0.33	0.36	0.40	0.36
2000	0.27	d0.09	0.31	0.29
2001	0.28	0.28	0.30	0.26
2002	0.28	0.32	0.30	0.35
2003	0.33	...	...	...

INTERIM DIVIDENDS (Per Share):

Amt.	Decl.	Ex.	Rec.	Pay.
0.18Q	4/24/02	6/19/02	6/21/02	7/11/02
0.185Q	7/24/02	9/18/02	9/20/02	10/10/02
0.185Q	10/16/02	12/18/02	12/20/02	1/16/03
0.185Q	1/22/03	3/19/03	3/21/03	4/17/03
0.185Q	4/23/03	6/18/03	6/20/03	7/17/03

Indicated div.: $0.74 (Div. Reinv. Plan)

CAPITALIZATION (12/31/02):

	($000)	(%)
Total Deposits	2,322,647	62.9
Long-Term Debt	1,042,440	28.3
Common & Surplus	324,686	8.8
Total	3,689,773	100.0

DIVIDEND ACHIEVER STATUS:

Rank: 69	10-Year Growth Rate: 14.48%
Total Years of Dividend Growth:	10

RECENT DEVELOPMENTS: For the three months ended 3/31/03, net income climbed 13.5% to $9.9 million from $8.8 million in the prior year. Interest income slipped 7.5% to $45.8 million, while interest expense fell 12.6% to $18.8 million. Net interest income slid 3.5% to $26.6 million from $27.6 million the previous year, primarily due to lower interest income on earning assets due to lower interest rates. Provision for loan losses was essentially unchanged at $2.1 million versus a year earlier. Non-interest income jumped 42.5% to $15.6 million from $10.9 million the year before. Non-interest expense was up 7.2% to $26.1 million from $24.3 million in 2002. Total assets increased 17.2% to $3.99 billion from $3.41 billion in the prior year. Total deposits were $2.49 billion, up 12.8% from $2.21 billion in the first quarter of 2002.

BUSINESS

FIRST CHARTER CORPORATION is a regional financial services company with assets of $3.99 billion as of 3/31/03. FCTR is the holding company for First Charter Bank, which operates 53 financial centers, five insurance offices and 93 ATMs located in 17 counties throughout the piedmont and western half of North Carolina. First Charter also operates one mortgage origination office in Virginia. The Company provides businesses and individuals with a broad range of financial services, including banking, financial planning, funds management, investments, insurance, mortgages and employee benefit programs.

ANNUAL FINANCIAL DATA

	12/31/02	12/31/01	12/31/00	12/31/99	12/31/98	12/31/97	12/31/96
Earnings Per Share	1.30	1.12	① 0.79	1.45	① 0.50	0.90	1.17
Tang. Book Val. Per Share	10.80	10.06	9.79	12.96	13.34	8.39	7.86
Dividends Per Share	0.73	0.72	0.69	0.68	0.58	0.52	0.48
Dividend Payout %	56.2	64.3	87.3	46.9	116.0	57.2	41.4
INCOME STATEMENT (IN MILLIONS)							
Total Interest Income	196.4	215.3	216.2	136.7	136.5	56.0	40.6
Total Interest Expense	83.2	109.9	108.3	67.3	70.6	24.8	17.3
Net Interest Income	113.2	105.4	107.9	69.4	65.9	31.2	23.3
Provision for Loan Losses	8.3	4.5	7.6	3.4	2.4	2.7	0.9
Non-Interest Income	47.6	38.8	30.6	18.2	13.7	9.5	6.3
Non-Interest Expense	97.8	87.6	92.7	45.9	59.2	25.6	16.1
Income Before Taxes	54.8	52.1	38.2	38.4	18.0	12.3	12.6
Net Income	39.8	35.3	① 24.8	26.1	① 9.2	8.4	8.9
Average Shs. Outstg. (000)	30,702	31,661	31,580	18,053	18,572	9,339	7,593
BALANCE SHEET (IN MILLIONS)							
Cash & Due from Banks	162.1	134.1	71.2	60.0	41.9	33.1	31.3
Securities Avail. for Sale	1,129.2	1,077.4	441.0	342.1	331.8	177.0	132.1
Total Loans & Leases	2,072.7	1,955.1	2,157.6	1,426.5	1,422.7	524.1	360.7
Allowance for Credit Losses	27.5	26.0	28.7	17.5	15.7	8.3	5.3
Net Loans & Leases	2,045.3	1,929.1	2,129.0	1,409.0	1,407.0	515.8	355.4
Total Assets	3,745.9	3,332.7	2,932.2	1,894.3	1,864.4	761.7	546.9
Total Deposits	2,322.6	2,162.9	1,998.2	1,149.5	1,123.0	621.4	455.2
Long-Term Obligations	1,042.4	808.5	570.0	492.0	469.9	53.3	27.3
Total Liabilities	3,421.3	3,023.4	2,622.9	1,666.6	1,618.4	683.9	487.4
Net Stockholders' Equity	324.7	309.3	309.3	227.7	246.0	77.8	59.4
Year-end Shs. Outstg. (000)	30,069	30,743	31,601	17,572	18,442	9,269	7,561
STATISTICAL RECORD:							
Return on Equity %	12.3	11.4	8.0	11.5	3.8	10.8	14.9
Return on Assets %	1.1	1.1	0.8	1.4	0.5	1.1	1.6
Equity/Assets %	8.7	9.3	10.5	12.0	13.2	10.2	10.9
Non-Int. Exp./Tot. Inc. %	60.8	60.8	67.0	52.3	74.4	63.1	54.3
Price Range	20.81-15.00	18.75-13.06	17.50-12.00	24.88-13.63	27.00-12.50	27.00-17.71	18.75-14.79
P/E Ratio	16.0-11.5	16.7-11.7	22.1-15.2	17.2-9.4	54.0-25.0	30.0-19.7	16.1-12.7
Average Yield %	4.1	4.5	4.7	3.5	2.9	2.3	2.9

Statistics are as originally reported. Adj. for 6-for-5 stk split, 1997. ① Incl. pre-tax restructuring and merger-related chgs. of $16.3 mill., 2000; $18.2 mill., 1998.

OFFICERS:
J. R. Davis, Jr., Chmn.
M. R. Coltrane, Vice-Chmn.
L. M. Kimbrough, Pres., C.E.O.
R. O. Bratton, Exec. V.P., C.F.O., Treas.

INVESTOR CONTACT: Robert O. Bratton, Chief Financial Officer, (704) 688-4473

PRINCIPAL OFFICE: 10200 David Taylor Drive, Charlotte, NC 28262-2373

TELEPHONE NUMBER: (704) 688-4300
FAX: (704) 788-0403
WEB: www.firstcharter.com

NO. OF EMPLOYEES: 902

SHAREHOLDERS: 7,883

ANNUAL MEETING: In Apr.

INCORPORATED: NC, 1983

INSTITUTIONAL HOLDINGS:
No. of Institutions: 69
Shares Held: 4,746,360
% Held: 15.8

INDUSTRY: National commercial banks (SIC: 6021)

TRANSFER AGENT(S): Registrar & Transfer Company, Cranford, NJ

NYSE SYMBOL FCF
Rec. Pr. 12.99 (5/31/03)

FIRST COMMONWEALTH FINANCIAL CORPORATION

YIELD 4.8%
P/E RATIO 15.3

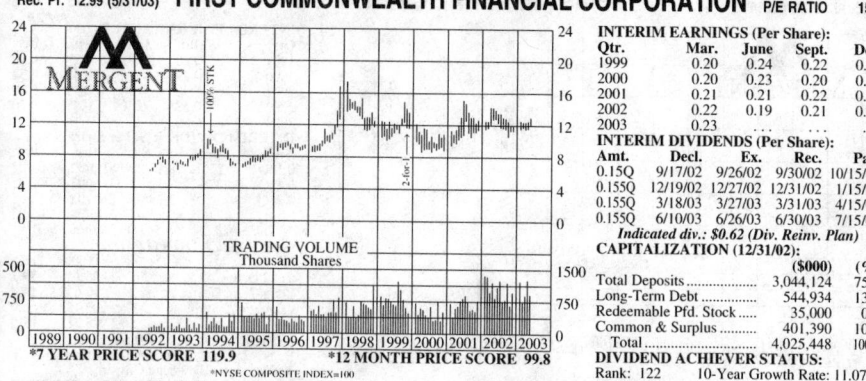

7 YEAR PRICE SCORE 119.9   **12 MONTH PRICE SCORE 99.8**
*NYSE COMPOSITE INDEX=100

INTERIM EARNINGS (Per Share):

Qtr.	Mar.	June	Sept.	Dec.
1999	0.20	0.24	0.22	0.21
2000	0.20	0.23	0.20	0.19
2001	0.21	0.21	0.22	0.23
2002	0.22	0.19	0.21	0.22
2003	0.23	...	...	...

INTERIM DIVIDENDS (Per Share):

Amt.	Decl.	Ex.	Rec.	Pay.
0.15Q	9/17/02	9/26/02	9/30/02	10/15/02
0.155Q	12/19/02	12/27/02	12/31/02	1/15/03
0.155Q	3/18/03	3/27/03	3/31/03	4/15/03
0.155Q	6/10/03	6/26/03	6/30/03	7/15/03

Indicated div.: $0.62 (Div. Reinv. Plan)

CAPITALIZATION (12/31/02):

	($000)	(%)
Total Deposits	3,044,124	75.6
Long-Term Debt	544,934	13.5
Redeemable Pfd. Stock	35,000	0.9
Common & Surplus	401,390	10.0
Total	4,025,448	100.0

DIVIDEND ACHIEVER STATUS:

Rank: 122   10-Year Growth Rate: 11.07%
Total Years of Dividend Growth: 15

RECENT DEVELOPMENTS: For the quarter ended 3/31/03, net income soared 74.2% to $13.3 million compared with $7.6 million in the corresponding period of 2002. Results for 2003 and 2002 included intangible amortization of $7,000 and $120,000, and litigation settlements of $610,000 and $8.0 million, respectively. Net interest income slipped 3.1% to $36.8 million from $38.0 million in the previous year. Provision for credit losses grew 18.6% to $3.5 million versus $2.9 million the year before.

PROSPECTS: Near-term results for net interest income may continue to be negatively affected by continued low or declining interest rates. In an attempt to partially mitigate its exposure to low and decreasing interest rates, the Company sold debt securities with an average remaining life of one year and the proceeds were reinvested in securities with an average life of three years. Meanwhile, FCF's provision for credit losses has risen due to higher loan values and continued economic uncertainty.

BUSINESS

FIRST COMMONWEALTH FINANCIAL CORPORATION is a financial services holding company with $4.53 billion in assets, as of 3/31/03. The Company operates in 18 counties in western and central Pennsylvania through First Commonwealth Bank, a Pennsylvania chartered bank. Financial services and insurance products are also provided by First Commonwealth Trust Company, First Commonwealth Financial Advisors, Inc. and First Commonwealth Insurance Agency. The Company also operates First Commonwealth Systems Corporation, a data processing subsidiary, First Commonwealth Professional Resources, Inc., a support services subsidiary, and jointly owns Commonwealth Trust Credit Life Insurance Company, a credit life reinsurance company.

ANNUAL FINANCIAL DATA

	12/31/02	12/31/01	12/31/00	12/31/99	12/31/98	12/31/97	12/31/96
Earnings Per Share	☐ 0.74	0.86	0.82	0.88	0.55	0.70	0.63
Tang. Book Val. Per Share	6.67	6.33	5.74	4.93	5.74	6.17	5.89
Dividends Per Share	0.60	0.58	0.56	0.49	0.44	0.40	0.36
Dividend Payout %	81.1	67.4	68.3	55.7	80.0	57.5	57.1
INCOME STATEMENT (IN MILLIONS):							
Total Interest Income	275.6	308.9	311.9	297.5	283.4	199.8	182.3
Total Interest Expense	122.7	167.2	174.5	152.7	148.3	102.8	88.3
Net Interest Income	152.9	141.7	137.3	144.9	135.1	97.1	94.0
Provision for Loan Losses	12.2	11.5	10.0	9.5	15.0	6.9	4.5
Non-Interest Income	28.9	32.4	33.4	25.9	26.3	19.8	13.7
Non-Interest Expense	125.4	105.0	99.5	93.6	100.2	65.9	63.6
Income Before Taxes	52.4	65.4	61.5	72.6	46.2	44.1	39.7
Net Income	☐ 43.5	50.2	47.2	53.0	34.0	30.5	27.6
Average Shs. Outstg. (000)	58,742	58,118	57,619	60,569	61,666	43,932	43,908
BALANCE SHEET (IN MILLIONS):							
Cash & Due from Banks	81.1	98.1	90.7	92.7	96.6	60.1	69.4
Securities Avail. for Sale	1,482.8	1,469.1	1,238.2	1,144.0	1,042.6	396.6	244.4
Total Loans & Leases	2,609.4	2,569.2	2,492.9	2,503.7	2,382.2	1,937.7	1,778.1
Allowance for Credit Losses	35.3	35.5	35.6	37.2	39.7	36.6	50.1
Net Loans & Leases	2,574.1	2,533.8	2,457.2	2,466.5	2,342.5	1,901.1	1,728.0
Total Assets	4,524.7	4,583.5	4,372.3	4,340.8	4,096.8	2,929.3	2,584.6
Total Deposits	3,044.1	3,093.2	3,064.1	2,948.8	2,931.1	2,242.5	2,104.8
Long-Term Obligations	544.9	629.2	621.9	603.4	630.9	193.1	40.9
Total Liabilities	4,123.4	4,213.5	4,038.2	4,054.2	3,741.4	2,657.5	2,323.3
Net Stockholders' Equity	401.4	370.1	334.2	286.7	355.4	271.8	261.4
Year-end Shs. Outstg. (000)	58,963	58,452	58,195	58,143	61,876	44,092	44,388
STATISTICAL RECORD:							
Return on Equity %	10.8	13.6	14.1	18.5	9.6	11.2	10.6
Return on Assets %	1.0	1.1	1.1	1.2	0.8	1.0	1.1
Equity/Assets %	8.9	8.1	7.6	6.6	8.7	9.3	10.1
Non-Int. Exp./Tot. Inc. %	69.0	60.3	58.2	54.8	62.1	56.4	59.0
Price Range	14.23-10.55	15.10-9.44	12.13-8.63	14.88-10.06	17.41-11.25	16.81-8.56	9.88-8.38
P/E Ratio	19.2-14.3	17.6-11.0	14.8-10.5	16.9-11.4	31.6-20.5	24.2-12.3	15.7-13.3
Average Yield %	16.7	14.3	12.7	14.2	26.0	18.3	14.5

Statistics are as originally reported. ☐ Incl. $6.1 mill. restr. chg. & $8.0 mill. litigation settlement.

OFFICERS:
E. J. Trimarchi, Chmn.
J. A. Glass, Vice-Chmn.
J. E. O'Dell, Pres., C.E.O.

INVESTOR CONTACT: Shareholder Relations, (800) 331-4107

PRINCIPAL OFFICE: 22 North Sixth Street, Indiana, PA 15701

TELEPHONE NUMBER: (724) 349-7220
WEB: www.fcfbank.com

NO. OF EMPLOYEES: 1,463

SHAREHOLDERS: 13,500 (approx.)

ANNUAL MEETING: In Apr.

INCORPORATED: PA, Nov., 1983

INSTITUTIONAL HOLDINGS:
No. of Institutions: 65
Shares Held: 11,443,872
% Held: 19.4

INDUSTRY: National commercial banks (SIC: 6021)

TRANSFER AGENT(S): The Bank of New York, New York, NY

FIRST FEDERAL CAPITAL CORP.

YIELD 2.8%
P/E RATIO 11.2

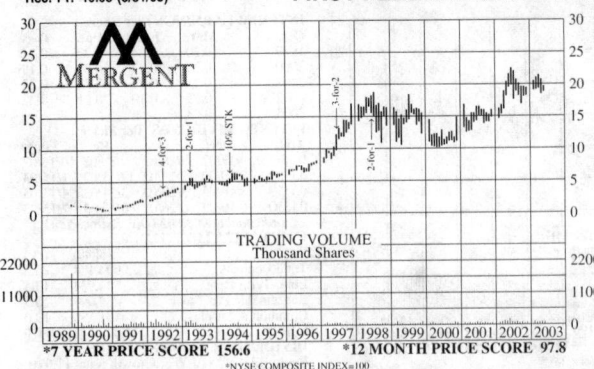

INTERIM EARNINGS (Per Share):

Qtr.	Mar.	June	Sept.	Dec.
1999	0.26	0.32	0.29	0.30
2000	0.29	0.30	0.32	0.34
2001	0.32	0.34	0.36	0.49
2002	0.38	0.40	0.45	0.50
2003	0.40	...	...	...

INTERIM DIVIDENDS (Per Share):

Amt.	Decl.	Ex.	Rec.	Pay.
0.13Q	7/25/02	8/13/02	8/15/02	9/05/02
0.13Q	10/22/02	11/12/02	11/14/02	12/05/02
0.13Q	1/30/03	2/18/03	2/20/03	3/13/03
0.14Q	4/23/03	5/13/03	5/15/03	6/05/03
Indicated div.: $0.56 (Div. Reinv. Plan)				

CAPITALIZATION (12/31/02):

	($000)	(%)
Total Deposits	2,355,148	79.1
Long-Term Debt	417,613	14.0
Common & Surplus	205,452	6.9
Total	2,978,213	100.0

TRADING VOLUME
Thousand Shares

*7 YEAR PRICE SCORE 156.6   *12 MONTH PRICE SCORE 97.8
*NYSE COMPOSITE INDEX=100

DIVIDEND ACHIEVER STATUS:
Rank: 25   10-Year Growth Rate: 20.42%
Total Years of Dividend Growth: 11

RECENT DEVELOPMENTS: For the three months ended 3/31/03, net income increased 4.5% to $8.0 million compared with $7.7 million in the corresponding year-earlier period. Net interest income slipped 1.9% to $18.3 million from $18.6 million the previous year. Provision for loan losses was $379,000 versus $647,000 the year before. Total non-interest income climbed 38.9% to $17.9 million. The significant gain in non-interest income primarily reflected a 72.4% increase in mortgage banking revenue, due to a 200.0% increase in loans sold during the quarter in

response to record low interest rates for single-family residential loans. Separately, on 4/10/03, FTFC announced an agreement to acquire Liberty Bancshares, Inc., of St. Paul, Minnesota, for approximately $78.0 million in stock and cash. FTFC expects to complete the transaction in the third quarter of 2003, subject to regulatory approvals. As of 3/31/03, Liberty had $405.0 million in assets, $259.0 million in loans, and $365.0 million in deposit liabilities. FTFC expects the transaction to be neutral to earnings per share in the first year and accretive thereafter.

BUSINESS

FIRST FEDERAL CAPITAL CORP., through its First Federal Capital Bank subsidiary, is a savings bank with assets of $3.09 billion, as of 3/31/03. FTFC's primary business is community banking, which includes attracting deposits from and making loans to the general public, businesses, government, and professional customers. The Company's primary market areas include communities located in the western, south-central, and eastern portions of Wisconsin and the northern portion of Illinois, as well as contiguous counties in Iowa and Minnesota. As of 4/17/03, FTFC maintained 91 retail and mortgage loan production offices, which included 49 in-store supermarket banking locations throughout its market areas.

ANNUAL FINANCIAL DATA

	12/31/02	12/31/01	12/31/00	12/31/99	12/31/98	12/31/97	12/31/96
Earnings Per Share	① 1.73	③ 1.51	② 1.25	1.17	③ 0.98	① 0.89	① ④ 0.50
Tang. Book Val. Per Share	6.67	6.81	6.09	5.06	4.80	4.74	4.26
Dividends Per Share	0.51	0.47	0.42	0.34	0.27	0.23	0.21
Dividend Payout %	29.5	31.1	33.6	29.1	27.5	26.4	41.1
INCOME STATEMENT (IN MILLIONS):							
Total Interest Income	161.3	171.5	161.4	130.1	118.7	115.0	104.0
Total Interest Expense	79.7	108.3	101.9	76.0	71.5	70.3	63.7
Net Interest Income	81.5	63.2	59.5	54.1	47.2	44.7	40.3
Provision for Loan Losses	3.5	1.8	1.0	0.4	0.3	0.5	...
Non-Interest Income	63.6	49.5	35.6	35.2	31.4	24.3	19.8
Non-Interest Expense	87.4	67.1	58.3	54.3	47.6	40.2	44.2
Income Before Taxes	54.3	43.8	35.9	34.6	30.7	28.3	15.9
Net Income	① 34.9	③ 28.4	② 23.1	22.4	③ 19.4	① 17.4	① ④ 10.1
Average Shs. Outstg. (000)	20,164	18,871	18,472	19,138	19,864	19,691	20,043
BALANCE SHEET (IN MILLIONS):							
Cash & Due from Banks	84.5	70.8	25.4	65.6	43.6	29.9	24.6
Total Loans & Leases	2,103.6	1,857.1	1,778.5	1,545.0	1,183.6	1,201.6	1,138.8
Allowance for Credit Losses	2.9	5.8	6.0	6.4	6.1	7.7	32.8
Net Loans & Leases	2,100.6	1,851.3	1,772.5	1,538.6	1,177.5	1,193.9	1,106.0
Total Assets	3,025.6	2,717.7	2,352.7	2,084.6	1,786.5	779.8	1,515.4
Total Deposits	2,355.1	2,029.3	1,699.3	1,471.3	1,460.1	382.0	1,024.1
Long-Term Obligations	417.6	467.4	370.8	469.6	189.8	275.8	383.6
Total Liabilities	2,820.2	2,525.3	2,206.2	1,957.3	1,663.8	670.4	1,420.0
Net Stockholders' Equity	205.5	192.4	146.5	127.3	122.7	109.4	95.4
Year-end Shs. Outstg. (000)	19,704	20,201	18,345	18,403	18,361	18,381	18,381
STATISTICAL RECORD:							
Return on Equity %	17.0	14.8	15.8	17.6	15.8	15.9	10.6
Return on Assets %	1.2	1.0	1.0	1.1	1.1	2.2	0.7
Equity/Assets %	6.8	7.1	6.2	6.1	6.9	14.0	6.3
Non-Int. Exp./Tot. Inc. %	60.2	59.5	61.2	60.8	60.6	58.3	73.6
Price Range	22.50-14.62	16.81-12.50	14.88-10.13	18.38-10.50	18.75-10.88	17.00-7.83	8.17-6.00
P/E Ratio	13.0-8.5	11.1-8.3	11.9-8.1	15.7-9.0	19.1-11.1	19.2-8.9	16.2-11.9
Average Yield %	2.7	3.2	3.4	2.4	1.8	1.9	2.9

Statistics are as originally reported. Adj. for stk. splits: 2-for-1, 6/98; 3-for-2, 6/97. ① Incl. loss on sale of invest. securities: $166,264, 2002; $725,000, 1997; $311,151, 1996; $28,580, 1995. ② Incl. gain on sale of real estate invests. of $1.2 mill. ③ Incl. gain on sale of invest. securities of $13,199, 2001; $343,000, 1998. ④ Incl. FDIC spec. assess. chrg. of $5.9 mill.

OFFICERS:
T. W. Schini, Chmn.
D. A. Nordeen, Vice-Chmn.
J. C. Rusch, Pres., C.E.O., C.O.O.

INVESTOR CONTACT: Michael Dosland, Sr. V.P., C.F.O., (608) 784-8000

PRINCIPAL OFFICE: 605 State Street, La Crosse, WI 54601-1868

TELEPHONE NUMBER: (608) 784-8000
FAX: (608) 784-6627
WEB: www.firstfed.com
NO. OF EMPLOYEES: 1,213
SHAREHOLDERS: 1,410 (record); 3,103 (approx. beneficial)
ANNUAL MEETING: In Apr.
INCORPORATED: WI, July, 1989

INSTITUTIONAL HOLDINGS:
No. of Institutions: 54
Shares Held: 5,362,336
% Held: 26.8

INDUSTRY: Federal savings institutions (SIC: 6035)

TRANSFER AGENT(S): Wells Fargo Shareowner Services, St. Paul, MN

FIRST FINANCIAL BANCORP

YIELD 3.6%
P/E RATIO 16.0

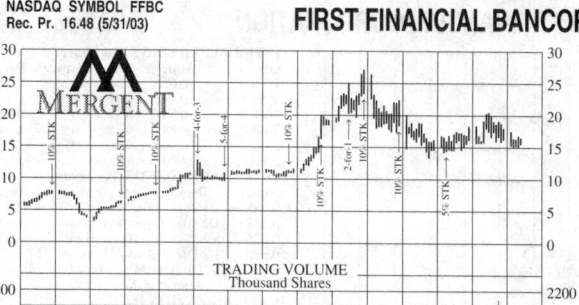

*7 YEAR PRICE SCORE 112.5   *12 MONTH PRICE SCORE 92.4

*NYSE COMPOSITE INDEX=100

INTERIM EARNINGS (Per Share):

Qtr.	Mar.	June	Sept.	Dec.
1999	0.27	0.18	0.30	0.29
2000	0.29	0.30	0.31	0.30
2001	0.29	0.21	0.26	0.16
2002	0.27	0.29	0.24	0.26
2003	0.24	...	...	...

INTERIM DIVIDENDS (Per Share):

Amt.	Decl.	Ex.	Rec.	Pay.
0.15Q	8/27/02	9/04/02	9/06/02	10/01/02
0.15Q	11/26/02	12/04/02	12/06/02	1/02/03
0.15Q	2/25/03	3/05/03	3/07/03	4/01/03
0.15Q	5/27/03	6/04/03	6/06/03	7/01/03

Indicated div.: $0.60 (Div. Reinv. Plan)

CAPITALIZATION (12/31/02):

	($000)	(%)
Total Deposits	2,922,434	81.2
Long-Term Debt	290,051	8.1
Redeemable Pfd. Stock	10,000	0.3
Common & Surplus	377,603	10.5
Total	3,600,088	100.0

DIVIDEND ACHIEVER STATUS:

Rank: 139   10-Year Growth Rate: 10.12%
Total Years of Dividend Growth: 19

RECENT DEVELOPMENTS: For the quarter ended 3/31/03, net earnings increased 14.3% to $10.6 million compared with $12.4 million in the corresponding period of the previous year. Total interest income decreased 14.2% to $53.8 million from $62.7 million in the year-earlier period. Total interest expense fell 23.4% to $16.6 million from $21.7 million the year before. Net interest income slipped 9.3% to $37.2 million from $41.0 million in the prior-year period, primarily due to net interest margin compression. Net inter-

est margin was 4.37% compared with 4.72% the previous year, a decrease of 35 basis points. The margin compression was due to continued downward repricing of assets. Provision of loan losses dropped 43.0% to $3.2 million from $5.6 million the year before. Total non-interest income declined 6.2% to $13.9 million from $14.8 million a year earlier. Total non-interest expense rose 1.0% to $31.8 million from $31.5 million in 2002.

BUSINESS

FIRST FINANCIAL BANCORP is a financial holding company that engages in the business of commercial banking and other financial activities through eight banking affiliates in Ohio, Michigan, Kentucky, and Indiana with a total of 105 retail banking centers as as an investment-advisor affiliate. The range of banking services provided by FFBC's subsidiaries to their customers include commercial lending, real estate lending, consumer credit, credit card, and other personal loan financing. In addition, the institutions offer deposit services that include interest-bearing and non-interest-bearing deposit accounts and time deposits. Most subsidiaries provide safe deposit facilities. Trust and asset management services are provided by FFBC's subsidiaries, excluding the savings banks, the finance company, the insurance agency, and the service corporation.

ANNUAL FINANCIAL DATA

	12/31/02	12/31/01	12/31/00	12/31/99	12/31/98	12/31/97	12/31/96
Earnings Per Share	③ 1.05	③ 0.91	② 1.19	① 1.02	1.05	0.96	0.91
Tang. Book Val. Per Share	7.58	7.47	7.77	6.75	6.20	6.80	6.92
Dividends Per Share	0.60	0.59	0.57	0.52	0.47	0.43	0.39
Dividend Payout %	57.1	65.1	48.0	51.0	45.1	44.9	42.7
INCOME STATEMENT (IN MILLIONS):							
Total Interest Income	241.0	289.7	315.5	282.4	219.5	192.2	171.3
Total Interest Expense	78.3	126.8	145.4	117.2	88.4	76.8	69.7
Net Interest Income	162.8	163.0	170.1	165.2	131.1	115.4	101.6
Provision for Loan Losses	16.2	26.8	11.3	9.2	6.1	4.7	3.4
Non-Interest Income	56.7	54.2	45.0	41.3	34.3	27.0	22.1
Non-Interest Expense	132.5	125.0	116.8	120.7	92.7	77.7	71.3
Income Before Taxes	70.8	65.4	87.0	76.6	66.6	59.9	49.0
Net Income	③ 48.2	③ 43.3	② 58.2	① 50.3	44.1	40.3	33.9
Average Shs. Outstg. (000)	46,001	47,479	48,862	49,335	42,014	42,196	37,127
BALANCE SHEET (IN MILLIONS):							
Cash & Due from Banks	181.8	211.1	182.1	225.8	136.5	142.3	110.8
Securities Avail. for Sale	605.3	595.6	564.8	490.1	313.2	332.6	290.7
Total Loans & Leases	2,748.6	2,874.2	3,012.1	3,040.5	2,269.5	1,978.6	1,701.7
Allowance for Credit Losses	48.7	48.8	43.4	43.5	32.3	29.1	24.1
Net Loans & Leases	2,699.9	2,825.5	2,968.7	2,997.0	2,237.2	1,949.5	1,677.6
Total Assets	3,730.0	3,854.8	3,932.5	3,940.7	2,871.1	2,636.1	2,261.7
Total Deposits	2,922.4	3,085.1	3,151.4	2,991.2	2,326.6	2,230.2	1,880.0
Long-Term Obligations	290.1	260.3	205.2	161.8	105.3	41.1	6.5
Total Liabilities	3,352.3	3,470.3	3,537.4	3,568.2	2,569.2	2,349.9	2,003.2
Net Stockholders' Equity	377.6	384.5	395.1	372.5	301.9	286.3	258.5
Year-end Shs. Outstg. (000)	45,004	46,600	45,987	49,213	41,813	42,071	37,358
STATISTICAL RECORD:							
Return on Equity %	12.8	11.3	14.7	13.5	14.6	14.1	13.1
Return on Assets %	1.3	1.1	1.5	1.3	1.5	1.5	1.5
Equity/Assets %	10.1	10.0	10.0	9.5	10.5	10.9	11.4
Non-Int. Exp./Tot. Inc. %	60.4	57.5	54.3	58.4	56.1	54.6	57.6
Price Range	20.50-15.61	18.25-14.17	20.12-13.33	26.41-17.32	27.17-18.89	19.97-10.91	11.63-10.25
P/E Ratio	19.5-14.9	20.1-15.6	16.9-11.2	25.9-17.0	25.9-18.0	20.9-11.4	12.7-11.2
Average Yield %	3.3	3.7	3.4	2.4	2.1	2.8	3.6

Statistics are as originally reported. Adj. for stk. splits: 2-for-1, 6/1/98; 10% div., 1/3/00, 10/1/97 & 11/1/96; 5%, 4/2/01. ① Incl. restr. chrg. of $6.9 mill. ② Incl. restr. credit of $353,000. ③ Incl. amort. of intangibles of $2.7 mill., 2001; $847,000, 2002.

OFFICERS:
B. E. Leep, Chmn.
S. N. Pontius, Pres., C.E.O.
C. D. Lefferson, Sr. V.P., C.F.O.

INVESTOR CONTACT: Richard E. Weinman, Sr. V.P., 425-7548

PRINCIPAL OFFICE: 300 High Street, Hamilton, OH 45011

TELEPHONE NUMBER: (513) 867-4700
FAX: (513) 425-7654
WEB: www.ffbc-oh.com

NO. OF EMPLOYEES: 1,815 (avg.)

SHAREHOLDERS: 4,547

ANNUAL MEETING: In Apr.

INCORPORATED: OH, Aug., 1982

INSTITUTIONAL HOLDINGS:
No. of Institutions: 63
Shares Held: 16,032,402
% Held: 35.6

INDUSTRY: National commercial banks
(SIC: 6021)

TRANSFER AGENT(S): Registrar and Transfer Company, Cranford, NJ

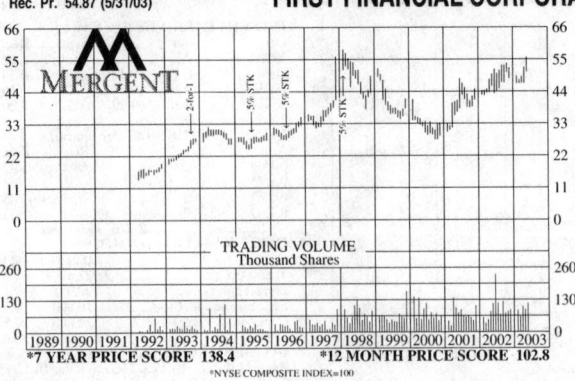

FIRST FINANCIAL CORPORATION

NASDAQ SYMBOL THFF
Rec. Pr. 54.87 (5/31/03)

YIELD 2.5%
P/E RATIO 13.5

7 YEAR PRICE SCORE 138.4   **12 MONTH PRICE SCORE 102.8**
*NYSE COMPOSITE INDEX=100

MERGENT

INTERIM EARNINGS (Per Share):

Qtr.	Mar.	June	Sept.	Dec.
1998	0.62	0.58	0.62	0.71
1999	0.71	0.77	0.80	0.83
2000	0.80	0.90	0.89	0.86
2001	0.88	0.85	0.92	0.91
2002	0.98	0.96	0.90	1.17
2003	1.04	...	...	...

INTERIM DIVIDENDS (Per Share):

Amt.	Decl.	Ex.	Rec.	Pay.
0.56S	5/16/01	6/08/01	6/12/01	7/02/01
0.58S	11/27/01	12/05/01	12/07/01	1/02/02
0.62S	5/22/02	6/10/02	6/12/02	7/02/02
0.62S	11/20/02	12/04/02	12/06/02	1/02/03
0.68S	5/22/03	6/09/03	6/11/03	7/01/03

Indicated div.: $1.36

CAPITALIZATION (12/31/02):

	($000)	(%)
Total Deposits	1,434,654	68.3
Long-Term Debt	423,290	20.2
Common & Surplus	241,971	11.5
Total	2,099,915	100.0

DIVIDEND ACHIEVER STATUS:

Rank: 9   10-Year Growth Rate: 24.93%
Total Years of Dividend Growth: 10

RECENT DEVELOPMENTS: For the three months ended 3/31/03, net income increased 4.5% to $7.0 million from $6.7 million in the corresponding period a year earlier. Net interest income slipped 2.8% to $18.9 million from $19.5 million the previous year. Provision for loan losses climbed 15.3% to $2.2 million from $1.9 million a year ago. Non-interest income jumped 30.9% to $8.1 million from $6.2 million the year before. This sharp increase was fueled by strong mortgage banking activity, which resulted in additional income from capitalized mortgage servicing rights and higher loan servicing and origination fees. Non-interest expense was $15.4 million, up 4.0% compared with $14.8 million in the prior year. Net interest margin declined to 4.02% versus 4.09% in 2002.

BUSINESS

FIRST FINANCIAL CORPORA-TION is a multi-bank holding company with $2.11 billion in assets as of 3/31/03. The Company offers a wide variety of financial services, including commercial, mortgage and consumer lending, lease financing, trust account services, and depositor services through its wholly-owned subsidiaries located in Indiana and Illinois. In May 2001, the Company acquired Forrest Sherer Inc., a full-line insurance agency headquartered in Terre Haute, Indiana.

ANNUAL FINANCIAL DATA

	12/31/02	12/31/01	12/31/00	12/31/99	12/31/98	12/31/97	12/31/96
Earnings Per Share	4.20	3.56	3.45	3.10	2.58	2.58	2.28
Tang. Book Val. Per Share	33.86	30.19	28.57	24.64	25.54	23.59	21.43
Dividends Per Share	1.20	1.12	1.02	0.88	0.79	0.67	0.54
Dividend Payout %	28.6	31.5	29.6	28.4	30.6	25.8	23.7
INCOME STATEMENT (IN MILLIONS):							
Total Interest Income	136.3	144.7	146.4	133.6	129.1	122.4	115.8
Total Interest Expense	58.1	74.1	80.6	66.8	66.4	62.1	57.8
Net Interest Income	78.2	70.5	65.8	66.8	62.7	60.3	58.0
Provision for Loan Losses	9.5	6.6	4.4	4.7	5.4	5.4	4.5
Non-Interest Income	30.5	21.5	13.6	12.0	10.6	9.0	7.8
Non-Interest Expense	63.3	53.3	42.7	43.5	42.6	39.6	39.3
Income Before Taxes	35.8	32.1	32.3	30.5	25.4	24.2	22.1
Net Income	28.6	24.2	23.2	21.6	18.6	18.1	16.0
Average Shs. Outstg. (000)	6,826	6,800	6,730	6,964	7,206	7,016	7,013
BALANCE SHEET (IN MILLIONS):							
Cash & Due from Banks	96.0	68.2	68.8	58.1	54.9	53.8	66.7
Securities Avail. for Sale	511.5	463.5	568.4	594.3	633.4	528.0	582.7
Total Loans & Leases	1,433.2	1,349.2	1,299.0	1,193.9	1,113.7	1,006.9	920.0
Allowance for Credit Losses	21.9	19.0	20.0	19.9	18.3	14.6	12.0
Net Loans & Leases	1,411.3	1,330.1	1,278.9	1,173.9	1,095.3	992.3	908.0
Total Assets	2,169.7	2,041.9	2,043.3	1,905.2	1,849.8	1,634.9	1,619.6
Total Deposits	1,434.7	1,313.7	1,322.6	1,256.1	1,260.4	1,194.5	1,175.2
Long-Term Obligations	423.3	426.1	489.1	382.3	96.1	37.2	70.6
Total Liabilities	1,927.8	1,824.4	1,852.0	1,736.5	1,667.6	1,469.5	1,469.3
Net Stockholders' Equity	242.0	217.5	191.2	168.7	182.2	165.5	150.4
Year-end Shs. Outstg. (000)	6,809	6,844	6,694	6,845	7,134	7,016	7,016
STATISTICAL RECORD:							
Return on Equity %	11.8	11.1	12.1	12.8	10.2	10.9	10.6
Return on Assets %	1.3	1.2	1.1	1.1	1.0	1.1	1.0
Equity/Assets %	11.2	10.7	9.4	8.9	9.8	10.1	9.3
Non-Int. Exp./Tot. Inc. %	58.3	58.0	53.8	55.3	58.1	57.2	59.6
Price Range	53.68-42.60	48.50-30.00	41.25-27.50	52.00-34.50	58.45-37.88	56.07-31.43	35.24-27.44
P/E Ratio	12.8-10.1	13.6-8.4	12.0-8.0	16.8-11.1	22.7-14.7	21.7-12.2	15.5-12.0
Average Yield %	2.5	2.9	3.0	2.0	1.6	1.5	1.7

Statistics are as originally reported. Adj. for 5% stk. div., 1/23/98 & 7/1/96.

OFFICERS:
D. E. Smith, Chmn., Pres., C.E.O.
N. L. Lowery, Vice-Chmn.
M. A. Carty, C.F.O., Treas.
J. W. Perry, Sec.

INVESTOR CONTACT: Michael A. Carty, Treasurer, (812) 238-6264

PRINCIPAL OFFICE: One First Financial Plaza, Terre Haute, IN 47807

TELEPHONE NUMBER: (812) 238-6000
FAX: (812) 232-5336
WEB: www.first-online.com

NO. OF EMPLOYEES: 834

SHAREHOLDERS: 1,000 (approx.)

ANNUAL MEETING: In Apr.

INCORPORATED: IN, Aug., 1984

INSTITUTIONAL HOLDINGS:
No. of Institutions: 40
Shares Held: 1,960,070
% Held: 28.0

INDUSTRY: State commercial banks (SIC: 6022)

TRANSFER AGENT(S): First Financial Corporation, Terre Haute, IN

FIRST FINANCIAL HOLDINGS, INC.

YIELD 2.6%
P/E RATIO 14.3

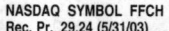

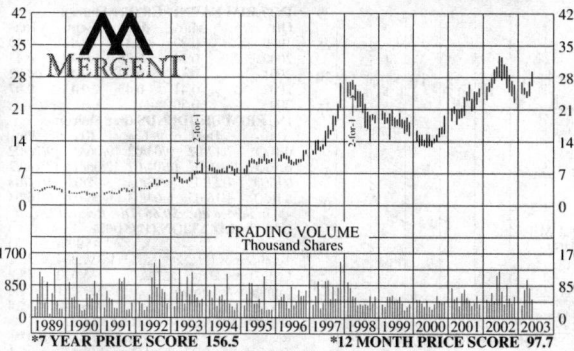

*7 YEAR PRICE SCORE 156.5   *12 MONTH PRICE SCORE 97.7
*NYSE COMPOSITE INDEX=100

INTERIM EARNINGS (Per Share):

Qtr.	Dec.	Mar.	June	Sept.
1999-00	0.35	0.36	0.38	0.38
2000-01	0.36	0.42	0.43	0.43
2001-02	0.49	0.54	0.51	0.50
2002-03	0.50	0.54	...	...

INTERIM DIVIDENDS (Per Share):

Amt.	Decl.	Ex.	Rec.	Pay.
0.17Q	4/26/02	5/08/02	5/10/02	5/24/02
0.17Q	7/26/02	8/07/02	8/09/02	8/23/02
0.19Q	10/25/02	11/06/02	11/08/02	11/22/02
0.19Q	2/03/03	2/05/03	2/07/03	2/21/03
0.19Q	4/25/03	5/07/03	5/09/03	5/23/03

Indicated div.: $0.76 (Div. Reinv. Plan)

CAPITALIZATION (9/30/02):

	($000)	(%)
Total Deposits	1,440,271	66.0
Long-Term Debt	577,000	26.4
Common & Surplus	165,648	7.6
Total	2,182,919	100.0

DIVIDEND ACHIEVER STATUS:
Rank: 44   10-Year Growth Rate: 17.46%
Total Years of Dividend Growth: 10

RECENT DEVELOPMENTS: For the three months ended 3/31/03, net income slipped 4.5% to $7.2 million compared with $7.5 million in the equivalent quarter of 2002. Results for 2003 and 2002 included net gains on the sale of loans of $2.6 million and $818,000, respectively. Results for 2003 also included a net gain on the sale of investments and mortgage-backed securities of $860,000. Net interest income declined 6.3% to $19.7 million from $21.0 million the previous year. Provision for loan losses was $1.7 mil-

lion versus $1.5 million in 2002. Total interest income was $33.8 million, down 12.3% from $38.6 million the year before. Total interest expense decreased 19.6% to $14.1 million versus $17.6 million in the prior-year period. Separately, on 3/24/03, the Company announced it acquired Woodruff and Company, Inc, a Columbia, South Carolina-based independent insurance agency that specializes in commercial property and casualty insurance accounts. Terms of the transaction were not disclosed.

BUSINESS

FIRST FINANCIAL HOLDINGS, INC., with assets of $2.21 billion as of 3/31/03, is a savings and loan holding company. Through its subsidiaries, First Federal Savings and Loan Association of Charleston, the Company offers a complete line of banking and related financial services to consumer and commercial customers through its 44 retail bank sales offices. The Company also engages in full-service brokerage, property, casualty, life and health insurance, third-party administrative services, trust and fiduciary services, reinsurance of private mortgage insurance and certain passive investment activities through its family of companies: First Southeast Investor Services, Inc., First Southeast Insurance Services, Inc. and First Southeast Fiduciary & Trust Services, Inc. FFCH's market area extends along the South Carolina coast from Hilton Head through Charleston and Myrtle Beach to coastal North Carolina and into Florence, South Carolina.

ANNUAL FINANCIAL DATA

	9/30/02	9/30/01	9/30/00	9/30/99	9/30/98	9/30/97	9/30/96
Earnings Per Share	2.04	1.64	1.47	1.40	①1.20	1.12	②0.56
Tang. Book Val. Per Share	12.55	11.71	10.35	9.43	9.16	8.21	7.45
Dividends Per Share	0.70	0.64	0.58	0.50	0.44	0.38	0.33
Dividend Payout %	34.3	38.7	39.5	35.7	36.7	33.6	59.4
INCOME STATEMENT (IN MILLIONS):							
Total Interest Income	154.0	173.3	161.6	140.8	136.3	121.8	111.1
Total Interest Expense	71.3	102.9	98.9	80.4	81.7	72.9	66.0
Net Interest Income	82.7	70.4	62.8	60.4	54.7	48.9	45.1
Provision for Loan Losses	5.9	5.0	2.7	2.8	2.4	2.4	1.8
Non-Interest Income	31.0	24.9	18.3	15.3	13.4	12.3	10.1
Non-Interest Expense	63.9	55.1	47.9	43.3	40.2	36.4	42.2
Income Before Taxes	43.8	35.2	30.4	29.7	25.5	22.4	11.1
Net Income	28.2	22.6	19.9	19.3	①16.9	14.1	②7.0
Average Shs. Outstg. (000)	13,832	13,733	13,559	13,786	14,101	12,678	12,690
BALANCE SHEET (IN MILLIONS):							
Total Loans & Leases	1,964.6	1,955.8	1,906.8	1,813.1	1,610.4	1,447.1	1,318.9
Allowance for Credit Losses	39.8	50.5	68.3	71.0	45.4	41.6	38.8
Net Loans & Leases	1,924.8	1,905.3	1,838.5	1,742.2	1,565.0	1,405.5	1,280.1
Total Assets	2,264.7	2,325.7	2,256.5	2,070.8	1,839.7	1,712.9	1,546.1
Total Deposits	1,440.3	1,395.8	1,241.3	1,219.8	1,164.4	1,069.3	1,061.6
Long-Term Obligations	577.0	625.0	766.5	594.5	471.5	439.3	332.2
Total Liabilities	2,099.0	2,168.8	2,118.7	1,944.9	1,714.5	1,608.1	1,451.4
Net Stockholders' Equity	165.6	156.9	137.9	125.9	125.2	104.8	94.8
Year-end Shs. Outstg. (000)	13,196	13,396	13,318	13,353	13,659	12,756	12,716
STATISTICAL RECORD:							
Return on Equity %	17.0	14.4	14.5	15.3	13.5	13.5	7.4
Return on Assets %	1.2	1.0	0.9	0.9	0.9	0.8	0.5
Equity/Assets %	7.3	6.7	6.1	6.1	6.8	6.1	6.1
Non-Int. Exp./Tot. Inc. %	56.3	57.9	59.1	57.1	59.0	59.5	76.5
Price Range	32.75-22.58	26.45-17.75	19.69-12.75	21.00-14.50	27.38-14.00	26.75-11.13	12.13-8.75
P/E Ratio	16.1-11.1	16.1-10.8	13.4-8.7	15.0-10.4	22.8-11.7	24.0-10.1	21.8-15.8
Average Yield %	2.5	2.9	3.5	2.8	2.1	2.0	3.2

Statistics are as originally reported. Adj. for 2-for-1 split, 3/30/98. ① Bef. $340,000 extraord. loss. ② Incls. special assessment chg. of $7.0 mill.

OFFICERS:
A. T. Hood, Pres., C.E.O.
S. E. Baham, Sr. V.P., C.F.O.

INVESTOR CONTACT: Susan E. Baham, Sr. V.P., C.F.O., (843) 529-5601

PRINCIPAL OFFICE: 34 Broad Street, Charleston, SC 29401

TELEPHONE NUMBER: (843) 529-5933
FAX: (843) 529-5929
WEB: www.firstfinancialholdings.com

NO. OF EMPLOYEES: 763

SHAREHOLDERS: 2,441 (approx., record)

ANNUAL MEETING: In Jan.

INCORPORATED: DE, Sept., 1987

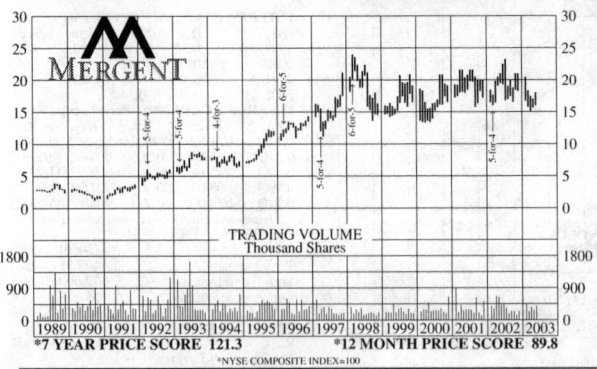

INTERIM EARNINGS (Per Share):

Qtr.	Mar.	June	Sept.	Dec.
1999	0.29	0.31	0.42	0.40
2000	0.34	0.38	0.40	0.43
2001	0.42	0.42	0.43	d0.02
2002	0.41	0.43	0.43	0.07
2003	0.30	…	…	…

INTERIM DIVIDENDS (Per Share):

Amt.	Decl.	Ex.	Rec.	Pay.
0.16Q	7/17/02	9/04/02	9/06/02	9/16/02
0.16Q	10/16/02	12/04/02	12/06/02	12/16/02
0.165Q	1/22/03	3/03/03	3/05/03	3/14/03
0.165Q	4/16/03	6/04/03	6/06/03	6/16/03

Indicated div.: $0.66 (Div. Reinv. Plan)

CAPITALIZATION (12/31/02):

	($000)	(%)
Total Deposits	1,339,204	70.2
Long-Term Debt	346,532	18.2
Common & Surplus	221,211	11.6
Total	1,906,947	100.0

DIVIDEND ACHIEVER STATUS:
Rank: 40   10-Year Growth Rate: 18.07%
Total Years of Dividend Growth: 11

TRADING VOLUME
Thousand Shares

*7 YEAR PRICE SCORE 121.3   *12 MONTH PRICE SCORE 89.8
*NYSE COMPOSITE INDEX=100

RECENT DEVELOPMENTS: For the three months ended 3/31/03, net earnings decreased 25.9% to $4.7 million compared with $6.4 million in the corresponding quarter of the previous year. Net interest income advanced 13.7% to $19.5 million from $17.2 million the year before. Provision for loan losses more than doubled to $6.2 million from $2.6 million in the year-earlier period. This increase was primarily attributed to the net charge-off of $2.5 million on a loan identified as non-performing in the fourth quarter of 2002 and the recent detection of the under-collateralization of a home builder's loan for which the provision for loan loss was increased. Total interest income declined 4.7% to $30.1 million from $31.6 million in the prior-year period. Total interest expense dropped 26.5% to $10.6 million from $14.4 million in 2002. Total non-interest income climbed 11.4% to $13.9 million from $12.5 million in the previous year. Total non-interest expense increased 15.6% to $19.8 million from $17.1 million the year before. Net interest margin increased to 3.73% versus 3.58% the year before.

BUSINESS

FIRST INDIANA CORPORATION is a full-service financial services company offering comprehensive financial solutions to businesses and individuals. FINB is the holding company for First Indiana Bank, N.A., a national bank headquartered in Indianapolis, and Somerset Financial Services, an accounting and consulting firm. As of 3/31/03, First Indiana Bank has $2.27 billion in assets and owned 33 offices in Central Indiana, plus construction and consumer loan offices in Indiana, Arizona, Florida, Illinois, North Carolina, and Ohio. The Company also originates consumer loans in 46 states through a national independent agent network. Through Somerset Financial Services and FirstTrust Indiana, a division of First Indiana Bank, the Company offers a full array of tax planning, accounting, consulting, wealth management, and investment advisory and trust services.

ANNUAL FINANCIAL DATA

	12/31/02	12/31/01	12/31/00	12/31/99	12/31/98	12/31/97	12/31/96
Earnings Per Share	1.34	1.25	1.55	1.42	1.15	1.09	① 0.85
Tang. Book Val. Per Share	13.40	12.69	11.87	11.31	10.45	9.66	8.43
Dividends Per Share	0.64	0.51	0.45	0.42	0.38	0.32	0.30
Dividend Payout %	47.8	41.0	28.9	29.4	33.3	29.4	35.3
INCOME STATEMENT (IN MILLIONS):							
Total Interest Income	125.9	157.1	172.8	146.0	135.8	127.3	125.5
Total Interest Expense	52.1	83.1	95.0	75.6	73.1	64.4	63.8
Net Interest Income	73.8	74.0	77.8	70.4	62.8	63.0	61.7
Provision for Loan Losses	20.8	15.2	9.8	9.4	9.8	10.7	10.8
Non-Interest Income	46.8	44.0	25.6	27.0	23.8	18.0	17.8
Non-Interest Expense	66.5	70.5	53.7	52.3	45.8	41.1	47.3
Income Before Taxes	33.3	32.3	39.9	35.6	31.0	29.2	21.5
Net Income	21.2	20.0	24.8	22.3	19.1	17.7	① 13.7
Average Shs. Outstg. (000)	15,809	15,999	15,997	16,050	16,571	16,314	16,146
BALANCE SHEET (IN MILLIONS):							
Securities Avail. for Sale	138.5	147.9	158.8	103.2	113.3	106.1	101.4
Total Loans & Leases	1,837.6	1,756.5	1,972.1	1,896.9	1,741.2	1,479.4	1,317.0
Allowance for Credit Losses	44.5	37.1	221.2	223.4	222.6	130.8	101.4
Net Loans & Leases	1,793.2	1,719.4	1,750.8	1,673.4	1,518.5	1,348.5	1,215.6
Total Assets	2,125.2	2,046.7	2,085.9	1,979.8	1,792.2	1,613.4	1,496.4
Total Deposits	1,339.2	1,379.5	1,400.0	1,312.1	1,227.9	1,107.6	1,095.5
Long-Term Obligations	346.5	296.6	336.8	366.9	327.2	257.5	215.5
Total Liabilities	1,904.0	1,837.6	1,887.1	1,802.7	1,626.2	1,455.6	1,352.1
Net Stockholders' Equity	221.2	209.0	198.8	177.1	166.0	153.0	138.7
Year-end Shs. Outstg. (000)	15,540	15,443	15,574	15,654	15,879	15,835	16,451
STATISTICAL RECORD:							
Return on Equity %	9.6	9.6	12.5	12.6	11.5	11.6	9.9
Return on Assets %	1.0	1.0	1.2	1.1	1.1	1.1	0.9
Equity/Assets %	10.4	10.2	9.5	8.9	9.3	9.5	9.3
Non-Int. Exp./Tot. Inc. %	55.2	59.7	52.0	53.7	52.9	50.8	59.4
Price Range	23.25-16.00	21.60-15.74	20.85-13.30	20.90-14.20	24.00-13.60	21.17-11.17	14.33-10.56
P/E Ratio	17.3-11.9	17.3-12.6	13.4-8.6	14.8-10.0	20.8-11.8	19.5-10.3	16.9-12.5
Average Yield %	3.3	2.7	2.6	2.4	2.0	2.0	2.4

Statistics are as originally reported. Adj. for stk. splits: 5-for-4, 2/02 & 2/97; 6-for-5, 3/98. ① Incl. gain of $1.2 mill. on the sale of subsidiary.

OFFICERS:
R. H. McKinney, Chmn.
M. M. McKinney, Vice-Chmn., C.E.O.
O. B. Melton Jr., Pres., C.O.O.
INVESTOR CONTACT: Investor Relations, (317) 472-2184
PRINCIPAL OFFICE: 135 North Pennsylvania Street, Indianapolis, IN 46204

TELEPHONE NUMBER: (317) 269-1200
FAX: (317) 269-1341
WEB: www.firstindiana.com
NO. OF EMPLOYEES: 723 (avg.)
SHAREHOLDERS: 1,752 (approx. record)
ANNUAL MEETING: In Mar.
INCORPORATED: IN, 1986

INSTITUTIONAL HOLDINGS:
No. of Institutions: 45
Shares Held: 3,563,158
% Held: 22.3
INDUSTRY: Federal savings institutions (SIC: 6035)
TRANSFER AGENT(S): Computershare Investor Services, Chicago, IL

FIRST MIDWEST BANCORP, INC.

YIELD	2.6%
P/E RATIO	15.4

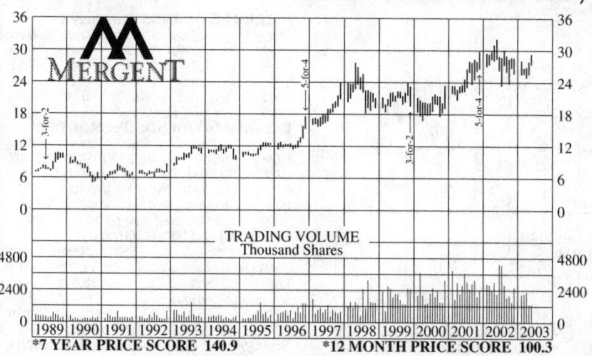

TRADING VOLUME Thousand Shares

*7 YEAR PRICE SCORE 140.9   ***12 MONTH PRICE SCORE 100.3**

INTERIM EARNINGS (Per Share):

Qtr.	Mar.	June	Sept.	Dec.
1999	0.35	0.34	0.34	0.31
2000	0.38	0.38	0.36	0.35
2001	0.43	0.42	0.40	0.38
2002	0.45	0.47	0.47	0.47
2003	0.48	...	...	...

INTERIM DIVIDENDS (Per Share):

Amt.	Decl.	Ex.	Rec.	Pay.
0.17Q	8/22/02	9/25/02	9/27/02	10/22/02
0.19Q	11/21/02	12/24/02	12/27/02	1/21/03
0.19Q	2/20/03	3/26/03	3/28/03	4/22/03
0.19Q	5/21/03	6/25/03	6/27/03	7/22/03

Indicated div.: $0.76 (Div. Reinv. Plan)

CAPITALIZATION (12/31/02):

	($000)	(%)
Total Deposits	4,172,954	70.7
Long-Term Debt	1,237,408	21.0
Common & Surplus	491,953	8.3
Total	5,902,315	100.0

DIVIDEND ACHIEVER STATUS:
Rank: 109   10-Year Growth Rate: 11.85%
Total Years of Dividend Growth: 10

RECENT DEVELOPMENTS: For the quarter ended 3/31/03, net income rose 3.0% to $22.7 million compared with $22.1 million in the corresponding year-earlier period. Net interest income fell 3.9% to $52.1 million, reflecting a decline in net interest margin. FMBI attributed the margin contraction to the repricing of earnings assets in the low interest rate environment and the acceleration of cash flows due to refinance-related prepayments on mortgage-backed securities. Provision for loan losses was $2.5 million versus $5.1 million in 2002. Total noninterest income rose 10.0%

to $17.8 million from $16.1 million the year before and included a nonrecurring gain of $1.2 million. Separately, on 4/15/03, FMBI announced that it has signed an agreement to acquire a branch of The Northern Trust Company, a subsidiary of Northern Trust Corporation. Going forward, earnings growth will rely upon FMBI maintaining favorable trends in asset generation, funding mix, asset quality, fee growth and expense management. Accordingly, FMBI anticipates mid-single digit growth in earnings per share for the full year 2003.

BUSINESS

FIRST MIDWEST BANCORP, INC. is a bank holding company with assets of approximately $6.05 billion as of 3/31/03. FMBI operates two wholly-owned subsidiaries, First Midwest Bank and First Midwest Insurance Company. First Midwest Bank is engaged in commercial and retail banking and offers a range of lending, depository, and related financial services including accepting deposits; commercial and industrial, consumer and real estate lending; collections; trust and investment management services; safe deposit box operations; and other banking services tailored for individual, commercial and industrial, and governmental customers. As of 4/23/03, First Midwest Bank operated 70 banking offices primarily in northern Illinois. First Midwest Insurance Company operates as a reinsurer of credit life, accident, and health insurance sold through First Midwest Bank, primarily in conjunction with the consumer lending operations.

ANNUAL FINANCIAL DATA

	12/31/01	12/31/00	12/31/99	12/31/98	12/31/97	12/31/96
Earnings Per Share	1.86	1.63	1.46	1.34	①0.98	①1.02	②1.05
Tang. Book Val. Per Share	10.07	9.18	8.75	7.19	8.32	8.97	8.27
Dividends Per Share	0.68	0.64	0.58	0.51	0.48	0.43	0.35
Dividend Payout %	36.6	39.3	39.3	38.3	48.9	41.7	33.3
INCOME STATEMENT (IN MILLIONS):							
Total Interest Income	329.7	385.2	421.5	361.3	364.6	270.5	237.2
Total Interest Expense	110.9	180.8	231.9	168.6	177.0	125.8	114.4
Net Interest Income	218.8	204.4	189.6	192.7	187.6	144.7	122.7
Provision for Loan Losses	15.4	19.1	9.1	5.8	5.5	8.8	7.5
Non-Interest Income	67.0	68.9	63.2	58.3	55.5	37.2	31.4
Non-Interest Expense	148.1	145.4	144.4	149.8	158.8	113.8	94.3
Income Before Taxes	122.3	108.8	99.3	95.4	78.7	59.4	52.4
Net Income	90.2	82.1	75.5	70.9	①54.7	①38.8	②33.7
Average Shs. Outstg. (000)	48,415	50,401	51,604	53,071	55,881	37,946	32,031
BALANCE SHEET (IN MILLIONS):							
Cash & Due from Banks	195.2	155.8	166.4	155.4	156.5	118.0	107.6
Securities Avail. for Sale	1,986.2	1,771.6	2,130.1	2,033.2	1,979.1	974.5	770.3
Total Loans & Leases	3,406.8	3,372.3	3,233.2	2,962.5	2,664.4	2,333.3	2,085.3
Allowance for Credit Losses	47.9	47.7	45.1	42.6	43.3	37.3	30.1
Net Loans & Leases	3,358.9	3,324.6	3,188.1	2,919.8	2,621.1	2,295.9	2,055.1
Total Assets	5,980.5	5,667.9	5,906.5	5,511.6	5,192.9	3,614.2	3,119.2
Total Deposits	4,173.0	4,193.9	4,252.2	4,001.2	4,050.5	2,796.0	2,260.7
Long-Term Obligations	1,237.4	971.9	1,145.9	1,077.7	623.9	438.0	493.1
Total Liabilities	5,488.6	5,220.7	5,459.8	5,142.3	4,740.0	3,276.7	2,857.1
Net Stockholders' Equity	492.0	447.3	446.7	369.3	452.9	337.5	262.1
Year-end Shs. Outstg. (000)	47,206	48,725	51,083	51,391	54,435	37,635	31,701
STATISTICAL RECORD:							
Return on Equity %	18.3	18.4	16.9	19.2	12.1	11.5	12.9
Return on Assets %	1.5	1.4	1.3	1.3	1.1	1.1	1.1
Equity/Assets %	8.2	7.9	7.6	6.7	8.7	9.3	8.4
Non-Int. Exp./Tot. Inc. %	51.8	53.2	57.1	59.7	65.3	62.6	61.2
Price Range	32.16-23.34	29.81-20.65	23.40-16.80	24.10-18.43	27.73-18.20	23.93-15.67	17.60-11.41
P/E Ratio	17.3-12.5	18.3-12.7	16.0-11.5	18.0-13.8	28.3-18.6	23.4-15.3	16.7-10.9
Average Yield %	2.5	2.5	2.9	2.4	2.1	2.2	2.4

Statistics are as originally reported. Adj. for 5-for-4 stk. split, 12/01; 3-for-2 split, 12/99. ① Incl. acquisition & restruct. chrgs.: $16.1 mill., 12/98; $5.4 mill., 12/97. ② Incl. acquisition & restruct. credit of $1.3 mill.

QUARTERLY DATA

(12/31/2002) ($000)	REV	INC
First Quarter	100,085	22,071
Second Quarter	100,599	22,934
Third Quarter	100,139	22,679
Fourth Quarter	95,372	22,466

OFFICERS:
R. P. O'Meara, Chmn.
J. M. O'Meara, Pres., C.E.O., C.O.O.
M. L. Scudder, Exec. V.P., C.F.O.

INVESTOR CONTACT: Barbara E. Briick, Investor Relations, (630) 875-7459

PRINCIPAL OFFICE: 300 Park Blvd., Suite 405, P.O. Box 459, Itasca, IL 60143-9768

TELEPHONE NUMBER: (630) 875-7450
FAX: (630) 357-3577
WEB: www.firstmidwest.com

NO. OF EMPLOYEES: 1,517

SHAREHOLDERS: 2,877 (record)

ANNUAL MEETING: In May

INCORPORATED: DE, Feb., 1982

INSTITUTIONAL HOLDINGS:
No. of Institutions: 116
Shares Held: 18,373,521
% Held: 39.1

INDUSTRY: National commercial banks (SIC: 6021)

TRANSFER AGENT(S): American Securities Transfer & Trust, Inc., Lakewood, CO

1ST SOURCE CORPORATION

YIELD 2.1%
P/E RATIO 31.2

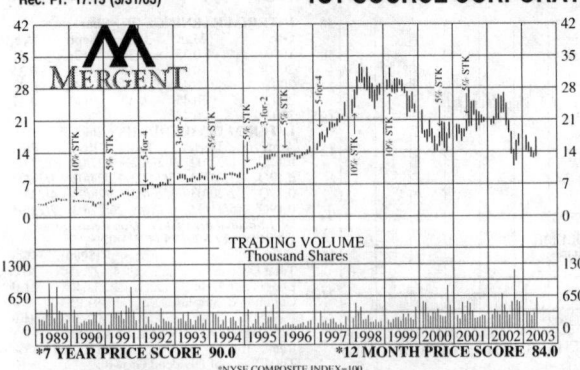

INTERIM EARNINGS (Per Share):

Qtr.	Mar.	June	Sept.	Dec.
1999	0.40	0.37	0.41	0.50
2000	0.41	0.43	0.44	0.51
2001	0.65	0.44	0.29	0.44
2002	0.20	0.13	0.10	0.11
2003	0.21	...	...	...

INTERIM DIVIDENDS (Per Share):

Amt.	Decl.	Ex.	Rec.	Pay.
0.09Q	7/17/02	8/01/02	8/05/02	8/15/02
0.09Q	10/15/02	11/01/02	11/05/02	11/15/02
0.09Q	1/20/03	2/03/03	2/05/03	2/14/03
0.09Q	4/22/03	5/01/03	5/05/03	5/15/03

Indicated div.: $0.36

CAPITALIZATION (12/31/02):

	($000)	(%)
Total Deposits	2,712,905	89.3
Long-Term Debt	16,878	0.6
Common & Surplus	309,429	10.2
Total	3,039,212	100.0

DIVIDEND ACHIEVER STATUS:
Rank: 96   10-Year Growth Rate: 12.49%
Total Years of Dividend Growth: 15

RECENT DEVELOPMENTS: For the quarter ended 3/31/03, net income grew 6.0% to $4.5 million compared with $4.2 million in the equivalent 2002 quarter. The improvement in earnings was attributed in part to an increase in the Company's number of customers served and market share gain by its retail branch network. Moreover, SRCE achieved solid growth in its investments under management, grew the client base in its trust department and experienced stronger results from its insurance and 401(k) management areas. Net interest income dipped 13.0% to $26.6 million

from $30.5 million the year before. Provision for loan losses plunged 53.0% to $5.6 million from $11.8 million in 2002. Total interest income declined 18.7% to $42.7 million from $52.5 million in the prior year. Total interest expense fell 26.5% to $16.2 million from $22.0 million in the previous year. Total non-interest income advanced 7.3% to $20.0 million from $18.7 million a year earlier. Total non-interest expense increased 7.9% to $34.8 million from $32.2 million the year before.

BUSINESS

1ST SOURCE CORPORATION is a registered bank holding company, with $3.28 billion in assets as of 3/31/03. Through its subsidiary, 1st Source Bank, it provides consumer and commercial banking services to individual and business customers through 60 banking locations, as of 4/30/03 in 15 counties in Indiana, Ohio and Michigan, seven Trustcorp Mortgage offices in Indiana, Ohio and Michigan, and 26 locations nationwide for the 1st Source Bank Specialty Finance Group. 1st Source Bank also competes for business nationwide by offering specialized financing services for used private and cargo aircraft, automobiles for leasing and rental agencies, heavy duty trucks, construction and environmental equipment.

ANNUAL FINANCIAL DATA

	12/31/02	12/31/01	12/31/00	12/31/99	12/31/98	12/31/97	12/31/96
Earnings Per Share	0.47	1.82	1.79	1.69	1.45	1.23	1.20
Tang. Book Val. Per Share	14.60	14.58	13.72	12.64	11.32	10.14	11.25
Dividends Per Share	0.36	0.35	0.33	0.28	0.25	0.23	0.20
Dividend Payout %	76.6	19.3	18.7	16.8	17.4	18.3	16.5
INCOME STATEMENT (IN MILLIONS):							
Total Interest Income	199.5	242.2	235.4	200.4	196.1	173.3	148.8
Total Interest Expense	80.8	123.4	130.4	100.7	102.2	87.3	73.4
Net Interest Income	118.7	118.8	105.0	99.7	93.9	86.0	75.4
Provision for Loan Losses	39.7	28.6	14.9	7.4	9.2	6.1	4.6
Non-Interest Income	73.1	92.8	73.9	63.3	51.5	35.7	25.5
Non-Interest Expense	140.7	121.2	104.0	99.0	85.5	73.0	60.6
Income Before Taxes	11.4	61.8	60.0	56.5	50.8	42.6	35.6
Net Income	10.0	40.7	40.0	38.0	33.2	28.2	23.2
Average Shs. Outstg. (000)	21,310	21,170	20,982	21,211	21,357	21,546	19,402
BALANCE SHEET (IN MILLIONS):							
Cash & Due from Banks	120.9	129.4	118.1	101.9	132.5	90.9	137.6
Securities Avail. for Sale	661.0	640.5	503.9	470.0	443.7	299.9	302.6
Total Loans & Leases	2,326.1	2,535.4	2,309.1	2,063.2	1,881.7	1,796.8	1,455.6
Allowance for Credit Losses	59.2	57.6	44.6	40.2	40.9	35.4	29.5
Net Loans & Leases	2,266.9	2,477.7	2,264.4	2,023.0	1,840.8	1,761.4	1,426.0
Total Assets	3,407.5	3,562.7	3,182.2	2,872.9	2,732.0	2,418.2	2,079.8
Total Deposits	2,712.9	2,882.8	2,462.7	2,127.5	2,177.1	1,891.8	1,634.0
Long-Term Obligations	16.9	11.9	12.1	12.2	13.2	16.7	18.6
Total Liabilities	3,098.0	3,211.8	2,866.9	2,589.4	2,471.4	2,178.5	1,907.9
Net Stockholders' Equity	309.4	306.2	270.6	238.8	215.9	195.0	171.8
Year-end Shs. Outstg. (000)	21,188	20,995	19,715	18,901	19,063	19,232	15,269
STATISTICAL RECORD:							
Return on Equity %	3.2	13.3	14.8	15.9	15.4	14.5	13.5
Return on Assets %	0.3	1.1	1.3	1.3	1.2	1.2	1.1
Equity/Assets %	9.1	8.6	8.5	8.3	7.9	8.1	8.3
Non-Int. Exp./Tot. Inc. %	73.4	57.4	58.9	60.8	58.5	59.8	60.2
Price Range	26.89-10.90	28.07-16.31	23.13-13.93	32.43-21.66	33.29-22.30	24.93-14.39	15.29-12.44
P/E Ratio	57.2-23.2	15.4-9.0	12.9-7.8	19.2-12.8	22.9-15.4	20.2-11.7	12.8-10.4
Average Yield %	1.9	1.6	1.8	1.0	0.9	1.2	1.4

Statistics are as originally reported. Adj. for stk. splits: 10% div., 2/12/99 & 2/13/98; 5-for-4, 2/14/97; 5% div., 5/15/01, 8/15/00, 2/15/96.

OFFICERS:
C. J. Murphy, III, Chmn., Pres., C.E.O.
L. E. Lentych, C.F.O., Treas.
J. B. Griffith, Sec., Gen. Couns.

INVESTOR CONTACT: Larry E. Lentych, C.F.O., Treas., (574) 235-2702

PRINCIPAL OFFICE: 100 North Michigan Street, South Bend, IN 46601

TELEPHONE NUMBER: (574) 235-5000
FAX: (574) 235-2912
WEB: www.1stsource.com

NO. OF EMPLOYEES: 1,233 (approx.)

SHAREHOLDERS: 1,086

ANNUAL MEETING: In Apr.

INCORPORATED: IN, Jan., 1922

INSTITUTIONAL HOLDINGS:
No. of Institutions: 40
Shares Held: 2,811,282
% Held: 13.4

INDUSTRY: State commercial banks (SIC: 6022)

TRANSFER AGENT(S): 1st Source Bank, South Bend, IN

FIRST VIRGINIA BANKS, INC.

YIELD		2.6%
P/E RATIO		16.3

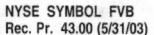

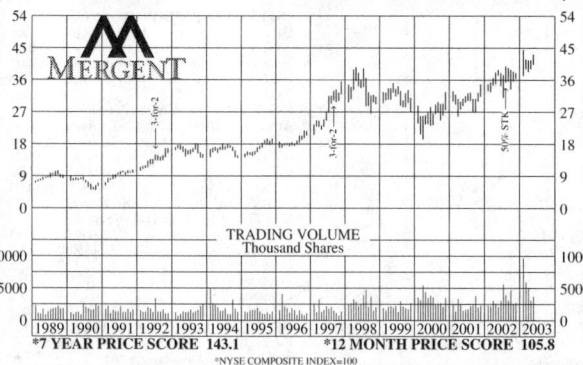

TRADING VOLUME
Thousand Shares

*7 YEAR PRICE SCORE 143.1 ***12 MONTH PRICE SCORE 105.8**
NYSE COMPOSITE INDEX=100

INTERIM EARNINGS (Per Share):

Qtr.	Mar.	June	Sept.	Dec.
2000	0.47	0.49	0.51	0.55
2001	0.58	0.54	0.55	0.56
2002	0.59	0.65	0.66	0.67
2003	0.66	...	...	...

INTERIM DIVIDENDS (Per Share):

Amt.	Decl.	Ex.	Rec.	Pay.
50% STK	5/29/02	8/19/02	7/31/02	8/16/02
0.273Q	8/28/02	9/26/02	9/30/02	10/25/02
0.28Q	11/20/02	12/27/02	12/31/02	1/13/03
0.28Q	2/26/03	3/27/03	3/31/03	4/25/03

Indicated div.: $1.12 (Div. Reinv. Plan)

CAPITALIZATION (12/31/02):

	($000)	(%)
Total Deposits	9,210,491	88.0
Long-Term Debt	13,488	0.1
Preferred Stock	381	0.0
Common & Surplus	1,237,964	11.8
Total	10,462,324	100.0

DIVIDEND ACHIEVER STATUS:
Rank: 151   10-Year Growth Rate: 9.69%
Total Years of Dividend Growth: 25

RECENT DEVELOPMENTS: For quarter ended 3/31/03, net income rose 9.5% to $46.2 million from $42.2 million in the equivalent quarter of 2002. Results for the 2003 and 2002 periods included amortization of intangibles of $2.2 million and $2.3 million, respectively. Results for 2003 also included securities gains of $5.8 million and merger-related expenses of $2.0 million. Net interest income slipped 2.3% to $115.7 million, while provision for loan losses dropped 68.1% to $1.1 million.

PROSPECTS: The proposed acquisition of the Company by BB&T Corporation is on schedule and expected to be completed in the third quarter of 2003. The acquisition will increase BB&T's assets to more than $91.00 billion and create the 11th largest financial institution in the U.S. The transaction is valued at $3.38 billion in stock. Separately, near-term results are expected to benefit from the Company's cost-reduction efforts, while synergies should provide opportunity for future operating improvements.

BUSINESS

FIRST VIRGINIA BANKS, INC., with assets of $11.25 billion as of 3/31/03, provides retail, commercial, international, and mortgage banking; insurance; trust and asset management services; and personal investment services through its subsidiaries. There are eight banks in the First Virginia group with 297 offices in Virginia, 55 offices in Maryland and 11 offices in East Tennessee. In addition, FVB operates a full-service insurance agency, First Virginia Insurance Services, Inc. On 7/2/01, FVB acquired James River Bankshares, Inc.

ANNUAL FINANCIAL DATA

	12/31/02	12/31/01	12/31/00	12/31/99	12/31/98	12/31/97	12/31/96
Earnings Per Share	④ 2.55	2.32	2.01	③ 2.00	1.69	② 1.63	① 1.56
Tang. Book Val. Per Share	14.78	13.27	12.05	11.66	10.71	10.75	10.65
Dividends Per Share	1.08	1.03	0.97	0.88	0.77	0.68	0.63
Dividend Payout %	42.3	44.3	48.5	44.0	45.8	41.6	40.6
INCOME STATEMENT (IN MILLIONS):							
Total Interest Income	627.4	653.3	643.8	640.6	663.6	631.1	587.2
Total Interest Expense	139.6	212.8	219.3	206.9	234.3	222.9	212.3
Net Interest Income	487.8	440.6	424.5	433.7	429.3	408.2	374.9
Provision for Loan Losses	10.0	6.8	9.4	14.2	20.8	17.2	17.7
Non-Interest Income	137.2	150.0	118.0	136.6	116.8	103.6	98.5
Non-Interest Expense	337.4	332.7	322.1	327.3	325.7	303.2	279.3
Income Before Taxes	277.7	251.1	211.0	228.8	199.6	191.3	176.3
Net Income	④ 183.9	164.5	142.0	③ 150.9	130.2	② 124.8	① 116.3
Average Shs. Outstg. (000)	72,109	70,976	70,886	75,357	77,294	76,320	74,858
BALANCE SHEET (IN MILLIONS):							
Cash & Due from Banks	370.4	386.2	323.0	441.8	377.4	386.8	378.2
Securities Avail. for Sale	1,136.0	1,553.6	301.4	227.0	286.1	243.2	323.6
Total Loans & Leases	6,377.9	6,510.6	6,366.5	6,385.4	6,093.2	5,938.0	5,364.8
Allowance for Credit Losses	71.0	71.9	70.3	70.1	70.3	68.1	62.8
Net Loans & Leases	6,306.9	6,438.6	6,296.2	6,315.3	6,022.9	5,869.9	5,302.0
Total Assets	11,227.6	10,623.0	9,516.5	9,451.8	9,564.7	9,011.6	8,236.1
Total Deposits	9,210.5	8,649.6	7,825.8	7,863.9	8,055.1	7,619.8	7,042.7
Long-Term Obligations	13.5	19.5	1.1	2.2	3.2	2.8	3.9
Total Liabilities	9,989.2	9,470.5	8,523.8	8,421.3	8,574.4	8,000.5	7,364.8
Net Stockholders' Equity	1,238.3	1,152.5	992.7	1,030.5	990.3	1,011.2	871.3
Year-end Shs. Outstg. (000)	70,899	71,741	69,245	73,743	75,141	77,726	72,918
STATISTICAL RECORD:							
Return on Equity %	14.9	14.3	14.3	14.6	13.1	12.3	13.4
Return on Assets %	1.6	1.5	1.5	1.6	1.4	1.4	1.4
Equity/Assets %	11.0	10.8	10.4	10.9	10.4	11.2	10.6
Non-Int. Exp./Tot. Inc. %	54.0	56.8	59.4	59.3	59.8	59.3	59.2
Price Range	39.98-30.93	34.77-25.69	32.63-19.33	35.09-27.00	39.63-26.46	35.59-20.56	21.78-17.00
P/E Ratio	15.7-12.1	15.0-11.1	16.3-9.6	17.5-13.5	23.5-15.7	21.8-12.6	14.0-10.9
Average Yield %	13.9	13.0	12.9	15.5	19.6	17.2	12.5

Statistics are as originally reported. Adj. for 3-for-2 splits, 8/02 & 9/97. ① Incl. one-time pre-tax SAIF chg. of $1.1 mill. ② Incl. $2.1 mill. gain fr. the sale of seven offices. ③ Incl. a pre-tax gain of $17.9 mill. fr. the sale of the Co.'s credit card portfolio. ④ Incl. $516,000 gain fr. securities.

OFFICERS:
B. J. Fitzpatrick, Chmn., Pres., C.E.O.
R. F. Bowman, Exec. V.P., C.F.O., Treas.
T. P. Jennings, Sr. V.P., Gen. Couns.

INVESTOR CONTACT: Barbara J. Chapman, V.P., Sec., (800) 995-9416

PRINCIPAL OFFICE: 6400 Arlington Boulevard, Falls Church, VA 22042-2336

TELEPHONE NUMBER: (703) 241-4000
FAX: (703) 241-3360
WEB: www.firstvirginia.com
NO. OF EMPLOYEES: 4,813 full-time; 432 part-time
SHAREHOLDERS: 19,813 (com.); 507 (preferred)
ANNUAL MEETING: In May
INCORPORATED: VA, Oct., 1949

INSTITUTIONAL HOLDINGS:
No. of Institutions: 201
Shares Held: 19,266,846
% Held: 27.9

INDUSTRY: State commercial banks (SIC: 6022)

TRANSFER AGENT(S): Registrar and Transfer Company, Cranford, NJ

FIRSTMERIT CORPORATION

YIELD 4.3%
P/E RATIO 13.1

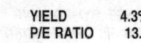

INTERIM EARNINGS (Per Share):

Qtr.	Mar.	June	Sept.	Dec
2000	0.45	0.45	0.45	0.45
2001	0.45	0.46	0.49	0.02
2002	0.51	0.49	0.38	0.43
2003	0.45	...	...	...

INTERIM DIVIDENDS (Per Share):

Amt.	Decl.	Ex.	Rec.	Pay.
0.25Q	8/15/02	8/22/02	8/26/02	9/16/02
0.25Q	11/21/02	11/27/02	12/02/02	12/16/02
0.25Q	2/20/03	2/27/03	3/03/03	3/17/03
0.25Q	5/15/03	5/22/03	5/27/03	6/16/03

Indicated div.: $1.00 (Div. Reinv. Plan)

CAPITALIZATION (12/31/02):

	($000)	(%)
Total Deposits	7,711,259	73.5
Long-Term Debt	1,821,120	17.3
Preferred Stock	1,093	0.0
Common & Surplus	963,564	9.2
Total	10,497,036	100.0

DIVIDEND ACHIEVER STATUS:
Rank: 164   10-Year Growth Rate: 9.07%
Total Years of Dividend Growth: 20

TRADING VOLUME
Thousand Shares

*7 YEAR PRICE SCORE 105.8   *12 MONTH PRICE SCORE 91.6
*NYSE COMPOSITE INDEX=100

RECENT DEVELOPMENTS: For the quarter ended 3/31/03, net income declined 11.9% to $38.3 million compared with $43.5 million in the corresponding period the previous year. Net interest income slipped 2.8% to $101.7 million from $104.7 million a year earlier, reflecting margin reduction, partially offset by an increase in average earning assets. Net interest margin was 4.21% compared with 4.48% in 2002. Provision for loan losses grew 21.7% to $23.5 million. Non-interest income rose 9.0% to $51.9 mil-

lion. Non-interest expenses grew 6.7% to $73.9 million, reflecting increases in operating costs due to higher salaries, wages, pension and benefits. Separately, the Company exceeded its mortgage projections by more than 40.0% in 2002. Moreover, FMER, which expects strong mortgage growth for 2003, exceeded its forecast by more than 30.0% as of 4/1/03. These increases resulted from FirstMerit Mortgage Corporation's expansion of its direct sales force, product offerings and geographic coverage.

BUSINESS

FIRSTMERIT CORPORATION is a multi-bank holding company with $10.56 billion in assets as of 3/31/03. The Company, through its affiliates, operates principally as a regional banking organization, providing banking, fiduciary, financial, insurance and investment services to corporate, institutional and individual customers throughout northeastern and Central Ohio and Western Pennsylvania counties. FirstMerit Bank, N.A., the Company's largest subsidiary, is the parent company of 16 wholly-owned subsidiaries. At 3/31/03, FirstMerit Bank, N.A. operated 157 full-service banking offices and 174 automated teller machines in 22 Ohio and western Pennsylvania counties. On 2/12/99, the Company acquired Signal Corp. On 10/31/01, FMER exited the manufactured housing lending business.

QUARTERLY DATA

12/31/2002 ($000)	REV	INC
1st Quarter	164,654	43,468
2nd Quarter	163,234	42,032
3rd Quarter	162,978	32,237
4th Quarter	157,147	36,629

ANNUAL FINANCIAL DATA

	12/31/02	12/31/01	12/31/00	12/31/99	12/31/98	12/31/97	12/31/96
Earnings Per Share	1.81	③ 1.42	1.80	② 1.31	1.34	1.36	1.09
Tang. Book Val. Per Share	9.68	9.06	10.48	9.39	10.39	8.56	8.19
Dividends Per Share	0.98	0.93	0.86	0.76	0.66	0.61	0.55
Dividend Payout %	54.1	65.5	47.8	58.0	49.3	44.8	50.5
INCOME STATEMENT (IN MILLIONS):							
Total Interest Income	648.0	726.9	791.5	684.9	503.1	407.8	411.7
Total Interest Expense	226.4	335.4	415.3	300.9	197.7	152.4	160.8
Net Interest Income	421.6	391.5	376.2	384.0	305.4	255.5	251.0
Provision for Loan Losses	98.6	61.8	32.7	37.4	28.4	21.6	17.8
Non-Interest Income	186.4	182.4	163.9	154.7	110.5	83.6	82.5
Non-Interest Expense	287.0	328.6	275.2	316.5	242.7	191.1	209.7
Income Before Taxes	222.3	183.5	232.2	184.8	144.8	126.4	106.0
Net Income	154.4	③ 122.6	159.8	② 125.7	97.5	86.4	70.9
Average Shs. Outstg. (000)	85,317	86,289	88,861	91,523	72,703	63,537	65,216
BALANCE SHEET (IN MILLIONS):							
Cash & Due from Banks	233.6	190.0	235.9	215.1	246.0	166.7	222.2
Total Loans & Leases	7,214.3	7,387.3	7,237.1	7,014.2	4,997.4	3,834.9	3,656.0
Allowance for Credit Losses	122.8	125.2	108.3	104.9	78.9	53.8	49.3
Net Loans & Leases	7,091.5	7,262.1	7,128.8	6,909.3	4,918.4	3,781.1	3,606.7
Total Assets	10,688.2	10,193.4	10,215.2	10,115.5	7,127.4	5,307.5	5,228.0
Total Deposits	7,711.3	7,539.4	7,614.9	6,860.1	5,461.6	4,255.2	4,204.9
Long-Term Obligations	1,821.1	1,588.3	1,563.4	2,281.2	807.4	441.8	423.7
Total Liabilities	9,723.5	9,282.6	9,300.3	9,260.5	6,358.7	4,777.1	4,704.3
Net Stockholders' Equity	964.7	910.8	914.9	833.6	768.6	530.3	523.7
Year-end Shs. Outstg. (000)	84,505	84,991	87,032	88,375	74,009	61,967	63,912
STATISTICAL RECORD:							
Return on Equity %	16.0	12.8	17.5	15.1	12.7	16.3	13.5
Return on Assets %	1.4	1.1	1.6	1.2	1.4	1.6	1.4
Equity/Assets %	9.0	8.9	9.0	8.2	10.8	10.0	10.0
Non-Int. Exp./Tot. Inc. %	47.2	57.3	50.9	58.8	58.4	56.4	62.9
Price Range	29.51-18.55	28.00-20.66	27.75-13.38	29.13-22.56	34.38-20.75	30.75-17.38	18.00-13.88
P/E Ratio	16.3-10.2	19.7-14.5	15.4-7.4	22.2-17.2	25.7-15.5	22.6-12.8	16.5-12.7
Average Yield %	4.1	3.8	4.2	2.9	2.4	2.5	3.5

Statistics are as originally reported. Adj. for stk. splits: 2-for-1, 9/29/97. ① Bef. extraord. credit $5.6 mill. ② Bef. extraord. chrg. of $5.8 mill. ③ Bef. acctg. change chrg. of $6.3 mill.; incl. one-time after-tax chrg. of $41.1 mill.

OFFICERS:
J. R. Cochran, Chmn., C.E.O.
T. E. Bichsel, Exec. V.P., C.F.O.
T. E. Patton, E.V.P., Gen. Couns., Sec.

INVESTOR CONTACT: Gary Elek, Exec. V.P., (330) 384-7136

PRINCIPAL OFFICE: III Cascade Plaza, 7th Floor, Akron, OH 44308-1103

TELEPHONE NUMBER: (330) 996-6300
FAX: (330) 384-7321
WEB: www.firstmerit.com

NO. OF EMPLOYEES: 2,300 (approx.)

SHAREHOLDERS: 9,441 (approx.)

ANNUAL MEETING: In April

INCORPORATED: OH, Nov., 1981

INSTITUTIONAL HOLDINGS:
No. of Institutions: 160
Shares Held: 27,771,329
% Held: 32.7

INDUSTRY: State commercial banks (SIC: 6022)

TRANSFER AGENT(S): FirstMerit Bank, N.A., Akron, Ohio

FLEETBOSTON FINANCIAL CORPORATION

YIELD 4.7%
P/E RATIO 22.9

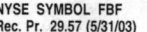

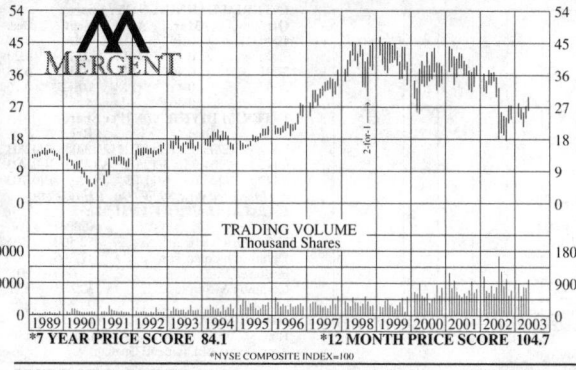

INTERIM EARNINGS (Per Share):

Qtr.	Mar.	June	Sept.	Dec.
2000	1.03	0.91	0.90	0.84
2001	0.12	0.48	0.70	d0.49
2002	0.70	d0.11	0.57	0.28
2003	0.55	...	...	...

INTERIM DIVIDENDS (Per Share):

Amt.	Decl.	Ex.	Rec.	Pay.
0.35Q	8/20/02	8/29/02	9/03/02	10/01/02
0.35Q	10/15/02	11/29/02	12/03/02	1/01/03
0.35Q	2/18/03	2/27/03	3/03/03	4/01/03
0.35Q	4/15/03	5/30/03	6/03/03	7/01/03

Indicated div.: $1.40 (Div. Reinv. Plan)

CAPITALIZATION (12/31/02):

	($000)	(%)
Total Deposits	125,814,000	77.1
Long-Term Debt	20,581,000	12.6
Preferred Stock	271,000	0.2
Common & Surplus	16,562,000	10.1
Total	163,228,000	100.0

DIVIDEND ACHIEVER STATUS:

Rank: 83   10-Year Growth Rate: 13.35%
Total Years of Dividend Growth: 10

TRADING VOLUME
Thousand Shares

*7 YEAR PRICE SCORE 84.1   *12 MONTH PRICE SCORE 104.7

*NYSE COMPOSITE INDEX=100

RECENT DEVELOPMENTS: For the quarter ended 3/31/03, FBF reported income from continuing operations of $577.0 million versus $736.0 million in the corresponding prior-year quarter. Results for the 2003 period included merger and restructuring costs of $5.0 million. Earnings for the 2003 and 2002 periods excluded losses from discontinued operations of $10.0 million and $1.0 million, respectively. Net interest income declined 6.4% to $1.62 billion.

PROSPECTS: FBF is having success in cross-selling products to both its consumer and commercial customers, which is helping to counter some of the revenue pressures from weakness in commercial loan demand and the equity markets. Meanwhile, core deposits and home equity loan levels continue to rise. Separately, FBF recently launched a Spanish-language informational Web site to complement its growing channels of outreach to Hispanic customers.

BUSINESS

FLEETBOSTON FINANCIAL CORPORATION (formerly Fleet Financial Group, Inc.), with assets of $199.79 billion and total deposits of $129.58 billion as of 3/31/03, is a diversified financial services firm with offices nationwide. The Company's products and services include: consumer banking, government banking, mortgage banking and commercial real estate lending, corporate finance, credit cards, insurance services, cash management, asset-based lending, equipment leasing, and investment management services. FBF operates one of the nation's largest discount brokerage firms through its subsidiary, Quick and Reilly, Inc. On 10/1/99, FBF acquired BankBoston Corporation.

ANNUAL FINANCIAL DATA

	12/31/02	12/31/01	12/31/00	12/31/99	12/31/98	12/31/97	12/31/96
Earnings Per Share	6 1.44	6 0.83	3 3.68	2 2.10	2.52	1 2.37	1.98
Tang. Book Val. Per Share	11.32	11.75	9.85	7.78	7.36	6.54	6.10
Dividends Per Share	1.40	1.32	1.20	1.08	0.98	0.90	0.86
Dividend Payout %	97.2	159.0	32.6	51.4	38.9	38.0	43.5
INCOME STATEMENT (IN MILLIONS):							
Total Interest Income	10,102.0	13,793.0	13,584.0	13,052.0	6,765.0	5,848.0	5,842.0
Total Interest Expense	3,682.0	6,396.0	7,063.0	6,310.0	2,896.0	2,221.0	2,439.0
Net Interest Income	6,420.0	7,397.0	6,521.0	6,742.0	3,869.0	3,627.0	3,403.0
Provision for Loan Losses	2,760.0	2,330.0	1,196.0	933.0	470.0	322.0	213.0
Non-Interest Income	5,036.0	5,340.0	9,024.0	6,974.0	3,237.0	2,247.0	2,201.0
Non-Interest Expense	6,404.0	8,913.0	8,633.0	9,357.0	4,129.0	3,381.0	3,460.0
Income Before Taxes	2,292.0	1,494.0	5,716.0	3,426.0	2,507.0	2,171.0	1,931.0
Net Income	6 1,524.0	6 931.0	3 3,420.0	2 2,038.0	1,532.0	1 1,303.0	1,139.0
Average Shs. Outstg. (000)	1,048,734	1,083,676	919,869	943,528	588,000	524,000	538,000
BALANCE SHEET (IN MILLIONS):							
Cash & Due from Banks	...	12,709.0	11,502.0	10,627.0	5,635.0	4,983.0	7,243.0
Securities Avail. for Sale	4,486.0	6,989.0	7,081.0	7,849.0	...	...	7,503.0
Total Loans & Leases	120,380.0	128,180.0	109,372.0	119,700.0	69,396.0	61,179.0	58,844.0
Allowance for Credit Losses	3,864.0	3,634.0	2,378.0	2,488.0	1,552.0	1,432.0	1,488.0
Net Loans & Leases	116,516.0	124,546.0	106,994.0	117,212.0	67,844.0	59,747.0	57,356.0
Total Assets	190,453.0	203,638.0	179,519.0	190,692.0	104,382.0	85,535.0	85,518.0
Total Deposits	125,814.0	129,337.0	101,290.0	114,896.0	69,678.0	63,735.0	67,071.0
Long-Term Obligations	20,581.0	25,530.0	28,357.0	25,349.0	8,820.0	4,500.0	5,114.0
Total Liabilities	173,620.0	186,030.0	163,347.0	175,385.0	94,973.0	77,501.0	78,103.0
Net Stockholders' Equity	16,833.0	17,608.0	16,172.0	15,307.0	9,409.0	8,034.0	7,415.0
Year-end Shs. Outstg. (000)	1,049,800	1,043,800	907,000	915,660	570,000	526,000	524,000
STATISTICAL RECORD:							
Return on Equity %	9.1	5.3	21.1	13.3	16.3	16.2	15.4
Return on Assets %	0.8	0.5	1.9	1.1	1.5	1.5	1.3
Equity/Assets %	8.8	8.6	9.0	8.0	9.0	9.4	8.7
Non-Int. Exp./Tot. Inc. %	55.9	70.0	55.5	68.2	58.1	57.6	61.7
Price Range	37.56-17.65	44.19-31.27	43.75-25.13	46.81-33.25	45.38-30.00	37.59-24.38	28.13-18.81
P/E Ratio	26.1-12.3	53.2-37.7	11.9-6.8	22.3-15.8	18.0-11.9	15.9-10.3	14.2-9.5
Average Yield %	5.1	3.5	3.5	2.7	2.6	2.9	3.7

Statistics are as originally reported. Adj. for 2-for-1 stk. split, 10/98. ⊡ Incl. pre-tax gain of $175.0 mill fr. the sale of bus. & pre-tax restr. chg. of $155.0 mill. ② Incl. aft.-tax merger & rel. chgs. of $760.0 mill. ③ Incl. aft.-tax BankBoston Corp. integration chgs. of $137.0 mill. & aft.-tax divest. gain of $420.0 mill. ④ Incl. the acq. of BankBoston Corp. on 10/1/99. ⑤ Incl. pre-tax merger chg. & loss on Fleet Mtge. of $1.07 bill. & pre-tax gains of $430.0 mill. on branch divests. ⑥ Bef. after-tax loss from disc. oper. of $336.0 mill.; incl. pre-tax merger & restr. chg. $71.0 mill.

QUARTERLY DATA

(12/31/2002)($000)	REV	INC
1st Quarter	4,074,000	735,000
2nd Quarter	3,877,000	(386,000)
3rd Quarter	3,665,000	579,000
4th Quarter	3,515,000	261,000

OFFICERS:
C. K. Gifford, Chmn., C.E.O.
T. J. Semrod, Vice-Chmn.
E. M. McQuade, Pres., C.O.O.

INVESTOR CONTACT: Investor Relations,
(617) 434-7858

PRINCIPAL OFFICE: 100 Federal Street,
Boston, MA 02110-2010

TELEPHONE NUMBER: (617) 434-2200
FAX: (617) 434-6943
WEB: www.fleet.com

NO. OF EMPLOYEES: 56,000 (approx.)

SHAREHOLDERS: 85,312

ANNUAL MEETING: In April

INCORPORATED: RI, May, 1970

INSTITUTIONAL HOLDINGS:
No. of Institutions: 675
Shares Held: 679,676,805
% Held: 64.7

INDUSTRY: National commercial banks
(SIC: 6021)

TRANSFER AGENT(S): EquiServe Trust
Company, Providence, RI

FLORIDA PUBLIC UTILITIES COMPANY

YIELD 3.9%
P/E RATIO 16.6

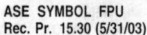
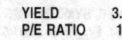
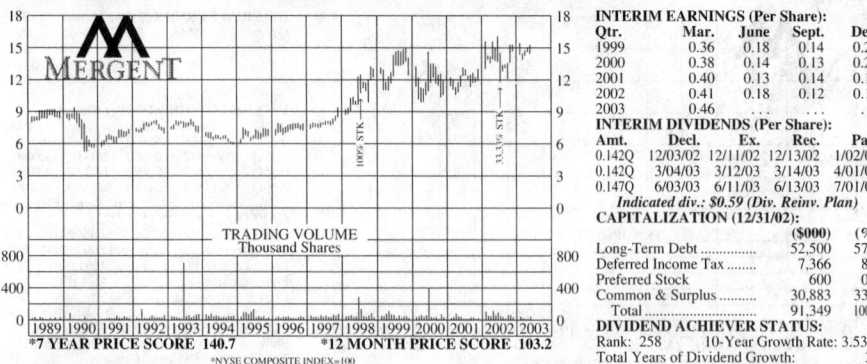

INTERIM EARNINGS (Per Share):

Qtr.	Mar.	June	Sept.	Dec.
1999	0.36	0.18	0.14	0.20
2000	0.38	0.14	0.13	0.23
2001	0.40	0.13	0.14	0.14
2002	0.41	0.18	0.12	0.16
2003	0.46	...	...	...

INTERIM DIVIDENDS (Per Share):

Amt.	Decl.	Ex.	Rec.	Pay.
0.142Q	12/03/02	12/11/02	12/13/02	1/02/03
0.142Q	3/04/03	3/12/03	3/14/03	4/01/03
0.147Q	6/03/03	6/11/03	6/13/03	7/01/03

Indicated div.: $0.59 (Div. Reinv. Plan)

CAPITALIZATION (12/31/02):

	($000)	(%)
Long-Term Debt	52,500	57.5
Deferred Income Tax	7,366	8.0
Preferred Stock	600	0.7
Common & Surplus	30,883	33.8
Total	91,349	100.0

DIVIDEND ACHIEVER STATUS:
Rank: 258   10-Year Growth Rate: 3.53%
Total Years of Dividend Growth: 34

TRADING VOLUME
Thousand Shares

*7 YEAR PRICE SCORE 140.7   *12 MONTH PRICE SCORE 103.2
*NYSE COMPOSITE INDEX=100

RECENT DEVELOPMENTS: For the quarter ended 3/31/03, income was $1.8 million, before income from discontinued operations of $9.9 million, versus income of $1.5 million, before income from discontinued operations of $108,000, in the prior-year quarter. Results for 2003 included a contract termination fee of $1.5 million and a one-time charge of $206,000 for an abandoned gas construction project. Total revenues increased 31.3% to $31.1 million from $23.7 million the previous year. Natural gas revenues climbed 57.0% to $18.4 million. Electric revenues were unchanged from the year-earlier period at $9.8 million. Propane gas revenues advanced 32.9% to $3.0 million. Gross profit improved 16.7% to $11.2 million. Operating income increased 30.8% to $4.1 million from $3.2 million in 2002. On 3/27/03, FPU completed the sale of its water assets to the City of Fernandina Beach. The transaction, which was valued at about $25.1 million, will allow FPU to focus on growing its core energy-related businesses. FPU's plan for growth involves expansion into new construction and acquisitions of smaller propane companies.

BUSINESS

FLORIDA PUBLIC UTILITIES COMPANY is regulated by the Florida Public Service Commission (except for propane gas service) and provides natural and propane gas service, electric service. The Company was comprised of the following five divisions as of 12/31/02: the South Florida division serves natural gas to 29,697 customers and propane gas to 6,288 customers; the Central Florida division serves 16,670 natural gas customers and 3,789 propane customers; the Northwest Florida division provides electricity to 12,335 customers; the Northeast Florida division serves 14,020 electric customers and 7,089 water customers and 1,456 propane customers; and the Nature Coast division serves propane gas to 1,207 customers. On 3/27/03, the Company sold the assets of its water utility system for about $25.1 million.

ANNUAL FINANCIAL DATA

	12/31/02	12/31/01	12/31/00	12/31/99	12/31/98	12/31/97	12/31/96
Earnings Per Share	[4] 0.70	[3] 0.80	0.87	[2] 0.88	0.77	[1] 0.80	0.69
Cash Flow Per Share	2.00	2.07	2.12	2.02	1.83	1.82	1.68
Tang. Book Val. Per Share	6.37	6.09	7.30	6.92	6.91	6.60	6.24
Dividends Per Share	0.56	0.55	0.53	0.50	0.47	0.45	0.446
Dividend Payout %	80.3	68.8	60.3	56.4	60.8	56.3	64.3
INCOME STATEMENT (IN THOUSANDS):							
Total Revenues	88,461	92,143	84,759	74,098	76,192	78,134	78,810
Costs & Expenses	73,115	77,872	70,520	60,608	63,220	66,075	66,780
Depreciation & Amort.	5,026	4,839	4,698	4,557	4,269	4,029	3,876
Maintenance Exp.	2,551	3,165	3,013	2,763	2,807	2,512	2,526
Operating Income	7,769	6,267	6,528	6,170	5,896	[1] 5,518	5,628
Net Interest Inc./(Exp.)	d4,513	d3,591	d3,487	d2,968	d2,840	d2,895	d2,858
Income Taxes	1,402	...	...	...	...	...	...
Net Income	[4] 2,761	[3] 3,052	3,288	[2] 3,529	3,068	[1] 3,191	2,751
Cash Flow	7,758	7,862	7,957	8,057	7,308	7,191	6,598
Average Shs. Outstg.	3,871	3,802	3,759	3,994	3,991	3,957	3,917
BALANCE SHEET (IN THOUSANDS):							
Gross Property	152,907	151,656	132,903	123,898	117,656	112,356	106,684
Accumulated Depreciation	54,952	54,327	48,703	45,626	42,429	39,632	36,808
Net Property	97,955	97,329	84,200	78,272	75,227	72,724	69,876
Total Assets	144,823	139,989	108,588	96,807	92,406	88,622	90,994
Long-Term Obligations	52,500	52,500	23,500	23,500	23,500	23,500	23,500
Net Stockholders' Equity	30,883	29,329	27,510	25,866	27,622	26,189	24,511
Year-end Shs. Outstg.	3,882	3,848	3,770	3,736	4,000	3,971	3,931
STATISTICAL RECORD:							
Operating Profit Margin %	8.8	6.8	7.7	8.3	7.7	7.1	7.1
Net Profit Margin %	3.1	3.3	3.9	4.8	4.0	4.1	3.5
Net Inc./Net Property %	2.8	3.1	3.9	4.5	4.1	4.4	3.9
Net Inc./Tot. Capital %	3.0	3.4	5.6	6.2	5.3	5.7	5.4
Return on Equity %	8.9	10.4	12.0	13.6	11.1	12.2	11.2
Accum. Depr./Gross Prop. %	35.9	35.8	36.6	36.8	36.1	35.3	34.5
Price Range	16.09-11.80	13.15-10.56	14.66-9.87	15.04-11.00	13.25-8.69	9.40-7.38	7.94-6.77
P/E Ratio	23.0-16.9	16.5-13.3	16.9-11.3	17.1-12.5	17.3-11.4	11.8-9.2	11.4-9.7
Average Yield %	4.0	4.6	4.3	3.8	4.2	5.4	6.1

Statistics are as originally reported. Adj. for stk. splits: 4-for-3, 7/02; 2-for-1, 7/98. Incl. after-tax gain fr. sale of prop. of $70,000. [1] Incl. non-recurr. credit $837,000 [2] Incl. non-recurr. credit of $134,000 [3] Incl. gain fr. sale of non-utility prop. of $15,000. [4] Bef. inc. fr. disc. opers. of $602,000; Incl. after-tax gain fr. sale of prop. of $70,000.

FRANKLIN RESOURCES, INC.

YIELD 0.8%
P/E RATIO 23.4

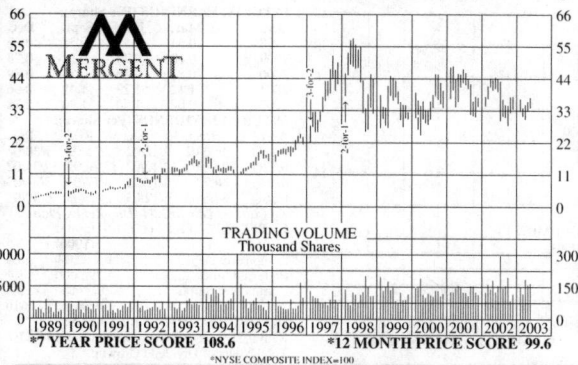

TRADING VOLUME
Thousand Shares

*7 YEAR PRICE SCORE 108.6   *12 MONTH PRICE SCORE 99.6
*NYSE COMPOSITE INDEX=100

INTERIM EARNINGS (Per Share):

Qtr.	Dec.	Mar.	June	Sept.
1999-00	0.55	0.58	0.58	0.58
2000-01	0.61	0.54	0.46	0.32
2001-02	0.45	0.46	0.48	0.26
2002-03	0.43	0.43	...	...

INTERIM DIVIDENDS (Per Share):

Amt.	Decl.	Ex.	Rec.	Pay.
0.07Q	3/13/02	3/26/02	3/29/02	4/16/02
0.07Q	6/27/02	7/03/02	7/08/02	7/16/02
0.07Q	9/26/02	10/03/02	10/07/02	10/15/02
0.075Q	12/11/02	12/27/02	12/31/02	1/15/03
0.075Q	3/14/03	3/27/03	3/31/03	4/15/03

Indicated div.: $0.30 (Div. Reinv. Plan)

CAPITALIZATION (9/30/02):

	($mill.)	(%)
Long-Term Debt	595.1	11.8
Deferred Income Tax	175.2	3.5
Common & Surplus	4,266.9	84.7
Total	5,037.3	100.0

DIVIDEND ACHIEVER STATUS:
Rank: 98   10-Year Growth Rate: 12.44%
Total Years of Dividend Growth: 13

RECENT DEVELOPMENTS: For the quarter ended 3/31/03, net income decreased 8.7% to $109.6 million compared with $120.0 million in the corresponding period of the year before. Total operating revenues slipped 2.1% to $613.1 billion. Investment management fees slid 4.9% to $347.9 million, while underwriting and distribution fees declined 1.7% to $194.2 million. However, shareholder servicing fees rose 15.2% to $55.3 million. Operating income decreased 5.6% to $139.7 million.

PROSPECTS: BEN continues to expand its relationships with clients as it promotes specialties such as domestic deep value, international value and small-cap growth. Moreover, BEN continues to attract new investors in the high net-worth arena, and expand its business development capabilities to support its growing client base. As of 3/31/03, BEN's total assets under management were comprised of 46.9% equity assets, 36.1% fixed-income assets, 14.8% hybrid assets, and 2.2% money.

BUSINESS

FRANKLIN RESOURCES, INC., operating as Franklin Templeton Investments, is engaged in providing investment management, marketing, distribution, transfer agency and other administrative services to the open-end investment companies of the Franklin Templeton Group and to U.S. and international managed and institutional accounts. The Company also provides investment management and related services to a number of closed-end investment companies. In addition, the Company provides investment management, marketing and distribution services to certain sponsored investment companies organized in the Grand Duchy of Luxembourg. Moreover, the Company provides advisory services, variable annuity products, and sponsors and manages public and private real estate programs. As of 3/31/03, BEN's subsidiaries had $252.38 billion in assets under management. On 4/10/01, BEN acquired Fiduciary Trust Company International for approximately $775.0 million.

ANNUAL FINANCIAL DATA

	9/30/02	9/30/01	9/30/00	9/30/99	9/30/98	9/30/97	9/30/96
Earnings Per Share	③ 1.65	① 1.91	2.28	② 1.69	1.98	1.72	1.26
Cash Flow Per Share	2.35	2.79	3.09	2.48	2.74	2.20	1.42
Tang. Book Val. Per Share	8.69	7.63	7.37	5.79	4.08	2.50	3.15
Dividends Per Share	0.28	0.26	0.24	0.22	0.20	0.17	0.15
Dividend Payout %	17.0	13.6	10.5	13.0	10.1	9.9	11.6
INCOME STATEMENT (IN MILLIONS):							
Total Revenues	2,518.5	2,354.8	2,340.1	2,262.5	2,577.3	2,163.3	1,522.6
Costs & Expenses	1,749.9	1,619.0	1,477.1	1,523.4	1,743.8	1,447.9	1,065.0
Depreciation & Amort.	183.1	223.8	199.6	200.0	191.4	123.9	40.5
Operating Income	585.5	512.0	663.4	539.1	642.1	591.5	417.1
Net Interest Inc./(Exp.)	d12.3	d10.6	d14.0	d21.0	d22.5	d25.3	d11.3
Income Before Income Taxes	578.3	637.8	739.6	574.1	676.3	615.7	456.2
Income Taxes	145.6	153.1	177.5	147.4	175.8	181.7	141.5
Net Income	③ 432.7	① 484.7	562.1	② 426.7	500.5	434.1	314.7
Cash Flow	615.8	708.6	761.7	626.7	691.8	558.0	355.2
Average Shs. Outstg. (000)	262,054	253,663	246,624	252,757	252,941	253,430	249,939
BALANCE SHEET (IN MILLIONS):							
Cash & Cash Equivalents	2,533.7	2,081.2	1,408.7	1,231.8	1,048.0	656.6	701.7
Total Current Assets	3,414.0	3,159.5	1,955.9	1,703.7	1,470.8	1,210.5	1,249.9
Net Property	394.2	449.6	444.7	416.4	349.2	...	...
Total Assets	6,422.7	6,265.7	4,042.4	3,666.8	3,480.0	3,095.2	2,374.2
Total Current Liabilities	1,339.0	1,528.1	728.5	662.9	655.5	709.9	551.7
Long-Term Obligations	595.1	566.0	294.1	294.3	494.5	493.2	399.5
Net Stockholders' Equity	4,266.9	3,977.9	2,965.5	2,657.0	2,280.8	1,854.2	1,400.6
Net Working Capital	2,075.1	1,631.4	1,227.3	1,040.8	815.3	500.6	698.2
Year-end Shs. Outstg. (000)	258,555	260,798	243,730	251,007	251,742	252,064	240,816
STATISTICAL RECORD:							
Operating Profit Margin %	23.2	21.7	28.4	23.8	24.9	27.3	27.4
Net Profit Margin %	17.2	20.6	24.0	18.9	19.4	20.1	20.7
Return on Equity %	10.1	12.2	19.0	16.1	21.9	23.4	22.5
Return on Assets %	6.7	7.7	13.9	11.6	14.4	14.0	13.3
Debt/Total Assets %	9.3	9.0	7.3	8.0	14.2	15.9	16.8
Price Range	44.48-27.90	48.30-30.85	45.63-24.63	45.00-27.00	57.88-25.75	51.91-22.08	24.92-15.46
P/E Ratio	27.0-16.9	25.3-16.2	20.0-10.8	26.6-16.0	29.2-13.0	30.3-12.9	19.8-12.3
Average Yield %	0.8	0.7	0.7	0.6	0.5	0.5	0.7

Statistics are as originally reported. Adj. for stk. splits: 3-for-2, 12/96; 2-for-1, 12/97. ① Incl. restr. chrg. $58.5 mill. ② Incl. one-time chrg. of $7.6 mill. ③ Incl. a chrg. of $60.1 mill. rel. to an unreal. loss in BEN's corp. investments.

OFFICERS:
C. B. Johnson, Chmn., C.E.O.
H. E. Burns, Vice-Chmn.
R. H. Johnson Jr., Vice-Chmn.
M. L. Flanagan, Pres., C.F.O.
INVESTOR CONTACT: Alan Weinfeld, Investor Relations, (650) 525-8900
PRINCIPAL OFFICE: One Franklin Parkway, San Mateo, CA 94403

TELEPHONE NUMBER: (650) 312-2000
FAX: (650) 312-3655
WEB: www.franklintempleton.com
NO. OF EMPLOYEES: 6,700 (approx.)
SHAREHOLDERS: 5,100 (approx.)
ANNUAL MEETING: In Jan.
INCORPORATED: DE, Nov., 1969

INSTITUTIONAL HOLDINGS:
No. of Institutions: 306
Shares Held: 104,530,485
% Held: 41.0

INDUSTRY: Investment advice (SIC: 6282)

TRANSFER AGENT(S): Bank of New York, New York, NY

FREDDIE MAC

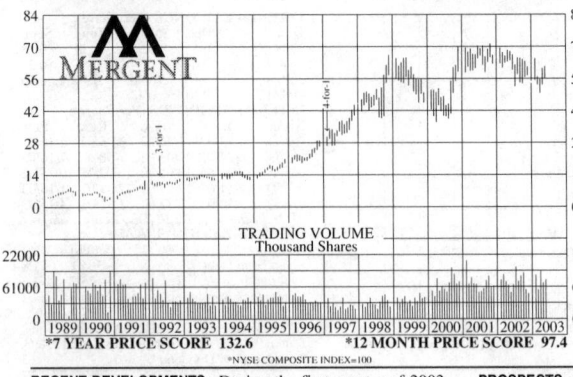

*7 YEAR PRICE SCORE 132.6   *12 MONTH PRICE SCORE 97.4

*NYSE COMPOSITE INDEX=100

INTERIM EARNINGS (Per Share):

Qtr.	Mar.	June	Sept.	Dec.
1998	0.54	0.56	0.58	0.62
1999	0.68	0.74	0.74	0.78
2000	0.81	0.83	0.86	0.89
2001	1.12	1.29	1.49	2.06
2002	2.07	1.50	1.90	2.38

INTERIM DIVIDENDS (Per Share):

Amt.	Decl.	Ex.	Rec.	Pay.
0.22Q	9/06/02	9/12/02	9/16/02	9/30/02
0.22Q	12/06/02	12/12/02	12/16/02	12/31/02
0.26Q	3/07/03	3/13/03	3/17/03	3/31/03
0.26Q	6/06/03	6/12/03	6/16/03	6/30/03

Indicated div.: $1.04 (Div. Reinv. Plan)

CAPITALIZATION (12/31/01):

	($000)	(%)
Long-Term Debt	314,733,000	95.3
Preferred Stock	4,596,000	1.4
Common & Surplus	10,777,000	3.3
Total	330,106,000	100.0

DIVIDEND ACHIEVER STATUS:
Rank: 51   10-Year Growth Rate: 16.57%
Total Years of Dividend Growth: 12

RECENT DEVELOPMENTS: During the first quarter of 2003, FRE's retained portfolio grew by $1.00 billion, representing annualized growth of 1.0%. This modest growth reflects a decline in the returns available on mortgage investments and high mortgage prepayments. FRE's total property/casualty portfolio declined by $9.00 billion, or at a 3.0% annualized rate, during the first quarter, primarily due to lower than typical market share, which is expected to return to more normal levels over the course of the year.

PROSPECTS: The Company is continuing with its previously announced restatement process in conjunction with the related re-audit by its new auditor. FRE continues to expect that the likely cumulative effect of the restatements will be to materially increase reported earnings for prior periods. The Company expects to release its restated results for 2002, 2001 and possibly 2000 shortly after the end of the second quarter of 2003. Immediately thereafter, FRE will release its first quarter 2003 earnings.

BUSINESS

FREDDIE MAC (formerly The Federal Home Loan Mortgage Corporation) is a federally chartered and stockholder-owned corporation. FRE purchases conventional residential mortgages from mortgage lending institutions and finances most of its purchases with sales of guaranteed mortgage securities called Mortgage Participation Certificates for which FRE ultimately assumes the risk of borrower default. FRE also maintains an investment portfolio that consists principally of federal funds sold, reverse repurchase agreements and tax-advantaged and other short-term investments. FRE's financial performance is driven primarily by the growth of its total servicing portfolio, the mix of sold versus retained portfolios, the spreads earned on the sold and retained portfolios and mortgage default costs.

ANNUAL FINANCIAL DATA

	p12/31/02	12/31/01	12/31/00	12/31/99	12/31/98	12/31/97	12/31/96
Earnings Per Share	④ 7.95	②③ 5.96	③ 3.39	③ 2.96	2.31	1.88	① 1.67
Tang. Book Val. Per Share	...	15.50	16.81	11.98	11.55	8.74	9.62
Dividends Per Share	0.88	0.80	0.68	0.60	0.48	0.40	0.35
Dividend Payout %	11.1	13.4	20.1	20.3	20.8	21.3	21.0

INCOME STATEMENT (IN MILLIONS):

	p12/31/02	12/31/01	12/31/00	12/31/99	12/31/98	12/31/97	12/31/96
Total Interest Income	36,773.0	34,288.0	28,350.0	22,753.0	16,638.0	13,001.0	10,783.0
Total Interest Expense	29,996.0	28,808.0	25,512.0	20,213.0	14,711.0	11,370.0	9,241.0
Net Interest Income	6,770.0	5,480.0	2,838.0	2,540.0	1,927.0	1,631.0	1,542.0
Provision for Loan Losses	...	45.0	40.0	60.0	190.0	310.0	320.0
Non-Interest Income	1,911.0	1,639.0	1,489.0	1,405.0	1,307.0	1,298.0	1,249.0
Non-Interest Expense	...	1,020.0	883.0	834.0	791.0	755.0	758.0
Income Before Taxes	...	6,300.0	3,534.0	3,161.0	2,356.0	1,964.0	1,797.0
Net Income	④ 5,764.0	②③ 4,373.0	③ 2,539.0	③ 2,218.0	1,700.0	1,395.0	① 1,258.0
Average Shs. Outstg. (000)	...	696,876	696,448	700,211	684,658	692,000	710,000

BALANCE SHEET (IN MILLIONS):

	p12/31/02	12/31/01	12/31/00	12/31/99	12/31/98	12/31/97	12/31/96
Total Loans & Leases	...	494,585.0	385,451.0	322,914.0	255,670.0	164,543.0	137,826.0
Allowance for Credit Losses	...	326.0	334.0	345.0	322.0	293.0	306.0
Net Loans & Leases	...	494,259.0	385,117.0	322,569.0	255,348.0	164,250.0	137,520.0
Total Assets	717,340.0	617,340.0	459,297.0	386,684.0	321,421.0	194,597.0	173,866.0
Long-Term Obligations	...	314,733.0	243,323.0	185,186.0	93,525.0	87,714.0	76,876.0
Total Liabilities	...	601,967.0	444,460.0	375,159.0	310,586.0	187,076.0	167,135.0
Net Stockholders' Equity	...	15,373.0	14,837.0	11,525.0	10,835.0	7,521.0	6,731.0
Year-end Shs. Outstg. (000)	...	695,304	692,584	695,091	695,179	679,000	695,000

STATISTICAL RECORD:

	p12/31/02	12/31/01	12/31/00	12/31/99	12/31/98	12/31/97	12/31/96
Return on Equity %	23.4	28.4	17.1	19.2	15.7	18.5	18.7
Return on Assets %	0.8	0.7	0.6	0.6	0.5	0.7	0.7
Equity/Assets %	3.4	2.5	3.2	3.0	3.4	3.9	3.9
Non-Int. Exp./Tot. Inc. %	18.1	14.3	20.4	21.1	24.5	25.8	27.2
Price Range	69.50-52.60	71.25-58.75	70.13-36.88	65.25-45.38	66.38-38.69	44.56-26.69	29.00-19.06
P/E Ratio	8.7-6.6	12.0-9.9	20.7-10.9	22.0-15.3	28.7-16.7	23.7-14.2	17.4-11.4
Average Yield %	1.4	1.2	1.3	1.1	0.9	1.1	1.5

Statistics are as originally reported. Adj. for stk. splits: 4-for-1, 1/97. ① Bef. extraord. chrg. $15.0 mill. ② Bef. acctg. change credit $5.0 mill. ③ Bef. extraord. gain $231.0 mill., 12/01; $8.0 mill., 12/00; $5.0 mill., 12/99 ④ Incl. special contributions chrg. $225.0 mill.

OFFICERS:
S. F. O'Malley, Chmn.
G. J. Parseghian, Pres., C.E.O.
M. F. Baumann, Exec. V.P., C.F.O.

INVESTOR CONTACT: Shareholder Relations, (800) 373-3343

PRINCIPAL OFFICE: 8200 Jones Branch Drive, McLean, VA 22102-3110

TELEPHONE NUMBER: (703) 903-2000
FAX: (703) 903-2759
WEB: www.freddiemac.com

NO. OF EMPLOYEES: 3,500 (approx.)

SHAREHOLDERS: 5,627 (approx.)

ANNUAL MEETING: In May

INCORPORATED: July, 1970

INSTITUTIONAL HOLDINGS:
No. of Institutions: 757
Shares Held: 591,937,245
% Held: 85.4

INDUSTRY: Federal & fed.-sponsored credit (SIC: 6111)

TRANSFER AGENT(S): EquiServe Trust Company, N.A., Jersey City, NJ

FRISCH'S RESTAURANTS, INC.

YIELD 1.9%
P/E RATIO 10.8

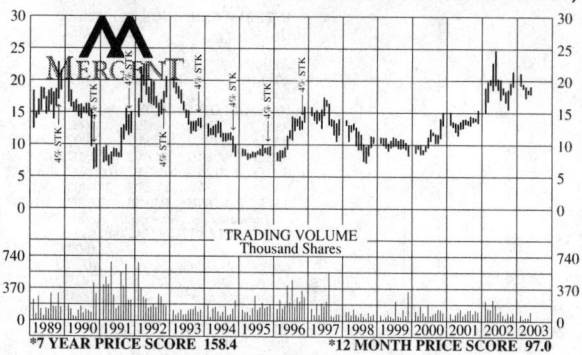

INTERIM EARNINGS (Per Share):

Qtr.	Sept.	Dec.	Feb.	May
1999-00	0.30	0.25	0.22	0.31
2000-01	0.45	0.38	0.24	0.42
2001-02	0.39	0.42	0.37	0.40
2002-03	0.58	0.44	0.32	...

INTERIM DIVIDENDS (Per Share):

Amt.	Decl.	Ex.	Rec.	Pay.
0.09Q	6/11/02	6/24/02	6/26/02	7/10/02
0.09Q	9/04/02	9/24/02	9/26/02	10/10/02
0.09Q	11/26/02	12/24/02	12/27/02	1/10/03
0.09Q	3/18/03	3/26/03	3/28/03	4/10/03
0.09Q	6/10/03	6/24/03	6/26/03	7/10/03

Indicated div.: $0.36

CAPITALIZATION (6/2/02):

	($000)	(%)
Long-Term Debt	35,905	35.4
Capital Lease Obligations..	4,246	4.2
Common & Surplus	61,230	60.4
Total	101,380	100.0

DIVIDEND ACHIEVER STATUS:
Rank: 212   10-Year Growth Rate: 6.20%
Total Years of Dividend Growth: 19

*7 YEAR PRICE SCORE 158.4   ***12 MONTH PRICE SCORE 97.0**

*NYSE COMPOSITE INDEX=100

RECENT DEVELOPMENTS: For the twelve weeks ended 3/9/03, net earnings declined 14.3% to $1.6 million compared with $1.9 million in the equivalent period of 2002. Results for 2003 included a charge of $145,000 for the impairment of long-lived assets. Total revenue climbed 8.1% to $51.9 million from $48.1 million a year earlier. Sales grew 8.2% to $51.7 million from $47.8 million in 2002. Same-store sales at the Company's Big Boy restaurants decreased 1.1% year over year. Separately, two Golden Corral restaurants are currently under construction and a third restaurant is expected to begin construction by the end of fiscal 2003. These three restaurants are scheduled to open in July, August and September of 2003, respectively. Plans for two more Golden Corral restaurants are underway. By the end of the third quarter of fiscal 2004, FRS expects to operate 25 Golden Corral restaurants. Meanwhile, construction of two new Big Boy restaurants are expected to begin later in 2003.

BUSINESS

FRISCH'S RESTAURANTS, INC. operated 88 family restaurants under the name of Frisch's Big Boy in Indiana, Kentucky and Ohio, and licensed another 34 restaurants to other Big Boy operators as of 4/8/03. In addition, the Company owns and operates 20 Golden Corral restaurants in greater Cincinnati and Dayton, Ohio and Louisville, Kentucky with plans to develop several more through 2007 in the Cincinnati, Dayton, Louisville, Cleveland and Toledo markets. Trademarks that the Company has the right to use include "Frisch's," "Big Boy," and "Golden Corral." In November 2000, the Company sold its Clarion Hotel Riverview for $12.0 million. In May 2001, FRS sold its Quality Hotel Central for $3.9 million.

ANNUAL FINANCIAL DATA

	6/2/02	6/3/01	5/28/00	5/30/99	5/31/98	6/1/97	6/2/96
Earnings Per Share	1.59	③ 1.27	② 1.08	① 0.74	0.73	0.17	0.32
Cash Flow Per Share	3.50	2.95	2.77	2.41	2.21	1.63	1.77
Tang. Book Val. Per Share	12.11	11.12	9.99	9.24	6.68	8.94	9.02
Dividends Per Share	0.33	0.32	0.29	0.28	0.24	0.23	0.22
Dividend Payout %	20.8	25.2	26.8	37.8	32.9	135.7	69.3

INCOME STATEMENT (IN THOUSANDS):

Total Revenues	211,758	190,030	167,200	159,551	152,222	165,931	166,945
Costs & Expenses	187,553	168,832	145,742	140,221	133,077	151,344	150,766
Depreciation & Amort.	9,551	8,599	9,621	9,937	9,256	10,486	10,350
Operating Income	14,654	12,599	11,837	9,394	9,889	4,101	5,829
Net Interest Inc./(Exp.)	d2,420	d2,607	d2,410	d2,437	d3,076	d2,373	d2,411
Income Before Income Taxes	12,234	9,992	9,426	6,957	6,813	1,728	3,417
Income Taxes	4,262	3,435	3,351	2,539	2,268	541	1,108
Net Income	7,971	③ 6,557	② 6,075	① 4,418	4,545	1,187	2,310
Cash Flow	17,522	15,156	15,696	14,355	13,801	11,673	12,660
Average Shs. Outstg.	5,013	5,144	5,658	5,967	6,238	7,151	7,157

BALANCE SHEET (IN THOUSANDS):

Cash & Cash Equivalents	671	280	565	200	84	231	135
Total Current Assets	7,487	6,965	20,778	6,924	6,508	6,882	8,564
Net Property	107,720	88,419	73,901	84,369	82,196	80,764	99,240
Total Assets	129,335	108,310	107,779	103,476	106,724	111,260	118,396
Total Current Liabilities	22,351	17,932	17,722	16,534	14,958	15,699	18,458
Long-Term Obligations	40,150	28,183	30,842	26,995	35,512	23,931	26,328
Net Stockholders' Equity	61,230	56,446	54,167	55,288	49,910	64,684	65,307
Net Working Capital	d14,864	d10,967	3,056	d9,610	d8,450	d8,816	d9,894
Year-end Shs. Outstg.	4,911	5,012	5,345	5,901	7,362	7,148	7,158

STATISTICAL RECORD:

Operating Profit Margin %	6.9	6.6	7.1	5.9	6.5	2.5	3.5
Net Profit Margin %	3.8	3.5	3.6	2.8	3.0	0.7	1.4
Return on Equity %	13.0	11.6	11.2	8.0	9.1	1.8	3.5
Return on Assets %	6.2	6.1	5.6	4.3	4.3	1.1	2.0
Debt/Total Assets %	31.0	26.0	28.6	25.5	33.3	21.5	22.2
Price Range	15.45-11.45	15.13-8.50	11.25-8.25	13.88-7.13	17.38-10.50	16.00-7.39	9.94-7.63
P/E Ratio	9.7-7.2	11.9-6.7	10.4-7.6	18.8-9.6	23.8-14.4	94.1-43.5	31.0-23.8
Average Yield %	2.5	2.7	3.0	2.7	1.7	2.0	2.5

Statistics are as originally reported. Adj. for stk. splits: 4% div., 12/27/96; 4% div., 12/27/95. ① Bef. extraord. gain of $3.7 mill. ② Bef. inc. from disc. opers. of $70,400. ③ Bef. inc. from disc. opers. of $1.1 mill.; incl. impairment chrg. of $1.5 mill.

OFFICERS:
J. C. Maier, Chmn.
C. F. Maier, Pres., C.E.O.
D. H. Walker, V.P., C.F.O., Treas.

INVESTOR CONTACT: Donald H. Walker, V.P., Treas., C.F.O., (513) 961-2660

PRINCIPAL OFFICE: 2800 Gilbert Avenue, Cincinnati, OH 45206-1206

TELEPHONE NUMBER: (513) 961-2660
FAX: (513) 559-5160
WEB: www.frischs.com

NO. OF EMPLOYEES: 4,400 full-time (approx.); 3,000 part-time (approx.)

SHAREHOLDERS: 2,300 (approx.)

ANNUAL MEETING: In Oct.

INCORPORATED: OH, Oct., 1947

INSTITUTIONAL HOLDINGS:
No. of Institutions: 23
Shares Held: 1,848,817
% Held: 37.0

INDUSTRY: Eating places (SIC: 5812)

TRANSFER AGENT(S): Continental Stock Transfer & Trust Company, New York, NY

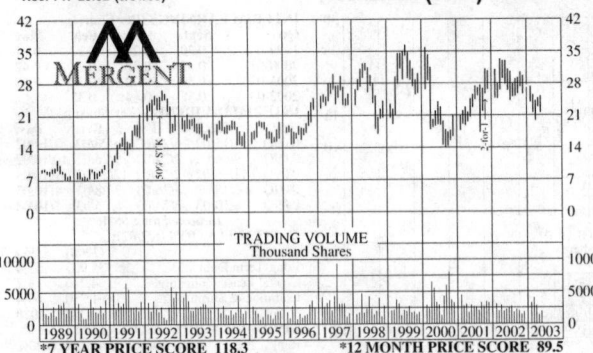

INTERIM EARNINGS (Per Share):

Qtr.	Feb.	May	Aug.	Nov.
2000	0.35	0.63	0.26	0.51
2001	0.20	0.42	0.52	0.46
2002	0.02	0.28	0.32	0.36
2003	0.11	...	...	...

INTERIM DIVIDENDS (Per Share):

Amt.	Decl.	Ex.	Rec.	Pay.
0.11Q	4/19/02	4/25/02	4/29/02	5/10/02
0.11Q	6/28/02	7/17/02	7/19/02	8/09/02
0.11Q	9/12/02	10/16/02	10/18/02	11/08/02
0.11Q	1/23/03	2/05/03	2/07/03	2/21/03
0.113Q	4/18/03	4/30/03	5/02/03	5/16/03

Indicated div.: $0.45 (Div. Reinv. Plan)

CAPITALIZATION (11/30/02):

	($000)	(%)
Long-Term Debt	161,763	25.9
Minority Interest	14,575	2.3
Common & Surplus	448,330	71.8
Total	624,668	100.0

TRADING VOLUME
Thousand Shares

*7 YEAR PRICE SCORE 118.3   *12 MONTH PRICE SCORE 89.5

*NYSE COMPOSITE INDEX=100

DIVIDEND ACHIEVER STATUS:
Rank: 209   10-Year Growth Rate: 6.56%
Total Years of Dividend Growth: 35

RECENT DEVELOPMENTS: For the 13 weeks ended 3/1/03, net income surged to $3.2 million compared with $666,000 in the corresponding period of the previous year. Earnings for 2003 and 2002 included after-tax charges of $3.1 million and $4.9 million, respectively, for severance and other costs related to the Company's restructuring initiative. Net sales grew slightly to $294.6 million from $293.2 million a year earlier, reflecting positive currency effects, partially offset by lower sales volumes and pricing.

PROSPECTS: The Company's restructuring initiative, which will be completed in the first half of 2003, is expected to result in annual operating savings of $10.0 million to $12.0 million, of which about $4.1 million were realized in 2002, and an incremental $6.0 million to $8.0 million is expected in 2003. Offsetting the restructuring savings are costs associated with FUL's pension and other postretirement benefit plans, which are expected to increase approximately $10.0 million compared with 2002.

BUSINESS

H.B. FULLER COMPANY and its subsidiaries are principally engaged in the manufacture and distribution of industrial adhesives, coatings, sealants, paints and other specialty chemical products worldwide. These products, in thousands of formulations, are sold to customers in a wide range of industries. Also, the Company is a producer and supplier of specialty chemical products for a variety of applications such as ceramic tile installation, HVAC insulation, powder coatings applied to metal surfaces such as office furniture, appliances and lawn and garden equipment, specialty hot melt adhesives for packaging applications, and liquid paint sold through retail outlets. As of 12/31/02, FULL had manufacturing operations in more than 36 countries in North and Latin America, Europe and the Asia/Pacific region.

ANNUAL FINANCIAL DATA

	12/31/02	12/1/01	12/2/00	11/27/99	11/28/98	11/29/97	11/30/96
Earnings Per Share	③ 0.98	① 1.59	1.74	② 1.58	② 0.58	① 1.43	1.61
Cash Flow Per Share	3.00	3.51	3.59	3.39	2.37	3.09	3.27
Tang. Book Val. Per Share	12.59	12.37	11.07	9.88	8.51	10.51	10.06
Dividends Per Share	0.44	0.43	0.42	0.41	0.39	0.36	0.33
Dividend Payout %	44.6	26.9	24.0	25.9	68.2	25.2	20.3
INCOME STATEMENT (IN MILLIONS):							
Total Revenues	1,256.2	1,274.1	1,352.6	1,364.5	1,347.2	1,306.8	1,275.7
Costs & Expenses	1,142.2	1,131.6	1,197.9	1,209.9	1,236.5	1,172.8	1,148.0
Depreciation & Amort.	57.5	54.4	52.2	50.8	49.5	46.8	47.0
Operating Income	56.4	88.1	102.5	103.7	61.2	87.3	80.8
Net Interest Inc./(Exp.)	d17.3	d21.2	d23.8	d26.8	d27.0	d19.8	d18.9
Income Before Income Taxes	40.3	63.5	76.9	74.4	32.8	65.3	76.6
Income Taxes	13.0	19.8	28.5	31.8	18.8	26.7	31.2
Equity Earnings/Minority Int.	0.8	1.3	0.7	1.5	2.0	1.6	0.1
Net Income	③ 28.2	① 44.9	49.2	② 44.1	② 16.0	① 40.3	45.4
Cash Flow	85.7	99.3	101.3	94.9	65.5	87.1	92.4
Average Shs. Outstg. (000)	28,601	28,330	28,206	27,956	27,688	28,200	28,228
BALANCE SHEET (IN MILLIONS):							
Cash & Cash Equivalents	3.7	11.5	10.5	5.8	4.6	2.7	3.5
Total Current Assets	408.9	403.9	435.1	440.1	457.9	409.2	388.2
Net Property	355.0	371.1	394.7	412.5	414.5	398.6	391.2
Total Assets	961.4	966.2	1,010.4	1,025.6	1,046.2	917.6	869.3
Total Current Liabilities	214.8	204.2	226.7	265.9	285.2	237.5	246.6
Long-Term Obligations	161.8	203.0	250.5	263.7	300.1	230.0	172.8
Net Stockholders' Equity	448.3	434.0	404.7	376.4	341.4	339.1	334.7
Net Working Capital	194.0	199.7	208.3	174.2	172.7	171.6	141.6
Year-end Shs. Outstg. (000)	28,362	28,281	28,240	28,080	27,965	27,682	28,132
STATISTICAL RECORD:							
Operating Profit Margin %	4.5	6.9	7.6	7.6	4.5	6.7	6.3
Net Profit Margin %	2.2	3.5	3.6	3.2	1.2	3.1	3.6
Return on Equity %	6.3	10.4	12.1	11.7	4.7	11.9	13.6
Return on Assets %	2.9	4.7	4.9	4.3	1.5	4.4	5.2
Debt/Total Assets %	16.8	21.0	24.8	25.7	28.7	25.1	19.9
Price Range	33.32-24.15	31.19-17.25	35.88-14.06	36.44-19.06	32.50-17.00	30.13-22.50	24.81-14.75
P/E Ratio	34.0-24.6	19.6-10.8	20.6-8.1	23.1-12.1	56.5-29.6	21.1-15.7	15.4-9.2
Average Yield %	1.5	1.8	1.7	1.5	1.6	1.4	1.7

Statistics are as originally reported. Adj. for 2-for-1 stk. split, 11/16/01. ① Bef. acctg. chrg.: 12/1/01, $501,000; 11/29/97, $3.4 mill.; 11/30/95, $2.5 mill. ② Incl. non-recurr. chrg. 11/27/99: $17.2 mill.; 11/28/98: $26.7 mill. ③ Incl. after-tax restructuring costs of $19.1 mill.

OFFICERS:
A. P. Stroucken, Chmn., Pres., C.E.O.
R. A. Tucker, Sr. V.P., C.F.O., Treas.
W. L. Gacki, V.P., Treas.
INVESTOR CONTACT: Scott Dvorak, Director of Investor Relations, (651) 236-5150
PRINCIPAL OFFICE: 1200 Willow Lake Blvd., Vadnais Heights, MN 55110-5101

TELEPHONE NUMBER: (651) 236-5900
FAX: (651) 236-5161
WEB: www.hbfuller.com
NO. OF EMPLOYEES: 4,900 (approx.)
SHAREHOLDERS: 3,606
ANNUAL MEETING: In April
INCORPORATED: MN, Dec., 1915

INSTITUTIONAL HOLDINGS:
No. of Institutions: 139
Shares Held: 18,232,369
% Held: 65.1
INDUSTRY: Adhesives and sealants (SIC: 2891)
TRANSFER AGENT(S): Wells Fargo Shareowner Services, Minnesota, MN

FULTON FINANCIAL CORPORATION

YIELD 3.1%
P/E RATIO 16.3

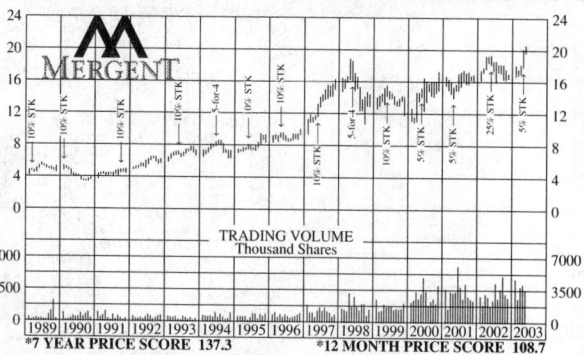

TRADING VOLUME
Thousand Shares

*7 YEAR PRICE SCORE 137.3   *12 MONTH PRICE SCORE 108.7

*NYSE COMPOSITE INDEX=100

INTERIM EARNINGS (Per Share):

Qtr.	Mar.	June	Sept.	Dec.
1999	0.23	0.24	0.24	0.25
2000	0.25	0.27	0.27	0.27
2001	0.26	0.28	0.22	0.29
2002	0.37	0.30	0.31	0.31
2003	0.34	...	...	...

INTERIM DIVIDENDS (Per Share):

Amt.	Decl.	Ex.	Rec.	Pay.
0.15Q	10/15/02	12/19/02	12/23/02	1/15/03
0.15Q	1/21/03	3/19/03	3/21/03	4/15/03
5% STK	4/15/03	4/28/03	4/30/03	5/23/03
0.16Q	4/15/03	6/19/03	6/23/03	7/15/03

Indicated div.: $0.64 (Div. Reinv. Plan)

CAPITALIZATION (12/31/02):

	($000)	(%)
Total Deposits	6,245,528	81.7
Long-Term Debt	535,555	7.0
Common & Surplus	863,742	11.3
Total	7,644,825	100.0

DIVIDEND ACHIEVER STATUS:
Rank: 155   10-Year Growth Rate: 9.51%
Total Years of Dividend Growth: 29

RECENT DEVELOPMENTS: For the quarter ended 3/31/03, net income rose 5.6% to $34.0 million compared with $32.2 million in the equivalent period of 2002. Results for 2003 and 2002 included investment securities gains of $2.2 million and $1.4 million, respectively. Results also included intangible amortization of $359,000 in both 2003 and 2002. Total interest income slipped 6.5% to $110.2 million from $117.8 million in the previous year. Total interest expense declined 16.7% to $34.5 million versus

$41.5 million a year earlier. Net interest income slipped 0.9% to $75.6 million compared with $76.3 million the year before. Provision for loan losses remained unchanged at $2.8 million versus the same period of the previous year. Total deposits increased 6.7% to $6.34 billion from $5.94 billion in 2002. Results benefited from strong performances in mortgage banking and investment management and trust services, partially offset by low interest rates and slow loan growth.

BUSINESS

FULTON FINANCIAL CORPORA-TION, with $8.28 billion in assets at 3/31/03, is a financial holding company. As of 4/15/03, the Company operated 189 banking offices in Delaware, Maryland, New Jersey and Pennsylvania through the following affiliates: Fulton Bank, Lebanon Valley Farmers Bank, Swineford National Bank, Lafayette Ambassador Bank, FNB Bank, Hagerstown Trust, Delaware National Bank, The Bank, The Peoples Bank of Elkton, and Skylands Community Bank. The Company's financial services affiliates include Fulton Financial Advisors, N.A., Fulton Insurance Services Group, Inc., and Dearden, Maguire, Weaver and Barrett, LLC. Residential mortgage lending is offered by all banks through Fulton Mortgage Company. On 1/2/01, FULT acquired investment management and advisory company, Dearden, Maguire, Weaver and Barrett, LLC. On 7/1/01, FULT acquired an $820.0 million bank holding company, Drovers Bancshares Corporation. On 2/18/03, Woodstown National Bank merged into The Bank, Woodsbury, NJ.

ANNUAL FINANCIAL DATA

	12/31/02	12/31/01	12/31/00	12/31/99	12/31/98	12/31/97	12/31/96
Earnings Per Share	1.29	① 1.04	1.05	0.97	0.88	0.73	0.72
Tang. Book Val. Per Share	7.46	6.81	6.86	6.20	6.07	5.35	5.34
Dividends Per Share	0.54	0.49	0.44	0.40	0.36	0.33	0.30
Dividend Payout %	41.9	47.0	41.8	40.9	40.8	44.6	41.1
INCOME STATEMENT (IN MILLIONS):							
Total Interest Income	469.3	518.2	462.6	418.9	409.3	319.6	268.7
Total Interest Expense	158.2	228.0	210.5	174.8	177.8	137.0	113.8
Net Interest Income	311.1	290.2	252.1	244.1	231.5	182.6	154.9
Provision for Loan Losses	11.9	14.6	8.6	8.2	5.6	7.7	4.2
Non-Interest Income	115.8	101.0	69.6	62.8	60.6	41.1	32.8
Non-Interest Expense	225.5	216.7	165.0	161.0	158.2	122.3	110.2
Income Before Taxes	189.4	160.0	148.0	137.7	128.3	93.6	73.3
Net Income	132.9	① 113.6	103.8	97.2	88.5	65.2	52.0
Average Shs. Outstg. (000)	108,474	109,136	98,748	100,368	100,547	89,450	72,124
BALANCE SHEET (IN MILLIONS):							
Cash & Due from Banks	314.9	356.5	267.2	245.6	247.6	172.4	165.0
Securities Avail. for Sale	2,383.6	1,687.8	1,140.6	1,137.8	1,206.1	597.4	317.1
Total Loans & Leases	5,326.7	5,373.0	4,879.7	4,432.0	4,040.5	3,317.2	2,783.6
Allowance for Credit Losses	81.5	71.9	73.2	67.3	67.5	56.6	48.2
Net Loans & Leases	5,245.1	5,301.1	4,806.5	4,364.8	3,973.0	3,260.6	2,735.4
Total Assets	8,387.8	7,770.7	6,571.2	6,070.0	5,838.7	4,460.8	3,769.4
Total Deposits	6,245.5	5,986.8	4,934.4	4,546.8	4,593.0	3,621.6	3,054.2
Long-Term Obligations	535.6	456.8	442.0	328.3	296.0	47.7	49.2
Total Liabilities	7,524.0	6,959.3	5,891.8	5,455.7	5,230.3	3,985.5	3,383.7
Net Stockholders' Equity	863.7	811.5	679.3	614.3	608.3	475.3	385.7
Year-end Shs. Outstg. (000)	106,155	108,413	99,087	99,049	100,257	88,863	72,275
STATISTICAL RECORD:							
Return on Equity %	15.4	14.0	15.3	15.8	14.5	13.7	13.5
Return on Assets %	1.6	1.5	1.6	1.6	1.5	1.5	1.4
Equity/Assets %	10.3	10.4	10.3	10.1	10.4	10.7	10.2
Non-Int. Exp./Tot. Inc. %	52.8	55.4	51.3	52.5	54.2	54.7	58.7
Price Range	19.41-15.91	17.52-13.92	17.32-10.89	15.55-11.75	18.91-10.68	16.34-9.37	10.02-8.31
P/E Ratio	15.0-12.3	16.8-13.3	16.5-10.3	16.1-12.1	21.5-12.1	22.3-12.8	13.9-11.5
Average Yield %	3.1	3.1	3.1	2.9	2.4	2.5	3.2

Statistics are as originally reported. Adj. for all stock splits through 5/03. ① Incl. merger-related expenses of $7.1 mill.

OFFICERS:
R. A. Fulton Jr., Chmn., C.E.O.
R. S. Smith Jr., Pres., C.O.O.
C. J. Nugent, Sr. Exec. V.P., C.F.O.

INVESTOR CONTACT: Corp. Comm. Dept., (717) 291-2739

PRINCIPAL OFFICE: One Penn Square, P.O. Box 4887, Lancaster, PA 17604

TELEPHONE NUMBER: (717) 291-2411
FAX: (717) 291-2695
WEB: www.fult.com

NO. OF EMPLOYEES: 2,906

SHAREHOLDERS: 29,860

ANNUAL MEETING: In Apr.

INCORPORATED: PA, 1982

INSTITUTIONAL HOLDINGS:
No. of Institutions: 122
Shares Held: 21,981,480
% Held: 21.8

INDUSTRY: National commercial banks (SIC: 6021)

TRANSFER AGENT(S): Stock Transfer Department, Lancaster, PA

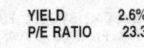

NYSE SYMBOL AJG
Rec. Pr. 27.25 (5/31/03)

GALLAGHER (ARTHUR J.) & COMPANY

YIELD 2.6%
P/E RATIO 23.3

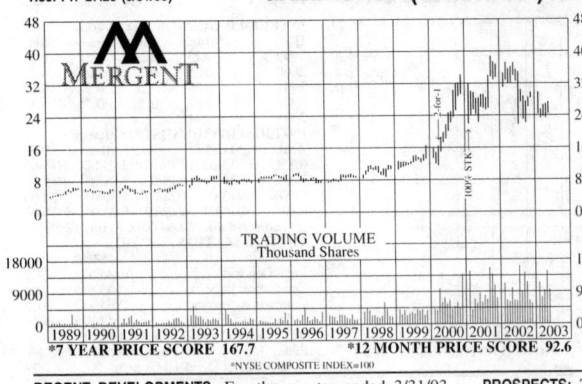

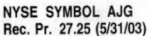

TRADING VOLUME
Thousand Shares

*7 YEAR PRICE SCORE 167.7   ***12 MONTH PRICE SCORE 92.6**

NYSE COMPOSITE INDEX=100

INTERIM EARNINGS (Per Share):

Qtr.	Mar.	June	Sept.	Dec.
1999	0.18	0.17	0.30	0.24
2000	0.20	0.19	0.37	0.28
2001	0.27	0.26	0.47	0.36
2002	0.37	0.37	0.25	0.42
2003	0.13	...	...	...

INTERIM DIVIDENDS (Per Share):

Amt.	Decl.	Ex.	Rec.	Pay.
0.15Q	5/14/02	6/26/02	6/28/02	7/15/02
0.15Q	9/12/02	9/26/02	9/30/02	10/15/02
0.15Q	11/21/02	12/27/02	12/31/02	1/15/03
0.18Q	1/23/03	3/27/03	3/31/03	4/15/03
0.18Q	5/21/03	6/26/03	6/30/03	7/15/03

Indicated div.: $0.72

CAPITALIZATION (12/31/02):

	($000)	(%)
Long-Term Debt	128,349	19.6
Common & Surplus	528,155	80.4
Total	656,504	100.0

DIVIDEND ACHIEVER STATUS:
Rank: 76   10-Year Growth Rate: 13.74%
Total Years of Dividend Growth: 18

RECENT DEVELOPMENTS: For the quarter ended 3/31/03, net income dropped 64.7% to $11.9 million from $33.7 million in the equivalent 2002 quarter. Results for 2003 included an after-tax charge of $19.3 million related to the Company's decision to exit from its investments in venture capital, development-stage companies and turn-arounds. Total revenues grew 6.4% to $254.3 million from $239.0 million the previous year. Commissions increased 17.8% to $168.6 million.

PROSPECTS: The Company should be well positioned for 2003 due to the current favorable rate environment and its full acquisition pipeline. Moreover, the hiring restrictions AJG implemented at the end of the third quarter of 2002 have been successful and remain in force. Meanwhile, the property/casualty portion of AJG's risk management segment continues to improve as new business production remains strong, claim counts have returned to favorable levels, and retention levels are exceeding 98.0%.

BUSINESS

ARTHUR J. GALLAGHER & COMPANY is engaged in providing insurance brokerage, risk management, employee benefit and other related services to clients in the United States and abroad. The Company's principal activity is the negotiation and placement of insurance for its clients. In addition, AJG specializes in furnishing risk management services that include assisting clients in analyzing risks and determining whether proper protection is best obtained through the purchase of insurance or through retention of those risks and the adoption of corporate risk management policies and cost-effective loss control and prevention programs. Risk management also includes claims management, loss control consulting and property appraisals. As of 4/23/03, the Company had offices in seven countries and served clients in more than 100 countries around the world through a network of correspondent brokers and consultants.

ANNUAL FINANCIAL DATA

	12/31/02	12/31/01	12/31/00	12/31/99	12/31/98	12/31/97	12/31/96
Earnings Per Share	☐ 1.41	1.39	1.05	0.88	0.78	0.78	0.66
Tang. Book Val. Per Share	4.44	3.60	3.75	3.14	2.69	2.31	1.89
Dividends Per Share	0.58	0.51	0.45	0.39	0.34	0.30	0.28
Dividend Payout %	41.1	36.3	42.4	44.0	43.9	38.9	42.5

INCOME STATEMENT (IN MILLIONS):

Total Revenues	1,101.2	910.0	740.6	605.8	540.7	488.0	456.7
Income Before Income Taxes	185.3	141.9	125.4	104.2	84.5	80.8	69.4
Income Taxes	55.6	16.6	37.6	36.5	28.0	27.5	23.6
Net Income	☐ 129.7	125.3	87.8	67.8	56.5	53.3	45.8
Average Shs. Outstg. (000)	91,861	90,127	83,924	77,132	72,824	68,152	71,100

BALANCE SHEET (IN MILLIONS):

Cash & Cash Equivalents	479.4	359.4	318.1	233.8	205.5	211.0	197.6
Premiums Due	1,183.7	555.3	405.2	364.9	288.3	217.6	237.6
Invst. Assets: Total	70.6	70.9	83.3	84.1	77.5	101.9	90.3
Total Assets	2,463.6	1,471.8	1,062.3	884.1	746.0	641.8	590.4
Long-Term Obligations	128.3	...	...	...	...	...	...
Net Stockholders' Equity	528.2	371.6	314.4	242.5	202.5	163.9	134.5
Year-end Shs. Outstg. (000)	88,548	85,111	79,497	73,680	70,580	66,364	65,172

STATISTICAL RECORD:

Return on Revenues %	11.8	13.8	11.9	11.2	10.5	10.9	10.0
Return on Equity %	24.6	33.7	27.9	27.9	27.9	32.5	34.0
Return on Assets %	5.3	8.5	8.3	7.7	7.6	8.3	7.8
Price Range	37.24-21.70	38.82-21.88	34.25-11.53	16.56-10.56	11.69-8.39	9.56-7.44	9.88-7.28
P/E Ratio	26.4-15.4	27.9-15.7	32.6-11.0	18.8-12.0	15.1-10.8	12.2-9.5	15.0-11.1
Average Yield %	2.0	1.7	1.9	2.9	3.4	3.6	3.3

Statistics are as originally reported. Adjusted for 2-for-1 stock split: 1/01 & 3/00. ☐ Incl. after-tax invest. chrg. $10.4 mill.

OFFICERS:
R. E. Gallagher, Chmn.
J. P. Gallagher, Jr., Pres., C.E.O.
D. K. Howell, C.F.O.

INVESTOR CONTACT: Marsha J. Akin, Investor Relations, (630) 773-3800

PRINCIPAL OFFICE: Two Pierce Place, Itasca, IL 60143-3141

TELEPHONE NUMBER: (630) 773-3800
FAX: (630) 285-4000
WEB: www.ajg.com
NO. OF EMPLOYEES: 7,100 (approx.)
SHAREHOLDERS: 700 (approx.)
ANNUAL MEETING: In May
INCORPORATED: IL, 1960; reincorp., DE, 1972

INSTITUTIONAL HOLDINGS:
No. of Institutions: 224
Shares Held: 61,297,769
% Held: 68.9

INDUSTRY: Insurance agents, brokers, & service (SIC: 6411)

TRANSFER AGENT(S): Computershare Investor Services, Chicago, IL

GANNETT CO., INC.

YIELD 1.2%
P/E RATIO 18.2

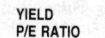
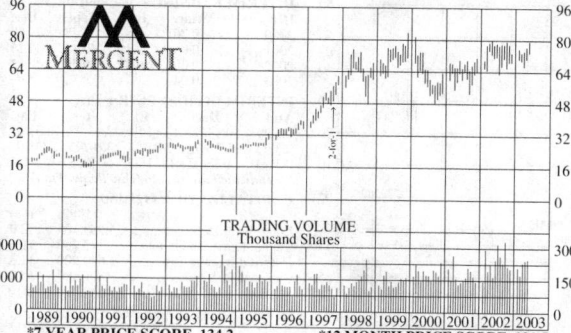

TRADING VOLUME Thousand Shares

*7 YEAR PRICE SCORE 134.2   *12 MONTH PRICE SCORE 101.5
*NYSE COMPOSITE INDEX=100

INTERIM EARNINGS (Per Share):

Qtr.	Mar.	June	Sept.	Dec.
2000	0.74	1.00	0.79	1.12
2001	0.66	0.88	0.66	0.93
2002	0.91	1.13	0.99	1.29
2003	0.93	...	...	...

INTERIM DIVIDENDS (Per Share):

Amt.	Decl.	Ex.	Rec.	Pay.
0.24Q	8/07/02	9/11/02	9/13/02	10/01/02
0.24Q	10/22/02	12/10/02	12/12/02	1/02/03
0.24Q	2/25/03	3/05/03	3/07/03	4/01/03
0.24Q	5/06/03	6/04/03	6/06/03	7/01/03

Indicated div.: $0.96 (Div. Reinv. Plan)

CAPITALIZATION (12/29/02):

	($000)	(%)
Long-Term Debt	4,547,265	37.5
Deferred Income Tax	678,541	5.6
Common & Surplus	6,911,795	56.9
Total	12,137,601	100.0

DIVIDEND ACHIEVER STATUS:

Rank: 251   10-Year Growth Rate: 4.05%
Total Years of Dividend Growth: 31

RECENT DEVELOPMENTS: For the quarter ended 3/30/03, net income climbed 2.6% to $249.8 million compared with $243.6 million in the corresponding period of 2002. Results included amortization of intangible assets of $1.8 million in both 2003 and 2002. Total operating revenues were $1.55 billion, up 2.6% from $1.51 billion in the previous year. Newspaper publishing revenues grew 3.6% to $1.39 billion. Operating income increased 2.1% to $411.0 million compared with $402.5 million the year before.

PROSPECTS: On 4/17/03, the Company announced the acquisition of a series of tourist magazines, ''101 Things to Do,'' in Hawaii. The transaction includes four quarterly magazines, the Web site, 101thingstodo.com, and the right to expand the franchise into other areas of the U.S. The acquisition enhances GCI's publications already in Hawaii and provides an opportunity to expand into other tourist markets. Separately, Gannett U.K. Limited agreed to acquire the Greater London regional publishing business.

BUSINESS

GANNETT CO., INC. is a diversified news and information company that publishes newspapers and operates broadcasting stations. GCI is also engaged in marketing, commercial printing, a newswire service, data services, and news programming. GCI has operations in 43 states, the District of Columbia, Guam, the United Kingdom, Belgium, Germany, Italy and Hong Kong. GCI is the largest U.S. newspaper group in terms of circulation, with 100 daily newspapers, including USA TODAY, more than 400 non-daily publications and USA WEEKEND, a weekly newspaper magazine. In the U.K., GCI subsidiary Newsquest plc publishes nearly 300 titles, including 17 daily newspapers. GCI owns and operates 22 television stations in major markets. Results for 2002 were derived: newspaper publishing, 88.0%; and television, 12.0%.

ANNUAL FINANCIAL DATA

	12/29/02	12/30/01	12/31/00	12/26/99	12/27/98	12/28/97	12/31/96
Earnings Per Share	4.31	3.12	④3.63	③3.26	②3.50	2.50	①2.22
Cash Flow Per Share	5.13	4.78	5.03	4.26	4.59	3.55	3.23
Tang. Book Val. Per Share	...	...	...	...	0.66	...	...
Dividends Per Share	0.93	0.89	0.85	0.81	0.80	0.73	0.70
Dividend Payout %	21.6	28.5	23.4	24.8	22.9	29.2	31.8
INCOME STATEMENT (IN MILLIONS)							
Total Revenues	6,422.2	6,344.2	6,222.3	5,260.2	5,121.3	4,729.5	4,421.1
Costs & Expenses	4,273.5	4,310.6	4,029.1	3,417.0	3,367.6	3,112.2	3,067.3
Depreciation & Amort.	222.4	443.8	375.9	280.1	310.2	301.0	287.4
Operating Income	1,926.3	1,589.8	1,817.3	1,563.1	1,443.5	1,316.3	1,066.4
Net Interest Inc./(Exp.)	d142.9	d217.2	d192.0	d88.9	d60.1	d91.7	d128.8
Income Before Income Taxes	1,764.5	1,370.6	1,608.8	1,527.2	1,669.4	1,209.0	1,086.7
Income Taxes	604.4	539.4	636.9	607.8	669.5	496.3	462.7
Net Income	1,160.1	831.2	④971.9	③919.4	②999.9	712.7	①624.0
Cash Flow	1,382.6	1,275.0	1,347.9	1,199.5	1,310.1	1,013.8	911.3
Average Shs. Outstg. (000)	269,286	266,833	268,118	281,608	285,711	285,610	281,782
BALANCE SHEET (IN MILLIONS)							
Cash & Cash Equivalents	90.4	140.6	193.2	46.2	66.2	52.8	31.2
Total Current Assets	1,133.1	1,178.2	1,302.3	1,075.2	906.4	884.6	766.6
Net Property	2,535.0	2,465.5	2,461.4	2,223.9	2,063.8	2,192.0	1,994.1
Total Assets	13,733.0	13,096.1	12,980.4	9,006.4	6,979.5	6,890.4	6,349.6
Total Current Liabilities	958.6	1,127.7	1,174.0	883.8	728.0	767.5	719.0
Long-Term Obligations	4,547.3	5,080.0	5,747.9	2,463.3	1,306.9	1,740.5	1,880.3
Net Stockholders' Equity	6,911.8	5,735.9	5,103.4	4,629.6	3,979.8	3,479.7	2,930.8
Net Working Capital	174.5	50.5	128.3	191.4	178.4	117.1	47.6
Year-end Shs. Outstg. (000)	267,910	265,797	264,272	277,926	279,001	283,874	282,636
STATISTICAL RECORD:							
Operating Profit Margin %	30.0	25.1	29.2	29.7	28.2	27.8	24.1
Net Profit Margin %	18.1	13.1	15.6	17.5	19.5	15.1	14.1
Return on Equity %	16.8	14.5	19.0	19.9	25.1	20.5	21.3
Return on Assets %	8.4	6.3	7.5	10.2	14.3	10.3	9.8
Debt/Total Assets %	33.1	38.8	44.3	27.3	18.7	25.3	29.6
Price Range	79.90-62.76	71.14-53.00	81.56-48.38	83.63-60.63	75.13-47.63	61.69-35.69	39.38-29.50
P/E Ratio	18.5-14.6	22.8-17.0	22.5-13.3	25.7-18.6	21.5-13.6	24.7-14.3	17.8-13.3
Average Yield %	1.3	1.4	1.3	1.1	1.3	1.5	2.0

Statistics are as originally reported. Adj. for 2-for-1 spl., 10/97. ① Excl. $294.6 mill. after-tx gain & $24.5 mill. inc. fr. disc. ops.; incl. $93.0 mill. after-tx gain. ② Incl. $184.0 mill. after-tax gain fr. disp. of five radio stations & alarm security bus. ③ Incl. $33.0 mill. net gain fr. exchange of TV stations & excl. $38.5 mill. gain fr. disc. ops. ④ Excl. $2.4 mill. net inc. fr. disc. ops. & $744.7 mill. net gain fr. sale of bus.

OFFICERS:
D. H. McCorkindale, Chmn., Pres., C.E.O.
G. Martore, Sr. V.P., C.F.O.

INVESTOR CONTACT: Gracia Martore, Sr. V.P., C.F.O., (703) 854-6918

PRINCIPAL OFFICE: 7950 Jones Branch Drive, McLean, VA 22107

TELEPHONE NUMBER: (703) 854-6000
FAX: (703) 364-0855
WEB: www.gannett.com
NO. OF EMPLOYEES: 51,000 (approx.)
SHAREHOLDERS: 13,100 (approx.)
ANNUAL MEETING: In May
INCORPORATED: NY, Dec., 1923; reincorp., DE, May, 1972

INSTITUTIONAL HOLDINGS:
No. of Institutions: 655
Shares Held: 212,515,030
% Held: 79.3

INDUSTRY: Newspapers (SIC: 2711)

TRANSFER AGENT(S): Wells Fargo Bank Minnesota, N.A., St. Paul, MN

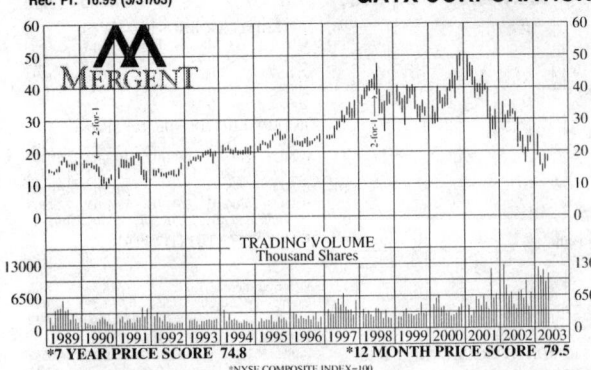

GATX CORPORATION

NYSE SYMBOL GMT
Rec. Pr. 16.99 (5/31/03)

YIELD 7.5%
P/E RATIO 70.8

7 YEAR PRICE SCORE 74.8   **12 MONTH PRICE SCORE 79.5**

NYSE COMPOSITE INDEX=100

INTERIM EARNINGS (Per Share):

Qtr.	Mar.	June	Sept.	Dec.
2000	0.76	0.67	0.78	d1.60
2001	0.09	0.46	d0.15	d0.25
2002	0.39	0.42	0.39	d0.61
2003	0.04	...	...	...

INTERIM DIVIDENDS (Per Share):

Amt.	Decl.	Ex.	Rec.	Pay.
0.32Q	10/11/02	12/11/02	12/13/02	12/31/02
0.32Q	1/30/03	3/05/03	3/07/03	3/31/03
0.32Q	4/25/03	6/11/03	6/13/03	6/30/03

Indicated div.: $1.28 (Div. Reinv. Plan)

CAPITALIZATION (12/31/02):

	($000)	(%)
Long-Term Debt	4,069,100	72.0
Capital Lease Obligations..	143,700	2.5
Deferred Income Tax	640,000	11.3
Common & Surplus	801,600	14.2
Total	5,654,400	100.0

DIVIDEND ACHIEVER STATUS:
Rank: 201   10-Year Growth Rate: 7.01%
Total Years of Dividend Growth: 17

RECENT DEVELOPMENTS: For the quarter ended 3/31/03, net income was $1.8 million versus income of $18.9 million a year earlier. The earnings decline was due to lower results from both the Company's Rail and Financial Services segments. Earnings for 2003 and 2002 included gains of $700,000 and $13.9 million on the extinguishment of debt, and asset impairment charges of $3.6 million and $2.6 million, respectively. Revenues fell 4.7% to $287.5 million.

PROSPECTS: GATX Rail's weak leasing rate pricing environment, coupled with ongoing weakness in Financial Services' core air and technology market, will likely restrain near-term results. However, GATX noted that its air fleet utilization as of 3/31/03 was 99.0%, it has placement or letters of intent on all six 2003 scheduled new aircraft deliveries, and placement or letters of intent on five of the eight 2003 scheduled existing lease renewals.

BUSINESS

GATX CORP. operates in two industry segments. GATX Rail is principally engaged in leasing rail equipment, including tank cars, freight cars and locomotives. As of 3/31/03, GMT owned or had an interest in about 106,000 railcars in North America. GATX Rail also owns Dyrekcja Eksploatacji Cystern, Poland's national tank car fleet, KVG Kesselwagen Vermietgesellschaft mbH, a German and Austrian-based tank car and specialty railcar leasing company, and a 37.5% interest in Switzerland-based AAE Cargo. The Financial Services segment provides financing for equipment and other capital assets on a worldwide basis and consists of four business units: Air, Technology, Venture Finance and Specialty Finance. In December 2002, GATX announced its intention to sell or otherwise run-off its Venture Finance business unit and curtail investment in its Specialty Finance business unit.

ANNUAL FINANCIAL DATA

	12/31/02	12/31/01	12/31/00	12/31/99	12/31/98	12/31/97	12/31/96
Earnings Per Share	④ 0.59	③ 0.15	② 0.63	3.01	2.62	① d1.27	2.19
Cash Flow Per Share	8.07	8.61	7.51	9.14	7.92	4.32	7.13
Tang. Book Val. Per Share	15.07	18.09	16.25	17.20	14.87	13.39	16.73
Dividends Per Share	1.28	1.24	1.20	1.10	1.00	0.92	0.86
Dividend Payout %	216.9	826.1	190.4	36.5	38.2	...	39.4
INCOME STATEMENT (IN MILLIONS):							
Total Revenues	1,274.3	1,488.6	1,311.8	1,773.0	1,763.1	1,701.9	1,414.4
Costs & Expenses	709.0	830.3	520.4	1,064.6	1,098.1	1,314.5	880.5
Depreciation & Amort.	368.1	415.9	334.8	308.2	267.5	252.3	202.4
Operating Income	197.2	242.4	377.6	400.2	397.5	135.1	331.5
Net Interest Inc./(Exp.)	d224.6	d249.9	d242.6	d232.2	d234.9	d222.4	d202.8
Income Before Income Taxes	39.0	5.6	53.5	253.9	162.6	d87.3	128.7
Income Taxes	10.0	cr1.9	22.7	102.6	74.3	cr5.5	54.4
Equity Earnings/Minority Int.	...	...	...	...	43.6	30.9	28.4
Net Income	④ 29.0	③ 7.5	② 30.8	151.3	131.9	① d50.9	102.7
Cash Flow	397.1	423.4	365.6	459.5	399.3	194.7	291.9
Average Shs. Outstg. (000)	49,177	49,202	48,753	50,301	50,426	45,084	40,966
BALANCE SHEET (IN MILLIONS):							
Cash & Cash Equivalents	372.0	347.3	173.6	102.5	94.5	77.8	46.2
Total Current Assets	1,534.8	1,823.0	1,684.5	1,144.1	1,032.4	1,168.5	1,039.1
Net Property	3,459.8	2,983.9	2,654.1	3,282.0	2,790.1	2,710.5	2,846.4
Total Assets	6,428.3	6,109.7	6,263.7	5,866.8	4,939.3	4,947.8	4,750.2
Total Current Liabilities	426.6	658.9	1,016.2	815.5	707.0	805.2	608.1
Long-Term Obligations	4,212.8	3,788.5	3,752.3	3,432.6	2,821.7	2,819.4	2,664.1
Net Stockholders' Equity	801.6	881.8	789.5	836.0	732.9	655.4	774.9
Net Working Capital	1,108.2	1,164.1	668.3	328.6	325.4	363.3	431.0
Year-end Shs. Outstg. (000)	49,048	48,756	48,599	48,599	49,284	48,942	46,128
STATISTICAL RECORD:							
Operating Profit Margin %	15.5	16.3	28.8	22.6	22.5	7.9	23.4
Net Profit Margin %	2.3	0.5	2.3	8.5	7.5	...	7.3
Return on Equity %	3.6	0.9	3.9	18.1	18.0	...	13.3
Return on Assets %	0.5	0.1	0.5	2.6	2.7	...	2.2
Debt/Total Assets %	65.5	62.0	59.9	58.5	57.1	57.0	56.1
Price Range	35.91-16.30	49.94-23.65	50.50-28.38	40.88-28.06	47.56-26.25	36.00-23.75	25.63-21.50
P/E Ratio	60.9-27.6	332.7-157.6	80.1-45.0	13.6-9.3	18.2-10.0	...	11.7-9.8
Average Yield %	4.9	3.4	3.0	3.2	2.7	3.1	3.6

Statistics are as originally reported. Adj. for 2-for-1 stk. split, 6/98 ① Incl. nonrecur. chrg. of $163.0 mill. ② Incl. chrg. of $160.5 mill.; bef. disc. ops. inc. of $35.8 mill. ③ Incl. job reduct. chrgs. of $13.4 mill., asset impair. chrgs. of $85.2 mill. & nonrecur. gain of $13.1 mill.; bef. disc. ops. inc. of $165.4 mill. ④ Incl. job reduct. chrgs. of $16.9 mill. & asset impair. chrgs. of $40.5 mill.; bef. disc. ops. inc. of $6.2 mill. & acctg. chge. chrg. of $34.9 mill.

OFFICERS:
R. H. Zech, Chmn., Pres., C.E.O.
B. A. Kenney, Sr. V.P., C.F.O.
R. J. Cinancio, V.P., Sec., Gen. Couns.

INVESTOR CONTACT: Irma Dominguez, Inv. Rel. Coord., (313) 621-8799

PRINCIPAL OFFICE: 500 West Monroe Street, Chicago, IL 60661-3676

TELEPHONE NUMBER: (312) 621-6200
FAX: (312) 621-6665
WEB: www.gatx.com

NO. OF EMPLOYEES: 2,800 (approx.)

SHAREHOLDERS: 3,663 (approx. record)

ANNUAL MEETING: In Apr.

INCORPORATED: NY, July, 1916

INSTITUTIONAL HOLDINGS:
No. of Institutions: 183
Shares Held: 44,901,072
% Held: 91.6

INDUSTRY: Rental of railroad cars (SIC: 4741)

TRANSFER AGENT(S): Mellon Investor Services, Ridgefield Park, NJ

GENERAL DYNAMICS CORPORATION

YIELD	1.9%
P/E RATIO	13.2

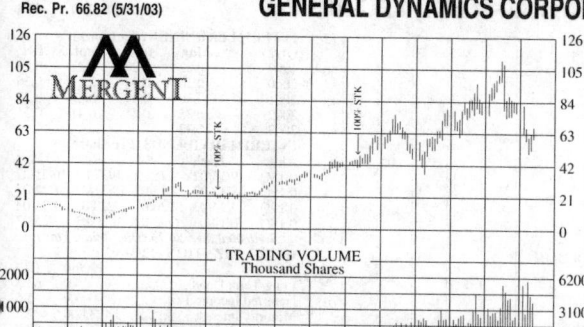

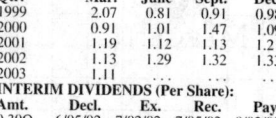

TRADING VOLUME
Thousand Shares

1989 1990 1991 1992 1993 1994 1995 1996 1997 1998 1999 2000 2001 2002 2003

*7 YEAR PRICE SCORE 144.8 *12 MONTH PRICE SCORE 78.6
*NYSE COMPOSITE INDEX=100

INTERIM EARNINGS (Per Share):

Qtr.	Mar.	June	Sept.	Dec.
1999	2.07	0.81	0.91	0.98
2000	0.91	1.01	1.47	1.09
2001	1.19	1.12	1.13	1.21
2002	1.13	1.29	1.32	1.33
2003	1.11	...	...	...

INTERIM DIVIDENDS (Per Share):

Amt.	Decl.	Ex.	Rec.	Pay.
0.30Q	6/05/02	7/02/02	7/05/02	8/02/02
0.30Q	8/07/02	10/09/02	10/11/02	11/15/02
0.30Q	12/04/02	1/15/03	1/17/03	2/07/03
0.32Q	3/05/03	4/09/03	4/11/03	5/09/03
0.32Q	6/04/03	7/02/03	7/07/03	8/08/03

Indicated div.: $1.28

CAPITALIZATION (12/31/02):

	($000)	(%)
Long-Term Debt	718,000	12.1
Common & Surplus	5,199,000	87.9
Total	5,917,000	100.0

DIVIDEND ACHIEVER STATUS:

Rank: 94	10-Year Growth Rate: 12.53%
Total Years of Dividend Growth:	11

RECENT DEVELOPMENTS: For the quarter ended 3/31/03, GD reported net income of $221.0 million versus income from continuing operations of $232.0 million the year before. Earnings for 2002 excluded a net loss of $3.0 million from discontinued operations. Net sales rose 10.3% to $3.42 billion. Information Systems and Technology segment sales improved 16.8% to $995.0 million, while Marine Systems segment sales grew 13.0% to $976.0 million.

PROSPECTS: On 3/3/03, GD acquired General Motors Defense in a cash transaction valued at $1.10 billion. GM Defense, with revenues of about $950.0 million, and a backlog of more than $1.40 billion as of 12/31/02, produces wheeled armored vehicles and turrets. Separately, GD continues to be awarded strategic contracts. For instance, GD was awarded a contract worth up to $473.0 million from the Israeli government to supply and support four Gulfstream G550 aircraft.

BUSINESS

GENERAL DYNAMICS CORPORATION is a major defense contractor operating in four business segments. Information Systems and Technology (26.6% of net sales for 2002) provides defense and commercial customers with infrastructure and systems integration skills required to process, communicate and manage information. Marine Systems (26.4%) provides the U.S. Navy with combat vessels, including nuclear submarines, surface combatants and auxiliary ships. The group also provides ship management services for the U.S. government and builds commercial ships. Aerospace (23.8%) designs, develops, manufactures, markets, and provides maintenance and support services for technologically advanced business jet aircraft. Combat Systems (21.1%) provides systems integration, design, development, production and support for armored vehicles, armaments, munitions and components. Other (2.1%) businesses consist of a coal mining operation, an aggregates operation and a leasing operation for liquefied natural gas tankers. On 1/26/01, GD acquired Primex Technologies, Inc.

ANNUAL FINANCIAL DATA

	12/31/02	12/31/01	12/31/00	12/31/99	12/31/98	12/31/97	12/31/96
Earnings Per Share	☑ 5.18	⬜ 4.65	⬜ 4.48	4.36	2.86	2.50	2.14
Cash Flow Per Share	6.23	5.98	5.60	5.35	3.86	3.20	2.67
Tang. Book Val. Per Share	5.62	3.84	6.43	3.27	5.46	5.64	13.60
Dividends Per Share	1.18	1.10	1.02	0.94	0.86	0.82	0.80
Dividend Payout %	22.8	23.7	22.8	21.6	30.2	32.8	37.6
INCOME STATEMENT (IN MILLIONS):							
Total Revenues	13,829.0	12,163.0	10,356.0	8,959.0	4,970.0	4,062.0	3,581.0
Costs & Expenses	12,034.0	10,407.0	8,801.0	7,556.0	4,302.0	3,525.0	3,161.0
Depreciation & Amort.	213.0	271.0	226.0	200.0	126.0	91.0	67.0
Operating Income	1,582.0	1,485.0	1,329.0	1,203.0	542.0	446.0	353.0
Net Interest Inc./(Exp.)	d45.0	d56.0	d60.0	d34.0	4.0	36.0	55.0
Income Before Income Taxes	1,584.0	1,424.0	1,262.0	1,126.0	549.0	479.0	409.0
Income Taxes	533.0	481.0	361.0	246.0	185.0	163.0	139.0
Net Income	☑ 1,051.0	⬜ 943.0	⬜ 901.0	880.0	364.0	316.0	270.0
Cash Flow	1,264.0	1,214.0	1,127.0	1,080.0	490.0	407.0	337.0
Average Shs. Outstg. (000)	202,852	202,907	201,262	202,057	127,000	127,000	126,000
BALANCE SHEET (IN MILLIONS):							
Cash & Cash Equivalents	328.0	442.0	177.0	270.0	220.0	441.0	894.0
Total Current Assets	5,098.0	4,893.0	3,551.0	3,491.0	1,873.0	1,689.0	1,858.0
Net Property	1,856.0	1,768.0	1,294.0	1,169.0	698.0	592.0	441.0
Total Assets	11,731.0	11,069.0	7,987.0	7,774.0	4,572.0	4,091.0	3,299.0
Total Current Liabilities	4,582.0	4,579.0	2,901.0	3,453.0	1,461.0	1,291.0	833.0
Long-Term Obligations	718.0	724.0	162.0	169.0	249.0	257.0	156.0
Net Stockholders' Equity	5,199.0	4,528.0	3,820.0	3,171.0	2,219.0	1,915.0	1,714.0
Net Working Capital	516.0	314.0	650.0	38.0	412.0	398.0	1,025.0
Year-end Shs. Outstg. (000)	200,993	200,746	200,502	201,013	127,000	126,000	126,000
STATISTICAL RECORD:							
Operating Profit Margin %	11.4	12.2	12.8	13.4	10.9	11.0	9.9
Net Profit Margin %	7.6	7.8	8.7	9.8	7.3	7.8	7.5
Return on Equity %	20.2	20.8	23.6	27.8	16.4	16.5	15.8
Return on Assets %	9.0	8.5	11.3	11.3	8.0	7.7	8.2
Debt/Total Assets %	6.1	6.5	2.0	2.2	5.4	6.3	4.7
Price Range	111.18-73.25	96.00-60.50	79.00-36.25	75.44-46.19	62.00-40.25	45.75-31.56	37.75-28.50
P/E Ratio	21.5-14.1	20.6-13.0	17.6-8.1	17.3-10.6	21.7-14.1	18.3-12.6	17.7-13.3
Average Yield %	1.3	1.4	1.8	1.5	1.7	2.1	2.4

Statistics are as originally reported. Adj. for 100% stk. div., 4/98. ⬜ Incl. research & dev. tax credit of $28.0 mill., 2001: $90.0 mill., 2000. ☑ Bef. a net loss of $134.0 mill. fr. disc. opers.

OFFICERS:
N. D. Chabraja, Chmn., C.E.O.
M. J. Mancuso, Sr. V.P., C.F.O.
D. H. Fogg, V.P., Treas.

INVESTOR CONTACT: R. Lewis, Inv. Rel., (703) 876-3195

PRINCIPAL OFFICE: 3190 Fairview Park Drive, Falls Church, VA 22042-4523

TELEPHONE NUMBER: (703) 876-3000
FAX: (703) 876-3125
WEB: www.generaldynamics.com

NO. OF EMPLOYEES: 57,000 (approx.)

SHAREHOLDERS: N/A

ANNUAL MEETING: In May

INCORPORATED: DE, Feb., 1952

INSTITUTIONAL HOLDINGS:
No. of Institutions: 596
Shares Held: 137,866,614
% Held: 70.0

INDUSTRY: Guided missiles and space vehicles (SIC: 3761)

TRANSFER AGENT(S): EquiServe Trust Company, N.A., Jersey City, NJ

GENERAL ELECTRIC COMPANY

YIELD 2.6%
P/E RATIO 19.4

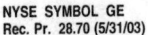

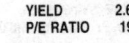

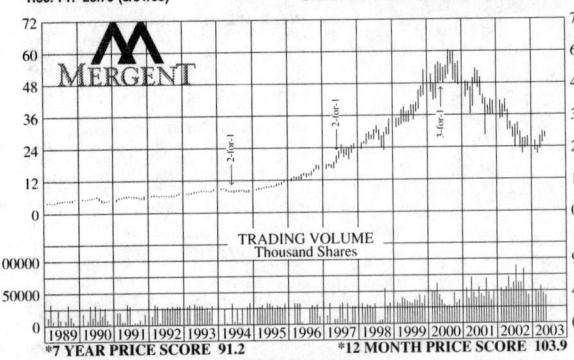

TRADING VOLUME
Thousand Shares

00000
50000

| 1989 | 1990 | 1991 | 1992 | 1993 | 1994 | 1995 | 1996 | 1997 | 1998 | 1999 | 2000 | 2001 | 2002 | 2003 |

*7 YEAR PRICE SCORE 91.2   *12 MONTH PRICE SCORE 103.9
*NYSE COMPOSITE INDEX=100

INTERIM EARNINGS (Per Share):

Qtr.	Mar.	June	Sept.	Dec.
1999	0.22	0.29	0.27	0.31
2000	0.26	0.34	0.32	0.36
2001	0.30	0.39	0.33	0.39
2002	0.35	0.44	0.41	0.31
2003	0.32	...	...	...

INTERIM DIVIDENDS (Per Share):

Amt.	Decl.	Ex.	Rec.	Pay.
0.18Q	9/13/02	9/25/02	9/27/02	10/25/02
0.19Q	12/13/02	12/27/02	12/31/02	1/27/03
0.19Q	2/14/03	2/26/03	2/28/03	4/25/03
0.19Q	6/13/03	6/26/03	6/30/03	7/25/03

Indicated div.: $0.76 (Div. Reinv. Plan)

CAPITALIZATION (12/31/02):

	($000)	(%)
Long-Term Debt	140,632,000	63.3
Deferred Income Tax	12,517,000	5.6
Minority Interest	5,473,000	2.5
Common & Surplus	63,706,000	28.7
Total	222,328,000	100.0

DIVIDEND ACHIEVER STATUS:
Rank: 70   10-Year Growth Rate: 14.45%
Total Years of Dividend Growth: 27

RECENT DEVELOPMENTS: For the quarter ended 3/31/03, income was $3.21 billion, before an accounting change charge of $215.0 million, versus income of $3.52 billion, before an accounting change charge of $1.02 billion, in the corresponding period of the previous year. Revenues slipped to $30.32 billion the year before, due to lower U.S. gas turbine sales and the absence of NBC Winter Olympic broadcast revenues in 2003.

PROSPECTS: Going forward, operating results should benefit from the introduction of new high-technology products and GE's continued effort to build its industrial growth platforms. Also, the Company continues to make strategic investments in its higher-return consumer finance and commercial finance businesses. For full-year 2003, the Company expect earnings to range from $1.55 to $1.70 per share.

BUSINESS

GENERAL ELECTRIC COMPANY'S businesses and their contributions to 2002 revenues are as follows: Financial Services (43.2%) are provided by GE Commercial Finance, GE Insurance, GE Consumer Finance and GE Equipment Management. The Materials, Power Systems, and Technical Products and Services (29.6%) sectors are providers of medical systems, power generation, motors and transportation systems. The Industrial Products and Systems segment (7.3%) includes transportation systems, industrial systems, and GE Supply. Aircraft Engines (8.3%) develops and manufactures engines for commercial aircraft. Consumer Products segment (6.3%) includes appliances and lighting. Broadcasting (5.3%) operations are conducted through NBC.

ANNUAL FINANCIAL DATA

	12/31/02	12/31/01	12/31/00	12/31/99	12/31/98	12/31/97	12/31/96
Earnings Per Share	② 1.51	② 1.41	1.27	1.07	0.93	① 0.82	0.73
Cash Flow Per Share	2.11	2.11	2.04	1.77	1.52	1.34	1.11
Tang. Book Val. Per Share	1.76	2.33	2.32	1.68	1.55	1.56	1.53
Dividends Per Share	0.72	0.64	0.55	0.47	0.40	0.35	0.31
Dividend Payout %	47.7	45.4	43.0	43.5	42.9	42.3	41.8

INCOME STATEMENT (IN MILLIONS):

	12/31/02	12/31/01	12/31/00	12/31/99	12/31/98	12/31/97	12/31/96
Total Revenues	131,698.0	125,913.0	129,853.0	111,630.0	100,469.0	90,840.0	79,179.0
Costs & Expenses	106,483.0	57,070.0	58,486.0	50,295.0	46,028.0	43,097.0	35,764.0
Depreciation & Amort.	5,998.0	7,089.0	7,736.0	6,691.0	5,860.0	5,269.0	3,785.0
Operating Income	19,217.0	61,754.0	63,631.0	54,644.0	48,581.0	42,474.0	39,630.0
Net Interest Inc./(Exp.)	10,216.0	d11,062.0	d11,720.0	d10,013.0	d9,753.0	d8,384.0	d7,904.0
Income Before Income Taxes	18,891.0	19,701.0	18,446.0	15,577.0	13,477.0	11,179.0	10,806.0
Income Taxes	3,758.0	5,573.0	5,711.0	4,860.0	4,181.0	2,976.0	3,526.0
Equity Earnings/Minority Int.	d326.0	d348.0	d407.0	d365.0	d265.0	d240.0	d269.0
Net Income	② 15,133.0	② 14,128.0	12,735.0	10,717.0	9,296.0	①8,203.0	7,280.0
Cash Flow	21,131.0	21,217.0	20,471.0	17,408.0	15,156.0	13,472.0	11,065.0
Average Shs. Outstg. (000)	10,028,000	10,052,000	10,057,000	9,996,000	9,990,000	10,035,000	9,924,000

BALANCE SHEET (IN MILLIONS):

	12/31/02	12/31/01	12/31/00	12/31/99	12/31/98	12/31/97	12/31/96
Cash & Cash Equivalents	125,772.0	110,099.0	99,534.0	90,312.0	83,034.0	76,482.0	64,080.0
Total Current Assets	145,700.0	128,254.0	116,848.0	105,850.0	97,307.0	91,301.0	77,257.0
Net Property	47,204.0	42,140.0	40,015.0	41,022.0	35,730.0	32,316.0	28,795.0
Total Assets	575,244.0	495,023.0	437,006.0	405,200.0	355,935.0	304,012.0	272,402.0
Total Current Liabilities	181,827.0	198,904.0	156,112.0	161,216.0	141,579.0	120,668.0	100,507.0
Long-Term Obligations	140,632.0	79,806.0	82,132.0	71,427.0	59,663.0	46,603.0	49,246.0
Net Stockholders' Equity	63,706.0	54,824.0	50,492.0	42,557.0	38,880.0	34,438.0	31,125.0
Net Working Capital	d36,127.0	d70,650.0	d39,264.0	d55,366.0	d44,272.0	d29,367.0	d23,250.0
Year-end Shs. Outstg. (000)	9,969,894	9,925,938	9,932,006	9,854,529	9,813,000	9,795,000	9,870,000

STATISTICAL RECORD:

	12/31/02	12/31/01	12/31/00	12/31/99	12/31/98	12/31/97	12/31/96
Operating Profit Margin %	14.6	49.0	49.0	49.0	48.4	46.8	50.1
Net Profit Margin %	11.5	11.2	9.8	9.6	9.3	9.0	9.2
Return on Equity %	23.8	25.8	25.2	25.2	23.9	23.8	23.4
Return on Assets %	2.6	2.9	2.9	2.6	2.6	2.7	2.7
Debt/Total Assets %	24.4	16.1	18.8	17.6	16.8	15.3	18.1
Price Range	41.84-21.40	53.55-28.50	60.50-41.64	53.16-31.35	34.64-23.00	25.52-15.98	17.69-11.58
P/E Ratio	27.7-14.2	38.0-20.2	47.6-32.8	49.5-29.2	37.1-24.6	31.1-19.5	24.1-15.8
Average Yield %	2.3	1.6	1.1	1.1	1.4	1.7	2.1

Statistics are as originally reported. Adj. for 3-for-1 stock split, 2/00; 2-for-1, 5/97. ① Incl. an after-tax gain of $1.50 bill. from the exchange of Lockheed Martin pfd. stk. & after-tax charges of $1.50 bill. for restruct. & oth. spec. matters. ② Bef. acctg. chng. chrg. of $444.0 mill., 2001; $1.02 bill., 2002.

OFFICERS:
J. R. Immelt, Chmn., C.E.O.
D. D. Dammerman, Vice-Chmn.
G. L. Rogers, Vice-Chmn.

INVESTOR CONTACT: David Frail, Shareholder Relations, (203) 373-2816

PRINCIPAL OFFICE: 3135 Easton Turnpike, Fairfield, CT 06828-0001

TELEPHONE NUMBER: (203) 373-2211
FAX: (203) 373-3131
WEB: www.ge.com
NO. OF EMPLOYEES: 315,000 (avg.)
SHAREHOLDERS: 669,000 (approx.)
ANNUAL MEETING: In Apr.
INCORPORATED: NY, Apr., 1892

INSTITUTIONAL HOLDINGS:
No. of Institutions: 1,320
Shares Held: 751,698,704
% Held: 50.5

INDUSTRY: Electric lamps (SIC: 3641)

TRANSFER AGENT(S): GE Share Owner Services, c/o The Bank of New York, New York, NY.

GENUINE PARTS COMPANY

YIELD 3.6%
P/E RATIO 15.5

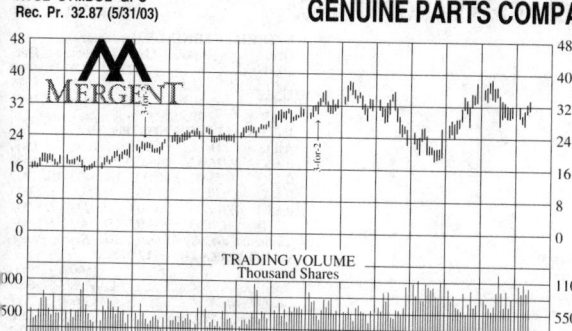

*7 YEAR PRICE SCORE 117.5   *12 MONTH PRICE SCORE 101.1

*NYSE COMPOSITE INDEX=100

INTERIM EARNINGS (Per Share):

Qtr.	Mar.	June	Sept.	Dec.
2000	0.52	0.55	0.53	0.61
2001	0.52	0.55	0.51	0.14
2002	0.50	0.55	0.54	0.52
2003	0.51	...	...	...

INTERIM DIVIDENDS (Per Share):

Amt.	Decl.	Ex.	Rec.	Pay.
0.29Q	8/19/02	9/04/02	9/06/02	10/01/02
0.29Q	11/18/02	12/04/02	12/06/02	1/02/03
0.295Q	2/17/03	3/05/03	3/07/03	4/01/03
0.295Q	4/17/03	6/04/03	6/06/03	7/01/03

Indicated div.: $1.18 (Div. Reinv. Plan)

CAPITALIZATION (12/31/02):

	($000)	(%)
Long-Term Debt	674,796	22.9
Deferred Income Tax	97,912	3.3
Minority Interest	47,408	1.6
Common & Surplus	2,130,009	72.2
Total	2,950,125	100.0

DIVIDEND ACHIEVER STATUS:
Rank: 220   10-Year Growth Rate: 5.74%
Total Years of Dividend Growth: 46

RECENT DEVELOPMENTS: For the quarter ended 3/31/03, income increased 1.6% to $88.4 million versus $87.0 million a year earlier. Results for 2003 and 2002 excluded accounting change charges of $19.5 million and $395.1 million, respectively. Net sales rose 2.2% to $2.02 billion from $1.98 billion a year earlier. Gross profit climbed 5.7% to $638.3 million, or 31.6% of net sales, from $604.0 million, or 30.5% of net sales, the previous year.

PROSPECTS: Demand for replacement parts is expected to grow due to anticipated slower sales of new cars, combined with other factors such as growing vehicle count, continuing increases in miles driven and accumulated mileage and the rising age of vehicles on the road. Meanwhile, the opening of new automotive plants in the southeastern area of the U.S. should provide a future avenue of growth for Motion Industries.

BUSINESS

GENUINE PARTS COMPANY is a service organization engaged in the distribution of automotive replacement parts, industrial replacement parts, office products and electrical and electronic materials throughout North America. GPC's Automotive Parts Group (52.3% of sales in 2002) distributes primarily NAPA automotive replacement parts and accessory items to independent and company-owned NAPA auto parts stores. The Industrial Parts Group's (27.1%) Motion Industries distributes industrial replacement parts including bearings, mechanical power transmission, electrical power transmission, hydraulic, pneumatic, and hose products. The Office Products Group's (16.8%) S.P. Richards Company distributes over 30,000 business products. The Electrical and Electronic Materials Group's (3.8%) EIS, Inc. distributes a range of materials and products for electrical and electronic apparatus.

ANNUAL FINANCIAL DATA

	12/31/02	12/31/01	12/31/00	12/31/99	12/31/98	12/31/97	12/31/96
Earnings Per Share	② 2.10	① 1.71	2.20	2.11	1.98	1.90	1.82
Cash Flow Per Share	2.50	2.21	2.72	2.61	2.36	2.23	2.10
Tang. Book Val. Per Share	11.88	10.97	10.50	9.80	9.52	10.39	9.62
Dividends Per Share	1.16	1.13	1.08	1.03	0.99	0.94	0.88
Dividend Payout %	55.0	66.1	49.3	48.8	50.0	49.6	48.3
INCOME STATEMENT (IN MILLIONS):							
Total Revenues	8,258.9	8,220.7	8,369.9	7,981.7	6,614.0	6,005.2	5,720.5
Costs & Expenses	7,583.0	7,638.9	7,630.8	7,263.7	5,955.6	5,380.8	5,124.8
Depreciation & Amort.	70.2	85.8	92.3	90.0	69.3	58.9	50.4
Operating Income	605.7	496.0	646.8	628.1	589.1	565.6	545.2
Income Before Income Taxes	605.7	496.0	646.8	628.1	589.1	565.6	545.2
Income Taxes	238.2	198.9	261.4	250.4	233.3	223.2	215.2
Net Income	② 367.5	① 297.1	385.3	377.6	355.8	342.4	330.1
Cash Flow	437.7	382.9	477.6	467.6	425.1	401.3	380.5
Average Shs. Outstg. (000)	175,104	173,633	175,327	179,238	180,081	180,165	181,568
BALANCE SHEET (IN MILLIONS):							
Cash & Cash Equivalents	20.0	85.8	27.7	45.7	85.0	72.8	67.4
Total Current Assets	3,335.8	3,146.2	3,019.5	2,895.2	2,683.4	2,093.6	1,937.6
Net Property	333.1	345.1	395.3	413.5	404.0	372.5	346.0
Total Assets	4,019.8	4,206.6	4,142.1	3,929.7	3,600.4	2,754.4	2,521.6
Total Current Liabilities	1,069.7	919.2	988.3	916.0	818.4	556.9	568.4
Long-Term Obligations	674.8	835.6	770.6	702.4	588.6	209.5	110.2
Net Stockholders' Equity	2,130.0	2,345.1	2,260.8	2,177.5	2,053.3	1,859.5	1,732.1
Net Working Capital	2,266.1	2,227.0	2,031.2	1,979.2	1,864.9	1,536.6	1,369.3
Year-end Shs. Outstg. (000)	174,381	173,474	172,390	177,276	179,505	178,948	180,048
STATISTICAL RECORD:							
Operating Profit Margin %	7.3	6.0	7.7	7.9	8.9	9.4	9.5
Net Profit Margin %	4.4	3.6	4.6	4.7	5.4	5.7	5.8
Return on Equity %	17.3	12.7	17.0	17.3	17.3	18.4	19.1
Return on Assets %	9.1	7.1	9.3	9.6	9.9	12.4	13.1
Debt/Total Assets %	16.8	19.9	18.6	17.9	16.3	7.6	4.4
Price Range	38.80-27.10	37.94-23.91	26.69-18.25	35.75-22.25	38.25-28.25	35.88-28.67	31.67-26.67
P/E Ratio	18.5-12.9	22.2-14.0	12.1-8.3	16.9-10.5	19.3-14.3	18.9-15.1	17.4-14.7
Average Yield %	3.5	3.7	4.8	3.6	3.0	2.9	3.0

Statistics are as originally reported. Adj. for stk. splits: 3-for-2, 4/97 ① Incl. after-tax non-recurr. chrg. $64.4 mill. ② Bef. acctg. change chrg. $395.1 mill.

OFFICERS:
L. L. Prince, Chmn., C.E.O.
T. C. Gallagher, Pres., C.O.O.
J. W. Nix, Exec. V.P., C.F.O.

INVESTOR CONTACT: Jerry Nix, Exec. V.P., Finance; C.F.O., (770) 953-1700

PRINCIPAL OFFICE: 2999 Circle 75 Parkway, Atlanta, GA 30339

TELEPHONE NUMBER: (770) 953-1700
FAX: (770) 956-2211
WEB: www.genpt.com

NO. OF EMPLOYEES: 30,700 (approx.)

SHAREHOLDERS: 7,773 (record)

ANNUAL MEETING: In April

INCORPORATED: GA, May, 1928

INSTITUTIONAL HOLDINGS:
No. of Institutions: 330
Shares Held: 125,942,356
% Held: 72.4

INDUSTRY: Motor vehicle supplies and new parts (SIC: 5013)

TRANSFER AGENT(S): Sun Trust Bank, Atlanta, GA

GLACIER BANCORP, INC.

YIELD	2.6%
P/E RATIO	13.7

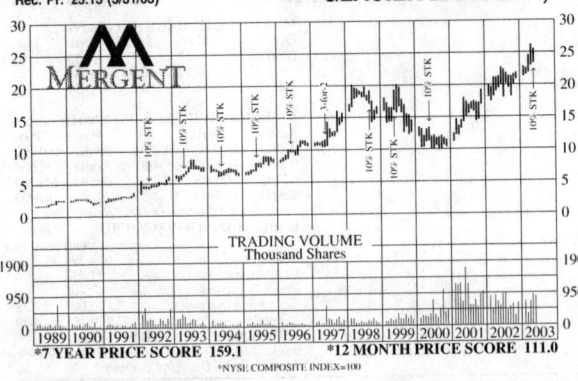

*7 YEAR PRICE SCORE 159.1 ***12 MONTH PRICE SCORE 111.0**
*NYSE COMPOSITE INDEX=100

INTERIM EARNINGS (Per Share):

Qtr.	Mar.	June	Sept.	Dec.
2000	0.25	0.25	0.30	0.29
2001	0.26	0.31	0.30	0.35
2002	0.36	0.43	0.45	0.45
2003	0.50	...	...	...

INTERIM DIVIDENDS (Per Share):

Amt.	Decl.	Ex.	Rec.	Pay.
0.16Q	6/26/02	7/05/02	7/09/02	7/18/02
0.17Q	9/25/02	10/04/02	10/08/02	10/17/02
0.18Q	12/30/02	1/10/03	1/14/03	1/23/03
0.18Q	3/14/03	4/04/03	4/08/03	4/17/03
10% STK	4/30/03	5/09/03	5/13/03	5/22/03

Indicated div.: $0.65 (adj.) (Div. Reinv. Plan)

CAPITALIZATION (12/31/02):

	($000)	(%)
Total Deposits	1,459,923	66.6
Long-Term Debt	483,660	22.1
Redeemable Pfd. Stock	35,000	1.6
Common & Surplus	212,249	9.7
Total	2,190,832	100.0

DIVIDEND ACHIEVER STATUS:

Rank: 47   10-Year Growth Rate: 17.22%
Total Years of Dividend Growth: 11

RECENT DEVELOPMENTS: For the first quarter ended 3/31/03, net earnings advanced 28.3% to $8.8 million compared with $6.9 million in the corresponding prior-year quarter. Net interest income increased 5.0% to $21.4 million from $20.4 million a year earlier. Total interest income decreased 4.4% to $31.6 million from $33.1 million the year before, while total interest expense fell 19.5% to $10.2 million from $12.7 million. Provision for loan losses amounted to $841,000 in 2003 versus $1.3 million in 2002.

Non-interest income climbed 27.7% to $7.5 million from $5.8 million, while non-interest expense rose 3.6% to $14.9 million from $14.4 million in the previous year. Return on average equity for the quarter was 16.41% versus 15.09% in 2002. On 4/24/03, the Company agreed to acquire Pend Oreille Bank in an all-cash transaction valued at $10.4 million. Pend Oreille branch locations will become branches of Mountain West Bank, thus expanding GBCI's coverage in northern Idaho and into Washington.

BUSINESS

GLACIER BANCORP, INC. is the parent holding company of its seven wholly-owned banking subsidiaries, Glacier Bank, First Security Bank of Missoula, Western Security Bank, Mountain West Bank in Idaho, Big Sky Western Bank, Valley Bank of Helena and Glacier Bank of Whitefish. GBCI provides commercial banking services in 27 communities through 51 banking offices in Montana, Idaho and Utah. The Company offers a range of banking products and services, including transaction and savings deposits, commercial, consumer and real estate loans, mortgage origination services, and retail brokerage services. As of 3/31/03, GBCI had assets of $2.32 billion and deposits of $1.48 billion. On 2/28/01, the Company acquired Western Security Bank for approximately 4.5 million common shares of GBCI and $37.3 million in cash.

ANNUAL FINANCIAL DATA

	12/31/02	12/31/01	12/31/00	12/31/99	12/31/98	12/31/97	12/31/96
Earnings Per Share	1.69	① 1.22	1.10	1.15	1.06	① 0.99	① 0.83
Tang. Book Val. Per Share	9.06	7.28	7.28	6.83	7.14	6.39	5.58
Dividends Per Share	0.58	0.55	② 0.562	0.52	0.38	0.31	0.28
Dividend Payout %	34.4	44.8	51.1	44.9	36.3	31.2	33.7
INCOME STATEMENT (IN MILLIONS):							
Total Interest Income	134.0	137.9	78.8	58.9	51.1	44.0	41.1
Total Interest Expense	47.5	65.5	37.4	25.6	22.2	19.9	18.6
Net Interest Income	86.5	72.4	41.5	33.3	28.9	24.1	22.6
Provision for Loan Losses	5.7	4.5	1.9	1.5	1.5	0.7	0.9
Non-Interest Income	25.9	23.3	13.3	11.1	11.3	8.3	8.3
Non-Interest Expense	57.8	57.4	31.3	24.0	21.5	17.2	17.5
Income Before Taxes	48.8	33.7	21.6	18.8	17.0	14.5	12.5
Net Income	32.4	① 21.7	14.0	12.2	10.7	① 9.2	① 7.4
Average Shs. Outstg. (000)	19,189	17,755	12,699	10,573	10,152	9,033	9,004
BALANCE SHEET (IN MILLIONS):							
Cash & Due from Banks	74.6	73.5	41.5	46.3	31.5	26.5	24.7
Securities Avail. for Sale	740.0	508.6	211.9	191.4	90.7	93.3	85.1
Total Loans & Leases	1,271.6	1,315.6	735.4	593.5	499.1	424.6	389.9
Allowance for Credit Losses	22.9	20.7	8.9	6.6	4.8	3.5	3.3
Net Loans & Leases	1,248.7	1,294.9	726.5	587.0	494.2	421.0	386.6
Total Assets	2,281.3	2,085.7	1,056.7	884.1	666.7	580.4	546.0
Total Deposits	1,459.9	1,446.1	720.6	576.3	444.5	346.8	321.7
Long-Term Obligations	483.7	367.3	196.8	194.7	120.6	139.3	143.3
Total Liabilities	2,069.1	1,908.8	958.6	805.3	591.7	520.8	494.0
Net Stockholders' Equity	212.2	177.0	98.1	78.8	74.9	59.6	51.9
Year-end Shs. Outstg. (000)	19,014	18,562	12,592	10,505	10,131	9,113	9,042
STATISTICAL RECORD:							
Return on Equity %	15.3	12.3	14.3	15.5	14.3	15.4	14.3
Return on Assets %	1.4	1.0	1.3	1.4	1.6	1.6	1.4
Equity/Assets %	9.3	8.5	9.3	8.9	11.2	10.3	9.5
Non-Int. Exp./Tot. Inc. %	51.4	60.0	57.1	54.1	53.5	52.8	56.5
Price Range	22.72-17.36	19.26-11.14	13.43-10.00	20.15-12.29	20.15-14.18	16.05-10.42	11.50-8.07
P/E Ratio	13.4-10.3	15.8-9.1	12.2-9.1	17.4-10.6	19.0-13.4	16.2-10.5	13.9-9.8
Average Yield %	2.9	3.6	4.8	3.2	2.2	2.3	2.8

Statistics are as originally reported. Adj. for stk splits: 10%, 5/03, 5/00, 5/99, 10/98; 3-for-2, 5/97. ① Incl. acquis. chrgs. of $563,000, 1996; $32,000, 1997; $2.0 mill., 2001. ② Incl. spec. div. of $0.041.

OFFICERS:
J. S. MacMillan, Chmn.
M. J. Blodnick, Pres., C.E.O.
J. H. Strosahl, Exec. V.P., C.F.O., Treas.

INVESTOR CONTACT: James H. Strosahl
(406) 756-4263

PRINCIPAL OFFICE: 49 Commons Loop, Kalispell, MT 59901

TELEPHONE NUMBER: (406) 756-4200
FAX: (406) 756-3518
WEB: www.glacierbancorp.com
NO. OF EMPLOYEES: 737 full-time; 72 part-time
SHAREHOLDERS: 8,713 (approx.)
ANNUAL MEETING: In April
INCORPORATED: DE, Dec., 1990

INSTITUTIONAL HOLDINGS:
No. of Institutions: 69
Shares Held: 7,010,792
% Held: 41.2

INDUSTRY: Federal savings institutions
(SIC: 6035)

TRANSFER AGENT(S): American Stock Transfer & Trust Company, New York, NY

GOLDEN WEST FINANCIAL CORPORATION

YIELD 0.4%
P/E RATIO 12.4

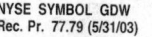
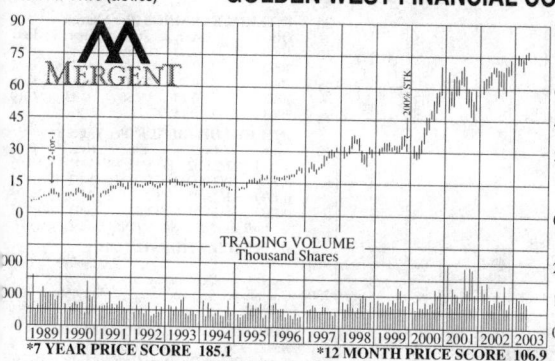

TRADING VOLUME
Thousand Shares

*7 YEAR PRICE SCORE 185.1   *12 MONTH PRICE SCORE 106.9
*NYSE COMPOSITE INDEX=100

INTERIM EARNINGS (Per Share):

Qtr.	Mar.	June	Sept.	Dec.
2000	0.78	0.84	0.86	0.93
2001	1.10	1.30	1.28	1.44
2002	1.51	1.44	1.56	1.60
2003	1.67	...	...	...

INTERIM DIVIDENDS (Per Share):

Amt.	Decl.	Ex.	Rec.	Pay.
0.072Q	4/30/02	5/13/02	5/15/02	6/10/02
0.072Q	7/25/02	8/13/02	8/15/02	9/10/02
0.085Q	10/25/02	11/13/02	11/15/02	12/10/02
0.085Q	1/31/03	2/12/03	2/15/03	3/10/03
0.085Q	4/29/03	5/13/03	5/15/03	6/10/03

Indicated div.: $0.34

CAPITALIZATION (12/31/02):

	($000)	(%)
Total Deposits	41,038,797	61.2
Long-Term Debt	21,034,581	31.3
Common & Surplus	5,025,250	7.5
Total	67,098,628	100.0

DIVIDEND ACHIEVER STATUS:

Rank: 67   10-Year Dividend Growth Rate: 14.71%
Total Years of Dividend Growth: 19

RECENT DEVELOPMENTS: For the quarter ended 3/31/03, net income increased 9.2% to $260.1 million from $238.1 million in the corresponding prior-year period. Results for 2003 and 2002 included gains on the sale of securities, mortgage-backed securities and loans of $15.3 million and $14.4 million, and pre-tax gains from changes in the fair value of derivatives of $2.9 million and $7.1 million, respectively. Net interest income advanced 13.2% to $528.7 million.

PROSPECTS: Demand for residential mortgages remains strong, supported by low interest rate environment. GDW's originations during the first quarter of 2003 outpaced repayments of existing loans, and as a result, its mortgage portfolio grew $2.10 billion versus an increase of $798.0 million in the corresponding prior-year period. New loans originated during the first quarter were comprised of 91.0% of adjustable rate mortgages, which helps limit GDW's earnings exposure once market interest rates rise.

BUSINESS

GOLDEN WEST FINANCIAL COR-PORATION, with assets of $70.00 billion as of 3/31/03, is the holding company of World Savings Bank, FSB, a federally chartered savings and lending institution. As of 3/31/03, GDW operated 472 savings and lending offices in 38 states under the World name. Also, the Company has two other subsidiaries, Atlas Advisers, Inc., and Atlas Securities, Inc., which provide services to Atlas Assets, Inc., a registered open-end management investment company sponsored by GDW. Atlas Advisers, Inc., is a registered investment adviser and the investment manager of Atlas Assets, Inc.'s portfolios. Atlas Securities, Inc., is a registered broker-dealer and the sole distributor of Atlas Fund shares.

ANNUAL FINANCIAL DATA

	12/31/02	12/31/01	12/31/00	12/31/99	12/31/98	12/31/97	12/31/96
Earnings Per Share	④ 6.12	③ 5.11	3.41	2.87	② 2.58	2.04	① 2.11
Tang. Book Val. Per Share	32.73	27.55	23.28	19.80	18.32	15.76	13.66
Dividends Per Share	0.30	0.26	0.22	0.19	0.17	0.15	0.13
Dividend Payout %	4.9	5.1	6.5	6.7	6.7	7.4	6.2
INCOME STATEMENT (IN MILLIONS):							
Total Interest Income	3,497.0	4,209.6	3,796.5	2,825.8	2,962.6	2,832.5	2,581.6
Total Interest Expense	1,566.7	2,578.3	2,645.4	1,822.4	1,995.2	1,942.0	1,750.6
Net Interest Income	1,930.3	1,631.3	1,151.2	1,003.5	967.3	890.5	831.0
Provision for Loan Losses	21.2	22.3	9.2	cr2.1	11.3	57.6	84.3
Non-Interest Income	247.0	236.7	160.8	143.3	137.6	81.3	74.9
Non-Interest Expense	601.5	513.8	424.8	386.1	354.5	327.0	453.4
Income Before Taxes	1,554.6	1,332.0	877.9	762.7	739.2	587.2	368.2
Net Income	④ 958.3	818.8	545.8	480.0	② 447.1	354.1	① 369.9
Average Shs. Outstg. (000)	156,682	160,358	160,278	166,951	173,462	173,319	173,967
BALANCE SHEET (IN MILLIONS):							
Securities Avail. for Sale	956.7	856.1	462.8	398.5	490.6	765.9	1,008.8
Total Loans & Leases	58,225.6	41,139.6	33,860.3	28,090.1	25,991.6	33,553.5	30,397.2
Allowance for Credit Losses	cr43.3	74.3	97.7	170.3	270.3	292.8	283.8
Net Loans & Leases	58,268.9	41,065.4	33,762.6	27,919.8	25,721.3	33,260.7	30,113.4
Total Assets	68,405.8	58,586.3	55,704.0	42,142.2	38,468.7	39,590.3	37,730.6
Total Deposits	41,038.3	34,472.6	30,047.9	27,714.9	26,219.1	24,109.7	22,099.9
Long-Term Obligations	21,034.6	18,835.2	20,330.6	9,728.2	7,075.2	9,627.1	10,122.4
Total Liabilities	63,380.6	54,302.1	52,016.7	38,947.4	35,344.4	36,892.2	35,380.1
Net Stockholders' Equity	5,025.3	4,284.2	3,687.3	3,194.9	3,124.3	2,698.0	2,350.5
Year-end Shs. Outstg. (000)	153,521	155,532	158,410	161,358	170,583	171,207	172,026
STATISTICAL RECORD:							
Return on Equity %	19.1	19.1	14.8	15.0	14.3	13.1	15.7
Return on Assets %	1.4	1.4	1.0	1.1	1.2	0.9	1.0
Equity/Assets %	7.3	7.3	6.6	7.6	8.1	6.8	6.2
Non-Int. Exp./Tot. Inc. %	27.6	27.5	32.4	33.7	32.1	33.6	50.1
Price Range	73.75-56.20	70.90-45.02	70.50-26.88	38.41-28.91	38.16-23.27	32.33-19.62	22.91-16.33
P/E Ratio	12.1-9.2	13.9-8.8	20.7-7.9	13.4-10.1	14.8-9.0	15.8-9.6	10.9-7.7
Average Yield %	0.5	0.4	0.5	0.6	0.6	0.6	0.7

Statistics are as originally reported. Adj. for stk. split: 3-for-1, 12/10/99. ① Bef. acct. chrg. of $205.2 mill. & incl. one-time SAIF chg. of $133.0 mill. & a tax benefit of $139.5 mill. ② Bef. extraord. loss of $12.5 mill. ③ Bef. acctg. chrg. of $6.0 mill. ④ Incl. a pre-tax gain fr. changes in the fair value of derivatives of $7.6 mill.

OFFICERS:
H. M. Sandler, Co-Chmn., Co-C.E.O.
M. O. Sandler, Co-Chmn., Co-C.E.O.
R. W. Kettell, Pres., C.F.O., Treas.

INVESTOR CONTACT: William C. Nunan, Group Senior Vice President, (510) 446-3614

PRINCIPAL OFFICE: 1901 Harrison Street, Oakland, CA 94612

TELEPHONE NUMBER: (510) 446-3420
FAX: (510) 446-3072
WEB: www.worldsavings.com

NO. OF EMPLOYEES: 6,839 full-time; 1,002 part-time

SHAREHOLDERS: 1,172

ANNUAL MEETING: In May

INCORPORATED: DE, May, 1959

INSTITUTIONAL HOLDINGS:
No. of Institutions: 350
Shares Held: 105,253,180
% Held: 68.8

INDUSTRY: Federal savings institutions (SIC: 6035)

TRANSFER AGENT(S): Mellon Investor Services, LLC, San Francisco, CA

GORMAN-RUPP COMPANY

YIELD	2.8%
P/E RATIO	25.5

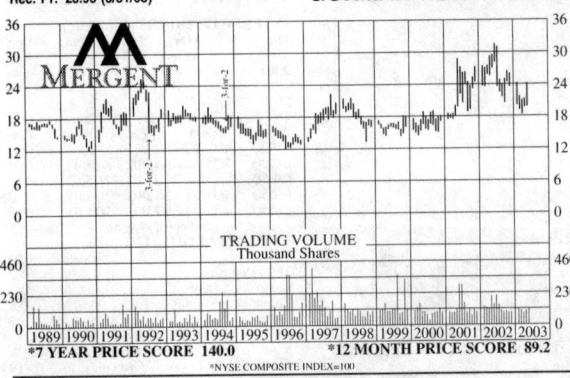

INTERIM EARNINGS (Per Share):

Qtr.	Mar.	June	Sept.	Dec.
1999	0.33	0.40	0.45	0.34
2000	0.48	0.42	0.37	0.34
2001	0.42	0.47	0.42	0.39
2002	0.25	0.38	0.23	0.19
2003	0.14	...	...	...

INTERIM DIVIDENDS (Per Share):

Amt.	Decl.	Ex.	Rec.	Pay.
0.16Q	7/25/02	8/13/02	8/15/02	9/10/02
0.17Q	10/24/02	11/13/02	11/15/02	12/10/02
0.17Q	1/23/03	2/12/03	2/14/03	3/10/03
0.17Q	4/24/03	5/13/03	5/15/03	6/10/03
Indicated div.: $0.68 (Div. Reinv. Plan)				

CAPITALIZATION (12/31/02):

	($000)	(%)
Long-Term Debt	291	0.3
Common & Surplus	111,456	99.7
Total	111,747	100.0

DIVIDEND ACHIEVER STATUS:
Rank: 256   10-Year Growth Rate: 3.62%
Total Years of Dividend Growth: 30

TRADING VOLUME Thousand Shares

*7 YEAR PRICE SCORE 140.0   ***12 MONTH PRICE SCORE 89.2**

NYSE COMPOSITE INDEX=100

RECENT DEVELOPMENTS: For the three months ended 3/31/03, net income dropped 44.2% to $1.2 million compared with $2.2 million in the corresponding quarter of 2002. Net sales were $43.8 million, down 3.3% from $45.3 million in the prior-year period. Gross profit declined 11.6% to $8.4 million, or 19.3% of net sales, from $9.5 million, or 21.1% of net sales, the previous year. Operating profit fell 51.7% to $1.7 million compared with $3.5 million the year before. Operating income was negatively affected by volume-related costs. In addition, margins at Patterson Pump Company, a wholly-owned subsidiary of GRC, were hampered by reduced production volumes related to cutbacks in demand for power generation equipment. Shipments of fabricated units to G.E. Power Systems were reduced by 78.0% due to the postponement and cancellation of orders resulting from lower demand for additional capacity in the power generation market.

BUSINESS

THE GORMAN-RUPP COMPANY is a manufacturer of pumps and related equipment for use in water and wastewater, construction, industrial, petroleum, original equipment, fire protection, government applications, and fabricated components for the power generation business. The types of pumps GRC produces include self-priming, centrifugal, magnetic drive centrifugal, rotary gear, diaphragm, bellows and oscillating. In 2002, the Company acquired American Machine and Tool Co., Inc. and Flo-Pak, Inc. in February and March, respectively.

ANNUAL FINANCIAL DATA

	12/31/02	12/31/01	12/31/00	12/31/99	12/31/98	12/31/97	12/31/96
Earnings Per Share	1.05	1.70	① 1.61	1.52	1.37	1.23	1.15
Cash Flow Per Share	1.87	2.54	2.41	2.28	2.10	1.92	1.81
Tang. Book Val. Per Share	13.05	12.64	11.67	10.74	9.75	9.07	8.44
Dividends Per Share	0.68	0.64	0.62	0.60	0.58	0.56	0.53
Dividend Payout %	64.8	37.6	38.5	39.5	42.3	45.5	46.1
INCOME STATEMENT (IN THOUSANDS):							
Total Revenues	194,075	203,813	191,484	180,165	172,246	165,568	155,678
Costs & Expenses	173,510	173,650	162,425	152,135	146,764	142,657	134,340
Depreciation & Amort.	7,035	7,128	6,863	6,489	6,330	5,959	5,675
Operating Income	13,530	23,035	22,196	21,541	19,152	16,952	15,663
Income Before Income Taxes	14,203	23,035	22,196	21,541	19,152	16,952	15,663
Income Taxes	5,267	8,450	8,400	8,460	7,400	6,340	5,735
Net Income	8,936	14,585	① 13,796	13,081	11,752	10,612	9,928
Cash Flow	15,971	21,713	20,659	19,570	18,082	16,571	15,603
Average Shs. Outstg.	8,539	8,556	8,583	8,586	8,600	8,609	8,617
BALANCE SHEET (IN THOUSANDS):							
Cash & Cash Equivalents	13,086	20,583	7,630	7,339	8,665	7,737	4,284
Total Current Assets	83,859	89,119	82,289	78,185	78,556	81,695	71,926
Net Property	57,757	53,895	57,885	53,609	43,916	40,919	40,549
Total Assets	152,846	148,113	145,881	136,875	127,477	127,865	117,650
Total Current Liabilities	19,282	18,103	19,079	17,439	17,431	17,036	15,199
Long-Term Obligations	291	...	3,413	3,107	783	6,689	3,796
Net Stockholders' Equity	111,456	107,910	99,999	92,295	83,706	78,060	72,737
Net Working Capital	64,577	71,016	63,210	60,746	61,125	64,659	56,727
Year-end Shs. Outstg.	8,541	8,538	8,566	8,592	8,581	8,609	8,618
STATISTICAL RECORD:							
Operating Profit Margin %	7.0	11.3	11.6	12.0	11.1	10.2	10.1
Net Profit Margin %	4.6	7.2	7.2	7.3	6.8	6.4	6.4
Return on Equity %	8.0	13.5	13.8	14.2	14.0	13.6	13.6
Return on Assets %	5.8	9.8	9.5	9.6	9.2	8.3	8.4
Debt/Total Assets %	0.2	...	2.3	2.3	0.6	5.2	3.2
Price Range	31.50-20.40	28.75-17.38	19.00-14.38	18.13-14.25	21.50-13.25	22.25-13.38	16.38-12.00
P/E Ratio	30.0-19.4	16.9-10.2	11.8-8.9	11.9-9.4	15.7-9.7	18.1-10.9	14.2-10.4
Average Yield %	2.6	2.8	3.7	3.7	3.3	3.1	3.7

Statistics are as originally reported. ① Incl. non-recur. chrg., $1.1 mill.

OFFICERS:
J. C. Gorman, Chmn.
J. S. Gorman, Pres., C.E.O.
R. E. Kirkendall, Sr. V.P., C.F.O.

INVESTOR CONTACT: Robert E. Kirkendall, Sr. V.P., C.F.O., (419) 755-1294

PRINCIPAL OFFICE: 305 Bowman St., Mansfield, OH 44903

TELEPHONE NUMBER: (419) 755-1011
FAX: (419) 755-1233
WEB: www.gormanrupp.com

NO. OF EMPLOYEES: 1,033 (approx.)

SHAREHOLDERS: 1,321

ANNUAL MEETING: In Apr.

INCORPORATED: OH, Apr., 1934

INSTITUTIONAL HOLDINGS:
No. of Institutions: 42
Shares Held: 3,839,096
% Held: 42.7

INDUSTRY: Pumps and pumping equipment (SIC: 3561)

TRANSFER AGENT(S): National City Bank, Cleveland, OH

GRAINGER (W.W.), INC.

YIELD 1.6%
P/E RATIO 19.0

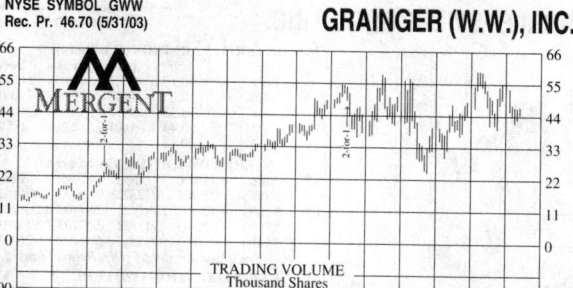

TRADING VOLUME
Thousand Shares

| 1989 | 1990 | 1991 | 1992 | 1993 | 1994 | 1995 | 1996 | 1997 | 1998 | 1999 | 2000 | 2001 | 2002 | 2003 |

*7 YEAR PRICE SCORE 122.2   ***12 MONTH PRICE SCORE 94.8**

*NYSE COMPOSITE INDEX=100

INTERIM EARNINGS (Per Share):

Qtr.	Mar.	June	Sept.	Dec.
1999	0.60	0.53	0.49	0.30
2000	0.44	0.59	0.51	0.51
2001	0.45	0.15	0.59	0.65
2002	0.61	0.57	0.64	0.68
2003	0.57	...	...	...

INTERIM DIVIDENDS (Per Share):

Amt.	Decl.	Ex.	Rec.	Pay.
0.18Q	7/31/02	8/08/02	8/12/02	9/01/02
0.18Q	10/30/02	11/06/02	11/11/02	12/01/02
0.18Q	1/29/03	2/06/03	2/10/03	3/01/03
0.18SQ	4/30/03	5/08/03	5/12/03	6/01/03

Indicated div.: $0.74

CAPITALIZATION (12/31/02):

	($000)	(%)
Long-Term Debt	119,693	6.7
Common & Surplus	1,667,698	93.3
Total	1,787,391	100.0

DIVIDEND ACHIEVER STATUS:
Rank: 180   10-Year Growth Rate: 8.20%
Total Years of Dividend Growth: 31

RECENT DEVELOPMENTS: For the quarter ended 3/31/03, net earnings totaled $52.4 million, down 10.4% versus earnings of $58.5 million, before a $23.9 million accounting change charge, the year before. Results for 2002 included a $7.3 million pre-tax gain from sales of investment securities. Net sales rose 1.2% to $1.14 billion from $1.13 billion a year earlier. Gross profit was $393.9 million, or 34.6% of net sales, versus $383.0 million, or 34.0% of net sales, in 2002. Operating earnings grew 1.6% to $91.4 million from $90.0 million the previous year.

PROSPECTS: On 4/14/03, the Company announced that its Lab Safety Supply subsidiary has completed its acquisition of the direct marketing business of Gempler's, Inc., a provider of tools, safety supplies, clothing and other equipment to the agricultural, horticultural, grounds maintenance and contractor markets. Terms of the transaction were not disclosed. Separately, the Company is projecting full-year 2003 sales growth of between 4.0% and 6.0%, and earnings of $2.50 to $2.65 per share.

BUSINESS

W.W. GRAINGER, INC. is a nationwide distributor of equipment, components, and supplies to the commercial, industrial, contractor and institutional markets. Products include motors, fans, blowers, pumps, compressors, air and power tools, heating and air conditioning equipment, as well as other items offered in its Grainger Industrial Supply Catalog and through its Grainger.com Web site. The Company serves its customers through its network of approximately 600 branches in the United States, Canada and Mexico. The Company also operates 17 distribution facilities throughout the U.S.

ANNUAL FINANCIAL DATA

	12/31/02	12/31/01	12/31/00	12/31/99	12/31/98	12/31/97	12/31/96
Earnings Per Share	③ 2.50	② 1.84	① 2.05	1.92	2.44	2.27	2.02
Cash Flow Per Share	3.49	2.93	3.18	2.96	3.24	3.05	2.74
Tang. Book Val. Per Share	16.59	15.09	14.08	13.47	11.39	11.13	11.65
Dividends Per Share	0.72	0.70	0.67	0.63	0.58	0.53	0.49
Dividend Payout %	28.8	38.0	32.7	32.8	24.0	23.3	24.3
INCOME STATEMENT (IN MILLIONS):							
Total Revenues	4,643.9	4,754.3	4,977.0	4,533.9	4,341.3	4,136.6	3,537.2
Costs & Expenses	4,157.3	4,312.5	4,535.0	4,118.4	3,854.4	3,663.8	3,117.4
Depreciation & Amort.	93.5	103.2	106.9	98.2	78.9	79.7	74.3
Operating Income	393.2	338.6	335.1	317.2	408.0	393.2	345.5
Net Interest Inc./(Exp.)	d1.6	d7.8	d22.5	d14.0	d5.1	d2.6	3.3
Income Before Income Taxes	397.8	297.3	331.6	303.8	400.8	389.6	348.9
Income Taxes	162.3	122.8	138.7	123.0	162.3	157.8	140.4
Net Income	③ 235.5	② 174.5	① 192.9	180.7	238.5	231.8	208.5
Cash Flow	329.0	277.7	299.8	279.0	317.4	311.5	282.8
Average Shs. Outstg. (000)	94,303	94,728	94,224	94,315	97,847	102,178	103,272
BALANCE SHEET (IN MILLIONS):							
Cash & Cash Equivalents	208.5	168.8	63.4	62.7	43.1	46.9	126.9
Total Current Assets	1,484.9	1,392.6	1,483.0	1,471.1	1,206.4	1,183.0	1,320.2
Net Property	736.8	689.7	676.4	697.8	660.5	592.9	551.0
Total Assets	2,437.4	2,331.2	2,459.6	2,564.8	2,103.9	1,997.8	2,119.0
Total Current Liabilities	586.3	553.8	747.3	870.5	664.5	533.9	616.1
Long-Term Obligations	119.7	118.2	125.3	124.9	122.9	131.2	6.2
Net Stockholders' Equity	1,667.7	1,603.2	1,537.4	1,480.5	1,278.7	1,294.7	1,462.7
Net Working Capital	898.7	838.8	735.7	600.6	541.9	649.1	704.2
Year-end Shs. Outstg. (000)	91,568	93,345	93,933	93,382	93,505	97,722	105,856
STATISTICAL RECORD:							
Operating Profit Margin %	8.5	7.1	6.7	7.0	9.4	9.5	9.8
Net Profit Margin %	5.1	3.7	3.9	4.0	5.5	5.6	5.9
Return on Equity %	14.1	10.9	12.5	12.2	18.7	17.9	14.3
Return on Assets %	9.7	7.5	7.8	7.0	11.3	11.6	9.8
Debt/Total Assets %	4.9	5.1	5.1	4.9	5.8	6.6	0.3
Price Range	59.40-39.20	48.99-29.51	56.88-24.31	58.13-36.88	54.72-36.44	49.88-35.25	40.75-31.31
P/E Ratio	23.8-15.7	26.6-16.0	27.7-11.9	30.3-19.2	22.4-14.9	22.0-15.5	20.2-15.5
Average Yield %	1.5	1.8	1.7	1.3	1.3	1.2	1.4

Statistics are as originally reported. Adj. for 2-for-1 stk. split, 6/98. ① Incl. $29.8 mil ($0.19/sh) one-time gain from the sale of an investment security. ② Incl. $39.1 mil restr. chg., a $20.1 mil loss fr. liquidation of equity in unconsol. subsid. and a $138,000 gain on invest. sale. ③ Bef. $23.9 mil ($0.26/sh) acctg. chrg., $1.9 mil restr. cr. & $7.3 mil gain on invest. sale.

OFFICERS:
R. L. Keyser, Chmn., C.E.O.
W. M. Clark, Pres., C.O.O.
P. O. Loux, Sr. V.P., C.F.O.
INVESTOR CONTACT: Robb Kristopher, Mgr., Inv. Rel., (847) 535-0879
PRINCIPAL OFFICE: 100 Grainger Parkway, Lake Forest, IL 60045-5201

TELEPHONE NUMBER: (847) 535-1000
FAX: (847) 535-0878
WEB: www.grainger.com
NO. OF EMPLOYEES: 13,183 full-time; 2,053 part-time
SHAREHOLDERS: 1,550 (approx.)
ANNUAL MEETING: In Apr.
INCORPORATED: IL, Dec., 1928

INSTITUTIONAL HOLDINGS:
No. of Institutions: 340
Shares Held: 59,242,301
% Held: 64.4
INDUSTRY: Electrical apparatus and equipment (SIC: 5063)
TRANSFER AGENT(S): BankBoston, N.A., Boston, MA

HARLEYSVILLE GROUP INC.

YIELD 2.7%
P/E RATIO 25.2

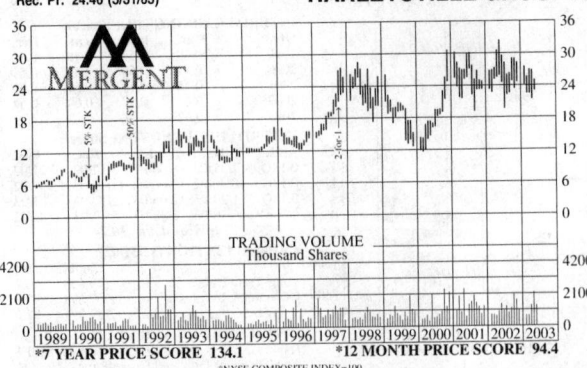

MERGENT

TRADING VOLUME
Thousand Shares

*7 YEAR PRICE SCORE 134.1   *12 MONTH PRICE SCORE 94.4
*NYSE COMPOSITE INDEX=100

INTERIM EARNINGS (Per Share):

Qtr.	Mar.	June	Sept.	Dec.
1999	0.50	0.52	d0.01	0.44
2000	0.25	0.37	0.45	0.60
2001	0.33	0.37	0.26	0.50
2002	0.44	0.01	0.50	0.57
2003	d0.11	...	...	...

INTERIM DIVIDENDS (Per Share):

Amt.	Decl.	Ex.	Rec.	Pay.
0.165Q	8/21/02	9/12/02	9/16/02	9/30/02
0.165Q	11/20/02	12/12/02	12/16/02	12/30/02
0.165Q	2/26/03	3/13/03	3/17/03	3/31/03
0.165Q	5/20/03	6/12/03	6/16/03	6/30/03

Indicated div.: $0.66 (Div. Reinv. Plan)

CAPITALIZATION (12/31/02):

	($000)	(%)
Long-Term Debt	95,620	13.1
Common & Surplus	632,112	86.9
Total	727,732	100.0

DIVIDEND ACHIEVER STATUS:
Rank: 161   10-Year Growth Rate: 9.25%
Total Years of Dividend Growth: 16

RECENT DEVELOPMENTS: For the quarter ended 3/31/03, net loss was $3.2 million versus net income of $13.3 million in the equivalent prior-year quarter. Results for 2003 included a $20.0 million pre-tax workers compensation reserve adjustment and a charge of $3.6 million for winter storm property catastrophe losses. Results were pressured by poor personal lines performance. This was partially offset by strong premium growth in its core commercial business segment. Total revenues increased 7.8% to $224.4 million from $208.2 million the previous year. Premiums

earned climbed 8.9% to $198.8 million from $182.5 million in 2002. Premiums earned in the commercial lines advanced 15.9% to $148.7 million, while premiums earned in the personal lines dropped 7.6% to $50.1 million. Net investment income slipped to $21.4 million from $21.5 million a year earlier. HGIC's combined ratio, a measure of underwriting losses and expenses per premium dollar earned, was 115.4% at 3/31/03 versus 103.3% at 3/31/02. Looking ahead, HGIC anticipates operating earnings per share for full-year 2003 in the range of $1.45 to $1.55.

BUSINESS

HARLEYSVILLE GROUP INC. is a regional insurance holding company headquartered in Pennsylvania engaged, through its subsidiaries, in the property and casualty insurance business. As of 12/31/02, the Company was approximately 56.0% owned by Harleysville Mutual Insurance Company. HGIC and Harleysville Mutual Insurance Company operate together as a network of regional insurance companies that underwrite personal and commercial coverages. As of 5/25/03, these insurance coverages were marketed in 32 eastern and midwestern states through approximately 1,900 local independent agencies. The companies include: Harleysville-Atlantic Insurance Company, Harleysville Insurance Company, Harleysville Insurance Company of New Jersey, Harleysville Insurance Company of New York, Harleysville Insurance Company of Ohio, Harleysville Lake States Insurance Company, Harleysville Preferred Insurance Company, Harleysville Worcester Insurance Company, and Mid-America Insurance Company. Additionally, the Company operates two limited partnerships: Harleysville Asset Management L.P. and Insurance Management Resources L.P.

ANNUAL FINANCIAL DATA

	12/31/02	12/31/01	12/31/00	12/31/99	12/31/98	12/31/97	12/31/96
Earnings Per Share	1.53	② 1.46	1.67	① 1.45	2.15	1.86	1.03
Tang. Book Val. Per Share	21.13	20.05	19.54	18.29	18.17	15.49	13.09
Dividends Per Share	0.63	0.58	0.55	0.52	0.48	0.44	0.40
Dividend Payout %	41.2	39.7	32.9	35.9	22.3	23.7	38.8
INCOME STATEMENT (IN MILLIONS):							
Total Premium Income	764.6	729.9	688.3	707.2	664.6	624.9	615.2
Net Investment Income	86.3	85.5	86.8	85.9	86.0	81.8	78.0
Other Income	d3.2	12.3	27.4	31.7	28.7	17.5	14.2
Total Revenues	847.7	827.8	802.6	824.8	779.3	724.2	707.4
Income Before Income Taxes	56.5	51.8	57.7	47.8	80.4	67.3	31.4
Income Taxes	10.2	8.3	9.0	4.9	17.0	13.2	2.7
Net Income	46.3	② 43.5	48.7	① 42.8	63.4	54.1	28.7
Average Shs. Outstg. (000)	30,296	29,819	29,136	29,565	29,520	29,032	27,844
BALANCE SHEET (IN MILLIONS):							
Cash & Cash Equivalents	92.6	38.5	52.3	79.5	18.8	29.8	37.3
Premiums Due	235.9	226.0	201.7	196.3	197.6	184.0	173.7
Invst. Assets: Equities	107.2	150.7	193.8	198.2	174.9	121.8	69.9
Invst. Assets: Total	1,706.9	1,611.1	1,599.1	1,604.0	1,579.6	1,451.6	1,291.3
Total Assets	2,311.5	2,045.3	2,021.9	2,020.1	1,934.5	1,801.2	1,622.6
Long-Term Obligations	95.6	96.1	96.5	96.8	97.1	97.4	97.7
Net Stockholders' Equity	632.1	590.3	566.6	526.9	529.7	446.5	370.2
Year-end Shs. Outstg. (000)	29,918	29,445	29,002	28,812	29,151	28,822	28,278
STATISTICAL RECORD:							
Return on Revenues %	5.5	5.3	6.1	5.2	8.1	7.5	4.1
Return on Equity %	7.3	7.4	8.6	8.1	12.0	12.1	7.7
Return on Assets %	2.0	2.1	2.4	2.1	3.3	3.0	1.8
Price Range	32.41-19.58	30.25-19.11	30.63-11.63	26.13-12.63	28.50-17.25	27.50-14.38	16.38-12.25
P/E Ratio	21.2-12.8	20.7-13.1	18.3-7.0	18.0-8.7	13.3-8.0	14.8-7.7	15.9-11.9
Average Yield %	2.4	2.4	2.6	2.7	2.1	2.1	2.8

Statistics are as originally reported. Adj. for stk. splits: 2-for-1, 10/6/97 ① Bef. acctg. change chrg. $2.9 mill., 12/99 ② Incl. non-recurr. chrg. $2.6 mill.

OFFICERS:
W. R. Bateman II, Chmn., C.E.O.
M. L. Patkus, Pres., C.O.O.
B. J. Magee, Sr. V.P., C.F.O.

INVESTOR CONTACT: Carol D. Manning, V.P., Inv. Rel., (215) 256-5020

PRINCIPAL OFFICE: 355 Maple Avenue, Harleysville, PA 19438-2297

TELEPHONE NUMBER: (215) 256-5000
FAX: (215) 256-5340
WEB: www.harleysvillegroup.com
NO. OF EMPLOYEES: 2,413 (avg.)
SHAREHOLDERS: 2,404 (approx.)
ANNUAL MEETING: In April
INCORPORATED: DE, May, 1986

INSTITUTIONAL HOLDINGS:
No. of Institutions: 91
Shares Held: 9,626,433
% Held: 32.1

INDUSTRY: Fire, marine, and casualty insurance (SIC: 6331)

TRANSFER AGENT(S): Mellon Investor Services, Ridgefield Park, NJ

HARLEYSVILLE NATIONAL CORP.

YIELD 2.7%
P/E RATIO 16.5

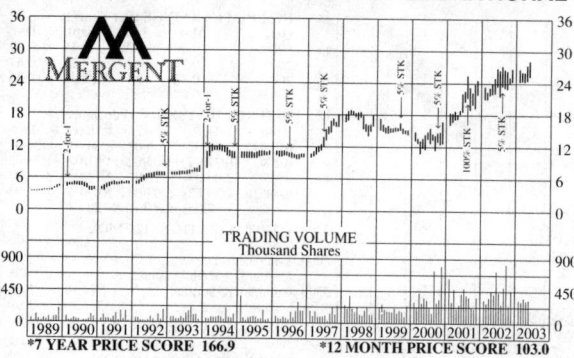

7 YEAR PRICE SCORE 166.9   *12 MONTH PRICE SCORE 103.0*
*NYSE COMPOSITE INDEX=100

INTERIM EARNINGS (Per Share):

Qtr.	Mar.	June	Sept.	Dec.
1999	0.29	0.33	0.34	0.31
2000	0.31	0.32	0.35	0.33
2001	0.33	0.36	0.39	0.38
2002	0.40	0.42	0.42	0.42
2003	0.43	...	...	...

INTERIM DIVIDENDS (Per Share):

Amt.	Decl.	Ex.	Rec.	Pay.
5% STK	8/08/02	8/29/02	9/03/02	9/16/02
0.18Q	11/15/02	11/26/02	11/29/02	12/16/02
0.03Sp	11/15/02	11/26/02	11/29/02	12/16/02
0.19Q	2/14/03	2/26/03	2/28/03	3/14/03
0.19Q	5/08/03	5/28/03	5/30/03	6/16/03

Indicated div.: $0.76 (Div. Reinv. Plan)

CAPITALIZATION (12/31/02):

	($000)	(%)
Total Deposits	1,979,822	84.3
Long-Term Debt	162,750	6.9
Common & Surplus	206,206	8.8
Total	2,348,778	100.0

DIVIDEND ACHIEVER STATUS:
Rank: 62   10-Year Growth Rate: 14.99%
Total Years of Dividend Growth: 16

RECENT DEVELOPMENTS: For the three months ended 3/31/03, net earnings climbed 8.3% to $8.5 million compared with $7.8 million in the corresponding quarter of the previous year. Interest income decrease 9.2% to $30.6 million from $33.7 million in the year-earlier period. Interest expense fell 13.0% to $11.4 million from $13.1 million in the prior-year quarter. Net interest income decreased 6.8% to $19.2 million from $20.6 million the year before. This decline was attributable to a decrease in net interest margin, which was 3.68% for the first quarter of 2003 versus 4.31% the year before. Provision for loan losses dropped 54.9% to $609,000 from $1.4 million in 2002 mainly due to small growth in loans and improved loan quality. Total non-interest income improved 30.6% to $7.2 million from $5.5 million in the previous year. Total non-interest expense increased 7.1% to $15.5 million from $14.5 million in the prior-year quarter.

BUSINESS

HARLEYSVILLE NATIONAL CORPORATION, is the parent bank holding company of Harleysville National Bank and Trust Company, Citizen's National Bank and Security National Bank. Through its banking subsidiaries, HNBC is engaged in the full-service commercial banking and trust business, including accepting time and demand deposits, making secured and unsecured commercial and consumer loans, financing commercial transactions, making construction and mortgage loans and performing corporate pension and personal investment and trust services. The Company operates 40 branch offices located in nine counties throughout Eastern Pennsylvania. As of 3/31/03, the Company had total assets of $2.47 billion.

ANNUAL FINANCIAL DATA

	12/31/02	12/31/01	12/31/00	12/31/99	12/31/98	12/31/97	12/31/96
Earnings Per Share	1.67	1.47	1.31	1.28	1.15	1.03	0.89
Tang. Book Val. Per Share	10.84	9.79	8.84	7.31	7.42	6.64	5.93
Dividends Per Share	0.71	0.62	0.54	0.49	0.43	0.39	0.35
Dividend Payout %	42.2	42.2	40.9	38.0	37.5	38.2	38.9
INCOME STATEMENT (IN MILLIONS):							
Total Interest Income	132.6	138.7	131.8	106.1	87.6	80.2	73.7
Total Interest Expense	52.6	64.9	65.8	46.9	37.8	33.9	30.9
Net Interest Income	80.0	73.7	66.0	59.2	49.8	46.4	42.8
Provision for Loan Losses	4.4	3.9	2.3	1.9	2.1	2.5	2.1
Non-Interest Income	22.5	22.2	12.2	10.1	9.8	7.4	5.1
Non-Interest Expense	56.3	55.0	44.7	38.4	32.6	28.5	25.9
Income Before Taxes	41.9	37.0	31.3	29.0	24.9	22.7	20.0
Net Income	32.9	28.8	25.6	22.3	18.8	16.7	14.4
Average Shs. Outstg. (000)	19,700	19,699	19,486	17,475	16,283	16,235	16,193
BALANCE SHEET (IN MILLIONS):							
Cash & Due from Banks	62.2	63.0	52.0	42.2	37.8	38.5	39.4
Total Loans & Leases	1,332.0	1,313.9	1,209.6	1,061.2	845.2	743.6	689.2
Allowance for Credit Losses	15.9	12.9	12.8	13.4	15.3	16.1	18.5
Net Loans & Leases	1,316.1	1,301.1	1,196.8	1,047.8	829.9	727.5	670.7
Total Assets	2,490.9	2,209.0	1,935.2	1,635.7	1,332.4	1,116.3	1,026.1
Total Deposits	1,979.8	1,746.9	1,489.1	1,231.3	1,034.0	919.1	847.7
Long-Term Obligations	162.8	127.8	110.8	130.3	93.5	17.0	35.0
Total Liabilities	2,284.7	2,019.6	1,761.7	1,506.0	1,209.6	1,006.5	928.5
Net Stockholders' Equity	206.2	189.3	173.5	129.7	122.8	109.8	97.6
Year-end Shs. Outstg. (000)	19,028	19,198	19,444	17,453	16,295	16,253	16,183
STATISTICAL RECORD:							
Return on Equity %	16.0	15.2	14.8	17.2	15.3	15.2	14.8
Return on Assets %	1.3	1.3	1.3	1.4	1.4	1.5	1.4
Equity/Assets %	8.3	8.6	9.0	7.9	9.2	9.8	9.5
Non-Int. Exp./Tot. Inc. %	54.9	57.4	57.1	55.4	54.7	53.1	54.0
Price Range	27.25-20.95	25.42-16.13	16.76-10.77	17.28-14.29	18.90-14.04	18.14-9.98	11.26-9.67
P/E Ratio	16.3-12.5	17.3-11.0	12.8-8.2	13.5-11.2	16.4-12.2	17.6-9.7	12.7-10.9
Average Yield %	2.9	3.0	3.9	3.1	2.6	2.8	3.3

Statistics are as originally reported. Adj. for 5.0% stk. split, 8/02; 10/00; 9/99; 6/97; 6/96; & 100.0% stk. split, 8/01

OFFICERS:
W. E. Daller Jr., Chmn., Pres., C.E.O.
G. J. Wagner, Exec. V.P., C.F.O.
V. L. Hunsberger, Treas.

INVESTOR CONTACT: Jo Anne M. Bynon, Sec., (800) 423-3955

PRINCIPAL OFFICE: 483 Main Street, Harleysville, PA 19438

TELEPHONE NUMBER: (215) 256-8851
FAX: (215) 256-1886
WEB: www.hncbank.com

NO. OF EMPLOYEES: 598 (approx.)

SHAREHOLDERS: 3,289

ANNUAL MEETING: In Apr.

INCORPORATED: PA, June, 1982

INSTITUTIONAL HOLDINGS:
No. of Institutions: 48
Shares Held: 3,158,275
% Held: 16.6

INDUSTRY: National commercial banks (SIC: 6021)

TRANSFER AGENT(S): American Stock Transfer & Trust Company, New York, NY

HAVERTY FURNITURE COMPANIES, INC.

YIELD 1.5%
P/E RATIO 15.1

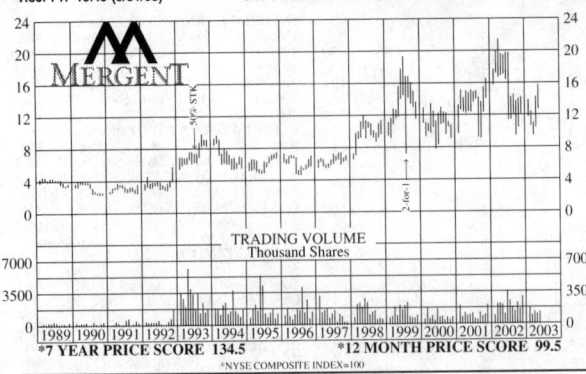

TRADING VOLUME
Thousand Shares

*7 YEAR PRICE SCORE 134.5   *12 MONTH PRICE SCORE 99.5

*NYSE COMPOSITE INDEX=100

INTERIM EARNINGS (Per Share):

Qtr.	Mar.	June	Sept.	Dec.
2000	0.30	0.28	0.35	0.39
2001	0.21	0.12	0.26	0.47
2002	0.30	0.17	0.27	0.36
2003	0.22	...	...	...

INTERIM DIVIDENDS (Per Share):

Amt.	Decl.	Ex.	Rec.	Pay.
0.058Q	7/25/02	8/06/02	8/08/02	8/22/02
0.058Q	10/31/02	11/06/02	11/11/02	11/25/02
0.058Q	2/03/03	2/12/03	2/14/03	2/26/03
0.058Q	4/25/03	5/07/03	5/09/03	5/23/03

Indicated div.: $0.23

CAPITALIZATION (12/31/02):

	($000)	(%)
Long-Term Debt	68,456	23.2
Capital Lease Obligations..	1,365	0.5
Common & Surplus	224,881	76.3
Total	294,702	100.0

DIVIDEND ACHIEVER STATUS:
Rank: 226   10-Year Growth Rate: 5.61%
Total Years of Dividend Growth: 32

RECENT DEVELOPMENTS: For the quarter ended 3/31/03, net income dropped 27.2% to $4.9 million compared with $6.7 million in the equivalent 2002 quarter. The decline in earnings was primarily attributed to soft sales due to macroeconomic issues, particularly white-collar job losses and lower consumer confidence. Net sales rose 0.2% to $175.4 million from $175.0 million a year earlier. Comparable-store sales declined 6.6% year over year.

PROSPECTS: Looking ahead, the Company will concentrate on enhancing all areas of operation while remaining committed to sustaining profitability. Meanwhile, the Company opened two key facilities as part of HVT's distribution strategy that requires fewer inventory stocking locations and reduces the number of centers needed to prep and load merchandise for home delivery. The increased costs associated with HVT's strategy are likely to be leveraged in the second quarter of 2003.

BUSINESS

HAVERTY FURNITURE COMPANIES, INC. is a full-service home furnishings retailer with 111 stores in 14 southern and central states as of 4/24/03. The Company's stores, primarily targeted at middle and upper-middle income families, offer a wide selection of well-known brand names of furniture, such as THOMASVILLE, BROYHILL, LANE/ACTION, LA-Z-BOY, BERNHARDT, and CLAYTON MARCUS. The Company has regional warehouses located in Charlotte, North Carolina, Jackson, Mississippi and Ocala, Florida serving all of the Company's local markets except for Dallas, Texas, and Atlanta, Georgia, which each have a metropolitan area warehouse.

ANNUAL FINANCIAL DATA

	12/31/02	12/31/01	12/31/00	12/31/99	12/31/98	12/31/97	12/31/96
Earnings Per Share	1.10	1.06	①1.31	1.19	0.72	0.57	0.53
Cash Flow Per Share	1.82	1.81	2.06	1.84	1.36	1.16	1.06
Tang. Book Val. Per Share	10.30	9.45	8.64	7.81	7.08	6.79	6.42
Dividends Per Share	0.22	0.21	0.20	0.19	0.17	0.16	0.15
Dividend Payout %	20.0	19.8	15.5	16.0	22.9	28.1	29.0
INCOME STATEMENT (IN THOUSANDS):							
Total Revenues	703,959	689,178	693,575	633,721	557,258	506,118	470,250
Costs & Expenses	652,640	622,276	619,117	560,744	496,428	449,650	419,777
Depreciation & Amort.	15,903	16,239	15,738	14,844	14,272	13,792	12,644
Operating Income	44,467	50,663	58,720	58,133	46,558	42,676	37,829
Net Interest Inc./(Exp.)	d6,561	d10,581	d11,707	d11,402	d13,183	d14,330	d14,463
Income Before Income Taxes	38,903	36,340	43,861	42,870	26,295	20,787	19,132
Income Taxes	14,588	13,630	16,010	15,470	9,460	7,400	6,885
Net Income	24,315	22,710	①27,851	27,400	16,835	13,387	12,247
Cash Flow	40,218	38,949	43,589	42,244	31,107	27,179	24,891
Average Shs. Outstg.	22,145	21,502	21,203	22,982	22,912	23,340	23,388
BALANCE SHEET (IN THOUSANDS):							
Cash & Cash Equivalents	3,764	727	3,256	1,762	1,874	390	414
Total Current Assets	263,825	305,755	295,992	271,678	278,177	289,629	283,130
Net Property	134,203	146,399	144,525	126,997	111,333	114,618	114,350
Total Assets	404,839	460,905	448,163	404,648	392,901	406,514	399,875
Total Current Liabilities	101,520	123,903	95,520	98,434	70,467	132,908	125,440
Long-Term Obligations	69,821	131,599	170,369	134,687	161,778	111,489	120,434
Net Stockholders' Equity	224,881	201,398	179,375	168,793	158,058	159,554	150,916
Net Working Capital	162,305	181,852	200,472	173,244	207,710	156,721	157,690
Year-end Shs. Outstg.	21,832	21,302	20,773	21,610	22,330	23,482	23,510
STATISTICAL RECORD:							
Operating Profit Margin %	6.3	7.4	8.5	9.2	8.4	8.4	8.0
Net Profit Margin %	3.5	3.3	4.0	4.3	3.0	2.6	2.6
Return on Equity %	10.8	11.3	15.5	16.2	10.7	8.4	8.1
Return on Assets %	6.0	4.9	6.2	6.8	4.3	3.3	3.1
Debt/Total Assets %	17.2	28.6	38.0	33.3	41.2	27.4	30.1
Price Range	21.45-9.40	16.55-9.10	13.44-7.75	19.33-7.19	12.00-6.50	7.38-5.44	7.31-4.63
P/E Ratio	19.5-8.5	15.6-8.6	10.3-5.9	16.2-6.0	16.7-9.0	12.9-9.5	13.9-8.8
Average Yield %	1.4	1.6	1.9	1.4	1.8	2.5	2.6

Statistics are as originally reported. Adj. for stk. split: 2-for-1, 8/25/99. ① Bef. $3.4 mil. ($0.16/sh) acctg. change chrg.

OFFICERS:
C. H. Ridley, Chmn.
C. H. Smith, Pres., C.E.O.
D. L. Fink, Exec. V.P., C.F.O.

INVESTOR CONTACT: Dennis L. Fink, Exec. V.P., C.F.O., (404) 443-2900

PRINCIPAL OFFICE: 780 Johnson Ferry Road, Suite 800, Atlanta, GA 30342

TELEPHONE NUMBER: (404) 443-2900
FAX: (404) 443-4180
WEB: www.havertys.com

NO. OF EMPLOYEES: 4,000 (approx.)

SHAREHOLDERS: 3,400 (approx. common); 200 (approx. class A)

ANNUAL MEETING: In May

INCORPORATED: MD, Sept., 1929

NYSE SYMBOL HCP
Rec. Pr. 39.21 (5/31/03)

HEALTH CARE PROPERTY INVESTORS, INC.

YIELD 8.5%
P/E RATIO 20.1

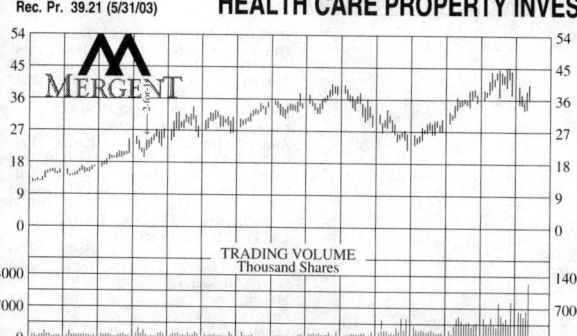

TRADING VOLUME
Thousand Shares

*7 YEAR PRICE SCORE 133.5   *12 MONTH PRICE SCORE 92.3
*NYSE COMPOSITE INDEX=100

INTERIM EARNINGS (Per Share):

Qtr.	Mar.	June	Sept.	Dec.
2000	0.52	0.55	0.46	0.60
2001	0.39	0.54	0.32	0.53
2002	0.42	0.55	0.54	0.39
2003	0.47	...	...	...

INTERIM DIVIDENDS (Per Share):

Amt.	Decl.	Ex.	Rec.	Pay.
0.82Q	7/25/02	8/01/02	8/05/02	8/20/02
0.83Q	10/29/02	11/06/02	11/08/02	11/20/02
0.83Q	1/27/03	2/04/03	2/06/03	2/20/03
0.83Q	4/23/03	5/01/03	5/05/03	5/20/03

Indicated div.: $3.32 (Div. Reinv. Plan)

CAPITALIZATION (12/31/02):

	($000)	(%)
Long-Term Debt	1,066,048	44.1
Minority Interest	71,535	3.0
Preferred Stock	274,487	11.3
Common & Surplus	1,006,402	41.6
Total	2,418,472	100.0

DIVIDEND ACHIEVER STATUS:
Rank: 208   10-Year Growth Rate: 6.57%
Total Years of Dividend Growth: 17

RECENT DEVELOPMENTS: For the quarter ended 3/31/03, income from continuing operations increased 9.7% to $34.3 million versus $31.3 million in the prior-year quarter. Earnings for 2003 and 2002 excluded losses from discontinued operations of $6.6 million and $842,000, respectively. Revenue advanced 15.5% to $92.1 million from $79.7 million a year earlier. Operating income increased 9.1% to $36.3 million. Diluted funds from operations grew 8.6% to $47.7 million from $43.9 million in 2002.

PROSPECTS: The Company expects earnings for 2003 to range from $2.05 to $2.08 per diluted share. Adjusting for real estate depreciation, real estate dispositions and dividends on operating partnership units, HCP projects diluted funds from operations to range between $3.51 and $3.59 per share. Separately, the Company has commitments to acquire or construct an additional $62.0 million of health care real estate and capital projects.

BUSINESS

HEALTH CARE PROPERTY INVESTORS, INC. is a real estate investment trust that invests in health-care-related facilities throughout the United States, including long-term care facilities, congregate care and assisted living facilities, acute care and rehabilitation hospitals, medical office buildings and physician group practice clinics. The Company's investment portfolio as of 3/31/03 included 453 facilities in 44 states. The Company's investments include 176 long-term care facilities, 126 retirement and assisted living facilities, 85 medical office buildings, 35 other health care facilities and 31 hospitals. On 11/4/99, HCP acquired American Health Properties, Inc. in a stock-for-stock transaction.

REVENUES

(12/31/2002)	($000)	(%)
Rental, Triple Leases.	240,537	66.9
Retnal, Managed Properties	91,200	25.4
Interest & Other Income	27,839	7.7
Total	359,576	100.0

ANNUAL FINANCIAL DATA

	12/31/02	12/31/01	12/31/00	12/31/99	12/31/98	12/31/97	12/31/96
Earnings Per Share	③ 1.93	① 1.78	② 2.13	① 2.25	① 2.54	① 2.19	2.12
Tang. Book Val. Per Share	16.92	17.24	17.10	17.99	13.15	12.72	11.74
Dividends Per Share	3.26	3.10	2.94	2.78	2.62	2.46	2.30
Dividend Payout %	168.9	174.1	138.0	123.6	103.1	112.3	108.5
INCOME STATEMENT (IN MILLIONS):							
Rental Income	331.7	310.6	306.8	199.6	138.4	113.9	104.6
Total Income	359.6	332.5	329.8	224.8	161.5	128.5	120.4
Costs & Expenses	138.3	121.8	129.8	85.5	50.4	36.4	33.2
Depreciation	75.7	84.1	72.6	47.9	32.5	25.7	23.1
Income Before Income Taxes	137.2	121.2	133.5	96.2	87.2	64.8	60.6
Net Income	③ 137.2	① 121.2	② 133.5	① 96.2	① 87.2	① 64.8	60.6
Average Shs. Outstg. (000)	58,147	53,975	51,100	34,861	33,664	28,994	28,652
BALANCE SHEET (IN MILLIONS):							
Cash & Cash Equivalents	8.5	8.4	58.6	7.7	4.5	4.1	2.8
Total Real Estate Investments	2,371.4	2,194.6	2,100.5	2,193.0	1,131.1	786.5	623.7
Total Assets	2,748.4	2,431.2	2,398.7	2,469.4	1,356.6	941.0	753.7
Long-Term Obligations	1,066.0	949.3	954.4	964.0	621.0	386.0	379.5
Total Liabilities	1,467.5	1,184.4	1,254.1	1,269.1	761.2	498.7	416.8
Net Stockholders' Equity	1,280.9	1,246.7	1,144.6	1,200.3	595.4	442.3	336.8
Year-end Shs. Outstg. (000)	59,470	56,387	50,874	51,421	30,987	30,216	28,678
STATISTICAL RECORD:							
Net Inc.+Depr./Assets %	7.7	8.4	8.6	5.8	8.8	9.6	11.1
Return on Equity %	10.7	9.7	11.7	8.0	14.6	14.6	18.0
Return on Assets %	5.0	5.0	5.6	3.9	6.4	6.9	8.0
Price Range	45.08-35.80	39.03-29.25	30.44-23.06	33.13-21.69	40.00-28.25	40.38-31.88	37.75-30.50
P/E Ratio	23.4-18.5	21.9-16.4	14.3-10.8	14.7-9.6	15.7-11.1	18.4-14.6	17.8-14.4
Average Yield %	8.1	9.1	11.0	10.1	7.7	6.8	6.7

Statistics are as originally reported. ① Incl non-recurr. credit: 12/31/01, $1.2 mill.; 12/31/99, $10.3 mill.; 12/31/98, $14.1 mill.; 12/31/97, $2.0 mill. ② Incls. net non-recurr. credit of $9.8 mill.; bef. extraord. gain of $274,000. ③ Bef. income fr. discont. opers. of $1.3 mill. & loss on real estate dispos. of $1.1 mill.; incl. impair. loss on real estate of $9.2 mill.

HEINZ (H.J.) COMPANY

NYSE SYMBOL HNZ
Rec. Pr. 33.07 (5/31/03)

YIELD 3.3%
P/E RATIO 15.7

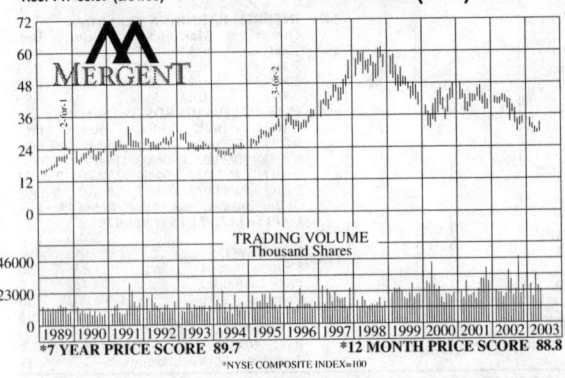

*7 YEAR PRICE SCORE 89.7   *12 MONTH PRICE SCORE 88.8

*NYSE COMPOSITE INDEX=100

INTERIM EARNINGS (Per Share):

Qtr.	July	Oct.	Jan.	Apr.
1999-00	0.57	1.14	0.47	0.27
2000-01	0.57	0.54	0.77	d0.49
2001-02	0.57	0.59	0.57	0.63
2002-03	0.50	0.60	0.37	...

INTERIM DIVIDENDS (Per Share):

Amt.	Decl.	Ex.	Rec.	Pay.
0.405Q	9/12/02	9/19/02	9/23/02	10/10/02
0.405Q	12/11/02	12/19/02	12/23/02	1/10/03
0.27Q	3/12/03	3/20/03	3/24/03	4/10/03
0.27Q	6/11/03	6/20/03	6/24/03	7/10/03

Indicated div.: $1.08 (Div. Reinv. Plan)

CAPITALIZATION (5/1/02):

	($000)	(%)
Long-Term Debt	4,642,968	64.5
Deferred Income Tax	394,935	5.5
Minority Interest	440,648	6.1
Preferred Stock	110	0.0
Common & Surplus	1,718,506	23.9
Total	7,197,167	100.0

DIVIDEND ACHIEVER STATUS:
Rank: 182   10-Year Dividend Growth Rate: 8.15%
Total Years of Dividend Growth: 39

RECENT DEVELOPMENTS: For the quarter ended 1/29/03, income from continuing operations was $129.8 million, down 19.5% versus income from continuing operations of $161.2 million the year before. Results for the recent period included a non-recurring after-tax charge of $61.6 million, primarily related to the spin-off of certain businesses to Del Monte Foods Company. Sales climbed 9.1% to $2.11 billion from $1.93 billion a year earlier.

PROSPECTS: Top-line growth is being driven by improved pricing, favorable foreign currency exchange rates and acquisitions, partially offset by lower sales volume. Meanwhile, the Company is planning several new product introductions in Europe, including HEINZ "BITE ME"® frozen snacks and SALAD HELPERS®, which come complete with tuna and dressings.

BUSINESS

H.J. HEINZ COMPANY manufactures and markets an extensive line of processed food products throughout the world, including ketchup and other sauces/condiments, frozen dinners, pet food, baby food, frozen potato products and canned soups, vegetables and fruits. Major U.S. brands include HEINZ, ORE-IDA, SMART ONES and BOSTON MARKET. Overseas, well-known brands include PLASMON, PUDLISZKI, ORLANDO, WATTIE'S, OLIVINE, FARLEY'S, ABC, and JURAN. Fiscal 2002 sales were derived: Ketchup, Condiments & Sauces, 28.3%; Frozen Foods, 21.2%; Convenience Meals, 12.6%; Seafood, 11.0%; Pet Products, 10.4%; Infant/Nutritional Foods, 9.5%; and Other, 7.0%. On 12/20/02, the Company completed the spin-off of its tuna, pet food, private-label soup and baby food businesses to Del Monte Foods Company.

ANNUAL FINANCIAL DATA

	5/1/02	5/2/01	5/3/00	4/28/99	4/29/98	4/30/97	5/1/96
Earnings Per Share	① 2.36	① 1.41	② 2.47	① 1.29	① 2.15	① 0.80	1.74
Cash Flow Per Share	3.22	2.28	3.32	2.11	2.99	1.72	2.66
Tang. Book Val. Per Share	...	...	...	...	...	0.03	0.87
Dividends Per Share	1.58	1.50	1.40	1.29	1.19	1.08	0.98
Dividend Payout %	67.1	106.0	56.5	99.8	55.1	135.6	56.6
INCOME STATEMENT (IN MILLIONS):							
Total Revenues	9,431.0	9,430.4	9,407.9	9,299.6	9,209.3	9,357.0	9,112.3
Costs & Expenses	7,538.8	8,148.9	7,368.4	7,888.1	7,375.3	8,260.2	7,480.9
Depreciation & Amort.	301.7	299.2	306.5	302.2	313.6	340.5	343.8
Operating Income	1,590.5	982.4	1,733.1	1,109.3	1,520.3	756.3	1,287.6
Net Interest Inc./(Exp.)	d266.8	d310.3	d244.4	d233.7	d226.0	d235.4	d232.6
Income Before Income Taxes	1,278.6	673.1	1,463.7	835.1	1,255.0	479.1	1,023.7
Income Taxes	444.7	178.1	573.1	360.8	453.4	177.2	364.3
Net Income	① 833.9	② 494.9	① 890.6	① 474.3	① 801.6	① 301.9	659.3
Cash Flow	1,135.6	794.1	1,197.0	776.5	1,115.2	642.3	1,003.1
Average Shs. Outstg. (000)	352,872	347,758	360,095	367,830	372,953	373,703	377,156
BALANCE SHEET (IN MILLIONS):							
Cash & Cash Equivalents	206.9	144.2	154.1	123.1	99.4	188.4	108.4
Total Current Assets	3,373.6	3,116.8	3,169.9	2,886.8	2,686.5	3,013.1	3,046.7
Net Property	2,250.1	2,168.4	2,358.8	2,171.0	2,394.7	2,479.2	2,616.8
Total Assets	10,278.4	9,035.2	8,850.7	8,053.6	8,023.4	8,437.8	8,623.7
Total Current Liabilities	2,509.2	3,655.1	2,126.1	2,786.3	2,164.3	2,880.4	2,715.1
Long-Term Obligations	4,643.0	3,014.9	3,935.8	2,472.2	2,768.3	2,284.0	2,281.7
Net Stockholders' Equity	1,718.6	1,373.7	1,595.9	1,803.0	2,216.5	2,440.4	2,706.8
Net Working Capital	864.4	d538.3	1,043.9	100.5	522.2	132.7	331.6
Year-end Shs. Outstg. (000)	350,904	348,949	347,443	359,128	363,418	367,184	368,598
STATISTICAL RECORD:							
Operating Profit Margin %	16.9	10.4	18.4	11.9	16.5	8.1	14.1
Net Profit Margin %	8.8	5.2	9.5	5.1	8.7	3.2	7.2
Return on Equity %	48.5	36.0	55.8	26.3	36.2	12.4	24.4
Return on Assets %	8.1	5.5	10.1	5.9	10.0	3.6	7.6
Debt/Total Assets %	45.2	33.4	44.5	30.7	34.5	27.1	26.5
Price Range	47.94-36.90	48.00-30.81	58.81-39.50	61.75-48.50	56.69-35.25	38.38-29.75	34.88-24.25
P/E Ratio	20.3-15.6	34.0-21.9	23.8-16.0	47.9-37.6	26.4-16.4	48.0-37.2	20.0-13.9
Average Yield %	3.7	3.8	2.8	2.3	2.6	3.2	3.3

Statistics are as originally reported. ① Incl. $8.9 mil ($0.03/sh) net chg., 2002; $34.7 mil ($0.10/sh) net chg., 2000; $408.2 mil ($1.11/sh) net chg., 1999; $12.5 mil net gain, 1998; $664.6 mil net chg., 1997. ② Bef. $16.9 mil ($0.05/sh) acctg. chg. & incl. $494.6 mil ($1.41/sh) net special chg. and $93.2 mil ($0.27/sh) tax gain.

OFFICERS:
W. R. Johnson, Chmn., Pres., C.E.O.
A. Winkleblack, Exec. V.P., C.F.O.
L. F. Stein, Sr. V.P., Gen. Couns.

INVESTOR CONTACT: Jack Runkel, V.P., Investor Relations, (412) 456-6034

PRINCIPAL OFFICE: 600 Grant Street, Pittsburgh, PA 15219

TELEPHONE NUMBER: (412) 456-5700
FAX: (412) 456-6128
WEB: www.heinz.com

NO. OF EMPLOYEES: 46,500 (approx.)

SHAREHOLDERS: 54,100 (approx. record)

ANNUAL MEETING: In Sept.

INCORPORATED: PA, July, 1900

INSTITUTIONAL HOLDINGS:
No. of Institutions: 524
Shares Held: 236,289,447
% Held: 67.3

INDUSTRY: Food preparations, nec (SIC: 2099)

TRANSFER AGENT(S): Mellon Investor Services, Ridgefield Park, NJ

HERSHEY FOODS CORPORATION

YIELD 1.8%
P/E RATIO 23.4

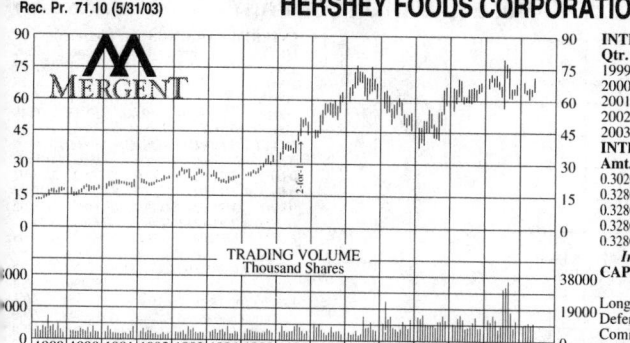

7 YEAR PRICE SCORE 126.7   **12 MONTH PRICE SCORE 105.1**

*NYSE COMPOSITE INDEX=100

INTERIM EARNINGS (Per Share):

Qtr.	Mar.	June	Sept.	Dec.
1999	1.57	0.35	0.62	0.70
2000	0.51	0.29	0.78	0.84
2001	0.57	0.38	0.88	d0.33
2002	0.63	0.46	0.89	0.96
2003	0.73	...	...	...

INTERIM DIVIDENDS (Per Share):

Amt.	Decl.	Ex.	Rec.	Pay.
0.302Q	4/30/02	5/22/02	5/24/02	6/14/02
0.328Q	8/06/02	8/21/02	8/23/02	9/13/02
0.328Q	10/01/02	11/20/02	11/22/02	12/13/02
0.328Q	2/12/03	2/21/03	2/25/03	3/14/03
0.328Q	4/22/03	5/21/03	5/23/03	6/13/03

Indicated div.: $1.31 (Div. Reinv. Plan)

CAPITALIZATION (12/31/02):

	($000)	(%)
Long-Term Debt	851,800	33.1
Deferred Income Tax	348,040	13.5
Common & Surplus	1,371,703	53.3
Total	2,571,543	100.0

DIVIDEND ACHIEVER STATUS:
Rank: 160   10-Year Growth Rate: 9.36%
Total Years of Dividend Growth: 28

RECENT DEVELOPMENTS: For the quarter ended 3/31/03, net income advanced 12.1% to $97.6 million compared with $87.0 million in the corresponding prior-year quarter. Results for 2002 included an after-tax business realignment charge of $5.7 million. Net sales decreased 3.6% to $953.2 million from $988.5 million a year earlier, primarily due to product line rationalization and product buy-in during the fourth quarter of 2002 ahead of price increases which were effective 1/1/03.

PROSPECTS: The Company's market position is strengthening due to solid gains from new products, more effective advertising and its continuing growth with convenience stores. The Company expects its value-enhancing strategy will help build momentum through the remainder of 2003. Sales on a comparable basis are expected to grow between 2.0% and 3.0% during 2003. In addition, HSY expects earnings growth to range from 9.0% to 11.0% in 2003.

BUSINESS

HERSHEY FOODS CORPORA-TION and its subsidiaries are engaged in the manufacture, distribution and sale of consumer food products including: chocolate and non-chocolate confectionery products sold in the form of bar goods, bagged items and boxed items; and grocery products sold in the form of baking ingredients, chocolate drink mixes, peanut butter, dessert toppings and beverages. HSY's products are marketed in over 90 countries worldwide under more than 50 brands. Principal confectionery brands include: HERSHEY'S, REESE'S, MR. GOODBAR, JOLLY RANCHER, KIT KAT, MILK DUDS, WHOPPERS, YORK, TWIZZLERS, and SUPER BUBBLE. Other confectionery products include ICE BREAKERS, BREATH SAVERS COOL BLASTS and BREATH SAVERS mints, and ICE BREAKERS, CARE*FREE, STICK*FREE, BUBBLE YUM, and FRUIT STRIPE gums. In January 1999, HSY sold a 94.0% majority interest in its former U.S. pasta business to New World, LLC. On 12/15/00, HSY acquired Nabisco, Inc.'s mints and gum businesses for $135.0 million.

ANNUAL FINANCIAL DATA

	12/31/02	12/31/01	12/31/00	12/31/99	12/31/98	12/31/97	12/31/96
Earnings Per Share	③2.93	②1.50	2.42	①3.26	2.34	2.23	1.77
Cash Flow Per Share	4.22	2.89	3.69	4.41	3.43	3.24	2.64
Tang. Book Val. Per Share	7.10	4.32	5.14	4.68	3.58	2.11	3.89
Dividends Per Share	1.26	1.17	1.08	1.00	0.92	0.84	0.76
Dividend Payout %	43.0	77.7	44.6	30.7	39.3	37.7	42.9
INCOME STATEMENT (IN MILLIONS):							
Total Revenues	4,120.3	4,557.2	4,221.0	3,970.9	4,435.6	4,302.2	3,989.3
Costs & Expenses	3,244.1	3,973.4	3,422.4	3,249.3	3,634.8	3,519.3	3,292.7
Depreciation & Amort.	177.9	190.5	176.0	163.3	158.2	152.8	133.5
Operating Income	698.3	393.4	622.7	558.4	642.7	630.2	563.1
Net Interest Inc./(Exp.)	d60.7	d69.1	d76.0	d74.3	d85.7	d76.3	d48.0
Income Before Income Taxes	637.6	343.5	546.6	727.9	557.0	554.0	479.7
Income Taxes	234.0	136.4	212.1	267.4	216.1	217.7	206.6
Net Income	③403.6	②207.2	334.5	①460.3	340.9	336.3	273.2
Cash Flow	581.5	397.7	510.5	623.6	499.0	489.0	406.7
Average Shs. Outstg. (000)	137,714	137,696	138,365	141,300	145,563	151,016	153,995
BALANCE SHEET (IN MILLIONS):							
Cash & Cash Equivalents	297.7	134.1	32.0	118.1	39.0	54.2	61.4
Total Current Assets	1,263.6	1,167.5	1,295.3	1,280.0	1,134.0	1,034.8	986.2
Net Property	1,486.1	1,534.9	1,585.4	1,510.5	1,648.1	1,648.2	1,601.9
Total Assets	3,480.6	3,247.4	3,447.8	3,346.7	3,404.1	3,291.2	3,184.8
Total Current Liabilities	546.8	606.4	766.9	712.8	814.8	795.7	817.3
Long-Term Obligations	851.8	877.0	877.7	878.2	879.1	1,029.1	655.3
Net Stockholders' Equity	1,371.7	1,147.2	1,175.0	1,098.6	1,042.3	852.8	1,161.0
Net Working Capital	716.8	561.1	528.4	567.2	319.1	239.1	169.0
Year-end Shs. Outstg. (000)	134,220	166,073	136,282	138,460	143,147	142,932	152,942
STATISTICAL RECORD:							
Operating Profit Margin %	16.9	8.6	14.8	14.1	14.5	14.6	14.1
Net Profit Margin %	9.8	4.5	7.9	11.6	7.7	7.8	6.8
Return on Equity %	29.4	18.1	28.5	41.9	32.7	39.4	23.5
Return on Assets %	11.6	6.4	9.7	13.8	10.0	10.2	8.6
Debt/Total Assets %	24.5	27.0	25.5	26.2	25.8	31.3	20.6
Price Range	79.49-56.45	70.15-55.13	66.44-37.75	64.88-45.75	76.38-59.69	63.88-42.13	51.75-31.94
P/E Ratio	27.1-19.3	46.8-36.7	27.5-15.6	19.9-14.0	32.6-25.5	28.6-18.9	29.2-18.0
Average Yield %	1.9	1.9	2.1	1.8	1.4	1.6	1.8

Statistics are as originally reported. Adj. for 2-for-1 split, 9/96. ① Incl. non-recurr. credit of $165.0 mill. ② Incl. pre-tax chrg. of $228.3 mill. for business realign. & asset impairmnts. and pre-tax gain of $19.2 mill. on sale of Luden's business. ③ Incl. pre-tax realign. chrg. of $34.0 mill. and bus. sale exploration chrg. of $17.2 mill.

OFFICERS:
R. H. Lenny, Chmn., Pres., C.E.O.
F. Cerminara, Sr. V.P., C.F.O.
B. H. Snyder, Sr. V.P., Gen. Couns., Sec.

INVESTOR CONTACT: James A. Edris, V.P., Investor Relations, (800) 539-0291

PRINCIPAL OFFICE: 100 Crystal A Drive, Hershey, PA 17033

TELEPHONE NUMBER: (717) 534-6799
FAX: (717) 534-7873
WEB: www.hersheys.com
NO. OF EMPLOYEES: 13,700 full-time (approx.); 1,700 part-time (approx.)
SHAREHOLDERS: 38,754 (com. & class B)
ANNUAL MEETING: In April
INCORPORATED: DE, Oct., 1927

INSTITUTIONAL HOLDINGS:
No. of Institutions: 408
Shares Held: 57,236,937
% Held: 43.0

INDUSTRY: Chocolate and cocoa products (SIC: 2066)

TRANSFER AGENT(S): Mellon Investor Services, LLC, Ridgefield Park, NJ

HILB, ROGAL & HAMILTON COMPANY

YIELD 1.1%
P/E RATIO 18.2

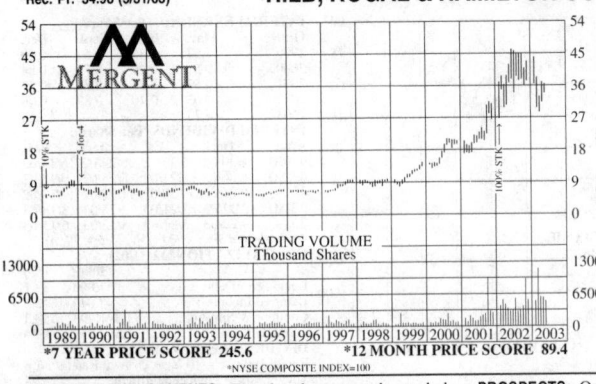

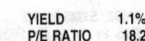

*7 YEAR PRICE SCORE 245.6   *12 MONTH PRICE SCORE 89.4
*NYSE COMPOSITE INDEX=100

INTERIM EARNINGS (Per Share):

Qtr.	Mar.	June	Sept.	Dec.
1999	0.30	0.12	0.21	0.12
2000	0.24	0.18	0.22	0.15
2001	0.27	0.27	0.32	0.12
2002	0.48	0.40	0.53	0.48
2003	0.51	...	...	...

INTERIM DIVIDENDS (Per Share):

Amt.	Decl.	Ex.	Rec.	Pay.
0.09Q	5/07/02	6/12/02	6/14/02	6/28/02
0.09Q	8/19/02	9/12/02	9/16/02	9/30/02
0.09Q	11/25/02	12/12/02	12/16/02	12/31/02
0.09Q	2/11/03	3/12/03	3/14/03	3/31/03
0.092Q	5/06/03	6/12/03	6/16/03	6/30/03

Indicated div.: $0.37

CAPITALIZATION (12/31/02):

	($000)	(%)
Long-Term Debt	177,151	36.3
Common & Surplus	310,648	63.7
Total	487,799	100.0

DIVIDEND ACHIEVER STATUS:
Rank: 221   10-Year Growth Rate: 5.72%
Total Years of Dividend Growth: 16

RECENT DEVELOPMENTS: For the three months ended 3/31/03, net income rose 19.2% to $18.1 million compared with income of $15.2 million, before an accounting change benefit of $3.9 million, in the same period of 2002. Results for 2003 and 2002 included amortization of intangibles of $2.2 million and $522,000, respectively. Results for 2003 also included a one-time, retirement benefit charge of $5.2 million. Total revenues were $142.0 million, up 42.2% from $99.9 million the previous year.

PROSPECTS: On 3/3/03, the Company completed the acquisition of Sheppard Riley Coughlin Insurance Agency, Inc., which operates insurance brokerage firms in the Northeast, for an undisclosed amount. The transaction strengthens the Company's position in the Greater Boston area. Separately, the Company plans to continue to focus on developing it sales team, step up the execution of its five-year strategic business plan, seek out strategic acquisitions, and create new product lines.

BUSINESS

HILB, ROGAL & HAMILTON COMPANY places various types of insurance, including property/casualty, marine, aviation and employee benefits, with insurance underwriters on behalf of its clients through the network of its wholly-owned subsidiary insurance agencies. The agencies operate in over 100 offices in the U.S., and the client base consists mainly of middle market commercial and industrial accounts. HRH also advises clients on risk management and employee benefits and provides claims administration and loss control consulting services to clients. On 7/1/02, the Company acquired Hobbs Group, LLC, an independent insurance broker that serves top-tier middle-market and risk management clients.

ANNUAL FINANCIAL DATA

	12/31/02	12/31/01	12/31/00	12/31/99	12/31/98	12/31/97	12/31/96
Earnings Per Share	③ 1.89	1.07	② 0.78	① 0.72	0.59	0.49	0.43
Cash Flow Per Share	2.54	1.91	1.33	1.24	1.04	0.93	0.82
Dividends Per Share	0.36	0.35	0.34	0.33	0.32	0.31	0.30
Dividend Payout %	18.9	35.7	43.6	45.8	54.2	63.3	69.8
INCOME STATEMENT (IN THOUSANDS):							
Total Revenues	452,726	330,267	262,119	227,226	175,364	173,709	158,243
Costs & Expenses	325,713	244,492	196,607	170,576	136,174	138,159	127,098
Depreciation & Amort.	13,091	19,984	17,596	15,191	11,509	11,667	10,856
Operating Income	113,922	65,792	47,917	41,458	27,681	23,882	20,290
Net Interest Inc./(Exp.)	d10,665	d9,062	d8,179	d6,490	d2,317	d2,037	d1,245
Income Before Income Taxes	103,257	56,730	39,737	33,069	25,364	21,845	19,045
Income Taxes	42,082	24,381	17,610	13,583	10,418	9,055	7,638
Net Income	③ 61,175	32,349	② 22,127	① 19,486	14,945	12,790	11,406
Cash Flow	74,266	52,332	39,723	34,677	26,454	24,457	22,262
Average Shs. Outstg.	29,240	27,411	29,784	28,014	25,418	26,430	26,986
BALANCE SHEET (IN THOUSANDS):							
Cash & Cash Equivalents	136,026	55,080	31,008	25,276	22,779	26,207	24,862
Total Current Assets	357,565	197,408	131,478	111,201	78,202	76,833	76,256
Net Property	20,386	19,485	16,495	15,413	12,387	11,762	16,092
Total Assets	833,024	499,301	353,371	317,981	188,066	181,607	181,475
Total Current Liabilities	324,045	225,045	151,001	124,307	88,505	88,273	89,112
Long-Term Obligations	177,151	114,443	103,113	111,826	43,658	32,458	27,196
Net Stockholders' Equity	310,648	142,801	88,222	71,176	45,710	51,339	55,298
Net Working Capital	33,520	d27,637	d19,523	d13,106	d10,303	d11,440	d12,856
Year-end Shs. Outstg.	33,484	28,311	26,560	26,118	24,234	25,626	26,642
STATISTICAL RECORD:							
Operating Profit Margin %	25.2	19.9	18.3	18.2	15.8	13.7	12.8
Net Profit Margin %	13.5	9.8	8.4	8.6	8.5	7.4	7.2
Return on Equity %	19.7	22.7	25.1	27.4	32.7	24.9	20.6
Return on Assets %	7.3	6.5	6.3	6.1	7.9	4.2	3.8
Debt/Total Assets %	21.3	22.9	29.2	35.2	23.2	10.8	9.0
Price Range	46.15-26.65	31.38-16.88	21.06-12.81	14.56-7.78	9.94-7.69	9.81-6.25	7.00-5.69
P/E Ratio	24.4-14.1	64.0-34.4	54.0-32.8	40.4-21.6	33.6-26.0	40.4-25.8	33.0-26.8
Average Yield %	1.0	1.4	2.0	2.9	3.6	3.9	4.8

Statistics are as originally reported. Adj. for 100% stk. div., 12/01. ① Incl. $1.9 mill. integration chg. & $4.9 mill. non-recur. gain. ② Excl. $325,000 cumulative effect of an acctg. chg. ③ Excl. $3.9 mill. cumulative effect of an acctg. gain.

OFFICERS:
A. L. Rogal, Chmn., C.E.O.
M. L. Vaughan III, Pres., C.O.O.
C. Jones, Sr. V.P., C.F.O., Treas.

INVESTOR CONTACT: Carolyn Jones, Sr. V.P., C.F.O., Treas., (804) 747-6500

PRINCIPAL OFFICE: 4951 Lake Brook Drive, Suite 500, Glen Allen, VA 23060

TELEPHONE NUMBER: (804) 747-6500
FAX: (804) 747-6046
WEB: www.hrh.com

NO. OF EMPLOYEES: 3,100 (approx.)

SHAREHOLDERS: 486

ANNUAL MEETING: In May

INCORPORATED: VA, 1982

INSTITUTIONAL HOLDINGS:
No. of Institutions: 183
Shares Held: 29,107,797
% Held: 85.6

INDUSTRY: Insurance agents, brokers, & service (SIC: 6411)

TRANSFER AGENT(S): Mellon Investor Services, LLC, Ridgefield Park, NJ

HILLENBRAND INDUSTRIES, INC.

YIELD 2.0%
P/E RATIO ...

*7 YEAR PRICE SCORE 126.3   *12 MONTH PRICE SCORE 95.4
*NYSE COMPOSITE INDEX=100

TRADING VOLUME
Thousand Shares

INTERIM EARNINGS (Per Share):

Qtr.	Feb.	May	Aug.	Nov.
1999-00	0.58	0.56	0.54	0.76
2000-01	0.40	0.65	0.65	1.01

Qtr.	Dec.	Mar.	June	Sept.
2001-02	1.00	0.85	0.52	d1.69
2002-03	0.12	1.00	...	...

INTERIM DIVIDENDS (Per Share):

Amt.	Decl.	Ex.	Rec.	Pay.
0.23Q	5/16/02	5/29/02	5/31/02	6/28/02
0.23Q	9/05/02	9/12/02	9/16/02	9/30/02
0.25Q	12/05/02	12/13/02	12/17/02	12/31/02
0.25Q	2/13/03	2/27/03	3/03/03	3/31/03
0.25Q	5/15/03	5/29/03	6/02/03	6/30/03

Indicated div.: $1.00 (Div. Reinv. Plan)

CAPITALIZATION (9/30/02):

	($000)	(%)
Long-Term Debt	322,000	24.2
Deferred Income Tax	10,000	0.8
Common & Surplus	999,000	75.1
Total	1,331,000	100.0

DIVIDEND ACHIEVER STATUS:
Rank: 136   10-Year Growth Rate: 10.38%
Total Years of Dividend Growth: 32

RECENT DEVELOPMENTS: For the second quarter ended 3/31/03, net income advanced 17.0% to $62.0 million compared with $53.0 million in the equivalent 2002 quarter. Total revenues increased 3.9% to $554.0 million from $533.0 million a year earlier. Health care sales climbed 11.5% to $213.0 million, while insurance revenues rose 2.1% to $97.0 million. Health care therapy rentals decreased 2.4% to $80.0 million, and funeral services sales slipped 0.6% to $164.0 million.

PROSPECTS: On 4/14/03, HB announced that its Hill-Rom health care unit established a new business structure to accelerate its strategy for strengthening its core businesses while investing in new revenue initiatives. Hil-Rom expects to eliminate between 250 and 300 salaried positions over the next 12 months. HB anticipates these actions will reduce net operating costs between $12.0 million and $14.0 million annually. For fiscal 2003, HB expects earnings to range from $3.84 to $3.90 per diluted share.

BUSINESS

HILLENBRAND INDUSTRIES, INC. is organized into two business groups. The Health Care Group (54.5% of fiscal 2002 revenues) consists of Hill-Rom, Inc., a manufacturer of equipment for the health care market and provider of wound care and pulmonary/trauma management services. Hill-Rom produces adjustable hospital beds, infant incubators, radiant warmers, hospital procedural stretchers, hospital patient room furniture, medical gas and vacuum systems and architectural systems designed to meet the needs of medical-surgical critical care, long-term care, home-care and prenatal providers. The Funeral Services Group consists of Batesville Casket Company, Inc. (29.0%), a manufacturer of caskets and other products for the funeral industry, and Forethought Financial Services, Inc. (16.5%), a provider of funeral planning financial products.

ANNUAL FINANCIAL DATA

	[5] 9/30/02	12/1/01	12/2/00	11/27/99	11/28/98	11/29/97	11/30/96
Earnings Per Share	[6] d0.16	[4] 2.71	[3] 2.44	[2] 1.87	[1] 2.73	2.28	2.02
Cash Flow Per Share	0.97	4.30	3.86	3.35	4.93	3.76	3.44
Tang. Book Val. Per Share	12.72	13.24	10.42	10.17	11.29	11.09	9.28
Dividends Per Share	[7] 1.02	0.84	0.80	0.78	0.72	0.66	0.62
Dividend Payout %	...	31.0	32.8	41.7	26.4	28.9	30.7
INCOME STATEMENT (IN MILLIONS):							
Total Revenues	1,757.0	2,107.0	2,096.0	2,047.0	2,001.0	1,776.0	1,684.0
Costs & Expenses	1,718.0	1,771.0	1,763.0	1,738.0	1,624.0	1,410.0	1,349.0
Depreciation & Amort.	71.0	100.0	89.0	98.0	149.0	102.0	99.0
Operating Income	d32.0	236.0	244.0	211.0	228.0	264.0	236.0
Net Interest Inc./(Exp.)	d14.0	d23.0	d27.0	d27.0	d27.0	d21.0	d22.0
Income Before Income Taxes	d35.0	223.0	240.0	195.0	293.0	259.0	233.0
Income Taxes	cr25.0	53.0	86.0	71.0	109.0	102.0	93.0
Net Income	[6] d10.0	[4] 170.0	[3] 154.0	[2] 124.0	[1] 184.0	157.0	140.0
Cash Flow	61.0	270.0	243.0	222.0	333.0	259.0	239.0
Average Shs. Outstg. (000)	62,922	62,814	62,913	66,296	67,578	68,796	69,474
BALANCE SHEET (IN MILLIONS):							
Cash & Cash Equivalents	296.0	284.0	132.0	170.0	297.0	364.0	266.0
Total Current Assets	958.0	868.0	724.0	782.0	858.0	821.0	694.0
Net Property	210.0	206.0	205.0	198.0	221.0	238.0	253.0
Total Assets	5,442.0	5,049.0	4,597.0	4,433.0	4,280.0	3,828.0	3,396.0
Total Current Liabilities	551.0	320.0	282.0	371.0	375.0	359.0	320.0
Long-Term Obligations	322.0	305.0	302.0	302.0	303.0	203.0	204.0
Net Stockholders' Equity	999.0	1,026.0	831.0	838.0	952.0	886.0	787.0
Net Working Capital	407.0	548.0	442.0	411.0	483.0	462.0	374.0
Year-end Shs. Outstg. (000)	61,702	62,467	62,404	63,547	66,759	68,511	68,786
STATISTICAL RECORD:							
Operating Profit Margin %	...	11.2	11.6	10.3	11.4	14.9	14.0
Net Profit Margin %	...	8.1	7.3	6.1	9.2	8.8	8.3
Return on Equity %	...	16.6	18.5	14.8	19.3	17.7	17.8
Return on Assets %	...	3.4	3.4	2.8	4.3	4.1	4.1
Debt/Total Assets %	5.9	6.0	6.6	6.8	7.1	5.3	6.0
Price Range	66.48-46.55	58.51-41.56	56.38-28.75	56.81-26.13	64.69-44.38	50.88-35.50	40.25-31.88
P/E Ratio	...	21.6-15.3	23.1-11.8	30.4-14.0	23.7-16.3	22.3-15.6	19.9-15.8
Average Yield %	1.8	1.7	1.9	1.9	1.3	1.5	1.7

Statistics are as originally reported. [1] Incl. non-recurr. chrg. of $66.0 mill. [2] Incl. unusual chrg. $38.0 mill. [3] Incl. non-recurr. chrgs. of $3.0 mill. [4] Incl. non-recurr. chrgs. of $32.0 mill. [5] For ten months [6] Incl. after-tax litigation chrg. of $158.0 mill. and oth. non-recurr. chrg. of $4.0 mill. [7] Incl. spec. div. of $0.08 per sh.

OFFICERS:
R. J. Hillenbrand, Chmn.
F. W. Rockwood, Pres., C.E.O.
S. K. Sorensen, V.P., C.F.O.

INVESTOR CONTACT: Mark R. Lanning, V.P., Treas., (812) 934-8400

PRINCIPAL OFFICE: 700 State Route 46 East, Batesville, IN 47006-8835

TELEPHONE NUMBER: (812) 934-7000
FAX: (812) 934-7364
WEB: www.hillenbrand.com

NO. OF EMPLOYEES: 10,300 (approx.)

SHAREHOLDERS: 17,600 (approx.)

ANNUAL MEETING: In April

INCORPORATED: IN, Aug., 1969

INSTITUTIONAL HOLDINGS:
No. of Institutions: 206
Shares Held: 25,647,366
% Held: 41.4

INDUSTRY: Furniture and fixtures, nec (SIC 2599)

TRANSFER AGENT(S): Computershare Investor Services, Chicago, IL

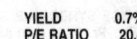

NYSE SYMBOL HD
Rec. Pr. 32.49 (5/31/03)

HOME DEPOT (THE), INC.

YIELD 0.7%
P/E RATIO 20.4

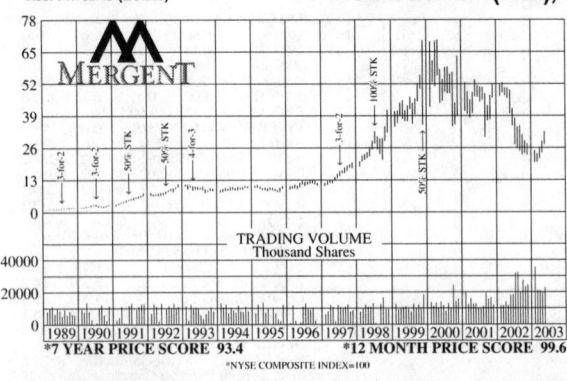

*7 YEAR PRICE SCORE 93.4 ***12 MONTH PRICE SCORE 99.6**
*NYSE COMPOSITE INDEX=100

INTERIM EARNINGS (Per Share):

Qtr.	Apr.	July	Oct.	Jan.
2000-01	0.27	0.36	0.28	0.20
2001-02	0.27	0.39	0.33	0.30
2002-03	0.36	0.50	0.40	0.30
2003-04	0.39	...	...	...

INTERIM DIVIDENDS (Per Share):

Amt.	Decl.	Ex.	Rec.	Pay.
0.05Q	5/29/02	6/11/02	6/13/02	6/27/02
0.05Q	8/22/02	9/03/02	9/05/02	9/19/02
0.06Q	11/21/02	12/03/02	12/05/02	12/19/02
0.06Q	2/27/03	3/11/03	3/13/03	3/27/03
0.06Q	5/29/03	6/10/03	6/12/03	6/26/03

Indicated div.: $0.24 (Div. Reinv. Plan)

CAPITALIZATION (2/2/03):

	($000)	(%)
Long-Term Debt	1,044,000	4.9
Capital Lease Obligations..	277,000	1.3
Deferred Income Tax	362,000	1.7
Common & Surplus	19,802,000	92.2
Total	21,485,000	100.0

DIVIDEND ACHIEVER STATUS:

Rank: 5   10-Year Growth Rate: 27.62%
Total Years of Dividend Growth: 15

RECENT DEVELOPMENTS: For the three months ended 5/4/03, net earnings grew 6.0% to $907.0 million from $856.0 million in the corresponding prior-year period. Net sales increased 5.8% to $15.10 billion from $14.28 billion a year earlier. Comparable-store sales were down 1.6% year-over-year. Gross profit totaled $4.83 billion, or 32.0% of net sales, versus $4.36 billion, or 30.5% of net sales, the year before. Operating income rose 6.3% to $1.45 billion from $1.36 billion the previous year.

PROSPECTS: The Company is projecting sales growth of between 9.0% and 12.0% and earnings growth of 9.0% to 14.0% during the current fiscal year. In addition, comparable-store sales are expected to be flat to slightly positive for the year. Meanwhile, HD is focused on increasing inventory levels and introducing new products to help boost sales amid increased competition in many of the Company's large U.S. markets. Separately, results should benefit from the Company's efforts to remodel many of its older stores.

BUSINESS

THE HOME DEPOT, INC. operated 1,568 retail warehouse stores as of 5/4/03 in the United States, Canada and Mexico that offer a wide assortment of building materials and home improvement products. The average Home Depot store has about 108,000 square feet of interior floor space and is stocked with approximately 40,000 to 50,000 separate items. Most stores have about 22,000 square feet of additional outdoor selling area for landscaping supplies. HD also operates 53 EXPO Design Center stores that sell products and services primarily for home decorating and remodeling projects, five Home Depot Supply stores, eight Home Depot Landscape Supply stores and one Home Depot Floor Store outlet.

ANNUAL FINANCIAL DATA

	2/2/03	2/3/02	1/28/01	1/30/00	1/31/99	2/1/98	2/2/97
Earnings Per Share	1.56	1.29	1.10	1.00	0.71	① 0.52	0.43
Cash Flow Per Share	1.95	1.62	1.35	1.19	0.86	0.63	0.53
Tang. Book Val. Per Share	8.39	7.53	6.32	5.22	3.83	3.17	2.71
Dividends Per Share	0.21	0.17	0.16	0.11	0.08	0.06	0.05
Dividend Payout %	13.5	13.2	14.5	11.3	10.8	12.2	11.9
INCOME STATEMENT (IN MILLIONS):							
Total Revenues	58,247.0	53,553.0	45,738.0	38,434.0	30,219.0	24,156.0	19,535.5
Costs & Expenses	51,514.0	47,857.0	40,946.0	34,176.0	27,185.0	21,961.0	17,769.5
Depreciation & Amort.	903.0	764.0	601.0	463.0	373.0	283.0	232.3
Operating Income	5,830.0	4,932.0	4,191.0	3,795.0	2,661.0	1,912.0	1,533.7
Net Interest Inc./(Exp.)	42.0	25.0	26.0	9.0	d7.0	2.0	9.5
Income Before Income Taxes	5,872.0	4,957.0	4,217.0	3,804.0	2,654.0	1,914.0	1,543.1
Income Taxes	2,208.0	1,913.0	1,636.0	1,484.0	1,040.0	738.0	597.0
Equity Earnings/Minority Int.	...	...	...	...	...	d16.0	d8.4
Net Income	3,664.0	3,044.0	2,581.0	2,320.0	1,614.0	① 1,160.0	937.7
Cash Flow	4,567.0	3,808.0	3,182.0	2,783.0	1,987.0	1,443.0	1,170.1
Average Shs. Outstg. (000)	2,344,000	2,353,000	2,352,000	2,342,000	2,320,000	2,286,000	2,194,884
BALANCE SHEET (IN MILLIONS):							
Cash & Cash Equivalents	2,253.0	2,546.0	177.0	170.0	62.0	174.0	558.4
Total Current Assets	11,917.0	10,361.0	7,777.0	6,390.0	4,933.0	4,460.0	3,709.4
Net Property	17,168.0	15,375.0	13,068.0	10,227.0	8,160.0	6,509.0	5,437.0
Total Assets	30,011.0	26,394.0	21,385.0	17,081.0	13,465.0	11,229.0	9,341.7
Total Current Liabilities	8,035.0	6,501.0	4,385.0	3,656.0	2,857.0	2,456.0	1,842.1
Long-Term Obligations	1,321.0	1,250.0	1,545.0	750.0	1,566.0	1,303.0	1,246.6
Net Stockholders' Equity	19,802.0	18,082.0	15,004.0	12,341.0	8,740.0	7,098.0	5,955.2
Net Working Capital	3,882.0	3,860.0	3,392.0	2,734.0	2,076.0	2,004.0	1,867.2
Year-end Shs. Outstg. (000)	2,293,000	2,345,888	2,323,747	2,304,317	2,213,178	2,196,324	2,162,318
STATISTICAL RECORD:							
Operating Profit Margin %	10.0	9.2	9.2	9.9	8.8	7.9	7.9
Net Profit Margin %	6.3	5.7	5.6	6.0	5.3	4.8	4.8
Return on Equity %	18.5	16.8	17.2	18.8	18.5	16.3	15.7
Return on Assets %	12.2	11.5	12.1	13.6	12.0	10.3	10.0
Debt/Total Assets %	4.4	4.7	7.2	4.4	11.6	11.6	13.3
Price Range	52.60-23.01	53.73-30.30	70.00-34.69	69.75-34.59	41.34-18.44	20.17-10.61	13.22-9.22
P/E Ratio	33.7-14.7	41.6-23.5	63.6-31.5	69.7-34.6	58.2-26.0	39.0-20.5	30.7-21.4
Average Yield %	0.6	0.4	0.3	0.2	0.3	0.4	0.5

Statistics are as originally reported. Adj. for 3-for-2 stk. split, 12/99; 100% stk. div., 7/98; 3-for-2 stk. split, 7/97. ① Incl. $104 mil pre-tax, non-recur. chg.

OFFICERS:
R. L. Nardelli, Chmn. Pres., C.E.O.
C. B. Tome, Exec. V.P., C.F.O.
F. Fernandez, Exec. V.P., Sec., Gen. Couns.

INVESTOR CONTACT: Investor Relations, (770) 384-2666

PRINCIPAL OFFICE: 2455 Paces Ferry Road N.W., Atlanta, GA 30339-4024

TELEPHONE NUMBER: (770) 433-8211
FAX: (770) 431-2707
WEB: www.homedepot.com
NO. OF EMPLOYEES: 168,000 full-time (approx.); 112,000 part-time (approx.)
SHAREHOLDERS: 207,516 (approx. record)
ANNUAL MEETING: In May
INCORPORATED: DE, June, 1978

INSTITUTIONAL HOLDINGS:
No. of Institutions: 1,062
Shares Held: 1,275,822,161
% Held: 55.6

INDUSTRY: Lumber and other building materials (SIC: 5211)

TRANSFER AGENT(S): EquiServe Trust Company, N.A., Providence, RI

HON INDUSTRIES INCORPORATED

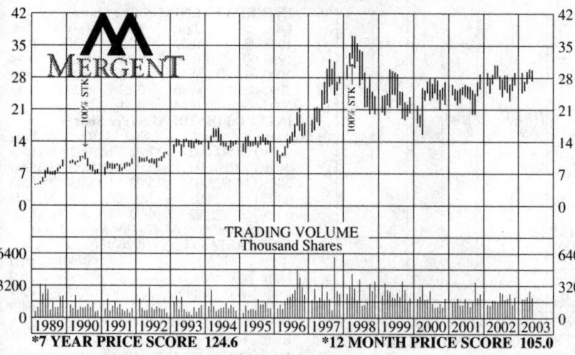

*7 YEAR PRICE SCORE 124.6   *12 MONTH PRICE SCORE 105.0
*NYSE COMPOSITE INDEX=100

INTERIM EARNINGS (Per Share):

Qtr.	Mar.	June	Sept.	Dec.
2000	0.41	0.39	0.57	0.40
2001	0.31	0.07	0.48	0.40
2002	0.27	0.34	0.46	0.48
2003	0.27	...	...	...

INTERIM DIVIDENDS (Per Share):

Amt.	Decl.	Ex.	Rec.	Pay.
0.125Q	8/05/02	8/13/02	8/15/02	8/30/02
0.125Q	11/07/02	11/13/02	11/15/02	11/27/02
0.13Q	2/12/03	2/19/03	2/21/03	2/28/03
0.13Q	5/06/03	5/13/03	5/15/03	5/30/03

Indicated div.: $0.52

CAPITALIZATION (12/28/02):

	($000)	(%)
Long-Term Debt	8,553	1.2
Capital Lease Obligations..	1,284	0.2
Deferred Income Tax	37,114	5.3
Common & Surplus	646,893	93.2
Total	693,844	100.0

DIVIDEND ACHIEVER STATUS:
Rank: 133   10-Year Growth Rate: 10.45%
Total Years of Dividend Growth: 14

RECENT DEVELOPMENTS: For the quarter ended 3/29/03, net income was flat at $15.9 million versus the equivalent quarter of 2002. Net sales fell 1.8% to $392.0 million, reflecting difficult market conditions resulting from geopolitical and economic uncertainty. Gross profit was 35.5% of net sales, versus 35.0% of net sales, the year before. The slight improvement in gross margin as a percentage of sales was primarily attributed to HNI's restructuring activities.

PROSPECTS: Looking ahead, the Company expects global economic and geopolitical uncertainty to continue to affect market conditions and challenge growth and profitability through the first half of the year. Accordingly, HNI will continue to focus on streamlining processes and operations, strengthening brands and maintaining a tight cost structure. HNI's cash position as of 3/29/03 was $114.0 million, including short-term investments.

BUSINESS

HON INDUSTRIES INCORPO-RATED manufactures and markets office furniture and hearth products. The Company's office furniture products (75.6% of 2002 net sales) are produced in four basic categories: storage, seating, office systems, and desks and related products. The office products are sold to dealers, wholesalers, warehouse clubs, retail superstores, end-user customers, and federal and state governments. HNI's hearth products (24.4%) include wood-burning, pellet-burning, gas-burning and electric factory-built fireplaces, fireplace inserts, stoves, and gas logs. The hearth products are sold through a national system of dealers, wholesalers, large regional contractors and Company-owned retail outlets. HNI has locations in the United States, Canada and Mexico.

ANNUAL FINANCIAL DATA

	12/28/02	12/29/01	12/30/00	1/1/00	1/2/99	1/3/98	12/28/96
Earnings Per Share	① 1.55	① 1.26	1.77	1.44	1.72	1.45	① 1.13
Cash Flow Per Share	2.71	2.64	3.08	2.51	2.58	2.05	1.55
Tang. Book Val. Per Share	7.79	6.45	5.97	6.45	5.77	4.59	3.39
Dividends Per Share	0.50	0.48	0.44	0.38	0.32	0.28	0.25
Dividend Payout %	32.3	38.1	24.9	26.4	18.6	19.3	22.1
INCOME STATEMENT (IN MILLIONS):							
Total Revenues	1,692.6	1,792.4	2,046.3	1,789.3	1,696.4	1,362.7	998.1
Costs & Expenses	1,481.2	1,588.0	1,789.2	1,577.4	1,464.3	1,181.9	866.7
Depreciation & Amort.	68.8	81.4	79.0	65.5	53.0	35.6	25.3
Operating Income	142.7	123.1	178.0	146.4	179.2	145.2	106.2
Net Interest Inc./(Exp.)	d2.1	d6.8	d12.1	d8.9	d9.1	d6.0	d0.9
Income Before Income Taxes	140.6	116.3	166.0	137.6	170.1	139.1	105.3
Income Taxes	49.2	41.9	59.7	50.2	63.8	52.2	37.2
Net Income	① 91.4	① 74.4	106.2	① 87.4	106.3	87.0	① 68.1
Cash Flow	160.1	155.8	185.3	152.8	159.3	122.6	93.3
Average Shs. Outstg. (000)	59,041	59,088	60,140	60,855	61,650	59,780	60,228
BALANCE SHEET (IN MILLIONS):							
Cash & Cash Equivalents	155.5	78.8	3.2	22.2	17.7	46.3	32.7
Total Current Assets	405.1	319.7	330.1	316.6	290.3	295.2	205.5
Net Property	353.3	405.0	454.3	455.6	444.2	341.0	234.6
Total Assets	1,020.6	961.9	1,022.5	906.7	864.5	754.7	513.5
Total Current Liabilities	298.7	230.4	264.9	225.1	217.4	200.8	152.6
Long-Term Obligations	9.8	80.8	128.3	124.2	135.6	134.5	97.8
Net Stockholders' Equity	646.9	592.7	573.3	501.3	462.0	381.7	252.4
Net Working Capital	106.4	89.2	65.3	91.4	72.9	94.4	53.0
Year-end Shs. Outstg. (000)	58,374	58,673	59,797	60,172	61,290	61,659	59,426
STATISTICAL RECORD:							
Operating Profit Margin %	8.4	6.9	8.7	8.2	10.6	10.7	10.6
Net Profit Margin %	5.4	4.2	5.2	4.9	6.3	6.4	6.8
Return on Equity %	14.1	12.6	18.5	17.4	23.0	22.8	27.0
Return on Assets %	9.0	7.7	10.4	9.6	12.3	11.5	13.3
Debt/Total Assets %	1.0	8.4	12.5	13.7	15.7	17.8	19.0
Price Range	30.85-22.88	28.85-19.96	27.88-15.56	29.88-18.75	37.19-20.00	32.13-16.00	21.38-9.25
P/E Ratio	19.9-14.8	22.9-15.8	15.7-8.8	20.7-13.0	21.6-11.6	22.2-11.0	18.9-8.2
Average Yield %	1.9	2.0	2.0	1.6	1.1	1.2	1.6

Statistics are as originally reported. Adj. for stk. split: 2-for-1, 3/27/98. ① Incl. non-recurr. chrg. $3.0 mill., 2002; $24.0 mill., 2001; net chrg. $12.5 mill., 1999; credit $3.2 mill., 1996.

OFFICERS:
J. D. Michaels, Chmn., Pres., C.E.O.
J. K. Dittmer, V.P., C.F.O.
J. I. Johnson, V.P., Sec., Gen. Couns.

INVESTOR CONTACT: Jerald K. Dittmer, V.P., C.F.O., (563) 264-7400

PRINCIPAL OFFICE: 414 East Third Street, P.O. Box 1109, Muscatine, IA 52761-0071

TELEPHONE NUMBER: (563) 264-7400
FAX: (563) 264-7217
WEB: www.honi.com

NO. OF EMPLOYEES: 8,500 full-time (approx.); 300 part-time (approx.)

SHAREHOLDERS: 6,777

ANNUAL MEETING: In May

INCORPORATED: IA, Jan., 1944

INSTITUTIONAL HOLDINGS:
No. of Institutions: 135
Shares Held: 27,489,824
% Held: 47.4

INDUSTRY: Office furniture, except wood (SIC: 2522)

TRANSFER AGENT(S): Computershare Investor Services, LLC, Chicago, IL

HORMEL FOODS CORPORATION

YIELD 1.8%
P/E RATIO 17.5

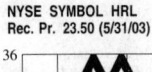

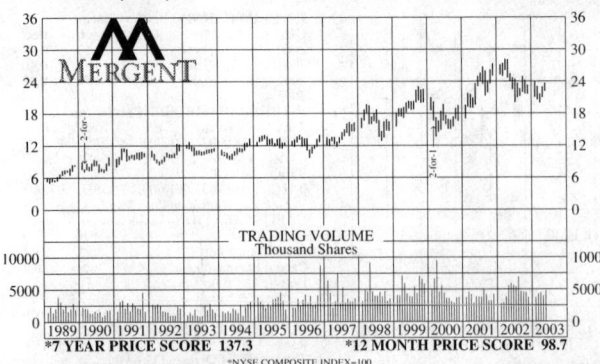

TRADING VOLUME
Thousand Shares

1989 | 1990 | 1991 | 1992 | 1993 | 1994 | 1995 | 1996 | 1997 | 1998 | 1999 | 2000 | 2001 | 2002 | 2003

*7 YEAR PRICE SCORE 137.3   ***12 MONTH PRICE SCORE 98.7**

*NYSE COMPOSITE INDEX=100

INTERIM EARNINGS (Per Share):

Qtr.	Jan.	Apr.	July	Oct.
1998-99	0.29	0.22	0.20	0.41
1999-00	0.30	0.26	0.21	0.44
2000-01	0.30	0.28	0.24	0.49
2001-02	0.36	0.24	0.27	0.49
2002-03	0.34	0.24	...	...

INTERIM DIVIDENDS (Per Share):

Amt.	Decl.	Ex.	Rec.	Pay.
0.098Q	5/24/02	7/17/02	7/20/02	8/15/02
0.098Q	10/01/02	10/16/02	10/19/02	11/15/02
0.105Q	11/25/02	1/15/03	1/18/03	2/15/03
0.105Q	3/24/03	4/15/03	4/19/03	5/15/03
0.105Q	5/22/03	7/16/03	7/19/03	8/15/03

Indicated div.: $0.42 (Div. Reinv. Plan)

CAPITALIZATION (10/26/02):

	($000)	(%)
Long-Term Debt	409,648	26.9
Common & Surplus	1,115,255	73.1
Total	1,524,903	100.0

DIVIDEND ACHIEVER STATUS:
Rank: 183   10-Year Growth Rate: 8.04%
Total Years of Dividend Growth: 35

RECENT DEVELOPMENTS: For the 13 weeks ended 4/26/03, net earnings grew 3.2% to $33.8 million from $32.7 million in the corresponding prior-year period. Net sales totaled $1.00 billion, up 5.0% compared with $954.6 million the previous year. Gross profit was $238.4 million, or 23.8% of net sales, versus $224.1 million, or 23.5% of net sales, the year before. Operating income rose 2.5% to $59.7 million from $58.2 million a year earlier. Earnings before income taxes increased 1.4% to $52.3 million from $51.6 million in the prior year.

PROSPECTS: Results are benefiting from increased volume of the Company's core grocery products including SPAM, DINTY MOORE stew, and HORMEL bacon bits and chili. Meanwhile, profitability is being negatively affected by an oversupply of turkey and pork in the market, which is pressuring market prices. HRL expects the U.S. pork market will return to more normal conditions in the second half of fiscal 2003; however, turkey market conditions remain uncertain.

BUSINESS

HORMEL FOODS CORPORATION (formerly Geo. A. Hormel & Co.) and its subsidiaries produce and market a variety of processed, packaged food products. The Company's main products include: meat and meat products, including hams, sausages, wieners, sliced bacon, luncheon meats, stews, chilies, hash and meat spreads. The products are sold fresh, frozen, cured, smoked, cooked or canned. The majority of its products are sold under the HORMEL name. Other trade names include: SPAM, LIGHT & LEAN, FARM FRESH, DINTY MOORE, BLACK LABEL, TOPSHELF, MARY KITCHEN, OLD SMOKEHOUSE and KID'S KITCHEN. Through its wholly-owned subsidiary, Jennie-O Foods, Inc., the Company is a producer and marketer of whole and processed turkey products.

ANNUAL FINANCIAL DATA

	10/26/02	10/27/01	10/28/00	10/30/99	10/31/98	10/25/97	10/26/96
Earnings Per Share	1.35	1.30	1.20	⑪ 1.11	⑪ 0.93	0.72	⑪ 0.52
Cash Flow Per Share	1.94	1.95	1.67	1.55	1.33	1.06	0.80
Tang. Book Val. Per Share	5.41	4.45	5.64	5.20	4.82	4.55	4.27
Dividends Per Share	0.39	0.37	0.35	0.33	0.32	0.31	0.30
Dividend Payout %	28.9	28.5	29.2	29.7	34.6	43.4	57.7
INCOME STATEMENT (IN MILLIONS):							
Total Revenues	3,910.3	4,124.1	3,675.1	3,357.8	3,261.0	3,256.6	3,098.7
Costs & Expenses	3,508.8	3,733.6	3,346.6	3,052.2	2,988.9	3,030.3	2,943.0
Depreciation & Amort.	83.2	90.2	65.9	64.7	60.3	52.9	42.7
Operating Income	318.3	300.3	262.6	240.9	211.9	173.3	113.0
Net Interest Inc./(Exp.)	d24.3	d18.2	1.3	3.6	d13.7	d15.0	d1.6
Income Before Income Taxes	294.0	285.0	264.4	251.5	217.3	170.9	125.5
Income Taxes	104.6	102.6	94.2	88.0	78.0	61.4	46.1
Net Income	189.3	182.4	170.2	⑪ 163.4	⑪ 139.3	109.5	⑪ 79.4
Cash Flow	272.6	272.6	236.1	228.1	199.6	162.4	122.1
Average Shs. Outstg. (000)	140,292	140,125	141,523	147,010	150,406	152,990	153,018
BALANCE SHEET (IN MILLIONS):							
Cash & Cash Equivalents	309.6	186.3	106.6	248.6	238.0	152.4	203.1
Total Current Assets	962.2	883.3	711.1	800.1	717.4	671.4	723.3
Net Property	652.7	679.9	541.5	505.6	486.9	488.7	421.5
Total Assets	2,220.2	2,162.7	1,641.9	1,685.6	1,555.9	1,528.5	1,436.1
Total Current Liabilities	410.1	420.2	342.6	385.4	267.7	260.6	266.4
Long-Term Obligations	409.6	462.4	145.9	184.7	204.9	198.2	127.0
Net Stockholders' Equity	1,115.3	995.9	873.9	841.1	813.3	802.2	785.6
Net Working Capital	552.1	463.1	368.5	414.7	449.7	410.8	456.9
Year-end Shs. Outstg. (000)	138,411	138,663	138,569	142,725	146,992	151,552	155,020
STATISTICAL RECORD:							
Operating Profit Margin %	8.1	7.3	7.1	7.2	6.5	5.3	3.6
Net Profit Margin %	4.8	4.4	4.6	4.9	4.3	3.4	2.6
Return on Equity %	17.0	18.3	19.5	19.4	17.1	13.6	10.1
Return on Assets %	8.5	8.4	10.4	9.7	9.0	7.2	5.5
Debt/Total Assets %	18.5	21.4	8.9	11.0	13.2	13.0	8.8
Price Range	28.20-20.02	27.35-17.00	20.97-13.63	23.09-15.50	19.69-12.84	16.38-11.75	14.00-9.69
P/E Ratio	20.9-14.8	21.0-13.1	17.5-11.4	20.8-14.0	21.3-13.9	22.9-16.4	26.9-18.6
Average Yield %	1.6	1.7	2.0	1.7	2.0	2.2	2.5

Statistics are as originally reported. Adj. for 2-for-1 stk. split, 2/15/07. ⑪ Incl. $3.8 mil ($0.03/sh) gain, 1999; $17.4 mil ($0.12/sh) after-tax gain, 1998; $5.4 mil ($0.04/sh) non-recur. chg., 1996.

OFFICERS:
J. W. Johnson, Chmn., Pres., C.E.O.
M. J. McCoy, Exec. V.P., C.F.O.
G. J. Ray, Exec. V.P.

INVESTOR CONTACT: Fred Halvin, Investor Relations, (507) 437-5007

PRINCIPAL OFFICE: 1 Hormel Place, Austin, MN 55912-3680

TELEPHONE NUMBER: (507) 437-5611
FAX: (507) 437-5489
WEB: www.hormel.com
NO. OF EMPLOYEES: 15,500 (approx.)
SHAREHOLDERS: 11,600 (approx.)
ANNUAL MEETING: In Jan.
INCORPORATED: DE, Sept., 1928

INSTITUTIONAL HOLDINGS:
No. of Institutions: 177
Shares Held: 33,638,333
% Held: 24.4

INDUSTRY: Meat packing plants (SIC: 2011)

TRANSFER AGENT(S): Wells Fargo Shareowner Services, South St. Paul, MN

HUDSON UNITED BANCORP

YIELD 3.4%
P/E RATIO 14.6

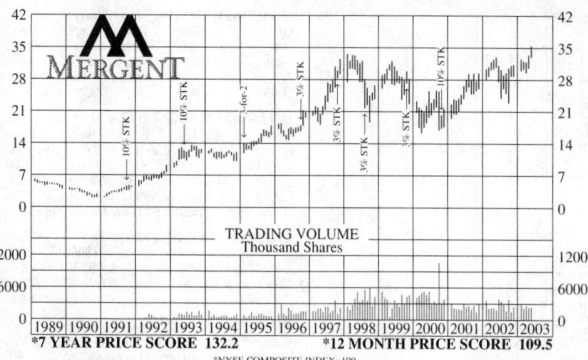

TRADING VOLUME
Thousand Shares

*7 YEAR PRICE SCORE 132.2   *12 MONTH PRICE SCORE 109.5

*NYSE COMPOSITE INDEX=100

INTERIM EARNINGS (Per Share):

Qtr.	Mar.	June	Sept.	Dec.
1999	0.48	0.49	0.50	d0.31
2000	0.53	d0.22	0.45	0.17
2001	0.46	0.49	0.51	0.54
2002	0.93	0.56	0.60	0.63
2003	0.63	...	...	...

INTERIM DIVIDENDS (Per Share):

Amt.	Decl.	Ex.	Rec.	Pay.
0.28Q	7/18/02	8/21/02	8/23/02	9/03/02
0.28Q	10/23/02	11/13/02	11/15/02	12/02/02
0.28Q	1/30/03	2/19/03	2/21/03	3/03/03
0.30Q	4/16/03	5/14/03	5/16/03	6/02/03

Indicated div.: $1.20 (Div. Reinv. Plan)

CAPITALIZATION (12/31/02):

	($000)	(%)
Total Deposits	6,199,701	89.7
Long-Term Debt	282,253	4.1
Common & Surplus	432,526	6.3
Total	6,914,480	100.0

DIVIDEND ACHIEVER STATUS:
Rank: 33   10-Year Growth Rate: 18.55%
Total Years of Dividend Growth: 12

RECENT DEVELOPMENTS: For the quarter ended 3/31/03, net income was $28.3 million versus $42.3 million in the corresponding year-earlier period. Results for 2002 included a non-recurring gain of $77.0 million received from Dime Bancorp Inc. related to the uncompleted merger of HU and Dime. Net interest income rose 5.1% to $75.2 million. Total provision for loan and lease losses fell to $7.0 million versus $28.8 million in 2002, due to a $21.3 million provision for loan and lease losses for 2002.

PROSPECTS: HU's results are benefiting from higher net interest income and increases in credit card fee income. Meanwhile, the Company has indicated that it intends to continue to seek opportunities to acquire other banks or financial services companies, and to acquire specific loans or other assets and/or to assume deposit or other liabilities of other banks or financial services companies, while continuing to focus on core business growth within its four state business area.

BUSINESS

HUDSON UNITED BANCORP (formerly HUBCO, Inc.) is a bank holding company for Hudson United Bank, a full-service commercial bank that operated 206 offices throughout New Jersey, Connecticut, New York, and Pennsylvania as of 3/31/03. The Company directly owns Hudson United Bank and four additional subsidiaries, which are HUBCO Capital Trust I, HUBCO Capital Trust II, JBI Capital Trust I and Jefferson Delaware Inc. The Company is also the indirect owner, through Hudson United Bank, of nine subsidiaries. At 3/31/03, HU, through its subsidiaries, had total deposits of $6.18 billion and total assets of $7.81 billion.

QUARTERLY DATA

(12/31/2002)($000)	REV	INC
1st Quarter	208,876	42,281
2nd Quarter	135,741	25,537
3rd Quarter	138,448	27,113
4th Quarter	136,203	28,275

ANNUAL FINANCIAL DATA

	12/31/02	12/31/01	12/31/00	12/31/99	12/31/98	12/31/97	12/31/96
Earnings Per Share	②③2.72	②2.00	①0.92	①1.18	①0.49	①1.80	①0.77
Tang. Book Val. Per Share	7.38	6.50	5.58	7.07	8.25	6.32	6.51
Dividends Per Share	1.10	1.01	0.93	0.88	0.78	0.65	0.57
Dividend Payout %	40.4	50.5	101.3	74.7	157.4	35.9	73.6
INCOME STATEMENT (IN MILLIONS):							
Total Interest Income	430.0	470.4	608.3	644.6	468.5	218.0	204.2
Total Interest Expense	129.2	185.0	288.6	301.5	214.4	77.8	72.8
Net Interest Income	300.8	285.4	319.7	343.1	254.2	140.2	131.4
Provision for Loan Losses	51.3	34.1	24.0	52.2	14.4	7.3	12.3
Non-Interest Income	185.1	109.4	31.1	88.7	33.3	41.1	30.3
Non-Interest Expense	247.1	227.2	250.0	271.3	232.1	93.6	116.2
Income Before Taxes	187.4	133.4	76.8	108.3	41.0	80.4	33.1
Net Income	②③123.2	②94.5	①49.8	①69.3	①23.2	①49.3	①21.5
Average Shs. Outstg. (000)	45,349	47,160	54,186	58,566	47,242	27,358	27,953
BALANCE SHEET (IN MILLIONS):							
Cash & Due from Banks	275.6	231.6	276.8	277.6	218.0	167.1	128.9
Total Loans & Leases	4,339.5	4,444.6	5,277.5	5,670.5	3,386.8	1,773.8	1,884.4
Allowance for Credit Losses	71.9	70.0	95.2	98.7	53.5	37.2	35.2
Net Loans & Leases	4,267.5	4,374.6	5,182.3	5,571.8	3,333.3	1,736.6	1,849.2
Total Assets	7,651.3	6,999.5	6,817.2	9,686.3	6,778.7	3,046.5	3,115.7
Total Deposits	6,199.7	5,983.5	5,813.3	6,455.3	5,051.4	2,314.4	2,592.1
Long-Term Obligations	282.3	123.0	123.0	132.0	100.0	100.0	100.0
Total Liabilities	7,218.7	6,615.6	6,448.8	9,167.1	6,321.8	2,860.4	2,909.4
Net Stockholders' Equity	432.5	383.9	368.5	519.2	456.8	186.1	206.3
Year-end Shs. Outstg. (000)	45,023	45,814	47,965	57,086	45,787	25,571	26,585
STATISTICAL RECORD:							
Return on Equity %	28.5	24.6	13.5	13.4	5.1	26.5	10.4
Return on Assets %	1.6	1.3	0.7	0.7	0.3	1.6	0.7
Equity/Assets %	5.7	5.5	5.4	5.4	6.7	6.1	6.6
Non-Int. Exp./Tot. Inc. %	50.9	55.6	71.3	62.8	80.7	51.6	71.9
Price Range	33.00-22.90	29.50-19.50	25.63-16.36	32.11-22.67	33.63-18.65	32.56-18.10	21.21-14.74
P/E Ratio	12.1-8.4	14.7-9.7	27.9-17.8	27.2-19.2	68.1-37.7	18.1-10.1	27.4-19.0
Average Yield %	3.9	4.1	4.4	3.2	3.0	2.5	3.2

Statistics are as originally reported. Adj. for all stk. splits thru 12/00. ① Incl. merger-rel. & restruct. costs of $15.0 mill., 2000; $32.0 mill., 1999; $66.4 mill., 1998; $270,000, 1997; $22.0 mill., 1996. ② Incl. trading asset gains of $197,000, 2002; $10.2 mill., 2001. ③ Incl. Dime Bancorp., Inc. merger termination payment of $77.0 mill., non-recurr. chrg. of $8.3 mill. & impairment chrgs. of $2.8 mill.

OFFICERS:
K. T. Neilson, Chmn., Pres., C.E.O.
W. A. Houlihan, Exec. V.P., C.F.O.
D. L. Van Borkulo-Nuzzo, Exec. V.P., Sec.

INVESTOR CONTACT: William A. Houlihan, Exec. V.P., C.F.O., (201) 236-2803

PRINCIPAL OFFICE: 1000 Macarthur Boulevard, Mahwah, NJ 07430

TELEPHONE NUMBER: (201) 236-2600
FAX: (201) 236-2649
WEB: www.hudsonunitedbank.com
NO. OF EMPLOYEES: 1,898
SHAREHOLDERS: 7,670 (approx.)
ANNUAL MEETING: In Apr.
INCORPORATED: NJ, June, 1982

INSTITUTIONAL HOLDINGS:
No. of Institutions: 173
Shares Held: 21,437,590
% Held: 47.6

INDUSTRY: State commercial banks (SIC: 6022)

TRANSFER AGENT(S): American Stock Transfer Company, New York, NY

ILLINOIS TOOL WORKS, INCORPORATED

YIELD 1.5%
P/E RATIO 20.3

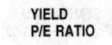
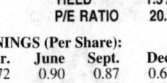
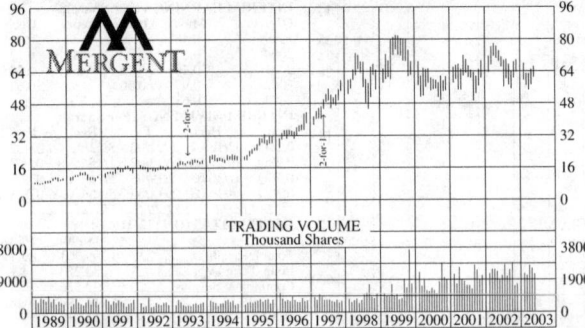

INTERIM EARNINGS (Per Share):

Qtr.	Mar.	June	Sept.	Dec.
2000	0.72	0.90	0.87	0.66
2001	0.60	0.76	0.65	0.61
2002	0.63	0.86	0.80	0.74
2003	0.65	...	...	...

INTERIM DIVIDENDS (Per Share):

Amt.	Decl.	Ex.	Rec.	Pay.
0.23Q	8/09/02	9/26/02	9/30/02	10/18/02
0.23Q	10/24/02	12/27/02	12/31/02	1/27/03
0.23Q	2/14/03	3/27/03	3/31/03	4/21/03
0.23Q	5/09/03	6/26/03	6/30/03	7/21/03

Indicated div.: $0.92 (Div. Reinv. Plan)

CAPITALIZATION (12/31/02):

	($000)	(%)
Long-Term Debt	1,460,381	18.0
Common & Surplus	6,649,071	82.0
Total	8,109,452	100.0

DIVIDEND ACHIEVER STATUS:
Rank: 66   10-Year Growth Rate: 14.74%
Total Years of Dividend Growth: 40

*7 YEAR PRICE SCORE 121.1   *12 MONTH PRICE SCORE 97.5
*NYSE COMPOSITE INDEX=100

RECENT DEVELOPMENTS: For the quarter ended 3/31/02, income from continuing operations advanced 2.6% to $199.5 million compared with income of $194.4 million in the equivalent 2002 quarter. Results for 2003 and 2002 included amortization and impairment of goodwill and other intangibles of $9.3 million and $4.9 million, respectively. Operating revenues climbed 5.0% to $2.31 billion from $2.20 billion the year before.

PROSPECTS: Looking ahead, the Company expects full-year 2003 income per diluted share from continuing operations in the range of $3.02 to $3.42. This outlook is based on the anticipated effect of uncertain economic conditions during 2003 on global end markets and profitability. Meanwhile, the Company expects second quarter 2003 earnings per diluted share from continuing operations of between $0.83 and $0.93.

BUSINESS

ILLINOIS TOOL WORKS, INCORPORATED manufactures and markets a variety of products and systems. As of 4/16/03, ITW had more than 600 operations in 44 countries. The Engineered Products-North America segment (30.9% of net sales for 2002) and the Engineered Products-International segment (15.9%) manufacture short lead-time components and fasteners, and specialty products. Specialty Systems-North America segment (34.1%) produces longer lead-time machinery and specialty equipment. The Specialty Systems-International segment (17.2%) manufactures longer lead-time machinery and specialty equipment for industrial spray coating and other applications. The Leasing and Investments segment (1.9%) makes investments in mortgage-related assets, equipment leases and property. ITW acquired Premark International, Inc. in November 1999 for $3.40 billion.

ANNUAL FINANCIAL DATA

	12/31/02	12/31/01	12/31/00	12/31/99	12/31/98	12/31/97	12/31/96
Earnings Per Share	③ 3.02	② 2.62	3.15	① 2.76	2.67	2.33	1.97
Cash Flow Per Share	4.02	3.88	4.50	3.89	3.50	3.07	2.68
Tang. Book Val. Per Share	13.12	10.82	9.64	9.27	8.59	8.14	6.80
Dividends Per Share	0.89	0.82	0.74	0.63	0.51	0.43	0.35
Dividend Payout %	29.5	31.3	23.5	22.8	19.1	18.5	17.8
INCOME STATEMENT (IN MILLIONS):							
Total Revenues	9,467.7	9,292.8	9,983.6	9,333.2	5,647.9	5,220.4	4,996.7
Costs & Expenses	7,656.2	7,600.4	8,006.8	7,584.5	4,356.8	4,107.8	4,017.9
Depreciation & Amort.	305.8	386.3	413.4	343.3	211.8	185.4	178.2
Operating Income	1,505.8	1,306.1	1,563.4	1,405.4	1,079.3	927.2	800.6
Net Interest Inc./(Exp.)	d68.5	d68.1	d72.4	d67.5	d14.2	d19.4	d27.8
Income Before Income Taxes	1,433.6	1,230.8	1,478.2	1,352.7	1,059.6	924.4	770.3
Income Taxes	501.8	428.4	520.2	511.6	386.8	337.4	284.0
Net Income	③ 931.8	② 802.4	958.0	① 841.1	672.8	587.0	486.3
Cash Flow	1,237.6	1,188.8	1,371.4	1,184.4	884.6	772.3	664.5
Average Shs. Outstg. (000)	308,045	306,306	304,414	304,649	252,443	251,760	247,556
BALANCE SHEET (IN MILLIONS):							
Cash & Cash Equivalents	1,057.7	282.2	151.3	233.0	93.5	185.9	137.7
Total Current Assets	3,878.8	3,163.2	3,329.1	3,272.9	1,834.5	1,858.6	1,701.1
Net Property	1,631.2	1,633.7	1,722.5	1,633.9	987.5	884.1	808.3
Total Assets	10,623.1	9,822.3	9,603.5	9,060.3	6,118.2	5,394.8	4,806.2
Total Current Liabilities	1,567.2	1,518.2	1,817.6	2,045.4	1,222.0	1,157.9	1,219.3
Long-Term Obligations	1,460.4	1,267.1	1,549.0	1,360.7	947.0	854.3	818.9
Net Stockholders' Equity	6,649.1	6,040.7	5,401.0	4,815.4	3,338.0	2,806.5	2,396.0
Net Working Capital	2,311.6	1,645.1	1,511.5	1,227.6	612.5	700.8	481.8
Year-end Shs. Outstg. (000)	306,826	305,169	302,449	300,569	250,128	249,598	247,772
STATISTICAL RECORD:							
Operating Profit Margin %	15.9	14.1	15.7	15.1	19.1	17.8	16.0
Net Profit Margin %	9.8	8.6	9.6	9.0	11.9	11.2	9.7
Return on Equity %	14.0	13.3	17.7	17.5	20.2	20.9	20.3
Return on Assets %	8.8	8.2	10.0	9.3	11.0	10.9	10.1
Debt/Total Assets %	13.7	12.9	16.1	15.0	15.5	15.8	17.0
Price Range	77.80-55.03	71.99-49.15	69.00-49.50	82.00-58.13	73.19-45.19	59.50-37.38	43.63-25.94
P/E Ratio	25.8-18.2	27.5-18.8	21.9-15.7	29.7-21.1	27.4-16.9	25.5-16.0	22.2-13.2
Average Yield %	1.3	1.4	1.2	0.9	0.9	0.9	1.0

Statistics are as originally reported. Adj. for stk. split: 2-for-1, 5/97. ① Incl. Premark International, Inc. merger-related costs of $81.0 mill. ② Excl. inc. from discont. oper. of $3.2 mill. ③ Excl. acctg. change charge of $221.9 mill., income from discont. oper. of $2.7 mill., but incl. amort. and impairment of goodwill & other intangibles of $27.9 mill.

OFFICERS: W. J. Farrell, Chmn., C.E.O.; F. S. Ptak, Vice-Chmn.; J. M. Ringer, Vice-Chmn.; J. C. Kinney, Sr. V.P., C.F.O. **INVESTOR CONTACT:** Investor Relations, (847) 724-7500 **PRINCIPAL OFFICE:** 3600 West Lake Avenue, Glenview, IL 60025-5811	**TELEPHONE NUMBER:** (847) 724-7500 **FAX:** (847) 657-4261 **WEB:** www.itw.com **NO. OF EMPLOYEES:** 48,700 (approx.) **SHAREHOLDERS:** 13,067 (approx. record) **ANNUAL MEETING:** In May **INCORPORATED:** DE, Jun., 1961	**INSTITUTIONAL HOLDINGS:** No. of Institutions: 592 Shares Held: 236,391,165 % Held: 77.0 **INDUSTRY:** Plastics products, nec (SIC: 3089) **TRANSFER AGENT(S):** Computershare Investor Service, L.L.C., Chicago, IL

IRWIN FINANCIAL CORP.

YIELD 1.1%
P/E RATIO 13.0

TRADING VOLUME
Thousand Shares

7 YEAR PRICE SCORE 107.8 *12 MONTH PRICE SCORE 123.7*
NYSE COMPOSITE INDEX=100

INTERIM EARNINGS (Per Share):

Qtr.	Mar.	June	Sept.	Dec.
2000	0.40	0.41	0.43	0.46
2001	0.40	0.56	0.50	0.53
2002	0.37	0.28	0.29	0.92
2003	0.41	...	...	...

INTERIM DIVIDENDS (Per Share):

Amt.	Decl.	Ex.	Rec.	Pay.
0.068Q	8/29/02	9/11/02	9/13/02	9/27/02
0.068Q	11/20/02	12/11/02	12/13/02	12/27/02
0.07Q	2/26/03	3/12/03	3/14/03	3/28/03
0.07Q	4/24/03	6/11/03	6/13/03	6/27/03

Indicated div.: $0.28 (Div. Reinv. Plan)

CAPITALIZATION (12/31/02):

	($000)	(%)
Total Deposits	2,694,344	72.6
Long-Term Debt	421,495	11.4
Redeemable Pfd. Stock	233,000	6.3
Common & Surplus	360,555	9.7
Total	3,709,394	100.0

DIVIDEND ACHIEVER STATUS:
Rank: 35   10-Year Growth Rate: 18.37%
Total Years of Dividend Growth: 13

RECENT DEVELOPMENTS: For the quarter ended 3/31/03, net income was $11.8 million versus income of $9.5 million, before an accounting change credit of $495,000, in the corresponding year-earlier period. IFC's earnings were favorably affected by growth in its loan and lease portfolios as well as strong mortgage banking originations. Net interest income rose 45.0% to $64.4 million. Provision for loan losses was $9.2 million versus $10.3 million in 2002. Non-interest income climbed 35.0% to $69.6 million.

PROSPECTS: IFC's bottom line is being driven by sharply higher results from the Company's mortgage banking operations, as evidenced by the 96.5% increase in net interest income to $16.1 million for the quarter ended 3/31/03. IFC attributed the significant increase largely to strong loan originations and sales, the result of favorable interest rate conditions and distribution channel expansion. Accordingly, IFC has increased its full-year 2003 earnings estimates to at least $2.25 per share.

BUSINESS

IRWIN FINANCIAL CORP. is a diversified financial services company with $5.37 billion in assets at 3/31/03. The Company operates five major lines of business through its direct and indirect subsidiaries. IFC's major lines of business are: mortgage banking, commercial banking, home equity lending, commercial finance and venture capital. Direct and indirect major subsidiaries include Irwin Union Bank and Trust, a commercial bank, which together with Irwin Union Bank, F.S.B., a federal savings bank, conduct IFC's commercial banking activities; Irwin Mortgage Corporation, a mortgage banking company; Irwin Home Equity Corporation, a consumer home equity lending company; Irwin Commercial Finance Corporation, a commercial finance subsidiary; and IrwinVentures LLC, a venture capital company.

ANNUAL FINANCIAL DATA

	12/31/02	12/31/01	12/31/00	12/31/99	12/31/98	12/31/97	12/31/96
Earnings Per Share	② 1.87	② 1.99	1.67	1.51	① 1.38	1.08	0.97
Tang. Book Val. Per Share	12.98	10.84	8.97	7.55	6.70	5.82	2.26
Dividends Per Share	0.27	0.26	0.24	0.20	0.16	0.14	0.12
Dividend Payout %	14.4	13.1	14.4	13.2	11.6	13.0	12.4

INCOME STATEMENT (IN MILLIONS):

Total Interest Income	311.4	268.2	184.5	126.6	122.4	99.4	89.4
Total Interest Expense	97.8	121.1	93.5	54.8	59.2	44.6	41.6
Net Interest Income	213.6	147.1	91.0	71.8	63.2	54.9	47.8
Provision for Loan Losses	44.0	17.5	5.4	4.4	6.0	6.2	4.5
Non-Interest Income	257.4	271.4	211.7	204.1	243.7	174.6	153.6
Non-Interest Expense	340.9	327.4	238.0	214.1	245.4	176.5	159.7
Income Before Taxes	86.2	73.6	59.3	57.3	55.5	46.7	37.3
Equity Earnings/Minority Int.	...	0.4	...	...	...	...	...
Net Income	② 52.8	② 45.3	35.7	37.9	① 35.1	28.9	22.4
Average Shs. Outstg. (000)	29,675	24,173	21,593	21,886	22,139	22,722	23,219

BALANCE SHEET (IN MILLIONS):

Total Loans & Leases	2,894.0	2,195.5	1,266.4	733.9	558.2	626.3	540.1
Allowance for Credit Losses	129.7	80.0	44.6	9.0	11.1	24.0	17.6
Net Loans & Leases	2,764.3	2,115.5	1,221.8	724.9	547.1	602.3	522.5
Total Assets	4,884.7	3,439.8	2,422.4	1,680.8	1,946.2	1,496.8	1,303.9
Total Deposits	2,694.3	2,309.0	1,443.3	870.3	1,009.2	719.6	640.2
Long-Term Obligations	421.5	29.7	29.6	29.8	2.8	7.1	17.6
Total Liabilities	4,523.3	3,207.5	2,232.5	1,521.6	1,800.9	1,368.8	1,185.0
Net Stockholders' Equity	360.6	232.3	189.9	159.3	145.2	128.0	118.9
Year-end Shs. Outstg. (000)	27,771	21,305	21,026	21,105	21,673	22,001	22,738

STATISTICAL RECORD:

Return on Equity %	14.7	19.5	18.8	23.8	24.2	22.6	18.9
Return on Assets %	1.1	1.3	1.5	2.3	1.8	1.9	1.7
Equity/Assets %	7.4	6.8	7.8	9.5	7.5	8.6	9.1
Non-Int. Exp./Tot. Inc. %	72.4	78.2	78.6	77.6	80.0	76.9	79.3
Price Range	20.60-13.20	27.70-14.49	22.00-13.25	28.88-16.00	37.00-19.50	21.56-12.00	12.38-8.94
P/E Ratio	11.0-7.1	13.9-7.3	13.2-7.9	19.1-11.2	26.8-14.1	20.1-11.2	12.8-9.3
Average Yield %	1.6	1.2	1.4	0.9	0.6	0.8	1.1

Statistics are as originally reported. Adj. for 2-for-1 stk. split, 5/98. ① Incl. gain from sale of leasing assets of $5.2 mill. ② Bef. acctg. chge. gain of $495,000, 12/02; $175,000, 12/01.

OFFICERS:
W. I. Miller, Chmn.
J. A. Nash, Pres.
G. F. Ehlinger, Sr. V.P., C.F.O.

INVESTOR CONTACT: Gregory F. Ehlinger, Sr. V.P., C.F.O., (812) 376-1020

PRINCIPAL OFFICE: 500 Washington Street, Columbus, IN 47201

TELEPHONE NUMBER: (812) 376-1909
FAX: (812) 376-1709
WEB: www.irwinfinancial.com

NO. OF EMPLOYEES: 3,288 (avg.)

SHAREHOLDERS: 1,856 (approx.)

ANNUAL MEETING: In Apr.

INCORPORATED: IN, May, 1972

INSTITUTIONAL HOLDINGS:
No. of Institutions: 98
Shares Held: 12,332,634
% Held: 44.0

INDUSTRY: State commercial banks (SIC: 6022)

TRANSFER AGENT(S): National City Bank, Cleveland, OH

MORGAN (J.P.) CHASE & COMPANY

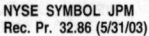
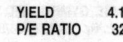
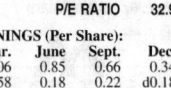
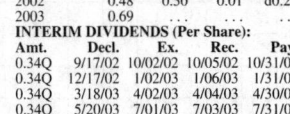

INTERIM EARNINGS (Per Share):

Qtr.	Mar.	June	Sept.	Dec.
2000	1.06	0.85	0.66	0.34
2001	0.58	0.18	0.22	d0.18
2002	0.48	0.50	0.01	d0.20
2003	0.69	...	...	...

INTERIM DIVIDENDS (Per Share):

Amt.	Decl.	Ex.	Rec.	Pay.
0.34Q	9/17/02	10/02/02	10/05/02	10/31/02
0.34Q	12/17/02	1/02/03	1/06/03	1/31/03
0.34Q	3/18/03	4/02/03	4/04/03	4/30/03
0.34Q	5/20/03	7/01/03	7/03/03	7/31/03

Indicated div.: $1.36 (Div. Reinv. Plan)

CAPITALIZATION (12/31/02):

	($000)	(%)
Total Deposits	304,753,000	77.7
Long-Term Debt	45,190,000	11.5
Preferred Stock	1,009,000	0.3
Common & Surplus	41,297,000	10.5
Total	392,249,000	100.0

DIVIDEND ACHIEVER STATUS:
Rank: 82   10-Year Growth Rate: 13.50%
Total Years of Dividend Growth: 11

TRADING VOLUME
Thousand Shares

*7 YEAR PRICE SCORE 71.8   *12 MONTH PRICE SCORE 113.8
°NYSE COMPOSITE INDEX=100

RECENT DEVELOPMENTS: For the quarter ended 3/31/03, net income advanced 42.6% to $1.40 billion versus $982.0 million in the equivalent 2002 quarter. Results for 2003 and 2002 included intangible amortization of $74.0 million and $69.0 million, respectively. Results for 2002 also included a merger and restructuring charge of $255.0 million. Net interest income increased 9.8% to $3.22 billion. Total non-interest income climbed 11.1% to $5.19 billion, while total non-interest expense grew 3.4% to $5.54 billion.

PROSPECTS: The Company is moving to align its investment banking cost structure with the weak revenue environment, committing to staff reductions, resizing JPM's business and geographic presence consistent with near-term opportunities, and taking certain cost-control measures. These actions are intended to generate approximately $700.0 million in gross savings. JPM is taking similar measures to improve results in its investment management and private banking businesses.

BUSINESS

J.P. MORGAN CHASE & COMPANY (formerly Chase Manhattan Corporation) is a global financial services firm with assets of $755.16 billion at 3/31/03. On 3/31/96, Chase Manhattan Corp. was acquired by Chemical Banking Corp., which then changed its name to Chase Manhattan Corp. JPM's present name was adopted as a result of the acquisition of J.P. Morgan & Co. Inc. by Chase Manhattan Corp. on 12/31/00. JPM conducts investment banking, asset management, private banking, private equity, custody and transaction services as well as retail and middle-market financial services. As of 4/16/03, JPM served more than 30.0 million customers throughout the U.S., and had offices in more than 50 countries. On 12/10/99, JPM acquired Hambrecht & Quist Group, Inc.

ANNUAL FINANCIAL DATA

	12/31/02	12/31/01	⑥ 12/31/00	④ 12/31/99	12/31/98	12/31/97	12/31/96
Earnings Per Share	⑥ 0.80	⑤ ⑥ 0.80	① 2.86	① 4.18	② 2.83	① 2.68	① 1.67
Tang. Book Val. Per Share	14.21	12.54	12.96	18.29	17.93	15.84	14.19
Dividends Per Share	1.36	1.34	1.23	1.06	0.93	0.81	0.73
Dividend Payout %	170.0	167.5	43.1	25.4	32.8	30.1	43.4

INCOME STATEMENT (IN MILLIONS):

Total Interest Income	25,284.0	32,181.0	36,643.0	20,237.0	22,289.0	21,756.0	19,909.0
Total Interest Expense	13,758.0	21,379.0	27,131.0	11,493.0	13,723.0	13,598.0	11,569.0
Net Interest Income	11,526.0	10,802.0	9,512.0	8,744.0	8,566.0	8,158.0	8,340.0
Provision for Loan Losses	4,331.0	3,185.0	1,377.0	1,621.0	1,554.0	804.0	897.0
Non-Interest Income	18,088.0	18,248.0	23,422.0	13,473.0	10,301.0	8,625.0	7,512.0
Non-Interest Expense	22,764.0	23,299.0	22,824.0	12,221.0	11,383.0	10,069.0	11,144.0
Income Before Taxes	2,519.0	2,566.0	8,733.0	8,375.0	5,930.0	5,910.0	3,811.0
Net Income	⑥ 1,663.0	⑤ 1,719.0	① 5,727.0	① 5,446.0	③ 3,782.0	③ 3,708.0	① 2,461.0
Average Shs. Outstg. (000)	2,009,000	1,972,400	1,969,000	1,285,500	1,303,950	1,317,600	1,339,200

BALANCE SHEET (IN MILLIONS):

Cash & Due from Banks	19,218.0	22,600.0	23,972.0	16,229.0	17,068.0	15,704.0	14,605.0
Securities Avail. for Sale	366,476.0	285,269.0	320,099.0	123,894.0	120,495.0	122,148.0	104,647.0
Total Loans & Leases	216,364.0	217,444.0	216,050.0	176,159.0	172,754.0	170,066.0	156,465.0
Allowance for Credit Losses	5,350.0	4,524.0	3,665.0	3,457.0	3,552.0	5,236.0	4,922.0
Net Loans & Leases	211,014.0	212,920.0	212,385.0	172,702.0	169,202.0	164,830.0	151,543.0
Total Assets	758,800.0	693,575.0	715,348.0	406,105.0	365,875.0	365,521.0	336,099.0
Total Deposits	304,753.0	293,650.0	279,365.0	241,745.0	212,437.0	193,688.0	180,921.0
Long-Term Obligations	45,190.0	43,622.0	47,238.0	20,140.0	18,375.0	15,127.0	13,314.0
Total Liabilities	716,494.0	651,926.0	672,460.0	381,938.0	341,487.0	343,229.0	314,555.0
Net Stockholders' Equity	42,306.0	41,099.0	42,338.0	23,617.0	23,838.0	21,742.0	20,994.0
Year-end Shs. Outstg. (000)	1,998,706	1,973,400	1,928,490	1,240,757	1,271,850	1,262,892	1,292,433

STATISTICAL RECORD:

Return on Equity %	3.9	4.2	13.5	23.1	15.9	17.1	11.7
Return on Assets %	0.2	0.2	0.8	1.3	1.0	1.0	0.7
Equity/Assets %	5.6	5.9	5.9	5.8	6.5	5.9	6.2
Non-Int. Exp./Tot. Inc. %	76.9	80.2	69.3	55.0	60.3	60.0	70.3
Price Range	39.68-15.26	57.33-29.04	67.17-32.38	60.75-43.88	51.71-23.71	42.19-28.21	31.96-17.38
P/E Ratio	49.6-19.1	71.7-36.3	23.5-11.3	14.5-10.5	18.3-8.4	15.8-10.5	19.1-10.4
Average Yield %	5.0	3.1	2.5	2.0	2.5	2.3	2.9

Statistics are as originally reported. Adj. for 3-for-2 split, 6/00; 2-for-1 split, 6/98. ① restruct. chrg.: $2.52 bill., 2001; $1.43 bill., 2000; $48.0 mill., 1999; $192.0 mill., 1997; $1.81 bill., 1996. ② Bef. acctg. chrg. $25.0 mill. ③ Incl. restruct. chrgs. of $529.0 mill. & prov. for risk mgmt. instrument cr. losses of $211.0 mill. ④ Results are for Chase Manhattan Corp. for 1999 and earlier. ⑤ Reflects merger with J.P. Morgan & Co. ⑥ Incl. surety settlement and litigation chrg. of $1.30 billion and a merger & restr. chrg. of $1.21

OFFICERS:
W. B. Harrison Jr., Chmn., C.E.O.
D. Dublon, Exec. V.P., C.F.O.
W. H. McDavid, Gen. Couns.
INVESTOR CONTACT: Ann Borowiec, (212) 270-7318
PRINCIPAL OFFICE: 270 Park Avenue, New York, NY 10017

TELEPHONE NUMBER: (212) 270-6000
FAX: (212) 270-1648
WEB: www.jpmorganchase.com
NO. OF EMPLOYEES: 94,335
SHAREHOLDERS: 126,759 (record)
ANNUAL MEETING: In May
INCORPORATED: DE, 1968

INSTITUTIONAL HOLDINGS:
No. of Institutions: 913
Shares Held: 1,309,774,658
% Held: 65.4
INDUSTRY: National commercial banks (SIC: 6021)
TRANSFER AGENT(S): Mellon Investor Services, LLC, Ridgefield Park, NJ

JACK HENRY & ASSOCIATES, INC.

YIELD 0.9%
P/E RATIO 26.5

7 YEAR PRICE SCORE 107.9 **12 MONTH PRICE SCORE 96.6**
*NYSE COMPOSITE INDEX=100

TRADING VOLUME
Thousand Shares

INTERIM EARNINGS (Per Share):

Qtr.	Sept.	Dec.	Mar.	June
1998-99	0.11	0.09	0.10	0.10
1999-00	0.11	0.10	0.12	0.13
2000-01	0.14	0.14	0.17	0.17
2001-02	0.16	0.14	0.15	0.17
2002-03	0.13	0.13	0.14	...

INTERIM DIVIDENDS (Per Share):

Amt.	Decl.	Ex.	Rec.	Pay.
0.035Q	4/26/02	4/30/02	5/02/02	5/17/02
0.035Q	8/28/02	9/04/02	9/06/02	9/20/02
0.035Q	10/30/02	11/15/02	11/19/02	12/03/02
0.035Q	1/27/03	2/10/03	2/12/03	2/27/03
0.035Q	4/25/03	4/29/03	5/01/03	5/16/03

Indicated div.: $0.14 (Div. Reinv. Plan)

CAPITALIZATION (6/30/02):

	($000)	(%)
Deferred Income Tax	15,800	4.4
Common & Surplus	340,739	95.6
Total	356,539	100.0

DIVIDEND ACHIEVER STATUS:
Rank: 31   10-Year Growth Rate: 18.93%
Total Years of Dividend Growth: 12

RECENT DEVELOPMENTS: For the three months ended 3/31/03, net income declined 9.2% to $12.3 million compared with $13.6 million in the corresponding quarter of 2002. Results continued to be hampered by declines in technology spending reflecting the slowdown in the capital goods markets. Total revenues slipped 0.9% to $98.9 million from $99.8 million a year earlier. Support and services revenues grew 18.2% to $59.2 million from $50.1 million in 2002. Licensing revenues dropped 40.8% to $10.4 mil-

lion from $17.7 million, while hardware sales decreased 12.7% to $21.7 million from $24.8 million a year earlier. Gross profit slipped 4.2% to $38.4 million, or 38.8% of total revenues, from $40.1 million, or 40.2% of total revenues, in the previous year. Operating income decreased 7.6% to $19.3 million compared with $20.9 million the year before. Backlog grew 26.6% to $172.8 million, which consisted of $64.2 million in-house and $108.5 million in outsourcing, versus $136.5 million in 2002.

BUSINESS

JACK HENRY & ASSOCIATES, INC. is a provider of integrated computer systems that perform data processing for banks and credit unions. The Company's proprietary applications software for IBM AS/400 computers is offered under two systems: CIF 20/20™ typically for banks with less than $400.0 million in assets, and the Silverlake System®, for banks with assets up to $10.00 billion. JKHY has developed several banking applications software systems that it markets, along with computer hardware, to financial institutions in the United States and overseas. As of 4/16/03, JKHY had more than 3,000 banks and credit unions as customers. JKHY also performs data conversion, software installation and software customization for the implementation of its systems, and provides continuing customer maintenance/support services. Additionally, JKHY processes ATM and debit card transactions through its subsidiary, CommLink Corp., and provides Internet banking applications for financial institutions.

ANNUAL FINANCIAL DATA

	6/30/02	6/30/01	6/30/00	6/30/99	6/30/98	6/30/97	6/30/96
Earnings Per Share	0.62	0.61	⑤ 0.41	⑤ 0.39	⑤ 0.28	⑤ 0.21	⑤ 0.16
Cash Flow Per Share	0.92	0.85	0.58	0.48	0.35	0.26	0.21
Tang. Book Val. Per Share	2.54	2.20	0.48	1.07	0.73	0.49	0.27
Dividends Per Share	0.14	0.12	0.10	0.08	0.07	0.055	0.047
Dividend Payout %	22.6	19.7	24.7	20.8	23.0	26.5	29.4

INCOME STATEMENT (IN THOUSANDS):

Total Revenues	396,657	345,468	225,300	184,497	113,423	82,600	67,558
Costs & Expenses	282,541	237,840	158,817	127,233	74,542	54,288	44,790
Depreciation & Amort.	27,470	21,888	15,473	7,858	5,105	4,071	3,562
Operating Income	86,646	85,740	51,010	49,406	33,776	24,241	19,206
Net Interest Inc./(Exp.)	1,827	466	d1,047	1,571	1,221	660	541
Income Before Income Taxes	88,473	86,923	51,765	51,347	35,344	25,087	19,873
Income Taxes	31,408	31,292	17,415	18,821	13,127	9,332	7,605
Net Income	57,065	55,631	⑤ 34,350	⑤ 32,526	⑤ 22,237	⑤ 15,755	⑤ 12,268
Cash Flow	84,535	77,519	49,823	40,384	27,342	19,826	15,830
Average Shs. Outstg.	92,367	91,344	85,278	84,448	79,044	76,288	74,904

BALANCE SHEET (IN THOUSANDS):

Cash & Cash Equivalents	18,762	19,574	6,132	9,887	26,523	13,867	8,080
Total Current Assets	179,977	172,050	104,000	79,842	69,138	42,729	28,146
Net Property	173,775	138,429	93,285	65,595	26,855	21,869	13,612
Total Assets	486,142	433,121	321,082	174,721	115,286	82,069	60,401
Total Current Liabilities	112,656	107,018	151,140	57,666	39,260	27,239	21,251
Long-Term Obligations	...	228	320	...	...	...	...
Net Stockholders' Equity	340,739	302,504	154,545	114,469	73,500	52,782	37,418
Net Working Capital	67,321	65,032	d47,140	22,176	29,878	15,490	6,895
Year-end Shs. Outstg.	88,951	88,847	82,716	80,400	75,740	74,068	71,208

STATISTICAL RECORD:

Operating Profit Margin %	21.8	24.8	22.6	26.8	29.8	29.3	28.4
Net Profit Margin %	14.4	16.1	15.2	17.6	19.6	19.1	18.2
Return on Equity %	16.7	18.4	22.2	28.4	30.3	29.8	32.8
Return on Assets %	11.7	12.8	10.7	18.6	19.3	19.2	20.3
Debt/Total Assets %	...	0.1	0.1	...	...	...	...
Price Range	24.49-7.24	33.24-18.56	33.13-12.06	14.13-6.61	13.75-6.19	7.56-4.38	6.96-3.40
P/E Ratio	39.5-11.7	54.5-30.4	81.8-29.8	36.7-17.2	48.7-21.9	36.5-21.1	42.7-20.8
Average Yield %	0.9	0.5	0.4	0.8	0.7	0.9	0.9

Statistics are as originally reported. Adj. for stk. splits: 2-for-1, 3/2/01; 100% div., 3/2/00; 3-for-2, 3/13/97. ⑤ Bef. disc. oper. loss 6/30/00: $332,000; 6/30/99: $758,000; 6/30/98: $668,000; 6/30/97: $450,000; 6/30/96: $2.6 mill.

OFFICERS:
M. E. Henry, Chmn., C.E.O.
T. W. Thompson, Pres.
K. D. Williams, C.F.O., Treas.

INVESTOR CONTACT: K. D. Williams, C.F.O., Treas., (417) 235-6652

PRINCIPAL OFFICE: 663 Highway 60, P.O. Box 807, Monett, MO 65708

TELEPHONE NUMBER: (417) 235-6652
FAX: (417) 235-4281
WEB: www.jackhenry.com
NO. OF EMPLOYEES: 2,093
SHAREHOLDERS: 45,597
ANNUAL MEETING: In Oct.
INCORPORATED: MO, Aug., 1977; reincorp., DE, Nov., 1985

INSTITUTIONAL HOLDINGS:
No. of Institutions: 151
Shares Held: 44,294,432
% Held: 50.3

INDUSTRY: Computer integrated systems design (SIC: 7373)

TRANSFER AGENT(S): UMB Bank, N.A. Kansas City, MO

JEFFERSON-PILOT CORP.

YIELD 3.1%
P/E RATIO 14.7

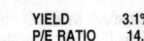
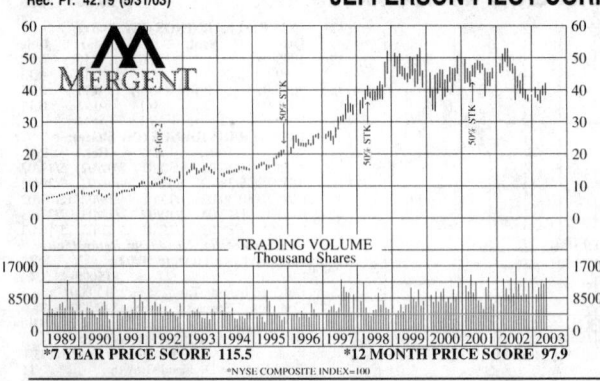

INTERIM EARNINGS (Per Share):

Qtr.	Mar.	June	Sept.	Dec.
1999	0.79	0.73	0.73	0.69
2000	0.89	0.83	0.83	0.73
2001	0.96	0.87	0.87	0.64
2002	0.92	0.84	0.81	0.46
2003	0.76	...	...	...

INTERIM DIVIDENDS (Per Share):

Amt.	Decl.	Ex.	Rec.	Pay.
0.302Q	8/05/02	11/20/02	11/22/02	12/05/02
0.302Q	11/04/02	2/19/03	2/21/03	3/05/03
0.33Q	2/10/03	5/21/03	5/23/03	6/05/03
0.33Q	5/05/03	8/20/03	8/22/03	9/05/03

Indicated div.: $1.32 (Div. Reinv. Plan)

CAPITALIZATION (12/31/02):

	($000)	(%)
Deferred Income Tax	385,000	9.8
Common & Surplus	3,540,000	90.2
Total	3,925,000	100.0

DIVIDEND ACHIEVER STATUS:
Rank: 107   10-Year Growth Rate: 11.87%
Total Years of Dividend Growth: 35

*7 YEAR PRICE SCORE 115.5   *12 MONTH PRICE SCORE 97.9
*NYSE COMPOSITE INDEX=100

RECENT DEVELOPMENTS: For the quarter ended 3/31/03, net income dropped 21.2% to $115.0 million from $146.0 million in the comparable prior-year quarter. Total revenue inched up to $888.0 million from $885.0 million the previous year. Revenue included a realized investment loss of $19.0 million in 2002 and a realized investment gain of $34.0 million in 2001. Revenue from premiums and other considerations advanced 14.5% to $426.0 million. Net investment income rose 0.7% to $407.0 million.

PROSPECTS: The Company continues to make progress in strengthening its operating performance. In the core individual life insurance business, JP continues to see solid results from its premier partnering strategy. In the first quarter, annualized first-year premiums, excluding small-case target marketing sales, grew 48.0% versus the year-earlier period. Life policyholder fund balance growth was also strong, improving 8.0% year-over-year to a record $10.40 billion.

BUSINESS

JEFFERSON-PILOT CORP. is a holding company that conducts insurance, investment, broadcasting and other business through its subsidiaries. Jefferson-Pilot Life Insurance Company offers both group and individual life insurance, health insurance, annuity and pension products. Other subsidiaries provide fire and casualty insurance, title insurance and mutual fund sales and management services. As of 4/28/03, Jefferson-Pilot Communications Company provided information and entertainment services through three network television and 17 radio stations, and produced and syndicated sports programming. Contributions to revenues in 2002 were as follows: net investment income, 46.4%; premiums & other, 24.0%; universal life and investment products, 20.6%; communications sales, 6.0%; broker-dealer concessions and other, 3.0%.

ANNUAL FINANCIAL DATA

	12/31/02	12/31/01	12/31/00	12/31/99	12/31/98	12/31/97	12/31/96
Earnings Per Share	3.04	⑪ 3.34	3.29	2.95	2.61	2.31	1.82
Tang. Book Val. Per Share	22.61	20.53	18.38	15.80	17.77	15.73	13.89
Dividends Per Share	1.18	1.07	0.96	0.86	0.77	0.69	0.62
Dividend Payout %	38.9	32.1	29.2	29.1	29.4	30.0	34.2
INCOME STATEMENT (IN MILLIONS)							
Total Premium Income	1,564.0	1,424.0	1,365.0	903.0	1,049.0	1,135.0	994.0
Net Investment Income	1,623.0	1,533.0	1,430.0	1,272.0	1,202.0	1,103.0	893.0
Other Income	293.0	373.0	443.0	386.0	359.0	340.0	238.0
Total Revenues	3,480.0	3,330.0	3,238.0	2,561.0	2,610.0	2,578.0	2,125.0
Policyholder Benefits	1,999.0	1,796.0	1,660.0	1,208.0	1,307.0	1,399.0	1,211.0
Income Before Income Taxes	710.0	800.0	814.0	751.0	670.0	591.0	443.0
Income Taxes	235.0	263.0	277.0	256.0	226.0	195.0	149.0
Net Income	475.0	⑪ 537.0	537.0	495.0	444.0	396.0	294.0
Average Shs. Outstg. (000)	148,222	153,411	155,922	159,348	160,578	160,189	159,917
BALANCE SHEET (IN MILLIONS)							
Cash & Cash Equivalents	67.0	139.0	26.0	62.0	21.0	9.0	105.0
Premiums Due	1,375.0	1,433.0	1,450.0	1,576.0	1,342.0	1,526.0	1,260.0
Invst. Assets: Fixed-term	19,501.0	17,467.0	16,108.0	15,182.0	14,503.0	13,945.0	10,550.0
Invst. Assets: Equities	409.0	511.0	551.0	737.0	949.0	893.0	929.0
Invst. Assets: Loans	4,203.0	4,005.0	3,694.0	3,449.0	3,408.0	3,138.0	2,535.0
Invst. Assets: Total	24,279.0	22,135.0	20,499.0	19,536.0	18,978.0	18,094.0	14,143.0
Total Assets	30,609.0	28,996.0	27,321.0	26,446.0	24,338.0	23,131.0	17,562.0
Long-Term Obligations	...	150.0	139.0	290.0	327.0	331.0	148.0
Net Stockholders' Equity	3,540.0	3,391.0	3,159.0	2,753.0	3,052.0	2,732.0	2,297.0
Year-end Shs. Outstg. (000)	142,799	150,007	154,306	155,016	158,844	159,417	159,179
STATISTICAL RECORD:							
Return on Revenues %	13.6	16.1	16.6	19.3	17.0	15.4	13.8
Return on Equity %	13.4	15.8	17.0	18.0	14.5	14.5	12.8
Return on Assets %	1.6	1.9	2.0	1.9	1.8	1.7	1.7
Price Range	53.00-36.35	49.67-38.00	50.59-33.25	53.09-40.79	52.25-32.45	38.56-22.89	26.50-20.06
P/E Ratio	17.4-12.0	14.9-11.4	15.4-10.1	18.0-13.8	20.0-12.4	16.7-9.9	14.6-11.0
Average Yield %	2.6	2.4	2.3	1.8	1.8	2.3	2.7

Statistics are as originally reported. Adj. for stk. splits: 3-for-2, 4/01, 4/98. ⑪ Bef. acctg. gain $1.0 mill.

OFFICERS:
D. A. Stonecipher, Chmn., C.E.O.
K. C. Mlekush, Vice-Chmn.
D. R. Glass, Pres., C.O.O.

INVESTOR CONTACT: Investor Relations,
(336) 691-3379

PRINCIPAL OFFICE: 100 North Greene
Street, Greensboro, NC 27401

TELEPHONE NUMBER: (336) 691-3000
FAX: (336) 691-3938
WEB: www.jpfinancial.com

NO. OF EMPLOYEES: 3,000 (approx.)

SHAREHOLDERS: 9,145

ANNUAL MEETING: In May

INCORPORATED: NC, Jan., 1968

INSTITUTIONAL HOLDINGS:
No. of Institutions: 354
Shares Held: 75,559,399
% Held: 52.8

INDUSTRY: Life insurance (SIC: 6311)

TRANSFER AGENT(S): Wachovia Bank,
N.A., Charlotte, NC

JOHNSON CONTROLS, INC.

YIELD 1.7%
P/E RATIO 12.3

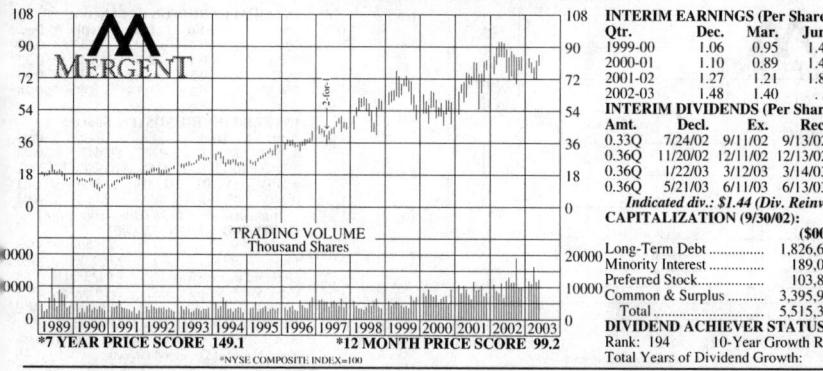

7 YEAR PRICE SCORE 149.1 **12 MONTH PRICE SCORE 99.2**
*NYSE COMPOSITE INDEX=100

INTERIM EARNINGS (Per Share):

Qtr.	Dec.	Mar.	June	Sept.
1999-00	1.06	0.95	1.45	1.63
2000-01	1.10	0.89	1.45	1.67
2001-02	1.27	1.21	1.85	2.02
2002-03	1.48	1.40	...	...

INTERIM DIVIDENDS (Per Share):

Amt.	Decl.	Ex.	Rec.	Pay.
0.33Q	7/24/02	9/11/02	9/13/02	9/30/02
0.36Q	11/20/02	12/11/02	12/13/02	1/02/03
0.36Q	1/22/03	3/12/03	3/14/03	3/31/03
0.36Q	5/21/03	6/11/03	6/13/03	6/30/03

Indicated div.: $1.44 (Div. Reinv. Plan)

CAPITALIZATION (9/30/02):

	($000)	(%)
Long-Term Debt	1,826,600	33.1
Minority Interest	189,000	3.4
Preferred Stock	103,800	1.9
Common & Surplus	3,395,900	61.6
Total	5,515,300	100.0

DIVIDEND ACHIEVER STATUS:

Rank: 194   10-Year Growth Rate: 7.51%
Total Years of Dividend Growth: 27

RECENT DEVELOPMENTS:

For the three months ended 3/31/03, net income rose 15.2% to $132.2 million compared with $114.8 million in the corresponding quarter of 2002. Net income benefited from a decrease in JCI's effective income tax rate. Net sales were $5.50 billion, up 14.4% from $4.81 billion in the prior-year period. Sales from the Automotive Systems Group grew 15.7% to $4.13 billion, while sales from the Controls Group rose 10.6% to $1.37 billion.

PROSPECTS:

The Company confirmed its guidance for consolidated sales growth for fiscal 2003 of between 5.0% and 10.0% over the prior year. In addition, the Company expects sales growth in the Automotive Systems Group to range from 5.0% to 10.0%, assuming North American light vehicle production of approximately 16.0 million to 16.1 million units, lower year-over-year European production and the positive effect of currency translation.

BUSINESS

JOHNSON CONTROLS, INC. operates in two business segments. The Automotive segment is engaged in the design and manufacture of complete seat systems, seating components and interior trim systems for North American and European manufacturers of cars, vans and light trucks. The Controls segment is a worldwide supplier of control systems, services and products providing energy management, temperature and ventilation control, security and fire safety for non-residential buildings. Revenues (and operating income) for fiscal 2002 were derived: Automotive Systems Group, 74.7% (76.9%); and Controls Group, 25.3% (23.1%).

ANNUAL FINANCIAL DATA

	9/30/02	9/30/01	9/30/00	9/30/99	9/30/98	9/30/97	9/30/96
Earnings Per Share	6.35	5.11	5.09	④ 4.48	③ 3.63	② 2.48	① 2.55
Cash Flow Per Share	11.79	10.60	10.06	9.25	7.78	6.67	6.49
Tang. Book Val. Per Share	4.48	3.41	3.65	0.45	...	...	9.70
Dividends Per Share	1.32	1.24	1.12	1.00	0.92	0.86	0.82
Dividend Payout %	20.8	24.3	22.0	22.3	25.3	34.7	32.2

INCOME STATEMENT (IN MILLIONS):

Total Revenues	20,103.4	18,427.2	17,154.6	16,139.4	12,586.8	11,145.4	9,210.0
Costs & Expenses	18,464.6	16,950.2	15,727.8	14,838.9	11,538.6	10,263.4	8,401.4
Depreciation & Amort.	516.8	515.9	461.8	445.6	384.2	354.9	329.7
Operating Income	1,122.0	961.1	965.0	854.9	664.0	527.1	478.9
Net Interest Inc./(Exp.)	d110.4	d110.0	d111.5	d136.0	d118.7	d112.8	d65.5
Income Before Income Taxes	1,006.0	835.3	855.7	769.9	616.8	425.6	421.5
Income Taxes	347.6	335.5	338.9	311.7	256.0	180.9	171.8
Equity Earnings/Minority Int.	d57.9	d53.3	d44.4	d38.6	d23.1	d24.1	d27.0
Net Income	600.5	478.3	472.4	④ 419.6	③ 337.7	② 220.6	① 222.7
Cash Flow	1,109.6	985.4	924.4	852.2	712.4	565.9	542.9
Average Shs. Outstg. (000)	94,100	93,000	91,900	92,100	91,600	84,800	83,600

BALANCE SHEET (IN MILLIONS):

Cash & Cash Equivalents	262.0	374.6	275.6	276.2	134.0	111.8	165.2
Total Current Assets	4,946.2	4,544.0	4,277.2	3,848.5	3,404.2	2,529.3	2,849.1
Net Property	2,445.5	2,379.8	2,305.0	1,996.0	1,882.9	1,533.0	1,320.2
Total Assets	11,165.3	9,911.5	9,428.0	8,614.2	7,942.1	6,048.6	4,991.2
Total Current Liabilities	4,806.2	4,579.7	4,510.0	4,266.6	4,288.4	2,972.7	2,182.6
Long-Term Obligations	1,826.6	1,394.8	1,315.3	1,283.3	997.5	706.4	752.2
Net Stockholders' Equity	3,499.7	2,985.4	2,576.1	2,270.0	1,941.4	1,687.9	1,507.8
Net Working Capital	140.0	d35.7	d232.8	d418.1	d884.2	d443.4	666.5
Year-end Shs. Outstg. (000)	88,880	87,499	85,989	85,395	84,700	84,100	83,000

STATISTICAL RECORD:

Operating Profit Margin %	5.6	5.2	5.6	5.3	5.3	4.7	5.2
Net Profit Margin %	3.0	2.6	2.8	2.6	2.7	2.0	2.4
Return on Equity %	17.2	16.0	18.3	18.5	17.4	13.1	14.8
Return on Assets %	5.4	4.8	5.0	4.9	4.3	3.6	4.5
Debt/Total Assets %	16.4	14.1	14.0	14.9	12.6	11.7	15.1
Price Range	93.20-69.10	82.70-51.94	65.13-45.81	76.69-49.00	61.88-40.50	51.00-35.38	42.69-31.25
P/E Ratio	14.7-10.9	16.2-10.2	12.8-9.0	17.1-10.9	17.0-11.2	20.6-14.3	16.7-12.3
Average Yield %	1.6	1.8	2.0	1.6	1.8	2.0	2.2

Statistics are as originally reported. Adj. for 100% stk. div., 3/97. ① Bef. $12.0 mill. chg. fr. disc. ops. ② Bef. $67.9 mill. disc. ops. ③ Incl. $35.0 mill. after-tax gain fr. sale of bus. ④ Incl. $32.5 mill. net one-time gain on sale of bus.

OFFICERS:
J. H. Keyes, Chmn.
J. M. Barth, Pres., C.E.O.
S. A. Roell, Sr. V.P., C.F.O.

INVESTOR CONTACT: Shareholder Services, (414) 524-2363

PRINCIPAL OFFICE: 5757 N. Green Bay Avenue, Milwaukee, WI 53201

TELEPHONE NUMBER: (414) 524-1200
FAX: (414) 524-3200
WEB: www.johnsoncontrols.com

NO. OF EMPLOYEES: 111,000 (approx.)

SHAREHOLDERS: 57,138

ANNUAL MEETING: In Jan.

INCORPORATED: WI, July, 1900

INSTITUTIONAL HOLDINGS:
No. of Institutions: 417
Shares Held: 58,748,271
% Held: 66.0

INDUSTRY: Public building & related furniture (SIC: 2531)

TRANSFER AGENT(S): Firstar Trust Company, Milwaukee, WI

JOHNSON & JOHNSON

YIELD 1.8%
P/E RATIO 23.5

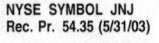
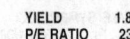

INTERIM EARNINGS (Per Share):

Qtr.	Mar.	June	Sept.	Dec.
1999	0.41	0.42	0.40	0.27
2000	0.47	0.40	0.45	0.32
2001	0.53	0.48	0.49	0.36
2002	0.59	0.54	0.60	0.48
2003	0.69	...	...	...

INTERIM DIVIDENDS (Per Share):

Amt.	Decl.	Ex.	Rec.	Pay.
0.205Q	7/15/02	8/16/02	8/20/02	9/10/02
0.205Q	10/15/02	11/15/02	11/19/02	12/10/02
0.205Q	1/06/03	2/13/03	2/18/03	3/11/03
0.24Q	4/24/03	5/16/03	5/20/03	6/10/03

Indicated div.: $0.96 (Div. Reinv. Plan)

CAPITALIZATION (12/29/02):

	($000)	(%)
Long-Term Debt	2,022,000	8.0
Deferred Income Tax	643,000	2.5
Common & Surplus	22,697,000	89.5
Total	25,362,000	100.0

DIVIDEND ACHIEVER STATUS:
Rank: 81   10-Year Growth Rate: 13.58%
Total Years of Dividend Growth: 40

TRADING VOLUME
Thousand Shares

*7 YEAR PRICE SCORE 142.6   ***12 MONTH PRICE SCORE 100.6**
*NYSE COMPOSITE INDEX=100

RECENT DEVELOPMENTS: For the quarter ended 3/31/03, net earnings increased 12.9% to $2.07 billion compared with $1.83 billion in the corresponding period of the previous year. Results for 2003 included after-tax special charges of $15.0 million, respectively, for in-process research and development costs associated with acquisitions. Sales advanced 12.3% to $9.82 billion from $8.74 billion in the year-earlier quarter.

PROSPECTS: On 4/29/03, the Company completed its acquisition of Scios Inc., a biopharmaceutical company that specializes in treatments for cardiovascular and inflammatory diseases, for approximately $2.40 billion. JNJ indicated the transaction would dilute earnings by $0.05 a share in 2003 and 2004. JNJ will also incur a one-time charge of about $700.0 million, or $0.23 a share, for in-process research and development.

BUSINESS

JOHNSON & JOHNSON is engaged in the manufacture and sale of a broad range of products in health care and other fields. The Pharmaceutical segment, (47.3% of 2002 sales), consists of prescription drugs in the antifungal, anti-infective, cardiovascular, dermatology, gastrointestinal, hematology, immunology, neurology, oncology, pain management, psychotropic and women's health fields. The Medical Devices and Diagnostics segment, (34.6%), includes a broad range of products used by or under the direction of health care professionals. The Consumer segment, (18.1%), consists of personal care and hygienic products. JNJ acquired ALZA Corp. on 6/22/01.

ANNUAL FINANCIAL DATA

	12/29/02	12/30/01	12/31/00	1/2/00	1/3/99	12/28/97	12/29/96
Earnings Per Share	⑤ 2.16	④ 1.84	③ 1.70	② 1.47	① 1.12	1.21	1.09
Cash Flow Per Share	2.70	2.35	2.23	1.98	1.57	1.60	1.68
Tang. Book Val. Per Share	4.53	4.97	4.15	3.11	2.37	3.38	2.90
Dividends Per Share	0.80	0.70	0.62	0.55	0.48	0.42	0.37
Dividend Payout %	36.8	38.0	36.5	37.1	43.5	35.3	33.9

INCOME STATEMENT (IN MILLIONS):

	12/29/02	12/30/01	12/31/00	1/2/00	1/3/99	12/28/97	12/29/96
Total Revenues	36,298.0	33,460.0	29,518.0	27,717.0	23,657.0	22,629.0	21,620.0
Costs & Expenses	24,891.0	23,514.0	21,114.0	20,101.0	17,979.0	16,940.0	16,308.0
Depreciation & Amort.	1,662.0	1,605.0	1,515.0	1,444.0	1,246.0	1,067.0	1,009.0
Operating Income	...	8,236.0	6,835.0	6,172.0	4,268.0	4,622.0	4,303.0
Net Interest Inc./(Exp.)	d160.0	d153.0	d146.0	d197.0	152.0	83.0	14.0
Income Before Income Taxes	9,291.0	7,898.0	6,622.0	5,753.0	4,269.0	4,576.0	4,033.0
Income Taxes	2,694.0	2,230.0	1,822.0	1,586.0	1,210.0	1,273.0	569.0
Net Income	⑤ 6,597.0	④ 5,668.0	③ 4,800.0	② 4,167.0	① 3,059.0	3,303.0	3,464.0
Cash Flow	8,259.0	7,273.0	6,315.0	5,611.0	4,305.0	4,370.0	4,473.0
Average Shs. Outstg. (000)	3,054,100	3,099,300	2,834,800	2,836,400	2,743,200	2,739,800	2,666,000

BALANCE SHEET (IN MILLIONS):

	12/29/02	12/30/01	12/31/00	1/2/00	1/3/99	12/28/97	12/29/96
Cash & Cash Equivalents	7,475.0	7,972.0	5,744.0	3,879.0	2,578.0	2,899.0	2,136.0
Total Current Assets	19,266.0	18,473.0	15,450.0	13,200.0	11,132.0	10,563.0	9,370.0
Net Property	8,710.0	7,719.0	6,971.0	6,719.0	6,240.0	5,810.0	5,651.0
Total Assets	40,556.0	38,488.0	31,321.0	29,163.0	26,211.0	21,453.0	20,010.0
Total Current Liabilities	11,449.0	8,044.0	7,140.0	7,454.0	8,162.0	5,283.0	5,184.0
Long-Term Obligations	2,022.0	2,217.0	2,037.0	2,450.0	1,269.0	1,126.0	1,410.0
Net Stockholders' Equity	22,697.0	24,233.0	18,808.0	16,213.0	13,590.0	12,359.0	10,836.0
Net Working Capital	7,817.0	10,429.0	8,310.0	5,746.0	2,970.0	5,280.0	4,186.0
Year-end Shs. Outstg. (000)	2,968,295	3,047,215	2,781,874	2,779,366	2,688,000	2,690,000	2,664,000

STATISTICAL RECORD:

	12/29/02	12/30/01	12/31/00	1/2/00	1/3/99	12/28/97	12/29/96
Operating Profit Margin %	...	25.0	23.2	22.3	18.2	20.4	19.9
Net Profit Margin %	18.2	17.2	16.3	15.0	13.0	14.6	16.0
Return on Equity %	29.1	23.4	25.5	25.7	22.5	26.7	32.0
Return on Assets %	16.3	14.7	15.3	14.3	11.7	15.4	17.3
Debt/Total Assets %	5.0	5.8	6.5	8.4	4.8	5.2	7.0
Price Range	65.89-41.40	60.97-40.25	52.97-33.06	53.44-38.50	44.88-31.69	33.66-24.31	27.00-20.78
P/E Ratio	30.5-19.2	33.1-21.9	31.2-19.4	36.3-26.2	40.2-28.4	27.9-20.2	24.9-19.2
Average Yield %	1.5	1.4	1.4	1.2	1.3	1.5	1.5

Statistics are as originally reported. Adjusted for 2-for-1 stock split, 6/96 & 6/01. ① Incl. a pre-tax in-process R&D chrg. $164.0 mill. and a pre-tax restruct. chrg. $613.0 mill. ② Incl. nonrecurr. after-tax chrg. of $42.0 mill. ③ Incl. pre-tax chrg. of $54.0 mill. for in-proc. res. & devel. ④ Incl. pre-tax chrg. of $105.0 mill. for in-proc. res. & devel. ⑤ Incl. after-tax spec. chrg. of $189.0 mill. in-processed R&D costs.

OFFICERS:
R. S. Larsen, Chmn., C.E.O.
R. N. Wilson, Sr. Vice-Chmn.
W. C. Weldon, Vice-Chmn.

INVESTOR CONTACT: Helen E. Short, V.P., (800) 950-5089

PRINCIPAL OFFICE: One Johnson & Johnson Plaza, New Brunswick, NJ 08933

TELEPHONE NUMBER: (732) 524-0400
FAX: (732) 214-0332
WEB: www.jnj.com

NO. OF EMPLOYEES: 108,300 (approx.)

SHAREHOLDERS: 103,300 (approx.)

ANNUAL MEETING: In Apr.

INCORPORATED: NJ, Nov., 1887

INSTITUTIONAL HOLDINGS:
No. of Institutions: 1,330
Shares Held: 1,811,167,544
% Held: 61.0

INDUSTRY: Pharmaceutical preparations (SIC: 2834)

TRANSFER AGENT(S): First Chicago Trust Company a Division of EquiServe, Jersey City, NJ

KEYCORP

YIELD 4.6%
P/E RATIO 11.9

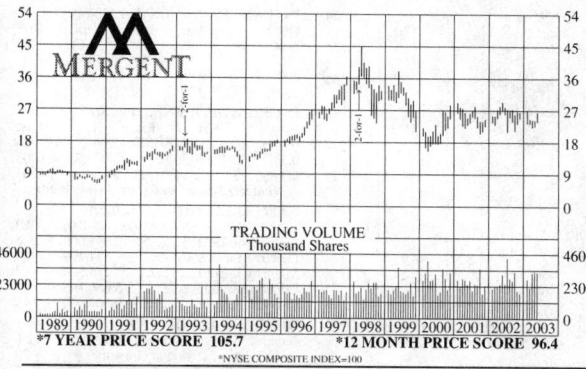

INTERIM EARNINGS (Per Share):

Qtr.	Mar.	June	Sept.	Dec.
2000	0.83	0.57	0.28	0.62
2001	0.51	d0.32	0.58	d0.41
2002	0.56	0.57	0.57	0.57
2003	0.51	...	...	...

INTERIM DIVIDENDS (Per Share):

Amt.	Decl.	Ex.	Rec.	Pay.
0.30Q	5/23/02	5/30/02	6/03/02	6/14/02
0.30Q	7/18/02	8/23/02	8/27/02	9/13/02
0.30Q	11/21/02	11/29/02	12/03/02	12/13/02
0.305Q	1/16/03	2/28/03	3/04/03	3/14/03
0.305Q	5/23/03	6/02/03	6/04/03	6/16/03

Indicated div.: $1.22 (Div. Reinv. Plan)

CAPITALIZATION (12/31/02):

	($000)	(%)
Total Deposits	49,346,000	68.7
Long-Term Debt	15,605,000	21.7
Common & Surplus	6,835,000	9.5
Total	71,786,000	100.0

DIVIDEND ACHIEVER STATUS:
Rank: 159   10-Year Growth Rate: 9.37%
Total Years of Dividend Growth: 23

RECENT DEVELOPMENTS: For the quarter ended 3/31/03, net income declined 9.6% to $217.0 million compared with $240.0 million in the corresponding period of the previous year. Net interest income rose 4.1% to $681.0 million from $654.0 million the year before. Provision for loan losses decreased 4.4% to $130.0 million. Total non-interest income declined 10.4% to $397.0 million due to lower income from trust and investment services and investment banking and capital market activities. Total non-interest expense slipped 0.6% to $657.0 million.

PROSPECTS: Net interest income continues to be negatively affected by contracting interest rate spreads and soft loan demand, while continued pressure on market-sensitive businesses is adversely affecting non-interest income. However, KEY expects modest improvement in the second quarter of 2003. For the full year, earnings per share are anticipated to range from $2.15 to $2.30. KEY will continue to focus on expense control, deposit growth and asset quality improvement. Meanwhile, KEY's nonperforming loans decreased by $39.0 million in the first quarter.

BUSINESS

KEYCORP (formerly Society Corporation) is a multi-line financial services company, with assets of $86.49 billion as of 3/31/03. The Company provides investment management, retail and commercial banking, retirement, consumer finance, and investment banking products and services to individuals and companies throughout the U.S. and, for certain businesses, internationally. The Company operates nationwide through 911 KeyCenters and offices, a network of 2,179 ATMs, a Web site named Key.com, and telephone banking centers. In October 1998, the Company acquired McDonald & Company Investments, Inc. On 1/31/00, the Company sold its credit card business.

ANNUAL FINANCIAL DATA

	12/31/02	12/31/01	12/31/00	12/31/99	12/31/98	12/31/97	12/31/96
Earnings Per Share	2.27	⑤0.37	④2.30	②③2.45	②2.23	②2.07	①1.69
Tang. Book Val. Per Share	13.35	11.85	12.42	11.14	10.30	9.14	7.97
Dividends Per Share	1.20	1.18	1.12	1.04	0.94	0.84	0.76
Dividend Payout %	52.9	318.8	48.7	42.4	42.2	40.6	45.1
INCOME STATEMENT (IN MILLIONS):							
Total Interest Income	4,366.0	5,627.0	6,277.0	5,695.0	5,525.0	5,262.0	4,951.0
Total Interest Expense	1,617.0	2,802.0	3,547.0	2,908.0	2,841.0	2,468.0	2,234.0
Net Interest Income	2,749.0	2,825.0	2,730.0	2,787.0	2,684.0	2,794.0	2,717.0
Provision for Loan Losses	553.0	1,350.0	490.0	348.0	297.0	320.0	197.0
Non-Interest Income	1,769.0	1,725.0	2,194.0	2,294.0	1,575.0	1,306.0	1,087.0
Non-Interest Expense	2,653.0	2,941.0	2,917.0	3,049.0	2,483.0	2,435.0	2,464.0
Income Before Taxes	1,312.0	259.0	1,517.0	1,684.0	1,479.0	1,345.0	1,143.0
Net Income	976.0	⑤157.0	④1,002.0	②⑥1,107.0	②996.0	②919.0	①783.0
Average Shs. Outstg. (000)	430,703	429,573	435,573	452,363	447,437	444,544	459,810
BALANCE SHEET (IN MILLIONS):							
Cash & Due from Banks	3,364.0	2,891.0	3,189.0	2,816.0	3,296.0	3,651.0	3,444.0
Securities Avail. for Sale	10,139.0	7,244.0	9,213.0	8,523.0	7,252.0	9,636.0	8,424.0
Total Loans & Leases	62,457.0	63,309.0	66,905.0	64,222.0	62,012.0	53,380.0	49,235.0
Allowance for Credit Losses	1,452.0	1,677.0	1,001.0	930.0	900.0	900.0	870.0
Net Loans & Leases	61,005.0	61,632.0	65,904.0	63,292.0	61,112.0	52,480.0	48,365.0
Total Assets	85,202.0	80,938.0	87,270.0	83,395.0	80,020.0	73,699.0	67,621.0
Total Deposits	49,346.0	44,795.0	48,649.0	43,233.0	42,583.0	45,073.0	45,317.0
Long-Term Obligations	15,605.0	14,554.0	14,161.0	15,881.0	12,967.0	7,446.0	4,213.0
Total Liabilities	78,367.0	74,783.0	80,647.0	77,006.0	73,853.0	67,768.0	62,240.0
Net Stockholders' Equity	6,835.0	6,155.0	6,623.0	6,389.0	6,167.0	5,181.0	4,881.0
Year-end Shs. Outstg. (000)	423,944	424,005	423,254	443,427	452,452	438,064	491,888
STATISTICAL RECORD:							
Return on Equity %	14.3	2.6	15.1	17.3	16.2	17.7	16.0
Return on Assets %	1.1	0.2	1.1	1.3	1.2	1.2	1.2
Equity/Assets %	8.0	7.6	7.6	7.7	7.7	7.0	7.2
Non-Int. Exp./Tot. Inc. %	58.7	64.6	59.2	60.0	58.3	59.4	64.8
Price Range	29.40-20.98	29.25-20.49	28.50-15.56	38.13-21.00	44.88-23.38	36.59-23.94	27.13-16.69
P/E Ratio	13.0-9.2	79.1-55.4	12.4-6.8	15.6-8.6	20.1-10.5	17.7-11.6	16.1-9.9
Average Yield %	4.8	4.7	5.1	3.5	2.8	2.8	3.5

Statistics are as originally reported. Adj. for 2-for-1 split, 3/98. ① Incl. pre-tax SAIF chg. & restr. chgs. totaling $17.0 mill. ② Incl. pre-tax gain fr. sale of branch: $148.0 mill., 1999; $89.0 mill., 1998; $151.0 mill., 1997. ③ Incl. various pre-tax net gains of $448.0 mill. & restr. chgs. of $98.0 mill. ④ Incl. pre-tax gains from divest. of $332.0 mill. & pre-tax restr. chgs. of $102.0 mill. ⑤ Bef. acctg. chrg. of $25.0 mill.; incl. pre-tax restr. gains of $4.0 mill.

OFFICERS:
H. L. Meyer III, Chmn., Pres., C.E.O.
T. C. Stevens, Vice-Chmn., C.A.O., Sec.
J. B. Weeden, C.F.O.
INVESTOR CONTACT: Bernon L. Patterson, Investor Relations, (216) 689-4520
PRINCIPAL OFFICE: 127 Public Square, Cleveland, OH 44114-1306

TELEPHONE NUMBER: (216) 689-6300
FAX: (216) 689-3595
WEB: www.key.com
NO. OF EMPLOYEES: 20,437
SHAREHOLDERS: 40,166
ANNUAL MEETING: In May
INCORPORATED: OH, Dec., 1958

INSTITUTIONAL HOLDINGS:
No. of Institutions: 428
Shares Held: 245,964,596
% Held: 58.1
INDUSTRY: National commercial banks (SIC: 6021)
TRANSFER AGENT(S): Computershare Investor Services, Chicago, IL

KIMBERLY-CLARK CORPORATION

YIELD 2.6%
P/E RATIO 16.4

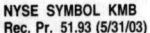

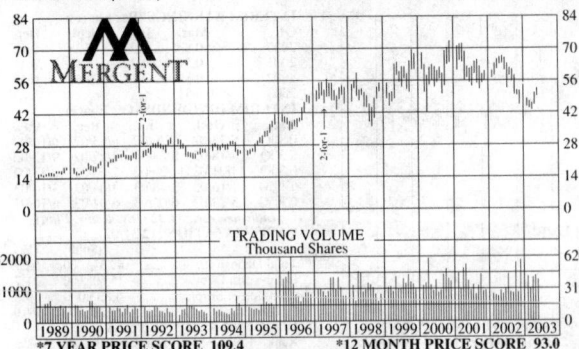

INTERIM EARNINGS (Per Share):

Qtr.	Mar.	June	Sept.	Dec.
2000	0.86	0.79	0.81	0.85
2001	0.81	0.78	0.79	0.68
2002	0.86	0.81	0.85	0.72
2003	0.78	...	...	...

INTERIM DIVIDENDS (Per Share):

Amt.	Decl.	Ex.	Rec.	Pay.
0.30Q	11/12/02	12/04/02	12/06/02	1/03/03
0.34Q	2/18/03	3/05/03	3/07/03	4/02/03
0.34Q	5/01/03	6/04/03	6/06/03	7/02/03

Indicated div.: $1.36 (Div. Reinv. Plan)

CAPITALIZATION (12/31/02):

	($000)	(%)
Long-Term Debt	2,844,000	29.6
Deferred Income Tax	854,200	8.9
Minority Interest	255,500	2.7
Common & Surplus	5,650,300	58.8
Total	9,604,000	100.0

TRADING VOLUME
Thousand Shares

*7 YEAR PRICE SCORE 109.4   *12 MONTH PRICE SCORE 93.0

*NYSE COMPOSITE INDEX=100

DIVIDEND ACHIEVER STATUS:
Rank: 255   10-Year Growth Rate: 3.71%
Total Years of Dividend Growth: 28

RECENT DEVELOPMENTS: For the quarter ended 3/31/03, net income declined 11.7% to $397.7 million compared with income of $450.6 million, before an accounting change charge of $11.4 million, in the equivalent 2002 quarter. The decline in earnings reflected a highly competitive environment, particularly in the diaper and training pant categories in North America. Net sales advanced 3.9% to $3.46 billion due to widespread volume growth.

PROSPECTS: The Company expects fiscal 2003 sales growth in the low-to-mid single digits. Meanwhile, in the second quarter of 2003, based on recent cost increases and competitive conditions, the Company expects earnings per share to be flat sequentially from the first quarter of 2003. In addition, second quarter results are expected to be impeded by inflationary pressures, which should be offset by pricing adjustments and expense reductions.

BUSINESS

KIMBERLY-CLARK CORPORATION is a global manufacturer of consumer products. The Company's global personal care, tissue and health care brands include HUGGIES, PULL-UPS, LITTLE SWIMMERS, GOODNITES, KOTEX, LIGHTDAYS, DEPEND, POISE, KLEENEX, SCOTT, COTTONELLE, VIVA, ANDREX, SCOTTEX, PAGE, KIMBERLY-CLARK, KIMWIPES, WYPALL, SURPASS, SAFESKIN, TECNOL, POPEE and KIMBEES. Kimberly-Clark also is a major producer of premium business, correspondence and technical papers. KMB had manufacturing operations in 43 countries and sells its products in more than 150 countries as of 4/22/03.

In fiscal 2002, net sales (and operating profit) were derived as follows: personal care, 37.2% (39.6%); consumer tissue, 36.6% (35.0%); and business-to-business, 26.2% (25.4%).

ANNUAL FINANCIAL DATA

	12/31/02	12/31/01	12/31/00	12/31/99	12/31/98	12/31/97	12/31/96
Earnings Per Share	[5][5] 3.24	[5] 3.02	3.31	[4] 3.09	[3] 2.13	[2] 1.58	[1] 2.49
Cash Flow Per Share	4.60	4.41	4.55	4.25	3.11	2.49	3.48
Tang. Book Val. Per Share	6.65	7.10	7.04	7.12	6.13	6.36	7.96
Dividends Per Share	1.18	1.11	1.07	1.03	0.99	0.95	0.92
Dividend Payout %	36.4	36.8	32.3	33.3	46.5	60.1	36.7

INCOME STATEMENT (IN MILLIONS):

Total Revenues	13,566.3	14,524.4	13,982.0	13,006.8	12,297.8	12,546.6	13,149.1
Costs & Expenses	10,395.9	11,446.6	10,674.8	9,943.4	10,079.2	10,735.7	10,534.4
Depreciation & Amort.	706.6	739.6	673.4	628.0	542.5	507.7	561.0
Operating Income	2,463.8	2,338.2	2,633.8	2,435.4	1,676.1	1,303.2	2,053.7
Net Interest Inc./(Exp.)	d166.4	d173.8	d197.8	d183.7	d174.4	d133.4	d158.6
Income Before Income Taxes	2,297.4	2,164.4	2,436.0	2,251.7	1,626.1	1,187.5	2,002.3
Income Taxes	666.6	645.7	758.5	730.2	561.9	433.1	700.8
Equity Earnings/Minority Int.	55.2	91.2	123.1	146.6	112.8	129.6	102.3
Net Income	[5][5] 1,686.0	[5] 1,609.9	1,800.6	[4] 1,668.1	[3] 1,177.0	[2] 884.0	[1] 1,403.8
Cash Flow	2,392.6	2,349.5	2,474.0	2,296.1	1,719.5	1,391.7	1,964.8
Average Shs. Outstg. (000)	520,000	533,200	543,800	540,100	553,100	559,300	564,000

BALANCE SHEET (IN MILLIONS):

Cash & Cash Equivalents	494.5	405.2	206.5	322.8	144.0	90.8	83.2
Total Current Assets	4,273.9	3,922.2	3,789.9	3,561.8	3,366.9	3,489.0	3,539.2
Net Property	7,619.4	7,326.5	6,918.5	6,222.0	5,845.0	5,600.6	6,813.3
Total Assets	15,585.8	15,007.6	14,479.8	12,815.5	11,510.3	11,266.0	11,845.7
Total Current Liabilities	4,038.3	4,168.3	4,573.9	3,845.8	3,790.7	3,698.3	3,686.9
Long-Term Obligations	2,844.0	2,424.0	2,000.6	1,926.6	2,068.2	1,803.9	1,738.6
Net Stockholders' Equity	5,650.3	5,646.9	5,767.3	5,093.1	3,887.2	4,133.3	4,483.1
Net Working Capital	235.6	d246.1	d784.0	d284.0	d423.8	d209.3	d147.7
Year-end Shs. Outstg. (000)	510,800	521,000	533,400	540,600	538,300	556,300	563,400

STATISTICAL RECORD:

Operating Profit Margin %	18.2	16.1	18.8	18.7	13.6	10.4	15.6
Net Profit Margin %	12.4	11.1	12.9	12.8	9.6	7.0	10.7
Return on Equity %	29.8	28.5	31.2	32.8	30.3	21.4	31.3
Return on Assets %	10.8	10.7	12.4	13.0	10.2	7.8	11.9
Debt/Total Assets %	18.2	16.2	13.8	15.0	18.0	16.0	14.7
Price Range	66.79-45.30	72.19-52.06	73.25-42.00	69.56-44.81	59.44-35.88	56.88-43.25	49.81-34.31
P/E Ratio	20.6-14.0	23.9-17.2	22.1-12.7	22.5-14.5	27.9-16.8	36.0-27.4	20.0-13.8
Average Yield %	2.1	1.8	1.9	1.8	2.1	1.9	2.2

Statistics are as originally reported. Adj. for stk. split: 2-for-1, 4/97. [1] Incl. gain $9.4 mill., 1993; $62.5 mill., 1994; $72.6 mill., 1996. [2] Bef. extraord. cr. $17.5 mill. & incl. restruct. chrg. $481.1 mill. [3] Bef. acctg. chrg. of $11.4 mill., 2002; $11.2 mill., 1998. [4] Incl. restruct. cr. $27.0 mill. [5] Incl. net chrg. of $95.5 mill., 2002; $179.7 mill., 2001.

OFFICERS:
T. J. Falk, Chmn., Pres., C.E.O.
M. A. Buthman, Sr. V.P., C.F.O.

INVESTOR CONTACT: Investor Relations, (972) 281-1200

PRINCIPAL OFFICE: P.O. Box 619100, Dallas, TX 75261-9100

TELEPHONE NUMBER: (972) 281-1200
FAX: (972) 281-1435
WEB: www.kimberly-clark.com

NO. OF EMPLOYEES: 63,900 (avg.)

SHAREHOLDERS: 37,731

ANNUAL MEETING: In Apr.

INCORPORATED: DE, June, 1928

INSTITUTIONAL HOLDINGS:
No. of Institutions: 807
Shares Held: 364,213,806
% Held: 71.3

INDUSTRY: Paper mills (SIC: 2621)

TRANSFER AGENT(S): Bank Boston, N.A., Boston, MA

KIMCO REALTY CORP.

YIELD 5.8%
P/E RATIO 16.6

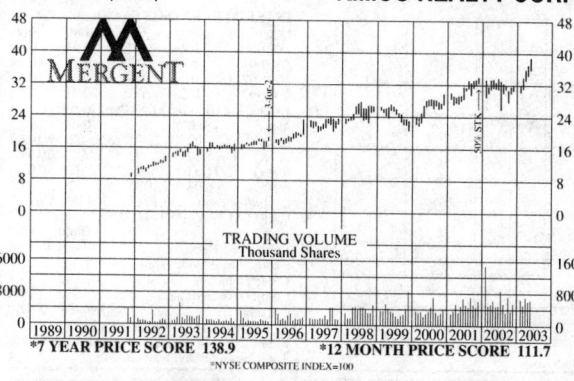

7 YEAR PRICE SCORE 138.9   **12 MONTH PRICE SCORE 111.7**

NYSE COMPOSITE INDEX=100

INTERIM EARNINGS (Per Share):

Qtr.	Mar.	June	Sept.	Dec.
1999	0.36	0.39	0.43	0.47
2000	0.46	0.48	0.47	0.49
2001	0.51	0.55	0.54	0.56
2002	0.53	0.53	0.53	0.60
2003	0.59	...	...	...

INTERIM DIVIDENDS (Per Share):

Amt.	Decl.	Ex.	Rec.	Pay.
0.52Q	6/17/02	7/01/02	7/03/02	7/15/02
0.52Q	9/16/02	10/01/02	10/03/02	10/15/02
0.54Q	10/28/02	12/30/02	1/02/03	1/15/03
0.54Q	3/17/03	4/01/03	4/03/03	4/15/03
0.54Q	6/16/03	7/01/03	7/03/03	7/15/03

Indicated div.: $2.16 (Div. Reinv. Plan)

CAPITALIZATION (12/31/02):

	($000)	(%)
Long-Term Debt	274,732	12.6
Preferred Stock	900	0.0
Common & Surplus	1,906,428	87.4
Total	2,182,060	100.0

DIVIDEND ACHIEVER STATUS:

Rank: 103   10-Year Growth Rate: 12.22%
Total Years of Dividend Growth: 10

RECENT DEVELOPMENTS: For the quarter ended 3/31/03, income from continuing operations was $66.3 million versus income of $55.5 million in the equivalent quarter of the previous year. Results for 2003 included a gain of $6.3 million the early extinguishment of debt and a gain of $1.2 million on the sale of properties and excluded a gain of $3.5 million from discontinued operations. Revenues from rental property advanced 10.7% to $124.1 million.

PROSPECTS: During the quarter, the Company acquired interests in 10 shopping center properties and three single tenant sites totaling 2.1 million square feet for an aggregate cost of approximately $246.1 million. In addition, the Company signed 97 new leases in the parent portfolio totaling 893,000 square feet with average base rent of approximately $7.49 per square foot.

BUSINESS

KIMCO REALTY CORP. is an owner and operator of neighborhood and community shopping centers. As of 4/28/03, the Company had interests in 630 properties totaling approximately 91.7 million square feet of leaseable space located in 41 states, Canada and Mexico. The Company's portfolio includes properties relating to the Kimco Income REIT, a joint venture arrangement with institutional investors established for the purpose of investing in retail properties financed primarily with individual non-recourse mortgages debt. Through its wholly-owned subsidiary, Kimco Developers Inc., KIM is engaged in the ground-up development of neighborhood and community shopping centers and sales thereof upon completion.

ANNUAL FINANCIAL DATA

	12/31/02	12/31/01	12/31/00	12/31/99	12/31/98	12/31/97	12/31/96
Earnings Per Share	③ 2.19	② 2.16	② 1.91	1.64	① 1.35	1.19	1.07
Tang. Book Val. Per Share	18.23	18.28	17.98	17.59	17.56	12.25	11.13
Dividends Per Share	2.08	1.92	1.77	1.58	1.31	1.15	1.04
Dividend Payout %	95.0	88.9	93.0	96.3	97.5	96.6	96.9
INCOME STATEMENT (IN MILLIONS):							
Rental Income	450.8	468.6	459.4	433.9	338.8	198.9	168.1
Total Income	450.8	468.6	459.4	433.9	338.8	198.9	168.1
Costs & Expenses	121.4	254.8	284.4	273.6	220.6	122.6	103.3
Income Before Income Taxes	261.5	255.9	205.0	176.8	127.2	85.8	73.8
Income Taxes	12.9	19.4	...	...	...	...	...
Net Income	③ 248.6	② 236.5	② 205.0	176.8	① 127.2	85.8	73.8
Average Shs. Outstg. (000)	105,969	101,163	93,653	91,466	75,961	56,775	53,859
BALANCE SHEET (IN MILLIONS):							
Cash & Cash Equivalents	103.0	176.8	19.1	28.1	43.9	31.0	37.4
Total Real Estate Investments	3,394.6	3,027.5	2,935.1	2,822.8	2,847.4	1,222.5	925.6
Total Assets	3,756.9	3,384.8	3,171.3	3,007.5	3,051.2	1,343.9	1,022.6
Long-Term Obligations	274.7	292.8	245.4	212.3	434.3	121.4	54.4
Total Liabilities	1,755.6	1,486.3	1,453.2	1,388.9	1,453.2	596.0	412.6
Net Stockholders' Equity	1,907.3	1,890.1	1,704.3	1,605.4	1,585.0	743.3	605.3
Year-end Shs. Outstg. (000)	104,602	103,353	94,717	91,193	90,201	60,592	54,323
STATISTICAL RECORD:							
Net Inc.+Depr./Assets %	8.6	7.0	6.5	5.9	4.2	6.4	7.2
Return on Equity %	13.0	12.5	12.0	11.0	8.0	11.5	12.2
Return on Assets %	6.6	7.0	6.5	5.9	4.2	6.4	7.2
Price Range	33.88-25.96	34.07-27.17	29.83-21.83	27.17-20.58	27.75-22.29	23.79-20.17	23.25-16.83
P/E Ratio	15.5-11.9	15.8-12.6	15.6-11.4	16.6-12.6	20.6-16.5	20.0-17.0	21.7-15.7
Average Yield %	7.0	6.3	6.9	6.6	5.2	5.2	5.2

Statistics are as originally reported. Adj. for 3-for-2 stk. spl., 12/01 ① Excl. extraord. chrg., 1998, $4.9 mill. ② Incl. gain on sales of shopping center prop. of $16.4 mill., 2001; $4.0 mill., 2000 ③ Bef. loss from disc. oper. of $2.9 mill. & incl. net gains of $22.4 mill.

OFFICERS:
M. Cooper, Chmn., C.E.O.
M. J. Flynn, Vice-Chmn., Pres., C.O.O.
D. B. Henry, Vice-Chmn., C.I.O.

INVESTOR CONTACT: Scott G. Onufrey, Investor Relations, (516) 869-7190

PRINCIPAL OFFICE: 3333 New Hyde Park Road, New Hyde Park. NY 11042-0020

TELEPHONE NUMBER: (516) 869-9000
FAX: (516) 869-9001
WEB: www.kimcorealty.com

NO. OF EMPLOYEES: 375

SHAREHOLDERS: 1,273 (record)

ANNUAL MEETING: In May

INCORPORATED: DE, 1973; reincorp., Aug., 1994

INSTITUTIONAL HOLDINGS:
No. of Institutions: 213
Shares Held: 60,129,384
% Held: 57.3

INDUSTRY: Real estate investment trusts (SIC: 6798)

TRANSFER AGENT(S): BankBoston, Boston, MA

LA-Z-BOY INCORPORATED

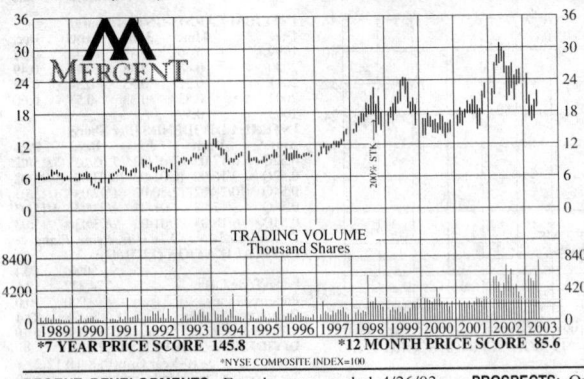

INTERIM EARNINGS (Per Share):

Qtr.	July	Oct.	Jan.	Apr.
1999-00	0.25	0.44	0.41	0.49
2000-01	0.21	0.48	0.27	0.17
2001-02	0.05	0.20	0.35	0.41
2002-03	0.32	0.50	0.41	0.45

INTERIM DIVIDENDS (Per Share):

Amt.	Decl.	Ex.	Rec.	Pay.
0.10Q	8/14/02	8/22/02	8/26/02	9/10/02
0.10Q	11/11/02	11/21/02	11/25/02	12/10/02
0.10Q	2/11/03	2/20/03	2/24/03	3/10/03
0.10Q	5/06/03	5/21/03	5/23/03	6/10/03

Indicated div.: $0.40 (Div. Reinv. Plan)

CAPITALIZATION (4/27/02):

	($000)	(%)
Long-Term Debt	137,444	15.3
Capital Lease Obligations	1,942	0.2
Deferred Income Tax	46,145	5.1
Common & Surplus	713,522	79.4
Total	899,053	100.0

TRADING VOLUME Thousand Shares

*7 YEAR PRICE SCORE 145.8   ***12 MONTH PRICE SCORE 85.6**

*NYSE COMPOSITE INDEX=100

DIVIDEND ACHIEVER STATUS:
Rank: 203   10-Year Growth Rate: 6.91%
Total Years of Dividend Growth: 21

RECENT DEVELOPMENTS: For the year ended 4/26/03, income jumped 55.6% to $96.1 million, before an accounting change charge of $59.8 million, compared with net income of $61.8 million in 2002. During the year, the Company experienced lower demand due to a drop in consumer confidence attributed to the relatively stagnant domestic economy and a wide variety of geopolitical uncertainties. Results for 2002 included a divestiture loss of $11.7 million. Sales slid 2.0% to $2.11 billion.

PROSPECTS: On 6/3/03, LZB announced a reorganization of its casegoods business group, including the establishment of a new global sourcing organization, and the closing of its plants in Morristown, Tennessee and in Monroe, NC. LZB expects the closure of the two facilities will result in the loss of approximately 480 manufacturing jobs, or 11.0% of the Casegoods Group's employee base. These actions should result in pre-tax charges of about $10.0 million in the first half of fiscal 2004.

BUSINESS

LA-Z-BOY INCORPORATED (formerly La-Z-Boy Chair Company) is one of the largest furniture manufacturers in the U.S. The Company is comprised of two business groups: upholstery and casegoods. The upholstery segment includes recliners, sofas, occasional chairs, reclining sofas and office and health care seating. The casegoods segment includes dining room tables and chairs, bed frames and bed boards, dressers, coffee tables and end tables manufactured using hardwood or hardwood veneer, as well as hospitality and assisted-living furniture. Brand names include LA-Z-BOY, ENGLAND, SAM MOORE, BAUHAUS, CENTURION, PENNSYLVANIA HOUSE, CLAYTON MARCUS, KINCAID, HAMMARY, ALEXVALE, AMERICAN DREW, LA-Z-BOY CONTRACT FURNITURE, AMERICAN OF MARTINSVILLE, and LEA. As of 5/28/03, LZB operated 314 La-Z-Boy Furniture Galleries® and 317 in-store galleries.

ANNUAL FINANCIAL DATA

	p4/26/03	4/27/02	4/28/01	4/29/00	4/24/99	4/25/98	4/26/97
Earnings Per Share	① 1.67	③ 1.01	② 1.13	1.60	1.24	0.93	0.83
Cash Flow Per Share	2.21	1.73	1.88	2.15	1.66	1.32	1.21
Tang. Book Val. Per Share	...	8.15	7.40	6.70	7.03	6.33	5.97
Dividends Per Share	0.39	0.36	0.34	0.32	0.30	0.28	0.25
Dividend Payout %	23.4	35.6	30.1	20.0	24.2	30.1	30.4
INCOME STATEMENT (IN MILLIONS):							
Total Revenues	2,111.8	2,154.0	2,256.2	1,717.4	1,287.6	1,108.0	1,005.8
Costs & Expenses	...	2,013.3	2,089.7	1,542.8	1,158.7	1,009.8	911.5
Depreciation & Amort.	30.7	44.0	45.7	30.3	22.1	21.0	20.4
Operating Income	162.9	96.7	120.8	144.3	106.8	77.2	73.9
Net Interest Inc./(Exp.)	d10.5	d8.7	d16.2	d7.7	d2.3	d2.1	d2.6
Income Before Income Taxes	155.0	88.9	112.0	140.3	107.2	79.3	73.8
Income Taxes	58.9	27.2	43.7	52.7	41.1	29.4	28.5
Net Income	① 96.1	③ 61.8	② 68.3	87.6	66.1	49.9	45.3
Cash Flow	...	105.7	114.0	118.0	88.2	70.9	65.7
Average Shs. Outstg. (000)	57,435	61,125	60,692	54,860	53,148	53,821	54,324
BALANCE SHEET (IN MILLIONS):							
Cash & Cash Equivalents	28.8	26.8	23.6	14.4	33.6	28.7	25.4
Total Current Assets	679.5	671.7	708.8	692.4	425.6	383.0	342.8
Net Property	209.4	205.5	230.3	227.9	126.0	121.8	114.7
Total Assets	1,123.1	1,160.8	1,222.5	1,218.3	629.8	580.4	528.4
Total Current Liabilities	214.6	226.9	249.9	237.0	132.4	108.3	97.7
Long-Term Obligations	222.4	139.4	199.4	236.1	62.7	67.3	54.7
Net Stockholders' Equity	609.9	713.5	695.1	663.1	414.9	388.2	359.3
Net Working Capital	464.9	444.8	458.9	455.4	293.2	274.7	245.1
Year-end Shs. Outstg. (000)	...	59,953	60,501	61,328	52,340	53,551	53,724
STATISTICAL RECORD:							
Operating Profit Margin %	7.7	4.5	5.4	8.4	8.3	7.0	7.4
Net Profit Margin %	4.6	2.9	3.0	5.1	5.1	4.5	4.5
Return on Equity %	15.8	8.7	9.8	13.2	15.9	12.9	12.6
Return on Assets %	8.6	5.3	5.6	7.2	10.5	8.6	8.7
Debt/Total Assets %	7.5	12.0	16.3	19.4	10.0	11.6	10.5
Price Range	30.94-19.25	23.30-14.70	17.81-13.00	24.56-15.38	22.63-14.08	14.96-9.88	11.33-8.96
P/E Ratio	18.5-11.5	23.1-14.6	15.8-11.5	15.4-9.6	18.2-11.4	16.1-10.6	13.6-10.8
Average Yield %	1.2	1.9	2.2	1.6	1.6	2.3	2.5

Statistics are as originally reported. Adj. for stk split: 200%, 9/98. ① *Bef. acctg. change chrg. $59.8 mill., 4/26/03* ② *Incl. restruct. chrg. of $11.2 mill.* ③ *Incl. a loss of $11.7 mill. on divestiture.*

OFFICERS:
P. H. Norton, Chmn.
G. L. Kiser, Pres., C.E.O.
D. M. Risley, Sr. V.P., C.F.O.

INVESTOR CONTACT: Gene M. Hardy, Sec., Treas., (737) 241-4414

PRINCIPAL OFFICE: 1284 North Telegraph Road, Monroe, MI 48162

TELEPHONE NUMBER: (734) 241-4414
FAX: (734) 241-4422
WEB: www.la-z-boy.com

NO. OF EMPLOYEES: 17,850 (approx.)

SHAREHOLDERS: 33,000 (approx.)

ANNUAL MEETING: In Aug.

INCORPORATED: MI, May, 1941

INSTITUTIONAL HOLDINGS:
No. of Institutions: 154
Shares Held: 26,601,767
% Held: 47.5

INDUSTRY: Wood household furniture (SIC: 2511)

TRANSFER AGENT(S): American Stock Transfer & Trust Company, New York, NY

LANCASTER COLONY CORPORATION

YIELD 2.1%
P/E RATIO 12.2

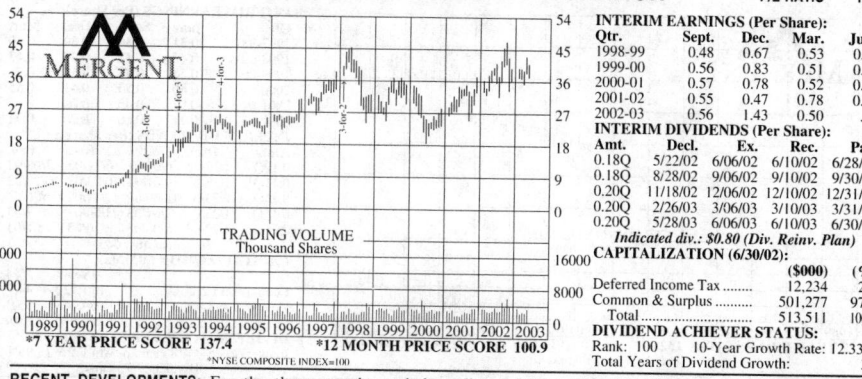

MERGENT

TRADING VOLUME
Thousand Shares

| 1989 | 1990 | 1991 | 1992 | 1993 | 1994 | 1995 | 1996 | 1997 | 1998 | 1999 | 2000 | 2001 | 2002 | 2003 |

*7 YEAR PRICE SCORE 137.4   ***12 MONTH PRICE SCORE 100.9**
*NYSE COMPOSITE INDEX=100

INTERIM EARNINGS (Per Share):

Qtr.	Sept.	Dec.	Mar.	June
1998-99	0.48	0.67	0.53	0.61
1999-00	0.56	0.83	0.51	0.61
2000-01	0.57	0.78	0.52	0.54
2001-02	0.55	0.47	0.78	0.69
2002-03	0.56	1.43	0.50	...

INTERIM DIVIDENDS (Per Share):

Amt.	Decl.	Ex.	Rec.	Pay.
0.18Q	5/22/02	6/06/02	6/10/02	6/28/02
0.18Q	8/28/02	9/06/02	9/10/02	9/30/02
0.20Q	11/18/02	12/06/02	12/10/02	12/31/02
0.20Q	2/26/03	3/06/03	3/10/03	3/31/03
0.20Q	5/28/03	6/06/03	6/10/03	6/30/03

Indicated div.: $0.80 (Div. Reinv. Plan)

CAPITALIZATION (6/30/02):

	($000)	(%)
Deferred Income Tax	12,234	2.4
Common & Surplus	501,277	97.6
Total	513,511	100.0

DIVIDEND ACHIEVER STATUS:
Rank: 100   10-Year Growth Rate: 12.33%
Total Years of Dividend Growth: 33

RECENT DEVELOPMENTS:

For the three months ended 3/31/03, net income totaled $18.0 million, down 37.4% compared with $28.8 million in the corresponding prior-year period. Earnings were hurt by unfavorable economic conditions, increased material costs, particularly soybean oil, and costs stemming from the introduction of new candle products. Results for 2003 included an $84,000 pre-tax restructuring and impairment gain, while results for 2002 included a one-time pre-tax gain of $15.6 million. Net sales slipped 4.2% to $259.5 million from $270.9 million a year earlier. Specialty foods net sales slid 1.7% to $141.0 million from $143.4 million the year before, while glassware and candles net sales fell 15.8% to $57.3 million from $68.0 million the previous year. Automotive net sales grew 3.0% to $61.3 million from $59.5 million the prior year. Gross profit totaled $53.6 million, or 20.6% of net sales, versus $57.5 million, or 21.2% of net sales, a year earlier. Operating income declined 7.8% to $29.0 million.

BUSINESS

LANCASTER COLONY CORPORATION operates in three business segments: Specialty Foods, Glassware and Candles, and Automotive. The Specialty Foods segment (51.3% of fiscal 2002 revenues) manufactures and sells salad dressings and sauces, frozen unbaked pies, frozen breads, refrigerated chip and produce dips, dairy snacks and desserts, premium dry egg noodles, frozen noodles, pastas and specialty items, croutons, and caviar. The Glassware and Candles segment (27.9%) produces a broad range of machine-pressed and machine-blown consumer glassware, technical glass products, and candles and other home fragrances of all sizes, forms and fragrance. The Automotive segment (20.8%) manufactures and sells rubber, vinyl and carpeted car mats, pickup truck bed mats, running boards, bed liners, tool boxes, and other accessories.

ANNUAL FINANCIAL DATA

	6/30/02	6/30/01	6/30/00	6/30/99	6/30/98	6/30/97	6/30/96
Earnings Per Share	2.49	① 2.40	2.51	2.28	2.22	2.01	1.71
Cash Flow Per Share	3.45	3.34	3.38	3.13	2.97	2.62	2.25
Tang. Book Val. Per Share	11.71	10.38	10.03	9.35	8.74	8.00	6.83
Dividends Per Share	0.74	0.69	0.65	0.61	0.57	0.51	0.46
Dividend Payout %	29.7	28.7	25.9	26.8	25.7	25.2	26.9
INCOME STATEMENT (IN MILLIONS)							
Total Revenues	1,129.7	1,098.5	1,104.3	1,045.7	1,008.8	922.8	855.9
Costs & Expenses	960.0	915.3	908.0	854.4	820.3	751.5	705.8
Depreciation & Amort.	35.3	35.5	34.3	35.6	32.6	27.0	24.4
Operating Income	134.4	147.7	161.9	155.7	155.9	144.4	125.7
Net Interest Inc./(Exp.)	d0.1	d1.2	d1.6	d2.7	d2.6	d2.6	d2.9
Income Before Income Taxes	149.3	145.9	160.2	153.5	155.4	142.5	123.2
Income Taxes	57.4	55.6	60.9	58.3	59.2	53.8	47.1
Net Income	91.9	① 90.2	99.3	95.1	96.1	88.7	76.1
Cash Flow	127.2	125.8	133.6	130.7	128.7	115.7	100.5
Average Shs. Outstg. (000)	36,910	37,636	39,554	41,799	43,364	44,108	44,624
BALANCE SHEET (IN MILLIONS)							
Cash & Cash Equivalents	83.4	4.9	2.7	18.9	23.2	32.1	4.7
Total Current Assets	366.1	317.6	315.9	328.4	311.5	308.8	273.3
Net Property	165.9	173.2	172.4	175.6	170.8	151.3	139.1
Total Assets	618.7	571.9	531.8	550.0	529.4	484.4	435.4
Total Current Liabilities	89.3	92.3	96.5	116.2	76.5	73.7	69.4
Long-Term Obligations	...	1.1	3.0	3.6	29.1	30.7	31.2
Net Stockholders' Equity	501.3	459.9	415.5	414.9	410.6	368.0	323.6
Net Working Capital	276.8	225.3	219.4	212.2	235.0	235.1	204.0
Year-end Shs. Outstg. (000)	36,598	37,253	37,962	40,548	42,753	43,526	44,345
STATISTICAL RECORD:							
Operating Profit Margin %	11.9	13.4	14.7	14.9	15.5	15.6	14.7
Net Profit Margin %	8.1	8.2	9.0	9.1	9.5	9.6	8.9
Return on Equity %	18.3	19.6	23.9	22.9	23.4	24.1	23.5
Return on Assets %	14.9	15.8	18.7	17.3	18.2	18.3	17.5
Debt/Total Assets %	...	0.2	0.6	0.6	5.5	6.3	7.2
Price Range	47.20-31.55	37.36-24.96	34.75-18.50	37.00-24.69	45.38-24.06	38.50-26.17	30.67-22.00
P/E Ratio	19.0-12.7	15.6-10.4	13.8-7.4	16.2-10.8	20.4-10.8	19.1-13.0	18.0-12.9
Average Yield %	1.9	2.2	2.4	2.0	1.6	1.6	1.7

Statistics are as originally reported. Adj. for stk. splits: 3-for-2, 1/27/98. ① Excl. accounting change chrg. $998,000.

OFFICERS:

J. B. Gerlach, Jr., Chmn., Pres., C.E.O.
J. L. Boylan, V.P., C.F.O., Treas., Asst. Sec.

INVESTOR CONTACT: Investor Relations, (614) 224-7141

PRINCIPAL OFFICE: 37 West Broad Street, Columbus, OH 43215

TELEPHONE NUMBER: (614) 224-7141
FAX: (614) 469-8219
WEB: www.lancastercolony.com
NO. OF EMPLOYEES: 5,900 (approx.)
SHAREHOLDERS: 11,700 (approx.)
ANNUAL MEETING: In Nov.
INCORPORATED: DE, 1961; reincorp., OH, Jan., 1992

INSTITUTIONAL HOLDINGS:
No. of Institutions: 166
Shares Held: 16,505,672
% Held: 45.8

INDUSTRY: Frozen specialties, nec (SIC: 2038)

TRANSFER AGENT(S): American Stock Transfer & Trust Company, New York, NY

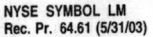

NYSE SYMBOL LM
Rec. Pr. 64.61 (5/31/03)

LEGG MASON, INC.

YIELD	0.7%
P/E RATIO	23.2

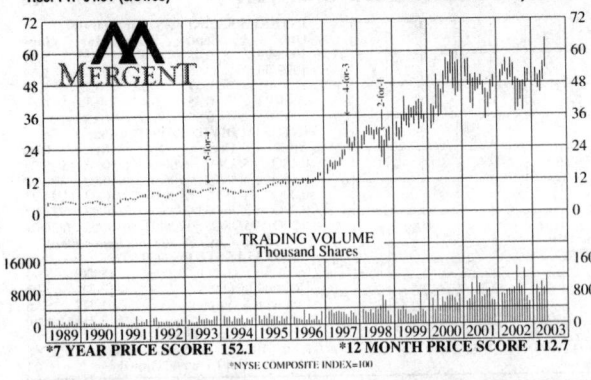

TRADING VOLUME
Thousand Shares

*7 YEAR PRICE SCORE 152.1   *12 MONTH PRICE SCORE 112.7

*NYSE COMPOSITE INDEX=100

INTERIM EARNINGS (Per Share):

Qtr.	June	Sept.	Dec.	Mar.
1997-98	0.31	0.36	0.39	0.40
1998-99	0.42	0.37	0.39	0.43
1999-00	0.54	0.47	0.55	0.78
2000-01	0.60	0.55	0.61	0.55
2001-02	0.52	0.55	0.60	0.67
2002-03	0.71	0.66	0.70	0.71

INTERIM DIVIDENDS (Per Share):

Amt.	Decl.	Ex.	Rec.	Pay.
0.10Q	4/23/02	6/07/02	6/11/02	7/08/02
0.11Q	7/23/02	10/01/02	10/03/02	10/21/02
0.11Q	10/23/02	12/09/02	12/11/02	1/06/03
0.11Q	1/23/03	3/04/03	3/06/03	4/07/03
0.11Q	4/22/03	6/06/03	6/10/03	7/07/03

Indicated div.: $0.44

CAPITALIZATION (3/31/02):

	($000)	(%)
Long-Term Debt	877,122	44.7
Common & Surplus	1,084,548	55.3
Total	1,961,670	100.0

DIVIDEND ACHIEVER STATUS:

Rank: 74   10-Year Growth Rate: 13.96%
Total Years of Dividend Growth: 19

RECENT DEVELOPMENTS: For the year ended 3/31/03, net income increased 24.8% to $190.9 million from $152.9 million the year before. Total revenues rose 2.3% to $1.62 billion from $1.58 billion in the prior year. Investment advisory and related fees improved 10.2% to $860.3 million from $780.6 million a year earlier. Principal transactions revenues grew 13.9% to $158.2 million, primarily due to increased fixed income transaction volume. Investment banking revenues increased 6.7% to $109.0 million.

PROSPECTS: Results continue to be driven by strong assets under management, which have increased by over $80.0 billion in the last three years, and totaled $192.20 billion as of 3/31/03. This increase reflected positive net client cash flows primarily from Western Asset, the Company's premier fixed income manager, and to a lesser degree, market appreciation. In addition, the Company should benefit from an increase in total client assets, which aggregated $250.30 billion at 3/31/03.

BUSINESS

LEGG MASON, INC. provides securities brokerage, investment advisory, corporate and public finance, and mortgage banking services to individuals, institutions, corporations and municipalities. As an investment advisor, the Company managed approximately $192.20 billion in assets as of 3/31/03. LM's mortgage-banking subsidiaries have direct and master servicing responsibility for commercial mortgages. For the fiscal year ended 3/31/03, revenues were derived as follows: investment advisory and related fees, 56.3%; commissions, 20.7%; principal transactions, 10.4%; investment banking, 7.1%; interest, 7.1%; and other, 4.1%. On 12/31/86, LM acquired Western Asset Management Co. On 5/26/00, LM acquired Perigee, Inc. During 2001, LM acquired Private Capital Management and Royce & Associates.

ANNUAL FINANCIAL DATA

	p3/31/03	3/31/02	3/31/01	3/31/00	3/31/99	3/31/98	3/31/97
Earnings Per Share	2.78	2.24	2.30	2.33	1.55	1.32	1.17
Cash Flow Per Share	...	3.05	2.84	2.83	1.92	1.69	1.53
Tang. Book Val. Per Share	...	2.28	12.38	10.60	8.83	7.97	7.33
Dividends Per Share	0.41	0.37	0.33	0.28	0.23	0.20	0.18
Dividend Payout %	14.7	16.5	14.3	11.8	14.8	15.3	15.7
INCOME STATEMENT (IN MILLIONS):							
Total Revenues	1,615.4	1,578.6	1,536.3	1,370.8	1,046.0	889.1	639.7
Costs & Expenses	...	1,135.5	1,105.8	991.7	682.2	594.4	425.1
Depreciation & Amort.	...	55.1	36.5	29.3	21.6	22.0	17.2
Operating Income	...	388.0	393.9	349.7	342.2	272.7	197.3
Net Interest Inc./(Exp.)	...	d127.3	d175.4	d134.3	d94.9	d73.7	d43.4
Income Before Income Taxes	308.3	253.2	265.8	239.1	148.8	128.4	95.2
Income Taxes	117.4	100.3	109.6	96.6	59.4	52.3	38.6
Net Income	190.9	152.9	156.2	142.5	89.3	76.1	56.6
Cash Flow	...	208.0	192.7	171.8	110.9	98.1	73.8
Average Shs. Outstg. (000)	68,760	68,262	67,916	60,787	57,657	58,006	48,157
BALANCE SHEET (IN MILLIONS):							
Cash & Cash Equivalents	...	3,095.0	2,627.5	2,058.1	1,740.6	1,334.3	793.1
Total Current Assets	...	4,458.4	4,087.8	3,813.4	2,805.9	2,129.2	1,399.4
Net Property	...	69.1	71.6	60.5	55.8	52.0	35.8
Total Assets	...	5,939.6	4,687.6	4,785.1	3,473.7	2,832.3	1,879.0
Total Current Liabilities	...	3,808.0	3,397.9	3,532.6	2,718.4	2,147.2	1,303.4
Long-Term Obligations	...	877.1	219.0	339.0	99.7	99.6	99.6
Net Stockholders' Equity	...	1,084.5	927.7	751.9	554.2	500.1	418.6
Net Working Capital	...	650.4	690.0	280.8	87.5	d18.1	96.0
Year-end Shs. Outstg. (000)	...	64,444	62,850	58,599	56,376	55,050	48,723
STATISTICAL RECORD:							
Operating Profit Margin %	...	24.6	25.6	25.5	32.7	30.7	30.8
Net Profit Margin %	...	9.7	10.2	10.4	8.5	8.6	8.8
Return on Equity %	...	14.1	16.8	19.0	16.1	15.2	13.5
Return on Assets %	...	2.6	3.3	3.0	2.6	2.7	3.0
Debt/Total Assets %	...	14.8	4.7	7.1	2.9	3.5	5.3
Price Range	57.15-37.11	56.99-34.25	60.25-30.69	42.88-26.44	32.28-17.31	33.97-14.16	14.77-9.94
P/E Ratio	20.6-13.3	25.4-15.3	26.2-13.3	18.4-11.3	20.8-11.2	25.8-10.8	12.6-8.5
Average Yield %	0.9	0.8	0.7	0.8	0.9	0.8	1.5

Statistics are as originally reported. Adj. for 2-for-1 split, 9/98; 4-for-3 split, 9/97.

OFFICERS:
R. A. Mason, Chmn., Pres., C.E.O.
C. J. Daley Jr., Sr. V.P., C.F.O., Treas.
R. F. Price, Sr. V.P., Sec., Gen. Couns.

INVESTOR CONTACT: F. Barry Bilson, Investor Relations, (410) 539-0000

PRINCIPAL OFFICE: 100 Light Street, Baltimore, MD 21202

TELEPHONE NUMBER: (410) 539-0000
FAX: (410) 539-8010
WEB: www.leggmason.com
NO. OF EMPLOYEES: 5,290 (approx.)
SHAREHOLDERS: 2,008
ANNUAL MEETING: In July
INCORPORATED: MD, 1981

INSTITUTIONAL HOLDINGS:
No. of Institutions: 228
Shares Held: 45,600,058
% Held: 70.2

INDUSTRY: Security brokers and dealers (SIC: 6211)

TRANSFER AGENT(S): Wachovia Bank, Charlotte, NC

LEGGETT & PLATT, INCORPORATED

	YIELD	2.4%
	P/E RATIO	19.4

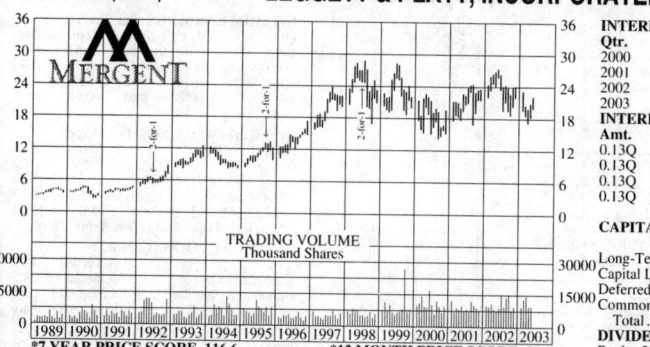

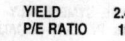

INTERIM EARNINGS (Per Share):

Qtr.	Mar.	June	Sept.	Dec.
2000	0.37	0.38	0.34	0.23
2001	0.23	0.25	0.28	0.18
2002	0.28	0.35	0.29	0.25
2003	0.25	...	...	...

INTERIM DIVIDENDS (Per Share):

Amt.	Decl.	Ex.	Rec.	Pay.
0.13Q	8/14/02	9/11/02	9/13/02	10/15/02
0.13Q	11/13/02	12/11/02	12/13/02	1/15/03
0.13Q	2/12/03	3/12/03	3/14/03	4/15/03
0.13Q	5/14/03	6/11/03	6/13/03	7/15/03

Indicated div.: $0.52

CAPITALIZATION (12/31/02):

	($000)	(%)
Long-Term Debt	768,900	26.8
Capital Lease Obligations..	39,700	1.4
Deferred Income Tax	79,400	2.8
Common & Surplus	1,976,900	69.0
Total	2,864,900	100.0

DIVIDEND ACHIEVER STATUS:
Rank: 55   10-Year Growth Rate: 15.85%
Total Years of Dividend Growth: 33

7 YEAR PRICE SCORE 116.6   **12 MONTH PRICE SCORE 93.5**
NYSE COMPOSITE INDEX=100

RECENT DEVELOPMENTS: For the quarter ended 3/31/03, net income declined 12.1% to $49.4 million compared with $56.2 million in the equivalent 2002 quarter, reflecting higher energy costs. Net sales advanced 1.5% to $1.04 billion. Sales for the Commercial Fixturing and Components segment grew 0.6% to $201.8 million, while sales for the Industrialized Materials segment climbed 5.9% to $91.1 million.

PROSPECTS: The Company expects second quarter 2003 sales in the range of $1.05 billion and $1.10 billion, with earnings per share in the range of $0.27 to $0.32. Based on weak market demand and its overall effect on the Company's revenues, LEG has narrowed its 2003 sales growth projection, excluding acquisitions, to between unchanged and 4.0%. This range yields earnings guidance of $1.15 to $1.30 per share for the full year.

BUSINESS

LEGGETT & PLATT, INCORPO-RATED is primarily engaged in the manufacture and distribution of metal stamping, forming, casting, machining, coating, welding, wire drawing, and assembly. The Company is an independent manufacturer of components for residential furniture and bedding; retail store fixtures and point of purchase displays; components for office furniture; non-automotive aluminum die castings; drawn steel wire; automotive seat support and lumbar systems; and bedding industry machinery for wire forming, sewing and quilting. Primary raw materials include steel and aluminum, followed by smaller amounts of chemicals, wood, and plastics. LEG's international division is involved primarily in the sale of machinery and equipment designed to manufacture LEG's MIRA-COIL innersprings. As of 4/16/03, LEG was composed of 29 business units and more than 300 facilities located in 18 countries. LEG operates through five segments: Residential Furnishings (50.4% of 2002 sales); Commercial Fixturing & Components (20.9%); Aluminum Products (11.1%); Industrial Materials (9.3%) and Specialized Products (8.3%).

ANNUAL FINANCIAL DATA

	12/31/02	12/31/01	12/31/00	12/31/99	12/31/98	12/31/97	12/31/96
Earnings Per Share	③ 1.17	③ 0.94	② 1.32	1.45	1.24	1.08	① 0.84
Cash Flow Per Share	1.99	1.92	2.18	2.19	1.87	1.62	1.34
Tang. Book Val. Per Share	5.36	4.81	4.58	4.50	4.59	3.88	3.37
Dividends Per Share	0.49	0.47	0.40	0.35	0.30	0.26	0.22
Dividend Payout %	41.9	50.0	30.3	24.1	24.6	24.1	26.3
INCOME STATEMENT (IN MILLIONS):							
Total Revenues	4,271.8	4,113.8	4,276.3	3,779.0	3,370.4	2,909.2	2,466.2
Costs & Expenses	3,689.9	3,555.4	3,616.4	3,129.4	2,815.6	2,441.9	2,070.4
Depreciation & Amort.	164.6	196.6	173.3	149.3	127.9	105.6	92.2
Operating Income	417.3	361.8	486.6	500.3	426.9	361.7	303.6
Net Interest Inc./(Exp.)	d37.1	d53.9	d62.2	d39.9	d33.5	d31.8	d30.0
Income Before Income Taxes	363.5	297.3	418.6	462.6	395.6	333.3	249.7
Income Taxes	130.4	109.7	154.5	172.1	147.6	125.0	96.7
Net Income	③ 233.1	③ 187.6	② 264.1	290.5	248.0	208.3	① 153.0
Cash Flow	397.7	384.2	437.4	439.8	375.9	313.9	245.2
Average Shs. Outstg. (000)	199,795	200,435	200,388	200,938	200,670	193,190	183,600
BALANCE SHEET (IN MILLIONS):							
Cash & Cash Equivalents	225.0	187.2	37.3	20.6	83.5	7.7	3.7
Total Current Assets	1,488.0	1,421.9	1,405.3	1,256.2	1,137.1	944.6	763.3
Net Property	960.7	961.9	1,018.4	915.0	820.4	693.2	582.9
Total Assets	3,501.1	3,412.9	3,373.2	2,977.5	2,535.3	2,106.3	1,712.9
Total Current Liabilities	598.0	457.0	476.6	431.5	401.4	372.5	292.8
Long-Term Obligations	808.6	977.6	988.4	787.4	574.1	466.2	388.5
Net Stockholders' Equity	1,976.9	1,866.6	1,793.8	1,646.2	1,436.8	1,174.0	941.1
Net Working Capital	890.0	964.9	928.7	824.7	735.7	572.1	470.5
Year-end Shs. Outstg. (000)	194,499	196,298	196,097	196,880	197,684	192,754	184,216
STATISTICAL RECORD:							
Operating Profit Margin %	9.8	8.8	11.4	13.2	12.7	12.4	12.3
Net Profit Margin %	5.5	4.6	6.2	7.7	7.4	7.2	6.2
Return on Equity %	11.8	10.1	14.7	17.6	17.3	17.7	16.3
Return on Assets %	6.7	5.5	7.8	9.8	9.8	9.9	8.9
Debt/Total Assets %	23.1	28.6	29.3	26.4	22.6	22.1	22.7
Price Range	27.40-18.60	24.45-16.85	22.56-14.19	28.31-18.63	28.75-16.88	23.88-15.75	17.38-10.31
P/E Ratio	23.4-15.9	26.0-17.9	17.1-10.7	19.5-12.8	23.2-13.6	22.1-14.6	20.8-12.3
Average Yield %	2.1	2.3	2.2	1.5	1.3	1.3	1.6

Statistics are as originally reported. Adj. for stk. split: 2-for-1, 6/98. ① Bef. extraord. chrg. $12.5 mill. ② Incl. pre-tax chrg. of $6.2 mill. for plant closures. ③ Incl. nonrecurr. chrg. of 2002, $15.0 mill.; 2001, $18.0 mill.

OFFICERS:
F. E. Wright, Chmn., C.E.O.
D. S. Haffner, Pres., C.O.O.
E. C. Jett, V.P., Sec., Gen. Couns.

INVESTOR CONTACT: David M. DeSonier, V.P., (417) 358-8131

PRINCIPAL OFFICE: No. 1 Leggett Road, Carthage, MO 64836

TELEPHONE NUMBER: (417) 358-8131
FAX: (417) 358-8449
WEB: www.leggett.com

NO. OF EMPLOYEES: 31,000 (approx.)

SHAREHOLDERS: 15,954

ANNUAL MEETING: In May

INCORPORATED: MO, 1901

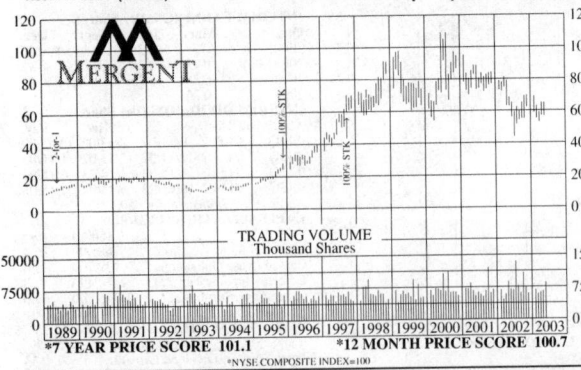

NYSE SYMBOL LLY
Rec. Pr. 59.77 (5/31/03)

LILLY (ELI) & COMPANY

YIELD 2.2%
P/E RATIO 26.0

INTERIM EARNINGS (Per Share):

Qtr.	Mar.	June	Sept.	Dec.
1999	0.40	0.52	0.67	0.73
2000	0.77	0.61	0.71	0.70
2001	0.74	0.76	0.54	0.54
2002	0.58	0.61	0.63	0.68
2003	0.38	...	...	...

INTERIM DIVIDENDS (Per Share):

Amt.	Decl.	Ex.	Rec.	Pay.
0.31Q	6/24/02	8/13/02	8/15/02	9/10/02
0.31Q	10/21/02	11/13/02	11/15/02	12/10/02
0.335Q	12/16/02	2/12/03	2/14/03	3/10/03
0.335Q	4/28/03	5/13/03	5/15/03	6/10/03

Indicated div.: $1.34 (Div. Reinv. Plan)

CAPITALIZATION (12/31/02):

	($000)	(%)
Long-Term Debt	4,358,200	34.5
Common & Surplus	8,273,600	65.5
Total	12,631,800	100.0

TRADING VOLUME
Thousand Shares

*7 YEAR PRICE SCORE 101.1   *12 MONTH PRICE SCORE 100.7
*NYSE COMPOSITE INDEX=100

DIVIDEND ACHIEVER STATUS:
Rank: 174   10-Year Growth Rate: 8.47%
Total Years of Dividend Growth: 35

RECENT DEVELOPMENTS: For the three months ended 3/31/03, net income decreased 35.3% to $407.0 million compared with $629.2 million in the corresponding quarter of the previous year. Results for 2003 included pre-tax asset impairment and other site charges of $353.9 million. Net sales increased 12.8% to $2.89 billion from $2.56 billion in the year-earlier period. Operating income declined 37.4% to $470.1 million.

PROSPECTS: Lilly ICOS LLC, a joint venture between ICOS Corporation and LLY, continues to anticipate U.S. approval for Cialis later in the second half of fiscal 2003. Cialis is an inhibitor developed for the treatment of erectile dysfunction. Meanwhile, during the quarter, Cialis was launched in Europe as well as Australia and New Zealand. Going forward, the Company expects earnings per share for full-year 2003 to be in the range of $2.50 to $2.60.

BUSINESS

LILLY (ELI) & COMPANY, discovers, develops, manufactures and markets pharmaceuticals and animal health products. Neuroscience products, (42.1% of 2002 sales), include PROZAC®, ZYPREXA®, DARVON®, PERMAX® and SARAFEM™. Endocrine products, (31.1%), include HUM-ULIN®, HUMALOG®, ILETIN®, ACTOS®, EVISTA® and HUMATROPE®. Anti-infective products, (5.2%), include CECLOR®, KEFLEX®, KEFTAB®, LORABID®, DYNABAC®, NEBCIN®, TAZIDIME®, KEFUROX®, KEFZOL® and VANCOCIN®. Animal Health products, (6.3%), include TYLAN®, RUMENSIN®, COBAN®, MONTEBAN®, MAX-IBAN®, APRALAN®, MICOTIL®, PULMOTIL® and PAYLEAN®. Cardiovascular products, (5.6%), consist primarily of REOPRO® and DOBUTREX®. Oncology products, (8.1%), include GEMZAR®, ONCOVIN®, VELBAN® and ELDISINE®, and other pharmaceutical products, (1.6%).

ANNUAL FINANCIAL DATA

	12/31/02	12/31/01	12/31/00	12/31/99	12/31/98	12/31/97	12/31/96
Earnings Per Share	⑥ 2.50	⑤ 2.58	④ 2.79	③ 2.30	② 1.87	① d0.35	1.39
Cash Flow Per Share	2.95	2.99	3.18	2.70	2.31	0.11	1.89
Tang. Book Val. Per Share	7.37	6.32	5.37	4.49	2.86	2.79	1.87
Dividends Per Share	1.24	1.12	1.04	0.92	0.80	0.74	0.69
Dividend Payout %	49.6	43.4	37.3	40.0	42.8	...	49.3
INCOME STATEMENT (IN MILLIONS):							
Total Revenues	11,077.5	11,542.5	10,862.2	10,002.9	9,236.8	8,517.6	7,346.6
Costs & Expenses	7,340.8	7,548.3	6,866.7	6,199.5	6,049.4	5,549.5	4,756.3
Depreciation & Amort.	493.0	454.9	435.8	439.7	490.4	509.8	543.5
Operating Income	3,243.7	3,539.3	3,559.7	3,363.7	2,697.0	2,458.3	2,046.8
Net Interest Inc./(Exp.)	d79.7	d146.5	d182.3	d183.8	d181.3	d234.1	d288.8
Income Before Income Taxes	3,457.7	3,552.1	3,858.7	3,245.4	2,665.0	510.2	2,031.3
Income Taxes	749.8	742.7	800.9	698.7	568.7	895.3	507.8
Net Income	⑥ 2,707.9	⑤ 2,809.4	④ 3,057.8	③ 2,546.7	② 2,096.3	① d385.1	1,523.5
Cash Flow	3,200.9	3,264.3	3,493.6	2,986.4	2,586.7	124.7	2,067.0
Average Shs. Outstg. (000)	1,085,088	1,090,793	1,097,725	1,106,055	1,121,486	1,101,099	1,093,654
BALANCE SHEET (IN MILLIONS):							
Cash & Cash Equivalents	3,654.7	3,731.0	4,618.2	3,836.0	1,597.1	2,024.6	955.1
Total Current Assets	7,804.1	6,938.9	7,943.0	7,055.5	5,406.8	5,320.7	3,891.3
Net Property	5,293.0	4,532.4	4,176.6	3,981.5	4,096.3	4,101.7	4,307.0
Total Assets	19,042.0	16,434.1	14,690.8	12,825.2	12,595.5	12,577.4	14,307.2
Total Current Liabilities	5,063.5	5,203.0	4,960.7	3,935.4	4,607.2	4,191.6	4,222.2
Long-Term Obligations	4,358.2	3,132.1	2,633.7	2,811.9	2,185.5	2,326.1	2,516.5
Net Stockholders' Equity	8,273.6	7,104.0	6,046.9	5,013.0	4,429.6	4,645.6	6,100.1
Net Working Capital	2,740.6	1,735.9	2,982.3	3,120.1	799.6	1,129.1	d330.9
Year-end Shs. Outstg. (000)	1,122,443	1,123,349	1,125,560	1,090,238	1,019,090	1,110,522	1,105,646
STATISTICAL RECORD:							
Operating Profit Margin %	29.3	30.7	32.8	33.6	29.2	28.9	27.9
Net Profit Margin %	24.4	24.3	28.2	25.5	22.7	...	20.7
Return on Equity %	32.7	39.5	50.6	50.8	47.3	...	25.0
Return on Assets %	14.2	17.1	20.8	19.9	16.6	...	10.6
Debt/Total Assets %	22.9	19.1	17.9	21.9	17.4	18.5	17.6
Price Range	81.09-43.75	95.00-70.01	109.00-54.00	97.75-60.56	91.31-57.69	70.31-35.56	40.19-24.69
P/E Ratio	32.4-17.5	36.8-27.1	39.1-19.4	42.5-26.3	48.8-30.8	...	28.9-17.8
Average Yield %	2.0	1.4	1.3	1.2	1.1	1.4	2.1

Statistics are as originally reported. Adj. for 2-for-1 stock split, 10/97. ① Incl. a net gain of $631.8 mill. & non-cash chg. of approx. $2.40 bill. ② Excl. net gain of $1.6 mill. fr. disc. opers.; incl. a pre-tax chg. of $127.5 mill. ③ Incl. net gain of $30.4 mill.; excl. a net gain of $174.3 mill. fr. disc. opers. ④ Incl. net one-time gain of $214.4 mill. fr. the sale of Kinetra. ⑤ Bef extraord. chrg. of $29.4 mill., incl. charges of $311.9 mill. ⑥ Incl. pre-tax acq. in-proc. R&D chrg. of $84.0 mill.

OFFICERS:
S. Taurel, Chmn., Pres., C.E.O.
C. E. Golden, Exec. V.P., C.F.O.
R. O. Kendall, Sr. V.P., Gen. Couns.

INVESTOR CONTACT: Terra L. Fox, Investor Relations, (317) 276-5795

PRINCIPAL OFFICE: Lilly Corporate Center, Indianapolis, IN 46285

TELEPHONE NUMBER: (317) 276-2000
FAX: (317) 276-6331
WEB: www.lilly.com
NO. OF EMPLOYEES: 43,700 (approx.)
SHAREHOLDERS: 56,200
ANNUAL MEETING: In Apr.
INCORPORATED: IN, Jan., 1901; reincorp., IN, Jan., 1936

INSTITUTIONAL HOLDINGS:
No. of Institutions: 810
Shares Held: 757,348,563
% Held: 67.4

INDUSTRY: Pharmaceutical preparations (SIC: 2834)

TRANSFER AGENT(S): Wells Fargo Shareowner Services, South St. Paul, MN

LINCOLN NATIONAL CORPORATION

YIELD 3.9%
P/E RATIO 165.7

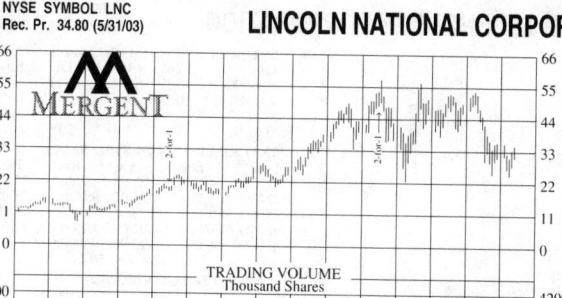
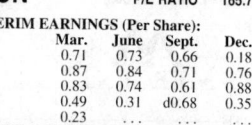

*7 YEAR PRICE SCORE 95.7   *12 MONTH PRICE SCORE 94.6
*NYSE COMPOSITE INDEX=100

INTERIM EARNINGS (Per Share):

Qtr.	Mar.	June	Sept.	Dec.
1999	0.71	0.73	0.66	0.18
2000	0.87	0.84	0.71	0.76
2001	0.83	0.74	0.61	0.88
2002	0.49	0.31	d0.04	0.35
2003	0.23	...	...	...

INTERIM DIVIDENDS (Per Share):

Amt.	Decl.	Ex.	Rec.	Pay.
0.32Q	8/08/02	10/08/02	10/10/02	11/01/02
0.335Q	11/14/02	1/08/03	1/10/03	2/01/03
0.335Q	3/13/03	4/07/03	4/09/03	5/01/03
0.335Q	5/09/03	7/08/03	7/10/03	8/01/03

Indicated div.: $1.34 (Div. Reinv. Plan)

CAPITALIZATION (12/31/02):

	($000)	(%)
Long-Term Debt	1,119,200	16.4
Redeemable Pfd. Stock	392,658	5.8
Preferred Stock	666	0.0
Common & Surplus	5,295,601	77.8
Total	6,808,125	100.0

DIVIDEND ACHIEVER STATUS:
Rank: 218   10-Year Growth Rate: 5.78%
Total Years of Dividend Growth: 19

RECENT DEVELOPMENTS: For the quarter ended 3/31/03, net income fell 51.4% to $41.6 million from $85.6 million in the equivalent prior-year quarter. Results for 2003 included restructuring charges of $3.6 million. Total revenue slid 2.4% to $1.10 billion from $1.13 billion the year before. Revenue for 2003 and 2002 included realized investment losses of $89.6 million and $103.5 million, and losses on derivatives of $1.9 million and $100,000, respectively. Comparisons were made with restated prior-year figures.

PROSPECTS: On 6/6/03, the Company announced that it will combine its life and annuity businesses into a single operating unit focused on providing wealth accumulation and protection, income distribution and wealth transfer products. The realignment is expected to significantly reduce operating expenses while positioning the Company to take advantage of the continuing market recovery. LNC also noted that it is exploring ways to capitalize on the combined strength of its currently separate employer-sponsored businesses.

BUSINESS

LINCOLN NATIONAL CORPORATION operates multiple insurance and investment management businesses, divided into four business segments. The Lincoln Retirement segment (38.6% of 2002 revenues) provides fixed and variable annuities products to the individual annuities and employer-sponsored markets. The Life Insurance segment (38.5%) provides life insurance products designed specifically for the high net-worth and affluent markets. The Investment Management segment (8.6%) provides investment products and services to both individual and institutional investors. The Lincoln UK segment (6.0%) provides life insurance products in the United Kingdom. Corporate and other operations accounted for 8.3% of 2002 revenues. In January 1998, the Company acquired the individual life insurance and annuities business of CIGNA Corporation for $1.40 billion. On 12/7/01, the Company sold Lincoln Re for $2.00 billion.

ANNUAL FINANCIAL DATA

	12/31/02	12/31/01	12/31/00	12/31/99	12/31/98	12/31/97	12/31/96
Earnings Per Share	⑤ 0.49	①②④ 3.05	① 3.19	① 2.30	2.51	③ 0.11	2.46
Tang. Book Val. Per Share	15.62	14.11	11.06	5.59	10.16	19.38	15.97
Dividends Per Share	1.28	1.22	1.16	1.10	1.04	0.98	0.92
Dividend Payout %	261.2	40.0	36.4	47.8	41.4	932.4	37.5
INCOME STATEMENT (IN MILLIONS):							
Total Premium Income	315.9	1,704.0	1,813.1	1,881.5	1,620.6	1,328.7	3,182.0
Other Income	4,319.5	4,676.6	5,038.4	4,922.2	4,466.4	3,569.7	3,539.3
Total Revenues	4,635.5	6,380.6	6,851.5	6,803.7	6,087.1	4,898.5	6,721.3
Policyholder Benefits	2,859.5	3,409.7	3,557.2	3,805.0	3,328.9	3,191.7	3,921.3
Income Before Income Taxes	1.6	764.1	836.3	570.0	697.4	34.9	712.3
Income Taxes	cr90.0	158.4	214.9	109.6	187.6	12.7	179.2
Equity Earnings/Minority Int.	...	...	...	...	...	...	d19.6
Net Income	⑤ 91.6	①②④ 605.8	① 621.4	① 460.4	509.8	③ 22.2	513.6
Average Shs. Outstg. (000)	185,596	193,303	194,921	200,418	203,262	207,992	209,122
BALANCE SHEET (IN MILLIONS):							
Cash & Cash Equivalents	1,690.5	3,095.5	1,927.4	1,895.9	2,433.4	3,794.7	1,231.7
Premiums Due	7,759.5	6,445.6	4,252.0	4,559.0	3,577.4	2,548.3	3,195.0
Invst. Assets: Fixed-term	32,767.5	28,345.7	27,449.8	27,688.6	30,232.9	24,066.4	27,906.4
Invst. Assets: Equities	337.2	470.5	549.7	604.0	542.8	660.4	992.7
Invst. Assets: Loans	6,151.1	6,475.2	6,623.9	6,627.8	6,233.1	4,051.3	4,031.1
Invst. Assets: Total	39,999.9	36,121.2	35,375.0	35,604.2	37,948.3	29,839.8	34,066.2
Total Assets	93,133.3	98,001.3	99,844.1	103,095.7	93,836.3	77,174.7	71,713.4
Long-Term Obligations	1,119.2	861.8	712.2	712.0	712.2	511.0	626.3
Net Stockholders' Equity	5,296.3	5,263.5	4,954.1	4,263.9	5,387.9	4,982.9	4,470.0
Year-end Shs. Outstg. (000)	177,308	186,944	190,748	195,495	202,112	201,718	207,318
STATISTICAL RECORD:							
Return on Revenues %	2.0	9.5	9.1	6.8	8.4	0.5	7.6
Return on Equity %	1.7	11.5	12.5	10.8	9.5	0.4	11.5
Return on Assets %	0.1	0.6	0.6	0.4	0.5	...	0.7
Price Range	53.65-25.11	52.75-38.00	56.38-22.63	57.50-36.00	49.44-33.50	38.56-24.50	28.50-20.38
P/E Ratio	109.5-51.2	17.3-12.5	17.7-7.1	25.0-15.7	19.7-13.3	366.9-233.1	11.6-8.3
Average Yield %	3.3	2.7	2.9	2.4	2.5	3.1	3.8

Statistics are as originally reported. Adj. for stk. split: 2-for-1, 6/99. ① Incl. non-recur. chrg. $24.6 mill., 12/01; $80.2 mill., 12/00; $18.9 mill., 12/99. ② Bef. acctg. change chrg. $15.6 mill. ③ Bef. disc. oper. gain $911.8 mill. ④ Incl. gain fr. sale of subsidiaries of $12.8 mill. ⑤ Incl. net non-recurr. chrg. of $24.5 mill, chrgs of $208.5 mill rel. to sale of reinsurance unit and restruct. chrgs. of $2.1 mill.

OFFICERS:
J. A. Boscia, Chmn., C.E.O.
R. C. Vaughan, Exec. V.P., C.F.O., Treas.
INVESTOR CONTACT: Priscilla Brown, V.P., Investor Relations, (215) 448-1422
PRINCIPAL OFFICE: 1500 Market Street, 39th Floor, Philadelphia, PA 19102-2112

TELEPHONE NUMBER: (215) 448-1400
FAX: (215) 448-6916
WEB: www.lfg.com
NO. OF EMPLOYEES: 5,830 (avg.)
SHAREHOLDERS: 10,381
ANNUAL MEETING: In May
INCORPORATED: IN, Jan., 1968

INSTITUTIONAL HOLDINGS:
No. of Institutions: 363
Shares Held: 125,062,375
% Held: 70.7
INDUSTRY: Life insurance (SIC: 6311)
TRANSFER AGENT(S): First Chicago Trust Company of New York, Jersey City, NJ

NASDAQ SYMBOL LLTC
Rec. Pr. 36.43 (5/31/03)

LINEAR TECHNOLOGY CORPORATION

YIELD 0.7%
P/E RATIO 51.3

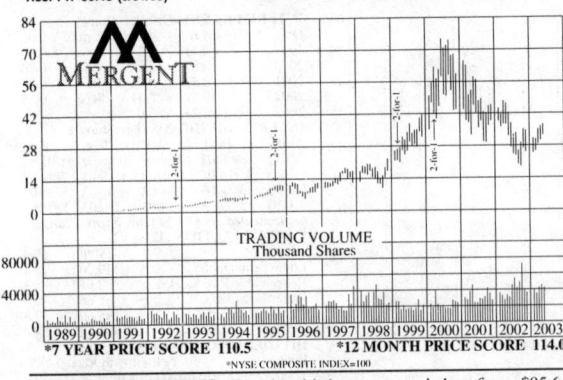

TRADING VOLUME
Thousand Shares

*7 YEAR PRICE SCORE 110.5   *12 MONTH PRICE SCORE 114.0
*NYSE COMPOSITE INDEX=100

MERGENT

INTERIM EARNINGS (Per Share):

Qtr.	Sept.	Dec.	Mar.	June
1999-00	0.18	0.20	0.23	0.27
2000-01	0.31	0.34	0.38	0.26
2001-02	0.14	0.14	0.16	0.17
2002-03	0.17	0.18	0.19	...

INTERIM DIVIDENDS (Per Share):

Amt.	Decl.	Ex.	Rec.	Pay.
0.05Q	4/16/02	4/24/02	4/26/02	5/15/02
0.05Q	7/23/02	7/31/02	8/02/02	8/21/02
0.05Q	10/15/02	10/23/02	10/25/02	11/13/02
0.05Q	1/14/03	1/22/03	1/24/03	2/12/03
0.06Q	4/15/03	4/23/03	4/25/03	5/14/03

Indicated div.: $0.24

CAPITALIZATION (6/30/02):

	($000)	(%)
Deferred Income Tax	37,982	2.1
Common & Surplus	1,781,454	97.9
Total	1,819,436	100.0

DIVIDEND ACHIEVER STATUS:
Rank: 2   10-Year Growth Rate: 40.70%
Total Years of Dividend Growth: 10

RECENT DEVELOPMENTS: For the third quarter ended 3/30/03, net income advanced 17.8% to $60.6 million compared with $51.5 million in the corresponding prior-year quarter. Net sales climbed 18.1% to $153.8 million from $130.2 million a year earlier. The increase in net sales was due to higher unit shipments, partially offset by a decrease in the average selling price, which resulted from a continuing change in mix to smaller package products slight price reductions. Gross profit increased 19.6% to $114.4 million

from $95.6 million the year before. Operating income jumped 26.5% to $75.8 million from $59.9 million in the 2002 quarter. Meanwhile, by focusing on unique, high-performance analog intensive markets the Company was able to produce a 39.4% return on sales during the quarter, despite an uncertain economic and geopolitical times. Looking ahead, LLTC estimates that fourth quarter sales and profits will grow about 5.0% to 8.0% sequentially.

BUSINESS

LINEAR TECHNOLOGY CORPORATION designs, manufactures and markets a broad line of standard high-performance linear integrated circuits. LLTC's products include operational, instrumentation and audio amplifiers, voltage regulators, power management devices, direct current to direct current converters and voltage references, comparators, monolithic filters, communications interface circuits, one-chip data acquisition sub-systems, pulse-width modulators and sample-and-hold devices, and high frequency devices. Applications for the Company's products include wireless and broadband telecommunications infrastructure, cellular telephones, networking products and satellite systems, notebook and desktop computers, computer peripherals, video/multimedia, industrial and medical instrumentation, automotive electronics, factory automation, process control, military and space systems, and high-end consumer products such as digital cameras, MP3 players and other electronic products.

ANNUAL FINANCIAL DATA

	6/30/02	7/1/01	7/2/00	6/27/99	6/28/98	6/29/97	6/30/96
Earnings Per Share	0.60	1.29	0.88	0.61	0.58	0.43	0.43
Cash Flow Per Share	0.74	1.39	0.95	0.68	0.63	0.47	0.46
Tang. Book Val. Per Share	5.63	5.59	4.20	2.95	2.46	1.94	1.47
Dividends Per Share	0.19	0.15	0.11	0.08	0.07	0.06	0.04
Dividend Payout %	31.7	11.6	12.5	12.7	11.2	12.8	10.5
INCOME STATEMENT (IN MILLIONS):							
Total Revenues	512.3	972.6	705.9	506.7	484.8	379.3	377.8
Costs & Expenses	240.9	390.6	306.6	226.8	217.1	178.4	176.8
Depreciation & Amort.	46.3	35.8	25.0	22.0	20.1	12.4	10.3
Operating Income	225.1	546.3	374.4	257.9	247.5	188.4	190.8
Net Interest Inc./(Exp.)	53.3	64.4	42.9	27.8	23.7	16.1	13.1
Income Before Income Taxes	278.4	610.7	417.3	285.7	271.3	204.5	203.9
Income Taxes	80.7	183.2	129.3	91.4	90.4	70.2	69.9
Net Income	197.6	427.5	287.9	194.3	180.9	134.4	134.0
Cash Flow	243.9	463.2	312.9	216.3	201.0	146.8	144.2
Average Shs. Outstg. (000)	328,538	332,527	328,002	317,888	319,876	314,180	311,552
BALANCE SHEET (IN MILLIONS):							
Cash & Cash Equivalents	1,552.0	1,549.0	1,175.6	786.7	637.9	443.4	322.5
Total Current Assets	1,727.6	1,727.8	1,310.1	905.1	768.2	559.3	418.9
Net Property	260.9	289.2	197.2	141.8	124.6	120.3	110.9
Total Assets	1,988.4	2,017.1	1,507.3	1,046.9	892.8	679.6	529.8
Total Current Liabilities	169.0	202.2	168.7	125.3	123.0	89.0	86.4
Net Stockholders' Equity	1,781.5	1,782.0	1,322.2	906.8	755.9	589.1	440.5
Net Working Capital	1,558.6	1,525.6	1,141.4	779.8	645.1	470.3	332.5
Year-end Shs. Outstg. (000)	316,150	318,908	315,167	307,462	307,292	303,824	298,648
STATISTICAL RECORD:							
Operating Profit Margin %	43.9	56.2	53.0	50.9	51.1	49.7	50.5
Net Profit Margin %	38.6	43.9	40.8	38.3	37.3	35.4	35.5
Return on Equity %	11.1	24.0	21.8	21.4	23.9	22.8	30.4
Return on Assets %	9.9	21.2	19.1	18.6	20.3	19.8	25.3
Price Range	47.50-18.92	65.13-29.45	74.75-35.06	41.59-20.88	22.63-9.78	18.75-10.13	12.56-5.44
P/E Ratio	79.2-31.5	50.5-22.8	84.9-39.8	68.2-34.2	39.0-16.9	43.8-23.7	29.2-12.6
Average Yield %	0.6	0.3	0.2	0.2	0.4	0.4	0.5

Statistics are as originally reported. Adj. for stk. splits: 2-for-1, 3/00 & 2/99.

OFFICERS:
R. H. Swanson Jr., Chmn., C.E.O.
D. Bell, Pres.
P. Coghlan, V.P., C.F.O.

INVESTOR CONTACT: Paul Coghlan, V.P., C.F.O., (408) 432-1900

PRINCIPAL OFFICE: 1630 McCarthy Blvd., Milpitas, CA 95035-7417

TELEPHONE NUMBER: (408) 432-1900
FAX: (408) 434-0507
WEB: www.linear.com
NO. OF EMPLOYEES: 2,691
SHAREHOLDERS: 1,838 (approx. record)
ANNUAL MEETING: In Nov.
INCORPORATED: CA, Sept. 1981; reincorp., DE, Jan., 2001

INSTITUTIONAL HOLDINGS:
No. of Institutions: 404
Shares Held: 262,593,025
% Held: 83.9

INDUSTRY: Semiconductors and related devices (SIC: 3674)

TRANSFER AGENT(S): EquiServe Trust Company, N.A., Providence, RI

LOWE'S COMPANIES, INC.

YIELD 0.2%
P/E RATIO 21.7

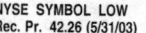

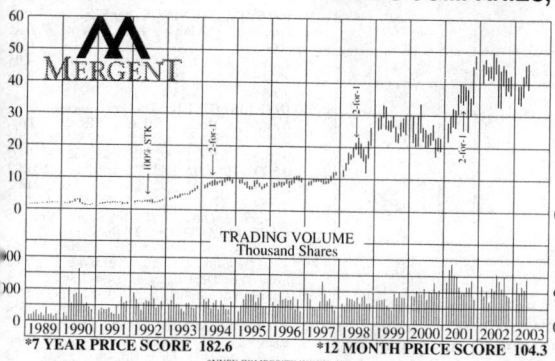

7 YEAR PRICE SCORE 182.6
*NYSE COMPOSITE INDEX=100
12 MONTH PRICE SCORE 104.3

TRADING VOLUME
Thousand Shares

INTERIM EARNINGS (Per Share):

Qtr.	Apr.	July	Oct.	Jan.
2000-01	0.25	0.37	0.27	0.19
2001-02	0.29	0.42	0.32	0.28
2002-03	0.44	0.59	0.43	0.40
2003-04	0.53	...	...	...

INTERIM DIVIDENDS (Per Share):

Amt.	Decl.	Ex.	Rec.	Pay.
0.02Q	5/31/02	7/17/02	7/19/02	8/02/02
0.02Q	9/30/02	10/16/02	10/18/02	11/01/02
0.025Q	12/06/02	1/15/03	1/17/03	1/31/03
0.025Q	4/04/03	4/15/03	4/17/03	5/02/03
0.025Q	5/30/03	7/16/03	7/18/03	8/01/03

Indicated div.: $0.10 (Div. Reinv. Plan)

CAPITALIZATION (1/31/03):

	($000)	(%)
Long-Term Debt	3,272,000	26.1
Capital Lease Obligations	464,000	3.7
Deferred Income Tax	478,000	3.8
Common & Surplus	8,302,000	66.3
Total	12,516,000	100.0

DIVIDEND ACHIEVER STATUS:

Rank: 170   10-Year Growth Rate: 8.62%
Total Years of Dividend Growth: 41

RECENT DEVELOPMENTS: For the quarter ended 5/2/03, net earnings advanced 21.7% to $421.0 million from $346.0 million in the corresponding period the previous year. Earnings for 2003 and 2002 included store opening costs of $19.0 million and $37.0 million, respectively. Net sales climbed 11.4% to $7.21 billion. Comparable-store sales increased 0.1% year over year. Gross margin totaled $2.24 billion, or 31.0% of net sales, compared with $1.92 billion, or 29.7% of net sales, a year earlier.

PROSPECTS: LOW continues to benefit from a strong housing market and improved consumer confidence despite the effect of the adverse weather and uncertain geopolitical events. For fiscal 2003, LOW expects to open 130 stores, reflecting total square footage growth of 15.0%. Total sales are expected to grow about 14.0% to 15.0% for the year, supported in part by an anticipated comparable-store sales increase of approximately 3.0% to 4.0%. Operating margin is expected to increase about 20 to 30 basis points.

BUSINESS

LOWE'S COMPANIES, INC. is a specialty retailer that combines the merchandise, sales and service of a home improvement center, a building materials supplier and a consumer-durables retailer to serve the do-it-yourself home improvement and construction markets. As of 5/19/03, LOW operated 875 stores in 45 states representing 97.2 million square feet of selling space. Each store is stocked with more than 40,000 separate items, while the Company's special order program features more than 400,000 additional items. On 4/2/99, the Company acquired Eagle Hardware & Garden, Inc.

ANNUAL FINANCIAL DATA

	1/31/03	2/1/02	2/2/01	1/28/00	1/29/99	1/30/98	1/31/97
Earnings Per Share	② 1.85	1.30	1.06	① 0.88	0.68	0.52	0.44
Cash Flow Per Share	2.64	1.96	1.59	1.32	1.07	0.86	0.73
Tang. Book Val. Per Share	10.62	8.60	7.17	6.14	4.45	3.71	3.20
Dividends Per Share	0.08	0.075	0.07	0.06	0.058	0.055	0.05
Dividend Payout %	4.3	6.2	6.6	6.8	8.5	10.6	11.4
INCOME STATEMENT (IN MILLIONS):							
Total Revenues	26,491.0	22,111.1	18,778.6	15,905.6	12,244.9	10,136.9	8,600.2
Costs & Expenses	23,305.0	19,779.2	16,966.8	14,419.8	11,139.5	9,271.7	7,897.8
Depreciation & Amort.	645.0	534.1	409.5	337.8	272.2	241.1	199.8
Operating Income	2,541.0	1,797.8	1,402.3	1,148.0	833.2	624.1	502.7
Net Interest Inc./(Exp.)	d182.0	d173.5	d120.8	d84.9	d74.7	d65.6	d49.1
Income Before Income Taxes	2,359.0	1,624.3	1,281.4	1,063.1	758.4	558.5	453.6
Income Taxes	888.0	601.0	471.6	390.3	276.0	201.1	161.5
Net Income	② 1,471.0	1,023.3	809.9	① 672.8	482.4	357.5	292.2
Cash Flow	2,116.0	1,557.4	1,219.4	1,010.6	754.6	598.6	491.9
Average Shs. Outstg. (000)	800,000	794,597	768,950	767,708	707,590	697,518	670,712
BALANCE SHEET (IN MILLIONS):							
Cash & Cash Equivalents	1,126.0	853.2	468.5	568.8	243.1	211.3	70.5
Total Current Assets	5,568.0	4,920.4	4,175.0	3,709.5	2,585.7	2,109.6	1,851.5
Net Property	10,352.0	8,653.4	7,035.0	5,177.2	3,636.9	3,005.2	2,494.4
Total Assets	16,109.0	13,736.2	11,375.8	9,012.3	6,344.7	5,219.3	4,435.0
Total Current Liabilities	3,5778.0	3,016.8	2,928.6	2,386.0	1,765.3	1,449.3	1,348.5
Long-Term Obligations	3,736.0	3,734.0	2,697.7	1,726.6	1,283.1	1,045.6	767.3
Net Stockholders' Equity	8,302.0	6,674.4	5,494.9	4,695.5	3,136.0	2,600.6	2,217.5
Net Working Capital	1,990.0	1,903.6	1,246.4	1,323.6	820.3	660.3	502.9
Year-end Shs. Outstg. (000)	781,900	775,714	766,484	764,718	705,286	701,264	693,616
STATISTICAL RECORD:							
Operating Profit Margin %	9.6	8.1	7.5	7.2	6.8	6.2	5.8
Net Profit Margin %	5.6	4.6	4.3	4.2	3.9	3.5	3.4
Return on Equity %	17.7	15.3	14.7	14.3	15.4	13.7	13.2
Return on Assets %	9.1	7.4	7.1	7.5	7.6	6.8	6.6
Debt/Total Assets %	23.2	27.2	23.7	19.2	20.2	20.0	17.3
Price Range	49.99-32.50	48.88-21.88	33.63-17.13	33.22-21.50	26.09-10.80	12.28-7.91	10.88-7.16
P/E Ratio	27.0-17.6	37.6-16.8	31.9-16.2	38.0-24.6	38.4-15.9	23.8-15.3	25.0-16.4
Average Yield %	0.2	0.2	0.3	0.2	0.3	0.5	0.6

Statistics are as originally reported. Adj. for 2-for-1 stk. split, 6/01 & 6/98. ① Incl. $24.4 mil pre-tax, non-recur. chg. ② Incl. store opening costs of $128.7 mill.

OFFICERS:
R. L. Tillman, Chmn., C.E.O.
R. A. Niblock, Exec. V.P., C.F.O.
S. A. Hellrung, Sr. V.P., Sec., Gen. Couns.

INVESTOR CONTACT: Paul Taaffe, Dir.-Inv. Rel., (336) 658-5239

PRINCIPAL OFFICE: 1605 Curtis Bridge Road, Wilkesboro, NC 28697

TELEPHONE NUMBER: (336) 658-4000
FAX: (336) 658-4766
WEB: www.lowes.com
NO. OF EMPLOYEES: 123,000 full-time (approx.); 30,000 part-time (approx.)
SHAREHOLDERS: 25,405
ANNUAL MEETING: In May
INCORPORATED: NC, Aug., 1952

INSTITUTIONAL HOLDINGS:
No. of Institutions: 732
Shares Held: 612,464,430
% Held: 78.5

INDUSTRY: Lumber and other building materials (SIC: 5211)

TRANSFER AGENT(S): EquiServe Trust Company, NA, Boston, MA

M&T BANK CORPORATION

YIELD 1.3%
P/E RATIO 17.3

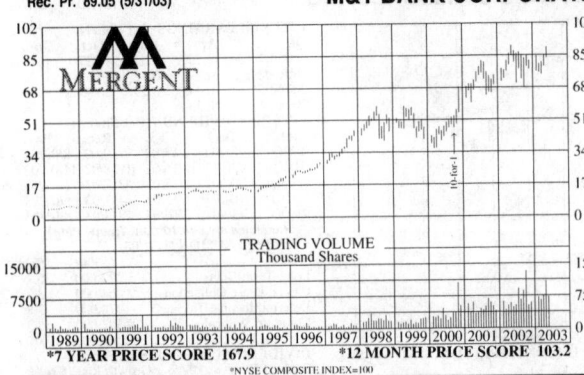

INTERIM EARNINGS (Per Share):

Qtr.	Mar.	June	Sept.	Dec.
2000	0.86	0.97	0.94	0.76
2001	1.14	0.94	0.98	1.05
2002	1.25	1.26	1.23	1.33
2003	1.34	...	...	...

INTERIM DIVIDENDS (Per Share):

Amt.	Decl.	Ex.	Rec.	Pay.
0.25Q	4/16/02	5/30/02	6/03/02	6/28/02
0.25Q	7/16/02	8/29/02	9/03/02	9/30/02
0.30Q	10/15/02	11/27/02	12/02/02	12/31/02
0.30Q	2/18/03	2/27/03	3/03/03	3/31/03
0.30Q	5/20/03	5/29/03	6/02/03	6/30/03

Indicated div.: $1.20 (Div. Reinv. Plan)

CAPITALIZATION (12/31/02):

	($000)	(%)
Total Deposits	21,664,923	73.8
Long-Term Debt	4,497,374	15.3
Common & Surplus	3,181,823	10.8
Total	29,344,120	100.0

DIVIDEND ACHIEVER STATUS:
Rank: 23   10-Year Growth Rate: 20.70%
Total Years of Dividend Growth: 22

TRADING VOLUME
Thousand Shares

*7 YEAR PRICE SCORE 167.9   *12 MONTH PRICE SCORE 103.2
*NYSE COMPOSITE INDEX=100

RECENT DEVELOPMENTS: For the quarter ended 3/31/03, net income increased 2.6% to $116.5 million from $113.6 million in the corresponding prior-year period. Interest income declined 5.6% to $435.6 million, while interest expense fell 25.3% to $119.6 million. Net interest income grew 5.0% to $316.0 million. Provision for credit losses rose 37.5% to $33.0 million. Total other income improved 6.9% to $132.8 million, while total other expense increased 3.9% to $242.3 million.

PROSPECTS: On 4/1/03, the Company acquired Allfirst Financial Inc. from Allied Irish Banks, p.l.c. (AIB) for 26.7 million shares of MTB common stock plus about $886.0 million in cash. As a result of the transaction, MTB is the 18th largest commercial bank headquartered in the U.S., and operates more than 700 branches and 1,600 ATMs in Maryland, New York, Pennsylvania, Virginia, West Virginia and the District of Columbia. Additionally, MTB will acquire AIB's branch office in New York City.

BUSINESS

M&T BANK CORPORATION, with assets of $33.44 billion as of 3/31/03, is a bank holding company with two wholly-owned bank subsidiaries, Manufacturers and Traders Trust Company and M&T Bank, National Association. The banks collectively offer commercial banking, trust and investment services to their customers. The Company's six reportable segments are Commercial Banking (17.3% of net interest income and 9.9% of non-interest income as of 12/31/02), Commercial Real Estate (14.0% and 1.4%), Discretionary Portfolio (5.5% and 7.5%), Residential Mortgage Banking (6.9% and 32.8%), Retail Banking (48.0% and 37.0%), and All Other (8.3% and 11.4%). On 2/10/01, the Company acquired Premier National Bancorp, Inc. On 4/1/03, MTB acquired Allfirst Financial Inc.

QUARTERLY DATA

(12/31/2002)($000)	REV	INC
1st Quarter	589,014	120,564
2nd Quarter	586,225	121,494
3rd Quarter	593,147	117,215
4th Quarter	599,693	125,819

ANNUAL FINANCIAL DATA

	12/31/02	12/31/01	12/31/00	12/31/99	12/31/98	12/31/97	12/31/96
Earnings Per Share	5.07	⏀3.82	⏀3.44	⏀3.28	⏀2.62	2.53	2.13
Tang. Book Val. Per Share	21.36	17.84	16.10	14.88	13.72	15.59	13.55
Dividends Per Share	1.05	1.00	0.63	0.45	0.38	0.32	0.28
Dividend Payout %	20.7	26.2	18.2	13.7	14.5	12.7	13.1
INCOME STATEMENT (IN MILLIONS):							
Total Interest Income	1,842.1	2,101.9	1,772.8	1,478.6	1,351.8	1,065.0	997.4
Total Interest Expense	594.5	943.6	918.6	719.2	687.5	508.1	466.4
Net Interest Income	1,247.6	1,158.3	854.2	759.4	664.3	556.9	531.0
Provision for Loan Losses	122.0	103.5	38.0	44.5	43.2	46.0	43.3
Non-Interest Income	511.9	477.4	324.7	282.4	270.6	193.1	170.2
Non-Interest Expense	921.0	948.3	694.5	579.0	566.1	421.8	409.0
Income Before Taxes	716.5	583.9	446.4	418.3	325.6	282.2	249.0
Net Income	485.1	⏀378.1	⏀286.2	⏀265.6	⏀208.0	176.2	151.1
Average Shs. Outstg. (000)	95,663	99,024	83,171	80,900	79,500	69,770	70,480
BALANCE SHEET (IN MILLIONS):							
Cash & Due from Banks	963.8	965.7	750.3	592.8	493.8	333.8	324.7
Securities Avail. for Sale	3,650.8	2,702.1	3,071.7	2,321.9	2,756.9	1,640.6	1,434.0
Total Loans & Leases	25,936.9	25,395.5	22,970.3	17,572.9	16,005.7	11,765.5	11,120.2
Allowance for Credit Losses	645.6	632.7	602.2	482.3	520.5	543.6	668.6
Net Loans & Leases	25,291.3	24,762.8	22,368.1	17,090.6	15,485.2	11,221.9	10,451.7
Total Assets	33,174.2	31,450.2	28,949.5	22,409.1	20,583.9	14,002.9	12,943.9
Total Deposits	21,664.9	21,580.4	20,232.7	15,373.6	14,737.2	11,163.2	10,514.5
Long-Term Obligations	4,497.4	3,461.8	3,414.5	1,775.1	1,567.5	427.8	178.0
Total Liabilities	29,992.7	28,510.7	26,249.0	20,612.1	18,981.5	12,972.7	12,038.3
Net Stockholders' Equity	3,181.8	2,939.5	2,700.5	1,797.0	1,602.4	1,030.3	905.7
Year-end Shs. Outstg. (000)	92,029	93,684	93,244	77,238	76,980	66,100	66,860
STATISTICAL RECORD:							
Return on Equity %	15.2	12.9	10.6	14.8	13.0	17.1	16.7
Return on Assets %	1.5	1.2	1.0	1.2	1.0	1.3	1.2
Equity/Assets %	9.6	9.3	9.3	8.0	7.8	7.4	7.0
Non-Int. Exp./Tot. Inc. %	52.3	58.0	58.9	55.6	60.6	56.2	58.3
Price Range	90.05-67.70	82.11-59.80	68.42-35.70	58.25-40.60	58.20-40.00	45.50-28.10	28.96-20.90
P/E Ratio	17.8-13.4	21.5-15.7	19.9-10.4	17.7-12.4	22.2-15.3	18.0-11.1	13.6-9.8
Average Yield %	1.3	1.4	1.2	0.9	0.8	0.9	1.1

Statistics are as originally reported. Adj. for 10-for-1 stk. split, 10/5/00. ⏀ Incl. after-tax nonrecurr. merger & acq. chrgs.: $4.8 mill., 2001; $16.4 mill. 2000; $3.0 mill., 12/31/99; $14.0 mill., 12/31/98.

OFFICERS:
R. G. Wilmers, Chmn., Pres., CEO
C. L. Campbell, Vice-Chmn.
M. P. Pinto, Exec. V.P., C.F.O.

INVESTOR CONTACT: M. S. Piemonte, Shldr. Rel./Corp. Fin. Dept., (716)842-5138

PRINCIPAL OFFICE: One M&T Plaza, 5th Floor, Buffalo, NY 14203

TELEPHONE NUMBER: (716) 842-5445
FAX: (716) 842-5177
WEB: www.mandtbank.com
NO. OF EMPLOYEES: 8,139 full-time; 1,152 part-time
SHAREHOLDERS: 12,565
ANNUAL MEETING: In April
INCORPORATED: NY, Nov., 1969

INSTITUTIONAL HOLDINGS:
No. of Institutions: 254
Shares Held: 52,076,601
% Held: 43.8

INDUSTRY: State commercial banks (SIC: 6022)

TRANSFER AGENT(S): BankBoston, N.A. c/o Equiserve, Boston, MA

MARSH & MCLENNAN COMPANIES, INC.

YIELD	2.5%
P/E RATIO	19.8

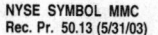
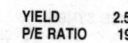
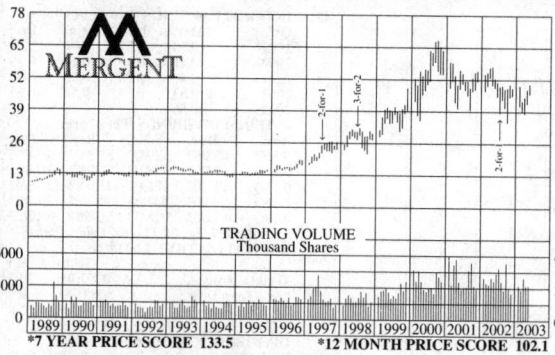

INTERIM EARNINGS (Per Share):

Qtr.	Mar.	June	Sept.	Dec.
1999	0.52	0.32	0.41	0.08
2000	0.60	0.48	0.49	0.49
2001	0.64	0.51	0.29	0.26
2002	0.74	0.60	0.55	0.57
2003	0.81	...	...	...

INTERIM DIVIDENDS (Per Share):

Amt.	Decl.	Ex.	Rec.	Pay.
0.28Q	9/19/02	10/10/02	10/15/02	11/15/02
0.28Q	11/21/02	1/02/03	1/06/03	2/14/03
0.28Q	3/20/03	4/07/03	4/09/03	5/15/03
0.31Q	5/15/03	7/07/03	7/09/03	8/15/03

Indicated div.: $1.24 (Div. Reinv. Plan)

CAPITALIZATION (12/31/02):

	($000)	(%)
Long-Term Debt	2,891,000	36.6
Common & Surplus	5,018,000	63.4
Total	7,909,000	100.0

DIVIDEND ACHIEVER STATUS:

Rank: 156   10-Year Growth Rate: 9.45%
Total Years of Dividend Growth: 41

*7 YEAR PRICE SCORE 133.5   ***12 MONTH PRICE SCORE 102.1**
*NYSE COMPOSITE INDEX=100

RECENT DEVELOPMENTS: For the quarter ended 3/31/03, net income increased 6.0% to $443.0 million from $418.0 million in the corresponding prior-year quarter. Total revenue advanced 8.2% to $2.85 billion from $2.64 billion the previous year. On a segment basis, operating income from risk and insurance services climbed 21.2% to $560.0 million. Operating income from investment management services dropped 41.1% to $103.0 million. Operating income from consulting services rose 12.2% to $83.0 million.

PROSPECTS: The Company should continue to benefit from revenue growth and increased profitability in risk and insurance services due to heightened demand for specialized services to reduce risk. Consulting revenues are likely to remain solid due to growth in retirement services and economic consulting along with significant improvements in health care and group benefits, human capital, and organizational change consulting. However, declines in U.S. equity markets may continue to challenge Putnum's performance.

BUSINESS

MARSH & MCLENNAN COMPANIES, INC. is engaged in the worldwide business of providing retail and wholesale insurance services, principally as a broker or consultant for insurers, insurance underwriters and other brokers. MMC's subsidiaries include Marsh Inc., a risk and insurance services firm; Putman Investments, one of the largest investment management companies in the U.S.; and Mercer Consulting Group, a major global provider of consulting services. Other subsidiaries render advisory services in the area of employee benefits and compensation consulting, management consulting, economic consulting and environmental consulting. Contributions to revenues by type of service in 2002 were as follows: insurance services, 56.7%; consulting, 22.6%; and investment management, 20.7%.

ANNUAL FINANCIAL DATA

	12/31/02	12/31/01	12/31/00	12/31/99	12/31/98	12/31/97	12/31/96
Earnings Per Share	2.45	① 1.70	2.05	② 1.31	1.49	① 0.80	1.06
Tang. Book Val. Per Share	...	...	...	...	...	1.53	3.10
Dividends Per Share	1.09	1.03	0.95	0.85	0.73	0.63	0.55
Dividend Payout %	44.5	60.8	46.3	64.9	49.2	79.5	52.0
INCOME STATEMENT (IN MILLIONS):							
Total Revenues	10,440.0	9,943.0	10,157.0	9,157.0	7,190.0	6,008.6	4,149.0
Income Before Income Taxes	2,133.0	1,590.0	1,955.0	1,247.0	1,305.0	662.4	668.0
Income Taxes	747.0	599.0	753.0	521.0	509.0	263.0	208.7
Net Income	1,386.0	① 991.0	1,202.0	② 726.0	796.0	① 399.4	459.3
Average Shs. Outstg. (000)	557,000	572,000	568,000	544,000	528,000	501,600	434,400
BALANCE SHEET (IN MILLIONS):							
Cash & Cash Equivalents	546.0	537.0	240.0	428.0	610.0	424.3	299.6
Premiums Due	2,478.0	2,692.0	2,812.0	2,323.0	1,909.0	1,498.2	1,085.8
Invst. Assets: Total	578.0	826.0	976.0	687.0	828.0	720.2	573.3
Total Assets	13,855.0	13,293.0	13,769.0	13,021.0	11,871.0	7,914.2	4,545.2
Long-Term Obligations	2,891.0	2,334.0	2,347.0	2,357.0	1,590.0	1,239.8	458.2
Net Stockholders' Equity	5,018.0	5,173.0	5,228.0	4,170.0	3,659.0	3,198.8	1,888.6
Year-end Shs. Outstg. (000)	538,200	548,654	552,053	534,052	514,000	509,850	433,914
STATISTICAL RECORD:							
Return on Revenues %	13.3	10.0	11.8	7.9	11.1	6.6	11.1
Return on Equity %	27.6	19.2	23.0	17.4	21.8	12.5	24.3
Return on Assets %	10.0	7.5	8.7	5.6	6.7	5.0	10.1
Price Range	57.30-34.61	59.03-39.50	67.84-35.25	48.38-28.56	32.16-21.69	26.67-17.10	19.15-14.04
P/E Ratio	23.4-14.1	34.8-23.3	33.1-17.2	36.9-21.8	21.6-14.6	33.5-21.5	18.1-13.3
Average Yield %	2.4	2.1	1.8	2.2	2.7	2.9	3.3

Statistics are as originally reported. Adj. for stk. split: 2-for-1, 7/02; 3-for-2, 6/98; 2-for-1, 6/97 ① Incl. non-recurr. chrg. 2001, $396.0 mill.; 1997, $296.8 mill. ② Incl. special chrg. $337.0 mill.

OFFICERS:
J. W. Greenberg, Chmn., Pres., C.E.O.
M. Cabiallavetta, Vice-Chmn.
C. A. Davis, Vice-Chmn.
INVESTOR CONTACT: J. Michael Bischoff, Inv. Rels., (212) 345-5475
PRINCIPAL OFFICE: 1166 Avenue Of The Americas, New York, NY 10036

TELEPHONE NUMBER: (212) 345-5000
FAX: (212) 345-4809
WEB: www.mmc.com
NO. OF EMPLOYEES: 59,500 (approx.)
SHAREHOLDERS: 10,666
ANNUAL MEETING: In May
INCORPORATED: DE, March, 1969

INSTITUTIONAL HOLDINGS:
No. of Institutions: 653
Shares Held: 354,934,557
% Held: 66.2
INDUSTRY: Insurance agents, brokers, & service (SIC: 6411)
TRANSFER AGENT(S): The Bank of New York, New York, NY

MARSHALL & ILSLEY CORPORATION

YIELD 2.4%
P/E RATIO 13.7

7 YEAR PRICE SCORE 122.7   **12 MONTH PRICE SCORE 100.7**
*NYSE COMPOSITE INDEX=100

INTERIM EARNINGS (Per Share):

Qtr.	Mar.	June	Sept.	Dec.
1999	0.38	0.39	0.41	0.41
2000	0.41	0.42	0.24	0.39
2001	0.40	0.28	0.38	0.49
2002	0.53	0.54	0.54	0.55
2003	0.56	...	...	...

INTERIM DIVIDENDS (Per Share):

Amt.	Decl.	Ex.	Rec.	Pay.
0.16Q	4/23/02	5/29/02	5/31/02	6/14/02
0.16Q	8/15/02	8/28/02	8/30/02	9/13/02
0.16Q	10/17/02	11/26/02	11/29/02	12/13/02
0.16Q	2/20/03	2/27/03	3/03/03	3/14/03
0.18Q	4/22/03	5/28/03	5/30/03	6/13/03

Indicated div.: $0.72 (Div. Reinv. Plan)

CAPITALIZATION (12/31/02):

	($000)	(%)
Total Deposits	20,393,706	79.3
Long-Term Debt	2,283,781	8.9
Common & Surplus	3,036,668	11.8
Total	25,714,155	100.0

DIVIDEND ACHIEVER STATUS:
Rank: 142   10-Year Growth Rate: 10.04%
Total Years of Dividend Growth: 30

RECENT DEVELOPMENTS: For the quarter ended 3/31/03, net income climbed 10.7% to $128.0 million versus $115.6 million in the same period of 2002. Results for 2003 and 2002 included a net gain of $1.6 million and a net loss of $700,000 from investment securities, and amortization of intangibles of $6.9 million and $4.3 million, respectively. Net interest income grew 9.7% to $272.5 million from $248.3 million, while provision for loan and lease losses jumped 69.1% to $25.7 million versus $15.2 million.

PROSPECTS: The Company anticipates net interest margin will decrease throughout much of the remainder of 2003. Net interest margin will likely continue to be affected by product spreads, loan and deposit growth and interest rates. Moreover, MI expects net charge-offs in 2003 for commercial loans to range between $18.0 million and $29.0 million, real estate loans in the range of $10.0 million and $16.0 million, and personal loans ranging from $6.0 million to $10.0 million.

BUSINESS

MARSHALL & ILSLEY CORPORATION, a multibank holding company with assets of $33.25 billion as of 3/31/03, is headquartered in Milwaukee, Wisconsin. The Company has 208 banking offices in Wisconsin, 25 locations throughout Arizona, 10 offices in Minneapolis/St. Paul, Minnesota, and locations in Duluth, Minnesota, Las Vegas, Nevada and Naples, Florida. The Company also provides trust and investment management, equipment leasing, mortgage banking, asset-based lending, financial planning, investments, and insurance services from offices throughout the U.S. and on the Internet. The Company's principal subsidiary is Metavante Corporation (formerly MI's M&I Data Services Division), a provider of integrated financial transaction processing, outsourcing services, software, and consulting services.

ANNUAL FINANCIAL DATA

	12/31/02	12/31/01	12/31/00	12/31/99	12/31/98	12/31/97	12/31/96
Earnings Per Share	2.16	①②1.55	①②1.46	1.57	②1.31	1.21	1.04
Tang. Book Val. Per Share	8.61	9.16	9.22	8.27	8.99	9.45	7.12
Dividends Per Share	0.63	0.57	0.52	0.47	0.43	0.39	0.36
Dividend Payout %	28.9	36.7	35.6	29.9	32.9	32.4	34.8
INCOME STATEMENT (IN MILLIONS):							
Total Interest Income	1,567.3	1,709.1	1,748.0	1,496.6	1,434.0	1,143.7	971.4
Total Interest Expense	561.0	866.3	1,075.0	791.3	758.0	579.6	465.7
Net Interest Income	1,006.5	842.8	673.0	705.3	676.1	564.0	505.7
Provision for Loan Losses	74.4	54.1	30.4	25.4	27.1	17.3	15.2
Non-Interest Income	1,082.7	1,002.8	928.4	845.8	1,424.2	598.9	503.3
Non-Interest Expense	1,296.0	1,290.4	1,100.7	997.7	944.9	775.4	680.7
Income Before Taxes	718.6	501.0	470.4	527.9	1,128.3	370.3	313.1
Net Income	480.3	①②337.9	①②317.4	354.5	②301.3	245.1	203.4
Average Shs. Outstg. (000)	222,048	218,264	217,766	226,010	230,480	203,020	196,964
BALANCE SHEET (IN MILLIONS):							
Cash & Due from Banks	1,012.1	617.2	760.1	705.3	760.4	800.1	780.6
Securities Avail. for Sale	4,391.9	4,216.8	4,801.2	4,477.0	4,247.2	4,182.2	3,213.9
Total Loans & Leases	23,908.8	19,295.4	17,587.1	16,335.1	13,996.2	12,542.3	9,301.9
Allowance for Credit Losses	338.4	268.2	235.1	225.9	226.1	202.8	155.9
Net Loans & Leases	23,570.4	19,027.2	17,352.0	16,109.2	13,770.1	12,339.5	9,146.0
Total Assets	32,874.6	27,253.7	26,077.7	24,369.7	21,566.3	19,477.5	14,763.3
Total Deposits	20,393.7	16,493.0	19,248.6	16,435.2	15,919.9	14,356.0	10,952.4
Long-Term Obligations	2,283.8	1,560.2	921.3	665.0	794.5	791.2	336.1
Total Liabilities	29,838.0	24,760.8	23,835.6	22,252.8	19,322.5	17,557.4	13,502.1
Net Stockholders' Equity	3,036.7	2,493.0	2,242.2	2,116.9	2,243.8	1,920.1	1,261.2
Year-end Shs. Outstg. (000)	226,233	207,898	205,693	211,632	212,206	203,074	177,168
STATISTICAL RECORD:							
Return on Equity %	15.8	13.6	14.2	16.7	13.4	12.8	16.1
Return on Assets %	1.5	1.2	1.2	1.5	1.4	1.3	1.4
Equity/Assets %	9.2	9.1	8.6	8.7	10.4	9.9	8.5
Non-Int. Exp./Tot. Inc. %	62.0	69.9	68.7	64.3	45.0	66.7	67.5
Price Range	32.12-23.11	32.12-23.54	31.13-19.13	36.38-27.19	31.13-19.69	30.25-16.19	17.81-12.19
P/E Ratio	14.9-10.7	20.8-15.2	21.4-13.1	23.2-17.3	23.8-15.1	25.0-13.4	17.2-11.8
Average Yield %	2.3	2.0	2.1	1.5	1.7	1.7	2.4

Statistics are as originally reported. Adj. for stk. splits: 2-for-1, 6/02. ① Bef. acctg. change chrg., $436,000, 2001; $2.3 mill., 2000. ② Incl. non-recur. net chrgs. of $68.1 mill., 2001; $16.7 mill., 2000; $23.4 mill., 1998.

OFFICERS:
J. B. Wigdale, Chmn.
D. J. Kuester, Pres., C.E.O.
M. F. Furlong, Exec. V.P., C.F.O.

INVESTOR CONTACT: M.A. Hatfield, Secretary, (414) 765-7801

PRINCIPAL OFFICE: 770 North Water Street, Milwaukee, WI 53202

TELEPHONE NUMBER: (414) 765-7801
FAX: (414) 765-8026
WEB: www.micorp.com
NO. OF EMPLOYEES: 12,625 (approx.)
SHAREHOLDERS: 19,141 (approx. record)
ANNUAL MEETING: In Apr.
INCORPORATED: WI, Feb., 1959

INSTITUTIONAL HOLDINGS:
No. of Institutions: 284
Shares Held: 87,571,569
% Held: 38.7

INDUSTRY: National commercial banks (SIC: 6021)

TRANSFER AGENT(S): Continental Stock Transfer & Trust Company, New York, NY

MASCO CORPORATION

	YIELD	2.3%
	P/E RATIO	18.1

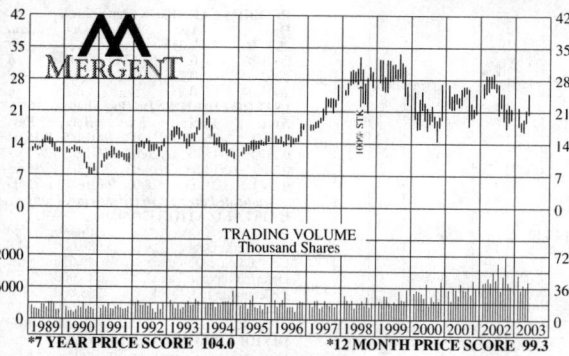

TRADING VOLUME
Thousand Shares

1989 1990 1991 1992 1993 1994 1995 1996 1997 1998 1999 2000 2001 2002 2003

*7 YEAR PRICE SCORE 104.0   ***12 MONTH PRICE SCORE 99.3**
*NYSE COMPOSITE INDEX=100

INTERIM EARNINGS (Per Share):

Qtr.	Mar.	June	Sept.	Dec.
1999	0.36	0.41	0.15	0.40
2000	0.39	0.41	0.41	0.10
2001	0.25	0.30	d0.39	0.26
2002	0.31	0.43	0.24	0.37
2003	0.32	...	...	...

INTERIM DIVIDENDS (Per Share):

Amt.	Decl.	Ex.	Rec.	Pay.
0.135Q	6/28/02	7/10/02	7/12/02	8/12/02
0.14Q	9/12/02	10/09/02	10/11/02	11/12/02
0.14Q	12/11/02	1/08/03	1/10/03	2/10/03
0.14Q	3/21/03	4/09/03	4/11/03	5/07/03

Indicated div.: $0.56 (Div. Reinv. Plan)

CAPITALIZATION (12/31/02):

	($000)	(%)
Long-Term Debt	4,316,470	44.9
Preferred Stock	20	0.0
Common & Surplus	5,293,820	55.1
Total	9,610,310	100.0

DIVIDEND ACHIEVER STATUS:
Rank: 216   10-Year Growth Rate: 5.98%
Total Years of Dividend Growth: 44

RECENT DEVELOPMENTS: For the quarter ended 3/31/03, net income climbed 10.4% to $165.8 million compared with income of $150.2 million, before an accounting change charge of $92.4 million, in the equivalent 2002 quarter. Results for 2003 included income of $13.5 million related to a litigation settlement. Net sales rose 19.0% to $2.50 billion due to acquisitions, including several home improvement products and service companies during 2002.

PROSPECTS: Based on present market conditions, the Company expects to achieve second quarter earnings in the range of $0.43 to $0.45 per common share. Meanwhile, the Company continues to expect record sales and earnings for 2003 with full-year earnings between $1.65 and $1.70 per common share. The Company's acquisitions continue to provide MAS with opportunities to broaden its product and service offerings and enter new markets.

BUSINESS

MASCO CORPORATION manufactures faucets, cabinets, architectural coatings, locks and other consumer brand-name home improvement and building products. MAS' principal product and service categories are kitchen and bathroom cabinets, faucets, other kitchen and bath products, architectural coatings, builders' hardware products and other specialty products and services. Brand-names include MERILLAT, KRAFTMAID, and QUALITY CABINETS kitchen and bathroom cabinets; DELTA and PEERLESS faucets; WEISER and BALDWIN locks; and BEHR architectural coatings. Sales in 2002 were derived as follows: cabinets and related products, 29.7%; plumbing products, 21.6%; installation and other services, 19.6%; decorative architectural products, 17.0%; and other specialty products, 12.1%.

ANNUAL FINANCIAL DATA

	12/31/02	12/31/01	12/31/00	12/31/99	12/31/98	12/31/97	12/31/96
Earnings Per Share	④ 1.33	③ 0.42	② 1.31	① 1.28	1.39	1.15	0.92
Cash Flow Per Share	1.76	0.99	1.84	1.68	1.78	1.48	1.23
Tang. Book Val. Per Share	1.31	1.30	2.78	3.14	4.99	4.53	4.30
Dividends Per Share	0.545	0.53	0.49	0.45	0.43	0.41	0.39
Dividend Payout %	41.0	125.0	37.4	35.2	30.9	35.2	41.8
INCOME STATEMENT (IN MILLIONS)							
Total Revenues	9,419.4	8,358.0	7,243.0	6,307.0	4,345.0	3,760.0	3,237.0
Costs & Expenses	7,868.0	7,048.7	6,038.0	5,213.8	3,528.2	3,056.9	2,656.8
Depreciation & Amort.	220.3	269.5	238.3	181.8	136.3	116.1	99.7
Operating Income	1,331.1	1,039.8	966.7	911.4	680.5	587.1	480.5
Net Interest Inc./(Exp.)	d236.9	d239.3	d191.4	d120.4	d85.3	d79.8	d74.7
Income Before Income Taxes	1,031.0	300.7	893.4	904.1	755.0	630.9	502.7
Income Taxes	348.9	102.2	301.7	334.5	279.0	248.5	207.5
Equity Earnings/Minority Int.	...	6.2	19.5	23.9	29.2	24.1	20.1
Net Income	④ 682.1	③ 198.5	② 591.7	① 569.6	476.0	382.4	295.2
Cash Flow	902.4	468.0	830.0	751.4	612.3	498.5	394.9
Average Shs. Outstg. (000)	514,100	474,900	451,800	446,200	343,700	337,600	321,200
BALANCE SHEET (IN MILLIONS)							
Cash & Cash Equivalents	1,066.6	312.0	169.4	230.8	541.7	441.3	473.7
Total Current Assets	3,949.8	2,626.9	2,308.2	2,109.8	1,862.6	1,626.7	1,429.8
Net Property	2,315.1	2,016.7	1,906.8	1,624.4	1,164.3	1,037.3	940.6
Total Assets	12,050.4	9,183.3	7,744.0	6,634.9	5,167.4	4,333.8	3,701.7
Total Current Liabilities	1,932.5	1,236.6	1,078.1	846.4	846.6	620.0	518.4
Long-Term Obligations	4,316.5	3,627.6	3,018.2	2,431.3	1,391.4	1,321.5	1,236.3
Net Stockholders' Equity	5,293.8	4,119.8	3,426.1	3,136.5	2,728.6	2,229.0	1,839.8
Net Working Capital	2,017.3	1,390.4	1,230.1	1,263.3	1,016.0	1,006.7	911.3
Year-end Shs. Outstg. (000)	488,890	459,050	444,750	443,510	339,330	331,140	321,740
STATISTICAL RECORD:							
Operating Profit Margin %	14.1	12.4	13.3	14.5	15.7	15.6	14.8
Net Profit Margin %	7.2	2.4	8.2	9.0	11.0	10.2	9.1
Return on Equity %	12.9	4.8	17.3	18.2	17.4	17.2	16.0
Return on Assets %	5.7	2.2	7.6	8.6	9.2	8.8	8.0
Debt/Total Assets %	35.8	39.5	39.0	36.6	26.9	30.5	33.4
Price Range	29.43-17.25	26.94-17.76	27.00-14.50	33.69-22.50	33.00-20.75	26.91-16.88	18.44-13.25
P/E Ratio	22.1-13.0	64.1-42.3	20.6-11.1	26.3-17.6	23.7-14.9	23.4-14.7	20.0-14.4
Average Yield %	2.3	2.4	2.4	1.6	1.6	1.9	2.4

Statistics are as originally reported. Adj. for stk. split: 2-for-1, 7/98. ① Incl. aftertax nonrecurr. chrg. of approx. $126.0 mill. ② Incl. pre-tax chrg. of $55.0 mill. for the write-down of assets and $90.0 mill. for the planned dispos. of assets. ③ Incl. a pretax, noncash write-down charge of $530.0 mill. ④ Incl. chrg. of $146.8 mill. for litigation settlement and gain of $15.6 mill. for reversal of planned disposition of business; Bef. acctg. change chrg. of $92.4 mill.

OFFICERS:
R. A. Manoogian, Chmn., C.E.O.
A. Barry, Pres., C.O.O.
T. Wadhams, V.P., Fin., C.F.O.

INVESTOR CONTACT: Investor Relations, (313) 274-7400

PRINCIPAL OFFICE: 21001 Van Born Road, Taylor, MI 48180

TELEPHONE NUMBER: (313) 274-7400
FAX: (313) 792-6135
WEB: www.masco.com
NO. OF EMPLOYEES: 61,000 (approx.)
SHAREHOLDERS: 6,000 (approx.)
ANNUAL MEETING: In May
INCORPORATED: MI, Dec., 1929; reincorp., DE, 1968

INSTITUTIONAL HOLDINGS:
No. of Institutions: 396
Shares Held: 377,047,582
% Held: 77.3

INDUSTRY: Plumbing fixture fittings and trim (SIC: 3432)

TRANSFER AGENT(S): Bank of New York, New York, NY

MAY DEPARTMENT STORES COMPANY (THE)

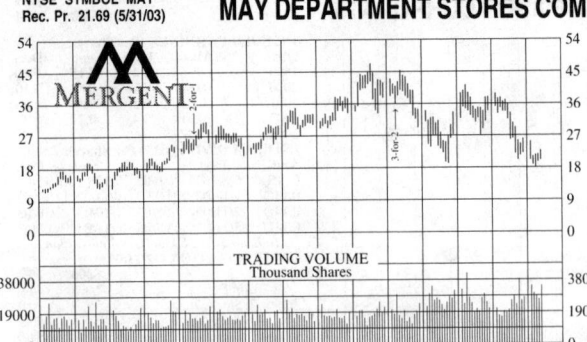

7 YEAR PRICE SCORE 83.5   **12 MONTH PRICE SCORE 85.3**
*NYSE COMPOSITE INDEX=100

INTERIM EARNINGS (Per Share):

Qtr.	Apr.	July	Oct.	Jan.
2000-01	0.35	0.41	0.27	1.59
2001-02	0.34	0.35	0.17	1.36
2002-03	0.23	0.22	0.05	1.26
2003-04	0.23	...	...	...

INTERIM DIVIDENDS (Per Share):

Amt.	Decl.	Ex.	Rec.	Pay.
0.237Q	8/16/02	8/28/02	9/01/02	9/15/02
0.237Q	11/15/02	11/26/02	12/01/02	12/15/02
0.24Q	2/13/03	2/26/03	3/01/03	3/15/03
0.24Q	3/21/03	5/28/03	6/01/03	6/15/03

Indicated div.: $0.96 (Div. Reinv. Plan)

CAPITALIZATION (2/1/03):

	($000)	(%)
Long-Term Debt	3,986,000	44.8
Capital Lease Obligations	49,000	0.6
Deferred Income Tax	710,000	8.0
Redeemable Pfd. Stock	265,000	3.0
Common & Surplus	3,883,000	43.7
Total	8,893,000	100.0

DIVIDEND ACHIEVER STATUS:
Rank: 225   10-Year Growth Rate: 5.62%
Total Years of Dividend Growth: 27

RECENT DEVELOPMENTS: For the 13 weeks ended 5/3/03, net earnings totaled $72.0 million, up 2.9% compared with $70.0 million in the corresponding prior-year period. Results for 2002 included a $40.0 million pre-tax charge stemming from the combination of certain divisions. Net sales slipped 7.2% to $2.87 billion from $3.10 billion the year before. Comparable-store sales declined 8.8% year-over-year. Earnings before income taxes slid 42.0% to $65.0 million from $112.0 million the previous year.

PROSPECTS: Results should benefit from the Company's store expansion program. In 2003, the Company expects to open nine additional department stores. During the first quarter, MAY opened two new department stores and completed the purchase of two department store locations in Columbus, Ohio. Meanwhile, MAY plans to open an additional 28 David's Bridal stores in 2003, excluding two that were opened in the first quarter, along with 15 After Hours Formalwear stores and two Priscilla of Boston stores.

BUSINESS

THE MAY DEPARTMENT STORES COMPANY operated 445 department stores in 45 states, the District of Columbia and Puerto Rico as of 5/13/03 under the following names: Lord & Taylor, Hecht's, Strawbridge's, Foley's, Robinsons-May, Filene's, Kaufmann's, Famous-Barr, L.S. Ayers, The Jones Store and Meier & Frank. In addition, MAY operated 183 David's Bridal stores, 235 After Hours stores and ten Priscilla of Boston stores. Thalhimers was acquired for $317.0 million in 1990, and was consolidated with the Hecht's division in January 1992. On 5/4/96, the Company completed its spin-off of Payless ShoeSource, Inc. On 8/11/00, MAY acquired David's Bridal, Inc.

ANNUAL FINANCIAL DATA

	2/1/03	2/2/02	2/3/01	1/29/00	1/30/99	1/31/98	2/1/97
Earnings Per Share	② 1.76	① 2.22	2.62	2.60	2.30	① 2.07	① 1.96
Cash Flow Per Share	3.57	3.98	4.18	3.93	3.51	3.19	3.01
Tang. Book Val. Per Share	7.61	7.76	8.53	9.51	8.67	8.82	8.09
Dividends Per Share	0.95	0.94	0.93	0.89	0.85	0.80	0.77
Dividend Payout %	54.0	42.3	35.5	34.2	36.8	38.6	39.3
INCOME STATEMENT (IN MILLIONS):							
Total Revenues	13,491.0	14,175.0	14,511.0	13,866.0	13,413.0	12,685.0	12,000.0
Costs & Expenses	11,769.0	12,123.0	12,253.0	11,587.0	11,301.0	10,695.0	10,118.0
Depreciation & Amort.	557.0	559.0	511.0	469.0	439.0	412.0	373.0
Operating Income	1,165.0	1,493.0	1,747.0	1,810.0	1,673.0	1,578.0	1,509.0
Net Interest Inc./(Exp.)	d345.0	d349.0	d345.0	d287.0	d278.0	d299.0	d277.0
Income Before Income Taxes	820.0	1,144.0	1,402.0	1,523.0	1,395.0	1,279.0	1,232.0
Income Taxes	278.0	438.0	544.0	596.0	546.0	500.0	483.0
Net Income	② 542.0	① 706.0	858.0	927.0	849.0	① 779.0	① 749.0
Cash Flow	1,081.0	1,246.0	1,351.0	1,377.0	1,270.0	1,173.0	1,104.0
Average Shs. Outstg. (000)	307,900	317,600	327,700	355,600	367,400	373,600	373,050
BALANCE SHEET (IN MILLIONS):							
Cash & Cash Equivalents	55.0	52.0	156.0	41.0	112.0	199.0	102.0
Total Current Assets	4,722.0	4,925.0	5,270.0	5,115.0	4,987.0	4,878.0	5,035.0
Net Property	5,466.0	5,264.0	4,899.0	4,769.0	4,513.0	4,224.0	4,159.0
Total Assets	11,936.0	11,920.0	11,574.0	10,935.0	10,533.0	9,930.0	10,059.0
Total Current Liabilities	2,666.0	2,538.0	2,214.0	2,415.0	2,059.0	1,866.0	1,923.0
Long-Term Obligations	4,035.0	4,403.0	4,534.0	3,560.0	3,825.0	3,512.0	3,849.0
Net Stockholders' Equity	4,035.0	3,841.0	3,855.0	4,077.0	3,836.0	3,809.0	3,650.0
Net Working Capital	2,056.0	2,387.0	3,056.0	2,700.0	2,928.0	3,012.0	3,112.0
Year-end Shs. Outstg. (000)	288,300	287,200	298,200	325,500	334,700	346,500	355,350
STATISTICAL RECORD:							
Operating Profit Margin %	8.6	10.5	12.0	13.1	12.5	12.4	12.6
Net Profit Margin %	4.0	5.0	5.9	6.7	6.3	6.1	6.2
Return on Equity %	13.4	18.4	22.3	22.7	22.1	20.5	20.5
Return on Assets %	4.5	5.9	7.4	8.5	8.1	7.8	7.4
Debt/Total Assets %	33.8	36.9	39.2	32.6	36.3	35.4	38.3
Price Range	38.86-20.10	41.25-27.00	33.94-19.19	45.38-29.19	47.25-33.17	38.09-29.08	34.84-26.67
P/E Ratio	22.1-11.4	18.6-12.2	13.0-7.3	17.5-11.2	20.5-14.4	18.4-14.0	17.8-13.6
Average Yield %	3.2	2.8	3.5	2.4	2.1	2.4	2.5

Statistics are as originally reported. Adj. for 3-for-2 stk. split, 3/99. ① Bef. $3 mil ($0.01/sh) extraord. loss, 2002; $4 mil extraord. loss, 1997; & bef. $5 mil extraord. loss & cr$11 mil from discont. opers., 1996. ② Incl. $76.0 mil ($0.24/sh) after-tax chg. for division combinations & $6.0 mil after-tax chg. fr. early debt redemption.

OFFICERS:
E. S. Kahn, Chmn., C.E.O.
J. L. Dunham, Pres.
T. D. Fingleton, Exec. V.P., C.F.O.

INVESTOR CONTACT: Sharon L. Bateman, Investor Relations, (314) 342-6494

PRINCIPAL OFFICE: 611 Olive Street, St. Louis, MO 63101

TELEPHONE NUMBER: (314) 342-6300
FAX: (314) 342-6497
WEB: www.maycompany.com
NO. OF EMPLOYEES: 116,000 (approx.)
SHAREHOLDERS: 40,000 (approx.)
ANNUAL MEETING: In May
INCORPORATED: NY, June, 1910; reincorp., DE, May, 1996

INSTITUTIONAL HOLDINGS:
No. of Institutions: 402
Shares Held: 232,178,918
% Held: 80.9

INDUSTRY: Department stores (SIC: 5311)

TRANSFER AGENT(S): The Bank of New York, New York, NY

MBIA INC.

YIELD 1.6%
P/E RATIO 11.3

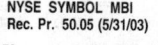

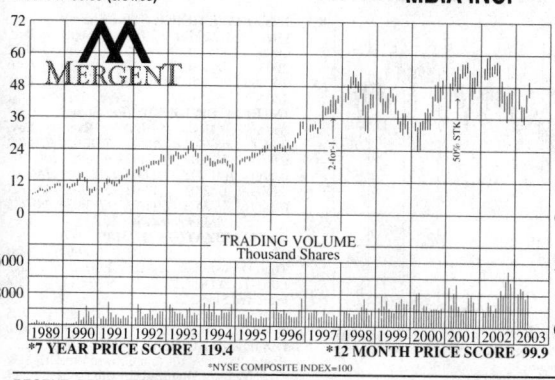

TRADING VOLUME
Thousand Shares

*7 YEAR PRICE SCORE 119.4   *12 MONTH PRICE SCORE 99.9
*NYSE COMPOSITE INDEX=100

INTERIM EARNINGS (Per Share):

Qtr.	Mar.	June	Sept.	Dec.
2000	0.89	0.87	0.88	0.92
2001	0.87	0.96	1.03	1.05
2002	1.07	0.96	1.10	0.84
2003	1.54	...	...	...

INTERIM DIVIDENDS (Per Share):

Amt.	Decl.	Ex.	Rec.	Pay.
0.17Q	6/13/02	6/24/02	6/26/02	7/15/02
0.17Q	9/13/02	9/20/02	9/24/02	10/15/02
0.17Q	12/06/02	12/17/02	12/19/02	1/15/03
0.20Q	3/20/03	3/27/03	3/31/03	4/15/03
0.20Q	6/13/03	6/23/03	6/25/03	7/15/03

Indicated div.: $0.80

CAPITALIZATION (12/31/02):

	($000)	(%)
Long-Term Debt	1,033,070	14.8
Deferred Income Tax	471,534	6.7
Common & Surplus	5,493,351	78.5
Total	6,997,955	100.0

DIVIDEND ACHIEVER STATUS:
Rank: 129   10-Year Growth Rate: 10.65%
Total Years of Dividend Growth: 15

RECENT DEVELOPMENTS: For the quarter ended 3/31/03, net income was $223.3 million versus income of $160.1 million, before an accounting change charge of $7.7 million, in the corresponding year-earlier period. Results for 2003 included a net realized gain of $30.2 million, while results for 2002 included a net realized loss of $836,000. Results for 2003 and 2002 also included gains of $60.2 million and $11.9 million related to changes in the fair value of derivative instruments. Total revenues increased 9.8% to $318.6 million.

PROSPECTS: MBIA's insurance operations continue to benefit from strong demand. Meanwhile, the ongoing difficult environment for equities is restraining the performance of MBI's investment management services operations. MBI noted that the decline in equity assets under management has only been partially offset by new fixed-income business. For instance, the market value of average assets under management as of 3/31/03 was down 9.3% from the prior year as equity assets dropped from $9.60 billion to $4.10 billion.

BUSINESS

MBIA INC. is engaged in providing financial guarantee insurance, investment management services and municipal services to public finance clients and financial institutions on a global basis. Financial guarantee insurance provides an unconditional and irrevocable guarantee of the payment of the principal of, and interest or other amounts owing on, insured obligations when due. MBI conducts its financial guarantee business through its wholly-owned subsidiary, MBIA Insurance Corporation. MBI also owns MBIA Assurance S.A., a French insurance company, which writes financial guarantee insurance in the countries of the European Community.

ANNUAL FINANCIAL DATA

	12/31/02	12/31/01	12/31/00	12/31/99	12/31/98	12/31/97	12/31/96
Earnings Per Share	① 3.98	① 3.82	3.55	③ 2.13	② 2.88	2.81	2.48
Tang. Book Val. Per Share	37.32	31.56	27.86	22.79	24.59	21.82	18.28
Dividends Per Share	0.66	0.59	0.55	0.53	0.52	0.51	0.47
Dividend Payout %	16.6	15.4	15.4	25.1	18.2	18.1	19.0
INCOME STATEMENT (IN MILLIONS):							
Total Premium Income	588.5	523.9	446.4	442.8	424.6	297.4	251.7
Net Investment Income	432.9	412.8	394.0	359.5	331.8	281.5	247.6
Other Income	195.9	199.2	184.2	162.2	164.7	75.1	46.3
Total Revenues	1,217.4	1,135.8	1,024.6	964.4	921.0	654.0	545.5
Policyholder Benefits	61.7	56.7	51.3	198.5	34.7	18.7	15.3
Income Before Income Taxes	792.6	791.0	714.9	387.9	565.0	479.6	408.1
Income Taxes	205.8	207.8	186.2	67.4	132.3	105.4	86.0
Net Income	① 586.8	① 583.2	528.6	③ 320.5	② 432.7	374.2	322.2
Average Shs. Outstg. (000)	147,574	149,283	148,669	150,604	150,245	133,121	130,044
BALANCE SHEET (IN MILLIONS):							
Invst. Assets: Fixed-term	8,093.7	7,421.0	6,740.1	5,784.0	5,884.1	4,867.3	4,149.7
Invst. Assets: Total	17,095.0	14,516.2	12,547.6	10,954.8	10,618.7	8,943.4	7,865.2
Total Assets	18,852.1	16,199.7	13,894.3	12,263.9	11,796.6	9,810.8	8,562.0
Long-Term Obligations	1,033.1	805.1	795.1	689.2	689.0	473.9	374.0
Net Stockholders' Equity	5,493.4	4,782.6	4,223.4	3,513.1	3,792.2	3,048.3	2,479.7
Year-end Shs. Outstg. (000)	144,774	148,434	147,846	149,328	149,322	134,192	129,882
STATISTICAL RECORD:							
Return on Revenues %	48.2	51.3	51.6	33.2	47.0	57.2	59.1
Return on Equity %	10.7	12.2	12.5	9.1	11.4	12.3	13.0
Return on Assets %	3.1	3.6	3.8	2.6	3.7	3.8	3.8
Price Range	60.11-34.93	57.49-36.00	50.79-24.21	47.92-30.08	53.96-30.71	44.84-30.29	34.88-23.33
P/E Ratio	15.1-8.8	15.0-9.4	14.3-6.8	22.5-14.1	18.7-10.7	15.9-10.8	14.1-9.4
Average Yield %	1.4	1.3	1.5	1.4	1.2	1.4	1.6

Statistics are as originally reported. Adj. for stk. splits: 3-for-2, 4/01; 2-for-1, 10/97. ① Bef. acctg. chrg. of $7.7 mill., 12/02; $3.9 mill., 12/01. ② Incl. non-recurr. chrg. of $36.1 mill. ③ Incl. non-recurr. chrg. of $105.0 mill.

OFFICERS:
J. W. Brown, Jr., Chmn., C.E.O.
G. C. Dunton, Pres.
N. G. Budnick, V.P., C.F.O.
INVESTOR CONTACT: Michael C. Ballinger, Inv. Rel., (914) 765-3893
PRINCIPAL OFFICE: 113 King Street, Armonk, NY 10504

TELEPHONE NUMBER: (914) 273-4545
FAX: (914) 765-3163
WEB: www.mbia.com
NO. OF EMPLOYEES: 694
SHAREHOLDERS: 828
ANNUAL MEETING: In May
INCORPORATED: CT, Nov., 1986

INSTITUTIONAL HOLDINGS:
No. of Institutions: 434
Shares Held: 131,340,014
% Held: 91.2

INDUSTRY: Surety insurance (SIC: 6351)

TRANSFER AGENT(S): Mellon Investor Services, LLC, Ridgefield Park, NJ

MBNA CORPORATION

YIELD 1.6%
P/E RATIO 14.4

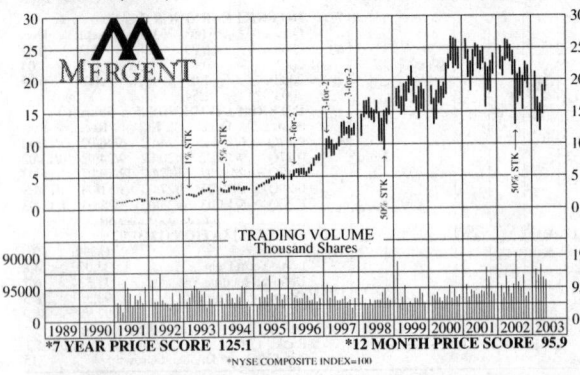

INTERIM EARNINGS (Per Share):

Qtr.	Mar.	June	Sept.	Dec.
2000	0.19	0.23	0.29	0.32
2001	0.23	0.29	0.36	0.40
2002	0.28	0.35	0.30	0.41
2003	0.33	...	...	...

INTERIM DIVIDENDS (Per Share):

Amt.	Decl.	Ex.	Rec.	Pay.
50% STK	6/06/02	7/16/02	7/01/02	7/15/02
0.07Q	7/16/02	9/12/02	9/16/02	10/01/02
0.07Q	10/17/02	12/11/02	12/13/02	1/01/03
0.08Q	1/23/03	3/12/03	3/15/03	4/01/03
0.08Q	4/23/03	6/11/03	6/13/03	7/01/03

Indicated div.: $0.32

CAPITALIZATION (12/31/02):

	($000)	(%)
Total Deposits	30,616,216	62.2
Long-Term Debt	9,538,173	19.4
Preferred Stock	86	0.0
Common & Surplus	9,101,233	18.5
Total	49,255,708	100.0

DIVIDEND ACHIEVER STATUS:
Rank: 85   10-Year Growth Rate: 13.31%
Total Years of Dividend Growth: 11

TRADING VOLUME
Thousand Shares

*7 YEAR PRICE SCORE 125.1   *12 MONTH PRICE SCORE 95.9
*NYSE COMPOSITE INDEX=100

RECENT DEVELOPMENTS: For the first quarter ended 3/31/03, net income advanced 16.9% to $432.5 million compared with $369.9 million in the corresponding prior-year quarter. Net interest income improved 8.2% to $555.6 million from $513.3 million a year earlier. Total interest income increased 3.1% to $944.0 million, while total interest expense declined 3.5% to $388.4 million. Provisions for possible credit losses grew 5.4% to $378.9 million from $359.4 million the year before.

PROSPECTS: KRB continues to expand and diversify its funding sources to support both current and future asset growth. KRB's funding sources include asset-backed securitizations, retail deposits, bank notes, brokered certificates of deposits, senior and subordinated debt, medium-term notes, trust preferred securities and preferred stock. Separately, KRB added 2.3 million new accounts, acquired 80 new credit card endorsements and renewed 232 group contracts during the first quarter.

BUSINESS

MBNA CORPORATION is a registered bank holding company, with assets of $54.57 billion as of 3/31/03. KRB is the parent of MBNA America Bank, N.A., which has two wholly-owned foreign bank subsidiaries, MBNA Europe Bank Limited, located in the United Kingdom, and MBNA Canada Bank. MBNA America Bank is also the parent of MBNA.com, a provider of credit card, consumer loan, retail deposit, travel and shopping services. The Company is an independent credit card lender and an issuer of affinity credit cards, marketed primarily to members of associations and customers of financial institutions. KRB offers credit cards in the U.S., the U.K., Ireland, Canada and Spain. In addition to its credit card lending, KRB also makes other consumer loans and offers insurance and deposit products.

QUARTERLY DATA

(12/31/2002)($000)	REV	INC
1st Quarter	2,511,967	369,910
2nd Quarter	2,529,247	457,842
3rd Quarter	2,555,568	398,042
4th Quarter	2,834,211	540,160

ANNUAL FINANCIAL DATA

	12/31/02	12/31/01	12/31/00	12/31/99	12/31/98	12/31/97	12/31/96
Earnings Per Share	② 1.34	1.28	1.02	0.81	0.65	0.51	① 0.39
Tang. Book Val. Per Share	4.63	4.08	3.03	3.49	2.12	1.75	1.51
Dividends Per Share	0.27	0.23	0.21	0.18	0.16	0.14	0.12
Dividend Payout %	20.1	18.2	20.3	22.3	24.0	27.1	31.1
INCOME STATEMENT (IN MILLIONS):							
Total Interest Income	3,678.1	3,205.1	2,775.7	2,262.3	1,966.2	1,711.0	1,383.4
Total Interest Expense	1,603.5	1,814.1	1,691.7	1,328.5	1,223.8	1,018.6	742.8
Net Interest Income	2,074.6	1,391.0	1,084.0	933.8	742.3	692.4	640.5
Provision for Loan Losses	1,340.2	1,140.6	409.0	408.9	310.0	260.0	178.2
Non-Interest Income	6,752.9	6,939.6	5,093.2	4,207.8	3,229.0	2,812.9	1,895.9
Non-Interest Expense	4,701.9	4,474.8	3,647.7	3,077.7	2,407.2	2,223.1	1,626.9
Income Before Taxes	2,785.4	2,715.2	2,120.4	1,655.0	1,254.1	1,022.1	731.3
Net Income	② 1,766.0	1,694.3	1,312.5	1,024.4	776.3	622.5	① 474.5
Average Shs. Outstg. (000)	1,277,787	1,314,230	1,269,797	1,255,557	1,184,132	1,184,702	1,167,710
BALANCE SHEET (IN MILLIONS):							
Cash & Due from Banks	722.0	962.1	971.5	488.4	382.9	263.1	225.1
Total Loans & Leases	17,696.9	14,703.6	11,682.9	7,971.1	11,776.1	8,261.9	7,659.1
Allowance for Credit Losses	1,111.3	833.4	386.6	356.0	216.9	162.5	118.4
Net Loans & Leases	16,585.6	13,870.2	11,296.3	7,615.1	11,559.2	8,099.4	7,540.7
Total Assets	52,856.7	45,447.9	38,678.1	30,859.1	25,806.3	21,305.5	17,035.3
Total Deposits	30,616.2	27,094.7	24,343.6	18,714.8	15,407.0	12,913.2	10,151.7
Long-Term Obligations	9,538.2	6,867.0	5,735.6	5,708.9	5,939.0	5,478.9	3,950.4
Total Liabilities	43,755.4	37,649.2	32,050.8	26,659.7	23,415.2	19,335.5	15,331.0
Net Stockholders' Equity	9,101.3	7,798.7	6,627.3	4,199.4	2,391.0	1,970.1	1,704.3
Year-end Shs. Outstg. (000)	1,277,672	1,277,672	1,277,706	1,202,672	1,127,694	1,127,673	1,127,672
STATISTICAL RECORD:							
Return on Equity %	19.4	21.7	19.8	24.4	32.5	31.6	27.8
Return on Assets %	3.3	3.7	3.4	3.3	3.0	2.9	2.8
Equity/Assets %	17.2	17.2	17.1	13.6	9.3	9.2	10.0
Non-Int. Exp./Tot. Inc. %	53.3	53.7	59.1	59.9	60.6	63.4	64.1
Price Range	26.30-12.95	26.38-15.62	26.75-13.00	22.17-13.88	17.25-9.00	13.59-7.96	8.64-4.48
P/E Ratio	19.6-9.7	20.6-12.2	26.2-12.7	27.5-17.2	26.7-13.9	26.6-15.6	21.9-11.4
Average Yield %	1.3	1.1	1.0	1.0	1.2	1.3	1.9

Statistics are as originally reported. Adj. for 3-for-2 splits: 7/02, 10/98, 10/97 & 2/97. ① Incl. pre-tax exp. fr. termination of mktg. agreement $54.3 mill. ② Incl. aft.-tax chrg. of $167.2 mill. rel. to implementation of the Federal Financial Institutions Examination Council for uncollectible interest and fees.

OFFICERS:
R. D. Lerner, Chmn.
C. M. Cawley, Pres., C.E.O.
V. H. Wright, C.F.O.

INVESTOR CONTACT: Brian D. Dalphon, Dir., Investor Relations, (800) 362-6255

PRINCIPAL OFFICE: 1100 North King Street, Wilmington, DE 19884-0141

TELEPHONE NUMBER: (302) 456-8588
FAX: (302) 456-8541
WEB: www.mbna.com
NO. OF EMPLOYEES: 28,000 (approx.)
SHAREHOLDERS: 2,743 (record)
ANNUAL MEETING: In May
INCORPORATED: MD, Dec., 1990

INSTITUTIONAL HOLDINGS:
No. of Institutions: 623
Shares Held: 903,822,121
% Held: 70.7

INDUSTRY: National commercial banks (SIC: 6021)

TRANSFER AGENT(S): National City Bank, Cleveland, OH

MCCORMICK & COMPANY, INC.

YIELD 1.6%
P/E RATIO 21.0

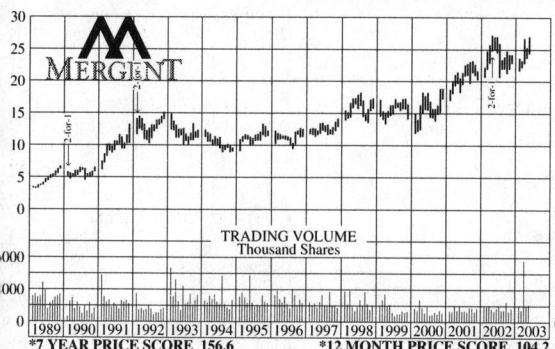

TRADING VOLUME
Thousand Shares

·000
·000

|1989|1990|1991|1992|1993|1994|1995|1996|1997|1998|1999|2000|2001|2002|2003|
*7 YEAR PRICE SCORE 156.6   *12 MONTH PRICE SCORE 104.2
*NYSE COMPOSITE INDEX=100

INTERIM EARNINGS (Per Share):

Qtr.	Feb.	May	Aug.	Nov.
1999-00	0.18	0.18	0.23	0.42
2000-01	0.19	0.19	0.25	0.42
2001-02	0.24	0.24	0.25	0.54
2002-03	0.25	...	...	...

INTERIM DIVIDENDS (Per Share):

Amt.	Decl.	Ex.	Rec.	Pay.
0.105Q	6/18/02	6/26/02	6/28/02	7/12/02
0.105Q	9/17/02	9/26/02	9/30/02	10/11/02
0.11Q	11/19/02	12/26/02	12/30/02	1/22/03
0.11Q	3/26/03	4/03/03	4/07/03	4/18/03

Indicated div.: $0.44 (Div. Reinv. Plan)

CAPITALIZATION (11/30/02):

	($000)	(%)
Long-Term Debt	453,900	43.4
Common & Surplus	592,300	56.6
Total	1,046,200	100.0

DIVIDEND ACHIEVER STATUS:
Rank: 177   10-Year Growth Rate: 8.26%
Total Years of Dividend Growth: 16

RECENT DEVELOPMENTS: For the three months ended 2/28/03, net income totaled $35.1 million, up 3.8% compared with $33.8 million a year earlier. Results included one-time pre-tax special charges of $78,000 and $367,000 in 2003 and 2002, respectively. Net sales rose 7.0% to $555.1 million from $518.9 million the year before. Gross profit was $199.8 million, or 36.0% of net sales, versus $185.3 million, or 35.7% of net sales, the prior year.

PROSPECTS: On 6/4/03, MKC announced that it has completed its acquisition of the Zatarain's business, which markets flavored rice, dinner mixes and food seasonings, from Citigroup Venture Capital and other investors for $180.0 million in cash. The acquisition is expected to add about $45.0 million to net sales and between $0.01 and $0.02 to earnings per share during the current fiscal year. MKC is targeting full-year 2003 sales growth of 6.0% to 9.0%.

BUSINESS

MCCORMICK & COMPANY, INC. is a diversified specialty food company primarily engaged in the manufacture of spices, seasonings, flavors and other specialty food products. The Company operates in three business segments: consumer, industrial, and packaging. The consumer segment (47.2% of 2002 revenues) sells spices, herbs, extracts, proprietary seasoning blends, sauces and marinades to the consumer food market under a variety of brands, including the MCCORMICK brand, the CLUB HOUSE brand in Canada, and the SCHWARTZ brand in the U.K. The industrial segment (45.5%) sells spices, herbs, extracts, proprietary seasonings, condiments, coatings and compound flavors to food processors, restaurant chains, distributors, warehouse clubs and institutional operations. The packaging segment (7.3%) sells plastic packaging products to the food, personal care and other industries, primarily in the U.S.

ANNUAL FINANCIAL DATA

	11/30/02	11/30/01	11/30/00	11/30/99	11/30/98	11/30/97	11/30/96
Earnings Per Share	⑤ 1.26	⑥ 1.05	⑦ 0.99	⑥ 0.72	⑥ 0.71	② 0.65	③ 0.27
Cash Flow Per Share	1.73	1.57	1.43	1.12	1.07	0.97	0.67
Tang. Book Val. Per Share	0.62	...	...	1.70	1.57	1.59	1.82
Dividends Per Share	0.42	0.40	0.38	0.34	0.32	0.30	0.28
Dividend Payout %	33.3	38.3	38.4	47.5	45.4	46.5	103.7
INCOME STATEMENT (IN MILLIONS):							
Total Revenues	2,320.0	2,372.3	2,123.5	2,006.9	1,881.1	1,801.0	1,732.5
Costs & Expenses	1,975.5	2,058.7	1,837.2	1,772.6	1,643.5	1,580.8	1,575.4
Depreciation & Amort.	66.8	73.0	61.3	57.4	54.8	49.3	63.8
Operating Income	277.7	240.6	225.0	176.9	182.8	170.8	93.3
Net Interest Inc./(Exp.)	d43.6	d52.9	d39.7	d32.4	d36.9	d36.3	d33.8
Income Before Income Taxes	234.8	190.4	186.0	150.0	152.5	142.3	61.7
Income Taxes	74.3	62.9	66.6	60.1	54.9	52.7	23.9
Equity Earnings/Minority Int.	19.3	19.1	18.1	13.4	6.2	7.8	5.6
Net Income	⑤ 179.8	⑥ 146.6	⑦ 137.5	⑥ 103.3	⑥ 103.8	② 97.4	③ 43.5
Cash Flow	246.6	219.6	198.8	160.7	158.6	146.8	107.3
Average Shs. Outstg. (000)	142,300	140,200	139,200	144,000	147,600	151,316	161,282
BALANCE SHEET (IN MILLIONS):							
Cash & Cash Equivalents	47.3	31.3	23.9	12.0	17.7	13.5	22.4
Total Current Assets	724.6	635.8	620.0	490.6	503.8	506.5	534.4
Net Property	468.3	424.5	373.0	363.3	377.0	380.0	400.4
Total Assets	1,930.8	1,772.0	1,659.9	1,188.8	1,259.1	1,256.2	1,326.6
Total Current Liabilities	673.4	713.7	1,027.2	470.6	518.0	498.2	499.3
Long-Term Obligations	453.9	454.1	160.2	241.4	250.4	276.5	291.2
Net Stockholders' Equity	592.3	463.1	359.3	382.4	388.1	393.1	450.0
Net Working Capital	51.2	d77.9	d407.2	20.0	d14.2	8.3	35.1
Year-end Shs. Outstg. (000)	140,000	138,400	136,600	140,800	145,000	148,048	156,410
STATISTICAL RECORD:							
Operating Profit Margin %	12.0	10.1	10.6	8.8	9.7	9.5	5.4
Net Profit Margin %	7.8	6.2	6.5	5.1	5.5	5.4	2.5
Return on Equity %	30.4	31.7	38.3	27.0	26.7	24.8	9.7
Return on Assets %	9.3	8.3	8.3	8.7	8.2	7.8	3.3
Debt/Total Assets %	23.5	25.6	9.7	20.3	19.9	22.0	22.0
Price Range	27.25-20.70	23.27-17.00	18.88-11.88	17.31-13.31	18.22-13.53	14.19-11.31	12.69-9.44
P/E Ratio	21.6-16.4	22.3-16.3	19.1-12.0	24.2-18.6	25.8-19.2	22.0-17.5	47.0-34.9
Average Yield %	1.8	2.0	2.5	2.2	2.0	2.4	2.5

Statistics are as originally reported. Adj. for 2-for-1 stk. split, 4/02. ⑤ Incl. $8.0 mill. pre-tax chrg., 2002; $10.8 mill. pre-tax chrg., 2001; $1.1 mil pre-tax chrg., 2000; $18.4 mill. after-tax chrg., 1999; $2.3 mill. pre-tax chrg., 1998. ② Bef. $1.0 mill. disc. oper. gain & incl. $3.2 mill. pre-tax credit. ③ Bef. $7.8 mill. extraord. chrg., $6.2 mill. disc. oper. gain & incl. $58.1 mill. pre-tax chrg.

OFFICERS:
R. J. Lawless, Chmn., Pres., C.E.O.
F. A. Contino, Exec. V.P., C.F.O.
C. J. Kurtzman, V.P., Treas.

INVESTOR CONTACT: Chris Kurtzman, V.P., Treas., (410) 771-7244

PRINCIPAL OFFICE: 18 Loveton Circle, P.O Box 6000, Sparks, MD 21152

TELEPHONE NUMBER: (410) 771-7301
FAX: (410) 771-7462
WEB: www.mccormick.com
NO. OF EMPLOYEES: 9,000 (approx.)
SHAREHOLDERS: 2,200 (approx. common); 9,900 (approx. non-voting common)
ANNUAL MEETING: In Mar.
INCORPORATED: MD, Nov., 1915

INSTITUTIONAL HOLDINGS:
No. of Institutions: 272
Shares Held: 94,801,352
% Held: 68.2

INDUSTRY: Food preparations, nec (SIC: 2099)

TRANSFER AGENT(S): Wells Fargo Shareowner Services, St. Paul, MN

MCDONALD'S CORPORATION

YIELD 1.3%
P/E RATIO 23.7

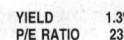

INTERIM EARNINGS (Per Share):

Qtr.	Mar.	June	Sept.	Dec.
2000	0.33	0.39	0.41	0.34
2001	0.29	0.34	0.42	0.21
2002	0.27	0.39	0.38	d0.27
2003	0.29	...	...	...

INTERIM DIVIDENDS (Per Share):

Amt.	Decl.	Ex.	Rec.	Pay.
0.225A	10/29/01	11/13/01	11/15/01	12/03/01
0.235A	10/22/02	11/13/02	11/15/02	12/02/02

Indicated div.: $0.23 (Div. Reinv. Plan)

CAPITALIZATION (12/31/02):

	($mill.)	(%)
Long-Term Debt	9,703.6	46.2
Deferred Income Tax	1,003.7	4.8
Common & Surplus	10,280.9	49.0
Total	20,988.2	100.0

DIVIDEND ACHIEVER STATUS:
Rank: 163   10-Year Growth Rate: 9.08%
Total Years of Dividend Growth: 26

TRADING VOLUME
Thousand Shares

*7 YEAR PRICE SCORE 74.6   *12 MONTH PRICE SCORE 86.6
*NYSE COMPOSITE INDEX=100

RECENT DEVELOPMENTS: For the quarter ended 3/31/03, MCD reported income of $364.2 million, before an accounting charge of $36.8 million, versus income of $351.7 million, before an accounting charge of $98.6 million, in the corresponding prior-year period. Systemwide sales improved 4.7% to $10.15 billion. Total revenues increased 5.6% to $3.80 billion, primarily reflecting restaurant expansion. Sales by Company-operated restaurants climbed 6.6% to $2.86 billion, while revenues from franchised and affiliated restaurants rose 2.7% to $943.6 million.

PROSPECTS: In 2003, the Company expects to open about 620 traditional restaurants and 340 satellite McDonald's restaurants, for a total of 960 new restaurants worldwide. Net of planned closings, worldwide restaurant additions are expected to total 360, with 200 net traditional and 160 net satellite restaurants. The Company expects sales from new restaurants to add approximately 2.0% to 3.0% to 2003 sales growth, and about 1.0% to 2004 sales growth. For 2005 and beyond, MCD is targeting annual systemwide sales growth in the range of 3.0% to 5.0%.

BUSINESS

MCDONALD'S CORPORATION develops, licenses, leases and services a worldwide system of restaurants. Units serve a standardized menu of moderately priced food consisting of hamburgers, cheeseburgers, chicken sandwiches, salads, desserts and beverages. As of 3/31/03, there were 17,816 units operated by franchisees, 9,147 units operated by the Company, and 4,209 units operated by affiliates. As of 12/31/02, MCD included in its restaurant units 662 Boston Markets, 232 Chipotle Mexican Grills, 181 Donatos Pizzas, and 8 Fazoli's. Systemwide sales in 2002 were derived from: franchised restaurants, 61.9%; Company-owned units' sales, 27.7%; and affiliated restaurants, 10.4%. On 5/26/00, MCD acquired approximately 750 Boston Market restaurants from Boston Chicken, Inc. In March 2002, MCD sold its Aroma Cafe business in the U.K.

ANNUAL FINANCIAL DATA

	12/31/02	12/31/01	12/31/00	12/31/99	12/31/98	12/31/97	12/31/96
Earnings Per Share	①③ 0.77	② 1.25	1.46	① 1.39	① 1.10	1.15	1.11
Cash Flow Per Share	1.59	2.08	2.20	2.07	1.73	1.73	1.66
Tang. Book Val. Per Share	6.88	6.30	5.95	6.20	6.26	4.83	5.48
Dividends Per Share	0.235	0.225	0.215	0.20	0.18	0.16	0.15
Dividend Payout %	30.5	18.0	14.7	14.0	16.0	14.1	13.2
INCOME STATEMENT (IN MILLIONS):							
Total Revenues	15,405.7	14,870.0	14,243.0	13,259.3	12,421.4	11,408.8	10,686.5
Costs & Expenses	12,242.0	10,829.3	10,099.0	9,107.5	8,678.6	7,920.2	7,356.8
Depreciation & Amort.	1,050.8	1,086.3	1,010.7	956.3	881.1	793.8	742.9
Operating Income	2,112.9	2,697.0	3,329.7	3,319.6	2,761.9	2,808.3	2,632.6
Net Interest Inc./(Exp.)	d374.1	d452.4	d429.9	d396.3	d413.8	d364.4	d342.5
Income Before Income Taxes	1,662.1	2,329.7	2,882.3	2,884.1	2,307.4	2,407.3	2,251.0
Income Taxes	670.0	693.1	905.0	936.2	757.3	764.8	678.4
Net Income	①③ 992.1	② 1,636.6	1,977.3	① 1,947.9	① 1,550.1	1,642.5	1,572.6
Cash Flow	2,042.9	2,722.9	2,988.0	2,904.2	2,431.2	2,411.0	2,287.9
Average Shs. Outstg. (000)	1,281,500	1,309,300	1,356,500	1,404,200	1,405,700	1,410,200	1,396,400
BALANCE SHEET (IN MILLIONS):							
Cash & Cash Equivalents	330.4	418.1	421.7	419.5	299.2	341.4	329.9
Total Current Assets	1,715.4	1,819.3	1,662.4	1,572.3	1,309.4	1,142.3	1,102.5
Net Property	18,583.4	17,289.5	17,047.6	16,324.5	16,041.6	14,961.4	14,352.1
Total Assets	23,970.5	22,534.5	21,683.5	20,983.2	19,784.4	18,241.5	17,386.0
Total Current Liabilities	2,422.3	2,248.3	2,360.9	3,274.3	2,497.1	2,984.5	2,135.3
Long-Term Obligations	9,703.6	8,555.5	7,843.9	5,632.4	6,188.6	4,834.1	4,830.1
Net Stockholders' Equity	10,280.9	9,488.4	9,204.4	9,639.1	9,464.7	8,851.6	8,718.2
Net Working Capital	d706.9	d429.0	d698.5	d1,702.0	d1,187.7	d1,842.2	d1,032.8
Year-end Shs. Outstg. (000)	1,268,200	1,280,700	1,304,900	1,350,800	1,356,200	1,660,600	1,389,200
STATISTICAL RECORD:							
Operating Profit Margin %	13.7	18.1	23.4	25.0	22.2	24.6	24.6
Net Profit Margin %	6.4	11.0	13.9	14.7	12.5	14.4	14.7
Return on Equity %	9.6	17.2	21.5	20.2	16.4	18.6	18.0
Return on Assets %	4.1	7.3	9.1	9.3	7.8	9.0	9.0
Debt/Total Assets %	40.5	38.0	36.2	26.8	31.3	26.5	27.8
Price Range	30.68-15.17	35.06-24.75	43.63-26.38	49.56-35.94	39.75-22.31	27.44-21.06	27.13-20.50
P/E Ratio	39.8-19.7	28.0-19.8	29.9-18.1	35.7-25.9	36.1-20.3	24.0-18.4	24.5-18.6
Average Yield %	1.0	0.8	0.6	0.5	0.6	0.7	0.6

Statistics are as originally reported. Adj. for stk. splits: 2-for-1, 3/99. ① Incl. after-tax non-recurr. chrg. of $699.9 mill., 2002; $18.9 mill., 1999; $321.6 mill., 1998. ② Incl. an after-tax gain on McDonald's Japan initial public offering of $137.1 million and after-tax non-recurring chrgs. totaling $279.6 mill. ③ Bef. acctg. change chrg. of $98.6 mill.

OFFICERS:
J. R. Cantalupo, Chmn., C.E.O.
C. Bell, Pres., C.O.O.
INVESTOR CONTACT: Investor Relations Service Center, (630) 623-7428
PRINCIPAL OFFICE: McDonald's Plaza, Oak Brook, IL 60523

TELEPHONE NUMBER: (630) 623-3000
FAX: (630) 623-5027
WEB: www.mcdonalds.com
NO. OF EMPLOYEES: 413,000 (approx.)
SHAREHOLDERS: 1,032,000 (approx.)
ANNUAL MEETING: In May
INCORPORATED: DE, Mar., 1965

INSTITUTIONAL HOLDINGS:
No. of Institutions: 727
Shares Held: 817,164,958
% Held: 64.4
INDUSTRY: Eating places (SIC: 5812)
TRANSFER AGENT(S): First Chicago Trust Company, Jersey City, NJ

NASDAQ SYMBOL MGRC
Rec. Pr. 25.90 (5/31/03)

MCGRATH RENTCORP

YIELD 3.1%
P/E RATIO 16.3

TRADING VOLUME
Thousand Shares

*7 YEAR PRICE SCORE 127.8   *12 MONTH PRICE SCORE 106.0
*NYSE COMPOSITE INDEX=100

INTERIM EARNINGS (Per Share):

Qtr.	Mar.	June	Sept.	Dec.
2000	0.45	0.52	0.73	0.50
2001	0.54	0.62	0.58	0.42
2002	d0.19	d0.10	0.68	0.61
2003	0.40	...	...	...

INTERIM DIVIDENDS (Per Share):

Amt.	Decl.	Ex.	Rec.	Pay.
0.18Q	9/20/02	10/10/02	10/15/02	10/31/02
0.18Q	12/23/02	1/13/03	1/15/03	1/31/03
0.20Q	3/21/03	4/11/03	4/15/03	4/30/03
0.20Q	5/28/03	7/11/03	7/15/03	7/31/03

Indicated div.: $0.80

CAPITALIZATION (12/31/02):

	($000)	(%)
Long-Term Debt	55,523	20.9
Deferred Income Tax	68,259	25.7
Minority Interest	3,107	1.2
Common & Surplus	139,019	52.3
Total	265,908	100.0

DIVIDEND ACHIEVER STATUS:
Rank: 68   10-Year Growth Rate: 14.54%
Total Years of Dividend Growth: 12

RECENT DEVELOPMENTS: For the three months ended 3/31/03, net income jumped to $4.9 million versus a net loss of $2.4 million in the corresponding period of 2002. Results for 2002 included an impairment related to rental equipment of $11.9 million. Total revenues slipped 13.5% to $27.5 million from $31.8 million a year earlier. Revenues from rental operations decreased 13.0% to $22.0 million from $25.3 million, while sales declined 14.1% to $5.3 million from $6.1 million in 2002. Revenues from other operations dropped 44.9% to $196,000 versus $356,000 the year before. Gross margin soared to $14.1 million from $3.1 million in the prior-year period. Income from operations increased to $8.7 million versus an operating loss of $2.9 million in the previous year. Separately, the Company reaffirmed its full-year 2003 earnings per share guidance of $2.12 to $2.17. This guidance is based on continued strong demand for modular classrooms in California, and timely delivery and installation of classroom rental products.

BUSINESS

MCGRATH RENTCORP is comprised of three business segments: Mobile Modular Management Corporation (MMMC), its modular building rental division; RenTelco, its electronic test equipment rental division; and Enviroplex, its majority-owned subsidiary portable classroom manufacturing business that sells directly to California public school districts. The Company owns 80.7% of Enviroplex. MMMC rents and sells modular buildings and accessories to fulfill customers' temporary and permanent space needs in California and Texas. RenTelco rents and sells electronic test equipment nationally from its two locations in Plano, Texas and Livermore, California.

ANNUAL FINANCIAL DATA

	12/31/02	12/31/01	12/31/00	12/31/99	12/31/98	12/31/97	12/31/96
Earnings Per Share	②1.00	2.14	2.19	①1.78	1.67	1.58	1.02
Cash Flow Per Share	2.42	4.51	4.26	3.39	2.98	2.62	1.88
Tang. Book Val. Per Share	11.13	10.67	8.99	7.60	7.54	6.79	5.99
Dividends Per Share	0.68	0.62	0.54	0.46	0.38	0.31	0.27
Dividend Payout %	68.0	29.0	24.7	25.8	22.8	19.6	26.6
INCOME STATEMENT (IN THOUSANDS):							
Total Revenues	145,086	159,394	164,158	129,962	135,428	134,976	89,005
Costs & Expenses	101,979	77,717	81,926	62,924	69,398	73,755	47,561
Depreciation & Amort.	17,872	29,632	25,716	21,474	18,794	15,771	13,285
Operating Income	25,235	52,045	56,516	45,564	47,236	45,450	28,159
Net Interest Inc./(Exp.)	d3,982	d7,078	d8,840	d6,606	d6,326	d4,070	d2,887
Income Before Income Taxes	21,253	44,967	47,676	38,958	40,910	41,379	25,272
Income Taxes	8,459	17,807	19,762	14,874	16,010	16,323	9,750
Equity Earnings/Minority Int.	d161	d482	d670	d251	d1,005	d1,011	...
Net Income	②12,633	26,678	27,244	①23,833	23,895	24,045	15,522
Cash Flow	30,505	56,310	52,960	45,307	42,689	39,816	28,807
Average Shs. Outstg.	12,619	12,495	12,428	13,383	14,349	15,181	15,306
BALANCE SHEET (IN THOUSANDS):							
Cash & Cash Equivalents	4	4	643	490	857	538	686
Total Current Assets	33,253	36,900	46,330	25,585	22,668	22,332	20,606
Net Property	270,278	307,304	299,938	268,149	250,441	223,503	177,032
Total Assets	313,134	354,884	357,246	297,722	278,676	252,392	200,035
Total Current Liabilities	29,889	30,745	37,012	24,811	22,964	27,047	15,281
Long-Term Obligations	55,523	104,140	126,876	110,300	97,000	82,000	53,850
Net Stockholders' Equity	139,019	131,595	108,958	95,403	105,394	98,646	88,808
Net Working Capital	3,364	6,155	9,318	774	d296	d4,715	5,326
Year-end Shs. Outstg.	12,490	12,335	12,125	12,546	13,970	14,522	14,820
STATISTICAL RECORD:							
Operating Profit Margin %	17.4	32.7	34.4	35.1	34.9	33.7	31.6
Net Profit Margin %	8.7	16.7	16.6	18.3	17.6	17.8	17.4
Return on Equity %	9.1	20.3	25.0	25.0	22.7	24.4	17.5
Return on Assets %	4.0	7.5	7.6	8.0	8.6	9.5	7.8
Debt/Total Assets %	17.7	29.3	35.5	37.0	34.8	32.5	26.9
Price Range	37.92-17.21	37.69-17.63	19.88-14.00	22.50-15.88	24.75-13.88	28.50-12.25	13.63-8.38
P/E Ratio	37.9-17.2	17.6-8.2	9.1-6.4	12.6-8.9	14.8-8.3	18.0-7.8	13.4-8.3
Average Yield %	2.5	2.2	3.2	2.4	2.0	1.5	2.5

Statistics are as originally reported. Adj. for stk. splits: 2-for-1, 4/25/97. ① Bef. acctg. chrg. of $1.4 mill. ② Incl. $24.1 mill. impair. of rental equip.

OFFICERS:
R. P. McGrath, Chmn.
D. C. Kakures, Pres., C.E.O.
T. J. Sauer, V.P., C.F.O.

INVESTOR CONTACT: Tom Sauer, V.P., C.F.O., (925) 606-9200

PRINCIPAL OFFICE: 5700 Las Positas Road, Livermore, CA 94550

TELEPHONE NUMBER: (925) 606-9200
FAX: (925) 276-3905
WEB: www.mgrc.com

NO. OF EMPLOYEES: 436 (avg.)

SHAREHOLDERS: 85 (record)

ANNUAL MEETING: In Sept.

INCORPORATED: CA, Mar., 1979

INSTITUTIONAL HOLDINGS:
No. of Institutions: 61
Shares Held: 6,197,759
% Held: 51.6

INDUSTRY: Equipment rental & leasing, nec (SIC: 7359)

TRANSFER AGENT(S): U.S. Stock Transfer, Glendale, CA

MCGRAW-HILL COMPANIES, INC. (THE)

YIELD 1.7%
P/E RATIO 21.0

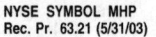

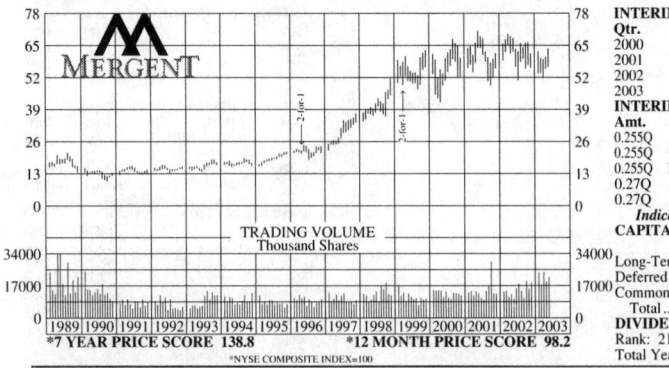

*7 YEAR PRICE SCORE 138.8   *12 MONTH PRICE SCORE 98.2
*NYSE COMPOSITE INDEX=100

INTERIM EARNINGS (Per Share):

Qtr.	Mar.	June	Sept.	Dec.
2000	0.29	0.55	1.11	0.50
2001	0.10	0.61	1.22	d0.01
2002	0.15	0.70	1.42	0.69
2003	0.20	...	...	...

INTERIM DIVIDENDS (Per Share):

Amt.	Decl.	Ex.	Rec.	Pay.
0.255Q	4/24/02	5/24/02	5/29/02	6/12/02
0.255Q	7/31/02	8/23/02	8/27/02	9/11/02
0.255Q	10/30/02	11/22/02	11/26/02	12/11/02
0.27Q	1/29/03	2/24/03	2/26/03	3/12/03
0.27Q	4/30/03	5/23/03	5/28/03	6/11/03

Indicated div.: $1.08 (Div. Reinv. Plan)

CAPITALIZATION (12/31/02):

	($000)	(%)
Long-Term Debt	458,923	16.2
Deferred Income Tax	200,114	7.1
Common & Surplus	2,165,822	76.7
Total	2,824,859	100.0

DIVIDEND ACHIEVER STATUS:
Rank: 213   10-Year Growth Rate: 6.18%
Total Years of Dividend Growth: 29

RECENT DEVELOPMENTS: For the quarter ended 3/31/03, MHP reported income from continuing operations of $38.2 million versus income of $28.6 million in the corresponding prior-year period. Earnings for 2003 and 2002 excluded gains of $57.2 million and $589,000, respectively, from discontinued operations. Operating revenue rose 1.9% to $846.5 million. Revenue from Financial Services grew 8.3% to $394.9 million, while revenue from McGraw-Hill Education slid 1.6% to $277.2 million.

PROSPECTS: The advertising market, which has been exacerbated by geopolitical events, continues to be sluggish. Meanwhile, the Company expects the kindergarten-through-twelfth grade market to grow in 2003 as new federal money is reaching the market and should help mitigate funding issues. For 2003, the Company anticipates modest growth in the second quarter followed by a pick-up in business in the second half. As a result, MHP expects earnings per share growth of 7.0% to 9.0% in 2003.

BUSINESS

THE MCGRAW-HILL COMPANIES, INC., a multimedia publishing and information services company, serves worldwide markets in education, finance and business information. As of 3/31/03, MHP operated more than 320 offices in 34 countries. The Company provides information in print through books, newsletters, and magazines, including Business Week; on-line over electronic networks; over the air by television, satellite and FM sideband; and on software, videotape, facsimile and compact disks. Among the Company's business units are Standard & Poor's Financial Information Services and Standard & Poor's Ratings Services divisions. Net sales for 2002 were derived as follows: McGraw-Hill Education, 49.2%; Financial Services, 33.9%; and Information and Media Services, 16.9%.

ANNUAL FINANCIAL DATA

	12/31/02	12/31/01	12/31/00	12/31/99	12/31/98	12/31/97	12/31/96
Earnings Per Share	⑤ 2.96	④ 1.92	③ 2.41	② 2.14	1.71	① 1.46	① 2.48
Cash Flow Per Share	5.07	4.07	4.25	3.70	3.22	2.93	3.67
Tang. Book Val. Per Share	1.88	0.18	0.33	2.24	1.48	0.64	0.28
Dividends Per Share	1.02	0.98	0.94	0.86	0.78	0.72	0.66
Dividend Payout %	34.5	51.0	39.0	40.2	45.8	49.5	26.6

INCOME STATEMENT (IN MILLIONS):

Total Revenues	4,787.7	4,645.5	4,281.0	3,992.0	3,729.1	3,534.1	3,074.7
Costs & Expenses	3,451.3	3,554.8	3,098.5	2,943.7	2,821.5	2,716.8	1,973.7
Depreciation & Amort.	408.8	420.6	362.3	308.3	299.2	293.5	238.6
Operating Income	927.6	670.1	820.2	740.0	608.4	523.8	862.5
Net Interest Inc./(Exp.)	d22.5	d55.1	d52.8	d42.0	d48.0	d52.5	d47.7
Income Before Income Taxes	905.1	615.1	767.3	698.0	560.4	471.3	814.8
Income Taxes	328.3	238.0	295.4	272.2	218.6	180.6	319.1
Net Income	⑤ 576.8	④ 377.0	③ 471.9	① 425.8	② 341.9	① 290.7	① 495.7
Cash Flow	985.5	797.6	834.2	734.1	641.1	584.2	734.3
Average Shs. Outstg. (000)	194,573	195,873	196,072	198,557	199,104	199,504	199,994

BALANCE SHEET (IN MILLIONS):

Cash & Cash Equivalents	58.2	53.5	3.2	6.5	10.5	4.8	3.4
Total Current Assets	1,674.3	1,812.9	1,801.7	1,553.7	1,428.8	1,464.4	1,349.6
Net Property	431.5	454.9	431.9	430.4	364.0	273.6	311.5
Total Assets	5,032.2	5,161.2	4,931.4	4,088.8	3,788.1	3,724.5	3,642.2
Total Current Liabilities	1,775.3	1,876.4	1,780.8	1,525.5	1,291.5	1,206.2	1,218.7
Long-Term Obligations	458.9	833.6	817.5	354.8	452.1	607.0	556.9
Net Stockholders' Equity	2,165.8	1,853.9	1,761.0	1,691.5	1,551.8	1,434.7	1,361.1
Net Working Capital	d101.0	d63.4	20.9	28.3	137.3	258.2	130.9
Year-end Shs. Outstg. (000)	191,833	193,218	194,285	195,709	197,111	198,204	199,062

STATISTICAL RECORD:

Operating Profit Margin %	19.4	14.4	19.2	18.5	16.3	14.8	28.1
Net Profit Margin %	12.0	8.1	11.0	10.7	9.2	8.2	16.1
Return on Equity %	26.6	20.3	26.8	25.2	22.0	20.3	36.4
Return on Assets %	11.5	7.3	9.6	10.4	9.0	7.8	13.6
Debt/Total Assets %	9.1	16.2	16.6	8.7	11.9	16.3	15.3
Price Range	69.70-50.71	70.87-48.70	67.69-41.88	63.13-47.13	51.66-34.25	37.38-22.44	24.63-18.63
P/E Ratio	23.5-17.1	36.9-25.4	28.1-17.4	29.5-22.0	30.2-20.0	25.7-15.4	9.9-7.5
Average Yield %	1.7	1.6	1.7	1.6	1.8	2.4	3.1

Statistics are as originally reported. Adj. for 2-for-1 split, 3/8/99. ① Incl. a one-time net gain of $24.2 mill., 1999; $40.1 mill., 1997; $260.5 mill., 1996. ② Bef. extraord. chrg. of $8.7 mill. ③ Bef. acctg. chrg. of $68.1 mill.; incl. a gain of $10.2 mill. fr. the sale of Tower Group Int'l. ④ Incl. a prov. of $159.0 mill. for restruct. & asset write-down & a pre-tax net chrg. of $7.1 mill. rel. to various one-time items. ⑤ Incl. a loss of $14.5 mill. fr. the sale of MMS Int'l.

OFFICERS:
H. McGraw III, Chmn., Pres., C.E.O.
R. J. Bahash, Exec. V.P., C.F.O.
F. D. Penglase, Sr. V.P.

INVESTOR CONTACT: Donald S. Rubin, Sr. V.P.-Inv. Rel., (212) 512-4321

PRINCIPAL OFFICE: 1221 Avenue Of The Americas, New York, NY 10020-1095

TELEPHONE NUMBER: (212) 512-2000
FAX: (212) 512-2305
WEB: www.mcgraw-hill.com
NO. OF EMPLOYEES: 16,505
SHAREHOLDERS: 5,115 (approx.)
ANNUAL MEETING: In April
INCORPORATED: NY, Dec., 1925

INSTITUTIONAL HOLDINGS:
No. of Institutions: 494
Shares Held: 132,613,172
% Held: 69.1

INDUSTRY: Book publishing (SIC: 2731)

TRANSFER AGENT(S): Mellon Investor Services, South Hackensack, NJ

MDU RESOURCES GROUP, INC.

YIELD 3.0%
P/E RATIO 15.3

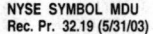

7 YEAR PRICE SCORE 124.9   **12 MONTH PRICE SCORE 114.3**
*NYSE COMPOSITE INDEX=100

TRADING VOLUME Thousand Shares

INTERIM EARNINGS (Per Share):

Qtr.	Mar.	June	Sept.	Dec.
2000	0.23	0.35	0.63	0.56
2001	0.49	0.63	0.74	0.42
2002	0.34	0.35	0.75	0.63
2003	0.37	...	...	...

INTERIM DIVIDENDS (Per Share):

Amt.	Decl.	Ex.	Rec.	Pay.
0.24Q	8/15/02	9/10/02	9/12/02	10/01/02
0.24Q	11/14/02	12/10/02	12/12/02	1/01/03
0.24Q	2/13/03	3/11/03	3/13/03	4/01/03
0.24Q	5/15/03	6/10/03	6/12/03	7/01/03

Indicated div.: $0.96 (Div. Reinv. Plan)

CAPITALIZATION (12/31/02):

	($000)	(%)
Long-Term Debt	819,558	32.9
Deferred Income Tax	374,097	15.0
Redeemable Pfd. Stock	1,200	0.0
Preferred Stock	15,000	0.6
Common & Surplus	1,283,745	51.5
Total	2,493,600	100.0

DIVIDEND ACHIEVER STATUS:

Rank: 254   10-Year Growth Rate: 3.74%
Total Years of Dividend Growth: 12

RECENT DEVELOPMENTS: For the three months ended 3/31/03, income was $27.7 million, before an accounting change charge of $7.6 million, versus net income of $23.7 million in the same period a year earlier. Results for 2002 included a non-recurring after-tax gain of $16.6 million. Operating revenues rose 22.5% to $467.8 million from $381.9 million the previous year. Operating income increased 15.5% to $52.9 million versus $45.8 million the year before.

PROSPECTS: On 4/11/03, MDU announced the acquisition of McElroy and Wilken, Inc., a privately-held ready mix and sand and gravel company serving northwestern Montana. Also on 4/11/03, MDU announced the acquisition of Atlas, Inc., a privately-held ready mix and concrete construction company, and Pioneer Construction, Inc., a privately-held aggregate company, for cash and stock. MDU now expects full-year 2003 earnings of between $2.00 and $2.25 per diluted share, before accounting changes.

BUSINESS

MDU RESOURCES GROUP, INC. is a diversified natural resource company. Montana-Dakota Utilities Co., a public utility division of MDU, generates, transmits and distributes electricity and distributes natural gas in the northern Great Plains. Great Plains Natural Gas Co., another public utility division of MDU, distributes natural gas in southeastern North Dakota and western Minnesota. These operations also supply related value-added products and services in the northern Great Plains. In addition, MDU, through its wholly-owned subsidiary, Centennial Energy Holdings, Inc., owns WBI Holdings, Inc., a provider of pipeline and energy services and a natural gas and oil producer; Knife River Corporation, a producer of construction materials; Utility Services, Inc., a utility infrastructure company; and Centennial Resources, which owns U.S. electric generating facilities. MDU also has an investment in an electric generating facility in Brazil through its wholly owned subsidiary, Centennial Energy Resources International Inc.

ANNUAL FINANCIAL DATA

	12/31/02	12/31/01	12/31/00	12/31/99	12/31/98	12/31/97	12/31/96
Earnings Per Share	2.07	2.29	1.80	1.52	▣ 0.66	1.24	1.05
Cash Flow Per Share	4.29	4.35	3.60	3.01	2.19	2.75	2.51
Tang. Book Val. Per Share	12.38	15.90	13.55	11.74	10.39	8.84	8.21
Dividends Per Share	0.93	0.89	0.85	0.81	0.78	0.75	0.73
Dividend Payout %	44.9	38.9	47.2	53.3	117.4	60.2	69.7
INCOME STATEMENT (IN MILLIONS):							
Total Revenues	2,031.5	2,223.6	1,873.7	1,279.8	896.6	607.7	514.7
Costs & Expenses	1,607.5	1,810.4	1,545.8	1,038.2	747.9	430.3	340.5
Depreciation & Amort.	158.0	139.9	110.9	81.8	77.8	65.8	62.7
Operating Income	266.1	273.3	217.0	159.8	70.9	111.6	111.5
Net Interest Inc./(Exp.)	d45.0	d45.9	d48.0	d36.0	d30.3	d30.2	d28.8
Income Taxes	86.2	98.3	69.7	49.3	17.5	30.7	16.1
Net Income	148.4	155.8	111.0	84.1	▣ 34.1	54.6	45.5
Cash Flow	305.6	295.0	221.2	165.1	111.1	119.6	107.3
Average Shs. Outstg. (000)	71,242	67,869	61,390	54,870	50,837	43,478	42,716
BALANCE SHEET (IN MILLIONS):							
Gross Property	3,004.0	2,756.7	2,496.1	2,042.3	1,810.8	1,510.3	1,370.3
Accumulated Depreciation	1,079.1	947.4	895.1	794.1	726.1	670.8	617.7
Net Property	1,924.9	1,809.3	1,601.0	1,248.2	1,084.7	839.5	752.6
Total Assets	2,937.2	2,623.1	2,313.0	1,766.3	1,452.8	1,113.9	1,205.4
Long-Term Obligations	819.6	783.7	728.2	563.5	413.3	298.6	280.7
Net Stockholders' Equity	1,298.7	1,124.7	896.0	684.4	565.7	401.2	365.6
Year-end Shs. Outstg. (000)	74,043	69,777	65,028	57,038	53,033	43,715	42,716
STATISTICAL RECORD:							
Operating Profit Margin %	13.1	12.3	11.6	12.5	7.9	18.4	21.7
Net Profit Margin %	7.3	7.0	5.9	6.6	3.8	9.0	8.8
Net Inc./Net Property %	7.7	8.6	6.9	6.7	3.1	6.5	6.0
Net Inc./Tot. Capital %	6.0	6.9	5.8	5.7	3.0	6.7	5.9
Return on Equity %	11.4	13.9	12.4	12.3	6.0	13.6	12.4
Accum. Depr./Gross Prop. %	35.9	34.4	35.9	38.9	40.1	44.4	45.1
Price Range	33.45-18.00	40.37-22.38	33.00-17.63	27.19-18.81	28.88-18.83	22.33-14.00	15.67-13.25
P/E Ratio	16.2-8.7	17.6-9.8	18.3-9.8	17.9-12.4	43.7-28.5	18.0-11.3	15.0-12.7
Average Yield %	3.6	2.8	3.4	3.5	3.2	4.1	5.0

Statistics are as originally reported. Adj. for 50% stk. div., 7/98. ▣ Incl. chrg. of $66.0 mill. related to write-downs of oil & gas prop.

OFFICERS:
M. A. White, Chmn., Pres., C.E.O.
W. L. Robinson, Exec. V.P., Treas., C.F.O.
L. H. Loble, II, V.P., Gen. Couns., Sec.

INVESTOR CONTACT: Cathi Christopherson, (701) 222-7959

PRINCIPAL OFFICE: Schuchart Building, 918 East Divide Avenue, Bismarck, ND 58506

TELEPHONE NUMBER: (701) 222-7900
FAX: (701) 222-7607
WEB: www.mdu.com
NO. OF EMPLOYEES: 6,983
SHAREHOLDERS: 14,000 (approx.)
ANNUAL MEETING: In Apr.
INCORPORATED: DE, Mar., 1924

INSTITUTIONAL HOLDINGS:
No. of Institutions: 178
Shares Held: 26,046,945
% Held: 35.2

INDUSTRY: Gas and other services combined (SIC: 4932)

TRANSFER AGENT(S): Wells Fargo Shareowner Services, St. Paul, MN

MEDTRONIC, INC.

YIELD 0.5%
P/E RATIO 37.2

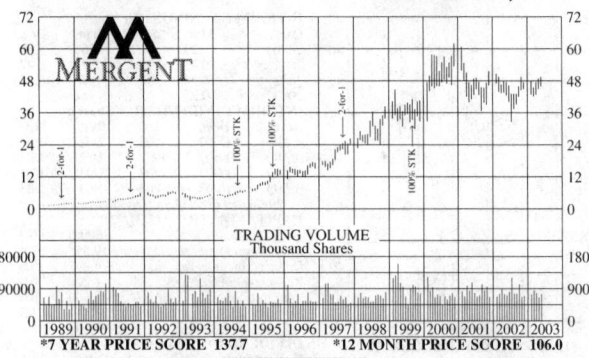

TRADING VOLUME
Thousand Shares

7 YEAR PRICE SCORE 137.7   *12 MONTH PRICE SCORE 106.0*

NYSE COMPOSITE INDEX=100

INTERIM EARNINGS (Per Share):

Qtr.	July	Oct.	Jan.	Apr.
1999-00	0.21	0.22	0.22	0.26
2000-01	0.24	0.26	0.25	0.12
2001-02	0.25	0.05	0.26	0.25
2002-03	0.31	0.25	0.35	0.40

INTERIM DIVIDENDS (Per Share):

Amt.	Decl.	Ex.	Rec.	Pay.
0.058Q	3/08/02	4/03/02	4/05/02	4/26/02
0.063Q	6/27/02	7/02/02	7/05/02	7/26/02
0.063Q	8/29/02	10/02/02	10/04/02	10/25/02
0.063Q	10/24/02	12/31/02	1/03/03	1/24/03
0.063Q	1/23/03	4/02/03	4/04/03	4/25/03

Indicated div.: $0.25 (Div. Reinv. Plan)

CAPITALIZATION (4/26/02):

	($000)	(%)
Long-Term Debt	9,500	0.1
Deferred Income Tax	233,800	3.5
Common & Surplus	6,431,100	96.4
Total	6,674,400	100.0

DIVIDEND ACHIEVER STATUS:
Rank: 15   10-Year Growth Rate: 22.13%
Total Years of Dividend Growth: 25

RECENT DEVELOPMENTS: For the year ended 4/25/03, net earnings leapt 62.6% to $1.60 billion versus $984.0 million the previous year. Results for 2003 and 2002 included pre-tax special charges of $2.5 million and $290.8 million, and pre-tax purchased in-process research and development charges of $114.2 million and $293.0 million, respectively. Net sales increased 19.6% to $7.67 billion.

PROSPECTS: MDT expects to benefit from strong revenues and earnings due to its broad product portfolio and new product pipeline. Meanwhile, MDT will continue to explore various strategic opportunities and the convergence of medical and information technologies. Separately, MDT announced approval in Europe for the Gatekeeper™ Reflux Repair System, a treatment for acid reflux, or gastroesophageal reflux disease.

BUSINESS

MEDTRONIC, INC. is a medical technology company operating in five operating segments that manufacture and sell device-based medical therapies. Cardiac Rhythm Management (47.3% of 2003 revenues) offers physicians and their patients a product line to treat bradycardia, tachyarrhythmias and heart failure. Cardiac Surgery (7.3%) offers a broad range of products for use by cardiac surgeons in the operating room. The Vascular segment (10.1%) offers minimally invasive products for the treatment of coronary vascular disease as well as diseases and conditions of the peripheral arteries. The Neurological and Diabetes segment (17.7%) offers products for the treatment of neurological disorders, diabetes, gastroenterology and urology conditions. The Spinal and Ear, Nose & Throat segment (17.6%) offers a range of products and therapies to treat a variety of disorders of the cranium, spine, ear, nose and throat.

ANNUAL FINANCIAL DATA

	4/26/02	4/27/01	4/30/00	4/30/99	4/30/98	4/30/97	4/30/96
Earnings Per Share	⑤ 0.80	①④ 0.85	③ 0.90	② 0.40	① 0.48	0.56	0.47
Cash Flow Per Share	1.07	1.10	1.10	0.57	0.63	0.68	0.59
Tang. Book Val. Per Share	1.10	3.53	2.61	1.99	1.68	1.34	1.41
Dividends Per Share	0.21	0.18	0.14	0.12	0.10	0.08	0.06
Dividend Payout %	26.9	21.2	16.1	30.4	21.3	14.4	12.4
INCOME STATEMENT (IN MILLIONS):							
Total Revenues	6,410.8	5,551.8	5,014.6	4,134.1	2,604.8	2,438.2	2,169.1
Costs & Expenses	4,515.8	3,714.9	3,157.7	3,121.2	1,744.0	1,536.9	1,410.2
Depreciation & Amort.	329.8	297.3	243.3	213.1	137.6	116.9	111.8
Operating Income	1,565.2	1,539.6	1,613.6	799.8	723.2	784.5	647.2
Net Interest Inc./(Exp.)	d6.6	74.2	15.4	22.2	14.8	24.7	21.2
Income Before Income Taxes	1,524.2	1,549.4	1,629.0	822.0	702.0	809.1	668.4
Income Taxes	540.2	503.4	530.5	353.6	244.6	279.2	230.6
Net Income	⑤ 984.0	①④ 1,046.0	③ 1,098.5	② 468.4	① 457.4	530.0	437.8
Cash Flow	1,313.8	1,343.3	1,341.8	681.5	594.9	646.9	549.6
Average Shs. Outstg. (000)	1,224,400	1,226,000	1,220,800	1,185,800	951,168	954,772	932,628
BALANCE SHEET (IN MILLIONS):							
Cash & Cash Equivalents	533.7	1,231.7	558.1	375.9	425.9	250.6	460.8
Total Current Assets	3,488.0	3,756.8	3,013.4	2,395.2	1,551.6	1,237.9	1,343.2
Net Property	1,451.8	1,176.5	946.5	748.8	508.8	487.2	415.3
Total Assets	10,904.5	7,038.9	5,669.4	4,870.3	2,774.7	2,409.2	2,503.3
Total Current Liabilities	3,984.9	1,359.3	991.5	990.3	572.0	518.7	525.0
Long-Term Obligations	9.5	13.3	14.1	17.6	16.2	14.0	15.3
Net Stockholders' Equity	6,431.1	5,509.5	4,491.5	3,654.6	2,044.2	1,746.2	1,789.3
Net Working Capital	d496.9	2,397.5	2,021.9	1,404.9	979.6	719.2	818.2
Year-end Shs. Outstg. (000)	1,215,209	1,209,515	1,197,698	1,170,452	938,090	935,256	937,272
STATISTICAL RECORD:							
Operating Profit Margin %	24.4	27.7	32.2	19.3	27.8	32.2	29.8
Net Profit Margin %	15.3	18.8	21.9	11.3	17.6	21.7	20.2
Return on Equity %	15.3	19.0	24.5	12.8	22.4	30.4	24.5
Return on Assets %	9.0	14.9	19.4	9.6	16.5	22.0	17.5
Debt/Total Assets %	0.1	0.2	0.2	0.4	0.6	0.6	0.6
Price Range	60.81-36.64	62.00-32.75	44.63-29.94	38.38-22.72	26.38-14.41	17.47-11.13	15.00-6.55
P/E Ratio	76.0-45.8	72.9-38.5	49.6-33.3	97.1-57.5	54.9-30.0	31.5-20.0	31.9-13.9
Average Yield %	0.4	0.4	0.4	0.4	0.5	0.6	0.5

Statistics are as originally reported. Adj. for 2-for-1 stk split, 9/99 & 9/97. ① Incl. a pre-tax chrg. of $169.3 mill., 1998; $338.8 mill., 2001. ② Incl. a pre-tax nonrecur. chg. of $371.3 mill. & a pre-tax chrg. of $150.9 mill. for pchsd. in-process R&D. ③ Incl. a pre-tax nonrecur. chrg. of $14.7 mill. for the Xomed acquis. ④ Incl. pre-tax spec. chrg. of $338.8 mill. ⑤ Incl. purch. in-process res. & dev. chrg. of $293.0 mill. & spec. chrg. of $290.8 mill.

OFFICERS:
A. D. Collins Jr., Chmn., Pres., C.E.O.
G. D. Nelson, Vice-Chmn

INVESTOR CONTACT: Rachael Scherer, Investor Relations, (763) 505-3035

PRINCIPAL OFFICE: 710 Medtronic Parkway, Minneapolis, MN 55432

TELEPHONE NUMBER: (763) 514-4000
FAX: (763) 514-4000
WEB: www.medtronic.com

NO. OF EMPLOYEES: 28,000 (approx.)

SHAREHOLDERS: 48,500 (approx. record)

ANNUAL MEETING: In Aug.

INCORPORATED: MN, 1957

INSTITUTIONAL HOLDINGS:
No. of Institutions: 941
Shares Held: 822,293,042
% Held: 67.4

INDUSTRY: Electromedical equipment (SIC: 3845)

TRANSFER AGENT(S): Wells Fargo Shareowner Services, St. Paul, MN

MERCANTILE BANKSHARES CORPORATION

YIELD 3.3%
P/E RATIO 14.6

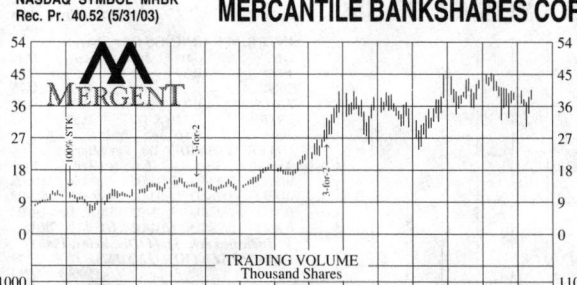

INTERIM EARNINGS (Per Share):

Qtr.	Mar.	June	Sept.	Dec.
2000	0.60	0.62	0.64	0.64
2001	0.65	0.62	0.65	0.63
2002	0.66	0.67	0.69	0.70
2003	0.71	...	...	...

INTERIM DIVIDENDS (Per Share):

Amt.	Decl.	Ex.	Rec.	Pay.
0.30Q	6/11/02	6/19/02	6/21/02	6/28/02
0.30Q	9/10/02	9/19/02	9/23/02	9/30/02
0.30Q	12/10/02	12/20/02	12/24/02	12/31/02
0.30Q	3/11/03	3/20/03	3/24/03	3/31/03
0.33Q	6/10/03	6/19/03	6/23/03	6/30/03

Indicated div.: $1.32 (Div. Reinv. Plan)

CAPITALIZATION (12/31/02):

	($000)	(%)
Total Deposits	8,260,940	83.7
Long-Term Debt	287,214	2.9
Common & Surplus	1,324,358	13.4
Total	9,872,512	100.0

DIVIDEND ACHIEVER STATUS:
Rank: 111   10-Year Growth Rate: 11.80%
Total Years of Dividend Growth: 26

TRADING VOLUME
Thousand Shares

*7 YEAR PRICE SCORE 126.7   ***12 MONTH PRICE SCORE 98.9**
*NYSE COMPOSITE INDEX=100

RECENT DEVELOPMENTS: For the three months ended 3/31/03, net income climbed 6.1% to $49.0 million compared with $46.2 million in the corresponding period of 2002. Results for 2003 and 2002 included a gain from investment securities of $815,000 and a loss of $2,000, and stock-based compensation expenses of $102,000 and $403,000, respectively. Total interest income declined 4.3% to $140.2 million from $146.5 million, while total interest expense fell 26.1% to $29.0 million from $39.3 million. Net interest income improved 3.7% to $111.1 million versus $107.2 million due to growth in average loans and average securities. Provision for loan losses slipped 2.2% to $3.0 million from $3.1 million in 2002. Total non-interest income grew 8.7% to $37.9 million, while total non-interest expenses rose 5.4% to $69.8 million. Separately, on 3/13/03, the Company announced a definitive agreement to acquire F&M Bancorp, a bank holding company, for $500.0 million in stock and cash.

BUSINESS

MERCANTILE BANKSHARES CORPORATION, with assets of $11.02 billion as of 3/31/03, is a bank holding company that owns substantially all of the outstanding shares of capital stock of twenty-one banks. The affiliated banks are engaged in the general commercial and retail banking business, including acceptance of demand, savings and time deposits and the making of various types of loans. Mercantile-Safe Deposit and Trust Company offers a full range of personal trust services, investment management services and, for corporate and institutional customers, investment advisory, financial and pension and profit sharing services, including Mercantile Capital Advisors, Inc. The Company also owns all of the outstanding shares of Mercantile Mortgage Corporation, a mortgage banking company, MBC Agency, Inc., an insurance agency, Hopkins Plaza Agency, Inc., an agent in the sale of fixed rate annuities, Hopkins Plaza Securities, Inc., a broker-dealer, MBC Leasing, Inc., a leasing company, and MBC Realty, LLC, which owns and operates various properties used by Mercantile Safe Deposit and Trust Company.

ANNUAL FINANCIAL DATA

	12/31/02	12/31/01	12/31/00	12/31/99	12/31/98	12/31/97	12/31/96
Earnings Per Share	2.72	2.55	2.51	2.25	2.04	1.84	1.64
Tang. Book Val. Per Share	17.64	16.03	15.03	13.51	13.36	12.50	11.35
Dividends Per Share	1.18	1.10	1.02	0.94	0.86	0.77	0.65
Dividend Payout %	43.4	43.1	40.6	41.8	42.2	42.0	39.8
INCOME STATEMENT (IN MILLIONS):							
Total Interest Income	586.4	649.8	646.5	559.2	555.4	534.0	498.1
Total Interest Expense	144.6	231.5	237.1	190.1	202.0	197.9	187.6
Net Interest Income	441.8	418.2	409.4	369.1	353.4	336.0	310.6
Provision for Loan Losses	16.4	13.4	17.2	12.1	11.5	13.7	14.7
Non-Interest Income	143.8	145.5	125.5	122.0	108.7	98.7	89.4
Non-Interest Expense	272.6	264.0	243.5	230.4	219.0	213.4	198.4
Income Before Taxes	296.6	286.3	274.2	248.6	231.6	207.6	186.9
Net Income	190.2	181.3	175.2	157.7	147.1	132.0	117.4
Average Shs. Outstg. (000)	70,067	71,199	69,719	70,020	72,237	71,904	71,477
BALANCE SHEET (IN MILLIONS):							
Cash & Due from Banks	281.1	290.2	244.9	219.4	255.0	337.2	257.3
Securities Avail. for Sale	2,511.2	2,288.7	1,676.6	1,743.9	1,880.5	1,607.3	1,596.7
Total Loans & Leases	7,312.0	6,906.2	6,693.3	5,718.9	5,220.9	4,978.5	4,582.7
Allowance for Credit Losses	138.6	141.5	138.6	118.0	112.4	106.1	97.7
Net Loans & Leases	7,173.4	6,764.8	6,554.7	5,600.9	5,108.5	4,872.4	4,485.0
Total Assets	10,790.4	9,928.8	8,938.0	7,895.0	7,609.6	7,170.7	6,642.7
Total Deposits	8,260.9	7,447.4	6,796.5	5,925.1	5,958.3	5,693.9	5,339.7
Long-Term Obligations	287.2	269.4	92.5	82.7	40.9	50.0	49.4
Total Liabilities	9,466.0	8,698.6	7,764.7	6,921.0	6,610.2	6,235.7	5,806.6
Net Stockholders' Equity	1,324.4	1,230.2	1,173.3	974.0	999.4	935.0	836.0
Year-end Shs. Outstg. (000)	68,836	69,776	71,099	68,646	71,027	71,874	71,153
STATISTICAL RECORD:							
Return on Equity %	14.4	14.7	14.9	16.2	14.7	14.1	14.0
Return on Assets %	1.8	1.8	2.0	2.0	1.9	1.8	1.8
Equity/Assets %	12.3	12.4	13.1	12.3	13.1	13.0	12.6
Non-Int. Exp./Tot. Inc. %	46.6	46.8	45.5	46.9	47.4	49.1	49.6
Price Range	45.36-32.07	44.50-33.63	45.13-23.75	39.94-30.00	40.25-25.25	40.25-21.17	22.50-16.50
P/E Ratio	16.7-11.8	17.5-13.2	18.0-9.5	17.7-13.3	19.7-12.4	21.9-11.5	13.7-10.1
Average Yield %	3.0	2.8	3.0	2.7	2.6	2.5	3.4

Statistics are as originally reported. Adj. for 3-for-2 stock split, 7/97.

OFFICERS:
E. J. Kelly III, Chmn., Pres., C.E.O.
T. L. Troupe, C.F.O., Treas.
J. L. Unger, Sec., Gen. Couns.

INVESTOR CONTACT: Investor Relations, (410) 347-8039

PRINCIPAL OFFICE: Two Hopkins Plaza, P.O. Box 1477, Baltimore, MD 21203

TELEPHONE NUMBER: (410) 237-5900
FAX: (410) 347-8493
WEB: www.mrbk.com

NO. OF EMPLOYEES: 2,885 (approx.)

SHAREHOLDERS: 9,166

ANNUAL MEETING: In Apr.

INCORPORATED: MD, May, 1969

INSTITUTIONAL HOLDINGS:
No. of Institutions: 188
Shares Held: 28,741,417
% Held: 41.7

INDUSTRY: State commercial banks (SIC: 6022)

TRANSFER AGENT(S): American Stock Transfer & Trust Company, New York, NY

MERCK & CO., INC.

YIELD	2.6%
P/E RATIO	17.4

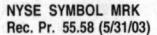

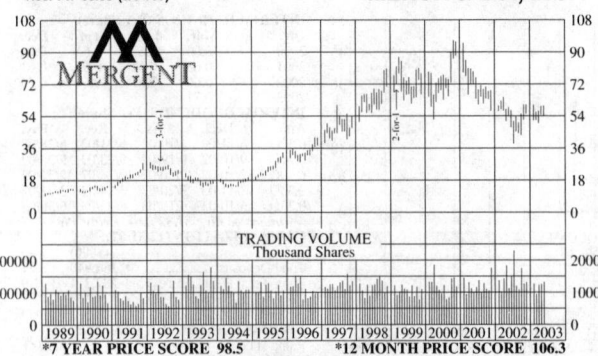

TRADING VOLUME
Thousand Shares

00000	20000
00000	10000
0	0

1989 1990 1991 1992 1993 1994 1995 1996 1997 1998 1999 2000 2001 2002 2003

*7 YEAR PRICE SCORE 98.5   ***12 MONTH PRICE SCORE 106.3**

*NYSE COMPOSITE INDEX=100

INTERIM EARNINGS (Per Share):

Qtr.	Mar.	June	Sept.	Dec.
1999	0.54	0.61	0.64	0.66
2000	0.63	0.73	0.78	0.75
2001	0.71	0.78	0.84	0.81
2002	0.71	0.77	0.83	0.83
2003	0.76	...	...	...

INTERIM DIVIDENDS (Per Share):

Amt.	Decl.	Ex.	Rec.	Pay.
0.36Q	7/23/02	9/04/02	9/06/02	10/01/02
0.36Q	11/26/02	12/04/02	12/06/02	1/02/03
0.36Q	2/25/03	3/05/03	3/07/03	4/01/03
0.36Q	5/27/03	6/04/03	6/06/03	7/01/03

Indicated div.: $1.44 (Div. Reinv. Plan)

CAPITALIZATION (12/31/02):

	($000)	(%)
Long-Term Debt	4,879,000	17.4
Minority Interest	4,928,300	17.6
Common & Surplus	18,200,500	65.0
Total	28,007,800	100.0

DIVIDEND ACHIEVER STATUS:

Rank: 108   10-Year Growth Rate: 11.85%
Total Years of Dividend Growth: 19

RECENT DEVELOPMENTS: For the quarter ended 3/31/03, net income climbed 5.3% to $1.71 billion compared with $1.63 billion in the year-earlier quarter. Results for 2003 included a pre-tax acquired research charge of $90.4 million. Sales climbed 10.0% to $13.39 billion primarily due to a 19.0% year-over-year aggregate sales increase of ZOCOR, FOSAMAX, COZAAR, HYZAAR, SINGULAIR and VIOXX.

PROSPECTS: The Company announced that Medco Health Solutions, Inc., its wholly owned pharmacy benefits management subsidiary, has filed a registration statement with the Securities and Exchange Commission for the 100.0 percent spin-off of shares of Medco Health common stock. MRK expects to complete the spin-off through a pro rata distribution during the third quarter of 2003 in a one-step transaction.

BUSINESS

MERCK & CO., INC. is a research pharmaceutical company that discovers, develops, manufactures and markets human and animal health products, directly and through its joint ventures, and provides pharmaceutical benefit services through Merck-Medco Managed Care LLC. The Merck Pharmaceuticals segment (41.4% of 2002 sales) consists of therapeutic and preventive agents, generally sold by prescription, for the treatment of human disorders. Human health products include ZOCOR, a cholesterol-lowering medicine, FOSAMAX, a treatment for osteoporosis, VIOXX, a prescription arthritis medicine, SINGULAIR, for the treatment of chronic asthma, and COZAAR and HYZAAR for the treatment of high blood pressure. The Medco Health Solutions, Inc. segment (58.6%) includes sales of non-Merck products and Merck-Medco pharmaceutical benefit services for more than 65.0 million customers.

ANNUAL FINANCIAL DATA

	12/31/02	12/31/01	12/31/00	12/31/99	12/31/98	12/31/97	12/31/96
Earnings Per Share	3.14	3.14	2.90	③ 2.45	② 2.15	① 1.87	1.60
Cash Flow Per Share	3.79	3.77	3.44	2.93	2.57	2.21	2.00
Tang. Book Val. Per Share	4.88	3.77	3.23	2.43	1.91	2.44	2.17
Dividends Per Share	1.41	1.37	1.21	1.10	0.94	0.84	0.71
Dividend Payout %	44.9	43.6	41.7	44.9	44.0	45.2	44.4

INCOME STATEMENT (IN MILLIONS):

Total Revenues	51,790.3	47,715.7	40,363.2	32,714.0	26,898.2	23,636.9	19,828.7
Costs & Expenses	39,784.6	36,193.5	29,677.7	23,708.7	20,282.3	16,936.1	13,916.9
Depreciation & Amort.	1,488.3	1,463.8	1,277.3	1,144.8	1,015.1	837.1	730.9
Operating Income	10,517.4	10,058.4	9,408.2	7,860.5	5,600.8	5,863.7	5,180.9
Income Before Income Taxes	10,213.6	9,716.7	9,059.2	7,857.5	7,248.8	5,734.4	5,180.9
Income Taxes	3,064.1	3,120.8	3,002.4	2,729.0	2,884.9	1,848.2	1,659.5
Equity Earnings/Minority Int.	644.7	685.9	764.9	762.0	884.3	727.9	600.7
Net Income	7,149.5	7,281.8	6,821.7	③ 5,890.5	② 5,248.2	① 4,614.1	4,122.1
Cash Flow	8,637.8	8,745.6	8,099.0	7,035.3	6,263.3	5,451.2	4,853.0
Average Shs. Outstg. (000)	2,277,000	2,322,300	2,353,200	2,404,600	2,441,100	2,469,400	2,427,200

BALANCE SHEET (IN MILLIONS):

Cash & Cash Equivalents	4,971.2	3,286.6	4,254.6	3,202.4	3,355.7	2,309.3	2,181.6
Total Current Assets	14,833.9	12,961.6	13,353.4	11,259.2	10,228.5	8,213.0	7,726.6
Net Property	14,195.6	13,103.4	11,482.1	9,676.7	7,843.8	6,609.4	5,926.7
Total Assets	47,561.2	44,006.7	39,910.4	35,634.9	31,853.4	25,811.9	24,293.1
Total Current Liabilities	12,375.2	11,544.2	9,709.6	8,758.8	6,068.8	5,568.6	4,829.2
Long-Term Obligations	4,879.0	4,798.6	3,600.7	3,143.9	3,220.8	1,346.5	1,155.9
Net Stockholders' Equity	18,200.5	16,050.1	14,832.4	13,241.6	12,801.8	12,613.5	11,970.5
Net Working Capital	2,458.7	1,417.4	3,643.8	2,500.4	4,159.7	2,644.4	2,897.4
Year-end Shs. Outstg. (000)	2,244,983	2,272,729	2,307,599	2,329,078	2,360,453	2,387,296	2,413,204

STATISTICAL RECORD:

Operating Profit Margin %	20.3	21.1	23.3	24.0	20.8	24.8	26.1
Net Profit Margin %	13.8	15.3	16.9	18.0	19.5	19.5	20.8
Return on Equity %	39.3	45.4	46.0	44.5	41.0	36.6	34.4
Return on Assets %	15.0	16.5	17.1	16.5	16.5	17.9	17.0
Debt/Total Assets %	10.3	10.9	9.0	8.8	10.1	5.2	4.8
Price Range	64.50-38.50	95.25-56.80	96.69-52.00	87.38-60.94	80.88-50.69	60.31-39.00	42.13-28.25
P/E Ratio	20.5-12.3	30.3-18.1	33.3-17.9	35.7-24.9	37.6-23.6	32.3-20.9	26.3-17.7
Average Yield %	2.7	1.8	1.6	1.5	1.4	1.7	2.0

Statistics are as originally reported. Adj. for 2-for-1 stock split, 2/99 ① Incl. a nonrecurr. pre-tax gain of $213.0 mill. & non-recurr. pre-tax chgs. totaling $207.0 mill. ② Incl. a pre-tax gain of $2.15 bill. from the sale of businesses, and a pre-tax charge of $1.04 bill. for acquired research and development. ③ Incl. a pre-tax chg. of $51.1 mill. for acquired research.

OFFICERS: R. V. Gilmartin, Chmn., Pres., C.E.O. J. C. Lewent, Exec. V.P., C.F.O. C. Dorsa, V.P., Treas. **INVESTOR CONTACT:** Mark Stejbach, Investor Relations, (908) 423-5185 **PRINCIPAL OFFICE:** One Merck Drive, Whitehouse Station, NJ 08889-0100	**TELEPHONE NUMBER:** (908) 423-1000 **FAX:** (908) 735-1500 **WEB:** www.merck.com **NO. OF EMPLOYEES:** 77,300 (avg.) **SHAREHOLDERS:** 246,300 **ANNUAL MEETING:** In Apr. **INCORPORATED:** NJ, June, 1927	**INSTITUTIONAL HOLDINGS:** No. of Institutions: 1,262 Shares Held: 1,315,077,068 % Held: 58.6 **INDUSTRY:** Pharmaceutical preparations (SIC: 2834) **TRANSFER AGENT(S):** Wells Fargo Shareowner Service, N.A., South St. Paul, MN

MERCURY GENERAL CORPORATION

YIELD 2.8%
P/E RATIO 32.7

TRADING VOLUME
Thousand Shares

*7 YEAR PRICE SCORE 125.4 *12 MONTH PRICE SCORE 103.6
*NYSE COMPOSITE INDEX=100

INTERIM EARNINGS (Per Share):

Qtr.	Mar.	June	Sept.	Dec.
1999	0.73	0.60	0.51	0.60
2000	0.55	0.48	0.51	0.48
2001	0.45	0.49	0.59	0.41
2002	0.53	0.02	0.34	0.32
2003	0.77	...	...	...

INTERIM DIVIDENDS (Per Share):

Amt.	Decl.	Ex.	Rec.	Pay.
0.30Q	4/29/02	6/12/02	6/14/02	6/27/02
0.30Q	7/26/02	9/11/02	9/13/02	9/26/02
0.30Q	10/25/02	12/11/02	12/13/02	12/26/02
0.33Q	1/31/03	3/13/03	3/17/03	3/27/03
0.33Q	4/28/03	6/11/03	6/15/03	6/30/03

Indicated div.: $1.32 (Div. Reinv. Plan)

CAPITALIZATION (12/31/02):

	($000)	(%)
Long-Term Debt	128,859	10.5
Common & Surplus	1,098,786	89.5
Total	1,227,645	100.0

DIVIDEND ACHIEVER STATUS:

Rank: 49   10-Year Growth Rate: 16.98%
Total Years of Dividend Growth: 16

RECENT DEVELOPMENTS: For the quarter ended 3/31/03, net income soared 45.4% to $42.1 million from $29.0 million in the equivalent prior-year quarter. Total revenues increased 26.7% to $528.1 million from $416.8 million the previous year. Revenues included a net realized investment loss of $759,000 in 2003 and a net realized investment gain of $238,000 in 2002. Net premiums written grew 27.8% to $538.8 million. Net premiums earned climbed 29.5% to $500.7 million from $386.6 million a year earlier.

PROSPECTS: Earnings growth is being driven primarily by increased policy sales in California, Florida and Texas. Separately, MCY announced that it has received approval from the California Department of Insurance to increase its personal automobile rates by 6.9% in Mercury Casualty Company and California Automobile Insurance Company and 3.8% in Mercury Insurance Company. MCY plans to implement these rate increases beginning in the second quarter of 2003.

BUSINESS

MERCURY GENERAL CORPORATION, through its subsidiaries, engages primarily in writing all risk classifications of automobile insurance in a number of states, principally in California. The Company offers automobile policyholders the following types of coverage: bodily injury liability, underinsured and uninsured motorist, personal injury protection, property damage liability, comprehensive, collision and other hazards specified in the policy. The Company sells its policies through independent agents in California, Florida, Georgia, Illinois, New York, Texas and Virginia. In addition, MCY writes other lines of insurance in various states, including mechanical breakdown and homeowners insurance. During 2002, approximately 85.1% of MCV's net premiums written were derived from California.

ANNUAL FINANCIAL DATA

	12/31/02	12/31/01	12/31/00	12/31/99	12/31/98	12/31/97	12/31/96
Earnings Per Share	1.21	1.94	2.02	2.44	3.21	2.82	1.93
Tang. Book Val. Per Share	20.21	19.71	19.06	16.71	16.78	14.51	11.66
Dividends Per Share	1.20	1.06	0.96	0.84	0.70	0.58	0.48
Dividend Payout %	99.2	54.6	47.5	34.4	21.8	20.6	24.9
INCOME STATEMENT (IN MILLIONS):							
Total Premium Income	1,741.5	1,380.6	1,249.3	1,188.3	1,121.6	1,031.3	754.7
Net Investment Income	113.1	114.5	106.5	99.4	96.2	86.8	70.2
Other Income	d68.3	11.9	10.3	d7.0	4.4	9.9	0.1
Total Revenues	1,786.3	1,507.0	1,366.0	1,280.7	1,222.1	1,127.9	825.0
Policyholder Benefits	1,268.2	1,010.4	901.8	789.1	684.5	654.7	501.9
Income Before Income Taxes	60.7	124.8	128.6	168.5	235.3	209.8	136.6
Income Taxes	cr5.4	19.5	19.2	34.8	57.8	53.5	30.8
Net Income	66.1	105.3	109.4	133.7	177.5	156.3	105.8
Average Shs. Outstg. (000)	54,502	54,382	54,258	54,815	55,354	55,383	54,794
BALANCE SHEET (IN MILLIONS):							
Cash & Cash Equivalents	300.0	75.8	38.9	51.6	47.9	62.8	69.7
Premiums Due	250.2	191.6	173.7	178.6	152.5	144.3	125.8
Invst. Assets: Fixed-term	1,632.9	1,586.4	1,509.5	1,322.1	1,324.9	1,215.0	954.1
Invst. Assets: Equities	231.0	277.8	252.5	209.8	219.7	173.5	148.1
Invst. Assets: Total	2,150.7	1,936.2	1,795.0	1,575.5	1,590.6	1,448.2	1,168.3
Total Assets	2,645.3	2,316.5	2,142.3	1,906.4	1,877.0	1,725.5	1,419.9
Long-Term Obligations	128.9	129.5	107.9	92.0	78.0	75.0	75.0
Net Stockholders' Equity	1,098.8	1,069.7	1,032.9	909.6	917.4	799.6	641.2
Year-end Shs. Outstg. (000)	54,362	54,277	54,193	54,425	54,684	55,125	55,014
STATISTICAL RECORD:							
Return on Revenues %	3.7	7.0	8.0	10.4	14.5	13.9	12.8
Return on Equity %	6.0	9.8	10.6	14.7	19.4	19.5	16.5
Return on Assets %	2.5	4.5	5.1	7.0	9.5	9.1	7.4
Price Range	51.15-37.25	44.50-32.00	44.88-21.06	45.50-20.94	70.00-33.00	54.44-26.13	29.13-19.88
P/E Ratio	42.3-30.8	22.9-16.5	22.2-10.4	18.6-8.6	21.8-10.3	19.3-9.3	15.1-10.3
Average Yield %	2.7	2.8	2.9	2.5	1.4	1.4	2.0

Statistics are as originally reported. Adj. for 2-for-1 stk. split, 10/97.

OFFICERS:
G. Joseph, Chmn., C.E.O.
G. Tirador, Pres., C.O.O.
T. R. Stalick, V.P., C.F.O.

INVESTOR CONTACT: Investor Relations, (323) 857-4973

PRINCIPAL OFFICE: 4484 Wilshire Boulevard, Los Angeles, CA 90010

TELEPHONE NUMBER: (323) 937-1060
FAX: (323) 857-7116
WEB: www.mercuryinsurance.com

NO. OF EMPLOYEES: 2,700 (approx.)

SHAREHOLDERS: 235 (approx.)

ANNUAL MEETING: In May

INCORPORATED: CA, 1961

INSTITUTIONAL HOLDINGS:
No. of Institutions: 126
Shares Held: 22,824,167
% Held: 42.3

INDUSTRY: Fire, marine, and casualty insurance (SIC: 6331)

TRANSFER AGENT(S): The Bank of New York, New York, NY

MGE ENERGY, INC.

YIELD 4.3%
P/E RATIO 19.8

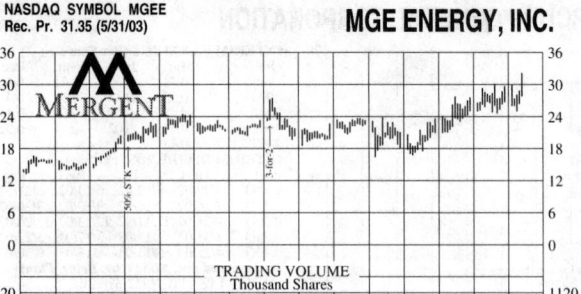

INTERIM EARNINGS (Per Share):

Qtr.	Mar.	June	Sept.	Dec.
2000	0.62	0.15	0.51	0.39
2001	0.58	0.32	0.36	0.37
2002	0.64	0.26	0.60	0.19
2003	0.53	...	...	...

INTERIM DIVIDENDS (Per Share):

Amt.	Decl.	Ex.	Rec.	Pay.
0.336Q	8/16/02	8/28/02	9/01/02	9/15/02
0.336Q	11/15/02	11/26/02	12/01/02	12/15/02
0.336Q	2/28/03	3/04/03	3/01/03	3/15/03
0.336Q	5/20/03	5/28/03	6/01/03	6/15/03

Indicated div.: $1.34 (Div. Reinv. Plan)

CAPITALIZATION (12/31/02):

	($000)	(%)
Long-Term Debt	192,149	39.9
Deferred Income Tax	62,450	13.0
Common & Surplus	227,370	47.2
Total	481,969	100.0

TRADING VOLUME
Thousand Shares

7 YEAR PRICE SCORE 137.3   **12 MONTH PRICE SCORE 103.7**
*NYSE COMPOSITE INDEX=100

DIVIDEND ACHIEVER STATUS:
Rank: 284   10-Year Growth Rate: 1.15%
Total Years of Dividend Growth: 27

RECENT DEVELOPMENTS: For the three months ended 3/31/03, net income declined 14.9% to $9.4 million compared with $11.0 million in the corresponding period of 2002. Total operating revenues jumped 30.8% to $128.5 million from $98.3 million a year earlier. Electric revenues were up $5.3 million as retail sales rose 2.4% and average rates were 3.9% higher. The Company sold 25 megawatts of electric capacity, for which the contract extends through August 2003. Gas revenues were up $24.9 million due to

colder weather, which increased retail gas deliveries by 20.0% and the average price of natural gas was 43.0% higher. Operating income decreased 13.9% to $17.5 million compared with $20.3 million in the previous year. Electric margins slipped 2.7 million due to an increase of $2.1 million for fuel costs for electric generation. The increase in fuel costs was due to substantially higher natural gas prices. Purchased power costs rose $5.9 million due to higher gas prices.

BUSINESS

MGE ENERGY, INC. (formerly Madison Gas & Electric Company) is the holding company for Madison Gas & Electric Company (MGEC), which is a public utility that generates and distributes electricity to nearly 130,000 customers in Dane County, Wisconsin as of 5/2/03. MGEE also purchases, transports and distributes natural gas to more than 126,000 customers in seven Wisconsin counties: Columbia, Crawford, Dane, Iowa, Juneau, Monroe and Vernon. Revenue for 2002 was comprised of: electric operations, 64.8%; and gas operations, 35.2%.

ANNUAL FINANCIAL DATA

	12/31/02	12/31/01	12/31/00	12/31/99	12/31/98	12/31/97	12/31/96
Earnings Per Share	1.69	① 1.63	1.67	1.48	1.38	1.40	0.40
Cash Flow Per Share	3.35	3.79	3.90	3.78	3.54	3.21	2.07
Tang. Book Val. Per Share	12.94	12.67	12.05	11.49	11.34	11.25	11.14
Dividends Per Share	1.34	1.33	1.32	1.31	1.30	1.29	1.27
Dividend Payout %	79.2	81.5	78.9	88.4	94.1	91.9	318.2
INCOME STATEMENT (IN THOUSANDS):							
Total Revenues	347,096	333,711	324,108	274,034	249,752	264,648	253,291
Costs & Expenses	260,124	248,302	228,927	191,127	170,014	191,842	182,545
Depreciation & Amort.	28,842	36,459	36,548	37,053	34,759	29,081	26,816
Maintenance Exp.	...	14,279	18,532	13,304	15,167	12,735	12,414
Operating Income	58,130	34,671	40,101	32,550	29,812	30,990	31,516
Net Interest Inc./(Exp.)	d12,545	d13,572	d14,129	d12,039	d10,855	d10,724	d10,891
Net Income	29,193	① 27,362	27,355	23,746	22,230	22,523	6,427
Cash Flow	58,035	63,821	63,903	60,799	56,989	51,604	33,243
Average Shs. Outstg.	17,311	16,819	16,382	16,084	16,080	16,080	16,080
BALANCE SHEET (IN THOUSANDS):							
Gross Property	825,571	741,909	952,035	879,253	814,286	770,695	739,514
Accumulated Depreciation	365,243	340,660	510,381	484,428	446,984	407,602	374,315
Net Property	460,328	401,249	441,654	394,825	367,302	363,093	365,199
Total Assets	628,953	541,451	571,604	495,510	466,265	471,790	484,169
Long-Term Obligations	192,149	157,600	183,437	148,599	159,761	129,923	128,886
Net Stockholders' Equity	227,370	216,292	200,312	185,686	182,275	180,923	179,089
Year-end Shs. Outstg.	17,575	17,072	16,619	16,161	16,080	16,080	16,080
STATISTICAL RECORD:							
Operating Profit Margin %	16.7	10.4	12.4	11.9	11.9	11.7	12.4
Net Profit Margin %	8.4	8.2	8.4	8.7	8.9	8.5	2.5
Net Inc./Net Property %	6.3	6.8	6.2	6.0	6.1	6.2	1.8
Net Inc./Tot. Capital %	6.1	6.4	6.4	6.3	5.8	6.3	1.8
Return on Equity %	12.8	12.7	13.7	12.8	12.2	12.4	3.6
Accum. Depr./Gross Prop. %	44.2	45.9	53.6	55.1	54.9	52.9	50.6
Price Range	30.14-24.62	27.80-20.88	23.69-16.75	23.88-16.38	23.75-20.63	22.75-18.50	27.50-19.63
P/E Ratio	17.8-14.6	17.1-12.8	14.2-10.0	16.1-11.1	17.2-14.9	16.2-13.2	68.7-49.1
Average Yield %	4.9	5.5	6.5	6.5	5.9	6.2	5.4

Statistics are as originally reported. ① Bef. acctg. change chrg. of $117,000.

OFFICERS:
G. J. Wolter, Chmn., Pres., C.E.O.
D. C. Mebane, Vice-Chmn.
T. A. Hanson, V.P., C.F.O., Sec.

INVESTOR CONTACT: Steve Kraus, Shareholder Services, (608) 252-7907

PRINCIPAL OFFICE: 133 South Blair Street, Madison, WI 53701-1231

TELEPHONE NUMBER: (608) 252-7000
FAX: (608) 252-7098
WEB: www.mge.com

NO. OF EMPLOYEES: 683

SHAREHOLDERS: 18,525 (approx.)

ANNUAL MEETING: In May

INCORPORATED: WI, Apr., 1896

INSTITUTIONAL HOLDINGS:
No. of Institutions: 68
Shares Held: 3,880,900
% Held: 21.6

INDUSTRY: Electric and other services combined (SIC: 4931)

TRANSFER AGENT(S): Continental Stock Transfer & Trust Company, New York, NY

MIDDLESEX WATER COMPANY

YIELD 3.7%
P/E RATIO 24.4

7 YEAR PRICE SCORE 104.2   **12 MONTH PRICE SCORE 99.0**
*NYSE COMPOSITE INDEX=100

INTERIM EARNINGS (Per Share):

Qtr.	Mar.	June	Sept.	Dec.
2000	0.11	0.17	0.19	0.19
2001	0.11	0.24	0.30	0.23
2002	0.16	0.24	0.32	0.25
2003	0.15	...	...	...

INTERIM DIVIDENDS (Per Share):

Amt.	Decl.	Ex.	Rec.	Pay.
0.21Q	8/02/02	8/13/02	8/15/02	9/03/02
0.215Q	10/28/02	11/13/02	11/15/02	12/02/02
0.215Q	1/23/03	2/12/03	2/14/03	2/28/03
0.215Q	4/24/03	5/13/03	5/15/03	6/02/03

Indicated div.: $0.86 (Div. Reinv. Plan)

CAPITALIZATION (12/31/02):

	($000)	(%)
Long-Term Debt	87,483	48.3
Deferred Income Tax	13,242	7.3
Preferred Stock	4,063	2.2
Common & Surplus	76,501	42.2
Total	181,290	100.0

DIVIDEND ACHIEVER STATUS:

Rank: 267   10-Year Growth Rate: 2.71%
Total Years of Dividend Growth: 30

RECENT DEVELOPMENTS: For the quarter ended 3/31/03, net income decreased 4.1% to $1.2 million compared with $1.3 million in the equivalent 2002 quarter. Revenues grew 5.6% to $15.0 million from $14.2 million a year earlier. Regulated revenues rose 3.4% to $12.9 million, while non-regulated revenues increased 19.5% to $2.0 million. The improvement in revenues was primarily attributed to higher base rates in Delaware Service territories as well as higher consumption and connection fees. In addition, consumption rose in the Company's New Jersey systems. Service fees

from the Company's operations and maintenance contracts rose as a result of an increase in fees under the city of Perth Amboy contract. Operating income slid 5.4% to $2.4 million from $2.5 million the year before. Looking ahead, the Company expects capital expenditures for 2003 of about $30.5 million, which includes $17.9 million for water system additions and improvements for its Delaware systems, and $3.0 million for the RENEW Program, which is MSEX's program to clean and cement line about nine miles of unlined mains in the Middlesex System.

BUSINESS

MIDDLESEX WATER COMPANY operates water utility systems in central and southern New Jersey and in Delaware as well as a wastewater utility in southern New Jersey. The Middlesex System treats, stores and distributes water for residential, commercial, industrial and fire prevention purposes, and produced approximately 73.0% of MSEX's total revenue in 2002. Water services are furnished to approximately 58,000 retail customers. Bayview Water Company provides water services to about 300 retail customers in Cumberland County, New Jersey. Pinelands Water Company and Pinelands Wastewater Company service approximately 2,400 retail customers and, under contract, one municipal wastewater system in Burlington County, New Jersey. Tidewater Utilities, Inc. provides water services to nearly 22,000 retail customers in Kent, Sussex and New Castle counties in Delaware. Utility Service Affiliates, Inc. provides contract operations and maintenance services for non-affiliated water and wastewater systems. Utility Service Affiliates (Perth Amboy) Inc. operates the water and wastewater utilities for the city of Perth Amboy, New Jersey. MSEX operates two business segments: regulated (87.8% of 2002 revenues) and non-regulated (12.2%).

ANNUAL FINANCIAL DATA

	12/31/02	12/31/01	12/31/00	12/31/99	12/31/98	12/31/97	12/31/96
Earnings Per Share	0.97	0.88	0.67	1.01	0.94	0.89	0.80
Cash Flow Per Share	1.57	1.53	1.28	1.54	1.46	1.34	1.28
Tang. Book Val. Per Share	9.85	9.48	9.33	9.40	9.08	8.00	7.80
Dividends Per Share	0.84	0.83	0.82	0.79	0.77	0.75	0.74
Dividend Payout %	87.1	94.3	121.3	78.3	81.6	84.5	92.1
INCOME STATEMENT (IN THOUSANDS):							
Total Revenues	61,933	59,638	54,477	53,497	43,058	40,294	38,025
Costs & Expenses	41,655	40,123	37,038	35,910	28,397	26,614	25,263
Depreciation & Amort.	4,963	5,304	4,945	4,303	3,797	3,145	3,011
Maintenance Exp.	2,847	2,719	2,555	2,619	1,715	1,741	1,528
Operating Income	12,467	11,493	9,938	10,665	9,149	8,793	8,222
Net Interest Inc./(Exp.)	d5,143	d5,042	d4,997	d4,695	d4,424	d3,337	d3,280
Net Income	7,765	6,953	5,305	7,881	6,521	5,861	5,167
Cash Flow	12,474	12,002	9,995	11,883	9,999	8,780	8,020
Average Shs. Outstg.	7,968	7,856	7,791	7,722	6,870	6,574	6,254
BALANCE SHEET (IN THOUSANDS):							
Gross Property	255,863	239,734	227,135	214,896	191,484	165,323	149,707
Accumulated Depreciation	47,920	43,671	38,875	35,175	32,368	30,252	28,463
Net Property	211,368	199,060	191,196	181,809	162,827	137,109	123,019
Total Assets	244,604	236,374	219,400	215,036	203,501	159,761	148,660
Long-Term Obligations	87,483	88,140	82,109	82,330	78,032	52,918	52,961
Net Stockholders' Equity	80,564	76,353	74,698	74,552	71,725	56,221	51,882
Year-end Shs. Outstg.	7,767	7,626	7,573	7,501	7,346	6,404	6,307
STATISTICAL RECORD:							
Operating Profit Margin %	20.1	19.3	18.2	19.9	21.2	21.8	21.6
Net Profit Margin %	12.5	11.7	9.7	14.7	15.1	14.5	13.6
Net Inc./Net Property %	3.7	3.5	2.8	4.3	4.0	4.3	4.2
Net Inc./Tot. Capital %	4.3	3.9	3.1	4.7	4.0	4.8	4.4
Return on Equity %	9.6	9.1	7.1	10.6	9.1	10.4	10.0
Accum. Depr./Gross Prop. %	18.7	18.2	17.1	16.4	16.9	18.3	19.0
Price Range	34.30-18.30	37.45-29.38	33.94-25.00	39.50-21.00	25.75-19.25	22.25-16.38	19.25-15.50
P/E Ratio	35.4-18.9	42.6-33.4	50.4-37.1	39.0-20.7	27.4-20.5	25.1-18.5	24.1-19.4
Average Yield %	3.2	2.5	2.8	2.6	3.4	3.9	4.2

Statistics are as originally reported. Adj. for 3-for-2 stk. split, 1/2/02.

OFFICERS:
J. R. Tompkins, Chmn.
D. G. Sullivan, Pres., C.E.O.
R. F. Williams, V.P., C.O.O.

INVESTOR CONTACT: Marion F. Reynolds, V.P., Sec. & Treas., (732) 634-1500

PRINCIPAL OFFICE: 1500 Ronson Road, Iselin, NJ 08830-3020

TELEPHONE NUMBER: (732) 634-1500
FAX: (732) 750-5981
WEB: www.middlesexwater.com
NO. OF EMPLOYEES: 147 (avg.)
SHAREHOLDERS: 2,073 (approx. common); 22 (approx. preferred)
ANNUAL MEETING: In May
INCORPORATED: NJ, 1897

INSTITUTIONAL HOLDINGS:
No. of Institutions: 41
Shares Held: 1,189,584
% Held: 14.9

INDUSTRY: Water supply (SIC: 4941)

TRANSFER AGENT(S): Registrar and Transfer Company, Cranford, NJ

MIDLAND COMPANY (THE)

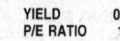

	YIELD	0.8%
	P/E RATIO	19.3

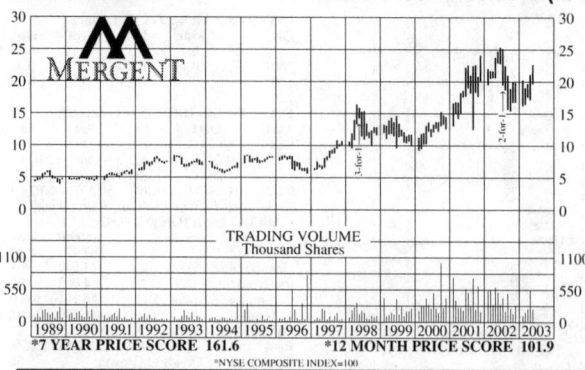

INTERIM EARNINGS (Per Share):

Qtr.	Mar.	June	Sept.	Dec.
1999	0.42	0.28	0.39	0.58
2000	0.49	0.39	0.42	0.60
2001	0.54	0.34	0.10	0.54
2002	0.53	0.33	d0.15	0.43
2003	0.56	...	...	...

INTERIM DIVIDENDS (Per Share):

Amt.	Decl.	Ex.	Rec.	Pay.
0.044Q	7/25/02	9/17/02	9/19/02	10/03/02
0.044Q	10/31/02	12/17/02	12/19/02	1/07/03
0.048Q	1/30/03	3/18/03	3/20/03	4/03/03
0.048Q	4/24/03	6/18/03	6/20/03	7/03/03

Indicated div.: $0.19 (Div. Reinv. Plan)

CAPITALIZATION (12/31/02):

	($000)	(%)
Long-Term Debt	47,163	12.0
Deferred Income Tax	35,642	9.1
Common & Surplus	308,908	78.9
Total	391,713	100.0

DIVIDEND ACHIEVER STATUS:
Rank: 189   10-Year Growth Rate: 7.69%
Total Years of Dividend Growth: 16

*7 YEAR PRICE SCORE 161.6   ***12 MONTH PRICE SCORE 101.9**
*NYSE COMPOSITE INDEX=100

RECENT DEVELOPMENTS: For the quarter ended 3/31/03, net income amounted to $10.0 million compared with income of $9.3 million, before an accounting change charge of $1.5 million, in the equivalent prior-year period. Total revenues grew 9.7% to $167.4 million from $152.5 million the previous year. Revenues for 2003 and 2002 included net realized investment losses of $1.8 million and $301,000, respectively. Premiums earned climbed 12.3% to $153.3 million from $136.5 million in 2002. Net investment income fell 3.6% to $8.4 million. Loss and loss

adjustment expenses advanced 13.0% to $78.6 million versus $69.6 million the year before. Separately, MLAN announced that earnings for the second quarter will likely be hurt by higher-than-normal catastrophe losses due to a series of severe weather storms that hit the midwestern, south central and southeastern U.S. Based on preliminary data and assuming a normal level of catastrophe losses for the remainder of the second quarter, MLAN is projecting pre-tax catastrophe losses could approach $21.0 million, or $0.76 per share on a diluted after-tax basis.

BUSINESS

THE MIDLAND COMPANY is a provider of specialty insurance products and services through two wholly-owned subsidiaries, American Modern Insurance Group and M/G Transport Group. American Modern, which accounted for approximately 96.0% of the Company's consolidated revenues in 2002, specializes in writing physical damage insurance and related coverages on manufactured housing and has expanded to other areas of insurance, including coverage for site-built homes, motorcycles, watercraft, snowmobiles, recreational vehicles, physical damage on long-haul trucks, extended service contracts, credit, life and related products, as well as collateral protection and mortgage fire products sold to financial institutions and their customers. The Company's other subsidiary, M/G Transport, charters barges and brokers freight for the movement of commodities on the inland waterways.

ANNUAL FINANCIAL DATA

	12/31/02	12/31/01	12/31/00	12/31/99	12/31/98	12/31/97	12/31/96
Earnings Per Share	② 1.14	1.52	1.89	1.65	1.43	① 1.31	0.06
Tang. Book Val. Per Share	17.59	16.53	15.73	13.56	13.30	10.56	8.75
Dividends Per Share	0.17	0.16	0.15	0.13	0.123	0.115	0.11
Dividend Payout %	16.0	10.4	7.7	8.0	8.6	8.8	183.6

INCOME STATEMENT (IN THOUSANDS):

Total Premium Income	577,668	508,233	456,120	400,991	375,478	311,159	303,175
Other Income	59,022	78,310	78,302	68,135	66,884	64,271	67,317
Total Revenues	636,690	586,543	534,422	469,126	442,362	375,430	370,492
Income Before Income Taxes	25,741	36,704	50,669	43,713	37,527	34,703	d769
Income Taxes	5,437	9,482	15,206	12,534	10,595	10,336	cr1,837
Net Income	② 20,304	27,222	35,463	31,179	26,932	① 24,367	1,068
Average Shs. Outstg.	17,789	17,990	18,758	18,926	18,824	18,582	18,198

BALANCE SHEET (IN THOUSANDS):

Cash & Cash Equivalents	745,733	715,295	701,048	620,957	593,857	504,106	404,079
Premiums Due	91,633	88,108	70,396	60,426	d753	58,739	57,949
Invst. Assets: Total	739,758	704,009	692,657	610,859	590,170	498,829	400,462
Total Assets	1,090,674	1,053,942	993,850	888,057	837,220	760,463	659,539
Long-Term Obligations	47,163	48,619	40,025	44,288	54,563	62,518	62,470
Net Stockholders' Equity	308,908	291,876	283,177	258,002	248,832	197,026	159,688
Year-end Shs. Outstg.	17,566	17,660	18,000	19,032	18,704	18,666	18,252

STATISTICAL RECORD:

Return on Revenues %	3.2	4.6	6.6	6.6	6.1	6.5	0.3
Return on Equity %	6.6	9.3	12.5	12.1	10.8	12.4	0.7
Return on Assets %	1.9	2.6	3.6	3.5	3.2	3.2	0.2
Price Range	25.38-15.40	24.14-12.50	15.25-9.25	14.66-9.63	16.42-9.58	10.85-6.17	8.46-5.63
P/E Ratio	22.3-13.5	15.9-8.3	8.1-4.9	8.9-5.8	11.5-6.7	8.3-4.7	145.6-96.8
Average Yield %	0.8	0.9	1.2	1.1	0.9	1.4	1.5

Statistics are as originally reported. Adj. for stk splits: 2-for-1, 7/02; 3-for-1, 5/98. ① Bef. loss from disc. ops. of $6.8 mill. ② Bef. acctg. chng. chrg. $1.5 mill.

OFFICERS:
J. P. Hayden III, Chmn., C.O.O.
J. W. Hayden, Pres., C.E.O.
J. I. Von Lehman, Exec. V.P., C.F.O., Sec.
INVESTOR CONTACT: James Von Lehman, Exec. V.P., C.F.O., (513) 943-7100
PRINCIPAL OFFICE: 7000 Midland Blvd., Amelia, OH 45102-2607

TELEPHONE NUMBER: (513) 943-7100
FAX: (513) 943-7111
WEB: www.midlandcompany.com
NO. OF EMPLOYEES: 1,011 (avg.)
SHAREHOLDERS: 2,100 (approx.)
ANNUAL MEETING: In April
INCORPORATED: OH, 1938

INSTITUTIONAL HOLDINGS:
No. of Institutions: 46
Shares Held: 4,024,424
% Held: 22.4
INDUSTRY: Insurance carriers, nec (SIC: 6399)
TRANSFER AGENT(S): Fifth Third Bank, Cincinnati, OH

MINE SAFETY APPLIANCES COMPANY

YIELD 2.0%
P/E RATIO 14.2

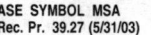
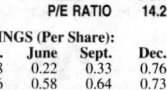
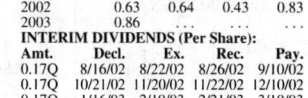

*7 YEAR PRICE SCORE 156.6   ***12 MONTH PRICE SCORE 103.3**

*NYSE COMPOSITE INDEX=100

TRADING VOLUME
Thousand Shares

INTERIM EARNINGS (Per Share):

Qtr.	Mar.	June	Sept.	Dec.
2000	0.58	0.22	0.33	0.76
2001	0.66	0.58	0.64	0.73
2002	0.63	0.64	0.43	0.83
2003	0.86	...	...	...

INTERIM DIVIDENDS (Per Share):

Amt.	Decl.	Ex.	Rec.	Pay.
0.17Q	8/16/02	8/22/02	8/26/02	9/10/02
0.17Q	10/21/02	11/20/02	11/22/02	12/10/02
0.17Q	1/16/03	2/19/03	2/21/03	3/10/03
0.20Q	5/08/03	5/19/03	5/21/03	6/10/03

Indicated div.: $0.80 (Div. Reinv. Plan)

CAPITALIZATION (12/31/02):

	($000)	(%)
Long-Term Debt	64,350	15.5
Deferred Income Tax	61,402	14.8
Preferred Stock	3,569	0.9
Common & Surplus	285,493	68.8
Total	414,814	100.0

DIVIDEND ACHIEVER STATUS:

Rank: 181   10-Year Growth Rate: 8.16%
Total Years of Dividend Growth: 32

RECENT DEVELOPMENTS: For the quarter ended 3/31/03, income was $10.5 million, before income from discontinued operations of $1.5 million, versus income of $7.7 million, before income from discontinued operations of $260,000, in the equivalent 2002 quarter. Total net sales grew 25.2% to $160.4 million. Net sales in North America increased 19.3% to $106.8 million, reflecting strong shipments of breathing apparatus to the fire service market and gas masks to military and homeland security markets. Net sales in Europe climbed 53.7% to $34.6 million, primarily due to favorable foreign currency translation and the inclusion of MSA Gallet, which was acquired during the second quarter of 2002. Other international sales rose 18.8% to $19.0 million. Gross profit grew 21.3% to $61.5 million from $50.7 million the year before. Going forward, MSA's outlook remains favorable as new product development and aggressive selling have helped MSA gain a solid share of U.S. Government funding. Meanwhile, MSA continues to explore strategic options, including the possible sale, of its Callery Chemical Division.

BUSINESS

MINE SAFETY APPLIANCES COMPANY manufactures and sells products designed to protect the safety and health of people throughout the world. The Company is organized into three geographic operating segments: North America (65.5% of sales in 2002), Europe (21.7%) and Other International (12.8%). MSA's principal products include respiratory protective equipment that is air-purifying, air-supplied and self-contained in design; instruments that monitor and analyze workplace environments and control industrial processes; thermal imaging cameras that enable firefighters and rescue workers to see through smoke and darkness; and personal protective products including head, eye and face, hearing protectors and fall protection equipment. Many of these products have wide application for workers in industries that include manufacturing, municipal and volunteer fire departments, public utilities, mining, chemicals, petroleum, construction, transportation, the military and hazardous materials clean-up. Consumer products target the do-it-yourself market and are available through select home center retail outlets under the MSA Safety Works™ brand. Other products manufactured and sold include boron-based and other specialty chemicals.

ANNUAL FINANCIAL DATA

	12/31/02	12/31/01	12/31/00	12/31/99	12/31/98	12/31/97	12/31/96
Earnings Per Share	③ 2.54	① 2.61	① 1.88	① 2 1.25	① 1.37	① 1.60	① 1.58
Cash Flow Per Share	4.29	4.81	3.87	3.07	3.05	3.18	3.12
Tang. Book Val. Per Share	19.87	17.87	18.85	18.55	18.21	17.79	17.20
Dividends Per Share	0.65	0.54	0.47	0.45	0.44	0.41	0.37
Dividend Payout %	25.6	20.7	25.2	36.3	32.4	25.8	23.2

INCOME STATEMENT (IN THOUSANDS):

Total Revenues	566,697	545,666	502,833	498,051	497,207	499,409	506,855
Costs & Expenses	492,129	459,051	440,168	447,662	443,028	438,833	445,485
Depreciation & Amort.	21,525	26,471	24,557	23,625	22,398	21,516	22,373
Operating Income	52,661	60,144	38,108	26,764	31,781	39,060	38,997
Net Interest Inc./(Exp.)	d4,769	d6,061	d4,502	d4,273	d3,258	d2,781	d1,595
Income Before Income Taxes	48,083	52,886	34,050	23,185	28,208	36,239	36,667
Income Taxes	16,870	21,255	10,811	6,859	9,933	14,385	13,606
Net Income	③ 31,213	① 31,631	① 23,239	① ② 16,326	① 18,275	① 21,854	① 23,061
Cash Flow	52,691	58,054	47,747	39,901	40,624	43,333	45,370
Average Shs. Outstg.	12,295	12,079	12,356	13,005	13,341	13,647	14,556

BALANCE SHEET (IN THOUSANDS):

Cash & Cash Equivalents	36,477	26,992	26,541	17,108	24,020	19,921	25,096
Total Current Assets	282,944	217,686	201,153	203,090	229,209	219,613	228,407
Net Property	125,605	152,968	159,586	163,509	164,561	155,184	147,058
Total Assets	579,765	520,698	489,683	451,741	456,716	406,404	407,682
Total Current Liabilities	99,700	82,500	86,978	80,005	110,006	103,240	91,814
Long-Term Obligations	64,350	61,477	71,806	36,550	11,919	15,220	13,278
Net Stockholders' Equity	289,062	253,504	226,465	242,457	242,846	241,449	241,432
Net Working Capital	183,244	135,186	114,175	123,085	119,203	116,373	136,593
Year-end Shs. Outstg.	12,207	12,101	11,828	12,875	13,137	13,368	13,833

STATISTICAL RECORD:

Operating Profit Margin %	9.3	11.0	7.6	5.4	6.4	7.8	7.7
Net Profit Margin %	5.5	5.8	4.6	3.3	3.7	4.4	4.5
Return on Equity %	10.8	12.5	10.3	6.7	7.5	9.1	9.6
Return on Assets %	5.4	6.1	4.7	3.6	4.0	5.4	5.7
Debt/Total Assets %	11.1	12.9	14.7	8.1	2.6	3.0	3.3
Price Range	50.50-28.20	51.90-22.00	26.50-18.63	27.00-16.83	29.00-19.08	24.58-17.83	18.50-13.67
P/E Ratio	19.9-11.1	19.9-8.4	14.1-9.9	21.6-13.5	21.2-14.0	15.4-11.1	11.7-8.6
Average Yield %	1.7	1.5	2.1	2.1	1.8	1.9	2.3

Statistics are as originally reported. Adj. for stk. split: 3-for-1, 5/24/00. ① Incl. restr. chrgs.: $2.3 mill., 12/31/01; $2.4 mill., 12/31/00; $4.0 mill., 12/31/99; $1.0 mill., 12/31/98; $2.2 mill., 12/31/97; $5.3 mill., 12/31/96; $730,000. ② Bef. acctg. chrg. of $1.2 mill. ③ Bef. inc. fr. disc. opers of $3.9 mill.

OFFICERS:
J. T. Ryan III, Chmn., C.E.O.
T. B. Hotopp, Pres.
D. L. Zeitler, V.P., Treas.

INVESTOR CONTACT: Investor Relations,
(412) 967-3000

PRINCIPAL OFFICE: 121 Gamma Drive,
RIDC Industrial Park, Pittsburgh, PA 15238

TELEPHONE NUMBER: (412) 967-3000
FAX: (412) 967-3451
WEB: www.msanet.com

NO. OF EMPLOYEES: 4,400 (approx.)

SHAREHOLDERS: 1,000 (approx.)

ANNUAL MEETING: In May

INCORPORATED: PA, Jan., 1917

INSTITUTIONAL HOLDINGS:
No. of Institutions: 53
Shares Held: 4,302,702
% Held: 35.9

INDUSTRY: Men's and boys' work clothing
(SIC: 2326)

TRANSFER AGENT(S): Mine Safety
Appliances Company, Pittsburgh, PA

MYERS INDUSTRIES, INC.

YIELD 2.0%
P/E RATIO 14.3

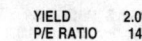

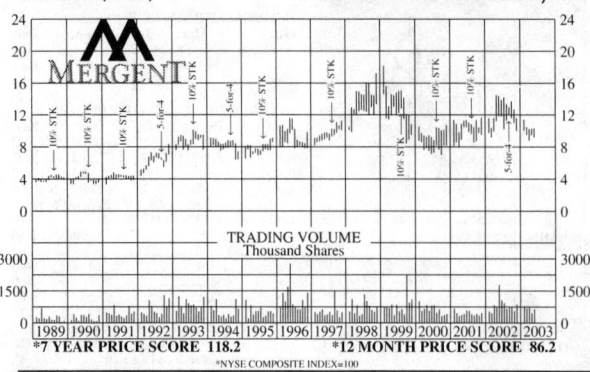

INTERIM EARNINGS (Per Share):

Qtr.	Mar.	June	Sept.	Dec.
1999	0.27	0.30	0.13	0.33
2000	0.28	0.27	0.11	0.15
2001	0.30	0.12	0.06	0.08
2002	0.34	0.22	0.10	0.13
2003	0.24	...	...	...

INTERIM DIVIDENDS (Per Share):

Amt.	Decl.	Ex.	Rec.	Pay.
0.05Q	6/26/02	9/04/02	9/06/02	10/01/02
0.05Q	9/19/02	12/04/02	12/06/02	1/02/03
0.05Q	2/13/03	3/05/03	3/07/03	4/01/03
0.05Q	4/23/03	6/11/03	6/13/03	7/01/03

Indicated div.: $0.20 (Div. Reinv. Plan)

CAPITALIZATION (12/31/02):

	($000)	(%)
Long-Term Debt	212,223	43.7
Deferred Income Tax	17,201	3.5
Common & Surplus	255,690	52.7
Total	485,113	100.0

DIVIDEND ACHIEVER STATUS:
Rank: 95   10-Year Growth Rate: 12.52%
Total Years of Dividend Growth: 26

TRADING VOLUME
Thousand Shares

*7 YEAR PRICE SCORE 118.2   *12 MONTH PRICE SCORE 86.2
*NYSE COMPOSITE INDEX=100

RECENT DEVELOPMENTS: For the quarter ended 3/31/03, net income fell 28.4% to $7.2 million compared with $10.0 million in the equivalent 2002 quarter. The decline in earnings was primarily attributed to substantially higher raw material costs, coupled with strong competition and excess capacity in the marketplace, which made it difficult to raise product prices. Net sales grew 9.6% to $163.2 million from $148.9 million a year earlier.

PROSPECTS: The Company continues to face increased competition and excess capacity in the marketplace, making it difficult to raise product pricing. In light of the continued difficult market environment, MYE is taking appropriate steps to mitigate pressure on margins. Additionally, MYE is concentrating on disciplined asset management, operating efficiency and is emphasizing debt reduction.

BUSINESS

MYERS INDUSTRIES, INC. is comprised of two segments: the manufacturing business (75.3% of 2002 sales) and the distribution business (24.7%). The manufacturing business designs, manufactures and markets plastic and rubber products for the industrial, agricultural, automotive, commercial and consumer markets. As of 4/23/03, MYE operated 25 manufacturing facilities in Europe and North America and marketed reusable plastics under the brand names NESTIER, AKROBINS and BUCKHORN. MYE also manufactures and sells molded rubber products and other materials used primarily in the tire and tire repair industries and for various other uses. As of 4/23/03, the distribution business, primarily conducted by the Myers Tire Supply division through 43 U.S. and five international branches, was engaged in the distribution of tools, equipment and supplies used for tire servicing and automotive underbody repair.

ANNUAL FINANCIAL DATA

	12/31/02	12/31/01	12/31/00	12/31/99	12/31/98	12/31/97	12/31/96
Earnings Per Share	0.80	0.51	① 0.81	1.03	0.94	0.73	0.68
Cash Flow Per Share	1.99	1.99	2.24	2.25	1.52	1.16	1.04
Tang. Book Val. Per Share	1.62	0.90	0.56	0.28	5.35	5.06	4.71
Dividends Per Share	0.19	0.18	0.16	0.15	0.13	0.11	0.09
Dividend Payout %	24.2	34.9	20.2	14.4	13.4	15.4	13.7
INCOME STATEMENT (IN THOUSANDS):							
Total Revenues	607,991	607,950	652,660	580,761	392,020	339,626	320,944
Costs & Expenses	520,106	518,106	546,563	473,711	325,129	288,098	273,733
Depreciation & Amort.	35,714	43,905	42,828	37,542	17,518	13,214	11,311
Operating Income	52,171	45,939	63,270	69,507	49,373	38,313	35,901
Net Interest Inc./(Exp.)	d11,810	d18,699	d22,360	d15,206	d888	d248	d285
Income Before Income Taxes	40,361	27,240	40,910	54,301	48,485	38,066	35,615
Income Taxes	16,401	12,049	16,909	23,125	19,806	15,727	14,612
Net Income	23,960	15,191	① 24,001	31,176	28,679	22,339	21,003
Cash Flow	59,674	59,096	66,828	68,719	46,197	35,553	32,314
Average Shs. Outstg.	29,972	29,752	29,828	30,502	30,455	30,731	30,978
BALANCE SHEET (IN THOUSANDS):							
Cash & Cash Equivalents	1,702	7,075	2,178	1,094	34,832	6,298	5,600
Total Current Assets	201,140	196,619	219,307	206,991	153,650	107,427	106,310
Net Property	190,795	190,736	204,198	189,496	104,433	90,551	80,660
Total Assets	602,482	582,166	624,797	600,410	306,708	224,078	207,122
Total Current Liabilities	117,369	104,899	115,583	102,244	51,234	39,644	36,853
Long-Term Obligations	212,223	247,145	284,273	280,104	48,832	4,261	4,569
Net Stockholders' Equity	255,690	217,526	213,903	207,747	202,689	176,677	162,445
Net Working Capital	83,771	91,719	103,724	104,747	102,417	67,783	69,457
Year-end Shs. Outstg.	30,072	29,810	29,686	30,231	30,510	30,412	30,846
STATISTICAL RECORD:							
Operating Profit Margin %	8.6	7.6	9.7	12.0	12.6	11.3	11.2
Net Profit Margin %	3.9	2.5	3.7	5.4	7.3	6.6	6.5
Return on Equity %	9.4	7.0	11.2	15.0	14.1	12.6	12.9
Return on Assets %	4.0	2.6	3.8	5.2	9.4	10.0	10.1
Debt/Total Assets %	35.2	42.5	45.5	46.7	15.9	1.9	2.2
Price Range	14.48-9.20	11.66-8.01	10.73-7.00	18.18-8.43	17.24-9.84	11.27-8.20	11.61-7.85
P/E Ratio	18.1-11.5	22.8-15.6	13.3-8.7	17.7-8.2	18.3-10.4	15.5-11.3	17.1-11.6
Average Yield %	1.6	1.8	1.8	1.1	0.9	1.2	1.0

Statistics are as originally reported. Adj. for stk. splits: 10% div., 8/01, 8/00, 8/99 & 8/97; 5-for-4, 8/02. ① Incl. an after-tax restructuring chrg. of $1.9 mill.

OFFICERS:
S. E. Myers, Pres., C.E.O.
J. C. Orr, C.O.O.
G. J. Stodnick, V.P., C.F.O.
M. I. Wiskind, Sr. V.P., Sec.

INVESTOR CONTACT: Gregory J. Stodnick, V.P., C.F.O., (330) 253-5592

PRINCIPAL OFFICE: 1293 South Main Street, Akron, OH 44301

TELEPHONE NUMBER: (330) 253-5592
FAX: (330) 761-6156
WEB: www.myersind.com

NO. OF EMPLOYEES: 4,293 (approx.)

SHAREHOLDERS: 2,214 (approx.)

ANNUAL MEETING: In Apr.

INCORPORATED: OH, Jan., 1955

INSTITUTIONAL HOLDINGS:
No. of Institutions: 93
Shares Held: 15,758,674
% Held: 52.5

INDUSTRY: Plastics products, nec (SIC: 3089)

TRANSFER AGENT(S): First Chicago Trust Company of New York, New York, NY

NACCO INDUSTRIES, INC.

YIELD	1.8%
P/E RATIO	10.3

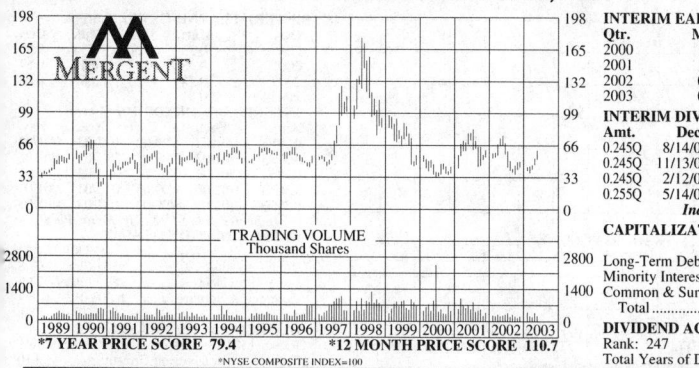

TRADING VOLUME
Thousand Shares

*7 YEAR PRICE SCORE 79.4   *12 MONTH PRICE SCORE 110.7
*NYSE COMPOSITE INDEX=100

INTERIM EARNINGS (Per Share):

Qtr.	Mar.	June	Sept.	Dec.
2000	1.13	1.67	1.09	0.75
2001	1.76	0.74	d3.36	d3.38
2002	0.77	0.34	0.98	3.97
2003	0.35	...	...	...

INTERIM DIVIDENDS (Per Share):

Amt.	Decl.	Ex.	Rec.	Pay.
0.245Q	8/14/02	8/29/02	9/03/02	9/16/02
0.245Q	11/13/02	11/27/02	12/02/02	12/16/02
0.245Q	2/12/03	2/26/03	2/28/03	3/14/03
0.255Q	5/14/03	5/29/03	6/02/03	6/16/03
Indicated div.: $1.02				

CAPITALIZATION (12/31/02):

	($000)	(%)
Long-Term Debt	681,600	54.9
Minority Interest	1,100	0.1
Common & Surplus	559,400	45.0
Total	1,242,100	100.0

DIVIDEND ACHIEVER STATUS:

Rank: 247   10-Year Growth Rate: 4.33%
Total Years of Dividend Growth: 19

RECENT DEVELOPMENTS: For the quarter ended 3/31/03, NC reported income of $2.9 million, before an accounting gain of $1.2 million, versus net income of $6.3 million in the prior-year quarter. Total revenues increased 7.5% to $619.9 million. Materials Handling group revenues jumped 12.7% to $419.0 million, primarily due to increased wholesale lift truck shipments. North American Coal Corporation revenues rose 2.2% to $84.9 million.

PROSPECTS: Lift truck markets in the Americas should improve in the second half of 2003, while the Europe and Asia-Pacific markets are expected to remain relatively flat. Meanwhile, the Housewares group expects previously implemented cost-saving and efficiency initiatives to benefit results in 2003. Separately, North American Coal Corporation anticipates higher lignite coal deliveries in 2003, primarily due to an expected rise in coal production.

BUSINESS

NACCO INDUSTRIES, INC., is a holding company with three principal businesses. NACCO Materials Handling Group (NMHG) (62.3% of 2002 revenue) designs, engineers, manufactures, sells, services and leases a full line of lift trucks and replacement parts marketed worldwide under the HYSTER™ and YALE™ brand names. NACCO Housewares Group (24.0%) consists of Hamilton Beach/Procter-Silex, Inc., a manufacturer and marketer of small household appliances and commercial products for restaurants, bars and hotels, and The Kitchen Collection, Inc., a national specialty retailer of brand-name kitchenware and electrical appliances. The North American Coal Corporation (13.7%) mines and markets lignite coal primarily as fuel for power generators.

ANNUAL FINANCIAL DATA

	12/31/02	12/31/01	12/31/00	12/31/99	12/31/98	12/31/97	12/31/96
Earnings Per Share	⑤ 6.05	④ d4.24	③ 4.63	② 6.66	① 12.53	① 7.55	5.67
Cash Flow Per Share	17.36	10.12	17.62	19.41	23.43	18.37	15.22
Tang. Book Val. Per Share	5.73	1.98	9.44	11.51	9.52	...	...
Dividends Per Share	0.97	0.93	0.89	0.85	0.81	0.77	0.74
Dividend Payout %	16.0	...	19.2	12.8	6.5	10.2	13.1
INCOME STATEMENT (IN MILLIONS):							
Total Revenues	2,548.1	2,637.9	2,871.3	2,602.8	2,536.2	2,246.9	2,273.2
Costs & Expenses	2,323.6	2,514.6	2,647.3	2,367.5	2,249.1	2,026.3	2,056.7
Depreciation & Amort.	92.7	117.6	106.1	104.0	89.0	88.6	85.3
Operating Income	131.8	5.7	117.9	131.3	198.1	132.0	131.2
Net Interest Inc./(Exp.)	d69.3	d56.9	d47.1	d43.3	d34.6	d36.6	d45.9
Income Before Income Taxes	59.7	d45.4	60.0	86.6	166.0	89.1	86.3
Income Taxes	11.3	cr9.0	22.3	31.7	60.7	26.4	34.3
Equity Earnings/Minority Int.	1.2	0.8	0.1	d0.6	d3.0	d0.9	d1.4
Net Income	⑤ 49.6	④ d34.7	③ 37.8	② 54.3	① 102.3	① 61.8	50.6
Cash Flow	142.3	82.9	143.9	158.3	191.3	150.4	135.9
Average Shs. Outstg. (000)	8,198	8,190	8,167	8,154	8,166	8,189	8,931
BALANCE SHEET (IN MILLIONS):							
Cash & Cash Equivalents	64.1	71.9	33.7	36.2	34.7	24.1	47.8
Total Current Assets	783.0	770.0	815.7	772.2	703.2	599.6	591.8
Net Property	658.0	732.0	710.7	625.4	593.4	541.7	550.3
Total Assets	2,123.9	2,161.9	2,193.9	2,013.0	1,898.3	1,729.1	1,708.1
Total Current Liabilities	596.2	874.3	650.2	583.1	548.6	506.5	416.0
Long-Term Obligations	681.6	519.4	732.7	615.5	569.6	558.2	674.8
Net Stockholders' Equity	559.4	529.3	606.4	562.2	518.3	425.1	379.3
Net Working Capital	186.8	d104.3	165.5	189.1	154.6	93.1	175.8
Year-end Shs. Outstg. (000)	8,201	8,196	8,171	9,804	8,120	8,154	8,186
STATISTICAL RECORD:							
Operating Profit Margin %	5.2	0.2	4.1	5.0	7.8	5.9	5.8
Net Profit Margin %	1.9	...	1.3	2.1	4.0	2.8	2.2
Return on Equity %	8.9	...	6.2	9.7	19.7	14.5	13.3
Return on Assets %	2.3	...	1.7	2.7	5.4	3.6	3.0
Debt/Total Assets %	32.1	24.0	33.4	30.6	30.0	32.3	39.5
Price Range	76.20-36.39	82.80-42.50	55.75-33.56	97.00-44.50	177.00-76.25	127.00-44.38	64.00-43.13
P/E Ratio	12.6-6.0	...	12.0-7.2	14.6-6.7	14.1-6.1	16.8-5.9	11.3-7.6
Average Yield %	1.7	1.5	2.0	1.2	0.6	0.9	1.4

Statistics are as originally reported. ① Incl. restruct. chrgs. $1.6 mill., 1998; $8.0 mill., 1997. ② Bef. acctg. chrg. $1.2 mill.; incl. one-time chrg. $1.9 mill. ③ Bef. extr. gain $29.9 mill.; incl. aft.-tax restr. chrg. $8.3 mill. & aft.-tax write-off of $1.5 mill. ④ Bef. acctg. chrg. $1.3 mill.; incl. restr. chrg. $21.5 mill., loss on sale of dealers $10.4 mill. & ins. recovery $8.0 mill. ⑤ Bef. extr. loss $7.2 mill.; incl. restr. chrg. $12.3 mill. & loss on sale of dealers $1.2 mill.

OFFICERS:
A. M. Rankin Jr., Chmn., Pres., C.E.O.
J. C. Butler Jr., V.P., Treas.
C. A. Bittenbender, V.P., Sec., Gen. Couns.

INVESTOR CONTACT: Ira Gamm, Manager, Investor Relations, (440) 449-9676

PRINCIPAL OFFICE: 5875 Landerbrook Drive, Mayfield Heights, OH 44124-4017

TELEPHONE NUMBER: (440) 449-9600
FAX: (440) 449-9607
WEB: www.nacco.com
NO. OF EMPLOYEES: 11,500 (approx.)
SHAREHOLDERS: 400 (cl. A com.); 300 (cl. B com.)
ANNUAL MEETING: In May
INCORPORATED: DE, 1986

INSTITUTIONAL HOLDINGS:
No. of Institutions: 60
Shares Held: 3,679,508
% Held: 46.0

INDUSTRY: Industrial trucks and tractors (SIC: 3537)

TRANSFER AGENT(S): National City Bank, Cleveland, OH

NATIONAL CITY CORPORATION

YIELD 3.6%
P/E RATIO 12.7

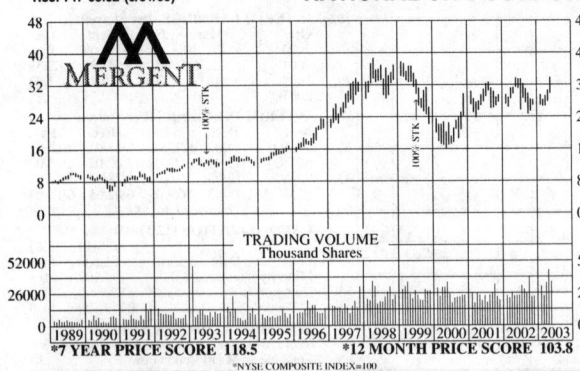

INTERIM EARNINGS (Per Share):

Qtr.	Mar.	June	Sept.	Dec.
2000	0.53	0.56	0.54	0.50
2001	0.55	0.57	0.58	0.57
2002	0.73	0.63	0.61	0.62
2003	0.81	...	...	...

INTERIM DIVIDENDS (Per Share):

Amt.	Decl.	Ex.	Rec.	Pay.
0.295Q	4/01/02	4/09/02	4/11/02	5/01/02
0.305Q	7/01/02	7/09/02	7/11/02	8/01/02
0.305Q	10/01/02	10/09/02	10/11/02	11/01/02
0.305Q	1/02/03	1/09/03	1/13/03	2/01/03
0.305Q	4/01/03	4/09/03	4/11/03	5/01/03

Indicated div.: $1.22 (Div. Reinv. Plan)

CAPITALIZATION (12/31/02):

	($000)	(%)
Total Deposits	65,118,768	67.8
Long-Term Debt	22,550,295	23.5
Common & Surplus	8,308,012	8.7
Total	95,977,075	100.0

DIVIDEND ACHIEVER STATUS:
Rank: 150   10-Year Growth Rate: 9.83%
Total Years of Dividend Growth: 10

*7 YEAR PRICE SCORE 118.5   *12 MONTH PRICE SCORE 103.8
*NYSE COMPOSITE INDEX=100

RECENT DEVELOPMENTS: For the quarter ending 3/31/03, net income increased 11.4% to $497.0 million versus $446.0 million in the corresponding prior-year period. Earnings for 2003 included severance and related costs of about $71.0 million, and charges of $42.0 million to recognize estimated impairment in automobile and aircraft lease residual values. Earnings for 2002 included net securities gains of $54.0 million. Net interest income improved 9.6% to $1.10 billion.

PROSPECTS: Although commercial loan demand continues to be weak and credit quality is improving more slowly than originally anticipated, the Company continues to perform well across its core businesses, especially retail, adding new accounts and customer relationships and gaining market share. Additionally, mortgage production and sales continue at high levels as low interest rates fuel mortgage demand, especially refinancing.

BUSINESS

NATIONAL CITY CORPORATION is a bank holding company, with total assets of $117.49 billion as of 3/31/03, providing financial services principally in Ohio, Pennsylvania, Kentucky, Michigan, Illinois, and Indiana. Its principal banking subsidiaries are National City Bank, Cleveland; BancOhio National Bank, Columbus; First National Bank of Louisville; and Merchants National Bank & Trust Co. of Indianapolis. NCC's primary businesses include commercial and retail banking, consumer finance, asset management, mortgage financing and servicing, and payment processing. As of 12/31/02, NCC owned 85.0% of National Processing Inc. In March 1998, NCC acquired Fort Wayne Corp. and First of America Bank Corp. On 9/1/99, NCC acquired First Franklin Financial Cos., Inc.

ANNUAL FINANCIAL DATA

	12/31/02	12/31/01	12/31/00	12/31/99	12/31/98	12/31/97	12/31/96
Earnings Per Share	⑤ 2.59	④ 2.27	2.13	③ 2.22	① 1.61	① 1.83	① 1.65
Tang. Book Val. Per Share	11.70	12.15	11.06	9.39	10.69	10.14	9.93
Dividends Per Share	1.20	1.16	1.14	1.06	0.94	0.83	0.73
Dividend Payout %	46.3	51.1	53.5	47.7	58.4	45.6	44.7
INCOME STATEMENT (IN MILLIONS):							
Total Interest Income	5,915.9	6,414.8	6,566.6	5,912.6	5,756.7	3,776.1	3,655.3
Total Interest Expense	1,910.5	2,975.9	3,608.2	2,912.6	2,845.0	1,833.3	1,712.8
Net Interest Income	4,005.4	3,438.8	2,958.4	3,000.0	2,911.6	1,942.8	1,942.6
Provision for Loan Losses	681.9	605.3	286.8	249.7	201.4	139.7	146.5
Non-Interest Income	2,812.0	2,677.8	2,484.2	2,380.8	2,314.1	1,375.9	1,273.0
Non-Interest Expense	3,729.6	3,344.9	3,183.9	2,982.5	3,377.1	2,010.6	2,010.7
Income Before Taxes	2,405.8	2,166.5	1,971.9	2,148.6	1,647.3	1,168.5	1,058.4
Net Income	⑤ 1,593.6	④ 1,388.1	1,302.4	③ 1,405.5	① 1,070.7	① 807.4	① 736.6
Average Shs. Outstg. (000)	616,174	611,937	612,625	632,452	665,720	441,380	445,348
BALANCE SHEET (IN MILLIONS):							
Cash & Due from Banks	3,756.4	4,404.0	3,535.2	3,480.8	4,783.5	2,967.2	2,935.3
Securities Avail. for Sale	10,080.4	10,291.7	10,592.3	15,135.4	16,337.5	8,929.0	9,381.4
Total Loans & Leases	72,134.4	68,040.6	65,604.4	60,203.9	58,011.2	38,442.2	35,495.3
Allowance for Credit Losses	1,098.6	997.3	928.6	970.5	970.2	698.4	705.9
Net Loans & Leases	71,035.8	67,043.3	64,675.9	59,233.4	57,040.9	37,743.8	34,789.4
Total Assets	118,258.0	105,816.7	88,534.6	87,121.5	88,245.6	54,683.5	50,855.8
Total Deposits	65,118.8	63,129.9	55,256.4	50,066.3	58,246.9	36,861.1	35,999.7
Long-Term Obligations	22,550.3	17,136.2	17,964.8	14,858.0	9,009.4	4,810.4	2,994.4
Total Liabilities	109,950.4	98,435.5	81,764.8	81,393.8	81,232.7	50,402.2	46,423.8
Net Stockholders' Equity	8,308.0	7,381.2	6,769.8	5,727.7	7,012.9	4,281.4	4,432.1
Year-end Shs. Outstg. (000)	611,491	607,355	609,189	607,058	652,654	422,196	446,396
STATISTICAL RECORD:							
Return on Equity %	19.2	18.8	19.2	24.5	15.3	18.9	16.6
Return on Assets %	1.3	1.3	1.5	1.6	1.2	1.5	1.4
Equity/Assets %	7.0	7.0	7.6	6.6	7.9	7.8	8.7
Non-Int. Exp./Tot. Inc. %	54.7	54.7	58.5	55.4	64.6	60.6	62.5
Price Range	33.70-24.60	32.70-23.69	29.75-16.00	37.81-22.13	38.75-28.47	33.78-21.25	23.63-15.31
P/E Ratio	13.0-9.5	14.4-10.4	14.0-7.5	17.0-10.0	24.1-17.7	18.5-11.6	14.4-9.3
Average Yield %	4.1	4.1	5.0	3.5	2.8	3.0	3.8

Statistics are as originally reported. Adj. for 2-for-1 stk. split, 7/99. ① Incl. pre-tax merger-related chgs. of $379.4 mill., 1998; $65.9 mill, 1997; $74.7 mill., 1996. ③ Results reflect the 3/31/98 acq. of First of America Bank Corp. ③ Incl. an after-tax non-recurring gain of $1.3 mill. ④ Incl. net ineffective hedge & oth. derivative gains of $362.9 mill. & write-downs to automobile lease residual values of $67.4 mill. ⑤ Incl. net hedge gains of $231.7 mill.

OFFICERS:
D. A. Daberko, Chmn., C.E.O.
W. E. MacDonald III, Vice-Chmn.
R. G. Siefers, Vice-Chmn.
J. D. Kelly, Exec. V.P., C.F.O.
INVESTOR CONTACT: Derek Green, V.P., Investor Relations, (800) 622-4204
PRINCIPAL OFFICE: 1900 East Ninth Street, Cleveland, OH 44114-3484

TELEPHONE NUMBER: (216) 222-2000
FAX: (216) 575-2353
WEB: www.nationalcity.com
NO. OF EMPLOYEES: 32,731
SHAREHOLDERS: 61,916
ANNUAL MEETING: In April
INCORPORATED: DE, Aug., 1972

INSTITUTIONAL HOLDINGS:
No. of Institutions: 474
Shares Held: 301,790,529
% Held: 49.4
INDUSTRY: National commercial banks (SIC: 6021)
TRANSFER AGENT(S): National City Bank Corporate Trust Operations, Cleveland, OH

NATIONAL COMMERCE FINANCIAL CORPORATION

YIELD 3.0%
P/E RATIO 15.1

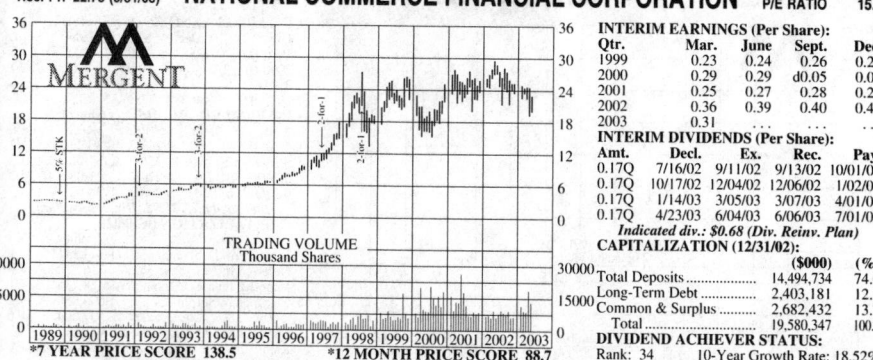

INTERIM EARNINGS (Per Share):

Qtr.	Mar.	June	Sept.	Dec.
1999	0.23	0.24	0.26	0.26
2000	0.29	0.29	d0.05	0.04
2001	0.25	0.27	0.28	0.29
2002	0.36	0.39	0.40	0.41
2003	0.31	...	...	...

INTERIM DIVIDENDS (Per Share):

Amt.	Decl.	Ex.	Rec.	Pay.
0.17Q	7/16/02	9/11/02	9/13/02	10/01/02
0.17Q	10/17/02	12/04/02	12/06/02	1/02/03
0.17Q	1/14/03	3/05/03	3/07/03	4/01/03
0.17Q	4/23/03	6/04/03	6/06/03	7/01/03

Indicated div.: $0.68 (Div. Reinv. Plan)

CAPITALIZATION (12/31/02):

	($000)	(%)
Total Deposits	14,494,734	74.0
Long-Term Debt	2,403,181	12.3
Common & Surplus	2,682,432	13.7
Total	19,580,347	100.0

DIVIDEND ACHIEVER STATUS:
Rank: 34   10-Year Growth Rate: 18.52%
Total Years of Dividend Growth: 28

TRADING VOLUME Thousand Shares

*7 YEAR PRICE SCORE 138.5   ***12 MONTH PRICE SCORE 88.7**
*NYSE COMPOSITE INDEX=100

RECENT DEVELOPMENTS: For the quarter ended 3/31/03, net income slid 14.4% to $64.1 million from $74.9 million in the prior year. Results for 2003 included a pre-tax litigation charge of $19.7 million, while results for 2002 included a pre-tax acquisition charge of $4.9 million. Net interest income was $177.4 million versus $178.7 million the year before. Total non-interest income grew 28.2% to $109.3 million, while total non-interest expense rose 24.3% to $148.6 million.

PROSPECTS: Going forward, the Company is focused on driving loan and deposit growth, along with lowering its sensitivity to interest rate fluctuations, to help boost profitability. In addition, NCF is taking steps to reduce expenses to help fund its aggressive expansion efforts in Atlanta, Georgia. In 2003, the Company plans to open twelve branches in Kroger locations in the Atlanta metro area, as well as four or five "hub" locations.

BUSINESS

NATIONAL COMMERCE FINANCIAL CORPORATION is a bank holding company with assets of $21.72 billion as of 3/31/03. The Company's banking subsidiaries, National Bank of Commerce (NBC) and NBC Bank, Federal Savings Bank (FSB), provide commercial and retail banking, savings and trust services through its Central Carolina Bank offices located in North Carolina and South Carolina and its National Bank of Commerce offices located in Tennessee, Mississippi, Arkansas, Georgia, Virginia and West Virginia. NBC Bank operates offices in DeSoto County, Mississippi. The Company also provides trust services through a subsidiary in Florida. As of 3/7/03, NCF owned 49.0% of First Market Bank, FSB. In addition to its banking subsidiaries, the Company operates several other non-banking financial businesses. In July 2000, the Company acquired CCB Financial Corporation. In 2001 NCF acquired SouthBanc Shares, Inc. and First Vantage-Tennessee.

ANNUAL FINANCIAL DATA

	12/31/02	12/31/01	[3]12/31/00	12/31/99	12/31/98	12/31/97	12/31/96
Earnings Per Share	[2]1.55	[2]1.09	[2]0.57	0.99	0.83	0.69	0.58
Tang. Book Val. Per Share	6.66	6.13	6.23	5.15	4.03	3.60	3.21
Dividends Per Share	0.62	0.54	0.45	0.36	0.29	0.22	0.19
Dividend Payout %	40.0	49.5	78.1	36.4	34.9	31.9	33.0
INCOME STATEMENT (IN MILLIONS):							
Total Interest Income	1,130.5	1,222.9	1,250.5	468.0	383.6	337.0	286.6
Total Interest Expense	396.9	571.8	664.7	231.5	191.0	174.2	151.1
Net Interest Income	733.6	651.1	585.7	236.5	192.6	162.8	135.5
Provision for Loan Losses	32.3	29.2	20.9	15.2	9.6	17.0	14.1
Non-Interest Income	391.0	324.9	247.5	92.5	84.9	82.4	70.9
Non-Interest Expense	618.2	588.1	627.9	155.3	140.3	123.5	105.2
Income Before Taxes	474.0	358.7	184.5	158.6	127.6	104.8	87.1
Net Income	[2]323.6	[2]225.3	[2]117.5	107.2	85.1	69.8	57.5
Average Shs. Outstg. (000)	208,144	207,484	207,496	108,823	102,884	101,368	100,196
BALANCE SHEET (IN MILLIONS):							
Cash & Due from Banks	517.3	561.4	446.7	179.1	224.9	206.2	164.9
Securities Avail. for Sale	117.0	197.2	74.4	30.3	62.7	98.3	31.8
Total Loans & Leases	12,937.5	11,991.7	11,050.2	3,988.6	3,200.1	2,611.2	2,348.0
Allowance for Credit Losses	177.0	173.4	160.5	62.4	51.5	45.5	35.5
Net Loans & Leases	12,760.5	11,818.4	10,889.6	3,926.2	3,148.6	2,565.7	2,312.5
Total Assets	21,472.1	19,273.7	16,553.5	6,806.2	5,811.1	4,692.0	4,200.4
Total Deposits	14,494.7	12,619.5	11,982.3	4,495.9	3,947.3	3,251.2	2,976.4
Long-Term Obligations	2,403.2	2,588.6	1,696.5	720.7	738.0	546.1	552.2
Total Liabilities	18,789.7	16,818.4	15,225.0	6,198.9	5,352.6	4,290.0	3,887.1
Net Stockholders' Equity	2,682.4	2,455.3	1,278.6	557.4	408.5	352.1	313.3
Year-end Shs. Outstg. (000)	205,408	205,059	205,246	108,223	101,443	97,704	97,540
STATISTICAL RECORD:							
Return on Equity %	12.1	9.2	9.2	19.2	20.8	19.8	18.4
Return on Assets %	1.5	1.2	0.7	1.6	1.5	1.5	1.4
Equity/Assets %	12.5	12.7	7.7	8.2	7.0	7.5	7.5
Non-Int. Exp./Tot. Inc. %	55.0	60.3	75.4	47.2	50.6	50.3	51.0
Price Range	29.60-21.27	27.88-20.00	25.19-15.19	26.50-17.50	27.38-13.38	17.88-8.94	9.75-6.38
P/E Ratio	19.1-13.7	25.6-18.3	44.2-26.6	26.8-17.7	33.0-16.1	25.9-13.0	17.0-11.1
Average Yield %	2.4	2.3	2.2	1.6	1.4	1.6	2.4

Statistics are as originally reported. Adj. for stock splits: 2-for-1, 7/98 & 5/97. [3] Reflects the 7/00 acquisition of CCB Financial Corp. [2] Incl. pre-tax acquisition chrg. of $4.9 mill., 2002; $11.4 mill., 2001; $122.9 mill., 2000.

OFFICERS:
E. C. Roessler, Chmn., Pres., C.E.O.
S. M. Fox, C.F.O.
W. R. Reed, Jr., C.O.O.

INVESTOR CONTACT: Jekka Pinckney, (901) 523-3525

PRINCIPAL OFFICE: One Commerce Square, Memphis, TN 38150

TELEPHONE NUMBER: (901) 523-3434
FAX: (901) 523-3310
WEB: www.ncbccorp.com

NO. OF EMPLOYEES: 5,490

SHAREHOLDERS: 12,875

ANNUAL MEETING: In Apr.

INCORPORATED: TN, Feb., 1966

INSTITUTIONAL HOLDINGS:
No. of Institutions: 241
Shares Held: 86,316,668
% Held: 41.9

INDUSTRY: National commercial banks (SIC: 6021)

TRANSFER AGENT(S): Bank of New York, New York, NY

NATIONAL FUEL GAS COMPANY

	YIELD	4.2%
	P/E RATIO	13.8

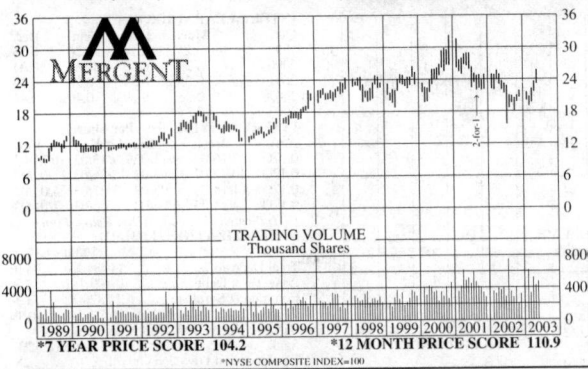

INTERIM EARNINGS (Per Share):

Qtr.	Dec.	Mar.	June	Sept.
1999-00	0.57	0.91	0.12	0.03
2000-01	0.66	0.94	0.45	d1.24
2001-02	0.41	0.77	0.22	0.06
2002-03	0.58	0.99	...	...

INTERIM DIVIDENDS (Per Share):

Amt.	Decl.	Ex.	Rec.	Pay.
0.26Q	9/12/02	9/26/02	9/30/02	10/15/02
0.26Q	12/12/02	12/27/02	12/31/02	1/15/03
0.26Q	3/17/03	3/27/03	3/31/03	4/15/03
0.27Q	6/05/03	6/26/03	6/30/03	7/15/03

Indicated div.: $1.08 (Div. Reinv. Plan)

CAPITALIZATION (9/30/02):

	($000)	(%)
Long-Term Debt	1,145,341	45.1
Deferred Income Tax	356,220	14.0
Minority Interest	28,785	1.1
Common & Surplus	1,006,858	39.7
Total	2,537,204	100.0

DIVIDEND ACHIEVER STATUS:
Rank: 264   10-Year Growth Rate: 3.31%
Total Years of Dividend Growth: 31

*7 YEAR PRICE SCORE 104.2   ***12 MONTH PRICE SCORE 110.9**

*NYSE COMPOSITE INDEX=100

RECENT DEVELOPMENTS: For the quarter ended 3/31/03, net income rose 30.1% to $80.5 million compared with $61.9 million in the same period a year earlier. Operating revenues climbed 69.5% to $809.1 million. NFG's results were fueled by higher commodity prices, colder-than-normal weather in its Pennsylvania service territory and the cancellation of a possible equity offering. Operating income grew 19.1% to $106.4 million, reflecting improved results from across the NFG's business segments.

PROSPECTS: On 3/10/03, NFG announced that its timber subsidiary signed a purchase agreement with an undisclosed buyer to sell approximately 70,000 acres of its timber property for $190.0 million. The sale, which represents about 50.0% of NFG's timber holdings, is expected to close by 7/31/03. Meanwhile, NFG has increased its full-year fiscal 2003 earnings guidance to between $1.75 and $1.85 per share, before recurring items.

BUSINESS

NATIONAL FUEL GAS COMPANY is a diversified energy company consisting of six business segments. The Utility segment operations (53.1% of 2002 revenues) are carried out by National Fuel Gas Distribution Corporation, which sells natural gas or provides natural gas transportation services to about 732,000 customers, as of 9/30/02, through a local distribution system located in western New York and northwestern Pennsylvania. The Exploration and Production segment operations (21.3%) are carried out by Seneca Resources Corporation. The Energy Marketing segment operations (10.4%) are carried out by National Fuel Resources, Inc. The International segment operations (6.5%) are carried out by Horizon Energy Development. The Pipeline and Storage segment operations (5.5%) are carried out by National Fuel Gas Supply Corporation. The Timber segment operations (3.2%) are carried out by Highland Forest Resources, Inc. and by a division of Seneca known as its Northeast Division.

ANNUAL FINANCIAL DATA

	9/30/02	9/30/01	9/30/00	9/30/99	9/30/98	9/30/97	9/30/96
Earnings Per Share	② 1.46	① 0.82	1.61	1.48	0.42	1.51	1.39
Cash Flow Per Share	3.70	2.99	3.40	3.13	1.95	2.97	2.70
Tang. Book Val. Per Share	12.44	12.63	12.55	12.09	11.38	12.02	11.31
Dividends Per Share	1.02	0.98	0.94	0.92	0.89	0.85	0.82
Dividend Payout %	70.2	120.1	58.9	62.0	210.7	56.8	59.3
INCOME STATEMENT (IN MILLIONS):							
Total Revenues	1,464.5	2,100.4	1,425.3	1,263.3	1,248.0	1,265.8	1,208.0
Costs & Expenses	1,051.8	1,746.1	1,041.4	917.7	1,019.4	960.2	925.9
Depreciation & Amort.	180.7	174.9	142.2	129.7	118.9	111.7	98.2
Maintenance Exp.	...	20.6	23.5	23.9	25.8	25.7	26.4
Operating Income	232.0	158.7	218.3	192.0	83.9	168.3	157.4
Net Interest Inc./(Exp.)	d120.6	d107.1	d100.1	d87.7	d85.3	d56.8	d56.6
Equity Earnings/Minority Int.	d0.7	d1.3	d1.4	d1.6	d2.2	...	...
Net Income	② 117.7	① 65.5	127.2	115.0	32.3	114.7	104.7
Cash Flow	298.4	240.4	269.4	244.7	151.2	226.3	202.9
Average Shs. Outstg. (000)	80,534	80,361	79,166	78,084	77,406	76,168	75,226
BALANCE SHEET (IN MILLIONS):							
Gross Property	4,512.7	4,273.7	3,829.6	3,383.5	3,186.9	2,668.5	2,471.1
Accumulated Depreciation	1,667.9	1,493.0	1,146.2	1,029.6	938.7	849.1	761.5
Net Property	2,844.7	2,780.7	2,683.4	2,353.9	2,248.1	1,819.4	1,709.6
Total Assets	3,401.3	3,445.6	3,236.9	2,842.6	2,669.9	2,271.5	2,149.8
Long-Term Obligations	1,145.3	1,046.7	953.6	822.7	692.7	581.6	574.0
Net Stockholders' Equity	1,006.9	1,002.7	987.4	939.3	875.6	917.9	856.0
Year-end Shs. Outstg. (000)	80,265	79,406	78,660	77,674	76,938	76,332	75,704
STATISTICAL RECORD:							
Operating Profit Margin %	15.8	7.6	15.3	15.2	6.7	13.3	13.0
Net Profit Margin %	8.0	3.1	8.9	9.1	2.6	9.1	8.7
Net Inc./Net Property %	4.1	2.4	4.7	4.9	1.4	6.3	6.1
Net Inc./Tot. Capital %	4.6	2.7	5.6	5.6	1.7	6.4	6.1
Return on Equity %	11.7	6.5	12.9	12.2	3.7	12.5	12.2
Accum. Depr./Gross Prop. %	37.0	34.9	29.9	30.4	29.5	31.8	30.8
Price Range	25.70-15.61	31.59-21.95	32.25-19.69	26.47-18.75	24.81-19.81	24.44-19.69	22.06-15.69
P/E Ratio	17.6-10.7	38.5-26.8	20.1-12.3	17.9-12.7	59.1-47.2	16.2-13.1	15.9-11.3
Average Yield %	5.0	3.7	3.6	4.0	4.0	3.9	4.4

Statistics are as originally reported. Adj. for 2-for-1 stk. split, 9/01. ① Incl. after-tax impairment chrg. of $104.0 mill. ② Incl. impairment of invest. in partnership chrg. of $15.2 mill.

OFFICERS:
P. C. Ackerman, Chmn., Pres., C.E.O.
W. E. DeForest, Sr. V.P.
J. P. Pawlowski, Treas.

INVESTOR CONTACT: Margaret M. Suto, Director, Investor Relations, (716) 857-6987

PRINCIPAL OFFICE: 10 Lafayette Square, Buffalo, NY 14203

TELEPHONE NUMBER: (716) 857-7000
FAX: (716) 541-7841
WEB: www.natfuel.com

NO. OF EMPLOYEES: 3,177

SHAREHOLDERS: 20,004

ANNUAL MEETING: In Feb.

INCORPORATED: NJ, Dec., 1902

INSTITUTIONAL HOLDINGS:
No. of Institutions: 192
Shares Held: 35,136,781
% Held: 43.4

INDUSTRY: Natural gas distribution (SIC: 4924)

TRANSFER AGENT(S): Mellon Investor Services, South Hackensack, NJ

NATIONAL PENN BANCSHARES, INC.

YIELD 3.1%
P/E RATIO 17.0

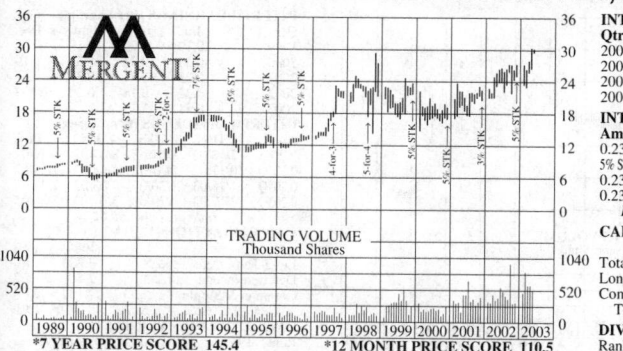

7 YEAR PRICE SCORE 145.4   **12 MONTH PRICE SCORE 110.5**

*NYSE COMPOSITE INDEX=100

INTERIM EARNINGS (Per Share):

Qtr.	Mar.	June	Sept.	Dec.
2000	0.39	0.37	0.35	0.33
2001	0.35	0.38	0.40	0.41
2002	0.41	0.43	0.44	0.44
2003	0.45	...	...	...

INTERIM DIVIDENDS (Per Share):

Amt.	Decl.	Ex.	Rec.	Pay.
0.23Q	9/25/02	10/29/02	10/31/02	11/17/02
5% STK	10/23/02	12/04/02	12/06/02	12/27/02
0.23Q	12/18/02	1/29/03	1/31/03	2/17/03
0.23Q	3/26/03	4/28/03	4/30/03	5/17/03

Indicated div.: $0.92 (Div. Reinv. Plan)

CAPITALIZATION (12/31/02):

	($000)	(%)
Total Deposits	2,112,640	84.3
Long-Term Debt	169,703	6.8
Common & Surplus	222,360	8.9
Total	2,504,703	100.0

DIVIDEND ACHIEVER STATUS:
Rank: 84   10-Year Growth Rate: 13.31%
Total Years of Dividend Growth: 24

RECENT DEVELOPMENTS: For the quarter ended 3/31/03, net income increased 18.5% to $10.4 million compared with $8.8 million in the corresponding year-earlier period. Net interest income rose 8.8% to $29.1 million from $26.8 million the previous year. Provision for loan losses was $2.3 million versus $4.0 million in 2002. Separately, on 5/1/03, NPBC announced the execution of a definitive agreement to acquire HomeTowne Heritage Bank for approximately $37.6 million in cash. Upon completion of the transaction, HomeTowne Heritage Bank will retain its name and operate as a division of NPBC, and expand to include the Company's community office located in New Holland, Pennsylvania. Additional community offices within Lancaster County are planned. NPBC expects that the transaction will close by 12/31/03. Also, during the first quarter of 2003, NPBC completed its acquisition of First-Service Bank of Doylestown, Pennsylvania and announced an agreement to sell its subsidiary, Panasia Bank, N.A., to Woori America Bank for $34.5 million.

BUSINESS

NATIONAL PENN BANCSHARES, INC., with total assets of $3.28 billion as of 3/31/03, is a bank holding company. As of 5/1/03, NPBC operated 65 community offices in southeastern Pennsylvania through National Penn Bank, including its FirstService Bank division, and two community offices in southeastern Pennsylvania through Panasia Bank N.A. Panasia Bank N.A. also operates four community offices in the northern New Jersey marketplace and one office in Annandale, Virginia. Trust and investment management services are provided through Investors Trust Company; brokerage services are provided through Penn Securities, Inc.; mortgage banking activities are provided through Penn 1st Financial Services, Inc.; equipment leasing services are provided through National Penn Leasing Company; and insurance products are provided through FirstService Insurance Agency, Inc.

ANNUAL FINANCIAL DATA

	12/31/02	12/31/01	12/31/00	12/31/99	12/31/98	12/31/97	12/31/96
Earnings Per Share	1.72	1.54	1.44	1.33	1.28	1.15	1.07
Tang. Book Val. Per Share	10.74	9.35	8.78	7.70	8.31	7.78	7.23
Dividends Per Share	0.85	0.79	0.71	0.66	0.61	0.52	0.44
Dividend Payout %	49.3	50.9	49.4	49.8	47.6	45.5	41.3
INCOME STATEMENT (IN MILLIONS):							
Total Interest Income	173.0	188.5	184.7	164.3	131.9	119.0	106.6
Total Interest Expense	63.4	92.5	99.7	82.8	67.0	54.6	46.0
Net Interest Income	109.6	96.0	85.0	81.5	64.9	64.4	60.5
Provision for Loan Losses	14.0	9.0	5.6	6.0	5.1	4.6	3.9
Non-Interest Income	39.8	34.5	27.2	23.3	17.0	12.1	9.1
Non-Interest Expense	89.8	80.7	70.8	65.7	51.3	46.1	41.3
Income Before Taxes	45.6	40.8	35.7	33.2	25.5	25.8	24.5
Net Income	36.2	32.7	29.2	27.4	20.5	18.6	16.9
Average Shs. Outstg. (000)	21,050	21,234	20,318	20,525	16,091	16,249	15,846
BALANCE SHEET (IN MILLIONS):							
Cash & Due from Banks	83.8	101.8	80.9	63.0	46.6	40.0	40.2
Securities Avail. for Sale	733.8	658.6	593.3	516.0	443.3	321.8	236.8
Total Loans & Leases	1,885.6	1,856.4	1,720.3	1,570.5	1,248.0	1,122.8	1,051.1
Allowance for Credit Losses	42.6	42.2	37.1	34.1	27.3	25.1	22.7
Net Loans & Leases	1,843.0	1,814.2	1,683.2	1,536.4	1,220.7	1,097.7	1,028.3
Total Assets	2,858.3	2,727.5	2,512.5	2,242.4	1,811.6	1,534.4	1,358.0
Total Deposits	2,112.6	2,076.8	1,814.3	1,593.3	1,208.1	1,115.6	980.8
Long-Term Obligations	169.7	140.0	146.4	223.1	248.5	155.5	76.1
Total Liabilities	2,635.9	2,531.8	2,335.1	2,094.7	1,681.4	1,411.2	1,243.3
Net Stockholders' Equity	222.4	195.7	177.4	147.7	130.5	123.2	114.7
Year-end Shs. Outstg. (000)	20,700	20,923	20,214	19,182	15,701	15,839	15,864
STATISTICAL RECORD:							
Return on Equity %	16.3	16.7	16.5	18.6	15.7	15.1	14.8
Return on Assets %	1.3	1.2	1.2	1.2	1.1	1.2	1.2
Equity/Assets %	7.8	7.2	7.1	6.6	7.2	8.0	8.4
Non-Int. Exp./Tot. Inc. %	60.1	61.9	63.1	62.7	62.6	60.3	59.3
Price Range	27.32-20.95	23.70-17.11	22.18-14.75	24.64-16.98	29.36-14.26	23.15-13.15	14.09-11.39
P/E Ratio	15.9-12.2	15.4-11.1	15.4-10.2	18.5-12.8	23.0-11.2	20.1-11.4	13.2-10.6
Average Yield %	3.5	3.9	3.9	3.2	2.8	2.9	3.5

Statistics are as originally reported. Adj. for stk. splits: 5% div., 12/02; 3% div., 12/01; 5% div., 12/00; 5% div., 12/99; 5-for-4, 7/98; 4-for-3, 7/97.

OFFICERS:
W. R. Weidner, Chmn., Pres., C.E.O.
G. L. Rhoads, C.F.O., Treas.
S. L. Spayd, Sec.

INVESTOR CONTACT: Gary L. Rhodes, C.F.O., Treas., (610) 369-6341

PRINCIPAL OFFICE: Philadelphia and Reading Avenues, Boyertown, PA 19512

TELEPHONE NUMBER: (610) 367-6001
FAX: (610) 369-6349
WEB: www.nationalpennbancshares.com
NO. OF EMPLOYEES: 952 (avg.)
SHAREHOLDERS: 3,338
ANNUAL MEETING: In Apr.
INCORPORATED: PA, Jan., 1982

INSTITUTIONAL HOLDINGS:
No. of Institutions: 52
Shares Held: 3,251,948
% Held: 14.1

INDUSTRY: National commercial banks (SIC: 6021)

TRANSFER AGENT(S): Mellon Investor Services, L.L.C., Ridgefield Park, NJ

NATIONAL SECURITY GROUP, INC. (THE)

YIELD 6.2%
P/E RATIO 35.6

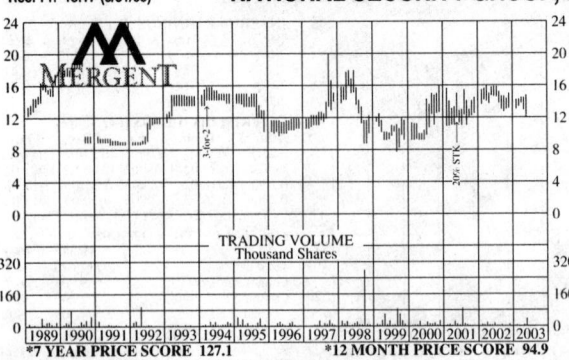

INTERIM EARNINGS (Per Share):

Qtr.	Mar.	June	Sept.	Dec.
1999	0.19	0.79	0.18	0.36
2000	0.45	0.33	0.57	0.19
2001	0.23	0.41	0.37	0.67
2002	0.31	0.18	0.25	d0.37
2003	0.31	...	...	...

INTERIM DIVIDENDS (Per Share):

Amt.	Decl.	Ex.	Rec.	Pay.
0.20Q	7/13/02	8/01/02	8/05/02	8/30/02
0.205Q	10/17/02	10/31/02	11/04/02	11/29/02
0.205Q	1/18/03	1/30/03	2/03/03	2/28/03
0.205Q	4/17/03	4/29/03	5/01/03	5/30/03

Indicated div.: $0.82

CAPITALIZATION (12/31/02):

	($000)	(%)
Long-Term Debt	3,380	7.0
Deferred Income Tax	2,501	5.2
Common & Surplus	42,159	87.8
Total	48,040	100.0

DIVIDEND ACHIEVER STATUS:
Rank: 193   10-Year Growth Rate: 7.55%
Total Years of Dividend Growth: 12

TRADING VOLUME
Thousand Shares

*7 YEAR PRICE SCORE 127.1   *12 MONTH PRICE SCORE 94.9
*NYSE COMPOSITE INDEX=100

RECENT DEVELOPMENTS: For the quarter ended 3/31/03, net income increased to $770.0 million versus $344.0 million in the corresponding year-earlier period. Total revenues climbed 29.7% to $11.4 million, led by a 37.1% gain in net insurance premiums earned. Premium revenue from NSEC's life, accident and health insurance business rose 2.4% to $1.4 million. Property and casualty insurance premium revenues advanced 45.3% to $8.5 million, driven by higher dwelling property premium revenue, reflecting increased marketing efforts, modernization of product lines including increases in policy limits, decreased competition in several markets, and rate increases implemented in several states. Separately, NSEC noted that due to adverse underwriting results in 2002, it has aggressively monitored rates on several insurance programs in several states. In an effort to improve underwriting results, NSEC raised homeowners rates by an average of 18.0% in Alabama and 15.0% in Georgia, in the first quarter of 2003. Similar increases are slated to take effect in the second and third quarters of 2003 in other lines of business.

BUSINESS

THE NATIONAL SECURITY GROUP, INC. is an insurance holding company that, through its subsidiaries, writes primarily dwelling fire and windstorm, homeowners, mobile homeowners, and personal non-standard automobile lines of insurance. The Company, through its life insurance subsidiary, offers a basic line of life, and health and accident insurance products. Property-casualty insurance is the most significant segment, accounting for 83.5% of total premium revenues as of 12/31/02. The Company's property and casualty insurance business is conducted through National Security Fire & Casualty Company, a wholly-owned subsidiary of the Company, and Omega One Insurance Company, a wholly-owned subsidiary of National Security Fire & Casualty Company.

ANNUAL FINANCIAL DATA

	12/31/02	12/31/01	12/31/00	12/31/99	12/31/98	12/31/97	12/31/96
Earnings Per Share	0.37	1.67	1.53	1.53	0.35	1.07	0.48
Tang. Book Val. Per Share	17.09	18.20	17.75	16.98	17.05	16.70	14.55
Dividends Per Share	0.81	0.76	0.71	0.68	0.64	0.58	0.54
Dividend Payout %	217.5	45.3	46.2	44.3	183.3	54.7	112.1
INCOME STATEMENT (IN THOUSANDS):							
Total Premium Income	32,631	25,357	22,921	25,936	28,451	31,156	26,654
Other Income	6,454	7,426	6,754	6,690	8,853	7,619	6,356
Total Revenues	39,085	32,783	29,675	32,626	37,304	38,775	33,010
Policyholder Benefits	22,763	13,516	14,125	17,275	22,880	22,995	19,677
Income Before Income Taxes	1,194	5,470	4,844	4,516	1,106	3,360	1,621
Income Taxes	422	1,392	1,068	760	176	362	265
Equity Earnings/Minority Int.	136	52	...	...	...	...	...
Net Income	908	4,130	3,776	3,756	930	2,998	1,356
Average Shs. Outstg.	2,467	2,467	2,467	2,467	2,675	2,780	2,808
BALANCE SHEET (IN THOUSANDS):							
Cash & Cash Equivalents	65,497	61,039	54,277	53,124	55,308	56,707	37,438
Premiums Due	4,597	3,824	3,677	4,687	7,223	8,889	12,746
Invst. Assets: Fixed-term	19,380	23,135	28,875	30,911	30,807	29,995	35,413
Invst. Assets: Loans	991	1,001	808	781	780	968	1,027
Invst. Assets: Total	87,558	85,196	84,575	84,990	87,741	88,951	75,390
Total Assets	101,602	99,484	97,563	98,105	103,973	106,958	98,219
Long-Term Obligations	3,380	2,108	2,401	2,672	3,004	...	...
Net Stockholders' Equity	42,159	44,884	43,780	41,888	41,968	46,352	40,519
Year-end Shs. Outstg.	2,467	2,467	2,467	2,467	2,461	2,776	2,784
STATISTICAL RECORD:							
Return on Revenues %	2.3	12.6	12.7	11.5	2.5	7.7	4.1
Return on Equity %	2.2	9.2	8.6	9.0	2.2	6.5	3.3
Return on Assets %	0.9	4.2	3.9	3.8	0.9	2.8	1.4
Price Range	16.00-12.68	15.62-10.89	16.04-9.17	12.50-7.71	17.92-8.75	20.00-10.62	11.87-9.69
P/E Ratio	43.2-34.3	9.4-6.5	10.5-6.0	8.2-5.1	51.2-25.0	18.7-10.0	24.6-20.1
Average Yield %	5.6	5.7	5.6	6.7	4.8	3.8	5.0

Statistics are as originally reported. Adj. for 20% stk. div., 5/01.

OFFICERS:
W. L. Brunson, Jr., Pres., C.E.O.
B. R. McLeod, C.F.O., Treas.

INVESTOR CONTACT: M. L. Murdock, Sr.
V.P., C.F.O., Treas., (334) 897-2273

PRINCIPAL OFFICE: 661 East Davis Street,
Elba, AL 36323

TELEPHONE NUMBER: (334) 897-2273
FAX: (334) 897-5694
WEB: www.nationalsecuritygroup.com
NO. OF EMPLOYEES: 22
SHAREHOLDERS: 1,100 (approx.)
ANNUAL MEETING: In Apr.
INCORPORATED: DE, Mar., 1990

INSTITUTIONAL HOLDINGS:
No. of Institutions: 3
Shares Held: 80,028
% Held: 4.0

INDUSTRY: Life insurance (SIC: 6311)

TRANSFER AGENT(S): The National Security
Group, Inc., Elba, AL

NICOR INC.

YIELD **5.2%**
P/E RATIO **11.2**

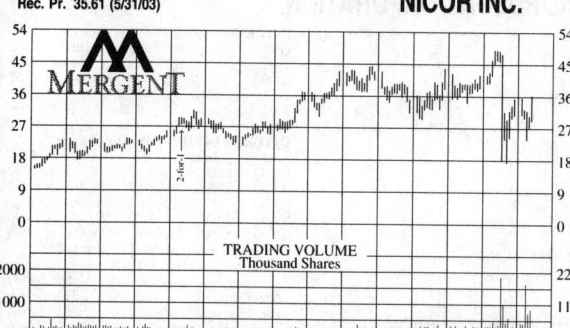

7 YEAR PRICE SCORE 97.6   **12 MONTH PRICE SCORE 96.4**
*NYSE COMPOSITE INDEX=100

INTERIM EARNINGS (Per Share):

Qtr.	Mar.	June	Sept.	Dec.
1999	0.82	0.56	0.42	0.83
2000	0.83	0.66	d1.37	0.87
2001	0.85	0.59	0.73	1.01
2002	0.90	0.46	0.68	0.89
2003	1.14	...	...	...

INTERIM DIVIDENDS (Per Share):

Amt.	Decl.	Ex.	Rec.	Pay.
0.46Q	7/18/02	9/26/02	9/30/02	11/01/02
0.46Q	11/21/02	12/27/02	12/31/02	2/01/03
0.465Q	3/20/03	3/27/03	3/31/03	5/01/03
0.465Q	4/30/03	6/26/03	6/30/03	8/01/03

Indicated div.: $1.86 (Div. Reinv. Plan)

CAPITALIZATION (12/31/02):

	($000)	(%)
Long-Term Debt	396,200	25.1
Deferred Income Tax	448,300	28.4
Redeemable Pfd. Stock	4,300	0.3
Common & Surplus	728,400	46.2
Total	1,577,200	100.0

DIVIDEND ACHIEVER STATUS:

Rank: 243   10-Year Growth Rate: 4.56%
Total Years of Dividend Growth: 15

RECENT DEVELOPMENTS: For the three months ended 3/31/03, income was $50.4 million, before an accounting change charge of $4.5 million, compared with net income of $36.5 million in the corresponding quarter of the previous year, due to impairment in both GAS' retail energy-related products and services businesses and its shipping segment, partially offset by higher utility operating and maintenance expenses. Operating revenues advanced 99.2% to $1.17 billion.

PROSPECTS: The Company should continue to benefit from favorable results in both its retail energy-related products and services businesses and its shipping segment. However, operating results may be pressured by higher costs in GAS' utility operations. The Company expects 2003 diluted earnings per share to range from $2.40 to $2.60, assuming normal weather for the remainder of the year.

BUSINESS

NICOR INC. is engaged in the purchase, storage, distribution, transportation, sale, and gathering of natural gas. The Company's natural gas unit, Northern Illinois Gas, is the largest gas distribution company in Illinois and one of the biggest in the nation. As of 12/31/02, Northern Illinois served more than 2.0 million customers in the northern third of the state, generally outside of Chicago. NICOR also owns Tropical Shipping Co., a transporter of containerized freight in the Caribbean. In 2002, operating revenues were derived: 83.1% gas distribution, 13.9% shipping and 3.0% other energy ventures.

ANNUAL FINANCIAL DATA

	12/31/02	12/31/01	12/31/00	12/31/99	12/31/98	12/31/97	12/31/96
Earnings Per Share	[4] 2.88	3.17	[3] 1.00	[2] 2.62	2.42	2.61	[1] 2.42
Cash Flow Per Share	6.38	6.46	4.12	5.58	5.25	5.29	4.92
Tang. Book Val. Per Share	16.55	16.39	15.56	16.80	15.97	15.43	14.74
Dividends Per Share	1.82	1.74	1.64	1.54	1.46	1.37	1.31
Dividend Payout %	63.2	54.7	163.5	58.8	60.3	52.5	54.1
INCOME STATEMENT (IN MILLIONS):							
Total Revenues	1,897.4	2,544.1	2,298.1	1,615.2	1,465.1	1,992.6	1,850.7
Costs & Expenses	1,515.9	2,151.8	2,059.7	1,262.9	1,120.0	1,631.6	1,492.3
Depreciation & Amort.	155.0	148.8	144.3	140.3	136.5	131.2	125.3
Operating Income	226.5	243.5	94.1	212.0	208.6	229.8	233.1
Net Interest Inc./(Exp.)	d38.5	d44.9	d48.6	d45.1	d46.6	d46.2	d46.2
Income Taxes	57.6	73.4	14.4	65.7	61.1	69.0	67.7
Net Income	[4] 128.0	143.7	[3] 46.7	[2] 124.4	116.4	127.9	[1] 121.2
Cash Flow	282.8	292.2	190.7	264.4	252.6	258.7	246.1
Average Shs. Outstg. (000)	44,300	45,200	46,300	47,400	48,100	48,900	50,000
BALANCE SHEET (IN MILLIONS):							
Gross Property	3,872.8	3,733.0	3,576.6	3,483.1	3,379.8	3,267.7	3,192.7
Accumulated Depreciation	2,076.0	1,964.4	1,847.0	1,747.9	1,648.0	1,531.9	1,420.8
Net Property	1,796.8	1,768.6	1,729.6	1,735.2	1,731.8	1,735.8	1,771.9
Total Assets	2,899.4	2,574.8	2,885.4	2,451.8	2,364.6	2,394.6	2,438.6
Long-Term Obligations	396.2	446.4	347.1	436.1	557.3	550.2	518.0
Net Stockholders' Equity	728.4	727.6	707.8	787.7	759.0	744.1	729.7
Year-end Shs. Outstg. (000)	44,011	44,398	45,491	46,890	47,514	48,217	49,492
STATISTICAL RECORD:							
Operating Profit Margin %	11.9	9.6	4.1	13.1	14.2	11.5	12.6
Net Profit Margin %	6.7	5.6	2.0	7.7	7.9	6.4	6.5
Net Inc./Net Property %	7.1	8.1	2.7	7.2	6.7	7.4	6.8
Net Inc./Tot. Capital %	8.1	9.1	3.3	7.9	7.1	8.0	7.8
Return on Equity %	17.6	19.7	6.6	15.8	15.3	17.2	16.6
Accum. Depr./Gross Prop. %	53.6	52.6	51.6	50.2	48.8	46.9	44.5
Price Range	49.00-17.25	42.38-34.00	43.88-29.38	42.94-31.19	44.44-37.13	42.94-30.00	37.13-25.38
P/E Ratio	17.0-6.0	13.4-10.7	43.9-29.4	16.4-11.9	18.4-15.3	16.5-11.5	15.3-10.5
Average Yield %	5.5	4.5	4.5	4.2	3.6	3.8	4.2

Statistics are as originally reported. [1] Bef. inc. fr. dis. ops. of $150.0 mill. [2] Incl. a pre-tax gain of $3.8 million on the sale of the Company's interest in QuickTrade. [3] Excls. one-time after-tax chrg. of $89.7 mill. [4] Incl. pre-tax gain of $4.1 mill. from the sale of prop.

OFFICERS:
T. L. Fisher, Chmn., C.E.O.
R. M. Strobel, Pres.
K. L. Halloran, Exec. V.P., C.F.O.

INVESTOR CONTACT: Mark Knox, Investor Relations, (305) 983-9500 ext.2529

PRINCIPAL OFFICE: 1844 Ferry Road, Naperville, IL 60563-9600

TELEPHONE NUMBER: (630) 305-9500
FAX: (630) 983-9328
WEB: www.nicorinc.com

NO. OF EMPLOYEES: 3,500 (approx.)

SHAREHOLDERS: 26,000 (approx.)

ANNUAL MEETING: In Apr.

INCORPORATED: IL, 1976

INSTITUTIONAL HOLDINGS:
No. of Institutions: 226
Shares Held: 23,693,810
% Held: 53.8

INDUSTRY: Natural gas distribution (SIC: 4924)

TRANSFER AGENT(S): Computershare Investor Services, Chicago, IL

NORDSON CORPORATION

YIELD 2.5%
P/E RATIO 37.1

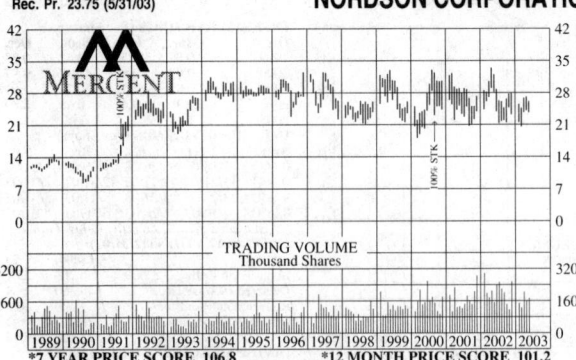

*7 YEAR PRICE SCORE 106.8　　***12 MONTH PRICE SCORE 101.2**

*NYSE COMPOSITE INDEX=100

INTERIM EARNINGS (Per Share):

Qtr.	Jan.	Apr.	July	Oct.
1999	0.21	0.39	0.40	0.43
2000	0.15	0.40	0.46	0.67
2001	0.23	0.27	0.17	0.07
2002	0.17	0.23	0.21	0.04
2003	0.15	0.24	...	...

INTERIM DIVIDENDS (Per Share):

Amt.	Decl.	Ex.	Rec.	Pay.
0.14Q	5/22/02	6/05/02	6/07/02	6/18/02
0.15Q	8/01/02	8/28/02	8/30/02	9/17/02
0.15Q	11/06/02	12/11/02	12/13/02	1/03/03
0.15Q	2/05/03	2/19/03	2/21/03	3/11/03
0.15Q	5/21/03	6/04/03	6/06/03	6/24/03

Indicated div.: $0.60 (Div. Reinv. Plan)

CAPITALIZATION (11/3/02):

	($000)	(%)
Long-Term Debt	171,314	38.6
Capital Lease Obligations..	3,581	0.8
Common & Surplus	268,890	60.6
Total	443,785	100.0

DIVIDEND ACHIEVER STATUS:

Rank: 146　　10-Year Growth Rate: 9.99%
Total Years of Dividend Growth: 22

RECENT DEVELOPMENTS: For the quarter ended 5/4/03, net income increased 4.0% to $8.1 million from $7.8 million in the corresponding prior-year period. Results for 2003 and 2002 included pre-tax severance and restructuring costs of $1.5 million and $814,000, respectively. Net sales rose 1.9% to $166.7 million, reflecting favorable currency effects due to the weaker U.S. dollar, partially offset by a decline in sales volume. On a segment basis, adhesive dispensing and nonwoven fiber systems sales grew 5.3% to

$109.6 million, while advanced technology systems sales improved 0.7% to $30.7 million. However, coating and finishing systems sales slipped 8.9% to $26.4 million. On a geographic basis, North America declined 5.2% to $69.1 million, while Pacific South sales slid 2.3% to $19.0 million. Meanwhile, sales in Europe improved 8.2% to $60.9 million, while sales in Japan advanced 18.8% to $17.7 million. Backlog at the end of the quarter was $66.4 million, up 46.3% from the beginning of the fiscal year.

BUSINESS

NORDSON CORPORATION designs, manufactures and markets precision dispensing systems that apply adhesives, sealants and coatings to a broad range of consumer and industrial products during manufacturing operations. The Company also manufactures technology-based systems for curing and surface treatment processes. NDSN's products are used in a diverse range of industries, including appliance, automotive, bookbinding, circuit board assembly, electronics, food and beverage, furniture, medical, metal finishing, nonwoven products, packaging, semiconductor and telecommunications. NDSN's three reportable segments are adhesive dispensing and nonwoven fiber systems (63.8% of net sales as of 11/3/02), advanced technology systems (18.6), and coating and finishing systems (17.6). The Company markets its products through a network of direct operations in 30 countries throughout North America, Europe, Japan, Asia, Latin America and Australia. More than 50.0% of the Company's revenues are generated outside the United States. NDSN has principal manufacturing facilities in Ohio, Georgia, Alabama, California, Rhode Island, Germany, the Netherlands, and the United Kingdom. The Company began a tradition of increasing its annual dividends as a private company in 1964.

ANNUAL FINANCIAL DATA

	11/3/02	10/28/01	10/29/00	10/31/99	11/1/98	11/2/97	11/3/96
Earnings Per Share	⊡ 0.66	⊡ 0.74	⊡ 1.67	⊡ 1.42	⊡ 0.63	1.45	1.49
Cash Flow Per Share	1.53	2.01	2.59	2.32	1.38	2.18	2.14
Tang. Book Val. Per Share	...	...	4.73	2.45	3.90	4.76	5.10
Dividends Per Share	0.57	0.56	0.52	0.48	0.44	0.40	0.36
Dividend Payout %	86.4	75.7	31.1	33.8	70.4	27.7	24.2
INCOME STATEMENT (IN THOUSANDS):							
Total Revenues	647,756	731,416	740,568	700,465	660,900	636,710	609,444
Costs & Expenses	565,250	630,024	618,791	594,180	590,826	537,344	501,661
Depreciation & Amort.	29,487	41,855	30,325	29,300	25,003	25,307	23,522
Operating Income	53,019	59,537	91,452	76,985	45,071	74,059	84,261
Net Interest Inc./(Exp.)	d21,713	d29,489	d11,665	d10,244	d9,647	d7,763	d5,955
Income Before Income Taxes	32,944	37,716	83,408	71,438	38,927	71,745	81,061
Income Taxes	10,872	13,106	28,776	23,932	18,102	21,778	27,990
Net Income	⊡ 22,072	⊡ 24,610	⊡ 54,632	⊡ 47,506	⊡ 20,825	49,967	53,071
Cash Flow	51,559	66,465	84,957	76,806	45,828	75,274	76,593
Average Shs. Outstg.	33,690	33,050	32,767	33,048	33,322	34,552	35,792
BALANCE SHEET (IN THOUSANDS):							
Cash & Cash Equivalents	5,897	7,943	815	16,060	6,850	1,717	9,531
Total Current Assets	274,573	362,177	369,238	341,316	328,476	318,815	317,702
Net Property	118,773	133,332	126,910	128,639	101,183	101,667	107,018
Total Assets	764,472	862,453	610,040	591,790	538,944	502,996	510,493
Total Current Liabilities	252,647	355,653	253,008	251,940	207,082	179,663	207,216
Long-Term Obligations	174,895	191,773	60,800	65,975	70,444	66,502	20,562
Net Stockholders' Equity	268,890	263,726	247,223	221,398	214,775	220,545	245,297
Net Working Capital	21,926	6,524	116,230	89,376	121,394	139,152	110,486
Year-end Shs. Outstg.	33,613	33,137	32,449	49,012	33,480	33,678	35,268
STATISTICAL RECORD:							
Operating Profit Margin %	8.2	8.1	12.3	11.0	6.8	11.6	13.8
Net Profit Margin %	3.4	3.4	7.4	6.8	3.2	7.8	8.7
Return on Equity %	8.2	9.3	22.1	21.5	9.7	22.7	21.6
Return on Assets %	2.9	2.9	9.0	8.0	3.9	9.9	10.4
Debt/Total Assets %	22.9	22.2	10.0	11.1	13.1	13.2	4.0
Price Range	33.40-21.31	33.25-20.67	32.99-18.06	32.97-21.50	26.19-21.13	32.50-22.19	32.50-22.75
P/E Ratio	50.6-32.3	43.6-27.9	19.8-10.8	23.2-15.1	41.9-33.8	22.5-15.4	21.9-15.3
Average Yield %	2.1	2.1	2.0	1.8	1.9	1.5	1.3

Statistics are as originally reported. Adj. for stk. split: 100% div., 9/12/00. ⊡ Incl. severance & restruct. costs of $2.5 mill., 11/02; $13.3 mill., 10/01; $9.0 mill., 10/00; $3.0 mill., 10/99; $26.0 mill., 11/98.

OFFICERS:
W. P. Madar, Chmn.
E. P. Campbell, Pres., C.E.O.
P. S. Hellman, Exec. V.P., C.F.O., C.A.O.

INVESTOR CONTACT: Bruce Waffen,
Investor Relations, (440) 414-5610

PRINCIPAL OFFICE: 28601 Clemens Road,
Westlake, OH 44145-4551

TELEPHONE NUMBER: (440) 892-1580
FAX: (440) 892-9507
WEB: www.nordson.com

NO. OF EMPLOYEES: 3,504

SHAREHOLDERS: 2,452 (approx.)

ANNUAL MEETING: In Mar.

INCORPORATED: OH, 1954

INSTITUTIONAL HOLDINGS:
No. of Institutions: 98
Shares Held: 12,830,200
% Held: 37.7

INDUSTRY: Adhesives and sealants (SIC: 2891)

TRANSFER AGENT(S): National City Bank,
Cleveland, OH

NORTHERN TRUST CORPORATION

YIELD 1.8%
P/E RATIO 20.7

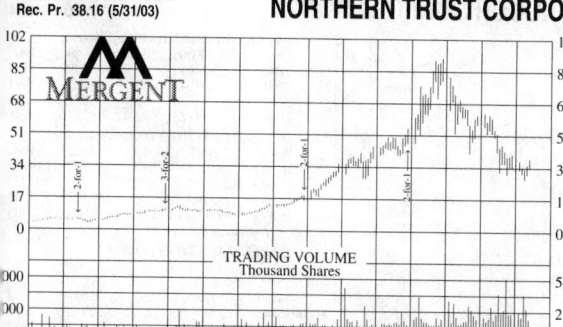

*7 YEAR PRICE SCORE 94.6   *12 MONTH PRICE SCORE 92.6
*NYSE COMPOSITE INDEX=100

TRADING VOLUME
Thousand Shares

MERGENT

INTERIM EARNINGS (Per Share):

Qtr.	Mar.	June	Sept.	Dec.
2000	0.49	0.53	0.53	0.54
2001	0.55	0.57	0.55	0.45
2002	0.56	0.56	0.43	0.43
2003	0.42	...	...	...

INTERIM DIVIDENDS (Per Share):

Amt.	Decl.	Ex.	Rec.	Pay.
0.17Q	7/16/02	9/06/02	9/10/02	10/01/02
0.17Q	11/19/02	12/06/02	12/10/02	1/02/03
0.17Q	2/18/03	3/06/03	3/10/03	4/01/03
0.17Q	4/16/03	6/06/03	6/10/03	7/01/03

Indicated div.: $0.68

CAPITALIZATION (12/31/02):

	($000)	(%)
Total Deposits	26,062,100	85.3
Long-Term Debt	1,483,600	4.9
Preferred Stock	120,000	0.4
Common & Surplus	2,879,800	9.4
Total	30,545,500	100.0

DIVIDEND ACHIEVER STATUS:

Rank: 58   10-Year Growth Rate: 15.57%
Total Years of Dividend Growth: 17

RECENT DEVELOPMENTS: For the quarter ended 3/31/03, net income decreased 25.8% to $94.7 million from $127.6 million in the corresponding prior-year period. Net interest income declined 4.6% to $153.5 million. Provision for credit losses was unchanged at $5.0 million. Total non-interest income slipped 6.5% to $373.1 million as trust fees slid 7.7% to $298.1 million, primarily due to the weak equity markets and lower securities lending fees, partially offset by net new business. Total non-interest expense grew 5.6% to $370.0 million. Net interest margin declined to

1.87% from 1.92% a year earlier, primarily due to a decline in the yield of the residential mortgage loan portfolio resulting from the impact of refinancing activity. Separately, on 4/30/03, NTRS completed its acquisition of Atlanta-based Legacy South, Inc., a private wealth management company with about $300.0 million in managed assets. As a result of the transaction, NTRS has a national office network of 83 offices in 13 states. Also, NTRS opened its first office in Tokyo, Japan in April 2003.

BUSINESS

NORTHERN TRUST CORPORATION is a Chicago-based multibank holding company. The Company's principal subsidiary is The Northern Trust Company, an Illinois banking corporation. NTRS also owns national bank subsidiaries in Arizona, California, Colorado, Florida and Texas; a federal savings bank with offices in Michigan, Missouri, Nevada, Ohio, Washington, Wisconsin, and Tokyo, Japan; a trust company in New York; and various other nonbank subsidiaries, including an investment management company owned through NTRS, a securities brokerage firm, an international investment consulting firm and a retirement services company. With total assets of $36.45 billion as of 3/31/03, NTRS offers financial services including fiduciary, banking, investment and financial consulting services for individuals as well as credit operating, trust and investment management services for corporations, institutions and organizations. The Company is a provider of personal fiduciary, master trust/custody and global custody, and treasury management services. NTRS and its subsidiaries also provide corporate banking, automated clearing house and leasing services.

ANNUAL FINANCIAL DATA

	12/31/02	12/31/01	12/31/00	12/31/99	12/31/98	12/31/97	12/31/96
Earnings Per Share	1.97	2.11	2.08	1.74	1.52	1.33	1.11
Tang. Book Val. Per Share	13.04	11.97	10.54	9.25	8.18	7.27	6.40
Dividends Per Share	0.68	0.62	0.54	0.48	0.42	0.36	0.31
Dividend Payout %	34.5	29.4	26.0	27.6	27.6	27.1	28.1
INCOME STATEMENT (IN MILLIONS):							
Total Interest Income	1,238.3	1,681.5	2,011.1	1,568.6	1,503.1	1,332.8	1,151.5
Total Interest Expense	636.5	1,086.2	1,442.5	1,049.8	1,025.9	894.6	763.2
Net Interest Income	601.8	595.3	568.6	518.8	477.2	438.2	388.3
Provision for Loan Losses	37.5	66.5	24.0	12.5	9.0	9.0	12.0
Non-Interest Income	1,536.8	1,580.1	1,537.0	1,235.2	1,071.6	934.5	777.9
Non-Interest Expense	1,432.1	1,376.9	1,351.5	1,125.0	997.1	891.8	766.8
Income Before Taxes	669.0	731.9	730.1	616.5	542.7	471.9	387.4
Net Income	447.1	487.5	485.1	405.0	353.9	309.4	258.8
Average Shs. Outstg. (000)	225,834	228,971	230,613	229,874	229,734	229,322	229,296
BALANCE SHEET (IN MILLIONS):							
Cash & Due from Banks	2,672.2	2,592.3	2,287.8	1,977.9	2,366.0	1,738.9	1,292.5
Securities Avail. for Sale	6,132.4	5,667.5	6,491.2	5,491.0	5,384.3	3,741.8	4,316.5
Total Loans & Leases	18,063.7	17,979.9	18,144.6	15,374.5	13,646.9	12,588.2	10,937.4
Allowance for Credit Losses	161.1	161.6	162.9	150.9	146.8	147.6	148.3
Net Loans & Leases	17,902.6	17,818.3	17,981.7	15,223.6	13,500.1	12,440.6	10,789.1
Total Assets	39,478.2	39,664.5	36,022.3	28,708.2	27,870.0	25,315.4	21,608.3
Total Deposits	26,062.1	25,019.3	22,827.9	21,371.0	18,202.7	16,360.0	13,796.2
Long-Term Obligations	1,483.6	1,484.5	1,405.7	1,426.9	1,425.6	1,491.9	732.8
Total Liabilities	36,478.4	36,891.0	33,560.1	26,533.5	25,929.7	23,576.4	20,064.2
Net Stockholders' Equity	2,999.8	2,773.5	2,462.2	2,174.7	1,940.3	1,739.0	1,544.1
Year-end Shs. Outstg. (000)	220,800	221,647	222,232	222,162	222,430	222,734	222,496
STATISTICAL RECORD:							
Return on Equity %	14.9	17.6	19.7	18.6	18.2	17.8	16.8
Return on Assets %	1.1	1.2	1.3	1.4	1.3	1.2	1.2
Equity/Assets %	7.6	7.0	6.8	7.6	7.0	6.9	7.1
Non-Int. Exp./Tot. Inc. %	67.0	63.3	64.2	64.1	64.4	65.0	65.8
Price Range	62.67-30.41	82.25-41.40	92.13-46.75	54.63-40.16	44.94-27.88	35.75-17.00	18.88-12.31
P/E Ratio	31.8-15.4	39.0-19.6	44.3-22.5	31.4-23.1	29.6-18.3	26.9-12.8	17.1-11.1
Average Yield %	1.5	1.0	0.8	1.0	1.2	1.4	2.0

Statistics are as originally reported. Adj. for stk. splits: 2-for-1, 12/9/96; 2-for-1, 12/11/99.

OFFICERS:

W. A. Osborn, Chmn., Pres., C.E.O.
P. R. Pero, Vice-Chmn., C.F.O.

INVESTOR CONTACT: Beverly J. Fleming, Dir., Inv. Rel., (312) 444-7811

PRINCIPAL OFFICE: 50 South La Salle Street, Chicago, IL 60675

TELEPHONE NUMBER: (312) 630-6000
FAX: (312) 444-7843
WEB: www.northerntrust.com
NO. OF EMPLOYEES: 9,317
SHAREHOLDERS: 3,136 (approx.)
ANNUAL MEETING: In April
INCORPORATED: DE, Aug., 1971

INSTITUTIONAL HOLDINGS:
No. of Institutions: 378
Shares Held: 144,269,643
% Held: 65.6
INDUSTRY: State commercial banks (SIC: 6022)
TRANSFER AGENT(S): Wells Fargo Shareowner Services, St. Paul, MN

NUCOR CORPORATION

YIELD 1.7%
P/E RATIO 23.4

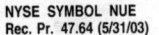

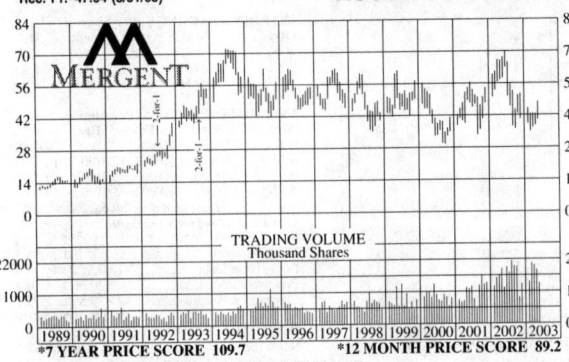

*7 YEAR PRICE SCORE 109.7 *12 MONTH PRICE SCORE 89.2
*NYSE COMPOSITE INDEX=100

TRADING VOLUME
Thousand Shares

INTERIM EARNINGS (Per Share):

Qtr.	Mar.	June	Sept.	Dec.
2000	0.94	0.98	0.85	1.03
2001	0.42	0.43	0.26	0.34
2002	0.26	0.76	0.50	0.55
2003	0.23	...	...	...

INTERIM DIVIDENDS (Per Share):

Amt.	Decl.	Ex.	Rec.	Pay.
0.19Q	9/04/02	9/25/02	9/27/02	11/08/02
0.19Q	12/10/02	12/27/02	12/31/02	2/11/03
0.20Q	3/06/03	3/27/03	3/31/03	5/12/03
0.20Q	6/03/03	6/26/03	6/30/03	8/11/03

Indicated div.: $0.80 (Div. Reinv. Plan)

CAPITALIZATION (12/31/02):

	($000)	(%)
Long-Term Debt	878,550	25.7
Minority Interest	216,655	6.3
Common & Surplus	2,322,989	68.0
Total	3,418,194	100.0

DIVIDEND ACHIEVER STATUS:
Rank: 37   10-Year Growth Rate: 18.33%
Total Years of Dividend Growth: 30

RECENT DEVELOPMENTS: For the thirteen weeks ended 4/5/03, net income fell 12.2% to $17.8 million from $20.3 million in the equivalent 2002 quarter. The decline in earnings was primarily attributed to higher raw material and energy costs. Net sales grew 37.0% to $1.48 billion. Total tons shipped to outside customers grew 33.6% to 4.0 million tons year-over-year, and steel production rose 31.5% to 4.3 million tons.

PROSPECTS: On 4/24/03, the Company and Companhia Vale do Rio Doce (CVRD) signed an agreement to construct and operate an environmentally friendly pig iron project in northern Brazil. NUE and CVRD will form a joint venture company to operate the facility. It is anticipated that NUE will purchase all of the production of the plant. Worth about $80.0 million, the ownership will be split 78.0% CVRD and 22.0% NUE.

BUSINESS

NUCOR CORPORATION is a recycler of steel products, with operating facilities in 14 states. The Company's manufactured products include carbon and alloy steel, for use in bars, beams, sheet and plate; steel joists and joist girders; steel deck; cold finished steel; steel fasteners; metal building systems; and light gauge steel framing. The primary raw material is ferrous scrap, which is acquired from numerous sources throughout the U.S. Hot-rolled and cold-rolled sheet steel are produced to customer orders. Other hot-rolled steel, cold-rolled steel, cold-finished steel and steel fasteners are manufactured in standard sizes and inventories are maintained. Steel joists, joist girders and steel deck are sold to general contractors and fabricators throughout the U.S. In December 2002, NUE acquired substantially all of the assets of Birmingham Steel Corporation for $615.0 million.

ANNUAL FINANCIAL DATA

	12/31/02	12/31/01	12/31/00	12/31/99	12/31/98	12/31/97	12/31/96
Earnings Per Share	☐ 2.07	☐ 1.45	3.80	2.80	3.00	3.34	2.83
Cash Flow Per Share	6.00	5.17	6.97	5.74	5.88	5.84	4.91
Tang. Book Val. Per Share	29.71	28.33	27.47	25.93	23.73	21.32	18.33
Dividends Per Share	0.74	0.66	0.58	0.51	0.46	0.38	0.31
Dividend Payout %	35.7	45.5	15.3	18.2	15.3	11.4	11.0
INCOME STATEMENT (IN MILLIONS):							
Total Revenues	4,801.8	4,139.2	4,586.1	4,009.3	4,151.2	4,184.5	3,647.0
Costs & Expenses	4,200.8	3,669.8	3,849.3	3,378.6	3,486.6	3,505.6	3,077.3
Depreciation & Amort.	307.1	289.1	259.4	256.6	253.1	218.8	182.2
Operating Income	293.9	180.4	477.5	374.1	411.5	460.1	387.5
Net Interest Inc./(Exp.)	d14.3	d6.5	0.8	5.1	3.8	...	0.3
Income Before Income Taxes	230.1	173.9	478.3	379.2	415.3	460.2	387.8
Income Taxes	68.0	60.9	167.4	134.6	151.6	165.7	139.6
Net Income	☐ 162.1	☐ 113.0	310.9	244.6	263.7	294.5	248.2
Cash Flow	469.2	402.0	570.3	501.2	516.8	513.2	430.4
Average Shs. Outstg. (000)	78,250	77,783	81,777	87,287	87,878	87,922	87,686
BALANCE SHEET (IN MILLIONS):							
Cash & Cash Equivalents	219.0	462.3	490.6	572.2	308.7	283.4	104.4
Total Current Assets	1,424.1	1,373.7	1,381.4	1,538.5	1,129.5	1,125.5	828.4
Net Property	2,932.1	2,365.7	2,340.3	2,191.3	2,097.1	1,858.9	1,791.2
Total Assets	4,381.0	3,759.3	3,721.8	3,729.8	3,226.5	2,984.4	2,619.5
Total Current Liabilities	591.5	484.2	558.1	531.0	486.9	524.5	465.7
Long-Term Obligations	878.6	460.5	460.5	390.5	215.5	168.0	152.6
Net Stockholders' Equity	2,323.0	2,201.5	2,131.0	2,262.2	2,072.6	1,876.4	1,609.3
Net Working Capital	832.6	889.5	823.4	1,007.5	642.6	601.1	362.7
Year-end Shs. Outstg. (000)	78,180	77,708	77,583	87,247	87,353	87,997	87,796
STATISTICAL RECORD:							
Operating Profit Margin %	6.1	4.4	10.4	9.3	9.9	11.0	10.6
Net Profit Margin %	3.4	2.7	6.8	6.1	6.4	7.0	6.8
Return on Equity %	7.0	5.1	14.6	10.8	12.7	15.7	15.4
Return on Assets %	3.7	3.0	8.4	6.6	8.2	9.9	9.5
Debt/Total Assets %	20.1	12.2	12.4	10.5	6.7	5.6	5.8
Price Range	70.15-36.00	56.50-33.45	56.44-29.60	61.81-41.63	60.63-35.25	62.94-44.75	63.00-45.1
P/E Ratio	33.9-17.4	39.0-23.1	14.9-7.8	22.1-14.9	20.2-11.7	18.8-13.4	22.3-15.9
Average Yield %	1.4	1.5	1.3	1.0	1.0	0.7	0.4

Statistics are as originally reported. ☐ Incl. chrg. of 2002, $87.8 mill.; 2001, $97.8 mill. for pre-operating and start-up costs of new facilities.

OFFICERS:
P. C. Browning, Chmn.
D. R. DiMicco, Vice-Chmn., Pres., C.E.O.
T. S. Lisenby, Exec. V.P., C.F.O., Treas.

INVESTOR CONTACT: Terry S. Lisenby, V.P., (704) 366-7000

PRINCIPAL OFFICE: 2100 Rexford Road, Charlotte, NC 28211

TELEPHONE NUMBER: (704) 366-7000
FAX: (704) 362-4208
WEB: www.nucor.com

NO. OF EMPLOYEES: 9,800

SHAREHOLDERS: 64,000

ANNUAL MEETING: In May

INCORPORATED: MI, Jan., 1940; reincorp., DE, Mar., 1958

INSTITUTIONAL HOLDINGS:
No. of Institutions: 325
Shares Held: 56,797,747
% Held: 72.8

INDUSTRY: Blast furnaces and steel mills (SIC: 3312)

TRANSFER AGENT(S): American Stock Transfer & Trust Company, New York, NY

NUVEEN INVESTMENTS, INC.

YIELD 2.0%
P/E RATIO 19.7

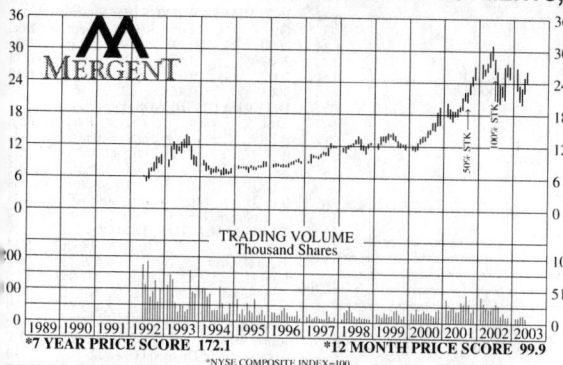

7 YEAR PRICE SCORE 172.1   **12 MONTH PRICE SCORE 99.9**

*NYSE COMPOSITE INDEX=100

INTERIM EARNINGS (Per Share):

Qtr.	Mar.	June	Sept.	Dec.
2000	0.26	0.26	0.26	0.27
2001	0.27	0.28	0.28	0.30
2002	0.30	0.31	0.33	0.35
2003	0.34	...	...	...

INTERIM DIVIDENDS (Per Share):

Amt.	Decl.	Ex.	Rec.	Pay.
100% STK	5/09/02	6/25/02	6/03/02	6/24/02
0.13Q	8/09/02	8/29/02	9/03/02	9/16/02
0.13Q	11/08/02	11/27/02	12/02/02	12/16/02
0.13Q	2/07/03	2/27/03	3/03/03	3/17/03
0.13Q	5/16/03	5/29/03	6/02/03	6/16/03

Indicated div.: $0.52

CAPITALIZATION (12/31/02):

	($000)	(%)
Common & Surplus	385,763	100.0
Total	385,763	100.0

DIVIDEND ACHIEVER STATUS:
Rank: 27   10-Year Growth Rate: 20.11%
Total Years of Dividend Growth: 10

RECENT DEVELOPMENTS: For the quarter ended 3/31/03, net income increased 8.8% to $32.6 million from $30.0 million in the previous year. Total operating revenues rose 9.7% to $101.5 million from $92.6 million a year earlier. Investment advisory fees from assets under management grew 11.8% to $95.2 million from $85.2 million the year before. Product distribution revenues fell 67.5% to $1.6 million from $4.9 million in 2001, while other revenue/performance fees jumped 74.9% to $4.7 million from $2.7 million the prior year.

PROSPECTS: Results are benefiting from positive net flows across all product lines, including managed accounts, closed-end exchange-traded funds and mutual funds. On 3/27/03, JNC raised approximately $1.30 billion in new assets through the initial public offering of common shares in the Nuveen Preferred and Convertible Income Fund. The expected issuance of FundPreferred™ shares, between six and eight weeks following the completion of the offering, could boost the total assets of the fund to more than $2.00 billion.

BUSINESS

NUVEEN INVESTMENTS, INC. (formerly The John Nuveen Company) is engaged in asset management and related research, as well as the development, marketing and distribution of investment products and services primarily targeted at affluent, high net-worth individuals and institutional markets. As of 3/31/03, total assets under management was approximately $81.36 billion. The Company distributes its investment products and services, including mutual funds, exchange-traded funds, defined portfolios and separately managed accounts through unaffiliated intermediary firms, including broker/dealers, commercial banks, affiliates of insurance providers, financial planners, accountants, consultants and investment advisors. The St. Paul Companies, Inc. owned approximately 79.0% of the Company's common stock as of 3/28/03.

ANNUAL FINANCIAL DATA

	12/31/02	12/31/01	12/31/00	12/31/99	12/31/98	12/31/97	12/31/96
Earnings Per Share	1.29	1.13	1.05	0.95	0.81	0.71	0.66
Cash Flow Per Share	1.40	1.27	1.16	1.07	0.93	0.79	0.72
Tang. Book Val. Per Share	...	0.01	2.40	1.58	1.07	0.67	2.74
Dividends Per Share	0.50	0.47	0.41	0.38	0.33	0.29	0.26
Dividend Payout %	38.8	41.3	38.8	39.6	40.3	41.3	39.4
INCOME STATEMENT (IN MILLIONS):							
Total Revenues	396.4	371.1	358.4	338.8	307.5	268.9	232.5
Costs & Expenses	173.5	167.6	178.2	176.7	155.1	134.0	105.9
Depreciation & Amort.	11.1	14.8	12.1	12.0	12.1	9.0	6.7
Operating Income	211.8	188.8	168.1	150.1	140.3	125.9	119.8
Net Interest Inc./(Exp.)	d4.9	d3.8	d3.0	d3.0	d2.6	d3.7	d2.3
Income Before Income Taxes	206.9	189.6	177.4	161.0	137.7	122.2	117.5
Income Taxes	80.7	74.9	70.7	63.7	54.1	48.0	45.0
Net Income	126.2	114.7	106.7	97.3	83.6	74.2	72.5
Cash Flow	137.3	129.5	118.7	109.3	95.8	83.2	79.2
Average Shs. Outstg. (000)	98,042	101,688	101,979	102,429	103,281	104,706	110,106
BALANCE SHEET (IN MILLIONS):							
Cash & Cash Equivalents	70.5	83.7	72.4	27.4	77.9	106.5	178.2
Total Current Assets	138.4	150.0	199.8	150.8	124.7	147.2	213.7
Net Property	31.3	28.4	25.5	14.5	12.8	14.8	14.1
Total Assets	841.0	696.6	607.0	541.0	468.0	492.2	355.3
Total Current Liabilities	373.7	228.7	52.8	52.7	63.8	126.6	47.8
Net Stockholders' Equity	385.8	406.3	402.9	346.1	304.1	273.1	271.9
Net Working Capital	d235.3	d78.7	147.0	98.1	60.9	20.6	166.0
Year-end Shs. Outstg. (000)	92,726	95,142	93,941	93,190	94,068	95,348	99,357
STATISTICAL RECORD:							
Operating Profit Margin %	53.4	50.9	46.9	44.3	45.6	46.8	51.5
Net Profit Margin %	31.8	30.9	29.8	28.7	27.2	27.6	31.2
Return on Equity %	32.7	28.2	24.6	28.1	27.5	27.2	26.7
Return on Assets %	15.0	16.5	17.6	18.0	17.9	15.1	20.4
Price Range	31.05-20.12	27.15-16.73	19.44-11.17	14.56-11.44	13.92-10.52	12.58-8.75	9.58-7.92
P/E Ratio	24.1-15.6	24.0-14.8	18.6-10.7	15.3-12.0	17.2-13.0	17.7-12.3	14.5-12.0
Average Yield %	2.0	2.1	2.7	2.9	2.7	2.7	3.0

Statistics are as originally reported. Adj. for 100% stk. div., 6/25/02; 50% stk. div., 9/28/01.

OFFICERS:
T. R. Schwertfeger, Chmn., C.E.O.
J. P. Amboian, Pres.
A. G. Berkshire, Sr. V.P., Gen. Couns.

INVESTOR CONTACT: Laurel O'Brien, (312) 917-8254

PRINCIPAL OFFICE: 333 West Wacker Drive, Chicago, IL 60606

TELEPHONE NUMBER: (312) 917-7700
FAX: (312) 917-8049
WEB: www.nuveen.com
NO. OF EMPLOYEES: 614
SHAREHOLDERS: 4,200 (approx., class A record)
ANNUAL MEETING: In May
INCORPORATED: DE, Mar., 1992

INSTITUTIONAL HOLDINGS:
No. of Institutions: 106
Shares Held: 11,911,473
% Held: 12.9
INDUSTRY: Security brokers and dealers (SIC: 6211)
TRANSFER AGENT(S): The Bank of New York, New York, NY

OLD NATIONAL BANCORP

YIELD 3.2%
P/E RATIO 13.4

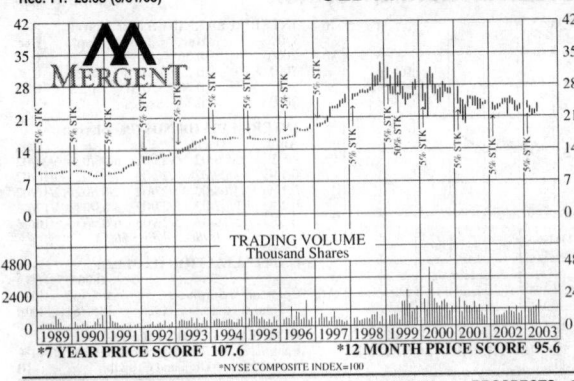

INTERIM EARNINGS (Per Share):

Qtr.	Mar.	June	Sept.	Dec.
2000	0.13	0.36	0.20	0.24
2001	0.33	0.30	0.41	0.38
2002	0.42	0.42	0.51	0.42
2003	0.41	...	...	...

INTERIM DIVIDENDS (Per Share):

Amt.	Decl.	Ex.	Rec.	Pay.
0.19Q	7/25/02	8/29/02	9/03/02	9/17/02
0.19Q	10/24/02	11/27/02	12/02/02	12/16/02
5% STK	12/06/02	1/02/03	1/06/03	1/27/03
0.19Q	1/23/03	2/27/03	3/03/03	3/17/03
0.19Q	4/24/03	5/29/03	6/02/03	6/16/03

Indicated div.: $0.76 (Div. Reinv. Plan)

CAPITALIZATION (12/31/02):

	($000)	(%)
Total Deposits	6,439,280	76.4
Long-Term Debt	1,247,857	14.8
Common & Surplus	740,710	8.8
Total	8,427,847	100.0

DIVIDEND ACHIEVER STATUS:
Rank: 190   10-Year Growth Rate: 7.67%
Total Years of Dividend Growth: 19

*7 YEAR PRICE SCORE 107.6   *12 MONTH PRICE SCORE 95.6

=NYSE COMPOSITE INDEX=100

RECENT DEVELOPMENTS: For the quarter ended 3/31/03, net income declined 5.7% to $26.3 million compared with $27.9 million in the corresponding period the prior year. Net interest income slipped 5.2% to $76.2 million from $80.3 million a year earlier. Provision for loan losses increased 20.0% to $9.0 million from $7.5 million the year before. Total non-interest income climbed 38.9% to $40.2 million, while other expense rose 14.5% to $70.2 million.

PROSPECTS: On 5/6/03, ONB acquired Evansville, Indiana-based James L. Will Insurance Agency, Inc., which focuses on commercial property and casualty as well as personal lines of insurance. The acquisition doubles the presence of ONB Insurance Group, a subsidiary of ONB, in the Evansville market. Separately, the Company continues to expand its presence in strong new markets such as Indianapolis and increase its marketing efforts.

BUSINESS

OLD NATIONAL BANCORP, with total assets of $9.73 billion as of 3/31/03, is a financial holding company headquartered in Evansville, Indiana with banking activity in Indiana, Illinois, Kentucky, Missouri, Tennessee, and Ohio. As of 12/31/02, the Company operated over 130 banking offices serving customers in both urban and rural markets. The Company's banking centers provide a wide range of financial services, such as commercial, real estate, and consumer loans; lease financing; checking, savings, time deposits and other depository accounts; letters of credit; cash management services; credit life, accident and health insurance; safe deposit facilities; investments and brokerage products; debit cards and other electronically accessed banking services; and Internet banking. The Company's non-bank affiliates provide additional financial or support services incidental to its operations, including issuance and reinsurance of credit life, accident, health, life, property, and casualty insurance; investment services; fiduciary and trust services; and property ownership.

ANNUAL FINANCIAL DATA

	12/31/02	12/31/01	12/31/00	12/31/99	12/31/98	12/31/97	12/31/96
Earnings Per Share	②1.84	①1.42	①0.93	1.44	1.32	1.11	1.10
Tang. Book Val. Per Share	9.12	9.95	9.42	9.00	9.46	9.53	8.52
Dividends Per Share	0.69	0.62	0.59	0.55	0.48	0.46	0.44
Dividend Payout %	37.3	43.5	62.9	37.8	36.3	41.3	39.8
INCOME STATEMENT (IN MILLIONS):							
Total Interest Income	547.4	629.7	638.3	488.9	437.9	429.4	394.4
Total Interest Expense	258.0	338.4	368.4	250.5	223.1	210.2	190.6
Net Interest Income	289.4	291.3	269.9	238.4	214.8	219.2	203.8
Provision for Loan Losses	33.5	28.7	29.8	11.5	11.4	27.0	11.0
Non-Interest Income	154.5	113.0	101.7	67.5	54.6	47.1	44.8
Non-Interest Expense	257.8	254.8	265.5	185.6	158.1	154.4	152.3
Income Before Taxes	152.6	120.8	76.2	108.8	99.9	85.0	85.3
Net Income	②117.9	①93.0	①61.7	82.7	71.7	60.7	60.2
Average Shs. Outstg. (000)	64,103	65,340	66,371	57,737	55,084	56,075	55,108
BALANCE SHEET (IN MILLIONS):							
Cash & Due from Banks	223.0	224.7	202.6	169.2	150.9	147.3	180.4
Securities Avail. for Sale	3,091.0	2,320.1	1,825.1	1,678.7	1,596.9	1,567.0	1,514.6
Total Loans & Leases	5,769.6	6,132.9	6,350.8	4,841.3	4,162.2	3,730.2	3,523.3
Allowance for Credit Losses	87.7	74.2	76.3	60.4	49.4	46.2	44.1
Net Loans & Leases	5,681.9	6,058.6	6,274.5	4,780.9	4,112.8	3,684.0	3,479.2
Total Assets	9,612.6	9,080.5	8,767.7	6,982.9	6,166.0	5,688.2	5,366.6
Total Deposits	6,439.3	6,616.4	6,583.9	5,071.3	4,443.5	4,298.7	4,268.0
Long-Term Obligations	1,247.9	1,000.0	863.2	663.0	629.9	388.8	74.6
Total Liabilities	8,871.8	8,441.2	8,141.4	6,490.2	5,671.4	5,211.0	4,908.1
Net Stockholders' Equity	740.7	639.2	626.3	492.7	494.6	477.2	458.5
Year-end Shs. Outstg. (000)	64,856	64,233	66,493	54,743	52,302	50,061	53,828
STATISTICAL RECORD:							
Return on Equity %	15.9	14.6	9.9	16.8	14.5	12.7	13.1
Return on Assets %	1.2	1.0	0.7	1.2	1.2	1.1	1.1
Equity/Assets %	7.7	7.0	7.1	7.1	8.0	8.4	8.5
Non-Int. Exp./Tot. Inc. %	58.1	63.0	71.5	60.7	58.7	58.0	61.3
Price Range	25.24-21.24	26.19-18.47	30.24-19.92	30.30-22.31	31.41-23.50	24.75-18.04	18.60-15.46
P/E Ratio	13.7-11.5	18.4-13.0	32.5-21.4	21.0-15.5	23.8-17.8	22.3-16.3	16.9-14.1
Average Yield %	3.0	2.8	2.4	2.1	1.7	2.2	2.6

Statistics are as originally reported. Adj. for 5% stk. div.: 1/03, 1/02, 1/01, 1/00, 1/98 & 1/97; 50% div., 5/24/99. ① Incl. after-tax merger and restruct. costs of $5.9 mill., 2001; $25.7 mill., 2000. ② Incl. after-tax gain of $8.3 mill. on branch sales.

OFFICERS:
J. A. Risinger, Chmn., Pres., C.E.O.
J. S. Poelker, Exec. V.P., C.F.O.

INVESTOR CONTACT: Lynell J. Walton, Asst. V.P., (812) 464-1366

PRINCIPAL OFFICE: 420 Main Street, Evansville, IN 47708

TELEPHONE NUMBER: (812) 464-1434
FAX: (812) 464-1567
WEB: www.oldnational.com

NO. OF EMPLOYEES: 2,741

SHAREHOLDERS: 25,718

ANNUAL MEETING: In April

INCORPORATED: IN, June, 1982

INSTITUTIONAL HOLDINGS:
No. of Institutions: 80
Shares Held: 6,522,274
% Held: 10.2

INDUSTRY: National commercial banks
(SIC: 6021)

TRANSFER AGENT(S): Old National Bancorp, Evansville, IN

NYSE SYMBOL ORI
Rec. Pr. 34.34 (5/31/03)

OLD REPUBLIC INTERNATIONAL CORPORATION

YIELD 2.0%
P/E RATIO 10.4

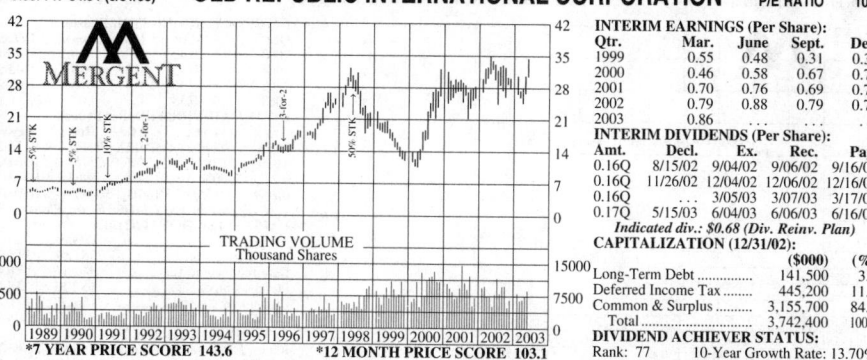

TRADING VOLUME
Thousand Shares

1989|1990|1991|1992|1993|1994|1995|1996|1997|1998|1999|2000|2001|2002|2003
*7 YEAR PRICE SCORE 143.6   *12 MONTH PRICE SCORE 103.1
*NYSE COMPOSITE INDEX=100

INTERIM EARNINGS (Per Share):

Qtr.	Mar.	June	Sept.	Dec.
1999	0.55	0.48	0.31	0.39
2000	0.46	0.58	0.67	0.77
2001	0.70	0.76	0.69	0.74
2002	0.79	0.88	0.79	0.77
2003	0.86	...	...	...

INTERIM DIVIDENDS (Per Share):

Amt.	Decl.	Ex.	Rec.	Pay.
0.16Q	8/15/02	9/04/02	9/06/02	9/16/02
0.16Q	11/26/02	12/04/02	12/06/02	12/16/02
0.16Q	...	3/05/03	3/07/03	3/17/03
0.17Q	5/15/03	6/04/03	6/06/03	6/16/03

Indicated div.: $0.68 (Div. Reinv. Plan)

CAPITALIZATION (12/31/02):

	($000)	(%)
Long-Term Debt	141,500	3.8
Deferred Income Tax	445,200	11.9
Common & Surplus	3,155,700	84.3
Total	3,742,400	100.0

DIVIDEND ACHIEVER STATUS:
Rank: 77   10-Year Growth Rate: 13.70%
Total Years of Dividend Growth: 21

RECENT DEVELOPMENTS: For the quarter ended 3/31/03, net income grew 9.2% to $104.3 million from $95.5 million in the comparable prior-year period. Results reflected pricing and risk selection improvements in ORI's three major business segments. Net revenues advanced 15.6% to $739.0 million. On a segment basis, operating income from the general insurance group climbed 48.1% to $59.4 million. Operating income in the mortgage guaranty group increased 8.0% to $75.9 million, while operating income from the title insurance group rose 27.9% to $25.7 million.

PROSPECTS: Going forward, operating results should remain favorable for ORI's General Insurance Group as ongoing price corrections and the application of more stringent underwriting standards in the last three years take hold. Meanwhile, ORI's mortgage guaranty and title insurance operations should continue to benefit from a continuation of positive market conditions in the housing sector, supported by the sale of new and used homes, and strong mortgage refinancing activity, which is being driven by the current low mortgage rate environment.

BUSINESS

OLD REPUBLIC INTERNATIONAL CORPORATION is a multiple line insurance holding company with assets of approximately $9.00 billion and total capitalization of $3.44 billion as of 3/31/03. The Company's subsidiaries market, underwrite, and manage a wide range of specialty and general insurance programs in the property & liability, title, mortgage guaranty insurance and life & health insurance businesses. The Company primarily serves the insurance and related needs of major financial services and industrial corporations, with an emphasis on energy services, construction and forest products, transportation and housing industries. In 2002, revenues were derived as follows: general insurance, 50.2%; title insurance, 30.5%; mortgage guaranty, 17.0%; life and health insurance, 2.1% and other, 0.2%.

ANNUAL FINANCIAL DATA

	12/31/02	12/31/01	12/31/00	12/31/99	12/31/98	12/31/97	12/31/96
Earnings Per Share	3.23	2.88	2.47	1.75	2.33	2.10	①1.64
Tang. Book Val. Per Share	25.49	22.78	20.08	14.03	17.27	15.59	14.57
Dividends Per Share	0.63	0.59	0.55	0.49	0.39	0.33	0.28
Dividend Payout %	19.5	20.5	22.3	28.0	16.6	15.9	16.9

INCOME STATEMENT (IN MILLIONS):

Total Premium Income	2,135.4	1,786.8	1,550.3	1,567.2	1,568.1	1,464.6	1,360.4
Net Investment Income	272.6	274.7	273.9	263.2	273.1	270.8	260.5
Other Income	348.2	311.7	246.1	271.5	330.3	227.2	182.7
Total Revenues	2,756.2	2,373.2	2,070.3	2,101.9	2,171.5	1,962.6	1,803.6
Policyholder Benefits	975.3	861.0	760.3	829.9	781.7	787.9	752.1
Income Before Income Taxes	560.8	503.8	426.2	317.0	466.8	426.1	342.2
Income Taxes	167.6	159.6	131.0	92.9	145.7	129.1	108.5
Equity Earnings/Minority Int.	d0.2	2.7	2.2	2.7	2.7	0.6	0.9
Net Income	393.0	346.9	297.5	226.8	323.8	297.6	①234.6
Average Shs. Outstg. (000)	121,549	120,328	120,197	129,787	139,150	141,768	140,438

BALANCE SHEET (IN MILLIONS):

Cash & Cash Equivalents	291.0	336.5	411.0	294.0	400.5	354.9	301.0
Premiums Due	2,004.8	1,835.3	1,660.4	1,626.3	1,572.2	1,634.3	1,677.9
Invst. Assets: Fixed-term	5,226.5	4,722.0	4,310.2	4,261.1	4,286.7	4,259.6	4,007.1
Invst. Assets: Equities	513.5	391.6	295.5	160.1	164.8	117.1	116.1
Invst. Assets: Total	6,051.2	5,472.9	5,038.9	4,739.4	4,854.2	4,720.1	4,414.0
Total Assets	8,714.7	7,919.8	7,280.9	6,938.4	7,019.7	6,922.8	6,656.2
Long-Term Obligations	141.5	159.0	238.0	208.3	145.1	142.9	154.0
Net Stockholders' Equity	3,155.7	2,783.9	2,439.3	2,199.1	2,305.4	2,153.0	1,901.1
Year-end Shs. Outstg. (000)	123,791	122,169	121,445	156,679	133,403	138,070	130,408

STATISTICAL RECORD:

Return on Revenues %	14.3	14.6	14.4	10.8	14.9	15.2	13.0
Return on Equity %	12.5	12.5	12.2	10.3	14.0	13.8	12.3
Return on Assets %	4.5	4.4	4.1	3.3	4.6	4.3	3.5
Price Range	35.00-24.40	31.56-21.20	32.06-10.63	22.75-12.06	32.25-17.94	26.79-16.42	18.50-13.50
P/E Ratio	10.8-7.6	11.0-7.4	13.0-4.3	13.0-6.9	13.8-7.7	12.8-7.8	11.3-8.2
Average Yield %	2.1	2.2	2.6	2.8	1.5	1.5	1.7

Statistics are as originally reported. Adj. for stk. splits: 50% div., 5/98. ① Bef. extraord. chrg. $4.4 mill.

OFFICERS:
A. C. Zucaro, Chmn., Pres., C.E.O.
J. S. Adams, Sr. V.P., C.F.O., Treas.
S. LeRoy III, Sr. V.P., Gen. Couns., Sec.
INVESTOR CONTACT: A. C. Zucaro, Chmn., Pres. & C.E.O., (312) 346-8100
PRINCIPAL OFFICE: 307 N. Michigan Ave., Chicago, IL 60601

TELEPHONE NUMBER: (312) 346-8100
FAX: (312) 726-0309
WEB: www.oldrepublic.com
NO. OF EMPLOYEES: 6,485 (approx.)
SHAREHOLDERS: 3,043
ANNUAL MEETING: In May
INCORPORATED: DE, 1969

INSTITUTIONAL HOLDINGS:
No. of Institutions: 273
Shares Held: 87,795,388
% Held: 72.6

INDUSTRY: Surety insurance (SIC: 6351)

TRANSFER AGENT(S): EquiServe, Jersey City, NJ

OTTER TAIL CORPORATION

YIELD 3.8%
P/E RATIO 15.9

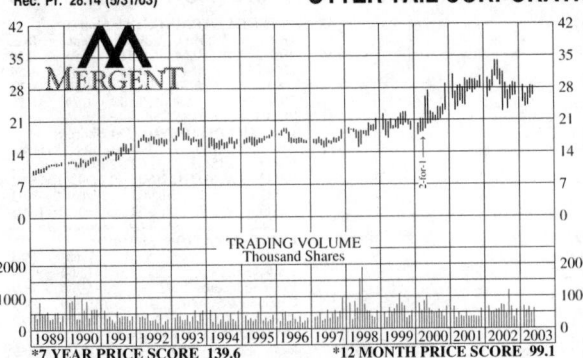

INTERIM EARNINGS (Per Share):

Qtr.	Mar.	June	Sept.	Dec.
2000	0.42	0.36	0.42	0.40
2001	0.45	0.34	0.43	0.43
2002	0.40	0.41	0.50	0.48
2003	0.38	...	...	...

INTERIM DIVIDENDS (Per Share):

Amt.	Decl.	Ex.	Rec.	Pay.
0.265Q	7/29/02	8/13/02	8/15/02	9/10/02
0.265Q	10/28/02	11/13/02	11/15/02	12/10/02
0.27Q	2/03/03	2/12/03	2/14/03	3/10/03
0.27Q	4/14/03	5/13/03	5/15/03	6/10/03

Indicated div.: $1.08 (Div. Reinv. Plan)

CAPITALIZATION (12/31/02):

	($000)	(%)
Long-Term Debt	258,229	37.9
Deferred Income Tax	94,147	13.8
Preferred Stock................	15,500	2.3
Common & Surplus	313,465	46.0
Total	681,341	100.0

DIVIDEND ACHIEVER STATUS:

Rank: 270   10-Year Growth Rate: 2.60%
Total Years of Dividend Growth: 27

TRADING VOLUME
Thousand Shares

*7 YEAR PRICE SCORE 139.6   *12 MONTH PRICE SCORE 99.1
*NYSE COMPOSITE INDEX=100

RECENT DEVELOPMENTS: For the three months ended 3/31/03, net income slipped 1.7% to $9.9 million compared with $10.0 million in the equivalent quarter of 2002. Results were hampered by difficult business conditions, particularly in the manufacturing and other businesses segments. Also, operating results were negatively affected by lower diagnostic imaging equipment sales volumes and higher operating expenses in the health services segment. Operating revenues rose 25.6% to $198.1 million from $157.7 million the year before, primarily due to increased contributions from each of OTTR's five business segments. Operating income decreased 3.3% to $18.3 million compared with $18.9 million a year earlier. Looking ahead, the Company is taking steps to bring operating expenses more in line with revenues within its health services segment, due to disappointing results. Also, the Company reaffirmed its earnings per share guidance for 2003 in the range of $1.80 to $1.85.

BUSINESS

OTTER TAIL CORPORATION (formerly Otter Tail Power Company) is an operating electric utility engaged in the production, transmission and distribution and sale of electric energy in 48 states and 6 Canadian provinces. OTTR's businesses are classified into five segments: electric (43.2% or revenues for 2002); manufacturing (20.0%); health services (13.2%); other businesses (11.9%); and plastics (11.7%). Electric includes the production, transmission, distribution and sale of electric energy in Minnesota, North Dakota and South Dakota. Manufacturing consists of the production of wind towers, frame-straightening equipment and accessories for the auto repair industry, custom plastic pallets, material and handling trays horticultural containers, fabrication of steel products, contract machining and metal parts stamping and fabrication. Health Services consists of businesses involved in the sale of diagnostic medical equipment, supplies and accessories. Other Business Operations consist of businesses in electrical and telephone construction contracting, transportation, telecommunications, entertainment and energy services and natural gas marketing. The Plastics segment consists of businesses producing polyvinyl chloride (PVC) pipe in the Upper Midwest and Southwest regions of the U.S.

ANNUAL FINANCIAL DATA

	12/31/02	12/31/01	12/31/00	12/31/99	12/31/98	12/31/97	12/31/96
Earnings Per Share	1.79	1.68	1.60	②1.79	①1.21	1.29	1.24
Cash Flow Per Share	3.47	3.37	3.20	3.25	2.68	2.98	2.79
Tang. Book Val. Per Share	9.51	9.31	9.06	9.32	8.58	8.07	7.64
Dividends Per Share	1.06	1.04	1.02	0.99	0.96	0.93	0.90
Dividend Payout %	59.2	61.9	63.7	55.3	79.7	72.1	72.9
INCOME STATEMENT (IN THOUSANDS):							
Total Revenues	710,116	654,132	559,445	464,577	431,078	394,279	361,739
Costs & Expenses	585,521	534,548	448,706	362,415	338,883	295,944	268,725
Depreciation & Amort.	42,613	42,100	38,249	34,796	34,965	39,302	34,788
Operating Income	81,982	77,484	72,490	67,366	57,230	59,033	58,226
Net Interest Inc./(Exp.)	d17,850	d15,991	d16,583	d14,771	d15,566	d18,519	d16,601
Income Taxes	20,061	20,083	17,515	23,915	15,140	14,308	14,040
Net Income	46,128	43,603	40,224	②44,977	①30,701	32,346	29,955
Cash Flow	88,005	83,710	76,595	77,545	63,308	69,290	62,385
Average Shs. Outstg.	25,397	24,832	23,928	23,831	23,596	23,278	22,364
BALANCE SHEET (IN THOUSANDS):							
Cash & Cash Equivalents	9,937	11,378	1,259	24,762	3,919	5,301	1,229
Gross Property	1,055,645	984,840	926,117	889,574	870,476	860,413	847,510
Accumulated Depreciation	467,759	441,863	410,188	386,618	370,290	350,647	327,672
Net Property	587,886	542,977	515,929	502,956	500,186	509,766	519,838
Total Assets	878,736	782,541	722,115	680,788	655,612	655,441	662,287
Long-Term Obligations	258,229	227,360	191,493	176,437	181,646	189,973	160,492
Net Stockholders' Equity	328,965	294,808	292,879	279,193	245,907	230,987	214,057
Year-end Shs. Outstg.	25,592	24,653	23,853	23,850	23,760	23,462	22,430
STATISTICAL RECORD:							
Operating Profit Margin %	11.5	11.8	13.0	14.5	13.3	15.0	16.1
Net Profit Margin %	6.5	6.7	7.2	9.7	7.1	8.2	8.3
Net Inc./Net Property %	7.8	8.0	7.8	8.9	6.1	6.3	5.8
Net Inc./Tot. Capital %	6.8	7.2	7.1	8.3	5.7	6.0	6.1
Return on Equity %	14.0	14.8	13.7	16.1	12.5	14.0	14.0
Accum. Depr./Gross Prop. %	44.3	44.9	44.3	43.5	42.5	40.8	38.7
Price Range	34.02-22.82	31.00-23.00	29.00-17.75	22.78-17.00	21.38-15.06	19.00-15.00	19.31-15.88
P/E Ratio	19.0-12.7	18.5-13.7	18.1-11.1	12.7-9.5	17.7-12.5	14.7-11.6	15.6-12.9
Average Yield %	3.7	3.9	4.4	5.0	5.3	5.5	5.1

Statistics are as originally reported. Adj. for stk. split: 2-for-1, 3/15/00. ① Incl. special chg. $9.5 mill. & bef. acctg. change credit $3.8 mill. ② Incl. net gain $8.1 mill.

OFFICERS:
J. C. MacFarlane, Chmn.
J. D. Erickson, Pres., C.E.O.
K. G. Moug, C.F.O., Treas.

INVESTOR CONTACT: Shareholder Services, (800) 664-1259

PRINCIPAL OFFICE: 215 South Cascade Street, P.O. Box 496, Fergus Falls, MN 56538-0496

TELEPHONE NUMBER: (866) 410-8780
FAX: (218) 998-3165
WEB: www.ottertail.com

NO. OF EMPLOYEES: 3,111

SHAREHOLDERS: 14,503

ANNUAL MEETING: In Apr.

INCORPORATED: MN, July, 1907

INSTITUTIONAL HOLDINGS:
No. of Institutions: 70
Shares Held: 5,639,183
% Held: 21.7

INDUSTRY: Electric services (SIC: 4911)

TRANSFER AGENT(S): Wells Fargo Bank, Minnesota, N.A., St. Paul, MN

PACIFIC CAPITAL BANCORP

YIELD 2.4%
P/E RATIO 14.1

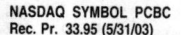
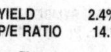
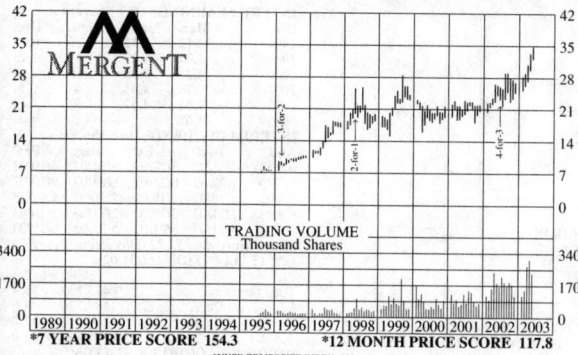

TRADING VOLUME
Thousand Shares

| | 1989 | 1990 | 1991 | 1992 | 1993 | 1994 | 1995 | 1996 | 1997 | 1998 | 1999 | 2000 | 2001 | 2002 | 2003 |

*7 YEAR PRICE SCORE 154.3   *12 MONTH PRICE SCORE 117.8
*NYSE COMPOSITE INDEX=100

INTERIM EARNINGS (Per Share):

Qtr.	Mar.	June	Sept.	Dec.
2000	0.58	0.34	0.19	0.35
2001	0.65	0.32	0.32	0.29
2002	0.79	0.43	0.50	0.42
2003	1.05	...	...	...

INTERIM DIVIDENDS (Per Share):

Amt.	Decl.	Ex.	Rec.	Pay.
4-for-3	4/23/02	6/12/02	5/21/02	6/11/02
0.18Q	7/01/02	7/19/02	7/23/02	8/13/02
0.18Q	10/01/02	10/18/02	10/22/02	11/12/02
0.18Q	1/01/03	1/16/03	1/21/03	2/11/03
0.20Q	4/02/03	4/17/03	4/22/03	5/15/03

Indicated div.: $0.80

CAPITALIZATION (12/31/02):

	($000)	(%)
Total Deposits	3,516,077	84.7
Long-Term Debt	264,969	6.4
Common & Surplus	371,075	8.9
Total	4,152,121	100.0

DIVIDEND ACHIEVER STATUS:

Rank: 41   10-Year Growth Rate: 17.94%
Total Years of Dividend Growth: 33

RECENT DEVELOPMENTS:

For the first quarter ended 3/31/03, net income advanced 32.3% to $36.4 million compared with $27.5 million in the corresponding prior-year quarter. Results for 2003 and 2002 included net gains on the sale of tax refund anticipation loans of $8.0 million and $10.2 million, respectively. Net interest income climbed 23.1% to $75.0 million from $61.0 million a year earlier. Total interest income increased 13.7% to $89.2 million, while total interest expense fell 18.9% to $14.2 million. Provision for credit losses declined 17.5% to $11.6 million from $14.1 million the year before. Total non-interest revenue rose 6.4% to $38.9 million, while total operating expense grew 13.6% to $44.4 million. Return on average equity increased to 39.25% from 33.96% in the year-earlier quarter. Looking ahead, the Company expects earnings for 2003 to range from $2.21 to $2.32 per share.

BUSINESS

PACIFIC CAPITAL BANCORP (formerly Santa Barbara Bancorp) is the parent of Pacific Capital Bank, N.A., a nationally chartered bank with four brands: Santa Barbara Bank and Trust, First National Bank of Central California, South Valley National Bank and San Benito Bank. As of 3/31/03, PCBC had assets of $4.42 billion and deposits of $3.64 billion. In 1998, Santa Barbara Bancorp merged with Pacific Capital Bancorp. Santa Barbara Bancorp was the surviving company, but took the name of Pacific Capital Bancorp. Pacific Capital Bank, N.A. is a 41-branch community bank network serving customers in six California central coast counties of Monterey, Santa Cruz, San Benito, Santa Barbara, Ventura and Santa Clara.

ANNUAL FINANCIAL DATA

	12/31/02	12/31/01	12/31/00	12/31/99	12/31/98	12/31/97	12/31/96
Earnings Per Share	☐ 2.14	1.58	1.45	1.34	0.91	0.97	0.77
Tang. Book Val. Per Share	9.75	9.33	8.39	7.17	6.63	5.81	5.32
Dividends Per Share	0.69	0.66	0.60	0.54	0.46	0.35	0.25
Dividend Payout %	32.2	41.7	41.4	40.2	50.4	35.6	32.0
INCOME STATEMENT (IN MILLIONS):							
Total Interest Income	266.7	291.1	290.9	211.6	193.5	114.9	89.6
Total Interest Expense	62.8	97.2	110.5	6.6	3.3	43.2	35.0
Net Interest Income	203.9	193.9	180.4	205.1	190.2	71.7	54.5
Provision for Loan Losses	19.7	26.7	14.4	6.4	9.1	7.0	4.3
Non-Interest Income	73.8	65.7	49.4	41.6	36.0	25.1	18.9
Non-Interest Expense	143.3	143.2	132.0	110.4	103.7	60.1	46.6
Income Before Taxes	114.7	89.8	83.4	129.9	113.3	29.8	22.6
Net Income	☐ 74.9	56.1	51.5	105.6	94.3	20.1	15.7
Average Shs. Outstg. (000)	34,990	35,519	35,479	33,053	32,596	20,779	20,360
BALANCE SHEET (IN MILLIONS):							
Cash & Due from Banks	151.5	136.5	176.3	121.5	114.2	67.8	51.2
Total Loans & Leases	3,019.8	2,799.1	2,517.1	1,981.9	1,582.8	881.5	684.2
Allowance for Credit Losses	53.8	48.9	35.1	28.7	29.3	21.1	16.6
Net Loans & Leases	2,966.0	2,750.2	2,482.0	1,953.2	1,553.5	860.4	667.6
Total Assets	4,219.2	3,960.9	3,677.6	2,879.3	2,649.4	1,592.4	1,301.3
Total Deposits	3,516.1	3,365.6	3,102.8	2,440.2	2,329.7	1,404.2	1,113.1
Long-Term Obligations	265.0	188.3	129.7	98.8	45.0	39.0	39.0
Total Liabilities	3,848.1	3,635.1	3,381.4	2,644.7	2,435.4	1,474.2	1,193.7
Net Stockholders' Equity	371.1	325.9	296.3	234.6	214.0	118.2	107.6
Year-end Shs. Outstg. (000)	34,550	34,943	35,308	32,739	32,279	20,323	20,235
STATISTICAL RECORD:							
Return on Equity %	20.2	17.2	17.4	45.0	44.1	17.0	14.6
Return on Assets %	1.8	1.4	1.4	3.7	3.6	1.3	1.2
Equity/Assets %	8.8	8.2	8.1	8.1	8.1	7.4	8.3
Non-Int. Exp./Tot. Inc. %	51.6	55.1	57.4	44.7	45.9	62.0	63.4
Price Range	29.10-20.43	22.97-18.07	23.06-16.03	28.50-15.09	25.78-16.50	18.38-10.31	10.78-7.41
P/E Ratio	13.6-9.5	14.5-11.4	15.9-11.1	21.2-11.2	28.4-18.2	19.0-10.7	14.0-9.6
Average Yield %	2.8	3.2	3.1	2.5	2.2	2.4	2.7

Statistics are as originally reported. Adj. for stk. split: 4-for-3, 6/02; 2-for-1, 4/98. ☐ Incl. net gain on the sale of tax refund anticipation loans of $10.2 mill.

OFFICERS:
D. W. Spainhour, Chmn.
D. V. Horton, Vice-Chmn.
C. C. Larson, Vice-Chmn.

INVESTOR CONTACT: Deborah Lewis Whiteley, Sr. V.P., Inv. Rel., (805) 884-6680

PRINCIPAL OFFICE: 1021 Anacapa Street, 3rd Floor, Santa Barbara, CA 93101

TELEPHONE NUMBER: (805) 564-6300
FAX: (805) 882-3856
WEB: www.pcbancorp.com

NO. OF EMPLOYEES: 1,225 (approx.)

SHAREHOLDERS: 9,000 (approx.)

ANNUAL MEETING: In April

INCORPORATED: CA, 1960

INSTITUTIONAL HOLDINGS:
No. of Institutions: 101
Shares Held: 8,630,535
% Held: 24.7

INDUSTRY: State commercial banks (SIC: 6022)

TRANSFER AGENT(S): Mellon Investor Services, South Hackensack, NJ

PARK NATIONAL CORPORATION

ASE SYMBOL PRK
Rec. Pr. 111.50 (5/31/03)

YIELD 3.0%
P/E RATIO 17.7

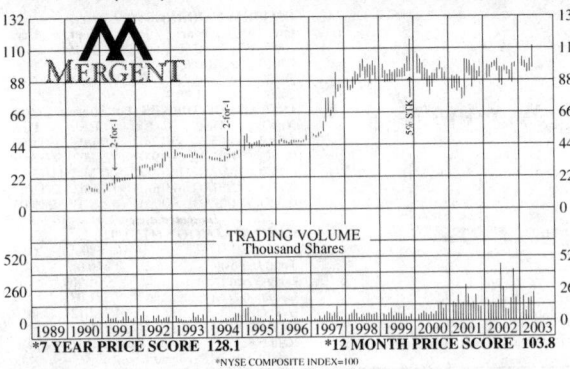

*7 YEAR PRICE SCORE 128.1   *12 MONTH PRICE SCORE 103.8

*NYSE COMPOSITE INDEX=100

INTERIM EARNINGS (Per Share):

Qtr.	Mar.	June	Sept.	Dec.
1998	1.12	1.17	1.15	0.99
1999	1.24	1.29	1.27	1.06
2000	1.27	1.33	1.30	1.20
2001	1.34	1.45	1.45	1.34
2002	1.53	1.57	1.59	1.45
2003	1.68	…	…	…

INTERIM DIVIDENDS (Per Share):

Amt.	Decl.	Ex.	Rec.	Pay.
0.76Q	4/15/02	5/22/02	5/24/02	6/10/02
0.76Q	7/22/02	8/21/02	8/23/02	9/10/02
0.83Q	11/18/02	12/18/02	12/20/02	1/02/03
0.83Q	1/21/03	2/19/03	2/21/03	3/10/03
0.83Q	4/21/03	5/21/03	5/23/03	6/10/03

Indicated div.: $3.32 (Div. Reinv. Plan)

CAPITALIZATION (12/31/02):

	($000)	(%)
Total Deposits	3,495,135	83.4
Long-Term Debt	187,226	4.5
Common & Surplus	509,292	12.2
Total	4,191,653	100.0

DIVIDEND ACHIEVER STATUS:
Rank: 52   10-Year Growth Rate: 16.55%
Total Years of Dividend Growth: 15

RECENT DEVELOPMENTS: For the three months ended 3/31/03, net income increased 8.0% to $23.2 million compared with $21.4 million in the corresponding year-earlier period. Net interest income of $52.2 million was essentially unchanged from the prior-year period. Provision for loan losses was $3.4 million versus $4.5 million the year before. Total non-interest income climbed 31.0% to $15.5 million compared with $11.8 million in 2002, primarily due to the increase in fee income earned from the origination and sale of fixed-rate mortgage loans and higher other income due to increased check and ATM transactions. PRK noted that this elevated level of mortgage loan production continued into the second quarter of 2003. Total other expense rose 2.9% to $30.1 million from $29.2 million a year earlier.

BUSINESS

PARK NATIONAL CORPORATION is a bank holding company with $5.11 billion in total assets at 3/31/03. Through its subsidiaries, the Company is engaged in the commercial banking and trust business, generally in small to medium population Ohio communities. The Company's subsidiaries provide the following services: the acceptance and servicing of demand, savings and time deposit accounts; commercial, industrial, consumer and real estate lending, including installment loans and automobile leasing, credit cards, home equity lines of credit and commercial and auto leasing; trust services; cash management; safe deposit operations; electronic funds transfers; online Internet banking with bill pay service; and a variety of additional banking-related services. On 3/23/01, the Company acquired Security Banc Corporation.

ANNUAL FINANCIAL DATA

	12/31/02	12/31/01	12/31/00	12/31/99	12/31/98	12/31/97	12/31/96
Earnings Per Share	6.15	5.58	5.10	4.67	4.22	3.81	3.43
Tang. Book Val. Per Share	36.93	33.60	29.66	24.60	23.50	22.52	19.89
Dividends Per Share	3.04	2.84	2.60	2.29	1.83	1.52	1.33
Dividend Payout %	49.4	50.9	51.0	48.9	43.3	40.0	38.9
INCOME STATEMENT (IN MILLIONS):							
Total Interest Income	287.9	320.3	249.3	191.9	185.9	180.5	122.3
Total Interest Expense	82.6	127.4	110.4	76.1	78.3	77.0	49.3
Net Interest Income	205.3	192.9	138.9	115.9	107.7	103.5	73.0
Provision for Loan Losses	15.0	13.1	8.7	7.0	6.8	7.0	4.5
Non-Interest Income	50.9	45.2	29.7	23.1	24.0	20.5	13.1
Non-Interest Expense	120.0	114.2	82.9	67.5	64.3	62.4	43.2
Income Before Taxes	121.2	110.9	76.9	64.4	60.5	54.6	38.3
Net Income	85.6	78.4	55.4	45.7	41.6	37.7	25.7
Average Shs. Outstg. (000)	13,910	14,051	10,877	9,811	9,856	9,908	7,494
BALANCE SHEET (IN MILLIONS):							
Cash & Due from Banks	157.1	169.1	109.9	104.2	100.3	93.6	61.5
Total Loans & Leases	2,701.2	2,806.3	2,293.0	1,850.7	1,654.0	1,603.6	1,123.6
Allowance for Credit Losses	71.0	70.5	63.7	58.0	50.5	47.3	38.8
Net Loans & Leases	2,630.2	2,735.8	2,229.3	1,792.7	1,603.5	1,556.3	1,084.8
Total Assets	4,446.6	4,569.5	3,211.1	2,634.3	2,460.8	2,288.4	1,614.8
Total Deposits	3,495.1	3,314.2	2,415.6	2,015.1	1,939.8	1,855.0	1,336.6
Long-Term Obligations	187.2	392.5	181.6	0.1	8.4	30.9	…
Total Liabilities	3,937.3	4,101.2	2,891.3	2,394.8	2,225.1	2,066.3	1,465.8
Net Stockholders' Equity	509.3	468.3	319.8	239.6	235.7	222.1	149.0
Year-end Shs. Outstg. (000)	13,792	13,941	10,779	9,740	10,031	9,862	7,490
STATISTICAL RECORD:							
Return on Equity %	16.8	16.7	17.3	19.1	17.6	17.0	17.2
Return on Assets %	1.9	1.7	1.7	1.7	1.7	1.6	1.6
Equity/Assets %	11.5	10.2	10.0	9.1	9.6	9.7	9.2
Non-Int. Exp./Tot. Inc. %	46.8	47.9	49.2	48.6	48.9	50.3	50.2
Price Range	102.45-84.01	102.50-74.50	106.00-77.50	116.00-86.67	102.62-80.95	93.87-48.69	50.60-44.17
P/E Ratio	16.7-13.7	18.4-13.4	20.8-15.2	24.8-18.6	24.3-19.2	24.6-12.8	14.8-12.9
Average Yield %	3.3	3.2	2.8	2.3	2.0	2.1	2.8

Statistics are as originally reported. Adj. for 5% stk. div. 12/99.

OFFICERS:
W. T. McConnell, Chmn.
H. O. Egger, Vice Chmn.
C. D. DeLawder, Pres., C.E.O.
J. W. Kozak, Sr. V.P., C.F.O.

INVESTOR CONTACT: David L. Trautman, Investor Relations, (740) 349-3927

PRINCIPAL OFFICE: 50 North Third Street, Newark, OH 43055

TELEPHONE NUMBER: (740) 349-8451
FAX: (740) 349-3765
WEB: www.parknationalcorp.com

NO. OF EMPLOYEES: 1,600

SHAREHOLDERS: 5,006

ANNUAL MEETING: In Apr.

INCORPORATED: DE, July, 1986; reincorp., OH, 1992

INSTITUTIONAL HOLDINGS:
No. of Institutions: 63
Shares Held: 3,976,274
% Held: 28.4

INDUSTRY: National commercial banks (SIC: 6021)

TRANSFER AGENT(S): First-Knox National Bank, Mount Vernon, OH

PAYCHEX, INC.

YIELD 1.4%
P/E RATIO 39.6

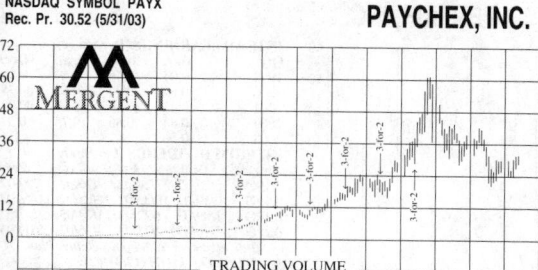

INTERIM EARNINGS (Per Share):

Qtr.	Aug.	Nov.	Feb.	May
1999-00	0.11	0.12	0.13	0.14
2000-01	0.16	0.16	0.18	0.18
2001-02	0.19	0.18	0.18	0.18
2002-03	0.20	0.20	0.19	...

INTERIM DIVIDENDS (Per Share):

Amt.	Decl.	Ex.	Rec.	Pay.
0.11Q	7/11/02	7/30/02	8/01/02	8/15/02
0.11Q	10/17/02	10/30/02	11/01/02	11/15/02
0.11Q	1/10/03	1/30/03	2/03/03	2/17/03
0.11Q	4/10/03	4/29/03	5/01/03	5/15/03

Indicated div.: $0.44 (Div. Reinv. Plan)

CAPITALIZATION (5/31/02):

	($000)	(%)
Common & Surplus	923,981	100.0
Total	923,981	100.0

DIVIDEND ACHIEVER STATUS:
Rank: 1   10-Year Growth Rate: 45.25%
Total Years of Dividend Growth: 14

TRADING VOLUME
Thousand Shares

*7 YEAR PRICE SCORE 121.5   *12 MONTH PRICE SCORE 108.0
*NYSE COMPOSITE INDEX=100

RECENT DEVELOPMENTS:

For the quarter ended 2/28/03, net income increased 6.8% to $71.5 million compared with $67.0 million in the corresponding period of the previous year. Revenues improved 18.5% to $287.8 million from $242.8 million in the year-earlier quarter. Payroll service revenues advanced approximately 20.0% to $235.8 million, supported by contributions from the acquisition Advantage Payroll Services, Inc. on 9/20/02. Revenues from human resources and benefits services climbed 21.0% to $39.0 million. Interest on funds held for clients decreased 9.1% to $13.5 million due to lower average interest rates earned in fiscal 2003 and a decrease in net realized gains on the sale of available-for-sale securities. Operating income rose 16.3% to $101.4 million from $87.2 million the year before. Separately, on 4/1/03, PAYX announced that it has completed the acquisition of InterPay, Inc., a wholly-owned subsidiary of FleetBoston Financial Corporation, for approximately $182.0 million.

BUSINESS

PAYCHEX, INC. is a national provider of payroll, human resource and benefits services for small-to-medium-sized businesses. The Company is based in Rochester, New York and has more than 100 locations around the country, serving over 440,000 clients nationwide. In 2002, the Company generated more than $890.0 million in service revenues. The company offers comprehensive payroll services, including payroll processing, payroll tax administration, and employee pay services, including direct deposit, check signing, and Readychex. Human resource and benefits outsourcing services include 401(k) plan recordkeeping, workers' compensation administration, section 125 plans, a professional employer organization, and other administrative services for business. On 9/20/02, PAYX acquired Advantage Payroll Services, Inc. for $240.0 million. On 4/1/03, PAYX acquired InterPay, Inc. for approximately $182.0 million.

ANNUAL FINANCIAL DATA

	5/31/02	5/31/01	5/31/00	5/31/99	5/31/98	5/31/97	5/31/96
Earnings Per Share	0.73	0.68	0.51	0.37	0.28	0.21	0.15
Cash Flow Per Share	0.85	0.78	0.60	0.46	0.35	0.27	0.19
Tang. Book Val. Per Share	2.43	2.00	1.50	1.17	0.90	0.69	0.55
Dividends Per Share	0.38	0.27	0.18	0.12	0.08	0.05	0.04
Dividend Payout %	52.0	39.7	35.3	32.2	29.0	25.8	23.4

INCOME STATEMENT (IN MILLIONS):

Total Revenues	954.9	869.9	728.1	597.3	493.7	734.7	325.3
Costs & Expenses	543.8	494.0	432.7	376.8	331.7	616.6	243.8
Depreciation & Amort.	47.4	39.1	36.5	32.9	27.3	21.4	13.9
Operating Income	363.7	336.7	258.9	187.6	134.7	96.6	67.5
Net Interest Inc./(Exp.)	31.3	27.3	16.5	12.6	9.5	7.0	...
Income Before Income Taxes	395.0	364.0	275.4	200.1	144.2	103.7	72.7
Income Taxes	120.5	109.1	85.4	61.0	42.0	28.5	20.4
Net Income	274.5	254.9	190.0	139.1	102.2	75.2	52.3
Cash Flow	321.9	294.0	226.5	172.0	129.5	96.6	66.3
Average Shs. Outstg. (000)	378,002	377,510	375,081	373,182	370,829	364,503	346,032

BALANCE SHEET (IN MILLIONS):

Cash & Cash Equivalents	2,669.3	2,655.0	2,236.5	1,704.8	1,405.0	1,079.6	117.2
Total Current Assets	2,814.6	2,791.3	2,362.6	1,793.1	1,478.8	1,140.7	165.3
Net Property	121.6	96.1	75.4	65.9	64.7	54.2	50.0
Total Assets	2,953.1	2,907.2	2,455.6	1,873.1	1,549.8	1,201.3	220.2
Total Current Liabilities	2,023.4	2,143.8	1,886.9	1,432.3	1,215.7	946.0	28.1
Net Stockholders' Equity	924.0	757.8	563.4	435.8	329.6	251.5	190.8
Net Working Capital	791.2	647.4	475.6	360.8	263.1	194.6	137.2
Year-end Shs. Outstg. (000)	375,859	373,647	371,769	369,489	367,173	366,252	347,784

STATISTICAL RECORD:

Operating Profit Margin %	38.1	38.7	35.6	31.4	27.3	13.2	20.8
Net Profit Margin %	28.7	29.3	26.1	23.3	20.7	10.2	16.1
Return on Equity %	29.7	33.6	33.7	31.9	31.0	29.9	27.4
Return on Assets %	9.3	8.8	7.7	7.4	6.6	6.3	23.8
Price Range	51.00-28.27	61.25-24.17	29.92-15.71	24.47-13.37	15.33-7.56	12.57-6.03	6.57-3.39
P/E Ratio	69.9-38.7	90.1-35.5	58.7-30.8	65.6-35.8	55.5-27.4	60.7-29.1	43.2-22.3
Average Yield %	1.0	0.6	0.8	0.6	0.7	0.6	0.7

Statistics are as originally reported. Adj. for stk. splits: 3-for-2, 5/15/00; 5/21/99; 5/22/98; 5/29/97; 5/23/96.

OFFICERS:
B. T. Golisano, Chmn., Pres., C.E.O.
J. M. Morphy, V.P., C.F.O., Sec.

INVESTOR CONTACT: John Morphy, V.P., C.F.O. & Sec., (585) 383-3406

PRINCIPAL OFFICE: 911 Panorama Trail South, Rochester, NY 14625-0397

TELEPHONE NUMBER: (585) 385-6666
FAX: (585) 383-3428
WEB: www.paychex.com

NO. OF EMPLOYEES: 7,100 full-time (approx.); 300 part-time (approx.)

SHAREHOLDERS: 16,842 (record)

ANNUAL MEETING: In Oct.

INCORPORATED: DE, June, 1979

INSTITUTIONAL HOLDINGS:
No. of Institutions: 407
Shares Held: 217,269,472
% Held: 57.8

INDUSTRY: Accounting, auditing, & bookkeeping (SIC: 8721)

TRANSFER AGENT(S): American Stock Transfer & Trust Co., New York, NY

PENTAIR, INC.

YIELD 2.2%
P/E RATIO 14.2

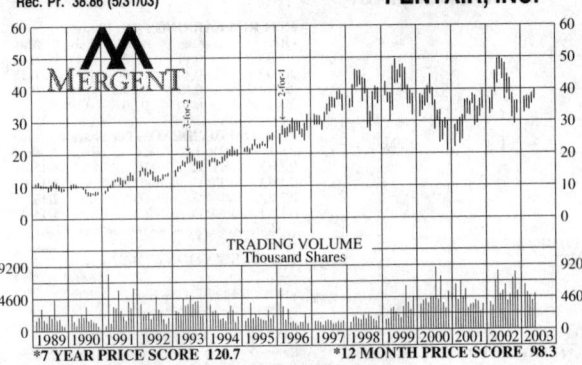

INTERIM EARNINGS (Per Share):

Qtr.	Mar.	June	Sept.	Dec.
1999	0.05	0.66	0.69	0.90
2000	0.69	0.79	0.58	d0.38
2001	0.42	0.58	0.50	d0.33
2002	0.43	0.86	0.75	0.57
2003	0.56	...	...	...

INTERIM DIVIDENDS (Per Share):

Amt.	Decl.	Ex.	Rec.	Pay.
0.19Q	6/25/02	7/24/02	7/26/02	8/09/02
0.19Q	10/10/02	10/23/02	10/25/02	11/08/02
0.19Q	1/09/03	1/22/03	1/24/03	2/07/03
0.21Q	2/26/03	4/23/03	4/25/03	5/09/03

Indicated div.: $0.84 (Div. Reinv. Plan)

CAPITALIZATION (12/31/02):

	($000)	(%)
Long-Term Debt	673,911	37.2
Deferred Income Tax	31,728	1.8
Common & Surplus	1,105,724	61.0
Total	1,811,363	100.0

DIVIDEND ACHIEVER STATUS:

Rank: 172   10-Year Growth Rate: 8.52%
Total Years of Dividend Growth: 26

| 1989 | 1990 | 1991 | 1992 | 1993 | 1994 | 1995 | 1996 | 1997 | 1998 | 1999 | 2000 | 2001 | 2002 | 2003 |

*7 YEAR PRICE SCORE 120.7   *12 MONTH PRICE SCORE 98.3

*NYSE COMPOSITE INDEX=100

RECENT DEVELOPMENTS: For the three months ended 3/31/03, net income increased 29.9% to $27.8 million compared with $21.4 million in the corresponding year-earlier period. Net sales advanced 5.7% to $637.5 million from $603.1 million the previous year. Excluding recent acquisitions, sales were flat compared with the first quarter of 2002. Operating income improved 14.1% to $52.2 million versus $45.7 million the year before.

PROSPECTS: PNR's near-term outlook is moderately positive. Going forward, the Company's Water segment should benefit from productivity improvements in the pump business, headcount reductions, and product line rationalization. Meanwhile, the Tools segment has announced plans to close its Tupelo, Mississippi operation and consolidate the manufacture of DELTA woodworking products into its Jackson, Tennessee, and Asian joint venture facilities. Accordingly, PNR has reaffirmed its earnings guidance for full-year 2003 of between $2.90 and $3.05 per share.

BUSINESS

PENTAIR, INC. is a diversified manufacturer operating in three segments on a global basis. The Tools segment (42.3% of 2002 sales), manufactures and markets tool products, woodworking machinery, portable power tools, power tool accessories, metal and stoneworking tools, pneumatic tools, compressors, generators, and pressure washers. The Water segment (36.1%), manufactures and markets water and wastewater pumps, control valves, pumps and pumping stations, storage tanks, filtration cartridges and systems, and pool and spa equipment and accessories. The Enclosures segment (21.6%), designs, manufactures, and markets standard, modified and custom enclosures that protect sensitive controls and components. Products include metallic and composite enclosures, cabinets, cases, subracks, backplanes, and associated thermal management systems.

ANNUAL FINANCIAL DATA

	12/31/02	12/31/01	12/31/00	12/31/99	12/31/98	12/31/97	12/31/96
Earnings Per Share	2.61	③ 1.17	② 1.68	2.33	2.46	① 2.11	① 1.83
Cash Flow Per Share	3.91	3.28	3.72	4.33	3.96	3.59	3.40
Tang. Book Val. Per Share	...	...	...	...	4.71	3.71	5.39
Dividends Per Share	0.74	0.70	0.66	0.64	0.60	0.54	0.50
Dividend Payout %	28.4	59.8	39.3	27.5	24.4	25.6	27.3
INCOME STATEMENT (IN MILLIONS):							
Total Revenues	2,580.8	2,615.9	2,748.0	2,367.8	1,937.6	1,839.1	1,567.1
Costs & Expenses	2,280.1	2,353.8	2,447.0	2,064.8	1,676.0	1,601.4	1,364.6
Depreciation & Amort.	64.7	104.3	99.0	88.6	68.4	67.8	59.5
Operating Income	236.0	157.8	202.0	214.3	193.2	169.8	142.9
Net Interest Inc./(Exp.)	d43.5	d61.5	d74.9	d47.8	d22.2	d21.7	d18.3
Income Before Income Taxes	192.4	93.3	127.1	166.5	170.9	158.4	124.6
Income Taxes	62.5	35.8	45.3	63.2	64.1	66.8	50.1
Net Income	129.9	③ 57.5	② 81.9	103.3	106.8	① 91.6	① 74.5
Cash Flow	194.6	161.9	180.9	192.0	171.0	154.6	129.1
Average Shs. Outstg. (000)	49,744	49,297	48,645	44,287	43,149	43,067	37,949
BALANCE SHEET (IN MILLIONS):							
Cash & Cash Equivalents	39.6	39.8	34.9	66.2	32.0	34.3	23.0
Total Current Assets	810.8	835.6	1,091.8	1,150.5	748.6	705.4	614.3
Net Property	351.3	329.5	353.0	403.8	308.3	293.6	298.8
Total Assets	2,514.5	2,372.2	2,612.4	2,803.0	1,554.7	1,472.9	1,289.0
Total Current Liabilities	476.2	428.4	648.8	760.9	394.8	392.2	301.6
Long-Term Obligations	673.9	715.0	781.8	857.3	288.0	294.5	279.9
Net Stockholders' Equity	1,105.7	1,015.0	1,010.6	993.2	709.4	630.6	563.9
Net Working Capital	334.6	407.2	443.0	389.5	353.8	313.2	312.6
Year-end Shs. Outstg. (000)	49,222	49,111	48,712	48,317	38,504	38,185	37,717
STATISTICAL RECORD:							
Operating Profit Margin %	9.1	6.0	7.4	9.1	10.0	9.2	9.1
Net Profit Margin %	5.0	2.2	3.0	4.4	5.5	5.0	4.8
Return on Equity %	11.7	5.7	8.1	10.4	15.1	14.5	13.2
Return on Assets %	5.2	2.4	3.1	3.7	6.9	6.2	5.8
Debt/Total Assets %	26.8	30.1	29.9	30.6	18.5	20.0	21.7
Price Range	49.84-29.02	39.60-21.88	44.63-20.63	49.44-29.88	46.25-26.75	39.88-27.25	32.25-22.89
P/E Ratio	19.1-11.1	33.8-18.7	26.6-12.3	21.2-12.8	18.8-10.9	18.9-12.9	17.6-12.5
Average Yield %	1.9	2.3	2.0	1.6	1.6	1.6	1.8

Statistics are as originally reported. ① Incl. non-recurr. credit 12/31/97: $10.3 mill.; credit 12/31/96: $12.1 mill. ② Incl. restruct. chrg. of $24.8 mill.; bef. loss fr. disc. ops. of $24.8 mill. ($0.51/sh.) & acctg. change chrg. of $1.2 mill. ($0.02/sh.) ③ Incl. restruct. chrg. of $40.1 mill.; bef. loss on sale of disc. ops. of $24.6 mill. ($0.50/sh.)

OFFICERS:
R. J. Hogan, Chmn., Pres., C.E.O.
D. D. Harrison, Exec. V.P., C.F.O.
L. L. Ainsworth, Sr. V.P., Gen. Couns., Sec.

INVESTOR CONTACT: Mark Cain, Investor Relations, (651) 639-5278

PRINCIPAL OFFICE: 1500 Country Road B2 West, Suite 400, St. Paul, MN 55113

TELEPHONE NUMBER: (651) 636-7920
FAX: (651) 639-5203
WEB: www.pentair.com
NO. OF EMPLOYEES: 11,900 (approx.)
SHAREHOLDERS: 4,092
ANNUAL MEETING: In May
INCORPORATED: MN, Aug., 1966

INSTITUTIONAL HOLDINGS:
No. of Institutions: 207
Shares Held: 34,456,261
% Held: 70.3

INDUSTRY: Woodworking machinery (SIC: 3553)

TRANSFER AGENT(S): Wells Fargo Shareowner Services, South St. Paul, MN

PEOPLES ENERGY CORPORATION

YIELD 5.0%
P/E RATIO 15.6

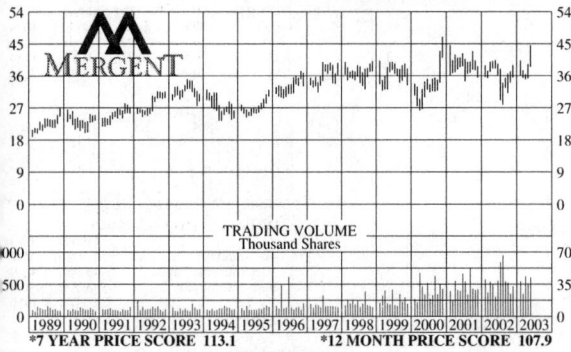

INTERIM EARNINGS (Per Share):

Qtr.	Dec.	Mar.	June	Sept.
1999-00	0.83	1.62	0.31	d0.32
2000-01	1.03	1.77	0.33	d0.38
2001-02	0.87	1.55	0.04	0.05
2002-03	0.87	1.77	...	...

INTERIM DIVIDENDS (Per Share):

Amt.	Decl.	Ex.	Rec.	Pay.
0.52Q	5/22/02	6/19/02	6/21/02	7/15/02
0.52Q	8/07/02	9/18/02	9/20/02	10/15/02
0.52Q	12/04/02	12/18/02	12/20/02	1/15/03
0.53Q	2/05/03	3/19/03	3/21/03	4/15/03
0.53Q	6/04/03	6/18/03	6/20/03	7/15/03

Indicated div.: $2.12 (Div. Reinv. Plan)

CAPITALIZATION (9/30/02):

	($000)	(%)
Long-Term Debt	554,014	31.9
Deferred Income Tax	378,225	21.8
Common & Surplus	806,324	46.4
Total	1,738,563	100.0

DIVIDEND ACHIEVER STATUS:
Rank: 277   10-Year Growth Rate: 1.69%
Total Years of Dividend Growth: 19

TRADING VOLUME
Thousand Shares

*7 YEAR PRICE SCORE 113.1   ***12 MONTH PRICE SCORE 107.9**
*NYSE COMPOSITE INDEX=100

RECENT DEVELOPMENTS: For the quarter ended 3/31/03, net income increased 15.4% to $63.5 million compared with $55.0 million in the equivalent period of the previous year. Total revenues advanced 72.9% to $903.8 million from $522.8 million in the year-earlier quarter. Operating income improved 15.7% to $114.5 million. Results benefited from significantly higher operating results from PGL's diversified energy businesses.

PROSPECTS: Going forward, the Company expects fiscal 2003 earnings in the range of $2.85 to $2.95 per diluted share, assuming normal weather conditions and average natural gas prices of $4.65 per million British thermal units for the remainder of the year. This represents an increase from the Company's previous guidance of between $2.70 and $2.80 per diluted share.

BUSINESS

PEOPLES ENERGY CORPORA-TION is a diversified energy company comprised of five primary business segments: gas distribution, power generation, midstream services, oil and gas production, and retail energy services. As of 4/25/03, these utilities distributed natural and synthetic gas to approximately 1.0 million customers in Chicago and northeastern Illinois. Other operations are conducted through PGL's subsidiaries engaged in non-regulated diversified energy operations. These subsidiaries consists of: Peoples District Energy Corp., a provider of district energy services; Peoples Energy Services, a provider of nonregulated retail energy sales; Peoples Energy Resources, a provider of gas-fired electric generation; Peoples NGV, a fueling station for natural gas-fueled vehicles; and Peoples Energy Production Company, which acquires investments in oil and gas production properties.

ANNUAL FINANCIAL DATA

	9/30/02	9/30/01	9/30/00	9/30/99	9/30/98	9/30/97	9/30/96
Earnings Per Share	[1] 2.51	[1] 2.74	2.44	2.61	2.25	2.81	2.96
Cash Flow Per Share	5.29	5.42	5.29	4.96	4.44	4.93	4.98
Tang. Book Val. Per Share	22.74	22.66	21.86	21.66	20.94	20.43	19.48
Dividends Per Share	2.07	2.03	1.99	1.95	1.91	1.87	1.83
Dividend Payout %	82.5	74.1	81.6	74.7	84.9	66.5	61.8
INCOME STATEMENT (IN MILLIONS):							
Total Revenues	1,482.5	2,270.2	1,417.5	1,194.4	1,138.1	1,274.4	1,198.7
Costs & Expenses	1,212.3	2,013.2	1,157.4	954.8	903.0	1,019.1	950.0
Depreciation & Amort.	98.9	95.0	100.9	83.5	77.2	74.1	70.6
Maintenance Exp.	...	...	...	...	44.0	47.6	45.6
Operating Income	171.3	162.0	159.2	156.0	113.8	133.5	132.4
Net Interest Inc./(Exp.)	d60.9	d72.1	d52.9	d39.5	d35.5	d33.1	d37.5
Income Taxes	46.3	51.4	43.3	52.6	0.5	1.8	5.8
Net Income	[1] 89.1	[1] 97.1	86.4	92.6	79.4	98.4	103.4
Cash Flow	187.9	192.1	187.4	176.2	156.6	172.5	174.1
Average Shs. Outstg. (000)	35,492	35,439	35,413	35,490	35,276	35,000	34,942
BALANCE SHEET (IN MILLIONS):							
Gross Property	2,794.6	2,703.6	2,517.1	2,330.9	2,210.0	2,117.5	2,046.2
Accumulated Depreciation	1,020.7	949.7	871.8	811.1	763.3	715.3	665.1
Net Property	1,773.9	1,753.9	1,645.3	1,519.8	1,446.7	1,402.2	1,381.1
Total Assets	2,723.6	2,994.1	2,501.9	2,100.2	1,904.5	1,820.8	1,783.8
Long-Term Obligations	554.0	643.3	419.7	521.7	516.6	527.0	527.1
Net Stockholders' Equity	806.3	805.5	777.1	768.7	741.4	716.5	681.2
Year-end Shs. Outstg. (000)	35,459	35,544	35,544	35,489	35,402	35,070	34,960
STATISTICAL RECORD:							
Operating Profit Margin %	11.6	7.1	11.2	13.1	10.0	10.5	11.0
Net Profit Margin %	6.0	4.3	6.1	7.8	7.0	7.7	8.6
Net Inc./Net Property %	5.0	5.5	5.3	6.1	5.5	7.0	7.5
Net Inc./Tot. Capital %	5.1	5.4	5.6	5.8	5.2	6.6	7.2
Return on Equity %	11.0	12.0	11.1	12.1	10.7	13.7	15.2
Accum. Depr./Gross Prop. %	36.5	35.1	34.6	34.8	34.5	33.8	32.5
Price Range	40.41-27.80	44.63-34.35	46.94-26.19	40.25-31.75	40.13-32.13	39.88-31.25	37.38-29.63
P/E Ratio	16.1-11.1	16.3-12.5	19.2-10.7	15.4-12.2	17.8-14.3	14.2-11.1	12.6-10.0
Average Yield %	6.1	5.1	5.4	5.4	5.3	5.3	5.5

Statistics are as originally reported. [1] Incls. special charges of $14.7 mill., 9/01; $17.0 mill., 9/02.

OFFICERS:
T. M. Patrick, Chmn., Pres., C.E.O.
T. M. Patrick, Pres., C.O.O.
T. A. Nardi, Sr. V.P., C.F.O.

INVESTOR CONTACT: Mary Ann Wall, Manager, Investor Relations, (312) 240-7534

PRINCIPAL OFFICE: 130 East Randolph Drive, 24th floor, Chicago, IL 60601-6207

TELEPHONE NUMBER: (312) 240-4000
FAX: (312) 240-4220
WEB: www.pecorp.com

NO. OF EMPLOYEES: 2,479

SHAREHOLDERS: 21,550

ANNUAL MEETING: In Feb.

INCORPORATED: IL, 1967

INSTITUTIONAL HOLDINGS:
No. of Institutions: 214
Shares Held: 16,612,056
% Held: 46.1

INDUSTRY: Natural gas distribution (SIC: 4924)

TRANSFER AGENT(S): Computershare Investor Services, Chicago, IL

PEPSICO INC.

YIELD 1.4%
P/E RATIO 22.8

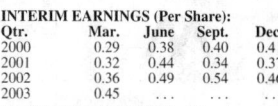

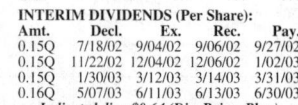

TRADING VOLUME
Thousand Shares

| | 1989 | 1990 | 1991 | 1992 | 1993 | 1994 | 1995 | 1996 | 1997 | 1998 | 1999 | 2000 | 2001 | 2002 | 2003 |

*7 YEAR PRICE SCORE 120.0   ***12 MONTH PRICE SCORE 99.4**

NYSE COMPOSITE INDEX=100

INTERIM EARNINGS (Per Share):

Qtr.	Mar.	June	Sept.	Dec.
2000	0.29	0.38	0.40	0.41
2001	0.32	0.44	0.34	0.37
2002	0.36	0.49	0.54	0.46
2003	0.45	...	...	...

INTERIM DIVIDENDS (Per Share):

Amt.	Decl.	Ex.	Rec.	Pay.
0.15Q	7/18/02	9/04/02	9/06/02	9/27/02
0.15Q	11/22/02	12/04/02	12/06/02	1/02/03
0.15Q	1/30/03	3/12/03	3/14/03	3/31/03
0.16Q	5/07/03	6/11/03	6/13/03	6/30/03

Indicated div.: $0.64 (Div. Reinv. Plan)

CAPITALIZATION (12/28/02):

	($000)	(%)
Long-Term Debt	2,187,000	16.6
Deferred Income Tax	1,718,000	13.0
Common & Surplus	9,298,000	70.4
Total	13,203,000	100.0

DIVIDEND ACHIEVER STATUS:

Rank: 166   10-Year Growth Rate: 8.97%
Total Years of Dividend Growth: 31

RECENT DEVELOPMENTS: For the 12 weeks ended 3/22/03, net income was $777.0 million versus $689.0 million in the same period a year earlier. Results for 2003 and 2002 included pre-tax merger-related costs of $11.0 million and $36.0 million, respectively. Results for 2003 also included an after-tax gain of $16.0 million on Quaker's Mission pasta business. Net sales grew 4.1% to $5.53 billion, and operating profit rose 13.5% to $1.14 billion.

PROSPECTS: PEP's solid near-term outlook is supported by the roll-out of new products and market programs designed to fuel growth over the balance of 2003. They include the introduction of MOUNTAIN DEW LIVEWIRE, an orange-flavored version of MOUNTAIN DEW that is expected to be available from Memorial Day through Labor Day; new packaging and re-designed graphics for PEPSI; and a number of new Quaker products.

BUSINESS

PEPSICO INC. is a worldwide consumer products company. Worldwide snacks (57.1% of 2002 division net sales and 56.4% of operating profit) manufactures, markets, sells and distributes primarily salty, sweet and grain-based snacks including such brands as LAY'S, DORITOS, CHEETOS, ROLD GOLD, SABRITAS and WALKERS. Worldwide beverages (36.9%, 34.6%) includes such brands as PEPSI, DIET PEPSI, MOUNTAIN DEW, MUG, AQUAFINA, SOBE, TROPICANA PURE PREMIUM, GATORADE and MIRINDA and 7-UP internationally. Quaker Foods North America (6.0%, 9.0%) manufactures, markets and sells a variety of food products. PEP also has various ownership interests in a number of bottling concerns. In August 2001, PEP acquired The Quaker Oats Company.

ANNUAL FINANCIAL DATA

	12/28/02	12/29/01	12/30/00	12/25/99	12/26/98	12/27/97	12/28/96
Earnings Per Share	[7] 1.85	[6] 1.47	1.48	[4] 1.37	[3] 1.31	[1] 0.95	[2] 0.72
Cash Flow Per Share	2.47	2.07	2.13	2.06	2.12	1.65	1.79
Tang. Book Val. Per Share	2.37	2.17	1.91	1.47	...	0.72	...
Dividends Per Share	0.59	0.57	0.55	0.53	0.51	0.48	0.43
Dividend Payout %	31.9	38.8	37.2	38.7	38.9	50.5	59.7
INCOME STATEMENT (IN MILLIONS):							
Total Revenues	25,112.0	26,935.0	20,438.0	20,367.0	22,348.0	20,917.0	31,645.0
Costs & Expenses	19,270.0	21,832.0	16,253.0	16,517.0	18,530.0	17,149.0	27,380.0
Depreciation & Amort.	1,112.0	1,082.0	960.0	1,032.0	1,234.0	1,106.0	1,719.0
Operating Income	4,730.0	4,021.0	3,225.0	2,818.0	2,584.0	2,662.0	2,546.0
Net Interest Inc./(Exp.)	d142.0	d152.0	d145.0	d245.0	d321.0	d353.0	d499.0
Income Before Income Taxes	4,868.0	4,029.0	3,210.0	3,656.0	2,263.0	2,309.0	2,047.0
Income Taxes	1,555.0	1,367.0	1,027.0	1,606.0	270.0	818.0	898.0
Net Income	[7] 3,313.0	[5] 2,662.0	2,183.0	[4] 2,050.0	[3] 1,993.0	[1] 1,491.0	[2] 1,149.0
Cash Flow	4,421.0	3,740.0	3,143.0	3,082.0	3,227.0	2,597.0	2,868.0
Average Shs. Outstg. (000)	1,789,000	1,807,000	1,475,000	1,496,000	1,519,000	1,570,000	1,606,000
BALANCE SHEET (IN MILLIONS):							
Cash & Cash Equivalents	1,845.0	1,649.0	1,330.0	1,056.0	394.0	2,883.0	786.0
Total Current Assets	6,413.0	5,853.0	4,604.0	4,173.0	4,362.0	6,251.0	5,139.0
Net Property	7,390.0	6,876.0	5,438.0	5,266.0	7,318.0	6,261.0	10,191.0
Total Assets	23,474.0	21,695.0	18,339.0	17,551.0	22,660.0	20,101.0	24,512.0
Total Current Liabilities	6,052.0	4,998.0	3,935.0	3,788.0	7,914.0	4,257.0	5,139.0
Long-Term Obligations	2,187.0	2,651.0	2,346.0	2,812.0	4,028.0	4,946.0	8,439.0
Net Stockholders' Equity	9,298.0	8,648.0	7,249.0	6,881.0	6,401.0	6,936.0	6,623.0
Net Working Capital	361.0	855.0	669.0	385.0	d3,552.0	1,994.0	...
Year-end Shs. Outstg. (000)	1,722,000	1,756,000	1,446,000	1,455,000	1,471,000	1,502,000	1,545,000
STATISTICAL RECORD:							
Operating Profit Margin %	18.8	14.9	15.8	13.8	11.6	12.7	8.0
Net Profit Margin %	13.2	9.9	10.7	10.1	8.9	7.1	3.6
Return on Equity %	35.6	30.8	30.1	29.8	31.1	21.5	17.3
Return on Assets %	14.1	12.3	11.9	11.7	8.8	7.4	4.7
Debt/Total Assets %	9.3	12.2	12.8	16.0	17.8	24.6	34.4
Price Range	53.50-35.01	50.46-40.25	49.94-29.69	42.56-30.13	44.81-27.56	41.31-28.25	35.88-27.25
P/E Ratio	28.9-18.9	34.3-27.4	33.7-20.1	31.1-22.0	34.2-21.0	43.5-29.7	49.8-37.8
Average Yield %	1.3	1.3	1.4	1.5	1.4	1.4	1.4

Statistics are as originally reported. [1] Incl. non-recurr. chrgs. of $290.0 mill.; bef. disc. oper. gain of $651.0 mill. [2] Incl. non-recurr. chrgs. of $716.0 mill. [3] Incl. non-recurr. chrg. of $288.0 mill. [4] Incl. non-recurr. chrg. of $65.0 mill. [5] Incl. after-tax merger-rel. chrgs. of $322.0 mill. and oth. asset impairmnt. & restruct. chrgs. of $19.0 mill. [6] Refl. 10/6/97 spin-off of TRICON Global Restaurants. [7] Incl. merger-rel. chrgs. of $224.0 mill.

OFFICERS:
S. S. Reinemund, Chmn., C.E.O.
I. K. Nooyi, Pres., C.F.O.
D. R. Andrews, Sr. V.P., Sec., Gen. Couns.

INVESTOR CONTACT: Kathleen Luke, V.P., Inv. Rel., (914) 253-3691

PRINCIPAL OFFICE: 700 Anderson Hill Road, Purchase, NY 10577-1444

TELEPHONE NUMBER: (914) 253-2000
FAX: (914) 253-2070
WEB: www.pepsico.com
NO. OF EMPLOYEES: 142,000 (approx.)
SHAREHOLDERS: 220,000 (approx.)
ANNUAL MEETING: In May
INCORPORATED: DE, Sept., 1919; reincorp., NC, Dec., 1986

INSTITUTIONAL HOLDINGS:
No. of Institutions: 1,072
Shares Held: 1,123,709,222
% Held: 65.4

INDUSTRY: Bottled and canned soft drinks (SIC: 2086)

TRANSFER AGENT(S): The Bank of New York, Newark, NJ

PFIZER INC.

YIELD 1.9%
P/E RATIO 20.4

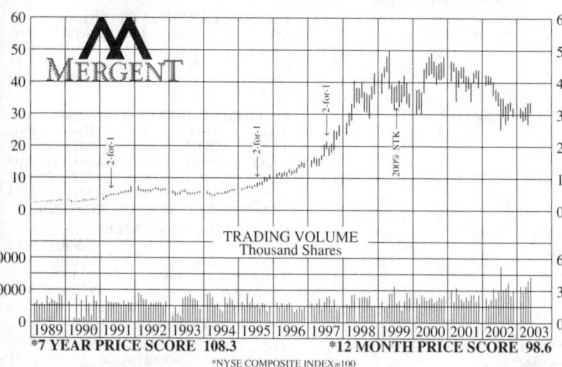

TRADING VOLUME
Thousand Shares

| 1989 | 1990 | 1991 | 1992 | 1993 | 1994 | 1995 | 1996 | 1997 | 1998 | 1999 | 2000 | 2001 | 2002 | 2003 |

*7 YEAR PRICE SCORE 108.3   ***12 MONTH PRICE SCORE 98.6**

*NYSE COMPOSITE INDEX=100

INTERIM EARNINGS (Per Share):

Qtr.	Mar.	June	Sept.	Dec.
1999	0.16	0.19	0.18	0.25
2000	0.31	0.18	0.21	0.23
2001	0.30	0.29	0.33	0.30
2002	0.37	0.32	0.38	0.42
2003	0.40	...	...	...

INTERIM DIVIDENDS (Per Share):

Amt.	Decl.	Ex.	Rec.	Pay.
0.13Q	6/27/02	8/14/02	8/16/02	9/05/02
0.13Q	10/24/02	11/13/02	11/15/02	12/05/02
0.15Q	12/16/02	1/15/03	1/17/03	2/14/03
0.15Q	4/24/03	5/14/03	5/16/03	6/05/03

Indicated div.: $0.60 (Div. Reinv. Plan)

CAPITALIZATION (12/31/02):

	($000)	(%)
Long-Term Debt	3,140,000	13.4
Deferred Income Tax	364,000	1.6
Common & Surplus	19,950,000	85.1
Total	23,454,000	100.0

DIVIDEND ACHIEVER STATUS:
Rank: 59   10-Year Growth Rate: 15.48%
Total Years of Dividend Growth: 35

RECENT DEVELOPMENTS: For the quarter ended 3/31/03, income was $2.46 billion, before an accounting change charge of $30.0 million and a gain of $2.24 billion from discontinued operations, versus income of $2.31 billion, before an accounting change charge of $410.0 million and a gain of $61.0 million from discontinued operations, in the prior year. Results for 2003 and 2002 included pre-tax merger-related costs of $91.0 million and $109.0 million, respectively. Revenues rose 10.0% to $8.53 billion.

PROSPECTS: On 4/16/03, PFE completed the acquisition of Pharmacia Corporation for approximately $54.00 billion. The acquisition is expected to expand PFE's global pharmaceutical position, broaden its product base and boost its research and development capacity. PFE also expects merger-related cost savings of $2.50 billion in 2005. Separately, on 3/31/03, PFE announced that it has completed the sale of its Adams confectionery business for about $4.20 billion in cash

BUSINESS

PFIZER INC. is a research-based, global pharmaceutical company that discovers, develops, manufactures and markets medicines for humans and animals. The products include NORVASC, a once-a-day calcium channel blocker for treatment of angina and hypertension, ZYRTEC, an anti-allergy medicine, VIAGRA, an oral medication for the treatment of erectile dysfunction, ZOLOFT, a selective serotonin re-uptake inhibitor for the treatment of depression, ZITHROMAX, an oral or injectable antibiotic, DIFLUCAN, used to treat various fungal infections, as well as non-prescription self-medications. The animal health segment includes anti-parasitic, anti-infective and anti-inflammatory medicines, and vaccines. Revenues for 2002 were derived as follows: pharmaceutical segment, 92.2% and consumer product segment, 7.8%. PFE acquired Warner-Lambert Co. on 6/19/00. On 4/16/03, PFE acquired Pharmacia Corporation for about $54.00 billion.

ANNUAL FINANCIAL DATA

	12/31/02	12/31/01	12/31/00	12/31/99	12/31/98	12/31/97	12/31/96
Earnings Per Share	④ 1.47	③ 1.22	③ 0.59	② 0.82	① 0.49	0.57	0.50
Cash Flow Per Share	1.64	1.39	0.74	0.96	0.62	0.69	0.61
Tang. Book Val. Per Share	3.04	2.64	2.26	2.11	2.06	1.71	1.43
Dividends Per Share	0.52	0.44	0.36	0.31	0.25	0.23	0.20
Dividend Payout %	35.4	36.1	61.0	37.4	51.7	40.0	40.2

INCOME STATEMENT (IN MILLIONS):

Total Revenues	32,373.0	32,259.0	29,574.0	16,204.0	13,544.0	12,504.0	11,306.0
Costs & Expenses	19,541.0	20,862.0	22,825.0	11,214.0	10,461.0	8,914.0	8,072.0
Depreciation & Amort.	1,036.0	1,068.0	968.0	542.0	489.0	502.0	430.0
Income Before Income Taxes	11,796.0	10,329.0	5,781.0	4,448.0	2,594.0	3,088.0	2,804.0
Income Taxes	2,609.0	2,561.0	2,049.0	1,244.0	642.0	865.0	869.0
Net Income	④9,181.0	③7,752.0	③3,718.0	②3,199.0	①1,950.0	2,213.0	1,929.0
Cash Flow	10,217.0	8,820.0	4,686.0	3,741.0	2,439.0	2,715.0	2,359.0
Average Shs. Outstg. (000)	6,241,000	6,361,000	6,368,000	3,884,000	3,945,000	3,909,000	3,864,000

BALANCE SHEET (IN MILLIONS):

Cash & Cash Equivalents	12,551.0	8,615.0	6,863.0	4,442.0	3,929.0	1,589.0	1,637.0
Total Current Assets	24,781.0	18,450.0	17,187.0	11,191.0	9,931.0	6,820.0	6,468.0
Net Property	10,712.0	10,415.0	9,425.0	5,343.0	4,415.0	4,137.0	3,850.0
Total Assets	46,356.0	39,153.0	33,510.0	20,574.0	18,302.0	15,336.0	14,667.0
Total Current Liabilities	18,555.0	13,640.0	11,981.0	9,185.0	7,192.0	5,305.0	5,640.0
Long-Term Obligations	3,140.0	2,609.0	1,123.0	525.0	527.0	729.0	687.0
Net Stockholders' Equity	19,950.0	18,293.0	16,076.0	8,887.0	8,810.0	7,933.0	6,954.0
Net Working Capital	6,226.0	4,810.0	5,206.0	2,006.0	2,739.0	1,515.0	828.0
Year-end Shs. Outstg. (000)	6,162,000	6,277,000	6,314,000	3,847,000	3,883,000	3,882,000	3,870,000

STATISTICAL RECORD:

Operating Profit Margin %	36.4	32.0	19.5	27.5	19.2	24.7	24.8
Net Profit Margin %	28.4	24.0	12.6	19.7	14.4	17.7	17.1
Return on Equity %	46.0	42.4	23.1	36.0	22.1	27.9	27.7
Return on Assets %	19.8	19.8	11.1	15.5	10.7	14.4	13.2
Debt/Total Assets %	6.8	6.7	3.4	2.6	2.9	4.8	4.7
Price Range	42.46-25.13	46.75-34.00	49.25-30.00	50.04-31.54	42.98-23.69	26.66-13.44	15.21-10.04
P/E Ratio	28.9-17.1	38.3-27.9	83.5-50.8	61.0-38.5	87.7-48.3	47.0-23.7	30.5-20.2
Average Yield %	1.5	1.1	0.9	0.8	0.8	1.1	1.6

Statistics are as originally reported. Adj. for stock splits: 200% div., 6/30/99; 2-for-1, 9/97. ① Incl. unus. & nonrecurr. pre-tax chgs. total. $1.06 bill.; excl. a $1.40 bill. gain from disc. opers. ② Incl. a one-time after-tax chrg. of $1.37 bill. for TROVAN inv. ③ Bef. inc. from disc. opers. of $355.0 mill., 2002; $36.0 mill., 2001; $8.0 mill., 2000 & incl. merger-rel. costs of $630.0 mill., 2002; $839.0 mill., 2001; $3.26 bill. 2000. ④ Bef. acctg. chng. chrg. of $410.0 mill.

OFFICERS:
H. A. McKinnell, Chmn., Pres., C.E.O.
J. F. Niblack, Vice-Chmn.
D. L. Shedlarz, Exec. V.P., C.F.O.

INVESTOR CONTACT: Investor Relations, (212) 573-2323

PRINCIPAL OFFICE: 235 East 42nd Street, New York, NY 10017-5755

TELEPHONE NUMBER: (212) 573-2323
FAX: (212) 573-2641
WEB: www.pfizer.com

NO. OF EMPLOYEES: 98,000 (approx.)

SHAREHOLDERS: 214,810 (approx.)

ANNUAL MEETING: In Apr.

INCORPORATED: DE, 1942

INSTITUTIONAL HOLDINGS:
No. of Institutions: 1,388
Shares Held: 3,042,223,755
% Held: 49.4

INDUSTRY: Pharmaceutical preparations (SIC: 2834)

TRANSFER AGENT(S): EquiServe Trust Company, N.A., Jersey City, NJ

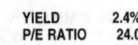

NYSE SYMBOL PSC
Rec. Pr. 23.52 (5/31/03)

PHILADELPHIA SUBURBAN CORPORATION

YIELD 2.4%
P/E RATIO 24.0

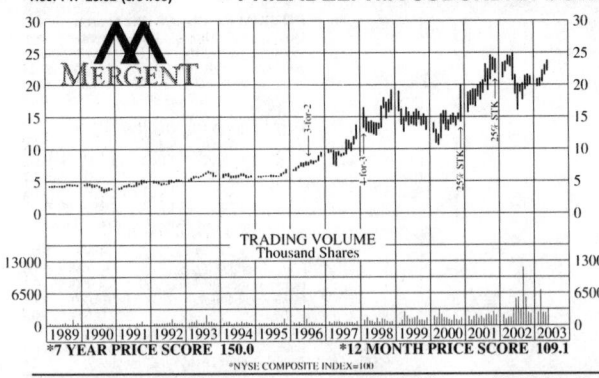

INTERIM EARNINGS (Per Share):

Qtr.	Mar.	June	Sept.	Dec.
2000	0.16	0.21	0.25	0.18
2001	0.19	0.22	0.28	0.18
2002	0.17	0.21	0.31	0.27
2003	0.19	...	...	...

INTERIM DIVIDENDS (Per Share):

Amt.	Decl.	Ex.	Rec.	Pay.
0.133Q	8/06/02	8/14/02	8/16/02	9/01/02
0.14Q	8/06/02	11/13/02	11/15/02	12/01/02
0.14Q	2/04/03	2/12/03	2/14/03	3/01/03
0.14Q	5/06/03	5/13/03	5/15/03	6/01/03

Indicated div.: $0.56 (Div. Reinv. Plan)

CAPITALIZATION (12/31/02):

	($000)	(%)
Long-Term Debt	582,910	54.2
Redeemable Pfd. Stock	172	0.0
Common & Surplus	493,097	45.8
Total	1,076,179	100.0

DIVIDEND ACHIEVER STATUS:
Rank: 238   10-Year Growth Rate: 4.91%
Total Years of Dividend Growth: 11

*7 YEAR PRICE SCORE 150.0   *12 MONTH PRICE SCORE 109.1
*NYSE COMPOSITE INDEX=100

RECENT DEVELOPMENTS: For the quarter ended 3/31/03, net income grew 12.1% to $13.3 million compared with $11.9 million in the equivalent 2002 quarter. Results for 2003 and 2002 included a gain on the sale of other assets of $55.0 million and $349.0 million, respectively. Operating revenues climbed 12.3% to $80.5 million from $71.7 million a year earlier due to rate relief and customer growth in various states in which the Company operates.

PROSPECTS: On 5/21/03, PSC completed the regulatory approval process for the pending acquisition of AquaSource Inc.'s investor-owned water and wastewater systems. In total, PSC received required regulatory approvals in ten states. The agreement provides for a target cash purchase price of about $205.0 million. The acquisition, which is expected to close during the third quarter, will increase PSC's customer base by more than 20.0% and expand its service territory to 13 states.

BUSINESS

PHILADELPHIA SUBURBAN CORPORATION is a holding company for regulated utilities providing water or wastewater services to approximately 2.0 million people in Pennsylvania, Illinois, Ohio, New Jersey, Maine, and North Carolina as of 5/7/03. PSC's two primary subsidiaries are Pennsylvania Suburban Water Company, a regulated public utility that provides water or wastewater services to about 1.3 million residents in the suburban areas north and west of the City of Philadelphia and in ten other counties in Pennsylvania, and Consumers Water Company, a holding company for several regulated public utility companies that provide water or wastewater service to about 700,000 residents in various communities in four states. In addition, PSC provides water and wastewater service to about 35,000 people through operating and maintenance contracts with municipal authorities and other parties close to its operating companies' service territories. Some of PSC's subsidiaries provide wastewater collection, treatment and disposal services, primarily residential, to about 40,000 people in Pennsylvania, Illinois, New Jersey and North Carolina.

ANNUAL FINANCIAL DATA

	12/31/02	12/31/01	12/31/00	12/31/99	12/31/98	12/31/97	12/31/96
Earnings Per Share	⑧ 0.97	② 0.87	③ 0.81	① ⑤ 0.56	0.66	0.56	④ 0.67
Cash Flow Per Share	1.61	1.46	1.33	1.06	1.03	0.92	1.11
Tang. Book Val. Per Share	7.26	1.46	1.33	5.73	5.34	4.46	5.98
Dividends Per Share	0.54	0.50	0.47	0.45	0.43	0.40	0.38
Dividend Payout %	55.4	58.0	58.1	79.6	64.6	70.8	57.0
INCOME STATEMENT (IN MILLIONS):							
Total Revenues	322.0	307.3	275.5	257.3	151.0	136.2	122.5
Costs & Expenses	137.2	132.8	123.1	124.4	68.2	64.8	59.9
Depreciation & Amort.	44.3	40.2	34.1	31.9	16.1	14.6	13.3
Operating Income	140.5	134.3	118.3	101.0	66.7	56.8	49.3
Net Interest Inc./(Exp.)	d40.4	d39.9	d40.4	d33.7	d19.0	d17.9	d15.3
Income Taxes	32.8	34.2	26.5	19.6	15.9	14.0	
Net Income	⑧ 67.2	② 60.1	③ 52.9	① ⑤ 36.4	28.8	23.2	④ 19.8
Cash Flow	111.5	100.2	86.9	68.2	44.7	37.6	33.1
Average Shs. Outstg. (000)	69,231	68,755	65,414	64,539	43,556	41,052	29,770
BALANCE SHEET (IN MILLIONS):							
Gross Property	1,836.9	1,677.1	1,536.2	1,393.0	745.5	656.0	612.8
Accumulated Depreciation	346.1	308.9	284.7	257.7	135.7	121.5	109.9
Net Property	1,490.8	1,368.1	1,251.4	1,135.4	609.8	534.5	502.9
Total Assets	1,717.1	1,560.3	1,414.0	1,280.8	701.5	618.5	582.9
Long-Term Obligations	582.9	516.5	468.8	413.8	261.8	232.5	217.5
Net Stockholders' Equity	493.1	473.0	429.5	366.3	234.8	194.7	180.0
Year-end Shs. Outstg. (000)	67,916	68,386	67,095	64,082	43,323	42,970	29,588
STATISTICAL RECORD:							
Operating Profit Margin %	43.6	43.7	42.9	39.3	44.2	41.7	40.2
Net Profit Margin %	20.9	19.6	19.2	14.1	19.1	17.0	16.1
Net Inc./Net Property %	4.5	4.4	4.2	3.2	4.7	4.3	3.9
Net Inc./Tot. Capital %	6.2	6.1	5.0	4.0	4.9	4.5	4.1
Return on Equity %	13.6	12.7	12.3	9.9	12.3	11.9	11.0
Accum. Depr./Gross Prop. %	18.8	18.4	18.5	18.5	18.2	18.5	17.9
Price Range	25.00-16.02	24.64-15.65	19.95-10.56	19.04-12.64	19.24-12.08	13.77-7.53	9.54-6.56
P/E Ratio	25.8-16.5	28.3-18.0	24.7-13.1	33.8-22.4	29.2-18.3	24.5-13.0	14.3-9.9
Average Yield %	2.6	2.5	3.1	2.8	2.7	3.8	4.7

Statistics are as originally reported. Adj. for stk. splits: 25% div., 11/01 & 12/00; 4-for-3, 1/98; 3-for-2, 7/96. ① Incl. restruct. recovery costs of $3.8 mill. ② Incl. gain on the sale of other assets of $3.4 mill. ③ Incl. restruct. recovery gain of $1.1 mill., merger transaction recovery costs of $2.9 mill., gain on the sale of other assets of $5.1 mill. ④ Incl. reversal of reserve for discont. oper. of $965,000. ⑤ Incl. merger transaction costs of $6.3 mill. ⑧ Incl. a net gain on sale of water system & other assets of $7.8 mill.

OFFICERS:
N. DeBenedictis, Chmn., Pres.
D. P. Smeltzer, Sr. V.P., C.F.O.
R. H. Stahl, Exec. V.P., Sec., Gen. Couns.

INVESTOR CONTACT: Donna Alston, (610) 645-1095

PRINCIPAL OFFICE: 762 W. Lancaster Avenue, Bryn Mawr, PA 19010-3489

TELEPHONE NUMBER: (610) 527-8000
FAX: (610) 527-1061
WEB: www.suburbanwater.com

NO. OF EMPLOYEES: 971

SHAREHOLDERS: 21,600 (approx. record)

ANNUAL MEETING: In May

INCORPORATED: PA, May, 1969

PIEDMONT NATURAL GAS COMPANY, INC.

YIELD 4.2%
P/E RATIO 19.2

7 YEAR PRICE SCORE 128.3   **12 MONTH PRICE SCORE 104.6**
*NYSE COMPOSITE INDEX=100

TRADING VOLUME
Thousand Shares

INTERIM EARNINGS (Per Share):

Qtr.	Jan.	Apr.	July	Oct.
1999-00	1.40	1.18	d0.32	d0.23
2000-01	1.56	1.23	d0.52	d0.24
2001-02	1.26	1.27	d0.27	d0.36
2002-03	1.74	0.93	...	...

INTERIM DIVIDENDS (Per Share):

Amt.	Decl.	Ex.	Rec.	Pay.
0.40Q	8/23/02	9/20/02	9/24/02	10/15/02
0.40Q	12/13/02	12/20/02	12/24/02	1/15/03
0.415Q	2/28/03	3/21/03	3/25/03	4/15/03
0.415Q	5/30/03	6/20/03	6/24/03	7/15/03

Indicated div.: $1.66 (Div. Reinv. Plan)

CAPITALIZATION (10/31/02):

	($000)	(%)
Long-Term Debt	462,000	38.2
Deferred Income Tax	158,275	13.1
Common & Surplus	589,596	48.7
Total	1,209,871	100.0

DIVIDEND ACHIEVER STATUS:
Rank: 222   10-Year Growth Rate: 5.71%
Total Years of Dividend Growth: 23

RECENT DEVELOPMENTS: For the three months ended 4/30/03, net income decreased 25.9% to $31.0 million compared with $41.8 million in the equivalent quarter of the previous year. The decrease in net income was largely due to higher cost of gas related to volumes delivered but not yet billed, higher operations and maintenance expenses and lower other income. Operating revenues jumped 38.8% to $407.8 million from $293.9 million in the year-earlier period.

PROSPECTS: The Company expects earnings per share for full-year 2003 to range from $2.22 to $2.32, including the one-time, non-recurring effect of recording revenues for volumes delivered but not yet billed. This earnings guidance includes the positive effect of new customer billing rates in North Carolina and South Carolina effective 11/1/02, and the estimated dilutive impact of integrating North Carolina Natural Gas (NCNG) during fiscal year 2003.

BUSINESS

PIEDMONT NATURAL GAS COMPANY, INC. is engaged in the transportation, distribution and sale of natural gas to over 740,000 residential, commercial and industrial customers in North Carolina, South Carolina and Tennessee. Non-utility subsidiaries and divisions are involved in the exploration, development, marketing and transportation of natural gas, oil, and propane. PNY's utility operations are subject to regulation by the North Carolina Utilities Commission, the Tennessee Public Service Commission and the Public Service Commission of South Carolina. PNY also owns Tennessee Natural Resources, Inc., and its subsidiaries.

ANNUAL FINANCIAL DATA

	10/31/02	10/31/01	10/31/00	10/31/99	10/31/98	10/31/97	10/31/96
Earnings Per Share	1.89	2.02	2.01	1.86	1.96	① 1.81	1.67
Cash Flow Per Share	3.64	3.64	3.64	3.38	3.45	3.24	3.02
Tang. Book Val. Per Share	17.82	17.26	16.52	15.71	14.91	13.90	13.07
Dividends Per Share	1.58	1.52	1.44	1.36	1.28	1.21	1.15
Dividend Payout %	83.9	75.2	71.6	73.1	65.3	66.6	68.6
INCOME STATEMENT (IN MILLIONS):							
Total Revenues	832.0	1,107.9	830.4	686.5	765.3	775.5	685.1
Costs & Expenses	663.1	942.3	672.1	531.8	613.9	632.5	555.1
Depreciation & Amort.	57.8	52.5	51.5	47.4	45.6	42.9	39.5
Maintenance Exp.	21.0	19.1	17.1	15.6	14.7	16.2	15.8
Operating Income	90.1	94.0	89.7	91.7	91.2	84.0	74.6
Net Interest Inc./(Exp.)	d40.6	d39.4	d40.3	d32.4	d33.2	d34.0	d31.1
Income Taxes	9.0	7.3	...	...	...	...	...
Net Income	62.2	65.5	64.0	58.2	60.3	① 54.1	48.6
Cash Flow	120.1	118.0	115.6	105.6	105.9	97.0	88.1
Average Shs. Outstg. (000)	32,937	32,420	31,779	31,242	30,717	29,883	29,161
BALANCE SHEET (IN MILLIONS):							
Gross Property	1,731.0	1,626.2	1,534.0	1,441.3	1,345.9	1,256.5	1,168.4
Accumulated Depreciation	572.4	511.5	463.0	420.1	381.6	342.4	306.4
Net Property	1,159.6	1,115.9	1,072.0	1,047.0	990.6	941.7	889.1
Total Assets	1,445.1	1,393.7	1,445.0	1,288.7	1,162.8	1,098.2	1,064.9
Long-Term Obligations	462.0	509.0	451.0	423.0	371.0	381.0	391.0
Net Stockholders' Equity	589.6	560.4	527.4	491.7	458.3	419.8	386.1
Year-end Shs. Outstg. (000)	33,090	32,463	31,914	31,295	30,738	30,193	29,549
STATISTICAL RECORD:							
Operating Profit Margin %	10.8	8.5	10.8	13.4	11.9	10.8	10.9
Net Profit Margin %	7.5	5.9	7.7	8.5	7.9	7.0	7.1
Net Inc./Net Property %	5.4	5.9	6.0	5.6	6.1	5.7	5.5
Net Inc./Tot. Capital %	5.1	5.4	5.7	5.6	6.4	6.0	5.6
Return on Equity %	10.6	11.7	12.1	11.8	13.2	12.9	12.6
Accum. Depr./Gross Prop. %	33.1	31.5	30.2	29.1	28.4	27.2	26.2
Price Range	38.00-27.35	38.00-29.19	39.44-23.69	36.63-28.63	36.13-27.88	36.44-22.00	25.75-20.50
P/E Ratio	20.1-14.5	18.8-14.4	19.6-11.8	19.7-15.4	18.4-14.2	20.1-12.2	15.4-12.3
Average Yield %	4.9	4.5	4.6	4.2	4.0	4.1	5.0

Statistics are as originally reported. ① Incl. pre-tax restruct. chg. of $1.8 mill.

OFFICERS:
J. H. Maxheim, Chmn.
T. E. Skains, Pres., C.E.O.
D. J. Dzuricky, Sr. V.P., C.F.O.

INVESTOR CONTACT: Stephen D. Connor, Investor Relations, (704) 364-3483 ext.6205

PRINCIPAL OFFICE: 1915 Rexford Road, Charlotte, NC 28211

TELEPHONE NUMBER: (704) 364-3120
FAX: (704) 365-8515
WEB: www.piedmontng.com
NO. OF EMPLOYEES: 1,715 (avg.)
SHAREHOLDERS: 16,186 (record)
ANNUAL MEETING: In Feb.
INCORPORATED: NY, May, 1950; reincorp., NC, Mar., 1994

INSTITUTIONAL HOLDINGS:
No. of Institutions: 143
Shares Held: 9,054,191
% Held: 27.4

INDUSTRY: Natural gas distribution (SIC: 4924)

TRANSFER AGENT(S): Wachovia Bank of North Carolina, NA, Boston, MA

PIER 1 IMPORTS, INC.

YIELD 1.2%
P/E RATIO 15.0

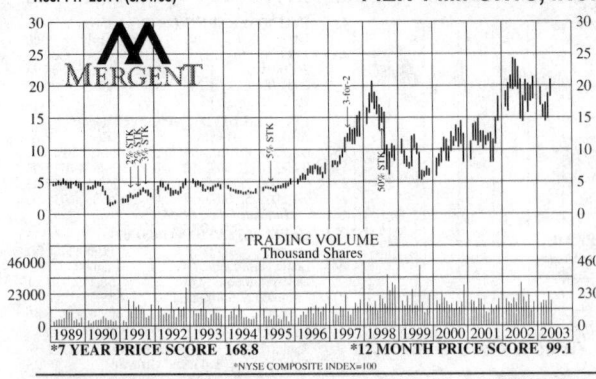

TRADING VOLUME
Thousand Shares

| 1989 | 1990 | 1991 | 1992 | 1993 | 1994 | 1995 | 1996 | 1997 | 1998 | 1999 | 2000 | 2001 | 2002 | 2003 |

*7 YEAR PRICE SCORE 168.8   ***12 MONTH PRICE SCORE 99.1**
*NYSE COMPOSITE INDEX=100

INTERIM EARNINGS (Per Share):

Qtr.	May	Aug.	Nov.	Feb.
1999-00	0.13	0.12	0.16	0.34
2000-01	0.17	0.18	0.24	0.38
2001-02	0.13	0.14	0.26	0.51
2002-03	0.23	0.23	0.33	0.57
2003-04	0.21	...	...	...

INTERIM DIVIDENDS (Per Share):

Amt.	Decl.	Ex.	Rec.	Pay.
0.05Q	4/05/02	5/06/02	5/08/02	5/22/02
0.05Q	6/27/02	8/05/02	8/07/02	8/21/02
0.05Q	9/26/02	11/04/02	11/06/02	11/20/02
0.06Q	12/05/02	2/03/03	2/05/03	2/19/03
0.06Q	3/27/03	5/05/03	5/07/03	5/21/03

Indicated div.: $0.24 (Div. Reinv. Plan)

CAPITALIZATION (3/1/03):

	($000)	(%)
Long-Term Debt	25,000	3.7
Common & Surplus	643,936	96.3
Total	668,936	100.0

DIVIDEND ACHIEVER STATUS:
Rank: 7   10-Year Growth Rate: 25.86%
Total Years of Dividend Growth: 11

RECENT DEVELOPMENTS: For the quarter ended 5/31/03, net income declined 14.1% to $19.1 million from $22.2 million in the corresponding prior-year quarter. Net sales grew 4.8% to $402.7 million from $384.4 million the previous year. Comparable-store sales were down 3.6% year over year. Cost of sales, including buying and store occupancy costs, increased 6.4% to $234.5 million. Results reflected the slowdown in the economy, geopolitical instability, and adverse weather conditions.

PROSPECTS: The Company expects to benefit from the new tax bill that provides rebates as well as changes in overall tax rates, which should result in higher take-home pay for families. PIR believes this will have a positive impact on Pier 1 and Cargokids stores as they begin the annual Back-to-School selling season in July. Looking ahead, PIR expects diluted earnings per share for the second quarter of fiscal 2004 ranging from $0.21 to $0.25, and between $1.45 and $1.50 for the full year.

BUSINESS

PIER 1 IMPORTS, INC. is a retailer of decorative home furnishings, furniture, dining and kitchen goods, bath and bedding accessories and other specialty items for the home imported from over 40 countries. As of 3/1/03, PIR operated more than 1,000 stores in 50 states, Canada, Puerto Rico, the United Kingdom and Mexico. The Company's stores operate under the "Pier 1 Imports" and "Cargokids!" names, as well as under the name "The Pier" in the United Kingdom. Also, PIR supplies merchandise and licenses the Pier 1 Imports name to Sears Mexico and Sears Puerto Rico, which sell Pier 1 merchandise in a "store-within-a-store" format in 17 Sears Mexico stores and in seven Sears Puerto Rico stores. In 1997, PIR acquired a national bank and its assets in Omaha, Nebraska, which operates under the name of Pier 1 National Bank and holds the credit card accounts for the Company's proprietary credit card.

ANNUAL FINANCIAL DATA

	3/1/03	3/2/02	3/3/01	2/26/00	2/27/99	2/28/98	3/1/97
Earnings Per Share	1.36	1.04	0.97	0.75	0.77	① 0.72	② 0.49
Cash Flow Per Share	1.84	1.49	1.41	1.11	1.02	0.90	0.69
Tang. Book Val. Per Share	7.10	6.27	5.53	4.70	4.14	3.86	3.19
Dividends Per Share	0.19	0.16	0.14	0.12	0.11	0.08	0.07
Dividend Payout %	14.0	15.4	14.4	16.0	14.3	11.4	14.5
INCOME STATEMENT (IN MILLIONS):							
Total Revenues	1,754.9	1,548.6	1,411.5	1,231.1	1,138.6	1,075.4	947.1
Costs & Expenses	1,503.8	1,346.9	1,216.8	1,067.9	972.8	929.7	837.1
Depreciation & Amort.	46.4	42.8	43.2	40.0	31.1	23.9	19.8
Operating Income	204.7	158.8	151.5	123.2	134.7	121.7	90.2
Net Interest Inc./(Exp.)	d2.3	d2.3	d3.1	d6.9	d7.9	d8.7	d9.9
Income Before Income Taxes	205.4	159.0	150.2	118.6	129.6	124.0	80.3
Income Taxes	76.0	58.8	55.6	43.9	49.3	46.0	32.1
Net Income	129.4	100.2	94.7	74.7	80.4	① 78.0	② 48.2
Cash Flow	175.8	143.0	137.8	114.7	111.5	102.0	68.0
Average Shs. Outstg. (000)	95,305	96,185	97,952	103,297	108,864	112,880	98,285
BALANCE SHEET (IN MILLIONS):							
Cash & Cash Equivalents	242.1	235.6	46.8	50.4	41.9	80.7	32.3
Total Current Assets	663.6	605.2	477.1	415.3	381.9	402.4	285.5
Net Property	254.5	210.0	211.8	213.0	226.3	216.3	216.8
Total Assets	967.5	862.7	735.7	670.7	654.0	653.4	570.3
Total Current Liabilities	243.6	208.4	144.1	176.0	129.8	121.6	110.4
Long-Term Obligations	25.0	25.4	25.0	25.0	96.0	114.9	111.3
Net Stockholders' Equity	643.9	585.7	531.9	440.7	403.9	392.7	323.0
Net Working Capital	420.0	396.8	333.0	239.3	252.1	280.8	175.1
Year-end Shs. Outstg. (000)	90,734	93,417	96,160	93,830	97,672	101,855	101,223
STATISTICAL RECORD:							
Operating Profit Margin %	11.7	10.3	10.7	10.0	11.8	11.3	9.5
Net Profit Margin %	7.4	6.5	6.7	6.1	7.1	7.3	5.1
Return on Equity %	20.1	17.1	17.8	17.0	19.9	19.9	14.9
Return on Assets %	13.4	11.6	12.9	11.1	12.3	11.9	8.5
Debt/Total Assets %	2.6	2.9	3.4	3.7	14.7	17.6	19.5
Price Range	24.35-14.35	18.30-7.97	14.50-5.88	12.38-5.25	20.75-6.06	15.96-7.22	7.95-4.61
P/E Ratio	17.9-10.6	17.6-7.7	14.9-6.1	16.5-7.0	26.9-7.9	22.2-10.0	16.2-9.4
Average Yield %	1.0	1.2	1.4	1.4	0.8	0.7	1.1

Statistics are as originally reported. Adj. for 3-for-2 stk. split, 7/98 & 7/97. ① Incl. $9.1 mil ($0.08/sh) gain. ② Bef. $4.1 mil extraord. chg.

OFFICERS:
M. J. Girouard, Chmn., C.E.O.
C. H. Turner, Exec. V.P., C.F.O., Treas.
J. R. Lawrence, Exec. V.P., Sec.

INVESTOR CONTACT: Cary Turner, Investor Relations, (817) 252-8400

PRINCIPAL OFFICE: 301 Commerce Street, Suite 600, Fort Worth, TX 76102

TELEPHONE NUMBER: (817) 252-8000
FAX: (817) 334-0191
WEB: www.pier1.com
NO. OF EMPLOYEES: 8,000 full-time (approx.); 9,100 part-time (approx.)
SHAREHOLDERS: 40,000 (approx.)
ANNUAL MEETING: In June
INCORPORATED: GA, May, 1978; reincorp., DE, April, 1979

INSTITUTIONAL HOLDINGS:
No. of Institutions: 272
Shares Held: 71,771,762
% Held: 78.9

INDUSTRY: Furniture stores (SIC: 5712)

TRANSFER AGENT(S): Mellon Investor Services, Ridgefield Park, NJ

PITNEY BOWES INC.

YIELD 3.1%
P/E RATIO 21.8

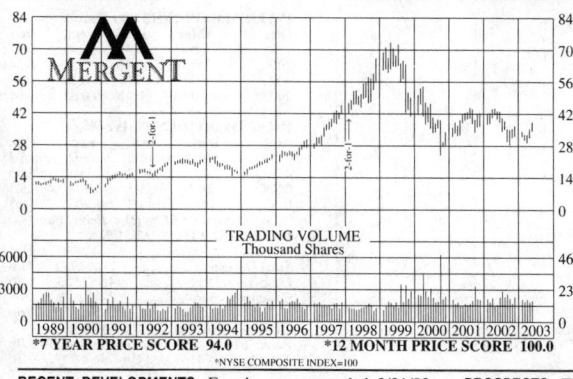

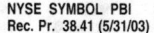

*7 YEAR PRICE SCORE 94.0   *12 MONTH PRICE SCORE 100.0
*NYSE COMPOSITE INDEX=100

INTERIM EARNINGS (Per Share):

Qtr.	Mar.	June	Sept.	Dec.
2000	0.57	0.64	0.63	0.55
2001	0.42	0.76	0.49	0.41
2002	0.53	0.59	0.61	0.08
2003	0.48	...	...	...

INTERIM DIVIDENDS (Per Share):

Amt.	Decl.	Ex.	Rec.	Pay.
0.295Q	7/08/02	8/21/02	8/23/02	9/12/02
0.295Q	11/11/02	11/20/02	11/22/02	12/12/02
0.30Q	1/28/03	2/19/03	2/21/03	3/12/03
0.30Q	4/14/03	5/21/03	5/23/03	6/12/03

Indicated div.: $1.20 (Div. Reinv. Plan)

CAPITALIZATION (12/31/02):

	($000)	(%)
Long-Term Debt	2,316,844	49.2
Deferred Income Tax	1,535,618	32.6
Preferred Stock	1,456	0.0
Common & Surplus	851,871	18.1
Total	4,705,789	100.0

DIVIDEND ACHIEVER STATUS:
Rank: 112   10-Year Growth Rate: 11.71%
Total Years of Dividend Growth: 19

RECENT DEVELOPMENTS: For the quarter ended 3/31/03, net income slid 12.1% to $113.9 million from $129.5 million in the prior year. Results for 2003 included a pre-tax restructuring charge of $21.3 million. Total revenue climbed 3.9% to $1.09 billion from $1.05 billion a year earlier. Revenues in the Global Mailing and Enterprise Solutions segments rose 5.0% to $747.9 million and 4.1% to $303.2 million, respectively, while Capital Services segment revenue slipped 13.8% to $39.7 million.

PROSPECTS: The Company is implementing restructuring initiatives expected to boost long-term operating profitability. PBI anticipates after-tax charges related to the initiatives of approximately $100.0 million through 2004. Separately, the Company is targeting full-year 2003 earnings in the range of $2.38 to $2.45 per share. In addition, PBI anticipates revenue growth of between 2.0% and 4.0% during the year.

BUSINESS

PITNEY BOWES INC. and its subsidiaries operate within three industry segments: Global Mailing, Enterprise Solutions, and Capital Services. Global Mailing, 68.3% of 2002 revenue (84.9% of operating profit), includes the sale, rental, and financing of mail finishing, mail creation and shipping equipment, related supplies and services, postal payment services, and software. Enterprise Solutions, 27.6% (7.9%), includes facilities management, through Pitney Bowes Management Services, Inc., and sales, service and financing of high-speed, software-enabled production mail systems, sorting equipment, incoming mail systems, electronic statement, billing and payment services, and mailing software. Capital Services, 4.1% (7.2%), includes large-ticket financing programs for a broad range of products.

ANNUAL FINANCIAL DATA

	12/31/02	12/31/01	12/31/00	12/31/99	12/31/98	12/31/97	12/31/96
Earnings Per Share	⑤1.81	④2.08	③2.18	①2.42	①2.03	1.80	②1.56
Cash Flow Per Share	1.60	3.36	3.42	3.94	3.32	2.82	2.51
Tang. Book Val. Per Share	0.10	1.05	4.34	5.28	5.26	5.96	6.86
Dividends Per Share	1.18	1.16	1.14	1.02	0.90	0.80	0.69
Dividend Payout %	65.2	55.8	52.3	42.1	44.3	44.4	44.2
INCOME STATEMENT (IN MILLIONS):							
Total Revenues	4,409.8	4,122.5	3,880.9	4,432.6	4,220.5	4,100.5	3,858.6
Costs & Expenses	3,346.9	3,192.6	2,564.5	2,906.2	2,845.8	2,796.5	2,698.8
Depreciation & Amort.	264.3	317.4	321.2	412.1	361.3	300.1	278.2
Operating Income	798.6	612.5	995.2	1,114.3	1,013.4	1,003.8	881.6
Net Interest Inc./(Exp.)	d179.2	d184.2	d192.4	d179.3	d149.2	d200.7	d197.2
Income Before Income Taxes	619.4	766.4	802.8	984.6	864.2	803.1	684.4
Income Taxes	181.7	252.1	239.7	325.4	296.2	277.1	215.0
Net Income	⑤437.7	④514.3	③563.1	①659.2	①567.9	526.0	①469.4
Cash Flow	701.8	831.6	884.1	1,071.1	929.1	825.9	747.4
Average Shs. Outstg. (000)	241,484	247,616	258,602	272,006	279,657	292,517	298,234
BALANCE SHEET (IN MILLIONS):							
Cash & Cash Equivalents	318.6	233.4	213.5	256.7	129.0	138.8	136.8
Total Current Assets	2,552.6	2,556.6	2,626.7	3,342.6	2,509.0	2,463.5	2,222.1
Net Property	1,046.9	1,008.3	1,114.5	1,306.1	1,287.8	1,289.7	1,307.2
Total Assets	8,732.3	8,318.5	7,901.3	8,222.7	7,661.0	7,893.4	8,155.7
Total Current Liabilities	3,350.3	3,083.0	2,881.6	2,872.8	2,721.8	3,373.2	3,305.3
Long-Term Obligations	2,316.8	2,419.2	1,881.9	1,997.9	1,712.9	1,068.4	1,300.4
Net Stockholders' Equity	853.3	891.4	1,285.0	1,625.6	1,648.0	1,872.6	2,239.0
Net Working Capital	d797.7	d526.4	d254.9	469.8	d212.8	d909.7	d1,083.2
Year-end Shs. Outstg. (000)	235,374	242,028	248,800	264,695	270,378	279,674	295,960
STATISTICAL RECORD:							
Operating Profit Margin %	18.1	14.9	25.6	25.1	24.0	24.5	22.8
Net Profit Margin %	9.9	12.5	14.5	14.9	13.5	12.8	12.2
Return on Equity %	51.3	57.7	43.8	40.5	34.5	28.1	21.0
Return on Assets %	5.0	6.2	7.1	8.0	7.4	6.7	5.8
Debt/Total Assets %	26.5	29.1	23.8	24.3	22.4	13.5	15.9
Price Range	44.41-28.55	44.70-32.00	54.13-24.00	73.31-40.88	66.38-42.22	45.75-26.81	30.69-20.94
P/E Ratio	24.5-15.8	21.5-15.4	24.8-11.0	30.3-16.9	32.7-20.8	25.4-14.9	19.7-13.4
Average Yield %	3.2	3.0	2.9	1.8	1.7	2.2	2.7

Statistics are as originally reported. Adj. for 2-for-1 stk. split, 1/98. ① Bef. discont. opers. chg. $22.9 mil, 1999; $8.5 mil, 1998. ② Incl. $30 mil restr. chg. ③ Bef. $64.1 mil discont. oper. gain & $4.7 mil acctg. chg. ④ Bef. $26.0 mil ($0.10/sh) discont. oper. chg. & incl. $268.3 mil chg for new mailing technology, $116.1 mil restr. chg. and $338.1 mil gain fr. a lawsuit settlement. ⑤ Bef. $38.0 mil ($0.16/sh) discont. oper. gain & incl. $213.2 mil non-recur. chg.

OFFICERS:
M. J. Critelli, Chmn., C.E.O.
B. P. Nolop, Exec V.P., C.F.O.
G. E. Buoncontri, Sr. V.P., Chief Info Off.
INVESTOR CONTACT: Charles F. McBride, Exec. Dir., Invest. Rel., (203) 351-6349
PRINCIPAL OFFICE: One Elmcroft Road, Stamford, CT 06926-0700

TELEPHONE NUMBER: (203) 356-5000
FAX: (203) 351-7336
WEB: www.pb.com
NO. OF EMPLOYEES: 25,188 (avg.)
SHAREHOLDERS: 27,418
ANNUAL MEETING: In May
INCORPORATED: DE, Apr., 1920

INSTITUTIONAL HOLDINGS:
No. of Institutions: 493
Shares Held: 174,711,080
% Held: 74.3
INDUSTRY: Office machines, nec (SIC: 3579)
TRANSFER AGENT(S): EquiServe, Jersey City, NJ

POPULAR, INC.

INTERIM EARNINGS (Per Share):

Qtr.	Mar.	June	Sept.	Dec.
1999	0.45	0.46	0.46	0.47
2000	0.46	0.46	0.51	0.54
2001	0.53	0.55	0.55	0.54
2002	0.63	0.72	0.65	0.61
2003	0.74	...	...	...

INTERIM DIVIDENDS (Per Share):

Amt.	Decl.	Ex.	Rec.	Pay.
0.20Q	8/14/02	9/11/02	9/13/02	10/01/02
0.20Q	11/13/02	12/11/02	12/13/02	1/02/03
0.20Q	2/12/03	3/05/03	3/07/03	4/01/03
0.27Q	4/30/03	6/11/03	6/13/03	7/01/03

Indicated div.: $1.08 (Div. Reinv. Plan)

CAPITALIZATION (12/31/02):

	($000)	(%)
Total Deposits	17,614,740	71.6
Long-Term Debt	4,567,853	18.6
Common & Surplus	2,410,879	9.8
Total	24,593,472	100.0

TRADING VOLUME
Thousand Shares

*7 YEAR PRICE SCORE 141.7   ***12 MONTH PRICE SCORE 107.9**
*NYSE COMPOSITE INDEX=100

DIVIDEND ACHIEVER STATUS:
Rank: 64   10-Year Growth Rate: 14.87%
Total Years of Dividend Growth: 10

RECENT DEVELOPMENTS: For the three months ended 3/31/03, net income was $99.1 million versus $89.0 million in the corresponding year-earlier period. Results included a loss of $10.7 million for 2003 and a gain of $511,000 for 2002 on derivatives. Net interest income rose 8.5% to $309.8 million from $285.4 million the previous year. Provision for loan losses was $48.2 million versus $54.5 million the year before. Total non-interest income grew 1.3% to $132.2 million, due in part to an increase in other service fees of $4.7 million, mainly debit and credit card fees, insurance agency commissions and check cashing fees. Total operating expenses climbed 8.9% to $263.6 million, primarily due to an increase in personnel costs. Separately, BPOP stated that it is seeing substantial growth from its U.S. business. BPOP also indicated that it will continue to invest in efforts to build its brand and enhance the Company's electronic platform to drive further expansion in these areas.

BUSINESS

POPULAR, INC. (formerly Banponce Corporation) is a diversified, publicly-owned bank holding company incorporated under the laws of Puerto Rico. As of 3/31/03, BPOP had total assets of $33.16 billion. Banco Popular de Puerto Rico is the Company's full-service commercial bank and operates 200 branches. The bank also operates seven branches in the U.S. Virgin Islands, one branch in the British Islands and one branch in New York. The Bank has the largest retail finance franchise and the largest trust operation in Puerto Rico. BPOP has three other principal subsidiaries; Popular Securities, Inc., Popular International Bank, Inc. and GM Group, Inc. Popular Securities Incorporated is a securities broker-dealer in Puerto Rico with financial advisory, investment and security brokerage operations for institutional and retail customers. Popular International Bank, Inc. owns all of the outstanding stock of Popular North America, Inc., ATH Costa Rica, CreST and Popular Insurance V.I., Inc., an insurance agency. In addition, as of 12/31/02, BPOP had an 85.0% investment in Levitt Mortgage Corporation, a mortgage loan company with operations in Puerto Rico.

ANNUAL FINANCIAL DATA

	12/31/02	12/31/01	12/31/00	12/31/99	12/31/98	12/31/97	12/31/96
Earnings Per Share	2.61	2.17	1.97	1.84	1.65	1.50	1.34
Tang. Book Val. Per Share	16.56	14.04	11.85	9.26	9.85	8.65	7.80
Dividends Per Share	0.80	0.72	0.64	0.58	0.47	0.38	0.33
Dividend Payout %	30.7	33.2	32.5	31.5	28.5	25.3	24.6
INCOME STATEMENT (IN MILLIONS):							
Total Interest Income	2,023.8	2,095.9	2,150.2	1,851.7	1,651.7	1,491.3	1,272.9
Total Interest Expense	843.5	1,018.9	1,167.4	897.9	778.7	707.3	591.5
Net Interest Income	1,180.3	1,077.0	982.8	953.7	873.0	784.0	681.3
Provision for Loan Losses	205.6	213.3	194.6	148.9	137.2	110.6	88.8
Non-Interest Income	523.7	465.5	465.1	372.9	291.2	247.6	205.5
Non-Interest Expense	1,029.0	920.1	877.5	837.5	720.4	636.9	541.9
Income Before Taxes	469.4	409.1	375.7	340.2	306.7	284.0	256.0
Equity Earnings/Minority Int.	d0.2	...	1.2	2.5	0.3	...	...
Net Income	351.9	303.9	276.1	257.6	232.3	209.6	185.2
Average Shs. Outstg. (000)	133,915	136,238	135,907	135,586	135,532	134,036	132,044
BALANCE SHEET (IN MILLIONS):							
Cash & Due from Banks	652.6	606.1	726.1	663.7	667.7	463.2	492.4
Securities Avail. for Sale	11,042.2	9,554.6	8,857.6	7,561.6	7,339.1	5,461.3	3,708.1
Total Loans & Leases	18,775.8	17,556.0	15,580.4	14,659.4	12,783.6	11,457.7	9,854.9
Allowance for Credit Losses	659.5	663.6	637.8	663.0	616.2	557.9	516.6
Net Loans & Leases	18,116.4	16,892.4	14,942.5	13,996.4	12,167.4	10,899.8	9,338.3
Total Assets	33,660.4	30,744.7	28,057.1	25,460.5	23,160.4	19,300.5	16,764.1
Total Deposits	17,614.7	16,370.0	14,804.9	14,173.7	13,672.2	11,749.6	10,763.3
Long-Term Obligations	4,567.9	4,009.2	1,451.9	2,127.6	1,582.2	1,678.7	1,141.7
Total Liabilities	31,248.3	28,470.9	26,062.5	23,776.9	21,423.7	17,797.4	15,501.6
Net Stockholders' Equity	2,410.9	2,272.8	1,993.6	1,661.0	1,709.1	1,503.1	1,262.5
Year-end Shs. Outstg. (000)	132,439	136,362	135,999	135,586	135,532	135,366	132,178
STATISTICAL RECORD:							
Return on Equity %	14.6	13.4	13.8	15.5	13.6	13.9	14.7
Return on Assets %	1.0	1.0	1.0	1.0	1.0	1.1	1.1
Equity/Assets %	7.2	7.4	7.1	6.5	7.4	7.8	7.5
Non-Int. Exp./Tot. Inc. %	60.4	60.7	60.6	63.1	61.9	61.7	61.1
Price Range	36.10-27.39	36.60-25.25	28.75-18.13	37.88-24.94	37.50-23.00	28.50-16.44	17.50-9.63
P/E Ratio	13.8-10.5	16.9-11.6	14.6-9.2	20.6-13.6	22.7-13.9	19.0-11.0	13.1-7.2
Average Yield %	2.5	2.3	2.7	1.8	1.6	1.7	2.4

Statistics are as originally reported. Adj. for 2-for-1 stk. split, 7/1/98.

OFFICERS:
R. L. Carrion, Chmn., Pres., C.E.O.
A. L. Ferre, Vice-Chmn.

INVESTOR CONTACT: Jorge A. Junquera, Sr.
Exec. V.P., C.F.O., (787) 754-1685

PRINCIPAL OFFICE: Popular Center
Building, 209 Munoz Rivera Avenue, Hato
Rey, San Juan, PR 00918

TELEPHONE NUMBER: (787) 765-9800
FAX: (787) 759-7803
WEB: www.popularinc.com
NO. OF EMPLOYEES: 10,959
SHAREHOLDERS: 11,117 (record)
ANNUAL MEETING: In Apr.
INCORPORATED: PRI, 1893; reincorp., PRI,
Nov., 1984

INSTITUTIONAL HOLDINGS:
No. of Institutions: 117
Shares Held: 29,888,374
% Held: 22.5

INDUSTRY: State commercial banks (SIC: 6022)

TRANSFER AGENT(S): Banco Popular de
Puerto Rico, San Juan, PR

PPG INDUSTRIES, INC.

YIELD 3.5%
P/E RATIO ...

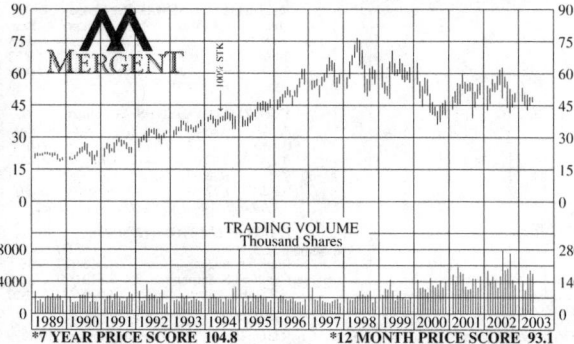

*7 YEAR PRICE SCORE 104.8   *12 MONTH PRICE SCORE 93.1
*NYSE COMPOSITE INDEX=100

INTERIM EARNINGS (Per Share):

Qtr.	Mar.	June	Sept.	Dec.
2001	0.33	0.92	0.55	0.49
2002	0.25	d2.03	0.87	0.55
2003	0.49	...	...	...

INTERIM DIVIDENDS (Per Share):

Amt.	Decl.	Ex.	Rec.	Pay.
0.43Q	7/18/02	8/08/02	8/12/02	9/12/02
0.43Q	10/17/02	11/07/02	11/12/02	12/12/02
0.43Q	1/16/03	2/13/03	2/18/03	3/12/03
0.43Q	4/17/03	5/08/03	5/12/03	6/12/03

Indicated div.: $1.72 (Div. Reinv. Plan)

CAPITALIZATION (12/31/02):

	($000)	(%)
Long-Term Debt	1,699,000	43.4
Deferred Income Tax	64,000	1.6
Common & Surplus	2,150,000	54.9
Total	3,913,000	100.0

DIVIDEND ACHIEVER STATUS:
Rank: 215   10-Year Growth Rate: 6.10%
Total Years of Dividend Growth: 31

RECENT DEVELOPMENTS: For the quarter ended 3/31/03, income was $84.0 million, before an accounting change charge of $6.0 million, versus income of $43.0 million, before an accounting change charge of $9.0 million, in 2002. Earnings benefited from strong commodity chemical prices, significant growth from new products in the Company's optical business and modest volume gains in most of PPG's coatings businesses. Net sales climbed 10.5% to $2.07 billion.

PROSPECTS: Going forward, the Company will continue its research and development efforts. In addition, PPG will focus on initiatives to generate cash and lower debt, while capitalizing on opportunities to enhance growth. Separately, on 4/9/03, PPG Architectural Finishes, a subsidiary of PPG, introduced Coraflon™ Air-Dried System coatings, a new line of colorful fluoropolymer coatings that are designed for structurally sound surfaces.

BUSINESS

PPG INDUSTRIES, INC. is a supplier of products for manufacturing, construction, automotive, chemical processing and numerous other world industries. The diversified global manufacturer makes protective and decorative coatings, flat glass, fabricated glass products, continuous-strand fiberglass, and industrial and specialty chemicals. PPG operates 170 manufacturing facilities in countries including Canada, China, England, France, Germany, Ireland, Italy, Mexico, the Netherlands, Portugal, Spain, Taiwan, and the U.S. In 2002, revenues (and operating income) were derived: coatings, 55.6% (69.4%); glass, 25.7% (16.4%); and chemicals, 18.8% (14.2%).

ANNUAL FINANCIAL DATA

	12/31/02	12/31/01	12/31/00	12/31/99	12/31/98	12/31/97	12/31/96
Earnings Per Share	[7] d0.36	[6] 2.29	[4] 3.57	[3] 3.23	[2] 4.48	[1] 3.94	3.96
Cash Flow Per Share	1.99	4.96	6.19	5.62	6.63	5.99	5.89
Tang. Book Val. Per Share	3.48	9.12	8.61	8.30	13.17	21.29	13.55
Dividends Per Share	1.70	1.68	1.60	1.52	1.42	1.33	1.26
Dividend Payout %	...	73.4	44.8	47.1	31.7	33.8	31.8

INCOME STATEMENT (IN MILLIONS):

Total Revenues	8,067.0	8,169.0	[5] 8,629.0	7,757.0	7,510.0	7,379.0	7,218.1
Costs & Expenses	7,697.0	6,726.0	6,907.0	6,418.0	5,851.0	5,690.0	5,561.3
Depreciation & Amort.	398.0	447.0	447.0	419.0	383.0	373.0	362.6
Operating Income	d28.0	996.0	1,275.0	1,158.0	1,276.0	1,316.0	1,294.2
Net Interest Inc./(Exp.)	d28.0	d241.0	d250.0	d182.0	d137.0	d105.0	d85.0
Income Before Income Taxes	cr7.0	666.0	1,017.0	973.0	1,294.0	1,175.0	1,239.6
Income Taxes	d39.0	247.0	369.0	377.0	466.0	435.0	471.0
Net Income	[7] d60.0	[6] 387.0	[4] 620.0	[3] 568.0	[2] 801.0	[1] 714.0	744.0
Cash Flow	338.0	834.0	1,067.0	987.0	1,184.0	1,087.0	1,106.6
Average Shs. Outstg. (000)	169,900	168,300	172,300	175,500	178,700	181,500	187,800

BALANCE SHEET (IN MILLIONS):

Cash & Cash Equivalents	117.0	108.0	111.0	158.0	128.0	129.0	69.6
Total Current Assets	2,945.0	2,703.0	3,093.0	3,062.0	2,660.0	2,584.0	2,296.4
Net Property	2,632.0	2,752.0	2,941.0	2,933.0	2,905.0	2,855.0	2,913.5
Total Assets	7,863.0	8,452.0	9,125.0	8,914.0	7,387.0	6,868.0	6,441.4
Total Current Liabilities	1,920.0	1,955.0	2,543.0	2,384.0	1,912.0	1,662.0	1,768.9
Long-Term Obligations	1,699.0	1,699.0	1,810.0	1,836.0	1,081.0	1,257.0	833.9
Net Stockholders' Equity	2,150.0	3,080.0	3,097.0	3,106.0	2,880.0	2,509.0	2,482.6
Net Working Capital	1,025.0	748.0	550.0	678.0	748.0	922.0	527.5
Year-end Shs. Outstg. (000)	169,442	168,713	168,222	173,988	175,000	117,826	183,215

STATISTICAL RECORD:

Operating Profit Margin %	...	12.2	14.8	14.9	17.0	17.8	17.9
Net Profit Margin %	...	4.7	7.2	7.3	10.7	9.7	10.3
Return on Equity %	...	12.6	20.0	18.3	27.8	28.5	30.0
Return on Assets %	...	4.6	6.8	6.4	10.8	10.4	11.6
Debt/Total Assets %	21.6	20.4	19.8	20.6	14.6	18.3	12.9
Price Range	62.86-41.39	59.75-38.99	65.06-36.00	70.75-47.94	76.63-49.13	67.50-48.63	62.25-42.88
P/E Ratio	...	26.1-17.0	18.2-10.1	21.9-14.8	17.1-11.0	17.1-12.3	15.7-10.8
Average Yield %	3.3	3.4	3.2	2.6	2.3	2.3	2.4

Statistics are as originally reported. [1] Incl $102 mil nonrecur. p-tx chg & $59 mil p-tx gain dvst chem bus. [2] Incl $85.0 mill. p-tax gain fr. sale of bus. & $27.0 mill. p-tax restr. chg. and oth. chgs. [3] Incl $110.0 mill. in p-tax chgs. [4] Incl $5.0 mill. one-time chg. fr. bus. divest & realign. [5] Bef outgoing freight costs. Prior years' revs are net of these costs. [6] Incl $103.0 mil bus. align. [7] Incl $755.0 mil asbestos settlmt, $77.0 mil bus align. & excl $9.0 mil acctg chg.

OFFICERS:
R. W. LeBoeuf, Chmn., C.E.O.
C. E. Bunch, Pres., C.O.O.

INVESTOR CONTACT: Douglas B. Atkinson, Investor Relations, (412) 434-2120

PRINCIPAL OFFICE: One PPG Place, Pittsburgh, PA 15272

TELEPHONE NUMBER: (412) 434-3131
FAX: (412) 434-2571
WEB: www.ppg.com
NO. OF EMPLOYEES: 34,100 (avg.)
SHAREHOLDERS: 28,704
ANNUAL MEETING: In Apr.
INCORPORATED: PA, Nov., 1883; reincorp., PA, Nov., 1920

INSTITUTIONAL HOLDINGS:
No. of Institutions: 418
Shares Held: 95,976,760
% Held: 56.5
INDUSTRY: Paints and allied products (SIC: 2851)
TRANSFER AGENT(S): Mellon Investor Services LLC, Ridgefield Park, NJ

PRAXAIR, INC.

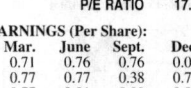
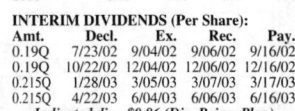

YIELD 1.4%
P/E RATIO 17.9

INTERIM EARNINGS (Per Share):

Qtr.	Mar.	June	Sept.	Dec.
2000	0.71	0.76	0.76	0.03
2001	0.77	0.77	0.38	0.72
2002	0.77	0.91	0.80	0.85
2003	0.79	…	…	…

INTERIM DIVIDENDS (Per Share):

Amt.	Decl.	Ex.	Rec.	Pay.
0.19Q	7/23/02	9/04/02	9/06/02	9/16/02
0.19Q	10/22/02	12/04/02	12/06/02	12/16/02
0.215Q	1/28/03	3/05/03	3/07/03	3/17/03
0.215Q	4/22/03	6/04/03	6/06/03	6/16/03
Indicated div.: $0.86 (Div. Reinv. Plan)				

TRADING VOLUME
Thousand Shares

CAPITALIZATION (12/31/02):

	($000)	(%)
Long-Term Debt	2,510,000	51.8
Common & Surplus	2,340,000	48.2
Total	4,850,000	100.0

*7 YEAR PRICE SCORE 133.1   ***12 MONTH PRICE SCORE 104.4**
*NYSE COMPOSITE INDEX=100

DIVIDEND ACHIEVER STATUS:
Rank: 28   10-Year Growth Rate: 19.78%
Total Years of Dividend Growth: 10

RECENT DEVELOPMENTS: For the quarter ended 3/31/03, net income climbed 2.4% to $130.0 million compared with income of $127.0 million, before an accounting change charge of $139.0 million, in the same period of 2002. Sales grew 8.5% to $1.34 billion from $1.23 billion in the prior-year period, primarily due to growth in refinery hydrogen and healthcare in North America. Sales in Europe benefited from a stronger Euro and price and volume gains.

PROSPECTS: PX expects sales growth for the second quarter of 2003 to be up 5.0% from the same period of 2002, and diluted earnings per share in the range of $0.84 to $0.89. Looking ahead, the Company expects the remainder of 2003 to benefit from the stabilization of energy markets and improvements in U.S. operating margins. As a result, the Company expects earnings per share for full-year 2003 to be in the range of $3.40 to $3.60.

BUSINESS

PRAXAIR, INC. is one of the largest suppliers of industrial gases worldwide, particularly in North and South America. PX serves industries through the production, sale and distribution of industrial gases and high-performance surface coatings, along with related services, materials and systems. Praxair's primary products are atmospheric gases (oxygen, nitrogen, argon, and rare gases) and process gases (carbon dioxide, helium, hydrogen, electronics gases, and acetylene). PX also designs, engineers, and supervises construction of cryogenic and non-cryogenic supply systems. PX's surface technology applies metallic and ceramic coatings and powders to metal surfaces in order to resist wear, high temperatures, and corrosion. Sales in North America accounted for 65.3% of revenues in 2002.

ANNUAL FINANCIAL DATA

	12/31/02	12/31/01	12/31/00	12/31/99	12/31/98	12/31/97	12/31/96
Earnings Per Share	⑥ 3.33	⑥ 2.64	⑤ 2.25	④ 2.72	③ 2.60	② 2.53	① 1.77
Cash Flow Per Share	6.26	5.69	5.18	5.46	5.46	5.24	4.41
Tang. Book Val. Per Share	8.04	15.28	14.79	14.40	14.80	13.48	5.56
Dividends Per Share	0.76	0.68	0.62	0.56	0.50	0.44	0.38
Dividend Payout %	22.8	25.8	27.6	20.6	19.2	17.4	21.5
INCOME STATEMENT (IN MILLIONS):							
Total Revenues	5,128.0	5,124.0	5,043.0	4,639.0	4,833.0	4,735.0	4,449.0
Costs & Expenses	3,770.0	3,825.0	3,823.0	3,440.0	3,552.0	3,515.0	3,409.0
Depreciation & Amort.	483.0	499.0	471.0	445.0	467.0	444.0	420.0
Operating Income	923.0	800.0	707.0	831.0	856.0	838.0	647.0
Net Interest Inc./(Exp.)	d206.0	d224.0	d224.0	d204.0	d260.0	d216.0	d195.0
Income Before Income Taxes	717.0	576.0	483.0	627.0	596.0	622.0	452.0
Income Taxes	158.0	135.0	103.0	152.0	127.0	151.0	110.0
Equity Earnings/Minority Int.	d11.0	d9.0	d17.0	d34.0	d44.0	d55.0	d60.0
Net Income	⑥ 548.0	⑥ 432.0	⑤ 363.0	④ 441.0	③ 425.0	② 416.0	① 282.0
Cash Flow	1,031.0	931.0	834.0	886.0	892.0	860.0	702.0
Average Shs. Outstg. (000)	164,745	163,507	161,092	162,222	163,356	164,053	159,038
BALANCE SHEET (IN MILLIONS):							
Cash & Cash Equivalents	39.0	39.0	31.0	76.0	34.0	43.0	63.0
Total Current Assets	1,286.0	1,276.0	1,361.0	1,335.0	1,394.0	1,497.0	1,666.0
Net Property	4,666.0	4,817.0	4,771.0	4,720.0	4,875.0	4,607.0	4,269.0
Total Assets	7,401.0	7,715.0	7,762.0	7,722.0	8,096.0	7,810.0	7,161.4
Total Current Liabilities	1,100.0	1,194.0	1,439.0	1,725.0	1,289.0	1,366.0	2,550.0
Long-Term Obligations	2,510.0	2,725.0	2,641.0	2,111.0	2,895.0	2,874.0	1,703.0
Net Stockholders' Equity	2,340.0	2,477.0	2,357.0	2,290.0	2,332.0	2,122.0	1,924.0
Net Working Capital	186.0	82.0	d78.0	d390.0	105.0	131.0	d884.0
Year-end Shs. Outstg. (000)	162,268	162,143	159,379	159,048	157,571	157,333	157,749
STATISTICAL RECORD:							
Operating Profit Margin %	18.0	15.6	14.0	17.9	17.7	17.7	14.5
Net Profit Margin %	10.7	8.4	7.2	9.5	8.8	8.8	6.3
Return on Equity %	23.4	17.4	15.4	19.3	18.2	19.6	13.8
Return on Assets %	7.4	5.6	4.7	5.7	5.2	5.3	3.9
Debt/Total Assets %	33.9	35.3	34.0	27.3	35.8	36.8	22.6
Price Range	61.11-44.55	55.92-36.50	54.94-30.31	58.13-32.00	53.88-30.69	58.00-39.25	50.13-31.50
P/E Ratio	18.4-13.4	21.2-13.8	24.4-13.5	21.4-11.8	20.7-11.8	22.9-15.5	28.3-17.8
Average Yield %	1.4	1.5	1.5	1.2	1.2	0.9	0.9

Statistics are as originally reported. ① Incl. $53.0 mill. integra. chg. ② Incl. $10.0 mill. pre-tax restr. chg. & $11.0 mill. pre-tax profit fr. settlemnt. ③ Incl. $8.0 mill. acq.-rel. chg. for exps. & $29.0 mill. spl chgs. for impair. loss & prov. loss fr. sale of plant equip. ④ Incl. $14.0 mill. after-tax non-recur. gain & excl. d$10.0 mill. acct. chg. ⑤ Incl. $117.0 mill. after-tax chg. for reposit. prog., $44.0 mill. chg. for consol. costs, & $67.0 mill. write-off of assets. ⑥ Excl. $139.0 mill. acctg. change chg., 2002; $2.0 mill., 2001.

OFFICERS:
D. H. Reilley, Chmn., Pres., C.E.O.
J. S. Sawyer, V.P.,C.F.O.
INVESTOR CONTACT: Elizabeth T. Hirsch, Director, Inv. Rel., (203) 837-2354
PRINCIPAL OFFICE: 39 Old Ridgebury Rd., Danbury, CT 06810-5113

TELEPHONE NUMBER: (203) 837-2000
FAX: (203) 837-2450
WEB: www.praxair.com
NO. OF EMPLOYEES: 25,010 (avg.)
SHAREHOLDERS: 24,770
ANNUAL MEETING: In Apr.
INCORPORATED: DE, Oct., 1988

PROCTER & GAMBLE COMPANY (THE)

YIELD 1.8%
P/E RATIO 25.2

TRADING VOLUME
Thousand Shares

| 1989 | 1990 | 1991 | 1992 | 1993 | 1994 | 1995 | 1996 | 1997 | 1998 | 1999 | 2000 | 2001 | 2002 | 2003 |

*7 YEAR PRICE SCORE 128.8   ***12 MONTH PRICE SCORE 101.5**

*NYSE COMPOSITE INDEX=100

INTERIM EARNINGS (Per Share):

Qtr.	Sept.	Dec.	Mar.	June
1998-99	0.80	0.78	0.72	0.29
1999-00	0.80	0.78	0.52	0.55
2000-01	0.82	0.84	0.63	d0.23
2001-02	0.79	0.93	0.74	0.64
2002-03	1.04	1.06	0.91	…

INTERIM DIVIDENDS (Per Share):

Amt.	Decl.	Ex.	Rec.	Pay.
0.41Q	7/09/02	7/17/02	7/19/02	8/15/02
0.41Q	10/08/02	10/16/02	10/18/02	11/15/02
0.41Q	1/14/03	1/22/03	1/24/03	2/14/03
0.41Q	4/07/03	4/15/03	4/17/03	5/15/03

Indicated div.: $1.64 (Div. Reinv. Plan)

CAPITALIZATION (6/30/02):

	($000)	(%)
Long-Term Debt	11,201,000	43.1
Deferred Income Tax	1,077,000	4.1
Preferred Stock	1,634,000	6.3
Common & Surplus	12,072,000	46.5
Total	25,984,000	100.0

DIVIDEND ACHIEVER STATUS:

Rank: 119   10-Year Growth Rate: 11.39%
Total Years of Dividend Growth: 49

RECENT DEVELOPMENTS: For the quarter ended 3/31/03, net income climbed 22.5% to $1.27 billion from $1.04 billion in the equivalent prior-year quarter. Results for 2003 and 2002 included after-tax restructuring charges of $66.0 million and $147.0 million, respectively. Net sales advanced 7.6% to $10.66 billion from $9.90 billion the previous year, boosted by double-digit growth in the health-care business and stronger results in Asia and Central and Eastern Europe.

PROSPECTS: On 3/18/03, PG announced that it signed an agreement to purchase a controlling interest from the majority shareholders of Wella AG, a German-based beauty care company. The cash purchase will give PG 77.6% of Wella's voting shares. Also, PG announced that it intends to make a tender offer for the remaining voting and preference shares of Wella. In addition to the tender offer, PG will assume net debt of about $1.10 billion, bringing the acquisition value to about $6.60 billion.

BUSINESS

THE PROCTER & GAMBLE COMPANY manufactures and markets nearly 300 brands of consumer products including laundry, cleaning and personal-care products, pharmaceuticals, foods and beverages, and business and industrial products. Leading brands are: DOWNY and TIDE cleansing compounds, BOUNTY paper towels, CREST toothpastes, ALWAYS sanitary napkins, HEAD AND SHOULDERS and PANTENE PROV shampoos. Other products include VICK'S cough and cold remedies, WHISPER sanitary pads, LENOR fabric conditioner, CHARMIN toilet tissue, PAMPERS diapers, OIL OF OLAY skin products, FOLGER'S coffee, PRINGLES potato chips, ACTONEL, a post-menopausal drug, and IAMS pet food, and CLAIROL NICE 'N EASY hair coloring products. As of 4/28/03, PG had operations in over 80 countries and marketed to consumers in more than 160 countries. On 11/15/01, PG acquired the Clairol hair care business for $4.95 billion.

ANNUAL FINANCIAL DATA

	6/30/02	6/30/01	6/30/00	6/30/99	6/30/98	6/30/97	6/30/96
Earnings Per Share	☐ 3.09	☐ 2.07	☐ 2.47	☐ 2.59	2.56	2.43	2.15
Cash Flow Per Share	4.21	3.61	3.94	4.01	3.60	3.60	3.21
Tang. Book Val. Per Share	…	1.55	1.35	2.62	2.55	4.59	4.05
Dividends Per Share	1.58	1.46	1.34	1.21	1.07	0.95	0.85
Dividend Payout %	51.1	70.5	54.2	46.7	42.0	39.3	39.6

INCOME STATEMENT (IN MILLIONS):

Total Revenues	40,238.0	39,244.0	39,951.0	38,125.0	37,154.0	35,764.0	35,284.0
Costs & Expenses	31,867.0	32,237.0	31,806.0	29,724.0	29,501.0	28,789.0	29,111.0
Depreciation & Amort.	1,693.0	2,271.0	2,191.0	2,148.0	1,598.0	1,487.0	1,358.0
Operating Income	6,678.0	4,736.0	5,954.0	6,253.0	6,055.0	5,488.0	4,815.0
Net Interest Inc./(Exp.)	d603.0	d794.0	d722.0	d650.0	d548.0	d457.0	d484.0
Income Before Income Taxes	6,383.0	4,616.0	5,536.0	5,838.0	5,708.0	5,249.0	4,669.0
Income Taxes	2,031.0	1,694.0	1,994.0	2,075.0	1,928.0	1,834.0	1,623.0
Net Income	☐ 4,352.0	☐ 2,922.0	☐ 3,542.0	☐ 3,763.0	3,780.0	3,415.0	3,046.0
Cash Flow	5,921.0	5,072.0	5,618.0	5,802.0	5,274.0	4,798.0	4,301.0
Average Shs. Outstg. (000)	1,404,900	1,405,600	1,427,200	1,446,800	1,465,500	1,360,000	1,372,000

BALANCE SHEET (IN MILLIONS):

Cash & Cash Equivalents	3,623.0	2,518.0	1,600.0	2,800.0	2,406.0	3,110.0	2,520.0
Total Current Assets	12,166.0	10,889.0	10,069.0	11,358.0	10,577.0	10,786.0	10,807.0
Net Property	13,349.0	13,095.0	13,692.0	12,626.0	12,180.0	11,376.0	11,118.0
Total Assets	40,776.0	34,387.0	34,194.0	32,113.0	30,966.0	27,544.0	27,730.0
Total Current Liabilities	12,704.0	9,846.0	10,065.0	10,761.0	9,250.0	7,798.0	7,825.0
Long-Term Obligations	11,201.0	9,792.0	8,916.0	6,231.0	5,765.0	4,143.0	4,670.0
Net Stockholders' Equity	13,706.0	12,010.0	12,287.0	12,058.0	12,236.0	12,046.0	11,722.0
Net Working Capital	d538.0	1,043.0	4.0	597.0	1,327.0	2,988.0	2,982.0
Year-end Shs. Outstg. (000)	1,300,800	1,295,700	1,305,900	1,319,800	1,337,400	1,360,000	1,372,000

STATISTICAL RECORD:

Operating Profit Margin %	16.6	12.1	14.9	16.4	16.3	15.3	13.6
Net Profit Margin %	10.8	7.4	8.9	9.9	10.2	9.5	8.6
Return on Equity %	31.8	24.3	28.8	31.2	30.9	28.3	26.0
Return on Assets %	10.7	8.5	10.4	11.7	12.2	12.4	11.0
Debt/Total Assets %	27.5	28.5	26.1	19.4	18.6	15.0	16.8
Price Range	94.75-74.08	81.72-55.96	118.38-52.75	115.63-82.00	94.81-65.13	83.44-51.81	55.50-39.69
P/E Ratio	30.7-24.0	39.5-27.0	47.9-21.4	44.6-31.7	37.0-25.4	34.3-21.3	25.9-18.5
Average Yield %	1.9	2.1	1.6	1.2	1.3	1.4	1.8

Statistics are as originally reported. Adj. for stk. splits: 2-for-1, 9/97. ☐ Incl. after-tax chrg. for organization 2005, $706.0 mill., 6/02; $1.48 billion, 6/01; $688.0 mill., 6/00; $385.0 mill., 6/99.

OFFICERS:
A. G. Lafley, Chmn., Pres., C.E.O.
B. Byrnes, Vice-Chmn.
R. K. Clark, Vice-Chmn.

INVESTOR CONTACT: Shareholder Services, (513) 983-3034

PRINCIPAL OFFICE: One Procter & Gamble Plaza, Cincinnati, OH 45202

TELEPHONE NUMBER: (513) 983-1100
FAX: (513) 983-2062
WEB: www.pg.com

NO. OF EMPLOYEES: 102,000 (approx.)

SHAREHOLDERS: 1,004,000 (approx.)

ANNUAL MEETING: In Oct.

INCORPORATED: OH, May, 1905

INSTITUTIONAL HOLDINGS:
No. of Institutions: 1,086
Shares Held: 712,192,149
% Held: 55.1

INDUSTRY: Soap and other detergents (SIC: 2841)

TRANSFER AGENT(S): The Procter and Gamble Company, Cincinnati, OH

PROGRESS ENERGY, INC.

YIELD 4.8%
P/E RATIO 16.9

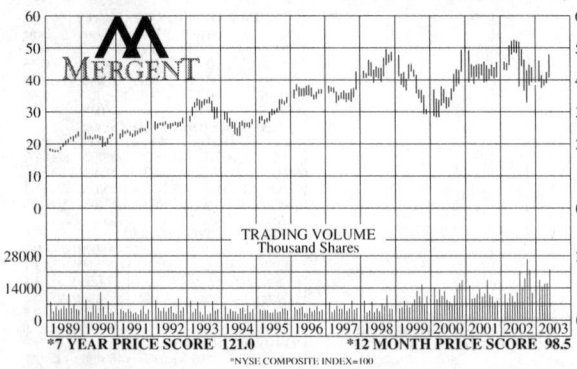

*7 YEAR PRICE SCORE 121.0 ***12 MONTH PRICE SCORE 98.5**

NYSE COMPOSITE INDEX=100

INTERIM EARNINGS (Per Share):

Qtr.	Mar.	June	Sept.	Dec.
2000	0.56	0.70	1.93	d0.07
2001	0.77	0.56	1.77	d0.42
2002	0.58	0.56	0.72	0.66
2003	0.84	...	...	...

INTERIM DIVIDENDS (Per Share):

Amt.	Decl.	Ex.	Rec.	Pay.
0.545Q	5/08/02	7/08/02	7/10/02	8/01/02
0.545Q	9/20/02	10/08/02	10/10/02	11/01/02
0.56Q	12/11/02	1/08/03	1/10/03	2/01/03
0.56Q	3/19/03	4/08/03	4/10/03	5/01/03
0.56Q	5/14/03	7/08/03	7/10/03	8/01/03

Indicated div.: $2.24 (Div. Reinv. Plan)

CAPITALIZATION (12/31/02):

	($000)	(%)
Long-Term Debt	9,747,293	55.9
Deferred Income Tax	932,813	5.3
Preferred Stock	92,831	0.5
Common & Surplus	6,677,009	38.3
Total	17,449,946	100.0

DIVIDEND ACHIEVER STATUS:

Rank: 265   10-Year Growth Rate: 3.27%
Total Years of Dividend Growth: 14

RECENT DEVELOPMENTS: For the quarter ended 3/31/01, income from continuing operations jumped 58.7% to $196.9 million from $124.1 million in the prior-year quarter. Earnings for 2003 and 2002 excluded income from discontinued operations of $11.3 million and $8.5 million, respectively. Results for 2003 benefited from favorable weather, customer growth, higher sales to other utilities and lower interest expense. Total operating revenues advanced 12.8% to $2.02 billion from $1.79 billion a year earlier.

PROSPECTS: On 3/21/03, PGN announced that Progress Ventures had agreed with Williams Energy Marketing and Trading to acquire a full-requirements power supply agreement from Jackson Electric Membership Corporation in Georgia for $188.0 million. The transaction will result in contractual coverage for a majority of Progress Ventures' power generation assets in Georgia. Separately, PGN expects full-year 2003 earnings to range from $3.60 to $3.80 per share.

BUSINESS

PROGRESS ENERGY, INC. (formerly CP&L Energy, Inc.) is a full-service utility holding company with more than 21,900 megawatts of generating capacity as of 4/23/03. PGN's utility segment (83.1% of 2002 revenues) includes two major electric utilities, Progress Energy Carolinas, Inc. and Progress Energy Florida, Inc. At 4/23/03, PGN's electric utilities served more than 2.8 million customers in North Carolina, South Carolina and Florida. PGN's diversified businesses (16.9%) include Progress Telecommunications Corporation, Progress Rail Services Corporation and Progress Ventures, Inc. Progress Ventures manages fuel extraction, manufacturing and delivery; merchant generation; and energy marketing and trading. On 11/30/00, the Company acquired Progress Energy Florida for about $5.40 billion.

ANNUAL FINANCIAL DATA

	12/31/02	12/31/01	12/31/00	12/31/99	12/31/98	12/31/97	12/31/96
Earnings Per Share	④ 2.53	③ 2.64	② 3.03	① 2.55	2.75	2.66	2.66
Cash Flow Per Share	7.57	8.46	8.36	10.44	10.74	10.32	9.35
Tang. Book Val. Per Share	12.43	10.58	8.60	19.57	19.49	18.63	17.77
Dividends Per Share	2.18	2.12	2.06	2.00	1.94	1.88	1.82
Dividend Payout %	86.2	80.3	68.0	78.4	70.5	70.7	68.4

INCOME STATEMENT (IN MILLIONS):

Total Revenues	7,945.1	8,461.5	4,118.9	3,357.6	3,130.0	3,024.1	2,995.7
Costs & Expenses	5,841.5	6,028.5	2,564.4	1,928.9	1,654.2	1,663.2	1,765.4
Depreciation & Amort.	1,099.1	1,189.2	835.0	588.1	578.3	565.2	446.5
Operating Income	1,004.5	1,243.8	719.6	840.5	897.5	795.6	783.9
Net Interest Inc./(Exp.)	d618.9	d662.6	d235.3	d169.1	d164.7	d139.6	d167.5
Income Taxes	cr157.8	cr151.6	202.8	258.4	257.5	253.0	269.8
Net Income	④ 552.2	③ 541.6	② 478.4	① 382.3	399.2	388.3	391.3
Cash Flow	1,651.3	1,730.8	1,313.3	967.4	974.6	947.5	828.2
Average Shs. Outstg. (000)	218,166	204,683	157,169	148,344	143,941	143,645	143,621

BALANCE SHEET (IN MILLIONS):

Gross Property	21,137.1	21,011.3	19,786.9	11,740.2	10,796.2	10,474.6	10,196.5
Accumulated Depreciation	10,480.9	10,096.4	9,350.2	4,975.4	4,496.6	4,181.4	3,796.6
Net Property	10,656.2	10,914.9	10,436.7	6,764.8	6,299.5	6,293.2	6,399.9
Total Assets	21,352.7	20,739.8	20,091.0	9,494.0	8,347.4	8,220.7	8,369.2
Long-Term Obligations	9,747.3	9,483.7	5,890.1	3,028.6	2,614.4	2,415.7	2,525.6
Net Stockholders' Equity	6,769.8	6,096.4	5,517.0	3,472.0	3,008.7	2,878.2	2,834.3
Year-end Shs. Outstg. (000)	237,993	218,725	206,089	159,600	151,338	151,340	151,416

STATISTICAL RECORD:

Operating Profit Margin %	12.6	14.7	17.5	25.0	28.7	26.3	26.2
Net Profit Margin %	6.9	6.4	11.6	11.4	12.8	12.8	13.1
Net Inc./Net Property %	5.2	5.0	4.6	5.7	6.3	6.2	6.1
Net Inc./Tot. Capital %	3.2	3.2	3.6	8.1	5.5	5.5	5.4
Return on Equity %	8.2	8.8	8.7	9.1	13.3	13.5	13.8
Accum. Depr./Gross Prop. %	49.6	48.1	47.3	42.4	41.7	39.9	37.2
Price Range	52.60-32.84	49.25-38.78	49.38-28.25	47.88-29.25	49.63-39.19	42.69-32.75	38.75-33.75
P/E Ratio	20.8-13.0	18.7-14.7	16.3-9.3	18.8-11.5	18.0-14.2	16.0-12.3	14.6-12.7
Average Yield %	5.1	4.8	4.7	5.3	5.2	4.4	5.0

Statistics are as originally reported. ① Incl. one-time chrg. of $29.0 mill. related to storm damage. ② Incl. after-tax nonrecurr. chrg. of $118.3 mill. & an after-tax gain of $121.1 mill. fr. sale of an investment. ③ Incl. non-recurr. impairment chrg. of $209.0 mill. ④ Incl. asset impair. chrg. of $363.8 mill. & invest. impair. chrg. of $25.0 mill.; bef. a loss of $23.8 mill. from disc. ops.

OFFICERS:
W. Cavanaugh III, Chmn., C.E.O.
R. B. McGehee, Pres., C.O.O.
P. M. Scott III, Exec. V.P., C.F.O.

INVESTOR CONTACT: Robert F. Drennan Jr., Mgr., Investor Relations, (919) 546-7474

PRINCIPAL OFFICE: 410 South Wilmington Street, Raleigh, NC 27601-1748

TELEPHONE NUMBER: (919) 546-6111
FAX: (919) 549-7678
WEB: www.progress-energy.com
NO. OF EMPLOYEES: 15,300 (approx.)
SHAREHOLDERS: 72,380
ANNUAL MEETING: In May
INCORPORATED: NC, April, 1926

INSTITUTIONAL HOLDINGS:
No. of Institutions: 391
Shares Held: 131,990,890
% Held: 55.0

INDUSTRY: Electric services (SIC: 4911)

TRANSFER AGENT(S): EquiServe Trust Company, N.A., Providence, RI

PROGRESSIVE CORPORATION (THE)

YIELD 0.1%
P/E RATIO 20.5

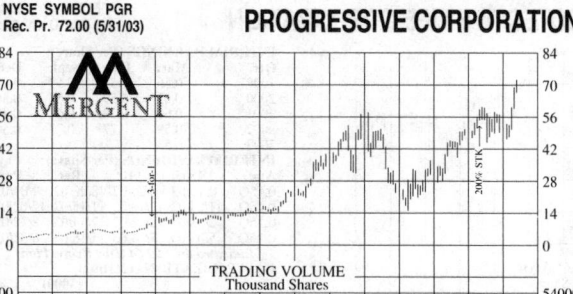

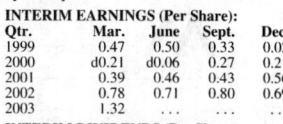

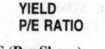

TRADING VOLUME
Thousand Shares

*7 YEAR PRICE SCORE 164.4   ***12 MONTH PRICE SCORE 119.4**
*NYSE COMPOSITE INDEX=100

INTERIM EARNINGS (Per Share):

Qtr.	Mar.	June	Sept.	Dec.
1999	0.47	0.50	0.33	0.02
2000	d0.21	d0.06	0.27	0.21
2001	0.39	0.46	0.43	0.56
2002	0.78	0.71	0.80	0.69
2003	1.32	...	...	...

INTERIM DIVIDENDS (Per Share):

Amt.	Decl.	Ex.	Rec.	Pay.
0.025Q	8/23/02	9/11/02	9/13/02	9/30/02
0.025Q	10/18/02	12/11/02	12/13/02	12/31/02
0.025Q	1/31/03	3/12/03	3/14/03	3/31/03
0.025Q	4/18/03	6/11/03	6/13/03	6/30/03

Indicated div.: $0.10

CAPITALIZATION (12/31/02):

	($000)	(%)
Long-Term Debt	1,489,000	28.3
Common & Surplus	3,768,000	71.7
Total	5,257,000	100.0

DIVIDEND ACHIEVER STATUS:

Rank: 248   10-Year Growth Rate: 4.31%
Total Years of Dividend Growth: 33

RECENT DEVELOPMENTS: For the quarter ended 3/31/03, net income advanced 65.4% to $291.5 million from $176.2 million in the comparable 2002 quarter. Total revenues climbed 31.5% to $2.72 billion from $2.07 billion the previous year. Revenues for 2003 and 2002 included net realized security losses of $3.1 million and $14.8 million, respectively. Net premiums written grew 31.7% to $2.88 billion, while premiums earned increased 32.1% to $2.60 billion. PGR's combined ratio improved to 85.5% from 89.3% the year before.

PROSPECTS: The Company anticipates solid growth for the full-year 2003 based on its strong first quarter results. Premium growth was widespread during the first quarter of 2003, with most states experiencing over 20.0% growth. Moreover, policies in force for the combined personal lines and commercial auto businesses increased 24.0% over the prior year. Meanwhile, PGR continued to report favorable loss ratios. However, PGR does not believe that this decreasing frequency trend is sustainable and expects a return to more historic levels.

BUSINESS

THE PROGRESSIVE CORPORA-TION, through its subsidiaries and affiliates, provides personal automobile insurance and other specialty property-casualty insurance and related services throughout the United States. PGR's personal lines business units write insurance for private passenger automobiles and recreation vehicles. PGR's commercial auto business unit writes insurance for automobiles and trucks owned by small businesses for primary liability, physical damage and other auto-related insurance coverages. PGR's other businesses primarily include writing lenders' collateral protection and directors' and officers' liability insurance and providing insurance-related services, primarily processing business for Commercial Auto Insurance Procedures, which are state supervised plans serving the involuntary market. The Company ranks fourth in the nation for auto insurance based on premiums written, offering its products by phone, on-line and through more than 30,000 independent insurance agencies.

ANNUAL FINANCIAL DATA

	12/31/02	12/31/01	12/31/00	12/31/99	12/31/98	12/31/97	12/31/96
Earnings Per Share	2.99	1.83	①0.21	1.32	2.04	1.77	1.38
Tang. Book Val. Per Share	15.62	13.32	11.61	10.99	10.38	8.65	6.88
Dividends Per Share	0.097	0.093	0.090	0.087	0.083	0.080	0.077
Dividend Payout %	3.2	5.1	43.5	6.6	4.1	4.5	5.6
INCOME STATEMENT (IN MILLIONS):							
Total Premium Income	8,883.5	7,161.8	6,348.4	5,683.6	4,948.0	4,189.5	3,199.3
Other Income	410.9	326.4	422.6	440.6	344.4	418.7	279.1
Total Revenues	9,294.4	7,488.2	6,771.0	6,124.2	5,292.4	4,608.2	3,478.4
Policyholder Benefits	6,299.1	5,264.1	5,279.4	4,256.4	3,376.3	2,967.5	2,236.1
Income Before Income Taxes	981.4	587.6	31.8	412.2	661.1	578.5	441.7
Income Taxes	314.1	176.2	cr14.3	117.0	204.4	178.5	128.0
Net Income	667.3	411.4	①46.1	295.2	456.7	400.0	313.7
Average Shs. Outstg. (000)	223,200	225,300	222,900	223,800	224,100	225,900	222,600
BALANCE SHEET (IN MILLIONS):							
Cash & Cash Equivalents	584.7	238.6	195.7	243.2	460.5	432.7	175.1
Premiums Due	1,958.5	1,698.6	1,804.7	2,015.5	1,737.2	1,478.3	1,130.8
Invst. Assets: Fixed-term	7,712.5	5,949.0	4,784.1	4,532.7	4,219.0	3,891.4	3,409.2
Invst. Assets: Equities	1,347.3	1,336.0	1,198.7	1,243.6	636.9	620.8	540.1
Invst. Assets: Total	10,284.3	8,226.3	6,983.3	6,427.7	5,674.3	5,270.4	4,450.6
Total Assets	13,564.4	11,122.4	10,051.6	9,704.7	8,463.1	7,559.6	6,183.9
Long-Term Obligations	1,489.0	1,095.7	748.8	1,048.6	776.6	775.9	775.7
Net Stockholders' Equity	3,768.0	3,250.7	2,869.8	2,752.8	2,557.1	2,135.9	1,676.9
Year-end Shs. Outstg. (000)	218,000	220,200	220,500	219,300	217,500	216,900	214,500
STATISTICAL RECORD:							
Return on Revenues %	7.2	5.5	0.7	4.8	8.6	8.7	9.0
Return on Equity %	17.7	12.7	1.6	10.7	17.9	18.7	18.7
Return on Assets %	4.9	3.7	0.5	3.0	5.4	5.3	5.1
Price Range	60.49-44.75	50.59-27.37	37.00-15.00	58.08-22.83	57.33-31.33	39.75-20.50	24.08-13.46
P/E Ratio	20.2-15.0	27.7-15.0	178.6-72.4	44.0-17.3	28.1-15.4	22.5-11.6	17.4-9.8
Average Yield %	0.2	0.2	0.3	0.2	0.2	0.3	0.4

Statistics are as originally reported. Adj. for stk. split: 200% div., 4/02 ① Incl. non-recurr. chrg. $4.2 mill.

OFFICERS:
P. B. Lewis, Chmn.
G. M. Renwick, Pres., C.E.O.
W. T. Forrester, C.F.O.
INVESTOR CONTACT: Investor Relations, (440) 446-7165
PRINCIPAL OFFICE: 6300 Wilson Mills Road, Mayfield Village, OH 44143

TELEPHONE NUMBER: (440) 461-5000
FAX: (440) 446-7168
WEB: www.progressive.com
NO. OF EMPLOYEES: 22,974
SHAREHOLDERS: 3,586
ANNUAL MEETING: In April
INCORPORATED: OH, Feb., 1965

INSTITUTIONAL HOLDINGS:
No. of Institutions: 343
Shares Held: 151,621,288
% Held: 69.6
INDUSTRY: Fire, marine, and casualty insurance (SIC: 6331)
TRANSFER AGENT(S): National City Bank, Cleveland, OH

PROTECTIVE LIFE CORPORATION

YIELD 2.3%
P/E RATIO 10.9

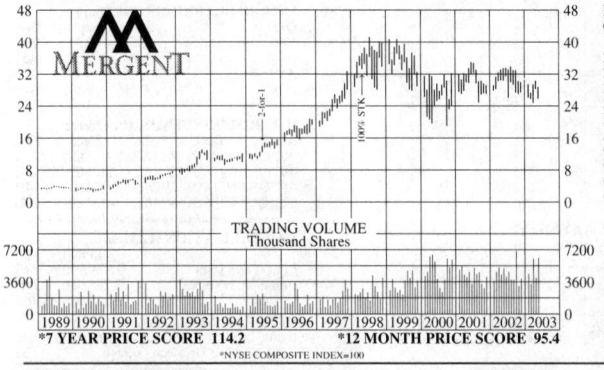

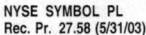

INTERIM EARNINGS (Per Share):

Qtr.	Mar.	June	Sept.	Dec.
1999	0.56	0.54	0.57	0.62
2000	0.65	0.59	0.52	0.56
2001	0.67	0.38	0.61	0.38
2002	0.59	0.77	0.73	0.50
2003	0.53	...	...	...

INTERIM DIVIDENDS (Per Share):

Amt.	Decl.	Ex.	Rec.	Pay.
0.15Q	8/12/02	8/21/02	8/23/02	9/03/02
0.15Q	11/04/02	11/13/02	11/15/02	12/02/02
0.15Q	2/03/03	2/12/03	2/14/03	2/28/03
0.16Q	5/05/03	5/14/03	5/16/03	6/02/03

Indicated div.: $0.64 (Div. Reinv. Plan)

CAPITALIZATION (12/31/02):

	($000)	(%)
Long-Term Debt	406,110	17.1
Deferred Income Tax	242,593	10.2
Common & Surplus	1,720,702	72.6
Total	2,369,405	100.0

*7 YEAR PRICE SCORE 114.2 *12 MONTH PRICE SCORE 95.4
*NYSE COMPOSITE INDEX=100

DIVIDEND ACHIEVER STATUS:
Rank: 138   10-Year Growth Rate: 10.12%
Total Years of Dividend Growth: 13

RECENT DEVELOPMENTS: For the three months ended 3/31/03, net income decreased 9.4% to $37.7 million compared with $41.6 million in the corresponding quarter of the previous year. Results for 2003 and 2002 included after-tax realized investment gains of $8.1 million and $2.6 million, respectively. Total revenues inched up to $472.8 million from $471.5 million in the year-earlier period.

PROSPECTS: The Company's focus over the next several quarters will be on continuing its strong growth momentum in the life insurance segment, maintaining a strong balance sheet and high credit quality in its investment portfolios, stabilizing and improving margins in its spread businesses, controlling expenses and increasing the profit contribution from the asset protection segment's continuing operations.

BUSINESS

PROTECTIVE LIFE CORPORATION is a holding company that provides financial services through the production, distribution and administration of insurance and investment products. The Company operates several divisions whose strategic focuses can be grouped into three segments: life insurance, specialty insurance products and retirement savings and investment products. The life insurance segment (86.4% of 2002 pre-tax operating income) includes the individual life, West Coast and acquisitions divisions. The retirement savings and the investment products segment (22.7%) includes the Stable Value products division, which markets guaranteed investment contracts, and investment products division, which sells variable annuities. The specialty insurance products segment (-9.1%) includes the financial institutions divisions, which markets credit life and disability insurance products.

ANNUAL FINANCIAL DATA

	12/31/02	12/31/01	12/31/00	12/31/99	12/31/98	12/31/97	12/31/96
Earnings Per Share	③ 2.54	② 2.01	2.32	① 2.32	2.04	1.78	1.47
Tang. Book Val. Per Share	24.37	19.72	13.38	10.03	11.51	12.30	9.99
Dividends Per Share	0.59	0.55	0.51	0.47	0.43	0.39	0.35
Dividend Payout %	23.2	27.4	22.0	20.3	21.1	21.9	23.8

INCOME STATEMENT (IN MILLIONS):

Total Premium Income	783.1	618.7	833.7	761.3	662.8	522.3	494.2
Net Investment Income	1,031.2	884.0	737.3	676.4	636.4	591.4	517.5
Other Income	106.3	111.5	163.0	96.2	67.2	33.6	26.4
Total Revenues	1,920.7	1,614.2	1,734.0	1,533.9	1,366.4	1,147.3	1,038.0
Policyholder Benefits	1,162.2	972.6	989.6	864.6	785.8	683.1	645.0
Income Before Income Taxes	267.2	209.6	253.8	255.8	220.7	179.4	139.7
Income Taxes	88.4	68.5	90.9	92.1	77.8	61.0	47.5
Equity Earnings/Minority Int.	...	...	d9.5	d10.6	d12.1	d6.4	d3.2
Net Income	③ 178.8	② 141.1	153.5	① 153.1	130.8	112.0	89.0
Average Shs. Outstg. (000)	70,463	69,950	66,281	66,161	64,088	62,850	61,608

BALANCE SHEET (IN MILLIONS):

Cash & Cash Equivalents	550.4	363.7	244.7	165.3	225.7	123.6	235.3
Premiums Due	2,477.9	2,239.2	1,185.4	940.3	797.2	639.4	380.0
Invst. Assets: Fixed-term	11,664.1	9,838.1	7,415.8	6,311.8	6,437.8	6,374.3	4,686.1
Invst. Assets: Equities	64.5	76.8	58.7	36.4	12.3	15.0	35.3
Invst. Assets: Total	15,481.5	13,317.7	10,241.4	8,722.0	8,606.6	8,049.4	6,552.2
Total Assets	21,953.0	19,718.8	15,145.6	12,994.2	11,989.5	10,511.6	8,263.2
Long-Term Obligations	406.1	376.2	306.1	181.0	152.3	120.0	168.2
Net Stockholders' Equity	1,720.7	1,400.1	1,114.1	865.2	944.2	758.2	615.3
Year-end Shs. Outstg. (000)	68,676	68,555	64,558	64,502	64,435	61,642	61,608

STATISTICAL RECORD:

Return on Revenues %	9.3	8.7	8.9	10.0	9.6	9.8	8.6
Return on Equity %	10.4	10.1	13.8	17.7	13.9	14.8	14.5
Return on Assets %	0.8	0.7	1.0	1.2	1.1	1.1	1.1
Price Range	33.90-26.00	35.00-24.80	32.25-19.00	40.75-27.81	41.25-28.00	32.75-18.81	20.81-15.06
P/E Ratio	13.3-10.2	17.4-12.3	13.9-8.2	17.6-12.0	20.2-13.7	18.4-10.6	14.2-10.2
Average Yield %	2.0	1.8	2.0	1.4	1.2	1.5	2.0

Statistics are as originally reported. Adj. for 100% stk. split, 4/98. ① Bef. extraord. loss of $1.8 mill. ② Bef. acctg. change chrg. $7.6 mill. & loss fr. disc. opers. of $30.5 mill. ③ Bef. extraord. loss of $1.4 mill.

OFFICERS:
J. D. Johns, Chmn., Pres., C.E.O.
A. Ritchie, Exec. V.P., C.F.O.

INVESTOR CONTACT: Allen Ritchie, Exec. V.P., C.F.O., (205) 268-1000

PRINCIPAL OFFICE: 2801 Highway 280 South, Birmingham, 35223

TELEPHONE NUMBER: (205) 268-1000
FAX: (205) 868-3541
WEB: www.protective.com

NO. OF EMPLOYEES: 2,438 (approx.)

SHAREHOLDERS: 2,250 (approx.)

ANNUAL MEETING: In May

INCORPORATED: DE, Feb., 1981

INSTITUTIONAL HOLDINGS:
No. of Institutions: 226
Shares Held: 52,042,037
% Held: 75.4

INDUSTRY: Life insurance (SIC: 6311)

TRANSFER AGENT(S): Bank of New York, New York, NY

QUAKER CHEMICAL CORPORATION

YIELD 3.7%
P/E RATIO 14.2

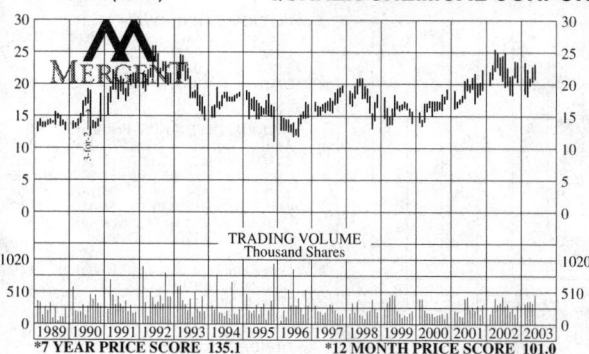

*7 YEAR PRICE SCORE 135.1
*12 MONTH PRICE SCORE 101.0
*NYSE COMPOSITE INDEX=100

INTERIM EARNINGS (Per Share):

Qtr.	Mar.	June	Sept.	Dec.
1999	0.34	0.42	0.48	0.51
2000	0.49	0.53	0.53	0.53
2001	0.45	0.45	0.12	d0.17
2002	0.26	0.35	0.45	0.46
2003	0.33	...	...	...

INTERIM DIVIDENDS (Per Share):

Amt.	Decl.	Ex.	Rec.	Pay.
0.21Q	9/25/02	10/15/02	10/17/02	10/31/02
0.21Q	11/20/02	1/15/03	1/17/03	1/31/03
0.21Q	3/19/03	4/14/03	4/16/03	4/30/03
0.21Q	5/14/03	7/15/03	7/17/03	7/31/03

Indicated div.: $0.84 (Div. Reinv. Plan)

CAPITALIZATION (12/31/02):

	($000)	(%)
Long-Term Debt	16,590	15.6
Deferred Income Tax	1,518	1.4
Common & Surplus	88,055	82.9
Total	106,163	100.0

DIVIDEND ACHIEVER STATUS:
Rank: 250   10-Year Growth Rate: 4.08%
Total Years of Dividend Growth: 31

RECENT DEVELOPMENTS: For the first quarter ended 3/31/03, net income jumped 31.8% to $3.1 million compared with $2.4 million in the corresponding quarter of 2002. Net sales were $73.4 million, up 22.4% from $59.9 million in the prior-year period. Sales benefited from favorable foreign currency translation, acquisitions completed in 2002 and improvements in both volume and price/mix in all regions except Europe. Gross profit rose 16.5% to $28.4 million from $24.4 million a year earlier.

PROSPECTS: Despite the strong start for the year, the Company's outlook for 2003 remains unclear due to shifting and uncertain manufacturing demand. In addition, the Company is seeing some softness in key markets that may hamper volumes, and increased raw material costs may continue to be a factor. However, near-term results should benefit from the effects of a stronger Euro and continued cost reductions. As a result, the Company expects year-over-year earnings growth in 2003.

BUSINESS

QUAKER CHEMICAL CORPORA-TION develops, produces, and markets a wide range of formulated chemical specialty products for various heavy industrial and manufacturing applications and, in addition, offers and markets chemical management services. The Company operates in three segments: metalworking process chemicals; coatings; and other chemical products. KWR's principal product lines include rolling lubricants, corrosion preventives, hydraulic fluids, machining and grinding compounds, forming compounds, chemical milling maskants, metal finishing compounds, technology for the removal of hydrogen sulfides, construction products and programs to provide chemical management services. In 2002, KWR acquired The United Lubricants Corporation and Epmar Corporation.

ANNUAL FINANCIAL DATA

	12/31/02	12/31/01	12/31/00	12/31/99	12/31/98	12/31/97	12/31/96
Earnings Per Share	1.51	⑤ 0.84	④ 1.93	③ 1.74	③ 1.20	② 1.45	① d0.88
Cash Flow Per Share	2.17	1.54	2.70	2.52	2.00	2.28	0.13
Tang. Book Val. Per Share	6.47	7.06	7.63	7.30	7.01	7.01	6.00
Dividends Per Share	0.83	0.82	0.79	0.77	0.73	0.70	0.69
Dividend Payout %	55.3	97.6	40.9	44.0	60.8	48.6	...

INCOME STATEMENT (IN THOUSANDS):

	12/31/02	12/31/01	12/31/00	12/31/99	12/31/98	12/31/97	12/31/96
Total Revenues	274,521	251,074	267,570	258,461	257,100	241,534	240,251
Costs & Expenses	244,311	230,503	235,610	224,224	232,719	213,122	235,574
Depreciation & Amort.	6,237	6,380	6,812	6,956	7,111	7,264	8,708
Operating Income	23,973	14,191	25,148	27,281	17,270	21,148	d4,031
Net Interest Inc./(Exp.)	d790	d850	d1,096	d1,992	d1,589	d1,218	d1,474
Income Before Income Taxes	24,318	14,430	26,486	27,151	16,797	19,735	d3,997
Income Taxes	7,782	4,473	8,211	10,860	6,719	7,893	466
Equity Earnings/Minority Int.	d2,239	d2,292	d1,112	d640	572	769	d3,136
Net Income	14,297	⑤ 7,665	④ 17,163	③ 15,651	③ 10,650	② 12,611	① d7,599
Cash Flow	20,534	14,045	23,975	22,607	17,761	19,875	1,109
Average Shs. Outstg.	9,474	9,114	8,896	8,975	8,860	8,707	8,635

BALANCE SHEET (IN THOUSANDS):

	12/31/02	12/31/01	12/31/00	12/31/99	12/31/98	12/31/97	12/31/96
Cash & Cash Equivalents	13,857	20,549	16,552	8,677	10,213	18,416	8,525
Total Current Assets	103,673	92,087	103,181	96,241	96,068	98,126	86,552
Net Property	48,512	38,244	42,459	44,752	49,622	40,654	43,960
Total Assets	213,858	170,387	188,161	182,213	189,903	170,640	165,608
Total Current Liabilities	66,144	44,663	50,200	44,657	50,432	47,759	64,034
Long-Term Obligations	16,590	19,380	22,295	25,122	25,344	25,203	5,182
Net Stockholders' Equity	88,055	80,899	84,907	81,199	83,735	75,642	74,254
Net Working Capital	37,529	47,424	52,981	51,584	45,636	50,367	22,518
Year-end Shs. Outstg.	9,322	9,137	8,851	8,934	8,894	8,720	9,664

STATISTICAL RECORD:

	12/31/02	12/31/01	12/31/00	12/31/99	12/31/98	12/31/97	12/31/96
Operating Profit Margin %	8.7	5.7	9.4	10.6	6.7	8.8	...
Net Profit Margin %	5.2	3.1	6.4	6.1	4.1	5.2	...
Return on Equity %	16.2	9.5	20.2	19.3	12.7	16.7	...
Return on Assets %	6.7	4.5	9.1	8.6	5.6	7.4	...
Debt/Total Assets %	7.8	11.4	11.8	13.8	13.3	14.8	3.1
Price Range	25.50-18.22	22.30-16.12	19.25-13.38	18.38-13.50	21.00-13.00	19.81-15.00	17.25-11.75
P/E Ratio	16.9-12.1	26.5-19.2	10.0-6.9	10.6-7.8	17.5-10.8	13.7-10.3	...
Average Yield %	3.8	4.3	4.8	4.8	4.3	4.1	4.7

Statistics are as originally reported. ① Incl. $16.9 mill. aft-tax spl. chg. ② Incl. $1.7 mill. aft-tax gain fr. sale of European bus. & $1.3 mill. aft-tax chg. for litigation. ③ Incl. $5.3 mill. aft-tax chgs. for reposit. and integration, 1998; $314,000, 1999. ④ Incl. $27,000 non-recur. gain. ⑤ Incl. $5.9 mill. restr. chg. & environmental chg. of $500,000.

OFFICERS:
R. J. Naples, Chmn., C.E.O.
J. W. Bauer, Pres., C.O.O.
M. F. Barry, V.P., C.F.O., Treas.
INVESTOR CONTACT: Michael F. Barry, V.P., C.F.O., Treas., (610) 832-8500
PRINCIPAL OFFICE: One Quaker Park, 901 Hector Street, Conshohocken, PA 19428

TELEPHONE NUMBER: (610) 832-4000
FAX: (610) 832-8682
WEB: www.quakerchem.com
NO. OF EMPLOYEES: 1,038
SHAREHOLDERS: 872
ANNUAL MEETING: In May
INCORPORATED: PA, 1930

INSTITUTIONAL HOLDINGS:
No. of Institutions: 66
Shares Held: 4,804,769
% Held: 53.4
INDUSTRY: Lubricating oils and greases (SIC: 2992)
TRANSFER AGENT(S): American Stock Transfer & Trust Company, New York, NY

QUESTAR CORPORATION

	YIELD	2.3%
	P/E RATIO	14.0

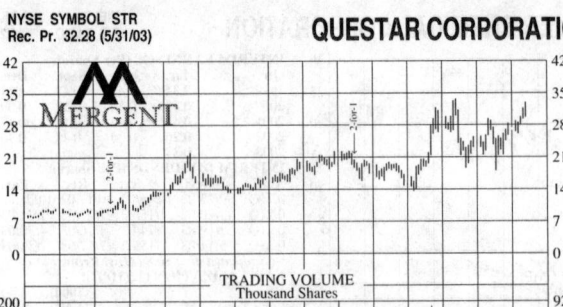

MERGENT

TRADING VOLUME
Thousand Shares

| 1989 | 1990 | 1991 | 1992 | 1993 | 1994 | 1995 | 1996 | 1997 | 1998 | 1999 | 2000 | 2001 | 2002 | 2003 |

*7 YEAR PRICE SCORE 138.3   ***12 MONTH PRICE SCORE 115.6**

*NYSE COMPOSITE INDEX=100

INTERIM EARNINGS (Per Share):

Qtr.	Mar.	June	Sept.	Dec.
1999	0.52	0.28	0.18	0.21
2000	0.62	0.33	0.34	0.65
2001	0.85	0.30	0.27	0.52
2002	0.61	0.36	0.28	0.82
2003	0.84	...	...	...

INTERIM DIVIDENDS (Per Share):

Amt.	Decl.	Ex.	Rec.	Pay.
0.18Q	8/13/02	8/21/02	8/23/02	9/16/02
0.185Q	10/24/02	11/20/02	11/22/02	12/16/02
0.185Q	2/11/03	2/19/03	2/21/03	3/17/03
0.185Q	5/20/03	5/28/03	5/30/03	6/16/03

Indicated div.: $0.74 (Div. Reinv. Plan)

CAPITALIZATION (12/31/02):

	($000)	(%)
Long-Term Debt	1,145,180	42.9
Deferred Income Tax	377,717	14.1
Minority Interest	10,025	0.4
Common & Surplus	1,138,761	42.6
Total	2,671,683	100.0

DIVIDEND ACHIEVER STATUS:
Rank: 261   10-Year Growth Rate: 3.38%
Total Years of Dividend Growth: 23

RECENT DEVELOPMENTS: For the quarter ended 3/31/03, income was $70.2 million compared with income of $50.2 million in the corresponding year-earlier period. Results for 2003 and 2002 excluded accounting change charges of $5.6 million and $15.3 million, respectively. STR attributed the higher earnings to increased nonregulated natural gas and oil prices and improved results from regulated businesses. Total revenues rose 16.7% to $469.8 million. Operating income advanced 41.8% to $127.9 million.

PROSPECTS: STR's prospects appear solid. As a result of favorable natural gas and oil prices and strong nonregulated production volumes, STR has increased its earnings guidance for 2003. The Company now expects full-year 2003 earnings to range between $2.05 and $2.20 per share, up from its previous guidance of $1.95 to $2.10 per share. In addition, STR has indicated that the Company remains on schedule with its plans to accelerate its drilling program on the Pinedale Anticline in western Wyoming.

BUSINESS

QUESTAR CORPORATION is a diversified energy services holding company with two divisions. Market Resources engages in energy development and production; gas gathering and processing; and wholesale gas and hydrocarbon liquids marketing, risk management, and storage. Regulated Services, through two subsidiaries, conducts interstate gas transmission and storage activities and retail gas distribution services. The Company is also involved in providing integrated information technology and communication data-hosting services.

ANNUAL FINANCIAL DATA

	12/31/02	12/31/01	12/31/00	12/31/99	12/31/98	12/31/97	12/31/96
Earnings Per Share	⑤ 2.07	④ 1.94	③ 1.94	① 1.20	② 0.93	1.26	1.20
Cash Flow Per Share	4.42	3.88	3.76	2.95	2.48	2.82	2.55
Tang. Book Val. Per Share	12.81	12.14	12.01	11.37	10.62	10.30	9.41
Dividends Per Share	0.73	0.70	0.69	0.67	0.65	0.62	0.59
Dividend Payout %	35.0	36.3	35.3	55.8	70.2	49.2	49.8
INCOME STATEMENT (IN MILLIONS):							
Total Revenues	1,200.7	1,439.4	1,266.2	924.2	906.3	933.3	818.0
Costs & Expenses	732.1	1,006.2	858.6	599.6	644.8	634.6	536.4
Depreciation & Amort.	194.4	159.0	147.6	144.7	128.7	128.5	110.0
Operating Income	274.2	274.1	259.9	179.9	132.8	170.2	171.6
Net Interest Inc./(Exp.)	d81.1	d64.8	d63.5	d53.9	d48.0	d43.8	d41.1
Income Taxes	91.1	88.3	85.4	47.8	29.0	45.6	45.4
Net Income	⑤ 170.9	④ 158.2	③ 156.7	① 98.8	② 76.9	104.8	98.1
Cash Flow	365.3	317.2	304.4	243.5	205.6	233.1	207.8
Average Shs. Outstg. (000)	82,573	81,658	80,915	82,676	82,817	82,668	81,656
BALANCE SHEET (IN MILLIONS):							
Gross Property	4,211.6	4,089.4	3,544.3	3,258.8	3,104.5	2,741.9	2,575.0
Accumulated Depreciation	1,593.8	1,524.3	1,590.3	1,471.9	1,356.9	1,210.7	1,097.6
Net Property	2,617.8	2,565.1	1,954.0	1,786.9	1,747.6	1,531.2	1,477.3
Total Assets	3,067.9	3,235.7	2,539.0	2,238.0	2,161.3	1,945.0	1,816.2
Long-Term Obligations	1,145.2	997.4	714.5	735.0	615.8	542.0	555.5
Net Stockholders' Equity	1,138.8	1,080.8	991.1	925.8	878.0	845.8	772.1
Year-end Shs. Outstg. (000)	82,054	81,523	80,818	81,419	82,632	82,142	82,050
STATISTICAL RECORD:							
Operating Profit Margin %	22.8	19.0	20.5	19.5	14.7	18.2	21.0
Net Profit Margin %	14.2	11.0	12.4	10.7	8.5	11.2	12.0
Net Inc./Net Property %	6.5	6.2	8.0	5.5	4.4	6.8	6.6
Net Inc./Tot. Capital %	6.4	6.5	8.0	5.3	4.5	6.5	6.4
Return on Equity %	15.0	14.6	15.8	10.7	8.8	12.4	12.7
Accum. Depr./Gross Prop. %	37.8	37.3	44.9	45.2	43.7	44.2	42.6
Price Range	29.45-18.01	33.75-18.58	31.88-13.56	19.94-14.75	22.38-15.81	22.31-17.13	20.69-15.44
P/E Ratio	14.2-8.7	17.4-9.6	16.4-7.0	16.6-12.3	24.1-17.0	17.7-13.6	17.3-12.9
Average Yield %	3.1	2.7	3.0	3.9	3.4	3.1	3.3

Statistics are as originally reported. Adj. for 2-for-1 stk. split, 6/98. ① Incl. write-down of invst. in partnerships of $49.7 mill. ② Incl. $34.0 mill. write-down of oil & gas prop. ③ Incl. aft.-tax gain of $16.3 mill. secur. sales. ④ Incl. aft.-tax loss of $905,000 on secur. sales & aft.-tax gain of $13.5 mill. on sales of nonstrategic prop. ⑤ Bef. acctg. chge. chrg. of $15.3 mill.

OFFICERS:
K. O. Rattie, Chmn., Pres., C.E.O.
S. E. Parks, Sr. V.P., C.F.O., Treas.
C. C. Holbrook, Sr. V.P., Gen. Coun., Sec.

INVESTOR CONTACT: Stephen E. Parks, Sr. V.P., C.F.O., Treas., (801) 324-5497

PRINCIPAL OFFICE: 180 East 100 South Street, Salt Lake City, UT 84145-0433

TELEPHONE NUMBER: (801) 324-5000
FAX: (801) 324-5483
WEB: www.questar.com
NO. OF EMPLOYEES: 2,225 (avg.)
SHAREHOLDERS: 10,826 (record); 30,000-35,000 (approx. beneficial)
ANNUAL MEETING: In May
INCORPORATED: UT, Oct., 1984

INSTITUTIONAL HOLDINGS:
No. of Institutions: 239
Shares Held: 51,561,050
% Held: 62.9

INDUSTRY: Gas transmission and distribution (SIC: 4923)

TRANSFER AGENT(S): Questar Corp., Salt Lake City, UT

NASDAQ SYMBOL RAVN
Rec. Pr. 19.56 (5/31/03)

RAVEN INDUSTRIES, INC.

YIELD 1.6%
P/E RATIO 15.2

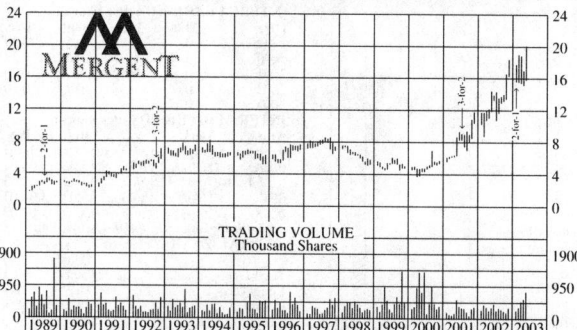

TRADING VOLUME
Thousand Shares

*7 YEAR PRICE SCORE 215.3   *12 MONTH PRICE SCORE 109.9
*NYSE COMPOSITE INDEX=100

INTERIM EARNINGS (Per Share):

Qtr.	Apr.	July	Oct.	Jan.
1999-00	0.11	0.14	0.18	0.11
2000-01	0.15	0.12	0.17	0.20
2001-02	0.24	0.22	0.27	0.22
2002-03	0.37	0.25	0.35	0.24
2003-04	0.45	...	...	...

INTERIM DIVIDENDS (Per Share):

Amt.	Decl.	Ex.	Rec.	Pay.
0.14Q	11/18/02	12/20/02	12/24/02	1/15/03
2-for-1	11/18/02	1/16/03	12/24/02	1/15/03
0.08Q	3/17/03	3/26/03	3/28/03	4/15/03
0.08Q	5/22/03	6/23/03	6/25/03	7/15/03

Indicated div.: $0.32 (Div. Reinv. Plan)

CAPITALIZATION (1/31/03):

	($000)	(%)
Long-Term Debt	151	0.3
Common & Surplus	58,236	99.7
Total	58,387	100.0

DIVIDEND ACHIEVER STATUS:

Rank: 114   10-Year Growth Rate: 11.61%
Total Years of Dividend Growth: 15

RECENT DEVELOPMENTS: For the quarter ended 4/30/03, net income increased 21.0% to $4.2 million compared with $3.5 million in the equivalent 2002 quarter. Results for 2003 included a gain of $9.0 million on the sale of businesses and assets. Net sales grew 19.3% to $36.9 million from $31.0 million a year earlier. On a segment basis, net sales of Engineered Films grew 35.5% to $11.1 million from $8.2 million the year before due to new extrusion capacity added in 2002. Net sales of Electronic Systems

rose 34.3% to $10.1 million, while net sales of Flow Controls remained unchanged at $11.8 million. Net sales of Aerostar leapt 64.1% to $4.0 million. Gross profit advanced 15.8% to $9.4 million from $8.2 million the year before. Operating income rose 23.4% to $6.5 million from $5.3 million in 2002. On 3/18/03, the Company announced that it was awarded a U.S. government contract to manufacture cargo parachutes for the U.S. Army for $7.8 million over the course of a year.

BUSINESS

RAVEN INDUSTRIES, INC. is a manufacturing company that operates through four core divisions. The Engineered Films division (33.4% of sales for fiscal 2003) produces rugged reinforced plastic sheeting for manufactured housing and recreational vehicles, temporary grain covers for agriculture, temporary building construction enclosures, and pond lining and containment for oil exploration. This segment also manufactures high-altitude research balloons for NASA and universities. The Electronics Systems unit (32.3%) provides electronic manufacturing services primarily for industrial original equipment manufacturers in North America and companies that contract their small-volume, high-mix production. The Flow Controls division (23.8%) develops global positioning systems-based control systems, computerized control hardware and software for precision farming, and systems for the precision application of insecticides, fertilizer and road de-icers. Aerostar International Inc. (10.5%) produces custom-shaped advertising inflatables, hot-air sport balloons, and specialized sewing applications.

ANNUAL FINANCIAL DATA

	1/31/03	1/31/02	1/31/01	1/31/00	1/31/99	1/31/98	1/31/97
Earnings Per Share	1.20	0.93	① 0.62	0.52	0.43	0.55	0.54
Cash Flow Per Share	1.62	1.26	0.97	0.89	0.79	0.90	0.86
Tang. Book Val. Per Share	5.67	5.65	5.06	3.87	4.42	4.25	3.79
Dividends Per Share	0.28	0.25	0.23	0.22	0.20	0.18	0.16
Dividend Payout %	22.9	26.9	37.1	41.9	46.9	32.7	30.4
INCOME STATEMENT (IN THOUSANDS):							
Total Revenues	120,903	118,515	132,858	147,906	152,798	149,619	139,441
Costs & Expenses	99,872	102,195	118,443	132,445	137,992	133,920	122,904
Depreciation & Amort.	3,966	3,145	3,667	4,884	5,133	5,137	4,566
Operating Income	17,065	13,175	10,748	10,577	9,673	10,562	11,971
Net Interest Inc./(Exp.)	d63	d129	d258	d418	d474	d323	d310
Income Before Income Taxes	17,254	13,565	10,924	10,503	9,649	12,540	11,915
Income Taxes	6,069	4,718	4,513	3,741	3,467	4,478	4,227
Net Income	11,185	8,847	① 6,411	6,762	6,182	8,062	7,688
Cash Flow	15,151	11,992	10,078	11,646	11,315	13,199	12,254
Average Shs. Outstg.	9,348	9,492	10,338	13,116	14,271	14,673	14,265
BALANCE SHEET (IN THOUSANDS):							
Cash & Cash Equivalents	9,217	7,478	10,673	5,707	5,335	2,850	3,439
Total Current Assets	49,351	45,308	52,236	55,371	60,861	57,831	56,696
Net Property	16,455	14,059	11,647	15,068	19,563	19,817	18,142
Total Assets	72,816	67,836	65,656	74,047	83,674	82,590	80,662
Total Current Liabilities	13,167	13,810	13,935	14,702	16,792	19,375	20,016
Long-Term Obligations	151	280	2,013	3,024	4,572	1,128	3,181
Net Stockholders' Equity	58,236	52,032	47,989	54,519	62,293	61,563	56,729
Net Working Capital	36,184	31,498	38,301	40,669	44,069	38,456	36,680
Year-end Shs. Outstg.	9,066	9,211	9,478	14,082	14,082	14,472	14,508
STATISTICAL RECORD:							
Operating Profit Margin %	14.1	11.1	8.1	7.2	6.3	7.1	8.6
Net Profit Margin %	9.3	7.5	4.8	4.6	4.0	5.4	5.5
Return on Equity %	19.2	17.0	13.4	12.4	9.9	13.1	13.6
Return on Assets %	15.4	13.0	9.8	9.1	7.4	9.8	9.5
Debt/Total Assets %	0.2	0.4	3.1	4.1	5.5	1.4	3.9
Price Range	18.40-8.74	11.80-5.58	6.95-3.71	6.08-4.50	7.58-5.08	8.58-6.50	7.67-5.33
P/E Ratio	15.3-7.3	12.7-6.0	11.2-6.0	11.8-8.7	17.5-11.7	15.6-11.8	14.3-9.9
Average Yield %	2.0	2.9	4.3	4.1	3.2	2.4	2.5

Statistics are as originally reported. Adj. for stk. split: 2-for-1, 1/03; 3-for-2, 7/01. ① Incl. gain on sale of assets of $367,000, 1/01; $3.5 mill., 1/00.

OFFICERS:
C. Hoigaard, Chmn.
R. M. Moquist, Pres., C.E.O.
T. Iacarella, V.P., C.F.O., Treas., Sec.

INVESTOR CONTACT: Investor Relations, (605) 336-2750

PRINCIPAL OFFICE: 205 E. 6th Street, P.O. Box 5107, Sioux Falls, SD 57117-5107

TELEPHONE NUMBER: (605) 336-2750
FAX: (605) 335-0268
WEB: www.ravenind.com

NO. OF EMPLOYEES: 765 (approx.)

SHAREHOLDERS: 2,781

ANNUAL MEETING: In May

INCORPORATED: SD, Feb., 1956

INSTITUTIONAL HOLDINGS:
No. of Institutions: 30
Shares Held: 3,083,277
% Held: 34.3

INDUSTRY: Fabricated textile products, nec (SIC: 2399)

TRANSFER AGENT(S): Wells Fargo Shareowner Services, St. Paul, MN

REGIONS FINANCIAL CORPORATION

YIELD	3.4%
P/E RATIO	12.6

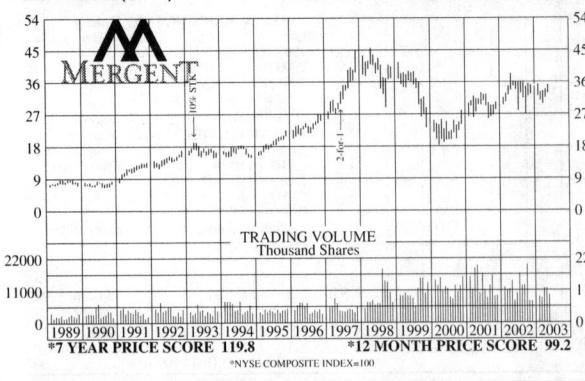

*7 YEAR PRICE SCORE 119.8   *12 MONTH PRICE SCORE 99.2
*NYSE COMPOSITE INDEX=100

INTERIM EARNINGS (Per Share):

Qtr.	Mar.	June	Sept.	Dec.
1999	0.61	0.63	0.59	0.59
2000	0.66	0.57	0.58	0.58
2001	0.57	0.49	0.59	0.60
2002	0.66	0.67	0.70	0.70
2003	0.71	...	...	...

INTERIM DIVIDENDS (Per Share):

Amt.	Decl.	Ex.	Rec.	Pay.
0.29Q	5/20/02	6/12/02	6/14/02	7/01/02
0.29Q	7/18/02	9/11/02	9/13/02	10/01/02
0.29Q	10/16/02	12/11/02	12/13/02	1/02/03
0.30Q	1/16/03	3/12/03	3/14/03	4/01/03
0.30Q	5/15/03	6/11/03	6/13/03	7/01/03

Indicated div.: $1.20 (Div. Reinv. Plan)

CAPITALIZATION (12/31/02):

	($000)	(%)
Total Deposits	32,926,201	77.5
Long-Term Debt	5,386,109	12.7
Common & Surplus	4,178,422	9.8
Total	42,490,732	100.0

DIVIDEND ACHIEVER STATUS:
Rank: 149   10-Year Growth Rate: 9.84%
Total Years of Dividend Growth: 31

RECENT DEVELOPMENTS: For the quarter ended 3/31/03, net income increased 2.9% to $158.6 million from $154.1 million the prior year. Net interest income slipped 2.7% to $359.9 million from $369.8 million the year before. Provision for loan losses rose 5.0% to $31.5 million from $30.0 million the previous year. Total non-interest income advanced 22.6% to $341.6 million, while total non-interest expense climbed 11.4% to $448.2 million.

PROSPECTS: Results are benefiting from strong revenue and earnings growth at Morgan Keegan, fueled by higher commissions and fees in the fixed-income capital markets segment, and from the Company's insurance operations. In addition, earnings are being positively affected by strong mortgage banking activity, particularly single-family residential mortgage loan production, which is being driven by increased levels of refinancings.

BUSINESS

REGIONS FINANCIAL CORPORATION (formerly First Alabama Bancshares, Inc.) is a regional financial holding company with assets of $48.46 billion as of 3/31/03. Serving customers throughout the South, RF provides traditional commercial and retail banking services and other financial services in the fields of investment banking, asset management, trust, mutual funds, securities brokerage, insurance, leasing and mortgage banking. RF's banking affiliate, Regions Bank, offers banking services from more than 680 full-service banking offices in Alabama, Arkansas, Florida, Georgia, Louisiana, North Carolina, South Carolina, Tennessee and Texas. RF also provides investment and brokerage services from more than 140 offices of Morgan Keegan & Company, Inc., which was acquired in March 2001. Morgan Keegan is one of the South's largest investment firms. On 4/2/02, the Company acquired Brookhollow Bancshares, Inc.

ANNUAL FINANCIAL DATA

	12/31/02	12/31/01	12/31/00	12/31/99	12/31/98	12/31/97	12/31/96
Earnings Per Share	2.72	2.24	2.38	2.35	⊡ 1.88	2.15	⊡ 1.85
Tang. Book Val. Per Share	18.88	17.54	15.73	13.89	13.61	13.99	12.76
Dividends Per Share	1.15	1.11	1.06	0.98	0.89	0.78	0.69
Dividend Payout %	42.3	49.6	44.5	41.7	47.3	36.0	37.3
INCOME STATEMENT (IN MILLIONS):							
Total Interest Income	2,537.0	3,055.6	3,234.2	2,854.7	2,597.8	1,653.1	1,386.1
Total Interest Expense	1,039.4	1,630.1	1,845.4	1,428.8	1,273.0	824.2	685.7
Net Interest Income	1,497.6	1,425.5	1,388.8	1,425.9	1,324.8	828.9	700.5
Provision for Loan Losses	127.5	165.4	127.1	113.7	60.5	41.8	29.0
Non-Interest Income	1,258.9	981.9	601.2	537.1	474.7	258.6	220.7
Non-Interest Expense	1,759.7	1,524.0	1,121.2	1,064.3	1,103.7	600.3	553.8
Income Before Taxes	869.2	718.0	741.7	785.0	635.3	445.3	338.4
Net Income	619.9	508.9	527.5	525.4	⊡ 421.7	299.7	⊡ 229.7
Average Shs. Outstg. (000)	227,639	227,063	221,989	223,967	223,781	139,421	124,272
BALANCE SHEET (IN MILLIONS):							
Cash & Due from Banks	1,577.5	1,239.6	1,210.9	1,393.4	1,619.0	726.1	774.8
Securities Avail. for Sale	9,747.7	8,555.0	5,468.4	6,873.3	4,893.4	1,576.6	1,797.5
Total Loans & Leases	31,230.3	31,137.0	31,472.7	28,221.2	24,430.1	16,427.6	13,335.5
Allowance for Credit Losses	681.7	670.8	472.7	414.9	379.9	227.0	199.8
Net Loans & Leases	30,548.6	30,466.2	31,000.0	27,806.3	24,050.2	16,200.6	13,135.6
Total Assets	47,938.8	45,382.7	43,688.3	42,714.4	36,831.9	23,034.2	18,930.2
Total Deposits	32,926.2	31,548.3	32,022.5	29,989.1	28,350.1	17,750.9	15,048.3
Long-Term Obligations	5,386.1	4,747.7	4,478.0	1,750.9	571.0	400.2	447.3
Total Liabilities	43,760.4	41,346.9	40,230.3	39,649.3	33,831.5	21,121.4	17,331.4
Net Stockholders' Equity	4,178.4	4,035.8	3,457.9	3,065.1	3,000.4	1,912.9	1,598.7
Year-end Shs. Outstg. (000)	221,337	230,081	219,769	220,636	220,454	136,696	125,310
STATISTICAL RECORD:							
Return on Equity %	14.8	12.6	15.3	17.1	14.1	15.7	14.4
Return on Assets %	1.3	1.1	1.2	1.2	1.1	1.3	1.2
Equity/Assets %	8.7	8.9	7.9	7.2	8.1	8.3	8.4
Non-Int. Exp./Tot. Inc. %	63.4	63.3	56.3	54.2	61.3	55.2	60.1
Price Range	38.40-27.10	32.99-25.73	28.00-18.31	41.63-23.19	45.63-28.88	45.00-25.69	27.00-20.25
P/E Ratio	14.1-10.0	14.7-11.5	11.8-7.7	17.7-9.9	24.3-15.4	20.9-11.9	14.6-10.9
Average Yield %	3.5	3.8	4.6	3.0	2.4	2.2	3.4

Statistics are as originally reported. Adj. for stk. splits: 2-for-1, 6/13/97. ⊡ Incl. merger and assessment expenses of $121.4 mill., 1998; $30.5 mill., 1996.

OFFICERS:
C. E. Jones, Jr., Chmn., Pres., C.E.O.
R. D. Horsley, Vice-Chmn., C.O.O.

INVESTOR CONTACT: Jenifer Goforth, Investor Relations, (205) 244-2823

PRINCIPAL OFFICE: 417 North 20th Street, Birmingham, AL 35203

TELEPHONE NUMBER: (205) 944-1300
FAX: (205) 326-7459
WEB: www.regions.com

NO. OF EMPLOYEES: 15,695

SHAREHOLDERS: 52,020 (record)

ANNUAL MEETING: In May

INCORPORATED: DE, June, 1970

INSTITUTIONAL HOLDINGS:
No. of Institutions: 271
Shares Held: 64,765,381
% Held: 29.2

INDUSTRY: National commercial banks (SIC: 6021)

TRANSFER AGENT(S): EquiServe, Jersey City, NJ

REPUBLIC BANCORP, INC.

YIELD 2.6%
P/E RATIO 10.5

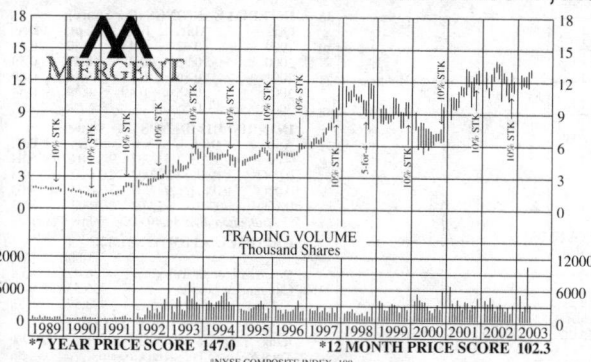

7 YEAR PRICE SCORE 147.0   *NYSE COMPOSITE INDEX=100*   **12 MONTH PRICE SCORE 102.3**

INTERIM EARNINGS (Per Share):

Qtr.	Mar.	June	Sept.	Dec.
2000	0.16	0.18	0.17	0.16
2001	Nil	0.32	0.20	0.19
2002	0.22	0.23	0.23	0.22
2003	0.58	...	...	...

INTERIM DIVIDENDS (Per Share):

Amt.	Decl.	Ex.	Rec.	Pay.
10% STK	10/18/02	11/06/02	11/08/02	12/02/02
0.085Q	11/22/02	12/11/02	12/13/02	1/06/03
0.085Q	2/21/03	3/12/03	3/14/03	4/07/03
0.085Q	5/15/03	6/04/03	6/06/03	7/07/03

Indicated div.: $0.34 (Div. Reinv. Plan)

CAPITALIZATION (12/31/02):

	($000)	(%)
Total Deposits	2,788,272	62.8
Long-Term Debt	1,321,443	29.7
Common & Surplus	332,728	7.5
Total	4,442,443	100.0

DIVIDEND ACHIEVER STATUS:
Rank: 20   10-Year Growth Rate: 20.92%
Total Years of Dividend Growth: 10

RECENT DEVELOPMENTS: For the quarter ended 3/31/03, net income advanced 49.4% to $10.0 million from $6.7 million in the corresponding prior-year period. Earnings for 2003 and 2002 included gains on the sale of loans of $5.4 million and $1.9 million, respectively. Net interest income increased 27.8% to $23.8 million from $18.6 million a year earlier, reflecting management strategies implemented in 2002 and an increase in Refund Anticipation loan volume. Provision for loan losses grew 61.0% to $4.3 million. Total

non-interest income jumped 54.2% to $11.7 million, and total non-interest expense rose 19.0% to $15.8 million. During the first quarter, RBNC opened its twenty-sixth banking center in Louisville, Kentucky and expects to expand its number of locations to over 30 by the end of 2003. Additionally, RBNC added 4,600 new personal checking accounts during the first quarter through new banking centers and by continuing to create full-bank relationships in conjunction with its fixed-rate loan promotion.

BUSINESS

REPUBLIC BANCORP, INC., with $1.81 billion in assets as of 3/31/03, is a bank holding company that provides retail, commercial and mortgage banking products and services through its wholly owned banking subsidiary, Republic Bank, a state-chartered banking corporation. As of 12/31/02, Republic Bank serves customers in Michigan, Ohio and Indiana with 96 retail, commercial and mortgage banking offices and 103 ATMs. In addition, the Company performs residential mortgage loan servicing for the benefit of others with responsibilities ranging from collecting and remitting loan payments to supervising foreclosure proceedings.

ANNUAL FINANCIAL DATA

	12/31/02	12/31/01	12/31/00	12/31/99	12/31/98	12/31/97	12/31/96
Earnings Per Share	0.96	⑤ 0.79	④ 0.76	④ 0.25	② 0.66	③ 0.54	① 0.41
Tang. Book Val. Per Share	5.79	5.17	4.06	3.30	2.63	2.17	2.39
Dividends Per Share	0.31	0.28	0.26	0.24	0.22	0.20	0.18
Dividend Payout %	32.2	35.5	33.6	96.4	33.3	36.8	42.7
INCOME STATEMENT (IN MILLIONS):							
Total Interest Income	284.7	333.4	348.3	299.7	146.0	118.9	99.1
Total Interest Expense	137.0	189.8	213.7	171.4	86.4	71.9	62.4
Net Interest Income	147.7	143.6	134.6	128.3	59.6	46.9	36.7
Provision for Loan Losses	16.0	8.7	6.5	11.7	4.0	3.0	0.3
Non-Interest Income	56.0	71.4	70.8	137.7	137.4	102.5	90.8
Non-Interest Expense	100.5	132.2	127.6	226.0	157.5	117.7	104.5
Income Before Taxes	87.2	74.1	71.3	28.4	35.6	28.7	22.8
Net Income	62.5	⑤ 48.4	④ 48.4	④ 17.6	② 22.9	③ 18.8	① 15.1
Average Shs. Outstg. (000)	59,025	60,522	60,379	60,906	34,983	34,900	35,407
BALANCE SHEET (IN MILLIONS):							
Cash & Due from Banks	75.5	75.3	76.6	74.4	17.6	27.5	33.6
Securities Avail. for Sale	248.9	364.6	211.9	206.5	47.3	119.9	228.6
Total Loans & Leases	3,656.5	3,458.4	3,771.7	3,373.4	1,212.4	1,095.7	784.6
Allowance for Credit Losses	36.1	29.2	28.5	27.1	10.5	7.3	4.7
Net Loans & Leases	3,620.5	3,429.2	3,743.2	3,346.3	1,202.0	1,088.4	779.9
Total Assets	4,778.2	4,740.6	4,610.6	4,301.6	2,196.1	1,874.5	1,495.3
Total Deposits	2,788.3	2,753.5	2,728.5	2,613.1	1,378.7	1,177.3	1,013.7
Long-Term Obligations	1,321.4	1,314.2	1,431.0	1,219.7	504.1	414.1	183.4
Total Liabilities	4,395.5	4,357.0	4,287.1	4,005.4	2,044.3	1,740.8	1,367.5
Net Stockholders' Equity	332.7	304.9	294.9	266.4	150.9	132.7	126.7
Year-end Shs. Outstg. (000)	57,441	58,483	59,803	60,275	34,777	34,184	34,483
STATISTICAL RECORD:							
Return on Equity %	18.8	16.9	16.4	6.6	15.2	14.2	11.9
Return on Assets %	1.3	1.1	1.0	0.4	1.0	1.0	1.0
Equity/Assets %	7.0	6.4	6.4	6.2	6.9	7.1	8.5
Non-Int. Exp./Tot. Inc. %	49.3	61.5	62.1	85.0	79.9	78.8	81.9
Price Range	14.00-10.21	13.31-8.52	9.71-5.26	10.59-7.68	11.95-7.60	11.68-5.77	6.21-4.74
P/E Ratio	14.6-10.6	16.8-10.8	12.8-6.9	42.7-31.0	18.2-11.6	21.6-10.7	15.1-11.5
Average Yield %	2.6	2.6	3.4	2.6	2.2	2.3	3.2

Statistics are as originally reported. Adj. for stk. splits: 10%, 12/02, 12/01, 12/00, 1/00, 12/97 & 12/96; 5-for-4, 9/98. ① Bef. extraord. loss of $388,000; incl. a gain on sale of loans of $1.2 mill. ② Incl. a gain on sale of loans of $2.1 mill. ③ Incl. a net gain on sale of loans & branches of $5.5 mill. ④ Incl. merger integr. & restruct. gain of $4.0 mill., 12/00; chrg. $31.5 mill., 12/99. ⑤ Incl. gain on sale of a subs. of $12.0 mill. & restruct. costs of $19.0 mill.

OFFICERS:
J. D. Campbell, Chmn.
S. Trager, Pres., C.E.O.
T. F. Menacher CPA, Exec. V.P., C.F.O., Treas., Sec.

INVESTOR CONTACT: Thomas Mehacher, Exec. V.P., Treas., C.F.O., (989) 725-7004

PRINCIPAL OFFICE: 1070 East Main Street, Owosso, MI 48867

TELEPHONE NUMBER: (989) 725-7337
FAX: (989) 723-8762
WEB: www.republicbancorp.com

NO. OF EMPLOYEES: 1,229

SHAREHOLDERS: 21,000 (approx.)

ANNUAL MEETING: In May

INCORPORATED: MI, Mar., 1985

INSTITUTIONAL HOLDINGS:
No. of Institutions: 94
Shares Held: 23,465,601
% Held: 40.5

INDUSTRY: National commercial banks (SIC: 6021)

TRANSFER AGENT(S): EquiServe Trust Company, N.A., Providence, RI

NYSE SYMBOL RLI
Rec. Pr. 29.58 (5/31/03)

RLI CORP.

YIELD 1.4%
P/E RATIO 14.3

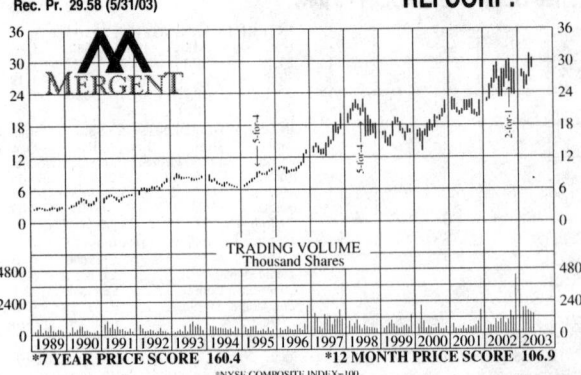

TRADING VOLUME
Thousand Shares

| | 1989 | 1990 | 1991 | 1992 | 1993 | 1994 | 1995 | 1996 | 1997 | 1998 | 1999 | 2000 | 2001 | 2002 | 2003 |

*7 YEAR PRICE SCORE 160.4   *12 MONTH PRICE SCORE 106.9
*NYSE COMPOSITE INDEX=100

INTERIM EARNINGS (Per Share):

Qtr.	Mar.	June	Sept.	Dec.
1999	0.32	0.44	0.42	0.37
2000	0.33	0.35	0.37	0.39
2001	0.36	0.37	0.40	0.39
2002	0.45	0.49	0.49	0.54
2003	0.55	...	...	...

INTERIM DIVIDENDS (Per Share):

Amt.	Decl.	Ex.	Rec.	Pay.
2-for-1	8/29/02	10/16/02	9/30/02	10/15/02
0.09Q	12/19/02	12/27/02	12/31/02	1/15/03
0.09Q	3/10/03	3/27/03	3/31/03	4/15/03
0.10Q	5/02/03	6/26/03	6/30/03	7/15/03

Indicated div.: $0.40 (Div. Reinv. Plan)

CAPITALIZATION (12/31/02):

	($000)	(%)
Deferred Income Tax	26,022	5.4
Common & Surplus	456,555	94.6
Total	482,577	100.0

DIVIDEND ACHIEVER STATUS:
Rank: 185   10-Year Growth Rate: 7.89%
Total Years of Dividend Growth: 26

RECENT DEVELOPMENTS: For the quarter ended 3/31/03, net income advanced 58.6% to $14.4 million compared with $9.1 million in the corresponding period of the previous year. Results excluded after-tax realized gains of $266,000 and $1.2 million in 2003 and 2002, respectively. Total revenues advanced 41.5% to $120.2 million from $85.0 million in the year-earlier quarter. Net premiums earned jumped 47.3% to $109.1 million.

PROSPECTS: Results are benefiting from favorable underwriting conditions and the Company's continuous effort to control expenses. The Company believes that the insurance marketplace will support continued growth in 2003 with some easing of rate increases seen in 2002. Furthermore, the Company should continue to benefit from significant momentum gained from last year's premium volume growth.

BUSINESS

RLI CORP. is a holding company composed primarily of four main insurance companies. RLI Insurance Company, the principal subsidiary, writes multiple lines of insurance on an admitted basis in all 50 states, the District of Columbia and Puerto Rico. Mt. Hawley Insurance Company, a subsidiary of RLI Insurance Company, writes surplus lines of insurance in all 50 states, the District of Columbia, Puerto Rico, the Virgin Islands and Guam. Underwriters Indemnity Company, a subsidiary of RLI Insurance Company, has authority to write multiple lines of insurance on an admitted basis in 33 states and the District of Colombia and surplus lines of insurance in Ohio. Planet Indemnity Company, a subsidiary of Mt. Hawley, has authority to write multiple lines of insurance on an admitted basis in 40 states and the District of Columbia. Other companies in the RLI Insurance Group include: Replacement Lens Inc., RLI Insurance Agency, Ltd., RLI Insurance Ltd., Underwriters Indemnity General Agency, Inc., and Safe Fleet Insurance Services, Inc.

ANNUAL FINANCIAL DATA

	12/31/02	12/31/01	12/31/00	12/31/99	12/31/98	12/31/97	12/31/96
Earnings Per Share	1.75	② 1.51	1.45	1.54	1.33	① 1.67	① 1.30
Tang. Book Val. Per Share	17.37	15.36	14.99	13.11	14.12	15.44	10.23
Dividends Per Share	0.34	0.31	0.29	0.27	0.25	0.23	0.22
Dividend Payout %	19.1	20.5	20.1	17.5	18.9	13.9	16.6

INCOME STATEMENT (IN THOUSANDS):

	12/31/02	12/31/01	12/31/00	12/31/99	12/31/98	12/31/97	12/31/96
Total Premium Income	348,065	273,008	231,603	195,274	142,324	141,884	130,656
Other Income	34,088	36,346	31,893	30,482	25,790	27,540	24,698
Total Revenues	382,153	309,354	263,496	225,756	168,114	169,424	155,354
Policyholder Benefits	203,122	155,876	124,586	96,457	64,728	61,251	68,261
Income Before Income Taxes	48,728	41,018	38,293	43,035	37,721	41,522	35,240
Income Taxes	12,876	10,771	9,600	11,584	9,482	11,351	9,544
Net Income	35,852	② 30,247	28,693	31,451	28,239	① 30,171	① 25,696
Average Shs. Outstg.	20,512	20,004	19,890	20,444	21,276	18,742	19,741

BALANCE SHEET (IN THOUSANDS):

	12/31/02	12/31/01	12/31/00	12/31/99	12/31/98	12/31/97	12/31/96
Cash & Cash Equivalents	47,889	53,648	48,095	64,092	51,917	18,697	40,824
Premiums Due	558,550	449,049	398,994	361,795	274,708	242,106	255,889
Invst. Assets: Fixed-term	724,496	462,273	401,822	342,513	328,856	333,700	308,187
Invst. Assets: Equities	227,342	277,621	306,194	284,639	296,521	251,460	188,935
Invst. Assets: Total	1,025,288	814,435	774,159	706,314	690,751	617,472	546,917
Total Assets	1,719,327	1,390,970	1,281,323	1,170,363	1,012,685	911,741	845,474
Long-Term Obligations	...	...	...	...	...	...	46,000
Net Stockholders' Equity	456,555	335,432	326,654	293,069	293,959	266,552	200,039
Year-end Shs. Outstg.	24,681	19,825	19,608	19,747	20,811	17,269	19,554

STATISTICAL RECORD:

	12/31/02	12/31/01	12/31/00	12/31/99	12/31/98	12/31/97	12/31/96
Return on Revenues %	9.4	9.8	10.9	13.9	16.8	17.8	16.5
Return on Equity %	7.9	9.0	8.8	10.7	9.6	11.3	12.8
Return on Assets %	2.1	2.2	2.2	2.7	2.8	3.3	3.0
Price Range	30.20-22.23	23.08-19.38	22.53-13.13	19.41-13.94	22.81-15.34	20.10-12.20	13.40-8.95
P/E Ratio	17.3-12.7	15.3-12.8	15.6-9.1	12.6-9.0	17.2-11.6	12.1-7.3	10.3-6.9
Average Yield %	1.3	1.5	1.6	1.6	1.3	1.4	1.9

Statistics are as originally reported. Adjusted for 2-for-1, 2002. ① Incl. net realized gains of $0.21 per share, 1997; $0.07 per share, 1996. ② Bef. acctg. credit of $800,000

OFFICERS:
G. D. Stephens, Chmn.
J. E. Michael, Pres., C.E.O.
J. E. Dondanville, V.P., C.F.O.

INVESTOR CONTACT: Mike Price, Treasurer, (309) 693-5880

PRINCIPAL OFFICE: 9025 North Lindbergh Drive, Peoria, IL 61615

TELEPHONE NUMBER: (309) 692-1000
FAX: (309) 692-1068
WEB: www.rlicorp.com

NO. OF EMPLOYEES: 515 full-time; 68 part-time

SHAREHOLDERS: 4,988

ANNUAL MEETING: In May

INCORPORATED: DE, May, 1984; reincorp., IL, May, 1993

ROHM & HAAS COMPANY

YIELD 2.6%
P/E RATIO 33.1

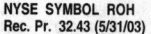
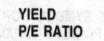

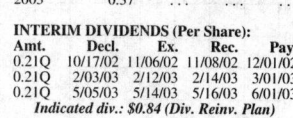

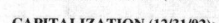

TRADING VOLUME
Thousand Shares

| 1989 | 1990 | 1991 | 1992 | 1993 | 1994 | 1995 | 1996 | 1997 | 1998 | 1999 | 2000 | 2001 | 2002 | 2003 |

*7 YEAR PRICE SCORE 115.0   ***12 MONTH PRICE SCORE 93.8**

*NYSE COMPOSITE INDEX=100

INTERIM EARNINGS (Per Share):

Qtr.	Mar.	June	Sept.	Dec.
2001	0.29	d0.94	0.24	0.17
2002	0.38	0.42	0.35	d0.16
2003	0.37	...	...	...

INTERIM DIVIDENDS (Per Share):

Amt.	Decl.	Ex.	Rec.	Pay.
0.21Q	10/17/02	11/06/02	11/08/02	12/01/02
0.21Q	2/03/03	2/12/03	2/14/03	3/01/03
0.21Q	5/05/03	5/14/03	5/16/03	6/01/03

Indicated div.: $0.84 (Div. Reinv. Plan)

CAPITALIZATION (12/31/02):

	($000)	(%)
Long-Term Debt	2,872,000	40.0
Deferred Income Tax	1,186,000	16.5
Common & Surplus	3,119,000	43.5
Total	7,177,000	100.0

DIVIDEND ACHIEVER STATUS:

Rank: 205   10-Year Growth Rate: 6.75%
Total Years of Dividend Growth: 25

RECENT DEVELOPMENTS: For the quarter ended 3/31/03, earnings from continuing operations were $82.0 million, before an accounting charge of $8.0 million, versus $79.0 million, before an accounting charge of $773.0 million, in 2002. Results for 2003 and 2002 included net non-recurring charges of $5.0 million and $6.0 million, respectively. Net sales rose 16.8% to $1.61 billion.

PROSPECTS: Severe raw material and energy increases may hamper results for the second quarter of 2003. However, the raw material/selling price gap is anticipated to narrow as the price increases that were implemented in an attempt to offset these increased costs take full effect. ROH expects full-year earnings from continuing operations in the range of $1.60 to $1.75.

BUSINESS

ROHM & HAAS COMPANY is a multinational producer of specialty polymers and biologically active compounds. Products range from basic petrochemicals such as propylene, acetone and styrene to differentiated specialty products. ROH has developed acrylic plastics, a field that it pioneered with its development of plexiglas, which is used in outdoor signs, industrial lighting, skylights, and boat windshields. Other products include polymers, resins and monomers geared toward a wide variety of industrial applications. ROH also manufactures industrial chemicals. Contributions to sales in 2002 were as follows: coatings, 29.4%; performance chemicals, 19.2%; electronic materials, 15.6%; monomers, 15.4%; salt, 11.1%; and adhesives and sealants, 9.3%.

ANNUAL FINANCIAL DATA

	12/31/02	12/31/01	12/31/00	⑥12/31/99	12/31/98	12/31/97	12/31/96
Earnings Per Share	⑦0.98	⑤d0.31	④1.61	③1.27	②2.52	2.13	①1.82
Cash Flow Per Share	3.04	2.18	4.39	3.19	4.02	3.55	3.15
Tang. Book Val. Per Share	...	...	...	...	9.66	9.15	8.44
Dividends Per Share	0.82	0.80	0.78	0.74	0.69	0.63	0.57
Dividend Payout %	83.7	...	48.4	58.3	27.5	29.7	31.6
INCOME STATEMENT (IN MILLIONS)							
Total Revenues	5,727.0	5,666.0	6,879.0	5,339.0	3,720.0	3,999.0	3,982.0
Costs & Expenses	4,838.0	5,013.0	5,510.0	4,260.0	2,822.0	3,103.0	3,153.0
Depreciation & Amort.	457.0	562.0	613.0	451.0	276.0	279.0	262.0
Operating Income	432.0	91.0	756.0	628.0	622.0	617.0	567.0
Net Interest Inc./(Exp.)	d132.0	d182.0	d241.0	d159.0	d34.0	d39.0	d32.0
Income Before Income Taxes	320.0	d76.0	581.0	464.0	700.0	611.0	530.0
Income Taxes	102.0	6.0	227.0	215.0	247.0	201.0	167.0
Equity Earnings/Minority Int.	...	18.0	19.0	7.0	2.0	11.0	d17.0
Net Income	⑦218.0	⑤d70.0	④354.0	③249.0	②453.0	410.0	①363.0
Cash Flow	675.0	480.0	967.0	698.0	723.0	682.0	618.0
Average Shs. Outstg. (000)	221,900	220,200	220,500	218,981	179,700	192,300	196,200
BALANCE SHEET (IN MILLIONS)							
Cash & Cash Equivalents	295.0	92.0	92.0	57.0	16.0	40.0	11.0
Total Current Assets	2,543.0	2,421.0	2,781.0	2,497.0	1,287.0	1,397.0	1,456.0
Net Property	2,974.0	2,916.0	3,339.0	3,496.0	1,908.0	2,008.0	2,066.0
Total Assets	9,706.0	10,350.0	11,267.0	11,256.0	3,648.0	3,900.0	3,933.0
Total Current Liabilities	1,621.0	1,624.0	2,194.0	2,510.0	875.0	850.0	886.0
Long-Term Obligations	2,872.0	2,720.0	3,225.0	3,122.0	409.0	509.0	562.0
Net Stockholders' Equity	3,119.0	3,815.0	3,653.0	3,475.0	1,561.0	1,797.0	1,728.0
Net Working Capital	922.0	797.0	587.0	d13.0	412.0	547.0	570.0
Year-end Shs. Outstg. (000)	221,132	220,427	219,937	218,981	154,000	182,700	189,300
STATISTICAL RECORD:							
Operating Profit Margin %	7.5	1.6	11.0	11.8	16.7	15.4	14.2
Net Profit Margin %	3.8	...	5.1	4.7	12.2	10.3	9.1
Return on Equity %	7.0	...	9.7	7.2	29.0	22.8	21.0
Return on Assets %	2.2	...	3.1	2.2	12.4	10.5	9.2
Debt/Total Assets %	29.6	26.3	28.6	27.7	11.2	13.1	14.3
Price Range	42.60-30.19	38.70-24.90	49.44-24.38	49.25-28.13	38.88-26.00	33.75-23.54	27.50-18.29
P/E Ratio	43.5-30.8	...	30.7-15.1	38.8-22.1	15.4-10.3	15.8-11.1	15.1-10.1
Average Yield %	2.3	2.5	2.1	1.9	2.1	2.2	2.5

Statistics are as originally reported. Adj. for 3-for-1 split, 9/98. ① Incl. $6.0 mil aft-tax non-recur chgs. ② Excl. $13.0 mil aft-tax extraord loss. ③ Incl. $105.0 mil R&D chg, $22.0 mill. loss fr disp & $36.0 mil restr chg. ④ Incl. $13.0 mil R&D chg & $13.0 mil restr chg. ⑤ Incl. $320.0 mil restr chg; Bef gain of $468.0 mil fr disc ops, $1.0 mil extraord loss & $2.0 mil acctg chg. ⑥ Results benef fr acqs of Morton International & LeaRonal. ⑦ Incl. $177.0 mil restr chg and excl. $7.0 mil disc ops, $8.0 mil extraord loss & $773.0 mil acctg chg.

OFFICERS:
R. L. Gupta, Chmn., C.E.O.
J. M. Fitzpatrick, Pres., C.O.O.

INVESTOR CONTACT: Laura L. Hadden, Mgr. Bus. & Fin., (215) 592-3052

PRINCIPAL OFFICE: 100 Independence Mall West, Philadelphia, PA 19106

TELEPHONE NUMBER: (215) 592-3000
FAX: (215) 592-3377
WEB: www.rohmhaas.com

NO. OF EMPLOYEES: 17,611 (avg.)

SHAREHOLDERS: 9,140

ANNUAL MEETING: In May

INCORPORATED: DE, Apr., 1917

INSTITUTIONAL HOLDINGS:
No. of Institutions: 312
Shares Held: 172,364,409
% Held: 78.0

INDUSTRY: Plastics materials and resins (SIC: 2821)

TRANSFER AGENT(S): EquiServe, LP, Boston, MA

ROPER INDUSTRIES, INC.

YIELD	1.0%
P/E RATIO	20.4

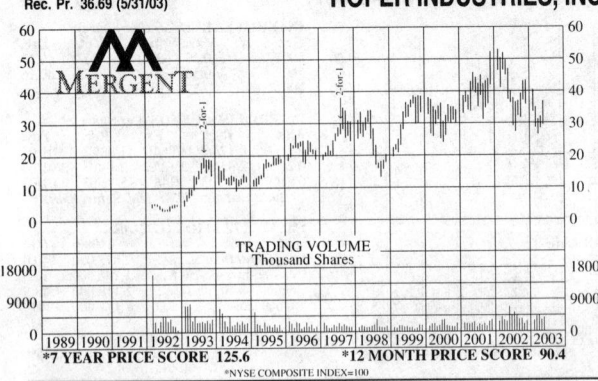

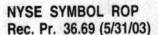

TRADING VOLUME
Thousand Shares

*7 YEAR PRICE SCORE 125.6   *12 MONTH PRICE SCORE 90.4

*NYSE COMPOSITE INDEX=100

INTERIM EARNINGS (Per Share):

Qtr.	Jan.	April	July	Oct.
1998-99	0.26	0.39	0.41	0.47
1999-00	0.31	0.44	0.36	0.48
2000-01	0.38	0.44	0.41	0.54
2001-02	0.46	0.55	0.47	0.60
2002-03	0.26	0.47	...	...

INTERIM DIVIDENDS (Per Share):

Amt.	Decl.	Ex.	Rec.	Pay.
0.083Q	5/23/02	7/12/02	7/16/02	7/31/02
0.083Q	9/03/02	10/10/02	10/15/02	10/31/02
0.087Q	11/20/02	1/15/03	1/17/03	1/31/03
0.087Q	3/24/03	4/14/03	4/16/03	4/30/03
0.087Q	5/28/03	7/15/03	7/17/03	7/31/03

Indicated div.: $0.35

CAPITALIZATION (10/31/02):

	($000)	(%)
Long-Term Debt	311,590	45.3
Common & Surplus	376,012	54.7
Total	687,602	100.0

DIVIDEND ACHIEVER STATUS:
Rank: 6   10-Year Growth Rate: 27.10%
Total Years of Dividend Growth: 10

RECENT DEVELOPMENTS: For the quarter ended 4/30/03, ROP reported earnings from continuing operations of $14.7 million versus $17.3 million in the equivalent 2002 quarter. Results for 2003 included a restructuring charge of about $2.0 million. Earnings excluded a loss of $616,000 in 2003 and income of $143,000 in 2002 from discontinued operations. Net sales advanced 9.7% to $165.5 million from $150.8 million in 2002. Gross profit increased 4.9% to $86.0 million from $82.0 million the year before.

PROSPECTS: The Company recently launched restructuring activities designed to generate as much as $15.0 million in annualized cost savings. The planned activities, including the integration of several of its business units and the shifting of certain production to low-cost countries including China and Mexico, are expected to be completed by the end of fiscal 2003. Separately, the Company anticipates fiscal 2003 earnings to range from $2.00 to $2.11 per diluted share.

BUSINESS

ROPER INDUSTRIES, INC. produces specialty industrial controls, fluid handling and analytical instrumentation products. The Instrumentation segment provides primarily test, inspection and measurement products for oil and gas, research and industrial markets under brands such as Acton Research, Antek, Gatan, Logitech, Struers and Uson. The industrial technology segment provides services for industrial, energy, commercial refrigeration, and water/wastewater markets under the brands, Abel Pump, AMOT Controls, Cornell Pump, Flow Technology, Fluid Metering, and Hansen. The Energy Systems and Controls segment provides control, monitoring and inspection systems for energy markets under the brands Compressor Controls, Petrotech, Metrix and Zetec. The Scientific and Industrial Imaging segment provides high-performance digital imaging products and equipment for industrial, medical and life and physical science applications under the brands Media Cybernetics, QImaging, Redlake, and Roper Scientific.

ANNUAL FINANCIAL DATA

	10/31/02	10/31/01	10/31/00	10/31/99	10/31/98	10/31/97	10/31/96
Earnings Per Share	① 2.08	1.77	1.58	1.53	1.24	1.16	0.94
Cash Flow Per Share	2.55	2.64	2.30	2.04	1.69	1.52	1.19
Tang. Book Val. Per Share	...	...	...	0.56	...	0.76	0.32
Dividends Per Share	0.33	0.30	0.28	0.26	0.24	0.20	0.16
Dividend Payout %	15.9	16.9	17.7	17.0	19.4	16.8	16.8
INCOME STATEMENT (IN THOUSANDS):							
Total Revenues	627,030	586,506	503,813	407,256	389,170	298,236	225,651
Costs & Expenses	497,025	460,623	393,319	313,335	308,644	225,966	170,528
Depreciation & Amort.	15,176	27,455	22,298	15,966	14,434	11,400	7,851
Operating Income	114,829	98,428	88,196	77,955	66,092	60,870	47,272
Net Interest Inc./(Exp.)	d18,506	d15,917	d13,483	d7,254	d7,856	d6,048	d3,282
Income Before Income Taxes	95,686	86,439	75,931	72,284	59,616	55,100	44,240
Income Taxes	29,663	30,600	26,653	24,938	20,300	18,750	15,383
Net Income	① 66,023	55,839	49,278	47,346	39,316	36,350	28,857
Cash Flow	81,199	83,294	71,576	63,312	53,750	47,750	36,708
Average Shs. Outstg.	31,815	31,493	31,182	30,992	31,717	31,458	30,882
BALANCE SHEET (IN THOUSANDS):							
Cash & Cash Equivalents	12,362	16,190	11,372	13,490	9,350	649	423
Total Current Assets	247,622	233,053	213,955	161,819	139,852	131,890	84,513
Net Property	51,339	51,887	48,907	34,797	31,905	31,395	23,959
Total Assets	828,973	762,122	596,902	420,163	381,533	329,320	242,953
Total Current Liabilities	130,231	103,880	84,492	72,243	57,578	44,936	39,506
Long-Term Obligations	311,590	323,830	234,603	109,659	120,307	99,638	63,373
Net Stockholders' Equity	376,012	323,506	270,191	231,968	197,033	177,869	137,396
Net Working Capital	117,385	129,173	129,463	89,576	82,274	86,954	45,007
Year-end Shs. Outstg.	31,363	30,879	30,599	30,282	30,343	30,920	30,322
STATISTICAL RECORD:							
Operating Profit Margin %	18.3	16.8	17.5	19.1	17.0	20.4	20.9
Net Profit Margin %	10.5	9.5	9.8	11.6	10.1	12.2	12.8
Return on Equity %	17.6	17.3	18.2	20.4	20.0	20.4	21.0
Return on Assets %	8.0	7.3	8.3	11.3	10.3	11.0	11.9
Debt/Total Assets %	37.6	42.5	39.3	26.1	31.5	30.3	26.1
Price Range	52.91-27.25	52.25-31.00	37.94-24.00	38.56-19.63	34.06-13.31	34.88-18.56	26.38-17.50
P/E Ratio	25.4-13.1	29.5-17.5	24.0-15.2	25.2-12.8	27.5-10.7	30.1-16.0	28.2-18.7
Average Yield %	0.8	0.7	0.9	0.9	1.0	0.7	0.7

Statistics are as originally reported. Adj. for stk. splits: 2-for-1, 8/97 ① Bef. acctg. change chrg. of $26.0 mill.; incl. Euro debt currency exchange loss of $4.1 mill.

OFFICERS:
D. N. Key, Chmn.
B. D. Jellison, Pres., C.E.O.
M. S. Headley, V.P., C.F.O.

INVESTOR CONTACT: Chris Hix, Dir., Investor Relations, (770) 495-5100

PRINCIPAL OFFICE: 2160 Satellite Boulevard, Suite 200, Duluth, GA 30097

TELEPHONE NUMBER: (770) 495-5100
FAX: (770) 495-5150
WEB: www.roperind.com

NO. OF EMPLOYEES: 3,100 (approx.)

SHAREHOLDERS: 203

ANNUAL MEETING: In March

INCORPORATED: DE, 1981

INSTITUTIONAL HOLDINGS:
No. of Institutions: 159
Shares Held: 27,470,522
% Held: 83.2

INDUSTRY: Pumps and pumping equipment (SIC: 3561)

TRANSFER AGENT(S): Wachovia Bank, N.A., Charlotte, NC

ROUSE COMPANY (THE)

YIELD 4.5%
P/E RATIO 24.6

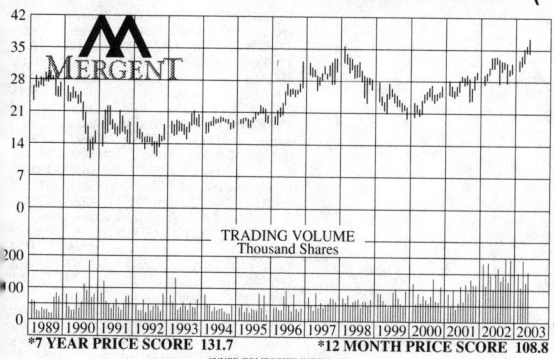

TRADING VOLUME
Thousand Shares

7 YEAR PRICE SCORE 131.7   **12 MONTH PRICE SCORE 108.8**
*NYSE COMPOSITE INDEX=100

INTERIM EARNINGS (Per Share):

Qtr.	Mar.	June	Sept.	Dec.
2000	0.40	0.44	0.96	0.41
2001	0.41	0.34	0.37	0.93
2002	0.20	1.04	0.33	d0.10
2003	0.24	...	...	...

INTERIM DIVIDENDS (Per Share):

Amt.	Decl.	Ex.	Rec.	Pay.
0.39Q	12/05/02	12/11/02	12/13/02	12/23/02
0.42Q	2/20/03	3/12/03	3/14/03	3/28/03
0.42Q	5/08/03	6/12/03	6/16/03	6/30/03
0.42Q	5/08/03	9/12/03	9/16/03	9/30/03

Indicated div.: $1.68 (Div. Reinv. Plan)

CAPITALIZATION (12/31/02):

	($000)	(%)
Long-Term Debt	4,441,477	80.0
Preferred Stock	41	0.0
Common & Surplus	1,112,043	20.0
Total	5,553,561	100.0

DIVIDEND ACHIEVER STATUS:

Rank: 143   10-Year Growth Rate: 10.03%
Total Years of Dividend Growth: 10

RECENT DEVELOPMENTS: For the three months ended 3/31/03, net earnings climbed 64.2% to $24.1 million compared with $14.7 million in the equivalent period of 2002. Results for 2003 included a curtailment loss on pension plans of $10.2 million and a provision for organizational changes, including early retirement and related costs, of $6.3 million. Results for 2002 included a net loss of $5.3 million from the early extinguishment of debt. Revenues grew 26.4% to $336.7 million.

PROSPECTS: The trend of strong demand for land in Summerlin, Nevada, Columbia, Maryland, and Fairwood, Maryland, the Company's three new community projects, continues. As a result, the Company expects its performance to remain solid throughout the remainder of the year. Separately, on 3/6/03, the Company announced that it has agreed to sell six properties, including five malls and an urban marketplace, in the Philadelphia area to Pennsylvania Real Estate Investment Trust.

BUSINESS

THE ROUSE COMPANY operated, as of 3/31/03, more than 150 properties encompassing retail, office, research and development, hotel and industrial space in 22 states. RSE owns and/or operates 38 regional retail centers and three community centers, with more than 45.0 million square feet and including about 137 nationally known department stores and 7,000 small merchants. RSE also owns and/or operates six mixed-use projects and an additional 2.7 million square feet of office/industrial space, mainly located either in the Baltimore-Washington corridor or in Las Vegas, Nevada. RSE, through its affiliates, is the developer of the cities of Columbia, Maryland and Summerlin, Nevada.

ANNUAL FINANCIAL DATA

	12/31/02	12/31/01	12/31/00	12/31/99	12/31/98	12/31/97	12/31/96
Earnings Per Share	[7] 1.15	[6] 1.42	[5] 2.21	[4] 1.77	[3] 1.34	[2] 2.59	[1] 0.14
Cash Flow Per Share	3.25	3.41	3.72	2.92	2.95	3.45	1.57
Tang. Book Val. Per Share	12.80	9.45	9.29	9.03	8.71	6.96	2.65
Dividends Per Share	1.56	1.42	1.32	1.20	1.12	1.00	0.88
Dividend Payout %	135.6	100.0	59.7	67.8	83.6	38.6	628.1
INCOME STATEMENT (IN MILLIONS):							
Total Revenues	1,104.7	966.3	633.7	715.7	692.6	916.8	831.9
Costs & Expenses	555.9	503.7	300.7	338.4	358.4	535.8	472.1
Depreciation & Amort.	162.9	125.5	90.3	100.3	84.1	82.9	80.0
Operating Income	385.9	337.1	242.7	276.9	250.1	298.0	279.9
Net Interest Inc./(Exp.)	d245.3	d228.8	d236.7	d244.5	d209.6	d207.5	d220.4
Income Before Income Taxes	102.7	108.3	5.8	32.4	40.6	90.5	59.5
Income Taxes	cr3.3	28.9	0.3	0.3	...	cr116.1	25.7
Equity Earnings/Minority Int.	6.8	32.8	129.6	76.5	75.8	6.8	...
Net Income	[7] 112.8	[6] 112.2	[5] 168.3	[4] 108.9	[3] 116.3	[2] 189.9	[1] 17.9
Cash Flow	263.6	225.6	213.3	196.8	188.3	286.0	103.2
Average Shs. Outstg. (000)	84,954	69,694	69,475	71,705	67,874	76,005	55,572
BALANCE SHEET (IN MILLIONS):							
Cash & Cash Equivalents	73.7	54.3	37.6	49.2	42.0	90.7	47.4
Total Current Assets	130.7	142.0	82.2	110.4	117.9	205.0	139.7
Total Assets	6,386.2	4,880.4	4,175.5	4,427.2	5,154.6	3,589.8	3,643.5
Long-Term Obligations	4,441.5	3,488.8	3,045.8	3,334.4	4,068.5	2,684.1	2,895.4
Net Stockholders' Equity	1,112.1	655.4	630.5	638.6	628.9	465.5	177.1
Net Working Capital	130.7	142.0	82.2	110.4	117.9	205.0	139.7
Year-end Shs. Outstg. (000)	86,910	69,354	67,880	70,694	72,225	66,911	66,743
STATISTICAL RECORD:							
Operating Profit Margin %	34.9	34.9	38.3	38.7	36.1	32.5	33.6
Net Profit Margin %	10.2	11.6	26.6	15.2	16.8	20.7	2.1
Return on Equity %	10.1	17.1	26.7	17.1	18.5	40.8	10.1
Return on Assets %	1.8	2.3	4.0	2.5	2.3	5.3	0.5
Debt/Total Assets %	69.5	71.5	72.9	75.3	78.9	74.8	79.5
Price Range	33.50-27.25	30.16-23.59	27.13-20.13	27.75-19.75	35.69-23.13	33.00-25.75	32.25-18.25
P/E Ratio	29.1-23.7	21.2-16.6	12.3-9.1	15.7-11.2	26.6-17.3	12.7-9.9	230.2-130.3
Average Yield %	5.1	5.3	5.6	5.1	3.8	3.4	3.5

Statistics are as originally reported. [1] Bef $1.5 mil extraord chg & incl $15.9 mil non-recur chg. [2] Bef $21.3 mil extraord chg and $1.2 mil acct chg & incl $23.5 mil non-recur chg. [3] Bef $4.4 mil extraord gain and $4.6 mil acct chg & incl $11.2 mil non-recur chg. [4] Bef $5.9 mil extraord chg & incl $32.6 mil non-recur gain. [5] Bef $2.2 mil extraord gain & incl $33.2 mil non-recur gain. [6] Incl $1.2 mil loss on prop and bef $696,000 extraord loss & $411,000 acct chg. [7] Incl $21.8 mil restr chg, $11.6 mil impair loss, $28.8 mil net gain.

OFFICERS:
A. W. Deering, Chmn., Pres., C.E.O.
T. J. DeRosa, Vice-Chmn., C.F.O.

INVESTOR CONTACT: David L. Tripp, Investor Relations, (410) 992-6546

PRINCIPAL OFFICE: 10275 Little Patuxent Parkway, Columbia, MD 21044-3456

TELEPHONE NUMBER: (410) 992-6000
FAX: (410) 992-6363
WEB: www.therousecompany.com
NO. OF EMPLOYEES: 3,453 (avg.)
SHAREHOLDERS: 2,245
ANNUAL MEETING: In May
INCORPORATED: MD, Oct., 1956

INSTITUTIONAL HOLDINGS:
No. of Institutions: 178
Shares Held: 77,136,970
% Held: 88.7
INDUSTRY: Nonresidential building operators (SIC: 6512)
TRANSFER AGENT(S): The Bank of New York, New York, NY

RPM INTERNATIONAL INC.

YIELD	4.2%
P/E RATIO	12.3

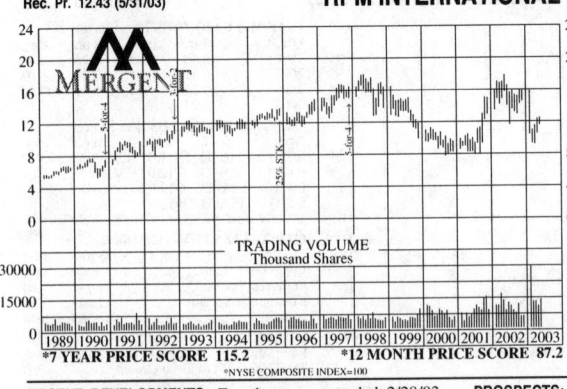

*7 YEAR PRICE SCORE 115.2   ***12 MONTH PRICE SCORE 87.2**

*NYSE COMPOSITE INDEX=100

INTERIM EARNINGS (Per Share):

Qtr.	Aug.	Nov.	Feb.	May
1998-99	0.29	0.20	0.06	0.32
1999-00	0.07	0.19	0.04	0.09
2000-01	0.28	0.17	d0.07	0.24
2001-02	0.36	0.24	0.03	0.33
2002-03	0.38	0.26	0.04	...

INTERIM DIVIDENDS (Per Share):

Amt.	Decl.	Ex.	Rec.	Pay.
0.125Q	7/01/02	7/10/02	7/12/02	7/31/02
0.13Q	10/11/02	10/17/02	10/21/02	10/31/02
0.13Q	1/09/03	1/09/03	1/13/03	1/31/03
0.13Q	4/04/03	4/10/03	4/14/03	4/30/03

Indicated div.: $0.52 (Div. Reinv. Plan)

CAPITALIZATION (5/31/02):

	($000)	(%)
Long-Term Debt	707,921	43.8
Deferred Income Tax	50,204	3.1
Common & Surplus	858,106	53.1
Total	1,616,231	100.0

DIVIDEND ACHIEVER STATUS:
Rank: 223   10-Year Growth Rate: 5.65%
Total Years of Dividend Growth: 29

RECENT DEVELOPMENTS: For the quarter ended 2/28/03, net income increased 49.1% to $4.9 million compared with $3.3 million in the equivalent 2002 quarter. The improvement in earnings was primarily attributed to strong operating earnings from its consumer and industrial segments and lower interest expense. Net sales rose 6.4% to $433.6 million from $407.5 million a year earlier. Gross profit advanced 4.7% to $187.0 million from $178.6 million the year before.

PROSPECTS: Looking ahead, the Company expects its third party insurance to be depleted in the coming months due to recent asbestos claims activity. Consequently, RPM will closely monitor federal and state legislative activities, and has begun a formal process to predict the cost of its future asbestos liabilities. The Company plans to complete it at the same time that it reports its fiscal 2003 results and accrue a liability sufficient to cover estimated asbestos costs.

BUSINESS

RPM INTERNATIONAL INC. (formerly RPM, Inc.) is a manufacturer of specialty coatings serving the industrial and consumer markets. The Company's industrial products include roofing systems, sealants, corrosion control coatings, flooring coatings and specialty chemicals. RPM's consumer products are used by professionals and do-it-yourselfers for home maintenance and improvement, automotive and boat repair and maintenance, and by hobbyists. Industrial brands include STONHARD, TREMCO, CARBOLINE, DAYGLO, EUCO and DRYVIT. Consumer brands include ZINSSER, RUST-OLEUM, DAP, VARATHANE, BONDO and TESTORS. As of 5/31/02, approximately 53.0% of RPM's sales were derived from the industrial market sectors, with the remainder in consumer products. On 8/31/99, RPM acquired DAP Products Inc. and DAP Canada Corp.

ANNUAL FINANCIAL DATA

	5/31/02	5/31/01	5/31/00	5/31/99	5/31/98	5/31/97	5/31/96
Earnings Per Share	0.97	①0.62	①0.38	0.86	0.84	0.80	0.72
Cash Flow Per Share	1.52	1.41	1.12	1.41	1.30	1.32	1.17
Tang. Book Val. Per Share	0.01	...	...	0.77	...	...	0.18
Dividends Per Share	0.50	0.49	0.47	0.45	0.42	0.39	0.36
Dividend Payout %	51.5	79.4	125.0	52.7	50.5	49.0	50.7

INCOME STATEMENT (IN MILLIONS):

Total Revenues	1,986.1	2,007.8	1,954.1	1,712.2	1,615.3	1,350.5	1,136.4
Costs & Expenses	1,734.7	1,759.6	1,699.5	1,457.6	1,372.0	1,131.1	948.1
Depreciation & Amort.	56.9	81.5	79.2	62.1	57.0	51.1	42.6
Operating Income	194.6	166.7	175.5	192.4	186.3	168.3	145.7
Net Interest Inc./(Exp.)	d40.5	d65.2	d51.8	d32.8	d36.7	d32.6	d25.8
Income Before Income Taxes	154.1	101.5	71.8	159.6	149.6	135.7	119.9
Income Taxes	52.6	38.5	30.8	65.1	61.7	57.4	51.0
Net Income	101.6	①63.0	①41.0	94.5	87.8	78.3	68.9
Cash Flow	158.4	144.5	120.1	156.7	144.8	129.5	111.5
Average Shs. Outstg. (000)	104,418	102,212	107,384	111,376	111,663	97,894	95,685

BALANCE SHEET (IN MILLIONS):

Cash & Cash Equivalents	42.2	23.9	31.3	19.7	40.8	37.4	34.3
Total Current Assets	801.3	819.4	785.1	705.4	672.5	720.3	465.1
Net Property	355.8	362.0	366.2	339.7	305.9	270.3	224.7
Total Assets	2,036.4	2,078.5	2,099.2	1,737.2	1,683.3	1,633.2	1,155.1
Total Current Liabilities	364.7	375.8	376.2	302.5	285.8	241.8	189.4
Long-Term Obligations	707.9	955.4	959.3	582.1	715.7	784.4	447.7
Net Stockholders' Equity	858.1	639.7	645.7	742.9	567.1	493.3	445.8
Net Working Capital	436.6	443.7	408.9	402.9	386.7	478.5	275.7
Year-end Shs. Outstg. (000)	114,696	102,211	103,134	109,443	100,254	98,029	96,811

STATISTICAL RECORD:

Operating Profit Margin %	9.8	8.3	9.0	11.2	11.5	12.5	12.8
Net Profit Margin %	5.1	3.1	2.1	5.5	5.4	5.8	6.1
Return on Equity %	11.8	9.8	6.3	12.7	15.5	15.9	15.5
Return on Assets %	5.0	3.0	2.0	5.4	5.2	4.8	6.0
Debt/Total Assets %	34.8	46.0	45.7	33.5	42.5	48.0	38.8
Price Range	15.05-7.91	11.31-7.75	16.50-9.94	18.00-12.75	16.80-12.50	14.90-11.50	13.80-11.30
P/E Ratio	15.5-8.2	18.2-12.5	43.4-26.1	20.9-14.8	20.0-14.9	18.6-14.4	19.2-15.8
Average Yield %	4.4	5.2	3.6	2.9	2.9	3.0	2.9

Statistics are as originally reported. Adj. for stk. splits: 5-for-4, 12/8/97. ① Incl. restruct chrg. of $52.0 million, 5/01; $45.0 mill., 5/00.

OFFICERS:
T. C. Sullivan, Chmn.
F. C. Sullivan, Pres., C.E.O.
R. L. Matejka, V.P., C.F.O., Contr.

INVESTOR CONTACT: Glenn R. Hasman, V.P.-Fin., (330) 273-8820

PRINCIPAL OFFICE: P.O. Box 777, 2628 Pearl Road, Medina, OH 44258

TELEPHONE NUMBER: (330) 273-5090
FAX: (330) 225-8743
WEB: www.rpminc.com

NO. OF EMPLOYEES: 7,687 (avg.)

SHAREHOLDERS: 40,230 (approx.)

ANNUAL MEETING: In Oct.

INCORPORATED: OH, May, 1947; reincorp., DE, Oct., 2002

INSTITUTIONAL HOLDINGS:
No. of Institutions: 253
Shares Held: 65,832,492
% Held: 56.8

INDUSTRY: Paints and allied products (SIC: 2851)

TRANSFER AGENT(S): Computershare Investor Services, Chicago, IL

S&T BANCORP, INC.

YIELD 3.5%
P/E RATIO 15.3

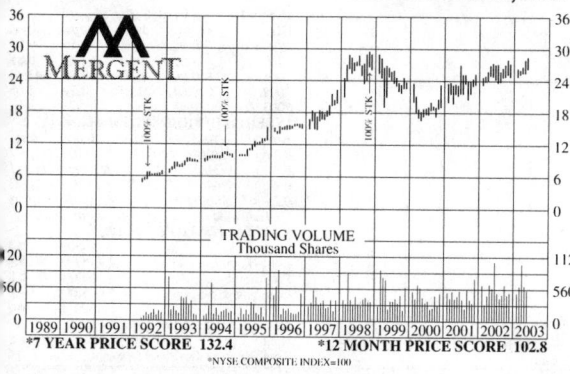

TRADING VOLUME
Thousand Shares

*7 YEAR PRICE SCORE 132.4   *12 MONTH PRICE SCORE 102.8
*NYSE COMPOSITE INDEX=100

INTERIM EARNINGS (Per Share):

Qtr.	Mar.	June	Sept.	Dec.
1999	0.37	0.37	0.37	0.39
2000	0.40	0.41	0.42	0.43
2001	0.43	0.44	0.51	0.44
2002	0.43	0.44	0.46	0.48
2003	0.47	...	...	...

INTERIM DIVIDENDS (Per Share):

Amt.	Decl.	Ex.	Rec.	Pay.
0.24Q	6/17/02	6/27/02	7/01/02	7/25/02
0.24Q	9/16/02	9/27/02	10/01/02	10/25/02
0.25Q	12/16/02	12/27/02	12/31/02	1/24/03
0.25Q	3/17/03	3/28/03	4/01/03	4/25/03
0.25Q	6/16/03	6/27/03	7/01/03	7/25/03

Indicated div.: $1.00 (Div. Reinv. Plan)

CAPITALIZATION (12/31/02):

	($000)	(%)
Total Deposits	1,926,119	78.8
Long-Term Debt	211,656	8.7
Common & Surplus	306,114	12.5
Total	2,443,889	100.0

DIVIDEND ACHIEVER STATUS:
Rank: 42   10-Year Growth Rate: 17.74%
Total Years of Dividend Growth: 13

RECENT DEVELOPMENTS: For the three months ended 3/31/03, net income climbed 9.3% to $12.5 million compared with $11.5 million in the equivalent quarter of 2002. Results for 2003 and 2002 included security gains of $1.0 million and $1.8 million, and amortization of intangibles of $87,000 and $112,000, respectively. Net interest income rose 21.2% to $26.4 million from $21.8 million in the previous year. Net interest and non-interest income benefited from the acquisitions of Peoples Financial Corpora-

tion and Evergreen Insurance, which were completed in the third quarter of 2002, and strong commercial lending and residential mortgage origination activities. Provision for loan losses more than doubled to $2.4 million from $1.0 million the year before. Total non-interest income grew 5.9% to $7.7 million from $7.3 million, and total non-interest expense rose 13.7% to $14.2 million from $12.5 million the year before.

BUSINESS

S&T BANCORP, INC. is a bank holding company with assets of $2.86 billion as of 3/31/03. The Company has three wholly-owned subsidiaries, S&T Bank, S&T Investment Company, Inc. and S&T Insurance Company, LLC. S&T Bank offers a variety of services including time and demand deposit accounts, secured and unsecured commercial and consumer loans, letters of credit, discount brokerage services, personal finance planning and credit card services. S&T Investment Company, Inc. is an investment holding company, which manages investments previously owned by the bank. The Company operates through a branch network of 46 offices in 8 counties of Pennsylvania. Commonwealth Trust Credit Life Insurance Company is a joint venture that reinsures credit life, accident and health insurance policies sold by S&T Bank.

ANNUAL FINANCIAL DATA

	12/31/02	12/31/01	12/31/00	12/31/99	12/31/98	12/31/97	12/31/96
Earnings Per Share	1.81	① 1.82	1.66	1.51	1.35	1.17	1.05
Tang. Book Val. Per Share	9.47	11.01	10.28	8.88	9.38	9.20	7.96
Dividends Per Share	0.96	0.90	0.82	0.74	0.63	0.53	0.45
Dividend Payout %	53.0	49.4	49.4	49.0	46.7	45.3	42.9
INCOME STATEMENT (IN MILLIONS):							
Total Interest Income	151.2	166.7	176.2	156.7	151.4	141.1	111.4
Total Interest Expense	56.3	76.7	86.1	69.9	69.2	62.3	51.5
Net Interest Income	94.9	90.0	90.0	86.8	82.3	78.8	59.9
Provision for Loan Losses	7.8	5.0	4.0	4.0	10.6	5.0	4.5
Non-Interest Income	32.7	31.2	22.2	20.1	24.4	16.4	11.2
Non-Interest Expense	51.8	47.0	45.7	43.5	42.0	43.2	35.5
Income Before Taxes	68.0	69.2	62.5	59.4	54.2	47.1	31.3
Net Income	48.6	① 49.2	45.0	41.4	38.0	33.4	23.2
Average Shs. Outstg. (000)	26,784	27,051	27,074	27,367	28,055	28,618	22,146
BALANCE SHEET (IN MILLIONS):							
Cash & Due from Banks	50.3	52.8	43.7	38.7	48.7	36.0	33.3
Securities Avail. for Sale	640.8	578.5	567.4	558.0	565.1	521.1	353.8
Total Loans & Leases	1,998.9	1,642.8	1,605.0	1,496.3	1,365.9	1,273.8	1,046.1
Allowance for Credit Losses	30.1	26.9	27.4	27.1	26.7	20.4	17.0
Net Loans & Leases	1,968.8	1,615.8	1,577.6	1,469.1	1,339.2	1,253.3	1,029.1
Total Assets	2,823.9	2,357.9	2,310.3	2,194.1	2,069.6	1,920.3	1,495.9
Total Deposits	1,926.1	1,611.3	1,525.3	1,435.1	1,380.1	1,284.7	1,032.3
Long-Term Obligations	211.7	251.2	378.0	364.1	240.1	144.2	136.6
Total Liabilities	2,517.8	2,064.5	2,033.2	1,954.4	1,810.0	1,660.2	1,319.7
Net Stockholders' Equity	306.1	293.3	277.1	239.7	259.6	260.1	176.3
Year-end Shs. Outstg. (000)	26,585	26,646	26,947	26,999	27,676	28,282	22,150
STATISTICAL RECORD:							
Return on Equity %	15.9	16.8	16.2	17.3	14.6	12.8	13.2
Return on Assets %	1.7	2.1	1.9	1.9	1.8	1.7	1.6
Equity/Assets %	10.8	12.4	12.0	10.9	12.5	13.5	11.8
Non-Int. Exp./Tot. Inc. %	40.6	38.7	40.7	40.7	39.4	45.3	50.0
Price Range	28.03-23.18	27.00-19.69	23.50-16.56	29.00-19.00	29.50-20.88	22.25-14.75	15.88-14.00
P/E Ratio	15.5-12.8	14.8-10.8	14.2-10.0	19.2-12.6	21.9-15.5	19.0-12.6	15.1-13.3
Average Yield %	3.7	3.9	4.1	3.1	2.5	2.9	3.0

Statistics are as originally reported. Adj. for 100% stk. split, 11/98. ① Excl. extraord. chrg. of $1.9 mill.

OFFICERS:
R. D. Duggan, Chmn.
J. C. Miller, Pres., C.E.O.
R. E. Rout, Exec. V.P., C.F.O., Sec.

INVESTOR CONTACT: Sandy Ingmire, (724) 465-1466

PRINCIPAL OFFICE: 43 South Ninth Street, Indiana, PA 15701

TELEPHONE NUMBER: (724) 465-1466
FAX: (724) 465-1488
WEB: www.stbank.com

NO. OF EMPLOYEES: 765

SHAREHOLDERS: 3,120 (record)

ANNUAL MEETING: In Apr.

INCORPORATED: PA, Mar., 1983

ST. PAUL COMPANIES, INC. (THE)

YIELD 3.2%
P/E RATIO 35.9

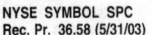
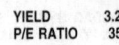
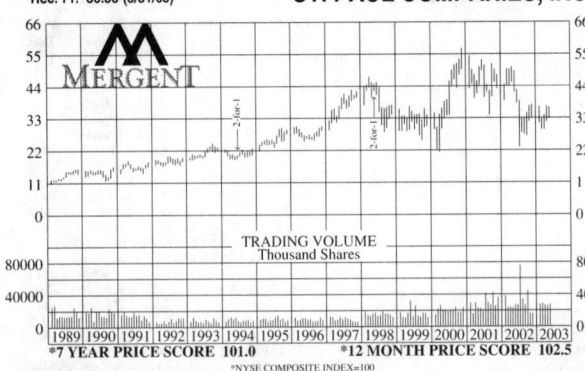

INTERIM EARNINGS (Per Share):

Qtr.	Mar.	June	Sept.	Dec.
1999	0.68	0.90	0.56	0.93
2000	1.53	0.95	0.98	0.86
2001	0.90	0.41	d2.86	d3.49
2002	0.67	d1.07	0.29	1.05
2003	0.75	...	...	...

INTERIM DIVIDENDS (Per Share):

Amt.	Decl.	Ex.	Rec.	Pay.
0.29Q	7/30/02	9/26/02	9/30/02	10/17/02
0.29Q	10/31/02	12/27/02	12/31/02	1/17/03
0.29Q	2/04/03	3/27/03	3/31/03	4/17/03
0.29Q	5/06/03	6/26/03	6/30/03	7/17/03

Indicated div.: $1.16 (Div. Reinv. Plan)

CAPITALIZATION (12/31/02):

	($000)	(%)
Long-Term Debt	2,713,000	32.1
Preferred Stock	65,000	0.8
Common & Surplus	5,681,000	67.2
Total	8,459,000	100.0

DIVIDEND ACHIEVER STATUS:
Rank: 230   10-Year Growth Rate: 5.51%
Total Years of Dividend Growth: 16

TRADING VOLUME Thousand Shares

7 YEAR PRICE SCORE 101.0   **12 MONTH PRICE SCORE 102.5**
*NYSE COMPOSITE INDEX=100

RECENT DEVELOPMENTS: For the quarter ended 3/31/03, net income was $181.0 million versus income of $142.0 million, before a loss from discontinued operations of $9.0 million, in the equivalent prior-year quarter. Total revenues declined 9.5% to $2.11 billion from $2.33 billion the previous year. Revenues for 2003 and 2002 included realized investment losses of $39.0 million and $38.0 million, respectively. Premiums earned fell 11.7% to $1.73 billion. Asset management revenues grew 8.5% to $102.0 million.

PROSPECTS: On 3/5/03, SPC announced a major new platform aimed at growing its business with small commercial enterprises. Features of the new approach include an underwriting technology, enhanced customer service capabilities, flexible and competitive insurance products, and a dedicated countrywide sales force. On 5/12/03, SPC announced that it had purchased the right to seek renewal of certain existing commercial insurance business written by the Kemper Insurance Companies in the U.S.

BUSINESS

ST. PAUL COMPANIES, INC. is a management company principally engaged in two industry segments: commercial property-liability insurance and nonlife reinsurance products and services. The Company also has a presence in the asset management industry through its 77.0% majority ownership of Nuveen Investments, Inc. As a management company, SPC oversees the operations of its subsidiaries and provides those subsidiaries with capital, management and administrative services. The primary business of the Company is underwriting, which produced 95.4% of consolidated revenues in 2002. The Company's investment banking-asset management operations accounted for 4.4% of consolidated revenues in 2002. In May 1997, the Company sold its insurance brokerage operation, The Minet Group. In April 1998, SPC acquired USF&G Corporation. In May 1997, the Company sold its insurance brokerage operation, The Minet Group. In April 1998, SPC acquired USF&G Corporation.

ANNUAL FINANCIAL DATA

	12/31/02	12/31/01	12/31/00	12/31/99	12/31/98	12/31/97	12/31/96
Earnings Per Share	⑤ 1.06	①④ d4.84	① 4.32	③ 3.19	② 0.32	① 4.20	① 3.25
Tang. Book Val. Per Share	20.58	21.03	30.54	26.42	25.79	25.09	22.87
Dividends Per Share	1.15	1.11	1.07	1.03	0.98	0.93	0.86
Dividend Payout %	108.5	...	24.8	32.3	307.7	22.0	26.5
INCOME STATEMENT (IN MILLIONS)							
Total Premium Income	7,390.0	7,296.0	5,898.0	5,290.0	6,944.6	4,616.5	4,448.2
Net Investment Income	1,169.0	1,217.0	1,616.0	1,557.0	1,585.0	886.2	807.3
Other Income	359.0	430.0	1,094.0	722.0	578.8	716.6	478.6
Total Revenues	8,918.0	8,943.0	8,608.0	7,569.0	9,108.4	6,219.3	5,734.2
Policyholder Benefits	5,995.0	7,479.0	4,407.0	4,087.0	5,876.3	3,345.2	3,318.3
Income Before Income Taxes	176.0	d1,431.0	1,453.0	1,017.0	d46.3	1,018.7	699.1
Income Taxes	cr73.0	cr422.0	440.0	238.0	cr135.6	245.5	141.3
Net Income	⑤ 249.0	①②④d1,009.0	① 1,013.0	③ 779.0	② 89.3	① 773.2	① 557.9
Average Shs. Outstg. (000)	227,000	212,000	233,000	246,000	238,682	184,522	168,838
BALANCE SHEET (IN MILLIONS)							
Cash & Cash Equivalents	2,467.0	2,304.0	1,347.0	1,583.0	1,209.2	552.9	470.6
Premiums Due	11,127.0	10,569.0	8,661.0	7,185.0	6,404.5	3,544.7	3,622.6
Invst. Assets: Fixed-term	17,188.0	15,911.0	20,470.0	19,329.0	21,056.3	12,449.8	11,944.1
Invst. Assets: Equities	394.0	1,410.0	1,466.0	1,618.0	1,258.5	1,033.9	808.2
Invst. Assets: Total	22,733.0	22,178.0	27,099.0	26,252.0	27,222.7	15,166.3	14,509.2
Total Assets	39,920.0	38,321.0	41,075.0	38,873.0	38,322.7	21,500.7	20,681.0
Long-Term Obligations	2,713.0	2,130.0	1,647.0	1,466.0	1,260.4	782.8	689.1
Net Stockholders' Equity	5,746.0	5,114.0	7,227.0	6,472.0	6,636.4	4,626.7	4,003.8
Year-end Shs. Outstg. (000)	226,798	207,624	218,308	224,830	233,750	167,456	167,032
STATISTICAL RECORD:							
Return on Revenues %	2.8	...	11.8	10.3	1.0	12.4	9.7
Return on Equity %	4.3	...	14.0	12.0	1.3	16.7	13.9
Return on Assets %	0.6	...	2.5	2.0	0.2	3.6	2.7
Price Range	50.60-23.00	54.44-34.00	57.00-21.31	37.06-25.38	47.19-28.06	42.75-28.81	30.38-25.00
P/E Ratio	47.7-21.7	...	13.2-4.9	11.6-8.0	147.4-87.7	10.2-6.9	9.4-7.7
Average Yield %	3.1	2.5	2.7	3.3	2.6	2.6	3.1

Statistics are as originally reported. Adj. for stk. split: 2-for-1, 5/98. ① Bef. disc. oper loss $79.6 mill., 12/01; $19.3 mill., 12/00; $67.8 mill., 12/97; $107.8 mill., 12/96 ② Incl. non-recurr. chrg. $221.0 mill. ③ Bef. acctg. change chrg. $29.9 mill. and excl. from disc. oper. $85.1 mill. ④ Incl. pre-tax restr. & goodwill chrgs. of $126.5 mill. ⑤ Bef. loss fr. disc. opers. of $25.2 mill. & acctg. chrg. $6.0 mill.; Incl. an after-tax settlement chrg. of $306.8 mill.

OFFICERS:
J. S. Fishman, Chmn., C.E.O.
T. A. Bradley, Sr. V.P., C.F.O.

INVESTOR CONTACT: Laura Gagon, Investor Relations, (651) 310-7696

PRINCIPAL OFFICE: 385 Washington Street, Saint Paul, MN 55102

TELEPHONE NUMBER: (651) 310-7911
FAX: (651) 310-3386
WEB: www.stpaul.com

NO. OF EMPLOYEES: 9,700 (approx.)

SHAREHOLDERS: 18,021

ANNUAL MEETING: In May

INCORPORATED: MN, May, 1853

INSTITUTIONAL HOLDINGS:
No. of Institutions: 391
Shares Held: 195,051,594
% Held: 85.9

INDUSTRY: Fire, marine, and casualty insurance (SIC: 6331)

TRANSFER AGENT(S): Wells Fargo Shareowner Services, South St. Paul, MN

SARA LEE CORPORATION

YIELD	3.4%
P/E RATIO	11.7

*7 YEAR PRICE SCORE 103.2   ***12 MONTH PRICE SCORE 87.8**
*NYSE COMPOSITE INDEX=100

INTERIM EARNINGS (Per Share):

Qtr.	Sept.	Dec.	Mar.	June
1999-00	0.28	0.42	0.29	0.35
2000-01	0.27	0.17	0.28	1.19
2001-02	0.30	0.20	0.31	0.43
2002-03	0.38	0.42	0.33	...

INTERIM DIVIDENDS (Per Share):

Amt.	Decl.	Ex.	Rec.	Pay.
0.15Q	4/25/02	5/30/02	6/03/02	7/01/02
0.15Q	6/27/02	8/29/02	9/03/02	10/01/02
0.155Q	10/31/02	11/27/02	12/02/02	1/02/03
0.155Q	1/30/03	2/27/03	3/03/03	4/01/03
0.155Q	5/08/03	5/29/03	6/02/03	7/01/03

Indicated div.: $0.62 (Div. Reinv. Plan)

CAPITALIZATION (6/29/02):

	($000)	(%)
Long-Term Debt	4,326,000	59.7
Deferred Income Tax	534,000	7.4
Minority Interest	632,000	8.7
Redeemable Pfd. Stock	226,000	3.1
Common & Surplus	1,534,000	21.2
Total	7,252,000	100.0

DIVIDEND ACHIEVER STATUS:

Rank: 162   10-Year Growth Rate: 9.15%
Total Years of Dividend Growth: 26

RECENT DEVELOPMENTS: For the quarter ended 3/29/03, net income rose 4.7% to $269.0 million from $257.0 million a year earlier. Results included pre-tax gains of $1.0 million and $5.0 million in 2003 and 2002, respectively, primarily related to restructuring and business dispositions. Net sales grew 3.6% to $4.35 billion from $4.20 billion the year before. Operating income climbed 7.3% to $328.0 million from $307.0 million the previous year.

PROSPECTS: Earnings should benefit from the aggressive implementation of cost-control initiatives, new product introductions, and increased marketing support for the Company's key brands. In an effort to improve the profitability of its bakery operations, SLE plans to eliminate approximately 60 regional fresh bread brands and close three manufacturing facilities in the U.S during the fourth quarter of fiscal 2003.

BUSINESS

SARA LEE CORPORATION is a global manufacturer and marketer of brand-name foods and consumer products. Intimates & Underwear (36.6% of fiscal 2002 sales) is comprised of SLE's intimates, knit products, legwear and accessories businesses. Well-known brands include BALI, HANES HER WAY, and PLAYTEX. Sara Lee Meats (21.0%) includes such brands as HILLSHIRE FARM, JIMMY DEAN, BALL PARK, and BRYAN. Sara Lee Bakery (16.9%) includes products sold under the EARTH GRAINS brand. Beverage (14.4%) includes such brands as HILLS BROS., CHOCK FULL O'NUTS, DOUWE EGBERTS, PICKWICK and MARCILLA. Household Products (11.1%) is comprised of shoe care, body care, insecticides, air fresheners, and SLE's direct sales operations. On 12/4/00, SLE sold PYA/Monarch, its U.S. foodservice distributor. On 8/7/01, SLE acquired The Earthgrains Company.

ANNUAL FINANCIAL DATA

	6/29/02	6/30/01	7/1/00	7/3/99	6/27/98	6/28/97	6/29/96
Earnings Per Share	⑤1.23	④1.87	③1.27	①1.26	②d0.57	1.02	0.92
Cash Flow Per Share	1.95	2.58	1.92	1.83	0.09	1.71	1.57
Tang. Book Val. Per Share	...	...	...	...	...	...	...
Dividends Per Share	0.60	0.58	0.54	0.50	0.46	0.35	0.46
Dividend Payout %	48.8	31.0	42.5	39.7	...	41.4	41.5
INCOME STATEMENT (IN MILLIONS):							
Total Revenues	17,628.0	17,747.0	17,511.0	20,012.0	20,011.0	19,734.0	18,624.0
Costs & Expenses	15,476.0	15,556.0	15,166.0	17,708.0	17,620.0	17,411.0	16,439.0
Depreciation & Amort.	582.0	599.0	602.0	553.0	618.0	680.0	634.0
Operating Income	1,570.0	1,592.0	1,743.0	1,751.0	1,773.0	1,643.0	1,551.0
Net Interest Inc./(Exp.)	d208.0	d180.0	d176.0	d141.0	d176.0	d159.0	d173.0
Income Before Income Taxes	1,185.0	1,851.0	1,567.0	1,671.0	d443.0	1,484.0	1,378.0
Income Taxes	175.0	248.0	409.0	480.0	80.0	475.0	462.0
Net Income	⑤1,010.0	④1,603.0	③1,158.0	①1,191.0	②d523.0	1,009.0	916.0
Cash Flow	1,592.0	2,202.0	1,748.0	1,732.0	81.0	1,663.0	1,523.0
Average Shs. Outstg. (000)	818,000	854,000	912,000	944,000	939,000	970,000	970,000
BALANCE SHEET (IN MILLIONS):							
Cash & Cash Equivalents	298.0	548.0	314.0	279.0	273.0	272.0	243.0
Total Current Assets	4,986.0	5,083.0	5,974.0	4,987.0	5,220.0	5,391.0	5,081.0
Net Property	3,155.0	2,146.0	2,319.0	2,169.0	2,090.0	3,079.0	3,007.0
Total Assets	13,753.0	10,167.0	11,611.0	10,521.0	10,989.0	12,953.0	12,602.0
Total Current Liabilities	5,463.0	4,958.0	6,759.0	5,953.0	5,733.0	5,016.0	4,642.0
Long-Term Obligations	4,326.0	2,640.0	2,248.0	1,892.0	2,270.0	1,933.0	1,842.0
Net Stockholders' Equity	1,534.0	1,122.0	1,234.0	1,266.0	1,816.0	4,280.0	4,320.0
Net Working Capital	d477.0	125.0	d785.0	d966.0	d513.0	375.0	439.0
Year-end Shs. Outstg. (000)	784,721	781,964	846,332	883,783	921,328	960,554	970,110
STATISTICAL RECORD:							
Operating Profit Margin %	8.9	9.0	10.0	8.7	8.9	8.3	8.3
Net Profit Margin %	5.7	9.0	6.6	6.0	...	5.1	4.9
Return on Equity %	65.8	142.9	93.8	94.1	...	23.6	21.2
Return on Assets %	7.3	15.8	10.0	11.3	...	7.8	7.3
Debt/Total Assets %	31.5	26.0	19.4	18.0	20.7	14.9	14.6
Price Range	23.84-16.15	24.75-18.26	25.31-13.38	28.75-21.06	31.81-22.16	28.91-18.25	20.25-14.94
P/E Ratio	19.4-13.1	13.2-9.8	19.9-10.5	22.8-16.7	...	28.5-18.0	22.1-16.3
Average Yield %	3.0	2.7	2.8	2.0	1.7	1.8	2.2

Statistics are as originally reported. Adj. for 2-for-1 stk. split, 12/98. ① Incl. $50 mil ($0.05/sh) net chg. from product recall & incl. $97 mil ($0.10/sh) net gain on sale of int'l tobacco opers. ② Incl. $1.60 bil ($1.72/sh) after-tax restr. chg. ③ Bef. $64.0 mil ($0.07/sh) income fr. disc. oper. ④ Bef. $663 mil ($0.78/sh) gain fr. disc. opers., incl. $967 mil pre-tax gain fr. disposal of Coach business & $554 mil of other one-time chgs. ⑤ Incl. $170 mil pre-tax chg.

OFFICERS:
C. S. McMillan, Chmn., Pres., C.E.O.
L. M. de Kool, Exec. V.P., C.F.O.
R. A. Palmore, Sr. V.P., Sec., Gen. Couns.
INVESTOR CONTACT: Janet Bergman, Sr. V.P., Corp. Rel., (312) 558-8651
PRINCIPAL OFFICE: Three First National Plaza, Suite 4600, Chicago, IL 60602-4260

TELEPHONE NUMBER: (312) 726-2600
FAX: (312) 558-4913
WEB: www.saralee.com
NO. OF EMPLOYEES: 154,900 (approx.)
SHAREHOLDERS: 74,500 (approx.)
ANNUAL MEETING: In Oct.
INCORPORATED: MD, Sept., 1941

INSTITUTIONAL HOLDINGS:
No. of Institutions: 630
Shares Held: 470,194,718
% Held: 60.1
INDUSTRY: Sausages and other prepared meats (SIC: 2013)
TRANSFER AGENT(S): Sara Lee Corp., Chicago, IL

SBC COMMUNICATIONS INC.

YIELD 4.4%
P/E RATIO 10.2

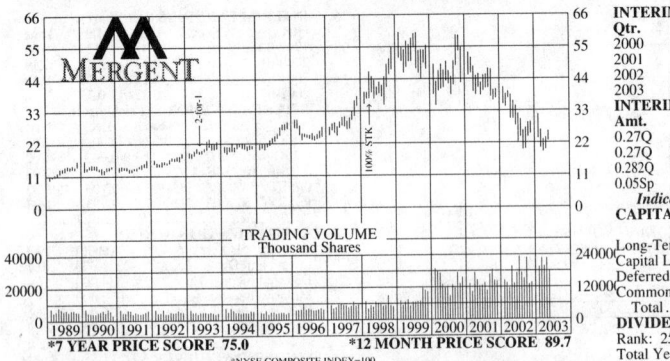

7 YEAR PRICE SCORE 75.0   **12 MONTH PRICE SCORE 89.7**
NYSE COMPOSITE INDEX=100

INTERIM EARNINGS (Per Share):

Qtr.	Mar.	June	Sept.	Dec.
2000	0.53	0.54	0.88	0.38
2001	0.54	0.61	0.61	0.37
2002	0.48	0.53	0.51	0.71
2003	0.74	...	...	...

INTERIM DIVIDENDS (Per Share):

Amt.	Decl.	Ex.	Rec.	Pay.
0.27Q	9/27/02	10/08/02	10/10/02	11/01/02
0.27Q	12/13/02	1/08/03	1/10/03	2/03/03
0.282Q	3/28/03	4/08/03	4/10/03	5/01/03
0.05Sp	3/28/03	4/08/03	4/10/03	5/01/03

Indicated div.: $1.13 (Div. Reinv. Plan)

CAPITALIZATION (12/31/02):

	($000)	(%)
Long-Term Debt	18,393,000	29.4
Capital Lease Obligations	143,000	
Deferred Income Tax	10,726,000	17.2
Common & Surplus	33,199,000	53.2
Total	62,461,000	100.0

DIVIDEND ACHIEVER STATUS:
Rank: 252   10-Year Growth Rate: 3.93%
Total Years of Dividend Growth: 18

RECENT DEVELOPMENTS: For the quarter ended 3/31/03, income was $2.46 billion compared with income of $1.63 billion in the same period a year earlier. Results for 2003 included an after-tax gain of $0.32 per diluted share related to the sale of SBC's interest in Cegetel. Results excluded a gain of $2.55 billion for 2003 and a charge of $1.82 for 2002 related to accounting changes. Total revenues slipped 1.8% to $10.33 billion.

PROSPECTS: SBC's near-term outlook is mixed. On one hand, SBC's top line continues to be pressured by the economic and competitive environments. On the other hand, the Company is seeing good growth from its digital subscriber line Internet service and long-distance operations. SBC expects to gain regulatory approvals to offer long-distance in its five remaining states in 2003.

BUSINESS

SBC COMMUNICATIONS INC. (formerly Southwestern Bell) is one of seven regional holding companies divested by AT&T in 1984. SBC offers a variety of products and services under the SBC Ameritech, SBC Nevada Bell, SBC Pacific Bell, SNET, and SBC Southwestern Bell brands, including local and long-distance voice, Internet services, telecommunications equipment, directory advertising and publishing. As of 1/28/03, SBC had 57.0 million network access lines in service and maintained a 60.0% equity interest in Cingular Wireless, which was formed in April 2000 and serves more than 22.0 million wireless customers. Internationally, SBC has telecommunications investments in 27 countries. On 4/1/97, SBC acquired Pacific Telesis Group. On 10/26/98, SBC acquired Southern New England Telecommunications Corporation. On 10/8/99, SBC acquired Ameritech Corp.

ANNUAL FINANCIAL DATA

	12/31/02	12/31/01	12/31/00	12/31/99	12/31/98	⑧12/31/97	12/31/96
Earnings Per Share	⑧2.23	⑦2.14	⑥2.32	⑤1.90	④2.05	③①0.80	1.73
Cash Flow Per Share	4.79	4.80	5.14	4.35	4.62	3.42	3.55
Tang. Book Val. Per Share	9.51	8.62	7.38	5.87	4.95	3.61	3.62
Dividends Per Share	1.07	1.02	1.00	0.96	0.93	0.89	0.85
Dividend Payout %	47.8	47.8	43.3	50.8	45.1	110.8	49.2

INCOME STATEMENT (IN MILLIONS):

Total Revenues	43,138.0	45,908.0	51,476.0	49,489.0	28,777.0	24,856.0	13,898.0
Costs & Expenses	25,967.0	25,987.0	31,056.0	29,423.0	16,786.0	16,845.0	8,134.0
Depreciation & Amort.	8,548.0	9,033.0	9,677.0	8,468.0	5,105.0	4,841.0	2,208.0
Operating Income	8,623.0	10,888.0	10,743.0	11,598.0	6,886.0	3,170.0	3,556.0
Net Interest Inc./(Exp.)	d821.0	d917.0	d1,313.0	d1,430.0	d993.0	d947.0	d472.0
Income Before Income Taxes	10,457.0	11,357.0	12,888.0	10,853.0	6,374.0	2,337.0	3,267.0
Income Taxes	2,984.0	4,097.0	4,921.0	4,280.0	2,306.0	863.0	1,166.0
Net Income	⑧7,473.0	⑦7,260.0	⑥7,967.0	⑤6,573.0	④4,068.0	③①1,474.0	2,101.0
Cash Flow	16,021.0	16,293.0	17,644.0	15,041.0	9,173.0	6,315.0	4,309.0
Average Shs. Outstg. (000)	3,348,000	3,396,000	3,433,000	3,458,000	1,984,000	1,844,000	1,214,000

BALANCE SHEET (IN MILLIONS):

Cash & Cash Equivalents	3,567.0	703.0	643.0	495.0	466.0	718.0	755.0
Total Current Assets	14,089.0	12,580.0	23,216.0	11,930.0	7,538.0	7,062.0	3,912.0
Net Property	48,490.0	49,827.0	47,195.0	46,571.0	29,920.0	27,339.0	14,007.0
Total Assets	95,057.0	96,322.0	98,651.0	83,215.0	45,066.0	42,132.0	23,449.0
Total Current Liabilities	14,683.0	23,948.0	30,357.0	19,313.0	9,989.0	10,252.0	5,820.0
Long-Term Obligations	18,536.0	17,133.0	15,492.0	17,475.0	11,612.0	12,019.0	5,505.0
Net Stockholders' Equity	33,199.0	32,491.0	30,463.0	26,726.0	12,780.0	9,892.0	6,835.0
Net Working Capital	d594.0	d11,368.0	d7,141.0	d7,383.0	d2,451.0	d3,190.0	d1,908.0
Year-end Shs. Outstg. (000)	3,318,000	3,354,216	3,386,709	3,395,272	1,959,000	1,837,000	1,200,000

STATISTICAL RECORD:

Operating Profit Margin %	20.0	23.7	20.9	23.4	23.9	12.8	25.6
Net Profit Margin %	17.3	15.8	15.5	13.3	14.1	5.9	15.1
Return on Equity %	22.5	22.3	26.2	24.6	31.8	14.9	30.7
Return on Assets %	7.9	7.5	8.1	7.9	9.0	3.5	9.0
Debt/Total Assets %	19.5	17.8	15.7	21.0	25.8	28.5	23.5
Price Range	40.99-19.57	53.06-36.50	59.00-34.81	59.94-44.06	54.88-35.00	38.06-24.63	30.13-23.00
P/E Ratio	18.4-8.8	24.8-17.1	25.4-15.0	31.5-23.2	26.8-17.1	47.6-30.8	17.4-13.3
Average Yield %	3.5	2.3	2.1	1.9	2.1	2.8	3.2

Statistics are as originally reported. Adj. 100% stk. div., 3/98. ① Incl. ops. of Pacific Telesis Group, acq. 4/97. ② Incl. nonrecur. chrgs. $1.89 bil. ③ Bef. extraord. chrg. of $2.82 bil. ④ Bef. extraord. loss of $60.0 mill.; bef. acctg. chg. cr. of $15.0 mill. ⑤ Bef. extraord. gain of $1.38 bil. & acctg. chg. cr. of $207.0 mill.; incl. nonrecur. chrgs. of $866.0 mill. ⑥ Incl. nonrecur. chrgs. of $659.0 mill. ⑦ Bef. extraord. chrg. of $18.0 mill.; incl. nonrecur. chrgs. of $1.14 bil. ⑧ Bef. acctg. chg. chrg. of $1.82 bil.

OFFICERS:
E. E. Whitacre, Jr., Chmn., C.E.O.
W. M. Daley, Pres.
S. Stephenson, Sr., Exec. V.P., C.F.O.

INVESTOR CONTACT: Larry L. Solomon, Investor Relations, (210) 351-3990

PRINCIPAL OFFICE: 175 E. Houston, P.O. Box 2933, San Antonio, TX 78299-2933

TELEPHONE NUMBER: (210) 821-4105
FAX: (210) 351-3553
WEB: www.sbc.com

NO. OF EMPLOYEES: 175,400 (approx.)
SHAREHOLDERS: 1,027,716
ANNUAL MEETING: In Apr.
INCORPORATED: DE, Oct., 1983

INSTITUTIONAL HOLDINGS:
No. of Institutions: 989
Shares Held: 1,646,019,862
% Held: 49.6

INDUSTRY: Telephone communications, exc. radio (SIC: 4813)

TRANSFER AGENT(S): EquiServe Trust Company, N.A., Jersey City, NJ

SCHERING-PLOUGH CORPORATION

YIELD 3.7%
P/E RATIO 16.3

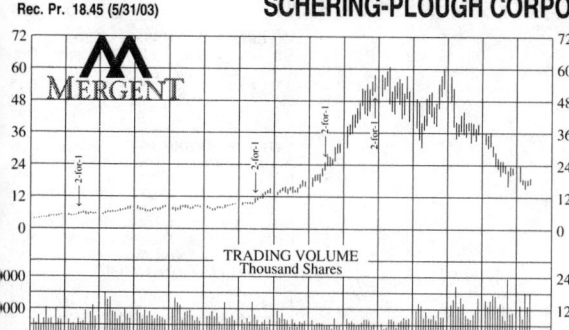

72 · 60 · 48 · 36 · 24 · 12 · 0

TRADING VOLUME
Thousand Shares

| 1989 | 1990 | 1991 | 1992 | 1993 | 1994 | 1995 | 1996 | 1997 | 1998 | 1999 | 2000 | 2001 | 2002 | 2003 |

*7 YEAR PRICE SCORE 66.5   ***12 MONTH PRICE SCORE 85.1**
*NYSE COMPOSITE INDEX=100

INTERIM EARNINGS (Per Share):

Qtr.	Mar.	June	Sept.	Dec.
1999	0.36	0.37	0.35	0.34
2000	0.42	0.43	0.40	0.39
2001	0.38	0.43	0.41	0.10
2002	0.41	0.43	0.29	0.29
2003	0.12	...	...	...

INTERIM DIVIDENDS (Per Share):

Amt.	Decl.	Ex.	Rec.	Pay.
0.17Q	4/23/02	5/01/02	5/03/02	5/28/02
0.17Q	6/25/02	7/31/02	8/02/02	8/27/02
0.17Q	10/22/02	10/30/02	11/01/02	11/26/02
0.17Q	1/28/03	2/05/03	2/07/03	2/28/03
0.17Q	4/22/03	4/30/03	5/02/03	5/27/03

Indicated div.: $0.68 (Div. Reinv. Plan)

CAPITALIZATION (12/31/02):

	($000)	(%)
Deferred Income Tax	358,000	4.2
Common & Surplus	8,142,000	95.8
Total	8,500,000	100.0

DIVIDEND ACHIEVER STATUS:
Rank: 80   10-Year Growth Rate: 13.58%
Total Years of Dividend Growth: 17

RECENT DEVELOPMENTS: For the three months ended 3/31/03, net income dropped 71.2% to $173.0 million compared with $600.0 million in the corresponding quarter of the previous year. The decline in earnings was largely due to the loss of U.S. sales and profits of the prescription CLARITIN line of nonsedating antihistimines, which resulted from its patent expiration and conversion from prescription to over-to-counter status in December 2002. Net sales decreased 18.9% to $2.07 billion.

PROSPECTS: In response to declining sales and earnings, SGP recently announced that it is installing a globalized management and systems structure that will introduce a new focus on cost management. The Company is also launching structural changes that should allow SGP to generate long-term growth. Meanwhile, SGP will work to contain or reduce overhead costs while channeling additional investment into key areas for growth, including the field force and product development and acquisition.

BUSINESS

SCHERING-PLOUGH CORPORATION is a is a global company primarily engaged in the discovery, development, manufacturing and marketing of pharmaceutical and consumer products. Pharmaceutical products include prescription drugs, over-the-counter medicines, vision-care products and animal health products promoted to the medical and allied professions. Prescription products include: CELESTAMINE, CLARINEX, CLARITIN, CLARITIN-D, CLARITIN SYRUP, NASONEX, POLARAMINE, PROVENTIL, and VANCERIL. The healthcare product segment consists of over-the-counter foot care products, including DR. SHOLLS, and sun care products, including COPPERTONE and BAIN DE SOLEIL. Healthcare products are sold primarily in the United States. In 2002, contributions to sales were pharmaceutical products, 85.9%; and healthcare products, 14.1%.

ANNUAL FINANCIAL DATA

	12/31/02	12/31/01	12/31/00	12/31/99	12/31/98	12/31/97	12/31/96
Earnings Per Share	② 1.35	① 1.32	1.64	1.42	1.18	0.97	0.83
Cash Flow Per Share	1.60	1.54	1.84	1.60	1.34	1.11	0.94
Tang. Book Val. Per Share	5.10	4.41	3.75	3.11	2.33	1.60	1.41
Dividends Per Share	0.67	0.62	0.55	0.48	0.42	0.37	0.32
Dividend Payout %	49.6	47.0	33.2	34.2	36.0	37.9	38.8

INCOME STATEMENT (IN MILLIONS):

	12/31/02	12/31/01	12/31/00	12/31/99	12/31/98	12/31/97	12/31/96
Total Revenues	10,180.0	9,802.0	9,815.0	9,176.0	8,077.0	6,778.0	5,656.0
Costs & Expenses	7,239.0	6,959.0	6,328.0	6,117.0	5,513.0	4,665.0	3,836.8
Depreciation & Amort.	372.0	320.0	299.0	264.0	238.0	200.0	173.2
Operating Income	2,569.0	2,523.0	3,188.0	2,795.0	2,326.0	1,913.0	1,646.0
Net Interest Inc./(Exp.)	47.0	...	...	...	...	...	...
Income Before Income Taxes	2,563.0	2,523.0	3,188.0	2,795.0	2,326.0	1,913.0	1,606.0
Income Taxes	589.0	580.0	765.0	685.0	570.0	469.0	393.0
Net Income	② 1,974.0	① 1,943.0	2,423.0	2,110.0	1,756.0	1,444.0	1,213.0
Cash Flow	2,346.0	2,263.0	2,722.0	2,374.0	1,994.0	1,644.0	1,386.2
Average Shs. Outstg. (000)	1,470,000	1,470,000	1,476,000	1,486,000	1,488,000	1,480,000	1,470,800

BALANCE SHEET (IN MILLIONS):

	12/31/02	12/31/01	12/31/00	12/31/99	12/31/98	12/31/97	12/31/96
Cash & Cash Equivalents	4,002.0	2,716.0	2,397.0	1,876.0	1,259.0	714.0	535.1
Total Current Assets	8,272.0	6,519.0	5,720.0	4,909.0	3,958.0	2,920.0	2,364.6
Net Property	4,236.0	3,814.0	3,362.0	2,939.0	2,675.0	2,526.0	2,246.3
Total Assets	14,136.0	12,174.0	10,805.0	9,375.0	7,840.0	6,507.0	6,253.2
Total Current Liabilities	4,729.0	3,917.0	3,645.0	3,209.0	3,032.0	2,891.0	3,454.2
Long-Term Obligations	...	...	...	...	...	46.0	46.4
Net Stockholders' Equity	8,142.0	7,125.0	6,119.0	5,165.0	4,002.0	2,821.0	2,059.9
Net Working Capital	3,543.0	2,602.0	2,075.0	1,700.0	926.0	29.0	d1,089.6
Year-end Shs. Outstg. (000)	1,468,000	1,465,000	1,463,000	1,472,000	1,472,000	1,466,000	1,461,468

STATISTICAL RECORD:

	12/31/02	12/31/01	12/31/00	12/31/99	12/31/98	12/31/97	12/31/96
Operating Profit Margin %	25.2	25.7	32.5	30.5	28.8	28.2	29.1
Net Profit Margin %	19.4	19.8	24.7	23.0	21.7	21.3	21.4
Return on Equity %	24.2	27.3	39.6	40.9	43.9	51.2	58.9
Return on Assets %	14.0	16.0	22.4	22.5	22.4	22.2	19.4
Debt/Total Assets %	...	...	...	...	...	0.7	0.7
Price Range	36.25-16.10	57.25-32.35	60.00-30.50	60.81-40.25	57.75-30.34	32.00-15.88	18.28-12.63
P/E Ratio	26.8-11.9	43.4-24.5	36.6-18.6	42.8-28.3	48.9-25.7	33.0-16.4	22.2-15.3
Average Yield %	2.6	1.4	1.2	1.0	1.0	1.5	2.1

Statistics are as originally reported. Adjusted for 2-for-1 stock split, 12/98 & 8/97. ① Incl. $500.0 mill. provision for a consent decree payment. ② Incl. pre-tax gain of $80.0 mill.

OFFICERS:
F. Hassan, Chmn., Pres., C.E.O.
J. L. Wyszomierski, Exec. V.P., C.F.O.

INVESTOR CONTACT: Geraldine U. Foster, Sr. V.P., (908) 298-4000

PRINCIPAL OFFICE: 2000 Galloping Hill Road, Kenilworth, NJ 07033-0530

TELEPHONE NUMBER: (908) 298-4000
FAX: (908) 822-7048
WEB: www.schering-plough.com

NO. OF EMPLOYEES: 30,500 (approx.)

SHAREHOLDERS: 30,500

ANNUAL MEETING: In Apr.

INCORPORATED: NJ, July, 1970

INSTITUTIONAL HOLDINGS:
No. of Institutions: 816
Shares Held: 1,037,200,959
% Held: 70.6

INDUSTRY: Pharmaceutical preparations (SIC: 2834)

TRANSFER AGENT(S): The Bank of New York, New York, NY

SEI INVESTMENTS COMPANY

YIELD 0.5%
P/E RATIO 22.9

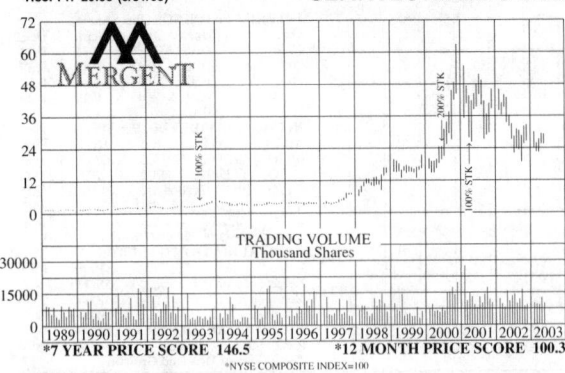

TRADING VOLUME
Thousand Shares

| 1989 | 1990 | 1991 | 1992 | 1993 | 1994 | 1995 | 1996 | 1997 | 1998 | 1999 | 2000 | 2001 | 2002 | 2003 |

*7 YEAR PRICE SCORE 146.5   ***12 MONTH PRICE SCORE 100.3**

*NYSE COMPOSITE INDEX=100

INTERIM EARNINGS (Per Share):

Qtr.	Mar.	June	Sept.	Dec.
1999	0.13	0.14	0.16	0.17
2000	0.18	0.20	0.24	0.25
2001	0.25	0.27	0.28	0.29
2002	0.30	0.31	0.32	0.32
2003	0.32	...	...	...

INTERIM DIVIDENDS (Per Share):

Amt.	Decl.	Ex.	Rec.	Pay.
0.05S	5/29/01	6/08/01	6/12/01	6/26/01
0.05S	12/13/01	1/02/02	1/04/02	1/22/02
0.06S	5/14/02	5/23/02	5/28/02	6/21/02
0.06S	12/10/02	12/31/02	1/03/03	1/21/03
0.07S	5/28/03	6/05/03	6/09/03	6/25/03

Indicated div.: $0.14

CAPITALIZATION (12/31/02):

	($000)	(%)
Long-Term Debt	33,500	10.2
Deferred Income Tax	6,393	1.9
Common & Surplus	290,007	87.9
Total	329,900	100.0

DIVIDEND ACHIEVER STATUS:
Rank: 10   10-Year Growth Rate: 24.29%
Total Years of Dividend Growth: 11

RECENT DEVELOPMENTS: For the quarter ended 3/31/03, net income increased 3.2% to $35.1 million from $34.0 million in the corresponding period the year before. Results for 2003 and 2002 included equity in earnings of an unconsolidated affiliate of $3.6 million and $2.7 million, respectively. Total revenues declined 5.4% to $150.6 million, resulting from difficult capital markets. On a segment basis, Private Banking and Trust revenue fell 7.3% to $76.9 million, primarily reflecting losses in the mutual fund processing business. Investment Advisors revenue slipped 7.7% to $35.9 million, while Enterprises revenue decreased 4.8% to $14.0 million. Revenues from Investment in New Business slid 3.3% to $11.4 million. However, Money Managers revenue grew 14.2% to $12.3 million. Operating and development expenses decreased 3.2% to $66.6 million compared with $68.7 million a year earlier. Going forward, the Company expects to accelerate its strategic new business initiatives in the second quarter of 2003.

BUSINESS

SEI INVESTMENTS COMPANY is a provider of asset management and investment technology services with operations in five business segments. The Private Banking & Trust segment (52.3% of 2002 operating profit) provides investment processing services, fund processing services, and investment management programs to banks and private trust companies. The Investment Advisors segment (24.0%, 33.6%) provides investment management programs and investment processing services to investors through a network of financial intermediaries. The Enterprises segment (9.0%, 9.4%) provides retirement and treasury business services for corporations, unions, foundations and endowments, and other institutional investors. The Money Managers segment (7.4%, 3.8%) provides business services to U.S. investment managers, mutual fund companies and alternative investment managers worldwide. Investments in New Businesses (7.3%, -6.3%) includes SEIC's global businesses, as well as initiatives in new U.S. markets. As of 4/17/03, SEIC operated 21 offices in ten countries.

ANNUAL FINANCIAL DATA

	12/31/02	12/31/01	12/31/00	12/31/99	12/31/98	12/31/97	12/31/96
Earnings Per Share	② 1.25	1.09	0.87	0.59	0.38	0.23	① 0.20
Cash Flow Per Share	1.41	1.26	1.02	0.73	0.51	0.35	0.29
Tang. Book Val. Per Share	2.66	2.38	1.70	0.60	0.40	0.26	0.37
Dividends Per Share	0.11	0.09	0.07	0.06	0.05	0.043	0.037
Dividend Payout %	8.8	8.3	8.4	10.2	13.3	18.6	18.3

INCOME STATEMENT (IN THOUSANDS):

	12/31/02	12/31/01	12/31/00	12/31/99	12/31/98	12/31/97	12/31/96
Total Revenues	620,819	658,013	598,806	456,192	366,119	292,749	247,817
Costs & Expenses	392,940	455,177	433,542	337,905	282,546	233,169	201,691
Depreciation & Amort.	18,060	19,650	17,305	15,793	15,688	14,068	10,039
Operating Income	209,819	183,186	147,959	102,494	67,885	45,512	36,087
Net Interest Inc./(Exp.)	2,937	4,796	4,126	d90	d1,017	d1,505	760
Income Before Income Taxes	223,048	198,324	159,618	109,169	69,883	44,007	37,944
Income Taxes	82,528	73,380	60,655	42,030	26,904	17,163	14,798
Net Income	② 140,520	124,944	98,963	67,139	42,979	26,844	① 23,146
Cash Flow	158,580	144,594	116,268	82,932	58,667	40,912	33,185
Average Shs. Outstg.	112,803	114,810	113,820	113,826	114,756	115,416	116,088

BALANCE SHEET (IN THOUSANDS):

	12/31/02	12/31/01	12/31/00	12/31/99	12/31/98	12/31/97	12/31/96
Cash & Cash Equivalents	175,724	173,685	159,576	73,206	52,980	16,891	13,167
Total Current Assets	134,247	266,142	249,031	146,992	113,509	83,995	64,956
Net Property	104,258	95,804	75,111	65,640	62,761	52,131	48,620
Total Assets	464,147	460,916	375,582	253,779	208,772	168,884	141,041
Total Current Liabilities	134,247	144,343	146,453	138,918	110,794	81,676	79,957
Long-Term Obligations	33,500	43,055	27,000	29,000	31,000	33,000	...
Net Stockholders' Equity	290,007	270,593	197,421	79,002	59,685	46,410	56,104
Net Working Capital	127,188	121,799	102,578	8,074	2,715	2,319	d15,001
Year-end Shs. Outstg.	109,180	109,180	108,560	106,152	107,166	106,602	110,988

STATISTICAL RECORD:

	12/31/02	12/31/01	12/31/00	12/31/99	12/31/98	12/31/97	12/31/96
Operating Profit Margin %	33.8	27.8	24.7	22.5	18.5	15.5	14.6
Net Profit Margin %	22.6	19.0	16.5	14.7	11.7	9.2	9.3
Return on Equity %	48.5	46.2	50.1	85.0	72.0	57.8	41.3
Return on Assets %	30.3	27.1	26.3	26.5	20.6	15.9	16.4
Debt/Total Assets %	7.2	9.3	7.2	11.4	14.8	19.5	...
Price Range	45.98-18.82	54.91-26.25	62.84-14.79	21.50-12.89	16.75-6.17	7.42-3.12	4.27-2.96
P/E Ratio	36.8-15.1	50.4-24.1	72.2-17.0	36.4-21.9	44.7-16.4	31.8-13.4	21.3-14.8
Average Yield %	0.3	0.2	0.2	0.3	0.4	0.8	1.0

Statistics are as originally reported. Adj. for 2-for-1 stk. split, 2/28/01. ① Bef. disc. oper. loss of $16.3 mill., 1996; $1.9 mill., 1995. ② Incl. a net loss on investments of $2.4 mill.

OFFICERS:
A. P. West Jr., Chmn., C.E.O.
D. J. McGonigle, Exec. V.P., C.F.O.
T. B. Cipperman, Sr. V.P., Gen. Couns.

INVESTOR CONTACT: Investor Relations, (610) 676-1000

PRINCIPAL OFFICE: 1 Freedom Valley Drive, Oaks, PA 19456-1100

TELEPHONE NUMBER: (610) 676-1000
FAX: (610) 676-1105
WEB: www.seic.com
NO. OF EMPLOYEES: 1,824 full-time; 66 part-time
SHAREHOLDERS: 700 (approx.)
ANNUAL MEETING: In May
INCORPORATED: PA, 1968

INSTITUTIONAL HOLDINGS:
No. of Institutions: 206
Shares Held: 51,034,980
% Held: 48.1

INDUSTRY: Security brokers and dealers (SIC: 6211)

TRANSFER AGENT(S): American Stock Transfer & Trust Co., New York, NY

SERVICEMASTER COMPANY (THE)

YIELD 4.0%
P/E RATIO 19.7

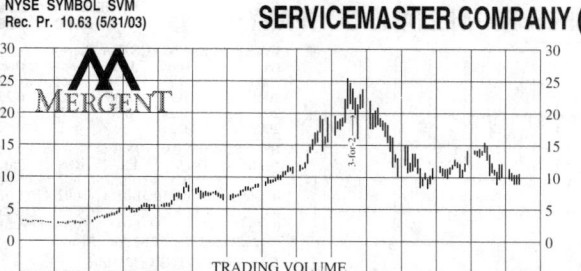

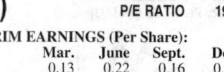

TRADING VOLUME
Thousand Shares

*7 YEAR PRICE SCORE 88.5 *12 MONTH PRICE SCORE 88.8

*NYSE COMPOSITE INDEX=100

INTERIM EARNINGS (Per Share):

Qtr.	Mar.	June	Sept.	Dec.
2000	0.13	0.22	0.16	0.11
2001	0.08	0.17	0.12	d0.86
2002	0.04	0.23	0.22	0.07
2003	0.02	...	...	...

INTERIM DIVIDENDS (Per Share):

Amt.	Decl.	Ex.	Rec.	Pay.
0.105Q	4/29/02	7/10/02	7/12/02	7/31/02
0.105Q	7/19/02	10/09/02	10/11/02	10/31/02
0.105Q	10/25/02	1/08/03	1/10/03	1/31/03
0.105Q	3/14/03	4/09/03	4/11/03	4/30/03
0.105Q	5/21/03	7/09/03	7/11/03	7/31/03

Indicated div.: $0.42 (Div. Reinv. Plan)

CAPITALIZATION (12/31/02):

	($000)	(%)
Long-Term Debt	804,340	34.4
Deferred Income Tax	312,500	13.4
Common & Surplus	1,218,700	52.2
Total	2,335,540	100.0

DIVIDEND ACHIEVER STATUS:
Rank: 239   10-Year Growth Rate: 4.79%
Total Years of Dividend Growth: 32

RECENT DEVELOPMENTS: For the first quarter ended 3/31/03, the Company reported net income of $4.7 million compared with income from continuing operations of $11.9 million, before a loss from discontinued operations of $217,000, in the corresponding prior-year quarter. Operating revenue increased slightly to $734.6 million from $734.3 million a year earlier. Operating income dropped 37.4% to $24.9 million from $39.7 million the year before. Comparisons were made with restated prior-year results.

PROSPECTS: The Company anticipates that, despite adverse economic and weather conditions, its business units will generate revenue and operating income growth in 2003. The Company believes it will continue to attract new customers and improve retention rates through the year. However, benefits from business growth are expected to be offset by increased costs stemming from a higher tax rate and investment in various marketing, technology and compliance initiatives.

BUSINESS

THE SERVICEMASTER COMPANY (formerly ServiceMaster L.P.) provides outsourcing services to residential and commercial customers worldwide. The TruGreen segment (38.3% of 2002 revenue) includes lawn care operations performed under the TruGreen ChemLawn and landscaping services provided under the TruGreen LandCare brands. The Terminix segment (25.8%) includes domestic termite and pest control services. The American Residential Services and American Mechanical Services (ARS/AMS) segment (20.0%) provides heating, ventilation, air conditioning and plumbing services under the ARS, AMS and Rescue Rooter brands. The American Home Shield segment (11.7%) offers warranty contracts on home systems and appliances and home inspection services through AmeriSpec. The Other Operations segment (4.2%) includes ServiceMaster Clean, Merry Maids and Furniture Medic franchise operations. On 11/30/01, SVM sold its management services business to ARAMARK Corp.

ANNUAL FINANCIAL DATA

	12/31/02	[4] 12/31/01	12/31/00	12/31/99	12/31/98	12/31/97	12/31/96
Earnings Per Share	[5] 0.56	[3] d0.54	[1] 0.61	[1] 0.55	0.64	0.55	0.76
Cash Flow Per Share	0.73	d0.14	1.12	0.99	0.99	1.41	0.99
Dividends Per Share	0.41	0.40	0.38	0.36	0.33	0.31	0.29
Dividend Payout %	73.2	...	62.3	65.4	51.6	56.4	38.2
INCOME STATEMENT (IN MILLIONS):							
Total Revenues	3,589.1	3,601.4	5,970.6	5,703.5	4,724.1	3,961.5	3,458.3
Costs & Expenses	3,189.9	3,561.9	5,396.0	5,181.9	4,223.1	3,524.5	3,084.1
Depreciation & Amort.	57.9	126.9	157.7	138.4	104.6	93.1	79.0
Operating Income	341.3	d87.4	416.9	383.2	396.4	343.9	295.2
Net Interest Inc./(Exp.)	d77.5	d125.1	d136.8	d109.0	d92.9	d76.4	d38.3
Income Before Income Taxes	263.6	d201.4	318.3	296.2	318.8	274.3	252.4
Income Taxes	93.5	cr29.6	133.3	122.6	128.8	cr54.8	7.3
Net Income	[5] 170.1	[3] d171.8	[1] 185.0	[1] 173.6	190.0	329.1	245.1
Cash Flow	228.0	d44.8	342.7	312.0	294.6	422.1	324.1
Average Shs. Outstg. (000)	314,112	311,408	305,518	314,406	298,887	299,640	326,403
BALANCE SHEET (IN MILLIONS):							
Cash & Cash Equivalents	302.6	483.1	100.9	114.2	120.4	124.1	114.4
Total Current Assets	919.2	1,150.7	984.8	959.2	670.2	594.1	499.3
Net Property	194.9	189.0	306.0	318.1	212.2	158.3	146.4
Total Assets	3,414.9	3,674.7	3,967.7	3,870.2	2,914.9	2,475.2	1,846.8
Total Current Liabilities	839.1	814.4	833.4	845.8	753.7	558.2	425.6
Long-Term Obligations	804.3	1,105.5	1,756.8	1,697.6	1,076.2	1,247.8	482.3
Net Stockholders' Equity	1,218.7	1,221.0	1,161.6	1,205.7	956.5	524.4	796.8
Net Working Capital	80.1	336.3	151.3	113.4	d83.5	35.9	73.8
Year-end Shs. Outstg. (000)	311,039	300,531	298,474	307,530	298,030	279,944	331,196
STATISTICAL RECORD:							
Operating Profit Margin %	9.5	...	7.0	6.7	8.4	8.7	8.5
Net Profit Margin %	4.7	...	3.1	3.0	4.0	8.3	7.1
Return on Equity %	14.0	...	15.9	14.4	19.9	62.7	30.8
Return on Assets %	5.0	...	4.7	4.5	6.5	13.3	13.3
Debt/Total Assets %	23.6	30.1	44.3	43.9	36.9	50.4	26.1
Price Range	15.50-8.89	14.20-9.84	14.94-8.25	22.00-10.13	25.50-16.00	19.67-10.95	11.83-8.63
P/E Ratio	27.7-15.9	...	24.5-13.5	40.0-18.4	39.8-25.0	35.9-20.0	15.7-11.4
Average Yield %	3.4	3.3	3.3	2.2	1.6	2.0	2.9

Statistics are as originally reported. Adj. for stk. splits: 3-for-2, 8/98, 6/97, 6/96. On 12/26/97, SVM converted from a publicly traded partnership to a taxable corp. Prior to that date, net income was not subject to federal and state taxes. [1] Bef. acctg. change chg. $11.2 mill. [2] Incl. non-recurr. chg. $85.5 mill. [3] Bef. income from discont. oper. of $330.2 mill. and extraord. chg. of $3.4 mill.; incl. impair. and oth. chrg. of $396.7 mill. [4] Refl. the sale of mgmt. svcs. business, incl. certain European pest control subs. and TruGreen LandCare Construction. [5] Bef. net disc. oper. loss $3.9 mill. and extr. loss $9.2 mill.; incl. impair. credit of $2.0 mill.

OFFICERS:
J. P. Ward, Chmn. , C.E.O.
E. J. Mrozek, Pres., C.O.O.

INVESTOR CONTACT: Bruce J. Byots, V.P.,
Investor Relations, (630) 663-2906

PRINCIPAL OFFICE: 2300 Warrenville Rd.,
Downers Grove, IL 60515-1700

TELEPHONE NUMBER: (630) 271-1300
FAX: (630) 271-2710
WEB: www.servicemaster.com
NO. OF EMPLOYEES: 40,000 (approx.)
SHAREHOLDERS: 32,000 (approx. record)
ANNUAL MEETING: In May
INCORPORATED: DE, Oct., 1986

INSTITUTIONAL HOLDINGS:
No. of Institutions: 237
Shares Held: 152,084,429
% Held: 50.9

INDUSTRY: Management svcs. (SIC: 8741)

TRANSFER AGENT(S): Computershare
Investor Services, Chicago, IL

SHERWIN-WILLIAMS COMPANY

YIELD 2.3%
P/E RATIO 13.6

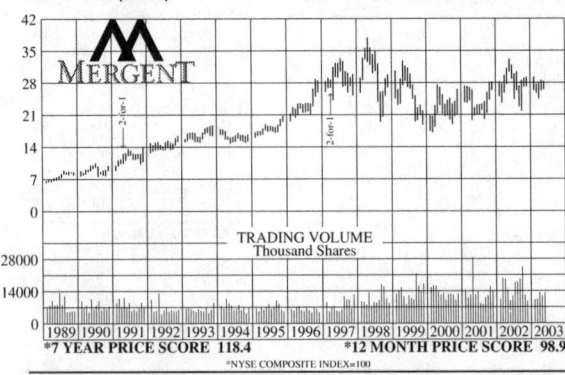

TRADING VOLUME
Thousand Shares

*7 YEAR PRICE SCORE 118.4   ***12 MONTH PRICE SCORE 98.9**
NYSE COMPOSITE INDEX=100

INTERIM EARNINGS (Per Share):

Qtr.	Mar.	June	Sept.	Dec.
2000	0.25	0.71	0.66	d1.55
2001	0.23	0.58	0.58	0.29
2002	0.23	0.70	0.73	0.38
2003	0.21	...	...	...

INTERIM DIVIDENDS (Per Share):

Amt.	Decl.	Ex.	Rec.	Pay.
0.15Q	7/24/02	8/21/02	8/23/02	9/06/02
0.15Q	10/18/02	10/31/02	11/04/02	11/18/02
0.155Q	2/05/03	2/20/03	2/24/03	3/10/03
0.155Q	4/23/03	5/21/03	5/23/03	6/06/03

Indicated div.: $0.62 (Div. Reinv. Plan)

CAPITALIZATION (12/31/02):

	($000)	(%)
Long-Term Debt ①	506,682	27.4
Preferred Stock	41,806	2.3
Common & Surplus	1,300,084	70.3
Total	1,848,572	100.0

DIVIDEND ACHIEVER STATUS:

Rank: 131   10-Year Growth Rate: 10.55%
Total Years of Dividend Growth: 23

RECENT DEVELOPMENTS: For the quarter ended 3/31/03, net income declined 11.5% to $30.8 million compared with income of $34.8 million, before an accounting change charge of $183.1 million, in the equivalent 2002 quarter. Net sales declined 0.1% to $1.15 billion due to the ongoing poor domestic industrial sector, unfavorable weather, changes in buying habits of some retail customers and weak currency exchange rates. Gross profit grew 2.0% to $646.7 million, or 43.7% of net sales, from $492.1 million, or 42.8% of net sales, a year earlier.

PROSPECTS: Net sales of the Paint Stores division should continue to benefit from strong architectural paint sales. Also, net sales of the Consumer segment are reflecting changes by some of its largest retail customers in their ordering or promotional patterns, the readjustment of store count by a major retailer and stringent inventory control relating to the slowdown in the domestic economy. Net sales of the Automotive Finishes segment should continue to benefit from improved foreign sales and a decline in the collision repair market in the U.S.

BUSINESS

SHERWIN-WILLIAMS COMPANY is engaged in the manufacture, distribution and sale of coatings and related products. The Paint Stores' division (63.7% of 2002 net sales) consisted of 2,651 company-operated specialty paint stores in the U.S., Canada, the Virgin Islands, Puerto Rico and Mexico, as of 3/31/03. The Consumer segment (22.8%) develops, manufactures and distributes a variety of paint, coatings and related products to third party customers and the Paint stores segment. The Automotive Finishes segment (8.8%) develops, manufactures and distributes motor vehicle finish products throughout North and South America, the Caribbean Islands and Italy. The International Coatings segment (4.7%) develops, licenses, manufactures and distributes a variety of paint, coatings and related products worldwide. SHW's brands include SHERWINWILLIAMS®, DUTCH BOY®, and KRYLON®.

ANNUAL FINANCIAL DATA

	12/31/02	12/31/01	12/31/00	12/31/99	12/31/98	12/31/97	12/31/96
Earnings Per Share	③ 2.04	1.68	② 0.10	1.80	1.57	1.50	1.34
Cash Flow Per Share	2.80	2.62	1.08	2.72	2.42	2.30	1.92
Tang. Book Val. Per Share	3.77	2.59	3.18	2.32	1.76	0.70	3.65
Dividends Per Share	0.60	0.58	0.54	0.48	0.45	0.40	0.35
Dividend Payout %	29.4	34.5	539.5	26.7	28.7	26.8	26.1

INCOME STATEMENT (IN MILLIONS):

	12/31/02	12/31/01	12/31/00	12/31/99	12/31/98	12/31/97	12/31/96
Total Revenues	5,184.8	5,066.0	5,211.6	5,003.8	4,934.4	4,881.1	4,132.9
Costs & Expenses	4,515.1	4,428.1	4,836.4	4,273.0	4,254.9	4,218.7	3,610.6
Depreciation & Amort.	115.6	148.1	160.0	155.7	147.9	139.2	103.6
Operating Income	554.1	489.8	215.2	575.1	531.6	523.2	418.6
Net Interest Inc./(Exp.)	d40.5	d54.6	d62.0	d61.2	d72.0	d80.8	d24.5
Income Before Income Taxes	497.2	424.4	143.4	490.1	440.1	427.3	371.1
Income Taxes	186.5	161.3	127.4	186.3	167.2	166.7	146.2
Net Income	③310.7	263.2	②16.0	303.9	272.9	260.6	224.9
Cash Flow	426.3	411.3	176.1	459.6	420.8	399.9	328.5
Average Shs. Outstg. (000)	152,435	156,894	162,695	169,026	173,536	174,032	171,117

BALANCE SHEET (IN MILLIONS):

	12/31/02	12/31/01	12/31/00	12/31/99	12/31/98	12/31/97	12/31/96
Cash & Cash Equivalents	164.0	118.8	2.9	18.6	19.1	3.5	1.9
Total Current Assets	1,506.0	1,506.9	1,551.5	1,597.4	1,547.3	1,532.3	1,416.2
Net Property	664.6	672.7	722.4	711.7	718.9	692.3	549.4
Total Assets	3,432.3	3,627.9	3,750.7	4,052.1	4,065.5	4,035.8	2,994.6
Total Current Liabilities	1,083.5	1,141.4	1,115.2	1,189.9	1,112.0	1,115.7	1,051.0
Long-Term Obligations	506.7	503.5	623.6	624.4	730.3	843.9	142.7
Net Stockholders' Equity	1,341.9	1,487.8	1,471.9	1,698.5	1,715.9	1,592.2	1,401.2
Net Working Capital	422.5	365.6	436.3	407.5	435.3	416.6	365.2
Year-end Shs. Outstg. (000)	148,910	153,978	159,558	165,664	171,033	172,907	171,831

STATISTICAL RECORD:

	12/31/02	12/31/01	12/31/00	12/31/99	12/31/98	12/31/97	12/31/96
Operating Profit Margin %	10.7	9.7	4.1	11.5	10.8	10.7	10.1
Net Profit Margin %	6.0	5.2	0.3	6.1	5.5	5.3	5.4
Return on Equity %	23.2	17.7	1.1	17.9	15.9	16.4	16.1
Return on Assets %	9.1	7.3	0.4	7.5	6.7	6.5	7.5
Debt/Total Assets %	14.8	13.9	16.6	15.4	18.0	20.9	4.8
Price Range	33.24-21.75	28.23-19.73	27.63-17.13	32.88-18.75	37.88-19.44	33.38-24.13	28.88-19.50
P/E Ratio	16.3-10.7	16.8-11.7	276.0-171.1	18.3-10.4	24.1-12.4	22.2-16.1	21.5-14.6
Average Yield %	2.2	2.4	2.4	1.9	1.6	1.4	1.4

Statistics are as originally reported. Adj. for stk. splits: 2-for-1, 3/97. ① Incl. debentures conv. into common. ② Incl. impairment of long-lived assets chrg. of $352.0 mill. ③ Excl. acctg. change chrg. of $183.1 mill.

OFFICERS:
C. M. Connor, Chmn., C.E.O.
J. M. Scaminace, Pres., C.O.O.
S. P. Hennessy, Sr. V.P., C.F.O., Treas.
INVESTOR CONTACT: Conway G. Ivy, Sr. V.P., (216) 566-2102
PRINCIPAL OFFICE: 101 Prospect Avenue, N.W., Cleveland, OH 44115-1075

TELEPHONE NUMBER: (216) 566-2000
FAX: (216) 566-3310
WEB: www.sherwin.com
NO. OF EMPLOYEES: 25,752 (avg.)
SHAREHOLDERS: 9,515
ANNUAL MEETING: In Apr.
INCORPORATED: OH, July, 1884

INSTITUTIONAL HOLDINGS:
No. of Institutions: 325
Shares Held: 102,327,789
% Held: 70.1
INDUSTRY: Paints and allied products (SIC: 2851)
TRANSFER AGENT(S): The Bank of New York, New York, NY

SIGMA-ALDRICH CORPORATION

YIELD 0.7%
P/E RATIO 19.7

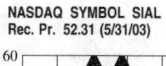

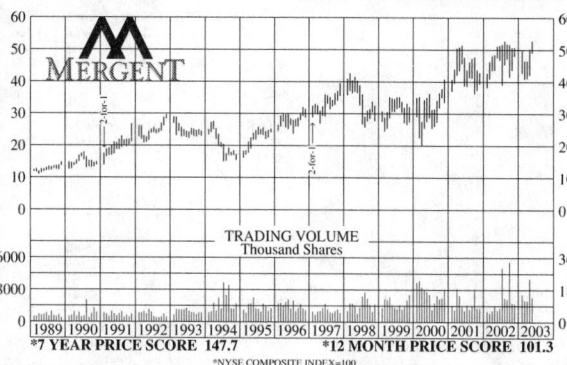

7 YEAR PRICE SCORE 147.7 **12 MONTH PRICE SCORE 101.3**
*NYSE COMPOSITE INDEX=100

INTERIM EARNINGS (Per Share):

Qtr.	Mar.	June	Sept.	Dec.
2000	0.45	0.45	0.35	0.40
2001	0.48	0.49	0.45	0.45
2002	0.54	0.58	0.55	0.84
2003	0.68	...	...	...

INTERIM DIVIDENDS (Per Share):

Amt.	Decl.	Ex.	Rec.	Pay.
0.085Q	8/13/02	8/28/02	8/30/02	9/13/02
0.09Q	11/12/02	12/11/02	12/13/02	1/02/03
0.09Q	2/11/03	2/26/03	2/28/03	3/14/03
0.09Q	5/06/03	5/28/03	5/30/03	6/13/03

Indicated div.: $0.36

CAPITALIZATION (12/31/02):

	($000)	(%)
Long-Term Debt	176,805	16.7
Common & Surplus	882,174	83.3
Total	1,058,979	100.0

DIVIDEND ACHIEVER STATUS:

Rank: 132   10-Year Growth Rate: 10.52%
Total Years of Dividend Growth: 21

RECENT DEVELOPMENTS: For the three months ended 3/31/03, income from continuing operations rose 14.7% to $48.9 million compared with $42.7 million in the corresponding period of 2002. Results for 2003 and 2002 excluded income of $2.6 million and a loss of $2.9 million, respectively, from discontinued operations. Net sales climbed 11.0% to $334.7 million from $301.6 million in the previous year. Gross profit grew 10.5% to $171.0 million from $154.8 million, but slipped as a percentage of net

sales to 51.1% from 51.3%, the year before. Overall results benefited from price gains, offset by a modest decrease in unit volumes. Looking ahead to 2003, the Company expects price gains to remain in line with first quarter results, while new sales and marketing efforts are expected to boost volume gains in the subsequent quarters of 2003. As a result, the Company raised its 2003 estimate of projected diluted earnings per share from continuing operations to a range of $2.60 to $2.65.

BUSINESS

SIGMA-ALDRICH CORPORATION develops, manufactures and distributes a broad range of biochemicals, organic chemicals, chromatography products and diagnostic reagents. These chemical products and kits are used in scientific and genomic research, biotechnology, pharmaceutical development, the chemical industry and for the diagnosis of disease. As of 4/22/03, the Company operated in 34 countries, offered more than 85,000 chemical products and distributes these products to over 150 countries. On 2/16/01, the Company acquired Isotec, Inc., a producer and supplier of stable isotopes and isotopically labeled compounds used in life science research, medical diagnostics and polyethlene terephthalate imaging applications.

ANNUAL FINANCIAL DATA

	12/31/02	12/31/01	12/31/00	12/31/99	12/31/98	12/31/97	12/31/96
Earnings Per Share	⑤ 2.54	④ 1.87	③ 1.66	①② 1.47	1.64	1.62	1.48
Cash Flow Per Share	3.45	2.82	2.47	2.13	2.25	2.08	1.93
Tang. Book Val. Per Share	10.90	9.34	9.72	11.89	10.96	9.73	9.41
Dividends Per Share	0.34	0.33	0.31	0.29	0.28	0.25	0.22
Dividend Payout %	13.4	17.6	18.7	19.7	17.1	15.4	14.9
INCOME STATEMENT (IN MILLIONS):							
Total Revenues	1,207.0	1,179.4	1,096.3	1,037.9	1,194.3	1,127.1	1,034.6
Costs & Expenses	854.7	889.9	819.2	767.3	889.9	826.3	759.7
Depreciation & Amort.	66.3	71.4	67.6	66.9	61.8	48.1	45.2
Operating Income	286.0	218.2	209.5	203.7	242.6	252.8	229.7
Net Interest Inc./(Exp.)	d13.8	d16.5	d6.6	...	...	...	...
Income Before Income Taxes	272.1	201.6	202.9	203.7	242.6	252.8	229.7
Income Taxes	85.4	60.9	63.9	55.1	76.2	86.7	81.8
Net Income	⑤ 186.7	④ 140.7	③ 139.1	①② 148.6	166.3	166.1	147.9
Cash Flow	253.1	212.1	206.6	215.5	228.2	214.1	193.1
Average Shs. Outstg. (000)	73,412	75,175	83,585	100,984	101,188	102,804	99,930
BALANCE SHEET (IN MILLIONS):							
Cash & Cash Equivalents	52.4	37.6	31.1	43.8	24.3	46.2	103.7
Total Current Assets	694.9	727.3	713.6	774.4	772.7	706.7	666.6
Net Property	535.8	542.1	493.0	481.7	518.7	438.9	379.1
Total Assets	1,389.7	1,439.8	1,347.7	1,432.0	1,432.8	1,243.8	1,100.0
Total Current Liabilities	265.7	397.6	335.3	105.6	142.4	119.5	110.3
Long-Term Obligations	176.8	177.7	100.8	0.2	0.4	0.6	3.8
Net Stockholders' Equity	882.2	809.7	859.3	1,259.4	1,216.4	1,060.3	942.3
Net Working Capital	429.2	329.7	378.3	669.0	630.3	587.2	556.3
Year-end Shs. Outstg. (000)	71,253	73,014	76,216	98,292	100,623	100,377	100,100
STATISTICAL RECORD:							
Operating Profit Margin %	23.7	18.5	19.1	19.6	20.3	22.4	22.2
Net Profit Margin %	15.5	11.9	12.7	14.3	13.9	14.7	14.3
Return on Equity %	21.2	17.4	16.2	11.8	13.7	15.7	15.7
Return on Assets %	13.4	9.8	10.3	10.4	11.6	13.4	13.4
Debt/Total Assets %	12.7	12.3	7.5	...	...	...	0.3
Price Range	52.80-38.16	51.49-36.25	40.88-20.19	35.25-24.50	42.75-25.75	39.63-26.88	32.06-23.75
P/E Ratio	20.8-15.0	27.5-19.4	24.6-12.2	24.0-16.7	26.1-15.7	24.5-16.6	21.7-16.0
Average Yield %	0.7	0.8	1.0	1.0	0.8	0.8	0.8

Statistics are as originally reported. Adj. for stk. splits: 2-for-1, 1/2/97. ① Bef. disc. oper. gain $23.7 mill. ② Incl. non-recurr. net gain $2.6 mill. ③ Incl. in-process res. & dev. chrg. $6.7 mill. ④ Incl. $1.2 mill. purch. in-process R&D chg. ⑤ Incl. $29.3 mill. gain fr. sale of facility & excl. $56.0 mill. loss fr. disc. ops.

OFFICERS:
D. R. Harvey, Chmn., Pres., C.E.O.
M. Hogan, C.F.O., C.A.O., Sec.
L. Blazevich, V.P., C.I.O.

INVESTOR CONTACT: Kirk A. Richter, Investor Relations, (314) 286-8004

PRINCIPAL OFFICE: 3050 Spruce Street, St. Louis, MO 63103

TELEPHONE NUMBER: (314) 771-5765
FAX: (314) 286-7874
WEB: www.sigma-aldrich.com

NO. OF EMPLOYEES: 5,940 (avg.)

SHAREHOLDERS: 1,107

ANNUAL MEETING: In May

INCORPORATED: DE, July, 1975

INSTITUTIONAL HOLDINGS:
No. of Institutions: 313
Shares Held: 54,928,157
% Held: 77.4

INDUSTRY: Chemicals & allied products, nec (SIC: 5169)

TRANSFER AGENT(S): Computershare Investor Services, Chicago, IL

SJW CORP.

YIELD	3.4%
P/E RATIO	14.7

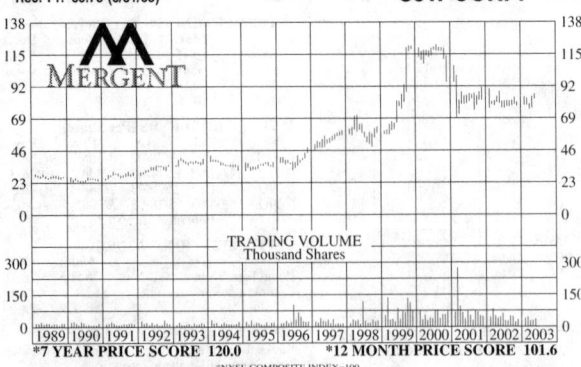

INTERIM EARNINGS (Per Share):

Qtr.	Mar.	June	Sept.	Dec.
1999	0.58	1.34	1.78	1.52
2000	0.44	0.89	1.63	0.54
2001	0.22	1.37	2.10	0.91
2002	0.57	1.31	1.90	0.89
2003	1.73	...	...	...

INTERIM DIVIDENDS (Per Share):

Amt.	Decl.	Ex.	Rec.	Pay.
0.69Q	7/18/02	7/30/02	8/01/02	9/01/02
0.69Q	10/24/02	11/01/02	11/05/02	12/01/02
0.728Q	1/29/03	2/06/03	2/10/03	3/01/03
0.728Q	4/29/03	5/08/03	5/12/03	6/01/03

Indicated div.: $2.91

CAPITALIZATION (12/31/02):

	($000)	(%)
Long-Term Debt	110,000	37.8
Deferred Income Tax	27,670	9.5
Common & Surplus	153,499	52.7
Total	291,169	100.0

DIVIDEND ACHIEVER STATUS:
Rank: 262   10-Year Growth Rate: 3.38%
Total Years of Dividend Growth: 36

7 YEAR PRICE SCORE 120.0   **12 MONTH PRICE SCORE 101.6**
=NYSE COMPOSITE INDEX=100

RECENT DEVELOPMENTS: For the three months ended 3/31/03, net income was $5.3 million compared with $1.7 million in the corresponding year-earlier period. Earnings for 2003 included an after-tax gain of $3.0 million on the sale of a SJW Land Company property. SJW noted that in April 2003 it reinvested the sale proceeds from the transaction in two income properties in a tax-deferred transaction. Operating revenues rose slightly to $27.8 million from $27.7 million the previous year. The Company attributed the rise in operating revenue primarily to a 4.0% rate increase that was largely offset by an approximately 7.0% decrease in customer consumption. Water production costs decreased 16.8% to $8.9 million, reflecting the aforementioned decline in customer consumption and an increase in less costly surface water supply. Operating income improved 17.9% to $4.0 million compared with $3.4 million the year before.

BUSINESS

SJW CORP. is a holding company with three subsidiaries. San Jose Water Company, is a public utility in the business of providing water service to a population of approximately 1.0 million people, as of 4/29/03, in an area comprising about 138 square miles in the metropolitan San Jose area. SJW Land Company owns and operates parking facilities adjacent to the Company's headquarters and the HP Pavilion in San Jose, California. As of 12/31/02, SJW Land Company also owned commercial buildings and other undeveloped land in the San Jose Metropolitan area, and a 70.0% limited partnership interest in 444 West Santa Clara Street, L.P. Crystal Choice Water Service LLC, a 75.0% owned limited liability subsidiary formed in January 2001, engages in the sale and rental of water conditioning and purification equipment. As of 12/31/02, SJW also owned 1,099,952 shares of California Water Service Group.

ANNUAL FINANCIAL DATA

	12/31/02	12/31/01	12/31/00	12/31/99	12/31/98	12/31/97	12/31/96
Earnings Per Share	4.67	4.60	②3.50	①②5.20	①5.05	4.80	①5.75
Cash Flow Per Share	9.28	8.95	7.39	8.55	8.08	7.59	8.44
Tang. Book Val. Per Share	48.69	47.27	45.57	45.35	43.29	40.21	35.87
Dividends Per Share	2.76	2.57	2.46	2.40	2.34	2.28	2.22
Dividend Payout %	59.1	55.9	70.3	46.2	46.3	47.5	38.6
INCOME STATEMENT (IN THOUSANDS):							
Total Revenues	145,652	136,083	123,157	117,001	106,010	110,084	102,593
Costs & Expenses	103,215	95,926	86,504	80,389	70,660	74,836	69,465
Depreciation & Amort.	14,013	13,240	11,847	10,235	9,594	8,847	8,671
Maintenance Exp.	7,866	7,090	6,881	6,638	6,909	7,087	6,851
Operating Income	20,558	19,827	17,925	19,739	18,847	19,314	17,606
Net Interest Inc./(Exp.)	d7,803	d6,737	d6,434	d6,552	d5,629	d5,695	d5,892
Net Income	14,232	14,017	②10,665	①②15,884	①16,018	15,216	①18,560
Cash Flow	28,245	27,257	22,512	26,119	25,612	24,063	27,231
Average Shs. Outstg.	3,045	3,045	3,045	3,055	3,170	3,170	3,227
BALANCE SHEET (IN THOUSANDS):							
Gross Property	541,919	507,227	462,892	432,262	403,227	371,200	342,368
Accumulated Depreciation	161,576	149,721	139,396	129,828	122,809	114,851	107,584
Net Property	390,830	367,815	333,475	312,567	291,778	263,650	242,071
Total Assets	453,223	431,017	391,930	372,427	359,380	323,223	296,536
Long-Term Obligations	110,000	110,000	90,000	90,000	90,000	75,000	75,000
Net Stockholders' Equity	153,499	149,354	144,325	143,894	143,149	133,553	120,028
Year-end Shs. Outstg.	3,045	3,045	3,045	3,045	3,168	3,170	3,170
STATISTICAL RECORD:							
Operating Profit Margin %	14.1	14.6	14.6	16.9	17.8	17.5	17.2
Net Profit Margin %	9.8	10.3	8.7	13.6	15.1	13.8	18.1
Net Inc./Net Property %	3.6	3.8	3.2	5.1	5.5	5.8	7.7
Net Inc./Tot. Capital %	4.9	4.9	4.2	6.1	6.2	6.6	8.8
Return on Equity %	9.3	9.4	7.4	11.0	11.2	11.4	15.5
Accum. Depr./Gross Prop. %	29.8	29.5	30.1	30.0	30.5	30.9	31.4
Price Range	90.40-76.00	107.00-69.50	122.00-95.00	121.00-57.25	71.50-48.50	60.50-46.00	48.25-32.00
P/E Ratio	19.4-16.3	23.3-15.1	34.9-27.1	23.3-11.0	14.2-9.6	12.6-9.6	8.4-5.6
Average Yield %	3.3	2.9	2.3	2.7	3.9	4.3	5.5

Statistics are as originally reported. ① Incl. non-recurr. gain $3.1 mill., 12/99; $1.6 mill., 12/98; $5.3 mill., 12/96. ② Incl. merger costs, 2000, $1.6 mill.; 1999, $1.6 mill.

OFFICERS:
D. Gibson, Chmn.
W. R. Roth, Pres., C.E.O.
A. Yip, C.F.O., Treas.

INVESTOR CONTACT: Richard Balocco, (408) 279-7933

PRINCIPAL OFFICE: 374 West Santa Clara Street, San Jose, CA 95196

TELEPHONE NUMBER: (408) 279-7800
FAX: (408) 279-7934
WEB: www.sjwater.com

NO. OF EMPLOYEES: 301 (avg.)

SHAREHOLDERS: 732

ANNUAL MEETING: In Apr.

INCORPORATED: CA, Feb., 1985

INSTITUTIONAL HOLDINGS:
No. of Institutions: 43
Shares Held: 643,487
% Held: 21.4

INDUSTRY: Water supply (SIC: 4941)

TRANSFER AGENT(S): Boston Equiserve, Boston, MA

SLM CORPORATION

YIELD 0.9%
P/E RATIO 24.4

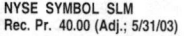

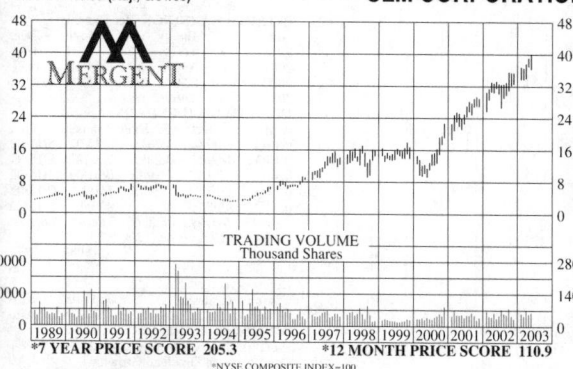

TRADING VOLUME
Thousand Shares

1989 1990 1991 1992 1993 1994 1995 1996 1997 1998 1999 2000 2001 2002 2003
*7 YEAR PRICE SCORE 205.3   *12 MONTH PRICE SCORE 110.9
*NYSE COMPOSITE INDEX=100

INTERIM EARNINGS (Per Share):

Qtr.	Mar.	June	Sept.	Dec.
1999	0.23	0.25	0.25	0.29
2000	0.31	0.24	0.18	0.19
2001	0.05	0.56	d0.42	0.56
2002	0.88	0.26	d0.14	0.64
2003	0.88	...	...	...

INTERIM DIVIDENDS (Per Share):

Amt.	Decl.	Ex.	Rec.	Pay.
0.25Q	1/29/03	3/05/03	3/07/03	3/21/03
0.25Q	5/15/03	6/04/03	6/06/03	6/20/03
0.26Q	5/29/03	6/04/03	6/08/03	6/20/03
200% STK	5/15/03	6/23/03	6/06/03	6/20/03

Indicated div.: $0.35 (Adj.; Div. Reinv. Plan)

CAPITALIZATION (12/31/02):

	($000)	(%)
Long-Term Debt	22,242,115	91.8
Preferred Stock	165,000	0.7
Common & Surplus	1,832,950	7.6
Total	24,240,065	100.0

DIVIDEND ACHIEVER STATUS:
Rank: 125   10-Year Growth Rate: 10.98%
Total Years of Dividend Growth: 22

RECENT DEVELOPMENTS: For the quarter ended 3/31/03, net income declined 1.4% to $416.5 million from $422.3 million in the equivalent 2002 quarter. Results reflected reduced interest earned on student loans and a decline in the value of SLM's investments. Earnings for 2003 and 2002 included derivative market value adjustment gains of $114.4 million and $288.4 million, respectively. Net interest income dropped 14.5% to $240.6 million. Provision for loan losses jumped 110.4% to $42.5 million. Total non-interest income grew 11.5% to $624.5 million.

PROSPECTS: On 4/2/03, the Company announced that it had completed the acquisition of Pioneer Mortgage, a Michigan-based mortgage banking company. This acquisition expands the fee-based, mortgage-banking services provided by its SLM Financial Corp. unit. Going forward, the Company should continue to benefit from a growing student loan market. During the first quarter, SLM's preferred-channel loan originations, a key measure of its market share success and an indicator of future loan acquisition volume, grew 22.0% year-over-year to more than $80.00 billion.

BUSINESS

SLM CORPORATION (formerly USA Education, Inc.) is a provider of education funding, managing nearly $81.00 billion in student loans for more than seven million borrowers. The Company primarily provides federally guaranteed student loans originated under the Federal Family Education Loan Program, and offers comprehensive information and resources to help guide students, parents and guidance professionals through the financial aid process. Through its subsidiaries and divisions, the Company also provides an array of consumer credit loans, including those for lifelong learning and K-12 education, and business and technical outsourcing services for colleges and universities. On 7/7/00, the Company acquired Student Loan Funding Resources, Inc. On 7/31/00, the Company completed the purchase of USA Group's guarantee servicing, student loan servicing and secondary market operations for $770.0 million in cash and stock.

ANNUAL FINANCIAL DATA

	12/31/02	12/31/01	12/31/00	12/31/99	12/31/98	12/31/97	12/31/96
Earnings Per Share	③ 1.64	⑤ 0.76	② 0.92	1.02	0.98	① 0.93	① 0.71
Tang. Book Val. Per Share	4.00	3.23	2.54	1.43	1.33	1.22	1.21
Dividends Per Share	0.28	0.24	0.22	0.20	0.19	0.17	0.16
Dividend Payout %	17.2	32.0	23.9	19.9	19.3	18.5	22.0

INCOME STATEMENT (IN MILLIONS):

	12/31/02	12/31/01	12/31/00	12/31/99	12/31/98	12/31/97	12/31/96
Total Interest Income	2,211.8	2,997.5	3,478.7	2,808.6	2,587.6	3,283.8	3,449.3
Total Interest Expense	1,202.6	2,124.1	2,836.9	2,114.8	1,925.0	2,526.2	2,582.9
Net Interest Income	1,009.1	873.4	641.8	693.8	662.7	757.7	866.4
Provision for Loan Losses	116.6	66.0	32.1	34.4	28.6	...	...
Non-Interest Income	1,020.7	517.6	687.6	450.8	477.0	500.9	146.9
Non-Interest Expense	689.8	707.7	585.7	358.6	360.9	493.8	405.7
Income Before Taxes	1,223.4	617.4	711.6	751.7	750.1	764.8	607.7
Equity Earnings/Minority Int.	...	d10.1	d10.7	d10.7	d10.7	d10.7	d10.7
Net Income	③ 792.0	③ 384.0	② 465.0	500.8	501.5	① 511.2	① 413.5
Average Shs. Outstg. (000)	474,519	490,200	493,065	489,474	510,198	548,823	583,398

BALANCE SHEET (IN MILLIONS):

	12/31/02	12/31/01	12/31/00	12/31/99	12/31/98	12/31/97	12/31/96
Net Loans & Leases	43,541.7	42,769.0	39,485.8	35,879.3	31,005.6	32,764.3	38,016.3
Total Assets	53,175.0	52,874.0	48,791.8	44,024.8	37,210.0	39,908.8	47,629.9
Long-Term Obligations	22,242.1	17,285.4	14,910.9	4,496.3	8,810.6	14,541.3	22,606.2
Total Liabilities	51,177.1	51,201.5	47,162.6	42,970.0	36,342.5	39,020.3	46,582.1
Net Stockholders' Equity	1,998.0	1,672.5	1,415.3	840.9	653.6	674.6	833.9
Year-end Shs. Outstg. (000)	457,740	466,485	492,435	472,730	492,381	550,899	689,802

STATISTICAL RECORD:

	12/31/02	12/31/01	12/31/00	12/31/99	12/31/98	12/31/97	12/31/96
Return on Equity %	39.6	23.0	32.9	59.6	76.7	75.8	49.6
Return on Assets %	1.5	0.7	1.0	1.1	1.3	1.3	0.9
Equity/Assets %	3.8	3.2	2.9	1.9	1.8	1.7	1.8
Non-Int. Exp./Tot. Inc. %	34.0	50.9	44.1	31.3	31.7	39.2	40.0
Price Range	35.65-25.67	29.33-18.63	22.75-9.27	17.98-13.17	17.13-9.17	15.73-8.48	9.36-6.02
P/E Ratio	21.7-15.6	38.6-24.5	24.7-10.1	17.6-12.9	17.4-9.3	16.8-9.1	13.2-8.5
Average Yield %	0.9	1.0	1.4	1.3	1.4	1.4	2.0

Statistics are as originally reported. Adj. for stk splits: 200% div., 6/03; 7-for-2, 1/98. ① Bef. chrgs. on debt extinguished, $3.3 mill., 12/97; $4.8 mill., 12/96. ② Incl. one-time integration chrg. $53.0 mill. ③ Incl. derivative mkt. value adjust. loss $203.9 mill., 12/02; $505.7 mill., 12/01.

OFFICERS:
E. A. Fox, Chmn.
A. L. Lord, Vice-Chmn., C.E.O.
T. J. Fitzpatrick, Pres., C.O.O.
INVESTOR CONTACT: Jeffrey R. Heinz, Dir., Inv. Rel., (703) 810-7751
PRINCIPAL OFFICE: 11600 Sallie Mae Drive, Reston, VA 20193

TELEPHONE NUMBER: (703) 810-3000
FAX: (703) 810-5074
WEB: www.salliemae.com
NO. OF EMPLOYEES: 6,705 (avg.)
SHAREHOLDERS: 547
ANNUAL MEETING: In May
INCORPORATED: DE, Feb., 1997

INSTITUTIONAL HOLDINGS:
No. of Institutions: 406
Shares Held: 429,101,775 (Adj.)
% Held: 94.1
INDUSTRY: Personal credit institutions (SIC: 6141)
TRANSFER AGENT(S): The Bank of New York, New York, NY

SMITH (A.O.) CORPORATION

YIELD 1.8%
P/E RATIO 17.3

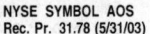
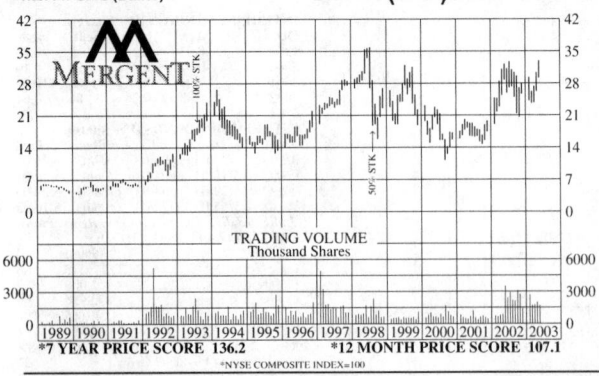

7 YEAR PRICE SCORE 136.2   **12 MONTH PRICE SCORE 107.1**
*NYSE COMPOSITE INDEX=100

INTERIM EARNINGS (Per Share):

Qtr.	Mar.	June	Sept.	Dec.
2000	0.60	0.74	0.31	0.11
2001	0.36	0.45	0.32	d0.21
2002	0.50	0.66	0.34	0.38
2003	0.46	...	...	...

INTERIM DIVIDENDS (Per Share):

Amt.	Decl.	Ex.	Rec.	Pay.
0.13Q	4/09/02	4/26/02	4/30/02	5/15/02
0.14Q	7/09/02	7/29/02	7/31/02	8/15/02
0.14Q	10/11/02	10/29/02	10/31/02	11/15/02
0.14Q	1/15/03	1/29/03	1/31/03	2/18/03
0.14Q	4/08/03	4/28/03	4/30/03	5/15/03

Indicated div.: $0.56 (Div. Reinv. Plan)

CAPITALIZATION (12/31/02):

	($000)	(%)
Long-Term Debt	239,084	31.6
Deferred Income Tax	7,512	1.0
Common & Surplus	511,052	67.5
Total	757,648	100.0

DIVIDEND ACHIEVER STATUS:
Rank: 195   10-Year Growth Rate: 7.31%
Total Years of Dividend Growth: 10

RECENT DEVELOPMENTS: For the quarter ended 3/31/03, net earnings advanced 13.1% to $13.7 million versus $12.1 million in the prior-year quarter. Earnings benefited from improved operating performance in the electrical products business as well as lower interest expense. Net sales increased 4.3% to $387.9 million from $371.9 million a year earlier. Electrical products sales climbed 8.6% to $213.1 million, while water systems sales slipped 0.4% to $174.8 million. Gross profit grew 1.7% to $78.2 million.

PROSPECTS: Despite weak consumer demand and an uncertain U.S. economy, AOS continues to expect earnings for full-year 2003 in the range of $2.05 to $2.25 per share. Lower pension income and increases in costs for medical benefits, liability insurance, and steel will adversely affect results throughout 2003, while benefits from the repositioning of the electrical products business, the integration of State Industries, and the introduction of new water heater products are weighted to the second half of the year.

BUSINESS

A.O. SMITH CORPORATION consists of two platforms, Electric Motor Technologies (53.8% of total 2002 net sales) and Water Systems Technologies (46.2%). The Electric Motor Technologies segment consists of A.O. Smith Electrical Products Company, which manufactures and markets hermetic motors directly to original equipment manufacturers and through a distributor network. The Water Systems Technologies segment consists of A.O. Smith Water Products Company, which manufactures residential and commercial gas and electric water heating systems and copper tube boilers. AOS operates facilities in the U.S., Canada, Mexico, England, Ireland, Hungary, the Netherlands and China. On 12/28/01, AOS acquired State Industries, Inc. for $117.2 million.

ANNUAL FINANCIAL DATA

	12/31/02	12/31/01	12/31/00	12/31/99	12/31/98	12/31/97	12/31/96
Earnings Per Share	1.86	④0.61	③1.76	②2.11	1.84	①1.33	①0.81
Cash Flow Per Share	3.69	2.57	3.66	3.68	3.13	2.26	1.52
Tang. Book Val. Per Share	6.95	6.30	8.64	7.69	10.93	10.69	13.52
Dividends Per Share	0.54	0.52	0.50	0.48	0.47	0.45	0.44
Dividend Payout %	29.0	85.2	28.4	22.7	25.4	34.0	54.5

INCOME STATEMENT (IN MILLIONS):

Total Revenues	1,469.1	1,151.2	1,247.9	1,039.3	917.6	832.9	781.2
Costs & Expenses	1,325.1	1,063.8	1,115.4	905.7	806.0	742.9	699.0
Depreciation & Amort.	50.7	47.1	45.1	37.3	31.2	26.3	22.6
Operating Income	93.3	40.3	87.5	96.3	80.4	63.7	59.6
Net Interest Inc./(Exp.)	d13.9	d16.4	d22.1	d11.4	d3.1	1.3	d8.1
Income Before Income Taxes	78.4	22.5	65.1	77.1	73.0	61.7	46.2
Income Taxes	27.0	8.0	23.4	26.8	25.3	21.4	17.1
Equity Earnings/Minority Int.	...	...	...	...	d3.2	d2.7	d3.9
Net Income	51.3	④14.5	③41.7	②50.3	44.5	①37.6	①25.2
Cash Flow	102.0	61.6	86.7	87.6	75.7	63.8	47.8
Average Shs. Outstg. (000)	27,649	23,915	23,691	23,787	24,184	28,191	31,383

BALANCE SHEET (IN MILLIONS):

Cash & Cash Equivalents	32.8	20.8	15.3	14.8	37.7	145.9	6.4
Total Current Assets	488.3	477.6	406.1	388.6	287.4	365.7	239.2
Net Property	362.7	355.3	282.8	283.5	248.8	207.8	182.6
Total Assets	1,224.9	1,293.9	1,059.2	1,064.0	767.4	716.5	885.0
Total Current Liabilities	261.7	256.0	170.4	168.4	132.2	127.9	138.4
Long-Term Obligations	239.1	390.4	316.4	351.3	131.2	101.0	238.4
Net Stockholders' Equity	511.1	451.9	448.4	431.1	401.1	399.7	424.6
Net Working Capital	226.6	221.6	235.7	220.2	155.2	237.8	100.8
Year-end Shs. Outstg. (000)	29,040	23,786	23,549	23,394	23,252	32,550	31,412

STATISTICAL RECORD:

Operating Profit Margin %	6.4	3.5	7.0	9.3	8.8	7.6	7.6
Net Profit Margin %	3.5	1.3	3.3	4.8	4.8	4.5	3.2
Return on Equity %	10.0	3.2	9.3	11.7	11.1	9.4	5.9
Return on Assets %	4.2	1.1	3.9	4.7	5.8	5.2	2.9
Debt/Total Assets %	19.5	30.2	29.9	33.0	17.1	14.1	26.9
Price Range	32.75-19.00	20.10-14.67	23.13-11.19	32.00-18.81	35.88-15.81	28.92-19.08	22.00-13.92
P/E Ratio	17.6-10.2	32.9-24.0	13.1-6.4	15.2-8.9	19.5-8.6	21.7-14.3	27.3-17.2
Average Yield %	2.1	3.0	2.9	1.9	1.8	1.9	2.5

Statistics are as originally reported. Adj. for stk. split: 3-for-2, 8/98. ① Bef. disc. opers. gain $15.2 mill. & gain of $101.0 mill. on disposition, 1997; $109.8 mill., 1996. ② Bef. loss from disc. opers. of $890,000 & loss of $7.0 mill. on disposition. ③ Bef. net loss of $11.9 mill. fr. disc. opers. ④ Incl. restr. chrg. of $9.4 mill.

OFFICERS:
R. J. O'Toole, Chmn., Pres., C.E.O.
K. W. Krueger, Sr. V.P., C.F.O.
W. D. Romoser, V.P., Sec., Gen. Couns.
INVESTOR CONTACT: Craig Watson, Dir., Investor Relations, (414) 359-4009
PRINCIPAL OFFICE: 11270 West Park Place, P.O. Box 245008, Milwaukee, WI 53224

TELEPHONE NUMBER: (414) 359-4000
FAX: (414) 359-4180
WEB: www.aosmith.com
NO. OF EMPLOYEES: 16,200 (approx.)
SHAREHOLDERS: 1,130 (com.); 457 (cl. A)
ANNUAL MEETING: In April
INCORPORATED: DE, Oct., 1986

INSTITUTIONAL HOLDINGS:
No. of Institutions: 129
Shares Held: 17,175,649
% Held: 59.2
INDUSTRY: Motors and generators (SIC: 3621)
TRANSFER AGENT(S): Wells Fargo Shareowner Services, South St. Paul, MN

SONOCO PRODUCTS COMPANY

YIELD 3.7%
P/E RATIO 16.6

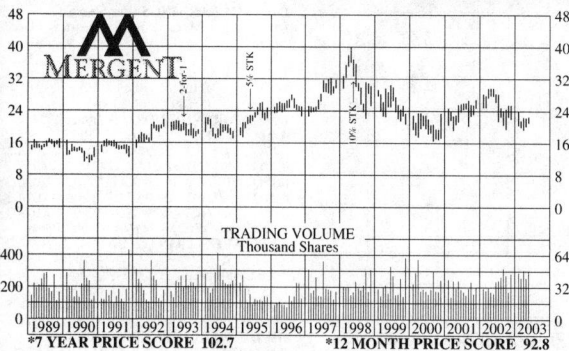

*7 YEAR PRICE SCORE 102.7 ***12 MONTH PRICE SCORE 92.8**
*NYSE COMPOSITE INDEX=100

INTERIM EARNINGS (Per Share):

Qtr.	Mar.	June	Sept.	Dec.
2000	0.45	0.47	0.39	0.37
2001	0.05	0.18	0.45	0.28
2002	0.35	0.39	0.30	0.36
2003	0.30	...	...	...

INTERIM DIVIDENDS (Per Share):

Amt.	Decl.	Ex.	Rec.	Pay.
0.21Q	7/17/02	8/14/02	8/16/02	9/10/02
0.21Q	10/16/02	11/13/02	11/15/02	12/10/02
0.21Q	2/05/03	2/19/03	2/21/03	3/10/03
0.21Q	4/16/03	5/14/03	5/16/03	6/10/03

Indicated div.: $0.84 (Div. Reinv. Plan)

CAPITALIZATION (12/31/02):

	($000)	(%)
Long-Term Debt	699,346	44.6
Common & Surplus	867,425	55.4
Total	1,566,771	100.0

DIVIDEND ACHIEVER STATUS:

Rank: 202   10-Year Growth Rate: 6.94%
Total Years of Dividend Growth: 19

RECENT DEVELOPMENTS: For the quarter ended 3/30/03, net income declined 13.6% to $29.0 million from $33.5 million in the equivalent 2002 quarter due to a negative price/cost relationship, mostly associated with lower average selling prices for global engineered carriers and higher costs for old corrugated containers, higher resin costs, and increased energy costs. Results for 2003 and 2002 included restructuring costs of $1.3 million and $1.4 million, respectively. Sales rose 4.2% to $681.4 million.

PROSPECTS: In light of uncertain economic conditions, SON expects second quarter 2003 earnings per share in the range of $1.46 to $1.50. Meanwhile, the Company continues to lower its cost structure and is initiating price increases to help offset higher raw material, energy and pension costs. Separately, on 4/22/03, SON completed the purchase of Australian Tube Company, a privately-held manufacturer of paper-based tubes and cores headquartered in Revsby, South Wales, Australia.

BUSINESS

SONOCO PRODUCTS COMPANY is a multinational manufacturer of industrial and consumer packaging products. SON is also vertically integrated into paperboard production and recovered-paper collection. The paperboard utilized in SON's packaging products is produced substantially from recovered paper. As of 4/16/03, SON operated approximately 300 facilities in 32 countries serving customers in some 85 nations. The industrial packaging segment (50.1% of 2002 sales) includes engineered carriers (paper and plastic tubes and cores), paper (paper manufacturing and recovered paper operations) and protective packaging (designed interior packaging and protective reels). The consumer packaging segment (49.9%) includes composite cans; flexible packaging (printing flexibles, high density bags and film products); and packaging services and specialty products (e-marketplace/supply chain management, graphics management, folding cartons, and paper glass covers and coasters).

ANNUAL FINANCIAL DATA

	12/31/02	12/31/01	12/31/00	12/31/99	12/31/98	12/31/97	12/31/96
Earnings Per Share	③ 1.39	③ 0.96	③ 1.66	1.83	② 1.84	① Nil	1.64
Cash Flow Per Share	3.03	2.61	3.17	3.25	3.24	1.43	3.08
Tang. Book Val. Per Share	5.27	4.64	5.94	6.37	6.40	6.69	3.49
Dividends Per Share	0.83	0.80	0.79	0.75	0.70	0.64	0.59
Dividend Payout %	59.7	83.3	47.6	41.0	38.2	...	35.8

INCOME STATEMENT (IN MILLIONS):

Total Revenues	2,812.2	2,606.3	2,711.5	2,546.7	2,557.9	2,847.8	2,788.1
Costs & Expenses	2,401.9	2,223.5	2,234.3	2,064.2	2,023.8	2,578.4	2,315.8
Depreciation & Amort.	159.3	158.6	150.8	145.8	145.7	153.5	142.9
Operating Income	251.0	224.2	326.4	336.7	388.5	115.9	329.4
Net Interest Inc./(Exp.)	d52.5	d48.4	d55.8	d47.2	d48.9	d52.2	d49.3
Income Before Income Taxes	198.5	175.8	270.6	289.6	339.6	63.7	280.1
Income Taxes	70.6	83.0	112.0	108.6	154.0	60.1	107.4
Equity Earnings/Minority Int.	7.4	d1.2	7.7	6.8	6.4	d1.0	d1.8
Net Income	③ 135.3	③ 91.6	③ 166.3	187.8	② 192.0	① 2.6	170.9
Cash Flow	294.6	250.2	317.1	333.7	337.7	153.1	306.6
Average Shs. Outstg. (000)	97,178	95,807	99,900	102,780	104,275	107,350	99,564

BALANCE SHEET (IN MILLIONS):

Cash & Cash Equivalents	31.4	36.1	35.2	36.5	57.2	53.6	71.3
Total Current Assets	663.3	665.2	695.8	723.1	661.4	873.0	737.6
Net Property	975.4	1,008.9	973.5	1,032.5	1,013.8	939.5	995.4
Total Assets	2,390.1	2,352.2	2,212.6	2,297.0	2,083.0	2,176.9	2,387.5
Total Current Liabilities	600.0	460.3	437.1	416.6	436.1	434.1	475.1
Long-Term Obligations	699.3	886.0	812.1	819.5	686.8	696.7	791.0
Net Stockholders' Equity	867.4	804.1	801.5	901.2	821.6	848.8	920.6
Net Working Capital	63.2	204.9	258.7	306.4	225.3	438.9	262.5
Year-end Shs. Outstg. (000)	96,380	95,453	95,006	101,448	101,683	105,417	98,850

STATISTICAL RECORD:

Operating Profit Margin %	8.9	8.6	12.0	13.2	15.2	4.1	11.8
Net Profit Margin %	4.8	3.5	6.1	7.4	7.5	0.1	6.1
Return on Equity %	15.6	11.4	20.7	20.8	23.4	0.3	18.6
Return on Assets %	5.7	3.9	7.5	8.2	9.2	0.1	7.2
Debt/Total Assets %	29.3	37.7	36.7	35.7	33.0	32.0	33.1
Price Range	29.70-19.45	26.88-19.20	23.50-16.56	30.50-20.69	40.00-22.13	32.27-22.61	28.07-22.61
P/E Ratio	21.4-14.0	28.0-20.0	14.2-10.0	16.7-11.3	21.7-12.0	...	17.1-13.8
Average Yield %	3.4	3.5	3.9	2.9	2.3	2.3	2.3

Statistics are as originally reported. Adj. for stk. splits: 10%, 6/98. ① Incl. non-recurr. after-tax chrg. $174.5 mill. for asset write-down. ② Bef. exraord. loss of $11.8 mill. and net gain on sale of divested assets of $85.4 mill. ③ Incl. nonrecurr. chrg. of $12.6 mill., 2002; $53.3 mill., 2001; $5.5 mill., 2000.

OFFICERS:
C. W. Coker, Chmn.
H. E. DeLoach, Jr., Pres., C.E.O.
C. J. Hupfer, V.P., C.F.O.

INVESTOR CONTACT: Allan V. Cecil, V.P.
Inv. Rel. & Corp. Affairs, (843) 383-7524

PRINCIPAL OFFICE: One North Second Street, Hartsville, SC 29550-3305

TELEPHONE NUMBER: (843) 383-7000
FAX: (843) 383-7008
WEB: www.sonoco.com

NO. OF EMPLOYEES: 17,400 (approx.)

SHAREHOLDERS: 50,000 (approx.)

ANNUAL MEETING: In Apr.

INCORPORATED: SC, May, 1899

INSTITUTIONAL HOLDINGS:
No. of Institutions: 2
Shares Held: 48,018,385
% Held: 49.5

INDUSTRY: Paperboard mills (SIC: 2631)

TRANSFER AGENT(S): EquiServe, Providence, RI

NASDAQ SYMBOL SOTR
Rec. Pr. 28.84 (5/31/03)

SOUTHTRUST CORPORATION

YIELD 2.9%
P/E RATIO 15.3

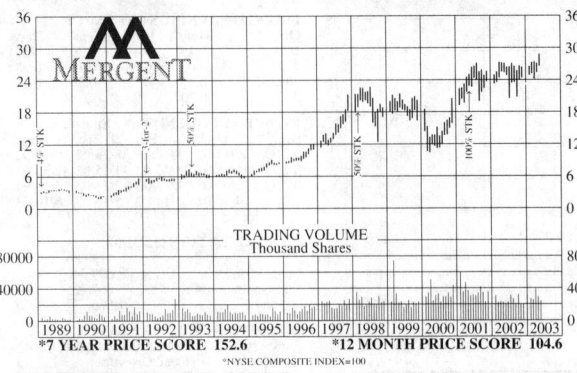

7 YEAR PRICE SCORE 152.6 **12 MONTH PRICE SCORE 104.6**
NYSE COMPOSITE INDEX=100

INTERIM EARNINGS (Per Share):

Qtr.	Mar.	June	Sept.	Dec.
1999	0.31	0.33	0.34	0.35
2000	0.35	0.36	0.36	0.37
2001	0.38	0.40	0.41	0.42
2002	0.44	0.45	0.47	0.48
2003	0.49	...	...	...

INTERIM DIVIDENDS (Per Share):

Amt.	Decl.	Ex.	Rec.	Pay.
0.17Q	4/17/02	5/29/02	5/31/02	7/01/02
0.17Q	7/17/02	8/21/02	8/23/02	10/01/02
0.17Q	10/16/02	11/20/02	11/22/02	1/02/03
0.21Q	1/15/03	2/19/03	2/21/03	4/01/03
0.21Q	4/16/03	5/21/03	5/23/03	7/01/03

Indicated div.: $0.84 (Div. Reinv. Plan)

CAPITALIZATION (12/31/02):

	($000)	(%)
Total Deposits	32,945,406	74.5
Long-Term Debt	6,652,838	15.0
Common & Surplus	4,627,581	10.5
Total	44,225,825	100.0

DIVIDEND ACHIEVER STATUS:
Rank: 73   10-Year Growth Rate: 14.35%
Total Years of Dividend Growth: 32

RECENT DEVELOPMENTS: For the three months ended 3/31/03, net income rose 8.6% to $171.3 million from $157.8 million in the corresponding prior-year period. Net interest income slipped 1.3% to $418.1 million from $423.8 million the year before. Provision for loan losses grew 6.3% to $29.4 million. Non-interest income, excluding securities transactions, rose 17.6% to $178.3 million, primarily due to increases in mortgage banking income, debit card fees, service charges, and investment fees. Non-interest expense declined 0.1% to $312.0 million from $312.3 million in 2002. Net interest margin declined to 3.69% from 3.87% the prior year. Total deposits amounted to $32.59 billion, up 3.4% compared with $31.51 billion a year earlier. Total loans and leases increased 4.6% to $34.40 billion from $32.90 billion the year before.

BUSINESS

SOUTHTRUST CORPORATION is a multibank holding company that operates 693 banking and loan offices and 871 automatic teller machines in Alabama, Florida, Georgia, Mississippi, North Carolina, South Carolina, Tennessee, Texas and Virginia. Consolidated total assets as of 3/31/03 amounted to $51.35 billion. The Company has four business segments: Regional Banking, Commercial Banking, Funds Management, and Capital Management. The Regional Banking segment (57.4% of 2002 net interest income and 77.4% of non-interest income) generates revenues from retail lending, depository services, and regional commercial lending. The Commercial Banking segment (16.7% and 5.6%) derives its revenues from commercial, industrial and commercial real estate customers. This business segment also provides cash management, international and commercial leasing services. The Funds Management segment (25.6% and 1.3%) is responsible for the Company's asset and liability management. The Capital Management segment (0.3% and 15.7%) provides trust, brokerage, investment, and insurance services.

ANNUAL FINANCIAL DATA

	12/31/02	12/31/01	12/31/00	12/31/99	12/31/98	12/31/97	12/31/96
Earnings Per Share	1.85	1.61	1.43	1.32	1.13	1.02	0.90
Tang. Book Val. Per Share	11.04	9.20	8.20	6.74	6.36	7.14	6.02
Dividends Per Share	0.65	0.55	0.48	0.42	0.37	0.32	0.29
Dividend Payout %	35.1	33.8	33.9	32.3	32.7	31.9	32.0
INCOME STATEMENT (IN MILLIONS):							
Total Interest Income	2,665.4	3,170.8	3,394.1	2,906.4	2,557.5	2,232.3	1,804.2
Total Interest Expense	960.3	1,642.7	2,008.4	1,539.5	1,386.3	1,186.1	938.2
Net Interest Income	① 1,705.1	1,528.1	① 1,385.7	1,366.9	1,171.2	1,046.2	866.0
Provision for Loan Losses	126.7	118.3	92.8	141.2	94.8	90.6	90.0
Non-Interest Income	661.0	571.0	505.7	443.6	386.1	270.5	254.8
Non-Interest Expense	1,276.9	1,153.4	1,087.2	1,010.5	914.4	748.2	643.3
Income Before Taxes	962.5	827.5	711.4	658.7	548.1	477.9	387.5
Net Income	649.9	554.5	482.3	443.2	368.9	306.7	254.7
Average Shs. Outstg. (000)	350,937	345,294	337,812	337,556	328,296	302,016	284,307
BALANCE SHEET (IN MILLIONS):							
Cash & Due from Banks	1,005.3	1,159.2	959.8	875.0	970.8	877.9	903.1
Securities Avail. for Sale	10,701.0	10,062.2	7,050.0	5,130.5	3,875.9	2,975.8	2,859.0
Total Loans & Leases	34,483.2	33,695.5	31,696.9	31,972.8	27,526.6	22,633.9	19,466.7
Allowance for Credit Losses	744.2	756.0	751.1	717.3	586.6	474.5	405.4
Net Loans & Leases	33,739.1	32,939.5	30,945.8	31,255.5	26,940.0	22,159.3	19,061.3
Total Assets	50,570.9	48,754.5	45,146.5	43,262.5	38,133.8	30,906.4	26,223.2
Total Deposits	32,945.4	32,634.1	30,702.5	27,739.3	24,839.9	19,586.6	17,305.5
Long-Term Obligations	6,652.8	5,484.5	4,178.1	4,655.8	3,935.3	3,888.8	2,727.4
Total Liabilities	45,943.3	44,792.2	41,794.1	40,335.1	35,395.5	28,711.8	24,488.3
Net Stockholders' Equity	4,627.6	3,962.4	3,352.5	2,927.4	2,738.3	2,194.6	1,734.9
Year-end Shs. Outstg. (000)	346,924	346,273	338,107	335,810	334,422	307,328	288,357
STATISTICAL RECORD:							
Return on Equity %	14.0	14.0	14.4	15.1	13.5	14.0	14.7
Return on Assets %	1.3	1.1	1.1	1.0	1.0	1.0	1.0
Equity/Assets %	9.2	8.1	7.4	6.8	7.2	7.1	6.6
Non-Int. Exp./Tot. Inc. %	54.0	54.9	57.5	55.8	58.7	56.8	57.4
Price Range	27.32-20.52	27.18-19.25	20.53-10.44	21.44-16.38	22.69-12.44	21.24-11.38	12.04-8.42
P/E Ratio	14.8-11.1	16.9-12.0	14.4-7.3	16.3-12.5	20.2-11.1	20.9-11.2	13.4-9.4
Average Yield %	2.7	2.3	3.1	2.2	2.1	2.0	2.8

Statistics are as originally reported. Adj. for stk. splits: 100% stk. div., 5/01; 3-for-2, 2/98. ① After a tax equivalent adjustment of $12.6 mill., 12/02; $14.5 mill., 12/00.

OFFICERS:
W. D. Malone, Jr., Chmn., C.E.O.
J. Banton, Pres., C.O.O.
A. E. Yother, Exec. V.P., Treas, Contr.

INVESTOR CONTACT: David Oliver, Corp. Commun., (205) 254-5523

PRINCIPAL OFFICE: 420 North 20th Street, Birmingham, AL 35203

TELEPHONE NUMBER: (205) 254-5000
FAX: (205) 254-5405
WEB: www.southtrust.com

NO. OF EMPLOYEES: 12,950 (approx.)

SHAREHOLDERS: 17,048 (approx., record)

ANNUAL MEETING: In Apr.

INCORPORATED: DE, 1968

INSTITUTIONAL HOLDINGS:
No. of Institutions: 376
Shares Held: 171,558,708
% Held: 50.2

INDUSTRY: National commercial banks (SIC: 6021)

TRANSFER AGENT(S): American Stock Transfer & Trust Company, New York, NY

STANLEY WORKS

YIELD 3.6%
P/E RATIO 15.4

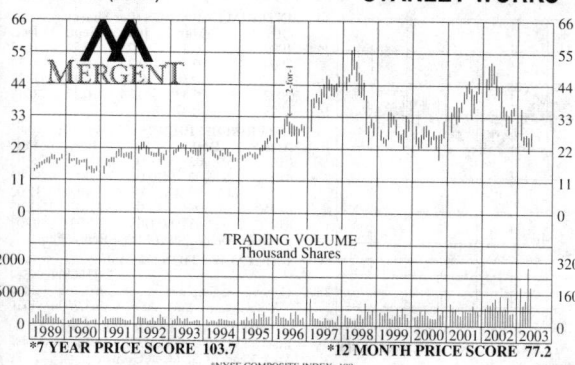

TRADING VOLUME
Thousand Shares

*7 YEAR PRICE SCORE 103.7   ***12 MONTH PRICE SCORE 77.2**
*NYSE COMPOSITE INDEX=100

INTERIM EARNINGS (Per Share):

Qtr.	Mar.	June	Sept.	Dec.
1999	0.34	0.28	0.56	0.49
2000	0.54	0.58	0.56	0.54
2001	0.54	0.58	0.62	0.07
2002	0.56	0.72	0.62	0.25
2003	0.22	...	...	...

INTERIM DIVIDENDS (Per Share):

Amt.	Decl.	Ex.	Rec.	Pay.
0.255Q	7/17/02	8/29/02	9/03/02	9/24/02
0.255Q	10/16/02	11/20/02	11/22/02	12/27/02
0.255Q	1/24/03	3/06/03	3/10/03	3/28/03
0.255Q	4/22/03	5/29/03	6/02/03	6/27/03

Indicated div.: $1.02 (Div. Reinv. Plan)

CAPITALIZATION (12/28/02):

	($000)	(%)
Long-Term Debt	564,300	36.5
Common & Surplus	983,800	63.5
Total	1,548,100	100.0

DIVIDEND ACHIEVER STATUS:
Rank: 245   10-Year Growth Rate: 4.46%
Total Years of Dividend Growth: 35

RECENT DEVELOPMENTS: For the quarter ended 3/29/03, net income decreased 60.7% to $19.2 million from $48.9 million in the equivalent 2002 quarter. Results for 2003 included pre-tax restructuring costs, impairment charges and other exit costs totaling $17.0 million. Net sales grew 8.0% to $666.2 million. Sales reflected the acquisition of Best Access Systems, a provider of security access control systems, in November 2002, partially offset by lower sales in the consumer channel.

PROSPECTS: On 4/9/03, SWK announced a restructuring plan, which includes a workforce reduction of over 1,000 people, closures of four manufacturing plants and five warehouses, and its exit from the Mac Tools retail channel. SWK expects that these actions will require severance payments and other exit costs, along with certain asset impairment charges. Excluding the Mac Direct exit, these actions are expected to require pre-tax charges of about $60.0 million during 2003.

BUSINESS

STANLEY WORKS is a worldwide producer of tools and door products for professional, industrial and consumer use. The Tools segment (75.4% of 2002 sales) manufactures and markets carpenters', mechanics', pneumatic and hydraulic tools as well as tool sets. The Company markets its carpenters' tools under the STANLEY®, FATMAX™, MAXGRIP™, POWERLOCK®, INTELLITOOLS™, CONTRACTOR GRADE™, DYNAGRIP®, ACCUSCAPE®, and GOLDBLATT® brands. The Doors segment (24.6%) manufactures and markets commercial and residential doors as well as closet doors and systems, home decor and door consumer hardware. Products in the Doors segment include residential insulated steel, reinforced fiberglass and wood entrance door systems. Door products are marketed under the STANLEY®, MAGICDOOR®, WELCOMEWATCH®, STANLEY-ACMETRACK™, MONARCH™ and ACME® brands. A substantial portion of SWK's products are sold through home centers and mass merchant distribution channels in the U.S.

ANNUAL FINANCIAL DATA

	12/28/02	12/29/01	12/30/00	1/1/00	1/2/99	1/3/98	12/28/96
Earnings Per Share	2.10	④ 1.81	2.22	③ 1.67	② 1.53	① d0.47	① 1.09
Cash Flow Per Share	2.90	2.76	3.17	2.62	2.41	0.34	1.93
Tang. Book Val. Per Share	5.05	7.04	6.58	6.19	5.32	5.67	7.68
Dividends Per Share	0.99	0.94	0.90	0.87	0.83	0.77	0.73
Dividend Payout %	47.1	51.9	40.5	52.1	54.2	...	67.0
INCOME STATEMENT (IN MILLIONS):							
Total Revenues	2,593.0	2,624.4	2,748.9	2,751.8	2,729.1	2,669.5	2,670.8
Costs & Expenses	2,233.2	2,284.5	2,324.8	2,410.0	2,397.8	2,577.2	2,377.1
Depreciation & Amort.	71.2	82.9	83.3	85.6	79.7	72.4	74.7
Operating Income	288.6	257.0	340.8	256.2	251.6	19.9	219.0
Net Interest Inc./(Exp.)	d24.5	d25.6	d27.1	d27.9	d23.1	d16.6	d22.5
Income Before Income Taxes	272.5	236.7	293.7	230.8	215.4	d18.6	174.2
Income Taxes	87.5	78.4	99.3	80.8	77.6	23.3	77.3
Net Income	185.0	④ 158.3	194.4	③ 150.0	② 137.8	① d41.9	① 96.9
Cash Flow	256.2	241.2	277.7	235.6	217.5	30.5	171.6
Average Shs. Outstg. (000)	88,246	87,467	87,668	89,887	90,193	89,469	88,824
BALANCE SHEET (IN MILLIONS):							
Cash & Cash Equivalents	121.7	115.2	93.6	88.0	110.1	152.2	84.0
Total Current Assets	1,190.4	1,141.4	1,094.3	1,091.0	1,086.4	1,005.3	910.9
Net Property	494.8	494.3	503.7	520.6	511.4	513.2	570.4
Total Assets	2,418.2	2,055.7	1,884.8	1,890.6	1,932.9	1,758.7	1,659.6
Total Current Liabilities	680.9	825.5	707.3	693.0	702.1	622.7	381.6
Long-Term Obligations	564.3	196.8	248.7	290.0	344.8	283.7	342.6
Net Stockholders' Equity	983.8	832.3	736.5	735.4	669.4	607.8	780.1
Net Working Capital	509.5	315.9	387.0	398.0	384.3	382.6	529.3
Year-end Shs. Outstg. (000)	86,835	84,659	85,188	88,945	88,772	88,788	88,720
STATISTICAL RECORD:							
Operating Profit Margin %	11.1	9.8	12.4	9.3	9.2	0.7	8.2
Net Profit Margin %	7.1	6.0	7.1	5.5	5.0	...	3.6
Return on Equity %	18.8	19.0	26.4	20.4	20.6	...	12.4
Return on Assets %	7.7	7.7	10.3	7.9	7.1	...	5.8
Debt/Total Assets %	23.3	9.6	13.2	15.3	17.8	16.1	20.6
Price Range	52.00-27.31	46.97-28.06	31.88-18.44	35.00-22.00	57.25-23.50	47.38-28.00	32.81-23.63
P/E Ratio	24.8-13.0	25.9-15.5	14.4-8.3	21.0-13.2	37.4-15.4	...	30.1-21.7
Average Yield %	2.5	2.5	3.6	3.1	2.1	2.0	2.6

Statistics are as originally reported. Adj. for stk. split: 2-for-1, 6/96. ① Incl. pretax restruct chrgs. of $238.5 mill., 1997; $47.8 mill., 1996. ② Incl. restruct. chrg. of $27.8 mill. ③ Incl. restruct. credit of $21.3 mill. ④ Incl. restruct. chrg. and asset write-offs of $72.4 mill.

OFFICERS:
J. M. Trani, Chmn., C.E.O.
J. M. Loree, Exec. V.P., C.F.O.
B. H. Beatt, V.P., Sec., Gen. Couns.

INVESTOR CONTACT: Investor Relations, (860) 225-5111

PRINCIPAL OFFICE: 1000 Stanley Drive, P.O. Box 7000, New Britain, CT 06053

TELEPHONE NUMBER: (860) 225-5111
FAX: (860) 827-3895
WEB: www.stanleyworks.com

NO. OF EMPLOYEES: 14,900 (approx.)

SHAREHOLDERS: 14,053

ANNUAL MEETING: In Apr.

INCORPORATED: CT, July, 1852

INSTITUTIONAL HOLDINGS:
No. of Institutions: 238
Shares Held: 60,798,224
% Held: 69.9

INDUSTRY: Hand and edge tools, nec (SIC: 3423)

TRANSFER AGENT(S): EquiServe Limited Partnership, Boston, MA

STATE AUTO FINANCIAL CORP.

YIELD	0.6%
P/E RATIO	21.6

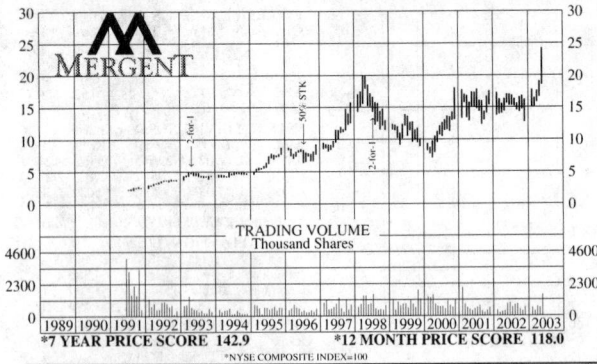

INTERIM EARNINGS (Per Share):

Qtr.	Mar.	June	Sept.	Dec.
1999	0.25	0.25	0.21	0.32
2000	0.35	0.32	0.20	0.34
2001	0.36	0.24	0.18	d0.27
2002	0.33	d0.04	0.15	0.49
2003	0.47	...	...	...

INTERIM DIVIDENDS (Per Share):

Amt.	Decl.	Ex.	Rec.	Pay.
0.033Q	5/23/02	6/10/02	6/12/02	6/28/02
0.035Q	8/16/02	9/10/02	9/12/02	9/30/02
0.035Q	11/22/02	12/11/02	12/13/02	12/31/02
0.035Q	3/07/03	3/13/03	3/17/03	3/31/03
0.035Q	5/23/03	6/11/03	6/13/03	6/30/03

Indicated div.: $0.14 (Div. Reinv. Plan)

CAPITALIZATION (12/31/02):

	($000)	(%)
Common & Surplus	463,769	100.0
Total	463,769	100.0

DIVIDEND ACHIEVER STATUS:
Rank: 134   10-Year Growth Rate: 10.44%
Total Years of Dividend Growth: 11

*7 YEAR PRICE SCORE 142.9   *12 MONTH PRICE SCORE 118.0
*NYSE COMPOSITE INDEX=100

RECENT DEVELOPMENTS: For the quarter ended 3/31/03, net income increased 60.0% to $21.1 million from $13.2 million in the equivalent 2002 quarter. Results benefited from higher earned premiums as well as a more favorable loss experience, driven mainly by a significant improvement in the underwriting results of the Meridian segment. Total revenue grew 10.2% to $253.4 million from $230.0 million the previous year. Revenue for 2002 and 2001 included net realized investment gains of $3.8 million and $1.3 million, respectively. Premiums earned climbed 9.2% to $232.4 million from $212.8 million in 2002. Net investment income increased 7.5% to $15.7 million. STFC announced that May 2003 storms would contribute about $23.0 million to $26.0 million in pre-tax losses in the second quarter, adding 10.0 to 11.0 direct loss ratio points to second quarter results. Separately, On 5/30/03, STFC reported that a minority shareholder has filed a proposal to buy its outstanding public shares at $27.50 a share. STFC has named a special committee and will evaluate the proposal.

BUSINESS

STATE AUTO FINANCIAL CORP., through its principal insurance subsidiaries, State Auto Property and Casualty Insurance Company (State Auto P&C), Milbank Insurance Company, Farmers Casualty Insurance Company and State Auto Insurance Company (SAIC), provides personal and commercial insurance. The Company's principal lines of business include personal and commercial auto, homeowners, commercial multi-peril, workers' compensation, general liability and fire insurance. STFC is a majority-owned subsidiary of State Automobile Mutual Insurance Company, an Ohio-domiciled property and casualty insurer. As of 5/20/03, STFC marketed its products through more than 22,000 independent agents associated with about 3,500 agencies in 26 states and the District of Columbia. The Company's products are marketed primarily in the central and eastern United States, excluding New York, New Jersey and the New England states.

ANNUAL FINANCIAL DATA

	12/31/02	12/31/01	12/31/00	12/31/99	12/31/98	12/31/97	12/31/96
Earnings Per Share	0.93	0.52	1.21	1.03	0.87	0.91	0.63
Tang. Book Val. Per Share	11.89	10.23	9.95	8.22	8.06	6.15	5.14
Dividends Per Share	0.135	0.125	0.115	0.105	0.095	0.085	0.077
Dividend Payout %	14.5	24.0	9.5	10.2	10.9	9.3	12.3
INCOME STATEMENT (IN MILLIONS):							
Total Premium Income	896.6	555.2	398.0	392.1	356.2	254.7	240.3
Other Income	70.9	68.1	64.8	48.8	45.8	34.3	33.3
Total Revenues	967.5	623.3	462.8	440.9	402.1	289.0	273.6
Policyholder Benefits	653.5	427.1	272.2	264.6	242.3	165.8	173.5
Income Before Income Taxes	37.8	18.0	61.4	57.0	49.6	47.1	30.1
Income Taxes	0.8	cr2.6	13.7	14.2	12.1	13.1	7.5
Net Income	37.0	20.6	47.7	42.8	37.5	34.0	22.6
Average Shs. Outstg. (000)	39,743	39,681	39,120	41,526	42,901	37,314	36,140
BALANCE SHEET (IN MILLIONS):							
Cash & Cash Equivalents	96.0	30.0	21.3	24.6	32.6	23.9	12.9
Premiums Due	23.0	13.9	9.3	10.8	22.7	12.1	9.7
Invst. Assets: Fixed-term	1,216.7	1,078.8	692.6	571.8	537.8	399.6	384.3
Invst. Assets: Equities	53.7	59.8	58.3	55.5	42.2	4.6	...
Invst. Assets: Total	1,272.3	1,138.7	750.9	627.3	580.0	404.2	384.3
Total Assets	1,593.0	1,367.5	898.1	759.9	709.8	493.2	453.1
Net Stockholders' Equity	463.8	400.2	386.1	317.7	340.8	225.5	186.5
Year-end Shs. Outstg. (000)	39,001	38,937	38,555	38,321	42,027	36,684	36,272
STATISTICAL RECORD:							
Return on Revenues %	3.8	3.3	10.3	9.7	9.3	11.8	8.3
Return on Equity %	8.0	5.2	12.4	13.5	11.0	15.1	12.1
Return on Assets %	2.3	1.5	5.3	5.6	5.3	6.9	5.0
Price Range	17.25-12.67	17.80-12.30	18.00-7.13	13.88-8.88	20.00-11.44	15.75-8.13	9.25-6.38
P/E Ratio	18.5-13.6	34.2-23.6	14.9-5.9	13.5-8.6	23.0-13.1	17.3-8.9	14.8-10.2
Average Yield %	0.9	0.8	0.9	0.9	0.6	0.7	1.0

Statistics are as originally reported. Adj. for stk. splits: 2-for-1, 7/98; 50% div., 7/96

OFFICERS:
R. H. Moone, Chmn., Pres., C.E.O.
S. J. Johnston, Sr. V.P., C.F.O., Treas.
J. R. Lowther, Sr. V.P., Sec., Gen. Couns.
INVESTOR CONTACT: Terrence Bowshier, V.P., Dir. Inv. Rel., (614) 464-5078
PRINCIPAL OFFICE: 518 East Broad Street, Columbus, OH 43215-3976

TELEPHONE NUMBER: (614) 464-5000
FAX: (614) 464-5374
WEB: www.stauto.com
NO. OF EMPLOYEES: 2,097
SHAREHOLDERS: 937
ANNUAL MEETING: In May
INCORPORATED: OH, April, 1990

INSTITUTIONAL HOLDINGS:
No. of Institutions: 40
Shares Held: 4,452,319
% Held: 11.4
INDUSTRY: Fire, marine, and casualty insurance (SIC: 6331)
TRANSFER AGENT(S): National City Bank, Cleveland, OH

STATE STREET CORPORATION

YIELD 1.4%
P/E RATIO 13.4

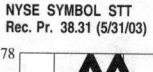

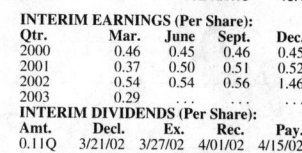

TRADING VOLUME
Thousand Shares

'000
'000

1989 1990 1991 1992 1993 1994 1995 1996 1997 1998 1999 2000 2001 2002 2003

*7 YEAR PRICE SCORE 117.9   ***12 MONTH PRICE SCORE 87.4**
*NYSE COMPOSITE INDEX=100

INTERIM EARNINGS (Per Share):

Qtr.	Mar.	June	Sept.	Dec.
2000	0.46	0.45	0.46	0.45
2001	0.37	0.50	0.51	0.52
2002	0.54	0.54	0.56	1.46
2003	0.29	...	...	...

INTERIM DIVIDENDS (Per Share):

Amt.	Decl.	Ex.	Rec.	Pay.
0.11Q	3/21/02	3/27/02	4/01/02	4/15/02
0.12Q	6/20/02	6/27/02	7/01/02	7/15/02
0.12Q	9/19/02	9/27/02	10/01/02	10/15/02
0.13Q	12/19/02	12/30/02	1/02/03	1/15/03
0.13Q	3/20/03	3/28/03	4/01/03	4/15/03

Indicated div.: $0.52 (Div. Reinv. Plan)

CAPITALIZATION (12/31/02):

	($000)	(%)
Total Deposits	45,468,000	88.2
Long-Term Debt	1,270,000	2.5
Common & Surplus	4,787,000	9.3
Total	51,525,000	100.0

DIVIDEND ACHIEVER STATUS:
Rank: 56   10-Year Growth Rate: 15.65%
Total Years of Dividend Growth: 22

RECENT DEVELOPMENTS: For the quarter ended 3/31/03, net income decreased 46.1% to $96.0 million from $178.0 million in the corresponding prior-year period. Earnings for 2003 included pre-tax merger and integration costs of $37.0 million and a one-time pre-tax charge of about $38.0 million related to tax legislation. Net interest revenue declined 27.4% to $204.0 million. Provision for loan losses amounted to $1.0 million in 2002. Total fee revenue grew 13.3% to $790.0 million. Servicing fees rose 18.7% to $438.0 million.

PROSPECTS: STT recently acquired a substantial portion of Deutsche Bank AG's Global Securities Services (GSS) business. Separately, on 4/10/03, STT announced cost reduction initiatives that will lower its operating expenses by about $125.0 million for the remainder of 2003. The first part of the expense reduction program is to reduce direct controllable expenses. The remainder of the reductions will be achieved through staff reductions of up to 1,800 people, in addition to the reduction of 1,000 people in connection with the GSS acquisition.

BUSINESS

STATE STREET CORPORATION (formerly State Street Boston Corporation), as of 3/31/03, is a bank holding company with $79.11 billion in assets that conducts business worldwide principally through its subsidiary, State Street Bank and Trust Company. The Company has two lines of business: services for institutional investors and investment management. Services for institutional investors are primarily accounting, custody and other services for large pools of assets. Investment management offers index and active equity strategies, short-term investment funds and fixed income products. As of 3/31/03, STT had $788.00 billion in assets under management. On 10/1/99, the Company sold its commercial lending business. On 2/8/01, STT acquired a majority interest in Bel Air Investment Advisors LLC. On 7/3/01, STT acquired DST Systems, Inc.'s portfolio accounting service business. On 12/31/02, STT sold its corporate trust business.

ANNUAL FINANCIAL DATA

	12/31/02	12/31/01	12/31/00	12/31/99	12/31/98	12/31/97	12/31/96
Earnings Per Share	[2] 3.10	1.90	1.82	[1] 1.89	1.33	1.16	0.90
Tang. Book Val. Per Share	12.92	11.88	10.09	8.31	7.19	5.97	5.47
Dividends Per Share	0.46	0.39	0.33	0.29	0.25	0.21	0.18
Dividend Payout %	14.8	20.5	18.2	15.3	18.8	18.1	20.6
INCOME STATEMENT (IN MILLIONS):							
Total Interest Income	1,974.0	2,855.0	3,256.0	2,437.0	2,237.0	1,755.0	1,443.0
Total Interest Expense	995.0	1,830.0	2,362.0	1,656.0	1,492.0	1,114.0	892.0
Net Interest Income	979.0	1,025.0	894.0	781.0	745.0	641.0	551.0
Provision for Loan Losses	4.0	10.0	9.0	14.0	17.0	16.0	8.0
Non-Interest Income	3,421.0	2,782.0	2,665.0	2,537.0	1,997.0	1,673.0	1,302.0
Non-Interest Expense	2,841.0	2,867.0	2,644.0	2,336.0	2,068.0	1,734.0	1,398.0
Income Before Taxes	1,555.0	930.0	906.0	968.0	657.0	564.0	447.0
Net Income	[2] 1,015.0	628.0	595.0	[1] 619.0	436.0	380.0	293.0
Average Shs. Outstg. (000)	327,477	330,492	328,088	327,502	327,854	327,578	326,532
BALANCE SHEET (IN MILLIONS):							
Cash & Due from Banks	1,361.0	1,651.0	1,618.0	2,930.0	1,365.0	2,411.0	1,623.0
Securities Avail. for Sale	29,055.0	21,775.0	14,744.0	15,489.0	10,072.0	10,580.0	9,642.0
Total Loans & Leases	4,174.0	5,341.0	5,273.0	4,293.0	6,309.0	5,562.0	4,713.0
Allowance for Credit Losses	61.0	58.0	57.0	48.0	84.0	83.0	73.0
Net Loans & Leases	4,113.0	5,283.0	5,216.0	4,245.0	6,225.0	5,479.0	4,640.0
Total Assets	85,794.0	69,896.0	69,298.0	60,896.0	47,082.0	37,975.0	31,524.0
Total Deposits	45,468.0	38,559.0	37,937.0	34,145.0	27,539.0	24,878.0	19,519.0
Long-Term Obligations	1,270.0	1,217.0	1,219.0	921.0	922.0	774.0	476.0
Total Liabilities	81,007.0	66,051.0	66,036.0	58,244.0	44,771.0	35,980.0	29,749.0
Net Stockholders' Equity	4,787.0	3,845.0	3,262.0	2,652.0	2,311.0	1,995.0	1,775.0
Year-end Shs. Outstg. (000)	324,927	323,670	323,422	319,180	321,390	334,446	324,616
STATISTICAL RECORD:							
Return on Equity %	21.2	16.3	18.2	23.3	18.9	19.0	16.5
Return on Assets %	1.2	0.9	0.9	1.0	0.9	1.0	0.9
Equity/Assets %	5.6	5.5	4.7	4.4	4.9	5.3	5.6
Non-Int. Exp./Tot. Inc. %	64.6	75.3	74.3	70.4	75.4	74.9	75.4
Price Range	58.36-32.11	63.93-36.25	68.40-31.22	47.63-27.75	37.16-23.94	31.84-15.66	17.13-10.44
P/E Ratio	18.8-10.4	33.6-19.1	37.7-17.2	25.2-14.7	27.9-18.0	27.4-13.5	19.1-11.6
Average Yield %	1.0	0.8	0.7	0.8	0.8	0.9	1.3

Statistics are as originally reported. Adj. for 2-for-1 stock splits, 5/01 & 5/97. [1] Incl. pre-tax net gain on the sale of Co.'s commercial banking business of $282.0 mill. [2] Incl. a net gain of $571.0 million related to various items.

OFFICERS:
D. A. Spina, Chmn., C.E.O
R. E. Logue, Pres., C.O.O.
E. J. Resch, Exec. V.P., C.F.O., Treas.
INVESTOR CONTACT: S. Kelley MacDonald, Sr. V.P.-Inv. Rel., (617) 664-3477
PRINCIPAL OFFICE: 225 Franklin Street, Boston, MA 02110

TELEPHONE NUMBER: (617) 786-3000
FAX: (617) 985-8055
WEB: www.statestreet.com
NO. OF EMPLOYEES: 18,952 full-time; 549 part-time
SHAREHOLDERS: 5,454
ANNUAL MEETING: In April
INCORPORATED: MA, Oct., 1969

INSTITUTIONAL HOLDINGS:
No. of Institutions: 538
Shares Held: 238,318,196
% Held: 71.8
INDUSTRY: State commercial banks (SIC: 6022)
TRANSFER AGENT(S): State Street Bank and Trust Company, Boston, MA

STEPAN COMPANY

YIELD 3.1%
P/E RATIO 13.0

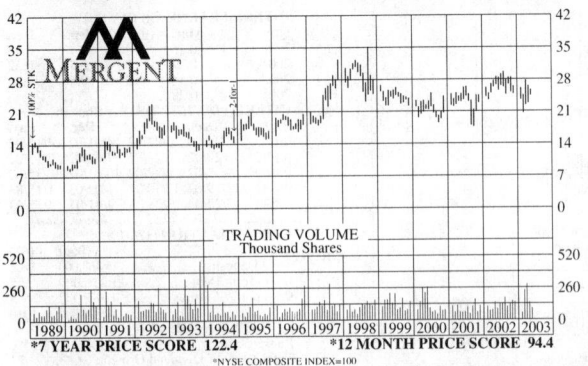

INTERIM EARNINGS (Per Share):

Qtr.	March	June	Sept.	Dec.
2000	0.41	0.64	0.61	d0.25
2001	0.36	0.61	0.44	0.18
2002	0.39	0.84	0.58	0.25
2003	0.23	...	...	...

INTERIM DIVIDENDS (Per Share):

Amt.	Decl.	Ex.	Rec.	Pay.
0.182Q	4/30/02	5/29/02	5/31/02	6/14/02
0.182Q	8/06/02	8/28/02	8/30/02	9/13/02
0.19Q	11/01/02	11/26/02	11/29/02	12/13/02
0.19Q	2/11/03	2/26/03	2/28/03	3/14/03
0.19Q	4/29/03	5/28/03	5/30/03	6/13/03

Indicated div.: $0.76

CAPITALIZATION (12/31/02):

	($000)	(%)
Long-Term Debt	104,304	36.8
Deferred Income Tax	20,065	7.1
Preferred Stock	14,566	5.1
Common & Surplus	144,263	50.9
Total	283,198	100.0

DIVIDEND ACHIEVER STATUS:
Rank: 197   10-Year Growth Rate: 7.14%
Total Years of Dividend Growth: 36

7 YEAR PRICE SCORE 122.4   **12 MONTH PRICE SCORE 94.4**

*NYSE COMPOSITE INDEX=100

RECENT DEVELOPMENTS: For the quarter ended 3/31/03, net income dropped 39.9% to $2.3 million from $3.8 million in the equivalent 2002 quarter. Earnings were adversely affected by higher energy costs coupled with higher freight, raw material and pension costs. Net sales increased 3.3% to $187.1 million from $181.2 million a year earlier, reflecting improved volume and favorable effects from foreign currency translation. Gross profit fell 12.5% to $25.4 million from $29.0 million in 2002.

PROSPECTS: The Company expects full-year 2003 earnings to be lower than earnings for 2002, primarily due to volatility in natural gas and raw material costs compounded by the weak economic environment. Effective 4/1/03, the Company raised prices in an attempt to restore its margins. Meanwhile, the Company is pursuing opportunities in several fabric softener products that are still expected to contribute to 2003 sales, although at a slower ramp-up than previously anticipated.

BUSINESS

THE STEPAN COMPANY is a producer of specialty and intermediate chemicals that are used in a variety of end products. The Company operates in three business segments: surfactants (80.0% of 2002 net sales), polymers (17.0%), and specialty products (3.0%). Surfactants are a principal ingredient in consumer and industrial cleaning products such as detergents, shampoos, lotions, toothpastes and cosmetics. Other applications include lubricating ingredients and emulsifiers for agricultural products, plastics and composites. Polymer products include phthalic anhydride, polyurethane systems and polyurethane polyols, which are used in construction materials and components of automotive, boating and other consumer products. Polyurethane systems provide thermal insulation. Polyurethane polyols are used in manufacturing laminate board. Specialty products include chemicals used in food, flavoring and pharmaceutical applications.

ANNUAL FINANCIAL DATA

	12/31/02	12/31/01	12/31/00	12/31/99	12/31/98	12/31/97	12/31/96
Earnings Per Share	2.05	1.59	1.47	① 2.08	2.12	1.86	1.80
Cash Flow Per Share	6.15	5.54	5.30	5.79	5.51	5.08	5.12
Tang. Book Val. Per Share	13.98	15.41	15.47	14.28	13.24	12.16	11.38
Dividends Per Share	0.74	0.71	0.66	0.61	0.56	0.51	0.48
Dividend Payout %	36.0	44.5	45.1	29.4	26.5	27.6	26.5
INCOME STATEMENT (IN THOUSANDS):							
Total Revenues	748,539	711,517	698,937	666,784	610,451	581,949	536,635
Costs & Expenses	674,492	640,320	627,632	585,554	527,681	502,298	464,111
Depreciation & Amort.	40,117	39,972	39,277	39,452	37,347	35,281	32,138
Operating Income	33,930	31,225	32,028	41,778	45,423	44,370	40,386
Net Interest Inc./(Exp.)	d7,239	d7,168	d8,328	d8,376	d7,453	d7,795	d7,243
Income Before Income Taxes	30,268	25,926	24,403	34,829	38,766	34,874	32,261
Income Taxes	10,139	9,774	9,395	12,700	15,312	14,464	13,194
Net Income	20,129	16,152	15,008	① 22,129	23,454	20,410	19,067
Cash Flow	59,444	55,322	53,470	60,723	59,905	50,649	46,427
Average Shs. Outstg.	9,802	10,133	10,236	10,632	11,043	10,959	10,002
BALANCE SHEET (IN THOUSANDS):							
Cash & Cash Equivalents	3,188	4,224	3,536	3,969	983	5,507	4,778
Total Current Assets	185,112	185,194	177,213	166,660	149,758	146,482	153,698
Net Property	211,050	212,433	199,147	209,491	215,096	206,601	207,159
Total Assets	439,667	435,488	415,049	414,576	404,361	374,936	381,012
Total Current Liabilities	105,017	109,730	108,341	98,045	87,944	82,693	83,376
Long-Term Obligations	104,304	109,588	96,466	107,420	107,708	94,898	102,567
Net Stockholders' Equity	158,829	159,729	154,176	155,064	147,984	137,598	131,615
Net Working Capital	80,095	75,464	68,872	68,615	61,814	63,789	70,322
Year-end Shs. Outstg.	8,881	9,420	9,024	9,488	9,693	9,692	9,817
STATISTICAL RECORD:							
Operating Profit Margin %	4.5	4.4	4.6	6.3	7.4	7.6	7.5
Net Profit Margin %	2.7	2.3	2.1	3.3	3.8	3.5	3.6
Return on Equity %	12.7	10.1	9.7	14.3	15.8	14.8	14.5
Return on Assets %	4.6	3.7	3.6	5.3	5.8	5.4	5.0
Debt/Total Assets %	23.7	25.2	23.2	25.9	26.6	25.3	26.9
Price Range	29.60-23.44	26.38-17.65	25.00-18.50	26.69-22.19	35.13-23.13	32.38-18.00	20.50-15.75
P/E Ratio	14.4-11.4	16.6-11.1	17.0-12.6	12.8-10.7	16.6-10.9	17.4-9.7	11.4-8.7
Average Yield %	2.8	3.2	3.0	2.5	1.9	2.0	2.6

Statistics are as originally reported. ① Incl. after-tax chrg. of $6.3 mill. related to a lawsuit settlement.

OFFICERS:
F. Q. Stepan, Chmn., C.E.O.
F. Q. Stepan Jr., Pres., C.O.O.
F. S. Eberts III, V.P., Gen Couns., Sec.
INVESTOR CONTACT: James E. Hurlbutt, V.P., Contr., (847) 501-2164
PRINCIPAL OFFICE: Edens & Winnetka Road, Northfield, IL 60093

TELEPHONE NUMBER: (847) 446-7500
FAX: (847) 446-2843
WEB: www.stepan.com
NO. OF EMPLOYEES: 1,529 (avg.)
SHAREHOLDERS: 1,392
ANNUAL MEETING: In April
INCORPORATED: IL, Jan., 1940; reincorp., DE, 1959

INSTITUTIONAL HOLDINGS:
No. of Institutions: 42
Shares Held: 3,114,583
% Held: 34.6
INDUSTRY: Surface active agents (SIC: 2843)
TRANSFER AGENT(S): Computershare Investor Services, Chicago, IL

STERLING FINANCIAL CORPORATION

YIELD 2.9%
P/E RATIO 15.4

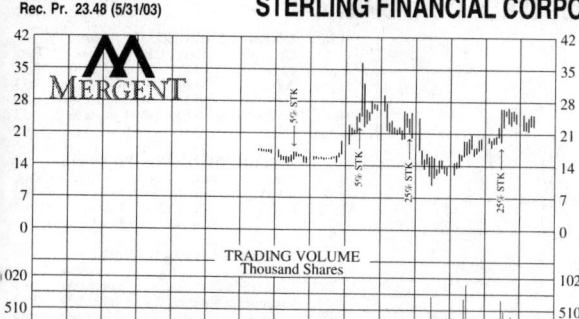

*7 YEAR PRICE SCORE 140.1   *12 MONTH PRICE SCORE 97.9
*NYSE COMPOSITE INDEX=100

TRADING VOLUME
Thousand Shares

INTERIM EARNINGS (Per Share):

Qtr.	Mar.	June	Sept.	Dec.
1999	0.30	0.32	0.29	0.28
2000	0.30	0.32	0.15	0.29
2001	0.30	0.34	0.32	0.34
2002	0.34	0.36	0.37	0.40
2003	0.39	...	...	...

INTERIM DIVIDENDS (Per Share):

Amt.	Decl.	Ex.	Rec.	Pay.
0.17Q	8/27/02	9/12/02	9/16/02	10/01/02
0.17Q	11/19/02	12/11/02	12/13/02	1/02/03
0.17Q	2/25/03	3/12/03	3/14/03	4/01/03
0.17Q	5/27/03	6/12/03	6/16/03	7/01/03

Indicated div.: $0.68 (Div. Reinv. Plan)

CAPITALIZATION (12/31/02):

	($000)	(%)
Total Deposits	1,702,302	82.1
Long-Term Debt	155,478	7.5
Redeemable Pfd. Stock	20,000	1.0
Common & Surplus	196,833	9.5
Total	2,074,613	100.0

DIVIDEND ACHIEVER STATUS:

Rank: 148   10-Year Growth Rate: 9.84%
Total Years of Dividend Growth: 15

RECENT DEVELOPMENTS: For the three months ended 3/31/03, net income climbed 20.0% to $6.6 million from $5.5 million in the corresponding prior-year period. Net interest income advanced 20.0% to $20.6 million from $17.1 million the previous year. Provision for loan losses totaled $1.0 million compared with $218,000 a year earlier. Non-interest income, excluding a $4,000 securities gain, grew 6.1% to $11.6 million from $10.9 million the year

before. Non-interest expense rose 6.7% to $22.1 million from $20.7 million in 2002. Separately, on 4/30/03, the Company announced that it plans to establish a banking presence in Berks County, Pennsylvania under the name PennSterling Bank, which will operate as a division of Bank of Lancaster County. PennSterling will initially focus on providing banking services to small and mid-sized businesses and private customers.

BUSINESS

STERLING FINANCIAL CORPORATION is a multi-bank financial holding company with $2.16 billion of assets as of 3/31/03. The Company provides a broad range of financial services, including personal and business banking, leasing, insurance and wealth management. As of 3/31/03, SLFI operated 51 branch banking offices in south central Pennsylvania and northern Maryland through its subsidiary banks, Bank of Lancaster County, N.A., Bank of Hanover and Trust Company, First National Bank of North East, and Bank of Lebanon County. The Company also operates financial services organizations including Town & County Leasing, LLC, Lancaster Insurance Group, LLC, Equipment Finance, LLC, Sterling Financial Settlement Services, and Sterling Financial Trust Company, which manages nearly $1.00 billion in assets as of 3/31/03.

ANNUAL FINANCIAL DATA

	12/31/02	12/31/01	12/31/00	12/31/99	12/31/98	12/31/97	12/31/96
Earnings Per Share	1.47	① 1.30	1.06	① 1.18	1.15	1.02	0.96
Tang. Book Val. Per Share	10.56	9.73	8.89	8.06	8.08	7.33	6.78
Dividends Per Share	0.65	0.62	0.60	0.56	0.52	0.49	0.42
Dividend Payout %	44.2	47.7	56.4	47.6	45.3	48.2	44.2

INCOME STATEMENT (IN MILLIONS):

Total Interest Income	123.6	115.9	113.3	67.7	60.1	56.5	52.6
Total Interest Expense	48.6	57.3	58.5	29.8	27.9	25.3	22.8
Net Interest Income	75.0	58.6	54.8	37.9	32.1	31.2	29.7
Provision for Loan Losses	2.1	1.2	0.6	0.4	0.9	1.1	0.6
Non-Interest Income	44.8	43.9	37.5	29.5	14.2	11.9	10.6
Non-Interest Expense	85.9	75.2	70.2	48.8	30.2	28.1	26.8
Income Before Taxes	31.8	26.2	21.5	18.2	15.2	13.9	13.0
Net Income	24.7	① 20.3	16.6	① 13.2	11.6	10.4	9.8
Average Shs. Outstg. (000)	16,823	15,725	15,696	11,169	10,122	10,182	10,229

BALANCE SHEET (IN MILLIONS):

Cash & Due from Banks	82.2	68.9	61.3	47.7	34.1	34.3	31.3
Securities Avail. for Sale	551.7	491.0	435.9	207.2	177.9	121.5	79.4
Total Loans & Leases	1,296.0	1,098.2	1,033.2	663.0	534.3	512.1	475.0
Allowance for Credit Losses	13.0	11.1	11.7	8.2	7.7	8.2	9.0
Net Loans & Leases	1,283.1	1,087.1	1,021.5	654.8	526.6	503.9	466.0
Total Assets	2,156.3	1,861.4	1,726.1	1,059.4	919.3	845.5	764.1
Total Deposits	1,702.3	1,535.6	1,420.3	892.4	781.4	718.7	647.0
Long-Term Obligations	155.5	121.1	113.9	34.3	34.1	32.3	30.4
Total Liabilities	1,959.5	1,709.3	1,586.8	969.4	838.0	771.5	694.9
Net Stockholders' Equity	196.8	152.1	139.3	90.0	81.3	74.0	69.2
Year-end Shs. Outstg. (000)	16,901	15,640	15,683	11,164	10,063	10,090	10,205

STATISTICAL RECORD:

Return on Equity %	12.6	13.4	11.9	14.7	14.3	14.1	14.2
Return on Assets %	1.1	1.1	1.0	1.2	1.3	1.2	1.3
Equity/Assets %	9.1	8.2	8.1	8.5	8.8	8.8	9.1
Non-Int. Exp./Tot. Inc. %	71.7	73.3	76.0	72.4	65.2	65.2	66.4
Price Range	26.79-17.98	20.80-12.10	24.40-9.80	29.44-19.68	36.48-18.59	19.35-14.63	17.41-14.48
P/E Ratio	18.2-12.2	16.0-9.3	23.1-9.3	24.9-16.6	31.8-16.2	18.9-14.3	18.2-15.1
Average Yield %	2.9	3.7	3.5	2.3	1.9	2.9	2.7

Statistics are as originally reported. Adj. for stk. splits: 25% div., 6/02; 25% div., 11/99; & 5% div., 6/98. ① Incl. pre-tax merger-related and restr. chrg., $2.9 mill. 2001; $423,000, 1999.

OFFICERS:
J. E. Stefan, Chmn.
J. R. Moyer, Jr., Pres., C.E.O.
J. B. Scovill, Sr. Exec. V.P., C.F.O., Treas.

INVESTOR CONTACT: Douglas P. Barton, (717) 581-6005

PRINCIPAL OFFICE: 101 North Pointe Blvd., Lancaster, PA 17601-4133

TELEPHONE NUMBER: (717) 581-6030
FAX: (717) 581-6033
WEB: www.sterlingfi.com

NO. OF EMPLOYEES: 748

SHAREHOLDERS: 4,700 (approx.)

ANNUAL MEETING: In Apr.

INCORPORATED: PA, Feb., 1987

INSTITUTIONAL HOLDINGS:
No. of Institutions: 36
Shares Held: 1,547,184
% Held: 9.1

INDUSTRY: National commercial banks (SIC: 6021)

TRANSFER AGENT(S): American Stock Transfer & Trust Company, New York, NY

STRYKER CORPORATION

	YIELD	0.2%
	P/E RATIO	37.2

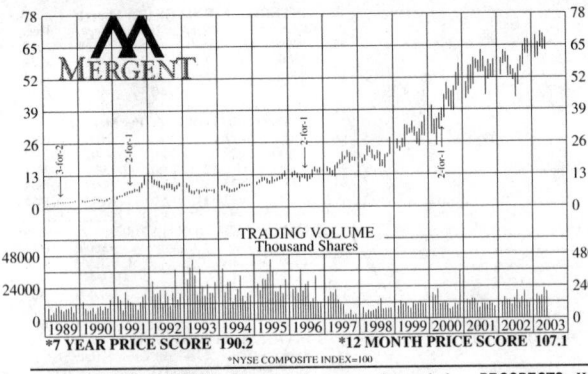

INTERIM EARNINGS (Per Share):

Qtr.	Mar.	June	Sept.	Dec.
1999	d0.11	d0.02	Nil	0.22
2000	0.26	0.26	0.25	0.33
2001	0.32	0.30	0.30	0.40
2002	0.40	0.42	0.36	0.52
2003	0.51	...	...	...

INTERIM DIVIDENDS (Per Share):

Amt.	Decl.	Ex.	Rec.	Pay.
0.10A	12/21/01	12/27/01	12/31/01	1/31/02
0.12A	12/03/02	12/27/02	12/31/02	1/31/03

Indicated div.: $0.12

CAPITALIZATION (12/31/02):

	($000)	(%)
Long-Term Debt	491,000	24.7
Common & Surplus	1,498,200	75.3
Total	1,989,200	100.0

DIVIDEND ACHIEVER STATUS:
Rank: 12   10-Year Growth Rate: 23.11%
Total Years of Dividend Growth: 10

TRADING VOLUME
Thousand Shares

*7 YEAR PRICE SCORE 190.2   *12 MONTH PRICE SCORE 107.1
*NYSE COMPOSITE INDEX=100

RECENT DEVELOPMENTS: For the three months ended 3/31/03, net income increased 28.4% to $104.1 million compared with $81.1 million in the corresponding quarter of the previous year. Net sales advanced 20.5% to $846.9 million. Orthopaedic implant sales jumped 24.3% to $490.8 million. MedSurg equipment sales climbed 17.6% to $304.1 million, while physical therapy services sales climbed 5.5% to $52.0 million.

PROSPECTS: Worldwide sales for the Medsurg Equipment segment are benefiting from elevated shipments of powered surgical instruments, endoscopic systems, hospital beds and stretchers and craniomaxillofacial implants. Separately, on 5/6/03, the Company announced that it has received clearance from the U.S. FDA to begin marketing and selling Simplex™ P with Tobramycin Bone Cement in the U.S.

BUSINESS

STRYKER CORPORATION and its subsidiaries develop, manufacture and market specialty surgical and medical products, including orthopaedic reconstructive, trauma, spinal and craniomaxillofacial implants, power surgical instruments, endoscopic systems, patient care and handling equipment for the global market and provides outpatient physical therapy services in the U.S. The Company, through its subsidiary, develops, builds, and markets video communications hardware and software for medical education. Revenues for 2002 were derived as follows: 56.6% from orthopaedic implants, 36.7% from MedSurg equipment, and 6.7% from physical therapy services. On 12/4/98, SYK acquired Howmedica, Inc., which was the orthopaedic division of Pfizer Inc.

ANNUAL FINANCIAL DATA

	12/31/02	12/31/01	12/31/00	12/31/99	12/31/98	12/31/97	12/31/96
Earnings Per Share	⑥ 1.70	④⑤ 1.34	④ 1.10	③ 0.10	② 0.20	0.64	① 0.54
Cash Flow Per Share	2.61	2.19	1.94	0.92	0.39	0.81	0.09
Tang. Book Val. Per Share	2.84	1.29	0.08	...	...	2.95	2.51
Dividends Per Share	0.10	0.08	0.07	0.06	0.055	0.05	0.02
Dividend Payout %	5.9	6.0	5.9	59.9	27.5	7.8	4.2
INCOME STATEMENT (IN MILLIONS):							
Total Revenues	3,011.6	2,602.3	2,289.4	2,103.7	1,103.2	980.1	910.1
Costs & Expenses	2,249.1	1,919.9	1,653.4	1,759.4	1,010.0	762.9	844.1
Depreciation & Amort.	186.1	172.0	168.6	162.8	37.6	33.3	34.7
Operating Income	576.4	510.4	467.4	181.5	55.6	184.0	31.3
Net Interest Inc./(Exp.)	d40.3	d67.9	d96.6	d122.6	...	...	...
Income Before Income Taxes	507.7	405.7	334.9	29.8	60.0	194.5	38.3
Income Taxes	161.1	133.9	113.9	10.4	20.4	70.0	61.7
Equity Earnings/Minority Int.	...	...	...	...	...	0.9	5.7
Net Income	⑥ 346.6	④⑤ 271.8	④ 221.0	③ 19.4	② 39.6	125.3	① d17.7
Cash Flow	532.7	443.8	389.6	182.2	77.2	158.6	16.9
Average Shs. Outstg. (000)	203,800	203,000	201,100	198,600	196,260	196,264	193,676
BALANCE SHEET (IN MILLIONS):							
Cash & Cash Equivalents	37.8	50.1	54.0	83.5	142.2	351.1	367.6
Total Current Assets	1,151.3	993.1	997.0	1,110.4	1,311.8	756.6	753.5
Net Property	519.2	444.0	378.1	391.5	429.5	163.9	172.3
Total Assets	2,815.5	2,423.6	2,430.8	2,580.5	2,885.9	985.1	993.5
Total Current Liabilities	707.5	533.4	617.4	669.6	699.5	303.0	251.7
Long-Term Obligations	491.0	720.9	876.5	1,181.1	1,488.0	4.4	89.5
Net Stockholders' Equity	1,498.2	1,056.2	854.9	671.5	652.1	612.8	530.4
Net Working Capital	443.8	459.7	379.6	440.8	612.4	453.6	501.8
Year-end Shs. Outstg. (000)	198,100	196,700	195,900	194,400	193,080	192,118	193,574
STATISTICAL RECORD:							
Operating Profit Margin %	19.1	19.6	20.4	8.6	5.0	18.8	3.4
Net Profit Margin %	11.5	10.4	9.7	0.9	3.6	12.8	...
Return on Equity %	23.1	25.7	25.9	2.9	6.1	20.5	...
Return on Assets %	12.3	11.2	9.1	0.8	1.4	12.7	...
Debt/Total Assets %	17.4	29.7	36.1	45.8	51.6	0.5	9.0
Price Range	67.47-43.85	63.20-43.30	57.75-24.44	36.63-22.22	27.88-15.50	22.66-12.13	16.06-9.94
P/E Ratio	39.7-25.8	47.2-32.3	52.5-22.2	365.9-222.0	139.3-77.5	35.4-18.9	29.7-18.4
Average Yield %	0.2	0.2	0.2	0.2	0.3	0.3	0.2

Statistics are as originally reported. Adj. for 2-for-1 stk. split 6/10/96 & 5/12/00. ① Incl. a pre-tax chg. of $41.8 mill. & a pre-tax gain of $61.1 mill. ② Incl. a pre-tax chg. of $83.3 mill. for purch. R&D & a pre-tax chg. of $49.9 mill. for acq.-rel. exps. ③ Incl. net nonrecurr. chrgs. of $141.1 mill. ④ Incl. pre-tax restruct. credit of $1.0 mill. ⑤ Bef. extraord. loss of $4.8 mill.; incl. pre-tax restruct. chrgs. of $600,000 ⑥ Incl. pre-tax restruct. chrgs. of $11.5 mill.

OFFICERS:
J. W. Brown, Chmn., C.E.O.
S. P. MacMillan, Pres. C.P.O.
D. H. Bergy, V.P., C.F.O., Sec.

INVESTOR CONTACT: Dean H. Bergy, V.P., C.F.O., & Sec., (269) 385-2600

PRINCIPAL OFFICE: P.O. Box 4085, Kalamazoo, MI 49003-4085

TELEPHONE NUMBER: (269) 385-2600
FAX: (269) 385-1062
WEB: www.strykercorp.com
NO. OF EMPLOYEES: 14,045 (avg.)
SHAREHOLDERS: 3,132 (record)
ANNUAL MEETING: In Apr.
INCORPORATED: MI, Feb., 1946

INSTITUTIONAL HOLDINGS:
No. of Institutions: 455
Shares Held: 133,740,769
% Held: 67.5

INDUSTRY: Surgical and medical instruments (SIC: 3841)

TRANSFER AGENT(S): National City Bank, Cleveland, OH

SUNTRUST BANKS, INC.

YIELD 3.0%
P/E RATIO 12.4

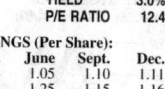
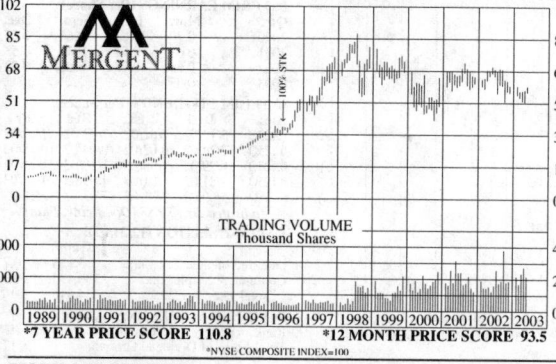

TRADING VOLUME
Thousand Shares

| 1989 | 1990 | 1991 | 1992 | 1993 | 1994 | 1995 | 1996 | 1997 | 1998 | 1999 | 2000 | 2001 | 2002 | 2003 |

*7 YEAR PRICE SCORE 110.8   ***12 MONTH PRICE SCORE 93.5**

*NYSE COMPOSITE INDEX=100

INTERIM EARNINGS (Per Share):

Qtr.	Mar.	June	Sept.	Dec.
2000	1.04	1.05	1.10	1.11
2001	1.14	1.25	1.15	1.16
2002	1.06	1.20	1.20	1.20
2003	1.17	...	...	...

INTERIM DIVIDENDS (Per Share):

Amt.	Decl.	Ex.	Rec.	Pay.
0.43Q	4/16/02	5/29/02	5/31/02	6/14/02
0.43Q	8/13/02	8/28/02	8/30/02	9/13/02
0.43Q	11/12/02	11/26/02	11/29/02	12/13/02
0.45Q	2/11/03	2/26/03	2/28/03	3/14/03
0.45Q	4/15/03	5/28/03	5/30/03	6/13/03

Indicated div.: $1.80 (Div. Reinv. Plan)

CAPITALIZATION (12/31/02):

	($000)	(%)
Total Deposits	79,706,628	80.8
Long-Term Debt	10,229,820	10.4
Common & Surplus	8,769,496	8.9
Total	98,705,944	100.0

DIVIDEND ACHIEVER STATUS:

Rank: 92   10-Year Growth Rate: 12.82%
Total Years of Dividend Growth: 17

RECENT DEVELOPMENTS:

For the quarter ended 3/31/03, net income was $327.8 million, up 7.5% versus $304.9 million the year before. Results for 2002 included an after-tax merger-related charge of $10.4 million. Net interest income grew 3.1% to $822.5 million from $798.1 million the previous year. Provision for loan losses fell 50.6% to $80.8 million from $163.6 million a year earlier. Total non-interest income slid 7.3% to $547.7 million from $590.5 million in 2002, while total non-interest expense was up 0.7% to $818.2 million from $812.9 million the prior year.

PROSPECTS:

On 4/17/03, the Company announced that it is expanding its insurance and financial planning services. In addition to traditional and variable life insurance, STI will now offer long-term care, disability income protection, estate planning and business continuity planning, which will be underwritten through nationally known insurance carriers such as John Hancock, Lincoln Life, Transamerica and Jefferson Pilot. Meanwhile, earnings are being positively affected by the Company's efforts to control costs and improve credit quality.

BUSINESS

SUNTRUST BANKS, INC., through its primary subsidiary, SunTrust Bank, provides deposit, credit, trust and investment services to a broad range of retail, business and institutional clients. Other subsidiaries provide mortgage banking, credit-related insurance, asset management, brokerage and capital market services. At 3/31/03, STI had total assets of $120.06 billion. The Company serves clients through its network of traditional and in-store branches and ATMs located in Florida, Georgia, Maryland, Tennessee, Virginia and the District of Columbia. In addition, STI provides customers with a full range of technology-based banking channels including Internet, personal computer and telephone banking.

ANNUAL FINANCIAL DATA

	12/31/02	12/31/01	12/31/00	12/31/99	12/31/98	12/31/97	12/31/96
Earnings Per Share	① 4.66	② 4.70	① 4.30	①② 3.50	① 3.04	3.13	2.76
Tang. Book Val. Per Share	26.56	26.67	25.07	23.24	22.99	23.38	20.87
Dividends Per Share	1.72	1.60	1.48	1.38	1.00	0.93	0.82
Dividend Payout %	36.9	34.0	34.4	39.4	32.9	29.6	29.9

INCOME STATEMENT (IN MILLIONS):

Total Interest Income	5,135.2	6,279.6	6,845.4	5,960.2	5,675.9	3,650.7	3,246.0
Total Interest Expense	1,891.5	3,027.0	3,737.0	2,814.8	2,746.8	1,756.4	1,461.8
Net Interest Income	3,243.7	3,252.6	3,108.4	3,145.5	2,929.1	1,894.4	1,784.2
Provision for Loan Losses	469.8	275.2	134.0	170.4	214.6	117.0	115.9
Non-Interest Income	2,391.7	2,155.8	1,773.6	1,660.0	1,716.2	934.2	818.0
Non-Interest Expense	3,342.3	3,113.5	2,828.5	2,939.4	2,932.4	1,685.6	1,583.1
Income Before Taxes	1,823.3	2,019.7	1,919.6	1,695.7	1,498.3	1,026.0	903.2
Net Income	① 1,331.8	② 1,369.2	① 1,294.1	①② 1,124.0	① 971.0	667.5	616.6
Average Shs. Outstg. (000)	286,052	291,584	300,956	317,079	319,711	213,480	223,486

BALANCE SHEET (IN MILLIONS):

Cash & Due from Banks	4,455.8	4,229.1	4,110.5	3,907.4	4,289.9	2,991.3	3,037.3
Securities Avail. for Sale	1,717.8	1,343.6	941.9	259.5	239.7	178.4	80.4
Total Loans & Leases	73,167.9	68,959.2	72,239.8	66,002.8	61,540.6	40,135.5	35,404.2
Allowance for Credit Losses	930.1	867.1	874.5	871.3	944.6	751.8	725.8
Net Loans & Leases	72,237.8	68,092.2	71,365.3	65,131.5	60,596.1	39,383.7	34,678.3
Total Assets	117,322.5	104,740.6	103,496.4	95,390.0	93,169.9	57,982.7	52,468.2
Total Deposits	79,706.6	67,536.4	69,533.3	60,100.5	59,033.3	38,197.5	36,890.4
Long-Term Obligations	10,229.8	11,010.6	7,895.4	4,967.3	4,757.9	3,171.8	1,565.3
Total Liabilities	108,553.0	96,381.1	95,257.2	87,763.1	84,991.3	52,783.4	47,588.3
Net Stockholders' Equity	8,769.5	8,359.6	8,239.2	7,626.9	8,178.6	5,199.4	4,880.0
Year-end Shs. Outstg. (000)	270,843	283,040	296,266	293,544	321,124	209,909	220,469

STATISTICAL RECORD:

Return on Equity %	15.2	16.4	15.7	14.7	11.9	12.8	12.6
Return on Assets %	1.1	1.3	1.3	1.2	1.0	1.2	1.2
Equity/Assets %	7.5	8.0	8.0	8.0	8.8	9.0	9.3
Non-Int. Exp./Tot. Inc. %	59.3	57.6	57.9	61.2	63.1	59.6	60.8
Price Range	70.20-51.48	72.35-57.29	68.00-41.63	79.81-60.44	87.75-54.00	75.25-44.13	52.50-32.00
P/E Ratio	15.1-11.0	15.4-12.2	15.8-9.7	22.8-17.3	28.9-17.8	24.0-14.1	19.0-11.6
Average Yield %	2.8	2.5	2.7	2.0	1.4	1.5	2.0

Statistics are as originally reported. Adj. for 2-for-1 stk. split, 5/96. ① Incl. pre-tax merger-related chrg.: $16.0 mill., 2002; $42.4 mill., 2000; $45.6 mill., 1999; $119.4 mill., 1998. ② Bef. extraord. gain of $6.3 mill., 2001; $202.6 mill., 1999.

OFFICERS:
L. P. Humann, Chmn., Pres., C.E.O.
J. W. Spiegal, Vice-Chmn., C.F.O.
T. J. Hoepner, Vice-Chmn.

INVESTOR CONTACT: Gary Peacock, Jr., Dir. of Inv. Rel., (404) 658-4879

PRINCIPAL OFFICE: 303 Peachtree Street N.E., Atlanta, GA 30308

TELEPHONE NUMBER: (404) 588-7711
FAX: (404) 827-6173
WEB: www.suntrust.com

NO. OF EMPLOYEES: 27,622

SHAREHOLDERS: 36,443 (approx.)

ANNUAL MEETING: In Apr.

INCORPORATED: GA, July, 1985

INSTITUTIONAL HOLDINGS:
No. of Institutions: 462
Shares Held: 131,056,686
% Held: 46.5

INDUSTRY: National commercial banks (SIC: 6021)

TRANSFER AGENT(S): SunTrust Bank Atlanta, GA

SUPERIOR INDUSTRIES INTERNATIONAL, INC.

YIELD 1.4%
P/E RATIO 12.7

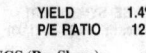

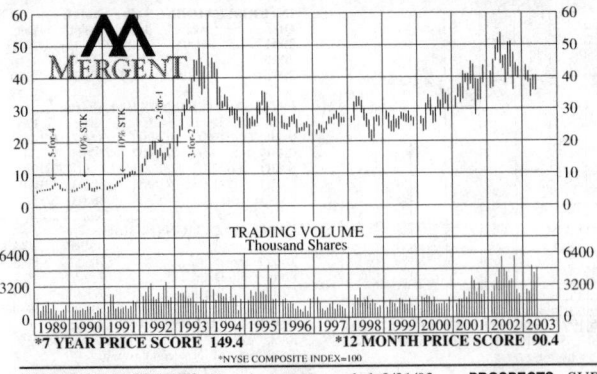

TRADING VOLUME
Thousand Shares

*7 YEAR PRICE SCORE 149.4   ***12 MONTH PRICE SCORE 90.4**
NYSE COMPOSITE INDEX=100

INTERIM EARNINGS (Per Share):

Qtr.	Mar.	June	Sept.	Dec.
2000	0.70	0.83	0.66	0.85
2001	0.61	0.51	0.41	0.58
2002	0.65	0.78	0.65	0.83
2003	0.83	...	...	...

INTERIM DIVIDENDS (Per Share):

Amt.	Decl.	Ex.	Rec.	Pay.
0.125Q	5/10/02	7/01/02	7/03/02	7/19/02
0.125Q	7/26/02	10/02/02	10/04/02	10/18/02
0.125Q	10/29/02	1/08/03	1/10/03	1/24/03
0.125Q	3/21/03	4/01/03	4/03/03	4/17/03
0.138Q	5/09/03	7/01/03	7/03/03	7/18/03

Indicated div.: $0.55 (Div. Reinv. Plan)

CAPITALIZATION (12/31/02):

	($000)	(%)
Deferred Income Tax	3,984	0.7
Common & Surplus	530,431	99.3
Total	534,415	100.0

DIVIDEND ACHIEVER STATUS:
Rank: 48   10-Year Growth Rate: 17.13%
Total Years of Dividend Growth: 17

RECENT DEVELOPMENTS: For the quarter ended 3/31/03, net income advanced 29.7% to $22.3 million versus $17.2 million in the prior-year quarter. Earnings for 2003 benefited from efficiency improvements at SUP's facilities in Mexico, as well as from a favorable mix of wheel production. Results for 2003 and 2002 included start-up costs related to the suspension components business of $2.5 million and $1.7 million, respectively. Net sales climbed 11.5% to $208.0 million from $186.5 million in 2002.

PROSPECTS: SUP is evaluating opportunities to produce wheels in Asia, both for export and for the rapidly growing Asian domestic markets. SUP continues to gain share in the aluminum wheel market, and based on new wheel supply programs already announced or in the pipeline, the Company is optimistic about results in the second half of 2003. However, production cut-backs for certain vehicle models recently announced by some of its OEM customers may adversely affect second quarter results.

BUSINESS

SUPERIOR INDUSTRIES INTERNATIONAL, INC. designs and manufactures automotive parts and accessories for original equipment manufacturers (OEMs) and for the automotive aftermarket. The OEM cast aluminum road wheels, the Company's primary product, are sold to General Motors and Ford, which together accounted for 87.0% of 2002 sales, as well as to DaimlerChrysler, Audi, BMW, Isuzu, Land Rover, Mazda, MG Rover, Mitsubishi, Nissan, Subaru, Toyota and Volkswagen, for factory installation as optional or standard equipment on selected vehicle models. SUP also manufactures aluminum suspension components, as well as aftermarket accessories including bed mats, exhaust extensions, license frames, lug nuts, springs and suspension products, steering wheel covers and other miscellaneous accessories. SUP operates manufacturing facilities in the U.S., Mexico and Hungary.

ANNUAL FINANCIAL DATA

	12/31/02	12/31/01	12/31/00	12/31/99	12/31/98	12/31/97	12/31/96
Earnings Per Share	③ 2.91	② 2.10	① 3.04	2.62	1.88	1.96	1.63
Cash Flow Per Share	4.12	3.18	4.07	3.67	2.84	2.92	2.58
Tang. Book Val. Per Share	19.96	17.30	15.45	13.35	11.42	10.30	8.87
Dividends Per Share	0.47	0.42	0.38	0.34	0.30	0.26	0.22
Dividend Payout %	16.2	20.0	12.5	13.0	16.0	13.3	13.5

INCOME STATEMENT (IN THOUSANDS):

Total Revenues	782,599	643,395	644,899	571,782	539,431	549,131	504,241
Costs & Expenses	640,527	538,901	496,474	438,051	432,387	434,030	395,129
Depreciation & Amort.	32,605	28,388	26,920	28,523	26,698	26,917	27,330
Operating Income	109,467	76,106	121,505	105,208	80,346	88,184	81,782
Net Interest Inc./(Exp.)	3,519	4,048	7,323	5,451	4,287	2,170	d326
Income Before Income Taxes	120,384	84,189	122,510	108,518	80,801	86,208	74,071
Income Taxes	42,134	28,835	42,573	37,710	28,482	30,819	27,221
Net Income	③ 78,250	② 55,354	① 79,937	70,808	52,319	55,389	46,850
Cash Flow	110,855	83,742	106,857	99,331	79,017	82,306	74,180
Average Shs. Outstg.	26,907	26,361	26,255	27,056	27,818	28,221	28,798

BALANCE SHEET (IN THOUSANDS):

Cash & Cash Equivalents	155,184	106,839	93,503	108,081	86,566	73,693	42,103
Total Current Assets	368,941	280,271	245,579	263,740	235,886	199,846	164,080
Net Property	235,566	228,181	218,713	163,113	158,194	147,989	161,670
Total Assets	645,796	540,838	491,664	460,468	427,430	382,679	357,590
Total Current Liabilities	97,123	71,137	75,022	86,847	91,111	65,415	76,369
Long-Term Obligations	...	...	...	340	673	1,344	1,940
Net Stockholders' Equity	530,431	448,741	399,319	353,086	312,034	287,416	251,111
Net Working Capital	271,818	209,134	170,557	176,893	144,775	134,431	87,711
Year-end Shs. Outstg.	26,573	25,933	25,840	26,454	27,312	27,902	28,324

STATISTICAL RECORD:

Operating Profit Margin %	14.0	11.8	18.8	18.4	14.9	16.1	16.2
Net Profit Margin %	10.0	8.6	12.4	12.4	9.7	10.1	9.3
Return on Equity %	14.8	12.3	20.0	20.1	16.8	19.3	18.7
Return on Assets %	12.1	10.2	16.3	15.4	12.2	14.5	13.1
Debt/Total Assets %	...	...	...	0.1	0.2	0.4	0.5
Price Range	53.80-35.79	44.85-28.00	36.00-22.94	29.38-22.75	33.88-20.06	29.50-22.13	28.38-21.63
P/E Ratio	18.5-12.3	21.4-13.3	11.8-7.5	11.2-8.7	18.0-10.7	15.1-11.3	17.4-13.3
Average Yield %	1.0	1.2	1.3	1.3	1.1	1.0	0.9

Statistics are as originally reported. ① Incl. non-recurr. chrg. $2.5 mill. ② Incl. non-recurr. start-up chrg. of $9.7 mill. ③ Incl. non-recurr. pre-production costs of $8.5 mill.

OFFICERS:
L. L. Borick, Chmn., C.E.O.
S. J. Borick, Pres., C.O.O.
R. J. Ornstein, V.P., C.F.O.

INVESTOR CONTACT: Cathy Buccieri, (818) 902-2701

PRINCIPAL OFFICE: 7800 Woodley Avenue, Van Nuys, CA 91406

TELEPHONE NUMBER: (818) 781-4973
FAX: (818) 780-3500
WEB: www.supind.com
NO. OF EMPLOYEES: 6,600 (approx.)
SHAREHOLDERS: 808 (approx.)
ANNUAL MEETING: In May
INCORPORATED: DE, June, 1969; reincorp., CA, June, 1994

INSTITUTIONAL HOLDINGS:
No. of Institutions: 166
Shares Held: 18,183,164
% Held: 67.3

INDUSTRY: Motor vehicle parts and accessories (SIC: 3714)

TRANSFER AGENT(S): Registrar and Transfer Company, Cranford, NJ

SUPERVALU INC.

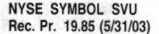

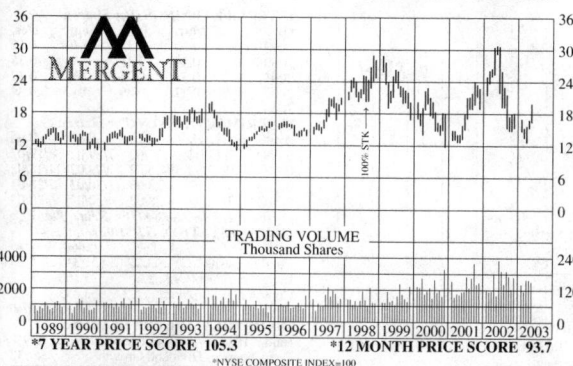

7 YEAR PRICE SCORE 105.3   **12 MONTH PRICE SCORE 93.7**
*NYSE COMPOSITE INDEX=100

INTERIM EARNINGS (Per Share):

Qtr.	May	Aug.	Nov.	Feb.
1999-00	0.55	0.37	0.42	0.52
2000-01	0.53	0.43	0.36	d0.70
2001-02	0.45	0.39	0.44	0.26
2002-03	0.57	0.44	0.43	0.48

INTERIM DIVIDENDS (Per Share):

Amt.	Decl.	Ex.	Rec.	Pay.
0.142Q	6/25/02	8/28/02	9/01/02	9/16/02
0.142Q	10/09/02	11/26/02	12/01/02	12/16/02
0.142Q	2/12/03	2/26/03	2/28/03	3/17/03
0.142Q	4/09/03	5/29/03	6/02/03	6/16/03

Indicated div.: $0.57 (Div. Reinv. Plan)

CAPITALIZATION (2/22/03):

	($000)	(%)
Long-Term Debt	1,474,929	35.6
Capital Lease Obligations	544,729	13.1
Deferred Income Tax	116,982	2.8
Common & Surplus	2,009,240	48.5
Total	4,145,880	100.0

DIVIDEND ACHIEVER STATUS:

Rank: 249   10-Year Growth Rate: 4.18%
Total Years of Dividend Growth: 30

RECENT DEVELOPMENTS: For the 52 weeks ended 2/22/03, net earnings climbed 29.6% to $257.0 million from $198.3 million in the corresponding period the year before. Results included after-tax restructuring and other charges of $1.8 million and $35.2 million in fiscal 2003 and fiscal 2002, respectively. Results for fiscal 2002 also included after-tax goodwill amortization of $11.6 million. Net sales slipped 5.6% to $19.16 billion from $20.29 billion a year earlier. Operating earnings rose 12.9% to $569.9 million.

PROSPECTS: The Company is targeting earnings per share of between $2.00 and $2.15 for the current fiscal year. Meanwhile, results should be positively affected by continued expansion of SVU's retail store network. The Company plans to open between 75 and 100 new Save-A-Lot food stores during the current fiscal year, along with eight to twelve new regional supermarkets. SVU also plans to convert its Baltimore-based Metro grocery stores to the Shopper's Food Warehouse banner.

BUSINESS

SUPERVALU INC. is a major food retailer and distributor to independently-owned retail food stores. The Company operates three principal store formats at retail and sells food and non-food products at wholesale. As of 2/22/03, SVU operated 1,150 Save-A-Lot limited assortment stores, including 783 licensed Save-A-Lot locations, 274 Company-owned stores and 93 Deals-Nothing Over a Dollar general merchandise stores; 267 regional supermarkets under the Cub Foods, Shop 'n Save, Shoppers Food Warehouse, Metro, bigg's, Farm Fresh, Scott's Foods, and Hornbacher's banners. Additionally, the Company is the primary supplier to approximately 2,460 retail grocery stores, as well as 29 of SVU's franchised Cub Foods locations and its 267 regional supermarkets, while serving as a secondary supplier to about 1,500 stores.

ANNUAL FINANCIAL DATA

	2/22/03	2/23/02	2/24/01	2/26/00	2/27/99	2/28/98	2/22/97
Earnings Per Share	③1.91	③1.53	③0.62	②1.87	1.57	①1.83	1.30
Cash Flow Per Share	4.14	4.11	3.24	4.06	3.45	3.64	3.03
Tang. Book Val. Per Share	3.24	2.90	1.64	1.58	6.09	5.80	6.06
Dividends Per Share	0.57	0.56	0.55	0.54	0.53	0.51	0.49
Dividend Payout %	29.8	36.3	87.9	28.6	33.4	27.9	38.1

INCOME STATEMENT (IN MILLIONS):

Total Revenues	19,160.4	20,908.5	23,194.3	20,339.1	17,420.5	17,201.4	16,551.9
Costs & Expenses	18,288.6	20,051.2	22,500.3	19,470.9	16,772.7	16,565.9	15,939.3
Depreciation & Amort.	301.8	340.9	348.8	285.3	229.6	230.1	232.1
Operating Income	569.9	516.5	345.2	582.8	418.2	405.4	380.5
Net Interest Inc./(Exp.)	d161.9	d172.8	d190.8	d135.4	d101.9	d114.0	d120.7
Income Before Income Taxes	408.0	343.7	154.4	447.5	316.3	291.4	259.8
Income Taxes	151.0	138.2	72.4	204.5	124.9	154.0	105.5
Equity Earnings/Minority Int.	...	...	...	...	...	93.4	20.7
Net Income	③257.0	③205.5	③82.0	②242.9	191.3	①230.8	175.0
Cash Flow	558.8	546.4	430.7	528.3	421.0	460.8	407.1
Average Shs. Outstg. (000)	134,877	133,978	132,829	130,090	121,961	126,550	134,510

BALANCE SHEET (IN MILLIONS):

Cash & Cash Equivalents	29.2	12.2	10.4	10.9	7.6	6.1	6.5
Total Current Assets	1,647.4	1,604.0	2,091.7	2,177.6	1,582.5	1,612.1	1,600.8
Net Property	2,220.9	2,208.6	2,232.8	2,168.2	1,699.0	1,589.6	1,648.5
Total Assets	5,896.2	5,824.8	6,407.2	6,495.4	4,265.9	4,093.0	4,283.3
Total Current Liabilities	1,525.3	1,701.5	2,341.2	2,509.6	1,521.9	1,457.2	1,369.1
Long-Term Obligations	2,019.7	1,875.9	2,008.5	1,953.7	1,246.3	1,260.7	1,420.6
Net Stockholders' Equity	2,009.2	1,916.7	1,793.5	1,821.5	1,305.6	1,201.9	1,307.4
Net Working Capital	122.1	d97.5	d249.5	d332.0	60.6	154.9	231.7
Year-end Shs. Outstg. (000)	133,688	132,889	132,374	134,662	120,109	120,368	133,764

STATISTICAL RECORD:

Operating Profit Margin %	3.0	2.5	1.5	2.9	2.4	2.4	2.3
Net Profit Margin %	1.3	1.0	0.4	1.2	1.1	1.3	1.1
Return on Equity %	12.8	10.7	4.6	13.3	14.7	19.2	13.4
Return on Assets %	4.4	3.5	1.3	3.7	4.5	5.6	4.1
Debt/Total Assets %	34.3	32.2	31.3	30.1	29.2	30.8	33.2
Price Range	30.81-14.75	24.10-12.60	22.88-11.75	28.88-16.81	28.94-20.19	21.09-14.06	16.50-13.56
P/E Ratio	16.1-7.7	15.8-8.2	36.9-18.9	15.4-9.0	18.4-12.9	11.6-7.7	12.7-10.4
Average Yield %	2.5	3.0	3.1	2.3	2.1	2.9	3.3

Statistics are as originally reported. Adj. for 100% stk. div., 8/98. ① Incl. $53.7 mil nonrecur net gain from sale of int. in ShopKo Stores, Inc. ② Incl. $163.7 pre-tax gain on sale of Hazelwood Farms Bakeries & incl. $103.6 pre-tax restr. chg. ③ Incl. after-tax restr. & other chgs $1.8 mil ($0.01/sh), 2003; $35.2 mil ($0.27/sh), 2002; $153.9 mil ($1.16/sh.), 2001.

OFFICERS:
J. Noddle, Chmn., Pres., C.E.O.
P. K. Knous, Exec. V.P., C.F.O.

INVESTOR CONTACT: Yolanda Scharton,
V.P., Investor Relations, (952) 828-4540

PRINCIPAL OFFICE: 11840 Valley View
Road, Eden Prairie, MN 55344

TELEPHONE NUMBER: (952) 828-4000
FAX: (952) 828-8998
WEB: www.supervalu.com
NO. OF EMPLOYEES: 57,400 (approx.)
SHAREHOLDERS: 7,038
ANNUAL MEETING: In May
INCORPORATED: DE, Dec., 1925

INSTITUTIONAL HOLDINGS:
No. of Institutions: 285
Shares Held: 101,199,744
% Held: 75.5

INDUSTRY: Groceries, general line (SIC: 5141)

TRANSFER AGENT(S): Wells Fargo
Shareowner Services, St. Paul, MN

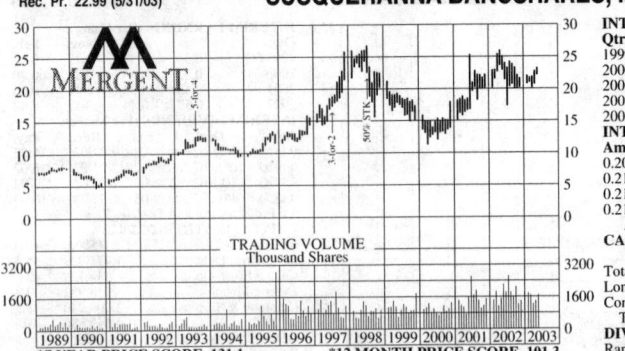

NASDAQ SYMBOL SUSQ
Rec. Pr. 22.99 (5/31/03)

SUSQUEHANNA BANCSHARES, INC.

YIELD 3.7%
P/E RATIO 14.6

INTERIM EARNINGS (Per Share):

Qtr.	Mar.	June	Sept.	Dec.
1999	0.32	0.33	0.40	0.12
2000	0.34	0.35	0.36	0.35
2001	0.32	0.36	0.36	0.37
2002	0.37	0.39	0.40	0.39
2003	0.40	...	...	...

INTERIM DIVIDENDS (Per Share):

Amt.	Decl.	Ex.	Rec.	Pay.
0.20Q	7/17/02	7/25/02	7/29/02	8/19/02
0.21Q	10/17/02	10/25/02	10/29/02	11/18/02
0.21Q	1/15/03	1/28/03	1/30/03	2/20/03
0.21Q	4/16/03	4/28/03	4/30/03	5/20/03

Indicated div.: $0.84 (Div. Reinv. Plan)

CAPITALIZATION (12/31/02):

	($000)	(%)
Total Deposits	3,831,344	75.3
Long-Term Debt	723,166	14.2
Common & Surplus	533,855	10.5
Total	5,088,365	100.0

DIVIDEND ACHIEVER STATUS:
Rank: 191   10-Year Growth Rate: 7.64%
Total Years of Dividend Growth: 32

*7 YEAR PRICE SCORE 131.1   *12 MONTH PRICE SCORE 101.3
*NYSE COMPOSITE INDEX=100

RECENT DEVELOPMENTS: For the three months ended 3/31/03, net income grew 8.4% to $16.1 million compared with $14.8 million in the corresponding period of 2002. Results for 2003 and 2002 included gains on the sale of loans and leases of $2.5 million and $1.4 million, and investment security gains of $90,000 and $141,000, respectively. Net interest income improved 6.4% to $47.3 million from $44.4 million in 2002. Provision for loan and lease losses rose 19.0% to $2.7 million. Total interest income slipped 5.7% to $74.2 million and total interest expense

decreased 21.5% to $26.9 million. Total non-interest income rose 4.4% to $25.5 million and total non-interest expense climbed 3.7% to $46.8 million. Total assets increased 11.0% to $5.72 billion, primarily due to core growth from SUSQ's focus on cross-selling multiple products to existing customers and expansion of its customer base through various commercial and retail sales efforts. Separately, SUSQ reaffirmed its diluted earnings per share guidance for 2003 of $1.62 to $1.68.

BUSINESS

SUSQUEHANNA BANCSHARES, INC. is a multi-state financial services holding company composed of eight commercial banks, a vehicle leasing company, a property and casualty insurance brokerage company, a trust and investment company, and an asset management company. As of 4/22/03, the Company's banking subsidiaries provided financial services at 159 locations in the mid-Atlantic region. As of 3/31/03, the Company had total assets of $5.72 billion, net loans and leases of $3.79 billion and total deposits of $3.94 billion. On 2/1/00, SUSQ acquired Boston Service Company, Inc., a provider of consumer automobile financing services. On 3/3/00, SUSQ acquired Valley Forge Asset Management Corp., an asset management company.

ANNUAL FINANCIAL DATA

	12/31/02	12/31/01	12/31/00	12/31/99	12/31/98	12/31/97	12/31/96
Earnings Per Share	1.55	1.41	⊡ 1.40	⊡ 1.17	1.26	1.20	1.01
Tang. Book Val. Per Share	11.96	12.54	11.56	10.92	10.91	10.25	9.87
Dividends Per Share	0.81	0.77	0.70	0.62	0.57	0.55	0.52
Dividend Payout %	52.3	54.6	50.0	53.0	45.2	45.6	51.3
INCOME STATEMENT (IN MILLIONS):							
Total Interest Income	316.7	341.3	353.4	299.8	292.8	264.1	231.8
Total Interest Expense	129.5	169.1	188.5	138.8	138.6	118.4	103.1
Net Interest Income	187.2	172.2	165.0	160.9	154.2	145.7	128.7
Provision for Loan Losses	10.7	7.3	3.7	7.2	5.2	4.6	4.6
Non-Interest Income	94.2	84.2	74.0	40.0	30.9	23.8	21.3
Non-Interest Expense	181.7	167.8	155.6	131.9	113.2	106.0	100.8
Income Before Taxes	89.1	81.3	79.7	61.8	66.7	58.8	44.6
Net Income	61.7	55.7	⊡ 55.0	⊡ 43.4	45.6	40.2	30.0
Average Shs. Outstg. (000)	39,932	39,593	39,365	37,137	36,179	33,495	29,612
BALANCE SHEET (IN MILLIONS):							
Cash & Due from Banks	156.3	149.2	129.1	144.5	105.3	97.3	98.5
Securities Avail. for Sale	52.6	88.6	59.0	17.7	76.0	41.9	96.1
Total Loans & Leases	3,831.0	3,519.5	3,433.6	2,995.2	2,773.6	2,569.6	2,173.1
Allowance for Credit Losses	39.7	37.7	37.2	37.2	35.2	34.6	31.9
Net Loans & Leases	3,791.3	3,481.8	3,396.4	2,957.9	2,738.4	2,535.1	2,141.1
Total Assets	5,544.6	5,051.1	4,792.9	4,310.6	4,064.8	3,524.9	3,038.5
Total Deposits	3,831.3	3,484.3	3,249.0	3,180.5	3,124.3	2,851.2	2,493.5
Long-Term Obligations	723.2	105.0	100.0	95.0	370.2	181.9	115.4
Total Liabilities	5,010.8	4,557.6	4,339.4	3,906.2	3,673.6	3,178.1	2,745.8
Net Stockholders' Equity	533.9	493.5	453.4	404.4	391.2	346.7	292.7
Year-end Shs. Outstg. (000)	39,638	39,344	39,221	37,022	35,857	33,833	29,657
STATISTICAL RECORD:							
Return on Equity %	11.6	11.3	12.1	10.7	11.6	11.6	10.2
Return on Assets %	1.1	1.1	1.1	1.0	1.1	1.1	1.0
Equity/Assets %	9.6	9.8	9.5	9.4	9.6	9.8	9.6
Non-Int. Exp./Tot. Inc. %	64.6	65.4	65.1	65.6	61.2	62.6	67.2
Price Range	26.00-17.25	37.99-15.00	17.98-11.25	21.25-14.88	26.75-15.50	25.83-14.33	15.89-11.56
P/E Ratio	16.8-11.1	26.9-10.6	12.8-8.0	18.2-12.7	21.2-12.3	21.5-11.9	15.7-11.4
Average Yield %	3.7	2.9	4.8	3.4	2.7	2.7	3.8

Statistics are as originally reported. Adj. for stk. splits: 50% div., 7/1/98; 3-for-2, 7/2/97.
⊡ Incl. restr. chg. of $7.4 million, 12/99; gain of $900,000, 12/00.

OFFICERS:
W. J. Reuter, Chmn., Pres., C.E.O.
D. K. Hostetter, Exec. V.P., C.F.O., Treas.
G. A. Duncan, Exec. V.P., C.O.O.
INVESTOR CONTACT: Alison van Harskamp, Investor Relations, (717) 625-6260
PRINCIPAL OFFICE: 26 North Cedar St., Lititz, PA 17543

TELEPHONE NUMBER: (717) 626-4721
FAX: (717) 626-1874
WEB: www.susqbanc.com
NO. OF EMPLOYEES: 1,733 full-time; 297 part-time
SHAREHOLDERS: 6,081
ANNUAL MEETING: In May
INCORPORATED: PA, Sept., 1982

INSTITUTIONAL HOLDINGS:
No. of Institutions: 115
Shares Held: 13,380,083
% Held: 33.5
INDUSTRY: National commercial banks (SIC: 6021)
TRANSFER AGENT(S): The Bank of New York, New York, NY

SYNOVUS FINANCIAL CORPORATION

YIELD 2.9%
P/E RATIO 18.3

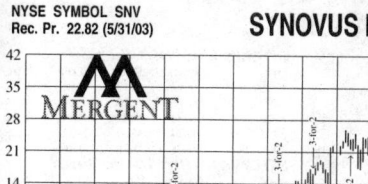

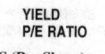

TRADING VOLUME
Thousand Shares

*7 YEAR PRICE SCORE 113.4   *12 MONTH PRICE SCORE 92.7
*NYSE COMPOSITE INDEX=100

INTERIM EARNINGS (Per Share):

Qtr.	Mar.	June	Sept.	Dec.
2000	0.22	0.22	0.23	0.26
2001	0.25	0.26	0.27	0.29
2002	0.28	0.29	0.31	0.35
2003	0.30	...	...	...

INTERIM DIVIDENDS (Per Share):

Amt.	Decl.	Ex.	Rec.	Pay.
0.14Q	6/11/02	6/18/02	6/20/02	7/01/02
0.14Q	8/19/02	9/17/02	9/19/02	10/01/02
0.14Q	11/20/02	12/18/02	12/20/02	1/02/03
0.165Q	3/04/03	3/18/03	3/20/03	4/01/03
0.165Q	6/10/03	6/18/03	6/20/03	7/01/03

Indicated div.: $0.66 (Div. Reinv. Plan)

CAPITALIZATION (12/31/02):

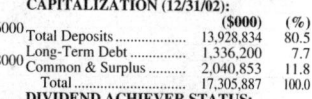

	($000)	(%)
Total Deposits	13,928,834	80.5
Long-Term Debt	1,336,200	7.7
Common & Surplus	2,040,853	11.8
Total	17,305,887	100.0

DIVIDEND ACHIEVER STATUS:
Rank: 26   10-Year Growth Rate: 20.41%
Total Years of Dividend Growth: 26

RECENT DEVELOPMENTS: For the quarter ended 3/31/03, net income climbed 8.7% to $89.9 million from $82.8 million the prior year. Net interest income grew 5.2% to $181.6 million from $172.6 million the year before. Provision for loan losses jumped 54.9% to $20.3 million from $13.1 million the previous year. Total non-interest income rose 12.5% to $325.3 million from $289.1 million a year earlier, while total non-interest expense was up 8.2% to $340.0 million from $314.3 million in 2002.

PROSPECTS: The Company continues to expand its operations through acquisitions. During the first quarter of 2003, the Company acquired United Financial Holdings, Inc., the parent company of United Bank and Trust Company in St. Petersburg, Florida and United Bank of the Gulf Coast in Sarasota, Florida. SNV also acquired FNB Bankshares, Inc. of Covington, Georgia during the quarter. Together, these acquisitions added $930.0 million in assets and 19 branch locations.

BUSINESS

SYNOVUS FINANCIAL CORPORATION, with assets of $20.60 billion as of 3/31/03, is a registered bank holding company engaged in two principal business segments: banking, which encompasses commercial banking, trust services, mortgage banking, credit card banking and certain securities brokerage operations, and bankcard data processing. SNV has 40 wholly-owned subsidiaries located in Georgia, Alabama, Florida, South Carolina, and Tennessee, offering a wide range of commercial banking services, including accepting customary types of demand and savings deposits; making individual, consumer, commercial, installment, first and second mortgage loans; and other fiduciary services. SNV also owns 81.0% of Total System Services, Inc.® (TSYS), an electronic transaction processing company.

ANNUAL FINANCIAL DATA

	12/31/02	12/31/01	12/31/00	12/31/99	12/31/98	12/31/97	12/31/96
Earnings Per Share	[1] 1.21	1.05	0.92	0.80	0.70	0.62	0.53
Tang. Book Val. Per Share	6.40	5.75	4.98	4.35	3.96	3.44	2.99
Dividends Per Share	0.57	0.49	0.42	0.34	0.28	0.23	0.19
Dividend Payout %	47.1	46.9	45.6	42.9	40.0	36.9	35.0
INCOME STATEMENT (IN MILLIONS)							
Total Interest Income	1,055.0	1,130.9	1,097.8	888.0	769.2	725.7	663.3
Total Interest Expense	337.5	501.1	535.5	374.7	328.7	313.3	288.4
Net Interest Income	717.5	629.8	562.3	513.3	440.5	412.4	374.9
Provision for Loan Losses	65.3	51.7	44.3	34.0	26.7	32.3	31.8
Non-Interest Income	1,234.8	937.7	833.5	739.8	562.0	489.2	425.4
Non-Interest Expense	1,299.5	1,006.0	923.3	856.5	673.6	601.3	541.6
Income Before Taxes	563.9	490.0	411.7	349.3	291.6	258.9	219.3
Net Income	[1] 365.3	311.6	262.6	225.3	187.1	165.2	139.6
Average Shs. Outstg. (000)	301,197	295,850	286,882	283,355	269,151	265,665	261,299
BALANCE SHEET (IN MILLIONS)							
Cash & Due from Banks	741.1	648.2	558.1	466.5	348.4	388.1	405.0
Securities Avail. for Sale	2,237.7	2,088.3	1,807.0	1,716.7	1,514.1	1,325.0	1,276.1
Total Loans & Leases	14,488.7	12,439.6	10,768.3	9,077.5	7,420.5	6,615.6	6,075.5
Allowance for Credit Losses	224.6	192.5	164.3	136.8	119.4	108.8	104.9
Net Loans & Leases	14,264.1	12,247.1	10,604.0	8,940.7	7,301.2	6,506.8	5,970.5
Total Assets	19,036.2	16,657.9	14,908.1	12,547.0	10,498.0	9,260.3	8,612.3
Total Deposits	13,928.8	12,146.2	11,161.7	9,440.1	8,542.8	7,707.9	7,203.0
Long-Term Obligations	1,336.2	1,052.9	840.9	318.6	127.0	7.2	97.3
Total Liabilities	16,878.3	14,963.0	13,490.9	11,320.3	9,426.4	8,237.7	7,828.6
Net Stockholders' Equity	2,040.9	1,694.9	1,417.2	1,226.7	1,070.6	903.7	783.8
Year-end Shs. Outstg. (000)	300,398	294,674	284,643	282,014	270,218	262,808	261,779
STATISTICAL RECORD:							
Return on Equity %	17.9	18.4	18.5	18.4	17.5	18.3	17.8
Return on Assets %	1.9	1.9	1.8	1.8	1.8	1.8	1.6
Equity/Assets %	10.7	10.2	9.5	9.8	10.2	9.8	9.1
Non-Int. Exp./Tot. Inc. %	66.5	64.2	66.2	68.4	67.3	66.7	67.7
Price Range	31.93-16.48	34.74-22.75	27.38-14.00	25.13-17.25	25.92-17.25	22.42-13.11	14.83-7.78
P/E Ratio	26.4-13.6	33.1-21.7	29.8-15.2	31.4-21.6	37.0-24.6	36.2-21.1	27.8-14.6
Average Yield %	2.4	1.7	2.0	1.6	1.3	1.3	1.7

Statistics are as originally reported. Adj. for stk. splits: 3-for-2, 5/98 & 4/97. [1] Incl. $8.4 mill. pre-tax impairment loss on a private equity investment.

OFFICERS:
J. H. Blanchard, Chmn., C.E.O.
J. D. Yancey, Pres., C.O.O.
T. J. Prescott, Exec. V.P., C.F.O.

INVESTOR CONTACT: Patrick A. Reynolds, Dir. of Inv. Rel., (706) 649-4973

PRINCIPAL OFFICE: 901 Front Avenue, P.O. Box 120, Columbus, GA 31902

TELEPHONE NUMBER: (706) 649-2401
FAX: (706) 641-6555
WEB: www.synovus.com

NO. OF EMPLOYEES: 10,406

SHAREHOLDERS: 27,266 (approx.)

ANNUAL MEETING: In Apr.

INCORPORATED: GA, June, 1972

INSTITUTIONAL HOLDINGS:
No. of Institutions: 240
Shares Held: 140,357,316
% Held: 46.8

INDUSTRY: National commercial banks (SIC: 6021)

TRANSFER AGENT(S): State Street Bank and Trust Company, Boston, MA

SYSCO CORPORATION

YIELD 1.4%
P/E RATIO 27.4

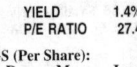
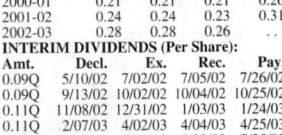
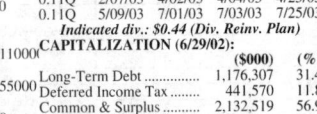

TRADING VOLUME
Thousand Shares

*7 YEAR PRICE SCORE 172.5 ***12 MONTH PRICE SCORE 99.1**
*NYSE COMPOSITE INDEX=100

INTERIM EARNINGS (Per Share):

Qtr.	Sept.	Dec.	Mar.	June
1998-99	0.13	0.13	0.11	0.18
1999-00	0.16	0.16	0.16	0.22
2000-01	0.21	0.21	0.21	0.26
2001-02	0.24	0.24	0.23	0.31
2002-03	0.28	0.28	0.26	…

INTERIM DIVIDENDS (Per Share):

Amt.	Decl.	Ex.	Rec.	Pay.
0.09Q	5/10/02	7/02/02	7/05/02	7/26/02
0.09Q	9/13/02	10/02/02	10/04/02	10/25/02
0.11Q	11/08/02	12/31/02	1/03/03	1/24/03
0.11Q	2/07/03	4/02/03	4/04/03	4/25/03
0.11Q	5/09/03	7/01/03	7/03/03	7/25/03

Indicated div.: $0.44 (Div. Reinv. Plan)

CAPITALIZATION (6/29/02):

	($000)	(%)
Long-Term Debt	1,176,307	31.4
Deferred Income Tax	441,570	11.8
Common & Surplus	2,132,519	56.9
Total	3,750,396	100.0

DIVIDEND ACHIEVER STATUS:
Rank: 24   10-Year Growth Rate: 20.67%
Total Years of Dividend Growth: 26

RECENT DEVELOPMENTS: For the 13 weeks ended 3/29/03, net earnings totaled $168.4 million, up 11.2% compared with $151.4 million in the corresponding prior-year period. Sales climbed 13.8% to $6.40 billion from $5.62 billion a year earlier. Cost of sales was $5.14 billion, or 80.4% of sales, versus $4.51 billion, or 80.2% of total sales, the year before. Earnings before income taxes advanced 11.2% to $272.7 million from $245.2 million the previous year.

PROSPECTS: In April 2003, SYY acquired the specialty meat cutting division of Auburndale, Florida-based Colorado Boxed Beef Company and its affiliated broadline foodservice operation, J&B Foodservice. Meanwhile, results should benefit from increased efficiencies and inventory reductions generated by a new distribution facility that is under construction in Front Royal, Virginia. The facility is expected to be operational by the summer of 2004.

BUSINESS

SYSCO CORPORATION is a major marketer and distributor of foodservice products. Included among its customers are about 415,000 restaurants, hotels, hospitals, schools and other institutions. The Company distributes entree items, dry and canned foods, fresh produce, beverages, dairy products and certain nonfood products, including paper products and cleaning supplies. Through its SYGMA Network, Inc. subsidiary, the Company serves pizza, chicken, steak and hamburgers to fast-food chains and other limited menu chain restaurants. SYY has three Canadian facilities located in Vancouver, Edmonton and Toronto. In fiscal 2002, the foodservice sales breakdown was: 63% restaurants; 10% hospitals and nursing homes; 6% schools and colleges; 6% hotels and motels; and 15% other.

ANNUAL FINANCIAL DATA

	6/29/02	6/30/01	7/1/00	7/3/99	6/27/98	6/28/97	6/29/96
Earnings Per Share	1.01	0.88	⑴ 0.68	0.54	⑴ 0.48	0.43	0.38
Cash Flow Per Share	1.42	1.27	1.01	0.84	0.74	0.65	0.58
Tang. Book Val. Per Share	1.85	2.07	1.90	1.71	1.57	1.67	1.70
Dividends Per Share	0.36	0.28	0.24	0.20	0.18	0.15	0.13
Dividend Payout %	35.6	31.8	35.3	37.0	37.4	35.3	34.2

INCOME STATEMENT (IN MILLIONS)

Total Revenues	23,350.5	21,784.5	19,303.3	17,422.8	15,327.5	14,454.6	13,395.1
Costs & Expenses	21,911.3	20,497.7	18,272.6	16,550.1	14,555.3	13,752.0	12,756.5
Depreciation & Amort.	278.3	248.2	220.7	205.0	181.2	160.3	144.7
Operating Income	1,161.0	1,038.5	810.0	667.7	591.0	542.3	494.0
Net Interest Inc./(Exp.)	d62.9	d71.8	d70.8	d72.8	d58.4	d46.5	d41.0
Income Before Income Taxes	1,100.9	966.7	737.6	593.9	532.5	496.0	453.9
Income Taxes	421.1	369.7	284.0	231.6	207.7	193.4	177.0
Net Income	679.8	596.9	⑴ 453.6	362.3	⑴ 324.8	302.5	276.9
Cash Flow	958.0	845.1	674.3	567.3	506.1	462.8	421.6
Average Shs. Outstg. (000)	673,446	667,949	669,556	673,594	686,880	708,940	730,396

BALANCE SHEET (IN MILLIONS)

Cash & Cash Equivalents	230.4	135.7	159.1	149.3	110.3	117.7	107.8
Total Current Assets	3,185.3	2,984.9	2,733.2	2,408.8	2,180.1	1,964.4	1,922.3
Net Property	1,697.8	1,518.6	1,344.7	1,227.7	1,151.1	1,058.4	990.6
Total Assets	5,989.8	5,468.5	4,814.0	4,096.6	3,780.2	3,436.6	3,325.4
Total Current Liabilities	2,239.4	2,089.9	1,782.9	1,427.5	1,324.2	1,113.8	1,037.5
Long-Term Obligations	1,176.3	961.4	1,023.6	997.7	867.0	685.6	581.7
Net Stockholders' Equity	2,132.5	2,147.5	1,761.6	1,427.2	1,356.8	1,400.5	1,474.7
Net Working Capital	945.9	895.0	950.3	981.2	855.9	850.6	884.8
Year-end Shs. Outstg. (000)	653,540	665,138	662,970	659,344	670,018	689,752	721,652

STATISTICAL RECORD:

Operating Profit Margin %	5.0	4.8	4.2	3.8	3.9	3.8	3.7
Net Profit Margin %	2.9	2.7	2.4	2.1	2.1	2.1	2.1
Return on Equity %	31.9	27.8	25.8	25.4	23.9	21.6	18.8
Return on Assets %	11.3	10.9	9.4	8.8	8.6	8.8	8.3
Debt/Total Assets %	19.6	17.6	21.3	24.4	22.9	20.0	17.5
Price Range	32.58-21.25	30.12-21.75	30.44-13.06	20.56-12.47	14.34-9.97	11.81-7.31	9.06-6.91
P/E Ratio	32.3-21.0	34.2-24.7	44.8-19.2	38.1-23.1	30.2-21.0	27.8-17.2	23.8-18.2
Average Yield %	1.3	1.1	1.1	1.2	1.5	1.6	1.4

Statistics are as originally reported. Adj. for 2-for-1 stk. split, 12/00 & 3/98. ⑴ Bef. $8.0 mil ($0.01/sh) chg. for acctg. adj., 2000; $28.1 mil ($0.04/sh), 1998.

OFFICERS:
R. J. Schnieders, Chmn., C.E.O.
T. E. Lankford, Pres., C.O.O.
J. K. Stubblefield, Exec. V.P.-Fin. & Admin.

INVESTOR CONTACT: John M. Palizza (281) 584-1308

PRINCIPAL OFFICE: 1390 Enclave Parkway, Houston, TX 77077-2099

TELEPHONE NUMBER: (281) 584-1390
FAX: (281) 584-1737
WEB: www.sysco.com

NO. OF EMPLOYEES: 47,000 (approx.)

SHAREHOLDERS: 15,583

ANNUAL MEETING: In Nov.

INCORPORATED: DE, May, 1969

INSTITUTIONAL HOLDINGS:
No. of Institutions: 650
Shares Held: 444,350,938
% Held: 67.9

INDUSTRY: Groceries, general line (SIC: 5141)

TRANSFER AGENT(S): EquiServe Trust Company, N.A., Providence, RI

T. ROWE PRICE GROUP, INC.

YIELD 1.9%
P/E RATIO 25.9

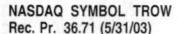
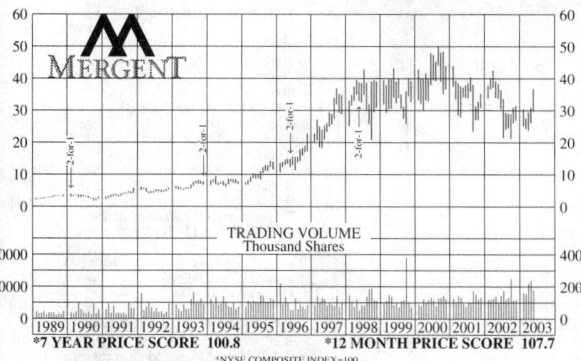

TRADING VOLUME
Thousand Shares

*7 YEAR PRICE SCORE 100.8   *12 MONTH PRICE SCORE 107.7
*NYSE COMPOSITE INDEX=100

INTERIM EARNINGS (Per Share):

Qtr.	Mar.	June	Sept.	Dec.
2000	0.58	0.54	0.53	0.43
2001	0.38	0.40	0.39	0.35
2002	0.41	0.40	0.34	0.37
2003	0.31	...	...	...

INTERIM DIVIDENDS (Per Share):

Amt.	Decl.	Ex.	Rec.	Pay.
0.16Q	9/05/02	9/25/02	9/27/02	10/11/02
0.17Q	12/12/02	12/24/02	12/27/02	1/13/03
0.17Q	3/10/03	3/19/03	3/21/03	4/04/03
0.17Q	6/05/03	6/18/03	6/20/03	7/07/03

Indicated div.: $0.68 (Div. Reinv. Plan)

CAPITALIZATION (12/31/02):

	($000)	(%)
Long-Term Debt	55,899	4.7
Common & Surplus	1,133,840	95.3
Total	1,189,739	100.0

DIVIDEND ACHIEVER STATUS:
Rank: 17   10-Year Growth Rate: 21.67%
Total Years of Dividend Growth: 16

RECENT DEVELOPMENTS: For the quarter ended 3/31/03, net income fell 26.9% to $38.8 million compared with $53.0 million in the equivalent 2002 quarter. Total revenues decreased 9.6% to $218.7 million from $242.0 million a year earlier. Investment advisory fees fell 12.8% to $164.4 million from $188.5 million the year before, primarily attributed to the decline in domestic and foreign equity markets, which lowered the Company's assets under management. Net operating income dropped 25.2% to $64.4 million from $86.2 million in 2002. Assuming some improvement in the financial markets over the remainder of 2003, TROW's margins should benefit accordingly. Progress has already been made in reducing compensation and related costs and lowering expenditures. Also, the Company expects second quarter of 2003 advertising and promotion expenditures to decline modestly year-over-year.

BUSINESS

T. ROWE PRICE GROUP, INC. (formerly T. Rowe Price Associates, Inc.) and its subsidiaries serve as investment adviser to the T. Rowe Price Mutual Funds, other sponsored investment portfolios, and private accounts of other institutional and individual investors primarily located in the U.S., including defined benefit and defined contribution plans, endowments, foundations, trusts and other mutual funds. TROW also provides investment advisory-related administrative services, including mutual fund transfer agent, accounting and shareholder services, participant record-keeping and transfer agent services for defined contribution retirement plans, discount brokerage, and trust services. On 12/28/00, T. Rowe Price Associates, Inc. shares were exchanged for shares of the Company effecting its structural change to a holding company. As of 3/31/03, total assets under management were $139.90 billion.

ANNUAL FINANCIAL DATA

	12/31/02	12/31/01	12/31/00	12/31/99	12/31/98	12/31/97	12/31/96
Earnings Per Share	1.52	1.52	2.08	1.85	1.34	1.13	0.80
Cash Flow Per Share	1.92	2.14	2.49	2.11	1.59	1.35	0.94
Tang. Book Val. Per Share	3.82	3.35	2.42	6.41	5.11	4.12	3.00
Dividends Per Share	0.64	0.60	0.52	0.40	0.34	0.26	0.21
Dividend Payout %	42.1	39.5	25.0	21.6	25.4	23.0	26.4
INCOME STATEMENT (IN MILLIONS):							
Total Revenues	925.8	1,027.5	1,212.3	1,036.4	886.1	755.0	586.1
Costs & Expenses	554.7	616.4	700.4	589.0	540.7	461.2	380.5
Depreciation & Amort.	50.6	80.5	53.7	32.6	32.6	29.0	18.1
Operating Income	320.5	330.6	458.2	414.8	312.8	264.8	187.5
Net Interest Inc./(Exp.)	d2.6	...	...	...	...	...	...
Income Before Income Taxes	309.6	330.6	458.2	414.8	312.8	264.8	187.5
Income Taxes	115.4	135.1	174.8	155.2	118.7	101.2	72.6
Equity Earnings/Minority Int.	...	0.4	d14.3	d20.2	d20.0	d19.2	d16.4
Net Income	194.3	195.9	269.0	239.4	174.1	144.4	98.5
Cash Flow	244.8	276.4	322.7	272.0	206.8	173.4	116.5
Average Shs. Outstg. (000)	127,706	129,045	129,600	129,200	129,952	128,073	123,884
BALANCE SHEET (IN MILLIONS):							
Cash & Cash Equivalents	111.4	79.7	80.5	358.5	283.8	200.4	114.6
Total Current Assets	208.2	183.7	211.6	480.1	384.5	287.2	187.8
Net Property	215.6	241.8	255.7	210.3	166.6	142.5	101.2
Total Assets	1,370.4	1,313.1	1,469.5	998.0	796.8	646.1	478.8
Total Current Liabilities	99.4	106.0	154.8	149.9	129.8	109.6	95.0
Long-Term Obligations	55.9	103.9	312.3	17.7	...	...	...
Net Stockholders' Equity	1,133.8	1,077.8	991.1	770.2	614.3	486.7	345.7
Net Working Capital	108.8	77.8	56.7	330.2	254.7	177.6	92.8
Year-end Shs. Outstg. (000)	122,649	123,089	122,439	120,108	120,183	118,195	115,146
STATISTICAL RECORD:							
Operating Profit Margin %	34.6	32.2	37.8	40.0	35.3	35.1	32.0
Net Profit Margin %	21.0	19.1	22.2	23.1	19.7	19.1	16.8
Return on Equity %	17.1	18.2	27.1	31.1	28.3	29.7	28.5
Return on Assets %	14.2	14.9	18.3	24.0	21.9	22.4	20.6
Debt/Total Assets %	4.1	7.9	21.3	1.8	...	...	...
Price Range	42.69-21.25	43.94-23.44	49.94-30.06	43.25-25.88	42.88-20.88	36.88-18.25	22.81-10.66
P/E Ratio	28.1-14.0	28.9-15.4	24.0-14.5	23.4-14.0	32.0-15.6	32.6-16.1	28.7-13.4
Average Yield %	2.0	1.8	1.3	1.2	1.1	0.9	1.3

Statistics are as originally reported. Adj. for 2-for-1 stock splits: 4/98, 12/96. ① Bef. extraord. chrg. $1.0 mill.

OFFICERS:
G. A. Roche, Chmn., Pres.
J. S. Riepe, Vice-Chmn.
C. Wasiak, C.F.O.

INVESTOR CONTACT: Steve Norwitz, Investor Relations, (410) 345-2124

PRINCIPAL OFFICE: 100 East Pratt Street, Baltimore, MD 21202

TELEPHONE NUMBER: (410) 345-2000
FAX: (410) 752-3477
WEB: www.troweprice.com

NO. OF EMPLOYEES: 3,710 (avg.)

SHAREHOLDERS: 3,900 (approx.)

ANNUAL MEETING: In Apr.

INCORPORATED: MD, Jan., 1947

INSTITUTIONAL HOLDINGS:
No. of Institutions: 271
Shares Held: 69,498,286
% Held: 57.0

INDUSTRY: Investment advice (SIC: 6282)

TRANSFER AGENT(S): Wells Fargo
Shareowner Services, N.A., St. Paul, MN

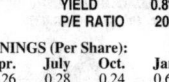

NYSE SYMBOL TGT
Rec. Pr. 36.63 (5/31/03)

TARGET CORPORATION

YIELD 0.8%
P/E RATIO 20.2

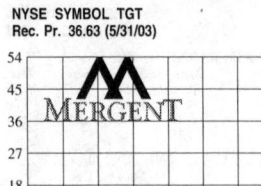

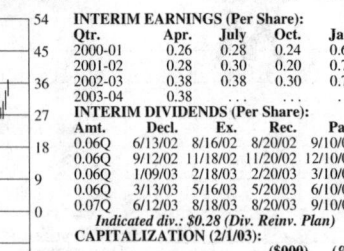

INTERIM EARNINGS (Per Share):

Qtr.	Apr.	July	Oct.	Jan.
2000-01	0.26	0.28	0.24	0.61
2001-02	0.28	0.30	0.20	0.73
2002-03	0.38	0.38	0.30	0.75
2003-04	0.38	...	...	...

INTERIM DIVIDENDS (Per Share):

Amt.	Decl.	Ex.	Rec.	Pay.
0.06Q	6/13/02	8/16/02	8/20/02	9/10/02
0.06Q	9/12/02	11/18/02	11/20/02	12/10/02
0.06Q	1/09/03	2/18/03	2/20/03	3/10/03
0.06Q	3/13/03	5/16/03	5/20/03	6/10/03
0.07Q	6/12/03	8/18/03	8/20/03	9/10/03

Indicated div.: $0.28 (Div. Reinv. Plan)

CAPITALIZATION (2/1/03):

	($000)	(%)
Long-Term Debt	10,042,000	51.2
Capital Lease Obligations..	144,000	0.7
Common & Surplus	9,443,000	48.1
Total	19,629,000	100.0

DIVIDEND ACHIEVER STATUS:
Rank: 207   10-Year Growth Rate: 6.60%
Total Years of Dividend Growth: 31

TRADING VOLUME
Thousand Shares

| 1989 | 1990 | 1991 | 1992 | 1993 | 1994 | 1995 | 1996 | 1997 | 1998 | 1999 | 2000 | 2001 | 2002 | 2003 |

*7 YEAR PRICE SCORE 135.8   *12 MONTH PRICE SCORE 101.4
*NYSE COMPOSITE INDEX=100

RECENT DEVELOPMENTS: For the three months ended 5/3/03, net earnings totaled $349.0 million, up 1.2% compared with $345.0 million a year earlier. Total revenues climbed 7.6% to $10.32 billion from $9.59 billion the previous year. Total comparable-store sales were down 0.1% year over year. Comparable-store sales growth of 1.1% at Target stores was more than offset by comparable-store sales declines at Mervyn's and Marshall Field's of 7.3% and 4.9%, respectively.

PROSPECTS: The Company anticipates fiscal 2003 earnings of approximately $2.03 per share, along with comparable-store sales growth of between 3.0% and 4.0% over the remainder of the year. Separately, during 2003, the Company plans to reduce the floor space its stores have allocated for men's apparel, home improvement, sporting goods and automotive products to make room for increased food offerings, including in-store cafes.

BUSINESS

TARGET CORPORATION (formerly Dayton Hudson Corporation) is a diversified general merchandise retailer. As of 5/3/03, the Company operated 1,494 stores in 47 states including 1,167 Target stores, 265 Mervyn's stores and 62 Marshall Field's stores. Target (85.0% of fiscal 2002 revenue) is a national discount store chain offering low prices with stores selling hardlines and fashion softgoods; Mervyn's (8.8%) is a moderate-priced department store chain specializing in active and casual apparel and home softlines. Marshall Field's (6.2%) is a full-service, full-line department store chain offering moderate to better merchandise.

ANNUAL FINANCIAL DATA

	2/1/03	2/2/02	2/3/01	1/29/00	1/30/99	1/31/98	2/3/97
Earnings Per Share	1.81	⑴ 1.51	1.38	⑵ 1.27	⑶ 1.02	⑷ 0.85	⑸ 0.52
Cash Flow Per Share	3.14	2.70	2.41	2.19	1.86	1.61	1.28
Tang. Book Val. Per Share	10.38	8.68	7.15	6.43	6.12	4.77	4.05
Dividends Per Share	0.24	0.22	0.21	0.20	0.18	0.17	0.15
Dividend Payout %	13.3	14.6	15.2	15.7	17.6	19.4	29.7

INCOME STATEMENT (IN MILLIONS):

Total Revenues	43,917.0	39,888.0	36,903.0	33,702.0	30,951.0	27,757.0	25,371.0
Costs & Expenses	39,441.0	36,129.0	33,485.0	30,519.0	28,217.0	25,322.0	23,496.0
Depreciation & Amort.	1,212.0	1,079.0	940.0	854.0	780.0	693.0	650.0
Operating Income	3,264.0	2,680.0	2,478.0	2,329.0	1,954.0	1,742.0	1,225.0
Net Interest Inc./(Exp.)	d588.0	d464.0	d425.0	d393.0	d398.0	d416.0	d442.0
Income Before Income Taxes	2,676.0	2,216.0	2,053.0	1,936.0	1,556.0	1,326.0	783.0
Income Taxes	1,022.0	842.0	789.0	751.0	594.0	524.0	309.0
Net Income	1,654.0	⑴ 1,374.0	1,264.0	⑵ 1,185.0	⑶ 962.0	⑷ 802.0	⑸ 474.0
Cash Flow	2,866.0	2,453.0	2,204.0	2,039.0	1,742.0	1,495.0	1,124.0
Average Shs. Outstg. (000)	914,000	909,800	913,000	931,400	934,600	927,400	874,800

BALANCE SHEET (IN MILLIONS):

Cash & Cash Equivalents	758.0	499.0	356.0	220.0	255.0	211.0	201.0
Total Current Assets	11,935.0	9,648.0	7,304.0	6,483.0	6,005.0	5,561.0	5,440.0
Net Property	15,307.0	13,533.0	11,418.0	9,899.0	8,969.0	8,125.0	7,467.0
Total Assets	28,603.0	24,154.0	19,490.0	17,143.0	15,666.0	14,191.0	13,389.0
Total Current Liabilities	7,523.0	7,054.0	6,301.0	5,850.0	5,057.0	4,556.0	4,111.0
Long-Term Obligations	10,186.0	8,088.0	5,634.0	4,521.0	4,452.0	4,425.0	4,808.0
Net Stockholders' Equity	9,443.0	7,860.0	6,519.0	5,862.0	5,311.0	4,460.0	3,790.0
Net Working Capital	4,412.0	2,594.0	1,003.0	633.0	948.0	1,005.0	1,329.0
Year-end Shs. Outstg. (000)	909,801	905,165	911,683	911,682	823,618	875,600	868,000

STATISTICAL RECORD:

Operating Profit Margin %	7.4	6.7	6.7	6.9	6.3	6.3	4.8
Net Profit Margin %	3.8	3.4	3.4	3.5	3.1	2.9	1.9
Return on Equity %	17.5	17.5	19.4	20.2	18.1	18.0	12.5
Return on Assets %	5.8	5.7	6.5	6.9	6.1	5.7	3.5
Debt/Total Assets %	35.6	33.5	28.9	26.4	28.4	31.2	35.9
Price Range	46.15-24.90	41.74-26.00	39.19-21.63	38.50-25.03	27.13-15.72	18.50-8.97	10.16-5.76
P/E Ratio	25.5-13.8	27.6-17.2	28.4-15.7	30.3-19.7	26.6-15.4	21.8-10.6	19.6-11.1
Average Yield %	0.7	0.6	0.7	0.6	0.8	1.2	1.9

Statistics are as originally reported. Adj. for 2-for-1 stk. split, 7/00 & 4/98. ⑴ Bef. $6 mil ($0.01/sh) extraord. chg. & incl. $67 mil pre-tax chg. ⑵ Bef. $41 mil ($0.05/sh) extraord. chg. ⑶ Bef. $27 mil ($0.03/sh) extraord. chg. ⑷ Bef. $51 mil ($0.06/sh) extraord. chg. & incl. $45 mil pre-tax gain. ⑸ Bef. $11 mil extraord. chg. & incl. $134 mil pre-tax chg.

OFFICERS:
R. J. Ulrich, Chmn., C.E.O.
G. L. Storch, Vice-Chmn.
D. A. Scovanner, Exec. V.P., C.F.O.

INVESTOR CONTACT: S.D. Kahn, V.P.-Inv. Rel., (612) 370-6736

PRINCIPAL OFFICE: 1000 Nicollet Mall, Minneapolis, MN 55403

TELEPHONE NUMBER: (612) 304-6948
FAX: (612) 370-5502
WEB: www.target.com

NO. OF EMPLOYEES: 252,000 (avg.)

SHAREHOLDERS: 15,773

ANNUAL MEETING: In May

INCORPORATED: MN, 1902

INSTITUTIONAL HOLDINGS:
No. of Institutions: 766
Shares Held: 754,249,935
% Held: 82.8

INDUSTRY: Variety stores (SIC: 5331)

TRANSFER AGENT(S): EquiServe, Jersey City, NJ

TCF FINANCIAL CORP.

YIELD	3.3%
P/E RATIO	12.3

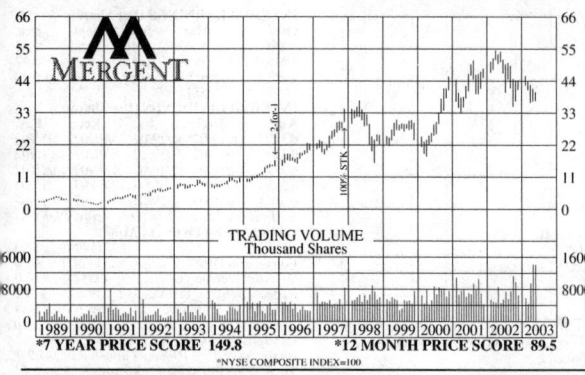

TRADING VOLUME
Thousand Shares

*7 YEAR PRICE SCORE 149.8   *12 MONTH PRICE SCORE 89.5

*NYSE COMPOSITE INDEX=100

INTERIM EARNINGS (Per Share):

Qtr.	Mar.	June	Sept.	Dec.
2000	0.51	0.59	0.59	0.66
2001	0.62	0.67	0.69	0.72
2002	0.75	0.78	0.80	0.82
2003	0.83	...	...	...

INTERIM DIVIDENDS (Per Share):

Amt.	Decl.	Ex.	Rec.	Pay.
0.287Q	4/29/02	5/08/02	5/10/02	5/31/02
0.287Q	7/23/02	7/31/02	8/02/02	8/30/02
0.287Q	10/21/02	10/30/02	11/01/02	11/29/02
0.325Q	1/15/03	2/05/03	2/07/03	2/28/03
0.325Q	4/21/03	4/30/03	5/02/03	5/30/03

Indicated div.: $1.30 (Div. Reinv. Plan)

CAPITALIZATION (12/31/02):

	($000)	(%)
Total Deposits	7,709,988	70.4
Long-Term Debt	2,268,244	20.7
Common & Surplus	977,020	8.9
Total	10,955,252	100.0

DIVIDEND ACHIEVER STATUS:

Rank: 8	10-Year Growth Rate: 25.49%	
Total Years of Dividend Growth:		11

RECENT DEVELOPMENTS: For the quarter ended 3/31/03, net income increased 6.8% to $60.1 million versus $56.3 million in the corresponding prior-year period. Results for 2003 and 2002 included net gains on sales of securities available for sale of $14.6 million and $6.0 million, respectively. Results for 2003 also included debt termination losses of $6.6 million. Net interest income slid 1.7% to $122.4 million, resulting from low interest rates and the refinancing of higher-yielding assets.

PROSPECTS: During the first quarter of 2003, the company opened three new branches, one in a Jewel-Osco® store in Illinois and two in Cub Foods® stores in Minnesota. TCF has opened 223 new branches since January 1998, which comprise 57.0% of all TCF branches. The Company plans to open 21 more new branches during the remainder of 2003, and closed five branches in Michigan and one supermarket branch in Colorado during the first quarter of 2003.

BUSINESS

TCF FINANCIAL CORP., with $12.13 billion in assets as of 3/31/03, is the holding company for two national banks. As of 3/31/03, TCB operated 392 banking offices, including 241 full-service supermarket branches, in Illinois, Indiana, Michigan, Minnesota, Wisconsin and Colorado. The Company's primary focus is lower- and middle-income customers and small- to medium-sized businesses in its markets. TCB's branches are typically open 12 hours a day, seven days a week and on holidays. TCB's products include commercial, consumer and residential mortgage loans and deposit and equipment finance, discount brokerage and investment and insurance sales products.

ANNUAL FINANCIAL DATA

	12/31/02	12/31/01	12/31/00	12/31/99	12/31/98	12/31/97	12/31/96
Earnings Per Share	②③ 3.15	② 2.70	2.35	2.00	1.76	1.69	① 1.21
Tang. Book Val. Per Share	10.31	9.91	9.29	7.78	7.74	7.94	7.36
Dividends Per Share	1.15	1.00	0.82	0.72	0.61	0.47	0.36
Dividend Payout %	36.5	37.0	35.1	36.2	34.8	27.7	29.7

INCOME STATEMENT (IN MILLIONS):

Total Interest Income	733.4	826.6	826.7	752.1	748.9	682.6	582.9
Total Interest Expense	234.1	345.4	388.1	327.9	323.2	289.0	242.7
Net Interest Income	499.2	481.2	438.5	424.2	425.7	393.6	340.1
Provision for Loan Losses	22.0	20.9	14.8	16.9	23.3	17.8	19.8
Non-Interest Income	418.8	354.9	325.2	306.6	280.3	215.0	147.8
Non-Interest Expense	538.4	502.0	462.5	452.8	428.7	361.6	341.1
Income Before Taxes	357.7	329.8	302.8	273.1	265.2	240.9	137.0
Net Income	②③ 232.9	② 207.3	186.2	166.0	145.6	145.1	① 85.7
Average Shs. Outstg. (000)	73,941	76,843	79,389	83,071	88,916	86,134	70,684

BALANCE SHEET (IN MILLIONS):

Cash & Due from Banks	416.4	386.7	392.0	429.3	420.5	297.0	238.7
Securities Avail. for Sale	2,426.8	1,584.7	1,403.9	1,521.7	1,677.9	1,430.2	1,003.5
Total Loans & Leases	8,121.1	8,244.2	8,546.7	7,895.7	7,141.2	7,174.9	5,080.1
Allowance for Credit Losses	77.0	75.0	66.7	55.8	80.0	188.3	154.9
Net Loans & Leases	8,044.1	8,169.2	8,480.0	7,840.0	7,061.2	6,986.6	4,925.2
Total Assets	12,202.1	11,358.7	11,197.5	10,661.7	10,164.6	9,744.7	7,091.0
Total Deposits	7,710.0	7,099.0	6,891.8	6,584.8	6,715.1	6,907.3	4,977.6
Long-Term Obligations	2,268.2	2,303.2	2,098.9	2,073.9	2,093.8	1,614.7	1,200.1
Total Liabilities	11,225.0	10,441.7	10,287.2	9,852.7	9,319.1	8,791.0	6,541.4
Net Stockholders' Equity	977.0	917.0	910.2	809.0	845.5	953.7	549.6
Year-end Shs. Outstg. (000)	73,941	76,932	80,289	81,941	85,569	92,822	69,514

STATISTICAL RECORD:

Return on Equity %	23.8	22.6	20.5	20.5	18.5	15.2	15.6
Return on Assets %	1.9	1.8	1.7	1.6	1.5	1.5	1.2
Equity/Assets %	8.0	8.1	8.1	7.6	8.3	9.8	7.8
Non-Int. Exp./Tot. Inc. %	58.8	60.3	61.6	63.5	62.9	60.8	70.3
Price Range	54.60-35.10	51.12-32.81	45.56-18.00	30.69-21.69	37.25-15.81	34.38-18.75	22.69-14.81
P/E Ratio	17.3-11.1	18.9-12.2	19.4-7.7	15.3-10.8	21.2-9.0	20.3-11.1	18.7-12.2
Average Yield %	2.6	2.4	2.6	2.8	2.3	1.8	1.9

Statistics are as originally reported. Adj. for 2-for-1 stk. split, 12/97. ① Incl. chrg. of $34.8 mill. for FDIC special assessment ② Incl. a pre-tax gain on the sale of branches of $2.0 mill., 2002; $3.3 mill., 2001. ③ Incl gains on sales of securities avail. for sale of $11.5 mill.

OFFICERS:
W. A. Cooper, Chmn., C.E.O.
L. A. Nagorske, Pres., C.O.O.
N. W. Brown, Exec. V.P., C.F.O., Treas.

INVESTOR CONTACT: Jason E. Korstange, Sr. V.P., Inv. Rel., (612) 745-2755

PRINCIPAL OFFICE: 200 Lake Street East, Wayzata, MN 55391-1693

TELEPHONE NUMBER: (612) 661-6500
FAX: (612) 332-1753
WEB: www.tcfbank.com

NO. OF EMPLOYEES: 5,400 full-time (approx.); 2,800 part-time (approx.)

SHAREHOLDERS: 11,000 (approx.)

ANNUAL MEETING: In May

INCORPORATED: DE, Nov., 1987

INSTITUTIONAL HOLDINGS:
No. of Institutions: 248
Shares Held: 46,424,722
% Held: 62.7

INDUSTRY: Federal savings institutions (SIC: 6035)

TRANSFER AGENT(S): BankBoston, N.A., Boston, MA

TECO ENERGY, INC.

YIELD 5.9%
P/E RATIO 9.2

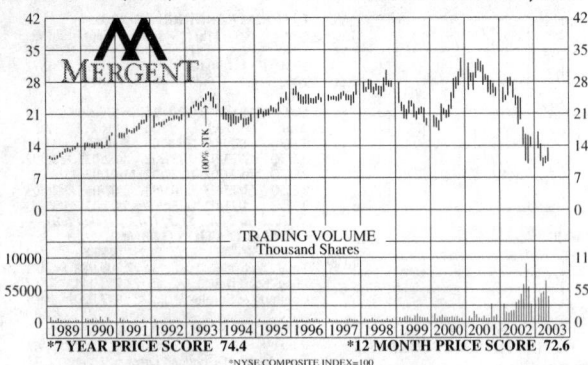

INTERIM EARNINGS (Per Share):

Qtr.	Mar.	June	Sept.	Dec.
2000	0.42	0.46	0.65	0.44
2001	0.53	0.52	0.71	0.47
2002	0.54	0.59	0.72	0.20
2003	d0.11	...	...	...

INTERIM DIVIDENDS (Per Share):

Amt.	Decl.	Ex.	Rec.	Pay.
0.355Q	4/17/02	4/29/02	5/01/02	5/15/02
0.355Q	7/17/02	7/30/02	8/01/02	8/15/02
0.355Q	10/16/02	10/30/02	11/01/02	11/15/02
0.355Q	1/28/03	2/05/03	2/07/03	2/15/03
0.19Q	4/10/03	4/29/03	5/01/03	5/15/03

Indicated div.: $0.76 (Div. Reinv. Plan)

CAPITALIZATION (12/31/02):

	($000)	(%)
Long-Term Debt	3,324,300	47.0
Deferred Income Tax	495,000	7.0
Redeemable Pfd. Stock	649,100	9.2
Common & Surplus	2,611,700	36.9
Total	7,080,100	100.0

TRADING VOLUME
Thousand Shares

*7 YEAR PRICE SCORE 74.4 ***12 MONTH PRICE SCORE 72.6**

*NYSE COMPOSITE INDEX=100

DIVIDEND ACHIEVER STATUS:
Rank: 241 10-Year Growth Rate: 4.62%
Total Years of Dividend Growth: 43

RECENT DEVELOPMENTS: For the quarter ended 3/31/03, TE reported a loss from continuing operations of $19.3 million, before an accounting change charge of $1.1 million, compared with income of $69.9 million the year before. Results for 2003 included an asset impairment charge of $104.5 million. Total revenues advanced 8.6% to $658.5 million. Regulated electric and gas revenues climbed 10.4% to $468.0 million, while revenues from unregulated operations increased 4.4% to $190.5 million.

PROSPECTS: On 4/11/03, TE announced the completion of its cash generation plan designed to raise cash and reduce spending. Under the plan, TE raised more than $950.0 million. The last two items put into place were the issuance of $250.0 million of long-term unsecured notes and the receipt of more than $50.0 million for the sale of half of TECO Coal's synthetic fuel production facilities. Negotiations are also underway to sell an additional 40.0% of the Company's synfuel production.

BUSINESS

TECO ENERGY, INC. is a public utility holding company. Tampa Electric Company (69.8% of 2002 revenues), consisting of TE's regulated operations, provides retail electric service to more than 575,000 customers in West Central Florida and gas to over 218,000 customers through its Peoples Gas System division, which is engaged in the purchase, distribution and marketing of natural gas. TE's unregulated operations (30.2%) include TECO Coal Corp., which owns mineral rights, and owns or operates surface and underground mines, synthetic fuel facilities, and coal processing and loading facilities in KY, TN and VA; TECO Power Services Corp. which has interests in independent power projects in AK, AZ, FL, MS, TX, VA, HI and Guatemala; TECO Transport Corp. which transports, stores and transfers coal and other dry-bulk commodities; and other diversified energy-related businesses.

ANNUAL FINANCIAL DATA

	12/31/02	12/31/01	12/31/00	12/31/99	12/31/98	12/31/97	12/31/96
Earnings Per Share	⑤ 1.95	④ 2.24	③ 1.97	①② 1.53	①② 1.52	② 1.61	1.71
Cash Flow Per Share	4.02	4.52	4.18	3.37	3.31	3.37	3.34
Tang. Book Val. Per Share	13.75	12.94	11.93	11.19	11.42	11.04	10.73
Dividends Per Share	1.41	1.37	1.33	1.28	1.23	1.17	1.10
Dividend Payout %	72.3	61.2	67.5	84.0	80.6	72.4	64.6
INCOME STATEMENT (IN MILLIONS):							
Total Revenues	2,675.8	2,648.6	2,295.1	1,983.0	1,958.1	1,862.3	1,473.0
Costs & Expenses	1,807.4	1,767.1	1,464.1	1,192.8	1,197.6	1,104.2	847.3
Depreciation & Amort.	317.3	307.7	277.4	241.3	236.1	231.3	190.6
Maintenance Exp.	162.1	151.3	140.0	125.3	128.9	114.2	92.2
Operating Income	389.0	422.5	413.6	423.6	395.5	412.6	342.9
Net Interest Inc./(Exp.)	d176.4	d180.8	d166.9	d123.7	d104.3	d105.8	d86.9
Income Taxes	cr38.4	cr10.1	18.5	87.0	81.0	94.7	71.4
Net Income	⑤ 298.2	④ 303.7	③ 250.9	①② 200.9	①② 200.4	② 211.4	200.7
Cash Flow	615.5	611.4	528.3	442.2	436.5	442.7	391.3
Average Shs. Outstg. (000)	153,300	135,400	126,300	131,200	131,700	131,200	117,200
BALANCE SHEET (IN MILLIONS):							
Gross Property	8,215.3	7,543.5	6,560.4	6,064.4	5,600.5	5,359.5	4,721.6
Accumulated Depreciation	2,751.3	2,705.2	2,590.3	2,436.6	2,292.9	2,123.0	1,765.0
Net Property	5,464.0	4,838.3	3,970.1	3,627.8	3,307.6	3,236.5	2,956.6
Total Assets	8,637.8	6,722.1	5,676.2	4,690.1	4,179.3	3,960.4	3,560.7
Long-Term Obligations	3,324.3	1,842.5	1,374.6	1,207.8	1,279.6	1,080.2	996.3
Net Stockholders' Equity	2,611.7	1,971.6	1,506.9	1,417.8	1,507.8	1,444.7	1,282.1
Year-end Shs. Outstg. (000)	175,800	139,600	126,300	126,700	132,000	130,900	117,600
STATISTICAL RECORD:							
Operating Profit Margin %	14.5	16.0	18.0	21.4	20.2	22.2	23.3
Net Profit Margin %	11.1	11.5	10.9	10.1	10.2	11.4	13.6
Net Inc./Net Property %	5.5	6.3	6.3	5.5	6.1	6.5	6.8
Net Inc./Tot. Capital %	4.2	6.7	7.1	6.4	6.1	7.1	7.4
Return on Equity %	11.4	15.4	16.7	14.2	13.3	14.6	15.7
Accum. Depr./Gross Prop. %	33.5	35.9	39.5	40.2	40.9	39.6	37.4
Price Range	29.05-10.02	32.97-24.75	33.19-17.25	28.00-18.38	30.63-24.75	28.00-22.75	27.00-23.00
P/E Ratio	14.9-5.1	14.7-11.0	16.8-8.8	18.3-12.0	20.1-16.3	17.4-14.1	15.8-13.4
Average Yield %	7.2	4.7	5.3	5.5	4.4	4.6	4.4

Statistics are as originally reported. ① Incl. non-recurr. chrg. $16.1 mill., 1999; $25.9 mill., 1998 ② Bef. disc. oper. loss $14.8 mill., 1999; gain $6.1 mill., 1998; loss $9.5 mill., 1997 ③ Incl. after-tax gain $8.3 mill. & nonrecurr. chrgs. $9.0 mill. ④ Incl. after-tax write-down of $6.1 mill. ⑤ Bef. gain from disc. opers. of $31.9 mill.; incl. aft.-tax chrgs. of $20.9 mill. for debt refin. and $5.8 mill. for asset valuation.

OFFICERS:
R. D. Fagan, Chmn., Pres., C.E.O.
G. L. Gillette, Sr. V.P., C.F.O.

INVESTOR CONTACT: Mark Kane, Investor Relations, (813) 228-1772

PRINCIPAL OFFICE: 702 N. Franklin Street, Tampa, FL 33602

TELEPHONE NUMBER: (813) 228-4111
FAX: (813) 228-1670
WEB: www.tecoenergy.com

NO. OF EMPLOYEES: 6,319

SHAREHOLDERS: 23,482 (approx.)

ANNUAL MEETING: In April

INCORPORATED: FL, Jan., 1981

INSTITUTIONAL HOLDINGS:
No. of Institutions: 340
Shares Held: 72,141,220
% Held: 41.0

INDUSTRY: Electric services (SIC: 4911)

TRANSFER AGENT(S): EquiServe, Trust Company, N.A., Providence, RI

TELEFLEX INC.

YIELD 1.9%
P/E RATIO 13.8

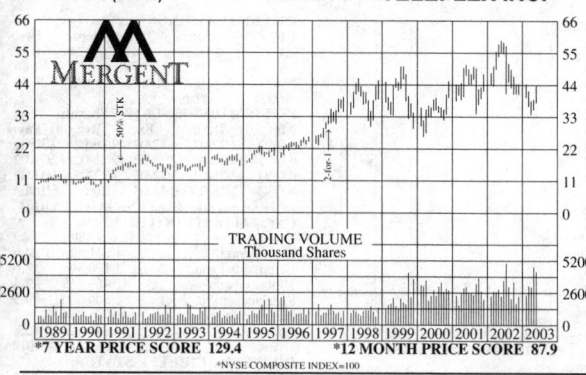

INTERIM EARNINGS (Per Share):

Qtr.	Mar.	June	Sept.	Dec.
2000	0.70	0.76	0.56	0.81
2001	0.77	0.79	0.56	0.74
2002	0.77	0.84	0.66	0.88
2003	0.74	...	...	...

INTERIM DIVIDENDS (Per Share):

Amt.	Decl.	Ex.	Rec.	Pay.
0.18Q	8/05/02	8/22/02	8/26/02	9/16/02
0.18Q	11/04/02	11/21/02	11/25/02	12/16/02
0.18Q	1/27/03	2/21/03	2/25/03	3/14/03
0.20Q	4/25/03	5/21/03	5/26/03	6/16/03

Indicated div.: $0.80 (Div. Reinv. Plan)

CAPITALIZATION (12/29/02):

	($000)	(%)
Long-Term Debt	240,123	20.8
Common & Surplus	912,281	79.2
Total	1,152,404	100.0

TRADING VOLUME
Thousand Shares

| 1989 | 1990 | 1991 | 1992 | 1993 | 1994 | 1995 | 1996 | 1997 | 1998 | 1999 | 2000 | 2001 | 2002 | 2003 |

*7 YEAR PRICE SCORE 129.4   *12 MONTH PRICE SCORE 87.9

*NYSE COMPOSITE INDEX=100

DIVIDEND ACHIEVER STATUS:
Rank: 88   10-Year Growth Rate: 13.09%
Total Years of Dividend Growth: 25

RECENT DEVELOPMENTS: For the quarter ended 3/30/03, net income slipped 3.9% to $29.2 million versus $30.4 million in the same period of 2002. Results for 2003 included a non-operating gain of $3.1 million. Revenues climbed 7.4% to $546.2 million from $508.4 million in the previous year. Commercial Products segment revenue grew 12.8% to $299.8 million, while Medical Products segment revenue climbed 10.1% to $118.1 million. Aerospace Products segment revenue declined 5.2% to $128.3 million.

PROSPECTS: Looking ahead, the Company expects challenging business conditions to continue for the remainder of 2003, particularly in the aerospace market. Nevertheless, the Company expects revenues and earnings to increase at a single-digit percentage rate in 2003 due to new product introductions. Going forward, the Company plans to continue to closely manage costs, while seeking strategic acquisitions. Separately, the integration of Megatech Electro, Inc. is progressing well.

BUSINESS

TELEFLEX INC. operates in three segments. Commercial Products (52.3% of 2002 sales and 48.4% of operating profit) designs and manufactures proprietary mechanical controls for the automotive market; mechanical, electrical and hydraulic controls, and electronics for the pleasure marine market; and proprietary products for fluid transfer and industrial applications. Medical Products (21.6%, 35.0%) manufactures and distributes a broad range of invasive disposable and reusable devices worldwide. Aerospace Products (26.1%, 16.6%) serves the aerospace and turbine engine markets. Its businesses design and manufacture precision controls and cargo systems for aviation; provide coating and repair services and manufactured components for users of both flight and land-based turbine engines.

ANNUAL FINANCIAL DATA

	12/29/02	12/30/01	12/31/00	12/26/99	12/27/98	12/28/97	12/29/96
Earnings Per Share	① 3.15	2.86	2.83	2.47	2.15	1.86	1.58
Cash Flow Per Share	5.54	5.21	4.83	4.22	3.71	3.13	2.65
Tang. Book Val. Per Share	16.61	19.99	18.01	15.85	14.21	12.49	11.30
Dividends Per Share	0.71	0.66	0.58	0.51	0.45	0.39	0.34
Dividend Payout %	22.5	23.1	20.5	20.4	20.7	20.8	21.5

INCOME STATEMENT (IN MILLIONS):

Total Revenues	2,076.2	1,905.0	1,764.5	1,601.1	1,437.6	1,145.8	931.2
Costs & Expenses	1,818.7	1,624.4	1,508.1	1,373.2	1,235.7	977.0	791.8
Depreciation & Amort.	95.1	92.4	77.4	67.4	60.1	47.9	38.8
Operating Income	162.4	188.2	179.0	160.5	141.8	120.8	100.7
Net Interest Inc./(Exp.)	...	d28.5	d20.8	d17.7	d17.1	d14.4	d13.9
Income Before Income Taxes	172.5	159.7	158.2	142.8	124.8	106.4	86.8
Income Taxes	47.2	47.4	49.0	47.5	42.2	36.3	29.6
Net Income	① 125.3	112.3	109.2	95.2	82.6	70.1	57.2
Cash Flow	220.4	204.7	186.6	162.6	142.7	118.0	95.9
Average Shs. Outstg. (000)	39,786	39,280	38,633	38,525	38,425	37,661	36,198

BALANCE SHEET (IN MILLIONS):

Cash & Cash Equivalents	44.5	46.9	45.1	29.0	66.7	30.7	68.6
Total Current Assets	837.9	747.5	662.0	604.9	616.9	566.5	466.0
Net Property	604.2	565.7	489.5	465.9	431.8	364.0	291.8
Total Assets	1,813.4	1,635.0	1,401.3	1,263.4	1,215.9	1,079.2	857.9
Total Current Liabilities	498.5	495.4	383.9	329.4	311.5	294.9	196.7
Long-Term Obligations	240.1	228.2	220.6	246.2	275.6	237.6	195.9
Net Stockholders' Equity	912.3	778.1	690.4	602.6	534.5	463.8	409.2
Net Working Capital	339.4	252.1	278.2	275.5	305.5	271.6	269.4
Year-end Shs. Outstg. (000)	39,398	38,933	38,344	38,019	37,615	37,118	36,222

STATISTICAL RECORD:

Operating Profit Margin %	7.8	9.9	10.1	10.0	9.9	10.5	10.8
Net Profit Margin %	6.0	5.9	6.2	5.9	5.7	6.1	6.1
Return on Equity %	13.7	14.4	15.8	15.8	15.4	15.1	14.0
Return on Assets %	6.9	6.9	7.8	7.5	6.8	6.5	6.7
Debt/Total Assets %	13.2	14.0	15.7	19.5	22.7	22.0	22.8
Price Range	59.35-40.64	50.99-34.00	45.38-26.13	50.44-28.88	46.38-29.50	39.75-23.19	26.13-18.94
P/E Ratio	18.8-12.9	17.8-11.9	16.0-9.2	20.4-11.7	21.6-13.7	21.4-12.5	16.5-12.0
Average Yield %	1.4	1.6	1.6	1.3	1.2	1.2	1.5

Statistics are as originally reported. Adj. for 2-for-1 split, 6/97. ① Incl. $10.1 mill. non-operating gain.

OFFICERS:
L. K. Black, Chmn.
J. P. Black, Pres., C.E.O.

INVESTOR CONTACT: Janine Dusossoit,
V.P., Investor Relations, (610) 834-6362

PRINCIPAL OFFICE: 630 West Germantown
Pike, Suite 450, Plymouth Meeting, PA
19462

TELEPHONE NUMBER: (610) 834-6301
FAX: (610) 834-8228
WEB: www.teleflex.com

NO. OF EMPLOYEES: 18,100 (approx.)

SHAREHOLDERS: 1,140 (approx.)

ANNUAL MEETING: In Apr.

INCORPORATED: DE, June, 1943

INSTITUTIONAL HOLDINGS:
No. of Institutions: 218
Shares Held: 24,905,471
% Held: 63.9

INDUSTRY: Surgical and medical
instruments (SIC: 3841)

TRANSFER AGENT(S): American Stock
Transfer & Trust Company, New York, NY

TELEPHONE AND DATA SYSTEMS, INC.

YIELD 1.3%
P/E RATIO ...

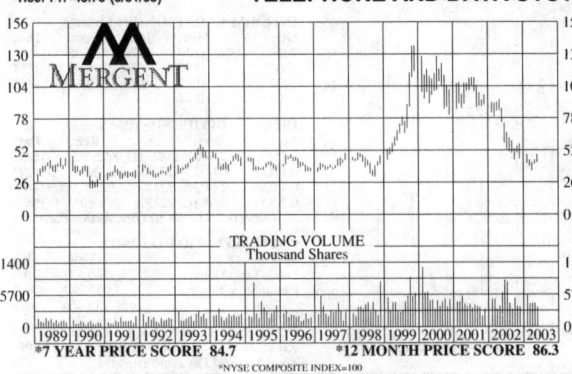

INTERIM EARNINGS (Per Share):

Qtr.	Mar.	June	Sept.	Dec.
2000	0.63	0.40	1.24	0.37
2001	0.52	d5.77	0.89	1.46
2002	0.23	d16.23	d0.35	d0.50
2003	d0.09	...	...	...

INTERIM DIVIDENDS (Per Share):

Amt.	Decl.	Ex.	Rec.	Pay.
0.145Q	8/27/02	9/12/02	9/16/02	9/30/02
0.145Q	11/18/02	12/12/02	12/16/02	12/30/02
0.155Q	2/28/03	3/13/03	3/17/03	3/31/03
0.155Q	5/15/03	6/12/03	6/16/03	6/30/03

Indicated div.: $0.62 (Div. Reinv. Plan)

CAPITALIZATION (12/31/02):

	($000)	(%)
Long-Term Debt	1,641,624	24.6
Deferred Income Tax	1,170,505	17.6
Minority Interest	489,735	7.4
Redeemable Pfd. Stock	300,000	4.5
Preferred Stock	6,954	0.1
Common & Surplus	3,052,623	45.8
Total	6,661,441	100.0

DIVIDEND ACHIEVER STATUS:
Rank: 214   10-Year Growth Rate: 6.13%
Total Years of Dividend Growth: 28

RECENT DEVELOPMENTS: For the quarter ended 3/31/03, TDS posted a net loss of $5.0 million versus income of $14.0 million, before an accounting change gain of $3.4 million, in the corresponding year-earlier period. Results for 2003 and 2002 included losses on marketable securities and other investments of $3.5 million and $37.4 million, respectively. Results for 2003 also included a pre-tax loss of $23.5 million on assets held for sale. Total operating revenues rose 21.4% to $807.4 million. U.S. Cellular reported an operating loss of $6.2 million versus operating profit of $79.7 million in 2002, reflecting increased expenses associated with expansion into new markets as well as the deployment of new technology. TDS Telecom operating income advanced 55.9% to $40.1 million.

BUSINESS

TELEPHONE AND DATA SYSTEMS, INC. is a diversified telecommunications service company with wireless telephone and wireline telephone operations. At 3/31/03, TDS served approximately 5.3 million customer/units in 34 states, including 4.2 million wireless customers, 669,900 telephone access lines, 118,100 Internet service accounts, 12,800 digital subscriber lines, and 202,100 long distance customers. TDS also owns a portfolio of investments in publicly traded telecommunications companies. TDS conducts substantially all of its wireless operations through its 82.2%-owned subsidiary, United States Cellular Corporation. TDS conducts substantially all of its wireline telephone operations through its wholly-owned subsidiary, TDS Telecommunications Corporation. U.S. Cellular provided 73.2% of TDS's consolidated revenues and 72.8% of consolidated operating income in 2002. TDS Telecom provided 26.8% of consolidated revenues and 27.2% of consolidated operating income in 2002.

ANNUAL FINANCIAL DATA

	12/31/02	12/31/01	12/31/00	12/31/99	12/31/98	12/31/97	12/31/96
Earnings Per Share	5 d16.85	4 d2.87	3 2.39	2 5.02	1.03	1 d0.19	1 2.08
Cash Flow Per Share	d8.15	4.80	8.97	10.62	7.00	4.64	5.92
Tang. Book Val. Per Share	54.63	56.36	67.07	39.81	36.58	32.49	33.23
Dividends Per Share	0.58	0.54	0.50	0.46	0.44	0.42	0.40
Dividend Payout %	...	...	20.9	9.2	42.7	...	19.2
INCOME STATEMENT (IN MILLIONS):							
Total Revenues	2,985.4	2,588.5	2,326.9	1,963.1	1,805.7	1,471.5	1,214.6
Costs & Expenses	2,088.6	1,702.4	1,507.6	1,239.4	1,417.2	1,173.7	829.0
Depreciation & Amort.	510.4	450.0	399.1	353.3	409.5	301.6	231.6
Operating Income	386.4	436.2	420.1	370.4	d20.9	d3.7	154.1
Net Interest Inc./(Exp.)	d132.2	d103.7	d100.6	d100.0	d126.4	d89.7	d42.9
Income Before Income Taxes	d1,555.7	d147.2	371.2	567.1	157.2	20.5	251.8
Income Taxes	cr577.0	cr44.9	149.5	228.2	69.3	28.6	123.6
Equity Earnings/Minority Int.	d33.9	d66.0	d76.2	d89.9	d52.0	d5.3	26.7
Net Income	5 d987.7	4 d168.2	3 145.5	2 314.2	64.4	1 d9.5	1 128.1
Cash Flow	d477.7	281.3	544.2	666.3	426.6	279.5	359.7
Average Shs. Outstg. (000)	58,644	58,661	60,636	62,736	60,982	60,211	60,732
BALANCE SHEET (IN MILLIONS):							
Cash & Cash Equivalents	1,298.9	140.7	102.6	116.0	55.4	75.6	119.3
Total Current Assets	1,948.0	674.4	527.1	508.0	405.4	408.3	346.1
Net Property	3,196.2	2,558.0	2,186.0	2,095.9	2,672.6	2,465.7	1,828.9
Total Assets	9,602.0	8,046.8	8,634.6	5,375.8	5,527.5	4,971.6	4,200.0
Total Current Liabilities	1,167.2	816.2	984.4	369.7	623.4	905.9	509.3
Long-Term Obligations	1,641.6	1,507.8	1,173.0	1,279.9	1,553.1	1,264.2	982.2
Net Stockholders' Equity	3,059.6	3,526.4	3,943.9	2,492.1	2,263.9	1,999.1	2,060.9
Net Working Capital	780.8	d141.9	d457.3	138.3	d217.9	d497.6	d163.2
Year-end Shs. Outstg. (000)	55,875	62,437	58,688	62,370	61,177	60,585	61,154
STATISTICAL RECORD:							
Operating Profit Margin %	12.9	16.8	18.1	18.9	...	...	12.7
Net Profit Margin %	...	...	6.3	16.0	3.6	...	10.5
Return on Equity %	...	...	3.7	12.6	2.8	...	6.2
Return on Assets %	...	...	1.7	5.8	1.2	...	3.1
Debt/Total Assets %	17.1	18.7	13.6	23.8	28.1	25.4	23.4
Price Range	93.15-44.10	111.25-85.16	128.50-80.60	137.00-44.13	50.13-30.63	49.94-34.50	48.88-34.75
P/E Ratio	...	...	53.8-33.7	27.3-8.8	48.7-29.7	...	23.5-16.7
Average Yield %	0.8	0.5	0.5	0.5	1.1	1.0	1.0

Statistics are as originally reported. 1 Incl. non-recurr. cr. 12/31/97: $41.4 mill.; cr. 12/31/96: $138.7 mill. 2 Incl. gain of $345.9 mill.; bef. disc. oper. loss of $142.3 mill. 3 Incl. gains on cellular & oth. invest. of $15.7 mill. 4 Incl. loss on marketable securities & oth. invest. of $548.3 mill.; bef. loss of $24.1 mill. on disp. of disc. ops. 5 Incl. loss on marketable securities & oth. invest. of $1.89 bill.; bef. acctg. chge. gain of $3.4 mill.

OFFICERS:
L. T. Carlson, Chmn.
L. T. Carlson, Jr., Pres., C.E.O.
S. L. Helton, Exec. V.P., C.F.O.
INVESTOR CONTACT: Julie Mathews,
Investor Services, (312) 630-1900
PRINCIPAL OFFICE: 30 North Lasalle Street,
Suite 400, Chicago, IL 60602

TELEPHONE NUMBER: (312) 630-1900
FAX: (312) 630-1908
WEB: www.teldta.com
NO. OF EMPLOYEES: 11,000 (approx.)
SHAREHOLDERS: 2,268
ANNUAL MEETING: In May
INCORPORATED: IA, Mar., 1968; reincorp.,
DE, May, 1998

INSTITUTIONAL HOLDINGS:
No. of Institutions: 216
Shares Held: 44,410,807
% Held: 75.3
INDUSTRY: Radiotelephone communications
(SIC: 4812)
TRANSFER AGENT(S): ComputerShare
Investor Services, Chicago, IL

TENNANT COMPANY

YIELD 2.4%
P/E RATIO 25.3

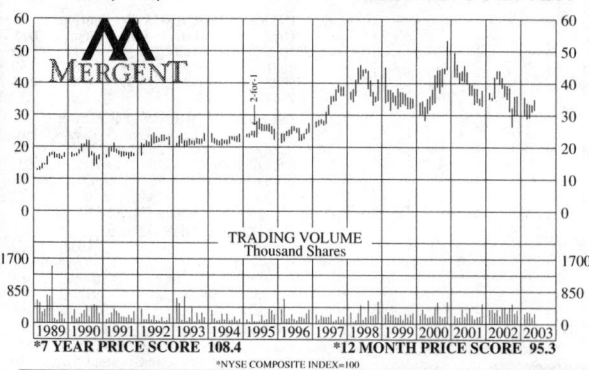

TRADING VOLUME
Thousand Shares

*7 YEAR PRICE SCORE 108.4   *12 MONTH PRICE SCORE 95.3
*NYSE COMPOSITE INDEX=100

INTERIM EARNINGS (Per Share):

Qtr.	Mar.	June	Sept.	Dec.
1999	0.53	0.66	0.35	0.61
2000	0.60	0.83	0.79	0.87
2001	0.02	0.14	0.32	0.04
2002	d0.15	0.32	0.30	0.48
2003	0.28	...	...	...

INTERIM DIVIDENDS (Per Share):

Amt.	Decl.	Ex.	Rec.	Pay.
0.21Q	8/15/02	8/28/02	8/30/02	9/16/02
0.21Q	11/14/02	11/26/02	11/29/02	12/16/02
0.21Q	2/20/03	2/26/03	2/28/03	3/14/03
0.21Q	5/01/03	5/28/03	5/30/03	6/13/03

Indicated div.: $0.84 (Div. Reinv. Plan)

CAPITALIZATION (12/31/02):

	($000)	(%)
Long-Term Debt	5,000	3.1
Common & Surplus	154,145	96.9
Total	159,145	100.0

DIVIDEND ACHIEVER STATUS:
Rank: 266   10-Year Growth Rate: 3.00%
Total Years of Dividend Growth: 30

RECENT DEVELOPMENTS: For the quarter ended 3/31/03, net income was $2.5 million versus a net loss of $1.4 million in the equivalent 2002 quarter. Results for 2003 included a net after-tax gain of $600,000. Results for 2002 included after-tax unusual charges of $3.3 million. Net sales increased 17.3% to $113.1 million, reflecting TNC's recognition of $6.4 million in deferred revenue and, to a lesser extent, strong new products and sales of cleaning equipment for commercial applications.

PROSPECTS: Despite the doubtful recovery in capital spending by customers in the industrial sector and the prevailing uncertainty in the global economy, the Company continues to expect 2003 earnings in the range of $1.43 to $1.76 per share, including unusual items. Going forward, the Company plans to concentrate on improving its operating effectiveness, expanding its presence in Europe and investing in the development of new products.

BUSINESS

TENNANT COMPANY is a manufacturer of nonresidential floor maintenance and outdoor cleaning equipment, floor coatings and related offerings. The Company's products include scrubbers, sweepers, extractors, buffers and other specialized floor cleaning equipment and supplies, plus an array of industrial floor coatings. The Company has manufacturing operations in Holland, Michigan and Uden, The Netherlands. TNC sells its products directly in ten countries and through distributors in 50 others. In January 1999, the Company acquired the business and assets of Paul Andra KG, a privately-owned manufacturer of commercial floor maintenance equipment in Germany.

ANNUAL FINANCIAL DATA

	12/31/02	12/31/01	12/31/00	12/31/99	12/31/98	12/31/97	12/31/96
Earnings Per Share	① 0.91	①② 0.52	3.09	① 2.15	2.67	2.41	2.10
Cash Flow Per Share	2.79	2.53	5.11	4.20	4.51	4.15	3.73
Tang. Book Val. Per Share	14.43	15.18	15.16	13.06	12.68	12.00	11.15
Dividends Per Share	0.82	0.80	0.78	0.76	0.74	0.72	0.69
Dividend Payout %	90.1	153.8	25.2	35.3	27.7	29.9	32.9
INCOME STATEMENT (IN THOUSANDS):							
Total Revenues	424,183	422,970	454,044	429,407	389,388	372,428	344,433
Costs & Expenses	391,660	391,047	392,129	379,478	334,489	318,872	296,415
Depreciation & Amort.	16,947	18,507	18,391	18,667	17,550	17,468	16,387
Operating Income	15,576	13,416	43,524	31,262	37,349	36,088	31,631
Net Interest Inc./(Exp.)	510	340	807	d1,097	1,479	2,678	1,768
Income Before Income Taxes	14,898	13,749	44,044	30,586	39,092	37,630	32,329
Income Taxes	6,633	8,945	15,794	10,893	13,767	13,425	11,302
Net Income	① 8,265	①② 4,804	28,250	① 19,693	25,325	24,205	21,027
Cash Flow	25,212	23,311	46,641	38,360	42,875	41,673	37,414
Average Shs. Outstg.	9,048	9,203	9,135	9,140	9,500	10,032	10,021
BALANCE SHEET (IN THOUSANDS):							
Cash & Cash Equivalents	16,356	23,783	21,512	14,928	17,693	16,279	9,881
Total Current Assets	162,901	152,387	171,628	165,093	150,868	143,105	126,481
Net Property	69,153	69,792	66,713	66,306	66,640	65,111	65,384
Total Assets	256,237	246,619	263,285	257,533	239,098	232,744	219,180
Total Current Liabilities	70,349	55,648	67,255	74,999	60,809	56,115	7,898
Long-Term Obligations	5,000	10,000	10,000	16,003	23,038	20,678	21,824
Net Stockholders' Equity	154,145	154,328	154,948	135,915	131,267	134,086	128,860
Net Working Capital	92,552	96,739	104,373	90,094	90,059	86,990	118,583
Year-end Shs. Outstg.	8,981	9,036	9,053	8,989	9,123	9,699	9,965
STATISTICAL RECORD:							
Operating Profit Margin %	3.7	3.2	9.6	7.3	9.6	9.7	9.2
Net Profit Margin %	1.9	1.1	6.2	4.6	6.5	6.5	6.1
Return on Equity %	5.4	3.1	18.2	14.5	19.3	18.1	16.3
Return on Assets %	3.2	1.9	10.7	7.6	10.6	10.3	9.2
Debt/Total Assets %	2.0	4.1	3.8	6.2	9.6	8.8	10.0
Price Range	44.00-26.35	49.56-32.80	53.38-28.25	45.00-31.44	45.75-33.00	39.63-26.13	27.50-21.25
P/E Ratio	48.3-29.0	95.3-63.1	17.3-9.1	20.9-14.6	17.1-12.4	16.4-10.8	13.1-10.1
Average Yield %	2.3	1.9	1.9	2.0	1.9	2.2	2.8

Statistics are as originally reported. ① Incl. non-recurr. chrg. $4.0 mill., 2002; $10.0 mill., 2001; $6.7 mill, 12/99; $4.1 mill., 12/93. ② Incl. pension settlement gain of $5.9 mill.

OFFICERS:
J. M. Dolan, Pres., C.E.O.
A. T. Brausen, V.P., C.F.O., Treas.
E. A. Blanchard, V.P., Gen. Couns., Sec.

INVESTOR CONTACT: Anthony T. Brausen, V.P., C.F.O. & Treas., (763) 540-1553

PRINCIPAL OFFICE: 701 North Lilac Drive, P.O. Box 1452, Minneapolis, MN 55440

TELEPHONE NUMBER: (763) 540-1208
FAX: (763) 540-1437
WEB: www.tennantco.com

NO. OF EMPLOYEES: 2,380 (avg.)

SHAREHOLDERS: 2,700 (approx.)

ANNUAL MEETING: In May

INCORPORATED: MN, Jan., 1909

INSTITUTIONAL HOLDINGS:
No. of Institutions: 60
Shares Held: 6,757,624
% Held: 75.1

INDUSTRY: Service industry machinery, nec (SIC: 3589)

TRANSFER AGENT(S): Wells Fargo Shareowner Services, N.A., St. Paul, MN

TEPPCO PARTNERS, L.P.

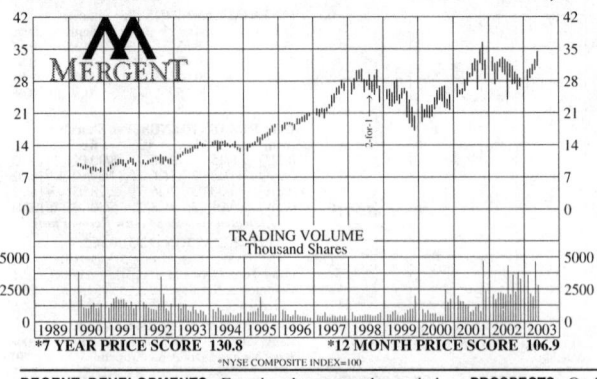

INTERIM EARNINGS (Per Share):

Qtr.	Mar.	June	Sept.	Dec.
2000	0.60	0.35	0.41	0.53
2001	0.55	0.89	0.35	0.40
2002	0.46	0.39	0.48	0.46
2003	0.43	...	...	...

INTERIM DIVIDENDS (Per Share):

Amt.	Decl.	Ex.	Rec.	Pay.
0.60Q	7/18/02	7/29/02	7/31/02	8/08/02
0.60Q	10/16/02	10/29/02	10/31/02	11/08/02
0.60Q	1/16/03	1/29/03	1/31/03	2/07/03
0.625Q	3/27/03	4/28/03	4/30/03	5/09/03

Indicated div.: $2.50

CAPITALIZATION (12/31/02):

	($000)	(%)
Long-Term Debt	1,377,692	58.1
Redeemable Pfd. Stock	103,363	4.4
Common & Surplus	891,842	37.6
Total	2,372,897	100.0

DIVIDEND ACHIEVER STATUS:
Rank: 185   10-Year Growth Rate: 7.89%
Total Years of Dividend Growth: 10

TRADING VOLUME
Thousand Shares

*7 YEAR PRICE SCORE 130.8   ***12 MONTH PRICE SCORE 106.9**
*NYSE COMPOSITE INDEX=100

RECENT DEVELOPMENTS: For the three months ended 3/31/03, net income increased 26.5% to $33.9 million compared with $26.8 million in the corresponding year-earlier period. Results for 2003 included the addition of the Val Verde Gas Gathering System that was acquired in July 2002. Earnings were also aided by higher downstream results, due to the cold winter weather in the Northeast and Midwest. Total operating revenues climbed 74.2% to $1.10 billion. Operating profit improved 36.4% to $51.3 million.

PROSPECTS: On 5/8/03, TPP announced two projects totaling $65.0 million that will expand both pipeline and processing capacity on the Company's Jonah Gas Gathering System in southwestern Wyoming. TPP expects the Phase III expansion to contribute more than $12.0 million to operating income during the first full year of operation. Separately, TPP expects full-year earnings to range between $1.40 and $1.65 per unit.

BUSINESS

TEPPCO PARTNERS, L.P. operates through three operating segments. The midstream segment, which comprised 88.2% of 2002 revenues and 15.5% of operating income, includes natural gas gathering services, and transportation and fractionation of natural gas liquids. The upstream segment (7.5%, 48.8%), includes crude oil transportation, storage, gathering and marketing activities, and distribution of lubrication oils and specialty chemicals. The downstream segment (4.3%, 35.7%), includes the transportation and storage of refined products, liquefied petroleum gases and petrochemicals. The Company, a master limited partnership formed in March 1990, operates through various subsidiaries. Texas Eastern Products Pipeline Company, LLC, a wholly-owned subsidiary of Duke Energy Field Services (DEFS), serves as the general partner of TPP. The assets of the midstream segment are managed and operated by DEFS under an agreement with TPP. In March 2002, TPP acquired the Chaparral and Quanah pipelines for about $132.0 million. In July 2002, TPP acquired the Val Verde Gathering System for $444.0 million.

ANNUAL FINANCIAL DATA

	12/31/02	12/31/01	12/31/00	12/31/99	12/31/98	12/31/97	12/31/96
Earnings Per Share	1.79	③ 2.18	1.89	1.91	② 1.61	① 1.95	1.89
Cash Flow Per Share	4.14	3.95	3.35	2.33	1.07	2.93	2.83
Tang. Book Val. Per Share	7.61	6.79	8.46	6.72	6.56	10.45	10.01
Dividends Per Share	2.35	2.15	2.00	1.85	1.75	1.55	1.45
Dividend Payout %	131.3	98.6	105.8	96.9	108.7	79.5	76.7
INCOME STATEMENT (IN MILLIONS):							
Total Revenues	3,242.2	3,556.4	3,087.9	1,934.9	429.6	222.1	216.0
Costs & Expenses	2,985.9	3,359.5	2,944.8	1,802.1	322.7	106.8	105.2
Depreciation & Amort.	86.0	45.9	35.2	32.7	26.9	23.8	23.4
Operating Income	170.2	151.0	108.0	100.1	80.0	91.6	87.4
Net Interest Inc./(Exp.)	d66.2	d62.1	d44.4	d29.4	d29.0	d32.2	d33.5
Income Before Income Taxes	105.9	92.5	66.0	72.9	53.9	61.9	59.2
Equity Earnings/Minority Int.	12.0	16.6	11.4	d0.7	d0.5	d0.6	d0.6
Net Income	117.9	③ 109.1	77.4	72.1	② 53.3	① 61.3	58.6
Cash Flow	203.9	155.0	112.5	104.8	80.3	85.1	82.1
Average Shs. Outstg. (000)	49,202	39,258	33,594	45,058	74,933	29,000	29,000
BALANCE SHEET (IN MILLIONS):							
Cash & Cash Equivalents	31.0	25.5	27.1	34.1	50.7	46.1	58.1
Total Current Assets	360.6	283.5	363.4	263.0	188.6	91.2	98.7
Net Property	1,587.8	1,180.5	949.7	720.9	671.6	567.7	561.1
Total Assets	2,770.6	2,065.3	1,622.8	1,041.4	915.0	673.9	671.2
Total Current Liabilities	366.8	668.8	358.3	243.5	148.2	53.9	47.6
Long-Term Obligations	1,377.7	730.5	835.8	455.8	427.7	309.5	326.5
Net Stockholders' Equity	891.8	543.2	315.1	229.8	227.2	303.0	290.3
Net Working Capital	d6.2	d385.4	5.1	19.5	40.4	37.3	51.2
Year-end Shs. Outstg. (000)	53,810	40,500	32,700	29,000	29,000	29,000	29,000
STATISTICAL RECORD:							
Operating Profit Margin %	5.3	4.2	3.5	5.2	18.6	41.2	40.5
Net Profit Margin %	3.6	3.1	2.5	3.7	12.4	27.6	27.1
Return on Equity %	13.2	20.1	24.6	31.4	23.5	20.2	20.2
Return on Assets %	4.3	5.3	4.8	6.9	5.8	9.1	8.7
Debt/Total Assets %	49.7	35.4	51.5	43.8	46.7	45.9	48.6
Price Range	33.25-23.90	36.50-24.38	27.00-19.00	28.25-17.13	30.69-23.25	28.25-19.81	21.06-17.13
P/E Ratio	18.6-13.4	16.7-11.2	14.3-10.1	14.8-9.0	19.1-14.4	14.5-10.2	11.1-9.1
Average Yield %	8.2	7.1	8.7	8.2	6.5	6.4	7.6

Statistics are as originally reported. Adj. for 2-for-1 stk. split, 8/98. ① Incl. gain on sale of inventory of $2.3 mill. ② Bef. extraord. loss of $72.8 mill. ③ Incl. net income of $18.9 mill. ($0.39/unit) fr. settlement of canceled transportation contract.

OFFICERS:
J. W. Mogg, Chmn.
B. R. Pearl, Pres., C.E.O., C.O.O.
C. H. Leonard, Sr. V.P., C.F.O., Treas.

INVESTOR CONTACT: Brenda J. Peters, Dir. of Inv. Relations, (713) 759-3954

PRINCIPAL OFFICE: 2929 Allen Pkwy., P.O. Box 2521, Houston, TX 77252-2521

TELEPHONE NUMBER: (713) 759-3636
FAX: (713) 759-3957
WEB: www.teppco.com

NO. OF EMPLOYEES: 970 (avg.)

SHAREHOLDERS: 51,300 (approx. benef.)

ANNUAL MEETING: N/A

INCORPORATED: DE, Mar., 1990

INSTITUTIONAL HOLDINGS:
No. of Institutions: 111
Shares Held: 10,670,304
% Held: 19.8

INDUSTRY: Refined petroleum pipelines (SIC: 4613)

TRANSFER AGENT(S): Mellon Investor Services, L.L.C., Ridgefield Park, NJ

3M COMPANY

YIELD 2.1%
P/E RATIO 24.6

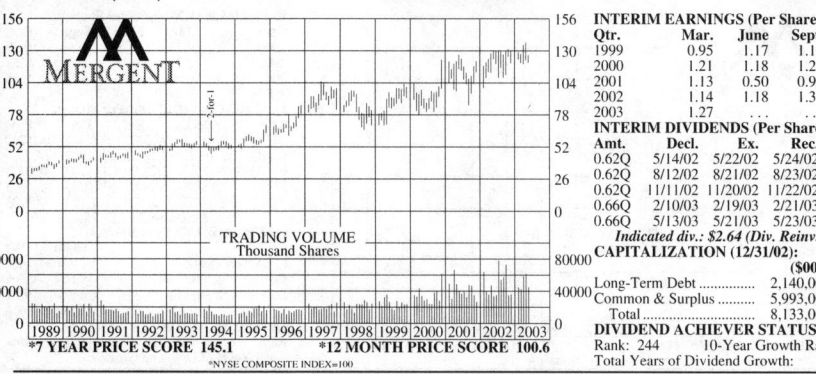

*7 YEAR PRICE SCORE 145.1   *12 MONTH PRICE SCORE 100.6
*NYSE COMPOSITE INDEX=100

TRADING VOLUME
Thousand Shares

INTERIM EARNINGS (Per Share):

Qtr.	Mar.	June	Sept.	Dec.
1999	0.95	1.17	1.13	1.10
2000	1.21	1.18	1.25	1.00
2001	1.13	0.50	0.99	0.96
2002	1.14	1.18	1.38	1.31
2003	1.27	...	...	...

INTERIM DIVIDENDS (Per Share):

Amt.	Decl.	Ex.	Rec.	Pay.
0.62Q	5/14/02	5/22/02	5/24/02	6/12/02
0.62Q	8/12/02	8/21/02	8/23/02	9/12/02
0.62Q	11/11/02	11/20/02	11/22/02	12/12/02
0.66Q	2/10/03	2/19/03	2/21/03	3/12/03
0.66Q	5/13/03	5/21/03	5/23/03	6/12/03

Indicated div.: $2.64 (Div. Reinv. Plan)

CAPITALIZATION (12/31/02):

	($000)	(%)
Long-Term Debt	2,140,000	26.3
Common & Surplus	5,993,000	73.7
Total	8,133,000	100.0

DIVIDEND ACHIEVER STATUS:

Rank: 244   10-Year Growth Rate: 4.48%
Total Years of Dividend Growth: 44

RECENT DEVELOPMENTS: For the quarter ended 3/31/03, net income increased 11.1% to $502.0 million from $452.0 million in the corresponding period the year before. Net sales grew 11.0% to $4.32 billion from $3.89 billion a year earlier. Transportation sales advanced 9.2% to $381.0 million. Health care sales rose 12.0% to $946.0 million, while industrial sales improved 9.0% to $821.0 million. Operating income grew 9.5% to $781.0 million.

PROSPECTS: On 4/4/03, MMM acquired GuardiaNet Systems, Inc., a software company serving the public library market. GuardiaNet's software and hardware manages access and collects fees for the use of library resources such as computers and printers. Looking ahead, second-quarter earnings for 2003 are anticipated to range between $1.47 and $1.53. In 2003, earnings per share are expected to range from $5.65 to $5.85, including special items.

BUSINESS

3M COMPANY (formerly Minnesota Mining and Manufacturing Company) is a worldwide producer of a diverse variety of industrial and consumer products. MMM has operations in more than 60 countries and serves customers in nearly 200 countries. 3M operates in seven business sectors: Health Care (21.8%) serves markets worldwide including medical, surgical, pharmaceutical, dental, health information systems and other markets; Industrial (19.3%) serves a broad range of industrial markets including aerospace, plastics, metalworking and packaging; Consumer and Office (15.0%) serves markets that include consumer, office, education, foodservice and other important markets; Display and Graphics (13.6%) serves markets that include electronic display, touch screen, and other major markets; Electro and Communications (11.2%) provides products that speed the delivery of information and ideas; Safety, Security and Protection Services (10.3%) provides products related to occupational health and safety, commercial care, and safety and security; Transportation (8.5%) serves automotive manufacturers, automotive body shops, and the aerospace and marine industries worldwide; and Corporate and Unallocated (0.3%).

ANNUAL FINANCIAL DATA

	12/31/02	12/31/01	12/31/00	12/31/99	12/31/98	12/31/97	12/31/96
Earnings Per Share	4.99	⑤ 3.58	④ 4.64	③ 4.34	② 2.97	① 5.06	3.63
Cash Flow Per Share	7.40	6.30	7.21	6.55	5.10	7.14	5.74
Tang. Book Val. Per Share	9.81	15.55	16.49	15.77	14.80	14.63	15.07
Dividends Per Share	2.48	2.40	2.32	2.24	2.20	2.12	1.92
Dividend Payout %	49.7	67.0	50.0	51.6	74.1	41.9	52.9

INCOME STATEMENT (IN MILLIONS):

Total Revenues	16,332.0	16,079.0	16,724.0	15,659.0	15,021.0	15,070.0	14,236.0
Costs & Expenses	12,332.0	12,717.0	12,641.0	11,803.0	12,116.0	11,525.0	10,862.0
Depreciation & Amort.	954.0	1,089.0	1,025.0	900.0	866.0	870.0	883.0
Operating Income	3,046.0	2,273.0	3,058.0	2,956.0	2,039.0	2,675.0	2,491.0
Net Interest Inc./(Exp.)	d41.0	d87.0	d111.0	d109.0	d139.0	d94.0	d79.0
Income Before Income Taxes	3,005.0	2,186.0	2,974.0	2,880.0	1,952.0	3,440.0	2,479.0
Income Taxes	966.0	702.0	1,025.0	1,032.0	685.0	1,241.0	886.0
Equity Earnings/Minority Int.	d65.0	d54.0	d92.0	d85.0	d54.0	d78.0	d77.0
Net Income	1,974.0	⑤ 1,430.0	④ 1,857.0	③ 1,763.0	② 1,213.0	① 2,121.0	1,516.0
Cash Flow	2,928.0	2,519.0	2,882.0	2,663.0	2,079.0	2,991.0	2,399.0
Average Shs. Outstg. (000)	395,500	399,900	399,900	406,500	408,000	419,000	418,000

BALANCE SHEET (IN MILLIONS):

Cash & Cash Equivalents	618.0	616.0	302.0	441.0	448.0	477.0	744.0
Total Current Assets	6,059.0	6,296.0	6,379.0	6,066.0	6,318.0	6,168.0	6,486.0
Net Property	5,621.0	5,615.0	5,823.0	5,656.0	5,566.0	5,034.0	4,844.0
Total Assets	15,329.0	14,606.0	14,522.0	13,896.0	14,153.0	13,238.0	13,364.0
Total Current Liabilities	4,457.0	4,509.0	4,754.0	3,819.0	4,386.0	3,983.0	3,606.0
Long-Term Obligations	2,140.0	1,520.0	971.0	1,480.0	1,614.0	1,015.0	851.0
Net Stockholders' Equity	5,993.0	6,086.0	6,531.0	6,289.0	5,936.0	5,926.0	6,284.0
Net Working Capital	1,602.0	1,787.0	1,625.0	2,247.0	1,932.0	2,185.0	2,880.0
Year-end Shs. Outstg. (000)	390,196	391,304	396,085	398,700	401,000	405,000	417,000

STATISTICAL RECORD:

Operating Profit Margin %	18.7	14.1	18.3	18.9	13.6	17.8	17.5
Net Profit Margin %	12.1	8.9	11.1	11.3	8.1	14.1	10.6
Return on Equity %	32.9	23.5	28.4	28.0	20.4	35.8	24.1
Return on Assets %	12.9	9.8	12.8	12.7	8.6	16.0	11.3
Debt/Total Assets %	14.0	10.4	6.7	10.7	11.4	7.7	6.4
Price Range	131.55-100.00	127.00-85.86	122.94-78.19	103.38-69.31	97.88-65.63	105.50-80.00	85.88-61.25
P/E Ratio	26.4-20.0	35.5-24.0	26.5-16.9	23.8-16.0	33.0-22.1	20.8-15.8	23.7-16.9
Average Yield %	2.1	2.3	2.3	2.6	2.7	2.3	2.6

Statistics are as originally reported. ① Incl. $803.0 mill. gain fr. sale of outdoor adver. bus. ② Bef. extraord. chrg. of $38.0 mill.; incl. pre-tax restruct. chrg. of $493.0 mill. & a gain on divest. of $10.0 mill. ③ Incl. a one-time net gain of $100.0 mill. related to various items. ④ Incl. a net after-tax chrg. of $15.0 mill. & excl. an acctg. chrg. of $75.0 mill. ⑤ Incl. non-recurr. net chrgs. of $504.0 mill. rel. to various items.

OFFICERS:
W. J. McNerney Jr., Chmn., C.E.O.
P. D. Campbell, Sr. V.P., C.F.O.

INVESTOR CONTACT: Matt Ginter, Director, Investor Relations, (651) 733-8206

PRINCIPAL OFFICE: 3M Center, St. Paul, MN 55144

TELEPHONE NUMBER: (651) 733-1110
FAX: (651) 733-9973
WEB: www.3m.com
NO. OF EMPLOYEES: 68,774 (avg.)
SHAREHOLDERS: 125,216
ANNUAL MEETING: In May
INCORPORATED: MN, July, 1902; reincorp., DE, June, 1929

INSTITUTIONAL HOLDINGS:
No. of Institutions: 919
Shares Held: 277,338,052
% Held: 71.1

INDUSTRY: Adhesives and sealants (SIC: 2891)

TRANSFER AGENT(S): Wells Fargo Shareowner Services, St. Paul, MN

NYSE SYMBOL TR
Rec. Pr. 29.65 (5/31/03)

TOOTSIE ROLL INDUSTRIES, INC.

YIELD 0.9%
P/E RATIO 24.3

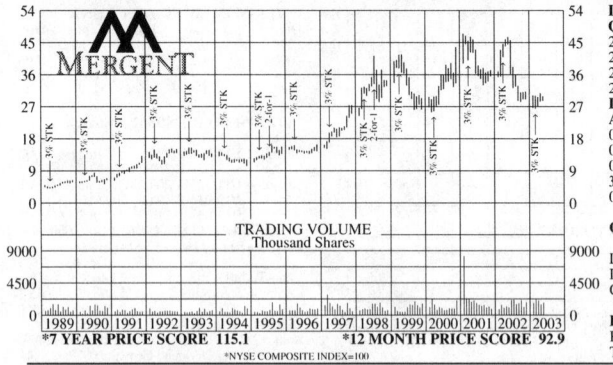

*7 YEAR PRICE SCORE 115.1   ***12 MONTH PRICE SCORE 92.9**
*NYSE COMPOSITE INDEX=100

INTERIM EARNINGS (Per Share):

Qtr.	Mar.	June	Sept.	Dec.
2000	0.23	0.29	0.58	0.29
2001	0.23	0.26	0.50	0.23
2002	0.24	0.23	0.50	0.28
2003	0.21	...	...	...

INTERIM DIVIDENDS (Per Share):

Amt.	Decl.	Ex.	Rec.	Pay.
0.07Q	9/17/02	9/25/02	9/27/02	10/10/02
0.07Q	12/10/02	12/18/02	12/20/02	1/07/03
0.07Q	2/18/03	2/28/03	3/04/03	4/03/03
3% STK	2/18/03	2/28/03	3/04/03	4/16/03
0.07Q	6/02/03	6/13/03	6/17/03	7/08/03

Indicated div.: $0.28

CAPITALIZATION (12/31/02):

	($000)	(%)
Long-Term Debt	7,500	1.4
Deferred Income Tax	19,654	3.5
Common & Surplus	526,740	95.1
Total	553,894	100.0

DIVIDEND ACHIEVER STATUS:

Rank: 38   10-Year Growth Rate: 18.30%
Total Years of Dividend Growth: 39

RECENT DEVELOPMENTS: For the quarter ended 3/29/03, net earnings declined 14.6% to $10.9 million versus $12.8 million in the corresponding 2002 quarter. Earnings for 2003 were adversely affected by higher ingredient costs and a customer bankruptcy. Net sales decreased 4.3% to $75.6 million. Lower net sales resulted from the timing of Easter seasonal product shipments, fewer shipping days in the quarter, and higher sales in the fourth quarter of 2002 due to January 2003 price increases.

PROSPECTS: TR is experiencing higher ingredient costs for nearly all of its principal ingredients, including sugar, corn syrup, vegetable oil, cocoa and chocolate. Although price increases were initiated on many of the Company's products in January 2003, additional price increases and bag weight declines on certain items are being further phased-in through the balance of 2003 to mitigate some of these higher costs. Meanwhile, TR had an increase in the carryover of open orders into the second quarter of 2003.

BUSINESS

TOOTSIE ROLL INDUSTRIES, INC. is engaged in the manufacture and sale of candy. The majority of the Company's products are sold under the following registered trademarks: TOOTSIE ROLL, TOOTSIE ROLL POPS, CHILD'S PLAY, CARAMEL APPLE POPS, CHARMS, BLOW-POP, BLUE RAZZ, ZIP-A-DEE-DOO-DA POPS, CELLA'S, MASON DOTS, MASON CROWS, JUNIOR MINT, CHARLESTON CHEW, SUGAR DADDY, SUGAR BABIES, ANDES and FLUFFY STUFF cotton candy. In September 1988, the Company acquired Charms Company for approximately $65.0 million. On 5/12/00, the Company acquired the assets of Andes Candies Inc. The Company has manufacturing facilities in Illinois, New York, Tennessee, Massachusetts, Wisconsin, Maryland and Mexico.

ANNUAL FINANCIAL DATA

	12/31/02	12/31/01	12/31/00	12/31/99	12/31/98	12/31/97	12/31/96
Earnings Per Share	1.25	① 1.23	1.40	1.30	1.22	1.08	0.84
Cash Flow Per Share	1.48	1.54	1.65	1.48	1.45	1.31	1.06
Tang. Book Val. Per Share	8.03	7.31	6.30	6.33	5.73	4.70	3.91
Dividends Per Share	0.27	0.26	0.24	0.20	0.16	0.13	0.11
Dividend Payout %	21.6	21.2	17.1	15.5	13.1	11.8	12.9
INCOME STATEMENT (IN THOUSANDS):							
Total Revenues	393,185	423,496	427,054	396,750	388,659	375,594	340,909
Costs & Expenses	284,162	312,852	303,011	282,252	274,587	272,688	257,309
Depreciation & Amort.	12,354	16,700	13,314	9,979	12,807	12,819	12,068
Operating Income	96,669	93,944	110,729	104,519	101,265	90,087	71,532
Net Interest Inc./(Exp.)	5,244	...	...	...	...	...	2,389
Income Before Income Taxes	100,688	100,787	117,808	111,447	106,063	95,361	75,098
Income Taxes	34,300	35,100	42,071	40,137	38,537	34,679	27,891
Net Income	66,388	① 65,687	75,737	71,310	67,526	60,682	47,207
Cash Flow	78,742	82,387	89,051	81,289	80,333	73,501	59,275
Average Shs. Outstg.	53,100	53,523	54,018	55,087	55,692	55,966	56,158
BALANCE SHEET (IN THOUSANDS):							
Cash & Cash Equivalents	146,244	175,161	132,487	159,506	163,920	142,280	144,157
Total Current Assets	224,948	246,096	203,211	224,532	228,539	206,961	201,513
Net Property	128,869	132,575	131,118	95,897	83,024	78,364	81,687
Total Assets	646,080	618,676	562,442	529,416	487,423	436,742	391,456
Total Current Liabilities	63,096	57,846	57,446	56,109	53,384	53,606	48,184
Long-Term Obligations	7,500	7,500	7,500	7,500	7,500	7,500	7,500
Net Stockholders' Equity	526,740	508,461	458,696	430,646	396,457	351,163	312,881
Net Working Capital	161,852	188,250	145,765	168,423	175,155	153,355	153,329
Year-end Shs. Outstg.	50,952	53,475	53,533	54,592	53,840	55,484	56,158
STATISTICAL RECORD:							
Operating Profit Margin %	24.6	22.2	25.9	26.3	26.1	24.0	21.0
Net Profit Margin %	16.9	15.5	17.7	18.0	17.4	16.2	13.8
Return on Equity %	12.6	12.9	16.5	16.6	17.0	17.3	15.1
Return on Assets %	10.3	10.6	13.5	13.5	13.9	13.9	12.1
Debt/Total Assets %	1.2	1.2	1.3	1.4	1.5	1.7	1.9
Price Range	46.61-28.25	47.53-33.00	43.76-25.44	41.71-26.10	41.30-24.37	27.38-15.15	16.42-13.77
P/E Ratio	37.2-22.6	38.8-26.9	31.3-18.2	32.2-20.1	34.0-20.0	25.2-13.9	19.6-16.5
Average Yield %	0.7	0.6	0.7	0.6	0.6	0.6	0.7

Statistics are as originally reported. Adj. for all stk. splits and divs. through 4/03. ① Incl. a nonrecurr. chrg. of $0.04 per sh. for the closing & consol. of a manufac. plant & for inventory adjustments.

OFFICERS:
M. J. Gordon, Chmn., C.E.O.
E. R. Gordon, Pres., C.O.O.
G. H. Ember Jr., V.P., C.F.O.

INVESTOR CONTACT: Investor Relations, (800) 851-9677

PRINCIPAL OFFICE: 7401 South Cicero Avenue, Chicago, IL 60629

TELEPHONE NUMBER: (773) 838-3400
FAX: (773) 838-3534
WEB: www.tootsie.com

NO. OF EMPLOYEES: 1,950 (avg.)

SHAREHOLDERS: 5,000 (approx. com. & cl. B com.)

ANNUAL MEETING: In May
INCORPORATED: VA, June, 1919

INSTITUTIONAL HOLDINGS:
No. of Institutions: 136
Shares Held: 11,911,652
% Held: 23.4

INDUSTRY: Candy & other confectionery products (SIC: 2064)

TRANSFER AGENT(S): Mellon Investor Services, LLC, Ridgefield Park, NJ

TRANSATLANTIC HOLDINGS, INC.

YIELD 0.6%
P/E RATIO 20.4

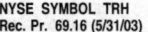

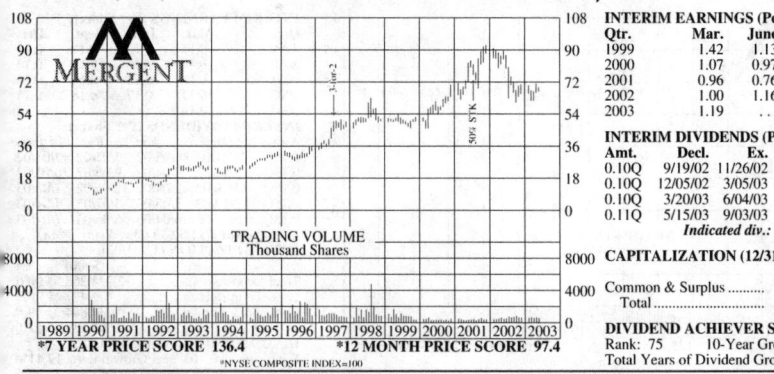

TRADING VOLUME
Thousand Shares

*7 YEAR PRICE SCORE 136.4   ***12 MONTH PRICE SCORE 97.4**

*NYSE COMPOSITE INDEX=100

INTERIM EARNINGS (Per Share):

Qtr.	Mar.	June	Sept.	Dec.
1999	1.42	1.13	0.69	0.34
2000	1.07	0.97	1.02	0.97
2001	0.96	0.76	d1.49	0.12
2002	1.00	1.16	1.16	d0.12
2003	1.19	...	...	...

INTERIM DIVIDENDS (Per Share):

Amt.	Decl.	Ex.	Rec.	Pay.
0.10Q	9/19/02	11/26/02	11/29/02	12/13/02
0.10Q	12/05/02	3/05/03	3/07/03	3/21/03
0.10Q	3/20/03	6/04/03	6/06/03	6/13/03
0.11Q	5/15/03	9/03/03	9/05/03	9/12/03

Indicated div.: $0.44

CAPITALIZATION (12/31/02):

	($000)	(%)
Common & Surplus	2,030,767	100.0
Total	2,030,767	100.0

DIVIDEND ACHIEVER STATUS:
Rank: 75   10-Year Growth Rate: 13.90%
Total Years of Dividend Growth: 12

RECENT DEVELOPMENTS: For the quarter ended 3/31/03, net income increased 18.7% to $62.8 million from $52.9 million in the comparable prior-year quarter. Total revenues grew 23.5% to $757.3 million from $613.1 million the previous year. Revenues included a realized net capital gain of $538,000 in 2003 and a realized net capital loss of $4.9 million in 2002. Net premiums earned rose 24.5% to $692.2 million from $556.0 million a year earlier. The combined ratio, a measure of underwriting losses, improved to 97.4% versus 98.2% the year before.

PROSPECTS: The Company continues to capitalize on positive business momentum, accompanied by strong premium volumes, cash flow and an improved combined ratio. Notably, premium growth is strong in both TRH's domestic and international portfolios, as market conditions remain favorable. Going forward, the Company will continue to utilize its financial strength and broad global reach to further grow its market presence. As of 3/31/03, TRH's consolidated assets and stockholder's equity were $7.80 billion and $2.10 billion, respectively.

BUSINESS

TRANSLANTIC HOLDINGS, INC., through its wholly-owned subsidiaries Transatlantic Reinsurance Company, Trans Re Zurich and Putnam Reinsurance Company, offers reinsurance capacity for a full range of property and casualty products on a treaty and facultative basis, directly and through brokers, to insurance and reinsurance companies, in both the domestic and international markets. The Company's principal lines of reinsurance include auto liability, other liability, accident and health, medical malpractice, marine and aviation, and surety and credit in the casualty lines, and fire and allied in the property lines. As of 4/24/03, the Company had operations based in Chicago, Toronto, Miami (serving Latin America and the Caribbean), Buenos Aires, Rio de Janeiro, London, Paris, Zurich, Warsaw, Johannesburg, Sydney, Hong Kong, Shanghai and Tokyo.

ANNUAL FINANCIAL DATA

	12/31/02	12/31/01	12/31/00	12/31/99	12/31/98	12/31/97	12/31/96
Earnings Per Share	② 3.21	① 0.36	4.03	3.58	4.73	3.56	4.49
Tang. Book Val. Per Share	38.78	35.33	35.59	31.53	30.96	26.17	32.95
Dividends Per Share	0.39	0.37	0.35	0.31	0.28	0.25	0.21
Dividend Payout %	12.2	103.3	8.6	8.8	5.9	7.1	4.7
INCOME STATEMENT (IN MILLIONS):							
Total Premium Income	2,369.5	1,790.3	1,631.5	1,484.6	1,380.6	1,259.3	1,130.6
Net Investment Income	252.0	240.1	234.5	230.7	222.0	207.6	192.6
Other Income	d6.0	d0.2	...	...	...	...	...
Total Revenues	2,615.5	2,030.2	1,866.0	1,715.4	1,602.6	1,466.9	1,323.3
Policyholder Benefits	1,796.4	1,561.5	1,196.9	1,148.8	1,020.9	933.0	841.5
Income Before Income Taxes	188.3	d34.1	268.0	236.1	323.4	234.7	196.3
Income Taxes	19.0	cr53.0	56.3	48.7	75.8	49.2	41.5
Net Income	② 169.3	① 18.9	211.6	187.4	247.5	185.5	154.9
Average Shs. Outstg. (000)	52,755	52,736	52,476	52,323	52,298	52,127	34,475
BALANCE SHEET (IN MILLIONS):							
Cash & Cash Equivalents	487.9	559.5	157.3	110.0	95.6	87.5	136.7
Premiums Due	1,167.8	1,254.2	778.5	777.1	658.0	591.0	528.1
Invst. Assets: Fixed-term	4,361.5	3,653.9	3,427.8	3,462.1	3,533.5	3,400.2	3,060.8
Invst. Assets: Equities	433.7	512.6	545.7	537.1	511.4	458.2	386.7
Invst. Assets: Total	5,460.1	4,880.2	4,262.0	4,229.4	4,258.2	3,921.8	3,512.4
Total Assets	7,286.5	6,741.3	5,522.7	5,480.2	5,253.2	4,835.0	4,379.1
Net Stockholders' Equity	2,030.8	1,846.0	1,856.4	1,642.5	1,610.1	1,369.6	1,137.3
Year-end Shs. Outstg. (000)	52,361	52,256	52,160	52,092	52,000	51,845	34,520
STATISTICAL RECORD:							
Return on Revenues %	6.5	0.9	11.3	10.9	15.4	12.6	11.7
Return on Equity %	8.3	1.0	11.4	11.4	15.4	13.7	13.6
Return on Assets %	2.3	0.3	3.8	3.4	4.7	3.8	3.5
Price Range	91.00-60.25	92.75-62.00	70.59-45.84	53.67-46.04	63.00-45.84	51.04-33.89	36.11-27.72
P/E Ratio	28.3-18.8	257.6-172.2	17.5-11.4	15.0-12.9	13.3-9.7	14.3-9.5	8.0-6.2
Average Yield %	0.5	0.5	0.6	0.6	0.5	0.6	0.7

Statistics are as originally reported. Adj. for stk. splits: 50% div., 7/01; 3-for-2, 7/97 ① Incl. after-tax catastrophe losses of $139.8 mill. ② Incl. after-tax chrg. of $65.0 mill. for increase in reserves.

OFFICERS:
M. R. Greenberg, Chmn.
R. F. Orlich, Pres., C.E.O.
S. S. Skalicky, Exec. V.P., C.F.O.

INVESTOR CONTACT: Steven S. Skalicky, Exec. V.P., C.F.O., (212) 770-2040

PRINCIPAL OFFICE: 80 Pine Street, New York, NY 10005

TELEPHONE NUMBER: (212) 770-2000
FAX: (212) 785-7230
WEB: www.transre.com
NO. OF EMPLOYEES: 435 (approx.)
SHAREHOLDERS: 27,000 (approx.)
ANNUAL MEETING: In May
INCORPORATED: DE, 1986

INSTITUTIONAL HOLDINGS:
No. of Institutions: 99
Shares Held: 50,099,305
% Held: 96.3

INDUSTRY: Fire, marine, and casualty insurance (SIC: 6331)

TRANSFER AGENT(S): American Stock Transfer & Trust Company, New York, NY

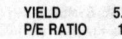

NASDAQ SYMBOL TRST
Rec. Pr. 11.46 (5/31/03)

TRUSTCO BANK CORP NY

YIELD 5.2%
P/E RATIO 16.9

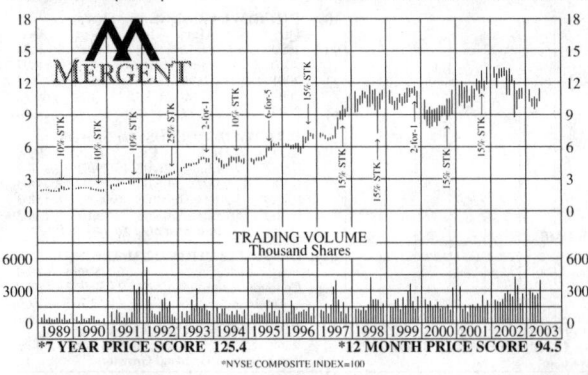

TRADING VOLUME
Thousand Shares

*7 YEAR PRICE SCORE 125.4   *12 MONTH PRICE SCORE 94.5
*NYSE COMPOSITE INDEX=100

INTERIM EARNINGS (Per Share):

Qtr.	Mar.	June	Sept.	Dec.
1999	0.13	0.13	0.14	0.13
2000	0.14	0.15	0.15	0.14
2001	0.16	0.16	0.14	0.16
2002	0.17	0.17	0.18	0.15
2003	0.18	...	...	...

INTERIM DIVIDENDS (Per Share):

Amt.	Decl.	Ex.	Rec.	Pay.
0.15Q	5/21/02	6/05/02	6/07/02	7/01/02
0.15Q	8/19/02	9/04/02	9/06/02	10/01/02
0.15Q	11/19/02	12/04/02	12/06/02	1/02/03
0.15Q	2/19/03	3/05/03	3/07/03	4/01/03
0.15Q	5/20/03	6/04/03	6/06/03	7/01/03

Indicated div.: $0.60 (Div. Reinv. Plan)

CAPITALIZATION (12/31/02):

	($000)	(%)
Total Deposits	2,274,268	90.6
Long-Term Debt	427	0.0
Common & Surplus	234,844	9.4
Total	2,509,539	100.0

DIVIDEND ACHIEVER STATUS:
Rank: 46   10-Year Growth Rate: 17.41%
Total Years of Dividend Growth: 26

RECENT DEVELOPMENTS: For the quarter ended 3/31/03, net income increased 6.7% to $13.2 million compared with $12.4 million in the corresponding period the year before. The increase in earnings was primarily due to higher average interest earning assets, a reduction in the provision for loan losses and an increase in non-interest income. Earnings included gains of $3.1 million and $1.9 million in 2003 and 2002, respectively, from securities transactions. Net interest income slipped to $23.7 million from $23.9 million in 2002. Provision for loan losses decreased 42.3% to $300,000 from $520,000 the previous year. Total non-interest income improved 16.2% to $7.9 million from $6.8 million in the prior year. Total non-interest expense grew 2.2% to $12.7 million from $12.4 million the year before. Net interest margin slid to 3.96% from 4.07% a year earlier. As of 3/31/03, total loans amounted to $1.35 billion and deposits were $2.30 billion.

BUSINESS

TRUSTCO BANK CORP NY is a multi-bank holding company for Trustco Bank, N.A. and Trustco Savings Bank. As of 3/31/03, assets totaled $2.71 billion. Trustco Bank provides a range of both personal and business banking services to individuals, partnerships, corporations, municipalities and governments of New York. As of 12/31/02, the bank operated 62 banking offices in Albany, Columbia, Dutchess, Greene, Montgomery, Rensselaer, Rockland, Saratoga, Schenectady, Schoharie, Warren, Washington, and Westchester counties in New York, and Bennington County in Vermont. The largest part of such business consists of accepting deposits and making loans and investments. Trustco Savings Bank operates one branch and one ATM, serving communities in Montgomery County, New York. In addition, the bank operates a full service trust department that has $897.0 million in assets under management. TRST also operates a non-bank subsidiary, ORE Subsidiary Corp., the manager of foreclosed properties acquired by the Bank.

ANNUAL FINANCIAL DATA

	12/31/02	12/31/01	12/31/00	12/31/99	12/31/98	12/31/97	12/31/96
Earnings Per Share	0.66	0.62	0.57	0.52	0.47	0.44	0.52
Tang. Book Val. Per Share	3.17	2.89	2.77	2.36	2.62	2.51	3.01
Dividends Per Share	0.60	0.52	0.45	0.42	0.36	0.31	0.27
Dividend Payout %	90.9	84.4	79.4	80.6	76.3	71.9	52.8
INCOME STATEMENT (IN MILLIONS):							
Total Interest Income	153.7	168.7	173.7	167.2	174.1	172.0	166.6
Total Interest Expense	58.0	72.8	75.6	74.0	88.3	86.5	82.3
Net Interest Income	95.7	95.9	98.1	93.2	85.7	85.5	84.3
Provision for Loan Losses	1.4	4.9	4.1	5.1	4.6	5.4	6.6
Non-Interest Income	27.3	25.8	16.4	15.4	22.1	17.2	10.3
Non-Interest Expense	55.3	51.3	47.8	45.6	48.8	46.2	42.0
Income Before Taxes	66.3	65.4	62.5	57.9	54.5	51.1	46.0
Net Income	49.2	45.5	41.7	38.2	35.0	32.2	28.7
Average Shs. Outstg. (000)	74,618	73,673	73,940	73,940	73,937	73,860	55,603
BALANCE SHEET (IN MILLIONS):							
Cash & Due from Banks	64.0	60.1	46.0	54.5	42.0	42.7	45.8
Securities Avail. for Sale	...	...	...	10.0	25.0	...	...
Total Loans & Leases	1,422.8	1,557.5	1,476.0	1,350.8	1,323.8	1,299.5	1,243.3
Allowance for Credit Losses	53.1	58.0	57.3	56.8	55.4	54.7	53.0
Net Loans & Leases	1,369.7	1,499.5	1,418.8	1,294.0	1,268.3	1,244.8	1,190.3
Total Assets	2,696.1	2,578.6	2,456.2	2,364.0	2,485.1	2,372.3	2,261.8
Total Deposits	2,274.3	2,092.9	2,011.0	1,994.9	2,107.4	2,021.9	1,953.1
Long-Term Obligations	0.4	0.6	0.9	...	...	...	...
Total Liabilities	2,461.2	2,372.8	2,260.4	2,197.7	2,299.2	2,193.4	2,099.4
Net Stockholders' Equity	234.8	205.8	195.8	166.4	185.8	178.8	162.4
Year-end Shs. Outstg. (000)	74,178	71,306	70,577	70,633	70,865	71,182	53,926
STATISTICAL RECORD:							
Return on Equity %	21.0	22.1	21.3	23.0	18.8	18.0	17.7
Return on Assets %	1.8	1.8	1.7	1.6	1.4	1.4	1.3
Equity/Assets %	8.7	8.0	8.0	7.0	7.5	7.5	7.2
Non-Int. Exp./Tot. Inc. %	47.9	43.8	40.0	40.0	45.6	44.9	42.4
Price Range	13.50-8.75	13.50-9.57	11.36-7.75	11.67-9.43	11.82-7.26	10.70-6.58	7.56-5.36
P/E Ratio	20.5-13.3	21.8-15.5	19.9-13.6	22.6-18.3	24.9-15.3	24.5-15.0	14.6-10.3
Average Yield %	5.4	4.5	4.7	3.9	3.8	3.6	4.2

Statistics are as originally reported. Adj. for stk. splits: 15% div., 11/01; 10/00; 2-for-1, 11/99; 15% div., 11/98; 15% div., 11/14/97; 15% div., 11/15/96.

OFFICERS:
J. A. Lucarelli, Chmn.
R. T. Cushing, Pres., C.E.O., C.F.O.
H. C. Collins, Sec.

INVESTOR CONTACT: William F. Terry, Sec., (518) 377-3311

PRINCIPAL OFFICE: 5 Sarnowski Drive, Glenville, NY 12302

TELEPHONE NUMBER: (518) 377-3311
FAX: (518) 381-3668
WEB: www.trustcobank.com
NO. OF EMPLOYEES: 488
SHAREHOLDERS: 13,621
ANNUAL MEETING: In May
INCORPORATED: NY, 1981

INSTITUTIONAL HOLDINGS:
No. of Institutions: 112
Shares Held: 18,935,886
% Held: 25.6

INDUSTRY: State commercial banks (SIC: 6022)

TRANSFER AGENT(S): Trustco Bank, Schenectady, NY

TRUSTMARK CORPORATION

YIELD	2.5%
P/E RATIO	13.9

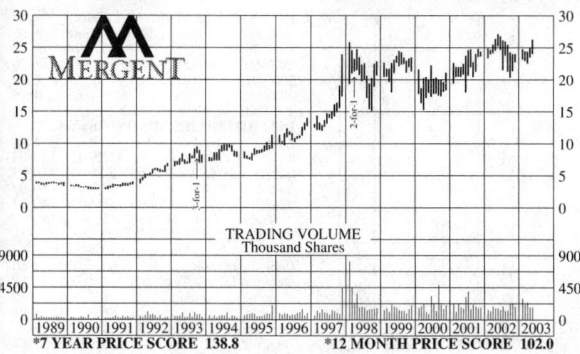

*7 YEAR PRICE SCORE 138.8 *12 MONTH PRICE SCORE 102.0
*NYSE COMPOSITE INDEX=100

INTERIM EARNINGS (Per Share):

Qtr.	Mar.	June	Sept.	Dec.
1999	0.33	0.34	0.35	0.34
2000	0.40	0.39	0.37	0.37
2001	0.40	0.41	0.45	0.46
2002	0.48	0.50	0.49	0.48
2003	0.41	...	...	...

INTERIM DIVIDENDS (Per Share):

Amt.	Decl.	Ex.	Rec.	Pay.
0.15Q	7/16/02	8/28/02	9/01/02	9/15/02
0.165Q	10/15/02	11/26/02	12/01/02	12/15/02
0.165Q	1/21/03	3/04/03	3/01/03	3/15/03
0.165Q	4/15/03	5/28/03	6/01/03	6/15/03

Indicated div.: $0.66 (Div. Reinv. Plan)

CAPITALIZATION (12/31/02):

	($000)	(%)
Total Deposits	4,686,296	80.2
Long-Term Debt	475,000	8.1
Common & Surplus	679,534	11.6
Total	5,840,830	100.0

DIVIDEND ACHIEVER STATUS:

Rank: 87	10-Year Growth Rate:	13.14%
Total Years of Dividend Growth:		29

RECENT DEVELOPMENTS: On 5/22/03, TRMK announced that it has signed a letter of intent to acquire seven branches in Florida, which reported total deposits of $205.0 million as of 3/31/03, from The Banc Corporation. The transaction is expected to close in the third quarter of 2003. Meanwhile, for the quarter ended 3/31/03, net income slid 19.3% to $24.5 million from $30.3 million in the corresponding period of the prior year. Earnings for 2003 and 2002 included security gains of $8.1 million and $140,000, amortization of intangible assets of $11.7 million and $986,000, and pre-tax gains on the sale of loans of $3.9 million and $1.5 million, respectively. Net interest income slipped 6.4% to $71.4 million from $76.3 million the year before. Provision for loan losses fell 30.3% to $3.0 million. Total non-interest income advanced 42.1% to $41.2 million, while total non-interest expense was up 34.1% to $69.7 million.

BUSINESS

TRUSTMARK CORPORATION is the holding company for Trustmark National Bank, along with its wholly-owned subsidiaries Trustmark Financial Services, Inc., Trustmark Investment Advisors, Inc. and The Bottrell Insurance Agency, Inc. The Company also provides banking services through its wholly-owned subsidiary, Somerville Bank & Trust Company. TRMK engages in business through four reportable segments: Retail Banking, Commercial Banking, Financial Services, and Treasury & Other. Retail Banking provides a full range of financial products and services to individuals and small business customers through over 130 offices in Mississippi and Tennessee. Commercial Banking provides various financial products and services to corporate and middle market clients through the Company's commercial lending, commercial real estate, indirect lending and private banking groups. Financial Services includes trust and fiduciary services, brokerage services, insurance services, as well as credit card and mortgage services. Included in Financial Services is TRMK's proprietary mutual fund family, The Performance Funds. Treasury & Other consists of the Company's internal operations.

ANNUAL FINANCIAL DATA

	12/31/02	12/31/01	12/31/00	12/31/99	12/31/98	12/31/97	12/31/96
Earnings Per Share	1.94	1.72	① 1.53	1.36	1.14	0.98	0.93
Tang. Book Val. Per Share	9.25	8.93	8.70	8.39	8.29	7.61	6.95
Dividends Per Share	0.62	0.56	0.51	0.44	0.35	0.29	0.25
Dividend Payout %	32.0	32.3	33.3	32.4	30.9	29.8	26.9
INCOME STATEMENT (IN MILLIONS):							
Total Interest Income	406.0	477.8	488.8	448.5	420.1	376.9	358.1
Total Interest Expense	113.8	209.2	255.2	205.1	191.9	172.9	164.0
Net Interest Income	292.2	268.6	233.6	243.4	228.2	204.0	194.1
Provision for Loan Losses	14.1	13.2	10.4	9.1	7.8	4.7	5.8
Non-Interest Income	141.9	132.0	124.5	101.9	89.1	75.6	67.0
Non-Interest Expense	233.8	215.9	189.4	187.1	180.4	167.9	157.8
Income Before Taxes	186.1	171.4	158.3	149.2	129.1	107.0	97.4
Net Income	121.1	111.3	① 104.2	98.0	83.3	71.1	65.1
Average Shs. Outstg. (000)	62,416	64,877	67,929	71,921	72,946	72,786	69,822
BALANCE SHEET (IN MILLIONS):							
Cash & Due from Banks	357.4	328.8	298.7	280.0	312.5	292.6	337.1
Securities Avail. for Sale	1,262.6	1,061.5	1,120.6	783.2	776.0	610.6	528.0
Total Loans & Leases	4,617.4	4,524.4	4,143.9	4,014.9	3,702.3	2,983.7	2,634.6
Allowance for Credit Losses	74.8	75.5	65.9	65.9	66.2	64.1	63.0
Net Loans & Leases	4,542.6	4,448.8	4,078.1	3,949.1	3,636.2	2,919.6	2,571.6
Total Assets	7,138.7	7,180.3	6,887.0	6,743.4	6,355.2	5,545.2	5,193.7
Total Deposits	4,686.3	4,613.4	4,058.4	3,924.8	3,946.4	3,818.9	3,597.4
Long-Term Obligations	475.0	225.0	250.0	...	...	...	...
Total Liabilities	6,459.2	6,494.9	6,257.3	6,087.6	5,703.3	4,951.5	4,669.5
Net Stockholders' Equity	679.5	685.4	629.6	655.8	651.9	593.6	524.2
Year-end Shs. Outstg. (000)	60,517	63,706	64,755	70,424	72,532	72,740	69,822
STATISTICAL RECORD:							
Return on Equity %	17.8	16.2	16.5	14.9	12.8	12.0	12.4
Return on Assets %	1.7	1.5	1.5	1.5	1.3	1.3	1.3
Equity/Assets %	9.5	9.5	9.1	9.7	10.3	10.7	10.1
Non-Int. Exp./Tot. Inc. %	53.9	53.9	52.9	54.2	56.9	60.1	60.5
Price Range	27.14-20.35	24.82-18.00	22.25-15.25	24.50-18.00	25.88-15.13	24.00-12.00	14.00-9.75
P/E Ratio	14.0-10.5	14.4-10.5	14.5-10.0	18.0-13.2	22.7-13.3	24.5-12.2	15.1-10.5
Average Yield %	2.6	2.6	2.7	2.1	1.7	1.6	2.1

Statistics are as originally reported. Adj. for stk. splits: 2-for-1, 3/30/98. ① Bef. acctg. change chrg. $2.5 mill. ($0.03/sh.)

OFFICERS:
R. G. Hickson, Chmn., Pres., C.E.O.
Z. L. Wasson, Jr., Treas.
T. H. Collier, III, Sec.

INVESTOR CONTACT: Joseph Rein, Vice Pres., Inv. Rel., (601) 949-6898

PRINCIPAL OFFICE: 248 East Capitol Street, Jackson, MS 39201

TELEPHONE NUMBER: (601) 354-5111
FAX: (601) 354-5053
WEB: www.trustmark.com

NO. OF EMPLOYEES: 2,443

SHAREHOLDERS: 4,600 (approx.)

ANNUAL MEETING: In Apr.

INCORPORATED: MS, Aug., 1968

INSTITUTIONAL HOLDINGS:
No. of Institutions: 92
Shares Held: 9,519,772
% Held: 16.1

INDUSTRY: National commercial banks (SIC: 6021)

TRANSFER AGENT(S): Trustmark National Bank, Jackson, MS

NYSE SYMBOL UGI
Rec. Pr. 34.20 (5/31/03)

UGI CORPORATION

YIELD 3.3%
P/E RATIO 14.2

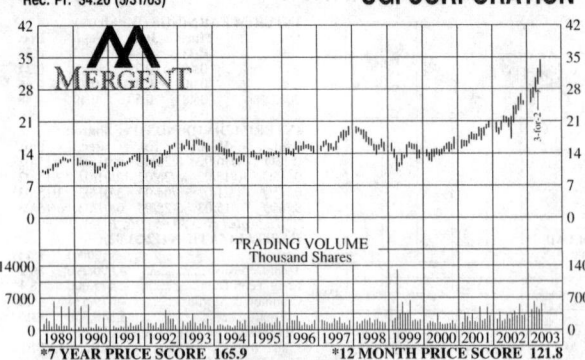

TRADING VOLUME
Thousand Shares

| 1989 | 1990 | 1991 | 1992 | 1993 | 1994 | 1995 | 1996 | 1997 | 1998 | 1999 | 2000 | 2001 | 2002 | 2003 |

*7 YEAR PRICE SCORE 165.9   *12 MONTH PRICE SCORE 121.8
*NYSE COMPOSITE INDEX=100

INTERIM EARNINGS (Per Share):

Qtr.	Dec.	Mar.	June	Sept.
1998-99	0.37	0.76	0.24	d0.21
1999-00	0.51	0.95	d0.11	d0.26
2000-01	0.67	1.11	d0.11	d0.40
2001-02	0.58	1.28	0.09	d0.16
2002-03	0.86	1.62	...	...

INTERIM DIVIDENDS (Per Share):

Amt.	Decl.	Ex.	Rec.	Pay.
0.412Q	10/29/02	11/26/02	11/29/02	1/01/03
0.427Q	1/29/03	2/26/03	2/28/03	4/01/03
3-for-2	1/29/03	4/02/03	2/28/03	4/01/03
0.285Q	4/29/03	5/28/03	5/30/03	7/01/03

Indicated div.: $1.14 (Div. Reinv. Plan)

CAPITALIZATION (9/30/02):

	($000)	(%)
Long-Term Debt	1,127,000	68.5
Deferred Income Tax	200,200	12.2
Common & Surplus	317,300	19.3
Total	1,644,500	100.0

DIVIDEND ACHIEVER STATUS:
Rank: 271   10-Year Growth Rate: 2.50%
Total Years of Dividend Growth: 15

RECENT DEVELOPMENTS: For the quarter ended 3/31/03, net income was $69.8 million versus $54.0 million in the corresponding year-earlier period. Results for 2003 included a pre-tax loss of $3.0 million on the extinguishment of debt. Total revenues climbed 48.7% to $1.14 billion. UGI attributed the improved results, in part, to the continuation of colder weather patterns over the course of the heating season. Operating income rose 22.5% to $184.4 million.

PROSPECTS: During the quarter ended 3/31/03, UGI announced that its electricity generation subsidiary, UGI Development Company, has signed a definitive agreement to acquire the 83 megawatt ownership interest in the Conemaugh generating station of Allegheny Energy Supply Company, LLC for about $51.3 million. Also, UGI's energy marketing subsidiary, UGI Energy Services, Inc., has agreed to acquire the gas marketing business of TXU Energy serving the northeast region of the United States.

BUSINESS

UGI CORPORATION is a holding company that operates propane distribution, gas and electric utility, energy marketing and related businesses through subsidiaries. The Company's majority-owned subsidiary AmeriGas Partners, L.P. conducts a retail propane distribution business. UGI Utilities, Inc. owns and operates a natural gas distribution utility and an electricity distribution utility in eastern Pennsylvania. UGI Enterprises, Inc., conducts domestic and international energy-related businesses through subsidiaries. Enterprises operates UGI Energy Services, which markets natural gas, oil and electricity, and UGI HVAC Enterprises, Inc., a heating and cooling installation and services business in the Mid-Atlantic region. Additionally, Enterprises owns FLAGA GmbH, which is engaged in the distribution of propane in Austria, the Czech Republic, and Slovakia. Enterprises also participates in a propane distribution joint venture in China.

ANNUAL FINANCIAL DATA

	9/30/02	9/30/01	9/30/00	9/30/99	9/30/98	9/30/97	9/30/96
Earnings Per Share	1.80	② 1.27	1.09	① 1.16	0.81	1.05	0.79
Cash Flow Per Share	4.03	3.83	3.48	3.03	2.58	2.78	2.52
Dividends Per Share	1.08	1.05	1.02	0.98	0.97	0.95	0.94
Dividend Payout %	60.2	82.9	93.0	84.5	118.9	91.0	118.5
INCOME STATEMENT (IN MILLIONS):							
Total Revenues	2,213.7	2,468.1	1,761.7	1,383.6	1,439.7	1,642.0	1,557.6
Costs & Expenses	1,867.6	2,135.5	1,473.0	1,118.0	1,181.7	1,356.0	1,311.9
Depreciation & Amort.	93.5	105.2	97.5	89.7	87.8	86.1	86.0
Operating Income	252.6	227.4	191.2	175.9	170.2	199.9	159.7
Net Interest Inc./(Exp.)	d109.1	d104.8	d98.5	d84.6	d84.4	d83.1	d79.5
Income Before Income Taxes	122.4	97.4	84.8	98.9	74.7	95.7	73.1
Income Taxes	46.9	45.4	40.1	43.2	34.4	43.6	33.6
Net Income	75.5	② 52.0	44.7	① 55.7	40.3	52.1	39.5
Cash Flow	169.0	157.2	142.2	145.4	128.1	138.2	125.5
Average Shs. Outstg. (000)	41,907	41,060	40,883	48,024	49,685	49,698	49,713
BALANCE SHEET (IN MILLIONS):							
Cash & Cash Equivalents	194.3	91.1	101.7	55.6	148.4	129.4	97.1
Total Current Assets	530.0	458.9	426.1	290.9	350.6	403.9	381.6
Net Property	1,271.9	1,268.0	1,073.2	1,084.1	999.0	987.2	974.6
Total Assets	2,614.4	2,550.2	2,278.8	2,135.9	2,074.6	2,151.7	2,144.9
Total Current Liabilities	586.4	567.5	539.4	402.3	321.8	404.5	369.2
Long-Term Obligations	1,127.0	1,196.9	1,029.7	989.6	890.8	844.8	845.2
Net Stockholders' Equity	317.3	255.6	247.2	249.2	367.1	376.1	377.6
Net Working Capital	d56.4	d108.6	d113.3	d111.4	28.8	d0.6	12.4
Year-end Shs. Outstg. (000)	41,552	40,945	40,491	40,906	49,235	49,799	49,704
STATISTICAL RECORD:							
Operating Profit Margin %	11.4	9.2	10.9	12.7	11.8	12.2	10.3
Net Profit Margin %	3.4	2.1	2.5	4.0	2.8	3.2	2.5
Return on Equity %	23.8	20.3	18.1	22.4	11.0	13.9	10.5
Return on Assets %	2.9	2.0	2.0	2.6	1.9	2.4	1.8
Debt/Total Assets %	43.1	46.9	45.2	46.3	42.9	39.3	39.4
Price Range	26.99-17.11	21.02-15.00	17.54-12.13	16.46-10.00	19.83-13.67	19.92-14.42	16.58-13.33
P/E Ratio	15.0-9.5	16.6-11.8	16.0-11.1	14.2-8.6	24.4-16.8	19.0-13.8	20.9-16.8
Average Yield %	4.9	5.8	6.9	7.4	5.8	5.6	6.3

Statistics are as originally reported. Adj. for 3-for-2 split, 4/03. Incl. results of AP Propane on a consolidated basis for all yrs. shown. ① Incl. non-recurr. chrg. of $1.6 mill. ② Incl. non-recurr. chrg. of $8.5 mill.; bef. acctg. chge. gain of $4.5 mill.

OFFICERS:
L. R. Greenberg, Chmn., Pres., C.E.O.
A. J. Mendicino, Sr. V.P., C.F.O.
B. P. Bovaird, V.P., Gen. Couns.

INVESTOR CONTACT: Robert W. Krick, Treas., (610) 337-1000, ext. 3141

PRINCIPAL OFFICE: 460 North Gulph Road, King of Prussia, PA 19406

TELEPHONE NUMBER: (610) 337-1000
FAX: (610) 992-3254
WEB: www.ugicorp.com

NO. OF EMPLOYEES: 6,300 (approx.)

SHAREHOLDERS: 10,054 (record)

ANNUAL MEETING: In Feb.

INCORPORATED: PA, 1991

UNITED BANKSHARES, INC.

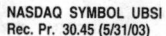

YIELD 3.3%
P/E RATIO 14.6

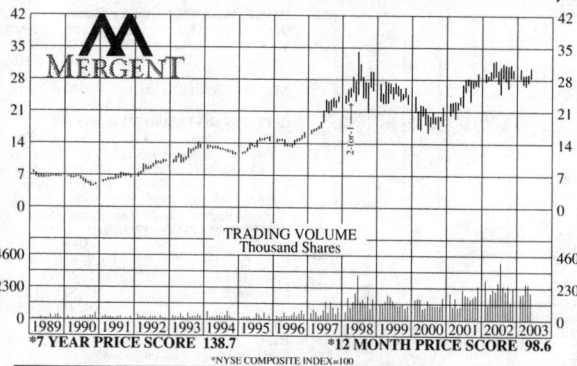

	42
	35
	28
	21
	14
	7
	0

TRADING VOLUME
Thousand Shares

4600
2300
0

1989 1990 1991 1992 1993 1994 1995 1996 1997 1998 1999 2000 2001 2002 2003

7 YEAR PRICE SCORE 138.7   **12 MONTH PRICE SCORE 98.6**
*NYSE COMPOSITE INDEX=100

INTERIM EARNINGS (Per Share):

Qtr.	Mar.	June	Sept.	Dec.
2000	0.42	0.43	0.44	0.11
2001	0.46	0.47	0.48	0.49
2002	0.50	0.51	0.52	0.53
2003	0.53	...	...	...

INTERIM DIVIDENDS (Per Share):

Amt.	Decl.	Ex.	Rec.	Pay.
0.24Q	8/26/02	9/11/02	9/13/02	10/01/02
0.25Q	11/25/02	12/11/02	12/13/02	1/02/03
0.25Q	2/24/03	3/12/03	3/14/03	4/01/03
0.25Q	5/19/03	6/11/03	6/13/03	7/01/03

Indicated div.: $1.00 (Div. Reinv. Plan)

CAPITALIZATION (12/31/02):

	($000)	(%)
Total Deposits	3,900,848	76.2
Long-Term Debt	679,712	13.3
Common & Surplus	541,539	10.6
Total	5,122,099	100.0

DIVIDEND ACHIEVER STATUS:
Rank: 176   10-Year Growth Rate: 8.27%
Total Years of Dividend Growth: 21

RECENT DEVELOPMENTS: For the quarter ended 3/31/03, net income rose 3.3% to $22.5 million from $21.8 million in the corresponding prior-year period. Earnings included a gain of $866,000 in 2003 and a loss of $304,000 in 2002 on security transactions. Total interest income declined 9.4% to $79.8 million, while total interest expense fell 14.4% to $29.6 million. Net interest income slipped 6.0% to $47.6 million. Provision for loan losses declined 34.7% to $1.5 million. Total non-interest income advanced 9.9% to $10.8 million, primarily due to increased mortgage-banking income and fees from deposit services. Total non-interest expense rose 17.3% to $37.6 million, reflecting increased employee salaries and related benefits. Separately, on 4/7/03, UBSI signed a definitive agreement to acquire Sequoia Bancshares, Inc., which has $547.0 million in assets, for about $109.0 million. As a result of the acquisition, which is expected to be completed during the fourth quarter of 2003, UBSI will have consolidated assets of over $6.40 billion with 97 full service offices in West Virginia, Virginia, Maryland, Ohio and Washington, D.C.

BUSINESS

UNITED BANKSHARES, INC. is a bank holding company with assets of $5.82 billion as of 3/31/03. UBSI, through its subsidiaries, United National Bank and United Bank, engages primarily in community banking and mortgage banking and additionally offers most types of business permitted by law and regulation. Included among the banking services offered are the acceptance of deposits in checking, savings, time and money market accounts; the making and servicing of personal, commercial, floor plan and student loans; and the making of construction and real estate loans. UBSI also owns nonbank subsidiaries that engage in mortgage banking, asset management, investment banking and financial planning. As of 4/17/03, the Company operated 85 offices in West Virginia, Virginia, Maryland, Ohio, and Washington. Net interest income (non-interest income) for 2002 were derived as follows: community banking, 92.8% (50.7%); mortgage banking, 6.1% (49.2%); and general corporate and other, 1.1% (0.1%).

ANNUAL FINANCIAL DATA

	12/31/02	12/31/01	12/31/00	12/31/99	12/31/98	12/31/97	12/31/96
Earnings Per Share	2.06	1.90	1.40	1.61	1.02	1.35	1.00
Tang. Book Val. Per Share	10.73	11.80	10.32	9.32	9.75	9.32	8.57
Dividends Per Share	0.93	0.89	0.84	0.81	0.72	0.66	0.61
Dividend Payout %	45.1	46.8	60.0	50.3	70.6	48.9	61.0
INCOME STATEMENT (IN MILLIONS):							
Total Interest Income	339.5	360.6	377.8	354.7	325.6	190.3	172.4
Total Interest Expense	132.6	175.5	197.8	174.4	155.4	84.5	73.2
Net Interest Income	206.9	185.1	180.1	180.3	170.3	105.8	99.2
Provision for Loan Losses	7.9	12.8	15.7	8.8	12.2	3.1	2.6
Non-Interest Income	73.5	62.2	33.8	51.1	41.8	19.7	14.2
Non-Interest Expense	144.1	115.7	110.4	117.5	138.0	59.9	63.5
Income Before Taxes	128.3	118.7	87.7	105.0	61.9	64.2	47.2
Net Income	88.9	80.0	59.0	70.2	44.4	40.9	30.5
Average Shs. Outstg. (000)	43,113	42,065	42,260	43,722	43,461	30,272	30,506
BALANCE SHEET (IN MILLIONS):							
Cash & Due from Banks	162.3	156.1	142.8	131.1	124.6	80.4	86.3
Securities Avail. for Sale	1,022.3	1,147.3	865.3	1,207.4	565.2	273.9	161.6
Total Loans & Leases	3,576.3	3,505.4	3,197.5	3,177.4	2,659.3	2,060.5	1,851.3
Allowance for Credit Losses	50.5	50.5	45.5	46.9	46.1	31.8	27.4
Net Loans & Leases	3,525.8	3,454.9	3,152.0	3,130.5	2,613.2	2,028.7	1,823.8
Total Assets	5,792.0	5,631.8	4,904.5	5,069.2	4,567.9	2,699.8	2,326.9
Total Deposits	3,900.8	3,787.8	3,391.4	3,261.0	3,493.1	2,106.0	1,827.6
Long-Term Obligations	679.7	736.5	706.5	953.3	345.9	142.7	132.6
Total Liabilities	5,250.5	5,125.2	4,473.7	4,673.2	4,146.4	2,420.4	2,068.4
Net Stockholders' Equity	541.5	506.5	430.9	395.9	421.5	279.4	258.5
Year-end Shs. Outstg. (000)	42,032	42,927	41,765	42,487	43,256	29,968	30,180
STATISTICAL RECORD:							
Return on Equity %	16.4	15.8	13.7	17.7	10.5	14.7	11.8
Return on Assets %	1.5	1.4	1.2	1.4	1.0	1.5	1.3
Equity/Assets %	9.3	9.0	8.8	7.8	9.2	10.4	11.1
Non-Int. Exp./Tot. Inc. %	51.4	46.8	51.6	50.8	65.1	47.8	56.1
Price Range	32.25-24.88	29.50-19.44	24.44-16.38	27.69-22.63	34.19-20.75	24.38-16.13	16.50-13.13
P/E Ratio	15.7-12.1	15.5-10.2	17.5-11.7	17.2-14.1	33.5-20.3	18.1-11.9	16.5-13.1
Average Yield %	3.3	3.6	4.1	3.2	2.6	3.3	4.1

Statistics are as originally reported. Adj. for 2-for-1 stk. split, 3/98.

OFFICERS:
R. M. Adams, Chmn., C.E.O.
S. E. Wilson, C.F.O., Chief Acctg. Officer

INVESTOR CONTACT: Steven E. Wilson, C.F.O. & C.A.O., (304) 424-8704

PRINCIPAL OFFICE: 300 United Center, 500 Virginia Street East, Charleston, WV 25301

TELEPHONE NUMBER: (304) 424-8800
FAX: (304) 424-8758
WEB: www.ubsi-wv.com
NO. OF EMPLOYEES: 1,460 (approx.)
SHAREHOLDERS: 12,278 (approx.)
ANNUAL MEETING: In May
INCORPORATED: WV, Mar., 1982

UNITED DOMINION REALTY TRUST, INC.

YIELD 6.7%
P/E RATIO 81.4

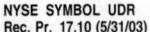
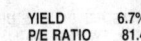
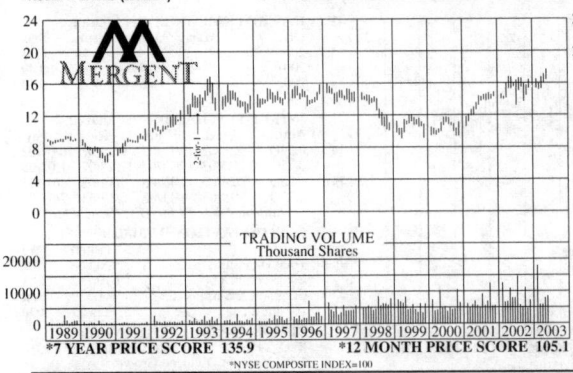

INTERIM EARNINGS (Per Share):

Qtr.	Mar.	June	Sept.	Dec.
1999	0.19	0.39	0.10	0.21
2000	0.18	0.12	0.20	0.07
2001	0.06	0.32	0.14	0.13
2002	0.07	0.07	0.03	0.06
2003	0.05	...	...	...

INTERIM DIVIDENDS (Per Share):

Amt.	Decl.	Ex.	Rec.	Pay.
0.278Q	9/26/02	10/09/02	10/11/02	10/31/02
0.278Q	12/05/02	1/15/03	1/17/03	1/31/03
0.285Q	3/13/03	4/09/03	4/11/03	4/30/03
0.285Q	6/12/03	7/16/03	7/18/03	7/31/03

Indicated div.: **$1.14** (Div. Reinv. Plan)

CAPITALIZATION (12/31/02):

	($000)	(%)
Long-Term Debt	2,057,640	67.3
Preferred Stock	310,400	10.1
Common & Surplus	690,871	22.6
Total	3,058,911	100.0

DIVIDEND ACHIEVER STATUS:
Rank: 233   10-Year Growth Rate: 5.34%
Total Years of Dividend Growth: 17

TRADING VOLUME
Thousand Shares

| 1989 | 1990 | 1991 | 1992 | 1993 | 1994 | 1995 | 1996 | 1997 | 1998 | 1999 | 2000 | 2001 | 2002 | 2003 |

*7 YEAR PRICE SCORE 135.9   ***12 MONTH PRICE SCORE 105.1**

*NYSE COMPOSITE INDEX=100

RECENT DEVELOPMENTS: For the quarter ended 3/31/03, the Company reported income of $12.0 million, before income from discontinued operations of $1.5 million, versus a loss of $2.6 million, before income from discontinued operations of $891,000, in the equivalent prior-year quarter. Results included a gain on the early retirement of debt of $182,000 in 2003 versus a loss of $15.8 million in 2002. Also, results for 2002 included a gain on the sale of depreciable property of $1.2 million. Rental income increased 3.9% to $151.4 million from $145.7 million a year earlier.

PROSPECTS: Earnings continue to reflect weak fundamentals in the apartment sector. However, the Company is experiencing signs that indicate some of its markets are beginning to stabilize. During the first quarter, average physical occupancy at same-property communities increased to 93.5% from 93.3% in the fourth quarter of 2002. Moreover, rent concessions as a percentage of gross potential rent declined to 2.9% from 3.1%. Given current expectations, UDR remains confident that it can achieve funds from operations for 2003 of $1.51 to $1.59 per share.

BUSINESS

UNITED DOMINION REALTY TRUST, INC. is a self-administered equity real estate investment trust with activities related to the ownership, development, acquisition, renovation, management, marketing and strategic disposition of multifamily apartment communities nationwide. At 3/31/03, UDR's apartment portfolio included 258 communities located in 19 states, with a total of 74,262 completed apartment homes. In addition, the Company had 1,120 apartment homes under development. The Company's apartment communities consist primarily of upper- and middle-income garden and townhouse communities that make up the broadest segment of the apartment market. UDR has regional offices in Richmond, Dallas and Atlanta.

ANNUAL FINANCIAL DATA

	12/31/02	12/31/01	12/31/00	12/31/99	12/31/98	12/31/97	12/31/96
Earnings Per Share	①③ 0.21	①② 0.27	① 0.41	①② 0.54	①② 0.49	①② 0.60	①② 0.49
Tang. Book Val. Per Share	6.48	7.10	7.91	8.59	9.11	9.01	9.09
Dividends Per Share	1.10	1.08	1.07	1.06	1.04	1.00	0.94
Dividend Payout %	524.8	398.9	260.3	195.8	212.2	166.2	192.8

INCOME STATEMENT (IN MILLIONS):

Rental Income	594.3	618.6	616.8	618.7	478.7	386.7	242.1
Total Income	596.1	623.2	622.2	620.7	482.1	387.8	243.8
Costs & Expenses	257.2	278.7	260.0	280.4	225.3	172.2	110.5
Depreciation	156.3	155.3	157.4	126.2	103.2	78.8	48.7
Interest Expense	131.0	144.4	156.0	153.7	106.2	79.0	50.8
Income Before Income Taxes	53.0	69.5	80.2	98.4	74.0	70.5	38.1
Equity Earnings/Minority Int.	d2.9	d4.2	d4.4	d5.7	d1.5	d0.3	d0.1
Net Income	①③ 50.1	①② 65.3	① 75.8	①② 92.7	①② 72.5	①② 70.2	①② 38.0
Average Shs. Outstg. (000)	106,952	101,037	103,208	103,639	100,062	87,339	57,482

BALANCE SHEET (IN MILLIONS):

Cash & Cash Equivalents	14.9	31.5	55.2	64.6	76.9	17.6	13.5
Total Real Estate Investments	3,165.9	3,212.2	3,252.1	3,204.7	3,362.6	2,080.9	1,834.3
Total Assets	3,276.1	3,348.1	3,454.0	3,688.3	3,762.9	2,313.7	1,966.9
Long-Term Obligations	2,057.6	2,064.2	1,992.3	2,127.3	2,117.7	1,156.2	1,044.8
Total Liabilities	2,205.6	2,229.7	2,146.7	2,283.9	2,273.4	1,240.7	1,114.5
Net Stockholders' Equity	1,001.3	1,042.7	1,218.9	1,310.2	1,374.1	1,058.4	850.4
Year-end Shs. Outstg. (000)	106,605	103,133	102,219	102,741	103,639	89,168	81,983

STATISTICAL RECORD:

Net Inc.+Depr./Assets %	6.3	6.6	6.8	5.9	4.7	6.4	4.4
Return on Equity %	5.0	6.3	6.2	7.1	5.3	6.6	4.5
Return on Assets %	1.5	2.0	2.2	2.5	1.9	3.0	1.9
Price Range	16.81-13.18	14.85-10.56	11.75-9.38	12.06-9.06	14.81-10.06	16.00-13.33	15.81-13.13
P/E Ratio	80.0-62.7	55.0-39.1	28.7-22.9	22.3-16.8	30.2-20.5	26.7-22.3	32.3-26.8
Average Yield %	7.4	8.5	10.1	10.0	8.4	6.8	6.5

Statistics are as originally reported. ① Bef. extraord. chrg. $33.8 mill., 12/02; $3.5 mill., 12/01; gain, $831,000, 12/00; $927,000, 12/99; chrg. $138,000, 12/98; chrg. $50,000, 12/97; $23,000, 12/96. ② Incl. non-recurr. chrg. $10.8 mill., 12/01; $19.3 mill., 12/99; $15.6 mill., 12/98; $1.4 mill., 12/97; $290,000, 12/96. ③ Bef. inc. fr. disc. opers of $36.9 mill.

OFFICERS:
R. Larson, Chmn.
T. W. Toomey, Pres., C.E.O.
C. Genry, C.F.O.

INVESTOR CONTACT: Ella Neyland, Investor Relations, (720) 283-6144

PRINCIPAL OFFICE: 1745 Shea Center Dr., Ste. 200, Highland Ranch, CO 80129

TELEPHONE NUMBER: (720) 283-6120
FAX: (720) 283-2454
WEB: www.udrt.com

NO. OF EMPLOYEES: 1,909

SHAREHOLDERS: 7,464

ANNUAL MEETING: In May

INCORPORATED: VA, Dec., 1984

INSTITUTIONAL HOLDINGS:
No. of Institutions: 196
Shares Held: 60,292,913
% Held: 55.3

INDUSTRY: Real estate investment trusts (SIC: 6798)

TRANSFER AGENT(S): Mellon Investor Services, Pittsburgh, PA

Price to Earnings

Price to Sales

Price to Cash Flow

Earnings per share

Return on Equity

Return on assets

UNITED MOBILE HOMES, INC.

YIELD 5.7%
P/E RATIO 18.9

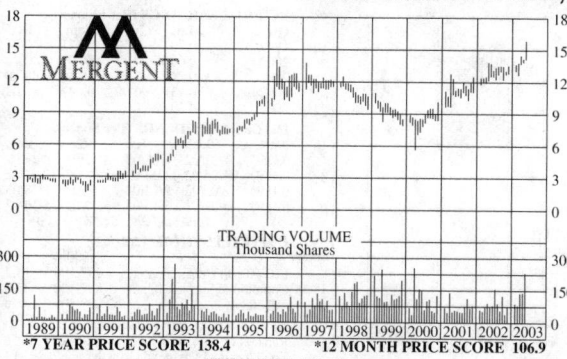

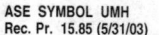

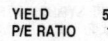

INTERIM EARNINGS (Per Share):

Qtr.	Mar.	June	Sept.	Dec.
1999	0.15	0.15	0.15	0.18
2000	0.20	0.17	0.18	0.16
2001	0.19	0.22	0.23	0.10
2002	0.24	0.20	0.19	0.22
2003	0.23	...	...	...

INTERIM DIVIDENDS (Per Share):

Amt.	Decl.	Ex.	Rec.	Pay.
0.215Q	3/15/02	5/13/02	5/15/02	6/17/02
0.217Q	6/20/02	8/13/02	8/15/02	9/16/02
0.22Q	9/27/02	11/13/02	11/15/02	12/16/02
0.223Q	1/16/03	2/13/03	2/18/03	3/17/03
0.225Q	3/15/03	5/13/03	5/15/03	6/16/03

Indicated div.: $0.90 (Div. Reinv. Plan)

CAPITALIZATION (12/31/02):

	($000)	(%)
Long-Term Debt	43,322	59.3
Common & Surplus	29,736	40.7
Total	73,058	100.0

DIVIDEND ACHIEVER STATUS:
Rank: 71   10-Year Growth Rate: 14.42%
Total Years of Dividend Growth: 12

TRADING VOLUME
Thousand Shares

*7 YEAR PRICE SCORE 138.4   *12 MONTH PRICE SCORE 106.9
*NYSE COMPOSITE INDEX=100

RECENT DEVELOPMENTS: For the quarter ended 3/31/03, net income declined 2.7% to $1.8 million versus $1.9 million in the corresponding year-earlier period. Results for 2003 and 2002 included gains on investment property and equipment of $6,302 and $3,327, respectively. Total revenues rose 9.6% to $7.8 million. Rental and related income grew 3.3% to $5.1 million, primarily due to rental increases to residents. UMH noted that it has been raising rental rates by about 3.0% to 4.0% annually. Revenues included inter-est and dividend income of $885,361 and $618,115, respectively. Funds from operations (FFO) slipped 1.5% to $2.5 million. FFO is defined as net income excluding gains or losses from sales of depreciable assets, plus depreciation. Separately, on 5/15/03, UMH acquired Northway Manor Mobile Home Park in West Monroe, New York, a community consisting of 150 manufactured home sites of which 65 are currently occupied. The community was purchased for a price of approximately $900,000.

BUSINESS

UNITED MOBILE HOMES, INC., a real estate investment trust, owned and operated 26 manufactured home communities containing over 6,000 sites, as of 5/28/03. The communities are located in New Jersey, New York, Ohio, Pennsylvania, and Tennessee. The Company's primary business is leasing manufactured home spaces on a month-to-month basis to private manufactured home owners. UMH also leases manufactured homes to residents.

ANNUAL FINANCIAL DATA

	12/31/02	12/31/01	12/31/00	12/31/99	12/31/98	12/31/97	12/31/96
Earnings Per Share	③ 0.85	①② 0.74	①② 0.71	①② 0.63	③ 0.60	② 0.63	③ 0.61
Tang. Book Val. Per Share	3.88	3.71	3.09	2.93	3.20	3.03	2.55
Dividends Per Share	0.86	0.80	0.76	0.75	0.74	0.70	0.60
Dividend Payout %	99.5	108.4	106.7	119.0	122.9	111.1	98.3
INCOME STATEMENT (IN THOUSANDS):							
Total Income	29,424	26,882	20,645	18,807	17,193	15,664	14,627
Costs & Expenses	20,654	18,531	12,710	11,719	10,496	9,297	9,169
Depreciation	2,923	2,772	2,708	2,530	2,509	2,159	2,007
Inc. bef. gain (loss) on invest. prop. & equip.	5,848	5,579	5,227	4,558	4,189	4,208	3,396
Inc. (loss) on sale of assets	665	d28	d37	d2	13	d11	334
Net Income	③ 6,512	①② 5,550	①② 5,189	①② 4,556	③ 4,202	② 4,197	③ 3,730
Average Shs. Outstg.	7,677	7,496	7,341	7,268	7,061	6,680	6,073
BALANCE SHEET (IN THOUSANDS):							
Cash & Cash Equivalents	35,124	27,486	16,894	13,519	8,585	3,739	2,636
Total Real Estate Investments	39,866	40,681	38,418	39,193	36,252	35,293	27,724
Total Assets	89,027	80,335	62,946	58,575	50,047	43,599	35,875
Long-Term Obligations	43,322	38,652	32,056	30,419	21,412	20,111	17,351
Total Liabilities	59,290	52,370	40,106	37,184	26,834	22,769	19,449
Net Stockholders' Equity	29,736	27,965	22,839	21,391	23,213	20,831	16,426
Year-end Shs. Outstg.	7,671	7,542	7,394	7,313	7,247	6,865	6,434
STATISTICAL RECORD:							
Net Inc.+Depr./Assets %	10.6	10.4	12.5	12.1	13.4	14.6	16.0
Return on Equity %	21.9	19.8	22.7	21.3	18.1	20.1	22.7
Return on Assets %	7.3	6.9	8.2	7.8	8.4	9.6	10.4
Price Range	13.85-11.77	12.75-9.63	10.13-5.63	10.94-7.88	12.50-9.38	13.75-10.88	14.00-9.63
P/E Ratio	16.1-13.7	17.2-13.0	14.3-7.9	17.4-12.5	20.8-15.6	21.8-17.3	22.9-15.8
Average Yield %	6.7	7.2	9.6	8.0	6.7	5.7	5.1

Statistics are as originally reported. ① Incls. gains on the sale of securities of $530,324, 12/01; $257,142, 12/00; $53,473, 12/99 ② Incls. losses on the sale of assets of $28,264, 12/01; $37,318, 12/00; $1,964, 12/99; $10,546, 12/97. ③ Incls. gains on the sale of assets of $664,546, 12/02; $13,095, 12/98; $333,647, 12/96.

OFFICERS:
E. W. Landy, Chmn.
S. A. Landy, Pres.
A. T. Chew, V.P., C.F.O.

INVESTOR CONTACT: Rosemarie Faccone,
Investor Relations, (732) 577-9997

PRINCIPAL OFFICE: 3499 Route 9 North,
Suite 3-C, Freehold, NJ 07728

TELEPHONE NUMBER: (732) 577-9997
FAX: (732) 577-9980
WEB: www.umh.com

NO. OF EMPLOYEES: 100 (approx.)

SHAREHOLDERS: 1,000 (approx. record)

ANNUAL MEETING: In May

INCORPORATED: NJ, 1968

INSTITUTIONAL HOLDINGS:
No. of Institutions: 16
Shares Held: 526,169
% Held: 6.6

INDUSTRY: Real estate investment trusts
(SIC: 6798)

TRANSFER AGENT(S): Mellon Investor
Services, New York, NY

NYSE SYMBOL UTR
Rec. Pr. 26.18 (5/31/03)

UNITRIN, INC.

YIELD 6.3%
P/E RATIO ...

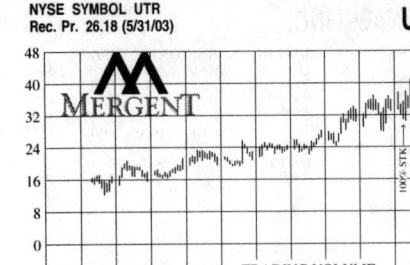

7 YEAR PRICE SCORE 100.9   **12 MONTH PRICE SCORE 83.8**
*NYSE COMPOSITE INDEX=100

INTERIM EARNINGS (Per Share):

Qtr.	Mar.	June	Sept.	Dec.
1999	0.70	0.50	0.71	0.84
2000	0.60	0.37	d0.07	0.41
2001	0.24	5.25	0.30	d0.18
2002	0.13	0.06	d0.27	d0.05
2003	0.20	...	...	...

INTERIM DIVIDENDS (Per Share):

Amt.	Decl.	Ex.	Rec.	Pay.
0.415Q	7/31/02	8/08/02	8/12/02	8/23/02
0.415Q	11/06/02	11/14/02	11/18/02	12/02/02
0.415Q	2/05/03	2/12/03	2/17/03	2/28/03
0.415Q	5/07/03	5/15/03	5/19/03	5/30/03

Indicated div.: $1.66

CAPITALIZATION (12/31/02):

	($000)	(%)
Long-Term Debt	297,100	14.2
Common & Surplus	1,802,400	85.8
Total	2,099,500	100.0

DIVIDEND ACHIEVER STATUS:
Rank: 113   10-Year Growth Rate: 11.68%
Total Years of Dividend Growth: 12

RECENT DEVELOPMENTS: For the quarter ended 3/31/03, net income grew 45.7% to $13.4 million from $9.2 million the previous year. Improved results in UTR's multi lines insurance, specialty lines insurance and consumer finance segments were partially offset by a loss from its Kemper Auto and Home segment and lower net income from the life and health insurance segment. Total revenues advanced 35.9% to $695.6 million from $511.9 million a year earlier. Premiums climbed 40.1% to $581.1 million. Consumer finance revenues rose 16.8% to $46.6 million.

PROSPECTS: The Company continues to evaluate strategic alternatives for its commercial lines of business. While evaluating these alternatives, the Company expects to continue reducing policies in force in certain commercial lines through extensive re-underwriting of contractors and related industries, program business, workers compensation, and product liability. Going forward, earnings for the remainder of 2003 should continue to benefit from the implementation of premium rate increases in most of the Company's product lines.

BUSINESS

UNITRIN, INC. is engaged, through its subsidiaries, in the property and casualty insurance, life and health insurance and consumer finance businesses. UTR conducts its operations through six operating segments: Multi Lines Insurance, which offers preferred and standard risk automobile, homeowners, fire, commercial liability and workers compensation; Specialty Lines Insurance, which offers automobile, motorcycle and watercraft insurance; Kemper Auto and Home, which offers personal automobile and homeowners' insurance; Life and Health Insurance, which offers individual life, accident, health and hospitalization insurance as well as property insurance products; Consumer Finance, which offers consumer loans primarily for the purchase of used automobiles as well as thrift products in the form of investment certificates and savings accounts; and Unitrin and Kemper Direct, which offers personal automobile insurance marketed through direct mail, radio and television advertising and over the Internet.

ANNUAL FINANCIAL DATA

	12/31/02	12/31/01	12/31/00	12/31/99	12/31/98	12/31/97	12/31/96
Earnings Per Share	d0.12	5.60	1.32	2.74	6.51	1.56	1.76
Tang. Book Val. Per Share	21.56	23.27	19.93	18.98	20.06	17.24	16.77
Dividends Per Share	1.66	1.60	1.50	1.40	1.30	1.20	1.10
Dividend Payout %	...	28.6	113.6	51.1	20.0	77.2	62.7
INCOME STATEMENT (IN MILLIONS):							
Total Premium Income	1,878.0	1,568.0	1,447.9	1,373.3	1,228.3	1,222.0	1,220.3
Other Income	420.2	965.8	505.3	440.3	857.6	308.1	302.8
Total Revenues	2,298.2	2,533.8	1,953.2	1,813.6	2,085.9	1,530.1	1,523.1
Policyholder Benefits	1,432.3	1,217.1	1,039.6	889.1	781.8	780.1	799.7
Income Before Income Taxes	d24.6	542.5	152.2	237.0	687.1	139.8	122.1
Income Taxes	cr18.3	190.3	54.4	77.9	238.6	47.1	40.2
Equity Earnings/Minority Int.	d1.9	28.7	d6.8	41.9	62.3	25.2	50.6
Net Income	d8.2	380.9	91.0	201.0	510.8	117.9	132.5
Average Shs. Outstg. (000)	67,700	67,900	68,800	73,100	78,200	75,200	75,442
BALANCE SHEET (IN MILLIONS):							
Cash & Cash Equivalents	16.9	27.9	23.3	24.1	8.6	14.5	17.0
Premiums Due	1,499.9	1,181.0	1,101.6	971.6	822.8	879.0	984.7
Invst. Assets: Fixed-term	3,023.0	2,926.4	2,733.2	2,651.8	2,557.3	2,315.4	2,207.4
Invst. Assets: Total	5,303.8	5,127.5	4,233.5	4,096.8	4,304.2	3,448.5	3,291.4
Total Assets	7,705.6	7,133.7	6,164.8	5,934.8	5,909.9	4,920.7	4,871.1
Net Stockholders' Equity	1,802.4	1,916.8	1,701.2	1,717.0	1,822.4	1,533.0	1,480.3
Year-end Shs. Outstg. (000)	67,596	67,547	67,648	70,993	76,000	75,170	74,682
STATISTICAL RECORD:							
Return on Revenues %	...	15.0	4.7	11.1	24.5	7.7	8.7
Return on Equity %	...	19.9	5.3	11.7	28.0	7.7	9.0
Return on Assets %	...	5.3	1.5	3.4	8.6	2.4	2.7
Price Range	42.80-27.85	41.95-33.90	41.13-27.19	42.38-30.50	37.06-27.78	34.25-24.25	28.19-22.13
P/E Ratio	...	7.5-6.1	31.2-20.6	15.5-11.1	5.7-4.3	22.0-15.6	16.1-12.6
Average Yield %	4.7	4.2	4.4	3.8	4.0	4.1	4.4

Statistics are as originally reported. Adj. for stk. split: 2-for-1, 3/26/99.

OFFICERS:
R. C. Vie, Chmn., C.E.O.
D. G. Southwell, Pres., C.O.O.

INVESTOR CONTACT: Edward J. Konar, Investor Relations, (312) 661-4930

PRINCIPAL OFFICE: One East Wacker Drive, Chicago, IL 60601

TELEPHONE NUMBER: (312) 661-4600
FAX: (312) 661-4690
WEB: www.unitrin.com

NO. OF EMPLOYEES: 8,700 (approx.)
SHAREHOLDERS: 7,500 (approx.)
ANNUAL MEETING: In May
INCORPORATED: DE, Feb., 1990

INSTITUTIONAL HOLDINGS:
No. of Institutions: 137
Shares Held: 16,930,616
% Held: 24.9

INDUSTRY: Fire, marine, and casualty insurance (SIC: 6331)

TRANSFER AGENT(S): Wachovia Bank, N.A., Charlotte, NC

UNIVERSAL CORPORATION

YIELD 3.4%
P/E RATIO 11.4

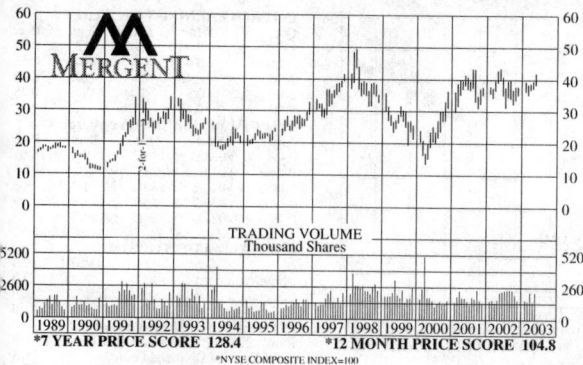

INTERIM EARNINGS (Per Share):

Qtr.	Sept.	Dec.	Mar.	June
1998-99	0.78	1.23	0.88	0.91
1999-00	0.93	0.85	1.29	0.69
2000-01	0.89	1.01	1.31	0.87
2001-02	1.04	1.09	1.26	0.61
2002-03	1.09	1.04	0.94	...

INTERIM DIVIDENDS (Per Share):

Amt.	Decl.	Ex.	Rec.	Pay.
0.34Q	8/01/02	10/10/02	10/15/02	11/12/02
0.36Q	12/05/02	1/09/03	1/13/03	2/10/03
0.36Q	2/06/03	4/10/03	4/14/03	5/12/03
0.36Q	5/01/03	7/10/03	7/14/03	8/11/03

Indicated div.: $1.44 (Div. Reinv. Plan)

CAPITALIZATION (6/30/02):

	($000)	(%)
Long-Term Debt	435,592	40.8
Deferred Income Tax	16,640	1.6
Minority Interest	28,300	2.6
Common & Surplus	587,995	55.0
Total	1,068,527	100.0

DIVIDEND ACHIEVER STATUS:
Rank: 231   10-Year Growth Rate: 5.45%
Total Years of Dividend Growth: 32

*7 YEAR PRICE SCORE 128.4   *12 MONTH PRICE SCORE 104.8
*NYSE COMPOSITE INDEX=100

RECENT DEVELOPMENTS: For the quarter ended 3/31/03, net income was $23.8 million versus $33.1 million in the corresponding year-earlier period. Results for 2003 included a restructuring charge of $1.3 million. Sales and other operating revenues rose 8.5% to $593.8 million. Tobacco operating profit slid 15.5% to $53.9 million. Lumber/building product operating profit fell 35.7% to $3.0 million, attributable to the sluggish Dutch economy. Agri-products operating profit declined 13.6% to $2.6 million.

PROSPECTS: UVV continues to progress with the streamlining and consolidation of its U.S. operations in order to compete more effectively in the U.S. market. The Company believes that U.S. crops will decline further as customers continue to seek more competitively priced leaf supplies in other areas where the Company has operations. Also, UVV is progressing with the restructuring of its operations in Zimbabwe in response to expectations of smaller crops in the future.

BUSINESS

UNIVERSAL CORPORATION is an independent leaf tobacco merchant with additional operations in agri-products and the distribution of lumber and building products. UVV's tobacco business involves selecting, buying, shipping, processing, packing, storing and financing leaf tobacco in the U.S. and other tobacco growing countries for the account of, or for resale to, manufacturers of tobacco products throughout the world. The agri-products operations involve the selecting, buying, shipping, processing, storing, financing, distribution, importing, and exporting of a number of products including tea, rubber, sunflower seeds, nuts, dried fruit, and canned and frozen foods. The lumber and building products operations involve distribution to the building and construction trade in the Netherlands, Belgium and other countries in Europe. In fiscal 2002, contributions to revenues (and operating income) were tobacco, 62.4% (84.5%); lumber and building products, 20.6% (10.3%); and agri-products, 17.0% (5.2%).

ANNUAL FINANCIAL DATA

	6/30/02	6/30/01	6/30/00	6/30/99	6/30/98	6/30/97	6/30/96
Earnings Per Share	4.00	④4.08	③3.77	②3.80	3.99	2.88	①2.04
Cash Flow Per Share	6.06	6.12	5.49	5.38	5.43	4.35	3.54
Tang. Book Val. Per Share	17.64	15.77	13.04	12.47	11.71	9.37	7.64
Dividends Per Share	1.36	1.28	1.24	1.20	1.12	1.06	1.02
Dividend Payout %	34.0	31.4	32.9	31.6	28.1	36.8	50.0

INCOME STATEMENT (IN MILLIONS):

Total Revenues	2,500.1	3,017.6	3,402.0	4,004.9	4,287.2	4,112.7	3,570.2
Costs & Expenses	2,244.6	2,722.4	3,116.0	3,697.6	3,957.7	3,824.3	3,325.2
Depreciation & Amort.	55.0	56.4	52.0	52.8	51.1	51.6	52.5
Operating Income	200.5	238.8	233.9	254.6	278.4	236.8	192.5
Net Interest Inc./(Exp.)	d47.8	d61.6	d56.9	d56.8	d64.0	d64.9	d68.8
Income Before Income Taxes	171.0	187.4	189.6	211.8	248.0	171.9	123.7
Income Taxes	59.8	66.3	68.2	76.0	98.7	68.8	49.5
Equity Earnings/Minority Int.	d4.5	d8.4	d7.6	d8.5	d8.1	d2.3	d2.9
Net Income	106.7	④112.7	③113.8	②112.3	141.3	100.9	①71.4
Cash Flow	161.6	169.1	165.8	180.0	192.3	152.4	123.9
Average Shs. Outstg. (000)	26,680	27,645	30,205	33,477	35,388	35,076	35,038

BALANCE SHEET (IN MILLIONS):

Cash & Cash Equivalents	58.0	109.5	61.4	92.8	79.8	109.1	214.8
Total Current Assets	1,105.0	1,132.6	1,088.2	1,170.3	1,430.3	1,431.2	1,329.0
Net Property	392.5	338.1	347.3	348.3	329.8	309.7	320.4
Total Assets	1,844.4	1,782.4	1,748.1	1,823.1	2,056.7	1,982.0	1,889.5
Total Current Liabilities	673.4	581.8	883.2	898.5	1,101.5	1,083.7	1,029.2
Long-Term Obligations	435.6	515.3	223.3	221.5	263.1	291.6	309.5
Net Stockholders' Equity	588.0	552.1	497.8	539.0	547.9	469.6	417.3
Net Working Capital	431.6	550.9	204.9	271.8	328.8	347.5	299.8
Year-end Shs. Outstg. (000)	26,225	27,185	28,147	32,091	34,866	35,139	35,056

STATISTICAL RECORD:

Operating Profit Margin %	8.0	7.9	6.9	6.4	6.5	5.8	5.4
Net Profit Margin %	4.3	3.7	3.3	3.2	3.3	2.5	2.0
Return on Equity %	18.1	20.4	22.9	23.6	25.8	21.5	17.1
Return on Assets %	5.8	6.3	6.5	7.0	6.9	5.1	3.8
Debt/Total Assets %	23.6	28.9	12.8	12.2	12.8	14.7	16.4
Price Range	43.50-31.15	43.37-29.75	36.38-13.50	35.75-19.44	49.50-31.50	41.69-27.88	32.75-22.25
P/E Ratio	10.9-7.8	10.6-7.3	9.6-3.6	9.4-5.1	12.4-7.9	14.5-9.7	16.1-10.9
Average Yield %	3.6	3.5	5.0	4.3	2.8	3.0	3.7

Statistics are as originally reported. ① Bef. extraord. gain of $900,000. ② Incl. gain of $16.7 mill. fr. sale of invest. ③ Incl. after-tax restruct. chrg.: 2001, $6.0 mill.; 2000, $7.0 mill. ④ Incl. pre-tax restruct. costs of $8.7 mill.

OFFICERS:
H. H. Harrell, Chmn.
A. B. King, Pres., C.E.O., C.O.O.
H. H. Roper, V.P., C.F.O.

INVESTOR CONTACT: Karen M. L. Whelan, V.P., Treas., (804) 254-8689

PRINCIPAL OFFICE: 1501 North Hamilton Street, Richmond, VA 23230

TELEPHONE NUMBER: (804) 359-9311
FAX: (804) 254-3594
WEB: www.universalcorp.com

NO. OF EMPLOYEES: 26,000 (approx.)

SHAREHOLDERS: 2,457

ANNUAL MEETING: In Oct.

INCORPORATED: VA, Jan., 1918

INSTITUTIONAL HOLDINGS:
No. of Institutions: 149
Shares Held: 18,010,895
% Held: 72.0

INDUSTRY: Farm-product raw materials, nec (SIC: 5159)

TRANSFER AGENT(S): Wells Fargo Shareowner Services, St. Paul, MN

UNIVERSAL HEALTH REALTY INCOME TRUST

YIELD 7.3%
P/E RATIO 15.2

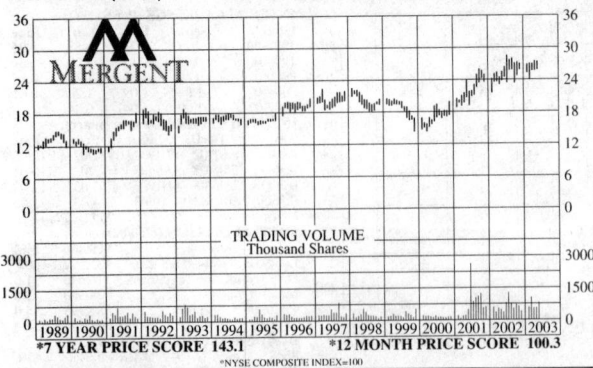

7 YEAR PRICE SCORE 143.1 **12 MONTH PRICE SCORE 100.3**
NYSE COMPOSITE INDEX=100

TRADING VOLUME
Thousand Shares

INTERIM EARNINGS (Per Share):

Qtr.	Mar.	June	Sept.	Dec.
1999	0.44	0.42	0.25	0.44
2000	0.44	0.42	0.43	0.52
2001	0.46	0.44	0.42	0.43
2002	0.53	0.44	0.43	0.43
2003	0.48	...	...	...

INTERIM DIVIDENDS (Per Share):

Amt.	Decl.	Ex.	Rec.	Pay.
0.48Q	6/03/02	6/12/02	6/14/02	6/28/02
0.48Q	9/05/02	9/12/02	9/16/02	9/30/02
0.485Q	12/02/02	12/13/02	12/17/02	12/31/02
0.485Q	3/03/03	3/13/03	3/17/03	3/31/03
0.49Q	6/02/03	6/12/03	6/16/03	6/30/03

Indicated div.: $1.96 (Div. Reinv. Plan)

CAPITALIZATION (12/31/02):

	($000)	(%)
Minority Interest	40	...
Common & Surplus	148,862	100.0
Total	148,902	100.0

DIVIDEND ACHIEVER STATUS:
Rank: 278   10-Year Growth Rate: 1.65%
Total Years of Dividend Growth: 15

RECENT DEVELOPMENTS: For the quarter ended 3/31/03, net income decreased 9.7% to $5.7 million compared with $6.3 million in the corresponding period of the previous year. Results for 2003 included a pre-tax loss of $35,000 on derivatives, a straight-line rent recognition charge of $105,000, and a pre-tax gain of $365,000 from the sale of real property. Total revenues rose to $7.2 million from $7.1 million in the year-earlier quarter.

PROSPECTS: The Company is benefiting from strong bonus rental revenue growth from UHS facilities. Meanwhile, UHT's hospital facilities continue to experience an increase in outpatient revenues, which is primarily the result of advances in medical technologies and pharmaceutical improvements that allow more services to be provided on an outpatient basis.

BUSINESS

UNIVERSAL HEALTH REALTY INCOME TRUST is an organized Maryland real estate investment trust (REIT). As of 12/31/02, the Trust had investments in 42 facilities located in 15 states consisting of investments in healthcare and human service related facilities including acute care hospitals, behavioral healthcare facilities, rehabilitation hospitals, sub-acute care facilities, surgery centers, childcare centers and medical office buildings. Six of the Trust's hospital facilities and three medical office buildings are leased to subsidiaries of Universal Health Services, Inc. (UHS). As of 12/31/02, UHS owned 6.6% of the Company's outstanding shares.

ANNUAL FINANCIAL DATA

	12/31/02	12/31/01	12/31/00	12/31/99	12/31/98	12/31/97	12/31/96
Earnings Per Share	④ 1.84	④ 1.74	③⑤ 1.81	①② 1.56	1.76	1.56	1.58
Tang. Book Val. Per Share	12.73	12.85	11.05	11.09	11.32	11.47	11.62
Dividends Per Share	1.92	1.88	1.84	1.81	1.75	1.71	1.70
Dividend Payout %	104.3	107.8	101.7	116.0	99.7	109.3	107.3
INCOME STATEMENT (IN THOUSANDS):							
Rental Income	28,429	27,574	27,315	23,584	23,123	22,180	21,172
Interest Income	...	...	...	281	111	584	751
Total Income	28,429	27,574	27,315	23,865	23,234	22,764	21,923
Costs & Expenses	4,678	4,555	4,153	3,003	3,065	2,524	2,193
Depreciation	4,431	4,401	4,461	3,857	3,879	3,775	3,636
Interest Expense	2,403	3,896	6,114	4,004	3,490	2,943	2,565
Income Before Income Taxes	16,700	14,739	14,482	11,418	12,800	13,522	13,529
Equity Earnings/Minority Int.	4,923	3,610	1,774	2,554	1,537	445	629
Net Income	④ 21,623	④ 18,349	③⑤ 16,256	①② 13,972	14,337	13,967	14,158
Average Shs. Outstg.	11,750	10,536	9,003	8,977	8,974	8,967	8,960
BALANCE SHEET (IN THOUSANDS):							
Cash & Cash Equivalents	598	629	294	852	572	1,238	137
Total Real Estate Investments	134,886	139,215	143,108	141,367	129,838	133,486	139,434
Total Assets	185,117	187,904	183,658	178,821	169,406	146,755	148,566
Long-Term Obligations	...	1,446	1,359	1,289	1,216	1,147	1,082
Total Liabilities	36,255	37,870	84,401	79,146	68,058	44,063	44,584
Net Stockholders' Equity	148,862	150,034	99,257	99,675	101,348	102,692	103,982
Year-end Shs. Outstg.	11,698	11,679	8,980	8,991	8,955	8,955	8,952
STATISTICAL RECORD:							
Net Inc.+Depr./Assets %	14.1	12.1	11.3	10.0	10.8	12.1	12.0
Return on Equity %	14.5	12.2	16.4	14.0	14.1	13.6	13.6
Return on Assets %	11.7	9.8	8.9	7.8	8.5	9.5	9.5
Price Range	28.50-21.40	26.00-18.75	19.88-14.25	20.50-14.25	22.50-17.94	22.38-18.38	20.63-17.38
P/E Ratio	15.5-11.6	14.9-10.8	11.0-7.9	13.1-9.1	12.8-10.2	14.3-11.8	13.1-11.0
Average Yield %	7.7	8.4	10.8	10.4	8.7	8.4	8.9

Statistics are as originally reported. ① Incl. a provision of $1.6 mill. for investment losses. ② Incl. pre-tax nonrecurr. chrgs. of $5.3 mill. ③ Incl. a gain on the sale of real prop. to UHS of $1.2 mill., 2002; $1.9 mill., 2000. ④ Incl. a gain on derivatives of $17,000, 2001 & loss of $217,000, 2002.

OFFICERS:
A. B. Miller, Chmn., C.E.O.
K. E. Gorman, Pres., C.F.O., Sec.

INVESTOR CONTACT: Investor Relations, (610) 265-0688

PRINCIPAL OFFICE: Universal Corporate Center, 367 South Gulph Road, King of Prussia, PA 19406-0958

TELEPHONE NUMBER: (610) 265-0688
FAX: (610) 768-3336
WEB: www.uhrit.com

NO. OF EMPLOYEES: N/A

SHAREHOLDERS: 700 (approx. record).

ANNUAL MEETING: In June

INCORPORATED: MD, July, 1986

INSTITUTIONAL HOLDINGS:
No. of Institutions: 81
Shares Held: 3,927,512
% Held: 32.7

INDUSTRY: Real estate investment trusts (SIC: 6798)

TRANSFER AGENT(S): EquiServe Trust Company, N.A., Providence, RI

UNIZAN FINANCIAL CORP.

YIELD 3.1%
P/E RATIO 11.8

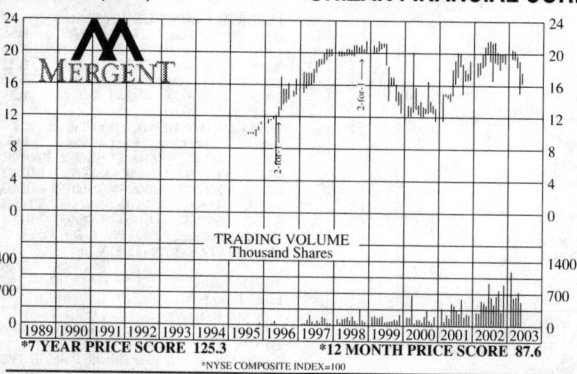

TRADING VOLUME
Thousand Shares

| 1989 | 1990 | 1991 | 1992 | 1993 | 1994 | 1995 | 1996 | 1997 | 1998 | 1999 | 2000 | 2001 | 2002 | 2003 |

*7 YEAR PRICE SCORE 125.3   ***12 MONTH PRICE SCORE 87.6**
*NYSE COMPOSITE INDEX=100

INTERIM EARNINGS (Per Share):

Qtr.	Mar.	June	Sept.	Dec.
2001	0.41	0.35	0.33	0.36
2002	d0.08	0.40	0.40	0.37
2003	0.32	...	...	...

INTERIM DIVIDENDS (Per Share):

Amt.	Decl.	Ex.	Rec.	Pay.
0.13Q	5/24/02	6/19/02	6/21/02	6/28/02
0.13Q	8/23/02	9/19/02	9/23/02	9/30/02
0.13Q	11/22/02	12/13/02	12/17/02	12/31/02
0.135Q	2/21/03	3/13/03	3/17/03	3/31/03
0.135Q	5/23/03	6/12/03	6/16/03	6/30/03

Indicated div.: $0.54 (Div. Reinv. Plan)

CAPITALIZATION (12/31/02):

	($000)	(%)
Total Deposits	1,931,615	75.2
Long-Term Debt	331,746	12.9
Capital Lease Obligations	165	0.0
Common & Surplus	304,290	11.9
Total	2,567,816	100.0

DIVIDEND ACHIEVER STATUS:

Rank: 118   10-Year Growth Rate: 11.44%
Total Years of Dividend Growth: 18

RECENT DEVELOPMENTS:

For the quarter ended 3/31/03, net income was $7.0 million compared with income of $140,000, before an accounting change charge of $1.4 million, in the equivalent 2002 quarter. Results for 2002 included $6.6 million for one-time after-tax acquisition-related and restructuring charges and provision expense related to the completion of UNIZ being formed as a result of the acquisition of BancFirst Ohio Corp. by UNB Corp. on 3/7/02. Total interest income advanced 29.2% to $37.4 million from $29.0 million a year earlier. Total interest expense rose 10.1% to $16.1 million from $14.6 million the year before. Net interest income surged 48.7% to $21.3 million from $14.3 million in 2002. Provision for loan losses amounted to $1.3 million versus $5.6 million the year before. Total other expenses increased 27.1% to $16.7 million from $13.1 million a year earlier. At 3/31/03, total deposits amounted to $2.02 billion versus $1.86 billion the year before.

BUSINESS

UNIZAN FINANCIAL CORP. is a financial services company with total assets of $2.80 billion at March 31, 2003. UNIZ was formed as a result of the acquisition of BancFirst Ohio Corp. by UNB Corp. on 3/7/02. As of 4/21/03, the Company operated 45 full-service retail financial centers in five metropolitan markets in Ohio: Canton, Columbus, Dayton, Newark and Zanesville. Additionally, through the Company's subsidiaries, Unizan Bank, National Association; Unizan Financial Services Group, National Association; Unizan Banc Financial Services, Inc.; and Unizan Financial Advisors, Inc., UNIZ offers its client base corporate and retail banking, wealth management products and services, Internet banking and niche businesses in government guaranteed loan programs and aircraft lending.

ANNUAL FINANCIAL DATA

	12/31/02	12/31/01	12/31/00	12/31/99	12/31/98	12/31/97	12/31/96
Earnings Per Share	⑴ 1.28	1.45	1.35	1.28	0.94	0.76	0.69
Tang. Book Val. Per Share	8.62	7.98	7.04	6.26	6.07	6.15	5.62
Dividends Per Share	0.52	0.50	0.48	0.47	0.36	0.33	0.29
Dividend Payout %	40.6	34.5	35.6	36.7	38.8	42.8	42.7
INCOME STATEMENT (IN MILLIONS):							
Total Interest Income	146.7	81.2	80.7	68.9	66.0	63.4	59.2
Total Interest Expense	65.5	38.2	42.7	31.4	30.6	30.3	27.8
Net Interest Income	81.2	43.0	37.9	37.4	35.4	33.0	31.4
Provision for Loan Losses	7.9	2.8	1.0	2.4	2.7	2.9	3.1
Non-Interest Income	25.6	15.5	12.6	14.1	10.9	7.2	6.4
Non-Interest Expense	60.7	32.3	27.7	27.5	27.0	23.5	22.2
Income Before Taxes	38.2	23.3	21.8	21.6	16.6	13.8	12.4
Net Income	⑴ 26.5	15.3	14.3	14.1	10.9	9.0	8.2
Average Shs. Outstg. (000)	20,778	10,604	10,608	10,982	11,639	11,786	11,818
BALANCE SHEET (IN MILLIONS):							
Total Loans & Leases	1,906.4	878.8	872.0	774.8	671.4	630.4	617.6
Allowance for Credit Losses	25.3	12.8	12.8	13.2	11.2	9.7	8.3
Net Loans & Leases	1,881.1	866.0	859.3	761.6	660.3	620.8	609.3
Total Assets	2,691.9	1,096.8	1,053.9	970.5	868.7	826.3	810.0
Total Deposits	1,931.6	819.5	827.6	764.2	685.5	649.5	600.7
Long-Term Obligations	331.9	114.8	61.2	54.3	41.6	35.7	62.6
Total Liabilities	2,387.6	1,011.5	978.0	899.9	797.0	749.8	738.6
Net Stockholders' Equity	304.3	85.4	75.9	70.7	71.7	76.5	71.3
Year-end Shs. Outstg. (000)	22,070	10,440	10,437	10,752	11,099	11,568	11,571
STATISTICAL RECORD:							
Return on Equity %	8.7	18.0	18.8	19.9	15.2	11.8	11.4
Return on Assets %	1.0	1.4	1.4	1.4	1.3	1.1	1.0
Equity/Assets %	11.3	7.8	7.2	7.3	8.3	9.3	8.8
Non-Int. Exp./Tot. Inc. %	56.8	55.3	54.8	53.4	58.3	58.4	58.7
Price Range	21.64-16.60	20.12-11.50	20.13-11.50	21.50-12.50	21.50-19.56	20.50-15.00	17.00-6.00
P/E Ratio	16.9-13.0	13.9-7.9	14.9-8.5	16.8-9.8	22.9-20.8	27.0-19.7	24.6-8.7
Average Yield %	2.7	3.2	3.0	2.8	1.8	1.8	2.6

Statistics are as originally reported. Results prior to 3/7/02 reflect UNB Corp. ⑴ Bef. acctg. change chrg. of $1.4 mill.; incl. merger-related after-tax chrg. of $6.6 mill.

OFFICERS:

R. L. Mann, Chmn., Pres., C.E.O.
E. L. D'Atri, Vice-Chmn.
J. J. Pennetti, Exec. V.P., C.F.O.

INVESTOR CONTACT: James J. Pennetti, Exec. V.P., C.F.O., (330) 438-1118

PRINCIPAL OFFICE: 220 Market Avenue South, Canton, OH 44702

TELEPHONE NUMBER: (330) 438-1118
FAX: (330) 438-1815
WEB: www.unbcorp.com

NO. OF EMPLOYEES: 733

SHAREHOLDERS: 3,399 (record); 3,569 (approx. beneficial)

ANNUAL MEETING: In Apr.

INCORPORATED: OH, 1983

INSTITUTIONAL HOLDINGS:
No. of Institutions: 59
Shares Held: 5,673,400
% Held: 25.8

INDUSTRY: National commercial banks (SIC: 6021)

TRANSFER AGENT(S): United National Bank & Trust Co., Canton, OH

VALLEY NATIONAL BANCORP

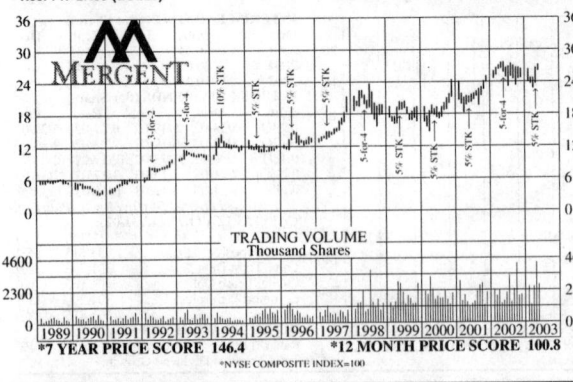

TRADING VOLUME
Thousand Shares

*7 YEAR PRICE SCORE 146.4   *12 MONTH PRICE SCORE 100.8
*NYSE COMPOSITE INDEX=100

INTERIM EARNINGS (Per Share):

Qtr.	Mar.	June	Sept.	Dec.
1999	0.30	0.29	0.31	0.30
2000	0.31	0.32	0.32	0.32
2001	0.28	0.33	0.35	0.36
2002	0.38	0.40	0.40	0.39
2003	0.40	...	...	...

INTERIM DIVIDENDS (Per Share):

Amt.	Decl.	Ex.	Rec.	Pay.
0.225Q	8/20/02	9/04/02	9/06/02	10/01/02
0.225Q	11/19/02	12/04/02	12/06/02	1/02/03
0.225Q	2/27/03	3/06/03	3/10/03	4/01/03
5% STK	4/09/03	4/30/03	5/02/03	5/16/03
0.225Q	5/22/03	6/04/03	6/06/03	7/01/03

Indicated div.: $0.90 (Div. Reinv. Plan)

CAPITALIZATION (12/31/02):

	($000)	(%)
Total Deposits	6,683,387	79.2
Long-Term Debt	1,119,642	13.3
Common & Surplus	631,738	7.5
Total	8,434,767	100.0

DIVIDEND ACHIEVER STATUS:
Rank: 135   10-Year Growth Rate: 10.43%
Total Years of Dividend Growth: 11

RECENT DEVELOPMENTS: For the quarter ended 3/31/03, net income slid 1.6% to $38.0 million from $38.6 million in the corresponding prior-year period. Results for 2003 and 2002 included net gains of $7.3 million and $3.6 million, respectively, related to various items. Results also included charges for distribution on capital securities of $3.9 million for 2003 and 2002. Net interest income grew 6.1% to $93.2 million. Provision for loan losses fell 12.1% to $3.3 million.

PROSPECTS: During the first quarter of 2003, total loans increased to $5.97 billion from $5.34 billion the year before as VLY continued to achieve strong increases in residential and commercial mortgages and commercial loans. Also, non-interest income continues to benefit from contributions from Master Coverage Corp., an all-line insurance agency, NIA/Lawyers Title Agency, LLC and Glen Rauch Securities, all recent acquisitions.

BUSINESS

VALLEY NATIONAL BANCORP, with $9.46 billion in assets as of 3/31/03, is a bank holding company. The Company's principal subsidiary is Valley National Bank (VNB). VNB is a national banking association, which provides a full range of commercial and retail banking services through 127 branch offices located in 82 communities serving 11 counties throughout northern New Jersey and Manhattan. These services include the following: the acceptance of demand, savings and time deposits; extension of consumer, real estate, Small Business Administration and other commercial credits; title insurance; investment services; and full personal and corporate trust, as well as pension and fiduciary services. On 1/19/01, the Company acquired Merchants New York Bancorp, Inc. for $375.0 million.

ANNUAL FINANCIAL DATA

	12/31/02	12/31/01	12/31/00	12/31/99	12/31/98	12/31/97	12/31/96
Earnings Per Share	④1.57	④1.32	③1.27	②1.26	②1.21	1.38	1.21
Tang. Book Val. Per Share	6.65	6.76	6.59	7.06	6.95	7.76	7.17
Dividends Per Share	0.83	0.78	0.74	0.69	0.62	0.54	0.49
Dividend Payout %	53.0	59.3	58.0	54.9	51.2	39.1	40.4
INCOME STATEMENT (IN MILLIONS):							
Total Interest Income	517.4	553.5	460.9	427.5	389.7	368.3	324.3
Total Interest Expense	157.7	218.7	202.8	169.2	160.1	156.0	145.5
Net Interest Income	359.7	334.8	258.1	258.4	229.6	212.3	178.8
Provision for Loan Losses	13.6	15.7	6.1	9.1	12.4	12.3	2.4
Non-Interest Income	81.2	68.5	50.9	47.3	43.1	42.3	26.3
Non-Interest Expense	208.0	188.2	141.0	137.9	134.8	123.2	101.2
Income Before Taxes	219.3	199.4	161.8	158.5	125.5	119.2	101.4
Net Income	④154.6	④135.2	③106.8	②106.3	②97.3	85.0	67.5
Average Shs. Outstg. (000)	98,357	102,426	84,216	84,487	80,465	61,597	55,746
BALANCE SHEET (IN MILLIONS):							
Cash & Due from Banks	243.9	311.9	186.7	161.6	175.8	148.2	162.9
Securities Avail. for Sale	2,140.4	2,171.7	1,035.8	1,005.4	929.1	1,017.2	950.2
Total Loans & Leases	5,762.5	5,331.8	4,661.4	4,554.8	3,977.9	3,622.3	3,177.2
Allowance for Credit Losses	64.1	63.8	53.7	55.1	49.9	46.4	41.2
Net Loans & Leases	5,698.4	5,268.0	4,607.7	4,499.6	3,928.0	3,576.0	3,136.0
Total Assets	9,134.7	8,583.8	6,425.8	6,360.4	5,541.2	5,090.7	4,686.7
Total Deposits	6,683.4	6,307.0	5,123.7	5,051.3	4,674.7	4,403.0	4,176.2
Long-Term Obligations	1,119.6	975.7	591.8	564.9	...	...	...
Total Liabilities	8,302.9	7,705.4	5,880.8	5,806.9	4,985.4	4,615.3	4,290.1
Net Stockholders' Equity	631.7	678.4	545.1	553.5	555.8	475.4	396.5
Year-end Shs. Outstg. (000)	95,050	100,364	82,739	78,347	79,972	61,296	55,310
STATISTICAL RECORD:							
Return on Equity %	24.5	19.9	19.6	19.2	17.5	17.9	17.0
Return on Assets %	1.7	1.6	1.7	1.7	1.8	1.7	1.4
Equity/Assets %	6.9	7.9	8.5	8.7	10.0	9.3	8.5
Non-Int. Exp./Tot. Inc. %	47.2	46.7	45.6	45.1	49.4	48.4	49.3
Price Range	27.66-23.09	25.11-18.18	24.40-14.64	20.39-16.13	23.70-15.63	21.26-12.73	14.92-11.34
P/E Ratio	17.6-14.7	19.0-13.8	19.2-11.5	16.2-12.8	19.6-12.9	15.4-9.2	12.3-9.4
Average Yield %	3.3	3.6	3.8	3.8	3.1	3.2	3.7

Statistics are as originally reported. Adj. for stk. splits: 5-for-4, 5/02 & 5/98; 5%, 5/03, 5/01, 5/00, 5/99, 5/97 & 5/96. ① Excl. an acctg. change chrg. $402,000. ② Incl. merger-related chrg., 1999, $3.0 mill.; 1998, $4.5 mill. ③ Incl. net gain on sale of loans of $2.0 mill. ④ Incl. a net charge of $2.1 mill., 2002; net gain of $3.7 mill., 2001.

OFFICERS:
G. H. Lipkin, Chmn., Pres., C.E.O.
S. B. Witty, Vice-Chmn.
A. D. Eskow, Exec. V.P., C.F.O.

INVESTOR CONTACT: Dianne M. Grenz, Investor Relations, (973) 305-8800

PRINCIPAL OFFICE: 1455 Valley Road, Wayne, NJ 07470

TELEPHONE NUMBER: (973) 305-8800
FAX: (973) 305-1605
WEB: www.valleynationalbank.com
NO. OF EMPLOYEES: 2,257
SHAREHOLDERS: 9,375
ANNUAL MEETING: In April
INCORPORATED: NJ, 1982

INSTITUTIONAL HOLDINGS:
No. of Institutions: 105
Shares Held: 11,122,077
% Held: 11.8

INDUSTRY: National commercial banks (SIC: 6021)

TRANSFER AGENT(S): American Stock Transfer & Trust Company, New York, NY

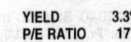

VALSPAR CORPORATION (THE)

YIELD 1.4%
P/E RATIO 18.6

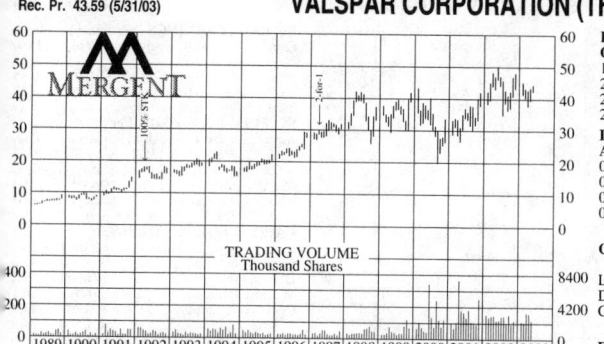

7 YEAR PRICE SCORE 138.7   **12 MONTH PRICE SCORE 99.5**
*NYSE COMPOSITE INDEX=100

INTERIM EARNINGS (Per Share):

Qtr.	Jan.	Apr.	July	Oct.
1999-00	0.26	0.59	0.59	0.56
2000-01	0.10	0.44	0.51	0.05
2001-02	0.25	0.67	0.74	0.68
2002-03	0.30	0.62	...	...

INTERIM DIVIDENDS (Per Share):

Amt.	Decl.	Ex.	Rec.	Pay.
0.14Q	8/14/02	9/27/02	10/01/02	10/15/02
0.15Q	12/11/02	12/27/02	12/31/02	1/15/03
0.15Q	2/26/03	3/28/03	4/01/03	4/15/03
0.15Q	6/12/03	6/27/03	7/01/03	7/15/03

Indicated div.: $0.60 (Div. Reinv. Plan)

CAPITALIZATION (10/25/02):

	($000)	(%)
Long-Term Debt	885,819	49.1
Deferred Income Tax	180,592	10.0
Common & Surplus	737,253	40.9
Total	1,803,664	100.0

DIVIDEND ACHIEVER STATUS:

Rank: 105   10-Year Growth Rate: 12.02%
Total Years of Dividend Growth: 24

RECENT DEVELOPMENTS: For the quarter ended 4/25/03, net income slid 6.9% to $32.2 million compared with $34.5 million in the equivalent 2002 quarter. Net sales advanced 1.4% to $561.8 million from $554.0 million a year earlier. Gross profit as a percentage of net sales decreased to 31.7% from 33.4% due to changes in product mix and increases in raw material costs. Total cost of sales grew 1.8 percentage points to 68.3% from 66.5% in the prior-year period. Income from operations slid 6.3% to $63.7 million.

PROSPECTS: VAL expects results for its industrial coatings product line to gradually improve throughout the remainder of 2003 despite the weak economy. Meanwhile, architectural and packaging coatings sales should continue to contribute to overall results. Results should also be enhanced by the realization of the benefits associated with VAL's cost-control initiatives. Moreover, VAL is currently concentrating on improving margins with actions to offset raw material increases.

BUSINESS

THE VALSPAR CORPORATION is a global paint and coatings manufacturer. The Company manufactures and distributes a broad portfolio of coatings products. The Industrial product line includes decorative and protective coatings for wood, metal, plastic and glass. The Architectural, Automotive and Specialty product line includes interior and exterior decorative paints, primers, varnishes and specialty decorative products, such as enamels, aerosols and faux finishes for the do-it-yourself and professional markets, as well as automotive refinish and high performance floor coatings. The Packaging Coatings product line includes coatings and inks for rigid packaging containers. The Other category includes specialty polymers, composites and colorants, which are used internally and sold to other coatings manufacturers. In December 2000, VAL acquired Lilly Industries, Inc.

ANNUAL FINANCIAL DATA

	10/25/02	10/26/01	10/27/00	10/29/99	10/30/98	10/31/97	10/25/96
Earnings Per Share	2.34	①1.10	②2.00	①1.87	1.63	1.49	1.26
Cash Flow Per Share	3.33	2.67	3.05	2.78	2.32	2.07	1.76
Tang. Book Val. Per Share	...	...	5.39	4.07	5.70	5.68	5.79
Dividends Per Share	0.56	0.54	0.52	0.46	0.42	0.36	0.33
Dividend Payout %	23.9	49.1	26.0	24.6	25.8	24.2	26.2
INCOME STATEMENT (IN MILLIONS):							
Total Revenues	2,126.9	1,921.0	1,483.3	1,387.7	1,155.1	1,017.3	859.8
Costs & Expenses	1,826.1	1,687.0	1,274.1	1,202.9	1,002.7	879.5	742.5
Depreciation & Amort.	51.1	73.1	45.2	39.8	30.7	25.8	22.3
Operating Income	249.6	160.9	163.9	145.0	121.7	112.0	95.0
Net Interest Inc./(Exp.)	d48.7	d72.6	d22.0	d19.1	d10.7	d5.3	d3.0
Income Before Income Taxes	198.5	91.2	141.7	135.1	118.8	109.2	93.0
Income Taxes	78.4	39.7	55.3	52.9	46.7	43.3	37.2
Net Income	120.1	①51.5	②86.5	①82.1	72.1	65.9	55.9
Cash Flow	171.3	124.6	131.7	121.9	102.9	91.6	78.2
Average Shs. Outstg. (000)	51,370	46,658	43,196	43,836	44,320	44,233	44,402
BALANCE SHEET (IN MILLIONS):							
Cash & Cash Equivalents	22.7	20.1	20.9	33.2	15.0	11.1	7.1
Total Current Assets	701.8	661.5	533.9	514.9	426.1	356.8	275.2
Net Property	402.5	411.2	298.7	312.1	233.5	185.7	153.8
Total Assets	2,419.6	2,226.1	1,125.0	1,110.7	801.7	615.5	486.4
Total Current Liabilities	503.9	475.1	334.3	374.7	268.0	259.4	179.1
Long-Term Obligations	885.8	1,006.2	300.3	298.9	164.8	35.8	31.9
Net Stockholders' Equity	737.3	654.6	437.6	393.8	340.2	295.1	253.7
Net Working Capital	197.9	186.4	199.6	140.2	158.1	97.4	96.1
Year-end Shs. Outstg. (000)	50,104	49,482	42,481	42,983	43,418	43,678	43,854
STATISTICAL RECORD:							
Operating Profit Margin %	11.7	8.4	11.1	10.4	10.5	11.0	11.0
Net Profit Margin %	5.6	2.7	5.8	5.9	6.2	6.5	6.5
Return on Equity %	16.3	7.9	19.8	20.9	21.2	22.3	22.0
Return on Assets %	5.0	2.3	7.7	7.4	9.0	10.7	11.5
Debt/Total Assets %	36.6	45.2	26.7	26.9	20.6	5.8	6.6
Price Range	50.15-34.80	42.00-26.48	43.31-19.75	41.88-29.25	42.13-25.75	33.06-26.81	29.31-20.94
P/E Ratio	21.4-14.9	38.2-24.1	21.7-9.9	22.4-15.6	25.8-15.8	22.2-18.0	23.3-16.6
Average Yield %	1.3	1.6	1.6	1.6	1.3	1.2	1.3

Statistics are as originally reported. Adj. for stk. splits: 2-for-1, 3/97. ① Incl. restruct. chrg. of $8.3 mill., 1999; $21.9 mill., 2001. ② Incl. restr. credit of $1.2 mill.

OFFICERS:
R. M. Rompala, Chmn., C.E.O.
J. M. Ballbach, Pres., C.O.O.
P. C. Reyelts, Sr. V.P., C.F.O.
R. Engh, Sec.

INVESTOR CONTACT: Rolf Engh, Sec., (612) 332-7371

PRINCIPAL OFFICE: 1101 Third Street South, Minneapolis, MN 55415

TELEPHONE NUMBER: (612) 332-7371
FAX: (612) 375-7723
WEB: www.valspar.com

NO. OF EMPLOYEES: 7,058 (avg.)

SHAREHOLDERS: 1,642

ANNUAL MEETING: In Feb.

INCORPORATED: DE, Dec., 1934

INSTITUTIONAL HOLDINGS:
No. of Institutions: 192
Shares Held: 31,060,396
% Held: 62.1

INDUSTRY: Paints and allied products (SIC: 2851)

TRANSFER AGENT(S): Mellon Investor Services LLC, Ridgefield Park, NJ

VECTREN CORPORATION

YIELD 4.4%
P/E RATIO 13.6

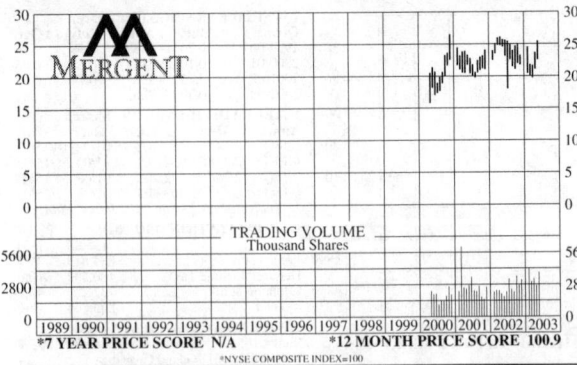

INTERIM EARNINGS (Per Share):

Qtr.	Mar.	June	Sept.	Dec.
2000	0.36	0.13	0.25	0.43
2001	0.61	d0.15	0.07	0.48
2002	0.67	0.18	0.20	0.62
2003	0.82	...	...	...

INTERIM DIVIDENDS (Per Share):

Amt.	Decl.	Ex.	Rec.	Pay.
0.265Q	7/24/02	8/13/02	8/15/02	9/01/02
0.275Q	11/01/02	11/13/02	11/15/02	12/02/02
0.275Q	1/29/03	2/12/03	2/14/03	3/03/03
0.275Q	4/23/03	5/13/03	5/15/03	6/02/03

Indicated div.: $1.10 (Div. Reinv. Plan)

CAPITALIZATION (12/31/02):

	($000)	(%)
Long-Term Debt	954,200	47.2
Deferred Income Tax	195,500	9.7
Minority Interest	1,900	0.1
Common & Surplus	869,900	43.0
Total	2,021,500	100.0

DIVIDEND ACHIEVER STATUS:
Rank: 259   10-Year Growth Rate: 3.47%
Total Years of Dividend Growth: 27

*7 YEAR PRICE SCORE N/A   ***12 MONTH PRICE SCORE 100.9**

*NYSE COMPOSITE INDEX=100

RECENT DEVELOPMENTS: For the quarter ended 3/31/03, net income advanced 22.2% to $55.7 million from $45.6 million in the prior-year quarter. Earnings for 2003 benefited from colder-than-normal weather and a strong wholesale power market. Total revenues increased 5.1% to $662.5 million. Gas utility revenues jumped 42.3% to $509.5 million, while electric utility revenues decreased 5.6% to $119.4 million. Energy services and other revenues dropped 76.9% to $33.6 million. Comparisons were made with restated 2002 results.

PROSPECTS: On 4/21/03, the Company and Citizens Gas and Coke Utility of Indianapolis announced the signing of a letter of intent to sell the assets of their jointly owned affiliate CIGMA, LLC to McJunkin Corporation. The transaction is expected to be completed in the second quarter of 2003. Separately, for full-year 2003, the Company expects earnings to range from $1.75 to $1.85 per share, including the effect of any permanent financing to be completed during the year.

BUSINESS

VECTREN CORPORATION was organized to reflect the merger on 3/31/00 of Indiana Energy, Inc. and SIGCORP, Inc., both of which were Dividend Achievers. VVC is an energy and applied technology holding company. The Company's energy delivery subsidiaries supply gas and/or electricity to nearly 1.0 million customers in adjoining service territories that cover nearly two-thirds of Indiana and west central Ohio. VVC's non-regulated subsidiaries and affiliates currently offer energy-related products and services, which include gas marketing and related services, coal mining and sales, broadband communications services and utility infrastructure services, which includes underground construction and repair, facilities locating and meter reading services. VVC has three reportable segments: gas utility services (48.6% of 2002 revenues) electric utility services (32.5%) and non-regulated operations (18.9%).

ANNUAL FINANCIAL DATA

	12/31/02	12/31/01	12/31/00	12/31/99	12/31/98
Earnings Per Share	1.68	② 1.01	① 1.17	1.48	1.40
Cash Flow Per Share	3.44	2.86	2.90	2.89	2.73
Tang. Book Val. Per Share	9.83	9.68	8.69	11.58	...
Dividends Per Share	1.07	1.03	0.98	...	...
Dividend Payout %	63.7	102.0	83.8	...	...
INCOME STATEMENT (IN MILLIONS):					
Total Revenues	1,804.3	2,170.0	1,648.7	1,068.4	997.7
Costs & Expenses	1,473.4	1,906.7	1,412.1	820.6	767.6
Depreciation & Amort.	119.6	123.7	105.7	87.0	81.6
Operating Income	211.3	139.6	130.9	160.8	148.5
Net Interest Inc./(Exp.)	d68.1	d82.6	d57.1	d42.9	d40.3
Income Taxes	38.9	18.6	34.2	45.7	42.3
Equity Earnings/Minority Int.	9.1	13.5	16.6	10.7	11.7
Net Income	114.0	② 67.4	① 72.0	90.7	86.6
Cash Flow	233.6	190.3	177.7	177.7	168.2
Average Shs. Outstg. (000)	67,900	66,900	61,380	61,430	61,578
BALANCE SHEET (IN MILLIONS):					
Gross Property	1,648.1	1,595.0	1,555.8	1,336.3	...
Net Property	1,876.1	1,776.7	1,659.2	1,400.8	...
Total Assets	2,926.5	2,856.8	2,909.2	1,980.5	...
Long-Term Obligations	954.2	1,014.0	632.0	486.7	...
Net Stockholders' Equity	869.9	848.6	731.7	709.8	...
Year-end Shs. Outstg. (000)	67,900	67,700	61,419	61,305	...
STATISTICAL RECORD:					
Operating Profit Margin %	11.7	6.4	7.9	15.0	14.9
Net Profit Margin %	6.3	3.1	4.4	8.5	8.7
Net Inc./Net Property %	6.1	3.8	4.3	6.5	...
Net Inc./Tot. Capital %	5.6	3.3	4.5	6.4	...
Return on Equity %	13.1	7.9	9.8	12.8	...
Price Range	26.10-17.95	24.44-19.76	26.50-15.75	...	...
P/E Ratio	15.5-10.7	24.2-19.6	22.6-13.5	...	...
Average Yield %	4.9	4.7	3.5	...	...

Statistics are as originally reported. ① Incl. nonrecurr. merger & integration chrg., $41.1 mill. ② Bef. extraord. loss of $7.7 mill. and acctg. change gain of $3.9 mill.; incl. pre-tax non-recurr. chrgs. of $21.9 mill.

OFFICERS:
N. C. Ellerbrook, Chmn., Pres., C.E.O.
J. A. Benkert Jr., Exec. V.P., C.F.O.
R. E. Christian, Sr. V.P., Gen. Couns., Sec.

INVESTOR CONTACT: Steven M. Schein, V.P., Investor Relations, (812) 491-4209

PRINCIPAL OFFICE: 20 N.W. Fourth Street, Evansville, IN 47708

TELEPHONE NUMBER: (812) 491-4000
FAX: (812) 491-4149
WEB: www.vectren.com

NO. OF EMPLOYEES: 1,876 (avg.)

SHAREHOLDERS: 13,460

ANNUAL MEETING: In May

INCORPORATED: IN, June, 1999

INSTITUTIONAL HOLDINGS:
No. of Institutions: 189
Shares Held: 27,161,163
% Held: 39.9

INDUSTRY: Gas and other services combined (SIC: 4932)

TRANSFER AGENT(S): National City Bank, Cleveland, OH

VF CORPORATION

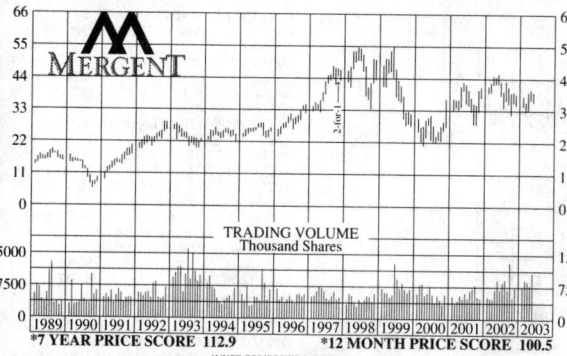

INTERIM EARNINGS (Per Share):

Qtr.	Mar.	June	Sept.	Dec.
2000	0.66	0.64	0.88	0.08
2001	0.67	0.60	0.90	d1.03
2002	0.69	0.79	1.15	0.63
2003	0.83	...	...	...

INTERIM DIVIDENDS (Per Share):

Amt.	Decl.	Ex.	Rec.	Pay.
0.24Q	7/17/02	9/06/02	9/10/02	9/20/02
0.25Q	10/17/02	12/06/02	12/10/02	12/20/02
0.25Q	2/11/03	3/06/03	3/10/03	3/20/03
0.25Q	4/22/03	6/06/03	6/10/03	6/20/03

Indicated div.: $1.00 (Div. Reinv. Plan)

CAPITALIZATION (1/4/03):

	($000)	(%)
Long-Term Debt	602,287	26.6
Common & Surplus	1,657,848	73.4
Total	2,260,135	100.0

DIVIDEND ACHIEVER STATUS:
Rank: 219   10-Year Growth Rate: 5.74%
Total Years of Dividend Growth: 30

TRADING VOLUME
Thousand Shares

1989|1990|1991|1992|1993|1994|1995|1996|1997|1998|1999|2000|2001|2002|2003
*7 YEAR PRICE SCORE 112.9   *12 MONTH PRICE SCORE 100.5
*NYSE COMPOSITE INDEX=100

RECENT DEVELOPMENTS: For the three months ended 4/5/03, net income rose 19.5% to $92.1 million compared with income from continuing operations of $77.0 million, before an accounting change charge of $527.3 million, in the equivalent period of 2002. Results benefited from the favorable effect of foreign currency translations and efficient cost management. Results for 2002 included a restructuring charge of $3.4 million and excluded a gain of $1.9 million from discontinued operations. Net sales climbed 3.1% to $1.25 billion versus $1.21 billion in 2002.

PROSPECTS: Operating results are benefiting from VFC's focus on tight cost management in this difficult business climate. Meanwhile, the Company expects sales in the second quarter of 2003 to be flat. Also, earnings per share for the second quarter may be flat to down 5.0%, excluding restructuring charges. Additionally, the Company expects earnings per share for full-year 2003 to increase in the range of 5.0% to 10.0% over 2002's $3.38 earnings per share from continuing operations.

BUSINESS

VF CORPORATION designs, manufactures and markets branded jeanswear, intimate apparel, playwear, workwear and daypacks. The Company's principal brands include: LEE®, RUSTLER® WRANGLER®, RIDERS®, VANITY FAIR®, VASSARETTE®, BESTFORM®, LILY OF FRANCE®, LEE SPORT® HEALTHTEX®, JANSPORT®, EASTPAK®, RED KAP® and THE NORTH FACE®. On 5/20/00, VFC acquired the Eastpak branded business and the CHIC jeans brand. On 8/16/00, VFC completed the acquisition of The North Face, Inc.

ANNUAL FINANCIAL DATA

	1/4/03	12/29/01	12/30/00	1/1/00	1/2/99	1/3/98	1/4/97
Earnings Per Share	③ 3.24	② 1.19	① 2.27	2.99	3.10	2.70	2.27
Cash Flow Per Share	4.22	2.67	3.76	4.37	4.40	3.91	3.61
Tang. Book Val. Per Share	10.91	9.97	12.56	10.08	9.33	8.68	8.68
Dividends Per Share	0.97	0.93	0.89	0.85	0.81	0.77	0.73
Dividend Payout %	29.9	78.1	39.2	28.4	26.1	28.5	32.2
INCOME STATEMENT (IN MILLIONS):							
Total Revenues	5,083.5	5,518.8	5,747.9	5,551.6	5,478.8	5,222.2	5,137.2
Costs & Expenses	4,351.9	5,002.6	5,064.5	4,731.6	4,633.3	4,460.9	4,419.3
Depreciation & Amort.	109.7	169.0	173.4	167.4	161.4	156.3	160.6
Operating Income	621.9	347.2	510.0	652.6	684.2	605.1	557.3
Net Interest Inc./(Exp.)	d63.9	d86.5	d81.0	d62.5	d55.9	d25.9	d49.4
Income Before Income Taxes	561.7	262.8	431.5	595.6	631.6	585.9	508.4
Income Taxes	197.3	125.0	164.4	229.3	243.3	234.9	208.9
Net Income	③ 364.4	② 137.8	① 267.1	366.2	388.3	350.9	299.5
Cash Flow	471.3	303.7	437.2	530.1	546.0	530.1	456.1
Average Shs. Outstg. (000)	112,336	114,764	117,218	122,258	124,995	129,720	127,292
BALANCE SHEET (IN MILLIONS):							
Cash & Cash Equivalents	496.4	332.0	118.9	79.9	63.2	124.1	270.6
Total Current Assets	2,074.5	2,031.4	2,110.1	1,877.4	1,848.2	1,601.5	1,706.3
Net Property	566.5	654.7	776.0	804.4	776.1	706.0	721.5
Total Assets	3,503.2	4,057.4	4,358.2	4,026.5	3,836.7	3,322.8	3,449.5
Total Current Liabilities	874.8	813.8	1,006.2	1,113.5	1,033.0	765.9	766.3
Long-Term Obligations	602.3	904.0	905.0	517.8	521.7	516.2	519.1
Net Stockholders' Equity	1,657.8	2,112.8	2,191.8	2,163.8	2,066.3	1,866.8	1,973.7
Net Working Capital	1,199.7	1,217.6	1,103.9	763.9	815.1	835.6	940.1
Year-end Shs. Outstg. (000)	108,525	109,998	86,807	116,205	119,466	121,225	127,816
STATISTICAL RECORD:							
Operating Profit Margin %	12.2	6.3	8.9	11.8	12.5	11.6	10.8
Net Profit Margin %	7.2	2.5	4.6	6.6	7.1	6.7	5.8
Return on Equity %	22.0	6.5	12.2	16.9	18.8	18.8	15.2
Return on Assets %	10.4	3.4	6.1	9.1	10.1	10.6	8.7
Debt/Total Assets %	17.2	22.3	20.8	12.9	13.6	15.5	15.0
Price Range	45.64-31.50	42.70-28.15	36.90-20.94	55.00-27.44	54.69-33.44	48.25-32.25	34.94-23.81
P/E Ratio	14.1-9.7	35.9-23.7	16.3-9.2	18.4-9.2	17.6-10.8	17.9-11.9	15.4-10.5
Average Yield %	2.5	2.6	3.1	2.1	1.8	1.9	2.5

Statistics are as originally reported. Adj. for stk. split: 2-for-1, 11/97. ① Incl. restr. costs of $119.9 mill.; bef. acctg. chge. chrg. of $6.8 mill. ② Incl. restr. costs of $236.8 mill. & a $0.06 per sh. gain fr. reversal of chrgs. ③ Excl. $8.3 mill. gain fr. disc. ops. & $527.3 mill. acctg. change chrg.

OFFICERS:
M. J. McDonald, Chmn., Pres., C.E.O.
R. K. Shearer, V.P., C.F.O.

INVESTOR CONTACT: Cindy Knoebel, Dir., Inv. Rel., (336) 547-6189

PRINCIPAL OFFICE: 105 Corporate Center Boulevard, Greensboro, NC 27408

TELEPHONE NUMBER: (336) 424-6000
FAX: (336) 547-7634
WEB: www.vfc.com

NO. OF EMPLOYEES: 56,000 (approx.)
SHAREHOLDERS: 6,022
ANNUAL MEETING: In Apr.
INCORPORATED: PA, Dec., 1889

INSTITUTIONAL HOLDINGS:
No. of Institutions: 287
Shares Held: 97,662,331
% Held: 89.6

INDUSTRY: Men's and boys' clothing, nec (SIC: 2329)

TRANSFER AGENT(S): First Chicago Trust Company of New York, Jersey City, NJ

VIRCO MFG. CORPORATION

YIELD 0.9%
P/E RATIO ...

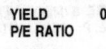

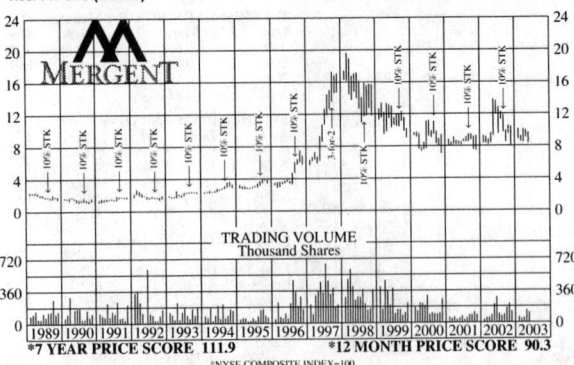

*7 YEAR PRICE SCORE 111.9   *12 MONTH PRICE SCORE 90.3

*NYSE COMPOSITE INDEX=100

INTERIM EARNINGS (Per Share):

Qtr.	Apr.	July	Oct.	Jan.
1999-00	d0.14	0.45	0.45	d0.05
2000-01	0.19	0.31	0.34	d0.53
2001-02	d0.27	0.33	0.29	d0.33
2002-03	d0.16	0.32	0.24	d0.39
2003-04	d0.31	...	...	...

INTERIM DIVIDENDS (Per Share):

Amt.	Decl.	Ex.	Rec.	Pay.
10% STK	8/22/02	9/06/02	9/06/02	9/30/02
0.02Q	8/22/02	10/09/02	10/11/02	10/31/02
0.02Q	12/11/02	12/24/02	12/31/02	1/31/03
0.02Q	2/14/03	3/27/03	3/31/03	4/30/03
0.02Q	6/10/03	6/26/03	6/30/03	7/31/03

Indicated div.: $0.08

CAPITALIZATION (1/31/02):

	($000)	(%)
Long-Term Debt	26,647	22.4
Deferred Income Tax	2,301	1.9
Common & Surplus	90,223	75.7
Total	119,171	100.0

DIVIDEND ACHIEVER STATUS:
Rank: 22   10-Year Growth Rate: 20.75%
Total Years of Dividend Growth: 20

RECENT DEVELOPMENTS: For the quarter ended 4/30/03, net loss widened to $4.0 million compared with $2.1 million in the equivalent 2002 quarter. Sales fell 24.3% to $31.2 million from $41.2 million a year earlier. The decline in results was primarily attributed to reduced orders as some of the Company's customers, including states, cities, counties, and school districts, are coping with restricted operating budgets. However, bond funding for public schools continues to be relatively strong. Looking ahead, the Company is pursuing all available business in its markets. The Company is particularly focusing on gaining market share via new product introductions. Also, VIR is evaluating different ways to contain spending. Furthermore, the Company will be able to reduce inventories by the end of the summer, and soon after, establish production levels appropriate for ongoing business activity.

BUSINESS

VIRCO MFG. CORPORATION is engaged in the design, production and distribution of furniture for contract and educational markets worldwide. The Company offers a broad product line of furniture for the education market, convention centers and arenas, the hospitality industry, government facilities, and places of worship. In addition, the Company sells to wholesalers, distributors, retailers and catalog retailers that serve these same markets. These products include student and teacher desks, computer stations, chairs, activity tables, and folding and stacking chairs for cafeteria and auditorium seating. The Company also produces a variety of tables, chairs and storage equipment. The Company's manufacturing and distribution facilities are located in California and Arkansas.

ANNUAL FINANCIAL DATA

	1/31/02	1/31/01	1/31/00	1/31/99	1/31/98	1/31/97	1/31/96
Earnings Per Share	② 0.02	① 0.31	0.72	1.20	0.94	0.64	0.36
Cash Flow Per Share	1.17	1.28	1.43	1.68	1.43	1.09	0.73
Tang. Book Val. Per Share	6.71	6.90	6.82	6.30	5.40	4.48	3.89
Dividends Per Share	0.07	0.068	0.062	0.055	0.051	0.043	0.02
Dividend Payout %	374.4	19.6	7.8	4.2	4.6	6.4	4.2

INCOME STATEMENT (IN THOUSANDS):

Total Revenues	257,462	287,342	266,641	273,620	258,194	236,277	224,349
Costs & Expenses	236,566	273,701	237,364	236,315	226,208	211,528	208,481
Depreciation & Amort.	15,813	13,412	9,993	7,132	7,110	6,541	5,364
Operating Income	5,083	229	19,284	30,173	24,876	18,208	10,504
Net Interest Inc./(Exp.)	d4,561	d4,962	d2,385	d1,111	d1,794	d2,507	d3,130
Income Before Income Taxes	436	6,986	16,693	28,902	22,604	15,054	8,413
Income Taxes	190	2,673	6,527	11,272	8,752	5,728	3,204
Net Income	② 246	① 4,313	10,166	17,630	13,852	9,326	5,209
Cash Flow	16,059	17,725	20,159	24,762	20,962	15,867	10,573
Average Shs. Outstg.	13,675	13,885	14,087	14,705	14,707	14,507	14,434

BALANCE SHEET (IN THOUSANDS):

Cash & Cash Equivalents	1,704	351	1,072	1,086	1,221	722	661
Total Current Assets	62,459	88,973	89,926	82,508	74,219	72,688	74,622
Net Property	83,406	94,645	87,937	59,320	39,563	37,478	36,955
Total Assets	161,372	199,549	190,863	151,380	122,015	118,020	119,225
Total Current Liabilities	27,995	45,800	38,503	35,103	30,187	27,545	23,302
Long-Term Obligations	26,647	43,741	46,027	21,344	9,459	21,513	35,909
Net Stockholders' Equity	90,223	94,141	93,834	88,923	77,325	63,965	55,461
Net Working Capital	34,464	43,173	51,423	47,405	44,032	45,143	51,320
Year-end Shs. Outstg.	13,445	13,652	13,750	14,120	14,313	14,268	14,268

STATISTICAL RECORD:

Operating Profit Margin %	2.0	0.1	7.2	11.0	9.6	7.7	4.7
Net Profit Margin %	0.1	1.5	3.8	6.4	5.4	3.9	2.3
Return on Equity %	0.3	4.6	10.8	19.8	17.9	14.6	9.4
Return on Assets %	0.2	2.2	5.3	11.6	11.4	7.9	4.4
Debt/Total Assets %	16.5	21.9	24.1	14.1	7.8	18.2	30.1
Price Range	9.45-7.41	11.18-7.02	13.36-9.02	19.64-10.94	17.31-5.64	7.50-2.87	4.00-2.74
P/E Ratio	522.4-409.3	35.6-22.4	18.5-12.5	16.3-9.1	18.3-6.0	11.7-4.5	11.1-7.6
Average Yield %	0.8	0.7	0.5	0.3	0.4	0.8	0.4

Statistics are as originally reported. Adj. for all stk. splits and divs. thru 9/02. ① Bef. acctg. change chrg. $297,000 ② Incl. a loss of $86,000 on the sale of fixed assets.

OFFICERS:
R. A. Virtue, Chmn., Pres., C.E.O.
R. E. Dose, V.P., Treas., Sec.
D. A. Virtue, Exec. V.P.

INVESTOR CONTACT: Investor Relations, (310) 533-0474

PRINCIPAL OFFICE: 2027 Harpers Way, Torrance, CA 90501

TELEPHONE NUMBER: (310) 533-0474
FAX: (310) 782-6098
WEB: www.virco.com
NO. OF EMPLOYEES: 2,000 (approx.)
SHAREHOLDERS: 350 (approx.); 1,500 (approx. beneficial)
ANNUAL MEETING: In June
INCORPORATED: CA, Feb., 1950; reincorp., DE, Apr., 1984

INSTITUTIONAL HOLDINGS:
No. of Institutions: 24
Shares Held: 3,026,107
% Held: 23.3

INDUSTRY: Public building & related furniture (SIC: 2531)

TRANSFER AGENT(S): Mellon Investor Services, Ridgefield Park, NJ

VULCAN MATERIALS COMPANY

YIELD 2.7%
P/E RATIO 20.8

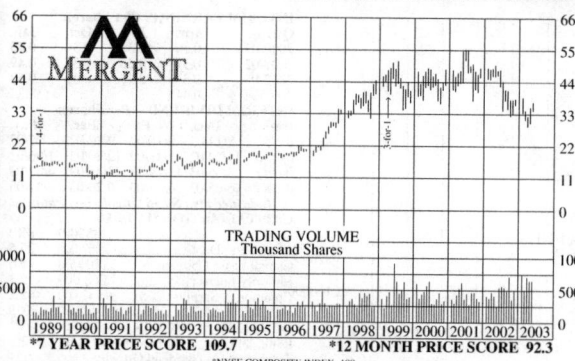

TRADING VOLUME	Thousand Shares

*7 YEAR PRICE SCORE 109.7   *12 MONTH PRICE SCORE 92.3

*NYSE COMPOSITE INDEX=100

INTERIM EARNINGS (Per Share):

Qtr.	Mar.	June	Sept.	Dec.
2000	0.23	0.75	0.84	0.34
2001	0.06	0.78	0.90	0.44
2002	0.11	0.64	0.75	0.36
2003	0.01	...	...	...

INTERIM DIVIDENDS (Per Share):

Amt.	Decl.	Ex.	Rec.	Pay.
0.235Q	5/10/02	5/22/02	5/24/02	6/10/02
0.235Q	7/12/02	8/23/02	8/27/02	9/10/02
0.235Q	10/11/02	11/22/02	11/26/02	12/10/02
0.245Q	2/14/03	2/26/03	2/28/03	3/10/03
0.245Q	5/09/03	5/21/03	5/23/03	6/10/03

Indicated div.: $0.98 (Div. Reinv. Plan)

CAPITALIZATION (12/31/02):

	($000)	(%)
Long-Term Debt	857,757	29.6
Deferred Income Tax	345,181	11.9
Common & Surplus	1,696,986	58.5
Total	2,899,924	100.0

DIVIDEND ACHIEVER STATUS:
Rank: 167   10-Year Growth Rate: 8.92%
Total Years of Dividend Growth: 10

RECENT DEVELOPMENTS: For the quarter ended 3/31/03, VMC reported income of $1.3 million, before an accounting change charge of $18.8 million, versus income of $11.6 million, before an accounting change charge of $20.5 million, in the corresponding prior-year period. Net sales grew 3.0% to $550.4 million. Construction materials net sales slid 2.1% to $392.0 million, reflecting poor weather and higher diesel and liquid asphalt costs. Chemicals net sales advanced 18.2% to $158.3 million.

PROSPECTS: In 2003, earnings per share are expected between $0.60 and $0.70 in the second quarter, and range from $1.85 to $2.15 for the full year, excluding an accounting change charge of $0.18. In 2003, Construction Material earnings are anticipated in the range of $350.0 million to $380.0 million. While residential construction is expected to remain at current strong levels with no year-over-year change in aggregates demand, nonresidential construction is projected to remain at current low levels.

BUSINESS

VULCAN MATERIALS COMPANY is engaged in the production, distribution and sale of construction materials and industrial and specialty chemicals. The Company is a producer of construction aggregates and other construction materials. The Company is also a chemicals manufacturer, supplying chloralkali and other industrial chemicals. Construction materials accounted for 77.8% of 2002 sales, while chemicals, such as chlorinated hydrocarbons, caustic soda and anhydrous ammonia, accounted for 22.2%. As of 12/31/02, VMC operated 220 permanent reserve-supplied aggregates production facilities in 17 states and Mexico.

ANNUAL FINANCIAL DATA

	12/31/02	12/31/01	12/31/00	12/31/99	12/31/98	12/31/97	12/31/96
Earnings Per Share	③ 1.86	2.17	② 2.16	2.35	2.50	2.03	① 1.79
Cash Flow Per Share	4.47	4.89	4.43	4.37	3.85	3.21	2.85
Tang. Book Val. Per Share	11.04	10.02	9.00	8.63	11.47	9.81	8.42
Dividends Per Share	0.94	0.90	0.84	0.78	0.69	0.63	0.56
Dividend Payout %	50.5	41.5	38.9	33.2	27.7	30.8	31.3
INCOME STATEMENT (IN MILLIONS):							
Net Sales	2,545.1	2,755.3	2,491.7	2,355.8	1,776.4	1,678.6	1,568.9
Costs & Expenses	2,236.2	2,371.4	1,918.9	1,790.6	1,295.8	1,274.4	1,181.9
Depreciation & Amort.	267.2	278.2	232.4	207.1	137.8	120.6	112.6
Operating Income	292.7	370.4	340.5	358.1	342.9	283.6	274.5
Net Interest Inc./(Exp.)	d51.5	d56.8	d43.4	d44.2	d0.1	d3.7	d5.5
Income Before Income Taxes	257.7	324.1	312.2	351.6	374.8	300.5	285.6
Income Taxes	67.2	101.4	92.3	111.9	118.9	91.4	97.0
Net Income	③ 190.4	222.7	② 219.9	239.7	255.9	209.1	① 188.6
Cash Flow	458.1	500.9	452.3	446.8	393.7	329.8	301.2
Average Shs. Outstg. (000)	102,515	102,497	102,012	102,190	102,177	102,849	105,519
BALANCE SHEET (IN MILLIONS):							
Cash & Cash Equivalents	170.7	100.8	55.3	52.8	180.6	128.6	50.8
Total Current Assets	789.7	730.0	694.5	624.7	576.4	487.1	394.0
Net Property	1,976.1	2,000.0	1,848.6	1,639.7	895.8	808.4	764.5
Total Assets	3,448.2	3,398.2	3,228.6	2,839.5	1,658.6	1,449.2	1,320.6
Total Current Liabilities	297.7	344.5	572.2	386.6	211.5	207.7	194.7
Long-Term Obligations	857.8	906.3	685.4	698.9	76.5	81.9	85.5
Net Stockholders' Equity	1,697.0	1,604.3	1,471.5	1,323.7	1,153.7	991.5	883.7
Net Working Capital	492.0	385.5	122.3	238.1	364.9	279.4	199.4
Year-end Shs. Outstg. (000)	101,557	101,320	101,044	100,735	100,596	101,061	104,913
STATISTICAL RECORD:							
Operating Profit Margin %	11.5	13.4	13.7	15.2	19.3	16.9	17.5
Net Profit Margin %	7.5	8.1	8.8	10.2	14.4	12.5	12.0
Return on Equity %	11.2	13.9	14.9	18.1	22.2	21.1	21.3
Return on Assets %	5.5	6.6	6.8	8.4	15.4	14.4	14.3
Debt/Total Assets %	24.9	26.7	21.2	24.6	4.6	5.7	6.5
Price Range	49.95-32.35	55.30-37.50	48.88-36.50	51.25-34.31	44.66-31.33	34.64-18.41	22.16-17.71
P/E Ratio	26.9-17.4	25.5-17.3	22.6-16.9	21.8-14.6	17.9-12.5	17.0-9.1	12.4-9.9
Average Yield %	2.3	1.9	2.0	1.8	1.8	2.4	2.8

Statistics are as originally reported. Adj. for 3-for-1 stk. split, 2/99. ① Incl. gain from sales of assets: $5.2 mill. ② Incl. a chrg. of $23.0 mill. from an arbitration settlement. ③ Bef. acctg. chrg. of $20.5 mill.

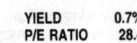

NYSE SYMBOL WMT
Rec. Pr. 52.61 (5/31/03)

WAL-MART STORES, INC.

YIELD 0.7%
P/E RATIO 28.4

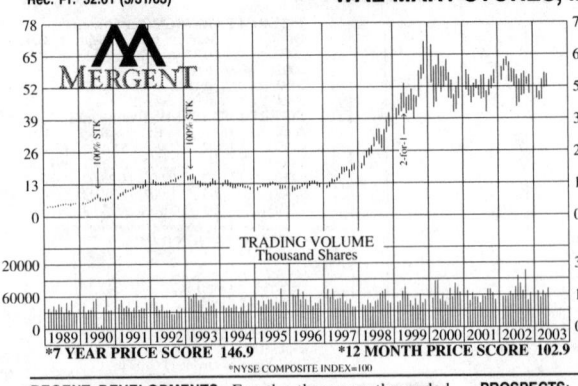

*7 YEAR PRICE SCORE 146.9   *12 MONTH PRICE SCORE 102.9
*NYSE COMPOSITE INDEX=100

INTERIM EARNINGS (Per Share):

Qtr.	Apr.	July	Oct.	Jan.
2000-01	0.30	0.36	0.31	0.45
2001-02	0.31	0.36	0.33	0.49
2002-03	0.37	0.46	0.41	0.57
2003-04	0.41	...	...	...

INTERIM DIVIDENDS (Per Share):

Amt.	Decl.	Ex.	Rec.	Pay.
0.075Q	8/14/02	9/18/02	9/20/02	10/07/02
0.075Q	11/14/02	12/18/02	12/20/02	1/06/03
0.09Q	3/06/03	3/19/03	3/21/03	4/07/03
0.09Q	6/05/03	6/18/03	6/20/03	7/07/03

Indicated div.: $0.36 (Div. Reinv. Plan)

CAPITALIZATION (1/31/03):

	($000)	(%)
Long-Term Debt	16,607,000	27.5
Capital Lease Obligations	3,001,000	5.0
Minority Interest	1,362,000	2.3
Common & Surplus	39,337,000	65.2
Total	60,307,000	100.0

DIVIDEND ACHIEVER STATUS:
Rank: 30   10-Year Growth Rate: 19.42%
Total Years of Dividend Growth: 21

RECENT DEVELOPMENTS: For the three months ended 4/30/03, income from continuing operations climbed 14.7% to $1.83 billion versus income from continuing operations of $1.60 billion a year earlier. Net sales increased 9.7% to $56.72 billion from $51.71 billion the year before. Comparable-store sales increased 2.2% year over year. Cost of sales totaled $43.92 billion, or 77.4% of net sales, compared with $40.14 billion, or 77.6% of net sales, the previous year.

PROSPECTS: On 5/2/03, the Company announced that it has entered into an agreement to sell its wholly-owned subsidiary McLane Company, Inc., a grocery and foodservice distributor with fiscal 2003 sales of about $14.90 billion, to Berkshire Hathaway Inc. The transaction is expected to be completed by the end of June 2003, subject to regulatory approval. Separately, the Company anticipates full-year 2003 earnings of between $2.00 and $2.05 per share.

BUSINESS

WAL-MART STORES, INC. operated 1,536 discount department stores, 1,309 Supercenters, 526 Sam's Clubs and 51 Neighborhood Markets in the United States as of 4/30/03. WMT also operated 602 Wal-Mart stores in Mexico, 259 in the United Kingdom, 213 in Canada, 92 in Germany, 54 in Puerto Rico, 23 in Brazil, 15 in Korea, and eleven in Argentina. WMT also operated 26 stores in China under joint venture agreements. WMT's stores offer a wide assortment of merchandise to satisfy most of the clothing, home, recreational and convenience needs of the family. Supercenters combine food, general merchandise, and services including pharmacy, dry cleaning, portrait studios, photo finishing, hair salons, and optical shops. WMT also operates McLane Company, Inc., a specialty distributor serving over 50,000 convenience stores, mass merchandisers, quick-service restaurants and movie theaters. In addition, WMT owns a 35.0% interest in Seiyu, Ltd., which operates over 400 stores throughout Japan.

ANNUAL FINANCIAL DATA

	1/31/03	1/31/02	1/31/01	1/31/00	1/31/99	1/31/98	1/31/97
Earnings Per Share	1.81	1.49	1.40	①1.25	0.99	0.78	0.67
Cash Flow Per Share	2.58	2.22	2.04	1.78	1.41	1.14	...
Tang. Book Val. Per Share	6.78	5.95	4.99	3.69	4.18	4.13	3.75
Dividends Per Share	0.29	0.27	0.23	0.19	0.15	0.13	0.10
Dividend Payout %	16.0	18.1	16.4	15.1	15.2	16.4	15.5

INCOME STATEMENT (IN MILLIONS):

	1/31/03	1/31/02	1/31/01	1/31/00	1/31/99	1/31/98	1/31/97
Total Revenues	246,525.0	219,812.0	193,295.0	166,809.0	139,208.0	119,299.0	106,146.0
Costs & Expenses	229,449.0	204,445.0	178,937.0	154,329.0	129,216.0	111,162.0	98,988.0
Depreciation & Amort.	3,432.0	3,290.0	2,868.0	2,375.0	1,872.0	1,634.0	1,463.0
Operating Income	13,644.0	12,077.0	11,490.0	10,105.0	8,120.0	6,503.0	5,695.0
Net Interest Inc./(Exp.)	d925.0	d1,326.0	d1,374.0	d1,022.0	d797.0	d784.0	d845.0
Income Before Income Taxes	12,719.0	10,751.0	10,116.0	9,083.0	7,323.0	5,719.0	4,850.0
Income Taxes	4,487.0	3,897.0	3,692.0	3,338.0	2,740.0	2,115.0	1,794.0
Equity Earnings/Minority Int.	d193.0	d183.0	d129.0	d170.0	d153.0	d78.0	...
Net Income	8,039.0	6,671.0	6,295.0	①5,575.0	4,430.0	3,526.0	3,056.0
Cash Flow	11,471.0	9,961.0	9,163.0	7,950.0	6,302.0	5,160.0	4,519.0
Average Shs. Outstg. (000)	4,446,000	4,481,000	4,484,000	4,474,000	4,485,000	4,533,000	...

BALANCE SHEET (IN MILLIONS):

	1/31/03	1/31/02	1/31/01	1/31/00	1/31/99	1/31/98	1/31/97
Cash & Cash Equivalents	2,758.0	2,161.0	2,054.0	1,856.0	1,879.0	1,447.0	883.0
Total Current Assets	30,483.0	28,246.0	26,555.0	24,356.0	21,132.0	19,352.0	17,993.0
Net Property	48,700.0	45,750.0	40,934.0	35,969.0	25,973.0	23,606.0	20,324.0
Total Assets	94,685.0	83,451.0	78,130.0	70,349.0	49,996.0	45,384.0	39,604.0
Total Current Liabilities	32,617.0	27,282.0	28,949.0	25,803.0	16,762.0	14,460.0	10,957.0
Long-Term Obligations	19,608.0	18,732.0	15,655.0	16,674.0	9,607.0	9,674.0	10,016.0
Net Stockholders' Equity	39,337.0	35,102.0	31,343.0	25,834.0	21,112.0	18,503.0	17,143.0
Net Working Capital	d2,134.0	964.0	d2,394.0	d1,447.0	4,370.0	4,892.0	7,036.0
Year-end Shs. Outstg. (000)	4,395,000	4,453,000	4,470,000	4,457,000	4,448,000	4,482,000	4,570,000

STATISTICAL RECORD:

	1/31/03	1/31/02	1/31/01	1/31/00	1/31/99	1/31/98	1/31/97
Operating Profit Margin %	5.5	5.5	5.9	6.1	5.8	5.5	5.4
Net Profit Margin %	3.3	3.0	3.3	3.3	3.2	3.0	2.9
Return on Equity %	20.4	19.0	20.1	21.6	21.0	19.1	17.8
Return on Assets %	8.5	8.0	8.1	7.9	8.9	7.8	7.7
Debt/Total Assets %	20.7	22.4	20.0	23.7	19.2	21.3	25.3
Price Range	63.94-43.72	58.75-41.50	69.00-41.44	70.25-38.69	41.38-18.78	20.97-11.00	14.13-9.55
P/E Ratio	35.3-24.2	39.4-27.9	49.3-29.6	56.2-30.9	41.8-19.0	26.9-14.1	21.2-14.4
Average Yield %	0.5	0.5	0.4	0.3	0.5	0.8	0.9

Statistics are as originally reported. Adj. for 100% stk. div., 4/99. ① Bef. $198.0 mil ($0.04/sh) acctg. chg.

OFFICERS:
S. R. Walton, Chmn.
H. L. Scott, Jr., Pres., C.E.O.
T. M. Schoewe, Exec. V.P., C.F.O.

INVESTOR CONTACT: Investor Relations, (479) 273-8446

PRINCIPAL OFFICE: 702 S.W. Eighth Street, Bentonville, AR 72716

TELEPHONE NUMBER: (479) 273-4000
FAX: (479) 273-1986
WEB: www.wal-mart.com

NO. OF EMPLOYEES: 1,400,000 (approx.)

SHAREHOLDERS: 330,000

ANNUAL MEETING: In June

INCORPORATED: DE, Oct., 1969

INSTITUTIONAL HOLDINGS:
No. of Institutions: 1,103
Shares Held: 1,572,027,492
% Held: 35.8

INDUSTRY: Variety stores (SIC: 5331)

TRANSFER AGENT(S): EquiServe Trust Company, N.A., Providence, RI

WALGREEN CO.

YIELD 0.5%
P/E RATIO 28.8

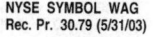

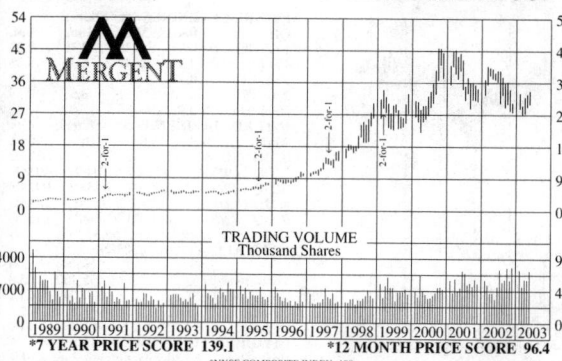

TRADING VOLUME
Thousand Shares

*7 YEAR PRICE SCORE 139.1   *12 MONTH PRICE SCORE 96.4
*NYSE COMPOSITE INDEX=100

INTERIM EARNINGS (Per Share):

Qtr.	Nov.	Feb.	May	Aug.
1998-99	0.11	0.20	0.16	0.16
1999-00	0.13	0.23	0.19	0.21
2000-01	0.15	0.29	0.21	0.21
2001-02	0.18	0.32	0.25	0.24
2002-03	0.22	0.36	...	...

INTERIM DIVIDENDS (Per Share):

Amt.	Decl.	Ex.	Rec.	Pay.
0.036Q	7/10/02	8/16/02	8/20/02	9/12/02
0.037Q	10/09/02	11/14/02	11/18/02	12/12/02
0.037Q	1/08/03	2/13/03	2/18/03	3/12/03
0.037Q	4/09/03	5/19/03	5/21/03	6/12/03

Indicated div.: $0.15 (Div. Reinv. Plan)

CAPITALIZATION (8/31/02):

	($000)	(%)
Deferred Income Tax	176,500	2.8
Common & Surplus	6,230,200	97.2
Total	6,406,700	100.0

DIVIDEND ACHIEVER STATUS:

Rank: 183   10-Year Growth Rate: 8.04%
Total Years of Dividend Growth: 27

RECENT DEVELOPMENTS:

For the three months ended 2/28/03, net earnings grew 13.6% to $370.9 million from $326.6 million in the corresponding prior-year period. Net sales totaled $8.45 billion, up 12.8% compared with $7.49 billion the previous year. Comparable-store sales increased 7.7% year over year. Prescription sales, which accounted for approximately 59.0% of sales in the second quarter of fiscal 2003, climbed 17.8%.

PROSPECTS:

During the first half of fiscal 2003, WAG opened 154 new stores, with a net gain of 115 stores after relocations and closings. The Company anticipates opening 425 new stores, or a net increase of about 345 stores after closings and relocations, during the current fiscal year. One of the key areas WAG is focusing its expansion efforts is Southern California, where the Company operates more than 90 stores as of 3/24/03.

BUSINESS

WALGREEN CO. operated 4,029 drugstores located in 43 states and Puerto Rico as of 4/30/03. The drugstores sell prescription and nonprescription drugs in addition to other products including general merchandise, cosmetics, toiletries, household items, food and beverages. Customer prescription purchases can be made at the drugstores as well as through the mail, telephone and the Internet. The Company's retail drugstore operations are supported by twelve distribution centers and a mail service facility located in Beaverton, Oregon. Prescription drugs comprised 60% of fiscal 2002 total sales; general merchandise, 29%; and nonprescription drugs, 11%.

ANNUAL FINANCIAL DATA

	8/31/02	8/31/01	8/31/00	8/31/99	8/31/98	8/31/97	8/31/96
Earnings Per Share	② 0.99	② 0.86	② 0.76	0.62	① 0.54	0.44	0.38
Cash Flow Per Share	1.29	1.12	0.99	0.82	0.72	0.60	0.52
Tang. Book Val. Per Share	6.08	5.11	4.19	3.47	2.86	2.40	2.08
Dividends Per Share	0.146	0.141	0.136	0.131	0.126	0.121	0.113
Dividend Payout %	14.8	16.4	17.9	21.1	23.3	27.5	29.7

INCOME STATEMENT (IN MILLIONS):

	8/31/02	8/31/01	8/31/00	8/31/99	8/31/98	8/31/97	8/31/96
Total Revenues	28,681.1	24,623.0	21,206.9	17,838.8	15,307.0	13,363.0	11,778.4
Costs & Expenses	26,749.6	22,955.5	19,752.7	16,613.3	14,283.0	12,491.0	11,027.0
Depreciation & Amort.	307.3	269.2	230.1	210.1	189.0	164.0	147.3
Operating Income	1,624.2	1,398.3	1,224.1	1,015.4	835.0	708.0	604.1
Net Interest Inc./(Exp.)	6.9	2.3	5.7	11.9	5.0	4.0	2.9
Income Before Income Taxes	1,637.3	1,422.7	1,263.3	1,027.3	877.0	712.0	606.9
Income Taxes	618.1	537.1	486.4	403.2	340.0	276.0	235.2
Net Income	② 1,019.2	② 885.6	② 776.9	624.1	① 537.0	436.0	371.7
Cash Flow	1,326.5	1,154.8	1,007.0	834.2	726.0	600.0	519.1
Average Shs. Outstg. (000)	1,032,271	1,028,947	1,019,889	1,014,282	1,005,692	996,670	993,744

BALANCE SHEET (IN MILLIONS):

	8/31/02	8/31/01	8/31/00	8/31/99	8/31/98	8/31/97	8/31/96
Cash & Cash Equivalents	449.9	16.9	12.8	141.8	144.0	73.0	8.8
Total Current Assets	5,166.5	4,393.9	3,550.1	3,221.7	2,623.0	2,326.0	2,019.0
Net Property	4,591.4	4,345.3	3,428.2	2,593.9	2,144.0	1,754.0	1,448.4
Total Assets	9,878.8	8,833.8	7,103.7	5,906.7	4,902.0	4,207.0	3,633.6
Total Current Liabilities	2,955.2	3,011.6	2,303.7	1,923.8	1,580.0	1,439.0	1,182.0
Long-Term Obligations	...	...	...	...	...	...	10.1
Net Stockholders' Equity	6,230.2	5,207.2	4,234.0	3,484.3	2,849.0	2,373.0	2,043.1
Net Working Capital	2,211.3	1,382.3	1,246.4	1,297.9	1,043.0	887.0	837.1
Year-end Shs. Outstg. (000)	1,024,908	1,019,425	1,010,819	1,004,022	996,488	987,580	984,564

STATISTICAL RECORD:

	8/31/02	8/31/01	8/31/00	8/31/99	8/31/98	8/31/97	8/31/96
Operating Profit Margin %	5.7	5.7	5.8	5.7	5.5	5.3	5.1
Net Profit Margin %	3.6	3.6	3.7	3.5	3.5	3.3	3.2
Return on Equity %	16.4	17.0	18.3	17.9	18.8	18.4	18.2
Return on Assets %	10.3	10.0	10.9	10.6	11.0	10.4	10.2
Debt/Total Assets %	...	...	...	...	...	...	0.3
Price Range	40.70-27.70	45.29-28.70	45.75-22.06	33.94-22.69	30.22-14.78	16.81-9.63	10.91-7.28
P/E Ratio	41.1-28.0	52.7-33.4	60.2-29.0	54.7-36.6	56.5-27.6	38.2-21.9	29.1-19.4
Average Yield %	0.4	0.4	0.4	0.4	0.5	0.6	0.9

Statistics are as originally reported. Adj. for 2-for-1 stk. split, 2/99 & 8/97. ① Bef. $26.4 mil ($0.03/sh) chg. for acctg. adj. & incl. $23.0 mil ($0.03/sh) after-tax gain. ② Incl. $6.2 mil ($0.01/sh) pre-tax gain from partial payment of a prescription-drug antitrust settlement, 2002; $22.1 mil ($0.01/sh), 2001; $33.5 mil ($0.02/sh), 2000.

OFFICERS:
D. W. Bernauer, Chmn., C.E.O.
J. A. Rein, Pres., C.O.O.
R. L. Polark, Sr. V.P., C.F.O.
J. W. Gleeson, V.P., Treas.

INVESTOR CONTACT: John M. Palizza, Asst. Treas., (847) 940-2935

PRINCIPAL OFFICE: 200 Wilmot Road, Deerfield, IL 60015

TELEPHONE NUMBER: (847) 940-2500
FAX: (847) 914-2654
WEB: www.walgreens.com

NO. OF EMPLOYEES: 93,000 full-time (approx.); 48,000 part-time (approx.)

SHAREHOLDERS: 96,976

ANNUAL MEETING: In Jan.

INCORPORATED: IL, Feb., 1909

INDUSTRY: Drug stores and proprietary stores (SIC: 5912)

TRANSFER AGENT(S): Computershare Investor Services, Chicago, IL

WASHINGTON FEDERAL, INC.

YIELD	3.6%
P/E RATIO	11.1

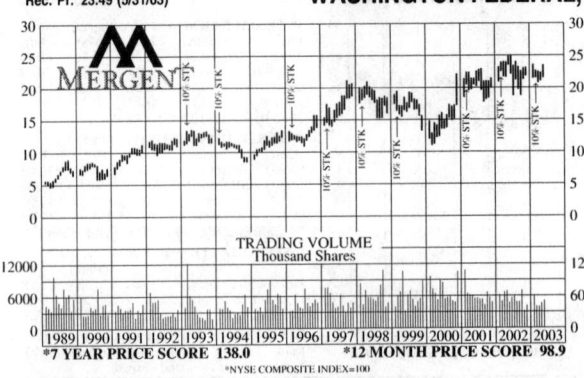

INTERIM EARNINGS (Per Share):

Qtr.	Dec.	Mar.	June	Sept.
1998-99	0.37	0.38	0.39	0.39
1999-00	0.38	0.38	0.37	0.36
2000-01	0.35	0.39	0.42	0.45
2001-02	0.50	0.51	0.51	0.53
2002-03	0.53	0.54	...	...

INTERIM DIVIDENDS (Per Share):

Amt.	Decl.	Ex.	Rec.	Pay.
0.23Q	6/24/02	7/02/02	7/05/02	7/19/02
0.23Q	9/23/02	10/02/02	10/04/02	10/18/02
0.23Q	12/23/02	12/31/02	1/03/03	1/17/03
10% STK	1/21/03	2/05/03	2/07/03	2/21/03
0.21Q	3/24/03	4/02/03	4/04/03	4/18/03

Indicated div.: **$0.84**

CAPITALIZATION (9/30/02):

	($000)	(%)
Total Deposits	4,452,250	63.0
Long-Term Debt	1,650,000	23.4
Common & Surplus	960,718	13.6
Total	7,062,968	100.0

DIVIDEND ACHIEVER STATUS:
Rank: 168   10-Year Growth Rate: 8.91%
Total Years of Dividend Growth: 19

TRADING VOLUME
Thousand Shares

*7 YEAR PRICE SCORE 138.0   *12 MONTH PRICE SCORE 98.9

*NYSE COMPOSITE INDEX=100

RECENT DEVELOPMENTS: For the three months ended 3/31/03, net income was $37.7 million compared with $35.8 million in the same period a year earlier. Results for 2003 included a pre-tax gain of $3.4 million on the sale of real estate. Net interest income declined 5.1% to $65.3 million from $68.8 million the previous year. Provision for loan losses was $150,000 versus $2.0 million the year before. Other income, which included the aforementioned gain on the sale of real estate, surged to $5.6 million from $1.5 million in 2002. Other expense declined 5.3% to $12.4 million. Separately, on 5/20/03, WFSL announced the signing of a definitive agreement to acquire United Savings and Loan Bank. Under the terms of the agreement, shareholders of United Savings will receive aggregate consideration of $65.0 million. The transaction is expected to close by 9/30/03, pending certain approvals. The combined company will have 119 offices in eight western states.

BUSINESS

WASHINGTON FEDERAL, INC. is a non-diversified unitary savings and loan holding company. WFSL conducts its operations through its federally insured savings and loan association subsidiary, Washington Federal Savings and Loan Association. The Company's business consists primarily of attracting savings deposits from the general public and investing these funds in loans secured by first mortgage liens on single-family dwellings, including loans for the construction of such dwellings, and loans on multi-family dwellings. WFSL also originates other types of loans for its portfolio and invests in certain United States Government and agency obligations and other investments permitted by applicable laws and regulations. As of 4/17/03, WFSL had 115 offices located in eight states in the western United States. In addition, through its subsidiaries, WFSL is engaged in real estate development and insurance brokerage activities.

QUARTERLY DATA

(9/30/02)	REV	INC
1st Quarter	66,555	35,385
2nd Quarter	68,798	35,759
3rd Quarter	68,260	35,883
4th Quarter	68,763	36,.927

ANNUAL FINANCIAL DATA

	9/30/02	9/30/01	9/30/00	9/30/99	9/30/98	9/30/97	9/30/96
Earnings Per Share	2.05	1.61	1.50	1.54	1.44	1.37	1.06
Tang. Book Val. Per Share	13.23	13.17	10.34	9.73	10.42	8.61	8.40
Dividends Per Share	0.82	0.77	0.74	0.67	0.61	0.56	0.51
Dividend Payout %	39.9	48.0	49.0	43.8	42.5	40.6	47.7
INCOME STATEMENT (IN MILLIONS):							
Total Interest Income	507.3	536.4	498.0	455.6	460.6	459.0	404.2
Total Interest Expense	234.9	320.1	299.5	244.5	252.2	257.4	228.7
Net Interest Income	272.4	216.3	198.5	211.1	208.4	201.6	175.5
Provision for Loan Losses	7.0	1.9	...	0.7	0.7	0.8	3.8
Non-Interest Income	8.2	10.1	11.3	12.8	11.3	7.0	6.0
Non-Interest Expense	51.2	49.1	46.6	46.1	45.1	44.4	53.2
Income Before Taxes	222.4	175.5	163.2	177.1	173.8	163.3	124.5
Net Income	144.0	113.6	105.7	114.3	111.8	105.1	79.9
Average Shs. Outstg. (000)	70,523	70,462	70,430	74,279	77,404	76,493	75,185
BALANCE SHEET (IN MILLIONS):							
Securities Avail. for Sale	918.8	1,079.9	1,178.5	1,169.9	764.2	672.1	533.6
Total Loans & Leases	4,292.0	4,207.8	5,280.0	4,730.1	4,452.2	4,469.8	3,723.0
Allowance for Credit Losses	...	...	330.8	351.3	308.7	279.0	...
Net Loans & Leases	4,292.0	4,207.8	4,949.2	4,378.7	4,143.5	4,190.8	3,723.0
Total Assets	7,392.4	7,026.7	6,719.8	6,163.5	5,637.0	5,719.6	5,115.0
Total Deposits	4,452.3	4,251.1	3,375.0	3,291.9	3,071.2	2,905.4	2,423.9
Long-Term Obligations	1,650.0	1,637.5	1,209.0	1,454.0	1,356.5	1,601.0	1,162.0
Total Liabilities	6,431.7	6,152.7	5,960.7	5,413.5	4,869.8	5,001.8	4,537.3
Net Stockholders' Equity	960.7	874.0	759.2	750.0	767.2	717.7	577.7
Year-end Shs. Outstg. (000)	69,895	63,648	69,373	72,183	68,475	76,514	65,540
STATISTICAL RECORD:							
Return on Equity %	15.0	13.0	13.9	15.2	14.6	14.6	13.8
Return on Assets %	1.9	1.6	1.6	1.9	2.0	1.8	1.6
Equity/Assets %	13.0	12.4	11.3	12.2	13.6	12.5	11.3
Non-Int. Exp./Tot. Inc. %	18.3	21.7	22.3	20.6	20.6	21.5	29.3
Price Range	25.05-18.64	22.94-17.69	22.12-10.99	19.44-13.24	21.00-15.20	21.19-13.89	15.74-10.87
P/E Ratio	12.2-9.1	14.2-11.0	14.7-7.3	12.6-8.6	14.6-10.5	15.4-10.1	14.8-10.2
Average Yield %	3.7	3.8	4.4	4.1	3.4	3.2	3.8

Statistics are as originally reported. Adj. for 10.0% stk. divs., 2/03; 2/02; 2/01; 2/99; 2/98; 2/97.

OFFICERS:
G. C. Pinkerton, Chmn.
R. M. Whitehead, Vice Chmn., Pres., C.E.O.
R. L. Saper, Exec. V.P., C.F.O.

INVESTOR CONTACT: Cathy Cooper, V.P.,
(206) 777-8246

PRINCIPAL OFFICE: 425 Pike Street, Seattle,
WA 98101

TELEPHONE NUMBER: (206) 624-7930
FAX: (206) 624-2334
WEB: www.washingtonfederal.com
NO. OF EMPLOYEES: 726 full-time
(approx.); 25 part-time (approx.)
SHAREHOLDERS: 2,533 (approx.)
ANNUAL MEETING: In Jan.
INCORPORATED: WA, Feb., 1995

INSTITUTIONAL HOLDINGS:
No. of Institutions: 175
Shares Held: 35,651,257
% Held: 50.9

INDUSTRY: Federal savings institutions
(SIC: 6035)

TRANSFER AGENT(S): Mellon Investor
Services, LLC, Ridgefield Park, NJ

WASHINGTON MUTUAL, INC.

YIELD 2.9%
P/E RATIO 9.9

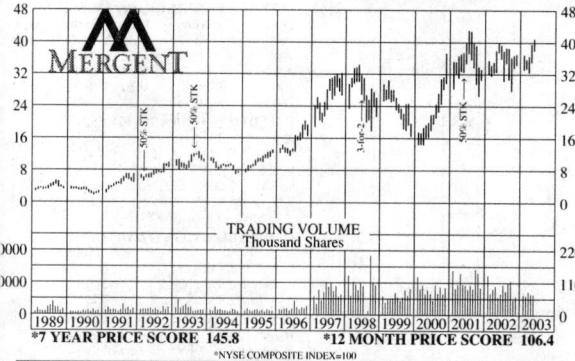

TRADING VOLUME
Thousand Shares

| 1989 | 1990 | 1991 | 1992 | 1993 | 1994 | 1995 | 1996 | 1997 | 1998 | 1999 | 2000 | 2001 | 2002 | 2003 |

*7 YEAR PRICE SCORE 145.8   *12 MONTH PRICE SCORE 106.4
*NYSE COMPOSITE INDEX=100

INTERIM EARNINGS (Per Share):

Qtr.	Mar.	June	Sept.	Dec.
2000	0.56	0.61	0.57	0.63
2001	0.76	0.91	0.85	0.62
2002	0.93	1.01	1.01	1.03
2003	1.07	...	...	...

INTERIM DIVIDENDS (Per Share):

Amt.	Decl.	Ex.	Rec.	Pay.
0.26Q	4/16/02	4/26/02	4/30/02	5/15/02
0.27Q	7/16/02	7/29/02	7/31/02	8/15/02
0.28Q	10/15/02	10/29/02	10/31/02	11/15/02
0.29Q	1/21/03	1/29/03	1/31/03	2/14/03
0.30Q	4/15/03	4/28/03	4/30/03	5/15/03

Indicated div.: $1.20 (Div. Reinv. Plan)

CAPITALIZATION (12/31/02):

	($000)	(%)
Total Deposits	155,516,000	64.2
Long-Term Debt	66,529,000	27.5
Common & Surplus	20,134,000	8.3
Total	242,179,000	100.0

DIVIDEND ACHIEVER STATUS:

Rank: 16   10-Year Growth Rate: 21.76%
Total Years of Dividend Growth: 13

RECENT DEVELOPMENTS: For the quarter ended 3/31/03, net income increased 4.9% to $1.00 billion from $956.0 million in the corresponding prior-year period. Earnings for 2003 and 2002 included net nonrecurring gains of $889.0 million and $63.0 million, respectively, from various items. Net interest income fell 15.8% to $2.02 billion, due to higher interest rate levels. Provision for loan and lease losses decreased 28.6% to $125.0 million. Total non-interest income advanced 74.0% to $1.41 billion.

PROSPECTS: During the first quarter, WM reported continued growth in checking accounts, which increased by more than 200,000 year over year. Also, WM opened 33 new financial center stores and three new home loan stores nationwide. WM is on schedule to open about 250 financial center stores and 70 home loans stores in 2003 as it continues to expand its national franchise. Looking ahead, WM expects another record year in 2003, reflecting its strong business fundamentals and steady credit quality.

BUSINESS

WASHINGTON MUTUAL, INC. is a holding company for both banking and nonbanking subsidiaries. The Company's primary banking subsidiaries are Washington Mutual Bank, FA (formerly Washington Mutual Savings Bank), Washington Mutual Bank and Washington Mutual Bank fsb. These organizations provide consumer banking, full-service securities brokerage, mutual fund management, and travel and insurance underwriting services. As of 3/31/03, WM and its subsidiaries had assets of $276.97 billion and operated more than 2,500 offices nationwide. In February 2001, WM acquired the residential mortgage banking business of PNC Financial Services Group and Bank United Corp. On 1/7/02, WM acquired Dime Bancorp. On 10/1/02, WM acquired the parent company of HomeSide Lending, Inc., the U.S. mortgage unit of the National Australia Bank Ltd., for about $1.30 billion.

ANNUAL FINANCIAL DATA

	12/31/02	12/31/01	12/31/00	12/31/99	12/31/98	12/31/97	12/31/96
Earnings Per Share	⑧ 4.05	⑦⑧ 3.15	⑤ 2.36	④ 2.11	③ 1.71	②⑧ 0.83	⑧ 0.38
Tang. Book Val. Per Share	9.03	6.29	9.96	8.41	8.85	7.97	7.98
Dividends Per Share	1.06	0.90	0.76	0.65	0.55	0.47	0.40
Dividend Payout %	26.2	28.5	32.2	31.0	32.0	57.0	105.8
INCOME STATEMENT (IN MILLIONS):							
Total Interest Income	14,247.0	15,065.0	13,783.0	12,062.2	11,221.5	6,811.0	3,149.2
Total Interest Expense	5,906.0	8,189.0	9,472.0	7,610.4	6,929.7	4,154.5	1,958.2
Net Interest Income	8,341.0	6,876.0	4,311.0	4,451.8	4,291.7	2,656.5	1,191.0
Provision for Loan Losses	595.0	575.0	185.0	167.1	162.0	207.1	201.5
Non-Interest Income	4,790.0	2,627.0	1,984.0	1,509.0	1,577.0	750.9	259.3
Non-Interest Expense	6,382.0	4,617.0	3,126.0	2,909.6	3,337.3	2,299.1	1,025.3
Income Before Taxes	6,154.0	4,311.0	2,984.0	2,884.2	2,369.5	901.1	223.5
Equity Earnings/Minority Int.	...	...	...	...	...	...	d13.6
Net Income	⑧ 3,896.0	①⑧ 2,732.0	⑤ 1,899.0	④ 1,817.1	③ 1,486.9	② 481.8	⑧ 114.3
Average Shs. Outstg. (000)	960,152	864,700	804,695	861,830	867,843	555,852	253,933
BALANCE SHEET (IN MILLIONS):							
Total Loans & Leases	147,528.0	132,991.0	119,626.0	113,745.7	107,612.2	67,124.9	30,694.2
Allowance for Credit Losses	1,653.0	1,404.0	1,014.0	1,041.9	1,067.8	670.5	590.8
Net Loans & Leases	145,875.0	131,587.0	118,612.0	112,703.7	106,544.4	66,454.4	30,103.4
Total Assets	268,298.0	242,506.0	194,716.0	186,513.6	165,493.3	96,981.1	44,551.9
Total Deposits	155,516.0	107,182.0	79,574.0	81,129.8	85,492.1	50,986.0	24,080.1
Long-Term Obligations	66,529.0	73,758.0	67,785.0	63,297.3	45,198.1	22,991.3	7,918.5
Total Liabilities	248,164.0	228,341.0	184,550.0	177,461.0	156,148.9	91,672.0	42,154.0
Net Stockholders' Equity	20,134.0	14,063.0	10,166.0	9,052.7	9,344.4	5,309.1	2,397.9
Year-end Shs. Outstg. (000)	944,047	873,089	809,784	857,384	890,112	579,510	283,820
STATISTICAL RECORD:							
Return on Equity %	19.4	19.4	18.7	20.1	15.9	9.1	4.8
Return on Assets %	1.5	1.1	1.0	1.0	0.9	0.5	0.3
Equity/Assets %	7.5	5.8	5.2	4.9	5.6	5.5	5.4
Non-Int. Exp./Tot. Inc. %	48.6	48.6	49.7	48.8	56.9	67.5	70.7
Price Range	39.98-27.80	42.99-26.52	37.29-14.42	30.50-16.46	34.45-17.83	32.28-18.78	20.39-11.61
P/E Ratio	9.9-6.9	13.6-8.4	15.8-6.1	14.5-7.8	20.2-10.4	39.0-22.7	53.9-30.7
Average Yield %	3.1	2.6	2.9	2.8	2.1	1.8	2.5

Statistics are as originally reported. Adj. for stk. 3-for-2 splits: 5/01, 6/98. ① Bef. extraord. gain of $382.0 mill. ② Incl. various pre-tax net exps. of $403.7 mill.; 1997: $256.7 mill., 1996. ③ Incl. net pre-tax non-recurr. gains of $316.0 mill. & a write-down of $52.9 mill. ④ Incl. trans.-rel. exp. of $95.7 mill. ⑤ Incl. a pre-tax gain on the sale of mtge. loans of $967.0 mill., 2001; $261.6 mill., 2000. ⑥ Reflects the acq. of Great Western Financial Corp. on 7/1/97. ⑦ Reflects acq. of H. F. Ahmanson & Co. on 10/1/98. ⑧ Incl. net nonrecurr. gains of $3.83 bill.

OFFICERS:
K. K. Killinger, Chmn., Pres., C.E.O.
T. W. Casey, Exec. V.P., C.F.O.

INVESTOR CONTACT: JoAnn DeGrande, First Vice Pres, (206) 461-3186

PRINCIPAL OFFICE: 1201 Third Avenue, Seattle, WA 98101

TELEPHONE NUMBER: (206) 461-2000
FAX: (206) 554-2778
WEB: www.wamu.com

NO. OF EMPLOYEES: 52,459

SHAREHOLDERS: 45,385

ANNUAL MEETING: In April

INCORPORATED: WA, Nov., 1994

INSTITUTIONAL HOLDINGS:
No. of Institutions: 754
Shares Held: 712,008,220
% Held: 76.2

INDUSTRY: Savings institutions, except federal (SIC: 6036)

TRANSFER AGENT(S): Mellon Investor Shareholder Services, LLC, Ridgefield Park, NJ

WASHINGTON REAL ESTATE INVESTMENT TRUST

YIELD 5.4%
P/E RATIO 23.1

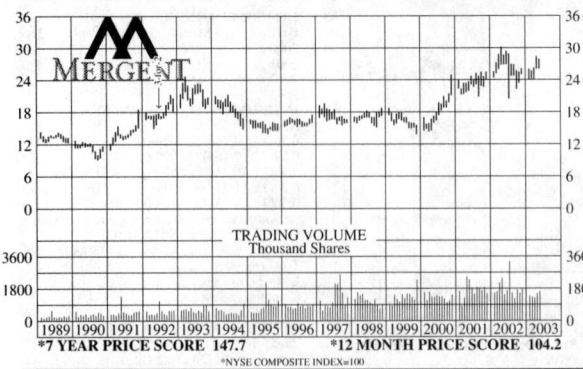

TRADING VOLUME
Thousand Shares

*7 YEAR PRICE SCORE 147.7   ***12 MONTH PRICE SCORE 104.2**

*NYSE COMPOSITE INDEX=100

INTERIM EARNINGS (Per Share):

Qtr.	Mar.	June	Sept.	Dec.
1999	0.46	0.25	0.25	0.29
2000	0.31	0.28	0.36	0.32
2001	0.30	0.33	0.43	0.32
2002	0.42	0.30	0.30	0.31
2003	0.28	...	...	...

INTERIM DIVIDENDS (Per Share):

Amt.	Decl.	Ex.	Rec.	Pay.
0.352Q	8/08/02	9/12/02	9/16/02	9/30/02
0.352Q	11/20/02	12/13/02	12/17/02	12/31/02
0.352Q	2/20/03	3/13/03	3/17/03	3/31/03
0.372Q	5/12/03	6/12/03	6/16/03	6/30/03

Indicated div.: $1.49 (Div. Reinv. Plan)

CAPITALIZATION (12/31/02):

	($000)	(%)
Long-Term Debt	402,701	55.2
Common & Surplus	326,177	44.8
Total	728,878	100.0

DIVIDEND ACHIEVER STATUS:
Rank: 234   10-Year Growth Rate: 5.21%
Total Years of Dividend Growth: 41

RECENT DEVELOPMENTS: For the quarter ended 3/31/03, net income was $11.2 million versus income of $12.6 million, before a net gain of $3.8 million from discontinued operations, in the corresponding quarter of the previous year. Total revenue rose 2.4% to $39.1 million. Operating income slipped to $27.4 million versus $27.5 million the year before. Funds from operations declined to $19.3 million from $19.5 million in 2002.

PROSPECTS: The Company may continue to experience unfavorable results due to the struggling economy. The office and industrial properties are being hardest hit, while the multifamily and retail portfolios are performing relatively well. However, WRE's geographic focus in the greater Washington/Baltimore metropolitan region, diversified real estate portfolio and strong balance sheet should bode well for long-term results.

BUSINESS

WASHINGTON REAL ESTATE INVESTMENT TRUST is a self-administered qualified equity real estate investment trust. The trust's business consists of the ownership and operation of income-producing real estate properties principally in the Greater Washington, D.C.-Baltimore, MD area. Upon the purchase of a property, WRE begins a program of improving the real estate to increase the value and to improve the operations, with the goals of generating higher rental income and reducing expenses. As of 4/21/03, the trust owned a diversified portfolio consisting of 11 retail centers, 24 office buildings, nine multifamily buildings and 16 industrial properties. WRE's principal objective is to invest in high-quality real estate in prime locations and to monitor closely the management of these properties, which includes active leasing and ongoing capital improvement programs.

ANNUAL FINANCIAL DATA

	12/31/02	12/31/01	12/31/00	12/31/99	12/31/98	12/31/97	12/31/96
Earnings Per Share	② 1.22	① 1.38	① 1.26	① 1.24	① 1.15	0.90	0.88
Tang. Book Val. Per Share	8.33	8.33	7.24	7.20	7.11	7.07	6.15
Dividends Per Share	1.39	1.31	1.23	1.16	1.11	1.07	1.03
Dividend Payout %	113.9	104.8	108.8	93.3	96.5	118.9	117.0
INCOME STATEMENT (IN THOUSANDS):							
Total Income	153,609	148,424	134,732	118,975	103,597	79,429	65,541
Costs & Expenses	48,480	48,247	45,849	41,454	37,672	29,702	25,027
Depreciation	29,200	26,735	22,723	19,590	15,399	10,911	7,784
Interest Expense	27,849	27,071	25,531	22,271	17,106	9,691	5,474
Net Income	② 48,080	① 52,353	① 45,139	① 44,301	① 41,064	30,136	27,964
Average Shs. Outstg.	39,281	37,951	35,872	35,700	35,700	33,400	31,800
BALANCE SHEET (IN THOUSANDS):							
Cash & Cash Equivalents	13,076	26,441	6,426	4,716	4,595	7,908	1,676
Total Real Estate Investments	706,790	651,961	597,607	578,296	530,573	448,300	305,940
Total Assets	755,997	707,935	632,047	608,480	558,707	468,571	318,488
Long-Term Obligations	402,701	359,726	351,260	297,038	238,912	107,461	107,590
Total Liabilities	428,266	382,717	371,833	349,769	303,447	216,483	122,865
Net Stockholders' Equity	326,177	323,607	258,656	257,189	253,733	252,088	195,623
Year-end Shs. Outstg.	39,168	38,829	35,740	35,721	35,692	35,678	31,803
STATISTICAL RECORD:							
Net Inc.+Depr./Assets %	10.2	11.2	10.7	10.5	10.1	8.8	11.2
Return on Equity %	14.7	16.2	17.5	17.2	16.2	12.0	14.3
Return on Assets %	6.4	7.4	7.1	7.3	7.3	6.4	8.8
Price Range	30.15-20.42	25.52-20.80	25.00-14.31	18.75-13.81	18.75-15.06	19.63-15.50	17.50-15.25
P/E Ratio	24.7-16.7	20.4-16.6	22.1-12.7	15.1-11.1	16.3-13.1	21.8-17.2	19.9-17.3
Average Yield %	5.5	5.7	6.3	7.1	6.6	6.1	6.3

Statistics are as originally reported. ① Incl. gain on sale of investment $4.3 mill.; 2001; $3.6 mill., 2000; $7.9 mill., 1999; $6.8 mill., 1998. ② Bef. inc. of $3.8 mill. from disc. ops.

OFFICERS:
E. B. Cronin Jr., Chmn., Pres., C.E.O.
L. M. Franklin, Sr. V.P., Corp. Sec.
S. Grootwassink, C.F.O.

INVESTOR CONTACT: Investor Relations, (301) 984-9400

PRINCIPAL OFFICE: 6110 Executive Boulevard, Rockville, MD 20852-3927

TELEPHONE NUMBER: (301) 984-9400
FAX: (301) 984-9610
WEB: www.writ.com

NO. OF EMPLOYEES: 286 (avg.)

SHAREHOLDERS: 37,000 (approx.)

ANNUAL MEETING: In May

INCORPORATED: DC, Nov., 1960; reincorp., MD, Jun., 1996

INSTITUTIONAL HOLDINGS:
No. of Institutions: 125
Shares Held: 11,556,960
% Held: 29.6

INDUSTRY: Real estate investment trusts (SIC: 6798)

TRANSFER AGENT(S): EquiServe Trust Company N.A., Providence, RI

WEBSTER FINANCIAL CORPORATION

YIELD 2.2%
P/E RATIO 11.2

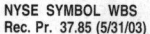

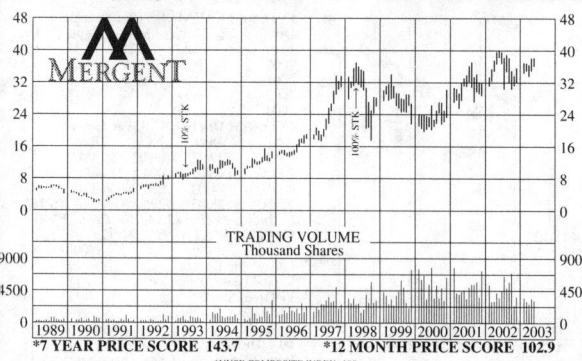

INTERIM EARNINGS (Per Share):

Qtr.	Mar.	June	Sept.	Dec.
1999	0.54	0.56	0.57	0.43
2000	0.61	0.66	0.64	0.64
2001	0.54	0.69	0.70	0.74
2002	0.65	0.82	0.84	0.85
2003	0.86	...	...	...

INTERIM DIVIDENDS (Per Share):

Amt.	Decl.	Ex.	Rec.	Pay.
0.19Q	7/23/02	8/01/02	8/05/02	8/19/02
0.19Q	10/22/02	10/31/02	11/04/02	11/18/02
0.19Q	1/29/03	2/06/03	2/10/03	2/24/03
0.21Q	4/22/03	5/01/03	5/05/03	5/19/03

Indicated div.: $0.84 (Div. Reinv. Plan)

CAPITALIZATION (12/31/02):

	($000)	(%)
Total Deposits	7,606,122	58.1
Long-Term Debt	4,455,669	34.0
Common & Surplus	1,035,458	7.9
Total	13,097,249	100.0

DIVIDEND ACHIEVER STATUS:
Rank: 117   10-Year Growth Rate: 11.54%
Total Years of Dividend Growth: 10

RECENT DEVELOPMENTS: For the quarter ended 3/31/03, net income rose 0.8% to $39.9 million compared with income of $39.6 million, before an accounting change charge of $7.3 million, in the equivalent 2002 quarter. The improvement in earnings was primarily due to strong revenue growth, which benefited from the expansion of noninterest income, which increased 28.1% to $11.7 million. Total interest expense decreased 13.2% to $64.8 million. Net interest income rose 8.5% to $104.7 million.

PROSPECTS: On 6/5/03, WBS agreed to acquire North American Bank and Trust Company, a state-chartered, commercial bank with $195.0 million in assets and eight offices in the Greater Waterbury region of Connecticut, in a combination cash and stock transaction value at about $30.0 million. Subject to approval, the purchase is expected to close in the fourth quarter of 2003. Separately, commercial and consumer loans accounted for 57.0% of total loans at 3/31/03 versus 50.0% a year earlier.

BUSINESS

WEBSTER FINANCIAL CORPORATION, through its subsidiaries, Webster Bank and Webster Insurance, Inc., delivers business and consumer banking, mortgage, insurance, trust and investment services with $14.36 billion in assets as of 3/31/03. As of 4/15/03, the Company provided its services through more than 110 banking offices, 219 ATMs, a Connecticut-based call center and the Internet. The Company has three segments: Retail Banking (78.0% of net interest income), Commercial Banking (21.4%), and Trust and Investment Services (0.6%). The Company is the majority owner of Chicago-based Duff & Phelps, LLC, a financial advisory service. Webster Bank owns the asset-based lending firm, Whitehall Business Credit Corporation, Budget Installment Corp., Center Capital Corporation, an equipment financing company headquartered in Farmington, Connecticut and Webster Trust Company, N.A.

ANNUAL FINANCIAL DATA

	12/31/02	12/31/01	12/31/00	12/31/99	12/31/98	12/31/97	12/31/96
Earnings Per Share	⑤ 3.31	④ 2.68	2.55	③ 2.10	③ 1.83	② 1.22	① 1.49
Tang. Book Val. Per Share	16.18	13.97	11.53	10.98	12.77	12.20	10.22
Dividends Per Share	0.74	0.67	0.62	0.47	0.43	0.39	0.34
Dividend Payout %	22.4	25.0	24.3	22.4	23.5	32.0	22.9
INCOME STATEMENT (IN MILLIONS):							
Total Interest Income	692.0	757.2	738.9	645.8	622.5	445.8	265.5
Total Interest Expense	286.3	389.8	412.4	342.3	377.0	253.9	149.7
Net Interest Income	405.7	367.5	326.5	303.5	245.4	191.9	115.8
Provision for Loan Losses	29.0	14.4	11.8	9.0	6.8	15.8	4.0
Non-Interest Income	185.6	162.1	128.8	92.6	74.2	36.0	25.5
Non-Interest Expense	328.3	308.9	267.1	244.5	197.8	158.5	97.2
Income Before Taxes	234.0	206.2	176.4	142.7	115.0	53.5	40.1
Net Income	⑤ 160.0	④ 136.8	118.3	③ 95.4	③ 70.5	③ 33.8	① 25.6
Average Shs. Outstg. (000)	48,392	42,743	46,428	45,393	38,571	27,656	16,578
BALANCE SHEET (IN MILLIONS):							
Cash & Due from Banks	266.5	218.9	265.0	245.8	173.9	122.3	85.2
Securities Avail. for Sale	4,119.2	3,999.1	3,143.3	2,700.6	2,969.8	2,290.3	573.6
Total Loans & Leases	7,912.6	6,967.2	7,053.9	6,204.4	5,128.1	3,907.4	2,569.3
Allowance for Credit Losses	116.8	97.3	234.7	182.2	134.6	82.8	43.7
Net Loans & Leases	7,795.8	6,869.9	6,819.2	6,022.2	4,993.5	3,824.6	2,525.5
Total Assets	13,468.0	11,857.4	11,249.5	9,931.7	9,033.9	7,019.6	3,917.6
Total Deposits	7,606.1	7,066.5	6,941.5	6,191.1	5,651.3	4,365.8	3,095.9
Long-Term Obligations	4,455.7	3,533.4	2,380.1	1,714.4	1,774.6	1,071.6	407.7
Total Liabilities	12,301.7	10,691.3	10,159.6	9,096.5	8,279.5	6,487.9	3,711.3
Net Stockholders' Equity	1,035.5	1,006.5	890.4	635.7	554.9	382.2	206.3
Year-end Shs. Outstg. (000)	45,626	49,149	48,939	45,243	37,327	27,306	15,852
STATISTICAL RECORD:							
Return on Equity %	15.5	13.6	13.3	15.0	12.7	8.8	12.4
Return on Assets %	1.2	1.2	1.1	1.0	0.8	0.5	0.7
Equity/Assets %	7.7	8.5	7.9	6.4	6.1	5.4	5.3
Non-Int. Exp./Tot. Inc. %	55.5	58.3	58.7	61.7	61.9	69.6	68.8
Price Range	40.10-30.28	37.10-25.50	30.19-19.69	34.13-21.56	37.00-17.50	33.75-17.31	19.13-13.38
P/E Ratio	12.1-9.1	13.8-9.5	11.8-7.7	16.2-10.3	20.2-9.6	27.7-14.2	12.9-9.0
Average Yield %	2.1	2.1	2.5	1.7	1.6	1.5	2.1

Statistics are as originally reported. ① Incl. non-recurr. chrgs. $5.2 mill. ② Incl. merger and acquis. chrg. of $27.1 mill. ③ Incl. acquis.-related chrg. of $9.5 mill., 1999; $17.4 mill., 1998. ④ Bef. extraord. chrg. of $1.2 mill. on early debt retirement and an acctg. change chrg. of $2.4 mill. ⑤ Incl. acq. related chrgs. of $2.0 mill.; bef. acctg. chge. chrg. of $7.3 mill.

OFFICERS:
J. C. Smith, Chmn., C.E.O.
W. T. Bromage, Pres., C.O.O.
W. J. Healy, Exec. V.P., C.F.O.

INVESTOR CONTACT: James M. Sitro, Sr. V.P., Inv. Rel., (203) 578-2399

PRINCIPAL OFFICE: Webster Plaza, Waterbury, CT 06702

TELEPHONE NUMBER: (203) 753-2921
FAX: (203) 755-5539
WEB: www.websterbank.com
NO. OF EMPLOYEES: 2,428 full-time; 280 part-time
SHAREHOLDERS: 11,000 (approx.)
ANNUAL MEETING: In Apr.
INCORPORATED: DE, Sept. 1986

INSTITUTIONAL HOLDINGS:
No. of Institutions: 175
Shares Held: 27,634,625
% Held: 60.1

INDUSTRY: Federal savings institutions (SIC: 6035)

TRANSFER AGENT(S): American Stock Transfer & Trust Co., New York, NY

WEINGARTEN REALTY INVESTORS

YIELD 5.7%
P/E RATIO 26.0

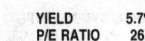

INTERIM EARNINGS (Per Share):

Qtr.	Mar.	June	Sept.	Dec.
1999	0.22	0.23	0.24	0.57
2000	0.24	0.25	0.25	0.24
2001	0.30	0.29	0.31	0.33
2002	0.31	0.34	0.43	0.34
2003	0.48	...	...	...

INTERIM DIVIDENDS (Per Share):

Amt.	Decl.	Ex.	Rec.	Pay.
0.555Q	7/29/02	8/09/02	8/13/02	9/13/02
0.555Q	10/28/02	11/06/02	11/08/02	12/16/02
0.585Q	2/24/03	3/05/03	3/07/03	3/17/03
0.585Q	4/28/03	5/29/03	6/02/03	6/16/03

Indicated div.: $2.34 (Div. Reinv. Plan)

CAPITALIZATION (12/31/02):

	($000)	(%)
Long-Term Debt	1,296,907	57.3
Capital Lease Obligations..	33,462	1.5
Preferred Stock	263	0.0
Common & Surplus	933,150	41.2
Total	2,263,782	100.0

DIVIDEND ACHIEVER STATUS:
Rank: 235   10-Year Growth Rate: 5.02%
Total Years of Dividend Growth: 14

*7 YEAR PRICE SCORE 143.7   *12 MONTH PRICE SCORE 107.6

°NYSE COMPOSITE INDEX=100

RECENT DEVELOPMENTS: For the three months ended 3/31/03, income was $29.0 million, before a gain of $886,000 from discontinued operations, compared with income of $27.5 million, before a gain of $1.9 million from discontinued operations, in the equivalent quarter of the previous year. Results for 2003 included a gain of $9,000 from the sale of properties. Total revenues increased 16.4% to $98.2 million from $84.4 million the year before.

PROSPECTS: On 5/13/03, the Company announced that it has completed the acquisition of a supermarket-anchored shopping center in Hollywood, Florida and an industrial property in Tampa, Florida. Including these properties, WRE has completed five acquisitions in 2003 representing an addition of 1.6 million square feet to its portfolio and aggregating an investment of $85.5 million.

BUSINESS

WEINGARTEN REALTY INVESTORS is a self-administered and self-managed real estate investment trust that acquires, develops and manages real estate, primarily anchored neighborhood and community shopping centers and, to a lesser extent, industrial properties. As of 2/24/03, the Company owned or operated under long-term leases interests in 306 developed income-producing real estate projects. WRI owned 247 shopping centers located in the Houston metropolitan area and in other parts of Texas and in California, Louisiana, Arizona, Nevada, Arkansas, New Mexico, Oklahoma, Tennessee, Kansas, Colorado, Missouri, Illinois, Florida, North Carolina, Georgia, Mississippi and Maine. WRI also owned 58 industrial projects located in Tennessee, Nevada, Georgia, Florida and Houston, Austin and Dallas, Texas. Also, WRI owned one office building.

ANNUAL FINANCIAL DATA

	12/31/02	12/31/01	12/31/00	12/31/99	12/31/98	12/31/97	12/31/96
Earnings Per Share	③ 1.75	② 1.84	② 1.46	①② 1.91	① 1.39	1.37	1.35
Tang. Book Val. Per Share	17.92	17.87	15.59	16.12	13.32	9.75	10.06
Dividends Per Share	2.22	2.11	2.00	1.89	1.79	1.71	1.65
Dividend Payout %	126.8	114.5	137.0	99.3	128.8	124.8	122.2
INCOME STATEMENT (IN MILLIONS):							
Rental Income	359.0	309.5	264.6	225.2	194.6	169.0	145.3
Interest Income	1.1	1.2	5.6	5.0	2.1	2.5	3.1
Total Income	365.4	314.9	273.4	230.3	198.1	174.5	151.1
Costs & Expenses	177.0	151.4	128.2	105.1	95.6	84.9	69.0
Depreciation	78.5	68.3	58.5	49.6	41.9	38.0	33.8
Income Before Income Taxes	110.1	103.5	87.0	96.1	61.4	55.0	53.9
Equity Earnings/Minority Int.	0.5	5.1	d8.0	0.2	0.3	...	...
Net Income	③ 110.6	② 108.5	② 79.0	①② 96.3	① 61.8	55.0	53.9
Average Shs. Outstg. (000)	53,360	48,369	40,397	40,335	40,304	40,157	39,833
BALANCE SHEET (IN MILLIONS):							
Cash & Cash Equivalents	27.4	12.4	14.8	5.8	16.6	15.1	14.0
Total Assets	2,423.9	2,095.7	1,646.0	1,309.4	1,107.0	946.8	831.1
Long-Term Obligations	1,330.4	1,070.8	869.6	594.2	516.4	507.4	389.2
Total Liabilities	1,435.5	1,170.8	943.5	663.5	573.9	556.8	430.1
Net Stockholders' Equity	933.4	921.1	629.9	645.9	533.2	390.0	401.0
Year-end Shs. Outstg. (000)	52,076	51,521	40,382	40,043	40,010	39,990	39,864
STATISTICAL RECORD:							
Net Inc.+Depr./Assets %	7.8	8.4	8.4	11.1	9.4	9.8	10.6
Return on Equity %	11.9	11.8	12.5	14.9	11.6	14.1	13.5
Return on Assets %	4.6	5.2	4.8	7.4	5.6	5.8	6.5
Price Range	39.20-29.29	33.77-25.85	30.00-23.04	30.42-24.67	31.25-23.96	30.42-25.83	27.17-22.83
P/E Ratio	22.4-16.7	18.4-14.1	20.5-15.8	15.9-12.9	22.5-17.3	22.3-18.9	20.1-16.9
Average Yield %	6.5	7.1	7.5	6.9	6.5	6.1	6.6

Statistics are as originally reported. Adj. for 50.0%, 4/02. ① Bef. extraord. chrg., 1999, $190,000; 1998, $1.4 mill. ② Incl. gain on sales of prop. of $8.3 mill, 2001; $382,000, 2000; $20.6 mill., 1999. ③ Bef. inc. of $21.3 mill. from disc. ops. & incl. gain of $188,000 from sale of prop.

OFFICERS:
S. Alexander, Chmn.
M. Debrovner, Vice-Chmn.
A. M. Alexander, Pres., C.E.O.

INVESTOR CONTACT: Tracey Pursell, Investor Relations, (713) 866-6050

PRINCIPAL OFFICE: 2600 Citadel Plaza Drive, P.O. Box 924133, Houston, TX 77292-4133

TELEPHONE NUMBER: (713) 866-6000
FAX: (713) 866-6049
WEB: www.weingarten.com

NO. OF EMPLOYEES: 265

SHAREHOLDERS: 3,366 (record)

ANNUAL MEETING: In Apr.

INCORPORATED: TX, 1948

INSTITUTIONAL HOLDINGS:
No. of Institutions: 183
Shares Held: 19,784,407
% Held: 38.0

INDUSTRY: Real estate investment trusts (SIC: 6798)

TRANSFER AGENT(S): Mellon Investor Services, Ridgefield Park, NJ

WELLS FARGO & COMPANY

YIELD 2.5%
P/E RATIO 14.2

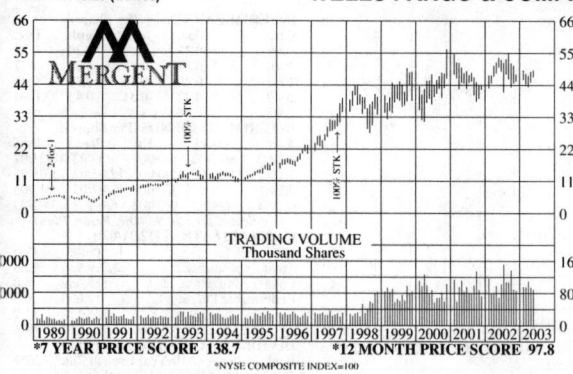

7 YEAR PRICE SCORE 138.7   **12 MONTH PRICE SCORE 97.8**

NYSE COMPOSITE INDEX=100

TRADING VOLUME
Thousand Shares

INTERIM EARNINGS (Per Share):

Qtr.	Mar.	June	Sept.	Dec.
2000	0.61	0.63	0.64	0.65
2001	0.67	d0.05	0.67	0.69
2002	0.80	0.82	0.84	0.86
2003	0.88	...	...	...

INTERIM DIVIDENDS (Per Share):

Amt.	Decl.	Ex.	Rec.	Pay.
0.28Q	7/23/02	8/07/02	8/09/02	9/01/02
0.28Q	10/22/02	11/06/02	11/08/02	12/01/02
0.30Q	1/28/03	2/05/03	2/07/03	3/01/03
0.30Q	4/22/03	5/07/03	5/09/03	6/01/03

Indicated div.: $1.20 (Div. Reinv. Plan)

CAPITALIZATION (12/31/02):

	($000)	(%)
Total Deposits	216,916,000	73.6
Long-Term Debt	47,302,000	16.1
Capital Lease Obligations	21,000	0.0
Preferred Stock	251,000	0.1
Common & Surplus	30,107,000	10.2
Total	294,597,000	100.0

DIVIDEND ACHIEVER STATUS:

Rank: 60   10-Year Growth Rate: 15.08%
Total Years of Dividend Growth: 15

RECENT DEVELOPMENTS: For the quarter ended 3/31/03, WFC reported net income of $1.49 billion versus income of $1.38 billion, before an accounting charge of $276.0 million, in the same prior-year period. Results included a net loss of $80.0 million in 2003 and a net gain of $18.0 million in 2002 related to various items. Net interest income rose 7.4% to $3.93 billion due to growth in earnings assets and core deposits.

PROSPECTS: Net interest income continues to grow at a solid and steady pace. During the past several quarters, WFC has shortened the duration of its investment portfolio through sales and prepayments of longer-term mortgage-backed securities. While this has had a modest adverse impact on net interest margin, it should provide greater flexibility to add securities in the event that interest rates rise and the mortgage warehouse begins to decline.

BUSINESS

WELLS FARGO & COMPANY (formerly Norwest Corporation), with $369.67 billion in assets as of 3/31/03, is a diversified financial services company providing banking, insurance, investments, mortgage and consumer finance through more than 5,600 financial services stores and the Internet across North America and elsewhere internationally. In early November 1998, the former Wells Fargo & Company merged with WFC Holdings, a subsidiary of Norwest Corp., with WFC Holdings as the surviving corporation. In connection with the merger, Norwest changed its name to Wells Fargo & Company. On 10/25/00, WFC acquired First Security, creating the largest banking franchise in the western region of the U.S.

ANNUAL FINANCIAL DATA

	12/31/02	12/31/01	12/31/00	12/31/99	12/31/98	12/31/97	12/31/96
Earnings Per Share	⑤ 3.32	③④ 1.97	③ 2.33	③ 2.23	② 1.17	1.75	① 1.54
Tang. Book Val. Per Share	11.56	9.71	9.11	7.87	6.71	8.90	7.88
Dividends Per Share	1.10	1.00	0.90	0.79	0.70	0.61	0.53
Dividend Payout %	33.1	50.8	38.6	35.2	59.8	35.1	34.2
INCOME STATEMENT (IN MILLIONS):							
Total Interest Income	18,832.0	19,201.0	18,725.0	14,375.0	14,055.0	6,697.4	6,318.3
Total Interest Expense	3,977.0	6,741.0	7,860.0	5,020.0	5,065.0	2,664.0	2,617.0
Net Interest Income	14,855.0	12,460.0	10,865.0	9,355.0	8,990.0	4,033.4	3,701.3
Provision for Loan Losses	1,733.0	1,780.0	1,329.0	1,045.0	1,545.0	524.7	394.7
Non-Interest Income	9,641.0	7,690.0	8,843.0	7,420.0	6,427.0	2,962.3	2,564.6
Non-Interest Expense	13,909.0	12,891.0	11,830.0	9,782.0	10,579.0	4,421.3	4,089.7
Income Before Taxes	8,854.0	5,479.0	6,549.0	5,948.0	3,293.0	2,049.7	1,781.5
Net Income	⑤ 5,710.0	③④ 3,423.0	③ 4,026.0	③ 3,747.0	② 1,950.0	1,351.0	① 1,153.9
Average Shs. Outstg. (000)	1,718,000	1,726,900	1,718,400	1,665,200	1,641,800	750,059	739,400
BALANCE SHEET (IN MILLIONS):							
Cash & Due from Banks	17,820.0	16,968.0	16,978.0	13,250.0	12,731.0	4,912.1	4,856.6
Securities Avail. for Sale	27,947.0	40,308.0	38,655.0	38,518.0	31,997.0	18,470.8	16,433.6
Total Loans & Leases	196,634.0	172,499.0	161,124.0	119,464.0	107,994.0	44,634.1	41,154.2
Allowance for Credit Losses	3,862.0	3,761.0	3,719.0	3,170.0	3,134.0	3,346.4	2,814.0
Net Loans & Leases	192,772.0	168,738.0	157,405.0	116,294.0	104,860.0	41,287.7	38,340.2
Total Assets	349,259.0	307,569.0	272,426.0	218,102.0	202,475.0	88,540.2	80,175.4
Total Deposits	216,916.0	182,266.0	169,559.0	132,708.0	136,788.0	55,457.1	50,130.2
Long-Term Obligations	47,320.0	36,095.0	32,046.0	23,375.0	19,709.0	12,766.7	13,082.2
Total Liabilities	318,904.0	280,355.0	245,938.0	195,971.0	181,716.0	81,518.0	74,111.2
Net Stockholders' Equity	30,358.0	27,214.0	26,488.0	22,131.0	20,759.0	7,022.2	6,064.2
Year-end Shs. Outstg. (000)	1,685,907	1,695,495	1,714,646	1,626,850	1,644,058	758,619	737,406
STATISTICAL RECORD:							
Return on Equity %	18.8	12.6	15.2	16.9	9.4	19.2	19.0
Return on Assets %	1.6	1.1	1.5	1.7	1.0	1.5	1.4
Equity/Assets %	8.7	8.8	9.7	10.1	10.3	7.9	7.6
Non-Int. Exp./Tot. Inc. %	56.8	64.0	60.0	58.3	68.6	63.2	65.3
Price Range	54.84-41.50	54.81-38.25	56.38-31.38	49.94-32.19	43.88-27.50	39.50-21.38	23.44-15.25
P/E Ratio	16.5-12.5	27.8-19.4	24.2-13.5	22.4-14.4	37.5-23.5	22.6-12.2	15.3-9.9
Average Yield %	2.3	2.1	2.1	1.9	2.0	2.0	2.7

Statistics are as originally reported. Adj. for 2-for-1 stk. split, 10/97. Reflects 11/98 merger with Norwest Corp. & name change to Wells Fargo & Co. Yrs. prior to 12/31/98 rep. the results of Norwest Corp. only. ① Incl. one-time SAIF pre-tax chrg. of $19.0 mill. ② Incl. a one-time net loss rel. to various items of $1.85 bill. ③ Incl. pre-tax net gain on dispos. of premises of $21.0 mill., 2001; $58.0 mill., 2000; $16.0 mill., 1999. ④ Incl. net venture capital losses of $1.63 billion. ⑤ Bef. acctg. chrg. of $276.0 mill.; incl. one-time net loss rel to var. items of $86.0 mill.

OFFICERS:
R. M. Kovacevich, Chmn., Pres., C.E.O.
H. I. Atkins, Exec. V.P., C.F.O.

INVESTOR CONTACT: Robert S. Strickland, Sr. V.P., (415) 396-0523

PRINCIPAL OFFICE: 420 Montgomery Street, San Francisco, CA 94163

TELEPHONE NUMBER: (800) 411-4932
FAX: (651) 450-4033
WEB: www.wellsfargo.com

NO. OF EMPLOYEES: 127,500

SHAREHOLDERS: 97,002

ANNUAL MEETING: In April

INCORPORATED: DE, Jan., 1929

INSTITUTIONAL HOLDINGS:
No. of Institutions: 972
Shares Held: 1,095,217,393
% Held: 65.4

INDUSTRY: National commercial banks (SIC: 6021)

TRANSFER AGENT(S): Wells Fargo Shareowners Services, St. Paul, MN

WESBANCO, INC.

YIELD 3.8%
P/E RATIO 14.7

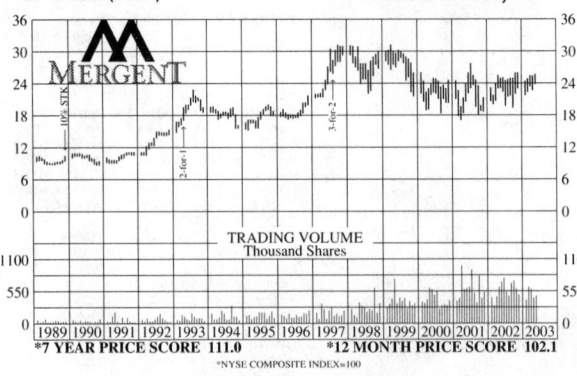

*7 YEAR PRICE SCORE 111.0   *12 MONTH PRICE SCORE 102.1
*NYSE COMPOSITE INDEX=100

INTERIM EARNINGS (Per Share):

Qtr.	Mar.	June	Sept.	Dec.
1999	0.33	0.40	0.30	0.34
2000	0.35	0.35	0.34	0.37
2001	0.40	0.40	0.39	0.41
2002	0.42	0.41	0.43	0.44
2003	0.44	...	...	...

INTERIM DIVIDENDS (Per Share):

Amt.	Decl.	Ex.	Rec.	Pay.
0.235Q	8/22/02	9/04/02	9/06/02	10/01/02
0.235Q	11/20/02	12/04/02	12/06/02	1/02/03
0.24Q	2/20/03	3/05/03	3/07/03	4/01/03
0.24Q	5/21/03	6/04/03	6/06/03	7/01/03

Indicated div.: $0.96 (Div. Reinv. Plan)

CAPITALIZATION (12/31/02):

	($000)	(%)
Total Deposits	2,399,956	82.4
Long-Term Debt	175,634	6.0
Redeemable Pfd. Stock	12,650	0.4
Common & Surplus	325,171	11.2
Total	2,913,411	100.0

DIVIDEND ACHIEVER STATUS:

Rank: 196   10-Year Growth Rate: 7.22%
Total Years of Dividend Growth: 17

RECENT DEVELOPMENTS: For the quarter ended 3/31/03, net income rose 10.2% to $8.9 million versus $8.1 million in the equivalent quarter of 2002. Results for 2003 and 2002 included net securities gains of $1.0 million and $1.2 million, and merger-related expenses of $92,000 and $1.1 million, respectively. Net interest income grew 2.4% to $24.8 million from $24.3 million the year before due to earning asset growth, partially offset by a decrease in net interest margin. Provision for loan losses slipped 11.6% to

$2.0 million versus $2.2 million in the previous year. Total non-interest income grew 16.1% to $8.2 million from $7.1 million a year earlier, reflecting growth in deposit activity fees, increases in ATM fees and debit card interchange fees and an increase in bank-owned life insurance income. Total non-interest expense increased 12.8% to $20.1 million, mainly due to an increase in operational costs related to additional banking offices and related expenses acquired in the acquisition of American Bancorporation on 3/1/02.

BUSINESS

WESBANCO, INC. is a bank holding company. The Company offers a range of financial services including retail banking, corporate banking, personal and corporate trust services, brokerage, mortgage banking and insurance. The Company's primary business function is the operation of a commercial bank through 72 offices located in West Virginia, Ohio and Pennsylvania. On 1/14/00, the Company restructured its banking and mortgage operations by merging all of its banking subsidiaries and its mortgage subsidiary into one state member banking corporation, WesBanco Bank, Inc. The Company also offers services through its non-banking affiliates. WesBanco Insurance Services, Inc. is a multi-line insurance agency specializing in property, casualty and life insurance for personal and commercial clients. WesBanco Securities, Inc. is a full service broker-dealer, which also offers discount brokerage services. WSBC also serves as investment adviser to a family of mutual funds under the name WesMark Funds, which include the WesMark Growth Fund, the WesMark Balanced Fund, the WesMark Bond Fund, the WesMark West Virginia Municipal Bond Fund, and the WesMark Small Company Growth Fund. On 3/1/02, WSBC acquired American Bancorporation.

ANNUAL FINANCIAL DATA

	12/31/02	12/31/01	12/31/00	12/31/99	12/31/98	12/31/97	12/31/96
Earnings Per Share	☐ 1.70	1.60	1.41	1.37	1.36	1.40	1.39
Tang. Book Val. Per Share	13.02	14.46	12.31	13.63	14.35	15.58	14.42
Dividends Per Share	0.93	0.92	0.89	0.87	0.83	0.77	0.70
Dividend Payout %	54.7	57.2	63.1	63.5	61.0	55.2	50.5
INCOME STATEMENT (IN MILLIONS):							
Total Interest Income	176.2	163.9	163.1	155.9	162.7	124.5	112.9
Total Interest Expense	72.6	76.4	79.6	69.2	73.9	55.8	48.2
Net Interest Income	103.6	87.6	83.5	86.6	88.8	68.8	64.7
Provision for Loan Losses	9.4	6.0	3.2	4.3	4.4	4.3	4.3
Non-Interest Income	27.9	24.6	23.4	24.6	25.7	14.7	12.3
Non-Interest Expense	76.6	64.9	64.5	67.8	68.3	48.7	43.2
Income Before Taxes	45.4	41.3	39.2	39.1	41.8	30.4	29.5
Net Income	☐ 34.8	29.0	26.9	27.6	28.3	22.3	21.2
Average Shs. Outstg. (000)	20,459	18,124	19,093	20,230	20,867	15,868	15,254
BALANCE SHEET (IN MILLIONS):							
Cash & Due from Banks	80.1	81.6	72.8	67.2	63.0	56.4	58.8
Securities Avail. for Sale	694.7	517.5	350.3	354.7	465.7	342.5	276.2
Total Loans & Leases	1,816.2	1,534.2	1,588.3	1,513.7	1,363.7	1,021.3	1,026.4
Allowance for Credit Losses	25.1	20.8	20.0	19.8	19.1	15.5	15.5
Net Loans & Leases	1,791.1	1,513.4	1,568.3	1,493.9	1,344.6	1,005.7	1,010.8
Total Assets	3,297.2	2,474.5	2,310.1	2,269.7	2,242.7	1,789.3	1,677.8
Total Deposits	2,400.0	1,913.5	1,870.4	1,814.0	1,787.6	1,414.3	1,342.8
Long-Term Obligations	175.6	279.1	159.3	41.6	22.2	...	...
Total Liabilities	2,972.1	2,216.3	2,051.6	2,000.1	1,946.2	1,539.7	1,450.2
Net Stockholders' Equity	325.2	258.2	258.5	269.7	296.5	249.6	227.5
Year-end Shs. Outstg. (000)	20,462	17,854	20,997	19,790	20,660	16,016	15,783
STATISTICAL RECORD:							
Return on Equity %	10.7	11.2	10.4	10.2	9.5	8.9	9.3
Return on Assets %	1.1	1.2	1.2	1.2	1.3	1.2	1.3
Equity/Assets %	9.9	10.4	11.2	11.9	13.2	13.9	13.6
Non-Int. Exp./Tot. Inc. %	58.3	57.9	60.3	61.0	59.7	58.4	56.0
Price Range	26.00-19.32	27.75-17.00	26.06-18.31	31.25-21.50	31.13-22.00	31.25-21.17	21.67-17.17
P/E Ratio	15.3-11.4	17.3-10.6	18.5-13.0	22.8-15.7	22.9-16.2	22.3-15.1	15.6-12.4
Average Yield %	4.1	4.1	4.0	3.3	3.1	3.0	3.6

Statistics are as originally reported. Adj. for 3-for-2 stk. split 8/1/97. ☐ Incl. $1.9 mill. net sec. gain & $2.5 mill. non-recur. exp.

OFFICERS:
J. C. Gardill, Chmn.
P. M. Limbert, Pres., C.E.O.
R. H. Young, Exec. V.P., C.F.O.

INVESTOR CONTACT: Investor Relations, (304) 234-9000

PRINCIPAL OFFICE: 1 Bank Plaza, Wheeling, WV 26003

TELEPHONE NUMBER: (304) 234-9000
FAX: (304) 232-9060
WEB: www.wesbanco.com

NO. OF EMPLOYES: 1,156 (approx.)

SHAREHOLDERS: 6,528 (approx.)

ANNUAL MEETING: In Apr.

INCORPORATED: WV, 1977

INSTITUTIONAL HOLDINGS:
No. of Institutions: 53
Shares Held: 5,282,783
% Held: 26.4

INDUSTRY: National commercial banks (SIC: 6021)

TRANSFER AGENT(S): WesBanco, Inc. c/o Corporate Trust Services, Cincinnati, OH

WESCO FINANCIAL CORPORATION

YIELD 0.4%
P/E RATIO 42.5

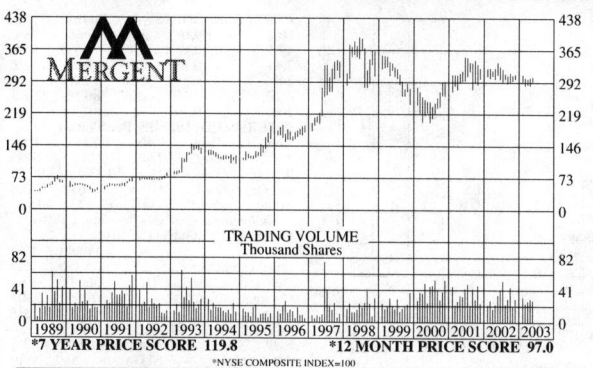

°NYSE COMPOSITE INDEX=100

INTERIM EARNINGS (Per Share):

Qtr.	Mar.	June	Sept.	Dec.
1999	1.49	1.56	1.54	3.01
2000	18.64	41.87	62.24	6.81
2001	2.78	2.12	1.57	0.91
2002	2.03	2.09	2.12	1.16
2003	1.76	...	...	...

INTERIM DIVIDENDS (Per Share):

Amt.	Decl.	Ex.	Rec.	Pay.
0.325Q	3/21/02	5/06/02	5/08/02	6/05/02
0.325Q	7/18/02	8/05/02	8/07/02	9/05/02
0.325Q	9/19/02	11/04/02	11/06/02	12/04/02
0.335Q	1/16/03	2/03/03	2/05/03	3/05/03
0.335Q	3/20/03	5/05/03	5/07/03	6/04/03

Indicated div.: $1.34

CAPITALIZATION (12/31/02):

	($000)	(%)
Long-Term Debt	32,481	1.6
Common & Surplus	1,958,162	98.4
Total	1,990,643	100.0

DIVIDEND ACHIEVER STATUS:
Rank: 253   10-Year Growth Rate: 3.75%
Total Years of Dividend Growth: 31

RECENT DEVELOPMENTS: For the three months ended 3/31/03, net income totaled $12.5 million, down 13.4% compared with $14.4 million in the corresponding prior-year period. Results for 2003 included an after-tax realized investment gain of $527,000. Total revenues climbed 8.7% to $155.8 million from $143.3 million the previous year. Furniture rental segment revenues slipped 6.8% to $93.4 million from $100.2 million, primarily due to lower furniture rentals. Insurance segment revenues advanced 59.2%

to $48.4 million from $30.4 million in 2002, while revenues in the industrial segment rose 4.7% to $12.3 million from $11.8 million a year earlier. WSC's cost of products and services sold declined 2.8% to $38.2 million from $39.4 million the year before. Insurance losses, loss adjustment and underwriting expenses more than doubled to $26.5 million versus $11.9 million the prior year. Income before income taxes slid 16.6% to $18.5 million from $22.2 million the previous year.

BUSINESS

WESCO FINANCIAL CORPORATION is engaged in three principal businesses: the insurance business, through Wesco-Financial Insurance Company, which engages in the property and casualty insurance business, and The Kansas Bankers Surety Company, which provides specialized insurance coverages for banks; the furniture rental business, through CORT Business Services Corporation, a provider of rental furniture, accessories and related services in the rent-to-rent segment of the furniture industry; and the steel service center business, through Precision Steel Warehouse, Inc. The Company's operations also include, through MS Property Company, the ownership and management of commercial real estate property, and the development and liquidation of foreclosed real estate. Since 1973, the Company has been 80.1%-owned by Blue Chip Stamps, a wholly-owned subsidiary of Berkshire Hathaway Inc.

ANNUAL FINANCIAL DATA

	12/31/02	12/31/01	12/31/00	12/31/99	12/31/98	12/31/97	12/31/96
Earnings Per Share	7.40	7.38	⊡129.56	7.60	10.08	14.30	4.30
Tang. Book Val. Per Share	237.64	231.46	241.16	262.20	308.20	243.56	171.36
Dividends Per Share	1.30	1.26	1.22	1.18	1.14	1.10	1.06
Dividend Payout %	17.6	17.1	0.9	15.5	11.3	7.7	24.7
INCOME STATEMENT (IN MILLIONS):							
Total Premium Income	64.6	43.0	23.8	17.7	15.9	11.5	10.1
Net Investment Income	70.7	71.0	59.8	49.7	40.5	36.6	33.3
Other Income	440.4	447.1	1,740.4	78.4	119.7	171.0	64.6
Total Revenues	575.7	561.1	1,824.0	145.7	176.2	219.1	108.0
Income Before Income Taxes	80.9	81.3	1,418.4	74.8	102.3	152.8	39.5
Income Taxes	28.2	28.8	495.9	20.7	30.5	51.0	8.9
Net Income	52.7	52.5	⊡922.5	54.1	71.8	101.8	30.6
Average Shs. Outstg. (000)	7,120	7,120	7,120	7,120	7,120	7,120	7,120
BALANCE SHEET (IN MILLIONS):							
Cash & Cash Equivalents	349.8	120.8	153.8	66.3	320.0	10.7	23.0
Premiums Due	67.4	43.9	38.4	...	...	7.1	7.9
Invst. Assets: Fixed-term	827.5	924.2	839.7	310.0	66.6	279.7	176.9
Invst. Assets: Total	1,454.3	1,591.4	1,673.6	2,524.9	2,845.2	2,509.8	1,725.7
Total Assets	2,407.0	2,319.7	2,460.9	2,652.2	3,228.4	2,588.1	1,818.4
Long-Term Obligations	32.5	33.6	56.0	3.6	33.6	33.6	37.2
Net Stockholders' Equity	1,958.2	1,912.4	1,977.0	1,895.4	2,223.8	1,764.3	1,251.0
Year-end Shs. Outstg. (000)	7,120	7,120	7,120	7,120	7,120	7,120	7,120
STATISTICAL RECORD:							
Return on Revenues %	9.2	9.4	50.6	37.2	40.8	46.5	28.3
Return on Equity %	2.7	2.7	46.7	2.9	3.2	5.8	2.4
Return on Assets %	2.2	2.3	37.5	2.0	2.2	3.9	1.7
Price Range	338.00-290.00	350.00-270.00	294.00-200.00	354.00-241.50	395.00-280.00	343.00-180.00	194.00-155.00
P/E Ratio	45.7-39.2	47.4-36.6	2.3-1.5	46.6-31.8	39.2-27.8	24.0-12.6	45.1-36.0
Average Yield %	0.4	0.4	0.5	0.4	0.3	0.4	0.6

Statistics are as originally reported. ⊡ Incl. after-tax realized securities gains of $1.31 bill.

OFFICERS:
C. T. Munger, Chmn., C.E.O.
R. H. Bird, Pres.
J. L. Jacobson, V.P., C.F.O.
INVESTOR CONTACT: Investor Relations,
(626) 585-6700
PRINCIPAL OFFICE: 301 East Colorado
Boulevard, Suite 300, Pasadena, CA 91101-1901

TELEPHONE NUMBER: (626) 585-6700
FAX: (626) 449-1455
NO. OF EMPLOYEES: 2,981 (avg.)
SHAREHOLDERS: 600 (approx.); 5200
(approx. beneficial)
ANNUAL MEETING: In May
INCORPORATED: DE, Mar., 1959

INSTITUTIONAL HOLDINGS:
No. of Institutions: 71
Shares Held: 6,242,305
% Held: 89.2
INDUSTRY: Metals service centers and
offices (SIC: 5051)
TRANSFER AGENT(S): Mellon Investor
Services, South Hackensack, NJ

WEST PHARMACEUTICAL SERVICES, INC.

YIELD 3.2%
P/E RATIO 35.9

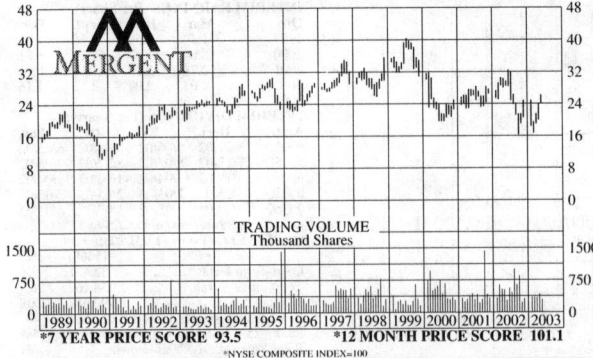

*7 YEAR PRICE SCORE 93.5   *12 MONTH PRICE SCORE 101.1

*NYSE COMPOSITE INDEX=100

INTERIM EARNINGS (Per Share):

Qtr.	Mar.	June	Sept.	Dec.
1999	0.63	0.69	0.57	0.68
2000	0.35	0.35	0.32	d0.91
2001	0.37	0.20	0.40	0.41
2002	0.45	0.37	d0.16	0.23
2003	0.26	...	...	...

INTERIM DIVIDENDS (Per Share):

Amt.	Decl.	Ex.	Rec.	Pay.
0.19Q	6/18/02	7/22/02	7/24/02	8/07/02
0.20Q	7/30/02	10/21/02	10/23/02	11/06/02
0.20Q	10/29/02	1/17/03	1/22/03	2/05/03
0.20Q	3/24/03	4/21/03	4/23/03	5/07/03

Indicated div.: $0.80 (Div. Reinv. Plan)

CAPITALIZATION (12/31/02):

	($000)	(%)
Long-Term Debt	159,200	38.2
Deferred Income Tax	56,200	13.5
Common & Surplus	201,500	48.3
Total	416,900	100.0

DIVIDEND ACHIEVER STATUS:

Rank: 204   10-Year Growth Rate: 6.77%
Total Years of Dividend Growth: 10

RECENT DEVELOPMENTS: For the three months ended 3/31/03, net income was $3.8 million compared with income of $6.3 million, before a loss of $200,000 from discontinued operations, in the equivalent quarter of the previous year. Results for 2003 included pre-tax charges of $5.1 million associated with a plant explosion. Net sales increased 15.8% to $117.8 million from $101.7 million the year before. Pharmaceutical systems net sales advanced 17.3% to $116.2 million.

PROSPECTS: Due to the strong results in the Pharmaceutical Systems Division and the progress in Drug Delivery, WST expects sales growth for the full-year 2003 in the range of 7.0% to 9.0%, without regard to favorable foreign currency effects for the remainder of the year, when compared to 2002. However, WST believes it cannot offer more detailed earnings guidance for 2003, due to risks associated with its Kinston-related interim production plans and a number of other factors.

BUSINESS

WEST PHARMACEUTICAL SERVICES, INC. (formerly The West Company, Inc.) is involved in drug formulation research and development, clinical research and laboratory services, and the design, development, and manufacture of components and systems for dispensing and delivering pharmaceutical, healthcare, and consumer products. Operations are divided into two business segments. The Pharmaceutical Systems segment (98.4% ot 2002 sales) designs, manufactures and sells stoppers, closures, medical device components and assemblies made from elastomers, metal, and plastics and provides contract laboratory services for testing injectable drug packaging. The Drug Delivery Systems segment (1.6%) identifies and develops drug delivery systems for biopharmaceutical and other drugs to improve therapeutic performance and/or method of administration. This segment also provides clinical research for Phase I, II and III studies and clinical and marketing research services mostly for consumer products organizations.

ANNUAL FINANCIAL DATA

	12/31/02	12/31/01	12/31/00	12/31/99	12/31/98	12/31/97	12/31/96
Earnings Per Share	④ 0.89	④ 1.37	③ 0.11	② 2.57	① 0.40	2.68	① 1.00
Cash Flow Per Share	3.17	3.60	2.68	4.94	2.36	4.60	2.87
Tang. Book Val. Per Share	10.84	10.05	10.65	11.23	11.24	13.65	11.79
Dividends Per Share	0.77	0.73	0.69	0.65	0.61	0.57	0.53
Dividend Payout %	86.5	53.3	626.7	25.3	152.5	21.3	53.0
INCOME STATEMENT (IN MILLIONS):							
Total Revenues	419.7	396.9	430.1	469.1	449.7	452.5	458.8
Costs & Expenses	360.0	323.6	377.9	366.5	382.4	357.6	395.4
Depreciation & Amort.	33.0	32.0	37.0	35.7	32.3	31.9	30.7
Operating Income	26.7	41.3	15.2	66.9	35.0	63.0	32.7
Net Interest Inc./(Exp.)	d9.5	d13.5	d13.1	d10.4	d7.2	d5.6	d6.9
Income Before Income Taxes	17.2	27.8	2.1	56.5	27.8	57.4	25.8
Income Taxes	4.1	8.6	1.5	18.4	21.2	13.3	10.8
Equity Earnings/Minority Int.	d0.3	0.4	1.0	0.6	0.1	0.3	1.4
Net Income	④ 12.8	④ 19.6	③ 1.6	② 38.7	① 6.7	44.4	① 16.4
Cash Flow	45.8	51.6	38.6	74.4	39.0	76.3	47.1
Average Shs. Outstg. (000)	14,434	14,348	14,409	15,048	16,504	16,572	16,418
BALANCE SHEET (IN MILLIONS):							
Cash & Cash Equivalents	33.2	42.1	42.7	45.3	31.3	52.3	27.3
Total Current Assets	161.3	158.5	173.1	184.7	159.7	170.7	156.7
Net Property	223.3	210.3	235.8	227.6	220.3	202.2	210.3
Total Assets	536.8	511.3	557.4	551.8	505.6	477.9	477.4
Total Current Liabilities	87.7	75.3	79.3	104.0	104.2	58.0	65.6
Long-Term Obligations	159.2	184.3	195.8	141.5	105.0	87.4	95.5
Net Stockholders' Equity	201.5	176.8	204.8	231.2	230.1	277.7	252.0
Net Working Capital	73.6	83.2	93.8	80.7	55.5	112.7	91.1
Year-end Shs. Outstg. (000)	14,480	14,344	14,310	14,664	15,026	16,568	16,383
STATISTICAL RECORD:							
Operating Profit Margin %	6.4	10.4	3.5	14.3	7.8	13.9	7.1
Net Profit Margin %	3.0	4.9	0.4	8.2	1.5	9.8	3.6
Return on Equity %	6.4	11.1	0.8	16.7	2.9	16.0	6.5
Return on Assets %	2.4	3.8	0.3	7.0	1.3	9.3	3.4
Debt/Total Assets %	29.7	36.0	35.1	25.6	20.8	18.3	20.0
Price Range	32.50-16.25	28.35-22.75	31.88-19.63	40.44-30.88	35.69-25.75	35.06-27.00	30.00-22.13
P/E Ratio	36.5-18.3	20.7-16.6	289.5-178.2	15.7-12.0	89.2-64.4	13.1-10.1	30.0-22.1
Average Yield %	3.2	2.9	2.7	1.8	2.0	1.8	2.0

Statistics are as originally reported. ① Incl. nonrecurr. chrgs. of $32.2 mill., 1998; $21.5 mill., 1996. ② Incl. restruct. chrg. of $700,000. ③ Incl. restruct. chrg. of $2.9 mill. & excl. loss of $24.8 mill. from disc. oper. ④ Incl. restruct. chrg. of $9.9 mill., 2002; $2.9 mill., 2001 & excl. inc. of $5.6 mill., 2002 & loss of $24.9 mill., 2001, resp. from disc. oper.

OFFICERS:
D. E. Morel Jr., Chmn., Pres., C.E.O.
L. R. Altemus, V.P., C.F.O.

INVESTOR CONTACT: Michael A.
Andserson, V.P. & Treas., (610) 594-2900

PRINCIPAL OFFICE: 101 Gordon Drive, P.O.
Box 645, Lionville, PA 19341-0645

TELEPHONE NUMBER: (610) 594-2900
FAX: (610) 594-3000
WEB: www.westpharma.com
NO. OF EMPLOYEES: 3,960
SHAREHOLDERS: 1,792 (of record); 2197
(nominee holders)
ANNUAL MEETING: In Apr.
INCORPORATED: PA, 1923

INSTITUTIONAL HOLDINGS:
No. of Institutions: 70
Shares Held: 10,215,214
% Held: 73.0

INDUSTRY: Fabricated rubber products, nec
(SIC: 3069)

TRANSFER AGENT(S): American Stock
Transfer & Trust Company, New York, NY

WESTAMERICA BANCORPORATION

YIELD 2.2%
P/E RATIO 17.0

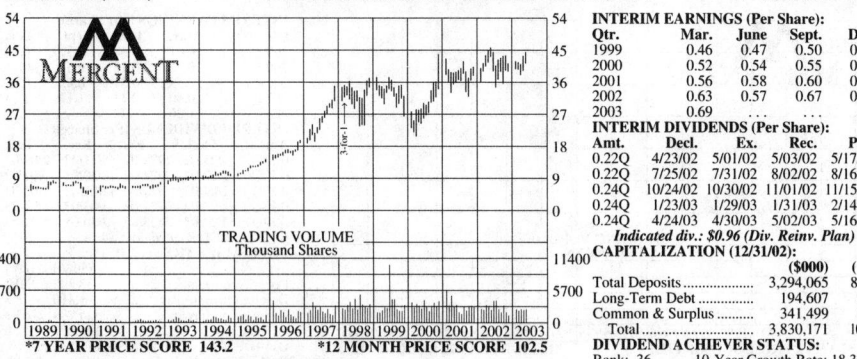

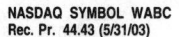

*7 YEAR PRICE SCORE 143.2   *12 MONTH PRICE SCORE 102.5
*NYSE COMPOSITE INDEX=100

INTERIM EARNINGS (Per Share):

Qtr.	Mar.	June	Sept.	Dec.
1999	0.46	0.47	0.50	0.51
2000	0.52	0.54	0.55	0.56
2001	0.56	0.58	0.60	0.62
2002	0.63	0.57	0.67	0.68
2003	0.69	...	...	...

INTERIM DIVIDENDS (Per Share):

Amt.	Decl.	Ex.	Rec.	Pay.
0.22Q	4/23/02	5/01/02	5/03/02	5/17/02
0.22Q	7/25/02	7/31/02	8/02/02	8/16/02
0.24Q	10/24/02	10/30/02	11/01/02	11/15/02
0.24Q	1/23/03	1/29/03	1/31/03	2/14/03
0.24Q	4/24/03	4/30/03	5/02/03	5/16/03

Indicated div.: $0.96 (Div. Reinv. Plan)

CAPITALIZATION (12/31/02):

	($000)	(%)
Total Deposits	3,294,065	86.0
Long-Term Debt	194,607	5.1
Common & Surplus	341,499	8.9
Total	3,830,171	100.0

DIVIDEND ACHIEVER STATUS:
Rank: 36   10-Year Growth Rate: 18.37%
Total Years of Dividend Growth: 13

RECENT DEVELOPMENTS: For the first quarter ended 3/31/03, net income increased 6.2% to $23.0 million compared with $21.7 million in the corresponding prior-year quarter. Net interest income rose 1.8% to $49.4 million from $48.5 million a year earlier. Total interest income decreased 3.1% to $57.1 million from $58.9 million, while total interest expense fell 25.8% to $7.7 million from $10.4 million the year before. Provision for loan losses remained unchanged versus the prior-year period at $900,000. Total non-interest income climbed 3.8% to $10.4 million, primarily due to higher fees on deposits, debit card and automated teller machine fees, mortgage banking income and other fees, partially offset by lower trust fees and financial services commissions. Meanwhile, total non-interest expense declined 0.6% to $25.5 million.

BUSINESS

WESTAMERICA BANCORPORA-TION, parent of Westamerica Bank, provides a full range of banking services to individual and corporate customers. The Company is a regional community bank with 89 branches serving 23 counties in northern and central California. At 3/31/03, the Company had total assets of $4.39 billion and total deposits of $3.33 billion. In addition, WABC also owns Community Banker Services Corporation, which is engaged in providing the Company and its subsidiaries data processing services and other support functions. On 7/31/00, the Company opened three Money Outlet Inc., stores, a subsidiary created to engage in the business of selling checks, drafts, or money orders, or receiving money as agent of an obligor. On 8/17/00, WABC finalized the acquisition of First Counties Bank, a five-branch financial institution headquartered in Lake County, California. On 6/21/02, WABC acquired Kerman State Bank.

QUARTERLY DATA

(12/31/2002)($000)	REV	INC
1st Quarter	73,132	21,659
2nd Quarter	69,209	19,347
3rd Quarter	75,368	22,877
4th Quarter	73,732	23,255

ANNUAL FINANCIAL DATA

	12/31/02	12/31/01	12/31/00	12/31/99	12/31/98	12/31/97	12/31/96
Earnings Per Share	⑴ 2.55	2.36	2.16	1.94	1.73	1.10	1.31
Tang. Book Val. Per Share	10.22	9.19	9.32	8.10	9.25	9.51	8.44
Dividends Per Share	0.90	0.82	0.74	0.66	0.52	0.36	0.30
Dividend Payout %	35.3	34.7	34.3	34.0	30.1	32.7	22.6
INCOME STATEMENT (IN MILLIONS):							
Total Interest Income	237.6	257.1	269.5	257.7	266.8	270.7	174.3
Total Interest Expense	39.2	68.9	88.6	78.5	86.7	88.1	60.9
Net Interest Income	198.5	188.2	180.9	179.2	180.2	182.6	113.3
Provision for Loan Losses	3.6	3.6	3.7	4.8	5.2	7.6	4.6
Non-Interest Income	36.6	42.7	41.1	40.2	37.8	37.0	22.0
Non-Interest Expense	103.3	102.7	100.2	100.1	101.4	137.9	75.6
Income Before Taxes	128.1	124.6	118.2	114.5	111.4	74.1	55.2
Net Income	⑴ 87.1	84.3	79.8	76.1	73.4	48.1	37.7
Average Shs. Outstg. (000)	34,225	35,748	36,936	39,194	42,524	43,827	28,839
BALANCE SHEET (IN MILLIONS):							
Cash & Due from Banks	...	...	...	...	...	...	149.4
Securities Avail. for Sale	948.5	949.5	921.5	982.6	987.9	1,003.5	696.9
Total Loans & Leases	2,494.9	2,485.3	2,484.5	2,325.0	2,304.2	2,270.2	1,453.8
Allowance for Credit Losses	54.5	52.9	54.6	55.7	57.6	58.9	44.5
Net Loans & Leases	2,440.4	2,432.4	2,429.9	2,269.3	2,246.6	2,211.3	1,409.3
Total Assets	4,224.9	3,928.0	4,031.4	3,893.2	3,844.3	3,848.4	2,548.5
Total Deposits	3,294.1	3,234.6	3,236.7	3,065.3	3,189.0	3,078.5	2,081.4
Long-Term Obligations	194.6	27.8	31.0	41.5	47.5	52.5	42.5
Total Liabilities	3,883.4	3,613.6	3,693.6	3,592.6	3,475.7	3,441.3	2,309.5
Net Stockholders' Equity	341.5	314.4	337.7	300.6	368.6	407.2	238.9
Year-end Shs. Outstg. (000)	33,411	34,220	36,251	37,125	39,828	42,799	28,305
STATISTICAL RECORD:							
Return on Equity %	25.5	26.8	23.6	25.3	19.9	11.8	15.8
Return on Assets %	2.1	2.1	2.0	2.0	1.9	1.3	1.5
Equity/Assets %	8.1	8.0	8.4	7.7	9.6	10.6	9.4
Non-Int. Exp./Tot. Inc. %	44.0	44.5	45.1	45.6	46.5	62.8	55.9
Price Range	45.78-34.50	42.64-31.92	43.94-20.75	37.50-26.38	37.25-23.63	35.00-18.43	19.75-14.17
P/E Ratio	18.0-13.5	18.1-13.5	20.3-9.6	19.3-13.6	21.5-13.7	31.8-17.1	15.1-10.8
Average Yield %	2.2	2.2	2.3	2.1	1.7	1.3	1.7

Statistics are as originally reported. Adj. for 3-for-1 stk. split, 2/25/98. ⑴ Incl. invest. impair. chrg. of $4.3 mill.

OFFICERS:
D. L. Payne, Chmn., Pres., C.E.O.
J. J. Finger, Sr. V.P., C.F.O.
R. A. Thorson, Sr. V.P., Treas.

INVESTOR CONTACT: Robert A. Thorson, (707) 863-6840

PRINCIPAL OFFICE: 1108 Fifth Avenue, San Rafael, CA 94901

TELEPHONE NUMBER: (415) 257-8000
WEB: www.westamerica.com

NO. OF EMPLOYEES: 1,050

SHAREHOLDERS: 9,000 (approx.)

ANNUAL MEETING: In April

INCORPORATED: CA, Feb., 1972

INSTITUTIONAL HOLDINGS:
No. of Institutions: 138
Shares Held: 14,194,482
% Held: 43.0

INDUSTRY: National commercial banks (SIC: 6021)

TRANSFER AGENT(S): Computershare Investor Services LLC, Chicago, IL

WEYCO GROUP, INC.

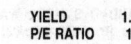

YIELD	1.1%
P/E RATIO	12.5

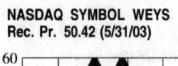

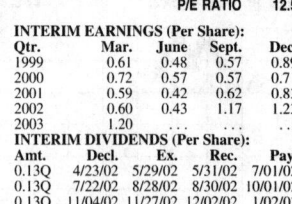

INTERIM EARNINGS (Per Share):

Qtr.	Mar.	June	Sept.	Dec.
1999	0.61	0.48	0.57	0.89
2000	0.72	0.57	0.57	0.71
2001	0.59	0.42	0.62	0.83
2002	0.60	0.43	1.17	1.23
2003	1.20	...	...	...

INTERIM DIVIDENDS (Per Share):

Amt.	Decl.	Ex.	Rec.	Pay.
0.13Q	4/23/02	5/29/02	5/31/02	7/01/02
0.13Q	7/22/02	8/28/02	8/30/02	10/01/02
0.13Q	11/04/02	11/27/02	11/27/02	1/02/03
0.13Q	1/27/03	2/27/03	3/03/03	4/01/03
0.14Q	4/22/03	5/28/03	5/30/03	7/01/03

Indicated div.: $0.56

CAPITALIZATION (12/31/02):

	($000)	(%)
Long-Term Debt	37,802	30.0
Deferred Income Tax	3,416	2.7
Common & Surplus	84,784	67.3
Total	126,002	100.0

DIVIDEND ACHIEVER STATUS:
Rank: 179   10-Year Growth Rate: 8.23%
Total Years of Dividend Growth: 22

*7 YEAR PRICE SCORE 172.2   ***12 MONTH PRICE SCORE 125.8**

*NYSE COMPOSITE INDEX=100

RECENT DEVELOPMENTS: For the three months ended 3/31/03, net income more than doubled to $4.7 million from $2.3 million in the corresponding prior-year period. Earnings were fueled by the acquisition of the domestic wholesale business and twenty-three retail stores of the Florsheim Group, Inc. on 5/20/02. Net sales climbed 69.0% to $60.4 million from $35.7 million the previous year. Net sales related to Florsheim's wholesale and retail operations were $18.2 million and $4.9 million, respectively. The Company's Nunn Bush and Stacy Adams divisions also contributed to the increases with sales for the first quarter up 10.0% and 6.0%, respectively. Wholesale net sales increased 58.1% to $54.7 million from $34.6 million in 2002. Retail sales soared to $5.7 million from $1.1 million a year earlier. Operating income amounted to $7.7 million, up 135.2% from $3.3 million the year before.

BUSINESS

WEYCO GROUP, INC. is engaged in the manufacture, purchase and distribution of men's footwear. The Company's products consist of both mid-priced leather dress shoes and lower-priced casual footwear. These shoes are sold under various brand names. The principal brands of shoes sold are FLORSHEIM, NUNN BUSH, NUNN BUSH NXXT, BRASS BOOT, STACY ADAMS and SAO BY STACY ADAMS. The Company's wholesale division, which generated approximately 91.2% of total sales in 2002, markets footwear through more than 10,000 shoe, clothing and department stores across the U.S. As of 12/31/02, the retail division consisted of 30 Company-operated stores in the U.S and three retail stores in Europe. On 5/21/02, the Company acquired Florsheim Group Inc.'s domestic wholesale business, related assets and 23 retail stores.

ANNUAL FINANCIAL DATA

	12/31/02	12/31/01	12/31/00	12/31/99	12/31/98	12/31/97	12/31/96
Earnings Per Share	3.44	2.46	2.59	① 2.55	2.07	1.88	1.66
Cash Flow Per Share	4.02	2.88	2.95	2.84	2.20	2.05	1.87
Tang. Book Val. Per Share	19.52	19.63	17.96	16.28	14.73	13.96	12.41
Dividends Per Share	0.50	0.46	0.42	0.38	0.34	0.30	0.29
Dividend Payout %	14.5	18.7	16.2	14.9	16.4	16.1	17.3
INCOME STATEMENT (IN THOUSANDS):							
Total Revenues	181,200	131,693	148,155	133,498	127,074	127,029	129,314
Costs & Expenses	157,563	116,730	130,693	117,033	112,647	113,561	116,605
Depreciation & Amort.	2,231	1,609	1,490	1,242	626	821	1,045
Operating Income	21,406	13,354	15,972	15,223	13,801	12,646	11,664
Net Interest Inc./(Exp.)	d436	726	479	831	1,419	1,475	...
Income Before Income Taxes	20,988	14,701	16,472	16,958	15,255	14,133	12,790
Income Taxes	7,800	5,200	5,850	5,900	5,450	5,065	4,718
Net Income	13,188	9,501	10,622	① 11,058	9,805	9,068	8,072
Cash Flow	15,419	11,110	12,112	12,300	10,431	9,890	9,117
Average Shs. Outstg.	3,836	3,862	4,108	4,339	4,731	4,825	4,871
BALANCE SHEET (IN THOUSANDS):							
Cash & Cash Equivalents	9,400	20,118	11,210	8,704	13,094	10,684	15,017
Total Current Assets	95,544	61,720	51,670	53,093	48,051	42,912	47,813
Net Property	22,160	15,337	16,272	16,594	13,801	2,313	2,653
Total Assets	146,235	97,954	91,943	95,919	92,782	82,204	73,077
Total Current Liabilities	20,233	20,911	17,758	26,253	26,387	14,643	13,973
Long-Term Obligations	37,802	...	...	...	...	...	...
Net Stockholders' Equity	84,784	73,592	71,345	67,751	65,148	66,677	59,104
Net Working Capital	75,311	40,810	33,912	26,840	21,664	28,269	33,840
Year-end Shs. Outstg.	3,789	3,749	3,973	4,161	4,424	4,775	4,762
STATISTICAL RECORD:							
Operating Profit Margin %	11.8	10.1	10.8	11.4	10.9	10.0	9.0
Net Profit Margin %	7.3	7.2	7.2	8.3	7.7	7.1	6.2
Return on Equity %	15.6	12.9	14.9	16.3	15.0	13.6	13.7
Return on Assets %	9.0	9.7	11.6	11.5	10.6	11.0	11.0
Debt/Total Assets %	25.9	...	...	...	...	...	...
Price Range	40.99-25.35	26.00-22.90	26.63-22.50	27.00-21.63	29.00-21.00	34.00-13.42	14.33-12.50
P/E Ratio	11.9-7.4	10.6-9.3	10.3-8.7	10.6-8.5	14.0-10.1	18.1-7.1	8.6-7.5
Average Yield %	1.5	1.9	1.7	1.6	1.4	1.3	2.1

Statistics are as originally reported. Adj. for 3-for-1 stock split, 10/1/97. ① Incl. after-tax gain of $496,000 on the sale of assets.

OFFICERS:
T. W. Florsheim Jr., Chmn., C.E.O.
J. W. Florsheim, Pres., C.O.O.
J. F. Wittkowske, Sr. V.P., C.F.O., Sec.

INVESTOR CONTACT: Investor Relations, (414) 908-1600

PRINCIPAL OFFICE: 333 W. Estabrook Blvd., P.O. Box 1188, Milwaukee, WI 53201

TELEPHONE NUMBER: (414) 908-1600
FAX: (414) 908-1601
WEB: www.weycogroup.com

NO. OF EMPLOYEES: 484 (approx.)

SHAREHOLDERS: 286; 118 (cl. B)

ANNUAL MEETING: In April

INCORPORATED: WI, June, 1906

INSTITUTIONAL HOLDINGS:
No. of Institutions: 17
Shares Held: 535,312
% Held: 13.4

INDUSTRY: Men's footwear, except athletic (SIC: 3143)

TRANSFER AGENT(S): American Stock Transfer & Trust Company, New York, NY

WGL HOLDINGS, INC.

YIELD 4.6%
P/E RATIO 14.2

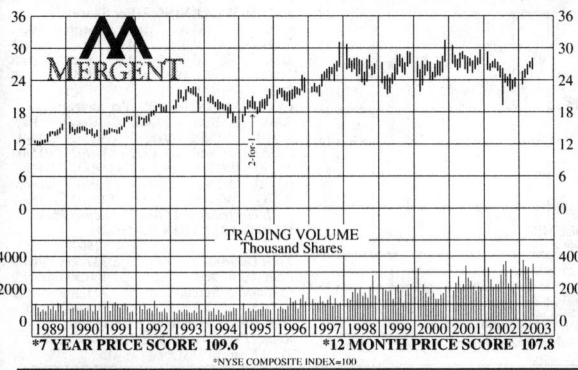

*7 YEAR PRICE SCORE 109.6   *12 MONTH PRICE SCORE 107.8
*NYSE COMPOSITE INDEX=100

TRADING VOLUME
Thousand Shares

INTERIM EARNINGS (Per Share):

Qtr.	Dec.	Mar.	June	Sept.
1999-00	0.85	1.39	d0.12	d0.33
2000-01	1.08	1.44	d0.15	d0.48
2001-02	0.62	0.94	d0.29	d0.47
2002-03	1.06	1.66	...	...

INTERIM DIVIDENDS (Per Share):

Amt.	Decl.	Ex.	Rec.	Pay.
0.318Q	6/26/02	7/08/02	7/10/02	8/01/02
0.318Q	9/25/02	10/08/02	10/10/02	11/01/02
0.318Q	12/20/02	1/08/03	1/10/03	2/01/03
0.32Q	3/05/03	4/08/03	4/10/03	5/01/03

Indicated div.: $1.28 (Div. Reinv. Plan)

CAPITALIZATION (9/30/02):

	($000)	(%)
Long-Term Debt	667,951	39.9
Deferred Income Tax	212,631	12.7
Preferred Stock	28,173	1.7
Common & Surplus	766,403	45.8
Total	1,675,158	100.0

DIVIDEND ACHIEVER STATUS:
Rank: 276   10-Year Growth Rate: 1.76%
Total Years of Dividend Growth: 26

RECENT DEVELOPMENTS: For the quarter ended 3/31/03, net income leapt 76.9% to $81.0 million compared with $45.8 million in the equivalent period of the previous year. Results for 2002 included a nonrecurring charge of $9.4 million. Utility revenues advanced 63.5% to $620.2 million from $379.4 million in the year-earlier quarter. Utility net revenues jumped 33.1% to $237.4 million from $178.4 million the year before.

PROSPECTS: The Company increased its earnings estimate for fiscal 2003 to a new range of $2.07 to $2.17 per share. This range includes the $0.02 per share and the $0.05 per share gains from the sale of land and headquarters property in the first and second quarters of fiscal 2003, respectively. This range also reflects certain assumptions including the resolution of the pending rate case in Virginia and normal weather patterns for the remainder of the fiscal year.

BUSINESS

WGL HOLDINGS, INC., (formerly Washington Gas Light Company), through its subsidiaries, engages in the sale and distribution of natural gas and other energy-related products and services. Washington Gas Light Company is a regulated natural gas utility serving over 963,000 customers in Washington D.C., Virginia and Maryland as of 4/30/03. Hampshire Gas Company is a regulated natural gas storage business, serving Washington Gas Light Company. Washington Gas Energy Services, Inc. sells natural gas and electricity to the Washington D.C. area as well as Baltimore, Maryland and Richmond, Virginia. Washington Gas Energy Systems, Inc. designs cost-saving energy systems for the commercial and government markets. American Combustion Industries, Inc. is a contractor for the installation and service of heating, ventilating and air-conditioning (HVAC) systems. Other nonregulated activities include consumer financing and land development. WGL owned a 50.0% interest in Primary Investors, LLC at 12/31/02.

ANNUAL FINANCIAL DATA

	9/30/02	9/30/01	9/30/00	9/30/99	9/30/98	9/30/97	9/30/96
Earnings Per Share	⑤ 0.80	⑤ 1.75	④ 1.79	③ 1.47	② 1.54	1.85	① 1.85
Cash Flow Per Share	2.39	3.29	3.27	2.88	2.90	3.13	3.09
Tang. Book Val. Per Share	15.78	16.24	15.31	14.72	13.83	13.48	12.79
Dividends Per Share	1.27	1.25	1.24	1.22	1.20	1.18	1.14
Dividend Payout %	158.4	71.7	69.0	82.6	77.6	63.8	61.3
INCOME STATEMENT (IN MILLIONS):							
Total Revenues	1,570.0	1,933.0	1,248.0	1,112.2	1,040.6	1,055.8	969.8
Costs & Expenses	1,366.2	1,683.8	1,018.9	903.6	840.8	847.7	770.1
Depreciation & Amort.	77.0	72.4	68.9	65.2	59.4	55.9	53.5
Maintenance Exp.	40.8	36.8	31.2	35.6	38.5	36.9	33.1
Operating Income	86.0	140.0	128.9	107.8	102.0	115.3	113.1
Net Interest Inc./(Exp.)	d45.9	d50.0	d43.7	d37.0	d37.7	d34.1	d30.6
Net Income	40.4	⑤ 83.8	④ 84.6	③ 68.8	② 68.6	82.0	① 81.6
Cash Flow	116.1	154.8	152.2	132.6	126.7	136.6	133.8
Average Shs. Outstg. (000)	48,563	47,120	46,473	45,984	43,691	43,706	43,360
BALANCE SHEET (IN MILLIONS):							
Gross Property	2,481.8	2,340.4	2,225.3	2,114.1	1,992.8	1,846.5	1,722.0
Accumulated Depreciation	875.0	820.7	765.0	711.3	673.3	629.3	591.4
Net Property	1,606.8	1,519.7	1,460.3	1,402.7	1,319.5	1,217.1	1,130.6
Total Assets	2,113.7	2,081.1	1,939.8	1,766.7	1,682.4	1,552.0	1,464.6
Long-Term Obligations	668.0	584.4	559.6	506.1	428.6	431.6	353.9
Net Stockholders' Equity	794.6	816.4	739.7	712.5	636.2	617.5	587.2
Year-end Shs. Outstg. (000)	48,565	48,543	46,470	46,473	43,955	43,700	43,704
STATISTICAL RECORD:							
Operating Profit Margin %	5.5	7.2	10.3	9.7	9.8	10.9	11.7
Net Profit Margin %	2.6	4.3	6.8	6.2	6.6	7.8	8.4
Net Inc./Net Property %	2.5	5.5	5.8	4.9	5.2	6.7	7.2
Net Inc./Tot. Capital %	2.4	5.2	5.8	5.0	5.7	6.9	7.6
Return on Equity %	5.1	10.3	11.4	9.7	10.8	13.3	13.9
Accum. Depr./Gross Prop. %	35.3	35.1	34.4	33.6	33.8	34.1	34.3
Price Range	29.31-19.25	30.50-25.26	31.50-21.75	29.44-21.31	30.75-23.06	31.13-20.88	25.00-19.13
P/E Ratio	36.6-24.1	17.4-14.4	17.6-12.2	20.0-14.5	20.0-15.0	16.8-11.3	13.5-10.3
Average Yield %	5.2	4.5	4.6	4.8	4.4	4.5	5.1

Statistics are as originally reported. ① Incl. a nonrecurr. after-tax chg. of $3.8 mill. assoc. with the Company's reorganization. ② Incl. a net gain of $1.6 mill. from the sale of investments in venture capital funds. ③ Incl. a nonrecurr. gain of $3.0 mill. from the sale of non-utility assets and a nonrecurr. chrg. of $2.9 mill. fr. the sale of utility property. ④ Incl. a nonrecurr. gain of $711,000 mill. fr. the sale of assets. ⑤ Incl. impairment provision of $9.4 mill., 9/02; $3.9 mill., 9/01.

OFFICERS:
J. H. DeGraffenreidt Jr., Chmn., C.E.O.
T. D. McCallister, Pres., C.O.O.
F. M. Kline, V.P., C.F.O.

INVESTOR CONTACT: Melissa Adams, Dir. Investor Relations, (202) 624-6410

PRINCIPAL OFFICE: 1100 H Street, N.W., Washington, DC 20080

TELEPHONE NUMBER: (703) 750-2000
FAX: (202) 624-6196
WEB: www.washgas.com

NO. OF EMPLOYEES: 2,205 (avg.)

SHAREHOLDERS: 17,960 (record)

ANNUAL MEETING: In Mar.

INCORPORATED: DC, Mar., 1957

INSTITUTIONAL HOLDINGS:
No. of Institutions: 144
Shares Held: 21,495,585
% Held: 43.9

INDUSTRY: Natural gas distribution (SIC: 4924)

TRANSFER AGENT(S): The Riggs National Bank, Washington, D.C.

WILMINGTON TRUST CORPORATION

YIELD 3.7%
P/E RATIO 14.7

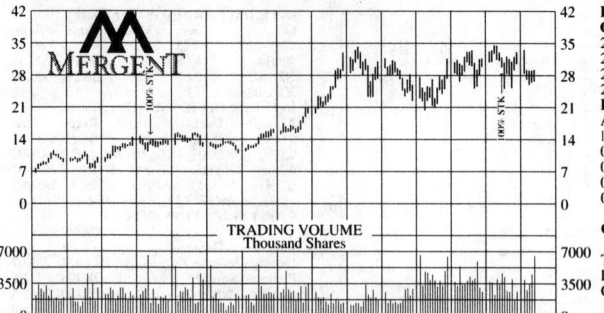

INTERIM EARNINGS (Per Share):

Qtr.	Mar.	June	Sept.	Dec.
2000	0.47	0.47	0.48	0.44
2001	0.46	0.47	0.48	0.48
2002	0.49	0.52	0.52	0.49
2003	0.44	...	...	...

INTERIM DIVIDENDS (Per Share):

Amt.	Decl.	Ex.	Rec.	Pay.
100% STK	4/18/02	6/18/02	6/03/02	6/17/02
0.255Q	7/18/02	7/30/02	8/01/02	8/15/02
0.255Q	10/17/02	10/30/02	11/01/02	11/15/02
0.255Q	1/16/03	1/30/03	2/03/03	2/17/03
0.27Q	4/17/03	4/29/03	5/01/03	5/15/03

Indicated div.: $1.08 (Div. Reinv. Plan)

CAPITALIZATION (12/31/02):

	($000)	(%)
Total Deposits	6,337,093	87.5
Long-Term Debt	160,500	2.2
Common & Surplus	741,269	10.2
Total	7,238,862	100.0

DIVIDEND ACHIEVER STATUS:
Rank: 171   10-Year Growth Rate: 8.61%
Total Years of Dividend Growth: 21

TRADING VOLUME
Thousand Shares

| 1989 | 1990 | 1991 | 1992 | 1993 | 1994 | 1995 | 1996 | 1997 | 1998 | 1999 | 2000 | 2001 | 2002 | 2003 |

*7 YEAR PRICE SCORE 123.1   ***12 MONTH PRICE SCORE 93.7**
*NYSE COMPOSITE INDEX=100

RECENT DEVELOPMENTS: For the quarter ended 3/31/03, net income declined 8.5% to $29.4 million from $32.1 million in the corresponding prior-year period. Net interest income improved 4.8% to $68.3 million. Provision for loan losses decreased 6.8% to $4.9 million. Total non-interest income slipped 5.4% to $61.2 million, while total non-interest expense increased 5.8% to $79.6 million. As of 3/31/03, combined assets under management were $28.89 billion, down 21.0% from $36.57 billion the year before.

PROSPECTS: WL's loan balances continue to increase, while revenue from its wealth advisory and corporate client businesses continue to rise. Growth continues to be particularly strong in total commercial loans, as low interest rates stimulate investment in real estate projects. Moreover, consumer loan balances continue to rise in WL's retail portfolio as collateral lending, primarily to wealth advisory clients, increase. Separately, WL will postpone certain capital expenditures in order to reduce expenses.

BUSINESS

WILMINGTON TRUST CORPORATION, with assets of $8.27 billion as of 3/31/03, is a financial services holding company with offices in California, Delaware, Florida, Georgia, Maryland, Nevada, New Jersey, New York, Pennsylvania, Tennessee, the Cayman and Channel Islands, Dublin, London, and Milan. The Company provides wealth management and specialized corporate services to clients throughout the United States and in more than 50 other countries, and commercial banking services throughout the Delaware Valley region. In addition, the Company is authorized to do business in Luxembourg and the Netherlands.

ANNUAL FINANCIAL DATA

	12/31/02	12/31/01	12/31/00	12/31/99	12/31/98	12/31/97	12/31/96
Earnings Per Share	2.01	☐ 1.89	1.85	1.61	1.67	1.54	1.42
Tang. Book Val. Per Share	7.31	7.25	6.48	5.17	6.07	7.51	6.86
Dividends Per Share	1.01	0.94	0.89	0.82	0.77	0.70	0.65
Dividend Payout %	50.2	50.1	47.8	51.4	45.8	45.8	45.6
INCOME STATEMENT (IN MILLIONS):							
Total Interest Income	392.9	468.8	530.5	462.2	456.9	430.6	402.9
Total Interest Expense	116.3	210.0	275.3	216.3	219.2	200.6	188.6
Net Interest Income	276.5	258.8	255.1	245.9	237.7	230.0	214.2
Provision for Loan Losses	22.0	19.9	21.9	17.5	20.0	21.5	16.0
Non-Interest Income	262.2	228.0	216.2	191.5	183.9	157.5	138.2
Non-Interest Expense	309.9	276.9	264.7	258.2	230.1	207.7	192.3
Income Before Taxes	206.8	190.0	184.8	161.7	171.5	158.4	144.1
Net Income	133.2	☐ 124.0	120.9	107.3	114.3	106.0	97.3
Average Shs. Outstg. (000)	66,301	65,942	65,360	66,766	68,550	68,932	68,798
BALANCE SHEET (IN MILLIONS):							
Cash & Due from Banks	248.9	210.1	223.8	225.1	204.6	239.4	231.2
Securities Avail. for Sale	1,343.9	1,264.8	1,440.1	1,686.3	1,298.7	1,316.4	798.5
Total Loans & Leases	6,025.5	5,488.8	5,189.0	4,821.6	4,324.4	4,004.8	3,783.9
Allowance for Credit Losses	85.5	81.7	77.3	78.4	76.7	74.6	66.8
Net Loans & Leases	5,939.9	5,407.2	5,111.7	4,743.2	4,247.7	3,930.1	3,717.1
Total Assets	8,131.3	7,518.5	7,321.6	7,201.9	6,300.6	6,122.4	5,564.4
Total Deposits	6,337.1	5,590.8	5,286.0	5,369.5	4,536.8	4,169.0	3,913.7
Long-Term Obligations	160.5	160.5	168.0	168.0	168.0	43.0	43.0
Total Liabilities	7,390.0	6,835.9	6,729.7	6,703.7	5,754.4	5,619.3	5,099.7
Net Stockholders' Equity	741.3	682.5	591.9	498.2	546.2	503.0	464.7
Year-end Shs. Outstg. (000)	65,628	65,400	64,787	64,706	66,658	66,956	67,786
STATISTICAL RECORD:							
Return on Equity %	18.0	18.2	20.4	21.5	20.9	21.1	20.9
Return on Assets %	1.6	1.6	1.7	1.5	1.8	1.7	1.7
Equity/Assets %	9.1	9.1	8.1	6.9	8.7	8.2	8.4
Non-Int. Exp./Tot. Inc. %	57.5	56.9	56.2	59.0	54.6	53.6	54.6
Price Range	34.63-25.05	33.50-25.10	31.69-20.28	31.75-22.38	34.25-23.19	33.00-19.63	20.88-15.13
P/E Ratio	17.2-12.5	17.8-13.3	17.1-11.0	19.8-13.9	20.5-13.9	21.4-12.7	14.8-10.7
Average Yield %	3.4	3.2	3.4	3.0	2.7	2.7	3.6

Statistics are as originally reported. Adj. for 2-for-1 stk. split, 6/02. ☐ Bef. an after-tax acctg. credit of $1.1 mill.

OFFICERS:
T. T. Cecala, Chmn., C.E.O.
R. V. Harra Jr., Pres., C.O.O., Treas.
D. R. Gibson, Sr. V.P., C.F.O.

INVESTOR CONTACT: Ellen Roberts, Media & Investor Relations, (302) 651-8069

PRINCIPAL OFFICE: Rodney Square North, 1100 North Market St., Wilmington, DE 19890-0001

TELEPHONE NUMBER: (302) 651-1000
FAX: (302) 651-8010
WEB: www.wilmingtontrust.com

NO. OF EMPLOYEES: 2,361

SHAREHOLDERS: 8,712

ANNUAL MEETING: In April

INCORPORATED: DE, Mar., 1901

INSTITUTIONAL HOLDINGS:
No. of Institutions: 200
Shares Held: 25,579,509
% Held: 38.8

INDUSTRY: State commercial banks (SIC: 6022)

TRANSFER AGENT(S): Wells Fargo Shareowner Services, St. Paul, MN

WPS RESOURCES CORPORATION

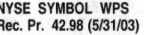

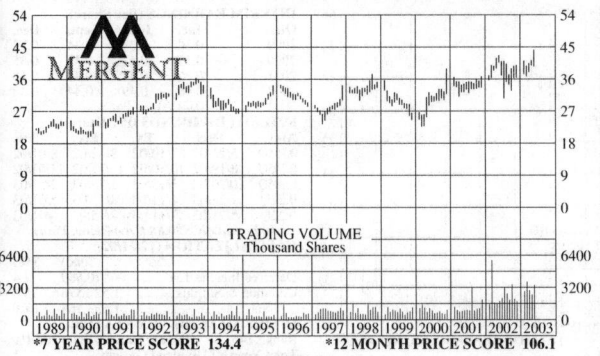

*7 YEAR PRICE SCORE 134.4   *12 MONTH PRICE SCORE 106.1*

NYSE COMPOSITE INDEX=100

INTERIM EARNINGS (Per Share):

Qtr.	Mar.	June	Sept.	Dec.
1999	0.86	0.38	0.52	0.48
2000	1.10	0.43	0.49	0.51
2001	0.89	0.41	0.76	0.70
2002	0.89	0.68	0.95	0.91
2003	0.92	...	...	...

INTERIM DIVIDENDS (Per Share):

Amt.	Decl.	Ex.	Rec.	Pay.
0.535Q	7/11/02	8/28/02	8/30/02	9/20/02
0.535Q	10/10/02	11/26/02	11/29/02	12/20/02
0.535Q	2/13/03	2/26/03	2/28/03	3/20/03
0.535Q	4/10/03	5/28/03	5/30/03	6/20/03

Indicated div.: $2.14 (Div. Reinv. Plan)

CAPITALIZATION (12/31/02):

	($000)	(%)
Long-Term Debt	824,400	49.0
Deferred Income Tax	73,700	4.4
Common & Surplus	782,800	46.6
Total	1,680,900	100.0

DIVIDEND ACHIEVER STATUS:
Rank: 273   10-Year Growth Rate: 2.11%
Total Years of Dividend Growth: 44

RECENT DEVELOPMENTS: For the three months ended 3/31/03, income was $29.8 million, before an accounting change credit of $3.2 million, compared with net income of $28.1 million in the equivalent quarter of the previous year. The improvement in earnings growth was primarily attributed to increased gas and electric margins at WPS Energy Services. Total revenues more than tripled to $1.28 billion from $397.1 million in the prior-year period.

PROSPECTS: WPS remains on target to achieve full-year 2003 earnings in the range of $2.75 to $2.95 per share, but may be at the lower end of the range due to its delayed rate case order. Earnings will reflect completion of WPS' pending Federal Energy Regulatory Commission rate case, successful execution of cost-control initiatives, normal weather patterns, and improvement in the economy.

BUSINESS

WPS RESOURCES CORPORATION (formerly Wisconsin Public Service Corp.) operates as a holding company with both regulated utility and non-regulated business units serving an 11,000 square mile service territory in northeastern Wisconsin and an adjacent portion of the Upper Peninsula of Michigan. The Company's principal wholly-owned subsidiaries are: Wisconsin Public Service Corporation (WPSC), a regulated electric and gas utility in Wisconsin and Michigan; Upper Peninsula Power Company, a regulated electric utility in Michigan; and WPS Energy Service, Inc. and WPS Power Development, Inc., both non-regulated subsidiaries. As of 12/31/02, WPSC served 407,696 electric retail and 295,816 gas retail customers.

ANNUAL FINANCIAL DATA

	12/31/02	12/31/01	12/31/00	12/31/99	12/31/98	12/31/97	12/31/96
Earnings Per Share	⚑ 3.42	⚑ 2.74	2.53	2.24	1.76	2.25	2.00
Cash Flow Per Share	8.14	6.35	7.05	5.94	5.63	6.11	5.93
Tang. Book Val. Per Share	24.43	22.73	20.21	19.97	19.48	20.00	19.56
Dividends Per Share	2.12	2.08	2.04	2.00	1.96	1.92	1.88
Dividend Payout %	62.0	75.9	80.6	89.3	111.4	85.3	94.0
INCOME STATEMENT (IN MILLIONS):							
Total Revenues	2,674.9	2,675.5	1,951.6	1,098.5	1,063.7	878.3	858.3
Costs & Expenses	2,375.2	2,466.1	1,646.1	819.5	808.3	644.4	617.2
Depreciation & Amort.	148.6	102.1	119.6	98.7	102.5	92.2	93.9
Maintenance Exp.	...	...	73.0	60.6	52.8	41.7	48.8
Operating Income	151.1	107.3	112.8	119.7	100.0	100.1	98.3
Net Interest Inc./(Exp.)	d58.1	d55.8	d50.8	d32.8	d28.6	d26.4	d25.0
Income Taxes	24.8	4.8	6.0	29.7	23.4	29.3	24.4
Equity Earnings/Minority Int.	...	...	...	...	0.6	0.8	0.3
Net Income	⚑ 112.5	⚑ 77.6	67.0	59.6	46.6	53.7	47.5
Cash Flow	258.0	179.7	186.6	158.3	149.2	145.9	141.6
Average Shs. Outstg. (000)	31,700	28,300	26,463	26,644	26,511	23,873	23,891
BALANCE SHEET (IN MILLIONS):							
Gross Property	3,161.1	2,954.0	2,547.7	2,429.2	2,197.6	1,899.4	1,825.8
Accumulated Depreciation	1,575.5	1,515.3	1,365.4	1,293.4	1,206.1	1,032.1	952.3
Net Property	1,610.2	1,463.6	1,198.3	1,150.9	1,010.2	886.4	892.9
Total Assets	3,207.9	2,870.0	2,816.1	1,816.5	1,510.4	1,299.6	1,330.7
Long-Term Obligations	824.4	727.8	587.0	510.9	343.0	304.0	305.8
Net Stockholders' Equity	782.8	715.9	593.9	587.5	568.4	529.0	518.7
Year-end Shs. Outstg. (000)	32,041	31,496	26,851	26,851	26,551	23,897	23,897
STATISTICAL RECORD:							
Operating Profit Margin %	5.6	4.0	5.8	10.9	9.4	11.4	11.5
Net Profit Margin %	4.2	2.9	3.4	5.4	4.4	6.1	5.6
Net Inc./Net Property %	7.0	5.3	5.6	5.2	4.6	6.1	5.0
Net Inc./Tot. Capital %	6.7	4.8	4.8	4.5	4.3	5.6	3.8
Return on Equity %	12.7	9.5	11.3	10.1	8.2	10.2	9.2
Accum. Depr./Gross Prop. %	49.8	51.3	53.6	53.2	54.9	54.3	52.2
Price Range	42.68-30.47	36.80-31.00	39.00-22.63	35.75-24.44	37.50-29.94	34.25-23.38	34.38-28.25
P/E Ratio	12.5-8.9	13.4-11.3	15.4-8.9	16.0-10.9	21.3-17.0	15.2-10.4	17.2-14.1
Average Yield %	5.8	6.1	6.6	6.6	5.8	6.7	6.0

Statistics are as originally reported. ⚑ Incl. after-tax gains of $22.8 mill., 2002; $1.3 mill., 2001, from the sale of part of the synthetic fuel operation of WPS Power Development

OFFICERS:
L. L. Weyers, Chmn., Pres., C.E.O.
J. P. O'Leary, Sr. V.P., C.F.O.
B. A. Johnson, Treas.

INVESTOR CONTACT: Donna M. Sheedy, Inv. Rel. Supervisor, (920) 433-1857

PRINCIPAL OFFICE: 700 North Adams Street, P.O. Box 19001, Green Bay, WI 54307-9001

TELEPHONE NUMBER: (920) 433-4901
FAX: (920) 433-1526
WEB: www.wpsr.com

NO. OF EMPLOYEES: 2,963

SHAREHOLDERS: 22,768

ANNUAL MEETING: In May

INCORPORATED: WI, July, 1883

INSTITUTIONAL HOLDINGS:
No. of Institutions: 160
Shares Held: 11,105,383
% Held: 34.7

INDUSTRY: Electric and other services combined (SIC: 4931)

TRANSFER AGENT(S): UAmerican Stock Transfer & Trust, Brooklyn, NY

WRIGLEY (WM.) JR. COMPANY

YIELD 1.6%
P/E RATIO 30.7

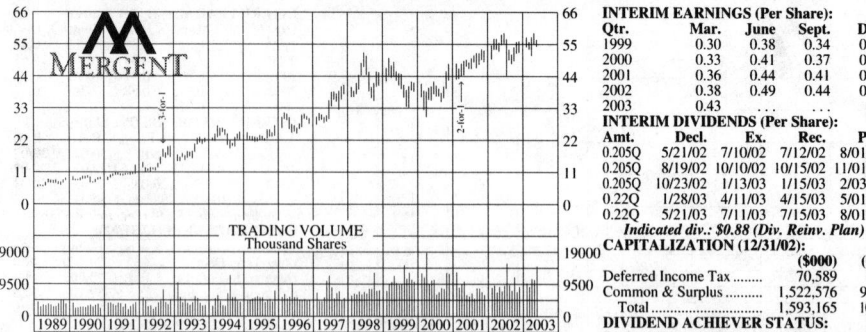

INTERIM EARNINGS (Per Share):

Qtr.	Mar.	June	Sept.	Dec.
1999	0.30	0.38	0.34	0.32
2000	0.33	0.41	0.37	0.35
2001	0.36	0.44	0.41	0.40
2002	0.38	0.49	0.44	0.48
2003	0.43	...	...	...

INTERIM DIVIDENDS (Per Share):

Amt.	Decl.	Ex.	Rec.	Pay.
0.205Q	5/21/02	7/10/02	7/12/02	8/01/02
0.205Q	8/19/02	10/10/02	10/15/02	11/01/02
0.205Q	10/23/02	1/13/03	1/15/03	2/03/03
0.22Q	1/28/03	4/11/03	4/15/03	5/01/03
0.22Q	5/21/03	7/11/03	7/15/03	8/01/03

Indicated div.: $0.88 (Div. Reinv. Plan)

CAPITALIZATION (12/31/02):

	($000)	(%)
Deferred Income Tax	70,589	4.4
Common & Surplus	1,522,576	95.6
Total	1,593,165	100.0

DIVIDEND ACHIEVER STATUS:
Rank: 145   10-Year Growth Rate: 10.01%
Total Years of Dividend Growth: 22

TRADING VOLUME
Thousand Shares

*7 YEAR PRICE SCORE 143.7   *12 MONTH PRICE SCORE 103.1
*NYSE COMPOSITE INDEX=100

RECENT DEVELOPMENTS: For the quarter ended 3/31/03, net earnings increased 13.7% to $97.0 million compared with $85.3 million in the corresponding prior-year quarter. Net sales advanced 12.2% to $672.4 million from $599.0 million a year earlier, primarily due to the effects of currency translation, as well as selected selling price increases, an improved product mix in WWY's international markets and higher unit volumes worldwide. Gross profit climbed 14.0% to $397.1 million from $348.3 million the year before.

PROSPECTS: In Asia, WWY is extending its JUICY FRUIT® brand with new fruit flavors. Meanwhile in Europe, WWY is increasing its distribution of ORBIT® DROPS, its sugar-free lozenges that are now available in four flavors. Also in Europe, WWY recently introduced EXTRA® THIN ICE™, its first international fresh breath strip product. In the U.S. the rollout of two additional fresh breath strip products, ECLIPSE® FLASH™ SPEARMINT and WINTERFRESH® THIN ICE, is nearing completion.

BUSINESS

WM. WRIGLEY JR. COMPANY is the world's largest chewing gum producer. Main brands are WRIGLEY'S SPEARMINT, DOUBLEMINT, JUICY FRUIT, WINTERFRESH, BIG RED, EXTRA, FREEDENT and ECLIPSE. Additional brands include ORBIT, HUBBA BUBBA®, AIRWAVES, ICEWHITE, EXCEL, ARROWMINT, COOL CRUNCH, P.K. and COOL AIR. Through its Amurol Confections Company subsidiary, the Company also manufactures and markets various non-gum items, such as a line of suckers, dextrose candy, liquid gel candy and hard roll candies. As of 12/31/02, Wrigley brands were produced in 14 factories, including three plants in North America four in Europe, one in Africa and five in the Asia/Pacific region. WWY's largest non-U.S. markets by shipments were Australia, Canada, China, France, Germany, Philippines, Poland, Russia, Taiwan and the United Kingdom.

ANNUAL FINANCIAL DATA

	12/31/02	12/31/01	12/31/00	12/31/99	12/31/98	12/31/97	12/31/96
Earnings Per Share	③1.78	1.61	1.45	1.33	②1.32	①1.17	①1.00
Cash Flow Per Share	2.16	1.91	1.70	1.59	1.55	1.39	1.20
Tang. Book Val. Per Share	6.77	5.67	4.87	4.97	4.98	4.25	3.87
Dividends Per Share	0.81	0.74	0.70	0.67	0.65	0.58	0.51
Dividend Payout %	45.2	46.3	48.3	50.0	49.4	50.0	51.3
INCOME STATEMENT (IN MILLIONS):							
Total Revenues	2,746.3	2,429.6	2,145.7	2,079.2	2,023.4	1,954.2	1,850.6
Costs & Expenses	2,075.7	1,848.0	1,624.6	1,572.9	1,526.1	1,508.5	1,443.1
Depreciation & Amort.	85.6	68.3	57.9	61.2	55.8	50.4	47.3
Operating Income	585.1	513.4	463.2	445.1	441.5	395.2	360.2
Net Interest Inc./(Exp.)	...	...	...	d0.7	d0.6	d1.0	d1.1
Income Before Income Taxes	583.4	527.4	479.3	444.4	440.9	394.2	359.1
Income Taxes	181.9	164.4	150.4	136.2	136.4	122.6	128.8
Net Income	③401.5	363.0	328.9	308.2	②304.5	①271.6	①230.3
Cash Flow	487.1	431.3	386.8	369.4	360.3	322.1	277.6
Average Shs. Outstg. (000)	225,145	225,349	227,036	231,722	231,928	231,928	231,966
BALANCE SHEET (IN MILLIONS):							
Cash & Cash Equivalents	304.9	333.2	329.9	306.9	351.7	327.4	300.6
Total Current Assets	1,006.3	913.8	828.7	803.7	843.2	797.7	729.4
Net Property	836.1	684.4	607.0	559.1	520.1	430.5	388.1
Total Assets	2,108.3	1,765.6	1,574.7	1,547.1	1,520.9	1,343.1	1,233.5
Total Current Liabilities	386.1	332.3	288.2	251.8	218.6	225.8	218.2
Net Stockholders' Equity	1,522.6	1,276.2	1,132.9	1,138.8	1,157.0	985.4	897.4
Net Working Capital	620.2	581.5	540.5	551.9	624.5	571.9	511.3
Year-end Shs. Outstg. (000)	225,056	224,950	232,442	228,992	232,220	231,938	231,940
STATISTICAL RECORD:							
Operating Profit Margin %	21.3	21.1	21.6	21.4	21.8	20.2	19.5
Net Profit Margin %	14.6	14.9	15.3	14.8	15.0	13.9	12.4
Return on Equity %	26.4	28.4	29.0	27.1	26.3	27.6	25.7
Return on Assets %	19.0	20.6	20.9	19.9	20.0	20.2	18.7
Price Range	58.90-44.21	53.30-42.94	48.31-29.94	50.31-33.25	52.16-35.47	41.03-27.28	31.44-24.19
P/E Ratio	33.1-24.8	33.1-26.7	33.3-20.6	37.8-25.0	39.7-27.0	35.1-23.3	31.6-24.3
Average Yield %	1.6	1.5	1.8	1.6	1.5	1.7	1.8

Statistics are as originally reported. Adj. for 2-for-1 stk. split, 2/01. ① Incls. non-recurring net chrg. 12/31/97: $3.3 mill.; chrg. 12/31/96: $13.0 mill. ② Incls. one-time gain of $10.4 mill. ③ Incl. business combination exploration chrg. of $10.0 mill.

OFFICERS:
W. Wrigley Jr., Pres., C.E.O.
R. V. Waters III, Sr. V.P., C.F.O.
A. J. Schneider, V.P., Treas.

INVESTOR CONTACT: Stockholder Relations, (800) 874-0474

PRINCIPAL OFFICE: 410 North Michigan Avenue, Chicago, IL 60611

TELEPHONE NUMBER: (312) 644-2121
FAX: (312) 644-0015
WEB: www.wrigley.com
NO. OF EMPLOYEES: 11,250 (approx.)
SHAREHOLDERS: 39,934 (com.); 3,085 (cl. B com.)
ANNUAL MEETING: In March
INCORPORATED: DE, Oct., 1927

INSTITUTIONAL HOLDINGS:
No. of Institutions: 411
Shares Held: 89,538,727
% Held: 39.8

INDUSTRY: Chewing gum (SIC: 2067)

TRANSFER AGENT(S): EquiServe Trust Company, N.A., Providence, RI